The Uniform Interpretation of the Brussels and Lugano Conventions

This work is a comparative examination of the uniform application of the Brussels and Lugano Conventions by courts in the UK, France, Germany, and various other European countries. It analyses evidence of inconsistent or divergent interpretations of certain contentious articles of these Conventions and the experience of litigation under them in other (French- and German-speaking) jurisdictions. The book acts as a unique repository of information and offers a detailed examination of both academic commentary and case-law from the Convention jurisdictions together with a critical appraisal of the jurisprudence of the European Court of Justice.

The Uniform Interpretation of the Brussels and Lugano Conventions

JUSTIN NEWTON
BA, LLB, LLM, D.Phil (Oxon)

HART PUBLISHING
OXFORD AND PORTLAND, OREGON
2002

Published in North America (US and Canada) by
Hart Publishing
c/o International Specialized Book Services
5804 NE Hassalo Street
Portland, Oregon
97213–3644
USA

Distributed in Netherlands, Belgium and Luxembourg by
Intersentia, Churchillaan 108
B2900 Schoten
Antwerpen
Belgium

Hart Publishing is a specialist legal publisher based in Oxford, England.
To order further copies of this book or to request a list of other publications
please write to:

Hart Publishing, Salters Boatyard, Folly Bridge,
Abingdon Rd, Oxford, OX1 4LB
Telephone: 144 (0)1865 245533 Fax: 144 (0) 1865 794882
email: mail@hartpub.co.uk
WEBSITE: http//:www.hartpub.co.uk

British Library Cataloguing in Publication Data
Data Available

ISBN 1–84113–323-X (hardback)

Typeset by J & L Composition, Filey, North Yorkshire
Printed and bound in Great Britain by
Biddles Ltd, www.biddles.co.uk

For my parents,
Ernest and Betty Newton

Acknowledgements

The greatest debt is owed primarily to my tutor Mr Adrian Briggs, Esq. Barrister, of St. Edmund Hall, Oxford, whose wisdom, ever-lucid comments and encouragement assisted in the completion of the thesis on which this work is based. Among the scholars at the University of Oxford, Mr. Edwin Peel of Keble College stands out for thanks for his encouragement in the early years of my D.Phil. Thanks are also due to Professor Ian Fletcher of Queen Mary and Westfield College, University of London and Mr. John Collier of Cambridge University for sparking my interest in the commercial conflict of laws.

For the research materials—in particular inter-library loans in French and German—I am grateful for the infinite patience and assistance of various librarians on two Continents: in the forefront of whom should be mentioned Ms. Elizabeth Martin, head of Reader Research Services at the St.Cross Building of the Bodleian Library, Ms. Angela de Souza of the University of Nottingham, the late David Rabasca and Mrs Edith Palmer, both of Law Reader Services at the Library of Congress, Washington, DC.

I am also grateful to the British Academy for funding, through its Humanities Research Board, the doctoral study on which this book is based.

Contents

2 Article 17

3 Article 24

4   Article 27(1), Public Policy

5 Article 27(2)

Updates to this work

Apart from the coming into force of the Brussels I Regulation 44/2001 on 1 March 2002, other important issues have arisen which the reader may wish to bear in mind when considering the material in the following account. Of general interest to the operation of the Brussels/Lugano Conventions, and now of the Brussels I Regulation itself, the following cases have come to the author's attention.

The vexed question of the inclusion by the English courts of the doctrine known as *forum non conveniens* into the Brussels Convention system (esp. with regard to Article 2) may finally be resolved by the European Court of Justice in the Court of Appeal's reference in *Owusu v Jackson t/a Villa Holiday Ball-Inn Villas & others* [2002] EWCA Civ 877, 19.6.2002, should the case not settle (as had happened with *Ladenimor SA v Intercomfinanz SA* (C–314/92) [1992] OJ C219/4, and [1994] OJ C103/9). *Owusu* involved the claimant's diving accident whilst on holiday in Jamaica, and his action in breach of contract and negligence against a number of co-defendants, the first of whom, a Mr. Jackson, was domiciled in England and therefore liable to be sued here under Article 2 Brussels Convention. Jackson had applied for a stay of proceedings (and his five co-defendants for orders that permission should not have been granted for service *ex juris* under CPR 6.20(3)) on *forum (non) conveniens* grounds, arguing that Jamaica was a clearly more appropriate forum for the trial of Owusu's action against the defendants. Court of Appeal authority already exists—*Re Harrods (Buenos Aires) Ltd* [1992] Ch 90, [1991] 4 All ER 334—to the effect that Article 2 is not mandatory in its application in disputes with no further connection to any other Contracting States. The Court of Appeal's reference in *Owusu* submitted essentially the question whether the availability of any discretionary remedy under national law (such as *forum non conveniens*) was compatible with the jurisdictional system under Title II of the Conventions.

In a similar vein to the frustration felt by the Court of Appeal and House of Lords in the *Turner v Grovit* saga, [1999] EWCA Civ 1532, [2000] 1 QB 345, CA, [2001] UKHL 65, [2002] 1 WLR 107, HL, reference made (C-159/02), [2002] OJ C169/18—that of commencing an action in another Contracting State with the perceived intention of harassing or oppressing a claimant already before the English courts—a recently reported French first instance court has also registered its disapproval, under Article 21, of what has become known as launching either a Belgian or Italian 'torpedo' in patent litigation: *Tribunal de grande instance de Paris* 9.3.2001 *Schaerer Schweiter Mettler AG v Fadis Spa* 2002 IIC 225. The court dismissed the plea put forward by Fadis that the French court should decline jurisdiction due to the fact that a court in Milan was already 'first seised' of the dispute under Article 21. The reason given, at p. 227, was interesting: 'Fadis has tried abusively to suspend any action for infringement in France and to consolidate before the Italian court several actions for declaration of non-infringement . . .'.

As far as updates are concerned to the various articles treated in detail in this work, the following should be noted whilst reading the chapters themselves.

It is somewhat ironic that an ECJ reference seeking a solution to the question left open in *Overseas Union Insurance Ltd & Others v New Hampshire Insurance Company* (C–351/89) [1991] ECR I–3317 and most emphatically answered by the English Court of Appeal in *Continental Bank N.A. v Aeakos Compania Naviera S.A. and others* [1994] 1 WLR 588—as to whether Article 17 'exclusive' jurisdiction prevails over the duty of a court 'second seised' under Article 21 to decline its jurisdiction—will not have come from an English court, but an Austrian—the recently reported reference in *Erich Gasser GmbH v MISAT Srl* (C-116/02), [2002] OJ C114/17, a reference from the *Oberlandesgericht Innsbruck*. In its question 2, the appeal court asked whether a *forum prorogatum* under an 'exclusive' Article 17 jurisdiction clause, yet 'second seised' under Article 21, may review the jurisdiction of the court 'first seised' (ambiguous in *Overseas Union Insurance*) or must apply Article 21 and ignore its own prorogated jurisdiction. Any answer to this question may well have a profound effect on the attitude of the English courts to Article 17 jurisdiction clauses/contract breakers who initiate actions in a Contracting State *forum derogatum*, in breach of such a clause (*Continental Bank N.A. v Aeakos Compania Naviera S.A. and others* [1994] 1 WLR 588, *OT Africa Line Ltd v Hijazy and others (The "Kribi")* [2001] 1 Lloyd's Rep. 76).

Of interest to chapter 3, dealing with Article 24, should be the effect of the *Van Uden Maritime* 'restrictions' on the jurisdiction to grant 'provisional, including protective measures' witnessed in the recently reported decision of the French *Cour de Cassation* in 11.12.2001 *Virgin Atlantic Airways Ltd et autres c/ G.I.E. Airbus Industries et autres* (2002) *Rev crit* 371, (2002) *JCP*, Juris., II 10107. The case centered around Virgin's application before the Paris Commercial Court for the appointment of technical experts to investigate an accident that occurred at Heathrow to an Airbus aircraft on 5 November 1997. Throughout the appeal court system, the French courts applied the *Van Uden Maritime* 'general restrictions' to jurisdiction to order provisional measures under Article 24, to the effect that there had to be 'a real connecting link between the subject matter of the measures sought and the territorial jurisdiction of the Contracting State of the court before which those measures [were] sought' (C-391/95) [1998] ECR I-7091, at p 7135 para 40. The *Cour de Cassation* therefore ruled that the French courts did not have jurisdiction under Article 24 to order the appointment of experts to investigate a crash occuring outside France, on the facts.

As regards 'public policy' under Article 27(1), three items are worthy of mention here. First is the decision of the Court of Session, Outer House, in Scotland: *SA Marie Brizzard et Roger International for Registration of a judgment* [2002] ScotSC 97, 5.4.2002, Lord Mackay of Drumadoon. This case will not only have an impact on the scope of public policy in Scotland under Article 27(1) , but also on this study as to the meaning of an Article 25 'judgment' for the purposes of recognition and enforcement, and the time of its rendition for transitional purposes.

Registration in Scotland had eventually been sought of a decision of the *Cour d'appel de Bordeaux* of 29 January 2001. The Scottish defender, William Grant and Sons International, resisted enforcement of this judgment on Article 27(1) public policy grounds on the basis of an action at first instance before the *Tribunal de Commerce de Bordeaux*, dated 27 January 1995. Their complaint was essentially premised on the (objectively biased) judicial composition of the French commercial court system, as the judge found, made up as it is by lay judges appointed from among prominent members of the local business community (of Bordeaux). By stating that the entire litigious episode of decisions—continuing up the chain of appeal court hierarchy, should be viewed in the round for enforcement purposes—the judge was able to side-step the unenviable and invidious task of having to declare that the composition of the courts of another Contracting State breached public policy under Article 27(1) and the right to a fair hearing under Article 6(1) ECHR. The decision of the *OLG Saarbrücken* 3.8.1987 (1989) *IPRax* 37, IPRspr. (1987) Nr. 156, (1988) *NJW* 3100 was not cited by the judge—finding nothing to cavil at in the lay court system in France. If, as was not decided, there had originally been a breach of Article 27(1) by the judicial composition of the first instance court, this aspect the judge would have found to have been 'laundered' by the rehearing of the entire case before the *Cour d'appel de Bordeaux*.

A second item that may be mentioned for the sake of completeness under Article 27(1) is the recent decision of the Court of Appeal in *Wim Harry Gerard Maronier v Bryan Larmer*, [2002] EWCA Civ 774, 29.5.2002. Enforcement was sought in England of a judgment of the District Court of Rotterdam dated 30 December 1999, in an action for professional negligence commenced in The Netherlands as long ago back as 12 March 1984. For various reasons, most apparently due to one of the parties' advisers and a bankruptcy, the action became stale for a long period, during which time the judgment debtor, Mr. Larmer, moved to England. Between 1998 and 1999 the action was re-activated, without notice of this fact being communicated to Mr. Larmer, who was served with the judgment of December 1999 at the beginning of 2000. In the exceptional circumstances of this case the Court of Appeal had no difficulty in declaring that there had been a breach of public policy under Article 27(1), in that Larmer had been denied a fair trial in Rotterdam, due to his ignorance of the re-activated proceedings.

The last item of interest to the study of 'public policy' and Article 27(1) is the issue of the recognition and enforcement of (US) judgments awarding punitive damages. In a recently published article, Triadafillidis, C. 'Anerkennung und Vollstreckung von "punitive damages" -Urteilen nach kontinentalem und insbesondere nach griechischem Recht' (2002) *IPRax* 236, the author informs us, at p 238, that the Supreme Court in Greece has refused to countenance enforcement of a US judgment awarding punitive damages, being a breach of Greek public policy, at autonomous law.

Under Article 27(2), two recently reported cases, one from Austria, the other from Germany deserve some attention when reading the corresponding chapter 5 in this work.

As we shall see, the sensitive question of the application of Article 27(2) to resist enforcement of a Contracting State judgment given after service of the document initiating the proceedings in the rendering court 'internally' by the method of *remise au parquet*, has provoked strong negative reactions in Germany. The same attitude is now in evidence in Austria—*Oberste Gerichtshof* decision *OGH* 11.7.2001 (2002) *ZfRV* 71. It has stated that in the absence of further (special) circumstances—which were not spelt out—such 'fictitious' service internally in the rendering Contracting State will be considered *never* to have been served 'in sufficient time' to enable a (presumably Austrian) defendant to defend himself adequately.

The interpretation of Article 27(2) in Germany has in the main been strict, and on occasion draconian. Readers of the German caselaw under Article 27(2) will therefore be surprised by the leniency of the interpretation of 'sufficient time' in *OLG Düsseldorf* 8.2.2002 (2002) *RIW* 558. In this case, due to the fact that the judgment debtor knew of the pending action, and more importantly of its exact content, the appeal court allowed a short period of one week to be considered as a sufficient period.

Table of Cases

European Court of Justice decisions on the Brussels Convention

Unreported cases, cases pending, and AGs' opinions

Withdrawn Cases

Individual Contracting State case law on the Brussels and Lugano Conventions

Belgian and Luxembourg Cases
Art.1

Cour d'appel de Bruxelles 24.2.2000 *SA Francesca Carrer c/ SRL Maglierie Alphaville* 2000 JT 468
Cour d'appel de Luxembourg 2.3.2000 *Vilain c/ Vilain* 2000 Pas. Lux., 282

Art.2

Trib.Prem instance Bruxelles 12.11.1999, unreported

Art.5(1)

Cour de Cassation/ Cour Supérieure de Justice

Cour de Cassation 6.4.1978, *Société de droit allemand 'Knauer und Co GmbH Maschinenfabrik' c/ Callens*, 1978 Pas., 871
Cour Supérieure de Justice 7.6.1978 *Gondert c/ Pultz* 1978–80 Pas Lux., 30
Cour de Cassation 28.6.1979 *Société 'Audi-NSU Auto Union AG' v Société 'Adelin Petit et Cie SA'* 1979 Pas., I, 1260, [1980] E.C.C. 235
Cour de Cassation 13.11.1981 *'Artus Metallwaren GmbH' c/ Société anonyme 'Werkhuizen Demeyere'* 1982 Pas., I, 363
Cour de Cassation 19.1.1984 *Carl Freudenberg KG c/ Société de Personnes à responsabilité Limitée 'Bureau R.C. Van Oppens'* 1984 Pas., I, 540
Cour de Cassation (Luxembourg) 25.6.1987 1987–1989 Pas. Lux., 122 *Charles Bernard v Marie-Louise Zwally* [1989] I.L.Pr. 137
Cour de Cassation *Leathertex Divisione Sinetici Spa v Bodetex* 4.12.1997, 1997 Pas., I, 530, [1998] I.L.Pr. 505
Cour de Cassation *Leathertex Divisione Sinetici Spa v Bodetex* 13.1.2000 2000 Rev. dr. comm. belge 179

Cours d'appel

Cour d'appel de Mons, 9.12.1975, *Société de Personnes à Responsabilité Limitée 'De Bloos' c/ Société en Commandite par Actions 'Bouyer'*, 1977 Pas., 1
Cour d'appel de Mons, 3.5.1977 *Ets. A. de Bloos S.P.R.L v Soc. en commandite par actions Bouyer*, 1978 Pas., II, 8
Cour d'appel de Liège *Audi NSU Auto Union AG c/ SA Adelin Petit et Cie* 12.5.1977 1979 JDI 193
Cour d'appel de Luxembourg 26.9.1980 *Smac c/ Thielen* 1981–83 Pas Lux., 134, 1983 ELR 281
Cour d'appel de Liège 4.11.1982 1984 JDI 397
Cour d'appel de Bruxelles 20.4.1987 1988 Annales de la Faculté de Droit de Liège 90
Cour d'appel de Mons, 4.5.1987 *S.I.P.A.L. Rexons Società Italiana Auto e Locomozione Spa v Sprl Gold's Products* [1990] I.L.Pr. 386
Cour d'appel de Luxembourg 3.12.1992 *Républiain Lorrain c/ Mancini* 1993–5 Pas Lux., 30
Cour d'appel de Luxembourg 8.3.1994 *Vesque c/ Badischer Winzerkeller E.G.* 1993–1995 Pas. Lux., 341

Cour d'appel de Bruxelles 19.6.2000 *S.A. Besix N.V. v WABAG Wasserreinigungsbau Alfred Kretzschmar GmbH,* http://curia.eu.int/common/recdoc/convention/en/2000/13–2000.htm

Tribunals

Tribunal de Liège 25.5.1979 1984 JDI 400
Tribunal de commerce de Bruxelles 2.9.1981 1984 JDI 396
Tribunal de commerce de Liège 4.1.1983 1984 JDI 398, *S.A. Jouets Eisemann v Geobra Brandstatter GmbH and another* [1985] E.C.C. 246
Tribunal de premiere instance, Bruxelles 9.3.1987 *Guy Barbier v Music for Pleasure Limited and another* [1990] I.L.Pr. 172
Tribunal de commerce de Liège, 9.1.1989, *S.P.R.L. Chesi / Budding,* 1991 Rev. dr. comm. belge 427
Tribunal de commerce de Bruxelles, 13.4.1989, *S.P.R.L. Linea Son Production/ Société de droit néerlandais Heuvelman B.V.* 1991 Rev. dr. comm. belge 430
Tribunal de commerce de Bruxelles, 22.6.1989, *S.P.R.L. Kheops/ S.A.R.L. Les Créations Ada Tuchbant,* 1990 Rev. dr. comm. belge 702
Tribunal de commerce de Bruxelles, 29.5.1990, *M.Filipson / Gebr.Herberg K.G.,* 1992 Rev. dr. comm. belge 907
Tribunal de commerce de Bruxelles, 10.9.1991, *Soc. dr. allemand Ravenstein Verlag c/ S.A. De Rouck,* 1994 Rev. dr. comm. belge 455
Rechtbank van Koophandel te Turnhout, 11.10.1993, *Grafix N.V. /GmbH Cantz'sche Druckerei,* 1994 Rev. dr. comm. belge 730
Hof van Beroep te Antwerpen, 3.1.1995, *Haesaerts Container International / Oy Fincarriers en Finnbelgia agencies,* 1995 Rev. dr. comm. belge 391
Tribunal de commerce de Liège, 18.5.1995 *S.A. Transports et Manutentions J. Germany / S.A. Satai Transports* 1996 Rev. dr. comm. belge 837
Tribunal de commerce de Liège, 19.6.1995 1996 Rev. dr. comm. belge 839
Tribunal de commerce d'Arlon, 12.9.1996, *Calorilux,* 1997 Rev. dr. comm. belge 321
Commerce Hasselt, 20.11.1996 *Metaalconstructie Vanacken B.V.B.A. / Installatietechniek Bitter B.V.* 1997 Rev. dr. comm. belge 200
Rechtbank van koophandel te Veurne 2.4.1997 *SARL Omicron distribution / BVBA Konstruktiewerkhuis en draineerbedrijf R. Vandezande* 1998 Rev. dr. comm. belge 401
Rechtbank van Koophandel te Gent 29.5.1997 *BVBA New Age t/ GmbH Hubermann & Sons Textil* 1998 Rev. dr. comm. belge 403
Hof van Beroep te Gent 26.6.1997 1998 Rev. dr. comm. belge 389
Rechtbank van koophandel Kortrijk 27.6.1997 *N.V. Silver International v Pochon Tissage S.A.,* unreported (http://www.cisg.law.pace.edu/cisg/wais/db/cases2/970627b1.html)

Art.5(2)

Cour de Cassation 29.3.2001 X.Y c/ G.C., unreported, *http://www.cass.be/cgi_juris/*

Art.5(3)

Cours d'appel

Cour d'appel de Liège 3.12.1990, *Perfetto c/ Parlapiano, et Sociétés de droit français 'Centrale Auto' et 'General Motors'* 1991 Pas., II, 84
Tribunal de commerce de Bruxelles 12.5.2000 *Röhm Enqyme GmbH v DSM N.V., BASF Belgium* 2001 IIC 571

Tribunals

Tribunal de commerce de Liège 4.1.1983 1984 JDI 398, *S.A. Jouets Eisemann v Geobra Brandstatter GmbH and another* [1985] E.C.C. 246
Amulum c/ Roquette 3.1.2000 2000 Rev. dr. comm. belge 242

Art.18

Cour de Cassation

Cours d'appel

Art.36

Art.38

Art.47

Protocol to Brussels Convention

French Cases
Art.1

Cour de Cassation

Cours d'appel

Cours d'appel

Cour d'appel de Versailles 23.11.1982, *ITW Ateco GmbH c/ International Technology S.A.R.L.*, 1983 Gazette du Palais, Juris., p.65
Cour d'appel de Paris 22.5.1991 *Société Tebe v Société Passiflore* [1993] I.L.Pr. 578

Art.4

Cour de Cassation

Cour de Cassation *Buchmann et autre c/ Steiner* 4.1.1984 1986 Rev. crit. 123
Cour de Cassation *Fondation Solomon R. Guggenheim c/ David Helion, Nicolas Helion et Sandro Rumney* 3.7.1996 1997 JDI 1016, [1997] I.L.Pr. 457, 1997 Rev. crit. 97

Cours d'appel

Cour d'appel de Paris 22.5.1991 *Société Tebe v Société Passiflore* [1993] I.L.Pr. 578
Cour d'appel de Paris *Société Fondation Solomon R. Guggenheim c/ David Helion, Nicolas Helion, et Sandro Rumney* 17.11.1993 1994 JDI 671

Art.5(1)

Cour de Cassation

Cour de Cassation *Société Julia c/ Société Sodevoc* 12.12.1978 1979 JDI 351
Cour de Cassation *Etablissements Carl Brehmer und Sohn c/ Baudoin* 23.1.1979 1979 JDI 333, 1979 Rev. crit. 816
Cour de Cassation *Dellinger c/ Société Leppak* 27.11.1979 1979 JDI 333, 1978 Gazette du Palais, Somm., 171
Cour de Cassation *Etablissements Malanca et autres c/ Société Savoye* 13.11.1980 1981 JDI 851
Cour de Cassation *Ivenel c/ Schwab* 2.4.1981 1981 JDI 849
Cour de Cassation *Société Socomo-Socotub c/ Société Reifenhauser* 2.6.1981 1983 JDI 395
Cour de Cassation *Société Ciatrans c/ Compagnie Le Monde* 3.6.1981 1983 JDI 398
Cour de Cassation *Société Technogel c/ Société Sodipe* 18.11.1981 1983 JDI 395
Cour de Cassation *Ossberger c/ Mauriès* 16.2.1982 1983 JDI 393
Cour de Cassation *Société Auminium Werke Wutoschingen c/ Société A.P. Landowksi-Samis* 10.3.1982 1983 JDI 393
Cour de Cassation 27.10.1982 *Soc. Wittels Albert Maschinen GmbH c/ Seel* 1983 Rev. crit. 661
Cour de Cassation *Soc K.D. Köln Düsseldorfer Deutsche Rheinschiffahrt c/ Soc. Transports et Voyages* 25.1.1984 1985 Rev. crit. 126
Cour de Cassation 4.3.1986 *Thompson Hayward Chemical Company and Impextraco v Soc. de Recherches de Nutrition animale Sirena and another* [1988] E.C.C. 319
Cour de Cassation *Ets Devriendt c/ Soc Roto Frank* 28.10.1986 1987 Rev. crit. 612
Cour de Cassation *Six Constructions Ltd c/ Paul Humbert* 14.1.1988 1989 JDI 91
Cour de Cassation 23.5.1989 *Société Europeenne d'Expansion (SEDEX) v Société Vetex* [1990] I.L.Pr. 254
Cour de Cassation 14.6.1989 *Six Constructions Ltd v Paul Humbert* [1990] I.L.Pr. 225
Cour de Cassation *Lejeune c/ Société F.A.I.S* 12.12.1989 1990 Rev. crit. 358
Cour de Cassation 8.1.1991 *Jakob Handte & Co. GmbH v Société Traitements Mecano-Chimiques des Surfaces (TMCS)* [1992] I.L.Pr. 428, 1991 Rev. crit. 411
Cour de Cassation *Soc Iris BV c/ Soc GAN* 19.3.1991 1992 Rev. crit. 708
Cour de Cassation *Société Svedex Holding B.V. v B.P. et autre* 3.3.1992 1993 Rev. crit. 692
Cour de Cassation 12.1.1993 *Hydro Gerätebau GmbH & Co. KG v Jean Besson International Sarl* [1994] I.L.Pr. 33
Cour de Cassation 27.1.1993 *Jakob Handte & Cie c/ Société Traitements Mecano-Chimiques des Surfaces (TMCS) et Soc. Bula et fils* 1993 Rev. crit. 485

Tribunals

Art.5(5)

Cour de Cassation

Cours d'appel

Art.6(1)

Cour de Cassation

Art.6 bis

Cour d'appel de Rouen 26.7.2000 *Navires Dafur et Happy Fellow* 2001 DMF 109

Art.7

Cour d'appel de Versailles 5.12.1998 *Société Group Josi Reinsurance Company SA v Compagnie d'Assurances Universal General Insurance Company UGIC* [1999] I.L.Pr.351

Art.8

Cour de Cassation

Cour de Cassation 22.2.2000 *Bonello c/ Crédit com. de France suisse* 2000 JCP, IV, 1622, 2001 JDI 143

Cours d'appel

Cour d'appel de Paris 19.2.1992 *Raphael Ben Lassin v Peter Payne and others* [1995] I.L.Pr. 17
Cour d'appel de Versailles 5.12.1998 *Société Group Josi Reinsurance Company SA v Compagnie d'Assurances Universal General Insurance Company UGIC* [1999] I.L.Pr.351

Art.9

Cours d'appel

Cour d'appel de Versailles 5.12.1998 *Société Group Josi Reinsurance Company SA v Compagnie d'Assurances Universal General Insurance Company UGIC* [1999] I.L.Pr.351

Tribunals

Tribunal de grande instance de Paris *Vasarely c/ Soc. Transport Yamato France et autres* 10.5.1985 1987 Rev. crit. 415

Art.10

Cours d'appel

Cour d'appel de Paris 13.12.1995 *ISEA Industrie SpA v S.A. LU* [1997] I.L.Pr. 823, *ISEA Industrie SpA c/ S.A. LU* 1997 JCP, II, 22772
Cour d'appel de Grenoble 29.4.1999 *Sté Rutschi Pumpen AG c/ SA Pompes Rutschi Mulhouse et a.* 2001 JCP, IV, 1466

Tribunals

Tribunal de grande instance de Paris *Vasarely c/ Soc. Transport Yamato France et autres* 10.5.1985 1987 Rev. crit. 415

Art.12

Tribunal de grande instance de Paris *Vasarely c/ Soc. Transport Yamato France et autres* 10.5.1985 1987 Rev. crit. 415

Art.13

Cour de Cassation

Cour de Cassation 18.7.2000 *SA Sté Générale de Banque c/ Epx Dumont* 2000 JCP, IV, 2579, 2001 JDI 140, 2001 Rev. crit. 142
Cour de Cassation 3.7.2001 *Launay c/ SARL Beton Feidt* 2001 JCP, IV, 2609

Cours d'appel

Art.22

Cour de Cassation

Cours d'appel

Art.24

Cour de Cassation

Cours d'appel

Tribunals

Tribunal de Grande Instance de Nîmes 9.6.1998 *Bechert, ès qual c/ Sté Proinbasa* 1999 Dalloz, Juris, 301

Art.25

Cour de Cassation

Cour de Cassation 17.11.1999 *M. Camenzuli c/ M.Désira* 2000 Rev. crit. 786

Cours d'appel

Cour d'appel de Paris 1.4.1997 *Sarl Ivresse v Société Tesserlana* [1999] I.L.Pr.332

Art.26

Cour de Cassation

Cour de Cassation *Klopp et autres c/ Holder* 28.2.1984 1985 Rev. crit. 131, 1984 Gazette du Palais, Juris., 350

Cours d'appel

Cour d'appel de Douai *Klopp et autres c/ Holder* 7.10.1982 1985 Rev. crit. 13
Cour d'appel de Paris *Bassil c/ Fidelity Bank London Branch* 14.12.1988, 1990 JDI 159

Tribunals

Tribunal de grande instance de Paris *Crédit Lyonnais Bank Nederland V. et autres c/ Giancarlo Parretto* 10.2.1993 1993 Rev. crit. 664

Art.27(1)

Cour de Cassation

Cour de Cassation *Office des Mineurs de Lahr c/ M.* 1.12.1976 1978 JDI 623
Cour de Cassation *P. c/ Office de jeunesse de Sieburg* 12.8.1977 1978 JDI 623
Cour de Cassation *Vanclef c/ Société Trans Traide International* 17.5.1978 1979 JDI 380
Cour de Cassation 19.10.1982 1983 Rev. crit. 721
Cour de Cassation *Klopp et autres c/ Holder* 28.2.1984 1985 Rev. crit. 131
Cour de Cassation *Société Polypétrol c/ Société générale routière* 9.10.1991 1993 JDI 157, 1992 Rev. crit. 516, *Sarl Polypetrol v Soc. Generale Routiere* [1993] I.L.Pr. 107
Cour de Cassation 13.10.1992 *J.L c/ Office cantonal de la jeunesse de Tübingen et Mme Ulricke G.* 1995 Rev. crit. 68
Cour de Cassation 5.5.1993, *Société Times Newspapers limited c/ Pordea*, 1994 Gazette du Palais, Juris., p.382, *Times Newspapers Limited v Gustave Pordea* [1994] I.L.Pr. 96
Cour de Cassation, 12.1.1994, *M. Tonon c/ Office cantonal de Tutlingen*, 1994 Rev. crit. 371, *M. Tonon v Office cantonal de Tutlingen* [1995] I.L.Pr. 23
Cour de Cassation 16.4.1996 *I.T.L. France S.A. v Medtrafina S.A.* [1996] I.L.Pr. 647
Cour de Cassation 14.5.1996 *Soc Brasserie du Pêcheur c/ La Kreissparkasse Main-Spessart* 1997 Gazette du Palais, Pan., 46 *Société Brasserie du Pecheur v Kreissparkasse Main-Spessart* [1997] I.L.Pr. 173
Cour de Cassation 11.3.1997 *Copraf SARL c/ Savict sas* 1997 JCP, IV, 149, 1997 RJDA 488, no.733
Cour de Cassation 13.1.1998 *Jean Pierre Mailliez c/ Soc. Norgrips et Soc. Redland plasterboard overseas Ltd*, unreported, http://curia.eu.int/common/recdoc/convention/en/1999/45–1999.htm
Cour de Cassation 16.3.1999 *Sieur Pordéa c/ Société Times Newspapers Limited* 1999 JDI 773, 2000 Rev.. crit. 223, [2000] I.L.Pr 763

Art.27(2)

Cour de Cassation

Art.28

Cour de Cassation

Cour de Cassation 3.4.1990 *Philippe Martin v Office de la Jeunesse Freiburg* [1991] I.L.Pr. 172
Cour de Cassation, 12.1.1994, *M. Tonon c/ Office cantonal de Tutlingen*, 1994 Rev. crit. 371
Cour de Cassation 14.5.1996 *Soc Brasserie du Pêcheur c/ La Kreissparkasse Main-Spessart* 1997
Gazette du Palais, Pan., 46, *Société Brasserie du Pecheur v Kreissparkasse Main-Spessart*
[1997] I.L.Pr. 173

Cours d'appel

Cour d'appel de Paris *Dame Schumann, sieur Halphen c/ dame Sanders-Polak* 16.12.1974
1975 JDI 146
Cour d'appel de Dijon *Société Sotalor c/ Société Kunststoffver Fahrenstechnik* 29.1.1975 1975
JDI 146
Cour d'appel de Douai 12.7.1978, *S.A.R.L. Defretin c/ S.A.R.L. Europlast* 1980 Gazette du
Palais, Somm., p.178
Cour d'appel de Douai 29.11.1978, *Vrammout c/ S.A.R.L. Westland*, 1980 Gazette du Palais,
Somm., p.178
Cour d'appel de Douai *Mme Tonnoir c/ Société anonyme Vanherf* 9.2.1989 1991 JDI 160

Tribunals

Tribunal de grande instance de Paris *Dietrich Garski c/ Brigitte Bolelli* 26.2.1980 1980 Rev.
crit. 782
Tribunal de grande instance de Paris *Société Unger Flugreisen c/ Société Diallo Voyages*
26.2.1980 1980 Rev. crit. 782

Art.29

Cour de Cassation

Cour de Cassation, 29.5.1985, *M. et Mme Yun c/ Soc. Seibo*, 1986 Rev. crit. 520
Cour de Cassation *Ph.Contant c/ G. Somers ès qualité* 13.4.1992 1993 Rev. crit. 67, *Philippe
Contant v Gaston Somers (Receiver of Vedette Sportswear Pvba)* [1993] I.L.Pr. 379
Cour de Cassation 14.5.1996 *Soc Brasserie du Pêcheur c/ La Kreissparkasse Main-Spessart* 1997
Gazette du Palais, Pan., 46, [1997] I.L.Pr. 173
Cour de Cassation 10.7.1996 *General Trading 5L SA c/ Claudio Bertini* 1996 Gazette du
Palais, II, Panor., 109
Cour de Cassation 8.2.2000 *Abadia Otin c/ SA Ateliers de la Chainette* 2000 JCP, IV, 1546

Art.31

Cour de Cassation

Cour de Cassation 9.1.1991 *Daniel Bassil v Fidelity Bank* [1992] I.L.Pr. 289

Cours d'appel

Cour d'appel de Paris 8.5.1979, *Mohammed Parang c/ Stimpfig et Gerlach*, 1979 Gazette du
Palais, Juris., p.344

Art.32

Cour de Cassation

Cour de Cassation *Office des Mineurs de Lahr c/ M.* 1.12.1976 1978 JDI 623

Art.54

Cours d'appel

Cour d'appel d'Angers *Société Van Pelt c/ Jedre* 29.1.1980 1980 JDI 889

Protocol to Brussels Convention

Cour de Cassation

Cour de Cassation 2.5.2001 *De Amorin Tavares c/ SA Nancéene Varin Bannier* 2001 JCP IV, 2122

German Cases

Art.1

Bundesgerichtshof (BGH)

BGH 30.4.1980 1980 NJW 2022, *De Cavel v De Cavel* [1980] E.C.C. 420
BGH 14.7.1993 1994 IPRax 447
BGH 16.9.1993 1994 IPRax 118, 1994 IPRax 118, IPRspr. 1993 Nr. 178, 1993 NJW 3269,
   123 BGHZ 268

Oberlandesgerichte (OLG)

OLG Saarbrücken 31.1.1989 *Re French Insolvency Proceedings* [1991] I.L.Pr. 459
OLG Zweibrücken 30.6.1992 IPRspr. 1992 Nr. 267
OLG Hamburg 21.9.1995 IPRspr. 1995 Nr. 169, 1996 NJW-RR 510
OLG Köln 6.6.1997 IPRspr. 1997 Nr. 148
OLG Jena 5.8.1998 1998 IPRspr. No.151, 1999 RIW 703
OLG Frankfurt/Main 5.11.1998 1998 IPRspr. Nr.192

Landgerichte/Amtsgerichte (LG/AG)

LG Stuttgart 23.8.1995 IPRspr. 1995 Nr. 150
LG München 2.6.1997 1998 IPRax 117
LG Bonn 20.1.1999 1999 RIW 879

Art.2

Bundesgerichtshof (BGH)

BGH 12.5.1993 1994 IPRax 115, 1993 NJW 2753, 1993 RIW 846, *Re a Counterclaim under
   Italian Law* [1995] I.L.Pr. 133
BGH 4.12.1997 IPRspr. 1997 Nr. 188, 1998 IPRax 205, BGH 4.12.1997 *Dieter Krombach* 1999
   EuZW 26, [1998] I.L.Pr. 681

Oberlandesgerichte (OLG)

OLG Hamm 11.7.1988 1989 IPRax 107
OLG Hamm 28.1.1994 1995 NJW-RR 187
OLG Frankfuhrt 17.10.1995 1998 IPRax 35, IPRspr. 1996 Nr. 137
OLG Oldenburg 15.3.1996 1997 IPRax 46
KG 17.11.1997 IPRspr. 1997 Nr. 162, 1999 IPRax 37
OLG Düsseldorf 25.8.1999 2000 IPRax 534

Landgerichte/Amtsgerichte (LG/AG)

LG Heidelberg 30.11.1982 1984 IPRax 99

Art.5(2)

Art.5(3)

Art.5(5)

Oberlandesgerichte (OLG)

OLG Düsseldorf 14.1.1994 1994 NJW-RR 1132
OLG Düsseldorf 26.5.1995 IPRspr. 1995 Nr.145
OLG München 29.5.1998 1998 IPRspr. No.144, 1999 RIW 872

Landgerichte/Amtsgerichte (LG/AG)

LG Wuppertal 8.9.1993 1994 NJW-RR 191
LG Berlin 28.9.1995 IPRspr. 1995 Nr. 154
LG Stuttgart 9.2.1996 1998 IPRax 100, IPRspr. 1996 Nr. 140
LG Krefeld 29.4.1996 *Richard Zellner v Phillip Alexander Securities and Futures Limited* [1997]
    I.L.Pr. 716
AG Hamburg 7.7.1999 2000 NJW-RR 352
LG München 19.8.1999 2000 NJW-RR 567

Art.6(1)

Bundesgerichtshof (BGH)

BGH 19.3.1987 IPRspr. Nr. 124, 1988 NJW 646
Landgerichte/Amtsgerichte (LG/AG)
LG Düsseldorf 16.1.1996 IPRspr. 1996 Nr. 138A

Art.6(2)

Bundesgerichtshof (BGH)

BGH 18.9.1997 IPRspr. 1997 Nr. 184, 1998 IPRax 205

Landgerichte/Amtsgerichte (LG/AG)

OLG Hamm 27.6.1996 1998 IPRax 202, IPRspr. 1996 Nr. 178

Art.6(3)

Bundesgerichtshof (BGH)

BGH 12.5.1993 IPRspr. 1993 Nr. 139, 1993 NJW 2753, 1993 RIW 846, IPRax 115, *Re a*
    Counterclaim under Italian Law [1995] I.L.Pr. 133

Oberlandesgerichte (OLG)

OLG München 25.3.1992 *Re a Counterclaim under Italian Law* [1993] I.L.Pr. 388
OLG Koblenz 17.9.1993 1993 IPRspr. Nr. 35, 1993 RIW 934

Landgerichte/Amtsgerichte (LG/AG)

AG Mainz 23.2.1983 IPRspr. 1983 Nr. 134a / *LG Mainz* 8.11.1983 IPRspr. 1983 Nr. 134b
LG Mainz 8.11.1983 1984 IPRax 100
LG München 20.3.1995 1996 IPRax 31
LG Kassel 15.2.1996 IPRspr. 1996 Nr. 30
LG Berlin 19.3.1996 IPRspr. 1996 Nr. 32
LG Duisburg 17.4.1996 IPRspr. 1996 Nr. 148
LG Köln 9.10.1996 IPRspr. 1996 Nr. 156

Landgerichte/Amtsgerichte (LG/AG)

Art.18

Bundesgerichtshof (BGH)

Oberlandesgerichte (OLG)

Landgerichte/Amtsgerichte (LG/AG)

Art.20

Bundesgerichtshof (BGH)

BGH 10.7.1986 1987 IPRax 172, IPRspr. 1986 Nr.172b, IPRspr. 1986 Nr. 182

Art.21

Bundesgerichtshof (BGH)

BGH 9.10.1985 IPRspr. 1985 Nr. 166, 1986 NJW 662, 1987 IPRax 314, 1986 JuS 481
BGH 10.10.1985 1986 NJW 2195
BGH 28.11.1985 1986 IPRax 293, *Re Proceedings in Two fora* [1987] E.C.C. 273
BGH 12.2.1992 1994 IPRax 40
BGH 8.2.1995 IPRspr. 1995 Nr. 165, 1995 NJW 1758, 1995 RIW 413, 1996 IPRax 192, *Re a
   Sale of Shares* [1996] I.L.Pr. 292
BGH 11.12.1996 1997 IPRax 348, 1997 RIW 421, 1997 WM 985, IPRspr. 1996 Nr. 171, 134
   BGHZ 201, 1997 NJW 870
OLG München 17.7.1997 IPRspr. 1997 Nr. 179

Oberlandesgerichte (OLG)

OLG München 31.10.1984 IPRspr. 1984 Nr. 169, 1986 RIW 815, 1985 IPRax 338
OLG Hamm 25.9.1985 1986 IPRax 233, 1986 RIW 383
OLG Hamm 6.7.1988 1988 NJW 3102
OLG Hamburg 25.10.1990 1990 IPRspr. Nr. 193
OLG Koblenz 30.11.1990 IPRspr. 1990 Nr. 194, 1991 RIW 63, *S.A. C.V. A Belgian Frim v S.
   GmbH* [1991] I.L.Pr. 588, 1991 EuZW 158
OLG Köln 13.12.1990 IPRspr. 1990 Nr. 195, 1991 NJW 1427, 1991 RIW 328, 1992 IPRax 89
OLG Hamm 25.11.1992 IPRspr. 1992 Nr. 214
OLG Hamm 3.12.1993 IPRspr. 1993 Nr. 164, 1995 IPRax 104
OLG München 22.12.1993 IPRspr. 1993 Nr. 165, 1994 RIW 511, 1994 IPRax 308, *Re a Clothing
   Sale Contract* [1995] I.L.Pr. 172
OLG München 17.7.1997 IPRspr. 1997 Nr. 179, *Re Termination of an Agency Contract* [1998]
   I.L.Pr. 815
OLG Köln 21.8.1997 IPRspr. 1997 Nr. 180
HansOLG Hamburg 6.2.1998 1998 IPRspr. No.175, 1999 IPRax 168, 1998 RIW 889, [2000]
   I.L.Pr. 249
OLG München 2.6.1998 1998 IPRspr. No.177, 1998 RIW 631, 1998 RIW 631, *Re Lifting of a
   Stay of Proceedings* [1999]. I.L.Pr. 291
OLG Stuttgart 24.11.1999 2000 RIW 954

Landgerichte/Amtsgerichte (LG/AG)

LG Frankfurt 22.2.1988 1989 IPRspr. Nr. 210a, 1989 IPRspr. Nr. 210b
LG München II 6.3.1997 IPRspr. 1997 Nr. 177, 1998 IPRax 477
LG Düsseldorf 27.1.1998 1998 IPRspr. No.174, 1999 RIW 147, 1998 GRUR Int. 803
LG Düsseldorf 27.2.1998 1998 GRUR Int. 804
OLG München 3.12.1999 2000 RIW 712

Art.22

Oberlandesgerichte (OLG)

OLG Hamm 18.10.1982 IPRspr. 1982 Nr. 19, 1983 NJW 523, 1983 RIW/AWD 56, 1983
   RIW/AWD 207
OLG Hamm 25.9.1985 IPRspr. 1985 Nr. 165, 1986 RIW 383

Art.24

Art.25

Art.26

Art.27(1)

Bundesgerichtshof (BGH)

Oberlandesgerichte (OLG)

Landgerichte/Amtsgerichte (LG/AG)

Art.27(2)

Bundesgerichtshof (BGH)

Landgerichte/Amtsgerichte (LG/AG)

Art.27(3)

Bundesgerichtshof (BGH)

Oberlandesgerichte (OLG)

Art.28

Bundesgerichtshof (BGH)

Oberlandesgerichte (OLG)

Art.29

Bundesgerichtshof (BGH)

BGH 16.5.1979 IPRspr. 1979 Nr. 199, 1980 NJW 528, 1979 NJW 2477, 1980 RIW/AWD 61,
   1979 RIW/AWD 570, 74 BGHZ 278, *Re Enforcement of a French Sequestration Order*
   [1979] E.C.C. 321
BGH 22.6.1983 1984 IPRax 202, IPRspr. 1983 Nr. 176, 1984 NJW 568, 1983 RIW 695,
   88 BGHZ 17
BGH 28.6.1984 1985 IPRax 101, IPRspr. 1984 Nr. 177
BGH 9.7.1992 1993 IPRax 244, 1992 RIW 1025

Art.31

Oberlandesgerichte (OLG)

OLG Hamm 6.12.1977 IPRspr. 1977 Nr. 168
OLG Frankfurt 31.7.1979 IPRspr. 1979 Nr. 202
OLG Hamm 10.9.1979 IPRspr. 1979 Nr. 203
OLG Koblenz 5.11.1985 1987 IPRax 24, IPRspr. 1985 Nr. 183, 1986 RIW 469
OLG Saarbrücken 11.8.1989 1990 IPRax 232, IPRspr. 1989 Nr. 217, *Re French Court Costs*
   [1992] I.L.Pr. 146
OLG Karlsruhe 3.12.1990 1991 RIW 859
OLG München 22.6.1992 IPRspr. 1992 Nr. 223
OLG Saarbrücken 1.10.1993 1995 IPRax 35, 1994 NJW-RR 636
OLG Saarbrücken 5.1.1994 1995 IPRax 244, 1994 RIW 1048, 1994 NJW-RR 638
OLG Karlsruhe 19.12.1994 IPRspr. 1995 Nr. 166
OLG Oldenburg 25.5.1995 IPRspr. 1995 Nr. 180
OLG Düsseldorf 23.8.1995 IPRspr. 1995 Nr. 168, 1996 RIW 67
OLG Düsseldorf 10.7.1996 1998 IPRax 279
OLG Stuttgart 15.5.1997 1997 RIW 684, 1998 NJW-RR 280
OLG Düsseldorf 18.7.1997 IPRspr. 1997 Nr. 173, 1998 NJW-RR 283
KG 28.11.1997 IPRspr. 1997 Nr. 187, 1998 RIW 630
KG 4.9.1998 1998 IPRspr. No.170, 2001 IPRax 236
OLG Düsseldorf 11.1.1999 1999 RIW 540

Landgerichte/Amtsgerichte (LG/AG)

LG Münster 21.6.1978 1980 NJW 1234, IPRspr. 1978 Nr. 153, 1978 RIW/AWD 686
LG Hamburg 31.8.1987 1989 IPRax 162, IPRspr. 1987 Nr. 156A
LG Stuttgart 28.3.1988 1989 IPRax 41, IPRspr. 1988 Nr. 207, 1988 RIW 563
LG Berlin 15.12.1988 1989 NJW 1434
LG Karlsruhe 7.12.1990 1992 IPRax 92, 1991 RIW 156
LG Darmstadt 8.12.1998 2000 IPRax 309

Art.32

Oberlandesgerichte (OLG)

OLG Stuttgart 25.1.1980 IPRspr. 1980 Nr. 163
OLG Düsseldorf 5.10.1983 IPRspr. 1983 Nr. 180
OLG Zweibrücken 14.9.1999 2001 NJW-RR 144
OLG Saarbücken 24.9.1992 IPRspr. 1992 Nr. 225, 1993 RIW 672
OLG Frankfurt/Main 2.12.1998 1998 IPRspr. Nr.195

Art.34

Oberlandesgerichte (OLG)

Art.36

Bundesgerichtshof (BGH)

Oberlandesgerichte (OLG)

Art.37

Bundesgerichtshof (BGH)

Oberlandesgerichte (OLG)

Art.38

Bundesgerichtshof (BGH)

Oberlandesgerichte (OLG)

OLG Koblenz 27.9.1976 IPRspr. 1976 Nr. 174, 1977 RIW/AWD 102
OLG Düsseldorf 19.9.1984 IPRspr. 1984 Nr. 190, 1985 RIW 492
OLG Düsseldorf 19.10.1984 1985 RIW 493, *Re the Enforcement of a French Judgment* [1986]
   E.C.C. 472
OLG Karlsruhe 29.1.1986 1987 IPRax 171, IPRspr. 1986 Nr. 172a, IPRspr. 1986 Nr.172b,
   1986 RIW 467
OLG Hamm 28.12.1993 1994 RIW 243, 1995 NJW-RR 189
OLG Düsseldorf 10.7.1996 1998 IPRax 279
OLG Stuttgart 15.5.1997 1997 RIW 684, 1998 NJW-RR 280

Art.39

Bundesgerichtshof (BGH)

BGH 25.2.1983 IPRspr. 1983 Nr. 174a, IPRspr. 1983 Nr.174b, 1983 NJW 1980 , 1983 NJW
   1979, 1983 RIW 290, 1983 RIW 535, 87 BGHZ 259

Oberlandesgerichte (OLG)

OLG Düsseldorf 27.1998 1998 IPRspr. Nr.187

Landgerichte/Amtsgerichte (LG/AG)

LG Stuttgart 28.3.1988 1989 IPRax 41, IPRspr. 1988 Nr. 207, 1988 RIW 563

Art.41

Bundesgerichtshof (BGH)

BGH 21.2.1985 1986 IPRax 157, IPRspr. 1985 Nr. 173

Oberlandesgerichte (OLG)

OLG Celle 29.2.1988 1988 RIW 565

Art.47

Oberlandesgerichte (OLG)

OLG Frankfurt 1.9.1987 IPRspr. 1987 Nr. 157
OLG Frankfurt 8.6.1988 IPRspr. 1988 Nr. 198
OLG Karlsruhe 3.12.1990 1991 RIW 859
OLG Oldenburg 22.8.1991 1991 RIW 950, 1991 IPRspr. Nr. 209
OLG Frankfuhrt/M 8.5.1992 *Re Enforcement of an Italian judgment* [1993] I.L.Pr. 353
OLG Köln 10.2.1993 IPRspr. 1993 Nr. 168
OLG Düsseldorf 27.11.1996 1997 RIW 330, 1998 IPRax 478, IPRspr. 1996 Nr. 183
OLG Hamm 11.2.1997 IPRspr. 1997 Nr. 170, *Re Curing a defective Service of Judgment* [1998] I.L.Pr.
   819
OLG Saarbrücken 24.11.1997 IPRspr. 1997 Nr. 186
OLG Franfurt a/M 9.4.1998 1998 IPRspr. No.184, 1998 RIW 474
OLG Frankfurt/Main 28.10.1998 1998 IPRspr. Nr.191

Art.50

Bundesgerichtshof (BGH)

BGH 26.6.1997 IPRspr. 1997 Nr. 183, 1998 RIW 146 *Unibank A/S v Fleming G. Christensen*
   [1998] I.L.Pr. 224

Oberlandesgerichte (OLG)

OLG *Koblenz* 5.11.1985 1987 IPRax 24, IPRspr. 1985 Nr. 183, 1986 RIW 469

Art.52

Landgerichte/Amtsgerichte (LG/AG)

LG *Darmstadt* 11.9.1996 1998 IPRax 198

Art.53

Landgerichte/Amtsgerichte (LG/AG)

LG *München* 19.8.1999 2000 NJW-RR 567

Art.54

OLG *Naumburg* 5.10.2000 2001 RIW 700

Art.57

Bundesgerichtshof (BGH)

BGH 10.10.1977 1978 NJW 1113, 1978 RIW/AWD 56

Oberlandesgerichte (OLG)

OLG *Düsseldorf* 1.3.1979 IPRspr. 1979 Nr. 157
OLG *Dresden* 24.11.1998 1998 IPRspr. No.162, 1999 RIW 968, 2000 IPRax 121

Landgerichte/Amtsgerichte (LG/AG)

LG *Aachen* 16.1.1976 IPRspr. 1976 Nr. 128, 1976 RIW/AWD 588
LG *Freiburg* 20.10.1994 IPRspr. 1995 Nr. 141a / OLG *Karlsruhe* 7.12.1995 IPRspr. 1995
    Nr. 141b
ArbG *Wiesbaden* 15.4.1998 1998 IPRspr. Nr.143

Italian, Dutch, Spanish, Norwegian and Swedish Cases
Art.1

Gerechtshof , The Hague 7.1.1987 *Menten v The Federal Republic of Germany* [1991]
    I.L.Pr. 259
Hoge Raad 30.11.1990 *Franciscus Maria Molenschot v Johannes Lambertus Molenschot* [1993]
    I.L.Pr. 81
Corte di Cassazione 25.1.1991 *Marc Rich & Co. AG. v Italimpianti SpA* [1993] I.L.Pr. 402
Arrodissementsrechtbank Amsterdam 14.6.1995 *Antonius van den Boogaard v Paula Laumen*
    [1996] I.L.Pr. 654
Norges Høyesterett 18.1.1996 *Norsk Hydro and Hydro Aluminium AS v Alumix Spa* [1998]
    I.L.Pr. 83

Art.2

Hoge Raad 13.2.1987 1988 Rev. crit. 555
Audencia Prov De Barcelona 15.2.1994 1995 R.E.D.I.211
District Court of the Hague 29.10.1997 *Julio Cesar Palmaz and ors. v Boston Scientific
    B.V. and ors.* [1998] FSR 199

Art.5(3)

Art.5(5)

Art.6(1)

Art.6(2)

Art.6(3)

Art.16(1)

Art.16(4)

Art.17

Art.18

Art.21

Art.22

Art.24

Art.25

Art.26

Art.27(1)

Art.27(2)

Art.27(3)

Art.31

Art.37

Tribunal Supremo 23.3.1999 *A.SA / I.* 1999 La Ley 14, no.4799

Art.41

Gerechtshof, Amsterdam 27.2.1992 *La medicale Equipex SA v Farmitalia Carlo Erba Srl* [1995] I.L.Pr. 577

Art.46

Corte di Cassazione 1.8.1997 *Commerzbank AG contro Critelli* 1998 Riv. dir int. priv e proc.570

Art.47

Arrondissementsrechtbank, Breda, 11.4.1984, *W.M. Brähmer as liquidator of Bekleidungswerke Wilhelm Cruse GmbH & Co. KG v Maria Louer- Van Loon and Cornelia Wigleven-Eijsermans* [1986] E.C.C. 178

Corte di Cassazione 1.8.1997 *Commerzbank AG contro Critelli* 1998 Riv. dir int. priv e proc.570

Art.50

Arrondissementsrechtbank Maastricht 11.11.1981 *Re Enforcement of a Foreign Bill of Costs* [1983] E.C.C. 551

Arrondissementsrechtbank, Roermond 18.12.1986 *Guyot de Mishaegen and another v Generale Bankmaatschappij N.V.* [1990] I.L.Pr. 349

Art.53

Gerechtshof, The Hague 29.2.1980 *Tropical Shipping Company v Dammers & Van der Heide's Scheepvaart en handelsbedrijf BV* [1982] E.C.C. 353

Tribunal Suprema 22.67.1999 *Intraensa c Herrera Serrano S.L.* 1999 REDI 733

Art.54

Corte di Cassazione 28.5.1998 *Fallimento Adorno contro Duménil Leblé* 1999 Riv. dir int. priv e proc.296

Art.57

Corte di Cassazione 28.10.1987 *Srl Siamar and Nedlloyd Lijnen B.V. v Srl Spedimex* [1990] I.L.Pr. 266

Hoge Raad 12.9.1997 *United Towing Ltd / Micoperi Offshore SpA* 1997 NJ 1644

Swiss and Austrian Cases

Art.1

Bundesgericht 18.1.1996 *Firma T S.r.l gegen Firma S.AG* 18.1.1996 122 BGE, III, 43 *Re the Supply of Equipment for the Purification of waste gases* [1998] I.L.Pr. 77

Bundesgericht 19.8.1998 *Dresdner Forfaitierungs AG gegen Sezione Speciale per l'assicurazione del credito all'esportazione* 124 BGE, III, 436

Bundesgericht 20.8.1998 *Banque Bruxelles Lambert Suisse SA et huit consorts contre République de Paraguay et Sezione speciale per l'assicurazione del credito all'esportazione* 124 BGE, III, 382

Art.5(2)

Art.5(3)

Art.5(5)

Art.6(1)

Art.6(2)

Art.7

Art.8

Art.11

Bundesgericht 20.8.1998 *Banque Bruxelles Lambert Suisse SA et huit consorts contre République de Paraguay et Sezione speciale per l'assicurazione del credito all'esportazione* 124 BGE, III, 382

Art.12

Bundesgericht 19.8.1998 *Dresdner Forfaitierungs AG gegen Sezione Speciale per l'assicurazione del credito all'esportazione* 124 BGE, III, 436

Bundesgericht 20.8.1998 *Banque Bruxelles Lambert Suisse SA et huit consorts contre République de Paraguay et Sezione speciale per l'assicurazione del credito all'esportazione* 124 BGE, III, 382

Art.13

Bundesgericht *Corinphila gegen Jaeger* 4.8.1995 121 BGE, III, 336
OGH 22.10.1997 1998 ZfRV 256

Art.14

Bundesgericht *Corinphila gegen Jaeger* 4.8.1995 121 BGE, III, 336
OGH 15.10.1996 *Entscheidungen des österreichischen Obersten Gerichtshofes in Zivil- und Justizverwaltungssachen* 69 Band, 1996, No.227, p.518
OGH 22.10.1997 1998 ZfRV 256

Art.16(1)

OGH 15.1.1998 *Entscheidungen des österreichischen Obersten Gerichtshofes in Zivil- und Justizverwaltungssachen* 71 Band, 1998, No.2, p.8, 1998 Juristische Blätter 380
OGH 25.6.1998 1998 Juristische Blätter 731
OGH 10.12.1998 *Entscheidungen des österreichischen Obersten Gerichtshofes in Zivil- und Justizverwaltungssachen* 71 Band, 1998, No.206/7, *OGH* 2000 RfRV 78
OGH 16.9.1999 2000 RfRV 79
OGH 29.9.1999 6 Ob 207/99f, unreported,
   http://curia.eu.int/common/recdoc/convention/en/2000/16–2000.htm
OGH 23.11.1999 2000 RfRV 114

Art.16(2)

OLG Wien 5.11.1998 1999 Juristische Blätter 259

Art.16(4)

Bundesgericht 21.8.1996 1999 GRUR Int. 187
Bundesgericht *Banque Audi Suisse S.A. contre Volkswagen Bank GmbH* 13.11.1998 124 BGE, III, 509

Art.16(5)

Bundesgericht 18.11.1998 124 BGE, III, 505
OGH 5.1.1998 1999 IPRax 47, 1998 Juristische Blätter 381

Art.17

Art.18

Art.21

Art.22

Art.24

Bundesgericht *SodaStream Ltd. gegen Urs Jäger AG* 17.9.1999 125 BGE, III, 451
OGH 12.4.2000 2000 ZfRV 231

Art.25

OGH 16.6.1999 2000 ZfRV 30
OGH 26.4.2000 2000 ZfRV 231
Bundesgericht *S contre X en liquidation* 8.2.2000 126 BGE III, 156
Bundesgericht 13.9.2001 *Z AG gegen Y. SpA*, unreported

Art.26

OGH 16.6.1999 2000 ZfRV 30

Art.27(1)

OGH 26.4.2000 2000 ZfRV 231
Bundesgericht *G Ltd contre K* 19.9.2000 126 BGE III, 534
Bundesgericht 5.7.2001 X *contrre l'arrêt rendu le 11.1.2001...Y Ltd*, unreported
Bundesgericht 23.7.2001 *M.R. gegen H AG*, unreported

Art.27(2)

Bundesgericht *X. Financial Services GmbH gegen W.* 12.6.1997, 123 BGE, III, 374
OGH 24.6.1998 *Entscheidungen des österreichischen Obersten Gerichtshofes in Zivil- und Justizverwaltungssachen* 71 Band, 1998, No.109, p.677, 1999 ZfRV 70
Bundesgericht *G contre S* 7.3.2000, unreported
OGH 12.7.2000 2001 ZfRV 68
OGH 12.7.2000 2001 ZfRV 68
OGH 20.9.2000 2001 ZfRV 114

Art.28

OGH 24.6.1998 *Entscheidungen des österreichischen Obersten Gerichtshofes in Zivil- und Justizverwaltungssachen* 71 Band, 1998, No.109, p.677, 1999 ZfRV 70

Art.29

OGH 19.10.2000 2001 ZfRV 72

Art.31

Bundesgericht 13.9.2001 Z AG gegen Y. SpA, unreported

Art.34

OGH 24.6.1998 *Entscheidungen des österreichischen Obersten Gerichtshofes in Zivil- und Justizverwaltungssachen* 71 Band, 1998, No.109, p.677, 1998 Juristische Blätter 729, 1999 ZfRV 70
OGH 12.7.2000 2001 ZfRV 68
OGH 12.7.2000 2001 ZfRV 68
OGH 20.9.2000 2001 ZfRV 114

Art.38

Bundesgericht 13.9.2001 Z AG gegen Y. SpA, unreported

Art.39

Bundesgericht 7.7.2000 *Soc S et Soc D contre Cour d'appel du Tribunal cantonal de Fribourg*, 126 BGE, III, 438
Bundesgericht 10.11.2000 X *gegen Urteil des Obergerichts*, unreported

Art.57

OGH 11.5.2000 2001 ZfRV 73

United Kingdom and Irish Cases

Art.1

Court of Appeal/Court of Session (Inner House)

Marc Rich & Co. A.G. v Societa Italiana Impianti P.A. (The 'Atlantic Emperor') [1989] 1 Lloyd's Rep. 548, CA
Aggeliki Charis Compania Maritima S.A. v Pagnan S.p.A (The 'Angelic Grace') [1995] 1 Lloyd's Rep. 87, CA
Firswood Ltd v Petra Bank [1996] CLC 608, CA
Philip Alexander Securities & Futures Ltd v Bamberger & Ors and related action [1996] CLC 1780, [1997] I.L.Pr. 73, CA
Alfred Toepfer International GmbH v Société Cargill France [1998] 1 Lloyd's Rep. 379
QRS 1 Aps and others v Frandsen [1999] 3 All ER 289, [1999] 1 WLR 2169, [1999] I.L.Pr. 432, [2000] I.L.Pr. 8, CA

High Court (First Instance)/Irish High Court/Court of Session (Outer House)

CFEM Facades S.A. v Bovis Construction Limited [1992] I.L.Pr. 561, QBD
Aiglon Ltd and another v Gau Shan Co Ltd Gau Shan Co Ltd v Aiglon Ltd and others [1993] BCLC 1321, QBD, Hirst J
Partenreederei M/S 'Heidberg' and ors v Grosvenor Grain and Feed Co. Ltd. (The 'Heidberg') [1994 2 Lloyd's Rep. 287, Diamond QC
Qingdao Ocean Shipping Co. v Grace Shipping Establishment (The 'Xing Su Hai') [1995] 2 Lloyd's Rep. 15, Rix J
Arab Business Consortium International Finance and Investment Co. v Banque Franco-Tunisienne [1996] 1 Lloyd's Rep. 485, Waller J
In re Hayward, deceased [1997] Ch. 45, Rattee J
Lexmar Corporation and Steamship Mutual Underwriting Association (Bermuda) Ltd v Nordisk Skibsrederforening and Northern Tankers (Cyprus) Ltd. [1997] 1 Lloyd's Rep. 289, Colman J
Philip Alexander Securities & Futures Ltd v Bamberger & Ors and related action [1996] CLC 1757, Waller J
Union de Remorquage et de Sauvetage S.A. v Lake Avery Inc. (The 'Lake Avery') [1997] 1 Lloyd's Rep. 540, [1997] CLC 683, QBD, Clarke J
Richard Zellner v Phillip Alexander Securities and Futures Limited [1997] I.L.Pr. 730, Jackson QC
UBS AG v Omni Holding AG (in liq.) [2000] 1 All ER (Comm) 42, [2000] 1 WLR 916, [2000] I.L.Pr. 51, Ch.D., Rimer J
R v Crown Court at Harrow and another, ex parte UNIC Centre Sarl [2000] All ER 449, QBD, Newman J
Ashurst v Pollard and another [2000] 2 All ER 772, Ch. D., Jacob J
Vale Do Rio Doce Navegacao v Shanghai Bao Steel Ocean Shipping Co. Ltd. [2000] 2 All ER (Comm) 70, Thomas J
Bruno Tassan Din and another v Banco Ambrosiano S.p.A [1991] 1 I.R. 569, HC
Credit Suisse & Credit Suisse Canada v CH (Ireland) Inc (in liquidation), 2.2.1996, Irish HC

Art.2

House of Lords/Irish Supreme Court

Court of Appeal/Court of Session (Inner House)

High Court (First Instance)/Irish High Court/Court of Session (Outer House)

Art.3

Court of Appeal/Court of Session (Inner House)

High Court (First Instance)/Irish High Court/Court of Session (Outer House)

Art.4

Court of Appeal/Court of Session (Inner House)

High Court (First Instance)/Irish High Court/Court of Session (Outer House)

Art.5(1)

House of Lords/Irish Supreme Court

Art.5(3)

House of Lords/Irish Supreme Court

Court of Appeal/Court of Session (Inner House)

Court of Appeal/Court of Session (Inner House)

Barclays Bank Plc v Glasgow City Council Kleinwort Benson Ltd v Glasgow City Council [1994]
  4 All ER 882, CA
Gascoine and another v Pyrah and another [1994] I.L.Pr. 82, CA
Fort Dodge Animal Health Limited v Akzo Nobel N.V. [1998] FSR 222
Canada Trust Co. and others v Stolzenberg and others (No.2) [1998] 1 WLR 547, [1998] 1
  All ER 318, CA
Pearce v Ove Arup Partnership Ldt and others [2000] Ch. 403, CA
Surzur Overseas Ltd v Koros & Ors [1999] CLC 801, CA
National Justice Compania Naviera S.A. v Prudential Assurance Co. Ltd. (The 'Ikarian Reefer'
  (No.2)) [2000] 1 Lloyd's Rep. 129, CA
Messier-Dowty Ltd and anor v Sabena S.A. and ors (No.2) [2000] 1 WLR 2040, [2000] 1 All
  ER (Comm) 833, [2000] 1 Lloyd's Rep. 428, CA
Brian Watson v First Choice Holidays and Flights Ltd and Aparta Hotels Caledonia S.A.,
  [2001] 2 Lloyd's Rep. 339

High Court (First Instance)/Irish High Court/Court of Session (Outer House)

Gascoine and another v Pyrah and another Independent 11.12.1991, QBD, Southwell QC
Barclays Bank Plc v Glasgow City Council; Kleinwort Benson Ltd v Glasgow City Council [1994]
  4 All ER 865, QBD, Hirst J
Aiglon Ltd and another v Gau Shan Co Ltd Gau Shan Co Ltd v Aiglon Ltd and others [1993]
  BCLC 1321, QBD, Hirst J
Qingdao Ocean Shipping Co. v Grace Shipping Establishment (The 'Xing Su Hai') [1995] 2
  Lloyd's Rep. 15, Rix J
Chiron Corporation v Evans Medical Ltd and others [1996] FSR 863, PCt, Walker J
Pearce v Ove Arup Partnership Ldt and others [1997] Ch. 293, [1997] 3 All ER 31, Ch.D.,
  Lloyd J
Coin Controls Ltd v Suzo International (UK) Ltd and others [1999] Ch. 33, [1997] 3 All ER 45,
  Ch.D, Laddie J
Petrotrade Inc and others v Smith and others [1998] 2 All ER 346, QBD
MacDonald v Federation International de Football Association 1999 SLT 1129, OH
Compagnie Commerciale Andre S.A. v Artibell Shipping Co. Ltd and Bank of Scotland [1999]
  SLT 1051, 1999 S.C.L.R 349, OH
Casio Computer Co. Ltd v Sayo and others [2001] I.L.Pr. 694, CA
Valerie Gannon v British and Irish Steam-packet Company Ltd, Landliner Travel Merseyside
  Limited and Edenderry Transport Ltd. [1993] 2 I.R. 359, [1995] IJEL 97, HC
Helen Kelly v Robert McCarthy and ors 1995 IJEL 91, Irish HC
Constance Short and ors v Ireland, The Attorney General & ors. [1996] 2 IR 188, HC

Art.6(2)

Court of Appeal/Court of Session (Inner House)

National Justice Compania Naviera S.A. v Prudential Assurance Co. Ltd. (The 'Ikarian Reefer'
  (No.2)) [2000] 1 Lloyd's Rep. 129, CA

High Court (First Instance)/Irish High Court/Court of Session (Outer House)

Société Commerciale de Réassurance and others v Eras International Ltd and others (No.2)
  [1995] 2 All ER 278, Potter J
Kinnear and others v Falconfilms NV and others (Hospital Ruber Internacional and another,
  third parties) [1994] 3 All ER 42, QBD, Phillips J
Hough v P & O Containers Ltd [1999] Q.B. 834, [1998] 2 All ER 978

Waterford Wedgwood plc & Anor v David Nagli Ltd & ors., [1998] CLC 1011, [1999] I.L.Pr.9,
    Ch.D, Aldous QC
*Trustor AB v Barclays Bank Plc (F Van Lanschot Bankiers (Luxembourg) SA (Part 20
    Defendant))*, 24.10.2000, Ch.D., Rimer J

Art.6(3)

House of Lords/Irish Supreme Court

*International Commercial Bank Plc v The Insurance Corporation of Ireland Plc, The Meadows
    Indemnity Company Ltd, third party* [1989] I.R. 453, SC

High Court (First Instance)/Irish High Court/Court of Session (Outer House)

*International Commercial Bank Plc v The Insurance Corporation of Ireland Plc, The Meadows
    Indemnity Company Ltd, third party* [1989] I.R. 453, HC

Art.8

House of Lords/Irish Supreme Court

Minister for Agriculture, Food and Forestry v Alte Leipziger Versicherung AG t/a Alte Leipziger
    [2001] 1 ILRM 519, SC

High Court (First Instance)/Irish High Court/Court of Session (Outer House)

S. & W. Berisford Plc and another v New Hampshire Insurance Co. [1990] 2 QB 631,
    Hobhouse J

Art.11

House of Lords/Irish Supreme Court

Jordan Grand Prix Ltd v Baltic Insurance Group and others [1999] 2 AC 127, [1999] 2 WLR
    134, HL
Agnew and others v Lansförsäkringsbolagens AB [2001] 1 AC 223, HL

Court of Appeal/Court of Session (Inner House)

New Hampshire Insurance Co. and others v Strabag Bau A.G. and others [1992] 1 Lloyd's Rep.
    361, CA
John Robert Charman and Mark E. Brockbank v WOC Offshore B.V. [1993] 2 Lloyd's Rep.
    551, CA
Agnew and others v Lansförsäkringsbolagens AB [1997] 4 All ER 937, CA
Jordan Grand Prix Ltd v Baltic Insurance Group and others [1998] 3 All ER 418, [1998] 1
    WLR 1049, CA

High Court (First Instance)/Irish High Court/Court of Session (Outer House)

John Robert Charman and Mark E. Brockbank v WOC Offshore B.V. [1993] 1 Lloyd's Rep.
    378, Hirst J
Agnew and others v Lansförsäkringsbolagens AB [1996] 4 All ER 978; [1996] Lloyd's Rep.
    IR 392, QBD
New Hampshire Insurance Co. and others v Strabag Bau A.G. and others [1990] 2 Lloyd's
    Rep. 61, QBD, Potter J,

Art.12

Court of Appeal/Court of Session (Inner House)

John Robert Charman and Mark E. Brockbank v WOC Offshore B.V. [1993] 2 Lloyd's Rep.
  551, CA

High Court (First Instance)/Irish High Court/Court of Session (Outer House)

John Robert Charman and Mark E. Brockbank v WOC Offshore B.V. [1993] 1 Lloyd's Rep.
  378, Hirst J
*The Charterers Mutual Assurance Association Limited v British & Foreign and T.M.M.
  Transcap* [1998] I.L.Pr. 838, QBD, Diamond QC

Art.12A

Court of Appeal/Court of Session (Inner House)

John Robert Charman and Mark E. Brockbank v WOC Offshore B.V. [1993] 2 Lloyd's Rep.
  551, CA

High Court (First Instance)/Irish High Court/Court of Session (Outer House)

John Robert Charman and Mark E. Brockbank v WOC Offshore B.V. [1993] 1 Lloyd's Rep.
  378, Hirst J
*The Charterers Mutual Assurance Association Limited v British & Foreign and T.M.M.
  Transcap* [1998] I.L.Pr. 838, QBD, Diamond QC

Art.13(1)

High Court (First Instance)/Irish High Court/Court of Session (Outer House)

Standard Bank London Ltd v Dimitrios and Styliani Apostolakis [2001] Lloyd's Rep. Bank
  240, [2000] I.L.Pr. 766, QBD, Longmore J

Art.16(1)

Court of Appeal/Court of Session (Inner House)

*Jarrett and another v Barclays Bank plc and another; Jones and another v First National
  Bank plc ; Peacock and another v First National Bank plc* [1999] Q.B. 1, [1997] 2 All ER 484
Ashurst v Pollard and another [2001] 2 WLR 722, CA

High Court (First Instance)/Irish High Court/Court of Session (Outer House)

Webb v Webb [1992] 1 All ER 17, Ch.D., Baker QC
Barratt International Resorts Ltd v Martin [1994] SLT 434, OH
In re Hayward, deceased [1997] Ch. 45, Rattee J
Ashurst v Pollard and another [2000] 2 All ER 772, Ch. D., Jacob J

Art.16(2)

High Court (First Instance)/Irish High Court/Court of Session (Outer House)

Newtherapeutics Ltd v Katz and another [1991] 2 All ER 151, Ch.D., Knox J
Re Fagin's Bookshop Plc [1992] BCLC 118, Ch.D., Harman J
*Grupo Torras S.A. and Torras Hostench London Ltd. v Sheikh Fahad Mohammed al-Sabah and
  others* [1995] 1 Lloyd's Rep. 374, QBD, Mance J

Art.18

House of Lords/Irish Supreme Court

Court of Appeal/Court of Session (Inner House)

Marc Rich & Co. A.G. v Societa Italiana Impianti P.A. (The 'Atlantic Emperor') (No.2) [1992]
1 Lloyd's Rep. 624, CA
Hewden Stuart Heavy Cranes Ltd v Leo Gottwald Kommanditgesellschaft & others, Lexis, CA
British Mensa Ltd v Gallant, 30.5.1999, CA,

High Court (First Instance)/Irish High Court/Court of Session (Outer House)

British Steel Corporation v Allivane International Ltd [1988] SCLR 562
Jenic Properties Ltd. v Andy Thornton Architectural Antiques 1992 SLT 5, (Sh.Ct.)
Kurz v Stella Musical Veranstaltungs GmbH [1992] 1 All ER 630, Ch.D., Hoffmann J
Caltex Trading PTE Ltd. v Metro Trading International Inc. and others [2000] 1 All ER
(Comm) 108, [1999] 2 Lloyd's Rep. 724, Rix J
Campbell International Trading House Limited v Peter Van Aart [1993] I.L.Pr. 314, Irish HC
Amstrad PLC v Mike Walker [1995] IJEL 94, HC
Jay Murray, Murray Telecommunications Group Ltd and others v Times Newspapers Ltd [1995]
3 I.R. 244, Irish HC

Art.19

High Court (First Instance)/Irish High Court/Court of Session (Outer House)

Coin Controls Ltd v Suzo International (UK) Ltd and others [1999] Ch. 33, [1997] 3 All ER 45,
Ch.D, Laddie J

Art.21

House of Lords/Irish Supreme Court

*International Commercial Bank Plc v The Insurance Corporation of Ireland Plc, The Meadows
Indemnity Company Ltd, third party* [1989] I.R. 453, SC

Court of Appeal/Court of Session (Inner House)

The 'Filiatra Legacy' [1994] 1 Lloyd's Rep. 513
Owens Bank Ltd v Bracco and others [1991] 4 All ER 833, CA
The 'Maciej Rataj' [1992] 2 Lloyd's Rep. 552, CA
Continental Bank N.A. v Aeakos Compania Naviera S.A. and others [1994] 1 WLR 588
Neste Chemicals S.A. and others v DK Line S.A. and Tokumaru Kaiun K.K. (The 'Sargasso')
[1994] 3 All ER 180, CA
*Grupo Torras S.A. and Torras Hostench London Ltd. v Sheikh Fahad Mohammed al-Sabah and
others* [1996] 1 Lloyd's Rep. 7, CA
Berkeley Administration Incorporated v McClelland and others [1996] I.L.Pr 772, CA
Bryan Francis Fox v Naser Taher and others [1997] I.L.Pr. 441, CA
Sarrio SA v Kuwait Investment Authority [1997] 1 Lloyd's Rep. 113, CA
The 'Happy Fellow' [1998] 1 Lloyd's Rep. 13, [1998] I.L.Pr.440, CA
Fort Dodge Animal Health Limited v Akzo Nobel N.V. [1998] FSR 222
Davy International Ltd and others v Voest Alpine Industrieanlagenbau GmbH and others
[1999] 1 All ER 103
Haji-Ioannou & ors v Frangos & ors. [1999] CLC 1075, [1999] 2 Lloyd's Rep. 337, CA
Turner v Grovit [2000] 1 QB 345, [1999] 3 All ER 616, [1999] I.L.Pr. 656, CA
Lough Neagh Exploration Ltd v Morrice and another [1999] NI 281
Molins Plc v G.D. S.p.A. [2000] 1 WLR 1741, [2000] 2 Lloyd's Rep. 234, CA
*SDL International Ltd v Centre de Co-operation Internationale en Recherche Agronomique
pour le Developpement* [2001] CLC 903

Art.22

House of Lords/Irish Supreme Court

Court of Appeal/Court of Session (Inner House)

High Court (First Instance)/Irish High Court/Court of Session (Outer House)

Art.24

Court of Appeal/Court of Session (Inner House)

Babanhaft International Co. S.A. v Bassatne and another [1989] 2 WLR 232, CA
Union Carbide Corporation v BP Chemicals Ltd 1995 SLT 972
Republic of Haiti and others v Duvalier and others [1990] 1 QB 202, [1989] 1 All ER 456, CA
Alltrans Inc v Interdom Holdings Ltd (Johnson Stevens Agencies Ltd and others, third parties)
    [1991] 4 All ER 458, CA
Balkanbank v Taher (No.2) [1995] 1 WLR 1067, CA
S & T Bautrading v Nordling [1997] 3 All ER 718, CA
Iomega Corporation v Myrica (U.K.) Limited 1999 SLT 796, 1998 SC 636
Crédit Suisse Fides Trust SA v Cuoghi [1998] QB 818, [1997] 3 All ER 724, CA
Fort Dodge Animal Health Limited v Akzo Nobel N.V. [1998] FSR 222
ICFI Corporate Securities Fund Plc v International Corporation for Finance and Investment,
    17.3.1999, CA
Refco Inc. and another v Eastern Trading Co. and others [1999] 1 Lloyd's Rep. 159
Surzur Overseas Ltd v Koros & Ors [1999] CLC 801, CA

High Court (First Instance)/Irish High Court/Court of Session (Outer House)

X v Y and anther [1990] 1 QB 220, Diamond QC
CFEM Facades S.A. v Bovis Construction Limited [1992] I.L.Pr. 561, QBD
G v Caledonian Newspapers Ltd 1995 SLT 559
State of Brunei Darussalam v Bolkiah, The Times, 5.9.2000, Jacob J
Ryan and another v Friction Dynamics Ltd and others 2.6.2000, Times Law Reports 14 June
    2000 459, Neuberger J
Phillips and others v Symes and another, 9.7.2001, Ch.D., Hart J

Art.25

Court of Appeal/Court of Session (Inner House)

Berkeley Administration Incorporated v McClelland and others [1995] I.L.Pr 201, CA
Landhurst Leasing Plc. v Marcq [1998] I.L.Pr. 822

High Court (First Instance)/Irish High Court/Court of Session (Outer House)

Virgin Aviation Services Ltd v CAD Aviation Services [1991] I.L.Pr. 79, QBD
EMI Records Ltd v Modern Music Karl Ulrich Walterbach GmbH [1992] 1 QB 115, [1992] 1
    All ER 616, Hobhouse J
CFEM Facades S.A. v Bovis Construction Limited [1992] I.L.Pr. 561, QBD
Barratt International Resorts Ltd v Martin [1994] SLT 434, OH
The 'Tjaskemolen' (No.2) [1997] 2 Lloyd's Rep. 476, Clarke J
Normaco and anor v Lundman and ors , Ch. D, 6.1.1999, Carnwath, J, The Times Law Reports
    6.1.1999
*Coca Cola Bottlers (Ulster) Ltd v The Concentrate Manufacturing Co. of Ireland (t/a Seven-up
    International),* 6.4.1990, Ch.D., Murray LJ
Société Lacoste SA and Papeteries Sibiline Stenay SA v Keeley Group Ltd [1999] 1 ILRM 510,
    HC

Art.26

Court of Appeal/Court of Session (Inner House)

Berkeley Administration Incorporated v McClelland and others [1996] I.L.Pr 772, CA

High Court (First Instance)/Irish High Court/Court of Session (Outer House)

Berkeley Administration Incorporated v McClelland and others [1995] I.L.Pr 201, CA

Art.31

High Court (First Instance)/Irish High Court/Court of Session (Outer House)

Selco Ltd v Mercier (No.2) 1997 SLT 687, OH
Elwyn (Cottons) Ltd v Pearle Designs Ltd [1989] I.R. 9, HC

Art.33

House of Lords/Irish Supreme Court

Brian Rhatigan v Textiles y Confecciones Europeas S.A., [1990] 1 I.R.125, SC [1992] I.L.Pr. 40,
   Irish SC

High Court (First Instance)/Irish High Court/Court of Session (Outer House)

Brian Rhatigan v Textiles y Confecciones Europeas S.A. [1990] I.L.Pr. 141, Irish HC

Art.34

House of Lords/Irish Supreme Court

Brian Rhatigan v Textiles y Confecciones Europeas S.A., [1990] 1 I.R.125, SC [1992] I.L.Pr. 40,
   Irish SC
Barnaby (London) Ltd v Desmond Mullen, [1997] 2 ILRM 341, [1998] IJEL 277, SC

High Court (First Instance)/Irish High Court/Court of Session (Outer House)

Brian Rhatigan v Textiles y Confecciones Europeas S.A. [1990] I.L.Pr. 141, Irish HC
Barnaby (London) Ltd v Desmond Mullen, [1996] 2 ILRM 24, Irish HC

Art.36

House of Lords/Irish Supreme Court

Barnaby (London) Ltd v Desmond Mullen, [1997] 2 ILRM 341, [1998] IJEL 277, SC

High Court (First Instance)/Irish High Court/Court of Session (Outer House)

Barnaby (London) Ltd v Desmond Mullen, [1996] 2 ILRM 24, Irish HC

Art.37

High Court (First Instance)/Irish High Court/Court of Session (Outer House)

Re Petition of Maire Brizard et Roger International S.A. [1997] I.L.Pr. 373

Art.38

Court of Appeal/Court of Session (Inner House)

Société d'Informatique Service Réalisation Organisation (SISRO) v Ampersand Software BV
   [1994] I.L.Pr 55, CA

Art.35 1979 Accession Convention

Court of Appeal/Court of Session (Inner House)

High Court (First Instance)/Irish High Court/Court of Session (Outer House)

Pre/Non-Convention Cases under autonomous laws/bilateral Treaties

Belgian Cases

Cour de Bruxelles 22.10.1831 1814–1840 Pas. Belge, 276

Cour d'appel de Bruxelles 5.4.1848 *Houdard c/ Badart* 1849 Pas. Belge, II, 139

Cassation 13.5.1871 *Voncken-Van Moorem c/ Meunier-Dubois* 1871 Jurisprudence du port d'Anvers, I, 191

Cassation 9.6.1871 *Th. Van Brabandt c/ Leysen Frères et De Ridder* 1871 Jurisprudence du port d'Anvers, I, 201

Cour de Liège 29.7.1871 *Chemin de Fer du Nord c/ Bastin* 1872 Jurisprudence du port d'Anvers, II, 50

Cour de Gand 2.12.1871 *Goorickx c/ Bauwens* 1872 Jurisprudence du port d'Anvers, II, 30

Cour de Bruxelles 8.8.1872 *Wéry c/ Leroy et Co.* 1873 Jurisprudence du port d'Anvers, II, 30

Cour de Bruxelles 24.7.1873 *Clauwaert c/ Petit* 1874 Jurisprudence du port d'Anvers, II, 114

Cassation 20.7.1874 *Gustave Jacob et Co. c/ J. Sam. Billing & Son* 1874 Jurisprudence du port d'Anvers, I, 310

Tribunal de Bruxelles 25.11.1880 *Piron c/ La Société anonyme la Compagnie de Bruxelles et la Compagnie suisse d'assurances l'Helvetia* 1880 Pas. Belge, III, 335

Tribunal de commerce de Liège 24.8.1882 *Wéry c/ Janssens* 1883 Jurisprudence des Tribunaux de premières instance, Cl. & B., 669

Cour d'appel de Liège 15.11.1883 *Parent Frères c/ Molttan* 1884 Pas. Belge, II, 26

Cour d'appel de Bruxelles 5.1.1887 *Personne c/ Best* 1886 Pas. Belge, II, 113

Cour d'appel de Liège 7.6.1888 *Société des sucreries centrales de Wanze c/ Massart* 1888 Pas. Belge, II, 363

Cour d'appel de Bruxelles 23.1.1889 *Société John Cockerill c/ Deutsche Transport Versicherungs Gesellschaft* 1890 Jurisprudence du port d'Anvers, I, 99

Tribunal de Commerce d'Alost 18.9.1889 *Foucquier c/ Callebaut Frères* 1890 Jurisprudence du port d'Anvers, II, 157

Tribunal de Commerce de Bruxelles 5.2.1890 *Grumieau c/ Van Wouwe* 1890 Jurisprudence du port d'Anvers, II, 65

Cassation 3.6.1890 *G. et C. Krelinger et autres c/ Capitaine Green* 1890 Jurisprudence du port d'Anvers, 1, 258

Cassation 2.2.1891 *A. Simkens c/ J.B. Schutijzer* 1893 Jurisprudence du port d'Anvers, I, 69

Cassation 3.9.1891 *Hertogs c/ Preud'Homme* 1893 Jurisprudence du port d'Anvers, I, 260

Cour d'appel de Bruxelles 3.1.1893 *Compagnie viennoise de réassurance c/ Simondet et Cie.* 1893 Pas. Belge, II, 292

Cassation 2.1.1894 *Veuve Janssens c/ Louis Lenoir* 1894 Jurisprudence du port d'Anvers, I, 319

Cassation 27.1.1894 *L. Baptiste Donckers c/ Brepols* 1895 Jurisprudence du port d'Anvers, I, 194

Tribunal civil de Verviers 29.1.1896 *Lejeune et Delebecque c/ Barry-Herfeldt* 1896 Jurisprudence des Tribunaux de premières instance, Cl. & B. , 255

Cassation 24.12.1896 *Pittoors et Pauli c/ Hermes et Zeynen* 1897 Jurisprudence du port d'Anvers, I, 102

Cassation 4.2.1897 *J.M. Steel et Co. c/ A. Gueur* 1897 Jurisprudence du port d'Anvers, I, 265

Cassation 15.5.1981 *Vindevogel c/ Société de personnes à responsabilité linitée Beheercentrale* 1981 Pas. Belge, I, 1073

French Cases

Tribunal de L'Empire 26.1.1892 *Willner c/ Schlesinger* 1893 JDI 905

Tribunal civil de la Seine 21.6.1901 *Vuille, Stouvenet et Dunant c/ Veuve Perret* 1901 JDI 934

Cour d'appel d'Alger 15.10.1902 *Heckmann c/ Compagnie Kohler* 1904 JDI 895

Cour de Besançon 1.3.1905 *Banque du Jura c/ Jobin* 1905 JDI 655

Cour de Besançon 13.8.1906 *Huguenin c/ Dames de Sainte-Ursule de Dôle* 1907 JDI 710

Cassation 6.6.1907 *Aimé et Auguste Hutt c/ Delarue, veuve Filoque* 1908 Rev. crit. 294

Cour de Paris 20.2.1908 *Reitlinger c/ Darlington Simpson* 1909 JDI 1071

Cassation 15.6.1909 *Samuel et comp. C. The marine insurance Co* 1911 Rev. crit. 339

Cour d'appel de Poitiers 11.5.1914 *Van den Berghe c/ Sœnem* 1914 Gazette du Palais, II, 144

Tribunal civil de la Seine 26.2.1924 *Meuter et Kramen c/ Sander Van de Smet* 1925 Rev. crit. 63

Cour de Lyon 20.3.1929 *Galland c/ Veuve Schelling* 1930 JDI 374

Cour de justice de Genève 14.2.1930 *Grenier c/ dame Grenier* 1931 JDI 522

Trib. civ Béthune 18.6.1930 *Vandaele c/ Méau* 1931 JDI 373

Trib. civ Seine 15.10.1931 *Klein c/ Niedermann* 1932 JDI 678

Cour de Cassation 9.12.1933 *Maerki* 1937 Rev. crit. 177

Cour de Douai 25.1.1935 *Hoedhaar c/ Faill. Mallet* 1939 JDI 606

Tribunal civil de Montpelier 11.12.1935 *Dame H c/ De H* 1936 JDI 364

Cassation 23.3.1936 *Sander c/ Meuter* 1937 Rev. crit. 198

Cour d'appel de Paris 20.7.1936 *Banque de Seguros c/ Soc. José Gamba et Cassa Navale* 1938 Rev. crit. 103

Cour de Colmar 26.11.1937 *Brasserie de Sarrebourg c/ Borsari et Cie* 1939 JDI 111

Tribunal de la Seine 20.11.1945 *Druart c/ Soc.Etabl. Ruinart* 1947 Rev. crit. 160

Cour d'appel de Paris 27.1.1955 *Soc. Jansen c/ Ste Heurtey* 1955 Rev. crit. 330

Cour d'appel d'Amiens 18.2.1958 *Forest c/ Punski* 1959 Rev. crit. 129

Cour d'appel de Paris 4.7.1958 *Bensa c/ Coleman* 1959 JDI 1122

Tribunal de grande instance de la Seine 8.12.1959 *Soc S.E.O. c/ Pons* 1960 JDI 1069

Tribunal de grande instance de Béthune 31.1.1961 *General Anders c/ Kwiakowski et Gas* 1961 JDI 1126

Cour d'appel de Paris 9.2.1962 *Lewis c/ époux Cunnington et Prince Tounsoun* 1963 JDI 148

Cassation 5.5.1962 *Dame Zins c/ Verdier* 1963 Rev. crit. 99

Tribunal de grande instance de la Seine 9.7.1962 *Soc. Exportazioni Oriente c/ dame Boghossian et autres* 1963 JDI 466

Cassation 8.1.1963 *Hohenzollern c/ Lambrino* 1963 Rev. crit. 109

Cour d'appel de Paris 18.11.1963 *Cts Brébart c/ Sacré* 1964 JDI 594, 1964 Gazette du Palais, Juris., 262

Tribunal de grande instance de la Seine 4.6.1964 *Fondation Pomorsko et autres c/ dame Vre Krolin* 1965 JDI 415

Cassation 9.12.1964 *Dame Foucquart c/ Foucquart* 1966 Rev. crit. 72, 1965 JDI 418

Cour d'appel de Paris 21.4.1967 *Rapetto c/ Demoiselle Borgstrom* 1968 JDI 345

Cassation 4.10.1967 *Bachir c/ Dame Bachir* 1968 Rev. crit. 98

Cassation 1.12.1969 *Soc. Anciens établ. Valla et Richard c/ Banque commerciale africaine* 1970 JDI 707

Tribunal de grande instance de Paris 18.4.1969 *Dlle Mitsouko Guy c/ Editions Vesco* 1971 Rev. crit. 281

Cour d'appel de Paris 17.12.1969 *Soc. mobile Parking c/ Soc. Cogepa et Garnier es –qualité* 1971 JDI 99

Tribunal de grande instance de Paris 14.1.1970 *Soc. Intrabank c/ veuve Beidas et autres* 1970 Rev. crit. 714

Art.14 Code Civil

Art.15 Code Civil

Art.46 NCPC

Art.48 NCPC

Other Provisions / Conventions

§32 ZPO

§38 I & II ZPO

Landgerichte/Amtsgerichte (LG/AG)

§39 ZPO

Bundesgerichtshof (BGH)

Oberlandesgerichte (OLG)

§40 ZPO

§182 ZPO

Oberlandesgerichte (OLG)

§261 III ZPO

Bundesgerichtshof (BGH)

Oberlandesgerichte (OLG)

Anerkennungs- und Vollstreckungsausführungsgesetz (AVAG)

Bundesgerichtshof (BGH)

BGH 30.4.1980 1980 NJW 2022, *De Cavel v De Cavel* [1980] E.C.C. 420
BGH 13.4.1983 1985 IPRax 154, IPRspr. 1983 Nr. 175, 1983 NJW 2773, 1983 RIW 615,
    Imef KG v Firma Herbert Fischer [1984] E.C.C. 128
BGH 16.5.1983 1985 IPRax 156, 1983 NJW 1979, 1983 RIW 535, 87 BGHZ 259
BGH 22.3.1984 1985 IPRax 101, IPRspr. 1984 Nr. 189, 1984 RIW 485, *In Re the Enforcement
    of Judgments Convention* [1985] E.C.C. 243
BGH 21.2.1985 1986 IPRax 157, IPRspr. 1985 Nr. 173
BGH 27.9.1990 IPRspr. 1990 Nr. 202
BGH 16.5.1991 1992 NJW 627
BGH 26.9.1997 IPRspr. 1997 Nr. 185, 1998 NJW-RR 141

Oberlandesgerichte (OLG)

OLG Zweibrücken 30.6.1992 IPRspr. 1992 Nr. 267
OLG Saarbücken 24.9.1992 IPRspr. 1992 Nr. 225, 1993 RIW 672
OLG Köln 4.1.1993 IPRspr. 1993 Nr. 167, 1993 RIW 498
OLG Frankfurt a. M. 25.5.1993 1993 RIW 676
OLG Hamburg 5.8.1993 IPRspr. 1993 Nr. 177, 1995 IPRax 391
OLG Köln 9.1.1995 IPRspr. 1995 Nr. 170
OLG Oldenburg 25.5.1995 IPRspr. 1995 Nr. 180
OLG Düsseldorf 27.11.1996 1997 RIW 330, 1998 IPRax 478, IPRspr. 1996 Nr. 183
OLG Stuttgart 15.5.1997 1997 RIW 684, 1998 NJW-RR 280
OLG Rostock 9.11.1998 2000 IPRax 214
OLG Zweibrücken 14.9.1999 2001 NJW-RR 144

Swiss Cases

Bundesgericht 9.2.1899 *Efpanet gegen Gève* BGE 25, I, 89
Bundesgericht 9.6.1909 *Alba contre Tognetti* BGE 35, I, 459
Cour de justice de Genève 7.6.1912 *Allemand c/ Soc. du Skating Palace* 1914 JDI 284
Bundesgericht 24.10.1912 *Behrendt & Cie gegen Lehner* BGE 38, I, 543
Bundesgericht 8.2.1919 *Walther gegen Jeschonek* BGE 45, I, 43
Bundesgericht 17.10.1924 *Geiger & Cie gegen Obergericht Luzern* BGE 50, I, 420, 1926 JDI
    1114
Cour de cassation zurichoise 9.4.1930 1931 JDI 778
Bundesgericht 4.12.1931 *Brüder Kronengold gegen Obergericht Aargau* BGE 57, I, 424
Tribunal fédérale Suisse 1.7.1932 *Dame Lanvin contre dame Quellien* 1933 JDI 237
Schuler gegen Schwyz Justizkommission 7.10.1932 58 BGE, I, 302
Fellheimer gegen Hausmann & Cie 15.12.1933 59 BGE, I, 290
Bundesgericht 13.2.1936 *Dame Rado contre Dame Biro* BGE 62, II, 20
Tribunal fédéral suisse 18.2.1938 *Constantin Mavromati c/ Vacher, syndic de faillite* 1938
    Rev. crit. 508
Obergericht 23.2.1939, *Blätter*, Band 38, 1939, 365, No. 151
I. Kammer 6.12.1940, *Blätter*, Band 43, 1944, 248, No.168
I. Kammer 26.3.1941, *Blätter*, Band 43, 1944, 248, No. 169
I. Kammer, 22.10.1941, *Blätter*, Band 43, 1944, 249, No. 170
Stevens gegen Frankenhauser 23.11.1942 68 BGE, I, 160
I. Kammer 3.7.1947, *Blätter*, Band 46, 1947, 117, No. 72
Obergericht 2.5.1949 *Blätter*, Band 48, 1949, 35, No. 16
Bundesgericht 23.6.1949 *Brönimann contre Tribunal cantonal vaudois et Société Universelle
    de Films* BGE 75, I, 146

English Cases

Conventions and Subsidiary Legislation

Brussels and Lugano Conventions

Convention on jurisdiction and the enforcement of judgments in civil and commercial matters of 27 September 1968, 30.10.78 [1978] OJ L304/36[1]

The Brussels Convention on jurisdiction and the enforcement of judgments in civil and commercial matters of 27 September 1968[2], [1978] OJ L304/77[3]

The Brussels Convention on jurisdiction and the enforcement of judgments in civil and commercial matters of 27 September 1968[4], 11.4.83, [1983] OJ C97/2

The Lugano Convention on jurisdiction and the enforcement of judgments in civil and commercial matters, Done at Lugano 16 September 1988, 25.11.1988, [1988] OJ L319/9

The Brussels Convention on jurisdiction and the enforcement of judgments in civil and commercial matters of 27 September 1968[5], 28.7.90 [1990] OJ C189/2

The Brussels Convention on jurisdiction and the enforcement of judgments in civil and commercial matters of 27 September 1968[6], 26.1.98, [1998] OJ C27/3

---

[1] Original French version 31.12.1972 [1972] JO L299/32

[2] As amended by the *Convention on the Accession of the Kingdom of Denmark, Ireland and the United Kingdom of Great Britain and Northern Ireland to the Convention on jurisdiction and the enforcement of judgments in civil and commercial matters and to the Protocol on its interpretation by the Court of Justice*, 9.10.1978, [1978] OJ L304/1('The 1978 Accession Convention')

[3] Came into force for the UK on 1st January 1987 (Civil Jurisdiction and Judgments Act 1982 (Commencement No.3) Order, SI 1986/2044; for Ireland on 1st April 1989 Jurisdiction of Courts and Enforcement of Judgments (European Communities) Act 1988 (Section 3)(Commencement) Order 1989 SI No.37 of 1989, replaced from 1.12.1999 by Jurisdiction of Courts and Enforcement of Judgments Act 1998, *Acts of Oireachtas*, No.52 of 1998; for Denmark on 1.11.1986 by Danish Law on the EC Judgments Convention of 4.6.1986 (Law Nr.324)

[4] As amended by the *Convention on the Accession of the Hellenic Republic to the Convention on jurisdiction and enforcement of judgments in civil and commercial matters and to the Protocol on its interpretation by the Court of Justice with the adjustments made to them by the Convention on the accession of the Kingdom of Denmark, of Ireland and of the United Kingdom of Great Britain and Northern Ireland*, 31.12.82, [1982] OJ L388/1 ('The 1982 Accession Convention')

[5] As amended by the *Convention on the accession of the Kingdom of Spain and the Portuguese Republic to the Convention on jurisdiction and enforcement of judgments in civil and commercial matters and to the Protocol on its interpretation by the Court of Justice with the adjustments made to them by the Convention on the accession of the Kingdom of Denmark, of Ireland and of the United Kingdom of Great Britain and Northern Ireland and the adjustments made to them by the Convention on the accession of the Hellenic Republic*, 3.10.89, [1989] OJ L285/1 ('The San Sebastian Convention' or 'The 1989 Accession Convention')

[6] As amended by the *Convention on the accession of the Republic of Austria, the Republic of Finland and the Kingdom of Sweden to the Convention on jurisdiction and enforcement of judgments in civil and commercial matters and to the Protocol on its interpretation by the Court of Justice with the adjustments made to them by the Convention on the accession of the Kingdom of Denmark, of Ireland and of the United Kingdom of Great Britain and Northern Ireland, by the Convention on the accession of the Hellenic Republic and by the Convention on the accession of the Kingdom of Spain and the Portuguese Republic*, 15.1.97, [1997] OJ C15/1 ('The 1996 Accession Convention')

Official Reports

Report on the Convention on jurisdiction and the enforcement of judgments in civil and commercial matters, by Mr. P. Jenard [1979] OJ C59/1, 'The Jenard Report'

Report on the Convention on the Association of the Kingdom of Denmark, Ireland and the United Kingdom of Great Britain and Northern Ireland to the Convention on jurisdiction and the enforcement of judgments in civil and commercial matters and to the Protocol on its interpretation by the Court of Justice, by Dr. P. Schlosser [1979] OJ C59/71, 'The Schlosser Report'

Report on the accession of the Hellenic Republic to the Community Convention on jurisdiction and the enforcement of judgments in civil and commercial matters, by Prof. D. Evrigenis and K. Kerameus [1986] OJ C298/1, 'The Evrigenis & Kerameus Report'

Report on the Convention on the accession of the Kingdom of Spain and the Portuguese Republic to the Convention on jurisdiction and the enforcement of judgments in civil and commercial matters and to the Protocol on its interpretation by the Court of Justice, by Mr.M. Almeida Cruz and Mr. M. Desantes Real and Mr. P. Jenard [1990] OJ C189/35, 'The Cruz Real & Jenard Report'

Report on the Convention on jurisdiction and the enforcement of judgments in civil and commercial matters done at Lugano on 16 September 1988, Report, by Mr. P. Jenard and Mr. G. Möller [1990] OJ C189/57, 'The Jenard & Möller Report'

Reforms of the Brussels Convention, and related Regulations

Preliminary Draft Convention on Jurisdiction and Foreign Judgments in civil and commercial matters, adopted by the Special Commission of the Hague Conference on Private International Law on 30 October 1999, amended version (new numbering of articles): on-line reference *http://www.hcch.net/e/conventions/draft36e.html*

The Commission's *Proposal for a Council Act establishing the Convention on Jurisdiction and Recognition and Enforcement of Judgments in Civil and Commercial Matters in the Member States of the European Union*, submitted on 22.12.1997, 31.1.98, [1998] OJ C33/20

Commission's *Proposal for a Council Regulation (EC) on jurisdiction and the enforcement of judgments in civil and commercial matters*, done at Brussels 14 July 1999 COM(1999) 348 final, 99/0154 (CNS), [1999] OJ C376 E, p.1, also available on-line at *http://europa.eu.int/ comm/sg/tfjai/unit/unit3_en.htm*

Commission's *Amended proposal for a Council Regulation on jurisdiction and the recognition and enforcement of judgments in civil and commercial matters*, done at Brussels 26.10.2000 COM(2000)689 final, 1999/0154 (CNS), [2001] OJ C062 243(E) 1

Commission's *Proposal for a Council Directive on the service in the Member States of judicial and extrajudicial documents in civil and commercial matters*, done at Brussels 4 May 1999 COM(1999) 219 final, 99/0102 (CNS), available on-line at *http://europa.eu.int/eur-lex/en/com/dat/1999/en_599PC0219.html*

Council Regulation (EC) 1346/2000 of 29 May 2000 on insolvency proceedings [2000] OJ L160/1

Council Regulation (EC) 1347/2000 of 29 May 2000 on jurisdiction and the recognition and enforcement of judgments in matrimonial matters and in matters of parental responsibility for children of both spouses [2000] OJ160/19

Council Regulation (EC) 1348/2000 of 29 May 2000 on the service in the Member States of judicial and extrajudicial documents in civil or commercial matters [2000] OJ160/37

Council Regulation (EC) No.44/2001 of 22 December 2000 on jurisdiction and the recognition and enforcement of judgments in civil and commercial matters [2001] OJ L12/1

Council Regulation (EC) 1206/2001 of 28 May 2001 on cooperation between the courts of the Member States in the taking of evidence in civil or commercial matters, 27.6.2001, [2001] OJ L174/1

Statement by the United Kingdom (Council Regulation (EC) No.44/2001 of 22 December 2000) (on the certification of the decisions of the courts of Gibraltar) [2001] OJ C13/1

Information communicated by Member States under Article 23 of Council Regulation (EC) No 1348/2000) of 29 May 2000 on the service in the Member States of judicial and extrajudicial documents in civil or commercial matters, 22 May 2001, [2001] OJ C151/4

First update of the information communicated by Member States under Article 23 of Council Regulation (EC) No 1348/2000) of 29 May 2000 on the service in the Member States of judicial and extrajudicial documents in civil or commercial matters, 18 July 2001, [2001] OJ C202/10

Corrigendum to the first update of the information communicated by Member States under Article 23 of Council Regulation (EC) No 1348/2000) of 29 May 2000 on the service in the Member States of judicial and extrajudicial documents in civil or commercial matters, 6.10.2001, [2001] OJ C282/15

Second update of the information communicated by Member States under Article 23 of Council Regulation (EC) No 1348/2000) of 29 May 2000 on the service in the Member States of judicial and extrajudicial documents in civil or commercial matters, 6 October 2001, [2001] OJ C282/2

UK and Ireland Implementing Legislation and its History

Civil Jurisdiction and Judgments Act 1982 (1982 c27)

Civil Jurisdiction and Judgments Act, s 53(1) & Sch.13, Part I, paras 1 and 2

The Civil Jurisdiction and Judgments Act 1982 (Commencement No.1) Order 1984, SI 1984/1553
The Civil Jurisdiction and Judgments Act 1982 (Commencement No.2) Order 1986, SI 1986/1781
The Civil Jurisdiction and Judgments Act 1982 (Commencement No.3) Order 1986, SI 1986/2044
The Civil Jurisdiction and Judgments Act 1982 (Amendment) Order 1989, SI 1989/1346
The Civil Jurisdiction and Judgments Act 1982 (Amendment) Order 1990, SI 1990/2591
The Civil Jurisdiction and Judgments Act 1982 (Amendment) Order 2000, SI 2000/1824

Civil Jurisdiction and Judgments Act 1991 (1991 c12)

The Civil Jurisdiction and Judgments Act 1991 (Commencement) Order 1992, SI 1992/745
The Civil Jurisdiction and Judgments Act 1982 (Interim Relief) Order 1997 SI 1997/302, in force 1.4.1997
The Civil Jurisdiction and Judgments Act 1982 (Provisional and Protective Measures) (Scotland) Order 1997 SI 1997/2780
The Civil Jurisdiction and Judgments Act 1982 (Gibraltar) Order 1997 SI 1997/2602
The Civil Procedure Rules 1998 SI1998/3132, as amended, esp. CPR 6.19–6.30, in *Civil Procedure 2000*, Vol.1, 2000
The Civil Procedure (Amendment) Rules 1999, SI 1999/1008
The Civil Procedure (Amendment) Rules 2000, SI 2000/221
The Civil Procedure (Amendment No.2) Rules 2000, SI 2000/940
The Civil Procedure (Amendment No.3) Rules 2000, SI 2000/1317
The Civil Procedure (Amendment No.2) Rules 2001, SI 2001/1388
The European Communities (Matrimonial Jurisdiction and Judgments) Regulations 2001, SI 2001/310
Civil Jurisdiction and Judgments Act 1982 (1982 c/ 27) 'Courts and Legal Services', Vol.11, *Halsbury's Statutes of England and Wales*, 4th ed., 2000 Reissue, p.1158; 'Judgments and Execution' Vol.22, *Halsbury's Statutes of England and Wales*, 4th ed., 1995 Reissue, p.509
'The Civil Jurisdiction and Judgments Act 1982' *The Laws of Scotland*, Vol. 4, 'Civil Jurisdiction', Stair Memorial Encyclopaedia, 1991, 1999 Cumulative Supplement
Select Committee on the European Communities EEC Jurisdiction Convention, House of Lords, 45th Report, 26.7.1977, Session 1976–77
Maxwell Report, Report of the Scottish Committee on Jurisdiction and Enforcement, HMSO, Edinburgh, 1980
House of Lords Debates: H.L. Vol. 425, cols 105, 1126, 1139; Vol. 426, col. 711; Vol. 427, cols 1032, 1383; Vol. 430, col. 1065; Vol. 432, col. 169; Vol. 524, cols 921
House of Commons Debates: H.C. Vol. 20, col. 942; Vol. 24, col. 594
Jurisdiction of Courts and Enforcement of Judgments (European Communities) Act, 1988, No.3 of 1988, 1988 *Acts of the Oireachtas* and Jurisdiction of Courts and Enforcement of Judgments Act, 1993, No.9 of 1993, 1993 *Acts of the Oireachtas*, consolidated by:
Jurisdiction of Courts and Enforcement of Judgments Act, 1998, No.52 of 1998, 1997 *Acts of the Oireachtas*

A sample of Former bilateral Conventions, now superseded

UK

Reciprocal Enforcement of Foreign Judgments (France) Order in Council 1936, SI 1936/609, incorporating the *Convention between His Majesty in respect of the United Kingdom and the President of the French Republic providing for the reciprocal enforcement of judgments in civil and commercial matters, with Protocol*

Reciprocal Enforcement of Foreign Judgments (Belgium) Order in Council, 1936 SI 1936/1169 incorporating the *Convention between His Majesty in respect of the United Kingdom and His Majesty the King of the Belgians providing for the reciprocal enforcement of judgments in civil and commercial matters, with Protocol*

Reciprocal Enforcement of Foreign Judgments (Germany) Order, 1961, SI 1961/1199, incorporating the *Convention between the United Kingdom of Great Britain and Northern Ireland and the Federal Republic of Germany for the reciprocal enforcement of judgments in civil and commercial matters*

Reciprocal Enforcement of Foreign Judgments (Norway) Order, 1962, SI 1962/636, incorporating the *Convention between the Government of the United Kingdom of Great Britain and Northern Ireland and the Government of the Kingdom of Norway providing for the reciprocal enforcement of judgments in civil and commercial matters*

Reciprocal Enforcement of Foreign Judgments (Austria) Order, 1962, SI 1962/1339, incorporating the *Convention between the United Kingdom of Great Britain and Northern Ireland and the Republic of Austria for the reciprocal enforcement of judgments in civil and commercial matters*

Reciprocal Enforcement of Foreign Judgments (The Netherlands) Order, 1969, SI 1969/1063, incorporating the *Convention between the United Kingdom of Great Britain and Northern Ireland and the Kingdom of the Netherlands providing for the reciprocal enforcement of judgments in civil and commercial matters*

Reciprocal Enforcement of Foreign Judgments (Italy) Order, 1973, SI 1973/1894, incorporating the *Convention between the United Kingdom of Great Britain and Northern Ireland and the Republic of Italy for the reciprocal enforcement of judgments in civil and commercial matters*

Belgium

Traité Franco-Belge 8 July 1899, 187 CTS (1898–1899), 378

Convention entre La Belgique et Les Pays-Bas sur la compétence judiciaire territoriale, sur la faillite, ainsi que sur l'autorité et l'exécution des décisions judiciaires, des sentences arbitrales et des actes authentiques, Signée à Bruxelles le 28 Mars 1925, 1929–1930 L.N.T.S., XCIII, 432

Convention entre le Royaume de Belgique et la République Fédérale d'Allemagne, concernant la reconnaissance et l'exécution réciproque, en matière civile ou commerciale, des décisions judiciaires, sentences arbitrales et actes authentiques, 30.6.1958, 1960 Pasinomie 1119

Convention entre Belgique et Italie concernant la reconnaissance et l'exécution des décisions judiciaires et d'autres titres exécutoires en matière civile et commerciale, 6 avril 1962, 490 UNTS, 7161

(Federal Republic of) Germany

Abkommen zwischen dem Deutschen Reich und der Schweizerischen Eidgenossenschaft über die gegenseitige Anerkennung und Vollstreckung von gerichtlichen Entscheidungen und Schiedssprüchen, 2.11.1929, RGBl, 1930, II, 1066, in force 1.12.1930

Abkommen zwischen dem Deutschen Reich und dem Königreich Italien über die Anerkennung und Vollstreckung gerichtlicher Entscheidungen Zivil- und Handelssachen, 9.3.1936, 1937 RGBl., II, 145, in force 19.6.1937, and again (post-war) on 1.10.1952

Gesetz zur Ausführung des Vertrages zwischen der Bundesrepublik Deutschland und der Republik Österreich vom 6.Juni 1959 über die gegenseitige Anerkennung und Vollstreckung von gerichtlichen Entscheidungen, Vergleichen und öffentlichen Urkunden in Zivil- und Handelssachen, 8.3.1960, BGBl., I, 169

Austria

Switzerland

Table of Abbreviations

Gaudemet-Tallon, 1996 . . . . Gaudemet-Tallon, H. *Les Conventions de Bruxelles et de Lugano*, 2ème éd., (LGDJ, Montchrestien, Paris, 1996)

Gaz. Pal., juris. . . . . *Gazette du Palais, jurisprudence*

Gaz. Pal., somm. . . . . *Gazette du Palais, sommaire*

Ga J Int'l Comp L . . . . *Georgia Journal of International and Comparative Law*

Geimer & Schütze, 1997 . . . . Geimer, R. & Schütze, R. *Europäisches Zivilverfahrensrech, Kommentar zum EuGVÜ und Lugano-Übereinkommen*, (C.H. Beck'sche Verlagsbuchhandlung, München, 1997)

Geo Wash J Int'l L & Econ . . . . *George Washington Journal of International Law and Economics*

GILSI . . . . *Gazette of the Incorporated Law Society of Ireland*

Gothot et Holleaux, 1985 . . . . Gothot, P. et Holleaux, D. *La Convention de Bruxelles du 27 septembre 1968: compétence judiciaire et effets des jugements dans la CEE*, (Editions Jupiter, Paris, 1985)

Grur. Int. . . . . *Gewerblicher Rechtsschutz und Urheberrecht— (Auslands- und) Internationaler Teil*

Hague Yrbk Int L . . . . *Hague Yearbook of International Law*

Harvard Int'l LJ . . . . *Harvard International Law Journal*

Harvard LR . . . . *Harvard Law Review*

Hastings Int'l & Comp L R . . . . *Hastings International and Comparative Law Review*

Hertz, 1998 . . . . Hertz, K. *Jurisdiction in Contract and Tort under the Brussels Convention*, Jurist-og Økonomforbundets Forlag, Copenhagen, 1998

Hill, 1998 . . . . Hill, J. *The Law relating to international commercial disputes*, 2nd ed., (Lloyd's of London Press, London, 1998)

IBL . . . . *International Business Lawyer*

ICCLR . . . . *International Company and Commercial Law Review*

ICLit . . . . *International Commercial Litigation*

ICLQ . . . . *International and Comparative Law Quarterly*

IHL . . . . *In-House Lawyer*

IIC . . . . *International Review of Industrial Property and Copyright Law*

IJEL . . . . *Irish Journal of European Law*

ILJ . . . . *Industrial Law Journal*

ILT . . . . *Irish Law Times*

I.L.Pr. . . . . *International Litigation Procedure*

ILRM . . . . Irish Law Reports Monthly

Ins L & P . . . . *Insurance Law and Practice*

Int F L R . . . . *International Financial Law Review*

Int ILR . . . . *International Insurance Law Review*

Int J IL . . . . *The International Journal of Insurance Law*

I J O S L . . . . *International Journal of Shipping Law*

Introduction

La Commission de la C.E.E. est d'avis[1] qu'il est, d'une manière générale, *pour éviter des perturbations et des difficultés dans l'économie de la Communauté*, très important que les décisions judiciaires . . . soient reconnus et exécutés dans tous les États membres. La protection juridique et, par là, la sécurité juridique . . . dépendent principalement d'un règlement satisfaisant des questions de reconnaissance et d'exécution. [2] [3]

Thus the seed for what, nine years later, would become the 'Convention on jurisdiction and the enforcement of judgments in civil and commercial matters'[4] was set.[5] It will be the aim of this work to test whether, and if so why, any (remaining

---

[1]   A similar view to this opinion is quoted (in English) by the 'Report on the Convention on jurisdiction and the enforcement of judgments in civil and commercial matters' by Mr. P. Jenard, 'The Jenard Report' [1979] OJ C59/1, at p.3; where necessary, and unless otherwise indicated, all translations are the writer's own, and all emphasis is added.

[2]   'The EEC Commission is of the opinion that, on the whole, to avoid the obstacles and difficulties in the economy of the Community, it is very important that judicial decisions . . . are recognised and enforced in all Member States. Judicial protection and thereby judicial security depend in the main on satisfactory rules on questions of recognition and enforcement.'

[3]   Response of the Commission of the European Economic Community on 17.10.1959 ([1959] JO, 2ᵉ Année No.56, 1123/59) to questions submitted to it by a member of the European Parliamentary Assembly, M Illerhaus, on 23.9.1959; these asked, in essence, whether a failure in the free movement of judgments represented an obstacle to the proper functioning of the Common market (at para. 2), and what initiatives the Commission had taken under Article 220 (now Article 293) (E)EC Treaty to address the problems (at paras. 3 and 4). An example Illerhaus gives (at para. 1), is the inability of German undertakings to enforce German judgments in their favour in The Netherlands, in actions against unlawful competition: written question No.39 of 23.9.1959 [1959] JO, 2ᵉ Année No.56, *Ibid*— also Ropers, J.-L. 'La reconnaissance et l'exécution reciproque des décisions de justice à l'intérieur du Marché Commun' (1962) *JCP*, I, *Doctr.*, 1679, regarding French judgments' traditionally hostile reception in Germany.

[4]   Original French version [1972] JO L299/32; reported as an English version at [1978] OJ L304/36, signed by the original Member States of (what was then) the European Economic Community in Brussels on 27 September 1968, and known as The 1968 Brussels Convention, as amended; unless otherwise more specifically indicated, references to 'The Brussels Convention' or 'the Conventions' include a reference to the current amended version of the Convention ([1998] OJ C27/3), as from 1.1.2001 until 1.3.2002 now in force in the UK *and* to the 1988 Lugano Convention ([1988] OJ L319/9); on 1.3.2002, the Brussels I Regulation 44/2001 will come into force, below. The necessary changes to the Civil Jurisdiction and Judgments Act 1982 and the Civil Procedure Rules on that date will be effected by The Civil Jurisdiction and Judgments Order 2001, SI 2001/3929, and The Civil Procedure (Amendment Nr. 5) Rules 2001, SI 2001/4015, respectively.

[5]   Although its inspiration was, according to Bellet, drawn from earlier efforts at *traités doubles*, especially in Articles 11(1) and 14(3) of the multilateral *Traité entre La Belgique, Les Pays-Bas et le Luxembourg sur la compétence judiciaire territoriale, sur la faillite, sur l'autorité et l'exécution des décisions judiciaires, des sentences arbitrales et des actes authentiques* (Benelux Treaty of 24.11.1961), 34

or new) 'perturbations' exist in the Convention's jurisdictional and recognition/ enforcement regimes in the Contracting States in civil and commercial matters.

The discussions that succeeded the Commission's impetus have been documented elsewhere;[6] it is not the intention of this treatment to dwell on them overlong. Sixteen plenary meetings of the commission of experts were held[7] at the offices of the EEC in Brussels: the first in July 1960 (at which the experts were first nominated)[8], and thereafter until the final sitting held between 5 and 15 July 1966. The commission was under the chairmanship of Professor A. Bülow, then Secretary of State for the German Ministry of Justice. A working group,[9] presided over by a *rapporteur* (Mr Jenard), with delegates from Italy, The Netherlands, France, Germany and the Community itself—together with observers from the Benelux Commission (Mme M. Weser), and two from the Hague Conference (one being G. Droz)—prepared, at its fifteenth session, a first official preliminary draft multilateral treaty[10] on 11 December 1964 for consideration, amendment and approval thereafter by the last committee session in July 1966. Their work was completed in November 1966.

The *raison d'être* for these discussions should detain our attention further. As was apparent from the tenor of M Illerhaus' questions, noted above, certain Member States of the Community had experienced difficulties in having their judgments enforced in other Member States.[11]

The prevailing contemporary regime[12] for the recognition and enforcement of judgments within the Community was (at best) an intricate network of inter-connecting bilateral recognition and enforcement Treaties,[13] or, (at worst), autonomous enforcement regimes, often necessitating lengthy *exequatur*

(1961) *Tractatenblad* No.163, and the *Convention entre La Belgique et Les Pays-Bas sur la compétence judiciaire territoriale, sur la faillite, ainsi que sur l'autorité et l'exécution des décisions judiciaires, des sentences arbitrales et des actes authentiques*, Signée à Bruxelles le 28 Mars 1925, 1929–1930 L.N.T.S., XCIII, 432; Bellet, P. 'L'élaboration d'une convention sur la reconnaissance des jugements dans le cadre du Marché Commun' (1965) *JDI* 833, at p.841; it also resembles, in its Title III, the construction of the *traité simple*, the *Convention on the recognition and enforcement of foreign judgements in civil and commercial matters*, signed at The Hague on 1.2.1971, 144 UNTS 249, especially Articles 1, 2, and 7–9 thereof.

[6] The Jenard Report [1979] OJ C59/1, at p.1 and p.3, and Weser, M. *Convention communautaire sur la compétence judiciaire et l'exécution des décisions*, 1975, at pp.205–06

[7] Arnold, H. 'Die Entwurf eines Gerichtsstands- und Vollstreckungsabkommens für die Europäische Wirtschaftsgemeinschaft' (1965) *AWD* 321.

[8] Scant details in Bülow, A. 'Vereinheitliches Internationales Zivilprozeßrecht in der Europäischen Wirtschaftsgemeinschaft' (1965) *RabelsZ* 473, at p.474.

[9] For details and *dramatis personae* of this Weser, 1975, at pp.205–06; also the Annex to the 'Report on the Convention on jurisdiction and the enforcement of judgments in civil and commercial matters', *Bulletin of the European Communities*, Supplement 12/72, at pp.112–13.

[10] The preliminary draft is set out by Prof. Bülow in (1965) *RabelsZ* 594; officially it is reported in *Documents de la Commission CEE* Nr.14, 371/IV/64, with an explanatory report at Nr.2, 449/IV/65; in English at 1966 Common Market Reports ¶6003.

[11] Above, n.3.

[12] For a general introduction and overview between 1959 and 1968, Mercier P. *Effets internationaux des jugements dans les Etats du Marché Commun*, 1965.

[13] Examples of these Treaties given above at pp.cxix–cxxi.

proceedings,[14] and of varying degrees of xenophobic severity and impenetrability. An expert of the Discussion group charged with reviewing this contemporary system, Martha Weser, produced a detailed report[15] illustrating the varying fate of a judgment rendered in one Member State of the EEC in the remainder. The anomalies she highlights had to be removed if the progress toward economic integration, envisaged in the 1957 Treaty of Rome, was to be nurtured and eventually achieved.

ARTICLE 293 (EX ARTICLE 220) EC AND THE BRUSSELS CONVENTION AS A COMMUNITY[16] INSTRUMENT

Some discussion has taken place[17] as to the exact nature of the Brussels Convention: as EC legislation (of some kind) or (ordinary) international treaty law.[18] Most commentators[19] agree that it is a hybrid of both, an international instrument under the auspices, and to be interpreted teleologically in the light of, Article 293 (ex Article 220) EC and the remaining articles of the EC Treaty.[20] The European

---

[14] An example being Articles 796 and 798 of the (former) Italian *Nuovo Codice di Procedura Civile*; the Jenard Report at p.5.

[15] It is unofficially to be found in various volumes of (1959) *Rev crit*, 613, (1960) *Rev crit*, p.21 onwards, p.151, p.313, p.533 following, and (1961) *Rev crit* p.105; and an English overview at Weser, M. 'Litigation on the Common Market Level' (1964) *AJIL* 44.

[16] Below on comments regarding Council Regulation (EC) No.44/2001 of 22 December 2000 on jurisdiction and the recognition and enforcement of judgments in civil and commercial matters (the 'Brussels I Regulation'), and its replacement of the 1968 Brussels Convention, below; on the interpretative consequences of the umbilical link, Donzallaz, Y. (2001) *AJP* 160, at p.166.

[17] Geimer, R. and Schütze, R. *Europäisches Zivilverfahrensrecht, Kommentar zum EuGVÜ und Lugano-Übereinkommen*, 1997, at p.7, para. 13 onwards; also Kerameus, K. 'Modern Perspectives of International Jurisdiction' in Fletcher, I., Mistelis, L., and Cremona, M. (eds) *Foundations and Perspectives of International Trade Law*, 2001, CH.16, p.237, at p.241, para. 16–009.

[18] On this aspect Brandes, F. *Der gemeinsame Gerichtsstand, Die Zuständigkeit im europäischen Mehrparteienprozeß nach Article 6 Nr.1 EuGVÜ/LÜ*, 1998, at pp.24–28; also Spellenberg, U. 'Der Gerichtsstand des Erfüllungsortes im europäischen Gerichtsstands- und Vollstreckungsübereinkommen' (1978) *ZZP* 38, p.39, an international law treaty on the basis of (what was) Article 220.

[19] The main commentaries in *English* are Stone, P. *The Conflict of Laws*, 1996; Beaumont P. *Civil Jurisdiction in Scotland—Brussels and Lugano Conventions*, 2nd edn, 1995; Briggs, A. *Civil Jurisdiction and Judgments*, 2nd edn, 1997; *Dicey and Morris on the Conflict of Laws*, 13th edn, 2000, Vol. I, especially pp.182–567.; *Cheshire and North's Private International Law*—North, P. and Fawcett, J.J., 13th edn, 1999; Hill, J. *The Law Relating to International Commercial Disputes*, 2nd edn, 1998; Kaye, P. *Law of the European Judgments Convention*, Vols. 1–5, 1999; in *French*, Gaudemet-Tallon, H. *Les Conventions de Bruxelles et de Lugano*, 2nd edn, 1996; *Nouveau Code de Procedure Civile*, Dalloz, 90ème édn, 1998, pp.685–715; Droz, G. *Compétence judiciare et effets des jugements dans le Marché Commun* (Études de la Convention de Bruxelles du 27 septembre 1968), Dalloz, 1972; Donzallaz, Y. *La Convention de Lugano*, Vol I, 1996, paras. 1–1736, Vol II, 1997, paras. 1737–4238, Vol III, 1998, paras. 4239–7164; in *German*, Kropholler, J. *Europäisches Zivilprozeßrecht: Kommentar zu EuGVÜ und Lugano-Übereinkommen*, 6 Aufl., 1998; Geimer, R. and Schütze, R. *Europäisches Zivilverfahrensrech, Kommentar zum EuGVÜ und Lugano-Übereinkommen*, 1997, 1997; Reithmann, C. and Martiny, D. (eds) *Internationales Vertragsrecht, Das internationale Privatrecht der Schuldverträge*, 5 Aufl., 1996.

[20] *Mund and Fester v Hatrex Internationaal Transport* (C-398/92) [1994] ECR I–467, and recently the Convention's expanded links with other international instruments, in *Dieter Krombach v Andre*

Court of Justice itself has, on a number of occasions,[21] had cause to refer back to the (E)EC Treaty's provisions, in the search for justification of a particular (autonomous)[22] interpretation of the terms of the Brussels Convention. A clear example of this occurred in *Mund & Fester v Hatrex Internationaal Transport*,[23] when the link between the Brussels Convention and the EEC Treaty was expressly spelt out. A provision of German law of *Arrest*[24] made the fact that enforcement abroad may have been necessary sufficient grounds for effecting an *Arrest*. Where enforcement of any eventual judgment may have been sought in another EC Member State/Brussels Contracting State, the question arose as to whether this amounted to a covert example of discrimination[25]—as the (Dutch) defendant argued—outlawed by Article 7 (then Article 6, now Article 12) EC Treaty. The Court of Justice thought so. For our purposes, it is the statement, at paragraph 12 of its judgment, that is revealing:

> the provisions of that [Brussels] Convention . . . and also the national provisions to which the Convention refers *are linked to the EEC Treaty*.[26]

It must be borne in mind when looking at the jurisprudence of the European Court, that it is an integrationalist Community instrument that is being

---

Bamberski (C-7/98), 28.3.2000, AG Antonio Saggio's opinion 23.9.1999; that European Community law has embraced measures taken under what once was the second 'pillar' in the Treaty of European Union—Justice and Home Affairs—is witnessed by the efforts of the Council of the EU, in its industrious output of Regulations under (the post-Treaty of Amsterdam) Title IV (ex Title IIIa) EC, Article 61(c), Article 65(a)(b), Article 67—for our purposes the Brussels I Regulation (44/2001), below. It is undeniable that this area of the conflict of laws is being engulfed by EC law.

[21] *Bavaria Fluggesellschaft Schwabe and Co. KG and Germanair Bedarfsluftfahrt GmbH and Co. KG v Eurocontrol* (C9 and 10/77) [1977] ECR 1517, at p.1525, para. 4; and *Somafer SA v Saar-Ferngas AG* (C33/78) [1978] ECR 2183, at p.2190, para. 4.

[22] Or the lack of uniformity justifying a departure from an autonomous interpretation: *Industrie Tessili Italiana Como v Dunlop AG* (C12/76) [1976] ECR 1473, at p.1484, para. 7; now *GIE Groupe Concorde and others v The master of the vessel 'Suhadiwarno Panjan'* (C-440/97) [1999] ECR I–6307, at p.6352, para. 30.

[23] (C-398/92) [1994] ECR I–467; also withdrawn reference in *Carmen Proetta v Andrew Neil* (C-60/99) from the Irish Supreme Court.

[24] §917(1)(2) ZPO, in detail below, Chapter 3, section 3.1(2)(i); also Kessedjian, C. *Note on Provisional and Protective Measures in Private International Law and Comparative Law*, Hague Conference on Private International Law, Prel. Doc. No.10 of October 1988, at pp.24–26.

[25] The courts have dealt with the question of discrimination in relation to security for costs: *Mary Pitt v James Bolger and Robert Barry* [1996] 2 ILRM 68, HC, *William Maher v Paschal Phelan* [1996] 1 ILRM 359, HC, *Carmen Proetta v Andrew Neil* [1996] 1 ILRM 457, HC; also *Nguyen v Searchnet Associates Ltd* 2000 SLT (Sh Ct) 83, at pp.86–87, and *Dieter Rossmeier v Mounthooly Transport and ors* [1999] (Scots CS) 216, *The Times* 7.2.2000, Crt. Sess. Inner House; *Fitzgerald v Williams* [1996] QB 657, and *Nasser v United Bank of Kuwait*, 11.4.2001, CA (Mance LJ, re interaction of Articles 6(1), 14 ECHR and CPR 25.13(2)(a)(b); a respondent's being ordinarily resident outside the Contracting States is the crucial factor, not whether he may have assets within them: *De Beer v Kanaar and Co.*, 9.8.2001, CA, (Jonathan Parker LJ), *Zappia Middle East Construction Company Ltd v Clifford Chance (a firm)*, 5.6.2001, CA (Robert Walker LJ); now *OGH* 16.6.1999 (2000) ZfRV 30 (Contracting State domiciliaries are released from security for costs orders under Austrian civil procedure code); Cebecioglu, T. *Stellung des Ausländers im Zivilprozeß*, 2000, at p.201 following; *Bundesgericht* 30.7.2001 *S contre Banque 3 et autre*, unreported.

[26] [1994] ECR I–467, at p.478.

construed, not a piece of domestic (English) legislation, with its own canons of construction.

As has been seen, Article 220 of the EEC Treaty and its (renumbered) successors exhorted the original six Member States to (what was then) the Treaty of Rome to enter into mutual discussions 'with a view to ensuring for the benefit of their nationals: . . . the simplification of the formalities governing the reciprocal recognition and execution of judicial decisions.' Yet the Committee of experts charged with this task went beyond the strict letter of Articled 220 in the draft Convention, produced in 1964,[27] by including a Title II, governing the occasions when a particular Member State would, and would not, be permitted to take jurisdiction over persons domiciled[28] or, *inter alia*, disputes concerning land[29] situated in, another Member State.[30]

At that stage in the evolution process of what would become the 1968 Convention, a fundamental principle made manifest in its preamble[31]—and bearing a heavy influence from other articles of the Treaty of Rome/EC Treaty[32]—was that of non-discrimination among Community nationals, and their assimilation[33] into the economic and legal structure of any other Member State in which they happened to be 'domiciled'. To this end, traditional bases of jurisdiction in the Member States, reposing, *inter alia*, merely on the nationality of one of the parties—commonly the plaintiff/claimant—had to be abrogated.[34]

More generally, the autonomous civil procedural codes of the Member States, while containing similarities in respect to certain jurisdictional rules,[35] could no longer, if non-discrimination was to be achieved, be invoked against other Member States' domiciliaries. In their stead, a uniform set of jurisdictional provisions[36] common to all the Member States would be inaugurated. Not only would non-discrimination of EEC domiciliaries be eradicated *inter se*, but in addition the number of defences to recognition and enforcement in Title III could, in consequence, be kept at an absolute minimum.

---

[27] A draft in German is reproduced by Bülow in 1965 *RabelsZ* 594, in English, above, at n.10.

[28] For a definition of this concept, and ss.41, 42 Civil Jurisdiction and Judgments Act 1982 ('CJJA 1982'), below at n. 263. Paras. 9–10 of Sch.1 to The Civil Jurisdiction and Judgments Order 2001 will apply from 1.3.2002 to identify the domicile of individuals and the seat of a company for the purposes of the Brussels I Regulation.

[29] Article 16(1); the remaining sub-paragraphs of Article 16 also contain important areas of exclusive jurisdiction.

[30] And also where there is a choice of court of a Contracting State, Article 17; below, chapter 2.

[31] Weser, M. 'Bases of Judicial Jurisdiction in the Common Market Countries' (1961) *Am J Comp L* 323, at p.339.

[32] Especially Article 7/6 (now Article 12 EC), and Articles 52, 59 and 60 EC (now Arts 43, 49 and 50, respectively).

[33] Comments of M. Goldman at meeting of 1 May 1969 of French private international law jurists in Weser, M. 'La libre circulation des jugements dans le Marché Commun' (1969) *Dr Intern Privé* 353, at p.366.

[34] Mercier, 1965, at p.159; also Weser, M. (1961) *Am J Comp L* 323, at p.328.

[35] Notably, the *actor sequitur forum rei* principle, now in Article 2.

[36] Articles 2, 5 and 7 of the draft, and considered by them to be 'reasonable' by Droz, G. 'Réflexions pour une réforme des articles 14 et 15 du Code civil français' (1975) *Rev crit* 1, at p.3

THE FORM OF THE BRUSSELS AND LUGANO CONVENTIONS THEMSELVES

The Brussels Convention has existed, or continues to exist, in one of five 'versions'—the earliest of which are now of historical interest only. The 'original'1968 Brussels Convention was the culmination of the work previously mentioned in the opening pages. It was signed by France, Germany, Belgium, The Netherlands, Luxembourg, and Italy on 26 September 1968 in Brussels, and came into force in those states on 1 February 1973. It is reported in English at [1978] OJ L304/36; its attendant report,[37] the 'Jenard Report'[38], explaining, *inter alia*, how the drafters envisioned its provisions to be understood, is available at [1979] OJ C59/1. Its second manifestation, the 1978 'version' of the Brussels Convention,[39] incorporated the changes[40] made to the original Convention by the 1978 Luxembourg Accession[41] Convention[42] ([1978] OJ L304/1), and is reported in the Official Journal at [1978] OJ L304/77. It came into force for the Accession States on 1 November 1986 for Denmark,[43] on 1 January 1987 for the UK,[44] and on 1 June 1988 in The Republic of Ireland.[45] Its own explanatory report, the 'Schlosser Report' is to be found at [1979] OJ C59/71.

Further formal alterations occurred on Greece's accession with the 1982 'version' of the Brussels Convention.[46] This again incorporated (minor) changes

---

[37] These *travaux préparatoires* are an innovation for the English court, as interpretative aids to the Conventions under ss.3(3) and 3B(2) CJJA 1982.

[38] 'Report on the Convention on jurisdiction and the enforcement of judgments in civil and commercial matters' by Mr. P. Jenard, 'The Jenard Report' [1979] OJ C59/1, one of the *travaux préparatoires* available for consultation by the Contracting State courts.

[39] The Brussels Convention on jurisdiction and the enforcement of judgments in civil and commercial matters of 27 September 1968 [1972] JO L299/32; English version at [1978] OJ L304/77.

[40] The material alterations effected to this Convention will be mentioned where they have a bearing on the Articles under discussion.

[41] Of Denmark, the UK and Ireland; for the UK implementing legislation, and subsequent amendments, 'Courts and Legal Services', Vol.11, *Halsbury's Statutes of England and Wales*, 4th ed., 2000 Reissue, p.1158 and 'Judgments and Execution' Vol.22, *Ibid*, 1995 Reissue, at p.509 onwards.

[42] Convention on the Accession of the Kingdom of Denmark, Ireland and the United Kingdom of Great Britain and Northern Ireland to the Convention on jurisdiction and enforcement of judgments in civil and commercial matters, 9.10.1978, [1978] OJ L304/1: ('The 1978 Luxembourg Accession Convention').

[43] §§ 1 and 2 the Danish implementing law Law Nr.324 of 4 June 1986, (in German translation) in Müller, H.B. *Die Umsetzung der europäischen Übereinkommen von Rom und Brüssel in das Recht der Mitgliedstaaten*, 1997, at p.283.

[44] Section 2(1), and ss.1, 2(2) CJJA 1982, which incorporated the 1978 Brussels Convention (in Sch.1) (and subsequent Accession Conventions, as defined in lengthening numbers in s.1(1)) into English law on that date: Article 2 Civil Jurisdiction and Judgments Act 1982 (Commencement No.3) Order 1986, SI 1986/2044.

[45] The (current) Irish implementing legislation is a new 1998 Act, in force 1.12.1999, incorporating the changes brought about by the 1996 Accession Convention (below)—Jurisdiction of Courts and Enforcement of Judgments Act 1998, *Acts of the Oeirachtas*, No. 52 of 1998; all (Accession) Conventions are set out in the First to Eighth Schedules.

[46] The Brussels Convention on jurisdiction and the enforcement of judgments in civil and commercial matters of 27 September 1968, 11.4.1983, [1983] OJ C97/2.

effected to the 1978 version by the 1982 Luxembourg Accession Convention[47] ([1982] OJ L388/1), and is reported at [1983] OJ C97/2. It came into force in the Acceding State, Greece, on 1 April 1989. Its report, the 'Evrigenis and Kerameus Report', is to be found at [1986] OJ C298/1.

More important changes were made in the 1989 'version' of the Brussels Convention,[48] incorporating alterations to the 1982 version by the 1989 Donostia—San Sebastián Accession[49] Convention[50] ([1989] OJ L285/1). It is reported at [1990] OJ C189/2. It came into force in the two Acceding States, Spain and Portugal, on 1 February 1991 and 1 July 1991, respectively. Its report, the 'Cruz, Real, Jenard Report', is at [1990] C189/35.

Yet further (formal) amendments to this 1989 Convention have been made by a 1996 'version' of the Brussels Convention.[51] This final, yet unfortunately not universally applicable[52] form of the Brussels Convention, incorporates the changes made to the 1989 version by the 1996 Brussels Accession[53] Convention[54] ([1997] OJ C15/1), and is reported with the amendments at [1998] OJ C27/3. It came into force for its Acceding States, Austria,[55] Sweden and Finland on 1 December 1998, 1 January 1999 and 1 April 1999 respectively, and in the UK on 1 January 2001.[56] A report is not yet available.

A 'Protocol on the interpretation by the Court of Justice of the Convention of 27 September 1968 on jurisdiction and the enforcement of judgments in civil and

---

[47] Convention on the Accession of the Hellenic Republic to the Convention on jurisdiction and enforcement of judgments in civil and commercial matters, 31.12.1982, [1982] OJ L388/1: ('The 1982 Luxembourg Accession Convention').

[48] The Brussels Convention on jurisdiction and the enforcement of judgments in civil and commercial matters of 27 September 1968, 28.7.1990 [1990] OJ C189/2, the version currently in force in the UK; on 1.3.2002 the Brussels I Regulation 44/2001 will come into force.

[49] Of Spain and Portugal.

[50] Convention on the accession of the Kingdom of Spain and the Portuguese Republic to the Convention on jurisdiction and enforcement of judgments in civil and commercial matters, 3.10.1989, [1989] OJ L285/1 ('The Donostia—San Sebastian Convention' or 'The 1989 Accession Convention').

[51] The Brussels Convention on jurisdiction and the enforcement of judgments in civil and commercial matters of 27 September 1968, 26.1.1998, [1998] OJ C27/3.

[52] As at 27.2.2002, it is in force throughout all 15 EU States, except Belgium.

[53] Of Austria, Finland and Sweden.

[54] Convention on the accession of the Republic of Austria, the Republic of Finland and the Kingdom of Sweden to the Convention on jurisdiction and enforcement of judgments in civil and commercial matters, 15.1.1997, [1997] OJ C15/1 ('The 1996 Accession Convention').

[55] Burgstaller, A. (ed) *Internationales Zivilverfahrensrecht*, 2000, at p.27 onwards for details and effects.

[56] As from 1.1.2001, a new Statutory Instrument—the CJJA 1982 (Amendment) Order 2000 SI 2000/1824, (Article 8 and Schs. 1 and 2)—substituted new Schedules 1 and 2 in, and added a new Schedule 3BB to, the CJJA 1982 (*London Gazette*, Friday 24.11.2000, No.56040, p.13274). Part II of the Order had from 1.8.2000 already made the necessary changes to the Lugano Convention to receive Poland as a 1988 Lugano Convention Contracting State: *Hansard* HL vol 614, No.111, col 1264 (30 June 2000); for Polish references *Dz. U.* No.10, items 132 and 133 (2000); Article 91(1) of the Polish Constitution provides that a ratified international agreement, such as the Lugano Convention, after its promulgation in the Official Gazette 'constitutes part of the domestic legal order and applies directly . . .'; the Czech Republic has also expressed an interest in adhering, apparently to the Swiss Embassy in Prague—(2001) *IPRax* 501, at p.510.

commercial matters', has, since coming into force on 1 September 1975, enabled the (ever increasing number of) Contracting State courts to request a preliminary ruling from the European Court of Justice on the interpretation of the Brussels Convention,[57] the various Accession Conventions, and the Protocol itself.[58] Article 2(1)(2)(3) of the Protocol sets out the Contracting State courts that may request a ruling, and, in Article 3(1), the circumstances[59] in which an Article 2(1) court (commonly the Contracting State's highest appellate court) *must* request one. Outside these circumstances these courts presumably have a discretion[60] to refer a question for interpretation.

The courts listed in Article 2(2)(3) (essentially appeal courts)[61], under Article 3(2), merely have *a discretion*[62] to refer a question for interpretation. To date[63] there have been 111[64] references for a preliminary ruling on the interpretation of the Conventions, strictly speaking, which have ended in a decision[65] by the European Court. Thirteen cases have been referred to the Court's docket, but were withdrawn[66] for various reasons. Eleven[67] cases are still pending a decision of the court.

Counting the total number of cases referred, ending either in withdrawal or decision, together with cases currently pending (with or, as yet, without an

---

[57] The English courts initially adopted a sparing, reticent attitude towards references under this Protocol: *Hamed El Chiaty and Co. v The Thomas Cook Group Ltd (The 'Nile Rhapsody')* [1994] 1 Lloyd's Rep. 382, at p.394 (Simon Brown LJ): litigation had consumed so much court time and legal expense; *Firswood Ltd v Petra Bank* [1996] CLC 608, at p.619 (Schiemann LJ), not troubling the ECJ with a reference at the expense of more important references; *In re Harrods (Buenos Aires) Ltd* [1992] Ch 90, at p.98, (Dillon LJ), not 'appropriate'; note recently a change in *Haji-Ioannou v Frangos* [1999] 2 Lloyd's Rep. 337, CA, and *Lubbe v Cape Plc* [2000] 1 WLR 1545, at p.1562 (Lord Bingham of Cornhill), *forum non conveniens* answer unclear.

[58] Article 1. But not, it seems, on (English) domestic legislation based on the Brussels Convention: *Kleinwort Benson Ltd v City of Glasgow District Council* (C–246/93) [1995] ECR I–615; but compare Sch.4 CJJA 1982 to Italian law *Riforma del sistema italiano di diritto internazionale privato* l.31 maggio 1995, n.218 Article 3(2).

[59] If the Article 2(1) court 'considers that a decision [of the European Court of Justice] on the question is necessary to enable it to give judgment'; on this aspect also the (English) jurisprudence built up around references under Article 177 (now Article 234) EC.

[60] Below, following footnote.

[61] *Christoph von Gallera v Gisèle Maître* (C–56/84) [1984] ECR 1769 and *Habourdin International SA and Banque Nationale de Paris v SpA Italocremona* (C–80/83) [1984] ECR 3639; for the notion of a 'court' in the reference procedure, AG Colomer's opinion of 28.6.2001 in *François de Coster v Collège des Bourgmestres et Echevins de Watermael-Boitsfort* (C–17/00), unreported.

[62] Under the same circumstances, as mentioned in n.61. Jayme, E. *Wiener Vorträge: Internationales Privat- und Verfahrensrecht Rechtsvergleichung Kunst-und Kulturrecht*, 2001, at pp.241–48.

[63] As at 27.2.2002.

[64] Out of a total of 137.

[65] The most recent of which are *Coreck Maritime GmbH v Handelsveem B.V., V. Berg and Sons Ltd, Man Producten Rotterdam B.V. and The Peoples Insurance Company of China* (C387–98) [2000] ECR I–9337, and *Richard Gaillard v Alaya Chekili* (C–518/99) [2000] OJ C63/18, ECJ judgment of 5.4.2001.

[66] P.xxv of case list above, for withdrawn cases; the most recent of which is *A.T. Van der Plast v W. Hartog Guis* (C-105/01), a reference from the *Hoge Raad*, removed from the register on 28.5.2001.

[67] The most recent being: *Freistaat Bayern v Jan Blijdenstein* (C–433/01) [2002] OJ C31/3, *Marseille Fret SA v Seatrano Shipping Company Ltd* (C–24/02), 22.1.2002, pending, and *Turner v Grovit and others* [2002] 1 WLR 107, a reference from the House of Lords.

Advocate General's opinion), the German courts have made most use[68] of this reference procedure, numbering somewhere approaching half of all references—52 out of 137; next comes The Netherlands with 24, then France with 20, the UK 14, Belgium 12, Italy 8, Austria 3,[69] Ireland two, with Denmark and Luxembourg one apiece.

'The Convention on jurisdiction and the enforcement of judgments in civil and commercial matters' signed at Lugano, Switzerland on 16 September 1988, and known as the Lugano Convention[70] is a multilateral Treaty, parallel[71] in form to the Brussels Convention. It links the members (or former members) of EFTA to the Brussels Convention Contracting States under a similar jurisdictional and enforcement instrument. It came into force in the UK on 1 May 1992,[72] and is reported in its official English version at [1988] OJ L319/9. It, too, has an accompanying report, the 'Jenard/Möller Report', located at [1990] OJ C189/57. The proceedings that lead up to its signature on 16 September 1988, and the discussions of the various delegates, have been collected together.[73] The process of negotiating this Treaty with non-(E)EC participants was instructive, as it highlighted certain weaknesses in the Brussels Convention itself (in its 1982 version), and gave voice to concerns of some EFTA States about the interpretation certain articles[74] of the Brussels Convention had received.

Its relationship with the Brussels Convention is governed by Article 54B(1)(2)(3) of the Lugano Convention. Of particular note should be the differences in wording between both Conventions, especially in Article 16(1)(b) and subtle differences in Article 5(1) (individual contracts of employment). Since the coming into force of the 1989 Brussels Convention, the distinction between jurisdiction clauses in 'international trade or commerce' (in Article 17(1)(c) Lugano) has disappeared.

---

[68] One contributory factor may well be Article 101 Abs. I of the German Constitution which states '[n]iemand darf seinem gesetzlichen Richter entzogen werden', that ('no-one can be deprived of his lawful judge'), even if a European Court of Justice variety: *Grundgesetz*, Lfg 22.4.1992 at §101, 291–92 : 'Article 101 Abs I, Satz 2 erstreckt sich auch auf die Befolgung der durch Article 177 EWGV begründeten Pflicht zur Einleitung eines Vorlageverfahrens . . .' ('Article 101 Abs. 1, second sentence also extends to following up the duty founded on Article 177 of the EEC Treaty to submit a reference for a preliminary ruling'); Starck, C. (ed) *Bonner Grundgesetz*, 4ᵉʳ Aufl., Band 3: Artikel 79–146, 2001.
[69] *Rudolf Gabriel v Schlank and Schick GmbH* (C-96/00), AG Jacob's opinion 13.12.2001, and *Verein für Konsumenteninformationen v Henkel* (C-96/00) [2000] OJ C192/11, pending; *Gantner Electronic GmbH v Basch Exploitatie Maatschappij B.V.* (C-111/01) [2001] OJ C134/10, pending.
[70] As regards its scope vis-à-vis the Brussels Convention *ratione personae/loci*, Article 54B(1)(2)(3) of the Lugano Convention; and on the differences in great detail Kohlegger, G. 'Ein Vergleich zwischen EuGVÜ und LGVÜ' (1999)*ÖJZ* 41.
[71] From an Austrian perspective Lechner, M. and Mayr, P. *Das Übereinkommen von Lugano*, 1996; Burgstaller, A. (ed) *Internationales Zivilverfahrensrecht*, 2000, at pp.31–33; also Klauser, A. *EuGVÜ und EVÜ*, 1999.
[72] As from 1.5.1992, s.1(1) of the Civil Jurisdiction and Judgments Act 1991 inserted into the CJJA 1982 a new s.3A and 3B, and Schedule 3C, to incorporate the Lugano Convention into English law: Article 2 Civil Jurisdiction and Judgments Act 1991 (Commencement) Order 1992 SI 1992/745.
[73] The 15 meetings between 8–9 October 1985–24–25 March 1988 are reported in *Convention de Lugano*, II. *Travaux Préparatoires*, Publications de l'Institut suisse de droit comparé, 1991.
[74] Notably Articles 5(1), 17, and 21.

Of some interest should be Article 57(4) of the Lugano Convention, which provides an additional ground to refuse recognition and enforcement in Title III;[75] special care also had to be exercised (before the end of 1999) regarding the taking of jurisdiction under Article 5(1) against Swiss domiciliaries—a reservation[76] in Article 1a of the Protocol 1 enabled the Swiss courts to refuse to recognise or enforce decisions of other Lugano Contracting States when jurisdiction was based solely on Article 5(1), if the defendant was a Swiss domiciliary, and the defendant objected to recognition or enforcement in Switzerland.

A notable absence from the Lugano Convention is a reference Protocol to the European Court of Justice; in its stead are (mutual) declarations,[77] in Article 1 of Protocol 2 on the Uniform interpretation of the Lugano Convention. These are attempts to harmonise as far as possible the interpretation of the terms of both Conventions.[78]

WHICH VERSION (IF ANY) OF THE BRUSSELS CONVENTION TO APPLY[79] IN THE UNITED KINGDOM:[80] THE APPLICABLE DATES[81]

A dispute as to jurisdiction (or for the recognition/enforcement of a Contracting State judgment) comes before the English courts, which may or may not involve the application of one or other version of the Brussels Convention against a defendant domiciled[82] in another Contracting State. Which version, if any, is to be applied?[83]

---

[75] A provision regarding judgments granted on jurisdiction taken under Article 57 conventions.

[76] It is not absolute: Article 1a(2) and (3). Since 31.12.1999 it has ceased to have effect, and can no longer prevent recognition or enforcement of judgments rendered before that date in contravention of its provisions: *Bundesgericht* 26.10.2000 *Heinz Fischer AG gegen Firma Alois Meier* BGE 126, III, 540, at p.543; *Bundesgericht* 23.7.2001 *M.R. gegen H AG*, unreported; Markus, A. 'Der schweizerische Vorbehalt nach Protokoll Nr.1 Lugano-Übereinkommen: Vollstreckungsaufschub oder Vollstreckungshindernis?' (1999) 135 *ZBJV* 57.

[77] Also the declarations, at [1988] OJ L319/37, and L319/40.

[78] For Swiss courts' use of this harmonising feature, *Bundesgericht* 26.9.1997 *A., B. und C. gegen D.* 123 BGE, III, 414 (citing the English Court of Appeal decision of *Dresser UK Ltd and others v Falcongate Freight Management Ltd and others (The 'Duke of Yare')* [1992] 2 All ER 450); also liasing in *OGH* 28.4.2000 (2001) *JBL* 117, at pp.118–19 and *Cour d'appel de Paris* 6.10.1999 *Sola c/ Soc La Tribune de Genève* (2001) *JDI* 146.

[79] We are assuming for the present that the Conventions apply *ratione materiae*, Article 1; as to which below.

[80] For jurisdiction *within* the UK, see Part II, ss.16–19 and Sch. 4 to the CJJA 1982—for some of the problems of intra-UK jurisdiction, the lack of any comparable *lis pendens* provisions in Articles 21/22 and *forum non conveniens*, *Norbrook Laboratories Ltd v Export Credits Guarantee Department*, 13.10.1992, N. Ireland CA; for (autonomous) jurisdictional provisions in civil (and presumably commercial) proceedings in Scotland see Part III, ss.20–23 and Sch 8 rr.1–8 of CJJA 1982.

[81] For the *point in time* which is crucial for the taking of jurisdiction, for the application of *lis alibi pendens*, or for the recognition or enforcement of a foreign judgment, refer to the next section.

[82] Or regarding land situated in another Contracting State, Article 16.

[83] Unfortunately the 1996 Accession Convention (of three of the former Lugano Contracting States) has still not yet, at 27.2.2002, come into force in Belgium; therefore the 1989 Brussels Convention continues to apply between Belgium and the UK (and other Contracting States), and the Lugano Convention between it and Austria, Finland and Sweden.

The process by which the various Accession Conventions have come into force has not been uniform throughout the European Union, so a little care is needed when seeking to apply the correct (or any) version *ratione temporis*. As far as the UK is concerned, the operative date for the application of the 1978 Brussels Convention is, as has been mentioned, 1 January 1987. From that date, the 1978 Brussels Convention has had[84] to be applied as against domiciliaries[85] from Denmark and all the other original Contracting States (France, Germany,[86] Belgium, The Netherlands, Luxembourg,[87] Italy)—except Ireland. The 1978 Brussels Convention only came into force in Ireland on 1 June 1988.

As far as the UK and the 1982 Brussels Convention are concerned, the operative date for the application of the 1982 Brussels Convention as against Greek domiciliaries[88] is 1 October 1989.[89]

The operative date for the application of the 1989 version of the Brussels Convention is a little more complex. It came into force in the UK on 1 December 1991.[90] As from this date in the UK, this version has therefore had to be applied to French, Dutch, and Spanish domiciliaries.[91] As from 1 February 1992, it has had to be applied to Luxembourg domiciliaries; from 1 May 1992 to Italian, and from 1 July 1992 to Greek and Portuguese domiciliaries. As regards German and Danish domiciliaries the dates are 1 December 1994 and 1 March 1996 respectively; and

---

[84] But Article 35 of the 1978 Accession Convention, which allows the UK/Irish courts to (continue to) take jurisdiction over Contracting State defendants if the parties had agreed *in writing* (before the Convention's entry into force) to submit their contract to the law of a part of the UK/Ireland: *New Hampshire Insurance Co. and others v Strabag Bau A.G. and others* [1992] 1 Lloyd's Rep. 361, CA.

[85] Note also too the exclusive competences in Article 16 (e.g. land in such other Contracting States), and to a choice of a Contracting State court under Article 17.

[86] Note German domiciliaries' rights to use German procedural law in § 68, §§72–74 of their ZPO is expressly reserved to them in Article V of the Protocol to the Brussels Convention.

[87] Care must be exercised with regard to the Luxembourgeois: Art I of the protocol (re Article 5(1))—and especially regarding the formalities in Article 17 jurisdiction clauses: *Porta-Leasing GmbH v Prestige International S.A.* (C784/79) [1980] ECR 1517 and their rigorous application in *Tribunal de première instance de Bruxelles* 13.12.1996 *S.A. Bureau Gerard et autres c/ Seligmann et Société de droit luxembourgeois S.A.R.L. Alfred Seligman et cie* 1996 *Pas. Belge*, III, 18 and *Rechtbank van koophandel te Veurne* 2.4.1997 *SARL Omicron distribution / BVBA Konstruktiewerkhuis en draineerbedrijf R. Vandezande* 1998 *Rev. dr. comm. belge* 401; *OGH* 16.1.2001 (2001) *ZfRV* 152; the Protocol has proved to be toothless in an enforcement context, however: (Luxembourg) *Cour Supérieure de Justice* 5.3.1974 *Mamer—Société Brand Ladenbau* 1972–1974 *Pas. Lux.* 425 (1975) *Rev crit* 660, *Cour Supérieure de Justice* 11.11.1975 *Soc. Weinor—S.A.R.L. Wiron Mod'Enfants* 1975–1977 *Pas. Lux.* 230, and *Cour d'appel de Luxembourg* 20.5.1999 *Entreprise de Constructions Pedinotti c/ Sollase* 2000 *Pas. Lux.* 200, at p.203 (breach of Protocol and Article 17 (by a French court) not a matter for subsequent censure in Luxembourg under Articles 28 and 27(1) in the enforcement context); Article 63(1)(2) of the Brussels I Regulation will ensure that the Article 5(1) and Article 23 anomalies will continue to exist under the Regulation as regards the Luxembourgeois.

[88] Again also Article 16 exclusive (Greek) competence and any Greek choice of court clause under Article 17.

[89] Civil Jurisdiction and Judgments Act 1982 (Amendment) Order 1989 SI 1989/1346, Article 1.

[90] Civil Jurisdiction and Judgments Act 1982 (Amendment) Order 1990 SI 1990/2591, Articles 1 and 12(1)–(3).

[91] For the sake of repetition, the same point can be made here under Articles 16 and 17.

the 1989 version has found belated application to Belgian domiciliaries as from 1 October 1997 in the UK courts.

The 1996 version of the Brussels Convention has had to be applied in the UK and throughout the European Union (except Belgium) since the 1 January 2001, most notably to defendants domiciled (and judgments[92] emanating from courts) in the former Lugano Contracting States of Austria, Finland and Sweden.

As far as the 1988 Lugano Convention itself is concerned, it came into force in the UK on 1 May 1992[93] and has had to be applied since then to domiciliaries in (and the decisions of courts from) Switzerland.[94] As regards Sweden, Finland and Austria,[95] as has been mentioned, from 1.1.2001, they are to be regarded as Brussels Convention Contracting States. The Lugano Convention has been applied in relations between the UK and Norway since 1 May 1993.

THE MECHANISMS BY WHICH A PARTICULAR VERSION (IF ANY) OF THE BRUSSELS CONVENTION IS TO BE APPLIED IN THE UNITED KINGDOM: THE INITIATION OF PROCEEDINGS, *LIS PENDENS* AND THE DATE A CONTRACTING STATE JUDGMENT WAS 'GIVEN'/RENDERED

Armed with the above dates, the courts in the UK can now seek to determine whether a particular date falls inside or outside a point in time ascertained by the following determining factors, set up by the various transitional provisions of the Conventions:

As regards the UK courts' taking jurisdiction[96] under Title II of (any or a particular version of) the Brussels Convention

Article 54 of all versions of the Brussels Conventions, Article 34(1) of the 1978 Accession Convention, Article 12(1) of the 1982 Accession Convention, Article 29(1) of the Donostia—San Sebastián Convention (and Article 13(1) of the 1996 Accession Convention),[97] all provide in similar wording when a particular

---

[92] For the sake of repetition, the same point can be made here under Articles 16 and 17, and n.85.

[93] Above text at n.72 and Civil Jurisdiction and Judgments Act 1991, and accompanying statutory instrument.

[94] Note the (former) caveats re Swiss domiciliaries, in Article 1 of the Protocol; and Walter, G. 'Wechselwirkungen zwischen europäischem und nationalem Zivilprozeßrecht: Lugano-Übereinkommen und Schweizer Recht' (1994) *ZZP* 301—yet Article Ia of the Protocol only prevented recognition and enforcement, not another Lugano Contracting State's taking jurisdiction over a Swiss domiciliary—*Cour d'appel de Paris* 13.10.1999 *Soc. Atlantic Ocean Line c/ Soc. Tati et Soc AIG Europe*, unreported Lexis.

[95] The dates for their former status as Lugano Contracting States: 1 January 1993, 1 July 1993 and 1 September 1996, respectively.

[96] Special provision for UK and Ireland re *lex causae* in contracts concluded before its entry into force—Article 35 1978 Accession Convention, and *New Hampshire Insurance Co. and others v Strabag Bau A.G. and others* [1990] 2 Lloyd's Rep. 61, QBD (Potter J) [1992] 1 Lloyd's Rep. 361, CA.

[97] Reproduced in Sch.3BB of the CJJA 1982 (as inserted by Article 8 and Sch.3 of The Civil Jurisdiction and Judgments Act 1982 (Amendment) Order 2000 SI 2000/1824, in force from 1.1.2001).

version of Brussels Convention, or, where relevant for an Acceding State, a particular Accession Convention is to be applied by the courts of the State of origin: only to legal proceedings 'instituted'[98] after the entry into force of the particular Convention in that Contracting State.[99]

As regards the UK's obligation to observe *lis pendens* in another Contracting State under Articles 21/22/23

Elsbeth Freifrau von Horn v Kevin Cinnamond[100] has given guidance to the Contracting State courts in the situation of the transitional application of the Conventions, and particularly Articles 21/22 thereof. If the Brussels Convention came into force between two Contracting States, in the interim period between the court first seised taking jurisdiction (under its national rules) and the court second seised taking jurisdiction (under the Brussels Convention), the second seised court is to apply Articles 21/22 if the court first seised has assumed jurisdiction on the basis of a rule that accords[101] with, *inter alia*,[102] the provisions of Title II of the Brussels Convention. The *lis pendens* provisions are, however, not to apply if *both* sets of proceedings were commenced[103] (under national rules) before the Brussels Convention came into force in the respective Contracting States.[104]

As regards the UK's obligation to recognise/enforce judgments of Contracting States under Title III of the Brussels Convention

Again, Article 54[II][105] of the Brussels Conventions, Article 34(3) (and Article 34(2)) of the 1978 Accession Convention, Article 12(2) of the 1982 Accession

---

[98] Thought to mean on the 'issue' of proceedings, not their service, Briggs, 1997, at p.28, n.109 and Briggs, A. *The Conflict of Laws*, 2002, at p.58: CPR 7.2(1) the 'start' of proceedings on 'issuing' the claim form—a view now provisionally supported by Lord Steyn in *Canada Trust Co. and others v Stolzenberg and others (Nr. 2)* [2002] 1 AC 1, at p.12; on 'issue' also the position in Austria, Burgstaller, A. (ed) *Internationales Zivilverfahrensrecht*, 2000, at p.41, para. 2.32; *contra*, 'service', Kropholler, 1998, at p.454, para. 2 'erhoben'; adopted as correct in *LG München* 29.5.1995 IPRspr. 1995 Nr. 146, at p.295; concurring in the 'service' view *OGH* 12.7.2000 (2001) *ZfRV* 68, at p.69; and Gaudemet-Tallon, 1996, at p.40, para. 52 'intentées'.

[99] I.e. the rendering court. At the time of writing there now appears in this regard to be a period of stability and uniformity in the UK: the 1996 version of the Brussels Convention is in force for all the Brussels Convention Contracting States, except Belgium; on 1.3.2002, the Brussels I Regulation 44/2001 will come into force—The Civil Jurisdiction and Judgments Order 2001, SI 2001/3929, and The Civil Procedure (Amendment Nr. 5) Rules 2001, SI 2001/4015.

[100] (C-163/95) [1997] ECR I–5451.

[101] For a possible meaning of this, below at n.108.

[102] Or under a bi-lateral recognition and enforcement Treaty previously in force between the two States.

[103] Note not at the date of the hearing of the challenge to jurisdiction, *Davy International Ltd and others v Voest Alpine Industrieanlagenbau GmbH and others* [1999] 1 All ER 103 (Mummery LJ) at p.114.

[104] *Davy International Ltd and others v Voest Alpine Industrieanlagenbau GmbH and others* [1999] 1 All ER 103, at p.114.

[105] Examples from German jurisprudence in a similar situation are *OLG München* 28.5.1974 IPRspr. 1974 Nr. 177, *OLG Koblenz* 27.9.1976 IPRspr. 1976 Nr. 174, for this transitional article in operation.

Convention, Article 29(2) of the Donostia—San Sebastián, (and Article 13(2) of the 1996 Accession Convention), provide in similar terms for one[106] particular scenario: 'judgments given[107] after the entry into force of . . . [a particular Convention in the rendering court of a Contracting State] in proceedings instituted [there] before that date': in this situation, Title III's liberal benefits must be extended to such a Contracting State judgment if 'jurisdiction was founded upon rules which accorded[108] with those provided for [*inter alia*] in Title II of [the Convention]'.

THE PAST, AND THE LEGAL POSITION OF THE CONTRACTING STATES IN SITUATIONS WHERE THE BRUSSELS/LUGANO CONVENTIONS DO NOT APPLY *RATIONE TEMPORIS/RATIONE MATERIAE*[109]

Prior to the entry into force of the Conventions, many of the Contracting States were inter-linked by a network of bilateral and multilateral recognition and enforcement Treaties,[110] listed in ever increasing numbers as they ceased to have

---

[106] By implication therefore, it is obvious that judgments given after the entry into force of a particular Convention in proceedings also 'instituted' after its entry into force are covered.

[107] Due to Article 25's wide definition of 'judgment', it seems a merely confirming (French) appeal court decision will have been 'given' (for transitional application) even if the lower court rendered judgment in the case prior to the Convention's coming into force: O'Sullivan J in *Société Lacoste SA and Papeteries Sibiline Stenay SA v Keeley Group Ltd* [1999] 1 ILRM 510, at p.516, Irish HC (appeal pending); similar outcome in *Cour d'appel de Luxembourg* 2.3.2000 *Vilain c/ Vilain* 2000 *Pas. Lux.* 282, where the relevant judgment filed for enforcement was, again, merely a confirming decision of the French *Cour d'appel de Douai, not* the first instance decision; the point seems to be whether the 'appeal' court merely confirms the lower court's decision, or substitutes its own: Jolowicz, J.A. *On Civil Procedure*, 2000, at p.275, p.279, and pp.300–01; cf *Guiard v De Clermond and Donner* [1914] 3 KB 145, at p.155: '[the] judgment now takes its whole force and effect not from the original [French] decision . . . but . . . from the judgment of the [French] Court of Appeal', (Lawrence J); cf. *De Santis v Russo* [2001] QCA 457, 26 October 2001, (McPherson JA).

[108] The meaning and exact extent of this phrase 'accorded' has never been examined by the European court (c.f. *Elsbeth Freifrau von Horn v Kevin Cinnamond* (C-163/95) [1997] ECR I–5451). The actual national jurisdictional base compared to Convention jurisdiction in *OLG München* 28.5.1974 IPRspr. 1974 Nr. 177, at p.467, but *not* in *OLG Celle* 8.12.1977 (1979) *RIW/AWD* 131, at p.131; *Cour d'appel de Paris Le Comptoir Commercial d'Orient S.A. c/ Medtrafina S.A.* 5.4.1994 (1995) *Rev crit* 573, at pp.586–87; also uncertain is the position where a defendant allegedly 'submitted' to the jurisdiction of the rendering court prior to the coming into force of the Convention, in circumstances similar or identical to those in Article 18 (and *Elefanten Schuh GmbH v Pierre Jacqmain* (C150/80) [1981] ECR 1671), *Caltex Trading PTE Ltd. v Metro Trading International Inc. and others* [1999] 2 Lloyd's Rep. 724, at p.732 (Rix J) (using national concepts of submission under Article 18); also Explanatory Report by Borrás, A. on the former Convention on jurisdiction and the recognition and enforcement of judgments in matrimonial matters, [1998] OJ C221/27, at p.59.

[109] Such a 'residual' situation occurred in the *Bavaria Fluggesellschaft Schwabe and Co. KG and Germanair Bedarfsluftfahrt GmbH and Co. KG v Eurocontrol* (C9 & 10/77) [1977] ECR 1517 case; on returning to the referring court, *BGH* 10.10.1977 1978 *NJW* 1113, it subsequently held that the matter was a 'civil and commercial' one under the relevant bilateral enforcement Treaty, and enforced the judgment; *Cour de Cassation* 5.5.1993, *Société Times Newspapers limited c/ Pordea*, 1994 *Gaz. Pal., juris*, p.382, [1994] I.L.Pr. 96.

[110] Certain provisions of the Brussels or Lugano Conventions are not innovative in their treatment of circumstances when a court can take jurisdiction over a case with an international element, nor when a court may refuse to recognise or enforce a foreign judgment. Direct (Article 4 of the 1925

effect, in Article 55 of the Brussels Convention. They have been superseded (without a residual role)[111] to the extent that[112] any particular dispute concerns 'civil and commercial matters', in Article 1 of the Brussels or Lugano Conventions, and as defined by the European Court of Justice.[113] Although it is no doubt dangerous[114] to invite too close a comparison between articles of these Treaties and the Brussels and Lugano Conventions (and the interpretations respectively placed on them), important parallels are nonetheless present, which may (or ought to have)[115] served as paradigms for the drafting, and potential interpretation, of similarly-worded provisions of the later Conventions. As will be seen, the defences of public policy in Article 27(1),[116] and respecting the rights of the defence, in Article 27(2),[117] have a relatively long provenance in such earlier instruments.

Without any attempt being made at an exhaustive treatment of these Treaties,[118] and of the expanse of material devoted to them,[119] only a small overview can be presented here. Of the Treaties concluded by France, the most influential (up to the signing of the Brussels Convention) have been the *Traité franco-suisse* of 1869,[120] the *Traité franco-belge* of 1899,[121] and the Convention between France and Spain of 28 May 1969.[122] Germany has concluded many such treaties with, *inter alia*, Belgium, The Netherlands and Spain;[123] the Lugano Contracting State,

---

Belgian/Netherlands Convention, 'où l'obligation est née, a été ou doit être exécutée' ('where the obligation arose, or was or was to be performed'), below) and indirect bases of jurisdiction were similar in many ways to those enumerated in the Brussels and Lugano Conventions; Article 5(1) introduced a rule of direct jurisdiction in contract in The Netherlands, however.

[111] *BGH* 23.1.1986, IPRspr. 1986 Nr. 171, [1987] E.C.C. 276; *BGH* 18.2.1993, IPRspr. 1993 Nr. 169, [1995] I.L.Pr. 523.

[112] They may still continue to have a function in transitional situations, above.

[113] As to which below.

[114] Due to the different integrationalist function of the Brussels and Lugano Conventions (*Somafer SA v Saar-Ferngas AG* (C33/78) [1978] ECR 2183, at p.2191, para. 7); although mentioned in *Firma Minalmet GmbH v. Firma Brandeis Ltd* (C-123/91) [1992] ECR I–5661, at no time has the ECJ sought a historical interpretation from these earlier bilateral Treaties: *Bavaria Fluggesellschaft Schwabe and Co. KG and Germanair Bedarfsluftfahrt GmbH and Co. KG v Eurocontrol* (C9 & 10/77) [1977] ECR 1517, *Firma Minalmet GmbH v Firma Brandeis Ltd* (C-123/91) [1992] ECR I–5661.

[115] As will be argued below, in respect primarily to Article 5(1) and Article 27(1) and (2).

[116] Sections 4.2.1–5.

[117] Section 5.1.1.

[118] In general in English Al Mulla, H. *The recognition and enforcement of foreign civil and commercial judgments under multilateral and bilateral conventions*, Ph.D. Thesis, Cambridge University, 1992.

[119] For a Continental overview Jellinek, W. *Die zweiseitigen Staatsverträge über Anerkennung ausländischer Zivilurteile*, Erstes Heft: Abhandlung, Zweites Heft: Vertragstexte und Register, 1953; Dutoit, Knoepler, Lalive, and Mercier (eds) *Répertoire de droit international privé suisse*, Vol.II, *Les Conventions bilatérales sur les conflits de juridictions, la reconnaissance et l'exécution des jugements étrangers*, 1983.

[120] Signed at Paris 15.6.1869 (1869) 139 CTS 329, 1848–1947 AS, 12ᵉ Vol., p. 315, in force 1.1.1870.

[121] (1898–1899) JO 1.8.1900, p.5029, 187 CTS 378, in force 25.8.1900.

[122] *Convention sur la reconnaissance et l'exécution des décisions judiciaires et arbitrales et des actes authentiques en matière civile et commerciale*, signée à Paris le 28 mai 1969, Décret n° 70–262 du 18 mars 1970, JO 25.3.1970, p.29, (1970) 746 UNTS, 183, in force 29 March 1970.

[123] Of 26.6.1959, 1959 BGBl., II, 766, UNTS 387, 245, in force from 27.1.1961; of 15.1.1965, 1965 BGBl., II, 27, UNTS 547, 173, in force 15.9.1965; of 14.1.1987, 1987 BGBl., II, 35, UNTS Reg. Nr. 25941, in force 18.4.1988, respectively.

Switzerland, has had treaties with Austria,[124] and Italy;[125] Austria with Italy[126] and France;[127] the UK, under the auspices of the Foreign Judgments (Reciprocal Enforcement) Act 1933, has concluded bilateral treaties with, *inter alia*, Norway and The Netherlands.[128]

A similar point concerning parallel historical interpretations can be advanced when a (cautious) comparison is made between certain rules of Title II of the Conventions and the (often historically now obsolete) civil procedure rules of certain Contracting States, governing the internal (and international) competence of their courts *ratione loci.*

A striking example of this is the Conventions' Article 5(1), governing jurisdiction 'in matters relating to a contract', which has, or has had, its (unintentional)[129] historical progenitors in the procedural codes of among others,[130] France,[131] Belgium[132] and Germany.[133] As will be seen, both Article 5(1) and these texts have revealed near *verbatim* similarities in their drafting and (perhaps therefore foreseeably) also their interpretation.[134]

---

[124] *Vertrag zwischen der Schweizerischen Eidgenossenschaft und der Republik Österreich über die Anerkennung und Vollstreckung gerichtlicher Entscheidungen*, 16.12.1960, AS 1962, 263, in force 12.5.1962.

[125] *Convention entre la Suisse et l'Italie sur la reconnaissance et l'exécution des décisions judiciaires*, 3.1.1933, 1848–1947 AS, Band 12, 338, in force 6.10.1933.

[126] *Abkommen zwischen der Republik Österreich und der Italienischen Republik über die Anerkennung und Vollstreckung von gerichtlichen Entscheidungen in Zivil- und Handelssachen, von gerichtlichen Vergleichen und von Nortariatsakten*, of 16.11.1971, 1974 BBl, 521, in force 2.10.1974.

[127] *Abkommen zwischen der Republik Österreich und der Französischen Republik über die Anerkennung und Vollstreckung von gerichtlichen Entscheidungen und öffentlichen Urkunden auf dem Gebiet des Zivil- und Handelsrechtes*, of 15.7.1966, 1967 BBl, 288, in force 13.8.1967.

[128] Reciprocal Enforcement of Foreign Judgments (Norway) Order, 1962, SI 1962/636, in force 6.4.1962; Reciprocal Enforcement of Foreign Judgments (The Netherlands) Order, 1969, SI 1969/1063, in force 21.9.1969, respectively.

[129] Except perhaps §29 ZPO, the German autonomous provision on jurisdiction in contractual matters, according to Droz, G. *Compétence judiciaire et effets des jugements dans le marché commun*, 1972, at p.58, para. 63.

[130] Up until 14 July 1920, the former English rule of RSC Ord. 11 r.1 (e) permitted service out when 'an action was founded on any breach within the jurisdiction . . . which . . . ought to be *performed within the jurisdiction*' *The Annual Practice*, 1920, 38th issue, at p.90; *Robey and Co. v The Snaefell Mining Company Limited* (1887) 20 QBD 152, and *The Eider* [1893] P. 119, CA.

[131] Article 420 of the *Code de procédure civile*, 1806: 'dans l'arrondissement duquel le paiement *devait être effectué', Les Codes Annotés*, 4ᵉ éd, 1905; the place of payment, thus expressed, dates back (in French procedural law) to Article 17 of an *ordonance* of March 1673—*Les Codes Français*, Tripier L. and Monnier, H, 1903, at p.65, and Roussel, J. *Les clauses attributives de compétence*, 1933, at pp.75–79, in more detail in Article 5(1) chapter below section 1.3.1.

[132] *Ibid* for Article 420 of the 1806 Belgian code of civil procedure (for commercial disputes)—*Les cinq codes en vigeur en Belgique*, Delebeque and Hoffman, 1872, at p.71–72; and thereafter the *Code de procédure civile*, loi 25 mars 1876, articles 42 and 53(3) 'ou dans lequel elle [obligation] doit être ou a été exécutée'—commentary Bormans, T. *Code de procédure civile belge*, Livre I, Titre premier, 2ᵉ éd, 1877, at pp.466–69; now unchanged in Article 635(3) *Code Judiciaire, Les Codes Larcier*, I, 1998.

[133] §29 *Zivilprozeßordnung—Zivilprozeßordnung, Beck'sche Kurz-Kommentare*, 59 Aufl., 2001, at pp.91–96.

[134] For determination of the place of performance of the obligation in question by the *lex causae*, and therefore the place of payment by the same method—*Cour de Bruxelles* 22.10.1831 1814–1840 *Pas. Belge*, 276; *Cassation* 13.5.1871 *Voncken-Van Moorem c/ Meunier-Dubois* 1871 *Jurisprudence du port d'Anvers*, I, 191; *Comm. Liège* 29.5.1908 *Pieper c/ La Société des Aciéries de Crefeld* 1909 P.P., No.242,

The essential purpose of an historical comparison, where appropriate, is to demonstrate the potential influence that the drafters of the Conventions, and the judges of the European Court of Justice—steeped in the conflict of laws systems of their respective Contracting States—brought respectively to the wording of the Conventions, and arguably therefore, also to their interpretation.[135]

THE FUTURE: COUNCIL REGULATION 44/2001 OF 22 DECEMBER 2000 ON JURISDICTION AND THE RECOGNITION AND ENFORCEMENT OF JUDGMENTS IN CIVIL AND COMMERCIAL MATTERS;[136] AND THE WORK OF THE SPECIAL COMMISSION OF THE HAGUE CONFERENCE ON PRIVATE INTERNATIONAL LAW

The Brussels I Regulation (44/2001)[137]

Despite the substantive amendments to the Brussels Convention in 1978 and 1989, dissatisfaction with certain aspects of the Convention remains,[138] as was evidenced by proposals for reform of the Brussels Convention at Community level,[139] from the European Commission: the first proposal of 22 December 1997[140] ('the December 1997 proposal'); the second, and later proposal for a Council Regulation[141] (EC) of

---

164; *Tribunal de Commerce de Bruxelles* 5.2.1890 *Grumieau c/ Van Wouwe* 1890 *Jurisprudence du port d'Anvers*, II, 65, at p.66; in all these cases Article 1247 of the (Belgian) Civil Code was used to determine the place of performance of the payment obligation under the place of performance jurisdictional articles of procedural codes.

[135] Again, below chapter 1 on Article 5(1).

[136] [2001] OJ L12/1, the 'Brussels I Regulation', or the 'Regulation'.

[137] The Brussels I Regulation, to come into force on 1.3.2002, Article 76; notable, apart from its firm basis in EC law, is the extension, in the Annexes, of the recognition/enforcement regime of the Regulation to Gibraltar, and the Regulation's exclusion of Denmark as a participant, in Article 1(3)—also Statement by the United Kingdom (Council Regulation (EC) No.44/2001 of 22 December 2000) (on the certification of the decisions of the courts of Gibraltar) [2001] OJ C13/1; Béraudo, J-P. (2001) *JDI* 1033, at pp.1034–35; Schs.1–2 of The Civil Jurisdiction and Judgments Order 2001, SI 2001/3929, and The Civil Procedure (Amendment Nr. 5) Rules 2001, SI 2001/4015.

[138] Explanatory Memorandum to the July 1999 proposal for a Council Regulation (EC) [1999] OJ C376 (E) 1–17, on-line reference below n.144—and an explicit example of this now para.15 of the preamble to the Brussels I Regulation, highlighting the problems surrounding the time when 'a case is regarded as pending'.

[139] The impetus for the recent proliferation of Community instruments in the surge towards the creation of an European 'judicial area' stems from a European Council meeting in Tampere on 15–16 October 1999—in the sphere of the mutual recognition and enforcement of judicial decisions, its conclusions in paras. 34 and 37 are especially important, SN 200/1/1999 Rev 1: http://europa.eu.int/council/off/conclu/oct1999/oct99_en.htm.

[140] The Commission's *Proposal for a Council Act establishing the Convention on Jurisdiction and Recognition and Enforcement of Judgments in Civil and Commercial Matters in the Member States of the European Union*, submitted on 22.12.1997, 31.1.1998, [1998] OJ C33/20.

[141] For the effect (in the UK) of the transformation and incorporation of the Brussels Convention into a Community Regulation, note the concerns of the Council Working Party on the revision of the Brussels and Lugano Conventions, *European Scrutiny Committee*, 25th Report, Session 1998–99, HC34–xxv, p.xiv, para. 2.11; and the written reply of the (then) Parliamentary Secretary at the Lord Chancellor's department, Mr K. Vaz, by letter of 28 September 1999 to the effect that the proposed

14 July 1999,[142] on the basis of Articles 61(c), 65 and 67 of the EC Treaty,[143] as amended, ('the July 1999 proposal').[144] The culmination of the work of the July 1999 proposal,[145] and the later amendment, is now embodied in the Brussels I Regulation 44/2001, which will come into force on 1 March 2002.[146] Most notable for present substantive purposes, and discussed in the appropriate chapters, are the

Regulation was not expected to be interpreted 'in a significantly different way' from the Brussels Convention: http://www.parliament.the-stationery-office.co.uk/pa/cm199899/cmselect/cmeuleg/34-xxxi/ 3413.htm.

[142] Done at Brussels 14 July 1999 COM(1999) 348 final, 99/0154 (CNS), [1999] OJ C376 E/01, available on-line at http://europa.eu.int/comm/sg/tfjai/unit/unit3_en.htm; this was a more cautious attempt at revision than the earlier proposal. Based on Article 61(c) in Title IV EC Treaty, the UK expressed willingness to be 'fully associated' with the initiative; on 1–2 March 2000 the Economic and Social Committee of the EU adopted an opinion on the draft proposed Regulation, [2000] OJ C-117/02.

[143] Measures under these articles (formerly Articles 73I and 73m) in Title IV EC (formerly Title IIIa) did not bind the UK, under Article 2 of the Protocol on the position of the UK and Ireland annexed to the Treaty establishing the European Community and to the Treaty on European Union—the UK may, in Articles 3 and 4 of this protocol 'opt in' to such measures, and has done so—p.5 of the accompanying explanatory memorandum to the July 1999 proposal told us that the UK only decided to participate fully on 12.3.1999; this eleventh-hour contribution, of course, probably explained the absence of reference to UK provisions in Annexes 1 and 4 of the July 1999 proposal- it may also reveal an explanation for a certain lack of rigorous and long-overdue clarification/redrafting of certain articles, especially Article 23 vis-à-vis 27 in the Brussels I Regulation. Article 1(3) of the Regulation, however, makes clear that Denmark has decided, under Article 2 of its particular Protocol to the above Treaties, not to become bound by measures taken under Title IV EC, and is not consequently to be regarded as a Brussels I Regulation 'Member State'; the Brussels Convention, in its 1996 form, will continue to apply to it and the UK: para. 22 preamble; Béraudo, J-P. (2001) *JDI* 1033, at p.1035; and para. 1 (b)(i), Sch.2 The Civil Jurisdiction and Judgments Order 2001.

[144] Following opinions of the European Parliament on 18.9.2000 and 21.9.2000, recommending a number of amendments (chiefly to the wording of the preamble, to consumer contracts, and to accommodate the UK's re-activated participation (A5–0254/2000)), the Commission issued a second amended proposal for a Council Regulation on jurisdiction and the recognition and enforcement of judgments in civil and commercial matters, 26.10.2000 COM(2000) 689 final, 1999/0154 (CNS), [2001] OJ C62/243(E): http://europa.eu.int/eur-lex/en/com/dat/2000/en_500PC0689.html; details of the entire evolution of the Regulation from December 1997 proposal to the Brussels I Regulation can be found at the European Parliament's website, section entitled 'The Legislative Observatory': http://wwwdb.europarl.eu.int/oeil/; Besse, D. *Die Vergemeinschaftung des EuGVÜ*, 1 Aufl., 2001.

[145] Reforms have already been proposed to the Brussels I Regulation, Council of the EU, 24.11.2000, JUSTCIV 130/13648/00.

[146] Article 76; Article 66 contains the transitional provisions familiar to the current Accession Conventions, and Article 66(2) will enact a rule that the recognition and enforcement regime in the Brussels I Regulation shall be used, *inter alia*, where proceedings in a Member State bound by the Brussels I Regulation will have been instituted before 1.3.2002, if the Brussels Conventions were previously in force and applied in both Member States concerned- significant, for our purposes, as far as changes to the default judgment defence are concerned, Article 34(2), below at pp.506–509.

changes[147] proposed by Regulation 44/2001 to the following Articles of the Brussels Convention: 5(1),[148] 17,[149] 24,[150] Article 27(1)[151] and 27(2).[152]

In addition, and of more general interest, is the metamorphosis[153] of the Brussels Conventions into an instrument, the form and effects of which will

---

[147] Apart from the changes in the text of the Brussels I Regulation, there will be a slight curtailment, in comparison to Article 234 (ex. Article 177) EC, in the ability of the courts of Member States against whose decisions there is no judicial remedy to request a preliminary ruling under Article 68(1) EC (the House of Lords essentially). Those courts must not automatically request a reference, but only when they consider that a decision on the question is necessary for them to give judgment; the power of the lower courts, (High Court/Court of Appeal) will remain untouched under Article 68(1) and Article 234 EC—the Regulation having been an act negotiated under Title IV (ex Title IIIa) EC.

[148] Special jurisdiction in contract was reduced by Article 5(1) of the December 1997 proposal simply to 'contract[s] for [the] sale of goods', when the defendant could be sued 'where delivery was or should have been carried out'; in contrast, Article 5(1) of the Brussels I Regulation retains Article 5(1) of the Brussels Convention—and the jurisprudence surrounding it—intact, *except* in two cases: Article 5(1)(b) 'the case of the sale of goods' and 'the case of the provision of services'. In these situations, the place of performance of the obligation in question is (unless otherwise agreed), respectively in the Member State where, 'under the contract', 'the goods were ... or should have been delivered,' or 'the services were ... or should have been provided'; also Bruneau, C. 'Les règles européennes de compétence en matière civile et commerciale' (2001) *JCP, Doctr.*, I, 304.

[149] The wording of Article 17 of the December 1997 proposal simplified the scope of Article 17 of the Brussels Convention *ratione materiae*—'[i]f the parties have agreed'—thus omitting any reference to the parties, domicile, and the problems associated with this, below Article 17 chapter; curiously therefore Article 23 of the Brussels I Regulation, headed 'prorogation of jurisdiction', re-introduces a minimum Member State domicile requirement of one of the parties, and will thereby perpetuate the idiosyncratic interpretations witnessed under Article 17 of the Brussels Convention— the judgment of the ECJ in *Coreck Maritime GmbH v Handelsveem B.V., V. Berg and Sons Ltd,* (C387–98) [2000] ECR I–9337, has unfortunately not clarified the point one way or the other; but AG Alber's opinion, of 23.2.2000, that either parties' Contracting State domicile will suffice for Article 17's scope *ratione materiae*.

[150] Was deleted and replaced by Article 18a of the December 1997 proposal; Article 31 of the Brussels I Regulation re-enacts *verbatim* Article 24 of the Brussels Convention, and therefore presumably represents approval of its recent interpretation in *Van Uden Maritime BV, trading as Van Uden Africa Line v Kommanditgesellschaft in Firma Deco Line, and another* (C-391/95) [1998] ECR I–7091 and *Hans-Hermann Mietz v Intership Yachting Sneek B.V.* (C-99/96) [1999] ECR I–2277.

[151] The defence of public policy was deleted in Article 37a1(1) of the December 1997 proposal, but reappears in Article 34(1) of the Brussels I Regulation as 'manifestly contrary to public policy', below chapter 4.

[152] Article 37a1(2) of the December 1997 proposal would have narrowed the defence in Article 27(2) of the Brussels Convention and would have reversed certain ECJ rulings; Article 34(2) of the Brussels I Regulation, dealing with defendants in default, omits any reference to 'due' service and reverses the effect of the *Firma Minalmet GmbH v Firma Brandeis Ltd* (C-123/91) [1992] ECR I–5661 decision, and encourages the lodging of an 'appeal'/'recours' in the rendering court; see below section 5.4.4 on the omission of 'due' service pp.506–509.

[153] Kennett, W. *Enforcement of Judgments in Europe*, 2000, at p.14 onwards; Béraudo, J-P. (2001) *JDI* 1033, at p.1034, observes that the Brussels Conventions will not disappear altogether, especially at n.2.

be more familiar to experts of the law of the European Union:[154] a Council Regulation.[155]

From Article 249 (ex Article 189) EC, we learn that such a Regulation is to have 'general application' and be 'binding in its entirety and directly applicable[156] in all Member States'. This means that the Brussels I Regulation (44/2001), unlike the Brussels Convention: does not require for its binding effect, (any) direct transposition into the law of the UK, in an additional schedule to the CJJA 1982; that judges of the High Court must take judicial notice of it, in its entirety;[157] and that it will produce vertical and horizontal direct effect[158] for individuals and companies, pre-empting national legislative competence.[159] Whatever the previous

---

[154] Articles 71 and 72 of the Brussels I Regulation will conserve the present bilateral arrangements negotiated under the present Article 59 of the Brussels Convention (mitigating the effect of enforcement of judgments based on Article 4, exorbitant grounds), and any that may have been negotiated before 1.3.2002; but there have been concerns expressed by the HC Select Committee that a provision has not been included to allow negotiation of arrangements *after that date*: *House of Commons European Scrutiny Committee*, 5th Report, Session 2000–01, HC, 28–v, at pp.51–52; also following n. and *Commission v Council (ERTA)* (C22/70) [1971] ECR 263.

[155] Kotuby, C. 'External Competence of the European Community in the Hague Conference on Private International Law: Community Harmonization and Worldwide Unification' (2001) *NILR* 1, commenting, at pp.16–17, upon the EU (external) competence—having thus now legislated in the sphere of Article 65 EC—to negotiate international agreements with non-Member States, particularly at the Hague Conference.

[156] Paragraph 6 of the preamble to the Brussels I Regulation re-iterates its directly applicable nature; this means that such a legal instrument will immediately become part of the domestic law of Member States, without the need, as at present in the UK with the Brussels Convention, for the intercession of implementing legislation, Arnull, A. *The European Union and its Court of Justice*, 1999, at p.107; Weatherill and Beaumont, *EU Law*, 3rd edn., 1999, at p.398; indeed, such implementation, unless authorised, appears to be impermissible: *Wyatt and Dashwood's European Union Law*, 4th edn., 2000, at p.86; for the necessary changes on 1.3.2002 to the CJJA 1982 and the CPR 1998, The Civil Jurisdiction and Judgments Order 2001, SI 2001/3929, and The Civil Procedure (Amendment Nr. 5) Rules 2001, SI 2001/4015, respectively.

[157] *Wyatt and Dashwood's European Union Law*, 2000, at p.89.

[158] Craig, P. and de Búrca, G. *The Evolution of EU Law*, 1999, at p.187; there is little doubt, in the clear and unambiguous language of the Brussels I Regulation, that it will produce both vertical and horizontal direct effect—as the Regulation, like the Brussels Convention before it, is clearly not merely a 'pious aspiration', that it is clear and unconditional, not contingent on any discretionary implementing measures, and that national rules cease to apply in its sphere of competence: *Consorzio de Prosciutto di Parma v Asda Stores Ltd* [2001] 1 CMLR 1103, at pp.1112–14, HL, (Lord Hoffmann), reference to ECJ pending on whether a Regulation at issue in that case produced direct effect.

[159] The uncertainty over the reception of *forum non conveniens* into the Brussels Convention system is likely to be increased when the Brussels I Regulation comes into force on 1 March 2002—compare certain CA authority, that for *forum non conveniens* to be excluded, the dispute must be firmly associated within the Contracting States—i.e. defendant domiciled in a Contracting State, and the courts of another Contracting State potentially involved as a *forum conveniens*—*Re Harrods (Buenos Aires) Ltd* [1992] Ch 90, at pp.96–97 (Dillon LJ): 'the Convention is merely an agreement between the contracting states among themselves . . .'; 'Convention is in no way concerned with national jurisdiction of contracting states' (Bingham LJ); Kennett, W. (2001) *ICLQ* 725, at p.727; *Re Polly Peck International Plc (in administration) (No.2)* [1998] 3 All ER 812, at pp.829–30, CA (Mummery LJ); *ACE Insurance SA-NV v Zurich Insurance Company* [2001] 1 Lloyd's Rep. 618, at pp.624–25, (Rix LJ, CA), and *Haji-Ioannou and ors v Frangos and ors.* [1999] 2 Lloyd's Rep. 337, at p.347: 'It does not . . . appear . . . that the exercise of jurisdiction to stay . . . is subversive of the Convention regime' (*obiter*, Lord Bingham of Cornhill, CJ)—the view of Dillon LJ will apply *a fortiori* with regard to the Regulation; *contra*, citing

debate over the exact status of the Brussels Convention, it is clear now that the Brussels I Regulation is a bold and decisive legislative statement, ensuring that jurisdiction and the recognition and enforcement of judgments in civil and commercial matters is firmly embedded within the control of the European Union. The exact repercussions of this shift of legislative emphasis to a Regulation may be hard to predict: it may be imperceptible,[160] or far-reaching, again depending on how the Brussels Convention was viewed. For the UK at least, one immediate question will be the Regulation's effect on our relations with non-Member State jurisdictions, in particular the notion of the compatibility (if at all) of *forum non conveniens*[161] with the Regulation itself.

The project for the Hague Worldwide Judgments Convention

On 5 May 1992 the Legal Advisor to the US State Department, E. Williamson, sent a letter to Mr G. Droz, then Secretary-General to the Hague Conference on Private International Law, outlining a proposal to consider a project for a Convention on recognition and enforcement of judgments.[162]

---

the wording in the Preamble Droz (2001) *Rev crit* 601, at pp.609–10. Jackson, D. 'Fitting English maritime jurisdiction into Europe—or vice versa?' (2001) *LMCLQ* 219, at pp.226–27; cf ECJ in *Ingmar GB Ltd v Eaton Leonard Technologies Inc.* (C-381/98), 9.11.2000, at paras. 21 and 25, on the mandatory application of Directive 86/653/EEC, for EC self-employed commercial agents' rights to compensation notwithstanding an (adverse Californian) choice of law clause; *Med-Eq A/S v Newlands Clinical Trials Ltd (t/a Medical Innovations) and others*, 12.12.2001, Ch.D (Evans-Lombe J).

[160] As mentioned, instead of the reference procedure in the Protocol, as at present, resort to the preliminary reference procedure in Article 234 (ex Article 177) will be necessary, limited by Article 68 (ex Article 73p) EC.

[161] *Quaere* the continued application and influence of s.49 CJJA 1982: if a national measure such as the application of s.49 CJJA 1982 'alters, obstructs or obscures the nature of the Community regulation' a breach of EU law will occur (Craig, P. and de Búrca, G. *EU Law, Text, Cases and Materials*, 1998, at p.177: *Amsterdam Bulb BV v Produktschap voor Siergewassen* (C50/76) [1977] ECR 137, at p.146, paras. 4–5: 'the direct application of a Community regulation means that its entry into force and *its application . . . are independent of any measure of reception into national law . . .*. Member States are under a duty not to obstruct the direct effect inherent in regulations . . .'.

[162] Extensive treatment in the Symposium reported in (1998) *Brook. J. Int'l L.* pp.1–220; also (1998) *Albany LR* at pp.78–80, pp.1207–67; for an adverse view of the draft: Newman (1998) *New York LJ* 3, at p.29, col.1, and A. Von Mehren (2000) *IPRax* 465, at pp.466–67; impetus, generally, seems apparently to have been the international isolationism felt by the US, generous in recognising and enforcing foreign judgments (see the 1962 Uniform Foreign Money-Judgments Recognition Act (UFMJRA) 13 Uniform Laws Annotated 263 (1986, and 2000 supplement), but receiving little reciprocal benefit abroad for US judgments—Colomb, A. 'Recognition of Foreign Money Judgments: A goal-orientated approach' (1969) 43 *St. John's LR* 604 at p.616 and p.635; Trooboff, P. D. 'International Law The Hague Conference' (2001) *The National Law Journal*, July 2001, A19; Smit, H. 'Federalizing International Civil Litigation in the United States' (1998) 8 *Transnational Law and Contemporary Problems* 57, at p.69; to avoid the jurisdiction under CPR 25.12, 25.13(2)(a) to order security for costs, a respondent must be ordinarily resident in another Contracting State, not merely have assets located there: *De Beer v Kanaar and Co.*, 9.8.2001, CA; Clermont, K. 'Jurisdiction salvation and the Hague Treaty' (1999) *Cornell LR* 89, at p.93–95; Zekoll, J. 'The role and status of American law in the Hague Judgments Convention project' (1998) *Alb LR* 1283, at p.1300; note Mance LJ in *Nasser v United Bank of Kuwait*, 11.4.2001, CA

At the Seventeenth Session of the Hague Conference, held between 10–29 May 1993, a decision was taken by a Final Act[163] to convene a Special Commission 'to study further the problems involved in drafting a new convention . . .'. To this end, this Commission has sat at various meetings in 1994, 1996–99, and has produced a number of conclusions[164] and syntheses[165] of these meetings. On 18 June 1999, the Special Commission provisionally adopted a document entitled 'Preliminary draft Convention on jurisdiction and the effects of judgments in civil and commercial matters'.[166] An amended version, with renumbered articles, which served as an *ad referendum* text for the Nineteenth Diplomatic Session, first part, of the Hague Conference, which took place between 6–20 June 2001,[167] was adopted on 30 October 1999[168] ('the October 1999 draft'). At this last Session, an unwieldy re-amended 'interim text' version emerged (the Commission II interim text),[169] representing the discussions in Commission II, with numerous alternatives and compromises to be proposed and agreed upon at a later date[170] in 2002.

(security for costs more likely to be ordered against US resident claimant, due to 'extra burden' of costs and delay in enforcement in US, and tailored in amount accordingly); judicial awareness of the draft Convention *Kam-Tech Systems Ltd v Rafael Yardem* 774 A.2nd 644 (N.J. Super. A.D.), at p.648; *Ahmed v Blackburn and Co. and others*, 31.1.2001, CA.

[163] 32 *ILM* 1134, at p.1145.

[164] *Conclusions of the second Special Commission meeting on the Recognition and Enforcement of foreign judgments in civil and commercial matters, Hague Conference on Private International Law*, Prel. Doc. No.12 August 1996.

[165] *Synthesis of the work of the Special Commission of March 1998 on International Jurisdiction and the Effects of Foreign Judgments in civil and commercial matters, Hague Conference on Private International Law*, Prel. Doc. No.9, July 1998, prepared by Kessedjian, C.

[166] Copy available from the Hague Conference web-site: http://www.hcch.net/e/workprog/jdgm.html; Kessedjian, C. 'The Hague Global Jurisdiction and Judgments Preliminary Draft Convention', in Fletcher et al (eds) *Foundations and Perspectives of International Trade Law*, 2001, Ch.15, p.233, following.

[167] According to information on the Hague Conference's website; further progress on the draft has been entrusted to the Commission on General Affairs and Policy, to meet in early 2002: http://www.hcch.net/e/events/events.html; Council of the European Union, JUSTCIV 96, 10844/01; an informal meeting was held in Edinburgh between 23–26 April 2001 to discuss such matters as activity-based and intellectual property jurisdiction: details of the draft agenda and the papers prepared by the various experts can be downloaded from the US Consumer Project on Technology's website: http://www.cptech.org/ecom/jurisdiction/.

[168] *Ad referendum, projet de convention* for future meetings: http://www.hcch.net/e/conventions/draft36e.html, also hard copy available at 2000 Yearbook of Private International Law 223; for a report of the Special Commission on the current text drawn up by Nygh, P. and Pocar, F. see online reference http://www.hcch.net/doc/jdgmpd11.doc (Nygh/Pocar report); stalemate was reached in these discussions: *Conclusions of the Special Commission of May 2000 on General Affairs and Policy of the Conference*, Prel. Doc. No 10, June 2000, at p.11: ftp://hcch.net/doc/concl_e.doc, Von Mehren, A. 'The Hague Jurisdiction and Enforcement Convention Project faces an impasse: a diagnosis and guidelines for a cure' (2000) *IPRax* 465.

[169] *Summary of the Outcome of the Discussion in Commission II of the First Part of the Diplomatic Conference 6–20 June 2001, Interim Text*; again, available from the Hague Conference's website; Wagner, R. (2001) *IPRax* 533

[170] A hearing of the Justice and Home Affairs department of the European Commission on the draft Hague Convention took place on 24 October 2001. The results of this hearing were, *inter alia*, various views on either a *convention simple* or *mixte*, and the way the Commission II interim text has diverged from the October 1999, more 'European', draft; also note the recent *Preliminary Doc-*

A European Council report, dated 18 April 2000,[171] revealed that the US State Department had grave reservations[172] with the October 1999 draft form of the Convention, and ensured[173] that progress towards finalisation of the October 1999 draft has been suspended for the time being.[174] A letter from Jeffrey Kovar, assistant legal advisor for Private International Law at the US State Department, revealed that the 'October 1999 draft presents a deal [sic] on jurisdiction that is heavily weighted against US jurisdiction practices. The Bar would reject it in this country.'[175]

Among general US concerns appeared to be the fact that the starting point for the model of the draft were the *traités doubles*, the Brussels and Lugano Conventions.[176] More specifically are:[177] the position, within Article 18(2)(e), of a general

ument No.16 of February 2002 for the attention of the Special Commission of April 2002 on general affairs and policy of the Conference, Hague Conference on Private International Law, Prel. Doc. No 16, Februrary 2002.

[171] Report of the Presidency of the Council of the European Union to the Permanent Representatives Committee, Justciv 44, 7855/00-on-line reference: http://register.consilium.eu.int/utfregister/frames/introfsEN.htm; it is clear that the EU has adopted a common negotiating position at the Hague Conference discussions: *Council of European Union*, 18.4.2000 7871/00 JUSTCIV 45; 20.9.2000 11332/00 JUSTCIV 91; 14.12.2000 14139/00 JUSTCIV 137 (Annex I); 16.5.2001 8398/01 JUSTCIV 59; 28.6.2001 10415/01 JAI 59, at p.13; the EU Commission meeting to discuss the Hague Convention on 24.10.2001 is now available online in French at http://europa.eu.int/comm/justice_home/unit/civil/audition10_01/compterendu_fr.htm; it is likely that there will be a Council Decision that will, in future, authorise the Member States to sign any Convention in the interests of the European Community, cf Council of the European Union 26.11.2001 14411/01, JUSTCIV 150.

[172] For details of the US' objections, see *International Jurisdiction and Judgments Project*, Report 14 April 2000, American Law Institute.

[173] The letter to the Secretary-General of the Hague Conference, Mr Van Loon, annexed to the report, also expresses disappointment at the hiatus, considering that it was on the US' initiative that the project was set up in the first place; the US is also negotiating from a (legally and historically) weak bargaining position, already providing an accommodating enforcement regime, often not reciprocated—Kovar, D. before the House of Representatives Subcommittee on courts and intellectual property of the H.Reps Committee on the Judiciary 29.6.2000: http://www.house.gov/judiciary/Kova0629.htm. *International Jurisdiction and Judgments Project*, at p.7, and Van Schaack, B. 'In defense of civil redress: the domestic enforcement of Human Rights norms in the context of the proposed Hague Judgments Convention' (2001) *Harvard Int'l LJ* 141, at p.176: 'a marginal increase in assurance that foreign judgments will be enforced here'; for traditional reluctance to become involved in such recognition and enforcement treaties, Brewster, B.H., *Official Opinions of the Attorneys-General*, (1890), v.18, 941, at p.86, penultimate para.

[174] Hau, W. 'Update on the Hague Convention on the recognition and enforcement of foreign judgments' (2000) 6 *Ann. Surv. Int'l. and Comp. L.* 1.

[175] Copy of the letter ('Kovar letter') can be consulted at http://www.cptech.org/ecom/jurisdiction/kovarletter.html; also Von Mehren, A. (2001) 49 *Am J Comp L* 191, at p.192.

[176] And its genesis in the Civil Law tradition. Von Mehren, A. 'La redaction d'une convention universellement acceptable sur la competence judiciaire internationale et les effets des jugements étrangers. Le project de la conference de la Haye peut-il aboutir?' (2001) *Rev crit* 85, at pp.93–94, inappropriate for countries who do not share the same legal, judicial and economic goals and traditions for participation in such a draft; whilst praising the initiative, sentiment echoed by Scoles, E. and Hay, P. *Conflict of Laws*, 3rd edn., 2000, at pp.1201–03.

[177] Silberman, L. and Lowenfeld, A. 'A different challenge for the ALI: Herein of Foreign Country Judgments, and International Treaty, and an American Statute' (2000) *Ind LR* 635, at p.642.

'doing business' jurisdictional provision[178] among the prohibited[179] bases of jurisdiction; jurisdictional problems that will be raised with regard to current US Antitrust practice;[180] the (potentially justified) concerns voiced by certain US human rights groups[181] that civil causes of action for breaches of fundamental human rights—for example under the Alien Tort Statute and Torture Victims Protection Act 1991, codified now 28 U.S.C. §1350 and note 1,[182] will be severely[183] curtailed by the jurisdictional limitations in the draft Convention, especially regarding 'tag' jurisdiction.[184]

The re-amended Commission II interim text, in its form, represents to some extent concessions made to the US delegation, whose influence can be felt in a number of alternatives added since the October 1999 draft.

Although at this stage only in this interim text form, the Convention even now continues to bear a more or less striking resemblance[185] to many of the provisions

---

[178] Such as that represented by the corporate, CPLR 301 'presence' doctrine/'doing business' test in New York jurisdictional practice: Siegel, D. *New York Practice*, 3rd edn., 1999, at pp.131–35—in an unpublished proposal of *The International Dispute Resolution Committee of the D.C. Bar, International Law Section*, on 6.12.2000, a compromise was discussed in a clause, which would attempt to codify current 'minimum contact'/due process jurisprudence of the Supreme Court: Article 1 'The plaintiff may bring a claim in the courts of a Contracting State when the defendant . . . has engaged in activity in that Contracting State, the claim arises out of that activity, and litigation in that Contracting State would not impose a manifestly unreasonable burden on the defendant . . . [or in Article 2] . . . has engaged in activity elsewhere that has an effect in that Contracting State, a) when the activity was intended to cause such an effect in that Contracting State, or b) when such an effect was reasonably certain to occur as a result of activity elsewhere directed at that Contracting State, and litigation in that Contracting State would not impose a manifestly unreasonable burden on the defendant.'

[179] Details in *International Jurisdiction and Judgments Project*, above n.172 at p.14; the possibility of moving this base into the Article 17 'grey list' (or at least removing it from Article 18), when other potential Contracting States may then have the option of recognising/enforcing such a judgment outside the regime of the Convention's Chapter III (Article 24) has not gathered momentum.

[180] Dodge, W. 'Antitrust and the draft Hague Judgments Convention' (2001) 32 *Law and Policy in International Business* 363; although Article 1(2)(i) of the Commission II interim text would now exclude 'antitrust or competition claims' from the Convention's ambit *ratione materiae*; for patent and trademark concerns, see the US Department of Commerce, Federal Register Vol.66, No.161, 20 August 2001, p.43575. For First Amendment free speech concerns, see Hudleston, S. (2001) 10 *Minn J Global Trade* 403.

[181] Lawyers Committee for Human Rights, *Draft Convention on Jurisdiction and Judgments: Human Rights Concerns*, June 1999, at pp.3–4; Article 18(3) of the Commission II interim text would exempt grave human rights abuse claims from the general prohibition on the use of national ('exorbitant') provisions.

[182] 'The district courts shall have original jurisdiction of any civil action by an alien for a tort only, committed in violation of the law of nations or a treaty of the United States'; (Swan, M). 'International Human Rights Tort Claims' in *Torture as Tort*, (Ed. Scott, C.), 2001, Ch.3, p.65, at pp.74–78.

[183] Van Schaack, B. (2001) *Harvard Int'l LJ* 141, at p.143: without a special article dealing with such causes of action, the draft Convention may 'severely hamper one of the most innovative developments in international law and unduly interfere . . . with [states'] duties under international treaty and customary law'; see Article 18(3) Commission II interim text.

[184] Examples especially in Van Schaack, B. at p.154, and p.180, n.213–14; *S.Kadic v Radovan Karadzic* 70 F.3d 232 (2nd Cir. 1995), especially at pp.246–47, personal service on defendant, Karadzic, whilst temporarily present in New York; also general 'doing business' jurisdiction invoked against two non-US companies, allegedly complicit in human rights abuses in Nigeria in *Wiwa v Royal Dutch Petroleum Co.* 226 F.3d 88 (2nd Cir. 2000), *cert. denied* (on *forum non conveniens* issue), No.00–1168, 26.3.2001, 2001 WL 69238; also Rogge, M. (2001) 36 *Texas Int'l LJ* 299.

[185] Although the draft is not merely a *traité double*—in addition to the foregoing bases of jurisdiction expected in 'classic' *traités doubles*, it permits in Article 17, rules of direct competence (which do

familiar[186] to European conflicts lawyers: Article 1(1) and Articles 1(2)(a)–(g), defining its scope *ratione materiae*,[187] will not present anything new[188], especially to English lawyers, particularly in the words of its draft Article 1(2)(g): the arbitration exclusion 'arbitration and *proceedings related thereto*'.[189] Other proposed exclusions, added in brackets to the interim text since the October 1999 draft, have yet to be agreed upon. Of particular interest here is the potential exclusion of provisional and protective measures, in Article 1(2)(k),[190] and Article 1(3), last subclause.[191]

not conflict *ratione materiae/personae* with Articles 4, 5, 7, 8, 12 and 13) under national law (so long as such are not prohibited by the list of so-called 'exorbitant' bases in Article 18). Judgments based on Article 17 will inhabit a nether world—unlike those based on Article 18, they will be excluded (*ratione materiae*) from the beneficial enforcement regime of Title III, by Article 24; their cross-border effectiveness, especially from a US perspective, must therefore be highly questionable, and do not represent a significant improvement on the current recognition and enforcement position.

[186] For US constitutional, 14th Amendment 'Due Process', concerns for a Hague Worldwide Judgments Convention: Borchers, P. 'Judgments Convention and minimum contacts' (1998) *Alb LR* 1161, at p.1168, and the Symposium reported therein—many provisions of the Brussels Convention and Hague draft 'focus on the nexus between the claim and the court, rather than on the nexus between the defendant and the court'; Brand, R. 'Due process, jurisdiction and a Hague Judgments Convention' (1999) *U Pitts LR* 661, at p.691, and pp.704–05; for concerns and uncertainties (at least of some 100 years antiquity—*International American Conference, Reports of Committees and Discussions thereon*, Vol. II, Washington, 1890, at p.924 (Delegate Quintana)) that ratification of any future Hague Convention—with the inevitable jurisdictional limitations therein—would unacceptably and unconstitutionally impinge on parochial US federalism, embodied in the Tenth Amendment, and its somewhat inconsistent interpretations, see Bradley, C. (1998) 97 *Mich LR* 390, especially at p.397, and pp.402–09; Nguyen, K. D. (2001) 28 *Hastings Constitutional Law Quarterly* 145; note Nadelmann's observation of the 'helpless and humiliating' position that the Constitution traditionally leaves the US in regards to implementation of Treaties on private international law: (1954) 102 *U Penn LR* 323 (1954), at p.339, p.357 and pp.359–61; for the impression that 'continued disparate [US] State practice' may, in today's 'global economy' have to change, Scoles, E. and Hay, P. *Conflict of Laws*, 3rd edn., 2000, at p.1151 and p.1198; Wagner, R. (2001) *IPRax* 533, at p.535.

[187] For the interim text's territorial scope, Article 2 should be consulted; Article 2(1)(a), dealing with a jurisdiction clause concluded between domestic parties for the courts of another Contracting State should be of particular note

[188] Article 1(2)(g) also excludes 'admiralty or maritime matters' from its scope-Theis, W. 'Admiralty proceedings and the proposed Hague Convention on Jurisdiction and Judgments' (2001) *J Mar L and C* 59.

[189] English courts have had to grapple with the Convention's arbitration exclusion on a number of occasions: *Marc Rich & Co. A.G. v Societa Italiana Impianti P.A. (The 'Atlantic Emperor')* [1989] 1 Lloyd's Rep. 548; *Aggeliki Charis Compania Maritima S.A. v Pagnan S.p.A (The 'Angelic Grace')* [1995] 1 Lloyd's Rep. 87, CA; *Union de Remorquage et de Sauvetage S.A. v Lake Avery Inc. (The 'Lake Avery')*, QBD, (Clarke J); *Alfred C. Toepfer International GmbH v Société Cargill France* [1998] 1 Lloyd's Rep. 379; *Lexmar Corporation and Steamship Mutual Underwriting Association (Bermuda) Ltd v Nordisk Skibsrederforening and Northern Tankers (Cyprus) Ltd.* [1997] 1 Lloyd's Rep. 289, (Colman J); *Partenreederei M/S 'Heidberg' and ors v Grosvenor Grain and Feed Co. Ltd. (The 'Heidberg')* [1994] 2 Lloyd's Rep. 287, (Diamond QC) and *Vale Do Rio Doce Navegacao v Shanghai Bao Steel Ocean Shipping Co. Ltd.* [2000] 2 All ER (Comm) 70, (Thomas J); *Navigation Maritime Bulgare v Rustal Trading Ltd. and others (The 'Ivan Zagubanski')* [2002] 1 Lloyd's Rep. 106, at p.122 (Aikens J): '[t]he principal focus or essential subject-matter of that claim [for an anti-suit injunction to compel the defendants domiciled in other Contracting States to arbitrate their claim] is. . .arbitration, because the claim is for relief to enforce the arbitration agreeement'.

[190] This was no consensus at the Session about this exclusion; Article 13 (the grant of provision and protective measures) and Article 23A (their recognition and enforcement) should also be consulted.

[191] Article 1(3), last sub-clause will enable a Contracting State court to refuse recognition/enforcement to a judgment given in another Contracting State in breach of an arbitration agreement; cf. s 32(1) CJJA 1982.

Article 3 embodies the provision of Article 2 of the Brussels Convention 'actor sequitur forum rei'. Yet in contrast to Article 2 of the Brussels Convention, Article 3 of the interim text only states that 'a defendant *may* be sued in the courts'. At first sight, Article 3(3)'s four alternatives under which (corporate) defendants 'may be sued', may well lead to an increase in the number of cases[192] similar to the situation that occurred in *In re Harrods (Buenos Aires) Ltd*[193]—until one reads in Article 22[194] that a court of a Contracting State, on application by a party, may suspend its proceedings '[i]n exceptional circumstances, when the jurisdiction of the court seised is not founded on a[] [valid Article 4] exclusive choice of court agreement . . . or on Article 7, 8 or 12 [jurisdiction in consumer, employment contracts and exclusive jurisdiction, respectively]'.[195]

Article 4[196] itself, dealing with jurisdiction clauses, draws heavily from Article 17 of the Brussels Convention, adding additional circumstances of formal validity in Article 4(2)(a),(b): '. . . or by any other means of communication which renders information accessible so as to be usable for subsequent reference; . . .' Article 5 deals with an appearance/submission by the defendant.

Article 6 of the interim text, governing 'action[s] in contract' now contains two alternatives. 'Alternative A', which will be more familiar to US practitioners, seems to represent the US delegation's attempt to foist in another guise a species of 'transacts any business' and/or 'contracts anywhere'[197] jurisdiction onto the remaining delegates; both Article 6(1)(a),(b) of Alternative A attempt to re-codify the confused position that is, *inter alia*, US state long-arm specific[198] jurisdiction in contract and constitutional due process standards.[199]

---

[192] Cf *The Deichland* [1990] 1 QB 361, CA at p.375 (Neill LJ), on the possibility of multiple company 'seats'.

[193] [1992] Ch 90, CA.

[194] A proposal manifest in Article 22(7) would limit its application in any event.

[195] This will no doubt be a novel and contentious article for those (European) countries that follow the Civil Law tradition: Article 22(2) attempts to codify the circumstances that courts in the UK (and the US) have traditionally considered on an application to stay proceedings on the ground of *forum non conveniens*; Article 22(3) is, no doubt, an attempt to reverse the discriminatory position of the *forum non conveniens* plea developed in US Supreme Court practice (where, despite assertions to the contrary in *Wiwa v Royal Dutch Petroleum Co.* 226 F.3d 88 (2nd Cir.2000) less deference shown to non US claimants): *Piper Aircraft Co. v Reyno* 454 US 235, at pp.255–56 (1981)—Fellas, J. In *International Commercial Litigation*, (Fellas, J.), 1999, at p.141; also Reed, A. (2000) 29 *Ga J Int'l and Comp L* 31, at p.60: 'foreign plaintiffs suing US defendants . . . are pejoratively relegated to the status of illegal immigrants . . .'; Kassel, B. (2001) *Der Betrieb* 1076, at p.1078; Hu Zhenjie (2001) *NILR* 143, at p.160 and at p.165.

[196] Article 4's wording *ratione materiae* does *not* refer to the habitual residence of either party (in contrast to Article 23 of the Brussels I Regulation); Article 2(1)(a) additionally provides that Article 4 shall still apply where both parties are habitually resident in the same Contracting State, but prorogate the courts of *another* Contracting State.

[197] In its requirement of conducting or directing, *inter alia*, 'significant activity', later defined in Article 6(2) variant 1 or variant 2; cf Wagner, R. (2001) *IPRax* 533, at p.539.

[198] The two possibilities of Alternative A, of Article 6(1)(a)(b) and the definitions of 'activity' in both variants of Article 6(2) appear at first to be an expression of a general, unrelated 'doing business' test; but the article continues and makes clear that 'the claim [is to be] based on a contract *directly related* to' the 'activities' mentioned in Article 6(1)(a)(b) of Alternative A.

[199] It is highly questionable that US jurisdictional practice should be even contemplated as a paradigm for such a Convention.

'Alternative B', more familiar to European jurists, and rescued from the earlier October 1999 draft, appears to limit a plaintiff/claimant's options to only two types of contractual disputes, both 'matters relating to the supply of goods . . . [and/or] to the provision of services'. An autonomous place of performance has been given in each case, a solution also adopted for such disputes by Article 5(1) of the Brussels I Regulation (44/2001).[200]

Article 7 concerns 'contracts concluded by consumers',[201] and Article 8 (which was not discussed at the 19th Session), in the October 1999 draft individual contracts of employment. Both articles contain the usual protective options for these categories of litigants (*inter alia*, against unfavourable jurisdiction clauses), perceived to be in (an economically) weaker position.

Article 9 addresses activities of branches, and Article 10, torts or delicts,[202] Article 11 trusts, and Article 12 exclusive jurisdiction—Articles 12(1)–(3) thereof being modelled heavily on Article 16 of the Brussels Convention.[203] Article 13 deals with provisional and protective measures, and in Alternative A (as its inspiration) appears to have taken into account in its drafting recent case law of the European Court of Justice.[204]

As regards jurisdiction based on national law as against a defendant habitually resident in another Contracting State,[205] Article 17 and Article 18 should be read together. Subject to the application of earlier articles, (Articles 4, 7, 8, 11(1), 12, 13), Article 17[206] does not prevent a Contracting State taking jurisdiction under national provisions,[207] so long as those provisions are not anathematised in Article 18.[208] Article 18(2) contains a non-exhaustive, illustrative list of prohibited grounds of jurisdiction—at one time so-called exorbitant/

---

[200] Below, chapter 1, section 1.2.7.

[201] I.e. those 'acting primarily for personal, family or household purposes' with another party 'acting for the purposes of its trade or profession'.

[202] For a possible clash between this and other draft Convention bases with US constitutional 'due process'/'minimum contacts' requirements: Weintraub, R.: '[c]an a convention permit United States courts to exercise tort long-arm jurisdiction beyond the limits that our Supreme Court has read into the Due Process Clause? [*Ashai Metal*]', (1998) *Albany LR* 1269, at p.1273; a proposed Article 10(2) attempts to deal with this.

[203] Article 12 also contains an innovative section (in proposed Alternatives) on exclusive jurisdiction for matters of 'intellectual property'.

[204] *Van Uden Maritime BV, trading as Van Uden Africa Line v Kommanditgesellschaft in Firma Deco Line, and another* (C–391/95) [1998] ECR I–7091 and *Hans-Hermann Mietz v Intership Yachting Sneek B.V.* (C–99/96) [1999] ECR I–2277, and below chapter 3, section 3.2.

[205] As against defendants habitually resident in non-Contracting States, Article 17 can presumably be read on its own, with no Article 18 restrictions on the 'exorbitant' measures that can be invoked over them; note Article 1 does not exclude the scope *ratione materiae/personae* of the Convention to defendants habitually resident in non-Contracting States.

[206] There is, however, no incentive for a plaintiff/claimant to use such a national base of jurisdiction under the Convention because a judgment based on it does not qualify for quasi-automatic recognition/enforcement under Title III, Article 24.

[207] Although judgments based on Article 17 competence are outside the scope of Chapter III's enforcement regime.

[208] Article 18(1) prohibits generally application of national rules in which there is 'no substantial connection' between Contracting State and the dispute and/or defendant.

extraordinary[209] jurisdictions: a selective number of the offending jurisdictional provisions from various civil codes, (US) state civil procedure codes[210] and the English common law[211] are represented and outlawed here.

A welcome inclusion in the Convention, both in its October 1999 draft and Commission II interim text, is Article 21[212]—a more precisely-drafted provision dealing with *lis pendens* than its counterpart in Articles 21/22 of the Brussels Convention. The new Article 21(5) defines clearly when a court will be deemed to be 'seised'[213] of an action,[214] for the application of *lis pendens*. Under Article 21(5)(a), seisin will occur, as a matter of English law, when 'the document instituting the proceedings . . . is lodged with the court.'[215] This will reverse the current English approach, laid down under Articles 21/22 of the Brussels Convention, that definitive seisin takes place upon service of the writ/claim form.[216]

Chapter III of the October 1999 draft and Article 23 onwards of the Commission II interim text, deal with recognition and enforcement. Notable additions[217]

---

[209] Now euphemistically expressed, in Article 18(1), to be bases of jurisdiction with 'no substantial connection between that State and the dispute'.

[210] Probably, for example, therefore *McKinneys' Consolidated Laws of New York Annotated*, CPLR § 302(a)(1) 'transacting any business' within the State of New York.

[211] Article 18(2)(f) prohibits 'the service of a writ [sic] upon the defendant in that State'; Article 18(1) may prohibit jurisdiction under English procedure CPR 6.20(5)(d) (c.f. *Amin Rasheed Shipping Corp. v Kuwait Insurance Co.* [1984] AC 50); Article 18(2)(j) would also seem to outlaw the use of CPR 6.20(5)(a) in certain circumstances.

[212] Although Article 21(6) of both forms of the Convention will exclude a situation of prior seisure (and therefore *lis pendens*) in one Contracting State of a negative declaration 'action' if 'an action seeking substantive relief is brought in the court second seised'.

[213] Problems have arisen under Articles 21/22 of the Brussels Convention as to when a court becomes seised of proceedings—*Siegfried Zelger v Sebastino Salinitri* (C129/83) [1984] ECR 2397 had told us that it was to be when an action became 'definitively pending', a concept to be left to national procedural law; for England, on service of the writ, and presumably now, also the claim form (rule unaffected by the 'start' of proceedings under CPR 7.2(1)); confirmed in *SDL International Ltd v Centre de Co-operation Internationale en Recherche Agronomique pour le Developpement* [2001] CLC 903, at p.911–13; *Dresser UK Ltd and others v Falcongate Freight Management Ltd and others (The 'Duke of Yare')* [1992] 1 QB 502 and *Neste Chemicals S.A. and others v DK Line S.A. and Tokumaru Kaiun K.K. (The 'Sargasso')* [1994] 3 All ER 180, CA; for Germany §§ 261 Abs. 1, 253 Abs.1 ZPO *on service* (after the 'Klageschrift' has been delivered to the court); for France, Article 857(1) NCPC in the *Tribunal de Commerce* the date of '*la remise au greffe*' (after service), *Cassation* 4.10.1994 *Soc Jacky Maeder GmbH c/ Compagnie maritime d'affrètement* 1994 Dalloz, IR., 255; for Switzerland, definitive pendency is a matter for the civil procedural codes of each (of the 26) individual Cantons/half Cantons, *A., B. und C. gegen D.* 26.9.1997 123 BGE, III, 414—Spühler, K. in *Der Einfluss des europäischen Rechts auf die Schweiz: Festschrift für Professor Roger Zäch zum 60. Geburtstag*, p.847, at p.852; for Austria §232 I öZPO *on service* (after delivery to the court)—*sed quaere*, Rüfner, T. (2001) *LMCLQ* 460 at p.463 and 465; note changes to Article 21 by Article 30 Brussels I Regulation, and Kennett, W. (2001) *ICLQ* 725, at p.732.

[214] Presumably 'on the merits'; for seisin and the problem of multiple defendants: *Grupo Torras S.A. and Torras Hostench London Ltd. v Sheikh Fahad Mohammed al-Sabah and others* [1995] 1 Lloyd's Rep. 374, QBD (Mance J), [1996] 1 Lloyd's Rep. 7, CA.

[215] Now in England and Wales under CPR Rule 7.2(1).

[216] *Ibid*; it is not believed that the 1998 CPR has changed this position under the Brussels Convention, merely the terminology—'started'.

[217] Article 23A, drafted as two alternatives, and although not forming a universal consensus, caters for Contracting State decisions ordering 'provisional and protective measures', as defined in Alternative A Article 23(2).

here are in Article 27(1): 'the court addressed shall verify the jurisdiction of the court of origin'; and among the standard defences[218] to recognition and enforcement is Article 28(1)(a), a provision dealing with a situation where the rendering court (second seised) has neglected to suspend or decline its proceedings under the *lis pendens* provisions of Article 21.[219]

Article 33 attempts to deal with the problem[220] of (US)[221] judgments for 'grossly excessive' punitive damages,[222] on which issue an earlier (draft) UK/US

---

[218] For public policy, and US examples, chapter 4, section 4.5.

[219] Tensions between courts will no doubt be increased by this provision: *Continental Bank N.A. v Aeakos Compania Naviera S.A. and others* [1994] 1 WLR 588; *Donohue v Armco Inc. and others* [2000] 1 All ER (Comm) 641, CA, [2002] 1 Lloyd's Rep. 425, HL; *Youell v Kara Mara Shipping Co. Ltd* [2000] 2 Lloyd's Rep. 102, Aikens J; *National Westminster Bank plc v Utrecht-America Finance Co.* [2001] 2 All ER (Comm) 7, at pp.18–19 (Clarke LJ).

[220] Letter of Mr Vaz on 28 September 1999, to the Chairman of the Select Committee on the European Communities, Lord Tordoff, annexed to the 31st Report of the House of Commons Select Committee on European Scrutiny, http://www.parliament.the-stationery-office.co.uk/pa/cm199899/cmselect/cmeuleg/34-xxxi/3413.htm, at p.7, penultimate paragraph; on the reaction of other potential Contracting States to the award of punitive damages, Braslow, N. 'The recognition and enforcement of common law punitive damages in a civil law system: some reflections on the Japanese experience' (1999) *Arizona Journal of International and Comparative Law* 285, especially at p.312, and Jung, K. 'How punitive damage awards affect US businesses in the international arena' (1999) 17 *Wis Int'l LJ* 489; Court of Appeal Larissa (316/1996) 1999 RHDI 564.

[221] Note the second reading of the Protection of Trading Interests Bill in the House of Commons' debate which exclusively singled out US anti-trust legislation for attack: 15.11.1979 HC, Vol.973, col. 1533. Article 33 of the Draft Convention does not appear to 'put in the boot' to such a great extent as would s. 5(1) Protection of Trading Interests Act 1980, HC, *Ibid.*, col. 1566, (Fletcher-Cooke, C., MP); also 'Blocking and clawback statutes: the United Kingdom approach' in Collins, L. *Essays in International Litigation and the Conflict of Laws*, 1994, p.333, at p.348.

[222] Although English law does currently award 'exemplary damages' in (Lord Devlin's) 3 limited categories (*Rookes v Barnard* [1964] AC 1129, at pp.1226–30, (with *Kuddus (AP) v Chief Constable of Leicestershire Constabulary* [2001] 2 WLR 1789, HL overruling *AB v South West Water Services* [1993] QB 507, CA)—chiefly, in the modern context, in causes of action for trespass, unlawful eviction of tenants, libel, false imprisonment and misconduct by the police (*Thompson v Commissioner of Police of the Metropolis* [1998] QB 498, at p.417, CA) and/or misfeasance in public office: *Kuddus (AP) v Chief Constable of Leicestershire Constabulary* [2001] 2 WLR 1789 HL—it is somewhat uncertain (despite Lord Denning's dictum in *S.A. General Textiles v Sun and Sand Ltd* [1978] 1 QB 279, at pp.299–300) that punitive damages awards in US (personal injury) claims would be enforced here, as being contrary to public policy, possibly a reflection of their exclusion in similar circumstances in English law, McGregor, H. *McGregor on Damages*, 16th edn., 1997, at pp.444–61; *contra Old North State Brewing Company, Inc. v Newlands Services Inc.* [1999] 4 WWR 573, at p.588, para. 53, BC CA (Finch J.A.); Sikora, D. *Die Anerkennung und Vollstreckung US-amerikanischer Urteile in England*, 1998, at p.75 onwards believes not; but cf. *Lancashire County Council v Municipal Mutual Insurance Ltd* [1997] QB 897, at p.908 (Simon Brown LJ), where insurance cover for the Chief Constable for (exemplary) damages (on basis of s 48 Police Act 1964) was *not* denied on the ground of public policy; the fact that domestic law recognised a similar remedy with a 'punitive' element was one reason why public policy may, in future, be rejected as a defence: Müller, P. 'Sind US-amerikanische Punitive-damages-Urteile in Deutschland vollstreckbar?' (2001) *Der Betrieb* 83; Müller, P. *Punitive Damages und deutsches Schadenersatzrecht*, 2000 at p.361 and for the proportionality principle, at pp.364–65; below, in Article 27(1) chapter 4, at p.382; also *T AG gegen S. Inc.* 12.6.1990 116 BGE, II, 376; for German view of Article 33, Wagner, R. (2001) *IPRax* 533, at p.545.

bilateral recognition and enforcement Treaty[223] was believed to have foundered.[224]

OVERVIEW OF BRUSSELS AND LUGANO CONVENTIONS THEMSELVES[225]

Title I: Scope

Title I, Article 1, defines the scope of the Brussels and Lugano Conventions *ratione materiae* for (1) the taking of jurisdiction 'on the merits' in Title II, Articles 2–18; (2) the obligation of one Contracting State court to decline to hear a case due to *lis pendens* under Articles 21–23;[226] (3) the ability of a Contracting State court to order provisional and protective measures under Article 24;[227] and (4) the recognition and enforcement of Contracting State court judgments under Title III,[228] Articles 25 *et seq.* Its interpretation is therefore a matter of some considerable importance. Yet commonly, in the desire to produce a unified concept of 'civil and commercial matters', or at least in defining the term *a contrario*, the consequences

---

[223] *Ad referendum* text, initialled in London on 26.10.1976, reported in (1977) 16 *ILM* 71; (defences in Articles 6–8 of this text), Article 8(c) would have provided a defence to 'recovery exceeding monetary limits upon liability fixed by a statute' of the enforcing State; such a statute only later appeared as s. 5(1) of the Protection of Trading Interests Act 1980—'clearly directed at the Clayton Act, s.4', *Current Law Statutes Annotated 1980*, 1981, section 11/5.

[224] At least this is the American perception: Fastiff, E. 'The Proposed Hague Convention on the Recognition and Enforcement of Civil and Commercial Judgments: A solution to Butch Reynold's Jurisdiction and Enforcement Problems' (1995) *Cornell Int'l LJ* 469, at p.471, n. 2; also Borchers, P. (1998) *Brook J Int'l L* 157, at pp.162–63; Scoles, E. and Hay, P. *Conflict of Laws*, 2nd edn., 1992, at p.961, para. 24.6; Weintraub, R. *Commentary on the Conflict of Laws*, 4th edn., 2001, at p.237.

[225] Innovations brought to English international civil procedure by the Conventions are: the availability of the so-called *travaux préparatoires* for consultation by the English courts in 'ascertaining the meaning or effect of any provision of' the Conventions, ss 3(3) and 3B(2) CJJA 1982; the reference procedure to the ECJ under the Protocol to the Brussels Convention; the judicial co-operation procedure under the Lugano Convention, s 3B(1) CJJA 1982 and Protocol No.2 to the Lugano Convention, above, and the methodology of interpretation of the Conventions, notably the 'teleological' method: Scholz, I. *Das Problem der autonomen Auslegung des EuGVÜ*, 1998—Kropholler, 1998, at p.41, para. 37; Briggs, A. 'Anti-Suit Injunctions in a Complex World' in F.D. Rose (ed) *Lex Mercatoria: Essays on International Commercial Law in Honour of Francis Reynolds*, 2000, p.219, at p.229.

[226] *Owens Bank Ltd v Fluvio Bracco and Others (No.2)* (C-129/92) [1994] ECR I–117; *Marc Rich and Co. A.G. v Societa Italiana Impianti P.A. (The 'Atlantic Emperor')* [1989] 1 Lloyd's Rep. 548, CA, at p.554; *Union de Remorquage et de Sauvetage S.A. v Lake Avery Inc. (The 'Lake Avery')* [1997] 1 Lloyd's Rep. 540, [1997] CLC 683, QBD (Clarke J).

[227] Article 24 is a special provision, outside the 'normal' rules of jurisdiction on the merits in Title II: *Van Uden Maritime BV, trading as Van Uden Africa Line v Kommanditgesellschaft in Firma Deco Line, and another* (C-391/95) [1998] ECR I–7091 and *Hans-Hermann Mietz v Intership Yachting Sneek B.V.* (C-99/96) [1999] ECR I–2277, discussed below.

[228] *LTU Lufttransportunternehmen GmbH and Co. KG v Eurocontrol* (C29/76) [1976] ECR 1541; unless Article 57 provides for an alternative enforcement regime (*Antonius van den Boogaard v Paula Laumen* (C-220/95) [1997] ECR I–1147, at p.1157, para. 27 (Advocate-General Jacobs), the system inaugurated by Title III, when applicable, must be resorted to, to the exclusion of any other (national procedure): *Jozef de Wolf v Harry Cox B.V.* (C42/76) [1976] ECR 1759.

themselves of Article 1's wide scope are sometimes overlooked:[229] notably the repercussions for the Contracting State courts,[230] when acceding to the Conventions, on their previous traditional civil procedural law.[231] These have proved to be enormous and fundamental. If, faced with jurisdictional questions, a court decides that the case involves 'civil and commercial matters', not in the excluded category of disputes, the Conventions will apply, to the exclusion of all other jurisdictional rules, unless, and to the extent that[232] the Conventions themselves permit their (re)-application:[233] if Article 1 means that the Conventions do apply to a particular dispute, the cry can never thereafter be heard that 'the Conventions do not/no longer apply'; they are all-embracing and pervasive in 'civil and commercial matters'. This should always be borne in mind when considering such Articles as Articles 2,[234] 4, 24, Articles 55–56[235] and 57.[236]

---

[229] Not in Briggs, 1997, at pp.3–5; an obvious example being where the Convention may permit jurisdiction over *each claim* (*Ocarina Marine Ltd and others v Marcard Stein & Co.* [1994] 2 Lloyd's Rep. 524, QBD, (Rix J)) to be taken against a (Part 20) defendant domiciled in another Contracting State, permission to serve such a party *ex juris* not being required—CPR 6.19(1): at least a modicum of care, to avoid either embarrassment and/or CPR 3.10, needs to be taken, however, to ensure the correct CPR PD 6B r.1 endorsement is included in the claim form, *Trustor AB v Barclays Bank Plc (F Van Lanschot Bankiers (Luxembourg) SA* (Part 20 Defendant)), 24.10.2000, Ch.D., Rimer J; also the effect of *lis pendens* provisions of Art.21: *Reichhold Norway ASA and another v Goldman Sachs International* [1999] 1 All ER (Comm) 40, at p.51 (Moore-Bick J); CPR 6.19(1) will be preserved for Denmark, and a new CPR 6.19(1A) will be inserted for proceedings to which the Brussels I Regulation will apply on 1.3.2002.

[230] Random examples being *Berliner Bank A.G. v Karageorgis and anor.* [1996] 1 Lloyd's Rep. 426 and *Johnson v Coburn*, 24.11.1999, CA (Kennedy LJ), where the English court adapted its own procedure in the light of repercussions such might have on the enforceability of its judgments abroad; on the hybrid nature of the English court, 'essentially civilian' in now dealing with the Convention, 'drafted in a civilian style'—Briggs, A. in Rose (ed) *Lex Mercatoria*, 2000, p.219, at p.229.

[231] The jurisdiction of the English court can now be asserted by service *ex juris* under what is now CPR 6.20; on or after 1.3.2002, proceedings to which the Brussels I Regulation apply, the CPR will be altered to insert CPR 6.19(1A) for service out of the jurisdiction such cases.

[232] For example under Article 4(1), or Article 24—*ibid*, Briggs, 1997, at pp.3–4, para. 1.02, (1999) 17 *BYIL* 319, at pp.327–28; but see *Intermetal Group Ltd and Anor v Worslade Trading Ltd* [1998] 2 IR 1.

[233] The stark question should therefore be: does the Convention apply once and for all, or not at all? Concurring in this view *Trib. de Bruxelles* 7.6.2000, unreported, re Article 4.

[234] Cf *Re Harrods (Buenos Aires) Ltd* [1992] Ch 90. Stay in favour of Texas despite jurisdiction apparently under Article 18/Article 5(1) as against Swiss defendant insurers in *ACE Insurance SA-NV v Zurich Insurance Company* [2000] 2 All ER (Comm) 449, at p.456 (Longmore J), *affm'd* [2001] 1 Lloyd's Rep. 618, CA., (Rix LJ); now *Lubbe v Cape Plc* [2000] 1 WLR 1545, at p.1562 (Lord Bingham of Cornhill).

[235] The Brussels Convention, when it applies *ratione temporis/personae/materiae*, supersedes earlier bilateral Conventions completely, with no remainder: *BGH* 23.1.1986 IPRspr. 1986 Nr. 171, at p.391, [1987] E.C.C. 276; *OLG Hamm* 3.8.1987 IPRspr. 1987 Nr. 155, at p.390; *BGH* 18.2.1993 IPRspr. 1993 Nr. 169, at p.378, [1995] I.L.Pr. 523; *Bavaria Fluggesellschaft Schwabe and Co. KG and Germanair Bedarfsluftfahrt GmbH and Co. KG v Eurocontrol* (C9 *and* 10/77) [1977] ECR 1517; *OLG München* 16.3.1999 IPRspr. 1999 Nr. 158, at p.378; (Belgian) *Cour de Cassation* 29.3.2001, *XY et autre c/ GC*, unreported, *http://www.cass.be/cgi_juris*.

[236] The *lacunae*-filling rôle of the Brussels Convention was highlighted in *The Maciej Rataj* (C-406/92) [1994] ECR I–5439; cf. *The 'Bergen'* [1997] 1 Lloyd's Rep. 380; *Frans Maas Logistics (UK) Ltd v CDR Trucking BV* [1999] 1 All ER (Comm) 737 (Colman J).

The actual interpretation of the constituent elements almost seems to pale into insignificance beside the effects of Title I's application, but interpreted they must be. Since the meaning of Article 1 is, in many respects of minor value to the Articles to be reviewed in this treatment, it will only be dealt with briefly here.[237] The European Court has been called upon to review the meaning of 'civil and commercial matters' in Article 1(1) directly in three cases: in *Netherlands State v Reinhold Rüffer*[238] for the purposes of Title II, and in *LTU Lufttransportunternehmen GmbH & Co. KG v Eurocontrol*[239] together with *Volker Sonntag v Hans Waidmann and others*[240] for Title III. The various exclusions, in the second paragraph of Article 1, have been interpreted in *Antonius van den Boogaard v Paula Laumen*[241] Article 1(1) '. . . rights in property arising out of a matrimonial relationship';[242] *Henri Gourdain v Franz Nadler*[243] Article 1(2) . . . proceedings relating to the winding-up of insolvent companies';[244] and *Marc Rich & Co. AG v Società*

---

[237] A more generous treatment is to be found in Kaye, P. *Law of the European Judgments Convention,* Vol I, 1999, Ch.6, pp.379–499; and Soltész, U. *Der Begriff der Zivilsache im Europäischen Zivilprozessrecht: zur Auslegung von Article 1 Abs. 1 EuGVÜ,* 1998.

[238] (C814/79) [1980] ECR 3807; cf. *R v Crown Court at Harrow and another, ex parte UNIC Centre Sarl* [2000] All ER 449, QBD (Newman J)—a 'civil matter' an application by a local authority under s 97 Trade Marks Act 1994 for forfeiture order in a magistrates' court.

[239] (C29/76) [1976] ECR 1541, at p.1551, para.5—both 'the legal relationships between the parties' and the 'subject matter of the action' will have a bearing on this 'civil and commercial' enquiry.

[240] (C-172/91) [1993] ECR I–1963.

[241] (C-220/95) [1997] ECR I–1147.

[242] *Jacques de Cavel v Luise de Cavel* (C143/78) [1979] ECR 1055; *OGH* 28.4.1999 *Entscheidungen* 72 Band, 1999, Nr. 80, p.514 (on the 'social security' exclusion, *sed quaere*); also *Swiss Bundesgericht* 27.5.1993 *R gegen R* reported in *Collection of jurisprudence of the European Court of Justice and of the highest courts of the States Parties concerning the Lugano Convention,* Vol.III, 1994, Publications of the Swiss Institute of Comparative Law, 1998, at p.431; *OGH* 21.10.1999 2 Ob 288/99p, unreported, http://www.curia.eu.int/common/recdoc/convention/en/2000/17–2000.htm, at p.9; such matters now dealt with in Article 1(1) Council Regulation (EC) 1347/2000 of 29 May 2000 on jurisdiction and the recognition and enforcement of judgments in matrimonial matters and in matters of parental responsibility for children of both spouses [2000] OJ160/19, in force on 1.3.2001; The European Communities (Matrimonial Jurisdiction and Judgments) Regulations 2001, SI 310/2001.

[243] (C133/78) [1979] ECR 733, at p.744, para. 4; *Ashurst v Pollard and another* [2001] 2 WLR 722, CA, at p.728 (Jonathan Parker LJ): 'Is bankruptcy the principal subject matter of the proceedings?'; see generally, Briggs, 1997, at p.31. Merely because a licensed insolvency practitioner happens to be one of the parties appears to be insufficient for the exclusion to operate. The question seems to be: is the legal foundation ('[t]he statutory basis upon which the action is founded', *Gerechtshof*, The Hague, 7.1.1987 *Menten v The Federal Republic of Germany* [1991] I.L.Pr. 259, at p.262) of the contested application based (and can only be based) on the law relating to bankruptcy/insolvency. One is put in mind of ss 238(2) and 239(2) Insolvency Act 1986—transactions at an undervalue and preferences and the officeholder/insolvency practitioner's application to the court; *OLG Saarbrücken* 31.1.1989 *Re French Insolvency Proceedings* [1991] I.L.Pr. 459, at p.461 and *Cour d'appel de Paris Pierrel c/ Ergur* 13.3.1991 (1992) *JDI* 187, [1993] I.L.Pr. 533; cf. *Jyske Bank (Gibraltar) Ltd v Spjeldnaes and others* [1999] 2 BCLC 101, at pp.119–23, (Evans-Lombe J); *Credit Suisse and Credit Suisse Canada v CH (Ireland) Inc (in liquidation),* 2.2.1996, Irish HC.

[244] Or, more precisely, the scope of the phrase 'relating to' winding up: *UBS v Omni Holding AG* [2000] 1 All ER (Comm) 42, Ch.D (Rimer J) at p.49—a claim capable of arising quite apart from any such winding-up held *not* within the exception; also *Firswood Ltd v Petra Bank* [1996] CLC 608, CA; *Cour d'appel de Luxembourg* 2.3.2000 *Vilain c/ Vilain* 2000 *Pas. Lux.,* 282, at p.286: 'il

Italiana Impianti PA[245] Article 1(4) 'arbitration'. The latter two occasionally arise for decision before the English courts, notably[246] in connection with the Article 1(4) arbitration exception.[247]

Since the decision of the European Court of Justice in *Van Uden Maritime BV, trading as Van Uden Africa Line v Kommanditgesellschaft in Firma Deco Line*,[248] the question of whether 'provisional, including protective measures' can be obtained under Article 24 in a 'civil and commercial' dispute—despite the fact that Article 1 may exclude proceedings entirely on the merits from the scope *ratione materiae* of the Convention—will now have to be borne in mind in addition.

Title II: (a) jurisdictional provisions, (b) *lis alibi pendens*, and (c) interim relief

(a) Jurisdictional provisions.

The jurisdictional provisions of the Conventions are for the most part[249] contained in Title II, and regulate the international (and, on occasion the internal[250]) competence of the Contracting State courts to decide civil and commercial issues on the merits[251] of a dispute. The provisions of Title II are somewhat complex, and the methodology of finding whether a particular court has jurisdiction is variously strewn throughout the Convention, with a distinct hierarchical[252] order among the articles.

---

n'est pas établi, au vu de l'arrêt, que les droits litigeux *soient nés indépendamment de la succession* à l'origine des difficultés' ('it was not established, in the case, that the rights in issue arose independently from the succession at the origin of the difficulties') (exception therefore applied); *Cour d'appel de Paris Dagmar Schieffer v Soc. Jacomo France* 9.5.1990 [1992] I.L.Pr. 25; see now the future scope *ratione materiae* of Council Regulation (EC) 1346/2000 of 29 May 2000 on insolvency proceedings [2000] OJ L160/1, to come into force 31.5.2002: Article 1 'collective insolvency proceedings which entail the partial or total divestment of a debtor and the appointment of a liquidator'.

[245] (C109/89) [1991] ECR I–3855.
[246] Also *QRS 1 Aps and others v Frandsen* [1999] 3 All ER 289, CA, Article 1(1) '. . . revenue . . . matters'
[247] *The 'Lake Avery'* [1997] 1 Lloyd's Rep. 540 (Clarke J); *The 'Heidberg'* [1994] 2 Lloyd's Rep. 287 (Diamond QC); *Vale Do Rio v Shanghai Bao Steel* [2000] 2 All ER (Comm) 70 (Thomas J).
[248] (C-391/95) [1998] ECR I–7091, reviewed in detail below chapter 3.
[249] Various other idiosyncratic articles, scattered throughout the Conventions, Accession Conventions and Protocols deal, or have dealt with, the taking of jurisdiction: Article 54a, Article 57, Articles I(1)(2), Article V and Art Vd of the Protocol; Article 35 of the 1978 Accession Convention (*New Hampshire Insurance Co. and others v Strabag Bau A.G. and others* [1990] 2 Lloyd's Rep. 61, QBD (Potter J) affm'd [1992] 1 Lloyd's Rep. 361, CA) and Article 54 III of the Lugano and 1996 Brussels Conventions.
[250] Especially re Article 5(1) in Continental procedure.
[251] Note now the effect of Article 24's *sui generis* competence to order interim relief, below, chapter 3.
[252] Also Briggs, 1997, at p.16 following; for the opportunities of avoiding having to sue under Article 2, Béraudo, J-P. 'Du bon usage des règles de compétence spéciales des Conventions de Bruxelles et de Lugano pour plaider chez soi' (2001) *JCP*, Doctr., 417, especially at pp.418–19, re Article 5(1).

The order of importance in rank appears to be as follows, always bearing in mind Article 19,[253] the 'special' procedure in Article 24,[254] and the *lis pendens* provisions of Articles 21–23:[255] subject to the 'exclusive'[256] jurisdictional categories in Article 16,[257] to jurisdiction taken under Article 57 'conventions on particular matters',[258] to 'submission' under Article 18,[259] to 'exclusive'[260] jurisdiction under Article 17, to the insurance[261] and consumer[262] provisions of sections 3 and 4, Articles

---

[253] Where a contracting state court must decline jurisdiction when it is seised of a claim which is principally concerned with a matter over which other Contracting State courts have exclusive jurisdiction.

[254] In *OLG München* 5.4.2000 (2000) *RIW* 464, a Greek court had ordered a provisional freezing order despite arbitration on the merits in Zürich, reviewed below, in chapter 3 at pp.321–322.

[255] Note also the effect of Article 20. It must also constantly be borne in mind that, except (perhaps contentiously) only in cases of exclusive jurisdiction under Article 16 (*Overseas Union Insurance Ltd and Others v New Hampshire Insurance Company* (C351/89) [1991] ECR I–3317), a particular court with jurisdiction under an article in the hierarchy must always decline jurisdiction under Article 21 if it is the court second seised (of an action between the same parties on the same cause of action), or may do so, if proceedings in both courts are related, under Article 22—for this duty in relation to 'a convention on a particular matter' under Article 57, *The Maciej Rataj* (C-406/92) [1994] ECR I–5439.

[256] This seems to mean that it takes precedence over jurisdictional provisions lower in the hierarchy; it is unclear whether Article 16 would have ascendancy over Article 57; questions 1–3 in withdrawn reference in *Boston Scientific Ltd v Cordis Corp.*(C-186/00) on the interpretation of, *inter alia*, Article 57 with regard to Articles 2 and 64 of the European Patent Convention, removed on 9.11.2000 [2001] OJ C118/27.

[257] For rights *in personam* of a trustee in bankruptcy against the bankrupt and co-owning spouse of immovable property located abroad (Portugal), arising from their personal relationship: *Ashurst v Pollard and another* [2001] 2 WLR 722, CA (Jonathan Parker LJ); also *George Lawrence Webb v Lawrence Desmond Webb* (C–294/92) [1994] ECR I–1717.

[258] For a comprehensive list of such conventions, Geimer, R. and Schütze, R. *Europäisches Zivilverfahrensrech, Kommentar zum EuGVÜ und Lugano-Übereinkommen*, 1997, at pp.625–31: *Hoge Raad* 12.9.1997 *United Towing Ltd/Micoperi Offshore SpA* 1997 *NJ* 1644; e.g. *OGH* 11.5.2000 (2001) *ZfRV* 73, at p.74; or jurisdiction under other 'Community' instruments: *ArbG Wiesbaden* 15.4.1998 (1998) IPRspr. Nr.143.

[259] To be judged according to *lex fori* of court reputedly seised: *OLG Dresden* 2.6.1999 IPRspr. (1999) Nr. 115, at p.286; as to what procedural steps will *not* amount to Art.18 submission, *Hewden Stuart Heavy Cranes Ltd v Leo Gottwald Kommanditgesellschaft & others*, 13.5.1992, CA, (Lloyd LJ): as long as the defendant maintains his position on challenging the assertion of jurisdiction at each and every stage, he may apply for an extension of time for service of a defence; apply for security for costs (on application to challenge (under CPR r.11)), and make submissions only on (potentially contrived) construction of claimant's case for jurisdictional purposes; cf *Corte di Cassazione* 22.5.1998 *Muller contro Fimiani R.* (1999) *Riv. dir. int. priv. e proc.* 966, where the challenge to jurisdiction was not repeated in the defence: still no submission under Art.18; however, a challenge appears to be *essential* in the defendant's *first* submissions, if any: *OLG Hamm* 2.10.1998 (1998) IPRspr. No.157, at pp.295–6, otherwise Art.18 will apply; also *BGH* 18.9.2001 (2001) *JZ* 484; *Med-Eq A/S v Newlands Clinical Trials Ltd (t/a Medical Innovations) and others*, 12.12.2001, Ch.D., (Evans-Lombe J).

[260] Over other articles (*Kurz v Stella Musical Veranstaltungs GmbH* [1992] Ch. 196, at p.203 (Hoffmann J)), except: Art.57 (*The Bergen*) [1997] 1 Lloyd's Rep. 380); Articles 16 and 18 (*Elefanten Schuh v Jacqmain* [1981] ECR 1671; *OLG Dresden* 2.6.1999 IPRspr. (1999) Nr. 115); *contra*, and almost certainly incorrect, *Cassation Ammerlaan Agroprojecten B.V* [1999] I.L.Pr. 627 (not over Art.6(1)); *Hough v P & O Containers Ltd* [1999] QB 834; *Corte di Cassazione* 11.6.2001 *Maritransport s.r.l. v Rewico Italia s.r.l. and Multiarredo s.r.l.* (2001) *ETL* 901.

[261] Fricke, M. 'Internationale Zuständigkeit und Anerkennungszuständigkeit in Versicherungssachen nach europäischem und deutschem Recht' (1997) *Versicherungsrecht* 399; Article 17 has only *limited* ascendancy over insurance/consumer matters.

[262] Schoibl, N. 'Die Zuständigkeit für Verbrauchersachen nach europäischem Zivilverfahrensrecht des Brüsseler und des Luganer Übereinkommens (EuGVÜ/LGVÜ)' (1998) *JBl* 700.

7–12a and 13–15, a defendant 'domiciled'[263] in a Contracting State *must* be sued[264] on the merits in the courts of the Contracting State of his/her/its domicile/ seat[265]—under Article 2—if 'special' jurisdiction in section 2, Articles 5–6, does not provide (for a plaintiff/claimant) an alternative base of jurisdiction in another Contracting State.

These are the only permitted bases of jurisdiction on the merits that may be invoked[266] against Contracting State domiciliaries[267] in civil and commercial matters: Article 3 lays down a rule that, as regards such defendants,[268] no other rules may be used against them, and '[i]n particular' the extraordinary, exorbitant

---

[263] 'Domicile' as defined in Articles 52 and 53, to be determined by national law: for the UK, ss 41, 42 Civil Jurisdiction and Judgments Act 1982 ('CJJA 1982'): *Petrotrade Inc and others v Smith and others* [1998] 2 All ER 346, *Canada Trust Co. and others v Stolzenberg and others (No.2)* [1998] 1 WLR 547, affm'd [2002] 1 AC 1, HL (time for ascertaining domicile for purposes of Articles 2, 6(1) on *issue* of proceedings); a good arguable case must be established for domicile in UK under Article 2-*Latchin t/a Dinka Latchin Associates v General Mediterranean Holidays SA and another*, 4.12.2001, QBD (A Smith J); and *The Deichland* [1990] 1 QB 361, CA, *Domansa and Ors v Derin Shipping and Trading Co. Inc.* [2001] Lloyd's Rep. 362, at p.366; for Ireland now as from 1 December 1999, s.15 (and Ninth Schedule) to the Jurisdiction of Courts and Enforcement of Judgments Act, 1998, *Acts of the Oireachtas*, 1998, No.52; for Germany especially in this context, §17 ZPO—*OLG Rostock* 11.11.1999 IPRspr. 1999 Nr. 132, at p.314-§§7 ff BGB and Kropholler, J. *Europäisches Zivilprozeßrecht: Kommentar zu EuGVÜ und Lugano-Übereinkommen*, 6 Aufl., 1998, at p.446, para. 7; for France Article 102 *Code Civil*, Dalloz, 1998, p.145 'principal établissement'; 'le siège social réel' in conjunction with Articles 42 and 43 NCPC 'au lieu où sont effectivement exercées . . . les fonctions de direction de la société', in *Nouveau Code de Procedure Civile*, Dalloz, 93ème éd, 2001, at pp.54–57, also Gaudemet-Tallon, 1996, at p.52, para. 71— *Cour de Cassation Fondation Solomon R. Guggenheim c/ David Helion, Nicolas Helion et Sandro Rumney* 3.7.1996 (1997) JDI 1016; for Austria, Burgstaller, A. (ed) *Internationales Zivilverfahrensrecht*, 2000, at p.46; Rammeloo, S. *Corporations in Private International Law*, 2001, esp.Ch.4, and at pp.274–76; note that the UK, as from 1.2.1998, is to treat Gibraltar (and persons domiciled there) as (a) separate Contracting State (parties): The Civil Jurisdiction and Judgments Act 1982 (Gibraltar) Order 1997 SI 1997/2602.

[264] 'Suing' appears to contemplate pursuing a substantive cause of action, Neill LJ in *The Deichland* [1990] 1 QB 361, CA, at p.374, (also *Alfred Toepfer International GmbH v Société Cargill France* [1998] 1 Lloyd's Rep. 379, at p.387 'whether a dispute as to jurisdiction can properly be categorised as 'cause of action'') (Phillips LJ); also therefore dicta by Waller LJ in *National Justice Compania Naviera S.A. v Prudential Assurance Co. Ltd. (The 'Ikarian Reefer' (No.2))* [2000] 1 Lloyd's Rep. 129, at p.137, who preferred a view that an application to the court for an order for costs under s 51 Supreme Court Act 1981 against a non-party domiciled in another Contracting State does not involve 'suing' that person; and now CPR 6.20(17).

[265] '[C]entral jurisdictional tenet' and the 'fundamental principle' (Advocate-General Fennelly) and ECJ in *Société Group Josi Reinsurance Company SA v Compagnie d'Assurances Universal General Insurance Company (UGIC)* (C-412/98) [2000] ECR I–5925, at p.5932, para. 16 and at p.5957, para. 55, respectively.

[266] The domicile of a plaintiff (in a non-Contracting State) is generally irrelevant to the scope *ratione personae* of the Convention, except in cases where the Convention explicitly declares it to be a relevant factor—AG Fennelly, in *Société Group Josi Reinsurance Company SA* (C-412/98) [2000] ECR I–5925, at p.5934, para. 22.

[267] As has been mentioned above, particular care must be taken with Luxembourg domiciled defendants under the Brussels Convention–*OGH* 16.1.2001 (2001) *ZfRV* 152 and Swiss domiciled defendants under the Lugano Convention (Article Ia Protocol, now otiose).

[268] Re-iteration of prohibition in *Cour de Cassation* 19.1.1999 *Soc. Transports La Mouette c/ Soc. De Transports NV Travacca*, unreported, http://curia.eu.int/common/recdoc/convention/en/1999/ 51–1999.htm and *OGH* 14.12.2000 (2001) *ZfRV* 150. Non-Contracting State domiciliaries have no such protection, Article 4, subject of course to Article 16.

autonomous jurisdictional regimes of the Contracting States, black-listed by way of example in Article 3 II.

(b) and *(c) lis alibi pendens* and interim relief.

The provisions on *lis alibi pendens*,[269] and the grant of 'provisional, including protective measures' under Article 24 are mentioned here for the sake of completeness. Article 24 has recently been elevated to a unique, *sui generis* status vis-à-vis Title II, and therefore merits a little attention here. *Van Uden Maritime BV v Kommanditgesellschaft in Firma Deco Line*[270] and *Hans-Hermann Mietz v Intership Yachting Sneek B.V.*[271] have shown us that Article 24 'adds a rule of jurisdiction falling outside the system set out in Articles 2 and 5 to 18'.[272] As long as the Convention applies *ratione materiae* to the application for provisional or protective measures, the judgments continue, it matters not:

(1) that proceedings on the merits are, or may be possible, in another Contracting State, (as we already knew), nor
(2) that *substantive proceedings on the merits,* under Articles 2 to 18 , are impossible[273] in any Contracting State—including in the one applied to, because Article 1 excludes such proceedings from the scope of the Convention *ratione materiae.*

Title III: Recognition and enforcement

This section of the Conventions lays down a simplified recognition and enforcement regime, at the heart of the Conventions' *raison d'être.*[274] Provided that the Contracting State court proceedings from which the Article 25 'judgment'[275]

[269] Articles 21/22/23; *The Maciej Rataj* (C-406/92) [1994] ECR I–5439; and *Grupo Torras v Sheikh Fahad Mohammed* [1995] 1 Lloyd's Rep. 374, QBD, [1996] 1 Lloyd's Rep. 7, CA.
[270] (C-391/95) [1998] ECR I–7091.
[271] (C-99/96) [1999] ECR I–2277, [1999] I.L.Pr. 541.
[272] [1998] ECR I–7091, at p.7130, para. 20; whether Articles 21/22 apply to Article 24's new-found independence is not known. *Mietz* has shown us, at para. 45, that even if a Contracting State defendant may be able to rely on Articles 13 and 14 of Title II to be sued *on the merits* as a consumer only in his/her domicile, this 'protection' (evident in Title III enforcement proceedings, Article 34 II), does *not* extend to 'actions' in another Contracting State for interim relief under Article 24.
[273] The Court in *Van Uden* found that 'provisional measures [were] not in principle ancillary to arbitration proceedings', *ibid,* at p.7133, para. 33.
[274] Cf AG Fennelly's view in *Société Group Josi Reinsurance Company SA* (C-412/98) [2000] ECR I–5925; *OLG München* 5.3.1999 IPRspr. (1999) Nr. 155, at p.369, where former enforcement procedure contrasted with that under the Lugano Convention.
[275] For a limited definition *Solo Kleinmotoren GmbH v Emilio Boch* (C-414/92) [1994] ECR I–2237, at p.2255, para. 17 ('decision must emanate from a judicial body . . . deciding on its own authority on the issues between the parties'), and *Bernard Denilauer v S.n.c. Couchet Frères* (C125/79) [1980] ECR 1553, at p.1568, paras. 8–9; *Eric Coursier v Fortis Bank and Martine Coursier, née Bellami* (C-267/97)

emanated fall within the Article 1 definition of civil and commercial matters,[276] such a judgment, *per* Article 26, must[277] be recognised,[278] or *per* Article 31, enforced,[279] in the other Contracting States. The grounds for refusal[280] of either step are curtailed to a minimum, as are the possibilities either for review of the jurisdiction of the rendering court (Article 28 I),[281] or a substantive re-examination of the merits of the judgment itself (Article 29).[282] Articles 31, 33, 35–41 represent an innovation[283] as regards the previous multilateral and

[1999] ECR I–2543, at pp.2571–72, paras. 29 and 32; *Cour d'appel de Bruxelles* 13.1.1998, http://www.cass.be/cgi_juris/: judicially-nominated collegiate 'decision' of experts not an Article 25 'judgment'; *CFEM Facades S.A. v Bovis Construction Limited* [1992] I.L.Pr. 561, at p.577, para. 61 (interlocutory decisions merely regulating procedural matters not within Title III) but a judgment entered on matters conceded is—according to Beldam LJ, in *Landhurst Leasing Plc. v Marcq* [1998] I.L.Pr. 822, at p.831, para. 37; not an *ex parte* Italian *decreto ingiunctivo* in *Cassation* 18.5.1994 *Giuseppe Micciche c/ Banco di Sicilia*, reported in *Collection*, Vol.III, 1994, Publications of the Swiss Institute of Comparative Law, 1998, at p.565; such a *decreto*, even if granted *incorrectly* after service on a defendant outside Italy, is still a 'judgment' capable of enforcement under the Brussels Convention regime: *OLG München* 24.3.1999 IPRspr. 1999 Nr. 159, at p.380; for critique of English default judgments, Cuniberti, G. (2000) *Rev crit* 786, at pp.789–91, reviewing *Cour de Cassation* 17.11.1999 *M. Camenzuli c/ M.Désira* (English 'writ' *not* the judgment for execution under Part III of the Convention); Kennett, W. *Enforcement of Judgments in Europe*, 2000, at pp.65–70; for enforcement of English (*inter partes*) *Mareva* injunction in Germany, *OLG Frankfurt/Main* 27.3.1998 (1998) IPRspr. Nr.182a.

[276] Wahl, N. *The Lugano Convention and Legal Integration*, 1990, at p.10.

[277] Subject to various (limited) defences in Articles 27, 28, 34 II, and the Protocols.

[278] Barnett, P. *Res judicata, estoppel, and foreign judgments*, 2001, at p.252, p.262, para. 7.31, and p.290, para. 7.99, and especially pp.294–95; the potential procedural reasons *why* a Contracting State judgment needs now swifter and easier recognition—e.g. for supporting pleas of issue/cause of action estoppel—remain, it is submitted, governed by English law, *qua lex fori*: *Hagen GmbH v Zeehaghe BV* (C-365/88) [1990] ECR I–1845; *Marc Rich and Co. A.G. v Societa Italiana Impianti P.A. (The 'Atlantic Emperor') (No.2)* [1992] 1 Lloyd's Rep. 624, at p.631 (Neill LJ, CA); *The 'Tjaskemolen'* [1997] 2 Lloyd's Rep. 476, at p.479 (Clarke J); *CHF Chevreau Haeute und Felle AG v Conceria Vignola Nobile*, 7.11.2000, QBD (Raymond Jack QC).

[279] Once registration in England and Wales under s 4 CJJA 1982 has been accomplished, the foreign judgment can only be subject to the same mode of execution, and the same limits as a domestic judgment: *Duer v Frazer* [2001] 1 WLR 919, at p.925, (Evans-Lombe J); also *Högsta Domstolens* 12.9.1995 *G. Preziosi di Gori and Nibi S.D.F. v Swiss Gold Imports Plc In Bankruptcy* [1997] I.L.Pr. 509, at p.511; in *Bundesgericht* 13.9.2001 *Z AG gegen Y. SpA*, unreported, a provisionally enforceable Lugano Contracting State judgment was placed on the same level, for domestic enforcement provisions (Article 80(1) SchKG) as an 'enforceable judicial judgment' for the purposes of proceedings for 'definitive Rechtsöffnung'.

[280] *Cour d'appel de Paris* 25.10.2001 *Soc. Altoun Contracting and Trading c/ Soc. Middle East Tankers et Freighters Sal* 2001 *Dalloz*, IR, 3491; very limited in comparison to earlier Treaties; for defences in Articles 27(1)(2), below, chapters 4 and 5, respectively.

[281] Exceptionally, e.g. breach of consumer provisions: *OLG Stuttgart* 4.8.2000 2001 NJW-RR 858; none otherwise—*OLG Frankfurt/Main* 27.3.1998 (1998) IPRspr. Nr.182a, at p.360; *Italian Leather SpA v WECO Polstermöbel GmbH & Co.* (C-80/00), [2000] OJ C149/22, AG Léger's opinion 21.2.2002, pending.

[282] Not permitted under any circumstances.

[283] Cf Jenard, P. *La Convention de Bruxelles du 27 septembre 1968 et ses prolongements*, Rép. Notarial, 1994, Tome XI, livre VI, 3e partie, 1994, at p.59, 7th principle enumerated there; the Title III procedure has had a revolutionary effect on the speed of Spanish *exequatur* proceedings, formerly applicable under the older regimes: Roca, S. in D. Campbell (Gen Ed) *International Judicial Assistance in Civil Matters*, 1999, at pp.274–75; Clare, T. 'Enforcement of foreign judgments in Spain' (1975) *Int'l Law*, 509, at pp.511–12.

bilateral[284] recognition and enforcement Conventions—a unified[285] procedure of applications and appeal structure.

THE AIMS OF THE CONVENTION, AND OF THIS WORK

A reading of the Preamble to the Brussels Convention reveals its umbilical link to Article 220 of the Treaty of Rome (now Article 293 EC).[286] It is evidently a product of a move towards greater harmonisation in 'the reciprocal recognition and enforcement of judgments.' But its concerns extend to strengthening 'the legal protection' of persons established in the Community; consequently,[287] provisions in Title II ensure, as regards defendants domiciled in Contracting States, that a uniform set of rules will be applied by each Contracting State, with few exceptions, autonomously interpreted in such a way that any which may deprive a defendant of the right[288] to be sued in the *forum rei*, Article 2, are uniformly (and restrictively) applied. As a particular, but non-exhaustive manifestation of this uniformity, certain bases of jurisdiction, in Article 3 II—and traditionally regarded as exorbitant—are not to be invoked[289] against a Contracting State defendant.

A direct correlation has been demonstrated[290] between the uniformity of jurisdictional provisions in Title II,[291] and the reduced number of defences to recognition and enforcement in Articles 27, 28 and 34 II. The complementary interplay

---

[284] So innovative that an Italian case applied the Title III structure to an English judgment before the Convention had come into force between the two Contracting States—Majoros, F. 'A propos de la procédure simplifiée de l'exequatur' (1978) *Rev crit* 45; of course, the internal procedure of each Contracting State, for recognition and enforcement will vary in ease or complexity: Nelle, A. *Anspruch, Titel und Vollstreckung im internationalen Rechtsverkehr*, 2000.

[285] *Jozef de Wolf v Harry Cox B.V.* (C42/76) [1976] ECR 1759; although the mechanics of execution are governed by the raft of attendant domestic procedures—*Cour d'appel de Bruxelles* 8.2.2000 *Lacaux Dominique c/ Sponsoring Development and Communication* 2000 JT 426, at p.427, para.[4]; *Duer v Frazer* [2001] 1 WLR 919, at p.925 ((Evans-Lombe J), under 1933 Act and RSC Ord.46 r.2.

[286] And to other general principles of EC Treaty law, and even human rights—*Dieter Krombach v Andre Bamberski* (C-7/98), 28.3.2000, AG Antonio Saggio's opinion 23.9.1999.

[287] 'for this purpose' in the Preamble.

[288] Article 2 is expressed as 'shall be sued . . .'; this right is not absolute, however. No breach of Article 6(1) ECHR (*in casu*, 'independent and impartial tribunal established by law') appears to occur if a defendant is not sued in the courts in which he would normally expect to be sued, under, most notably, Article 2 (that of his domicile) if another base of jurisdiction is given under the Brussels Convention, e.g. Articles 5(1), 6, 17: *OT Africa Line Ltd v Hijazy and others (The 'Kribi')* [2001] 1 Lloyd's Rep. 76, at pp.86–87, (Aikens J); *Société Commerciale de Réassurance and others v Eras International Ltd and others (No.2)* [1995] 2 All ER 278 (Potter J).

[289] The lingering effects of the exorbitant jurisdictions can still otherwise create problems: *Cour d'appel de Paris* 25.10.2001 *Mme 3 c/ X* 2002 *Dalloz*, IR, 41; noted by Rix LJ in *TSN Kunststoffrecycling GmbH v Jurgens* [2002] 1 All ER (Comm) 282, at p.284.

[290] Beaumont, P. *Civil Jurisdiction in Scotland—Brussels and Lugano Conventions*, 2nd edn, 1995, at p.14; Briggs, 1997, at p.1 n.2; also Lord Hailsham, HL Debates, 2nd reading, 3.12.1981, Vol. 425, at col.1128, penultimate full para; Jackson, D.C. *Enforcement of Maritime Claims*, 3rd edn., 2000, at p.99 para. 4.1; noted by Rix LJ in *TSN Kunststoffrecycling GmbH v Jurgens* [2002] 1 All ER (Comm) 282, at p.284.

[291] *Duijnstee v Goderbauer* (C288/82) [1983] ECR 3663, at p.3675, para. 14.

between Titles II and III seek to ensure one of the Convention's fundamental aims—the free and rapid[292] movement of Contracting State judgments[293] throughout the European Union,[294] under an exclusive and self-contained system,[295] with a unified procedure of applications, time limits, and mechanisms for appeal.[296] As the interpretative function of the European Court has progressed and developed—and the list of articles for which a preliminary reference has been sought, has increased—the Court itself has added further specific aims—which may or may not be a direct consequence of the desire to reach a unified application[297] of the Convention, or at least to curtail views that may hamper its ultimate realisation.

Such relevant and non-exhaustive examples of these aims are: 'to facilitate, to the greatest possible extent, the free movement of judgments by providing a simple and rapid enforcement procedure';[298] to promote legal certainty, or predictability[299] (for both plaintiffs/claimants[300] and defendants[301]) as regards the application of the jurisdictional rules; to ensure, as far as possible,[302] that in certain clearly defined cases the existence of a particularly close relationship between a dispute and the Court that may most conveniently be called upon to decide it;[303]

[292] *Société d'Informatique Service Réalisation Organisation (SISRO) v Ampersand Software BV* (C–432/93) [1995] ECR I–2269, at p.2299, para. 35.

[293] Same point made in *Solo Kleinmotoren GmbH v Emilio Boch* (C-414/92) [1994] ECR I–2237, at p.2256, para. 20.

[294] Again, a similar point made in *Hoffmann v Krieg* (C145/86) [1988] ECR 645, at p.666, para. 10.

[295] Recently *Eric Coursier v Fortis Bank and Martine Coursier, née Bellami* (C–267/97) [1999] ECR I–2543, at p.2571, para. 25; Kerameus, K., in Fletcher et al (eds) *Foundations and Perspectives of International Trade Law*, 2001, p.237, at p.238, para. 16–002.

[296] *(SISRO) v Ampersand Software* (C-432/93) [1995] ECR I–2269; *quaere*, therefore, correctness of Spanish *Tribunal Supremo* 23.3.1999 *A.SA / I.* 1999 La Ley 14, no.4799, where national procedural law (on appeals) granted *fewer procedural possibilities;* Kerameus, K. 66 (2002) *RabelsZ,* 1 at p.12.

[297] Its insistence, wherever possible, on an 'autonomous' interpretation to the Convention's terms; the 'autonomous' definition of a tort for Article 5(3) purposes—requiring a harmful event—meant that a claim for dishonest assistance, although not characterised as a tort in English law, could be brought under Article 5(3): *Casio Computer Co. Ltd v Sayo and others* [2001] I.L.Pr. 694, at pp.700–701, (Tuckey LJ), CA; in essence to remedy what Kerameus has termed the 'deficiency of common interpretation', in Fletcher et al (eds) *Foundations and Perspectives of International Trade Law*, 2001, p.237, at p.242, para.16–011.

[298] *Krombach v Bamberski* (C–7/98), 28.3.2000, at para. 19.

[299] Confirmed in *GIE Groupe Concorde and others v The master of the vessel "Suhadiwarno Panjan"* (C–440/97) [1999] ECR I–6307; also ensured by the oft-repeated invocation, where desirable, of an autonomous interpretation of the Convention's terms: *Richard Gaillard v Alaya Chekili* (C-518/99) [2000] OJ C63/18, 5.4.2001, at para.13.

[300] *Mulox IBC Ltd v Hendrick Geels* (C-125/92) [1993] ECR I–4075, at p.4103, para. 11; *Rutten v Cross Medical* (C-383/95) [1998] ECR I–75, para. 13.

[301] *Handte v (TMCS)* (C–26/91) [1992] ECR I–3967, at p.3995, para. 18; *Réunion Européenne SA* (C–51/97) [1998] ECR I–6511, at pp.6545–47.

[302] But not always so: *Custom Made Commercial* (C–288/92) [1994] ECR I–2913, a clash of Convention aims here, certainty versus proximity—certainty seems to have triumphed: *Concorde* (C-440/97) [1999] ECR I–6307, at p.6350, para. 23.

[303] *Tessili v Dunlop* (12/76) [1976] ECR 1473, at p.1473, para. 13; *Lloyd's Register of Shipping v Campenon Bernard* (C–439/93) [1995] ECR I–961, at p.981, para. 21; *Réunion Européenne SA* (C–51/97) [1998] ECR I–6511, at p.6544, para. 27 (re Article 5(3)).

to restrain[304] the use of the *forum actoris*, unless expressly provided for;[305] to instigate, and support,[306] an expeditious procedure for the enforcement of judgments;[307] and to ensure the rights of the defendant are effectively protected.[308]

Together with these should be included a list of so-called 'non-aims', that the Conventions do not seek to achieve. Although the Conventions are ambitious in ambit, to produce as far as possible[309] a unified European civil procedure[310] in jurisdiction and the enforcement of judgments, there are limits to their reach. The Brussels Convention has been expressed not to do certain things: notably not to unify[311] the substantive[312] nor internal[313] procedure of the different Contracting States.

---

[304] Tension here between *Bier v Mines de Potasse* (21/76) [1976] ECR 1735 and cases such as *Marinari v Lloyds Bank Plc* (C-364/93) [1995] ECR I–2719 and *Réunion Européenne SA* (C-51/97) [1998] ECR I–6511, regarding Article 5(3); *S.A. Besix N.V. v WABAG Wasserreinigungsbau Alfred Kretzschmar GmbH* (C-256/00), 19.2.2002, unreported, at para. 34.

[305] The 'hostility', evidenced in particular in Article 3 II, has commonly surfaced with regard to Article 5(3), and was recently confirmed in *Réunion Européenne SA* [1998] ECR I–6511, at p.6546, para. 34; also *Leathertex* (C-420/97) [1999] ECR I–6747; *Group Josi Reinsurance* (C-412/98) [2000] ECR I–5925, at p.5956, para. 50.

[306] By rejecting an interpretation which might jeopardise its attainment: *Solo Kleinmotoren v Boch* (C-414/92) [1994] ECR I–2237, at p.2256, para. 20; *Industrial Diamond Supplies v Luigi Riva* (C43/77) [1977] ECR 2175, at p.2189, para. 30.

[307] For a statement of this aim *Berend Jan Van Dalfsen and Others v Bernard Van Loon and Theodora Berendsen* (C-183/90) [1991] ECR I–4743, at p.4772, para. 19; *Cour d'appel d'Aix-en-Provence* 2.3.2000 *Soc.Frahuil c/ M.Astier, Banco Español de Credito et autres* (2001) *Rev crit* 163, at p.166; *Société Eram Shipping Co. Ltd v Compagnie Internationale de Navigation and ors*, 7.8.2001, (Mance LJ) CA.

[308] 'in the original proceedings' *Elefanten Schuh GmbH v Pierre Jacqmain* (C150/80) [1981] ECR 1671, at p.1685, para. 14; *Bernard Denilauer v S.n.c. Couchet Frères* (C125/79) [1980] ECR 1553, at p.1569, para. 13; regarding Article 40: *Firma P v Firma K* (178/83) [1984] ECR 3033, at p.3042, para. 11; and re Article 27(2), *Hendrikman v Magenta Druck* (C-78/95) [1996] ECR I–4943; applied by the *BGH* 24.2.1999 1999 IPRax 371, at p.373, now reported in English [2001] I.L.Pr. 425 (separate representation necessary where there may be a conflict of interest); and now of course *Krombach* (C-7/98), 28.3.2000.

[309] An uneasy balance exists between the (unified) jurisdictional rules of the Convention and 'the procedural rules of . . . national law . . . [governing whether an] action is admissible', *Hagen v Zeehaghe BV* (365/88) [1990] ECR I–1845, at p.1866, para. 22; *Kinnear v Falconfilms NV* [1994] 3 All ER 42, at p.48, regarding Article 6(2); also Spühler, K. in *Der Einfluss des europäischen Rechts auf die Schweiz: Festschrift für Professor Roger Zäch zum 60. Geburtstag*, 1999, p.847, at p.852 for the problems of the interplay between national and Convention/autonomous definitions of Convention terms (*in casu*, Article 21 'definitively pending'); *Turner v Grovit and others* [2002] 1 WLR 107, HL, reference made, at p.123 (Lord Hobhouse).

[310] Kropholler, 1998, at p.28, para. 7; termed by Briggs 'the fundamental jurisdictional statute', 1997, at p.11, para. 2.01.

[311] Except where this jeopardises the effective operation of the Convention: *Société d'Informatique Service Réalisation Organisation (SISRO) v Ampersand Software BV* (C-432/93) [1995] I–2269.

[312] *Fiona Shevill and Others v Presse Alliance SA* (C-68/93) [1995] ECR I–415, at p.463, paras. 35 and 37; differences in procedural rules and a judge's margin of appreciation of them, are inevitable—yet it is their ultimate object and influence on the effectiveness of the Convention that should concern us and the ECJ: *Italian Leather SpA v WECO Polstermöbel GmbH & Co.* (C-80/00) [2000] OJ C149/22, AG Léger's opinion 21.2.2002, pending.

[313] *Siegfried Zelger v Sebastino Salinitri* (C129/83) [1984] ECR 2397, at p.2408, para. 15 and *Roger Van der Linden v Berufsgenossenschaft der Feinmechanik und Elektrotechnik* (C-275/94) [1996] ECR I–1393, at p.1412, para. 14; it was not a sufficient argument to prohibit the grant by an English court of a

The upshot, or distillation, of a view of the Conventions' expressed aims is the confidence[314] that whenever a particular dispute is litigated in one Contracting State, it will apply rules of jurisdiction and recognition and enforcement common to all Contracting States. In theory at least, it matters little[315] before which Contracting State a jurisdictional dispute under the Convention comes; it should be decided in exactly the same way throughout the European Union.

Yet certain articles of the Conventions are more contentious in certain Contracting States, and have produced a greater number of (inconsistent) case law and commentary throughout the Community than others: Article 21 vis-à-vis Article 17 in the UK; Article 5(1) in France; Article 24 (it appears Community-wide); Article 17 in the UK, Germany and France; and Article 27(1)(2) in Germany. These articles will be discussed in greater detail in the chapters devoted to them in the main body of the text. All that need be said at the present juncture is that it is arguable that the Convention is by no means being applied in a uniform manner.

In the light of the above, it will be this work's aim to undertake a comparative analysis, mainly from case law and commentaries from France, Belgium, Germany, Austria, Switzerland and England, of Articles 17, 5(1), 24, 27(1) and 27(2) and to explore whether, and if so why, the text of each article, and the ECJ jurisprudence thereon, are not being uniformly interpreted[316] throughout the Contracting States. At its simplest, this will involve taking these articles and comparing the Contracting State courts' attitude and interpretation of them.

Without prejudice to the generality of the above, this treatment will also attempt to discover a more contentious issue, namely whether, if at all, any particular Contracting State courts are so interpreting the Brussels Convention so as to protect, in some way, either the economy of legal resources in (their own) particular Contracting States, or to ensure the perpetuation of cherished autonomous procedural provisions and/or positions of the nationals/domiciliaries of such States.

As an adjunct, various chapters will review, briefly, the long-established traditional codes of civil procedure and bilateral enforcement Conventions, to ascertain whether these have had, or ought to have had, an influence on the Brussels

---

restraint order/anti-suit injunction in Brussels Convention cases that other Contracting States do not exercise such a jurisdiction—*Turner v Grovit and others* [2002] 1 WLR 107, HL, at p.123, reference made.

[314] *OT Africa Line Ltd v Hijazy and others (The 'Kribi')* [2001] 1 Lloyd's Rep. 76 (Aikens J), still demonstrates the problems where one party to a contract commences proceedings in another Contracting State, considered, by the Contracting State chosen, to be a *forum derogatum*, in the light of Article 17; below on the more restrained attitude, at pp.92–93 of *The 'Kribi'*, to the grant of anti-suit injunctions in such a case.

[315] But note the analysis of Vial, E. *Die Gerichtsstandswahl und der Zugang zum internationalen Zivilprozeß im deutsch- italienischen Rechtsverkehr*, 1999, at pp.172–73 comparing time limits in various Contracting State courts.

[316] The 'perturbations' referred to on p.1 that the Brussels Convention was intended to eliminate—this occurs, and an explanation is therefore needed, when a court decides a case in an overtly/covertly different fashion from those of the UK, or in a way that appears to conflict with ECJ jurisprudence.

Convention's drafting, or a premonitory effect on the interpretation of similarly-worded provisions of the Brussels Convention.

In order to keep pace with recent changes mooted at Community level, and of the work latterly completed at the Hague Conference on Private International Law, where relevant, proposed alterations to the Brussels Convention that the former instruments will herald will be (briefly) discussed at the end of the pertinent sections.

This work will also attempt to provide, in a general fashion, and in a way that has not hitherto been attempted in any coherent fashion,[317] a comparative commentary, bibliography and repository of information concerning (continental) case law; and using primary and secondary sources written in French and German so as to be of use—it is hoped—to future scholars of European civil procedure.

---

[317] Despite excellent commentaries from individual Contracting States on their own reception of the Conventions and the increased citation of other Contracting State court decisions (thanks to publications such as the P. Kaye (ed) *International Litigation Procedure, European Case Law on the Judgments Convention,* 1998 and the recent ECJ case law website: http://curia.eu.int/common/convention/en/index.htm). In addition to the Articles, a non-exhaustive chronological list of cases interpreting the Convention Articles is given at the beginning of this work, and a similarly non-exhaustive bibliography of texts and articles at the end.

1

Article 5(1)[1]

INTRODUCTION

A PROVISION DEALING with jurisdiction in contract[2] seemed to be indispensable in a Convention governing 'commercial matters'[3]—especially given the integrationalist euphoria engendered by a single (economic) market. One could have imagined that the contract, if not already so, would become the most widely used device for intra-Community trade.

Yet which contractual connecting factor should be favoured[4] by the Brussels and Lugano Conventions? The national jurisdictional laws[5] of the Contracting States[6] had had various models for many years, in addition to the jurisdiction at the place of the defendant's domicile: from the place of formation[7] through to the place of its breach.[8] It appears that the drafters' hands were forced in an effort to

---

[1] *Dicey and Morris*, 13th edn., 2000, Vol. I, at pp.342–52; *Cheshire and North*, 13th edn., 1999, at pp.200–10.

[2] Caution also with Article 34 of the 1978 Accession Convention, and the reservations regarding Luxembourg—OGH 16.1.2001 (2001) *ZfRV* 152, (and formerly) Swiss domiciliaries in the Protocols to the Conventions.

[3] Droz, G. *Compétence judiciaire et effets des jugements dans le marché commun*, 1972, p.58, para. 64; for earlier bilateral Conventions Beck, H. *Die Anerkennung und Vollstreckung ausländischer gerichtlicher Entscheidungen in Zivilsachen nach den Staatsverträgen mit Belgien, Österreich, Grossbritannien und Griechenland*, 1967; also Brussels I Regulation (44/2001), Article 5(1), below.

[4] The variety of connecting factors in national codes proved to be the main reason why the *forum contractus* was omitted from a list of indirect competences for the 'Avant-projet de Convention adopté par la Commission spéciale', *Document préliminaire No.4, texte révisé de mai 1964*, the Fragistas Report, Conférence de La Haye de droit international privé, *Actes et documents de la Session extraordinaire 13 au 26 avril 1966, Exécution des jugements*, 1969, at p.35, para. 8(a).

[5] Article 46 NCPC *Nouveau Code de Procedure Civile*, Dalloz, 93ème éd, 2001, at p.57 with notes; §29 ZPO; Article 635(3) Belgian *Code judiciaire* (previously Articles 42 and 53 of the 1876 Law); Austrian §88(1) JN; now Article 113 (Swiss) IPRG 1987— Karrer, P., Arnold, K., Patocchi, P., *Switzerland's Private International Law*, 2nd edn., 1994, and also Walter, G. *Internationales Zivilprozessrecht der Schweiz, Ein Lehrbuch*, 2 Aufl., 1998 at p.144 onwards; for Greece Article 33 Cpc, Yessiou-Faltsi, P. *Civil Procedure in Hellas*, 1998, at pp.147–48; and Spain, Donzallaz, Y. *La Convention de Lugano*, Vol III, 1998 paras. 4239–7164, at p.109, para. 4348.

[6] Not in The Netherlands however, it appears.

[7] In Italy, prior to 1 September 1995, Article 4(2) CprC with the place of formation *or* place of performance; now Article 3(2) of the *Riforma del sistema italiano di diritto internazionale privato*, Legge 21 maggio 1995, n.218, *verbatim* with Article 5(1) Brussels Convention.

[8] In England and Wales, as from May 2000, CPR Rule 6.20(5) and (6); up until 1.8.1920 RSC Ord. XI r.1(e)—Dicey, A.V., *A Digest of the Law of England with reference to The Conflict of Laws*, 2nd edn., 1908, at p.233 onwards and *The Annual Practice 1920*, 38th issue, 1920, at pp.90–91; Ord 11 r.1(1)(d)(i) criticised by Schack, H. *Internationales Zivilverfahrensrecht*, 2. Auf., 1996, at p.101, para. 257.

find a balance[9]—an antidote[10] even—to Article 2, the Conventions' darling, the enshrining principle 'actor sequitur forum rei'. Any provision giving jurisdiction in contract would have to provide a viable,[11] alternative competence to Article 2, yet not overcompensate,[12] and stray into creating a *forum actoris,* autonomous national examples of which had already been outlawed in Article 3 [I] and [II] of the Brussels Convention.

It was thought that equilibrium[13] could be achieved by giving the plaintiff/claimant the option[14] of suing in 'the place of performance of the obligation in question'.[15] The Jenard Report[16] states that other (national) alternatives[17] were rejected, as being too prone to upsetting Article 2. Article 5(1)'s success[18] would have to be assessed by how often disputes fulfilled the *raison d'être* of the Article's inclusion, namely to provide

[9] In this sense Broggini, G. 'Zuständigkeit am Ort der Vertragserfüllung' in Schwander, I. (ed) *Das Lugano-Übereinkommen,* 1990, p.111, at p.118.

[10] In this sense Geimer, R. and Schütze, R. *Europäisches Zivilverfahrensrech, Kommentar zum EuGVÜ und Lugano-Übereinkommen,* 1997, at pp.123–24; this 'curative' aspect of the competence of the *forum destinatae solutionis* was recognised early on by Bernard, M. *De la compétence des tribunaux français a l'égard des étrangers et de l'exécution des jugements étrangers en France,* 1900, at p.105: 'Le système né de la règle *actor sequitur forum rei* est par trop simpliste. Il concentre toutes les actions concernant une personne en un lieu unique: son domicile. Toute question de compétence . . . est une question de *situation* . . .' ('The system born of the *actor sequitur forum rei* rule is far too simplistic. It focuses all actions regarding a person in one unique place: his domicile. Every question of competence . . . is a question of *location* . . .').

[11] *Six Constructions Ltd v Paul Humbert* (C-32/88) [1989] ECR 341, at p.357.

[12] The impression of favouring plaintiffs/claimants from certain Contracting States is perhaps why Article 5(1) has fallen out of favour in some jurisdictions, according to Huet and Jayme in *Civil Jurisdiction and Judgments in Europe*—Proceedings of the Colloquium on the Interpretation of the Brussels Convention by the Court of Justice considered in the context of the European Judicial Area, Luxembourg, 11 and 12 March 1991, 1992, at p.57 and p.78.

[13] Geimer, R. and Schütze, R., 1997, at p.124; also Weiß, J. *Die Konkretisierung der Gerichtsstandsregeln des EuGVÜ durch den EuGH,* 1997, at p.45; it appears that Article 5(1) will apply whenever jurisdiction is given to one particular Contracting State (as the place of performance of the obligation in question) over a defendant domiciled in another, irrespective of the 'internal/domestic' relations otherwise involved between the claimant (or its parent company) and the defendant: *Cour de Cassation* 30.1.2001 *ING Bank NV Paris c/ Soc. Mantel Holland Beheer BV* (2001) *Rev crit* 539, and at p.549, obs. Poillot-Peruzetto.

[14] Note Article I of the Protocol to the Brussels and Lugano Conventions, *Dicey and Morris,* 13th edn., 2000, at p.343, para. 11–240, and its application in *Rechtbank van koophandel te Veurne* 2.4.1997 *SARL Omicron distribution c/ BVBA Konstruktiewerkhuis en draineerbedrijf R. Vandezande* (1998) *Rev. dr. comm. belge* 401; on the (now otiose) Swiss reservation (*Bundesgericht* 26.10.2000 *Heinz Fischer AG gegen Firma Alois Meier* BGE 126, III, 540, at p.543), and, in some detail Kaye, P. *Law of the European Judgments Convention,* Vols. 1–5, 1999, at p.718 onwards.

[15] This treatment will not deal with the related issue of jurisdiction in individual contracts of employment nor consumer or insurance matters; on these topics, De Bra, P. *Verbraucherschutz durch Gerichtsstandsregelungen im deutschen u. europäischen Zivilprozeßrecht,* 1992 and Brulhart, V. *La compétence internationale en matière d'assurances dans l'espace judiciaire européen,* 1997.

[16] [1979] OJ C59/1, at p.23, re the jurisdiction where the obligation arose.

[17] Also rejected in the German-Belgian Convention *Abkommen zwischen der Bundesrepublik Deutschland und dem Königreich Belgien über die gegenseitige Anerkennung und Vollstreckung von gerichtlichen Entscheidungen, Schiedssprüchen und öffentlichen Urkunden in Zivil- und Handelssachen,* 26.6.1959, 1959 BGBl., II, 766—Geimer, R. and Schütze, R *Internationale Urteilsanerkennung*—Band. II, 1971, at p.280.

[18] Indeed the whole *rationale* behind the list of special jurisdictional provisions—ascertaining the place of performance of a contractual obligation by reference to the express or tacit intention of the

a close connecting factor between [these] dispute[s] and the court with jurisdiction to resolve [them].[19]

This enquiry will attempt to show that the jurisdictional process to be undergone in determining jurisdiction under Article 5(1) is a complex operation;[20] that the debate that has raged over its usefulness continues today,[21] and that after many references to the European Court of Justice, certain issues are far from settled.[22] It will attempt to demonstrate that the 'close connecting factor' has proved to be a chimera, especially with international payment obligations,[23] unless, of course, the random, selective and unlikely inauguration in certain Contracting States of a *forum actoris* for such actions could ever have been intended.[24]

This section will also attempt to demonstrate that the Article has also proved to be a fertile area for national concerns,[25] and does potentially raise the spectre of judicial protectionism,[26] mainly for plaintiffs, perceived nationally to be economically and/or legally[27] disadvantaged.

parties, or by operation of law, had been recognised and rejected as early as 1869 by Von Savigny, *A Treatise on the Conflict of Laws*, (trans.Guthrie, W.), at p.154 and pp.164–65.

[19] Jenard Report [1979] OJ C59/1; now recently invoked as a reason for the article's revision by AG Léger in *Leathertex Divisione Sintetici SpA v Bodetex BVBA* (C-420/97) [1999] ECR I-6747, also below; Geimer, R. and Schütze, 1997, at p.124, para. 3 consider it as reasonable that a defendant should be jurisdictionally accountable in the forum, where, by the *lex causae*, he is to perform the obligation in question—*contra*, AG Colomer in *GIE Groupe Concorde and others v The master of the vessel «Suhadiwarno Panjan»* (C-440/97) [1999] ECR I-6307, at p.6321, para. 44; opinion also not accepted in ECJ decision of 28.9.1999, below.

[20] Too complex in some Contracting States, according to AG Colomer in *GIE Groupe Concorde*, [1999] ECR I-6307, at p.6309, pp.6317–18, paras. 3, 28–30 respectively.

[21] One influential piece seems to be Overbeck, A. 'Interprétation traditionelle de l'article 5–1 des Conventions de Bruxelles et de Lugano: le coup de grâce?' in Borrás, Bucher, Struycken, Verwilghen (eds) *E Pluribus Unum, Liber Amicorum Georges A.L. Droz*, 1996, p.287, at pp.290–91.

[22] *Cour de Cassation* in *Sté Comptoir commercial d'Orient c/ Société Medtrafina* 11.3.1997 (1998) *JDI* 129, [1999] I.L.Pr. 336, and its reference in *Groupe Concorde et autres c/ Capitaine du Suhadiwarno Panjan et autres* 9.12.1997 (1998) *Rev crit* 117, challenging the correctness of *Custom Made Commercial Ltd v Stawa Metallbau GmbH* (C-288/92) [1994] ECR I-2913; the reasoning in *Custom Made Commercial* has recently been confirmed in the case referred, *GIE Groupe Concorde* (C-440/97) [1999] ECR I-6307 at p.6348 and p.6352, paras. 13, and 29, respectively; *S.A. Besix N.V. v WABAG Wasserreinigungsbau Alfred Kretzschmar GmbH* (C-256/00), 19.2.2002.

[23] Mayss, A. and Reed, A. *European Business Litigation*, 1998, at p.117; Walter, 2 Aufl., 1998, at p.171; *Dicey and Morris*, 13th edn., 2000, at p.351, para. 11–257.

[24] For those Contracting States whose laws allow recourse, *lege causae*—or in International Sales Conventions—to the *forum actoris* to sue for payment obligations, below section 1.3.

[25] Mezger, E. 'Über einige Lücken des EuGVÜ (Brüssel 1968) und des deutschen Ausführungsgesetzes' in Lüke, Ress, Will (eds) *Gedächtnisschrift für Constantinesco* 1983, p.503, at p.514—and such jurisdiction in contract will undergo further drafting revision yet again in Article 5(1)(2) of the Brussels I Regulation, below at pp.116–118.

[26] Noted by Reed, A. 'Special Jurisdiction and the Convention: the Case of *Domicrest Ltd v Swiss Bank Corporation*' (1999) *CJQ* 218, at p.232.

[27] 'legally' in those Contracting States whose substantive laws state payment is to be made at the debtor's domicile/place of business, which, according to AG Colomer, leads to 'une désaffection sensible des juridictions nationales', *GIE Groupe Concorde* [1999] ECR I-6307, at p.6321–22, para. 46; opinion not adopted by ECJ, below; Béraudo, J-P. 'Du bon usage des règles de compétence spéciales des Conventions de Bruxelles et de Lugano pour plaider chez soi' (2001) *JCP*, Doctr., 417, at p.418.

Yet the lingering irony of this whole enquiry will turn out to be its predictability: from an historical perspective,[28] it will be seen that clearer, more precise drafting,[29] not serendipity,[30] should have been the drafters' aims in creating a jurisdictional provision in contract. A brief historical excursus will attempt to show how these contemporary problems and criticisms could have been avoided. Indeed, Von Bar, in his published work in 1881, wrote of the *forum contractus*:

> ... den Ort der Erfüllung ... entspricht nicht den vernüftigen Erwartungen der Parteien und wird die Entscheidung oft einem Gerichte zuweisen, welches der einen Partei absolut ungelegen ... erschienen wird ...[31]

The outline of this chapter will therefore follow the, by now, classic line of enquiry that a Contracting State court must follow to discover whether it has jurisdiction under Article 5(1):[32] whether the dispute before it concerns a 'matter[] relating to a contract', what is the (principal) (contractual)[33] 'obligation in question', and where is its 'place of performance'. At each juncture, national caselaw will be proffered to demonstrate either mutual conformity, or disharmony, with comparable and compatriot decisions in other Contracting States, or with the jurisprudence of the ECJ itself—together with, where relevant, the proposals for reform made manifest in Article 5(1)(2) Brussels I Regulation. To counterbalance this enquiry, historical examples of jurisdiction for the place of performance (of payment obligations) will be given to show that the current problems raised today have a long history in private international law.

---

[28] For an early survey, Hackl, C. 'Örtliche Zuständigkeit gemäß Article 5(1) und (3) des Brüsseler EG-Übereinkommens vom 27.9.1968 über die gerichtliche Zuständigkeit und die Vollstreckung gerichtlicher Entscheidungen in Zivil- und Handelssachen' (1984) *ZfRV* 1.

[29] The uncertainty over the place of performance of the obligation in question's being left to the *lex causae* has, for two types of contract it appears, been removed by Article 5(1)(b) of the Brussels I Regulation, below sections 1.1.6, 1.2.7 and 1.4; Kropholler, 2002, pp.137–41, paras. 30–42.

[30] Trusting that a provision, so exactly mirroring earlier provisions (of for example, §29 ZPO), would not receive a similar interpretation by the ECJ; augments that are frequently used to the effect that if the Convention drafters had wanted to cover a particular 'contractual' situation, they would have legislated accordingly: *LG Frankfurt/Main* 5.10.1995 IPRspr. 1995 Nr. 155, Lord Goff in *Kleinwort Benson Ltd v Glasgow City Council* [1999] 1 AC 153, at p.167 and Peel, E. 'Jurisdiction under the Brussels Convention' in Rose, F.D. (ed) *Restitution and the Conflict of Laws*, 1995, p.1 at pp.46–47.

[31] ('the place of performance does not correspond to the reasonable expectations of the parties and often directs the decision to a court which, for one of the parties, is absolutely unsuitable . . .', Von Bar, K. L. *Theorie und Praxis des internationalen Privatrechts*, Band 2, 1966, at p.438; cf. *Industrie Tessili Italiana Como v Dulop AG* (C-12/76) [1976] ECR 1473, at p.1485, para. 14.

[32] For the English courts the relevant 'applicable principles' in Lord Goff's speech in *Kleinwort Benson Ltd* [1999] 1 AC 153, at pp.163–67; followed in *AIG Group (UK) Ltd and others v The Ethniki* [2000] All ER (Comm) 65, CA, at p.69 following (Evans LJ).

[33] Recently *Agnew and others v Lansförsäkringsbolagens AB* [2001] 1 AC 223, HL.

1.1   'IN MATTERS RELATING TO A CONTRACT'

The first task[34] of a national court, in determining whether it has jurisdiction[35] under Article 5(1),[36] is to see whether the case (as pleaded,[37] or the circumstances surrounding it)[38] relates in some way[39] to a contract.

Unfortunately neither the Convention, nor the ECJ itself (head on),[40] has defined this crucial opening phrase, nor the constituent elements within it. Several cases are usually[41] proffered in which the contractual 'matter'/nature of the dispute was in issue. Primary among these is *Martin Peters Bauunternehmung GmbH v Zuid Nederlandse Aannemers Vereniging,*[42] in which a Dutch contractors' association attempted to recover payments due under its internal rules[43] from one of its members, Peters, a German construction company. Two important issues arise from the case: firstly, so as to ensure as far as possible the uniform application of Article 5(1), the opening words of the article are to be interpreted autonomously,[44] not by any law of one particular Contracting State, *lege fori,* nor

---

[34] After having discounted, of course, whether the dispute falls under any other of the 'specialised' heads of Convention jurisdiction, e.g. consumer/employment/insurance contracts, Article 16 or Article 57—Stone, P. *The Conflict of Laws,* 1996, at p.167, and in more detail Geimer and Schütze, 1997, at pp.127–29.

[35] Note 'international' and 'internal' jurisdiction, Briggs, 1997, at p.91, para. 2.122 and Schack, 2.Auf., 1996, at p.102, para. 260 following.

[36] This chapter will not discuss disputes relating to individual contracts of employment under Article 5(1).

[37] *SPRL Arcado v SA Haviland* (C-9/87) [1988] ECR 1539, below p.48; *Bio-Medical Research Ltd. T/A Slendertone v Delatex S.A.* [2000] 4 IR 307, at pp.316–17, SC (Fennelly J) obligation to pay not the obligation in question in the indorsement of claim.

[38] In 'matters' is a vague word; exactly how close a relationship/connection to a contract is not spelt out, yet is an important consideration (esp. for pre-contractual 'duties' of utmost good faith in insurance contracts): *Agnew and others v Lansförsäkringsbolagens AB* [1997] 4 All ER 937, CA, affm'd (albeit by a 3:2 majority) [2001] 1 AC 223, HL, below; also *Strathaird Farms Ltd v G A Chattaway & Co.* 1993 SLT (Sh Ct) 36, at p.38; *Cour d'appel de Chambéry Société Péchiney Electrométallurgie PEM c/ Société Universal Ceramic Materials Plc UCM* 23.2.1998 (1999) *JDI* 188.

[39] *Ibid.,* the exact nature or degree of relationship to a contract is unclear—intimate, or 'vaguely connected with'; note the comment of Lord Clyde in *Kleinwort Benson Ltd v Glasgow City Council* [1999] 1 AC 153, HL, at p.180g: 'It is thus *not* enough for the invocation of jurisdiction under article 5(1) that some remote connection can be found between the point in dispute and a contractual relationship'; cf. *Engdiv Ltd v G. Percy Trentham Ltd* 1990 SLT 617, at p.621 'in matters relating to a [head construction] contract, although not directly for breach of contract'.

[40] Only couched in negative terms in *Jakob Handte & Co. GmbH v Société Traitements Mecano-Chimiques des Surfaces (TMCS)* (C-26/91) [1992] ECR I-3697 and *Réunion Européenne SA and others v Spliethoff's Bevrachtingskantoor BV, and the Master of the vessel Alblasgracht V002* (C-51/97) [1998] ECR I-6511.

[41] Briggs, 1997, at p.92, para. 2.126 onwards; Hill, J. *The Law Relating to International Commercial Disputes,* 2nd edn, 1998, at p.127, para. 5.6.13 onwards; Gaudemet-Tallon, H. *Les Conventions de Bruxelles et de Lugano,* 2ème éd., 1996, at p.108, para. 156 onwards.

[42] (C-34/82) [1983] ECR 987; this case was followed by the *Cour d'appel de Chambéry* in the similar factual situation in *Roth c/ Syndicat des copropriétaires de l'immeuble Saint-Georges I et II* 13.6.1989 (1991) *JDI* 149, at p.150, reviewed below.

[43] At p.1003, para. 18, this act of the association made no difference to the 'matters relating to a contract'.

[44] At p.1002, para. 9.

lege causae; secondly, that the links between an association and its individual members, although not seen in the case as strictly contractual, created between them 'close links of the same kind[45] as those which are created between the parties to a contract.'[46] The national court therefore had before it obligations which could 'be regarded as contractual for the purpose of . . . Article 5(1)'.[47] National notions of what constitutes a contract are therefore no longer a reliable, nor legitimate, guide for the application of Article 5(1). Obligations arising from close links between parties, akin to a contract, are an extra gloss on national expectations.

SPRL Arcado v SA Haviland[48] confirmed[49] the independent interpretation approach[50] to the analysis of Article 5(1). Of future interest[51] to this section, apart from the use of other Community legislation[52]/instruments[53] to help in the interpretation of Article 5(1), is the statement that the 'payment of commission due under an independent commercial agency agreement *finds its very basis* in that agreement'.[54] If the obligation(s) pleaded is/are grounded in an agreement, autonomously viewed,[55] then the claim will be one involving 'matters relating to a contract'. While concentrating on the fact that the claim must spring from the source of an agreement, the ECJ was no doubt concerned not with the word 'contract', but the words 'matters relating' to a contract.

Effer SpA v Hans-Joachim Kantner[56] did not strictly advance the definition of contract much further, but clarified[57] that jurisdiction under Article 5(1) is not destroyed merely by the defendant's allegations as to the non-existence of the contract.[58]

---

[45] Reasoning applied in *Roth c/ Syndicat des copropriétaires de l'immeuble Saint-Georges I et II* 13.6.1989 1991 *JDI* 149, at p.150, according to Huet—contractual link between a housing co-operative and one of its resident members.

[46] [1983] ECR 987, at p.1003, para. 13; however, the case is not authority for the proposition that for Article 5(1) there need be no contract according to national law: Lord Goff in *Kleinwort Benson Ltd v Glasgow City Council* [1999] 1 AC 153, at p.168.

[47] At p.1002, para. 13.

[48] (C-9/87) [1988] ECR 1539, at p.1554, para. 11—for the facts see the report at p.1540, point 2; the *Cour d'appel de Brussels* had hoped for a definition of 'matters relating to a contract' at p.1541, point 3. It was not forthcoming.

[49] At p.1554, para. 11.

[50] Amidst such an interpretative atmosphere: *Netherlands State v Reinhold Rüffer* (C-814/79) [1980] ECR 3807; *Somafer SA v Saar-Ferngas AG* (C-33/78) [1978] ECR 2183.

[51] For the consideration of pre-contractual remedies.

[52] Council directive 86/653 of 18.12.1986 regarding self-employed commercial agents, at p.1555, para. 14.

[53] Article 10 Rome Convention of 19 June 1908 on the Law Applicable to Contractual Obligations— *quaere* would the ECJ, unlike the House of Lords, use Article 10(1)(e) to rule that a claim in restitution would be a 'matter relating to a contract'?

[54] At p.1554, para. 12; important also in *Leathertex Divisione Sintetici SpA v Bodetex BVBA* (C-420/97) [1999] ECR I-6747, for a 'characteristic approach', not adopted by the ECJ in its ruling, discussed below.

[55] But as yet still undefined.

[56] (C-38/81) [1982] 825.

[57] *Ibid.* p.835, para. 8.

[58] Applied in *Soc. SBCN c/ M.B. Marine S.p.a. et autres.Compagnie Winterthur Milan c/ soc.Groupe Saltiel et autres* 18.10.1994 (1995) *Rev crit* 721, at p.724 and the *Cour d'appel de Paris* 16.9.1994 *Ste Stige*

Athanasios Kalfelis v Bankhaus Schröder, Munchmeyer, Hengst & Co. & Others[59] attempted, *inter alia*, to delimit the jurisdictional competence of Article 5(1) and Article 5(3); tort, for Article 5(3) purposes was said to cover 'all actions which [sought] to establish the liability of a defendant and which [were] not related[60] to a 'contract' within the meaning of Article 5(1)'.[61] To establish this boundary, an exclusionary contractual criterion must now be imposed; yet without any strict initial reference point.

A welcome breakthrough therefore came in *Jakob Handte & Co. GmbH v Société Traitements Mecano-Chimiques des Surfaces (TMCS).*[62] TMCS had purchased two polishing machines from a Swiss company. To these TMCS had a component fitted that was manufactured by the German defendant, Handte, and sold to, and installed for, TMCS by Handte France. The component proved defective. Questions arose over whether jurisdiction could be asserted over Handte under Article 5(1), this being an action of a sub-purchaser, TMCS against the manufacturer, Handte, directly,[63] for the defects in the goods.

The ECJ noted what was *not* covered by the phrase 'matters relating to a contract': 'a situation in which there [was] *no obligation freely assumed* by one party towards another.'[64] The emphasised words seem to suggest that there be knowledge of, and assent[65] to each (contractual) obligation *inter partes*, between

---

c/ Fossard, unreported, Juris-Data 94–22994—for when it is the plaintiff/claimant that is denying the existence of a contract: *Boss Group Ltd v Boss France SA* [1996] 4 All ER 970, CA; *USF Ltd (t/a USF Memcor) v Aqua Technology Hanson NV/SA* [2001] 1 All ER (Comm) 856, QBD (Aikens J); *Bio-Medical Research Ltd. T/A Slendertone v Delatex S.A.* [2000] 4 IR 307, SC.

[59] (C-189/87) [1988] ECR 5565.

[60] A claim which can be advanced in contract cannot therefore, according to *Athanasios Kalfelis v Bankhaus Schröder*, also be advanced simultaneously in tort: *Source Ltd v T.U.V. Rheinland Holding A.G. and others* [1998] QB 54, CA; *Rye Valley Foods Ltd v Fisher Frozen Foods Ltd*, 10.5.2000, Irish HC (O'Sullivan J); if the defendant is encouraged to believe that 'the place of performance' is outside the forum potentially seised, he will thus plead Article 5(1)'s preclusionary effect vis-à-vis Article 5(3)— *Réunion Européenne SA* below, and support in the same case by *Cour d'appel de Paris* 16.11.1994 1995 DMF 554; *Alfred Dunhill Ltd v Diffusion Internationale de Maroquinerie de Prestige SARL and others* [2001] CLC 949, at p.959 (K. Rokison QC).

[61] (C-189/87) [1988] ECR 5565, at p.5584, para. 18; for actions under Article 5(3), Briggs, 1997, at p.111, para. 2.144, *Dicey and Morris*, 13th edn., 2000, Vol 1, at p.352 onwards, Rule 38(3); *Cheshire and North*, 13th ed., 1999, at pp.211–19; Kropholler, J. *Europäisches Zivilprozeßrecht*: Kommentar zu EuGVÜ und Lugano-Übereinkommen, 6 Aufl., 1998, at p.123, para. 55 onwards; Gaudemet-Tallon, 1996, at p.136, para. 183 following.

[62] (C-26/91) [1992] ECR I-3697.

[63] French law admitted a contractual action in these circumstances. This, however, did not affect the autonomous interpretation of Article 5(1): *Soc. SBCN c/ M.B. Marine S.p.a. et autres.Compagnie Winterthur Milan c/ soc.Groupe Saltiel et autres* 18.10.1994 (1995) *Rev crit* 721 and *Cour de Cassation* 23.3.1999 *Soc. Rémi Claeys aluminium c/ Soc. Sermit et Soc Roubon* (2000) *Rev crit* 224.

[64] [1992] ECR I-3697, at p.3995, para. 15; applied in *Cour de Cassation* 6.7.1999 *Donovan Data Systems Europe c/ Dragon Rouge Holding* (2000) *Rev crit* 67, a *cassation* where the appeal court had failed to ascertain an obligation freely assumed between the parent English company (of the French defendant company, Donovan Informatique France) and the French plaintiff company, at p.68; OGH 28.6.2000 (2001) *ZfRV* 32.

[65] I.e, not becoming contractually bound *aliunde*, by operation of law; but assent as to liability to one's contracting partner; the fact that, by operation of a particular governing law, certain obligations are

contracting parties who both[66] know of each other's identity[67] for there to be a matter relating to a 'contract'. Since the manufacturer had not freely undertaken[68] any contractual obligation towards the sub-purchaser, there was no 'contractual' relationship *inter partes*.

A further reason given for denying the existence of jurisdiction under Article 5(1), in such circumstances, was based on a general Convention aim, newly emerged: that of legal certainty.[69] A defendant[70] must be able, when an interpretation of the special rules of jurisdiction is involved, 'reasonably to predict before which courts . . . he may be sued'.[71]

From now on, not only must the nature of the dispute be analysed, but the identity of the potential *dramatis personae* must be reasonably predictable *inter se*, for a matter to be considered to be 'contractual'. A manufacturer, the Court continued,[72] could not reasonably foresee where an action might be brought against him by a sub-purchaser, nor even the latter's identity.

This view in *Jakob Handte* has been confirmed by the European Court of Justice in *Réunion Européenne SA and others v Spliethoff's Bevrachtingskantoor BV, and the Master of the vessel Alblasgracht V002*,[73] with an equally restrictive[74] interpretation. Now, according to *Réunion Européenne SA*, knowledge or potential knowledge of the contractual *dramatis personae* is not the sole factor affecting whether or not an obligation was 'freely assumed by one party towards the other'.[75] In *Handte*, neither the plaintiff sub-purchaser nor the defendant manufacturer

---

subsequently imposed on the freely-contracting parties does not affect the application of Article 5(1): *LG Frankfurt/Main* 5.10.1995 IPRspr. 1995 Nr. 155 and *Viskase Ltd and another v Paul Kiefel GmbH* [1999] 1 WLR 1305, CA; *Agnew and others v Lansförsäkringsbolagens AB* [2001] 1 AC 223, HL, at p.253 (Lord Hope of Craighead); in *Rudolf Gabriel v Schlank & Schick GmbH* (C-96/00), AG Jacobs—opinion of 13.12.2001—took the view, at para. 58, that an action under Austrian consumer protection law came within Article 13 'proceedings concerning a contract [concluded by a consumer]', even though—as the German Government had argued—'liability [was not] based on the conclusion of a contract'.

[66] Now *Réunion Européenne SA and others v Spliethoff's Bevrachtingskantoor BV, and the Master of the vessel Alblasgracht V002* (C-51/97) [1998] ECR I-6511, post-reference decision *Cassation* 16.3.1999, [1999] I.L.Pr. 613.

[67] Strictly this was added later in the judgment.

[68] Because Handte could not reasonably have foreseen TMCS's identity; *sed quaere*, a subsidiary of Handte, Handte France, was selling Handte's products in France; *Handte* distinguished in *Rudolf Gabriel v Schlank & Schick GmbH* (C-96/00), AG Jacobs' opinion 13.12.2001, at para.54, as the particular Austrian consumer had been 'targeted' by the German company.

[69] Subsequent cases to take up the 'certainty' aim have been *Custom Made Commercial Ltd v Stawa Metallbau GmbH* (C-288/92) [1994] ECR I-2913, at p.2956, para. 18; *Mulox IBC Ltd v Hendrick Geels* (C-125/92) [1993] ECR I-4075, at p.4103, para. 11; *Antonio Marinari v Lloyds Bank Plc and Zubaidi Trading Co.* (C-364/93) [1995] ECR I-2719, 2741, para. 19 for Article 5(3) purposes; *GIE Groupe Concorde* (C-440/97) [1999] ECR I-6307, pp.6350–51, at para. 24.

[70] Who is 'normally well-informed', at p.3995, para. 18.

[71] *Ibid.*

[72] *Ibid.* at para. 19.

[73] (C-51/97) [1998] ECR I-6511.

[74] *Ibid* at p.6542, paras. 17–20.

[75] *Ibid.* at para. 17.

knew[76] of each other's identity. As a review of the facts of *Réunion Européenne SA* will show, one party at least, the Dutch defendants Spliethoff's, may well have had knowledge[77] from the bearer bill of lading of the existence and identity of the ultimate consignee, Brambi, to whose rights the plaintiff insurers were subrogated.[78]

These insurers, Réunion, had brought an action under the bill of lading issued by the carriers, an Australian company, against them for allegedly negligent transportation of a consignment of goods. The transport under the bill was between Sydney and Rotterdam, and then by road to France. Unknown to the consignees,[79] the actual carriers had been Splietfhoff's, the Dutch company, although this fact had not been mentioned[80] on the bill of lading. One of the questions referred by the French *Cour de Cassation*[81] was whether the insurers' action under the bill of lading between themselves and an un-nominated carrier was a matter 'relating to a contract' within Article 5(1).

Unusually[82] in this case, and unlike *Handte*, it was not the plaintiff insurers who were relying on the matter falling under Article 5(1), but the defendants.[83] The plaintiffs preferred to advance their claim in tort under Article 5(3).[84] The European Court held, at paras. 17–19, that the matter was not 'a matter relating to a contract'. The parties—Brambi (and therefore[85] its insurers) and Spliethoff's— had not freely assumed obligations towards each other,[86] as Brambi, for its part, did not know of Spliethoff's existence:

---

[76] At least from their respective contracts of sale.

[77] If the ultimate consignee had been endorsed on the bill; if not, the case is no different from *Handte*.

[78] On the issue of the identity of parties for subrogation purposes, *Drouot Assurances S.A. v Consoldidated Metallurgical, Protea Assurance and GIE Réunion Européenne* (C-351/96) [1998] ECR I-3075; *Rudolf Gabriel v Schlank & Schick GmbH* (C-96/00), AG Jacob's opinion 13.12.2001.

[79] For a case when they are known: *Corte di Cassazione 2.6.1992 Gracechurch Container Line Limited v SpA Assicurazioni Generali* [1994] I.L.Pr. 206, the Italian court finding it had no jurisdiction under Article 5(1) as the place of delivery of the goods was not within the jurisdiction.

[80] (C-51/97) [1998] ECR I-6511, at p.6539, para. 9.

[81] The French referring court's decision can be found at (1997) *Rev crit* 101, and in English at [1997] I.L.Pr. 711.

[82] As previously mentioned, Article 5(1) has a pre-emptory and exclusionary effect as regards tortious actions under Article 5(3): *Kalfelis v Bankhaus Schröder* (C-189/87) [1988] ECR 5565; *Rye Valley Foods Ltd v Fisher Frozen Foods Ltd*, 10.5.2000, Irish HC (O'Sullivan J). If the matter fell under Article 5(1), the insurers feared that the place of performance would have been Rotterdam (as the place of delivery), and so deprive them of the French *forum actoris* jurisdiction; this is exactly what the defendants hoped for—rightly, in their view, from the appeal court case in *La Réunion européenne Cour d'appel de Paris* 16.11.1994 1995 DMF, 554; in *Alfred Dunhill Ltd v Diffusion Internationale de Maroquinerie de Prestige SARL and others* [2001] CLC 949, claimant's action for negligent misrepresentation held to fall within Article 5(3).

[83] [1998] ECR I-6511, at pp.6543–44; *Cour d'appel de Chambéry Société Péchiney Electrométallurgie PEM c/ Société Universal Ceramic Materials Plc UCM* 23.2.1998 (1999) *JDI* 188.

[84] They unsuccessfully attempted to persuade the ECJ that the place where damage occurred was the place of discovery of the damage to the cargo, [1998] ECR I-6511, at p.6547, at para. 37.

[85] Now *Drouot Assurances S.A. v Consoldidated Metallurgical, Protea Assurance and GIE Réunion Européenne* (C-351/96) [1998] ECR I-3075.

[86] Cf. *Cheshire and North*, 13th edn., 1999, at p.202.

that bill of lading discloses no contractual relationship freely entered into between Brambi . . . and . . . Spliethoff's . . . who . . . were the actual maritime carriers of the goods.[87]

This case demonstrates that knowledge must be a mutual condition. Both parties must know of each other's existence—that one may know does not now seem to suffice for Article 5(1).[88]

These cases, some have argued,[89] will have a dramatic effect on assignees and those subrogated to others' rights. The European Court has already, in *Drouot Assurances S.A. v Consoldidated Metallurgical*,[90] had to rule on whether a subrogated insurer is the 'same party' as its assured for the purposes of Article 21 of the Convention. What effect will this decision have on a subrogated insurer's right of recourse against the alleged contract-breaker in contract under Article 5(1)? Should the alleged defendant know of the assured/indemnified party, he will not, of course, know whether, nor with whom, this party is insured. Following logically from *Drouot Assurances S.A.*, if the interests of insurer and assured in suing in contract 'are identical to and indissociable from'[91] each other, then the defendant will have to treat them as the same party (and possibly therefore as having the same (known) identity) for Article 5(1) purposes.

Conversely, if, for the application of Article 5(1), the defendant must be able to foresee the identity of his prospective[92] opponent and where he may be sued, this severely limits[93] the scope of Article 5(1) for plaintiff/claimant parties' succeeding,[94] without the original defendant's knowledge, to the rights of others.[95]

---

[87] *Réunion Européenne SA* (C-51/97) [1998] ECR I –6511, at p.6542, para. 19; for the effect of this ruling on an 'agreement' for purposes of Article 17, see below at p.250 following.

[88] Note the post-reference case, *Cassation* 16.3.1999, [1999] I.L.Pr. 613.

[89] Hartley, T. (1993) *ELR* 506 at p.516; and Briggs, 1997, at p.94, para. 2.128.

[90] (C-351/96) [1998] ECR I-3075.

[91] (C-351/96) [1998] ECR I-3075, at p.3098, at para. 23.

[92] It is more evident than ever that '[Article 5(1)] seems to have been drafted only so as to deal with the paradigmatic claim that the defendant is in breach of a single obligation contained in a contract whose validity and enforceability is not in doubt', Peel, E. 'Jurisdiction over restitutionary claims' [1998] *LMCLQ* 22, at p.27.

[93] *Quaere*, whether the defendant has freely to assume obligations to *someone* (presumably the other contracting party) not, necessarily however, the claimant third party himself.

[94] Also now the Contracts (Rights of Third Parties) Act 1999; s 1(3), identifying the third party 'expressly . . . by name, as a member of a class . . . but need not be in existence when the contract is entered into'; *Atlas Shipping Agency (UK) Ltd v Suisse Atlantique Société d'Armement Maritime S.A* [1995] 2 Lloyd's Rep. 188, QBD (Rix J); also *Coreck Maritime GmbH* (C387–98) [2000] ECR I-9337, reviewed below, at p.213, and the statements, at paras. 24–25, regarding third parties in bills of lading cases; even if, which is a moot point, the judgment extends beyond transmission in bills of lading cases, if a third party wishes to take advantage of a contractual term (for his benefit) in the 1999 Act, s 1(4) ensures that he may not do so 'otherwise than subject to and in accordance with *any other relevant terms* of the contract'; Andrews, N. (2001) *CLJ* 353, at pp.374–75; and *Bundesgericht 25.7.2000 Gerhard Pabst GmbH gegen Ivana Gillar-Kokrda*, unreported.

[95] Yet this would seem to be a very simplistic reading of *Jakob Handte & Co. GmbH*: that a claim ceases to be contractual simply because the party the defendant thought he had contracted with (and from whom he would normally expect any litigation to come from), drops from the picture on assignment, or on an exercise of subrogation rights—and an unforeseeable assignee/insurer succeeds to that

Yet reading *Jakob Handte & Co. GmbH* does seem to suggest that a defendant's prospective ability to trace the identity of his other contracting partner is a prerequisite for the application of Article 5(1). If this is so, there is an inconsistency between the Court's judgment in this case, and that in other cases, concerning other Convention articles.[96]

In *Partenreederei ms Tilly Russ and Ernest Russ v NV Haven- & Vervoerbedrijf Nova and NV Goeminne Hout*[97] the question before the European Court was whether a third party holder of a bill of lading could be bound by a jurisdiction clause under Article 17, contained in the contract between the carrier and the shipper. The answer given in no way suggests that a (statutory) assignee's rights and obligations under the bill of lading were no longer seen as being outside the sphere of contract. It was conceded that the obligation on the assignee/holder to respect, and become bound by, the jurisdiction clause was contractual[98] in origin:

> [t]he third party holder of the bill of lading . . . becomes subject to all the obligations, mentioned in the bill of lading.[99]

Yet the carrier may not be aware, in advance, who an ultimate consignee, or assignee, of the bill of lading may be. It is entirely inconsistent that a consignee may sue and be sued under Article 17,[100] but not under Article 5(1),[101] when the dispute will be under the (contractual) bill of lading:

> [t]he proposition that a claim ceases to be contractual when assigned to an assignee seems simply wrong . . .[102]

The 'foreseeable identity' or 'actual identity' reasoning of *Jakob Handte & Co. GmbH* and *Réunion Européenne SA* seem to crumble in the face of such cases as *Partenreederei ms Tilly Russ, Gerling Konzern Speziale Kreditversicheruns- AG & Others v Amministrazione del Tesoro dello Stato*,[103] and *Sherson Lehman Hutton Inc. v TVB Treuhandgesellschaft für Vermögensverwaltung und Beteiligungen mbH*.[104]

The other basis for the decisions in *Jakob Handte & Co. GmbH* and *Réunion Européenne SA* was that there was no 'obligation freely assumed'[105] between the

---

party's rights; this aspect of Article 5(1) shows the uneasy and ill-liaised relationship between 'matters relating to a contract' and Article 17 'agreements', under which, according to the *Tilly Russ*, there is no problem in the transmission or rights and obligations to (unforeseen) third parties.

[96] Article 21, 'the same parties' and *Drouot Assurances S.A. v Consoldidated Metallurgical, Protea Assurance and GIE Réunion Européenne* (C-351/96) [1998] ECR I-3075.

[97] (C-71/83) [1984] 2417.

[98] As it was contained in the bill of lading.

[99] At p.2435, para. 25.

[100] Although the Article 17 'agreement' only tested as against the original, presumably, 'contracting' parties.

[101] *Jakob Handte & Co. GmbH* interpreted literally may point to this anomaly; Hartley, (1993) *ELR* 506, at p.513.

[102] Briggs, 1997, at p.94, para. 2.128.

[103] (C-201/82) [1983] ECR 2503.

[104] (C-89/91) [1993] ECR I-139.

[105] *Jakob Handte* [1992] ECR I-3697, at p.3994, para. 15.

parties. Whether this means in some objective way that manufacturer and sub-purchaser, or carrier and consignee, did not freely contract with each other, or something more specific, is unclear. Certain contractual obligations *inter se* are not 'freely assumed', but imposed, *aliunde*, by the general law (of contract).[106] It is submitted that it is not at these that *Jakob Handte* and *Réunion Européenne SA* are aimed. What the cases must mean in this context is that the parties themselves must come together 'freely', not by operation of law.[107] What happens thereafter,[108] and whatever the law imposes on their consensual union,[109] in terms of obligations within this 'free' agreement, is irrelevant for the scope of Article 5(1) *ratione materiae*.

1.1.1   The different language versions of Article 5(1) and 'matters relating to a contract'[110]

The opening words of Article 5(1), 'in matters relating to a contract' are rendered in the equally authentic German version as the longer phrase 'wenn ein Vertrag[111] *oder* Ansprüche[112] aus einem Vertrag . . ?.[113]:

---

[106] By the *lex causae* or *fori*.

[107] Excluded therefore is a sub-purchaser's action in a chain of contracts in French law of contract; also see the German cases *LG Göttingen* 9.11.1976 IPRspr. 1976 Nr. 145; *LG Bayreuth* 29.6.1988 IPRspr. 1988 Nr. 159; *LG Frankfurt/Main* 5.10.1995 IPRspr. 1995 Nr. 155; *quaere* s 2(1) Carriage of Goods by Sea Act 1992.

[108] The distinction may not be so easily drawn as this phrase suggests, as regards the scope of Article 5(1) and restitutionary claims, Peel, E., in F.D. Rose (ed) *Restitution and the Conflict of Laws*, 1995, p.1, at p.8; note questions 1 and 2 in the reference *Rudolf Gabriel v Schlank & Schick GmbH* (C-96/00) [2000] OJ C149/25, reference reported [2000] I.L.Pr. 677: it is unclear, re Article 5(1) and Article 13 ('proceedings concerning a contract concluded by . . . [a] consumer'), whether the referring court is asking if the particular claim (under Austrian consumer protection law) is within these Articles' scope *ratione materiae* generally, or whether the claim itself must *thereafter also* be 'contractual'; AG Jacobs in his opinion of 13.12.2001 in *Rudolf Gabriel v Schlank & Schick GmbH* (C-96/00) did not draw this distinction, but found Gabriel's action within the scope *ratione materiae* of Article 13; the *Cour d'appel de Nancy* 2.10.2000 *SA Maison française de distribution c/ Claude* (2001) *JCP*, IV, 1956 has classified a similar claim, at French autonomous law, as a 'faute délictuelle'.

[109] For example, implied conditions as to fitness for purpose—*Viskase Ltd and another v Paul Kiefel GmbH* [1999] 1 WLR 1305, CA; *Rye Valley Foods Ltd v Fisher Frozen Foods Ltd*, 10.5.2000, Irish HC (O'Sullivan J); or implied terms of business efficacy *Raiffeisen Zentralbank Österreich Aktiengesellschaft v National Bank of Greece S.A.* [1999] 1 Lloyd's Rep. 408; *Agnew and others v Lansförsäkringsbolagens AB* [2001] 1 AC 223, at p.244 (Lord Woolf, MR), at p.264 (Lord Millett, of the minority).

[110] Note the differing English translations of the various language versions of Article 5(1) presented in Verheul, J. (1976) *NILR* 347, at p.348.

[111] Dealt with in this section.

[112] 'claims' dealt with in section 1.2 'obligations'.

[113] Verheul, J. (1976) *NILR* 347, at p.348; it will be immediately noticeable that the 'oder' gives two alternatives to the article's scope *ratione materiae*, and thereby alters slightly the (German) classification process; also it will be noticeable that the German phrase 'den Gegenstand des Verfahrens bilden' ('in question'), attaches itself to these two alternatives and not to the word obligation.

wenn ein Vertrag oder Ansprüche aus einem Vertrag den Gegenstand des Verfahrens bilden, vor dem Gericht des Ortes, an dem die Verpflichtung erfüllt worden ist oder zu erfüllen wäre;. . .[114]

The words 'wenn ein Vertrag' corresponds more closely with the English and French versions, in matters relating to a contract. The alternative '. . . oder Ansprüche aus einem Vertrag' has no such direct equivalent. A workable translation of this latter phrase would be 'or claims out of/arising out of a contract.'

As a second alternative, at least in comparison to the English version, it could thus be seen to have a dramatic impact on such claims as pre-contractual duties, or claims *culpa in contrahendo*. Whether this second alternative qualifies, or limits, the opening phrase[115] 'a contract' in any way, has not been explored in commentaries. Yet, it does strongly suggest to German interpreters of the phrase that claims under Article 5(1) must be 'contractual'[116] claims out of/arising out of a contract.

These alternative opening words of the German version also present a problem for this treatment. As part of the defining opening words of Article 5(1)'s scope *ratione materiae*, they naturally belong in this first section as 'matters relating to a contract'. But as they also refer to 'Ansprüche' ('claims'), they belong in the next section of the treatment, below 1.2, reviewing the meaning of the word 'obligation in question'.

In the English version of Article 5(1), the 'obligation' in question is left to the end of its section in Article 5(1):

> in matters relating to a contract, in the courts for the place of performance of the *obligation* in question.

The corresponding German version of the highlighted word obligation is 'die Verpflichtung': it can be seen that no 'in question' adjunct is appended to it.

The upshot of this mis-matched solecism in the different language versions of Article 5(1) is that the enquiry in this section, to a German view, straddles both[117] 'in matters relating to a contract' and 'the obligation in question'.[118]

---

[114] A free translation of which is '*when a contract or claims arising out of a contract* form the basis of the proceedings, before the court in which the obligation was, or was to be, fulfilled'.

[115] Lord Goff in *Kleinwort Benson Ltd v Glasgow City Council* [1999] 1 AC 153, whose view that the 'obligation in question' had to be contractual no doubt coloured his interpretation of 'matters relating to a contract'.

[116] I.e. not only post-formation, but *Handte v TMCS* [1992] ECR I-3967 obligations, freely-entered into. This would, of course, tilt the interpretative balance towards excluding unjust enrichment claims and possibly claims *culpa in contrahendo*, below, and *BGH* 28.2.1996 132 BGHZ 105; *contra LG Dortmund* 19.2.1998 1998 IPRspr. Nr.139; AG Geelhoed, in his opinion of 31.1.2002 in *Fonderie Officine Meccaniche Tacconi Spa v HWS Heinrich Wagner Sinto Maschinenfabrik GmbH* (C-334/00), pending, categorised pre-contractual actions into 3 stages, esp. at paras. 80–83: for claims strictly *culpa in contrahendo*—raising an expectation in one party that a contract will be concluded—he preferred to denominate as Art.5(3) tort actions, at para. 82.

[117] A more thorough and detailed (alternative) characterisation process is thus demanded in the German version of Article 5(1).

[118] And tends to suggest strongly that the Article 5(1) obligation must in addition be contractual.

That the German version is dissimilar to the others has been recognised in *Effer SpA v Hans-Joachim Kantner*.[119] What effect this different wording may have is examined below.[120] It also means that the German introductory words, unlike in the English and French versions, do not sit easily into the first two[121] of the three 'normal' sections traditionally associated with Article 5(1).

The confusion, for English eyes, that the German version causes—straddling as it does two stages of enquiry under Article 5(1)—is amply demonstrated by the decision of the *LG Frankfurt/Main*.[122] In this case a German holder of a bill of exchange attempted to sue the foreign issuer of the bill, a bank located in another Contracting State, under Article 5(1), and under the right of recourse action given under German law.[123] As perhaps one might have expected, after *Jakob Handte & Co. GmbH v Société Traitements Mecano-Chimiques des Surfaces (TMCS)*,[124] the LG found that the claim was not a 'matter relating to a contract', but a liability imposed as a matter of law. There is nothing exceptional in this, yet the way the opening qualifying words are used by the court and the commentator[125] is revealing, and somewhat confusing. According to the court, Article 5(1) could not apply because:

> es sich dabei nicht um eine vertragliche, sondern um eine gesetzliche Verpflichtung[126] handele.[127]

The commentator runs through the normal *De Bloos* and *Peters v ZNAV*[128] autonomous definition of 'matters relating to a contract'.[129] She then makes this revealing and ambiguous statement about the Article 5(1) qualification process:

> Es ist Sache der *lex causae*, die entsprechende Qualifikation vorzunehmen und zu entscheiden, ob es sich um einem *vertraglichen Anspruch*[130] . . . handelt . . . Zu klären ist

---

[119] (C-38/81) [1982] 825, at p.834, para. 5: 'the lack of uniformity between the different language versions'.
[120] Below, pp.57–58 and notes.
[121] 'Matters relating to a contract', and 'the obligation in question'.
[122] 5.10.1995 IPRspr. 1995 Nr. 155.
[123] Similar to that under English law ss 54–55 Bills of Exchange Act 1882.
[124] (C-26/91) [1992] ECR I-3697.
[125] Bachmann, (1997) *IPRax* 153, at p.154.
[126] This word 'Verplichtung' ('obligation') would logically presuppose that the first classification stage has been passed, (or would to English views).
[127] ('because what is concerned is a legal, not a contractual obligation'); IPRspr. 1995 Nr. 155, at p.314; cf. *obiter* observations in *Alfred Dunhill Ltd v Diffusion Internationale de Maroquinerie de Prestige SARL and others* [2001] CLC 949, at pp.960–61.
[128] (C-34/82) [1983] ECR 987.
[129] 'Anspruch[ ] aus einem Vertrag unterliegt nach der Rechtsprechung des EGH einer autonomen Auslegung' at p.154 ('According to ECJ jurisprudence, claims arising out of a contract are subject to an autonomous interpretation')
[130] The same word as used in the opening of Article 5(1), not 'Verpflichtung'.

daher nach der ... *lex causae*, ob die verschiedenen *wechselrechtlichen Ansprüche*[131] Gegenstand von Article 5 Nr.1 EuGVÜ sind.[132]

The quoted comment suggests that the 'Anspruch' (claim) must be considered as contractual by the *lex causae*. It should not. *Peters v ZNAV* has shown us that the phrase 'Ansprüche aus einem Vertrag' is to be interpreted autonomously.

As if to confirm this, the *LG Bayreuth*,[133] in an earlier case opposing the issuer of a bill of exchange and its holder, affirmed that the claim ('Anspruch') of the holder—the right of recourse action—was not contractual; although the reviewer, relying on *Peters v ZNAV*, thinks[134] that the case was far more akin to a contractual relationship than the *LG Bayreuth* made out.

A further German case grappling with the different[135] classification process, necessitated, it seems by the German version of Article 5(1), is *OLG Düsseldorf*.[136] A German plaintiff sought severance pay from his German employer, which was insolvent. He then attempted to sue its French parent company, under a liability imposed by German law, of the direct responsibility that a controlling shareholder[137] takes towards its company, if (*quaere* negligently) involved in its day-to-day management and control. Again, quite predictably, the appeal court held Article 5(1) to be inapplicable *ratione materiae*:

Zwar habe zwischen den Parteien kein Vertragsverhältnis bestanden, so daß sich ein *direkter vertraglicher Anspruch*[138] nicht ergebe. Der Kl. mache jedoch einen Anspruch[139] aus Durchgriffshaftung geltend ...[140]

The claim in this case simply did not satisfy the initial hurdle of 'a matter relating to a contract'. There was no question therefore in this case that the court

---

[131] Note, it is an autonomous qualification of the word 'Anspruch' that the German version requires, not *lege causae*, since the word 'Anspruch' forms part of the phrase 'in matters relating to a contract'.

[132] ('It is a matter for the *lex causae* to carry out the corresponding classification and to decide whether what is concerned is a *contractual claim*. The *lex causae* has to clarify whether the different *bill of exchange claims* are a matter for Article 5(1) Brussels Convention') (1997) *IPRax* 153, at p.154.

[133] 29.6.1988, (1989) *IPRax* 230.

[134] Furtak, (1989) *IPRax* 212, at p.212.

[135] At least to English expectations.

[136] (1998) *IPRax* 210.

[137] I.e. piercing the corporate veil, imposing liabilities on shadow directors.

[138] *Quaere*, an initial—autonomous—qualification of 'Anspruch', or subsequent *lex causae* qualification, as suggested by Bachmann, (1997) *IPRax* 153, at p.154. Zimmer suggests that the claim was not considered to be an 'Anspruch aus einem Vertrag'—'nicht vertagsrechtlich', at (1998) *IPRax* 187, at p.189.

[139] It seems as if the claim is first classified, by German law—as direct shareholder liability action—and *then* tested to see whether if fits into Article 5(1); also this methodology in *Kleinwort Benson Ltd v Glasgow City Council* [1999] 1 AC 153, HL.

[140] ('In fact, no contractual relationship was in existence between the parties, so that there was no *direct contractual claim* ... The plaintiff is however suing for a claim in shareholder liability ...'), (1998) *IPRax* 210, at p.210; concurring Kropholler, 2002, at p. 129, para. 11.

would or could have considered any further whether a (contractual) 'Verpflichtung' was involved.[141]

The German version of Article 5(1), it is submitted, forces a slightly different approach to the classification of claims, and a different emphasis regarding those claims than that which is evident[142] in England. The German version, unlike the English wording 'in matters relating to a contract' alternatively forces the German courts to characterise the actual claim (Anspruch) as pleaded as contractual or not. The wider, more nebulous English wording 'matters relating' to a contract allows the English court to look to the (objective)[143] surrounding, background circumstances of any 'contract' globally.[144] This in turn leads to a debate, and authorities, in England[145] discussing whether the 'obligation' must, in addition, be contractual.

1.1.2   'Matters relating to'[146] a contract

Although these three words are intimately bound up with the word 'contract', it is evident from the cases[147] that the dispute must in some way, however loosely, be connected with 'a contract'.[148] The division is not strictly made in some cases, because it is unnecessary, or classification is obvious; in others, concerned with

---

[141] Most recently *OLG Jena* 5.8.1998 (1999) *RIW* 703 and *OLG München* 25.6.1999 (1999) *RIW* 871—claims by liquidators against, respectively, sole corporate shareholders of insolvent German companies and the insolvent company's managing director—both held to be 'matters relating to a contract'.

[142] But Lord Goff in *Kleinwort Benson Ltd v Glasgow City Council* [1999] 1 AC 153, at p.167d: 'the claim . . . is simply a claim to restitution'.

[143] The German version appears to limit the qualification process to the actual claims as presented.

[144] Cf recently in Lord Woolf's speech in *Agnew and others v Lansförsäkringsbolagens AB* [2001] 1 AC 223, at pp.240–41

[145] There are, to the writer's knowledge, no authorities in Germany dealing with pre-contractual 'obligations' under the Brussels or Lugano Conventions; there has recently been reported a French case *Société Péchiney Electrométallurgie (PEM) c/ Société Universal Ceramic Materials Plc (UCM)* 23.2.1998 (1999) *JDI* 188, and *Bundesgericht* 11.7.2000 *Dörken-Gutta Pol gegen Gutta-Werke AG*, unreported, discussed below.

[146] This division is made despite Evans LJ' s preference not to separate the phrase up into 'two separate sub-issues' in *Agnew and others v Lansförsäkringsbolagens AB* [1997] 4 All ER 937, at p.941; Lord Clyde considered the phrase in *Kleinwort Benson Ltd v Glasgow City Council* [1999] 1 AC 153, at p.180; the HL has recently confirmed in the appeal in *Agnew* that the non-disclosure re-insurance dispute was clearly within the scope *ratione materiae* of Article 5(1), [2001] 1 AC 223.

[147] *Boss Group Ltd v Boss France SA* [1996] 4 All ER 970, CA; *USF Ltd (t/a USF Memcor) v Aqua Technology Hanson NV/SA* [2001] 1 All ER (Comm) 856; *Soc I.S.I. c/ Soc. De promotion des Centres privés audiovisuels* 25.1.1983 (1983) *Rev crit* 516; *Kleinwort Benson Ltd v Glasgow City Council* [1999] 1 AC 153, HL; *Trade Indemnity plc and others v Försäkringsaktiebolaget Njord (in liq)* [1995] 1 All ER 796, QBD (Rix J); *Agnew and others v Lansförsäkringsbolagens AB* [1996] 4 All ER 978, QBD (Mance J) *affm'd* [1997] 4 All ER 937, CA, [2001] 1 AC 223, HL.

[148] This individual word became important in *Kleinwort Benson Ltd v Glasgow City Council* where it was separated from the other words by Roch LJ [1996] 2 All ER 257, CA, at p.268.

pre-contractual liabilities,[149] and claims *culpa in contrahendo*,[150] the meaning and ambit of 'matters relating to' becomes crucial.

The scope of this phrase has been considered in relation to actions for declarations of non-liability. It received a wide interpretation in *Boss Group Ltd v Boss France SA*,[151] a case where the plaintiff manufacturer was seeking a (negative) declaration that no contract existed between it and its French distributor.[152] The words 'matters relating to' a contract, it seems, were fulfilled in that case due to the 'lively dispute between the parties as to whether there was a contract'[153] and the fact that Article 5(1) was not confined 'to actions to enforce a contract or to obtain recompense for its breach, but [referred] generally to "matters relating to a contract"'.[154]

Whether it is correct to say that any connection, however tenuous to a contractual[155] relationship will open out Article 5(1) *in limine* remains to be seen. The *Cour de Cassation* in *Soc I.S.I. c/ Soc. De promotion des Centres privés audiovisuels*[156] and *Société anversoise de dépôts et hypothèques c/ Richard*[157] has had to rule on an 'action en nullité d'un contrat' and a simultaneous action in damages under Article 5(1). The actions seemed to be to have a once valid contract annulled, rather than ruling (at the same time, or at all) on the financial and restitutionary consequences of such nullity.[158]

In *Soc I.S.I.*, a French company commenced an action to nullify a contract between it and its German company, having acquired from the latter the rights to use the latter's audio training system. This system was found to be a copy of another teaching method, and the French company asserted the contract's nullity on the ground of its illicit object. The court held that the lower courts were correct to have retained jurisdiction under Article 5(1). Gaudement-Tallon, the reviewer, quotes Huet as saying: 'un litige sur la validité du contrat est toujours un litige en matière contractuelle'.[159] [160]

---

[149] Such as the (mutual) duty of utmost good faith when concluding English contracts of insurance—now *Agnew and others v Lansförsäkringsbolagens AB*, [2001] 1 AC 223, HL.

[150] Below at pp.62–64 and *Société Péchiney Electrométallurgie (PEM) c/ Société Universal Ceramic Materials Plc (UCM)* 23.2.1998 (1999) JDI 188; LG Dortmund 19.2.1998 1998 IPRspr. Nr.139.

[151] [1996] 4 All ER 970, although the word contract also featured largely in the discussions.

[152] *Bio-Medical Research Ltd. T/A Slendertone v Delatex S.A.* [2000] 4 IR 307, SC, at p.314; no argument specifically addressed the point that dispute did not involve 'matters relating to a contract'.

[153] [1996] 4 All ER 970, at p.975 (Saville LJ).

[154] *Bio-Medical Research Ltd. T/A Slendertone v Delatex S.A.* [2000] 4 IR 307, SC, at p.314.

[155] In *Boss Group Ltd v Boss France SA* one party at least was able to assert the existence of the contract; in *Kleinwort Benson Ltd v Glasgow City Council* neither party could—the House of Lords, in a previous case, having declared the contract to have been void.

[156] 25.1.1983 (1983) *Rev crit* 516.

[157] *Cour de Cassation* 27.6.2000 *Société anversoise de dépôts et hypothèques c/ Richard* (2001) JDI 137, (2001) *Rev crit* 152.

[158] *Kleinwort Benson Ltd* would force an unjustified scission in these issues.

[159] ('an action on the validity of a contract is always an action in matters relating to a contract').

[160] (1983) *Rev crit* 516, at p.519; also Gothot, P. et Holleaux, D., 1985, at p.31, para. 63, who agree that a negative declaration reveals a 'matter relating to' a contract; Huet in *Civil Jurisdiction and Judgments in Europe—Proceedings of the Colloquium on the Interpretation of the Brussels Convention by the Court*

In *Société anversoise de dépôts et hypothèques c/ Richard*,[161] the French domiciliary Richard obtained a loan from a Belgian mortgage company; after default, the company took measures to take possession of the mortgaged property. Richard responded by seeking to annul the loan contract and claim damages as a result of its nullity. There was *not* a cassation in the case due to the lower court's application of Article 5(1) *ratione materiae* to an action 'en nullité d'un contrat', but for another reason. The comment[162] on the case notes the division in French academic circles as to whether an action to annul does fall within Article 5(1); and observes the following artificial situation—that an 'action en nullité' puts in question in the litigation *each and every obligation* of the contracting parties *inter se*, with jurisdiction therefore possible at the place of performance of any of them, even if[163] the basis for the action is either lack of consensus *ad idem*, a writing, illegality of object, or presumably therefore a failure to observe the dictates of utmost good faith.

1.1.3   Pre-contractual duties

It is with actions that relate to liability for pre-contractual duties[164] that the opening three words of Article 5(1)—'in matters relating'—come into their own.[165] In

---

of Justice considered in the context of the European Judicial Area, Luxembourg, 11 and 12 March 1991, Butterworths, 1992, at p.68 repeats his views on the 'action for the annulment of a contract' issue in the European Court of Justice's Colloquium discussions on the Brussels Convention. While mentioning both *SPRL Arcado v SA Haviland* (C-9/87) [1988] ECR 1539, at p.1555, para. 15 and Article 10 of the Rome Convention 1980, it is clear that he is only discussing the application for the annulment of the contract *simpliciter*, not of the consequences of an annulled/void contract. No support can be found in the passages in the discussion as to whether a *Kleinwort Benson* restitution-type action would or would not be included in Article 5(1).

[161]   27.6.2000 (2001) *JDI* 137, (2001) *Rev crit* 152.
[162]   (2001) *JDI* 137, at p.139.
[163]   At p.140—a lack of an 'obligation in question' in this situation is, according to some commentators, to be supplied by the place of performance of the *characteristic obligation*, presumably by analogy with Article 10 Rome Convention.
[164]   The exact legal nature of duty of utmost good faith uncertain in English law: (*The 'Sea Star'* [2001] 2 WLR 170, HL); and *K/S Merc-Scandia XXXII v Certain Lloyd's Underwriters* [2001] Lloyd's Rep IR 802, CA, at pp.813–15.
[165]   The problem in this area appears to stem from the concept of 'obligation': must it be, in addition, a 'contractual' obligation—i.e. post-formation (Lord Hope's view of the minority in *Agnew and others v Lansförsäkringsbolagens AB* [2001] 1 AC 223, at p.254, below), whether as a result of express and/or implied agreement, or imposed (as a matter of the *lex causae*)? Or something much wider—such as *any obligation*, including pre-formation 'duties' that are somehow present in the negotiation and/or conclusion of the contract. Viewed in this way, there is something to be said in support of the view of Lord Millett, of the minority, in *Agnew*, [2001] 1 AC 223, at p.265, that 'there is no contractual obligation not innocently to misrepresent the facts during contractual negotiations ... [nor is there an] 'obligation not to exercise undue influence [or duress or mistake] in order to persuade a party to enter into a contract'; and *obiter* support for this view in *Alfred Dunhill Ltd v Diffusion Internationale de Maroquinerie de Prestige SARL and others* [2001] CLC 949; an answer to this dilemma may come in *Fonderie Officine Meccaniche Tacconi Spa v HWS Heinrich Wagner Sinto Maschinenfabrik GmbH* (C-334/00) [2000] OJ C302/21, pending,—although it is submitted that nothing in AG Geelhoed's

Trade Indemnity plc and others v Försäkringsaktiebolaget Njord (in liq),[166] Rix J held that a re-insurer's action to avoid the re-insurance treaty for material misrepresentation and non-disclosure was a 'matter relating to' a contract within Article 5(1) Lugano Convention. Conversely, in *Agnew and others v Lansförsäkringsbolagens AB*,[167] Mance J was more forthright in accepting[168] the defendant's well-founded concession[169] that the dispute involved a 'matter relating to' a contract: 'The matter is on any objective appreciation intimately concerned with and closely related to the contracts . . .'.[170]

Evans LJ[171] in the Court of Appeal[172] introduced an interesting interpretation of our phrase, extending its ambit into the widest possible area—a link between the *raison d'être* of the pre-contractual obligation and the contract itself: 'it is meaningless to talk of the duty[173] *except by reference* to a particular contract.'[174]

These pre-contractual obligations, *ex hypothesi*, only arise because of the present intention[175] to conclude[176] a contract, and do not have any independent *raison d'être*, but are parasitic on a prospective contract. A matter will relate to a contract if it has existence by reference to a real contract, concluded in law.

---

opinion of 31.1.2002 reveals categorically one way or the other whether pre-contractual 'utmost good faith' actions are excluded from Art.5(1).

[166] [1995] 1 All ER 796, QBD (Rix J) under Article 5(1) of Lugano Convention. Nothing turns on this.

[167] [1996] 4 All ER 978, QBD (Mance J); affm'd [1997] 4 All ER 937, CA, affm'd (by a majority) [2001] 1 AC 223, HL.

[168] Again, the action concerned a re-insurer's declaration of non-liability—confirmed by unanimous decision of HL in *Agnew*, but divided as to whether the obligation had to arise 'under' a contract, below.

[169] [1996] 4 All ER 978, at p.985.

[170] *Ibid*; this despite the pre-contractual duties under the Marine Insurance Act 1906 arising, as a matter of English law (*Banque Financière de la Cité SA v Westgate Insurance Co. Ltd* [1990] 1 QB 665) outside the law of contract, at p.968e.

[171] [1997] 4 All ER 937, CA; Briggs, 1997 Brit Yrbk Int'l L 331, at p.336, and p.337; this decision may 'stand[] in need of reconsideration'.

[172] This aspect of the case was uncontroversial in the appeal in *Agnew and others v Lansförsäkringsbolagens AB* [2001] 1 AC 223, HL.

[173] Mutual 'duties' of utmost good faith owed by the contracting parties to each other, to avoid material mis-representations and non-disclosures under the Marine Insurance Act 1906.

[174] At p.941; also on this point Hill, 2nd edn., 1998, at p.131, para. 5.6.19; support now for the present position regarding pre-contractual duties can be found by (close) analogy with a statement by AG Jacobs in *Rudolf Gabriel v Schlank & Schick GmbH* (C-96/00), 13.12.2001, at para.35: an action under Austrian consumer protection legislation found to involve 'proceedings concerning a contract [in Article 13] . . . for the simple reason that the right of action is *closely connected with the underlying contract*'; and his rejection, at para. 58, of the view that this right of action had to be 'based on the conclusion of a contract'.

[175] In this case, both parties had the intention; part of the German law of *culpa in contrahendo* covers the case where only one party intends to contract, Markesinis, B.S., Lorenz, W., Dannemann, G. *The German Law of Obligations*, Volume 1, *The Law of Contracts and Restitution: A Comparative Introduction*, 1997, at p.69: 'reliance damages must be paid by a party who in the course of negotiations has made the other party believe that a contract will certainly be concluded . . .'; Geimer and Schütze, 1997, at p.127, para. 18; *Veco v Muenzing Chemie D Series* I-5.1.2.–B42; *Péchiney Electrométallurgie c/ UCM* (1999) JDI 188; LG Dortmund 19.2.1998 1998 IPRspr. Nr.139.

[176] Hill, 2nd edn., 1998, at para. 5.6.21 thinks that Article 5(1) probably depends on the conclusion of a valid contract.

1.1.4 'In matters relating to' and *culpa in contrahendo* claims

Geimer and Schütze agree[177] that *culpa in contrahendo* actions fall under Article 5(1) but without saying why.[178] Such actions in German law[179] represent a category of liability *sui generis*, and seem to inhabit a nebulous area between the law of contract and delict. One of the functions of such liability is to allow a plaintiff/claimant to recover for pre-contractual reliance loss when a contract is not eventually concluded, but in the conviction of one of the parties a valid contract has come about;[180] or when, in such circumstances, the defendant breaks off negotiations[181] arbitrarily, and without good reason. If, as Geimer and Schütze suggest, this action is caught by Article 5(1), the words 'matters relating to'[182] a contract have received a very wide[183] interpretation indeed.

Recent cases—*Cour d'appel de Chambéry, Société Péchiney Electrométallurgie (PEM) c/ Société Universal Ceramic Materials Plc (UCM)*[184] and *Dörken-Gutta Pol gegen Gutta-Werke AG*[185]—have had to come to terms with an action based on one company's alleged bad faith in pre-contractual negotiations, and breaking-off conclusion of an intended contract.

In *Société Péchiney Electrométallurgie (PEM)*, the French claimant company, Péchiney, had decided to transfer its business activities to some of its competitors, one of whom was the English defendant company, UCM. Discussions for the transfer took place, and a document in English entitled 'Heads of Agreement, subject to contract'[186] was signed. The board of UCM refused to accept the conditions in the Heads of Agreement, and no concluded business transfer was ever reached.

---

[177] Geimer and Schütze, 1997, at p.127, para. 18.

[178] Also Donzallaz, Y. *La Convention de Lugano*, Vol III, 1998 paras. 4239–7164, at p.158, para. 4534.

[179] Especially Markesinis, Lorenz and Dannemann above n 175, Volume 1, p.64 onwards.

[180] *Ibid*, at p.66.

[181] *Ibid*, at p.69; the 'second' phase identified by AG Geelhoed in his opinion of 31.1.2002 in *Fonderie Officine Meccaniche Tacconi Spa v HWS Heinrich Wagner Sinto Maschinenfabrik GmbH* (C-334/00), pending, in a brief comparative overview of Continental jurisprudence on *culpa in contrahendo* claims; in this 'second' phase the AG would place such claims under Art.5(3), at para. 82; only when the proto-contracting parties are already agreed on the essentials of the contract, or one party has embarked on part-performance can Art.5(1) become implicated, at para. 83; also an example in Zimmermann, R. and Whittaker, S. (eds) *Good Faith in European Contract Law*, 2000, at pp.236–57.

[182] But note, the German wording of Article 5(1) is different to the English and French versions.

[183] Consonant with Evans LJ in *Agnew and others v Lansförsäkringsbolagens AB* [1997] 4 All ER 937.

[184] 23.2.1998 (1999) *JDI* 188; similar conclusion reached by *Cour de Cassation* 5.10.1999 *Matussière et autres c/ Société Werk Waldhof Aschaffenburg Graphische Papiere (PWA) GmbH* (2001) *JDI* 133.

[185] *Bundesgericht* 11.7.2000, unreported; a first instance German decision, *LG Dortmund* 19.2.1998 1998 IPRspr. Nr.139 has recognised the (academic) controversy of whether claims *culpa in contrahendo* fall within Article 5(1), and has stated, at least in its non delictual aspects, that such claims *do* qualify *ratione materiae* in Article 5(1): 'eine Verletzung von Aufklärungs- oder Beratungspflichten oder, wie im vorliegenden Fall, ein Vertrauensmißbrauch . . .' ('a breach of duties of disclosure or giving advice, or, as in this case, a misuse of confidence . . .'), at p.255.

[186] In this agreement, any eventual sale was subject to a number of conditions, among which was UCM's board approval. Although AG Geelhoed's specific 'phases' of contracting and *culpa in contrahendo* claims generally are unfamiliar to English lawyers, it is probably clear that the AG would agree that a stage three phase had been reached here, justifying the application of Art.5(1), at para. 83.

The French company sued in Bonneville for damages against UCM 'pour avoir agi avec mauvaise foi et déloyauté dans les pourparlers ou avoir rompu ceux-ci brutalement et sans motif'.[187] [188] Although, according to the commentator, *culpa in contrahendo* claims were classed as delictual in France and contractual in Germany, could it be said,[189] on a necessarily autonomous view that, in general,[190] or in this case, the parties had freely assumed (any) obligation(s) towards each other.[191]

The appeal court held, in the circumstances of the Heads of Agreement, that UCM had agreed to acquire the business in circumstances outside those expressly reserved in the Heads of Agreement, and had therefore freely undertaken an obligation to the French company. The matter was therefore one which related to a contract within Article 5(1). The case's reviewer[192] preferred to see, in general, an obligation in the Heads of Agreement not to break off negotiations as a matter relating to a contract.

The case strongly suggests that, absent such Heads of Agreement, the court would not have been able to find in the pre-contractual negotiations any 'obligation' freely assumed *inter partes*, and therefore Article 5(1) would not have been applicable.

In *Dörken-Gutta Pol gegen Gutta-Werke AG*[193] the Swiss claimant, Gutta, demanded payment from the first defendant, a Polish company, Dörken-Gutta, for building materials supplied and invoices outstanding; and from the second defendant, the German company Ewald Dörken AG, damages (presumably equivalent to the unpaid invoices) on the grounds of *culpa in contrahendo* and 'erwecktes Vertrauen in das Kozernverhalten der Muttergesellschaft'[194]: both these latter causes of action arising from an agreement between the second defendant and Elda Holding B.V.—the Dutch parent/holding company of the claimant—to the effect that the second defendant would refinance the first

---

[187] ('to have acted in bad faith and disloyally in the preliminary negotiations, or to have broken these off abruptly and without justification').

[188] (1999) *JDI* 188, at p.189.

[189] *Ibid*, at p.189, where this question is asked.

[190] Where there is no 'Heads of Agreement' document reached.

[191] In *Jakob Handte v TMCS* (C-26/91) [1992] ECR I-3967 and *Réunion Européenne SA v Spliethoff's Bevrachtingskantoor BV* (C-51/97) [1998] ECR I-6511.

[192] *Ibid*, at p.190. Although the refinements of *culpa in contrahendo* claims are probably not appreciated by English lawyers, if AG Geelhoed's sliding scale of mutual contractual engagements are adopted by the ECJ (at paras. 81–83, 31.1.2002, his phases one, two and three) in *Fonderie Officine Meccaniche Tacconi Spa v HWS Heinrich Wagner Sinto Maschinenfabrik GmbH* (C-334/00), pending, the application of either Art.5(3) or Art.5(1) will depend on the proximity to the point of contracting the parties have reached; as already stated, his opinion does not appear to have a bearing on insurance claims/utmost good faith, or would fall into his third phase in Art.5(1) in any event.

[193] (Swiss) *Bundesgericht* 11.7.2000, unreported.

[194] ('expectance reliance in the corporate conduct of the holding company'); a recently-introduced liability under Swiss law, as such a species of *culpa in contrahendo* which the *Bundesgericht* in an earlier decision had yet to classify, as a matter of Swiss law, as contractual or delictual; this should not matter for the application of Article 5(1) however—*Jakob Handte & Co. GmbH v Société Traitements Mecano-Chimiques des Surfaces (TMCS)* (C-26/91) [1992] ECR I-3967.

defendant. This did not take place, and the claimant argued that it would never have supplied materials, unsecured, to the first Polish defendant without this agreement. The *Bundesgericht* noted that the phrase 'matters relating to a contract' was to be interpreted broadly:

> und darunter Ansprüche zu verstehen sind, die *im Zusammenhang mit* einem Akt freiwilliger Selbstbingung von zwei oder mehr Rechtssubjekten stehen.[195]

The court accept the majority view of German-speaking commentators[196] that claims *culpa in contrahendo* could fall within Article 5(1); and that the obligation in question was stated to be the agreement to refinance, found to be performed within the jurisdiction of the Swiss courts.

Another case to have considered the issue of *culpa in contrahendo*, where a 'preliminary contract' had been concluded, is the *Corte di Cassazione* 21.11.1983 in *Veco Sas v Muenzing Chemie GmbH*.[197] The report states that the defendant allegedly broke off negotiations for an agency contract, to be concluded at some future date. The plaintiff's case, in the *causa petendi*, was that the German defendant' s obligations to conclude the future contract were referable to the concluded preliminary contract. The case therefore seems to be at the other end of the scale as regards *culpa in contrahendo* claims, distinguishable from those cases where there is no concluded/signed (preliminary) agreement of any kind.

1.1.5   The meaning of 'a contract'[198]

If there is a dispute as to the existence of the contract, one party denying,[199] the other asserting its validity,[200] Article 5(1) continues to apply:

---

[195] ('and such claims are to be understood as including those *in connection with* an act of becoming consensually bound between two or more legal personalities').

[196] Also *LG Dortmund* 19.2.1998 1998 IPRspr. Nr.139.

[197] *D Series* I-5.1.2.–B42; probably concurring AG Geelhoed, opinion of 31.1.2002 in *Fonderie Officine Meccaniche Tacconi Spa v HWS Heinrich Wagner Sinto Maschinenfabrik GmbH* (C-334/00), at para. 83.

[198] At English law at least, there must have been at one time a valid contract in existence for the application of the word 'contract' in Article 5(1); a valid contract, in the sense that it must have been legally possible to conclude it *ab initio*. If one party was acting *ultra vires* in contracting, a valid contract could never have come into existence, irrespective of other issues such as the need for writing, or other aspects of formation.

[199] For an example when the defendant denies the existence of the contract: *Effer SpA v Hans-Joachim Kantner* (C-38/81) [1982] 825; for the plaintiff denying *Boss Group Ltd v Boss France SA* [1996] 4 All ER 970, CA; *USF Ltd (t/a USF Memcor) v Aqua Technology Hanson NV/SA* [2001] 1 All ER (Comm) 856; *Bio-Medical Research Ltd. T/A Slendertone v Delatex S.A.* [2000] 4 IR 307, SC.

[200] If, as in *Kleinwort Benson Ltd v Glasgow City Council* neither party could assert or deny the existence of the contract, Article 5(1) could not apply.

the plaintiff establishes a good arguable case that there is a matter relating to a contract by relying on the fact that this is what the defendant is contending against it.[201]

Where such assertions by either side are not possible,[202] because the contract was void *ab initio*, it has now been settled[203] as a matter of English law,[204] that such a case does not involve a 'matter relating to a contract'. Instead, a second, non-contractual stage has been reached, which Gaudemet-Tallon correctly calls 'les conséquences de la nullité ou de l'inexistence du contrat[205] [206]:

lorsqu'il s'agit des conséquences de cette décision[207] on ne se trouve plus 'en matière contractuelle'[208] puisque le contrat a été déclaré nul ou inexistant.[209] [210]

This leads us into the next sub-section concerning actions based on the consequences[211] of a 'void' contract.

---

[201] According to Saville LJ in *Boss Group Ltd v Boss France SA* [1996] 4 All ER 970, CA, at p.975; applied in *USF Ltd (t/a USF Memcor) v Aqua Technology Hanson NV/SA* [2001] 1 All ER (Comm) 856, at pp.862–63 (Aikens J)'.

[202] The clear distinction between an assertion and inescapably settled fact was recognised by Lord Hutton in *Kleinwort Benson Ltd v Glasgow City Council* [1999] 1 AC 153, at p.195.

[203] This interpretation is a result of the House of Lords in *Kleinwort Benson Ltd v Glasgow City Council* [1999] 1 AC 153, [1997] 3 WLR 923, HL, by a bare majority, Lords Nicholls and Mustill dissenting; but *Cheshire and North*, 1999, for its 'worrying implications', at p.203.

[204] The *Kleinwort Benson Ltd v Glasgow City Council* saga involved Article 5(1) of Sch.4, in Title II of the CJJA 1982, governing intra-UK jurisdiction, which was in all material respects identical to Article 5(1) Brussels Convention. Section 16(3)(a)(b) CJJA 1982 ensures regard is had to the principles and decisions of the ECJ, and that 'appropriate weight' is given to the s 3(3) Reports in the interpretation of Sch.4; Lord Goff made full use of the former in *Kleinwort Benson Ltd v Glasgow City Council* [1999] 1 AC 153, although so close an affinity between the two regimes would mean the ECJ caselaw could potentially supersede the House of Lords' interpretation in this and any future cases: Briggs (1997) 68 *BYBIL* 331, at p.332.

[205] ('the consequence of the contract's nullity or the non-existence of the contract').

[206] Gaudemet-Tallon, 1996, at pp.112–13, para. 159.

[207] On the consequences of the contract's nullity.

[208] *Contra* Lord Nicholls in *Kleinwort Benson Ltd v Glasgow City Council* [1999] 1 AC 153, at p.176: to him this distinction was artificial, capricious and unthinkable, at p.175.

[209] ('when it is a question of the consequences of this decision, a matter relating to a contract is no longer involved since the contract has been declared void or non-existant').

[210] *Ibid*; also Gothot, P. et Holleaux, D., 1985, at p.31, para. 62; cf, *Cour de Cassation 27.6.2000 Société anversoise de dépôts et hypothèques c/ Richard* (2001) *JDI* 137, (2001) *Rev crit* 152, an *action en nullité* and for damages, but an otherwise legally valid contract *ab initio*, above.

[211] It appears that an action to void an otherwise valid contract, for whatever reason, will be within Article 5(1): *Agnew and others v Lansförsäkringsbolagens AB* [2001] 1 AC 223, HL; cf. *obiter* observations in *Alfred Dunhill Ltd v Diffusion Internationale de Maroquinerie de Prestige SARL and others* [2001] CLC 949.

1.1.5(i)   The 'void contract'[212]

The consequences[213] of a contract, previously found to have been void *ab initio* for lack of capacity, were the subject of the action in *Kleinwort Benson Ltd v Glasgow City Council*.[214]

In the Court of appeal,[215] the distinction made by Gaudemet-Tallon above, between the action to nullify the contract, and an action dealing with its consequences,[216] was kept alive in the dissenting judgment of Leggatt LJ:

> the cause of action arises only because there proved *not* to be any contractual relationship between the parties.[217]

Roch LJ, of the majority, relied, *inter alia*, on: *Martin Peters Bauunternehmung GmbH v Zuid Nederlandse Aannemers Vereniging*,[218] a case which seemed to him to be similar, 'in that in that case, as in this, under the national law there was no contract';[219] and Article 10(1)(e) of the 1980 Rome Convention, to show that the consequences of a contract's nullity are, by European law,[220] to be seen as contractual. For Millett LJ, the opening classifying words of Article 5(1) were to be interpreted widely, not merely being 'equated with contractual causes of action ... or even "claims based on contract"'.[221] For him, 'contract' in Article 5(1) had tacitly included within it the term 'void contract'.[222]

The House of Lords, by a bare majority,[223] reversed the Court of Appeal's decision. Lord Goff began his speech by stating that the claim[224] was one in

---

[212] Although Lord Goff decided not to apply Article 5(1) because there was no 'contractual obligation', therefore, arguably, a separate section 1.3 question, below—'It [a claim] can only [fall within Article 5(1)] if it can properly be said to be based upon a particular contractual obligation', at p.167; Panagopoulos, G. *Restitution in Private International Law*, 2000, at pp.206–07.

[213] Not merely an action to have the contract declared void *ab initio*, although the distinction seems hard to countenance, according to Lord Nicholls, above.

[214] [1994] 4 All ER 865 (Hirst J) [1996] 2 All ER 257, CA, *revrs'd* [1999] 1 AC 153, HL.

[215] [1996] 2 All ER 257, Leggatt LJ dissenting.

[216] *Kleinwort Benson* may have limited application if it is only applicable to actions subsequent to finding a contract's nullity; but Briggs (1997) 68 *BYBIL* 331, at p.333.

[217] [1996] 2 All ER 257, at p.265, original emphasis.

[218] (C-34/82) [1983] ECR 987.

[219] [1996] 2 All ER 257, at p.269.

[220] UK's reservation, permitted by Article 22(1) of the 1980 Rome Convention, and exercised in s 2(2) of the Contracts (Applicable Law) Act 1990, to oust Article 10(1)(e)'s application.

[221] [1996] 2 All ER 257, at p.273.

[222] *Ibid.* at p.276.

[223] Lords Goff, Clyde and Hutton; Lords Nicholls and Mustill dissenting.

[224] Presumably by English law as *lex fori*, as a claim 'to restitution, which in English law, is based on the principle of unjust enrichment', at p.167; then attempted to fit the claim, thus classified, into Article 5(1) of Sch.4, with its own autonomous classifications. Is this the correct methodology? (Maher, G. (1998) *The Juridical Review* 131, clearly thinks national classifications of restitution were too influential in the case, at p.133). Can the phrase the 'contractual obligation in question' (in its 'contractual' context evident from phrases in *De Bloos v Bouyer*) have a limiting interpretative influence on the matters relating to a contract, or vice versa? Clearly Lords Goff and Hutton

restitution, based on the principle of unjust enrichment, to recover money paid under a void contract. This, he believed, made the claim fall outside Article 5(1), which concerned itself with contractual obligations:

> it seems impossible to say that the claim for the recovery of the money is based upon a particular contractual obligation.[225]

Lord Clyde agreed with the overall majority decision, but decided, at p.181, to concentrate on the words 'relating to', the present participle of which indicated to him that 'there [had to be] a relationship still continuing between the current issue and a contract'.[226] Lord Hutton thought that the phrase in Article 5(1) was wider than a potential paraphrasing of the article as 'may be sued on[227] a contract'.[228]

Lord Nicholls, of the minority, did not believe that in 'matters relating to a contract' was confined to 'contractual obligations'. For him:

> a dispute over the existence of a contract[229] and, if it is held to be void, over the consequences for payments already made . . . is as much a dispute 'relating to a contract' as a dispute over the existence of a contract.[230]

A sharp distinction has now to be made between a dispute as to the existence of a contract, and the consequences of a void contract.[231] While it is true that such a distinction will jurisdictionally fragment[232] the resolution of these two different claims, the majority decision forces a strict and literal reading of the word

---

thought so, at p.169 and p.189, respectively; Lord Nicholls, dissenting, did not, at p.175. Cf *Alfred Dunhill Ltd v Diffusion Internationale de Maroquinerie de Prestige SARL and others* [2001] CLC 949, *obiter*, that an 'obligation' not to induce a contract by misrepresentation is not 'a matter relating to a contract'. Is it right to pre-classify an action according to English notions, only then to see if Article 5(1)'s pre-requisites are then satisfied? This is courting a temptation to be lead astray, as Lord Goff continues: 'claims of this kind [i.e. claims to restitution] do not *per se* fall within Article 5(1)', at p.167.

[225] [1999] 1 AC 153, at p.167; *dubitante* Briggs, (1997) 68 *BYBIL* 331, at p.334.

[226] At p.181, referring to a Scottish decision, *Strathaird Farms Ltd v G A Chattaway & Co.* 1993 SLT (Sh Ct) 36, at p.39 decided under Article 5(1) of Sch.4 to the CJJA 1982—a Scottish pursuer's action to recover an overpayment from an English defender was not proceeding 'based upon contract': 'the existence of the contract between the parties is only part of *the historical background* explaining why the payment was made'; '[i]f there is no obligation because there has never been a contract then there is no jurisdiction under the article', at p.181.

[227] This has a bearing on pre-contractual duties.

[228] At p.186.

[229] Not, on the facts, actually before his Lordship in this case.

[230] At p.176; *contra* Gaudemet-Tallon, 1996, at pp.112–13, para. 159; his Lordship is concentrating on the phrase as a unit rather than considering the word 'contract' separately; this may be one of the reasons for his dissent.

[231] If an action combines pleas to have the contract declared void and to recover any sums paid over, a scission will now occur; the view that any declaration of invalidity and the consequences thereof should somehow be amalgamated for the sake of economy has been weakened by the ECJ in *Leathertex Divisione Sintetici SpA v Bodetex BVBA* (C-420/97) [1999] ECR I-6747, and its scission as to places of performance of payment obligations.

[232] Cf Gaudemet-Tallon, 1996, at p.113.

'contract'[233] in Article 5(1), and compels this 'channelling', or division upon (an English) court.

1.1.5(ii)   Restitution and 'a contract'[234]

In the Austrian *OGH* decision of 27 January 1998,[235] the court had to decide whether it had jurisdiction under Article 5(1) in an 'unjust enrichment' claim—a repayment claim of moneys advanced by the Austrian plaintiff to a German defendant on the basis of a transfer of a business owned by the defendant. The plaintiff claimed that they had been deceived into entering into the contract and initiated a 'Rückforderungsanspruch',[236] due to lack of agreement on its part to the contract. The obligation to make repayment was found to be an independent contractual obligation:

> Der Rückabwicklungsanspruch tritt nicht an die Stelle einer der beiden vertraglichen Hauptpflicht.[237]

The basis of the plaintiff's claim was the repayment claim itself.[238] There was no discussion in the case, as it seemed presumably to the court unarguable, that the claim was not one 'in matters relating to a contract.'[239] The fact that the court was dealing, at the same time, with the consequences of a 'void/voidable' contract did not provoke any discussion of Article 5(1) scope *ratione materiae*. A similar conclusion was reached by *OGH* 10 March 1998,[240] another claim for repayment in unjust enrichment, founded on the mutual dissolution of a contract. The fact that, as in the earlier decision, the claim was presented due to a lack of consent of one of the parties, was immaterial:

---

[233] The House of Lords' ruling will also have a knock-on effect for Article 11, and Articles 13–15, insurance and consumer 'contracts' respectively.

[234] *Bundesgericht* 10.5.2000 *Dame R contre Cour de justice civile du canton de Genève*, unreported; although it speaks of 'restitution' of moneys lent, this right was expressly reserved and stipulated in the loan document; restitution of money (over)paid in error, based on unjust enrichment *not* within Article 5(1) of Sch.4 in *Eddie v Alpa Srl* (2000) *SLT* 1062, at p.1068 (Lord Eassie); also considered in *BGH* 132 BGHZ 105, at p.108: German plaintiff sought the return of goods bought for, or transferred to, a Brazilian defendant, 'domiciled' in Spain, in contemplation of an intended marriage that never in fact took place—the views of the editors of the *Münchener-Kommentar* to the *Zivilprozeßordnung* adopted: 'Article 5(1) . . . does not apply to claims for unjust enrichment or to other relationships imposed by law', at p.108; for the 'void' contract the *Kleinwort Benson* saga, culminating in the House of Lord's decision [1999] 1 AC 153; Lord Goff thought it 'impossible to say that the claim for the recovery of money [was] based upon a particular contractual obligation', at p.167.

[235] (1998) *JBl* 515.

[236] ('a restitutionary claim').

[237] (1998) *JBl* 515, at p.516 ('the restitutionary obligation does not replace one of the two primary obligations').

[238] Austrian law, however, made the repayment obligation performable at the German debtor's domicile.

[239] Compare Lord Nicholls, of the minority in *Kleinwort Benson*, at pp.174–75: 'Part-payments made in advance in purported performance of a contractual obligation . . .'.

[240] (1998) *ZfRV* 161.

Der Rückstellungsanspruch[241] resultiert in beiden Fällen aus der Auflösung eines *bereits geschlossenen Vertrages.*[242]

These two cases are clearly distinguishable, to English lawyers,[243] from the claims in unjust enrichment resulting from a void contract, *ab initio*, in *Kleinwort Benson*. Yet here, at least, we have a judicial position that does not rule out restitutionary claims *tout court*.

A German case has also had to consider the question of an 'unjust enrichment' claim: *BGH*, 28 February 1996.[244] A German plaintiff sought the return of goods bought for, or transferred to, a Brazilian defendant, 'domiciled' in Spain in contemplation of an intended marriage,[245] that never in fact took place. Although the court found that the Convention did not apply *ratione temporis* nor *materiae*, it did adopt the views of the editors of the *Münchener-Kommentar* to the *Zivilprozeßordnung*[246] in concluding that:

> ... Article 5 Nr.1 ... gilt nicht für Bereicherungsansprüche oder sonstige gesetzliche Schuldverhältnisse.[247]

The court continued that the plaintiff's action did not fall within German autonomous law, §29 ZPO, 'Streitigkeiten aus einem Vertragsverhältnis' ('disputes arising from a contractual relationship') either:

> [only] schuldrechtliche[], auf eine Verpflichtung gerichtete[] Vereinbarungen [qualify, while]. . .gesetzliche Schuldverhältnisse, z.B. Ansprüche aus ... *ungerechtfertiger Bereicherung*, nicht darunter fallen.[248]

This case seems more in line with the majority speeches of their Lordships in *Kleinwort Benson*—after all, the marriage contract never existed. Should a case come before the German courts on similar facts as in *Kleinwort Benson*, it could be confidently stated that the court would (most likely) not consider that Article 5(1) could be used to found jurisdiction. The above quotation also shows that the German court has focussed on the fact that an unjust enrichment claim is not a

---

[241] The place of performance of the repayment claim, it was held, was not covered by the 1980 Vienna Convention—this only covered payment of the purchase price; Swiss law, *lege causae*, decided that the place of repayment was in Austria.

[242] ('the obligation to make reparation results in both cases from the dissolution of a contract, previously concluded'), (1998) *ZfRV* 161; this aspect distinguishes this case from *Kleinwort Benson*.

[243] But not sufficient reason for Lord Hutton.

[244] 132 BGHZ 105.

[245] It seems, on provisions of the *BGB*, akin to the old breach of promise cases known to English family law.

[246] The case was therefore decided under the similarly-worded §29 ZPO, but this distinction is immaterial for present purposes.

[247] ('Article 5(1) does not apply to claims in restitution nor other obligations imposed by operation of law'), 132 BGHZ 105, at p.108.

[248] ('[only] agreements under the law of obligations, directed at an obligation [qualify while] legal obligations imposed by law, such as claims arising out of unjust enrichment do not fall thereunder.'), *ibid*, at p.109; *OLG Düsseldorf* 26.10.1995 IPRspr. 1997 Nr. 135 has also opined that Article 5(1) does *not* cover, *inter alia*, unjust enrichment claims.

contractual obligation,[249] rather than simply stating that unjust enrichment falls, *tout court*, outside Article 5(1)'s scope *ratione materiae*.

1.1.6   Potential amendments to Article 5(1) ratione materiae by Article 5(1) of the Brussels I Regulation and the Hague draft Worldwide Judgments Convention

Unfortunately, the proposed amendments in Article 5(1) of the Brussels I Regulation, and Article 6 of the Hague draft Convention do not solve the problems of interpretation associated with the word 'contract',[250] void contracts, restitution and pre-contractual duties. Article 5(1)(a) of Regulation, and thence also Article 5(1)(b), continue to be premised on the fact that—as with the current version of Article 5(1)—a dispute in a Member State court still involves 'matters relating to a contract'. The whole raft of uncertainties, and comment, in the foregoing section will therefore be incorporated into any future interpretations of Article 5(1)(a)(b).

Article 6 of the Hague draft Convention is somewhat differently drafted *ratione materiae*, and perhaps more restrictively so. It speaks of jurisdiction regarding 'an action *in* contract'.[251] Whether this would cut out actions for breach of pre-contractual duties of utmost good faith is uncertain, but would, *prima facie*, seem to do so. The word 'in' could be said to narrow the field of claims further than the more liberal 'in matters relating to. . .' in Article 5(1) of the Brussels Convention.

1.2   THE 'OBLIGATION IN QUESTION'

The next, and second, task for a national court to undertake is whether the claim(s) advanced[252] by the plaintiff/claimant are within the Article 5(1)

---

[249] The main thrust of Lord Goff's speech in *Kleinwort Benson*.

[250] Difficulties in classification obvious in Nygh/Pocar report on the October 1999 draft: 'characterisation can only be made by a court . . . either according to its own law . . . or . . . its conflict of laws rules', at p.51.

[251] Compare therefore the dissenting minority speeches of Lords Millett and Hope of Craighead in *Agnew and others v Lansförsäkringsbolagens AB*, [2001] 1 AC 223, to the effect that an obligation had to spring from the contract itself, once concluded. The minority therefore did not consider that pre-contractual duties were Article 5(1) (contractual) obligations.

[252] Note not under the contract in general, below and *Corte di Cassazione* 21.6.1984 *Handelsagentur Dieter Nienaber GmbH & Co. KG v Impex-Euro Sr.* [1988] E.C.C. 150, at p.155 para. 10(a), *Source Ltd v T.U.V. Rheinland Holding A.G. and others* [1998] QB 54, CA; identification of the obligation in question thus depends crucially on the way in which the plaintiff has formulated his claim for relief, *Fisher and others v Unione Italiana de Riassicurazione SPA* [1999] Lloyd's Reins.L Rep. 215, at p.219 (Colman J); *Viskase Ltd and another v Paul Kiefel GmbH* [1999] 1 WLR 1305, at p.1318 (Chadwick LJ); *Barry and another v Bradshaw and others* [2000] CLC 455, CA, at p.457 (Aldous LJ); *Bio-Medical Research Ltd. T/A Slendertone v Delatex S.A.* [2000] 4 IR 307, SC (Fennelly J); important (the obligation to pay

definition[253] of the term 'obligation'.[254] If more than one 'obligation', so identified, is put forward,[255] it then has to find which,[256] if any, among them is the 'principal'[257] obligation.

This deceptively simple analysis belies a number of unsolved problems with Article 5(1), which will be discussed below. What is evident, and of importance for this work, is the potential for protectionist abuse, both in the classification process in general, examined here, and in allowing this classification of the claim(s) advanced to remain under the sole control[258] of the plaintiff/claimant, without court intervention. As a result, scrutiny will be necessary, by comparative analysis, to ascertain whether plaintiffs/claimants could, and do, so draft[259] their claims as to delimit them only to those obligations which are to be performed, on any

(under a letter of credit)) in *Chailease Finance Corporation v Credit Agricole Indosuez* [2000] 1 Lloyd's Rep. 348, CA, at p.354 (Potter LJ); *contra, semble,* Norwegian Supreme Court *Høyesteretts Kjaeremål-sutvalg* 27.1.1998 *Terje Karlung v Svensk Vägguide Comertex AB* [1999] I.L.Pr. 298, at p.301, para. 21.

[253] Only 'obligations' as autonomously defined in *Ets. A. de Bloos S.P.R.L v Soc. en commandite par actions Bouyer* (C-15/76) [1976] ECR 1497 have 'a place of performance'; this distinction proved crucial in the attempted reformulation of payment obligations by AG Léger—whose solution of reformulation was *not* subsequently adopted by the ECJ—in *Leathertex Divisione Sintetici SpA v Bodetex BVBA* (C-420/97) [1999] ECR I-6747, reviewed below sections 1.2.5, 1.3.9(ii), 1.3.10.

[254] As to whether the 'obligation' has, in addition, to be contractual, below section 1.2.6, at p.106; and now the important decision in the HL in *Agnew and others v Lansförsäkringsbolagens AB* [2001] 1 AC 223; Novy, D. 'Article 5(1) of the Brussels Convention (2000) 1 *Hibernian Law Journal* 69, at pp.80–81; for when the obligation is to refrain from doing something: *Boss Group Ltd v Boss France SA* [1996] 4 All ER 970 and *USF Ltd (t/a USF Memcor) v Aqua Technology Hanson NV/SA* [2001] 1 All ER (Comm) 856 (not to supply anyone else in a disputed exclusive distribution contract); or, as in *Kenburn Waste Management Ltd v Bergman*, 11.5.2001, Ch.D. (Pumfrey J), 30.1.2002, CA, where the obligation is to ensure a particular state of affairs persists in a particular place/Contracting State; in *S.A. Besix N.V. v WABAG Wasserreinigungsbau Alfred Kretzschmar GmbH* (C-256/00), 19.2.2002, at paras. 28–29, the application of Art.5(1) was held to be conditional on a literal interpretation of the text 'the *place* of performance', i.e., in the singular, at the very least in cases of the negative obligations in that case (that may potentially breached in any or all Contracting States).

[255] In the assessment of 'the obligation in question' only the claimant's pleadings are relevant—in *USF Ltd (t/a USF Memcor) v Aqua Technology Hanson NV/SA* [2001] 1 All ER (Comm) 856 (Aikens J) it is submitted, rejected the view that the defendant's pleadings in another Contracting State are relevant for this Article 5(1) analysis.

[256] Below, for section 1.2.2 on the possible methodologies for identification of the 'principal' obligation; obviously if only one 'obligation' forms the basis of the claim, the question does not arise: *Bundesgericht* 25.7.2000 *Gerhard Pabst GmbH gegen Ivana Gillar-Kokrda*, unreported.

[257] *Hassan Shenavai v Klaus Kreischer* (C-266/85) [1987] ECR 239; if a court cannot find/select one 'principal obligation' from among a number, it is now settled that each (principal) obligation has its own independent place of performance *lege causae: Leathertex Divisione Sintetici SpA v Bodetex BVBA* (C-420/97) [1999] ECR I-6747, esp. at p.6792, para. 40, below.

[258] The level of autonomy a plaintiff has, vis-à-vis the supervision of national courts, will also have to be examined, in section 1.2.3. Examples of the principal obligation turning simply on the relative value of the plaintiff's claim: *Pierre c/ Soc. de droit italien Vetrolan* 22.5.1991 1992 *Dalloz, som.com.,* 164 and *Cassation* 14.1.1998 *Société Productions S.C.A.P. c/ Roberto Faggioni,* unreported, Lexis and *Cour d'appel de Luxembourg* 8.3.1994 *Vesque c/ Badischer Winzerkeller E.G.* 1993–1995 *Pas. Lux.* 341.

[259] Below, especially *Source Ltd v T.U.V. Rheinland Holding A.G. and others* [1998] QB 54, CA; *AIG Group (UK) Ltd v 'The Ethniki'* [2000] All ER (Comm) 65, CA, (Evans LJ); also *Eddie v Alpa Srl* (2000) SLT 1062—despite averments in pleadings, simply because 'symbolic' delivery of bills of lading was within Scottish jurisdiction did not similarly make this extend to the place of delivery of the goods: 'a pursuer . . . should be able to set out, in averment, a *sufficient exposition* of contractual terms where

analysis,[260] in the *forum actoris*.[261] It will be equally important to examine whether it is open to particular national courts,[262] when classifying an 'obligation' or 'principal obligation', to adopt, from among a number of possible interpretations of these terms, that which either favours the retention of jurisdiction—usually again the *forum actoris*—or, with similar results, that which side-steps an interpretation[263] which otherwise would force[264] a domestic plaintiff/claimant to follow the place of performance (of a payment obligation) to another Contracting State.

As is traditional with commentaries on Article 5(1),[265] the current state of the European law on the subject of the article will be given in some (briefer) detail here: in the cases *Ets. A. de Bloos S.P.R.L v Soc. en commandite par actions Bouyer*[266] and *Hassan Shenavai v Klaus Kreischer*.[267]

from it can be seen that there is *an intellibible and stateable basis* for maintaining [the place of performance] . . . is within the territorial jurisdiction', at p.1067; and *Sté Filtertechniek Nederland BV c/ Johannes Hoff* 21.5.1997 (1998) *JDI* 133, *Cour de Cassation* 8.2.2000 (2000) *JCP*, IV, 1542.

[260] This should strictly be according to the law governing the obligation—effectively the *lex causae: Industrie Tessili Italiana Como v Dunlop AG* (C-12/76) [1976] ECR 1473, but has not always proved to be so—most recently in *Sté Comptoir commercial d'Orient c/ Société Medtrafina* 11.3.1997 1998 *JDI* 129, [1999] I.L.Pr. 336, and *Groupe Concorde et autres c/ Capitaine du Suhadiwarno Panjan et autres* 9.12.1997 1998 *Rev crit* 117; the ECJ ruling in *Groupe Concorde* (C-440/97) [1999] ECR I-6307 appears to have laid to rest any dissent, (*Cour de Cassation* 14.12.1999 *Soc. de droit allemand Edeka Frucht Kontor c/ Caisse regionale de Credit agricole*, (2001) *JDI* 133; *Cour de Cassation* 21.3.2000 *Soc. Maquet c/ Soc Becker Holding et autres* (2000) *Rev crit* 792; *Cour de Cassation GIE Groupe Concorde e.a. v Le capitaine commandant le navire «Suhadiwarno Panjan»* 20.6.2000 (2000) *JCP*, IV p.1306, (2000) *JDI* 547, (2001) *Rev crit* 156; *Cour de Cassation* (Ch.com.) 16.5.2000 *Thyssen Industrie AG c/ Soc. Kern et autre* (2001) *Rev crit* 155).

[261] The Convention's anathema: made plain in Article 3 [I] and [II] and in recent ECJ cases: *Antonio Marinari v Lloyds Bank Plc and Zubaidi Trading Co.* (C-364/93) [1995] ECR I-2719 at p.2739 para. 13; *Sherson Lehman Hutton Inc. v TVB Treuhandgesellschaft für Vermögensverwaltung und Beteiligungen mbH* (C-89/91) [1993] ECR I-139 at p.187 para. 17; and *Dumez France and Tracoba v Hessische Landesbank (Helaba) & Others* (C-220/88) [1990] I-49 at p.79 para. 16 and p.80 para. 19.

[262] Especially the French cases on independent commercial agents: *Dellinger c/ Société Leppak* 26.4.1978; *Dellinger c/ Société Leppak* 27.11.1979 (1980) *JDI* 333, *Sté Stoppani SPA c/ Sté Stoppani France* 18.3.1997 (1998) *JDI* 129 and Mourre, A. 'La compétence juridictionelle dans les litiges relatifs à la rupture d'un contrat de concession exclusive' (1992) *Gaz Pal*, Chron., 920, at p.924 onwards; note also the adverse German reaction to the French courts' perceived motivation in Storp, R. 'Internationale Zuständigkeit des Erfüllungsorts bei Verträgen mit französischen Vertretern' (1999) *RIW* 823, at p.824.

[263] One would expect this tendency to emerge most clearly from among those States where the material *lex causae* on the place of performance of (monetary) obligations forces the creditor (plaintiff/claimant), in the absence of agreement/circumstances to the contrary, to seek out his debtor: France Article 1247 *Code civil*, Germany §§269, 270 IV BGB; Austria §905 Abs.2 ABGB; Belgium Article 1247 *Code civil*. Such a tendency has not, however, emerged in Germany, nor, as yet, in Austria below p.139 following.

[264] The material *leges causae* of the countries in the preceding footnote have this effect.

[265] In more detail, Gaudemet-Tallon, 1996, pp.116–21, paras. 163–65; Geimer and Schütze, 1997, at pp.135–36, paras. 59–62; in some detail Hertz, K. *Jurisdiction in Contract and Tort under the Brussels Convention*, 1998, pp.88–101; Briggs, 1997, pp.99–105; *Cheshire and North*, 13th edn, 1999, at pp.200–11; Kropholler, 1998, at pp.104–07, paras. 14–17.

[266] (C-15/76) [1976] ECR 1497.

[267] (C-266/85) [1987] ECR 239; and now *Leathertex Divisione Sintetici SpA v Bodetex BVBA* (C-420/97) [1999] ECR I-6747.

The 'classic' starting point in identifying an Article 5(1) 'obligation' is the former, *Ets. A. de Bloos*. The European court approached the problem of an 'obligation' from three interrelated and unhelpful, self-paraphrasing angles. As is well known in the case, the French defendant company Bouyer had granted to the Belgian plaintiff company, de Bloos, the exclusive right to distribute Bouyer's products in, *inter alia*, Belgium and Luxembourg. De Bloos considered that Bouyer had terminated this concession unilaterally and without notice. It sued Bouyer in Belgium under Article 5(1), seeking in its action two things: firstly, a declaration of the contract's dissolution, on account of Bouyer's wrongful conduct; secondly, damages pursuant to a Belgian law[268] of 27 July 1961,[269] which had been specifically enacted to provide compensation to (Belgian) concessionaires in such circumstances. Due to differences[270] in the language versions of Article 5(1), the Belgian referring court[271] asked whether 'obligation' meant any obligation arising out of the contract, or more specifically the obligation in dispute.[272] If the latter were the correct interpretation, the court further asked whether 'obligation' meant the original obligation and/or the obligation to pay damages/compensation for its non-observance and/or the various compensatory obligations under Articles 2 and 3[273] of the Belgian Law of 27 July 1961. At paragraph 11,[274] the ECJ opted to interpret 'obligation' as referring to 'the contractual[275] obligation forming the basis of the legal proceedings.'[276] This was further defined, or paraphrased, shortly after as 'the obligation . . . which corresponds to the contractual right on which the plaintiff's claim[277] is

---

[268] Esp. on this law Weser, M. 'L'article 5, alinéa 1er de la Convention de Bruxelles du 27 septembre 1968 et la concession de vente exclusive' (1976) *Journal des Tribunaux* 323; Van Hille, P. 'Concessions de vente en Belgique et règles de compétence de la Convention C.E.E. du 27 septembre 1968' (1976) *Journal des Tribunaux* 733; Ledoux, R. 'Les concessions de vente en Belgique et règles de compétence de la C.E.E.' (1975) *Journal des Tribunaux* 217, and 'Examen de jurisprudence. La loi du 27 juillet 1961 relative à la résiliation unilatérale des concessions de vente exclusive à durée indéterminée (1992 à 1997)' (1998) *Rev. dr. comm. belge* 3, at p.41.

[269] As to which below and in general Rauscher, T. *Verpflichtung und Erfüllungsort in* Article *5(1) EuGVÜ*, 1984 especially p.14 onwards; for the Code *Les Codes Larcier*, I, Ed. 1995, p.650.

[270] Long since corrected, by the 1978 Accession Convention, in the French version.

[271] *Cour d'appel de Mons*; for the decision after the reference back: *Digest of case law relating to the European Communities*, D-Series, Issue 5, I-5.1.1–B6.

[272] At p.1501 of the report; from the Italian version of the Convention it was clear that this meant the obligation forming the basis of the proceedings.

[273] As to which Rauscher, 1984. Belgian case law has consistently held that the obligation under Article 2 of the 1961 law is not an autonomous/independent obligation: *Cassation* 6.4.1978, *Société de droit allemand «Knauer und Co GmbH Maschinenfabrik» c/ Callens*, 1978 *Pas. Belge*, 871, and Belgian *Cour de Cassation* 28.6.1979 *Audi-NSU Auto Union AG v Adelin Petit et Cie SA* [1980] E.C.C. 235; but that Article 3 *is* independent: Belgian *Cour de Cassation* 19.1.1984 *Carl Freudenberg KG c/ Société de Personnes à responsabilité Limitée «Bureau R.C. Van Oppens»* 1984 *Pas. Belge*, I, 540.

[274] P.1508 of the report.

[275] As to the relevance of this word, below at p.106 *et seq*.

[276] At p.1508.

[277] As to how much autonomy the plaintiff's claim, as pleaded, has, below at pp.96–99, and *Source Ltd v T.U.V. Rheinland Holding A.G. and others* [1998] QB 54, CA; and the cautionary observations in *Royal Bank of Scotland Plc v Cassa di Risparmio delle Province Lombard and others* [1992] BankLR 251, at

based.'[278] A claim for damages for failure to perform a contractual obligation could not therefore be considered as an 'obligation' for Article 5(1), because such a claim was dependent on, replaced,[279] and flowed from the 'support'[280] of the 'unperformed contractual obligation'.[281]

To conclude this already confused interpretation, the Court said that a comparison had to be drawn between 'the contractual right relied on by the grantee'[282] [283] and the 'contractual obligation of the grantor'.[284] Only if the grantor's contractual obligation coincided with, or 'mirrored', the grantee's corresponding contractual right (as formulated in his claim), would a court have jurisdiction over an 'obligation', thus autonomously defined, under Article 5(1).

A claim for payment of damages[285] could, on this analysis, either be 'an independent contractual obligation'—a distinct contractual obligation of the grantor;[286] or it could be contingent—as a matter of autonomous Community law—and therefore 'parasitic' on, an unperformed contractual obligation itself. Only the former—independent obligations—have a place of performance under Article 5(1). The latter were simply not seen as Article 5(1) 'obligations' at all.[287]

Turning away momentarily from the ECJ caselaw, and although only in a first instance English case on the point, a workable definition of 'the obligation in question' was given by Colman J in *Fisher and others v Unione Italiana de Riassicurazione SPA.*[288] In this case, plaintiff re-insurers sought a declaration of non-liability under Article 5(1) in a retrocession[289] contract with Italian defendants, alleging[290] the defendants were in breach of a warranty under the retrocession to retain part of the risk for themselves. Colman J had to ascertain the obligation in question[291] and its place of performance. After reviewing the usual

---

p.256 (Mustill LJ); *AIG Group (UK) Ltd and others v The Ethniki* [2000] All ER (Comm) 65, CA, at p.72 (Evans LJ); Briggs, A. 'Decisions of British courts during 1999—B. Private International Law' (1999) *BYBIL* 319, at p.325.

[278] At p.1508, para. 13
[279] P.1509, para. 17
[280] P.1508, para. 14, (a verb in the original text).
[281] P.1509, para. 17.
[282] Or more generally the plaintiff/claimant.
[283] At p.1509, para. 15.
[284] *Ibid*, for the grantor can be read more generally the defendant.
[285] If contractually-stipulated; otherwise payment is a remedial obligation, *Medway Packaging Ltd v Meurer Maschinen GmbH & Co. K.G.* [1990] 2 Lloyd's Rep. 112, CA.
[286] For the compensatory obligations under the Belgian law, below.
[287] The ECJ finally held that it was for the *lex causae* to decide whether compensation/damages claims were 'independent' or merely accessory.
[288] [1999] Lloyd's Rep. IR 215, at p.219.
[289] An insurance contract taken out between a reinsurer and another reinsurer.
[290] The plaintiff pleaded this point explicitly and this proved to be crucial.
[291] The pleaded basis of the plaintiff's claim for a negative declaration (on such actions in relation to (re)insurance: *Agnew and others v Lansförsäkringsbolagens AB* [2001] 1 AC 223, HL) was found to be the defendant's failure to retain part of the risk; this was therefore the 'obligation in question'. Its place of performance was found to be in Italy, and therefore the English court did not have jurisdiction under Article 5(1).

cases,[292] he came to the conclusion that 'the obligation in question' had the following three characteristics: '(1) it is a promissory term of or at least a duty closely connected with[293] a contract, such as the duty to disclose all material facts. . .(2) there is a dispute relating to its performance; (3) the plaintiff has formulated his claim for relief in the proceedings on the grounds of the performance or non-performance of that obligation'.[294]

Another English case shows how flexible the concept 'obligation' is perceived to be, at least by the English courts. In *Raiffeisen Zentralbank Österreich Aktiengesellschaft v National Bank of Greece S.A.*[295] the English court decided that an implied contractual obligation could be an 'obligation' for Article 5(1) purposes.[296] In *Raiffeisen* itself, the Greek defendant bank had agreed to make a loan to a Liberian company, Sea Nomad, to enable it to finance the purchase of a vessel. Money was to be advanced in a series of stages, referred to as 'drawdowns', as the work progressed. The plaintiff Austrian bank also made a series of bridging loans to Sea Nomad's parent company Halda, to be passed on to Sea Nomad. The last of these bridging loans was made on condition that Halda had first obtained from the defendant bank a letter containing an irrevocable undertaking that the Greek bank would pay the plaintiff the amount of the bridging loan, and confirmation that no event of default had occurred in the Greek bank's own loan agreement. This the Greek bank duly did in a letter of 17 June 1992. Consequently, Raiffeisen allowed its final loan to proceed to Halda. This last loan was not repaid. Raiffeisen commenced proceedings in England, *inter alia*, on the basis of an implied term in the June letter that if the Greek bank allowed its loan to proceed before becoming contractually bound to do so, they would make payments to the plaintiffs on that basis also.[297] After finding an implied term to this effect, the judge went on to say:

> there is no logical reason why a claim based on it should not be the principal[298] obligation in question . . . just because it is an implied term and therefore its existence cannot be shown as clearly as a claim based on an express term.[299]

---

[292] *Martin Peters Bauunternehmung GmbH v Zuid Nederlandse Aannemers Vereniging* (C-34/82) [1983] ECR 987; *Ets. A. de Bloos S.P.R.L v Soc. en commandite par actions Bouyer* (C-15/76) [1976] ECR 1497 and *Custom Made Commercial Ltd v Stawa Metallbau GmbH* (C-288/92) [1994] ECR I-2913; an 'authoritative summary' (*Viskase Ltd v Paul Kiefel* [1999] 1 WLR 1305, at p.1312, (Evans LJ)) of the effect of the ECJ cases under Article 5(1) is given in Lord Goff's speech in *Kleinwort Benson Ltd v Glasgow City Council* [1999] 1 AC 153, at pp.163–67; applied again by Evans LJ in *AIG Group (UK) Ltd v 'The Ethniki'* [2000] All ER (Comm) 65, CA.
[293] Above, section 1.1 on 'matters relating to a contract', and *Agnew and others v Lansförsäkringsbolagens AB* [2001] 1 AC 223, HL.
[294] [1999] LRLR 215, at p.219; *Bio-Medical Research Ltd. T/A Slendertone v Delatex S.A.* [2000] 4 IR 307, SC.
[295] [1999] 1 Lloyd's Rep. 408, QBD (Tuckey J).
[296] Even, indeed, the 'principal' obligation according to the case of *Hassan Shenavai v Klaus Kreischer* (C-266/85) [1987] ECR 239, discussed below, at p.76.
[297] Paraphrasing Tuckey J, at p.412.
[298] It was found to be the principal obligation because it was 'a payment obligation which gave [the plaintiffs] some security', at p.411.
[299] *Ibid.* at p.412.

Recently, the case of the *'Sea Maas'*[300] has, again, shown how fluid the concept of the (principal) obligation in question can be. In this case, Rix J held that when in a bill of lading case an action is brought under the Hague or Hague/Visby rules for damage to cargo, the principal obligation in question under Article 5(1) is the obligation to exercise 'due diligence'. This may, according to the bill of lading holder's claim, vary in its place of performance according to the species of alleged lack of due diligence.[301]

Before other national case law itself relating to the 'obligation in question' is examined in full- which will consider, *inter alia*, commercial agency contracts[302]—together with what is, and is not, to be classified as an 'independent'/'accessory' contractual obligation—it is necessary to complete this survey of the obligation in question by returning to the Community cases, and briefly review *Hassan Shenavai v Klaus Kreischer*.[303] This case resolved one question concerning multiple obligations in a plaintiff's claim, and exposed in the process further avenues of uncertainty, only recently illuminated.[304]

Shenavai v Kreischer concerned a claim for a payment obligation under Article 5(1). The German plaintiff sued Kreischer, the Dutch defendant, for payment of the former's architectural work commissioned by the defendant. For present purposes,[305] the Court admitted[306] that the *Ets. A. de Bloos* case did not provide any guidance when a plaintiff/claimant asserted various different obligations, so defined, in his claim. Its 'very helpful obiter remark'[307] on the subject is well known:

> where various obligations are at issue, it will be the principal obligation which will determine its jurisdiction.[308]

Yet no guidance is given in the case as to how, if at all,[309] any particular obligation is to be exalted above any other; nor until *Leathertex Divisione Sintetici SpA v Bodetex BVBA*,[310] what was to happen if this proved impossible.[311] Nothing was

---

[300] [1999] 2 Lloyd's Rep. 281 (Rix J).

[301] At p.284, *in casu*, a lack of due diligence in providing a seaworthy vessel at the commencement of the voyage (in Newport, Wales).

[302] For an historical analysis of this area Rauscher, 1984.

[303] (C-266/85) [1987] ECR 239.

[304] *Leathertex Divisione Sintetici SpA v Bodetex BVBA* (C-420/97) [1999] ECR I-6747.

[305] The other important point of the case more generally centred around the resolution of confusion between the application of two earlier cases, *Roger Ivenel v Helmut Schwab* (C-133/81) [1982] ECR 1891 or *Ets. A. de Bloos S.P.R.L v Soc. en commandite par actions Bouyer* (C-15/76) [1976] ECR 1497.

[306] [1987] ECR 239, at p.256, para. 19.

[307] According to Beaumont, *Civil Jurisdiction in Scotland—Brussels and Lugano Conventions*, 2nd edn, 1995, at p.99, para. 5.21.

[308] [1987] ECR 239, at p.256, para. 19.

[309] The obligatory nature of the *Shenavai* ruling has been commented upon: Briggs, 1997, at p.101, para. 2.132; also Hertz, 1998, at p.95, para. 2.2.2. and *Sté Filtertechniek Nederland BV c/ Johannes Hoff* 21.5.1997 (1998) *JDI* 133, at p.135 according to Huet; confirmed in *Cassation* 8.2.2000 *Hoff c/ Sté Filtertechniek Nederland BV* (2000) *JCP*, IV, 1542.

[310] (C-420/97) [1999] ECR I-6747, AG Léger's opinion 16.3.1999.

[311] *Ibid.*

said about having more than one principal obligation,[312] conceivably with different places of performance within, or outside, particular Contracting States. Unanswered[313] was also the question of what happens, on finding a principal obligation, to the jurisdictional status of the remaining obligations necessarily demoted to a secondary rank.[314] The following discussion of these problems, as well as that concerning the 'independent obligation' also reveals questions as to just how much control a plaintiff/claimant should exert over the drafting of his contractual claim.[315]

1.2.1 'Independent' or 'Dependent'/'Accessory' obligations, and the consequences of each

As we have seen, *de Bloos* excluded from the Article 5(1) definition of 'obligation' claims for the payment of damages or compensation, which, in their turn, flowed from the breach of an independent contractual obligation. Such payment claims could not, consequently, have a place of performance. This *De Bloos* distinction of independent/dependent obligations has proved especially significant,[316] and disadvantageous, for plaintiffs claiming monetary, (especially payment), obligations under Article 5(1), where the substantive law[317] of their *fori actoris* requires performance of (independent) monetary obligations[318] at the domicile of the debtor, typically therefore the defendant.

---

[312] Kropholler, 1998, at p.107, para. 16 briefly mentions the possibility. The court, he presumes, would only have jurisdiction over the principal obligation to be performed in its domain—this has been confirmed by *Leathertex Divisione Sintetici SpA v Bodetex BVBA* (C-420/97) [1999] ECR I-6747.

[313] But in France now *Sté Filtertechniek Nederland BV c/ Johannes Hoff* 21.5.1997 (1998) *JDI* 133.

[314] I.e. can a court, notwithstanding its lack of jurisdiction over the principal obligation, nonetheless take jurisdiction over secondary obligations? *Sté Filtertechniek Nederland BV* has demonstrated that a French court can.

[315] As to which below, *Fisher and others v Unione Italiana de Riassicurazione SPA* [1998] CLC 682, and *AIG Group (UK) Ltd and others v The Ethniki* [2000] All ER (Comm) 65, CA.

[316] Esp. Holleaux in *Société Van Pelt c/ Jedre* 29.1.1980 (1980) *JDI* 889, at p.890.

[317] For a comparison of these, an excellent survey in Schack, H. *Der Erfüllungsort im deutschen, ausländischen und internationalen Privat- und Zivilprozeßrecht*, 1985, p.20 onwards; for Germany §§269–270 IV BGB; inconvenient for creditors in France and Belgium Article 1247 *Code civil*; advantageous for creditors in, *inter alia*, Switzerland Article 74(2)(1) *Obligationenrecht*, Italy, Article 1182 [III] *Codice Civil*, Beltramo, Longio, and Merrymann (eds) *The Italian Civil Code*, 1993, Booklet 1, payment obligations at 'domicile of the creditor . . .'; in Denmark *Østre Landsrets* 1.12.1999 *PC Express AB v Columbus IT Partner A/S* [2001] I.L.Pr. 314; and in England, *inter alia, Robey & Co. v The Snaefell Mining Co. Ltd.* [1887] QB 152, at p.154 and *The Eider* [1893] P. 119, at p.131, (Lord Esher, MR): 'the debtor must follow his creditor . . .'; and July 1981 Law Commission Report, No.109, Cmnd. 8318, *Council of Europe Conventions on Foreign Money Liabilities (1967) and on the Place of Payment of Money Liabilities (1972)*, at pp.23–28.

[318] Holleaux, (1980) *JDI* 889, at p.892: 'ce qui a, il est vrai, l'inconvénient de ramener le problème de compétence à celui du caractère portable ou quérable du paiement.'('leading back, it is true, to the inconvenient situation of having jurisdiction from the 'portable' or 'quérable' nature of payment.) One solution was to demote payment obligations to 'dependent' obligations, AG Léger in *Leathertex Divisione Sintetici*, but *rejected* recently by the ECJ, at [1999] ECR I-6747.

Where possible, various ways[319] have been discovered to out-manoeuvre this unfortunate combination[320] of independent (payment) obligation and inconvenient *lex causae*. One obvious solution was to deny 'independent' status to payment 'obligations';[321] instead, rather to graft them on[322] to an 'obligation' which, *lege causae*, was clearly to be performed in the plaintiff/claimant's forum. Another was to subordinate[323] all 'obligations' to one principal obligation which, again, was invariably to be performed in the *forum actoris*. By having only one independent obligation,[324] all others would necessarily be 'dependent', and therefore not be subject[325] to the jurisdiction-founding vagaries of location *lege causae*.

Of the few commentators to have considered this section in any detail, Gothot and Holleaux[326] have said of the 'independent contractual obligation'[327] that it should be defined by having:

> des éléments générateurs propres, c'est-à-dire comme ne procédant pas, ou pas uniquement, de la transgression[328] du contrat.[329] [330]

Presumably, then, any compensatory damages claim, that is in some way contingent[331] on a breach of contract generally, or of a specific obligation therein, is not an Article 5(1) 'obligation'. Yet this over-comforting generalisation does not square easily with clauses in contracts concerning payments to be made at a contract's end by effluxion of time, or release fees/payments; nor does it accurately cover claims for compensation[332] (implied into contracts by law), payable by a

---

[319] For France *Etablissements Carl Brehmer und Sohn c/ Baudoin* 23.1.1979 / *Dellinger c/ Société Leppak* 26.4.1978 / *Dellinger c/ Société Leppak* 27.11.1979 (1979) *JDI* 333 and *Sociétés Rotaprint Export Ehmer et Rotaprint c/ Société Guyot Fourchault* 13.2.1981 (1981) *JDI* 849.

[320] For the historical connection between certain Civil Codes and Civil Procedural Codes below.

[321] The methodology preferred by AG Léger in his recent opinion in *Leathertex Divisione Sintetici SpA v Bodetex BVBA* (C-420/97) [1999] ECR I-6747, but rejected by the ECJ, below.

[322] *Soc K.D. Köln Düsseldorfer Deutsche Rheinschiffahrt c/ Soc. Transports et Voyages* 25.1.1984 (1985) *Rev crit* 126; *Sté Stoppani SPA c/ Sté Stoppani France* 18.3.1997 (1998) *JDI* 129.

[323] *Dellinger c/ Société Leppak* 26.4.1978 / *Dellinger c/ Société Leppak* 27.11.1979 (1979) *JDI* 333; also Mourre, reviewing *Cassation* 8.1.1985 *Sortimat Creuz*, at p.925.

[324] Which in essence, approached the 'characteristic performance' of the contract: Rauscher, 1984, at p.137; and Mourre, A. 'La compétence juridictionelle dans les litiges relatifs à la rupture d'un contrat de concession exclusive' (1992) *Gaz Pal*, Chron., 920, at p.925.

[325] The Jenard Report on this aspect has proved to be incorrect and highly ironic, [1979] OJ C59/1, at p.23: '[t]he court for the place of performance of the obligation will be useful in proceedings for the recovery of fees.'

[326] Gothot, P. et Holleaux, D. *La Convention de Bruxelles du 27 septembre 1968: compétence judiciaire et effets des jugements dans la CEE*, 1985.

[327] *Ets. A. de Bloos v Bouyer* (C-15/76) [1976] ECR 1497, at p.1509, para. 17.

[328] Penalty payments, contingent on breach of contract, although (usually) expressed in the contract itself, would therefore not be independent.

[329] ('its own self-generating elements, i.e. not proceeding, or not uniquely so, from the breach of contract').

[330] Gothot, P. et Holleaux, D., 1985, at p.33 para. 66; also Holleaux *Etablissements Carl Brehmer und Sohn c/ Baudoin* 23.1.1979 (1980) *JDI* 333, at p.337.

[331] I.e., according to Briggs, 1997, at p.102, 'a substituted, not an original obligation'.

[332] Esp. Arts 2 and 3 of the Belgian 'Loi relative à la résiliation unilatérale des concessions de vente exclusive à durée indéterminée', 27.7.1961, amended 13.4.1971, *Les Codes Larcier*, I, Ed. 1995, p.650 and

grantor of an exclusive sales/distribution contract to (Belgian) concessionaires for the premature ending of the contract for whatever reason.[333]

A refined approach is offered again by Gothot and Holleaux: they divide up obligations into (1) 'obligations originaires'[334] and 2(a) 'indemnités compensatoires non autonomes'[335] and 2(b) 'indemnités compensatoires autonomes'.[336] As we shall see, the French courts[337] have unfortunately not been consistent in the use of these categories, at times separating each one,[338] at others amalgamating[339] all three.[340]

Thus, it has been in the area of exclusive sales contracts that it can be argued that the greatest protectionist strains of (French and Belgian) national law have come to the fore. The problem has been mentioned before: the rulings in *de Bloos* and *Tessili*[341] have combined to disadvantage those exclusive sales agents claiming (independent) payment/compensatory obligations with a place of performance, *lege causae*, at the place of domicile of their principals, as debtors. The national reactions to *deBloos* and *Tessili* have therefore been threefold, the most worrying (for a uniform application of the Convention and avoidance of the *forum actoris*) coming from France.[342] There, as will be seen, the cases show a distinct departure from the ECJ jurisprudence, possible for their own protectionist[343] reasons.

Conversely, the German reaction to this 'independent payment' problem, regarding German commissionnaires, has been more or less conformist:

Cour de Cassation, Belgium 28.6.1979 *Audi-NSU Auto Union AG v Adelin Petit et Cie SA* [1980] E.C.C. 235.

[333] *Ibid.*

[334] (1980) *JDI* 889, at p.891; payment of purchase price, and (presumably) commission would fall within (1).

[335] *Ibid*; this would include damages for breach of contract.

[336] *Ibid*—those obligations, not dependent on an (antecedent) breach of contract, but implied by law, for example Article 3, para.1 of the Belgian law of 27 July 1961, where a sales concession is ended by the grantor (other than for 'faute grave') the payment of an 'indemnité' mandated.

[337] The Belgian courts have proved (somewhat) inconsistent in denying independent status to the obligations under Article 2 of Law 27 July 1961, instead subordinating it on occasion to the obligation to give notice (in Belgium).

[338] *Sté Filtertechniek Nederland BV c/ Johannes Hoff* 21.5.1997 (1998) *JDI* 133.

[339] Rauscher, 1984, at p.135 speaks of one obligation 'sucking up' all the others.

[340] *Ibid*, at p.96.

[341] Reviewed below, at pp.119–120.

[342] Confirmed by Storp, (1999) *RIW* 823, at p.824: [d]er französische Vertreter erhält somit alle Vorteile eines 'Heimatspiels' ('the French representative gains all the advantages of "playing at home"').

[343] Mourre supports this unfortunately stark view, (1992) *Gaz Pal*, Chron., 920, at p.926 and has no doubt that the *Cour de Cassation* has embarked on such a protectionist crusade: 'Il s'agit donc bien, pour protéger les concessionnaires français . . . de créer *à leur profit un véritable privilège de juridiction*'; early examples are *Dellinger c/ Société Leppak* 27.11.1979 (1979) *JDI* 333, at p.335 and *Etablissements Carl Brehmer und Sohn c/ Baudoin* 23.1.1979 (1979) *JDI* 333; it is too early to tell what effect *Leathertex Divisione* will have on these types of contracts, rejecting as it does a 'global', characteristic approach for the obligation in question, such as that beloved by the *Cour de Cassation* to 'respect the contract', below.

In der Entscheidung des OLG Frankfurht[344] wird nun klar, daß die deutschen Gerichte nicht bereit sind, der Tendenz französischer Gerichte zu einem einheitlichen VH-Vertragsgerichtsstand zu folgen.[345]

The Belgian courts have not gone as far as the French, but, in their own way, have ensured that their law of 27.7.1961 has not been deprived of its traditional (jurisdictionally) protectionist provision.[346] The way this has been done is in conformity with the *de Bloos* ruling, which leaves the determination of an obligation as either a 'dependent' or 'independent' obligation to the *lex causae*. The *Cour d'appel de Mons*, therefore classified the Articles 2 and 3 compensatory obligations as dependent on (breach of) the independent contractual obligation to give sufficient notice of the termination,[347] found to be performed in Belgium. The potential for accusations of protectionist leanings in the Belgian courts to their domestically-domiciled Belgian sales agents is evident from a decision of the *Tribunal de commerce de Liège*.[348] Rauscher,[349] in his comparative work, traces the Belgian jurisprudential developments both before and after *de Bloos*. He, too, remarks on the Belgian courts' so classifying Articles 2 and 3 of law 27 July 1961 as advantageously 'dependent' contractual obligations,[350] so as to avoid the unfortunate consequences of being forced to apply to the compensatory obligation expressed therein a place of performance, which, in Article 1247 Belgian *Code civil*, would invariably be outside Belgium. Of the above decisions he concludes:

> die belgischen Gerichte[351] auch . . . nicht den Schutz des belgischen VH . . . gefährdet sehen wollen.[352]

---

[344] 28.11.1979 (1980) *RIW* 585; also *OLG Düsseldorf* 24.4.1997 IPRspr. (1997) Nr. 145: 'Der Umstand, daß der Schwerpunkt der vertraglichen Beziehung im allgemeinen am Tätigkeitsort des Handelsvertreters [in Germany] . . . liegt, ist nicht ausreichend für die Annahme eines gemeinsamen Erfüllungsortes für die beidenseitigen Ansprüche aus dem Handelsvertretersverhältnis' ('the fact that the main focus of the contractual relationship lies, on the whole, at the place of the representative's activities [in Germany], is not sufficient to accept a general place of performance for the mutual obligations in the commercial agency contract').

[345] ('From the decision of the *OLG Frankfuhrt* it is now clear that the German courts are not ready to follow the French courts' tendency to create a unified jurisdiction for sales agents in contract') Rauscher, 1984, at p.117; the Austrian Federal Court has resisted the French temptation, too: *OGH* 20.1.1999 1999 *ÖJZ* 504, below.

[346] Article 4 of this Belgian provision creates a *forum actoris*, providing 'le concessionnaire lésé . . . peut en tout cas assigner le concédant, en Belgique, soit devant le juge *de son propre domicile . . .*', Les Codes Larcier, I, Ed. 1995, p.650; although a provision such as Article 4 is outlawed by Article 3 II Brussels Convention, it may be argued that a similar legacy is being preserved under Article 5(1).

[347] A similar approach to *Medway Packaging Ltd v Meurer Maschinen GmbH & Co. K.G.* [1990] 2 Lloyd's Rep. 112, CA.

[348] 1977 *JT* 710.

[349] Rauscher, 1984.

[350] Now *Leathertex Divisione Sintetici SpA v Bodetex BVBA* (C-420/97) [1999] ECR I-6747, AG Léger's opinion 16.3.1999 *not* adopted.

[351] A Luxembourg case—*Vesque c/ Badischer Winzerkeller E.G.* 1993–1995 *Pas. Lux.* 341—reviewed below, did not allow one out of eleven claims to be brought in Luxembourg due to the *de Bloos* analysis of independent payment obligations, at p.346.

[352] ('the Belgian courts also do not wish to see the protection of Belgian sales agents endangered'), Rauscher, 1984, at p.94.

Yet he is more critical[353] of what he believes to be the forthright and blatant protectionism displayed, after a conforming start, by the French *Cour de Cassation.*[354] His survey unfortunately finishes in 1984, but there are numerous French decisions concerning exclusive distribution/sales contracts thereafter—even post-dating *Hassan Shenavai v Klaus Kreischer*[355]—which decided the question of having more than one 'obligation' allegedly breached forming the basis of a claim.

It behoves this treatment to examine, in the next section, whether the trend identified by Rauscher, and engendered so early after *De Bloos*, has continued. It will also be seen in this treatment that the (French) rebellion[356] against the ECJ's jurisprudence has now spread beyond these specialist contracts to sale of goods contracts[357] in general.

1.2.1(i)   The French decisions on the 'obligation in question'

The French courts' (perceived) protectionist classification of 'the obligation in question'[358] has proved to be as subtle as adaptable: regarding exclusive sales contracts *sui generis*, French plaintiffs have either been vague in their claims, or very specific: on the one hand, French sales agents have merely alleged a breach, in the vaguest terms,[359] of the concession contractus; on the other,[360] they have claimed damages and compensation for breach of very specific[361] obligations. The French courts have been equal to this also.

The impression that a protectionist, 'homeward' interpretation of concession contracts is operating under Article 5(1) stems[362] from an early, yet post-*de Bloos*, decision of the *Cour de Cassation, Etablissements Carl Brehmer und Sohn c/ Baudoin.*[363] The French exclusive agent of the German defendant's products

---

[353] Also Mourre, A. 'La compétence juridictionelle dans les litiges relatifs à la rupture d'un contrat de concession exclusive' (1992) *Gaz Pal*, Chron., 920, at pp.925–26.

[354] Rauscher, 1984, at p.99, the decision which he feels marks the protectionist turning-point. In fact, Mourre, *ibid*, at p.924, traces the rebellion against *de Bloos* to an earlier decision of the *Cour d'appel de Paris*, 29.9.1978, unreported.

[355] (C-266/85) [1987] ECR 239, reviewed above at p.76.

[356] Identified by Droz, G. 'Delendum est forum contractus? (vingt ans après les arrêts *de Bloos* et *Tessili* interprétant l'article 5.1 de la Convention de Bruxelles du 27 septembre 1968' (1997) *Dalloz*, Chron., 351.

[357] The opposition to the *de Bloos* and *Tessili* jurisprudence, despite recent confirmation in *Custom Made Commercial Ltd v Stawa Metallbau GmbH* (C-288/92) [1994] ECR I-2913, comes from *Sté Comptoir commercial d'Orient c/ Société Medtrafina* 11.3.1997 1998 *JDI* 129, [1999] I.L.Pr. 336; and *Groupe Concorde et autres c/ Capitaine du Suhadiwarno Panjan et autres* 9.12.1997 1998 *Rev crit* 117, (C-440/97) [1999] ECR I-6307—below sections 1.3.9(i) and 1.3.10.

[358] The cynical may also find traces of it in the methodology employed to find the 'principal' obligation, below.

[359] Therefore to respect the contract's exclusivity.

[360] Which has happened in the most recent cases.

[361] Thereby forcing the French courts into the formulaic examination of independent obligation and place of performance.

[362] Audit, (1980) *Dalloz*, somm., 329, at p.330 calls it: 'une mise à l'écart aussi ouverte'.

[363] *Etablissements Carl Brehmer und Sohn c/ Baudoin* 23.1.1979 (1979) JDI 33.

claimed damages for breach of contract for the defendant's alleged supplying of a third party. In a non-specific claim such as this, the court approved[364] the lower courts for having considered the obligation in question to be 'beaucoup plus générale—de «respecter le contrat de concession»[365]'.[366] The obligation, if such it was, to 'respect the contract',[367] is invariably to be performed at the domicile of the (French) plaintiff concessionaire. The same formula, not following the *De Bloos* route, but of 'respecting the contract', was found in *Dellinger c/ Société Leppak.*[368]

Similarly, such 'generalisation' of exclusive distributorship contracts was continued by two *Cour d'appel de Paris* decisions: *Société Aluminium Werke Wutoschingen c/ Société A.P. Landowski Samis*[369] and *Sociétés Rotaprint Export Ehmer et Rotaprint c/ Société Guyot Fourchault.*[370] In the first there was, again, a claim by the French concessionaire and again:

> l'obligation litigieuse servant de base à la demande [était] celle du concédant de respecter le contrat [371] [372]

In the second, the French plaintiff additionally sought payment of commission[373] overdue. The Paris court permitted itself to become seised of both the specific and the general claim.

The break with *de Bloos* was re-inforced in *Sortimat Creuz c/ Monde Machines*,[374] which moved away from the obligation serving as the basis of the proceedings[375] to the characteristic obligation of the contract, finding that:

---

[364] (1980) *Dalloz*, somm., p.330.

[365] ('to respect the contract of concession'); in *Cour de Cassation* 15.5.2001 *SA Optelec c/ Sté Midtronics Bv* (2001) *JCP*, II, 10634, the court did not censure that part of the appeal court's decision finding the 'obligation in question' to be the Dutch defendant's 'characteristic obligation' to respect the exclusive distributorship contract, at pp.2213–14, obs. Raynard.

[366] *Ibid;* also *USF Ltd (t/a USF Memcor) v Aqua Technology Hanson NV/SA* [2001] 1 All ER (Comm) 856 (Aikens J); even though the obligation sued on under Art.5(1) in *Kenburn Waste Management Ltd v Bergman*, 11.5.2001, Ch.D., 30.1.2001, CA was the defendant's negative obligations in a 'contract of compromise' *not to communicate* with the (retail) clients of the claimant over alleged breaches of patents, this case would not, it is submitted, run counter to the ECJ judgment in *S.A. Besix N.V. v WABAG Wasserreinigungsbau Alfred Kretzschmar GmbH* (C-256/00), 19.2.2002—that Art.5(1) must designate only *one single place* of performance.

[367] Also Rauscher (1984) at pp.100–01.

[368] 27.11.1979 (1979) *JDI* 333; Audit, critical of the lack of reference to the law of the place of performance, as *Tessili* decided, observes that: '[o]n glissait ainsi de l'obligation litigieuse à *l'obligation principale* du contrat', (1979) *JDI* 333, at p.335.

[369] 13.11.1980 (1981) *JDI* 849.

[370] 13.2.1981 (1981) *JDI* 849.

[371] ('the obligation in question [was] that of the grantor to respect the contract').

[372] *Ibid*, at p.849; also *Cour de Cassation* 15.5.2001 *SA Optelec c/ Sté Midtronics Bv* (2001) *JCP*, II, 10634.

[373] *Quaere*, whether this obligation should have been regarded as an 'indemnités compensatoires autonomes', with its place of performance, in Article 1247 CC, outside France.

[374] 8.1.1985 *Bull.Cass* 1985.8, reviewed by Mourre, (1992) *Gaz Pal*, Chron., 920, at p.925.

[375] And thus from the French wording of Article 5(1) itself, amended in this form.

l'obligation caracteristique était celle incombant au concédant allemand de respecter la clause d'exclusivité.[376] [377]

Mourre tries to explain away the departure from the ECJ's jurisprudence, by the *Cour de Cassation*'s over-eager acceptance of concepts used in national procedural law, especially Article 46(2)[378] *Nouveau Code de Procédure Civile*, and national case law. Yet there is no avoiding the protectionist effect and motive in this ruling—its creation of a *forum actoris*[379] for French sales agents, and, of course, the disregarding of the ECJ's jurisprudence:

> [e]n définissant l'obligation servant de base à la demande non plus comme l'obligation litigieuse mais comme *l'obligation caractéristique*[380] du contrat.[381] [382]

Another method employed is the 'dwarfing' of claims by one 'independent' obligation. This is amply demonstrated by *Soc K.D. Köln Düsseldorfer Deutsche Rheinschiffahrt c/ Soc. Transports et Voyages.*[383] The German principal, it was claimed, had abusively terminated the (ticket-vending) agency contract with its French ticket agent. Here the *Cour de Cassation* expressly approved[384] the lower court for having considered the 'principal' obligation to be that 'de respecter un mandat'. Since this contract was concerned with France, its place of performance was there, more specifically in Paris, at the plaintiff's place of business. The interest of the case is that highlighted in the criticism by Gaudemet-Tallon. The court simply did not differentiate the plaintiff's individual claims, but merely concentrated on the contract *in toto*,

---

[376] ('the *characteristic obligation* was that resting on the German grantor to respect the exclusivity clause').
[377] *Bull.Cass* 1985.8, reviewed in (1992) *Gaz. Pal.*, Chron., 920; *Cour de Cassation* 15.5.2001 *SA Optelec c/ Sté Midtronics Bv* (2001) *JCP*, II, 10634.
[378] Which speaks of jurisdiction at the 'lieu de l'exécution de la prestation de service'('place of performance of the obligation to perform'); *Nouveau Code de Procedure Civile*, Dalloz, 93ème éd, 2001, at p.57 onwards; also now the reform of Article 5(1) by Article 5(1)(b) of the Brussels I Regulation, below and the inspiration it has drawn from Art.46 NCPC: Kropholler, 2002, p.137, para. 31.
[379] Mourre, (1992) *Gaz Pal*, Chron., 920, who is in no doubt of the protectionist motives, at p.926: '[o]n fait rentrer par la fenêtre l'Article 14 du Code civil que la Convention avait fait sortir par la porte.'('it is letting Article 14 Cc in by the back door that the Convention had forced out by the front').
[380] Support for such a finding now coming from AG Léger's opinion in *Leathertex Divisione Sintetici* (C-420/97), 16.3.1999, but this approach was *not* adopted by the ECJ's judgment [1999] ECR I-6747.
[381] ('by no longer defining the obligation forming the basis of the plaintiff's case as the obligation in question but as the characteristic obligation of the contract').
[382] (1992) *Gaz Pal*, Chron., 920; the ECJ in *Leathertex Divisione*, [1999] ECR I-6747, at pp.6788–9, para. 26, noted this tendency to find a 'characteristic performance' in concession contracts, but rejected their assimilation with contracts of employment, at p.6791, paras. 36–37; cf *Cour de Cassation* 15.5.2001 *SA Optelec c/ Sté Midtronics Bv* (2001) *JCP*, II, 10634, however.
[383] 25.1.1984 (1985) *Rev crit* 126.
[384] *Ibid*, at p.127.

[e]n effet, «l'obligation de respecter le contrat»[385] peut être entendue soit comme *englobant* toutes les obligations nées du contrat . . . l'obligation générale en cause dans tous les litiges portant sur l'exécution du contrat . . .[386] [387]

As has been mentioned earlier, such a methodology for defining the obligation necessarily subordinates all other claims—even if strictly 'independent contractual obligations' in their own right—to that of 'respecting the contract', to be performed in France.[388] The protection of domestic plaintiffs in the *forum actoris* is thereby assured. General claims[389] for abusive breach of contract can be advanced, safe in the knowledge that no other obligation that might possibly have a non-domestic place of performance will be considered: *Pierre c/ Société de droit italien Vetrolan.*[390]

A more recent, and by now, classic statement of the French position comes from the *Cour de Cassation* in *Société Gotz GmbH c/ Société Noge.*[391] The dispute concerned a disagreement between a French exclusive distributor and its German supplier. The French company sued 'en résiliation du contrat'. Having by-passed a German place of delivery and payment clause,[392] the only thing left for the court to declare was that

les obligations relevant du contrat d'exclusivité ne pouvaient être executées qu'en France.[393] [394]

In France it is safe to say that a similar position has been reached with regard to a concession contract's 'obligation in question' as with contracts of employment:[395] 'l'obligation principale découlant du contrat de concession. . ., à savoir l'exclusivité territoriale.'[396] [397]

---

[385] This is quite different from the individual obligations embedded in the contract, and presented in the plaintiff's claim—the only ones that ought to be relevant for Article 5(1): *Fisher and others v Unione Italiana de Riassicurazione SPA* [1998] CLC 682; *quaere Cour de Cassation* 15.5.2001 *SA Optelec c/ Sté Midtronics Bv* (2001) *JCP*, II, 10634.

[386] ('in effect the obligation to respect the contract can be understood as enveloping all the obligations under the contract . . . the principal obligation in question in all claims concerning the performance of the contract').

[387] (1985) *Rev crit* 126, at p.129; admittedly, though, the solutions advocated by the ECJ's jurisprudence leads to a fragmentation of payment obligations from the same contract, advanced in the same proceedings: *Leathertex Divisione Sintetici SpA v Bodetex BVBA* (C-420/97) [1999] ECR I-6747.

[388] The Belgian court in *Tribunal de commerce de Bruxelles*, 29.5.1990, *M.Filipson c/ Gebr.Herberg K.G.*, (1992) *Rev dr comm. belge* 907, at p.911 has come to the same view: 'l'obligation qui était à respecter était le contrat d'agence . . . [qui] s'exécutait sur le territoire belge.'('the obligation to be performed was the agency contract, that was performed on Belgian territory').

[389] In addition, *Gilbert Mayer c/ Société Charles Wednesbury Limited* 13.9.1995 (1997) *JDI* 170, at p.172.

[390] 22.5.1991 (1992) *Dalloz*, somm., 164, at p.165 (Audit).

[391] 27.2.1996 (1996) *Rev crit* 736.

[392] Found to apply to the underlying sales contracts.

[393] ('the obligation from the contract of exclusivity could only be performed in France').

[394] *Société Gotz GmbH c/ Société Noge* 27.2.1996 (1996) *Rev crit* 736, at p.741, (Gaudemet-Tallon).

[395] The former a product of French jurisprudence, the latter from *Roger Ivenel v Helmut Schwab* (C-133/81) [1982] ECR 1891 and post-San Sebastian Amendments [1989] OJ L285/1, Article 4. Also Rauscher, 1984, at p.137: 'nicht mehr die streitige Pflicht, sondern die vertragsprägende . . .'('no longer the obligation in question, but the characteristic one . . .').

[396] ('principal obligation ensuing from the concession contract . . . viz. the territorial exclusivity').

[397] (1996) *Rev crit* 736, at p.741.

It would be expected that a plaintiff/claimant who advances very specifically enumerated claims[398] would not benefit from this over-indulgent interpretation. In *Gilbert Mayer c/ Société Charles Wednesbury Limited*,[399] the French exclusive agent put in three specific claims:[400] for outstanding commission, and damages both for breach of the agency contract, and for loss of reputation and 'résistance abusive'. Taking as the principal obligation 'celle du mandant de livrer les marchandises à son représantant'[401] [402] the *Cour d'appel de Paris* recognised its competence over all three claims.

Another case to confirm this 'englobing' trend is *Sté Stoppani SPA c/ Sté Stoppani France*.[403] A general claim was advanced for breach of an exclusive distribution contract. The *Cour de Cassation* censured the lower court for not having used the *Tessili* formula for determining the place of performance,[404] yet said nothing about the lower court's amalgamation of two separate claims into one 'obligation in question', this being:

> à la fois celle d'approvisionner . . . le distributeur en produits *et* de respecter l'exclusivité de distribution[405] [406]

A later case to consider the issue is the *Cour d'appel de Paris* in *Printed Forms Equipment Limited c/ Soc. Materiel Auxiliaire d'Informatique 'MAI'*,[407] where 'l'obligation à prendre en considération est celle qui découle du contrat à la charge du concédant.'[408] [409]

Concession contracts, in whatever form, have been subjected to an objectively determined, 'global' obligation to respect the contract. *De Bloos*, which shows us that it is the plaintiff's claims,[410] not the obligations of the contract generally,

---

[398] *Gilbert Mayer c/ Société Charles Wednesbury Limited* 13.9.1995 1997 *JDI* 170; *Sté Stoppani SPA c/ Sté Stoppani France* 18.3.1997 1998 *JDI* 129; *Sté Filtertechniek Nederland BV c/ Johannes Hoff* 21.5.1997 (1998) *JDI* 133.

[399] 13.9.1995 (1997) *JDI* 170.

[400] Below, at pp.93–94.

[401] ('that of the principal to deliver products to his representative').

[402] (1997) *JDI* 170, at p.172, i.e. an objective, global, (characteristic) assessment, rather than on the basis of the pleaded case.

[403] 18.3.1997 (1998) *JDI* 129.

[404] This would have led to France in any event, below, next section on the 'place of performance'.

[405] ('*both* to supply the distributor with products *and* to respect the exclusivity of distribution').

[406] At p.130; the ECJ in *Leathertex Divisione v Bodetex* [1999] ECR I-6747, has recently shown that a strict 'individualisation' of obligations is mandated under Article 5(1), below.

[407] Unreported, Lexis, 14.10.1998.

[408] ('obligation to be taken into account is the one which stems from the contract for which the grantor is responsible').

[409] Again, inevitably, therefore, the obligation to respect the concession contract; in *Cour de Cassation* 8.2.2000 *Figot c/ Sté Leithauser GmbH and Co* (2000) *JCP*, IV, 1544 at p.606, (2000) *Rev Crit* 473, (2001) *JDI* 133, [2001] I.L.Pr. 28, the *Cour de Cassation* has continued this consistent line of jurisprudence in the case of a French commercial agent: 'l'obligation qui sert de base à la demande . . . est la sanction du contrat d'agence . . .'('the obligation in question . . . is the outcome of the agency contract').

[410] The generality of claim merely for breach of (the concession) contract no doubt has, in part, been responsible for this; *contra*, *Fisher and others v Unione Italiana de Riassicurazione SPA* [1998] CLC 682, at p.687 (Colman J): 'the plaintiff has formulated his claim for relief in the proceedings on the

that are the concern of Article 5(1), seems to have been overlooked. As Rauscher had pointed out earlier, the vague invocation of a respect for the contract is unsatisfactory within the elements of Article 5(1):

> Der Grundsatz 'pacta sunt servanda' ist weder im französischen noch im deutschen Recht eine konkret klagbare Vertragspflicht . . .[411]

Article 5(1) demands specificity of claims and corresponding 'obligations'. The French over-generalisation has led to a *forum actoris*:

> Da die 'obligation de respecter le contrat' die einzige ausschlaggebende Pflicht ist, wird immer der Erfüllungsortgerichtsstand beim VH begründet.[412]

The French courts have tried, in the area of commercial sales/agency contracts, to ensure as far as possible that a French *forum actoris* is available to French commercial agents by classifying the 'obligation' as one approaching a 'characteristic' one—to respect the contract. They have, by judicial activism, equated these agency contracts to contracts of employment.[413] Only the ECJ and the Convention's drafters can create such a 'protective' jurisdiction.[414]

1.2.2   Ascertaining the 'principal' obligation[415]

It is necessary to ascertain a principal obligation for the simple expedient of avoiding the founding of jurisdiction under Article 5(1) through any number of pleaded claims whatever, and howsoever trivial they may be *inter se*.

As the independence or otherwise of the obligation is to be determined[416] by the *lex causae*, it would seem logical[417] that the principal obligation among the plaintiff/claimant's claims should be determined likewise. The cases that have considered the question in any detail[418] have made no explicit

---

grounds of the performance or non-performance of that obligation [of the defendant to retain part of the risk].'

[411] ('the principle of *pacta sunt servanda* does not in itself form a concrete cause of action in contract either in French or German law'), Rauscher, 1984, at p.131; although still the prevalent view in France: *Cassation* 15.5.2001 *SA Optelec c/ Sté Midtronics Bv* (2001) *JCP*, II, 10634.

[412] ('Since the "obligation de respecter le contrat" is the only principal duty, jurisdiction at the place of performance is always founded with the commercial agent'), *ibid*, at p.135.

[413] Using terminology, and no doubt reasoning, similar to *Roger Ivenel v Helmut Schwab* (C-133/81) [1982] ECR 1891; also following n.414.

[414] The ECJ has recently refused to do so in commercial agency contracts in *Leathertex Divisione Sintetici SpA v Bodetex BVBA* (C-420/97) [1999] ECR I-6747, at p.6791, paras. 36–37.

[415] Donzallaz, 1998, Vol III, at p.197, para. 4647.

[416] *Ets. A. de Bloos v Bouyer* (C-15/76) [1976] ECR 1497, at p.1509, para. 17.

[417] *Contra* Kropholler, 1998, at p.107, para. 16, who thinks autonomously; unless this issue is the sole preserve of national procedural law—*Kongress Agentur Hagen GmbH v Zeehaghe BV* (C-365/88) [1990] ECR I-1845.

[418] English: *Union Transport Plc v Continental Lines S.A. and Conti Lines S.A.* affm'd [1992] 1 Lloyd's Rep. 229, HL, applied in *Ocarina Marine Ltd and others v Marcard Stein & Co.* [1994] 2 Lloyd's Rep. 524, QBD (Rix J); *Medway Packaging Ltd v Meurer Maschinen GmbH & Co. K.G.* [1990] 2 Lloyd's Rep.

mention[419] of this or any methodology. The English cases show a certain divergence[420] from those French cases to have raised the point. The former have preferred a test of relative importance among the claims advanced, while the latter a more subjective approach of comparative value or importance to the plaintiff/claimant.

1.2.2(i)   English cases on the 'principal' obligation[421]

In *Union Transport Plc v Continental Lines S.A. and Conti Lines S.A.*,[422] the plaintiff based its claim on the defendants' alleged failure to perform two obligations under a charterparty: the second of which, it was found, inevitably[423] followed on from breach of the first. The plaintiffs sued the Belgian shipowners under Article 5(1) in London. The defendants' obligations were to nominate a vessel,[424] and to provide the vessel at the loading port.[425] Both reported decisions[426] in the case considered that the principal obligation from among the two claimed was that of nominating the vessel, to be performed in London.[427] Evans J, at first instance, had considered, in the case of sequential obligations, the principal obligation to be the one that initially triggers the others:

the process could not begin[428] until the vessel was nominated.[429]

112, CA; *Source Ltd v T.U.V. Rheinland Holding A.G. and others* [1998] QB 54, CA, *Raiffeisen Zentralbank Österreich Aktiengesellschaft v National Bank of Greece S.A.* [1999] 1 Lloyd's Rep. 408, *The 'Sea Maas'* [1999] 2 Lloyd's Rep. 281 (Rix J) *Barry and another v Bradshaw and others* [2000] CLC 455, CA; French: *Sté Filtertechniek Nederland BV c/ Johannes Hoff* 21.5.1997 (1998) *JDI* 133; *Gilbert Mayer c/ Société Charles Wednesbury Limited* 13.9.1995 (1997) *JDI* 170.

[419] It was not obvious from the report of *OGH* 20.1.1999 1999 *ÖJZ* 504, at p.506 why the commission claim in that case was the principal obligation. We can only surmise that its value caused its ascendancy.

[420] But Lord Goff in *Union Transport Plc v Continental Lines S.A. and Conti Lines S.A.* [1992] 1 Lloyd's Rep. 229, at p.234.

[421] Note the UK Government's submissions in the *Leathertex Divisione Sintetici* [1999] ECR I-6747 reference, where, despite the order for reference, the Government sought to eke out a 'principal' obligation, at p.6787, para. 20.

[422] [1991] 2 Lloyd's Rep. 48, CA, affm'd [1992] 1 Lloyd's Rep. 229, HL.

[423] It may be argued therefore, that the case is (limited) authority on its facts for determining the principal obligation among a number of *sequential* obligations pleaded.

[424] To be performed in London; had the vessel already been nominated, the provision of the vessel would have been the 'obligation in question' (as the sole remaining one).

[425] To have been performed in Florida, USA.

[426] Evans J, at first instance, had found likewise.

[427] Perhaps this interpretation lends weight to the 'homeward trend' in jurisdiction cases; but this may be attempting to extract too much from the decisions.

[428] In the House of Lords, accidents of timing were not decisive for Lord Goff: [1992] 1 Lloyd's Rep. 229, at p.234.

[429] [1991] 2 Lloyd's Rep. 48, at p.51, quoted by Lloyd LJ in CA; it would seem on this analysis that any obligation—such as a *Johnson v Taylor Bros.* [1920] A.C. 144 obligation—following on as an inevitable consequence of breach of an earlier—will not be a 'principal obligation'.

Lloyd LJ preferred[430] a classification that gave the plaintiff/claimant a 'complete cause of action':[431]

> The very fact that a *complete cause of action* could have been based on the failure to nominate ... goes a long way to show that the failure to nominate was the principal obligation.[432]

In the House of Lords, Lord Goff agreed *verbatim* with the Court of Appeal, but did add a curiously subjective[433] gloss, as an element of his findings:

> the failure to nominate was *regarded by the respondents* as the principal ground of complaint, the failure to provide a vessel being added, it appears, because of some point which might be taken by the appellants.[434]

Union Transport Plc is instructive in the area of claims which are, in a sense, sequentially linked as a matter of causation. Outside this relatively limited sphere, it is of little help, unless Lord Goff's rather subjective 'principal ground for complaint' analysis should somehow[435] be decisive.

A second English case, pre-dating *Union Transport Plc*, which considered the 'principal obligation' issue is *Medway Packaging Ltd v Meurer Maschinen GmbH & Co. K.G.*[436] The case concerned what the plaintiff considered, and accepted as, a repudiatory breach of an exclusive distributorship contract by a German supplier. The plaintiff thus claimed damages for breach of two obligations: firstly, for failure to give reasonable notice of the determination; and secondly, (by appointing another English distributor) breach of the defendant's obligation to respect the contract's exclusivity. Fox LJ held that the failure to give reasonable notice was the principal obligation, 'because it is the giving of proper notice which brings the whole contract to an end.'[437]

Can this be propounded as a general test: the principal obligation being one which can (legitimately) end a (distributorship) contract? It may clearly be unworkable to formulate such a general definition of a principal obligation for each and every contract. Such obligations only[438] take on comparative importance

---

[430] [1991] 2 Lloyd's Rep. 48, at p.50.

[431] This supports the view that the case can only be taken as authority for sequential obligations; each unrelated, yet independent claim may represent a 'complete cause of action'.

[432] [1991] 2 Lloyd's Rep. 48, at p.51.

[433] For an objective/subjective ascertaining of the principal obligation see the French section below at pp.93–94, and comment by Huet, in *Sté Filtertechniek Nederland BV c/ Johannes Hoff* 21.5.1997 (1998) *JDI* 133, at p.134.

[434] [1992] 1 Lloyd's Rep. 229, at p.234, HL.

[435] This ground was followed by Rix J in *Ocarina Marine Ltd and others v Marcard Stein & Co.* [1994] 2 Lloyd's Rep. 524, at p.532; the court was to find the 'real ground for complaint'.

[436] [1990] 2 Lloyd's Rep. 112, CA.

[437] *Ibid*, at p.116; on this analysis had the recent case of *Bodetex Divisione* come before the English courts, it is likely that failure to pay commission—as an event considered by the plaintiff/claimant as terminating the contract—would have been regarded as the principal obligation.

[438] An important, unresolved issue at Community level is whether the national court is entitled to look behind the veil, as it were, of the plaintiff's claim(s) to the contract and its other obligations generally.

vis-à-vis each other in the plaintiff/claimant's claim, not the contract as a whole.[439] What, among a number of claims, may seem a principal ground for complaint in a statement of claim/claim form may diminish in stature when viewed[440] among the contractual obligations globally.[441]

Again, the ascertainment of the 'principal', among the numerous, obligations forming the basis of an English plaintiff re-insurer's claim, (*inter alia*, for a negative declaration of liability to indemnify a Greek reassured), proved vital for whether or not the English courts had jurisdiction under Article 5(1) in *AIG Group (UK) Ltd v The Ethniki*.[442] The treaty of reinsurance contained a 72 hour notification of loss clause, whereby the re-assured's compliance with this obligation was stated to be a condition precedent to any liability of the re-insurers. On the basis of non-compliance with this clause in the events of the case, the re-insurers sought their negative declaration of liability. Additionally,[443] and in the alternative, the plaintiffs sought damages for breach of an implied term[444] that the re-assured would take all necessary steps fairly and carefully to ascertain its loss. Both parties conceded that the former notification obligation was to be performed in London, while the latter was to be performed in Greece.

At first instance, Colman J, while not referring explicitly to *Union Transport Plc*, held, correctly, that compliance with the 72 hour notification clause was the 'principal' obligation under Article 5(1), since it 'operated as a complete bar to a claim':[445]

> once the 72 hours had elapsed without notice, it was not open to the defendant validly to claim under the reassurance, no matter whether they performed . . . the implied ascertainment of loss obligation.[446]

The judge's reasoning as to the principal obligation in *The Ethniki* was upheld on appeal.[447] Evans LJ, contrary to the arguments of counsel, did not believe the trial judge had picked out the breach of the notification clause as the principal obligation—upon which the plaintiff's claim for a negative declaration was

---

[439] But *Source Ltd v T.U.V. Rheinland Holding A.G. and others* [1998] QB 54, CA.

[440] *Quaere*, whether it is legitimate to consider all contractual obligations; *ibid.*

[441] The only danger (of fragmentation after *Leathertex v Bodetex*) that arises is that a court might be tempted first to where the various obligations are to be performed and then earmark the one to be performed in the forum as the principal one. This tendency should be resisted: *Gilbert Mayer c/ Société Charles Wednesbury Limited* 13.9.1995 (1997) *JDI* 170, at p.171, where the court, using a subjective/objective test, could thus subordinate a payment obligation, clearly to be performed outside the forum (in England, Article 1247 *Code civil*) to those to be performed in France.

[442] [1998] 4 All ER 301, QBD (Colman J) affm'd [2000] All ER (Comm) 65, CA, (Evans LJ).

[443] [1998] 4 All ER 301, at p.306.

[444] That an implied term can be a (principal) obligation under Article 5(1), *Raiffeisen Zentralbank Österreich Aktiengesellschaft v National Bank of Greece S.A.* [1999] 1 Lloyd's Rep. 408, QBD (Tuckey J).

[445] [1998] 4 All ER 301, at p.307; in the words of *Union Transport Plc*, as 'a complete cause of action'; or, as here, a prospective, 'complete defence' (to any potential payment action or counterclaim before the English court).

[446] *Ibid.*

[447] [2000] All ER (Comm) 65, CA (Evans LJ) (Thorpe LJ and Jonathan Parker J concurring).

based—because either it was 'primary', i.e. first in time, nor due to its prominent position in the pleaded points of claim; instead, he held, as had Colman J, that breach of the 72 hours notification clause, being a condition precedent to further liability, was 'the real ground of complaint'.[448] Of interest too, in the case—and in contrast to claims-drafting evidenced in the French decisions—is Evans LJ's attitude to whether a plaintiff/claimant can so arrange his pleadings as to influence, in some way, the court's choice of the principal obligation. He stated that the court's identifying task was an objective one:

> the plaintiff cannot camouflage the principal obligation by relegating it to a subordinate role by the way he chooses to express his claim. The court's decision does not rest in the plaintiff's hands.[449]

In words reminiscent of *Union Transport Plc*,[450] the English courts will regard any obligation as the 'principal' obligation if it can be shown that '[b]reaches of [a particular clause, such as prior notification] are deployed as the basis for the primary relief sought'[451] in the pleadings. The primary relief sought in *The Ethniki* was a negative declaration. The other claims were found to have been advanced merely for completeness, on the alternative footing that the re-insurers primary contentions had failed.

The ability to identify the obligation and/or principal obligation in question proved to be crucial to the acceptance or dismissal of jurisdiction in another decision of the Court of Appeal in *Viskase Ltd and another v Paul Kiefel GmbH*.[452] Here English claimants, plastics packaging companies, sued German defendant manufacturers, for breach of contract in regard to the latter's supply to the claimants of eight polystyrene thermoforming machines, allegedly unfit for commercial production purposes. The Court was divided as to whether the English court had jurisdiction under Article 5(1) in regard to an express term,[453] but unanimous as regards an implied term, that the machines would be reasonably fit for their intended purpose.

Evans LJ, of the minority on the following Article 5(1) point, saw that the plaintiff's case, as pleaded, concerned two 'obligation[s] in question': (1) 'an *express* undertaking by the defendant . . . that machines manufactured . . . to the specification which was later incorporated in the contracts, would achieve certain results. . .'[454] and (2) an implied term under s.14(3) of the Sale of Goods Act 1979. He thought that the express undertaking was 'the principal obligation',[455] which

---

[448] [2000] All ER (Comm) 65, CA (Evans LJ) (Thorpe LJ and Jonathan Parker J concurring), at p.73.
[449] *Ibid*, at p.72.
[450] '[t]he principal ground of complaint' at [1992] 1 Lloyd's Rep. 229, p.234, (Lord Goff).
[451] *AIG Group (UK) Ltd and others v The Ethniki* [1998] 4 All ER 301, at p.308 (Colman J).
[452] [1999] 1 WLR 1305.
[453] Evans LJ found an express term, while the majority (Morritt and Chadwick LJJ) could find no such term.
[454] [1999] 1 WLR 1305, at p.1314.
[455] *Ibid*, at p.1314—it may not be authority for the proposition that an express undertaking will always 'trump' an implied term to become a 'principal obligation'.

could only have been performed at the plaintiff's premises. Had he believed, however, that the second obligation—the implied term as to reasonable fitness—had been the 'sole or principal obligation',[456] he would have agreed with Chadwick LJ's analysis, of the majority, as to its place of performance (in Germany).

Unfortunately for the plaintiff, Chadwick LJ, for his part, could find no express obligation, nothing 'in the contractual documentation [revealing] any expressed warranty as to fitness for purpose'.[457] On this ground, therefore, the whole court was unanimous, that an implied term as to fitness for purpose was represented by 'an obligation which was to be performed, once and for all,[458] at the time of delivery',[459] ex works,[460] in Germany. The case illustrates that the English court did not have jurisdiction due to the choice of 'the [principal] obligation in question'.

In *Raiffeisen Zentralbank Österreich Aktiengesellschaft v National Bank of Greece S.A.*,[461] as already seen, an implied term was held to be the principal obligation. This term was to the effect that the defendant Greek bank would re-imburse any sums, under an inter-bank letter in a series of loan transactions, that the defendants had prematurely[462] released to the borrowers. It was found to be the principal obligation, as it was 'a payment obligation which gave [the plaintiffs] some security.'[463]

The principal obligation among a number of obligations of an accountant and tax adviser in his retainer towards his clients, as plaintiffs, was the subject of the CA decision in *Barry and another v Bradshaw and others*.[464] Here the plaintiffs' pleaded case was crucial, leading to the conclusion that the principal obligation was the alleged failure of the defendant, one Young, domiciled in Ireland 'to

---

[456] *Ibid*, at p.1315, there was no discussion as to the methodology used by his Lordship as to how he came to the principal obligation conclusion—unless an *express* term overrides one implied by law.

[457] *Ibid*, at p.1320.

[458] Not a continuing warranty for jurisdictional purposes—'a subsequent failure of the machine . . . is evidence of the antecedent breach . . .', at p.1321; *Rye Valley Foods Ltd v Fisher Frozen Foods Ltd*, 10.5.2000, Irish HC (O'Sullivan J): 'the alleged *manifestation of defects* in the goods supplied . . . which became apparent [in Ireland] . . . does not constitute . . . a breach of contract . . . occurring in [Ireland] . . . delivery was to occur in England'; cf where the defendant, in addition, undertakes to install machines at claimant's premises: *Corte di Cassazione* 10.3.2000 *Krauss Maffei Verfahrenstechnik GmbH contro Soc. Bristol Myers Squibb* 2000 *Il Foro Italiano* 2226, (2001) *RIW* 308, (2001) *RIW* 536.

[459] [1999] 1 WLR 1305, at p.1323; except in regards to one machine which was to be delivered in Birmingham; consistent with this is *Cour de Cassation* 8.2.2000 *SA LM Plast c/ SARL Fahr Bucher France* (2000) *JCP*, IV, 1545, (2001) *JDI* 133, [2001] I.L.Pr. 31, (2001) *Rev crit* 151.

[460] Contrast *MBM Fabri-Clad Limited v Eisen-und-Huttenwerke Thale AG* [2000] CLC 373, CA, at p.378, (Pill LJ), where the obligation to supply by delivery—this time not ex works—was held to be in England; also *Ferguson Shipbuilders Ltd v Voith Hydro GmbH & Co.* (2000) *SLT* 229, where delivery by the German defendant of a propeller system for installation into tugs was in the view of the Court of Session to be performed in Glasgow; *Cour de Cassation* 26.6.2001 *Anton Huber GmbH & Co c/ Soc. Polyspace*, (2001) *JCP*, IV, 2554, *Cour de Cassation* 26.6.2001 *Sté Ogosa destribuciones c/ SA Madrange* (2001) *JCP*, IV, 2556.

[461] [1999] 1 Lloyd's Rep. 408.

[462] I.e. at points in time when, and in conditions under which, they were not contractually bound to do so.

[463] [1999] 1 Lloyd's Rep. 408, at p.411.

[464] [2000] CLC 455.

represent, conduct and settle the tax affairs of the [plaintiffs]',[465] which was to be performed in England as the place where, *inter alia*, the Inland Revenue were situated.

Source Ltd v T.U.V. Rheinland Holding A.G. and others[466] raises an important issue[467] and a grave concern. An English importer engaged the defendant German companies to inspect goods manufactured in the Far East, and to issue certificates of quality, in order to release payment under a letter of credit. This the defendants did. The goods proved to be defective, and the plaintiffs commenced an action, *inter alia*, in contract,[468] alleging 'a breach of a contractual obligation to exercise reasonable skill and care in presenting[469] reports to the plaintiffs'.[470] Although the Court of Appeal was anxious to avoid drafting chicanery, the case does for all that raise two issues of concern for this analysis: firstly, the slightly confused wording, and application of *Hassan Shenavai v Klaus Kreischer*;[471] and secondly, as a result, the court's bypassing of the actual claim put forward by the plaintiff, and the substitution[472] of its own (objectively-assessed) obligation from the contract as a whole. Of *Shenavai*, it was said:

> Where more than one obligation has been breached [sic], jurisdiction under Article 5(1) for the claims in respect of all[473] the breaches of contract will be determined by the place of performance of the principal obligation breached [sic]. . . we have to decide which is *the principal obligation in this contract*.[474]

This incorrect analysis of *Shenavai* can no doubt be explained away by the court's desire not be seised of a claim, perhaps 'concocted' so as to be performed in England. Albeit that the plaintiff/claimant is fully at liberty to pick and choose which claims to advance in his action, blind reliance on the statement of claim, as

---

[465] [2000] CLC 455, at p.460, (Aldous LJ); *dubitante*, however, in general, Pill LJ at p.463.

[466] [1997] 3 WLR 365, CA.

[467] Regarding the level of autonomy and inviolability the plaintiff's claim has.

[468] Their alternative action in tort was held to be inadmissible—following the Continental doctrine of cumul and non-cumul. These terms, according to Lohse, M. *Das Verhältnis von Vertrag u. Delikt—eine rechtsvergleichende Studie zur vertragsautonomen Auslegung von* Article 5 Nr.1 u. Article 5 Nr.3 GVÜ, 1991, at p.86, merely reflect, in French law at least, whether or not 'dem Geschädigtem eine Wahlmöglichkeit (option) zwischen deliktischem und vertraglichem Anspruch zusteht.'('the victim has a legal choice (option) between a tortious or contractual claim').

[469] Presentation was to be made in England.

[470] [1997] 3 WLR 365, CA, at p.368, (Staughton LJ); the court was obviously not impressed with the presentation of this claim, which it no doubt considered to be a specious drafting device. The plaintiffs knew that (only) the presentation of reports was to be performed in England.

[471] (C-266/85) [1987] ECR 239.

[472] 'I have no doubt that the principal obligation should be characterised as the inspection of the goods' according to Staughton LJ at p.369; on the issue of court intervention in a plaintiff's claim below and (Belgian) *Cour de Cassation* 19.12.1985, (1986) JT p.281, at p.282, *Tribunal de commerce de Liège* 6.1.1986, (1986) *Ann Dr Liège* 275, at p.280, obs. Christians.

[473] *Sed quaere.*

[474] Staughton LJ, at p.369; yet *Shenavai* demonstrates what is to be identified as the principal obligation among the claims advanced, not the contract as a whole.

pleaded, would have lead to condoning the undesirable consequence of forum shopping here.[475]

While this area is left to national law,[476] without clarification of the meaning of the observations in *Shenavai,* the possibility for divergent national definitions of 'principal' obligations remains.

1.2.2(ii)   French cases on the 'principal' obligation

As far as can be gathered from reported cases, the French courts use both a subjective[477] and[478]/or objective[479] approach to classifying one of a number of pleaded claims as the 'principal' obligation. In the first, *Pierre c/ Société de droit italien Vertrolan,*[480] a French commercial agent sued his Italian supplier for outstanding commission, and damages for abusive breach of contract. The figure in francs claimed as damages outweighed the commission. The relative amounts therefore informed the 'principal obligation':

> ces éléments rélèvent *qu'aux yeux du demandeur*[481] l'obligation litigieuse principale est celle d'indemnité pour rupture abusive . . .[482] [483]

While this case clearly misapplies[484] the 'independent contractual obligation' criterion from *De Bloos,* what is decisive is the plaintiff/claimant's attitude towards the drafting of his claim, and, one can immediately foresee, the potential for drafting manipulation. Another clear example of this, again from the *Cour d'appel de Paris,* is *Gilbert Mayer c/ Société Charles Wednesbury Limited.*[485]

---

[475] Also Hertz, 1998, at p.96: 'A plaintiff who views the place of performance of the principal obligation as an inconvenient forum may prefer to abandon part of the claim and litigate only that part which can be brought in a more convenient forum'; *Royal Bank of Scotland Plc v Cassa di Risparmio delle Province Lombard and others,* [1992] 1 BankLR 251, at p.256 (Mustill LJ); Briggs, (1999) BYBIL 319, at p.325.

[476] In *Kongress Agentur Hagen GmbH v Zeehaghe BV* (C-365/88) [1990] ECR I-1845.

[477] By looking at the plaintiff's attitude to his case as pleaded; *Gilbert Mayer c/ Société Charles Wednesbury Limited* CA Paris, 13.9.1995 (1996) *Dalloz* somm., p.167, obs. Audit, CA Versailles 2.6.1988 (1990) *JDI* 147, compare Lord Goff in *Union Transport Plc* [1992] 1 Lloyd's Rep. 229, HL, at p.234.

[478] For a mixed approach *Sté Filtertechniek Nederland BV c/ Johannes Hoff* 21.5.1997 (1998) *JDI* 133; *cassation* rejected by *Cour de Cassation* 8.2.2000 *Hoff c/ Sté Filtertechniek Nederland BV* (2000) *JCP,* IV, 1542.

[479] By simply comparing the quantum of damages; this approach, too, can obviously be controlled by the plaintiff: *Pierre c/ Société de droit italien Vertrolan* CA Paris 22.5.1991, (1992) *Dalloz,* somm., p.164.

[480] CA Paris 22.5.1991, (1992) *Dalloz,* somm., p.164.

[481] Similar to Lord Goff's statement in *Union Transport Plc v Continental Lines S.A. and Conti Lines S.A.* [1992] 1 Lloyd's Rep. 229, at p.234.

[482] ('these elements show that in the *eyes of the plaintiff* the principal obligation is that for damages for wrongful breach').

[483] (1992) *Dalloz,* somm., p.164, at p.164.

[484] Audit, the reviewer is quite explicit in his condemnation, at p.165: 'En décidant que l'indemnité se substitue à l'obligation contractuelle inexécutée et que celle-ci se localisait en France, l'arrêt omet de préciser de quelle obligation il s'agissait.'

[485] 13.9.1995 (1997) *JDI* 170.

The plaintiff, Meyer, was for a number of years the French exclusive commercial agent for the English defendant. After relations deteriorated, Mayer sued in Paris for outstanding commission 'pour mémoire',[486] for damages for breach of the exclusive agency agreement[487] and damages for 'préjudice moral',[488] loss of reputation and 'résistance abusive'. The appeal court held[489] that the *TGI Paris* had correctly considered itself competent to hear the ensemble of claims. The principal obligation in question was found[490] to be the defendant's obligation to supply Mayer with products at his Paris domicile. For present purposes, the interest of the case lies in the fact that the principal obligation was found by default, negatively, by reason of the plaintiff/claimant's pleaded case. Its point of departure was the plaintiff/claimant's own attitude towards his claim for commission, showing its own relative unimportance[491] to him, and thus its secondary nature. It found:

> comme secondaire la demande relative aux commission . . . non pas pour une raison objective, tenant au quantum . . . mais subjective, à savoir *l'état d'esprit* de . . . Mayer qui l'a présentée «pour mémoire»[492] [493]

This trend has continued in *Sté Filtertechniek Nederland BV c/ Johannes Hoff.*[494] Again, a French commercial representative (of a Dutch company) sued on the basis of three claims: firstly for payment of an advanced notice indemnity (300,000 francs), for 'une indemnité de clientèle' (919,000 francs) and for supplementary damages for abusive termination. The principal obligation was found by the simple (objective)[495] expedient of the relative value of the three claims: the

---

[486] The actual sum was not stated. The phrase 'pour mémoire' is translated as 'for the record' and seems, in the court's eyes at least, to have trivialised this part of the claim so as not to be the principal obligation. Crucially perhaps, it would have had to have been performed in England in any case, at Wednesbury's domicile, Article 1247 *Code civil.*
[487] In the sum of 1.5 million francs.
[488] 750,000 francs.
[489] *Gilbert Mayer c/ Société Charles Wednesbury Limited* 13.9.1995 (1997) *JDI* 170, at p.171.
[490] No reference is made to the *lex causae* in its examination of the claims.
[491] The relative unimportance of the *de Bloos* ruling to the French courts in cases of exclusive distributorship contracts is evidenced by their continuance to find that the principal obligation is always that of the distributor to deliver the merchandise (to their French agents) or simply 'to respect the contract'; for this last aspect, and its historical developments, above; Rauscher, 1984, esp. at p.101.
[492] ('as secondary the obligation relating to commission, not for an objective reason relating to quantum, but subjective, viz. the state of mind of Mayer who advanced it "for the record"').
[493] (1997) *JDI* 170, at p.171; compare *AIG Group (UK) Ltd v The Ethniki* [1998] 4 All ER 301, [2000] All ER (Comm) 65, CA.
[494] 21.5.1997 (1998) *JDI* 133; now reported in English at [1998] I.L.Pr. 196; appeal in *cassation* dismissed by *Cour de Cassation* 8.2.2000 *Hoff c/ Sté Filtertechniek Nederland BV* (2000) *JCP*, IV, 1542, (2001) *JDI* 133, [2001] I.L.Pr. 82, (2001) *Rev crit* 150; (objective) value considerations were also important in *Cassation* 14.1.1998 *Société Productions S.C.A.P. c/ Roberto Faggioni*, unreported, Lexis.
[495] The reviewer thinks it is both objective and subjective, the amounts in the sovereign control of the plaintiff; in *So Re Tex* 16.6.1999, it was held that 'le montant est très nettement supérieur à celui des autres demandes'('the amount is quite clearly higher than that of the other claims'), incidentally to the detriment of the French claimant's ability to seise the French courts under Article 5(1).

'indemnité de clientèle' thus carried the day. Again, according to French law,[496] as the *lex causae*, this was to be payable at the debtor's domicile, *in casu* therefore, The Netherlands. Yet despite its lack of jurisdiction over this principal obligation, the court nevertheless[497] declared itself competent over the other two (secondary) claims under Article 5(1).

Audit is rightly critical[498] of both methods used by the *Cours d'appel*, since the (possibly exclusionary) 'principal obligation' should not be dependent on the whim, or drafting techniques,[499] of plaintiffs/claimants. It is submitted that to differentiate between objective and subjective criteria is artificial; both quantum of, and personal attitude to, claims, or indeed whether particular claims are ever even pleaded, lies solely in the discretion of plaintiffs. That said, however, this level of drafting control should not lead to jurisdictional manoeuvring:[500]

> il ne faudrait cependant pas que celle-ci [objective/subjective method] incite le cas échéant un plaideur à chiffrer une demande de dommages-intérêts de manière à faire basculer la compétence vers le for qui a sa préférence.[501] [502]

1.2.2(iii) Other Contracting States and the 'principal' obligation

The French methodology of the subjective/objective test for the ascertainment of the principal obligation seems to have been followed by the *Cour d'appel de Luxembourg* in *Vesque c/ Badischer Winzerkeller E.G.*[503] In this case the court had to qualify the principal obligation from among eleven claims made by a Luxembourg sole representative, Vesque, of a German defendant wine producer: one claim for an indemnity for lack of due notice, six claims for non-payment of various commissions/lost commission due, three for damages for loss of sales, and one claim for goodwill.[504] The (mixed) French approach was in evidence:

---

[496] Article 1247 *Code civil* states, after a number of exceptions—notably for an agreement on a place of performance—that 'le payement doit être fait au domicile du débiteur.' *Code civil*, 2ème éd., *Megacode*, Dalloz, 1997–8, pp.956–57.

[497] Below on the imperative nature of *Hassan Shenavai v Klaus Kreischer* (C-266/85) [1987] ECR 239; also *Cour de Cassation* 8.2.2000 *Hoff c/ Sté Filtertechniek Nederland BV* (2000) JCP, IV, 1542.

[498] (1992) *Dalloz*, somm., 164, at p.164.

[499] He would no doubt approve of *Source Ltd v T.U.V. Rheinland Holding A.G. and others* [1998] QB 54.

[500] (1992) *Dalloz*, somm., p.164; the case appears to be different under Article 5(3) because *Shevill v Presse Alliance SA* (C-68/93) [1995] ECR I-415 has shown us that a claimant may legitimately draft his claim in the tort of defamation to cover damage limited to particular Contracting States; *Hunter v Gerald Duckworth and Co. Ltd*, [2000] I.L.Pr. 229, Irish HC.

[501] ('however, it should not be that this encourages the plaintiff, as the case may be, to mark out a claim for damages in a way that tips jurisdiction towards his preferred forum').

[502] (1992) *Dalloz*, somm., 164, at p.164; recently comments by Evans LJ in *AIG Group (UK) Ltd v The Ethniki* [2000] All ER (Comm) 65, CA, at p.72: '[t]he plaintiff cannot camouflage the principal obligation by relegating it to a subordinate rôle by the way he chooses to express his claim. The court's decision does not rest in the plaintiff's hands.'

[503] 8.3.1994, 1993–95 *Pas. Lux.* 341.

[504] *Ibid*, at p.342–43.

on détermine l'obligation principale en fonction de l'importance qu'elle peut présenter pour le demandeur, en tenant compte en premier lieu de la valeur des différentes obligations . . .[505] [506]

In a recently reported Austrian case, *OGH* 20.1.1999[507]—where an Austrian sole representative agent of a Finnish company was suing the latter for commission, and damages for breach of due notice requirements—no methodology was mentioned at all:

Hauptpflicht ist hier aber zweifellos die vom Kl. geforderte Provision[508]

The current methodologies use by the English and French courts in determining the principal obligation are numerous and highly speculative. The former have tended towards a (controlled) 'legal consequence' or 'but for' , causation analysis; the latter a more simple test of relative merit (to the claimant). Surprisingly, there is a dearth of German caselaw and comment in this area. The concerns engendered by these approaches (for this treatment) are the ones which may fuel either drafting manipulation, or a Contracting State's ability favourably to promote an obligation to be performed domestically to a jurisdiction-founding status. The next section will deal with the attempts, or lack of them, the Contracting State courts have made to deal with these issues.

1.2.3   The court's level of control over a plaintiff/claimant's claim

It may now be apt to digress somewhat to an area relatively untouched by critical comment[509] or judicial decision:[510] the question of how much autonomy the plaintiff/claimant's claim has in the court's application of Article 5(1), or whether a court can, and should, of its own motion, intervene to 'modify' the pleadings in order to substitute[511] what it believes to be the correct principal 'obligation(s) in question'. The whimsical nature of the French test for the principal obligation

---

[505] ('the principal obligation is found according to the importance it may have for the plaintiff, taking account primarily of the value of the different obligations').
[506] *Ibid*, at p.345.
[507] 1999 *ÖJZ* 504.
[508] ('the principal obligation here is undoubtedly the commission claimed by the plaintiff'), *ibid*, at p.506.
[509] But note Christians' observations on *Tribunal de commerce de Liège* 6.1.1986 (1986) *Ann Dr Liège* 275, at p.280.
[510] The English attitude is represented by *Source Ltd v T.U.V. Rheinland Holding A.G. and others* [1998] QB 54 and Mustill LJ's comment at the end of his judgment in *Royal Bank of Scotland Plc v Cassa di Risparmio delle Province Lombard and others* [1992] 1 BankLR 251, at pp.255–56; also Briggs, (1999) *BYBIL* 319, at p.325: 'the obligation relied on as the foundation of the contractual claim cannot be artificially contrived'; note *Fisher and others v Unione Italiana de Riassicurazione SPA* [1998] CLC 682, QBD (Colman J) where the plaintiff's pleaded case caused him to be hoist by his own petard: the obligation pleaded in support of the negative declaration—that the defendant was, by warranty, to retain a portion of the risk—was to be performed in Italy.
[511] Christians (1986) *Ann Dr Liège* 275, at p.280.

would suggest that a level of control is necessary. *De Bloos* does make it clear that the 'raw material' for the court to work on is the claim *as presented*,[512] but the Court could surely not have meant to suggest that the claim was immutably cast in stone. At the other end of the spectrum, however, Hertz[513] undoubtedly goes too far when, in this regard, he states that:

> [j]urisdiction must be decided on the basis of the claim as actually argued by the plaintiff . . .[514]

That the court cannot, of its own motion, prevent spurious, jurisdiction-founding claims being advanced was no doubt part of the ruling in, or at least a reaction to, *Shenavai v Kreischer*.[515] The court must allow the plaintiff/claimant a certain degree of autonomy, until it senses that the plaintiff/claimant is seeking to elevate a claim/obligation—which would otherwise not qualify (under any test) as the 'principal obligation'—to avoid the unfortunate consequences of an unfavourable *lex causae*. Yet the dividing line between autonomy and intervention is a nebulous one. What may appear important to the plaintiff/claimant may not do so objectively to a court in the context of a contract as a whole.

The Italian *Corte di Cassazione* seems to have adopted the 'claim as presented' view in *Handelsagentur Dieter Nienaber GmbH & Co. KG v Impex-Euro Sr.*[516] as a principle of interpreting claims under Article 5(1). It is only those claims that are part of the *causa petendi*, not others that may incidentally also have to be performed under the same contract, that are jurisdictionally relevant.[517] The Norwegian Supreme Cour, in *Terje Karlung v Svensk Vägguide Comertex AB*[518] seems to have taken a different view (on the authority of *Effer v Kantner*). Here the belief was 'that the court should not automatically use the plaintiff's claims as a basis.'[519]

That the (English) courts are alive to this issue is represented by *Royal Bank of Scotland Plc v Cassa di Risparmio delle Province Lombard and others*.[520] Mustill LJ in the course of his judgment noted that the plaintiff confirming bank had—during the course of first instance proceedings—abandoned[521] one of the bases for its claims to repayment from the Italian defendant issuing banks, on the ground that re-imbursement under a letter of credit was to be made primarily via

---

[512] *Contra*, an example of 'piercing the pleadings': 'La Cour de Cassation énonce nettement que les juges du fond ne sont pas tenus de se limiter aux termes de l'acte introductif d'instance mais doivent rechercher quelles sont, *en realité*, toutes les obligations en cause . . .' (Gaudemet-Tallon), reviewing *Soc K.D. Köln Düsseldorfer Deutsche Rheinschiffahrt c/ Soc. Transports et Voyages* 25.1.1984 (1985) *Rev crit* 126, at p.129.

[513] Hertz, 1998.

[514] *Ibid*, at p.96.

[515] (C-266/85) [1987] ECR 239.

[516] 21.6.1984 [1988] E.C.C. 150.

[517] *Ibid*, at p.155, para. 10(a).

[518] *Høyesteretts Kjaeremålsutvalg* 27.1.1998 [1999] I.L.Pr. 298.

[519] *Ibid*, at p.301, para. 21.

[520] [1992] 1 BankLR 251; and *AIG Europe (UK) Ltd and others v The Ethniki* [2000] All ER (Comm) 65, CA.

[521] [1992] 1 BankLR 251, at p.255.

intermediary re-imbursing banks in New York. At the end of his judgment, his lordship found that abandoning this portion of their claim had not improved the plaintiff's jurisdictional position. This therefore made 'it unnecessary to consider whether this[522] [was] a legitimate way to invoke Article 5(1),' which suggests strongly, *a contrario*, some sort of control may otherwise have been exercised in different circumstances.

Certain cases in Belgium have ruled on both sides of the line. The Belgian *Cour de Cassation*[523] has pointed to the inviolability of the plaintiff's claim:

> la compétence doit s'apprécier en fonction non pas de l'objet réel du litige à rechercher par le tribunal, mais de la demande *telle qu'elle est forumulée* par le demandeur.[524] [525]

A different approach was taken in a first instance decision,[526] prompting Christians, the reviewer, to ask the same question answered so emphatically in *Source Ltd v T.U.V. Rheinland Holding A.G. and others:*[527]

> Quel est l'office du juge dans cette tâche de qualification? Cette détermination doit-elle se fonder uniquement sur le libellé de la demande telle qu'elle est énoncée par le demandeur . . . Dans quelle mesure ces éléments de fait permettent-ils au juge de déterminer l'objet d'une demande?[528] [529]

As *Kongress Agentur Hagen GmbH v Zeehaghe BV*[530] has shown us, it is for the individual Contracting State courts to regulate their own procedure, and the way a claim is presented; its admissibility and construction is intimately bound up *par excellence* with rules of internal court procedure. The potential for abuse, however, and the attendant tendency of an interpretation that favours a 'homeward trend',[531] remain, especially in those Contracting States, like France, which have adopted a liberal, subjective approach to classifying the principal obligation. Whether *Source Ltd v T.U.V. Rheinland Holding* goes beyond the bounds set in *De Bloos* and *Shenavai v Kreischer*—looking only to the claim(s) advanced by the plaintiff—in substituting its own view of the contract as a whole, is a moot point. The English court will no doubt, as in that case, continue[532] to take a pragmatic

---

[522] Presumably abandoning the original pleadings/statement of case as presented.

[523] 19.12.1985, 1986 JT 281, at p.282.

[524] ('jurisdiction must be assessed not according to the actual object of the case as found by the court, but to the claim such as it is formulated by the plaintiff').

[525] *Ibid.*

[526] *Tribunal de commerce de Liège* 6.1.1986 (1986) *Ann Dr Liège* 275, obs. Christians.

[527] [1997] 3 WLR 365, CA.

[528] ('what is the function of the judge in this task of qualification? Should this determination be based solely on the wording of the demand put forward by the plaintiff? To what extent do these factual elements permit the judge to determine the basis of the demand?').

[529] (1986) *Ann Dr Liège* 275, at p.280.

[530] (C-365/88) [1990] ECR I-1845.

[531] Although the court's vigilance in *Source Ltd v T.U.V. Rheinland Holding* ousted the plaintiff's claim.

[532] Instructive, by way of comparison may be the court's vigilance with regard to the service of multiple defendants and *lis pendens* under Articles 21/22: *Grupo Torras S.A. and Torras Hostench London Ltd. v Sheikh Fahad Mohammed al-Sabah and others* [1995] 1 Lloyd's Rep. 374, at p.420 (Mance J): 'I do not

and interventionist line.[533] There is however, no uniform interpretation of the issue. Unfortunately the reported German cases reveal no direct or indirect discussion on the point of how the principal obligation is to be found, nor of any indication of *sua sponte* interventionist control.[534] Why this might be, is not known. No methodology is suggested by any of the German commentators, neither Geimer and Schütze,[535] Schlosser,[536] nor Kropholler.[537]

1.2.4 Whether ascertaining the 'principal' obligation is possible, and obligatory;[538] and if so, is *Shenavai v Kreischer* imperative in its application?

As the previous sections show, where various 'contractual obligation[s]',[539] corresponding to 'contractual right[s]',[540] are causally linked, sequentially, one among them forming a complete cause of action,[541] it may be easy to point to a principal obligation; equally, if the plaintiff/claimant's attitude to one or more pleaded claims is explicitly obvious due to quantum claimed, the court's task is fairly straight-forward. However, it may not always be possible[542] to single out one pleaded obligation for elevation to a principal obligation. Is the application of *Shenavai* obligatory,[543] or only a contingent condition on a court's being able to find a principal obligation?

If it is obligatory, this would suggest that Article 5(1) should not apply[544] if a principal obligation is lacking: the *raison d'être* for the rule in *Shenavai*, after all, is to prevent a relatively insignificant obligation founding jurisdiction under Article 5(1). The language of *Hassan Shenavai v Klaus Kreischer*[545] is ambiguous at best. That the court 'will . . . be *guided* by the maxim'[546] suggests[547] that the rule is

---

think that the Convention falls to be construed on the basis of an assumption that parties will abuse its procedures. National courts must be assumed to be capable of dealing with abuse.'

[533] The Court of Appeal in *AIG Group (UK) Ltd and others v The Ethniki* [2000] All ER (Comm) 65.
[534] Nor of a court overriding the plaintiff's claim as pleaded.
[535] Geimer and Schütze R, 1997, at p.135 paras. 60–61.
[536] Schlosser, P. *EuGVÜ: Europäisches Gerichtsstands- und Vollstreckungsübereinkommen mit Luganer Übereinkommen*, 1996, at p.47, para. 7.
[537] Kropholler, 1998, at pp.106–07, para. 16.
[538] The Belgian appeal court in the reference in *Leathertex Divisione Sintetici* (C-420/97) thought not. It and the *Cassation* decision are reported at [1998] I.L.Pr. 505, and reviewed below.
[539] *Ets. A. de Bloos* v *Bouyer* (C-15/76) [1976] ECR 1497, at p.1509, para. 15.
[540] *Ibid.*
[541] *Union Transport Plc v Continental Lines S.A. and Conti Lines S.A.* [1992] 1 Lloyd's Rep. 229, HL.
[542] Briggs, 1997, at p.100, para. 2.132.
[543] I.e. must one of a number of obligations be squeezed into a principal rôle?
[544] Briggs, 1997, at p.100; confirmed in *Leathertex Divisione Sintetici SpA v Bodetex BVBA* (C-420/97) [1999] ECR I-6747.
[545] (C-266/85) [1987] ECR 239.
[546] [1987] ECR 239, at p.256, para. 19.
[547] To Lloyd LJ at least in *Union Transport Plc v Continental Lines S.A. and Conti Lines S.A.* [1991] 2 Lloyd's Rep. 48, at p.51.

not strictly compulsory; yet a few words later, 'it *will* be the principal obligation which *will* determine its jurisdiction'[548] suggests that it is. Lloyd LJ, stated, *obiter*, that caution should be exercised in not contorting the maxim[549] beyond its natural meaning as a (mere) guiding principle:

> The Court [in *Shenavai*] is not indicating that in every dispute there can only be one principal obligation. . .[I]f the obligations can be so characterised then the maxim will afford guidance[550]

Assuming that, by whatever method,[551] one among a number of obligations has been designated by the court as 'principal', the question still remains whether the maxim in *Shenavai* is imperative,[552] or merely optional.[553] This question of the exclusionary effect of *Shenavai* fell squarely for decision in *Sté Filtertechniek Nederland BV c/ Johannes Hoff*,[554] discussed above. The French distributor had made three claims: one 'principal', on account of its superior monetary value for 'indemnité de clientèle',[555] to be performed at the defendant's Dutch domicile according to French law (Article 1247 *Code civil*), *lege causae*; the other two, (thus necessarily) accessory monetary claims, the court held to be performed in France.

The question[556] as to whether *Shenavai* prevented[557] the French courts from assuming jurisdiction over the secondary claims is admirably summarised by the commentator:

> impératif, auquel cas la juridiction saisie, incompétente pour statuer sur l'obligation litigieuse principale, *l'est aussi, ipso facto,* pour connaître. . .[des] accessoires *alors même* que ces dernières seraient exécutables dans son ressort.[558] [559]

---

[548] [1987] ECR 239, at p.256, para. 19.

[549] *Union Transport Plc v Continental Lines S.A. and Conti Lines S.A.* [1991] 2 Lloyd's Rep. 48, at p.52; this is also the view taken by Stone, 1996, at p.169 who says it may be 'artificial or arbitrary [so] to select one'.

[550] [1991] 2 Lloyd's Rep. 48, at p.52.

[551] As to which above p.86 *et seq.*

[552] Better still, in the sense of exclusionary, excluding all other claims from consideration: *Sté Filtertechniek Nederland BV c/ Johannes Hoff* 21.5.1997 (1998) *JDI* 133, at p.135, Huet; also *Source Ltd v T.U.V. Rheinland Holding A.G. and others* [1998] QB 54.

[553] *Ibid,* and Briggs, 1997, at p.100 para. 2.132, suggesting a third possibility; also Stone, 1996, at p.169.

[554] 21.5.1997 (1998) *JDI* 133, confirmed by *Cour de Cassation* 8.2.2000 *Hoff c/ Sté Filtertechniek Nederland BV* (2000) *JCP*, IV, 1542; Huet clearly believes after this case that *Shenavai* is optional, rather than imperative, (2001) *JDI* 133, at p.135.

[555] One would have expected that the optional interpretation of *Shenavai* is more likely to occur in those Contracting States which consider such an indemnity obligation as a 'principal obligation' and consequentially have to bring their debtor-favouring Civil Codes to bear *lege causae*. The situation in Germany, however, does not coincide with the French position, below, section 1.3.6.

[556] The question also posed by Gaudemet-Tallon, 1996, at p.121, para. 165.

[557] I.e. is it imperative or optional?

[558] ('obligatory, in which case the jurisdiction seised (being unable to rule on the principal obligation in question) is also incompetent, *ipso facto*, to take cognizance of accessory ones, even though these latter are to be performed within its jurisdiction').

[559] *Sté Filtertechniek Nederland BV c/ Johannes Hoff* 21.5.1997 (1998) *JDI* 133, at p.135, (Huet).

Conversely, if *Shenavai* is only optional, it would not prevent a court having competence under Article 5(1), since the remaining accessory obligations were to be performed in the forum State. The *Cour d'appel* adopted[560] the latter (optional) approach,[561] and claimed jurisdiction over the accessory claims, even though it was incompetent for the principal obligation.

The English Court of Appeal's decision in *Source Ltd v T.U.V. Rheinland Holding A.G. and others*[562] could well be regarded as authority[563] pointing the other way. The plaintiff's first pleaded contractual cause of action, it will be remembered, centred on the German defendants' alleged failure to exercise reasonable skill and care in presenting reports to the plaintiffs.[564] In reality this in no way represented the (causative)[565] chain of events. The crux of why the plaintiffs had engaged the defendants was to inspect the goods and prepare certificates of appropriate quality for presentation to the supplier's (confirming) bank. Yet the negligent inspection itself was not pleaded by the plaintiffs, as its undoubted place of performance was in Hong Kong, and not in England; the plaintiffs wished only to rely on the presentation of the reports in England. The Court of Appeal did not allow them to do so, declaring 'the principal obligation in this contract [sic]'[566] was the inspection of the goods. *Shenavai*'s terminology,[567] of the principal obligation, was used in an imperative, exclusionary sense to undermine what the court saw as a manufactured obligation.

1.2.5 More than one 'principal' obligation, or no 'principal' obligation discernible: *Leathertex Divisione Sintetici SpA v Bodetex BVBA*[568]

In the unlikely event that, by either the French or English method, multiple principal obligations, or no principal obligation(s), are found to exist in a claim, what is to happen? For the sake of completeness, the situation is briefly discussed

---

[560] *Ibid*, at p.135; correct in Stone's view, 1996, at p.169—*Shenavai* is 'enabling rather than restrictive'.
[561] *Contra* Geimer and Schütze, 1997, at p.134, para. 57: 'Werden mehrere Hauptansprüche aus dem Vertragsverhältnis geltend gemacht, liegt aber der Erfüllungsort nur hinsichtlich einer Hauptverpflichtung im Gerichtsstaat, so darf . . . das Gericht nicht über die anderen Ansprüche befinden.' ('If several principal obligations in a contract are claimed, but only the place of performance of one principal obligation is in the Contracting State, the court may *not* take cognisance of the other claims').
[562] [1997] 3 WLR 365, CA.
[563] Unless this decision can be confined on its facts to a case where a plaintiff patently puts in a specious, jurisdiction-founding claim. The courts have to be alive to this possibility.
[564] [1997] 3 WLR 365, at p.368.
[565] In the sense of the proximate cause of the alleged breach of contract.
[566] At p.369 (Staughton LJ). Note that the principal obligation is to be found from among the claims advanced—not, as in that case, from the contract in general.
[567] *Quaere*, whether *Shenavai* should have been applied at all, because the plaintiffs had only advanced a single contractual obligation, not several.
[568] (C-420/97) [1999] ECR I-6747, AG Léger's opinion not referred to, 16.3.1999.

by German commentators[569]—who merely stress the individual place of performance for each principal obligation, and the fact that there is no accessory jurisdiction over all principal obligations, unless each and every obligation's place of performance is in the Contracting State of the forum.

The question submitted to the European Court for a ruling on the interpretation of Article 5(1) and *Shenavai*, in *Leathertex Divisione Sintetici SpA*, concerned the problem of neither of two independent contractual obligations being found to be a 'principal' obligation.[570] The reference seemed, *prima facie*, to centre on a specific issue concerning the (mandatory application or) interpretation of *Shenavai*: could a court take jurisdiction under Article 5(1) over an obligation which was neither the 'principal' obligation, nor to be performed with that Contracting State, when it *did* have jurisdiction over another obligation of 'equal weight'.[571]

As appears from the report, the Belgian appeal court favoured grouping the two claims together, albeit that one independent payment obligation was to be performed in Italy.[572] A Belgian commercial agent, sole representative of an Italian company in Belgium and Luxembourg, sued its 'principal' in Belgium for (1) outstanding commission due and (2) damages for wrongful termination (failure to give adequate notice of termination).[573] The referring court noted that the lower Belgian appeal court had made three findings on the facts of the case: (1) that neither of the two obligations, the payment of commission nor the failure to give notice, could be found[574] to be the 'principal' obligation under *Shenavai*; (2) that one obligation, to give adequate notice, was to be performed in Belgium, while the other—to pay outstanding commission—in Article 1247 of the Belgian Civil Code *lege causae*, fell to be performed at the debtor's (defendant's) place of business in Italy; and (3) in these circumstances, to avoid a scission in the two claims—both being 'of equal weight'[575]—the Belgian court had jurisdiction under Article 5(1) to hear *both* claims under the contract.[576]

The Belgian *Cour de Cassation* referred to the Court of Justice a question as to whether such a course of action were permissible under Article 5(1), when neither obligation could be considered to be superior:

---

[569] Kropholler, 1998 at p.107, para. 16: 'so ist für jede von ihnen [principal obligations] gesondert zu prüfen, ob der Erfüllungsort im Gerichtsstaat liegt' ('for every one of them it is to be specifically tested whether the place of performance lies in the Contracting State'); and Geimer and Schütze, 1997, at p.134, para. 57.

[570] Donzallaz, 1998, Vol. III, at p.198, para. 4650, simply argues that *Shenavai* does not apply and the claims become fragmented; the ECJ in *Leathertex Divisione* agreed.

[571] [1998] I.L.Pr. 505, at p.509, at para. 16, the referring court report.

[572] *Cour de Cassation* (Belgium) 4.12.1997 reported in English at [1998] I.L.Pr. 505.

[573] This compensatory obligation under autonomous Belgian law, has traditionally been seen as a dependent obligation: *Cour de Cassation* 19.1.1984 *Carl Freudenberg KG c/ Société de Personnes à responsabilité Limitée «Bureau R.C. Van Oppens»* 1984 *Pas. Belge*, I, 540, at p.545—censure has followed an attempt to amalgamate both types of claims—*Tribunal de commerce de Bruxelles*, 22.6.1989, S.P.R.L. *Kheops/ S.A.R.L. Les Créations Ada Tuchbant*, (1990) *Rev. dr. comm. belge* 702.

[574] The methodology or lack of it, was not mentioned in the case.

[575] [1998] I.L.Pr. 505, at p.506, para. 16.

[576] *Ibid*, para. 16.

[i]n this particular case, we are presented with a situation which does not allow a hierarchy[577] to be established within the obligations, since they are described as being of equal rank.[578]

As mentioned above, and from the thrust of the UK Government's arguments, it appeared as though the reference rested on whether *Shenavai* was imperative, and a 'principal' obligation had to eked out; or whether amalgamating claims of equal rank were permissible, *Shenavai* proving impossible to apply.

AG Léger's opinion steered an unusual course. He did not take the opportunity of (re-)examining *Shenavai*, but approached the question from the standpoint[579] of avoiding the possible fragmentation of proceedings between Belgium and Italy, consequent upon the current, and 'traditional', method of interpreting Article 5(1). He used the case of having two 'payment' obligations in the reference not only to review *Tessili*,[580] but to alter the emphasis[581] of *de Bloos* in regard to obligations that that case would class as 'independent' contractual obligations, with their own unique place of performance, *lege causae*. It is this latter aspect that will be examined here.

In the opening section of his opinion, the Advocate General reveals his disquiet at the distinction, regarding 'independent' and 'dependent' payment obligations, maintained since the decision in *de Bloos*. As will be recalled, *de Bloos* observed a different category (1) for 'independent' contractual obligations, which may involve the payment of money—such as commission[582] and the purchase price[583]—from (2) damages *strictu sensu*, replacing unperformed[584] contractual obligations. In a radical departure from this accepted view, the Advocate General thought that this traditional distinction should be dispensed with when (generic) payment obligations are concerned:

---

[577] Despite the UK Government's attempts to have the question referred reformulated so as enable the European Court, by some means, to find a 'principal' obligation: cf the findings of the CA in *Medway Packaging Ltd v Meurer Maschinen GmbH & Co. K.G.* [1990] 2 Lloyd's Rep. 112.

[578] AG Léger in *Leathertex Divisione v Bodetex* (C-420/97) [1999] ECR I-6747, at p.6760, para. 69.

[579] His analysis was coloured to a large extent by the desire, noted in the *Cour d'appel's cri de coeur*, to have both claims heard together.

[580] The *Tessili* aspects of his opinion will be noted below, section 1.3.9(ii).

[581] As will be seen, his review of *de Bloos* he felt was necessitated by the impracticability of finding an autonomous definition for 'the place of performance' of independent payment obligations.

[582] Of the many examples: *Rechtbank van Koophandel te Turnhout*, 11.10.1993, *Grafix N.V. /GmbH Cantz'sche Druckerei*, (1994) *Rev. dr. comm. belge* 730, *Tribunal de commerce de Liège*, 18.5.1995 (1996) *Rev. dr. comm. belge* 837; Austrian *OGH* 20.1.1999 1999 *ÖJZ* 504, *Tribunale di Milano* 4.12.1997 *Banca Agricola Milanese s.p.a c/ Commerzbank AG* (1999) *Riv. dir. int. priv. e proc.* 63; the post-*Shenavai* reference itself in *LG Kaiserslautern* 5.5.1987 IPRspr. (1987) Nr. 128.

[583] Of the innumerable cases, *OLG München* 11.11.1976 IPRspr. (1976) Nr. 146, and *Cour d'appel de Paris* 5.4.1995 *Mathis c/ Ste Baums Mang et autre*, unreported, Juris Data 95-21259.

[584] Specifically in commercial agency cases, in Belgium *Cour de Cassation* 28.6.1979 *Audi-NSU Auto Union AG c Adelin Petit et Cie SA* 1979 *Pas. Belge*, I, 1260, at p.1283, [1980] E.C.C. 235; and *Société Van Pelt c/ Jedre* 29.1.1980 (1980) *JDI* 889, (1981) *Rev crit* 118.

[t]here is no reason to draw a distinction[585] between these obligations since they come under the same category of obligations to make payment.[586]

A contractually stipulated payment—such as commission—should therefore no longer be regarded as an 'independent contractual obligation'. Instead, what should be considered the 'obligation in question'—(which has a place of performance)—is *the activity which produced the payment* of commission—i.e. the commercial agent's activity itself, or, as AG Léger phrased it:

> the commercial agent, *whose commission constitutes the consideration therefor.* . .[is] why I approve that view[587] and I consider that it should be transposed to a case where a claim is for payment of commission allegedly due in respect of the proper performance of the service provided as part of a commercial agency.[588]

So it is the 'contrepartie' of what formerly was the (independent) contractual obligation to pay—the purchase price,[589] and now, commission[590]—that according to the Advocate General, is now to be considered as 'the obligation in question', when the payment of money is involved.

Yet it is hard to see how this 'contrepartie' analysis will work in all cases, especially where the payment of money does not depend on some other activity,[591] but is the *raison d'être* of the contract itself, such as in a contract of guarantee,[592] or in documentary credit transactions.[593]

Demoting what once was an 'independent' contractual obligation to pay to merely a reflection, or 'contrepartie', of another (more important) 'background'

---

[585] The payment of damages (that *De Bloos* would say is a dependent obligation), had a 'contrepartie' in an unperformed contractual obligation (to give adequate notice). Therefore so should the payment of commission, below.

[586] *Leathertex Divisione Sintetici SpA* (C-420/97) [1999] ECR I-6747, at p.6772, para. 149.

[587] Of AG Lenz in *Custom Made Commercial.*

[588] (C-420/97) [1999] ECR I-6747, at p.6777, para. 181 and at p.6773, para. 153.

[589] Its 'contrepartie' would be performed at the place of delivery, as found by AG Lenz in *Custom Made Commercial.*

[590] The place where the agent carries out his activities, AG Léger, in *Leathertex Divisione Sintetici SpA.* Note cases such as the Swiss *Bundesgericht* 23.8.1996 *K contre Dames P et F* 122 BGE III 298 (commission), the *Cour d'appel de Luxembourg* 8.3.1994 *Vesque c/ Badischer Winzerkeller E.G.* 1993–95 *Pas. Lux.* 341 at p.346 and *Sté Filtertechniek Nederland BV c/ Johannes Hoff* 21.5.1997 (1998) *JDI* 133, at p.134, [1998] I.L.Pr. 196, at pp.198–99 *re, inter alia,* the payment of goodwill, appeal dismissed in *Cassation* 8.2.2000 *Hoff c/ Sté Filtertechniek Nederland BV* (2000) *JCP,* IV, 1542.

[591] Such as the delivery of goods in international sales transactions.

[592] *Société Le Crédit Suisse c/ Bouillon et Société pour l'aménagement et la promotion de la station d'Isola 2000* 12.10.1994 (1995) *JDI* 158 and *Marc Thomas c/ Sté Crédit de l'Est* 17.10.1996 (1998) *JDI* 144, under Article 5(1) Lugano Convention; also noted by Poillot-Perzuetto, reviewing *Cour de Cassation* 30.1.2001 *ING Bank NV Paris c/ Soc. Mantel Holland Beheer BV* (2001) *Rev crit* 539.

[593] *Royal Bank of Scotland Plc v Cassa di Risparmio* [1991] I.L.Pr. 411, QBD (Phillips J) affm'd [1992] 1 BankLR 251, CA and *Chailease Finance Corporation v Credit Agricole Indosuez* [2000] 1 Lloyd's Rep. 348, CA; although, arguably, presentation commonly triggers payment.

obligation also smacks of influence[594] from the interpretation[595] of Article 4(2) of the 1980 Rome Convention, and should be resisted. Taking the 'contrepartie' route in all cases will lead to the 'obligation in question' in Article 5(1) becoming indistinguishable from the 'characteristic obligation'[596] in Article 4(2) of the Rome Convention.

Yet it is in the very last paragraph of his opinion that the Advocate General reveals that his analysis of *De Bloos*, and the changes he advocates to *Tessili/Custom Made Commercial*, are only to apply if and when[597] a 'principal' obligation cannot be found:

> this policy does not exempt the referring court from first checking *whether a hierarchy can be established* between the contested obligations arising from the agreement, in order, as the Court has consistently held, to determine the principal obligation so as to designate the court which has jurisdiction.[598]

In *Leathertex Divisione Sintetici SpA v Bodetex BVBA* itself, it seemed highly unlikely, following the judgment of *Custom Made Commercial*, that the European Court of Justice would have dispensed with over twenty-five years of authority from the time of *De Bloos*. It is true that attaching a place of performance to (independent) payment obligations exposes them to the vicissitudes[599] of material *leges causae*, be debts 'quérables'[600] or 'portables';[601] but to sacrifice at least the

---

[594] The Swiss *Bundesgericht* recently toyed with the idea of applying the characteristic performance in *A.AG gegen B* 9.3.1998 124 BGE, III, 188, at p.191, but found the idea too controversial. It felt bound by the 'persuasive' authority of the ECJ's decision in *Custom Made Commercial* under the Declaration [1988] OJ L319/40 to the Lugano Convention 1988.

[595] Note that under Article 4(2), the 'characteristic performance', whatever else it is, is not normally the payment of money. 'It is the performance for which the payment is due, i.e. . . . the delivery of goods . . .' *Guiliano & Lagarde Report on the Convention on the law applicable to contractual obligations* [1980] OJ C282/1 at p.20, second column, penultimate paragraph; Moss, G.C. 'Performance of obligations as the basis of jurisdiction and choice of law (Lugano and Brussels Conventions Article 5(1) and Rome Convention Article 4)' (2000) *Nordic Journal of International Law* 379.

[596] Incidentally the solution preferred by AG Colomer in the other 'rebellious' opinion given in *GIE Groupe Concorde* (C-440/97) [1999] ECR I-6307, at p. pp.6338–39, at para. 103; the 'characteristic obligation' route was not taken in *OGH* 20.1.1999 1999 *ÖJZ* 504, at p.505; although amalgamation of the two concepts was the source of some confusion in the appeal court in *Cour de Cassation* 15.5.2001 *SA Optelec c/ Sté Midtronics Bv* (2001) *JCP*, II, 10634, at p.2214, obs. Raynard.

[597] The reason why the AG's opinion in *Leathertex Divisione Sintetici* is being included in this section.

[598] *Leathertex Divisione Sintetici SpA v Bodetex BVBA* (C-420/97) [1999] ECR I-6747.

[599] Critique of Article 5(1) from Reed, A. 'Special Jurisdiction and the Convention: the Case of *Domicrest Ltd v Swiss Bank Corporation*' (1999) *CJQ* 218, at p.233.

[600] I.e., in default of contrary agreement—*BayObLG* 26.4.2001 (2001) *RIW* 862—and the circumstances surrounding the transaction, the creditor must demand payment at the debtor's place of business, as in France, Belgium, Germany and Austria.

[601] I.e., in default of contrary agreement and the circumstances surrounding the transaction, the debtor must seek out his creditor at the latter's domicile/place of business, as in Switzerland, Italy, Greece and England—eg *Deutsche Rückversicherung AG v La Fondiara Assicurazioni SpA*. [2001] 2 Lloyd's Rep. 621 (David Steel J) at pp.625–26: 'the default rule must readily give way to the practical considerations of the relevant transaction'.

certainty of knowing that, given an express choice of performance[602]/law clause, a plaintiff/claimant will be able to predict, under Article 5(1), where he can reasonably be expected[603] to collect his debts, simply in order to amalgamate such claims with dependent contractual damages seemed to be too high a price. This was, indeed, how the ECJ effectively ruled in *Bodetex Divisione*, while avoiding direct confrontation with its *Tessili* jurisprudence, by its findings on the 'principal' obligation issue. These it confined to the end of its judgment in two short paragraphs, at p.6792, paras. 39–40. It simply stated that when a national court is confronted by obligations of 'equal rank', or, by implication therefore, finds it impossible to ascertain a principal obligation, then the *Shenavai* principle 'accessorium sequitur principale' cannot be applied; and despite the valiant submissions of Bodetex, and the Commission to the contrary, a fragmentation of the claims will occur, each obligation being sent independently to its own (different)[604] place of performance by (Belgian law as) the *lex causae*.

The bulk of the ECJ's judgment was taken up by Bodetex's argument that commercial agency contracts should be assimilated to contracts of employment[605]—together with the Commission's attempts to avoid the fragmentation of the claims to which a strict interpretation, and non-application of *Shenavai*—would inevitably lead.

The Court refused to place such contracts of representation on a jurisdictional par with Article 5(1) contracts of employment; nor did it condone an interpretation of Article 5(1) that would 'avoid in advance situations to which Article 22 of the Convention would be applicable.'[606]

1.2.6 A (tacit) requirement that the Article 5(1) obligation, in addition, be contractual?[607]

At first sight it seems that in an ordinary international sale of goods contract, the seller delivers, the buyer takes delivery and pays the price; disputes about any

---

[602] Subject now of course to *Mainschiffahrts-Genossenschaft eG (MSG) v Les Gravières Rhénanes SARL* (C-106/95) [1997] ECR I-911.

[603] Predictability for the plaintiff, after all, is now also a Convention aim: *Mulox IBC Ltd v Hendrick Geels* (C-125/92) [1993] ECR I-4075, at p.4103, para. 11.

[604] The only palliative for the plaintiff being to sue for the whole claim in the Article 2 jurisdiction of the debtor's domicile.

[605] After the San Sebastian Convention amendments to Article 5(1), to reflect caselaw of the ECJ (*Roger Ivenel v Helmut Schwab* (C-133/81) [1982] ECR 1891) jurisdiction is now given 'in matters relating to individual contracts of employment, [*inter alia*, to the] . . . place . . . where the employee habitually carries out his work . . .'; this amendment has not been without its problems: *Mulox IBC Ltd v Hendrick Geels* (C-125/92) [1993] ECR I-4075, *Petrus Wilhelmus Rutten v Cross Medical Ltd* (C-383/95) [1997] ECR I-57, *Giulia Pugliese v Finmeccanica SpA Alenia Aerospazio Division* (C-437/00) [2001] OJ C61/1, pending.

[606] (C-420/97) [1999] ECR I-6747, at pp.6789–90, para. 30.

[607] It was thought that Roch LJ's statement, in *Kleinwort Benson Ltd v Glasgow City Council* [1996] 2 All ER 257, CA, at p.270, that 'obligations' are not confined to contractual obligations, may have had

obligation[608] have their genesis within the strict confines of a contractual relationship. In some Contracting State[609] systems, mutual 'obligations' may be owed by both parties in the (negotiation) stages running up to the formal point of contracting. This may cause problems for classification of these pre-contractual[610] duties. For Article 5(1), it means that the word 'obligation' may or may not have to have a tacit 'contractual' adjunct appended to it.

1.2.6(i) The English cases

In England and Wales, at least, the problem of whether pre-contractual duties are nonetheless 'obligations' for the purposes of jurisdiction under Article 5(1) has been discussed in two cases,[611] *Trade Indemnity plc and others v Försäkringsaktiebolaget Njord (in liq)*[612] and *Agnew and others v Lansförsäkringsbolagens AB.*[613] These will be examined below. For now, it will be sufficient to identify a number of potential issues, should the word 'obligation' in Article 5(1) have an additional contractual tag. If the obligation itself must be 'contractual', how is its

to be re-assessed; Lord Goff stressed on a number of occasions that an Article 5(1) obligation had to be contractual; but now *Agnew and others v Lansförsäkringsbolagens AB* [2001] 1 AC 223, HL; cf *Alfred Dunhill Ltd v Diffusion Internationale de Maroquinerie de Prestige SARL and others* [2001] CLC 949.

[608] Excluding for now actions for misrepresentation, (*obiter* in *Alfred Dunhill Ltd v Diffusion Internationale de Maroquinerie de Prestige SARL and others* [2001] CLC 949), and *culpa in contrahendo*; in *Bundesgericht* 11.7.2000 *Dörken-Gutta Pol gegen Gutta-Werke AG*, unreported, the Swiss court was receptive to the idea that *culpa in contrahendo* claims could be accommodated within Article 5(1), but did not need to decide the issue; but *OGH* 18.7.2000 (2001) *ZfRV* 33 has categorically ruled that a *culpa in contrahendo* claim *can* be a 'contractual obligation', to be performed at the place of the contract's formation; also *LG Dortmund* 19.2.1998 1998 IPRspr. Nr.139. AG Geelhoed, in his opinion of 31.1.2002 in *Tacconi v Wagner*, noted at para. 82 that claims on the Continent, strictly known as claims *culpa in contrahendo*, would fall more naturally into Art.5(3)—his three 'phases' of pre-contractual activity, at paras. 81–83, each one edging closer to the time of actual contractual conclusion are nebulous, and not easy for an English lawyer to differentiate.

[609] Pre-contractual duties of utmost good faith in insurance contracts in England and Wales have provoked a discussion of 'contractual' obligations, in *Agnew and others v Lansförsäkringsbolagens AB* [2001] 1 AC 223, HL; *obiter*, an 'obligation' not to induce a contract by misrepresentation not a 'matter relating to a contract': *Alfred Dunhill Ltd v Diffusion Internationale de Maroquinerie de Prestige SARL and others* [2001] CLC 949.

[610] For the German attitude to claims *culpa in contrahendo*, Markesinis, Lorenz, and Dannemann Volume 1, 1997, at p.69 following; *LG Dortmund* 19.2.1998 1998 IPRspr. Nr.139; also Hill, 2nd edn., 1998, at p.131, para. 5.6.21—who is doubtful of jurisdiction under Article 5(1), where negotiations do not lead to a concluded contract.

[611] The findings and fortunes of the two cases cited have, to a large degree, been influenced by the changing judicial attitude to the word 'contract' in the saga of *Kleinwort Benson Ltd v Glasgow City Council* [1996] 2 All ER 257, CA; [1999] 1 AC 153, HL; also Rix J's acknowledgement in *Trade Indemnity plc and others v Försäkringsaktiebolaget Njord (in liq)* [1995] 1 All ER 796, at p.815: 'if restitutionary claims [are] . . . within Article 5(1), it would follow that the word 'obligation' must have a meaning which is wider than 'contractual obligation''; *Dicey and Morris*, 13th edn., Vol. I, 2000, at p.345, para. 11–245 is neutral as to the effect of the House of Lords' decision in *Kleinwort Benson Ltd*.

[612] [1995] 1 All ER 796, QBD (Rix J).

[613] [1996] 4 All ER 978, QBD (Mance J) affm'd [1997] 4 All ER 937, CA, affm'd HL [2001] 1 AC 223, (Lords Millett and Hope of Craighead dissenting).

contractual[614] nature to be classified? Must it arise 'under', or 'out of' a contract—in other words post-formation?[615] If, as seems logical, the 'contractual' nature of an obligation is to be judged in the same way as 'matters relating to a contract',[616] is it a correct proposition to state that once the hurdle of 'matters relating to a contract' is passed, *ex hypothesi*, the contractual nature[617] or not of the obligation can be assumed?[618] The problem will be shown to stem, at least in part, from the French and English versions of Article 5(1) of the Brussels Convention. The German version of Article 5(1),[619] for all its verbosity, provides clear evidence[620] that the claim must 'arise out of' a contract.[621] This too, together with limited German case law on the subject, will be examined below.

Were this area free from (English) authority,[622] an obvious answer, from even a cursory view of *De Bloos*, would be that the obligation must be 'contractual'. The two terms are used in conjunction on a number of occasions by the European Court.[623] It refers to 'the obligation . . . which arises *under*[624] the contract',[625] 'the *contractual* obligation of the grantor which corresponds to the *contractual* right

---

[614] One would have thought in the same way as the introductory words 'matters relating to a contract': *Martin Peters Bauunternehmung GmbH v Zuid Nederlandse Aannemers Vereniging* (C-34/82) [1983] ECR 987 and *Jakob Handte & Co. GmbH v Société Traitements Mecano-Chimiques des Surfaces (TMCS)* (C-26/91) [1992] ECR I-3697; *Alfred Dunhill Ltd v Diffusion Internationale de Maroquinerie de Prestige SARL and others* [2001] CLC 949, *obiter*.

[615] And also an obligation that refers to pre-formation duties?

[616] *Ibid.*

[617] The courts finding of the initial application of Article 5(1) 'matters relating to a contract' may act *qua res judicata* for the (contractual) obligation question: Lord Goff in *Kleinwort Benson* and Mance J in *Agnew and others v Lansförsäkringsbolagens AB* [1996] 4 All ER 978, at p.989.

[618] At first blush, support for this proposition seems to come from *Atlas Shipping Agency (UK) Ltd and United Shipping Services Ltd v Suisse Atlantique Société d'Armement Maritime S.A.* [1995] 2 Lloyd's Rep. 188, QBD (Rix J) at p.194, col.2, para. 1; the issue clearly involved 'matters relating to a contract' but an equitable remedy (obligation) was being enforced, although through a contract—but the dissenting speeches of Lords Millett and Hope of Craighead in *Agnew and others v Lansförsäkringsbolagens AB*; *Alfred Dunhill Ltd v Diffusion Internationale de Maroquinerie de Prestige SARL and others* [2001] CLC 949.

[619] Set out below, p.113.

[620] 'aus einem Vertrag' ('out of a contract').

[621] Compare the various English translations of Article 5(1) in (1976) *NILR* 347, at p.348 'claims *resulting from* a contract' for the German version.

[622] The authority of *Agnew and others v Lansförsäkringsbolagens AB* [1997] 4 All ER 937, CA, and its reliance on the reversed CA decision in *Kleinwort Benson Ltd v Glasgow City Council* [1996] 2 All ER 257 may have been seen by some to have been weakened by Lord Goff's speech in the House of Lords in the *Kleinwort Benson Ltd* case, *Cheshire and North*, 13th edn., 1999, at p.204; it was no doubt responsible for the two dissenting speeches in the recent House of Lords appeal in *Agnew* itself.

[623] Lord Goff, at p.168, in *Kleinwort Benson Ltd v Glasgow City Council* [1999] 1 AC 153, also relied on *de Bloos* and *Shenavai* to disagree with Roch LJ in the Court of Appeal. Roch LJ had supported a wider interpretation of the term 'obligation', presumably not confined to contractual obligations. Lord Goff was 'unable to agree; it is plain . . . that the word does indeed refer to the *contractual obligation* on which the claim is based.'

[624] *Quaere*, does this mean within the context of a concluded contract?

[625] *Ets. A. de Bloos S.P.R.L v Soc. en commandite par actions Bouyer* (C-15/76) [1976] ECR 1497, at p.1508, para. 14.

relied upon by the grantee'[626] and 'the obligation . . . is that which the *contract* imposes'.[627]

The first case to consider the issue of pre-contractual obligations under Article 5(1) was *Trade Indemnity plc and others v Försäkringsaktiebolaget Njord (in liq)*.[628] Rix J held[629] that the pre-contractual duties of disclosure, and avoidance of, material (mis)representations leading up to contracts of re-insurance were not within the term 'obligation[s] in question'.[630] In his view, previous authorities[631] emphasised a pre-requisite of 'a contract giving rise to contractual obligations, or at any rate consensual relations akin to contract giving rise to comparable obligations'.[632]

Mance J reached the opposite conclusion in a similar re-insurers' avoidance action in *Agnew and others v Lansförsäkringsbolagens AB*.[633] He quite correctly observed that in none of the authorities relied on by Rix J was 'the nature of the obligations embraced by Article 5(1) directly in issue'.[634] Continuing, he provided support for the proposition that whenever a dispute involves 'matters relating to a contract' an irrebuttable presumption[635] arises that all claims will relate to 'obligations' under Article 5(1):[636]

> Once it is concluded (as here) that the matter relates to a contract, the only[637] inquiries expressly required under Article 5(1) are whether the matter involves an obligation.[638]

---

[626] *Ibid*, at p.1509, para. 15.

[627] *Ibid*, at para. 16; this part of *de Bloos* had, at one stage, fallen out of favour with the English Court of Appeal in *Kleinwort Benson Ltd*, only to re-emerge in Lord Goff's speech in the House of Lords in the same case. After *Agnew and others v Lansförsäkringsbolagens AB* [2001] 1 AC 223, HL, it is questionable whether *Kleinwort Benson Ltd* can be seen as conclusive authority for pre-contractual 'duties', *strictu sensu*; although an 'obligation', if such it is, prior to the conclusion of a contract *not uberrimae fidei*—such as not to induce a contract by misrepresentation—is not 'a matter relating to a contract' for Article 5(1) purposes: *obiter* in *Alfred Dunhill Ltd v Diffusion Internationale de Maroquinerie de Prestige SARL and others* [2001] CLC 949, at p.961.

[628] [1995] 1 All ER 796, QBD (Rix J).

[629] *Ibid*, at p.819.

[630] The English reinsurers could not therefore obtain jurisdiction under Article 5(1) Lugano Convention for their avoidance action.

[631] *Ets. A. de Bloos S.P.R.L v Soc. en commandite par actions Bouyer* (C-15/76) [1976] ECR 1497 *Martin Peters Bauunternehmung GmbH v Zuid Nederlandse Aannemers Vereniging* (C-34/82) [1983] ECR 987; *SPRL Arcado v SA Haviland* (C-9/87) [1988] ECR 1539 and *Union Transport Plc v Continental Lines S.A. and Conti Lines S.A.* [1992] 1 Lloyd's Rep. 229, HL.

[632] [1995] 1 All ER 796, at p.818.

[633] [1996] 4 All ER 978, affm'd [1997] 4 All ER 937, CA, affm'd HL, [2001] 1 AC 223.

[634] [1996] 4 All ER 978, at p.987, a way to avoid the obvious 'contractual' context in *de Bloos*.

[635] Stating this at its highest.

[636] Less convincing was his argument about the Convention's drafters' omission of a special head of jurisdiction: a lucid comment on this aspect by Peel, E. 'Jurisdiction under the Brussels Convention' in F. Rose (ed) *Restitution and the Conflict of Laws*, 1995, 1, at p.16.

[637] The language used here suggests there is a presumption; the Court of Appeal decision in *Kleinwort Benson* must surely have been an influence here.

[638] [1996] 4 All ER 978, at p.989f.

The Court of Appeal[639] agreed,[640] and continued in the same vein.[641] The relationship between the characterisation of 'matters relating to a contract' and its subsequent preclusive,[642] defining influence on 'obligation' is emphasised by Evans LJ thus:

'the obligation in question' *refers back* to the requirement that the proceedings shall be 'in matters relating to a contract'. Since any proceedings of this sort will be to enforce or claim relief in respect of an obligation owed by the defendant . . . it follows that *the proceedings themselves*[643] will identify the 'obligation in question'.[644]

The Court of Appeal's wide view of obligations in this case was influenced by the expanded view of 'matters relating to a contract' in *Kleinwort Benson Ltd v Glasgow City Council*[645] in the same court.[646]

The appeal in *Agnew v Lansförsäkringsbolagens AB* was heard by the House of Lords, in which, by a bare majority,[647] their Lordships dismissed the Swedish insurance company's appeal—thereby permitting Agnew's representative claim to avoid the contract of reinsurance for material non-disclosures to proceed in England under Article 5(1) of the Lugano Convention.

---

[639] [1997] 4 All ER 937, CA.

[640] Also Merkin, *Insurance Contract Law*, 1997, Issue 35, D.4.1–116–17: 'it would be illogical to distinguish between cases in which there is a warranty' and those with none; also 'what is clear is that the usual reinsurance problem—that of utmost good faith—is an issue which falls within Article 5(1)'.

[641] '[T]he reference in Article 5(1) to "the obligation in question" ought not to be considered in isolation from the remaining words in Article 5(1)', at p.942 (Evans LJ).

[642] Cf Briggs, 1997, at p.104.

[643] *Quaere*, more evidence of a presumption?

[644] [1997] 4 All ER 937, at p.942: also Leggatt LJ in *Kleinwort Benson Ltd v Glasgow City Council*, dissenting, [1996] 2 All ER 257,at p.266: 'the phrase "performance of the obligation in question" most naturally refers to the performance prescribed by the contract of relevant contractual obligations'; it is submitted that Lord Goff's view (appending the word 'contractual' to 'obligation') can be confined to a 'contract', believed by the parties to be valid, but subsequently—and by mutual agreement—held to be void *ab initio*; he did not, it appears, wish to speak generally, but merely tried to emphasise that an obligation must have arisen in relation to a contract that once had legal effect. He should not be interpreted as laying down any general rule that precludes jurisdiction being taken under Article 5(1) over 'pre-contractual' obligations: Merkin, 1997, Issue 35, D.4.1–116–17, makes the point that pre-contractual duties of non-disclosure would otherwise be excluded, whereas similar post-contractual, continuing duties of utmost good faith (of *The Litsion Pride* [1985] 1 Lloyd's Rep. 437, *The Captain Panagos* [1986] 2 Lloyd's Rep. 470 type, as refined by *Manifest Shipping Co. Ltd v Uni-Polaris Shipping Co. Ltd (The 'Sea Star')* [2001] 2 WLR 170, HL, and *K/S Merc-Scandia XXXII v Certain Lloyd's Underwriters* [2001] Lloyd's Rep IR 802, CA, at pp.813–15) *would be* covered by Article 5(1), an illogical division—*contra*, and *obiter*, outside the insurance context *Alfred Dunhill Ltd v Diffusion Internationale de Maroquinerie de Prestige SARL and others* [2001] CLC 949.

[645] [1996] 2 All ER 257, CA.

[646] Lord Goff, [1999] 1 AC 153, HL reversed the lower court's findings that restitutionary obligations in consequence of a void contract were 'matters relating to a contract' for the purposes of Article 5(1) of Schedule 4 to the CJJA, echoing words used in *de Bloos* that 'the word does indeed refer to the *contractual* obligation on which the claim is based', at p.168.

[647] Lords Woolf MR, and Cooke of Thorndon, with whom Lord Nicholls of Birkenhead agreed; Lords Millett and Hope dissenting.

The source of the disagreement[648] between their Lordships centred on whether or not the 'obligation' in Article 5(1) had to arise variously from,[649] in, within, or under[650] a contract—all expressions indicating, to the minority, obligations of a *post-contractual* nature. Three categories of obligations appeared to need consideration: (1) express obligations of, and after, a concluded contract; (2) implied obligations (as a matter of law) of, and after, a concluded contract; and (3) 'obligations' (which the parties mutually owe each other), which arise, from whatever source, prior to contracting.

Lord Woolf,[651] in the absence of authority, would have found no difficulty—in the ordinary meaning of the language of Article 5(1)—in holding that there was 'an obligation' to disclose, which was 'in question': a 'common-sense answer to this case'.[652] He relied (perhaps too) heavily on the policy of the Convention, manifest in Article 5(1), namely a close connection[653] between the place of performance of that obligation (to disclose) and the court seised. The crucial word 'under' a contract, from statements of the ECJ in *de Bloos v Bouyer*, he felt did not have any particular, or decisive, impact one way or the other on the question whether pre-contractual obligations could be accommodated under Article 5(1). For him, there was no discernible distinction between obligations under a concluded contract, which were not express, and pre-contractual 'obligations'. He did not, with respect, focus directly on (mutual) 'obligations' which exist (by law or otherwise) *prior to*[654] contracting.

Lord Cooke of Thorndon, agreed:

> [w]hether it is a term or condition 'in' (or 'under') the contract is the kind of question which schoolmen might debate, but that is a refinement of linguistics which . . . should be avoided . . . in interpreting a modern convention . . .[655]

He, too, was influenced by the close connecting factor with the London insurance market.

Lords Hope and Millett,[656] in powerfully reasoned dissents, concluded that the duty of utmost good faith was not a 'contractual' obligation under Article 5(1), and could therefore not be brought here. For Lord Hope:

---

[648] All agreed that Article 11 (in matters relating to insurance) did not apply to reinsurance—a view confirmed recently in *Société Group Josi Reinsurance Company SA v Compagnie d'Assurances Universal General Insurance Company (UGIC)*, (C-412/98) [2000] ECR I-5925.

[649] A wider concept.

[650] The crucial word in this appeal, used by Lords Millett and Hope of the minority to allow the appeal and exclude pre-contractual obligations from Article 5(1); *obiter* in *Alfred Dunhill Ltd v Diffusion Internationale de Maroquinerie de Prestige SARL and others* [2001] CLC 949.

[651] His speech, too, was much influenced by seeking to distinguish *Kleinwort Benson Ltd v Glasgow City Council* [1999] 1 AC 153.

[652] [2001] 1 AC 223, at p.243.

[653] [2001] 1 AC 223, at pp.240–41; also Lord Cooke, who opined 'the natural place of trial is London', at p.247.

[654] Such as under ss.18 and 20 Marine Insurance Act 1906; also post-contractual duties *K/S Merc-Scandia XXXXII v Certain Lloyd's Underwriters* [2000] 2 All ER (Comm) 731.

[655] [2001] 1 AC 223, at pp.246–47.

[656] *Ibid* at p.247.

[t]he duties which the law implies at the stage when parties are in negotiation or are in the process of entering into the contract . . . fall into an entirely different category from the obligations which are created by or arise from the contract when it is made. . .[W]hen the [ECJ] uses the expression 'contractual obligation' it has in mind obligations which were created by or arose under the contract, not duties which were to be performed at or before the stage when it was entered into.[657]

For him, it would be a misuse of the language of Article 5(1) to describe the duty of utmost good faith as a 'contractual' obligation. For Lord Millett, the word:

'obligation in question'. . .must be limited to an obligation non-performance of which gives rise to contractual liability, [not one which is] merely a condition precedent to the formation of a fully binding contract.[658]

Again, failure to observe a duty of utmost good faith did not, for Lord Millett, constitute a breach of a contractual obligation.

From the point of view of the London insurance market, Lords Woolf and Cooke's views are probably to be preferred—but their analysis was too much influenced, *ab intitio*, by considerations of *forum conveniens*. For this insurance market, the minority speeches would be disastrous, forcing greater reliance, if possible, on Article 17 jurisdiction clauses, or on Article 2. Yet these dissents force an artificial rubicon between pre- and post-formation duties of utmost good faith,[659] by excluding the former, while, arguably, including the latter. Clearly on the same reasoning that the dissenting speeches excluded pre-contractual duties, post-contractual communication with insurers/reinsurers (such as submitting details of a loss[660]) would clearly come within Article 5(1).

1.2.6(ii)   *The German cases*

Before a number of German cases[661] are examined, it is as well to look again at the official[662] German version of Article 5(1) and its literal, (unofficial), translation. It reads:

---

[657] [2001] 1 AC 223, at pp.253–54.

[658] *Ibid* at p.266.

[659] Also of interest to practitioners should be Lord Millett's view of (continuing) express warranties (i.e. that the (re)assured warrants by an express clause in the contract that the pre-contractual duties have been complied with)—'in my opinion it would make no difference if *the contract contained* an express warranty on the part of the assured that it had made full disclosure of all relevant facts . . .', [2001] 1 AC 223, at p.266; it is submitted that if the contract contained such a clause, there should be nothing about their inclusion to cavil at under Article 5(1).

[660] *The Litsion Pride* [1983] 1 Lloyd's Rep. 437 and *The Captain Panagos* [1986] 2 Lloyd's Rep. 470, as tempered by *Manifest Shipping Co. Ltd v Uni-Polaris Shipping Co. Ltd (The 'Sea Star')* [2001] 2 WLR 170, HL and *K/S Merc-Scandia XXXII v Certain Lloyd's Underwriters* [2001] Lloyd's Rep IR 802, CA, at pp.813–15.

[661] The pre- *Jakob Handte & Co. GmbH v Société Traitements Mecano-Chimiques des Surfaces (TMCS)* cases of *LG Göttingen* 9.11.1976 IPRspr. 1976 Nr.145; *LG Bayreuth* 29.6.1988 IPRspr. 1988 Nr.159.

[662] The ECJ in *Effer SpA v Hans-Joachim Kantner* (C-38/81) [1982] 825, at p.834, para. 5, recognised the lack of uniformity between the language versions of Article 5(1).

wenn ein Vertrag oder Ansprüche aus[663] einem Vertrag den Gegenstand des Verfahrens bilden,[664] vor dem Gericht des Ortes, an dem die Verpflictung erfüllt worden ist[665] oder zu erfüllen wäre . . .

A literal translation would be:

when a contract or claims arising out of[666] a contract form the basis of the proceedings, before the court for the place where the obligation[667] was fulfilled or was to be fulfilled.

The English and French versions of Article 5(1), 'in matters relating to a contract', and 'en matière contractuelle' become, in the German version, 'wenn ein Vertrag oder Ansprüche aus einem Vertrag [den Gegenstand des Verfahrens bilden]'.[668] It is important to note that what forms the basis of the proceedings is not the 'obligation', as in the French[669] and English versions, but the opening, characterising phrase 'wenn ein Vertrag. . .'.[670] The word 'obligation', qualified in the English and French versions by 'in question' and 'qui sert de base à la demande' is simply rendered in German by 'die Verpflichtung' without any qualification.[671] The wording is materially different.[672]

What is undeniable is that the opening words of the German version of Article 5(1) obviate the need for a German court to consider, in addition, whether a particular obligation ('Verpflichtung') is contractual or not. *Ex hypothesi*, a claim ('Anspr[uch] aus einem Vertrag') which is not contractual will not reveal an obligation that is, arguably, not also contractual.[673] Such a combined classification at

---

[663] '[a]us' meaning 'out of' could also be translated as 'arising out of'—this has an important bearing on whether or not obligations must be contractual, the methodology adopted by Swiss *Bundesgericht* in 11.7.2000 *Dörken-Gutta Pol gegen Gutta-Werke AG*, unreported, available from *Bundesgericht*'s website: http://www.bger.ch/. In either sense, the German version here suggests that they do.

[664] O'Malley, S. and Layton, A. *European Civil Practice*, 1989, incorrect on this point at p.390 n.13.

[665] This wording, rendered in French as 'a été ou doit être exécutée' appears to give both this and the German version an added factual place of performance advantage over the English version.

[666] Above, n.663; translation in (1976) *NILR* 348, 'claims *resulting from* a contract'.

[667] Note in the free, unofficial translation of the German version the absence of the words 'in question'.

[668] The last five words in the square brackets (added), according to O'Malley, S. and Layton, A., 1989, at p.390 form part of the phrase 'matters relating to a contract'. They do not. They are rendered in the free English translation, above, as 'form the basis of the proceedings', or in Article 5(1) parlance, 'in question'.

[669] 'obligation qui sert de base à la demande'.

[670] 'In matters relating to a contract'; the odd statement of Bachmann (1997) *IPRax*, at p.154 'Der Anspruch kann gestetzlicher Natur sein'('the claim can be of a legal nature'), above.

[671] It is submitted therefore that what, for the English courts, becomes a two stage test: (although the order of steps (1) and (2) appears to be flexible: *Alfred Dunhill Ltd v Diffusion Internationale de Maroquinerie de Prestige SARL and others* [2001] CLC 949, *obiter*): (1) matters relating to a contract and (2) *then* seeing if there is a contractual obligation, becomes for the German courts a condensed, *single-stage* investigation. If the matter—as a single enquiry—is not contractual nor a contractual claim ('Anspr[uch] aus einem Vertrag'), then the investigation goes no further; it is irrelevant therefore whatever the 'Verpflichtung' is.

[672] To AG Reischl, in *Effer v Kantner* (C-38/81) [1982] 825, at p.838, point 1, the German version of Article 5(1) was, to him, the clearest in point, without explanation (apart from being a native speaker).

[673] Swiss *Bundesgericht* in 11.7.2000 *Dörken-Gutta Pol gegen Gutta-Werke AG*, unreported.

the outset, forced on the court by the German wording of Article 5(1) means, as the *LG Frankfuhrt*[674] and the *OLG Düsseldorf*[675] found, that the claims pleaded[676] by the plaintiff will have to satisfy the autonomous definition of a contract *ab initio*; by contrast, in the UK, the word 'relating' to a contract has been given quite a wide interpretation, carrying with it the notion of anything remotely connected with a foreseeable,[677] consensual[678] relationship[679] that, at one time at least, had existence in law,[680] albeit not in fact, nor in the minds of the 'contracting' parties. That the German version requires that the plaintiff's claims also be of a consensual[681] kind, and arise from within a (concluded) contract[682] would seem to limit the application of Article 5(1) severely in Germany.

As will be seen, claims[683] which arise by operation of law, or from express statutory wording would seem, through the German version of Article 5(1), to be excluded. The English view in *Agnew and others v Lansförsäkringsbolagens AB* that there is 'no further[684] requirement that the obligation itself be 'contractual' in any sense'[685] would probably not be shared in Germany,[686] no doubt due to its rather idiosyncratic wording in Article 5(1).

In *OLG Düsseldorf*,[687] it will be remembered, the German plaintiff sales manager had demanded severance pay from his German employer. It was insolvent. He attempted to sue its French parent company, the defendant, claiming it had been sufficiently[688] involved in the day-to-day management and/or running of its insolvent subsidiary so as to incur the subsidiaries' liabilities under German company law.[689] This action, invoking the direct liability of a controlling

---

[674] *LG Frankfurt/Main* 5.10.1995 IPRspr. 1995 Nr. 155.

[675] (1998) *IPRax* 210.

[676] The German version is stricter and more exclusionary than the more nebulous, and inclusionary word in English 'relating' to a contract. Relating to a contract could mean any tenuous connection to a consensual relationship. This would not be possible in the German version.

[677] An element of foreseeability, with whom one is contracting, is necessary: *Jakob Handte & Co. GmbH v Société Traitements Mecano-Chimiques des Surfaces (TMCS)* (C-26/91) [1992] ECR I-3967, at p.3995, para. 18.

[678] *Ibid.*

[679] Akin to a contract, as in *Martin Peters Bauunternehmung GmbH v Zuid Nederlandse Aannemers Vereniging* (C-34/82) [1983] ECR 987, at p.1002, para. 13.

[680] *Kleinwort Benson Ltd v Glasgow City Council* [1999] 1 AC 153, HL.

[681] Thus in *LG Frankfuhrt am Main* and *OLG Düsseldorf* not claims that arise by operation of law, below.

[682] 'aus einem Vertrag'; *quaere* therefore, pre-contractual duties.

[683] Note the distinction between *locus standi* to sue or be sued and the actual mechanics/details of liability itself; esp. Briggs, 1997, at p.95, para. 2.129 on liability under the Sale of Goods Act 1979.

[684] The German version necessitates a *single stage*, *Agnew* a double stage, 'test'; the resulting difference of approach naturally leads to disharmony.

[685] Briggs, 1997, at p.104, para. 2.134.

[686] The section on *culpa in contrahendo*; *Fonderie Officine Meccaniche Tacconi Spa v HWS Heinrich Wagner Sinto Maschinenfabrik GmbH* (C-334/00) [2000] OJ C302/21, qu.2 in reference pending, AG Geelhoed's opinion, 31.1.2002.

[687] 26.10.1995 (1998) *IPRax* 187.

[688] Similar to the liabilities of a 'shadow director', as defined in the English Companies Act 1985.

[689] §303 *Aktiengesetz*.

shareholder was held to be 'eine quasi-vertragliche Haftung aus einem gesetzlichen Schuldverhältnis',[690] and therefore not covered by Article 5(1). While conceding, as *Handte & Co. GmbH v Société Traitements Mecano-Chimiques des Surfaces (TMCS)* required, that the relationship between the parties was not one 'relating to a contract', the reviewer[691] also emphasises the non-contractual nature of the plaintiff/claimant's specific claim:

> die geltend gemachten Konzernhaftungsanspruch nicht vertragsrechtlich[692]

As has previously been examined, the specialised area of non-disclosure actions in English marine insurance law has neatly exposed a problem with Article 5(1): whether it is artificial to draw a line, for jurisdictional purposes in Title II, at the time of a contract's conclusion for certain mutual duties that are owed prior to contracting. It is uncertain whether the Conventions' framers ever envisaged the position of any such line. While the source of such duties is uncertain even in English law, this is not a solid foundation to attempt to classify, or accommodate them under Article 5(1); abetting the classification problem has been the 'contractual' background of statements in *de Bloos*, which the facts of the case demonstrate never appeared to have the definitional authority at times advocated. The same insurance law may also highlight the artificial nature of a strict contractual cut-off point for Article 5(1): with post-formation duties of utmost good faith, also controversial in their existence, and express contractual warranties that certain material facts have been made.[693]

The German version of Article 5(1) has also revealed problems for that Contracting State, not of contractual timing, but of obligations imposed by operation of law. For this Contracting State, the classification problem under Article 5(1) has become not 'is the pleaded claim a contractual one', but 'is it "a matter relating to a contract"' with its *Handte* and *Réunion* limitations—a condensed, single-stage investigation. Obligations, arising by or due to operation of law appear to have been held not to fall within Article 5(1) *ratione materiae*.

As even this brief overview of interpreting one word of a single Convention article has shown, the possibility for divergent interpretation is present, and its operation is equally as complex; as is the potential for judicial and self-protectionism, especially where payment obligations are concerned. To have included a special, autonomous obligation for all contracts, with a clearly defined (autonomous) place of performance would have been preferable to leaving such obligations to the vagaries of divergent *leges causae*.[694] Such a place however,

---

[690] ('a quasi-contractual liability resulting from an obligation imposed by operation of law').
[691] Zimmer (1998) *IPRax* 187, at pp.189–90.
[692] ('the claim sued upon for direct shareholder liability is not contractual'), *ibid.*
[693] *Agnew and others v Lansförsäkringsbolagens AB* [2001] 1 AC 223, at p.266 (Lord Millett), HL.
[694] Also Hertz, *Jurisdiction in Contract and Tort under the Brussels Convention*, 1998, at p.165, para. 5.2.4, n.302; he mentions that Denmark tabled a motion in the 1978 Accession Convention negotiations to restrict Article 5(1) to non-payment obligations.

would have either created a *forum actoris*, or replicated jurisdiction under Article 2 in any event.

Hertz[695] has gathered a list of commentators who have advocated the total repeal of Article 5(1), and others who have recommended the adoption of a 'characteristic'[696] obligation, instead of the specific obligation forming the basis of the proceedings. Apart from the uncertainties inherent in this classification, in sale of goods contracts, the 'characteristic obligation' is reckoned to be[697] that of the seller to deliver, which, in payment obligations, again singles out the *forum actoris*.

1.2.7   The reform of Article 5(1)'s 'obligation in question' and its 'place of performance'—Article 5(1) of the Brussels I Regulation, and Article 6 of the Hague draft Worldwide Judgments Convention

The greatest innovation for our purposes here brought by the Brussels I Regulation is now in the redrafted Article 5(1)—to correct what, in the explanatory memorandum to the former identically-worded July 1999 proposal, is termed the 'shortcomings'[698] of *Tessili*. In certain defined circumstances, it will produce an autonomous[699] place of performance of the 'obligation in question'.[700] The disadvantage of Regulation is that this autonomous interpretation only extends to two types of contract, identified in Article 5(1)(b)—'[a] case of the sale of goods[701]...[or]...[a] case of the provision of services'.[702] Outside these two 'specialised' areas, in Article 5(1)(c),[703] the general rule of jurisdiction in contract, retained in Article 5(1)(a)—and therefore the current position under the Brussels Convention—will reassert itself and prevail.

---

[695] *Ibid.*, at p.159, n.267.

[696] Thus achieving an amount of convergence between this and the Rome Convention 1980, Article 4(2); Moss (2000) *Nordic Journal of International Law* 379, at p.394; cf *Cour de Cassation* 15.5.2001 *SA Optelec c/ Sté Midtronics Bv* (2001) *JCP*, II, 10634.

[697] *Report on the Convention on the law applicable to contractual obligations*, (Giuliano and Lagarde Report), 31,10.1980 [1980] OJ C282/1, at p.20: 'It is the performance for which payment is due'.

[698] Available at http://europa.eu.int/comm/sg/tfjai/unit/unit3_en.htm at p.13.

[699] Subject to contrary intention, 'unless otherwise agreed'; recently, on a contractually-agreed place of delivery proving decisive for jurisdiction under Article 5(1), *BayObLG* 26.4.2001 (2001) *RIW* 862, at p.863.

[700] Huet, (2001) *JDI* 1121, at p.1128, observes that in Art.5(1)(b), the obligation in question is in the singular, and queries what will happen to locating this (autonomously) when more than one claim is brought forward; the solution may be to locate autonomously the 'principal obligation' retained from the earlier jurisprudence of *Hassan Shenavai v Klaus Kreischer* (C-266/85) [1987] ECR 239 and its progeny.

[701] Thought by Kropholler, 2002, at pp.137–138, paras. 31–32 to encompass the 'sale of goods' concept as understood by the 1980 Vienna Sales Convention.

[702] Huet, (2001) *JDI* 1121, at p.1127 and Béraudo, (2001) *JDI* 1033, at pp.1046–47, for the potential scope of Art.5(1)(b) *vis-à-vis* concession (and other types of distributorship) contracts.

[703] If, as it is submitted, Art.5(1)(c) is to be read as dividing Arts.5(1)(a) from 5(1)(b) *ratione materiae*; Kropholler, 2002, at p.133, para. 22—Art.5(1)(c) to apply when Art.5(1)(b) cannot be so.

In the specialised cases, however, and subject to contrary intention,[704] the (autonomous) place of performance in each respective case will be in the Member State where, 'under the contract', 'the goods were delivered or should have been delivered. . .[or] the services were provided or should have been provided.'

Disputes over international payment obligations in sales of goods cases have, at last, been freed from the ambivalent shackles of the place of performance *lege causae*; or so it appears.[705] The words 'under the contract' recall, it is submitted, a reliance on the *lex causae*,[706] in the absence of clear contractual drafting as to where the goods are to be delivered or services provided. It seems one problem over the place of performance of an obligation has, in certain cases, been exchanged for uncertainty over another (albeit autonomous) one.[707]

This said, in the vast majority of cases[708] (as under the current law), a seller's claim to the price of goods sold and delivered will in future, in cases governed by the 1980 Sales Convention,[709] under Article 5(1)(b), be brought in the *forum actoris*.

[704] It is likely that such contrary agreements on the place of performance will be subject to the ECJ's current findings on such clauses under Art.5(1) in *Mainschiffahrts-Genossenschaft eG (MSG) v Les Gravières Rhénanes SARL* (C-106/95) [1997] ECR I-911; Novy, D. 'Article 5(1) of the Brussels Convention' (2000) 1 *Hibernian Law Journal* 69, at pp.92–3; in Mayer, et Heuzé, *Droit International Privé*, 7ème éd, 2001, at p.226, para. 339, the authors fear there will be a regrettable rise in place of performance clauses due to the new version of Art.5(1); also Droz, G. and Gaudemet-Tallon, H. (2001) *Rev crit* 601, at pp.634–36.

[705] Béraudo, J-P. (2001) *JDI* 1033, at p.1045.

[706] Interpreting the French version of this phrase 'en vertu du contrat', Béraudo, (2001) *JDI* 1033, at pp.1044–45 believes it to mean either performance as determined by a place of performance clause, or by the *lex causae*, together with, potentially, the *forum actoris* of the seller under Article 31 Vienna Sales Convention; *contra*, Huet, (2001) *JDI* 1121, at pp.1128–29, who shuns the return to a *lex causae* influence, preferring, alternatively, 'en vertu du contrat' to mean from 'l'économie du contrat et aux circonstances de l'espèce' (a rather vague *forum conveniens* analysis rejected by the ECJ in *GIE Groupe Concorde e.a. v Le capitaine commandant le navire 'Suhadiwarno Panjan'* (C-440/97) [1999] ECR I-6307).

[707] Cf Harris, J. 'The Brussels Regulation' (2001) 20 *CJQ* 218, at p.220; Kubis, S. (2001) *ZeuP* 737, at p.751; also Markus, A. 'Revidierte Übereinkommen von Brüssel und Lugano: Zu den Hauptpunkten' (1999) *SZW* 205, at p.213; Ancel, (2001) *Rev crit* 150, at p.162; for the international sale of goods, governed by the 1980 Vienna Sales Convention, Article 31, in the absence of a contrary stipulation, a series of places of delivery are mandated—in Article 31(a)(b)(c); in the vast majority of cases (*OGH* 10.9.1998 *Entscheidungen* 71 Band, 1998, No.145) the *forum actoris* (for the Seller)—Schlechtriem, P (ed) *Commentary on the UN Convention on the International Sale of Goods (CISG)*, 2nd edn. (in translation), 1998, at p.230; Cf *Cour d'appel de Riom* 3.2.1999 *SA Bourbie c/ Société Thyssen Henschel GmbH* (2000) *JCP*, IV, 1704, at p.772; *Cour d'appel d'Orléans* 29.3.2001 *SARL TCE Diffusion c/ Soc. Elettrotecnica Ricci*, http://www.jura.uni-sb.de/CJFA; *Cour de Cassation* 26.6.2001 *Anton Huber GmbH & Co c/ Soc. Polyspace*, (2001) *JCP*, IV, 2554, *Cour de Cassation* 26.6.2001 *Sté Ogosa destribuciones c/ SA Madrange* (2001) *JCP*, IV, 2556; Heuzé, V. *La vente internationale de marchandises, Droit Uniforme*, 2000, at p.216.

[708] Unless such clauses as 'delivery ex works' or 'ex store' are included—such as in *Viskase Ltd and another v Paul Kiefel GmbH* [1999] 1 WLR 1305; and *Rye Valley Foods Ltd v Fisher Frozen Foods Ltd*, 10.5.2000, Irish HC (O'Sullivan J); these will no doubt become more common, to provide evidence of 'contrary intention'; *Cour de Cassation* 8.2.2000 *SA LM Plast c/ SARL Fahr Bucher France* (2000) *JCP*, IV, 1545, (2001) *JDI* 133, [2001] I.L.Pr. 31, (2001) *Rev crit* 151.

[709] The 'under the contract' phrase in Art.5(1)(b) will bring in the 1980 Vienna Convention, and its place of performance as it currently does under Art.5(1) Brussels Convention; *contra*, Kropholler, 2002, at p.140, para. 38; Béraudo, J-P. (2001) *JDI* 1033, at p.1045. For contracts governed by English law, the place of delivery and therefore jurisdiction will be governed by the terms of the contract, and

The Hague draft Worldwide Judgments Convention, Article 6,[710] appears to have a much more limited jurisdictional provision in contracts. It only applies to 'action[s] in contract' (a) 'in matters relating to the supply[711] of goods' or (b) 'the provision of services'. Again the jurisdictionally relevant Contracting State will be where those goods or[712] services were supplied[713] or provided, respectively.

It is arguable that the whole spectrum of conceivable contractual actions will not be accommodated[714] within Article 6(a), (b) or (c). International sales of goods will probably more naturally sit within Article 6(a), international commercial agency/representation, insurance and banking contracts in Article 6(b). But there may be cases which may be thought to fall through the scope of Article 6 *ratione materiae*, which disputes will have to find other bases of jurisdiction.

If sales of goods were to be included, this should have been stated explicitly, instead of awaiting potentially diverse, inconsistent, lengthy and costly litigation worldwide to settle on a definition *ratione materiae*, of 'the supply of goods' or 'the provision of services'.

The 'autonomising' of the 'obligation in question' in certain commonly-encountered situations is to be welcomed, in promoting greater certainty, as was the 1989 San-Sebastian amendments to the (new) individual contracts of employment provision.[715] The proposals for reform will avoid, to a large extent, the potential for either drafting chicanery by claimants, or the adoption of a beneficial selection/nomination of an 'obligation' that is clearly to be performed within the *forum actoris*. It should also avoid the unseemly selection of a 'principal' obligation merely via a highly questionable subjective test of comparable worth to claimants. Due account will also, in future, be taken in the proposals of the strenuous efforts of the AG in *Leathertex Divisione* to demote independent payment obligations, so as not to have to apply to them varying *leges causae* that may benefit some, but by no means all, Contracting State creditors' suing in the *forum actoris*.

---

in default of which s 29 Sale of Goods Act 1979; for a recently reported case under Art.32 of the Vienna Sales Convention (place of delivery), *Cour d'appel de Riom* 3.2.1999 *SA Bourbie c/ Société Thyssen Henschel GmbH* (2000) *JCP*, IV, 1704, at p.772; Kubis, S. (2001) *ZeuP* 737, at p.751.

[710] The version of Article 6 referred to here is that of the 1999 draft. It now forms, in the Commission II interim text, Alternative B in Article 6 behind Alternative A. This latter is a longer (US delegation influenced) version—that of a claim based on a contract directly related to an activity that is frequently and/or significantly conducted and/or directed in the potential forum of a Contracting State— together with what appears suspiciously like the constitutional scrutiny of a US 14th Amendment 'due process' analysis. This latter alternative is more general than focussing on two specific types of contract in Alternative B. It founds jurisdiction primarily on the defendant's (minimum) contacts with the forum, rather than the dispute's.

[711] This almost certainly includes a *sale* of goods.

[712] In 'mixed cases' of the supply of goods and services, the place of performance will be where 'the principal obligation took place', an unusually drafted compromise, *quaere* along *Shenavai* lines.

[713] *Quaere*, it may mean that where goods are *not* delivered, Article 6(a) will not apply.

[714] The fact that there is no general jurisdictional fall-back provision in contract may be a critical sign of disapproval of the current version of Art.5(1) Brussels Convention; Briggs, 2002, at p.74, gives certain examples of these.

[715] Which amalgamated both the obligation in question and its place of performance to where the employee habitually carries out his work.

1.3   THE 'PLACE OF PERFORMANCE'

la méconnaissance de la jurisprudence *Tessili* n'est pas sanctionnée que lorsqu'elle a pour effet de priver les tribunaux français de leur compétence internationale.[716] [717]

The third, and final, question facing the national court when deciding whether it has jurisdiction under Article 5(1) has also proved to be[718] a complex[719] and controversial[720] one, as one might have expected, given the interpretation and application of such a connecting factor in the conflict of laws. A 'place of performance' must be found for the (principal) obligation(s), previously identified.[721] The methodology[722] used by the Court of Justice for this task comes from the seminal case of *Industrie Tessili Italiana Como v Dunlop AG*,[723] confirmed[724] in *Custom Made Commercial Ltd v Stawa Metallbau GmbH*[725] and recently reaffirmed in *GIE Groupe Concorde and others v The master of the vessel 'Suhadiwarno Panjan'.*[726]

---

[716] ('ignoring the *Tessili* jurisprudence is only justified when the case has the effect of depriving French courts of their international competence').

[717] Watt reviewing *Soc. Comptoir des Plastiques de l'Ain c/ Soc. Novamec et autres* 9.2.1994 (1994) *Rev Crit* 577, at p.582, which serves as a *leitmotiv* for this section; also Mezger, E. 'L'unification du lieu du paiement des obligations monétaires' (1967) *JDI* 584, at p.596 believes (correctly) that the warning signs for the inauguration of a *forum actoris* for payment obligations was already evident in earlier bilateral Conventions, and autonomous civil procedure.

[718] It should have come as no surprise to the Convention's drafters—below on the historical precedents for Article 5(1).

[719] Involving, as it does, at the jurisdictional stage, in addition, ascertaining a choice of law and its application; the ECJ in its judgment of 19.2.2002 in *S.A. Besix N.V. v WABAG Wasserreinigungsbau Alfred Kretzschmar GmbH* (C-256/00) has ruled that the obligation in question can only have a single place of performance; a negative obligation not to contract with any other, nor to compete, did not have a prerequisite geographical limitation in a particular Contracting State, that the Court interpreted into Art.5(1); the cases, reviewed below, in which the place of performance of negative obligations (such as exclusive supply/sale/distribution or non-competition contracts) may have to be revisited and reassessed; but the authority of *Kenburn Waste Management Ltd v Bergman*, 11.5.2001, Ch.D., Pumfrey J, 30.1.2002, CA (where 'the negative obligation was to achieve a state of affairs *within* the United Kingdom') will remain unaffected by *S.A. Besix N.V. v WABAG*.

[720] Especially regarding the place of performance of independent payment obligations; the Advocate Generals' opinions in *Leathertex Divisione Sintetici SpA v Bodetex BVBA* (C-420/97) [1999] ECR I-6747, AG Léger's opinion 16.3.1999 and *GIE Groupe Concorde* (C-440/97) [1999] ECR I-6307, AG Colomer's opinion 16.3.1999, below; *Definitely Maybe (Touring) Ltd v Marek Lieberberg Konzertagentur GmbH* [2001] 1 WLR 1745, QBD (Morison J).

[721] In some detail, Kennett, W. 'Place of performance and predictability' (1995) *YEL* 193.

[722] In the absence of a (valid) (implied) place of performance clause (reflected in any case by the traditional Civil Codes of the Contracting States), *Hof van Beroep te Antwerpen*, 3.1.1995, *Haesaerts Container International c/ Oy Fincarriers en Finnbelgia agencies*, (1995) *Rev. dr. comm. belge* 391.

[723] (C-12/76) [1976] ECR 1473.

[724] The traditional methodology has been under attack in France from *Sté Comptoir commercial d'Orient c/ Société Medtrafina* 11.3.1997 (1998) *JDI* 129, [1999] I.L.Pr. 336, *Groupe Concorde et autres c/ Capitaine du Suhadiwarno Panjan et autres* 9.12.1997 1998 *Rev crit* 117, and Droz, G. 'Delendum est forum contractus? (vingt ans après les arrêts *de Bloos* et *Tessili* interprétant l'article 5.1 de la Convention de Bruxelles du 27 septembre 1968' (1997) *Dalloz*, Chron., 351.

[725] (C-288/92) [1994] ECR I-2913.

[726] (C-440/97) [1999] ECR I-6307; AG Colomer's opinion 16.3.1999.

Tessili involved an international sale of goods contract between a German (plaintiff) buyer, Dunlop, and an Italian (defendant) seller/supplier, Tessili. The goods supplied by Tessili proved defective and Dunlop commenced an action[727] before its local court in Hanau, Germany.

The well-known answer to the question of how a national court is to interpret the 'place of performance' was given in a (very terse)[728] judgment, for three reasons: one concerned with the Convention's article;[729] the second concerned with a lack of (unified) substantive contract law, and the last involved with an inescapable consequence[730] of the law of contract.[731]

The first reason—connected with the Convention article's aim—has proved to be over-optimistic and the subject of some cause for criticism,[732] even rebellion.[733] The other two remain. Subsequent cases,[734] especially *Custom Made Commercial*, *GIE Groupe Concorde* and *Leathertex Divisione Sintetici SpA v Bodetex BVBA*, have attempted to shore up *Tessili* with the addition of a fourth justification, that of foreseeability,[735] incidentally mentioned by AG Mayras, *en passant*, in *Tessili*[736] itself.

In any event, the methodology which has endured and become trite law, is assigned to the national court to

> determine in accordance with its own rules of conflict of laws what is the law applicable to the legal relationship in question and define in accordance with that law the place of performance . . .[737]

One can see immediately that the potential for divergent[738] interpretation exists, according to which court is seised, in its contractual choice of law rules[739] and resulting application of divergent *leges causae*.

While dealing with the prominent objections, and advantages, of this *lex causae* classification, the crux of the current examination will concentrate on the national

---

[727] AG Mayras notes, at p.1487, that the aim of Dunlop's action was not clear; on its return to the *OLG Frankfuhrt am Main*, its action proved to be for rescission of the sale contract, *Digest* I–5.1.2–B9.

[728] The material parts of the judgment are in paras. 13–14, at pp.1485–6; summarised by Kropholler, 2002, at p.131, para. 17.

[729] At para. 13

[730] Subsequently recognised in the Rome Convention 1980, Article 10.

[731] Mentioned by AG Mayras, at p.1491, 'those which result from a breach of the contract are created by law . . .'.

[732] Cf AG Lenz in *Custom Made Commercial* (C-288/92) [1994] ECR I-2913, at p.2933, para. 80.

[733] Below, and Droz, (1997) *Dalloz*, Chron., 351.

[734] Including *Hassan Shenavai v Klaus Kreischer* (C-266/85) [1987] ECR 239

[735] This Convention aim has recently come to the fore in cases such as *Jakob Handte & Co. GmbH v Société Traitements Mecano-Chimiques des Surfaces (TMCS)* (C-26/91) [1992] ECR I-3697, at p.3995, para. 18; *Mulox IBC Ltd v Hendrick Geels* (C-125/92) [1993] ECR I-4075, at p.4103, para. 11 and *Antonio Marinari v Lloyds Bank Plc and Zubaidi Trading Co.* (C-364/93) [1995] ECR I-2719, at p.2741, para. 19.

[736] At p.1490–91.

[737] At p.1485, para. 13, *in fine*.

[738] Briggs, 1997, at p.106.

[739] Not as problematical as when *Tessili* was decided, now the 1980 Rome Convention, and as from 1.4.1991, in UK the Contracts (Applicable Law) Act 1990—also the *Corte di Cassazione 6.8.1998 BS Electrodomesticos s.a. c/ Fallimento Sicentecnica s.p.a* (1999) *Riv. dir. int. priv. e proc.* 583, at p.585; *Hoge Raad 24.9.1997 Technisch Handelsbureau C. van Maanen BV / Construzioni Meccaniche Caorle SpA*

reactions to the *Tessili* decision, be they conformist or otherwise; and to focus on one area which has provoked special vilification[740] of *Tessili*, that of the place of performance of (independent) payment obligations.

What many commentators[741] are agreed upon is that the *Tessili* formula creates a *forum actoris* for claimants[742] in those Contracting States whose national law requires (in the absence of an agreement/circumstances to the contrary) performance of payment obligations at the creditor[743]/plaintiff/claimant's domicile,[744] and/or in those Contracting States which are also parties to certain international sales conventions.[745] It is pointed out that the Convention wished to abolish those (national) jurisdictional provisions, especially in Article 3 [II], which had the effect of creating a *forum actoris*. To this it can be objected that a certain amount of forum shopping by plaintiffs is inevitable in a Convention which provides for alternative bases of jurisdiction to the Article 2 'actor sequitur

---

1999 *NJ* 1734—it may be that the 1980 Rome Convention itself, esp. Art.4(1)(2), will not be uniformly interpreted throughout the Contracting States—cf application of Art.4(5) in *Ferguson Shipbuilders Ltd v Voith Hydro GmbH & Co.* (2000) *SLT* 229 and *Caledonia Subsea Ltd v Microperi Srl* [2001] SC 716, OH, *Cour de Cassation M.Robert Bismuth c/ Association d'Avenir Sportif de la Marsa et Société Olympique de Marseille* (2001) *JDI* 97, at p.102 and *Definitely Maybe (Touring) Ltd v Marek Lieberberg Konzertagentur GmbH* [2001] 1 WLR 1745, QBD, Morison J; Moss, 2000 Nordic Journal of International Law 379, at p.394; also *Samcrete Egypt Engineers and Contractors S.A.E. v Land Rover Exports Limited* [2002] CLC 533, CA.

[740] Droz criticisms early on in *Soc. Michael Horauf Maschinen c/ Soc. Leysens Meier* 14.6.1975 1976 *Rev crit* 117, at pp.124–26. Whether this criticism is justified and/or could have been predicted, given Article 5(1)'s ancestry, will have to be touched on.

[741] Esp. Gothot, P. et Holleaux, D., 1985, at p.41, para. 76.

[742] In *Definitely Maybe (Touring) Ltd v Marek Lieberberg Konzertagentur GmbH* [2001] 1 WLR 1745, QBD, at p.1747 (Morison J), the question of the jurisdiction of the English courts for an action for the payment of fees hinged on whether English or German law was found to be the *lex causae* of a touring contract for a group which allegedly (under)performed in Germany; the bulk of the court's judgment on jurisdiction was taken up with a discussion of various articles of the 1980 Rome Convention on the applicable law.

[743] Not the case in Germany, Markesinis, Lorenz, and Dannemann,Volume 1, 1997, at p.367: '[t]he most important consequence of the German rules contained in §270 IV is this: an unpaid creditor must bring his action against the defaulting debtor at the debtor's place of residence . . .'.

[744] For England, Proctor, C. *International Payment Obligations—a Legal Perspective*, 1997, at p.112 and *Robey & Co. v Snaefill Mining Co. Ltd* (1887) 20 QBD 752, *The Eider* [1893] P. 119: 'the debtor must follow his creditor . . .', at p.131 (Lord Esher); Italy Article 1182(3) *codice civile*: 'L'obbligazione avente per oggetto una somma di danaro deve essere adempiuta *al domicilio che il creditore* ha al tempo della scadneza'('The obligation having as its subject matter a sum of money shall be performed at the domicile of the creditor at the time the obligation matures'), translated by Beltramo, M. *The Italian Civil Code*, 1969, at p.314; in Switzerland Article 74(2)(1) *Obligationenrecht*.

[745] Holl, V. 'Der Gerichtsstand des Erfüllungsortes gemäß Article 5 Nr.1 EuGVÜ' (1995) *WB* 462, at p.464; *OLG Hamm* 5.11.1997 IPRspr. 1997 Nr. 160A, at p.326, BAG 17.7.1997 IPRspr. 1997 Nr. 154; also Goode, R. *Commercial Law*, 2nd edn, 1995, esp. p.928 onwards; on the 1980 Vienna Convention on International Sales: Schlechtriem, P (ed) *Commentary on the UN Convention on the International Sale of Goods (CISG)*, 2nd edn (in translation), 1998; Fogt, M. (2001) *IPRax* 358; also *Cour d'appel de Colmar La SARL Pelliculest c/ Soc Morton International GmbH, Cour d'appel de Paris 26.10.2000 Soc. Hind Livestock Exports Ltd c/ SARL Soviam, Cour d'appel d'Orléans 29.3.2001 Soc. TCE Diffusion c/ Soc. Elettrotecnica Ricci*, all reported on a CISG website at http://www.jura. uni-sb.de/CISG/decisions/).

forum rei' rule. A plaintiff/claimant will[746] bring an action in the *forum actoris* if possible.[747]

Yet the *forum actoris* objection may in some cases fail to take account of the original *raison d'être* of Article 5(1),[748] mentioned in the Jenard Report[749] and in *Tessili* itself: the

> particularly close relationship between a dispute and the court which may be called upon to take cognisance of [it][750]

A 'détour par le conflit de lois'[751] required by *Tessili* introduces an element of capriciousness into the proximity[752] equation, varying according to the particular place of performance determined by the *lex causae*.[753] The gradual reduction[754] and extinction[755] of Article 5(1)'s original purpose has provoked concerns about the inauguration[756] of the *forum actoris*, and the use of a new Convention aim, predictability,[757] to preserve the life of the *Tessili* jurisprudence.

Yet it is the 'selective'[758] benefit of Article 5(1) to certain Contracting State creditors and not to others that has proved to be the principal objection to the continued existence of the article. It no longer depends

> von einer zuständigkeitsrechtlichen Wertentscheidung ab, sondern vor dem Zufall, ob das ausländische Vertragsstatut die streitige Verpflichtung als Hol-oder Bringschuld ausgestaltet.[759]

---

[746] Kennett, W. 'Place of performance and predictability' (1995) *YEL* 193, at p.193 n.5; a plaintiff/claimant will in the vast majority of cases wish to sue in his *forum actoris* 'for compulsive psychological reasons' in *Società Kretschmer v Muratori, Corte di Cassazione*, 24.10.1988 [1991] I.L.Pr. 361, at p.367 para. 13.

[747] Also Allwood, W. 'Casenote: *Arcado v Haviland*' (1988) *ELR* 366, at p.368.

[748] Holleaux in *Société Gola Werke German Gotz c/ Barsaghian* 28.3.1979 (1980) *JDI* 888, at p.889.

[749] 5.3.1979, [1979] OJ C59/1, at p.23.

[750] (C-12/76) [1976] ECR 1473, at p.1485, para. 13.

[751] Gaudemet-Tallon, 1996, at p.126, para. 172; this detour took up a disproportionate amount of the Swiss court's judgment in *Firma T S.r.l gegen Firma S.AG* 18.1.1996 122 BGE, III, 43, at pp.45–46.

[752] One would have thought that either the plaintiff/claimant's or defendant's forum would be identified, but this is not necessarily so—*Royal Bank of Scotland Plc v Cassa di Risparmio* [1991] I.L.Pr. 411, QBD (Phillips J) aff'd [1992] 1 BankLR 251, CA.

[753] Occupying a prominent position in the judgment of Morison J in *Definitely Maybe (Touring) Ltd v Marek Lieberberg Konzertagentur GmbH* [2001] 1 WLR 1745, QBD; Novy, (2000) 1 *Hibernian Law Journal* 69, at p.86.

[754] In *Hassan Shenavai v Klaus Kreischer* (C-266/85) [1987] ECR 239, traced by Hill, J. 'Jurisdiction in matters relating to a contract under the Brussels Convention' (1995) *ICLQ* 591.

[755] *Custom Made Commercial Ltd v Stawa Metallbau GmbH* (C-288/92) [1994] ECR I-2913.

[756] Is it only now that the purpose of the Swiss and Luxembourg domiciliaries' reservation becomes clear?

[757] Dietze, J. 'Die aktuelle Rechtsprechung des EuGH zum EuGVÜ' (1995) *EuZW* 359, at p.360; other Convention aims have been emphasised by AG Léger in *Leathertex Divisione Sintetici SpA v Bodetex BVBA* (C-420/97) [1999] ECR I-6747.

[758] Schack, 2. Auf., 1996, at p.106, para. 269; also Hertz, 1998.

[759] ('on a jurisdictionally justified value judgment, but on pure chance, whether the foreign governing law classifies the obligation in question as a debt to be collected or brought.'), Schack, *ibid*, esp. if there is a fragmentation of obligations as in *Leathertex Divisione Sintetici SpA v Bodetex BVBA* (C-420/97) [1999] ECR I-6747.

A valid point can be made for Article 5(1)'s creation of a *forum actoris* for all Contracting State creditors or none. While the *Tessili* jurisprudence and divergent national laws of contract exist, some Contracting State plaintiff/claimants are either advantaged or disadvantaged.[760] The only thing that can be said for the current position is that, in the absence of express stipulation in the contract,[761] its arbitrariness[762] is at least reasonably foreseeable. Parties in those Contracting States at risk from disadvantageous *leges causae* should protect themselves with adequately drafted place of performance[763] and/or jurisdiction clauses.

Rather weak criticism[764] of Article 5(1) comes from those who state that the *Tessili* formula overcomplicates[765] what, after all, is a jurisdictional question:

> [l]e gros inconvénient de l'arrêt *Tessili* est d'obliger le juge saisi à examiner d'abord la loi applicable à l'obligation litigieuse avant de décider sa compétence . . .[766] [767]

It is an inescapable fact of the law of contract that, in the absence of agreement, the place and mode of performance is to be governed by the law of that contract, recognised by *Tessili*:

> the determination of the place of performance of obligations depends on the contractual context to which these obligations belong.[768]

The next section will attempt to show that the criticisms of the *lex causae* formulation of Article 5(1) come too late, given the diverse, and historical

---

[760] The critical distinction, brought about by different material laws, and observed by Purchas LJ in *Mercury Publicity Limited v Wolfgang Loerke GmbH* [1993] I.L.Pr. 142, CA, at p.150, Morison J in *Definitely Maybe (Touring) Ltd v Marek Lieberberg Konzertagentur GmbH* [2001] 1 WLR 1745, QBD, at p.1747 and *Tribunal de commerce de Liège*, 19.6.1995 (1996) *Rev. dr. comm. belge* 839, at p.841.

[761] Note *Tribunal de Commerce Hasselt*, 20.11.1996 *Metaalconstructie Vanacken B.V.B.A. c/ Installatietechniek Bitter B.V.* (1997) *Rev. dr. comm. belge* 200; an express place of performance clause (for example payment to be made at the seller's place of business/bank) is unlikely to fall foul of the recent restrictions placed on such clauses in *Mainschiffahrts-Genossenschaft v Les Gravières Rhénanes* (C-106/95) [1997] ECR I-911, at p.944, para. 34; cf *Cheshire and North*, 13th edn., 1999, at p.206; a place of performance can be stipulated by incorporation of standard terms: *OLG Dresden* 24.11.1998 (1999) *RIW* 968, at p.969, (unsuccessful *in casu*); however, successful agreement on place of delivery determinative in *BayObLG* 26.4.2001 (2001) *RIW* 862; or a clause can give the plaintiff/claimant the option of nominating and/or altering a place of performance (payment)—as in *Chailease Finance Corporation v Credit Agricole Indosuez* [2000] 1 Lloyd's Rep. 348, CA.

[762] Briggs, 1997, at p.107, para. 2.137.

[763] Noting the caveat to these clauses introduced by *Mainschiffahrts-Genossenschaft eG (MSG) v Les Gravières Rhénanes SARL* (C-106/95) [1997] ECR I-911.

[764] At least to English eyes: the former RSC Ord. 11 r.1(1)(d)(iii), now CPR Rule 6.20(5)(c); yet this was a particularly strong *leitmotiv* in AG Colomer's opinion in *GIE Groupe Concorde e.a.* (C-440/97) [1999] ECR I-6307, at p.6309, p.6317, pp.6321–23, p.6336 and p.6340, paras. 3, 28, 44–49, 95, and 107, respectively—passed over without comment by the ECJ's judgment.

[765] Droz, 1997 *Dalloz*, Chron., 351, at p.352 and Broggini, G. 'Zuständigkeit am Ort der Vertragserfüllung' in *Das Lugano-Übereinkommen*, (Hrsg. Schwander, I.), 1990, p.111, at p.121.

[766] ('the great drawback of the *Tessili* case is requiring the judge seised to examine first the applicable law of the obligation in question before deciding on his own competence').

[767] Gaudemet-Tallon, 1996, at p.126 para. 172.

[768] (C-12/76) [1976] ECR 1473, p.1485, para. 14 *in fine*; in this sense Briggs, A. 'The Brussels Convention' (1994) *YEL* 557, at p.574.

provenance that jurisdiction at the place of performance has enjoyed for almost two hundred years.

1.3.1   Historical precedents for 'the place of performance' under Article 5(1)— the civil codes of Europe[769]

Whatever the merits or demerits of the current position with regard to Article 5(1), and despite numerous clarifying references to the ECJ, the provision remains a contentious article. One is thus tempted to speculate on the original drafting of the article, its historical predecessors[770] and the interpretations[771] they received. If, as it will be attempted to demonstrate, the same problematical interpretations[772] were already in existence, the Convention's drafters should have been aware of the potential for historical repetition, and legislated accordingly.

A good example of belated criticism comes from Droz.[773] In his classic work of 1972,[774] he picks up on two points in Article 5(1): first, the close links between the dispute and tribunal[775] so as to justify the facultative jurisdiction under Article 5 generally; and secondly, the crucial[776] adoption by the Convention of jurisdiction in contract matters after German (procedural) law:

---

[769] The earlier French version of Article 420 of the *Code de procédure*: title XIX, Article 17 of the *Ordonnance sur le Commerce de 1673*, discussed in Roussel, J. *Les clauses attributives de compétence*, 1933, at p.75 onwards, with a jurisdictional place of payment provision; also a comparative analysis of European place of performance (payment) in procedural codes in Schmelcher, G. *Der Erfüllungsort von Geldschulden (Der Zahlungsort)—Eine rechtsvergleichende Darstellung*, Diss., Basel, 1972, at pp.3–11.

[770] Apart from the German model, below, at p.126, a similarly worded provision also appeared in Convention Franco-Belge du 8 Juillet 1899, Article 2 '. . . le demandeur belge ou français peut saisir . . . le juge du lieu où l'obligation est née, *a été ou doit être exécutée*'; in detail 1990 *Juris-Classeur, Droit International*, Fasc. 591, Watté, and Weser, M. *Traité Franco-belge du 8 Juillet 1899*, at pp.69–134.

[771] The German-Belgian Reciprocal Recognition and Enforcement Convention of 30.6.1958, BGBl 59 II, 766 at p.768, provided for an almost identical provision to Article 5(1) but in a rule of indirect (enforcement) jurisdiction, in its Article 3(1)(5): 'wenn ein Vertrag oder ein Anspruch aus einem Vertrag den Gegenstand der Klage gebildet hat..[wo] die Verpflichtung erfüllt worden ist oder zu erfüllen wäre'; also Article 4 of the Belgian-Dutch Convention of 28.3.1926, and Article 2(5) of the Belgian-Italian Convention.

[772] Especially regarding jurisdiction associated with payment obligations, below; even in England, Ord XI r.1(e) of the 1883 Rules of Court had provision for performance within the jurisdiction, Dicey, A.V. *A Digest of the Law of England with reference to the Conflict of Laws*, 1896, at p.248 and *The Yearly Supreme Court Practice 1899*, at p.164.

[773] In 1976, in *Soc. Michael Horauf Maschinen c/ Soc. Leysens Meier* 14.6.1975 (1976) *Rev crit* 117, at pp.124–26: 'le *forum solutionis* risque de perdre sa neutralité commerciale ou économique pour devenir un élément du *forum actoris* ou d'un for contractuel de mauvais aloi', at p.126.

[774] Droz, G. *Compétence judiciaire et effets des jugements dans le marché commun*, 1972.

[775] At p.56, para. 61.

[776] Crucial for at least two reasons: (1) contractual disputes would have the bulk of work under the Convention; and (2) German jurisdictional law, as the model for Article 5(1), already had a long provenance.

le système retenu dans la Convention est celui du droit allemand . . .[777] [778]

Yet reviewing a very early Convention case of the *Cour d'appel de Paris, Soc. Michael Horauf Maschinen c/ Soc. Leysens Meier,*[779] Droz suddenly raises fears,[780] not mentioned in his book, *inter alia*, of the arbitrary nature of jurisdiction under Article 5(1), due to the place of performance determined by divergent *leges causae*, and of the potential creation of a *forum actoris*:

> ce qui choquera[781] c'est que les buts[782] poursuivis par l'introduction du *forum contractus solutionis* risquent de n'être pas atteints, que le payement soit considéré comme portable ou quérable.[783] [784]

It behoves this analysis to turn to the legal background against which the Convention was drafted, to see the state of contemporary national jurisdictional regimes. Questions must be asked whether the jurisprudential *dénouements* surrounding Article 5(1) were at all foreseeable. To answer such questions, it is necessary to look at the historical development of Article 5(1)'s acknowledged forebear,[785] §29 of the German ZPO.

The Jenard Report has already made mention[786] that Article 5(1)'s inspiration[787] was §29 of the German *Zivilprozeßordnung* (ZPO).[788] This code has a comparatively

---

[777] ('the system retained in the Convention is that of German law').

[778] Droz, 1972, p.58, para. 63; also formerly Article 420 of the procedural codes of France and Belgium (later Article 46 and 42, of the Belgian *loi du 25 mars 1876*, below, combined with the place of payment provisions of Article 1247 of the (French/Belgian) *Code Civil*: *Tribunal de Commerce de Bruxelles* 5.2.1890 *Grumieau c/ Van Wouwe* 1890 Jurisprudence du port d'Anvers, II, 65, at p.66; *Comm. Liège* 29.5.1908 *Pieper c/ La Société des Aciéries de Crefeld* 1909 P.P., No.242, 164, at p.164, col. 2; for an historical Swiss example of jurisdiction for the place of payment from Article 74(2)(1) OR, *Obergericht* 23.2.1939, *Blätter für Zürcherische Rechtsprechung*, Band 38, 1939, 365, No. 151 and Egger, Escher, Haab, Oser (eds), *Kommentar zum Schweizerischen Zivilgestezbuch*, V Band: *Das Obligationenrecht, Erster Halbband*, 1929, at pp.470–75.

[779] 14.6.1975 (1976) *Rev crit* 117.

[780] At p.124.

[781] It should not have shocked, as German procedural history had shown.

[782] Below: the aims that a combination of *Zivilprozeßordnung* and *Bundesgesetzbuch* tried to achieve were slightly different from the original aim of Article 5(1); the former tried to eliminate what Droz now fears, the *forum actoris*. Why should this now come as such a surprise to him?

[783] ('what will be alarming is that the goals pursued by the introduction of the *forum contractus solutionis* are at risk of not being reached whether the payment is seen as 'portable' or 'quérable'').

[784] (1976) *Rev crit* 117, at p.125; experience has shown the almost naïve belief that there might be a close link between forum and dispute; and that plaintiffs would not try to take advantage of Article 5(1)—esp., in France, below p.142 *et seq.*

[785] Jurisdiction in contract, and more specifically at the place of performance, has had a long Bilateral Convention history; esp. Al Mulla, H. *The recognition and enforcement of foreign civil and commercial judgments under multilateral and bilateral conventions*, Ph.D Thesis, Cambridge University, 1992, esp. at p.119 onwards.

[786] 5.3.1979 [1979] OJ C59/1, at p.22; also Droz, 1972, at p.58, para. 63.

[787] Droz, *ibid.*

[788] For the most complete analysis of this massive piece of legislation, *Zivilprozeßordnung, Beck'sche Kurz-Kommentare*, 59 Aufl., 2001, esp., for §29, p.91 following.

long provenance,[789] and predates the Brussels Convention by some eighty-nine years. In this time, concepts which are now used in Article 5(1)[790] have received wide judicial and critical comment.[791] Although it is not within this treatment's ambit to engage in a detailed historical analysis of §29, and its effect on Article 5(1),[792] various problems and contentions with Article 5(1) can be examined against the background of §29 ZPO. It must also be borne in mind to what extent, if any, the provenance surrounding §29 ZPO was,[793] or should have been, taken into account when the Convention's drafters were considering jurisdiction in contractual matters under Article 5(1).

§29 [I] ZPO bears a remarkable comparison[794] to Article 5(1). Indeed, a free direct English translation of §29 [I] ZPO resembles more closely the official English version of Article 5(1) than does a free direct translation of the German version of Article 5(1). §29 [I] ZPO reads as follows:

> Für Streitigkeiten aus einem Vertragsverhältnis und über dessen Bestehen ist das Gericht des Ortes zuständig, an dem die streitige[795] Verpflichtung zu erfüllen ist.[796]

The interpretation of the above provision by the German courts over the years has revealed similar patterns of development and problems that would eventually manifest themselves with regard to Article 5(1). A brief examination of the cases will demonstrate the background against which Article 5(1) was, or should have been, drafted.

---

[789] Originally enacted in 30.1.1877, RGBl, s.83, and in force on 1.10.1879, as (materially) amended 12.9.1950, and 20.12.1974.

[790] For a comparative linguistic analysis of individual phrases in both §29 and Article 5(1), this page.

[791] For a detailed historical analysis of both, esp. Schack, 1985, at pp.128–35 and more generally: Schack, 2. Aufl., 1996 at pp.100–109, Nagel, H. *Internationales Zivilprozeßrecht*, 3 Aufl., 1991, at p.56 onwards, and Linke, H. *Internationales Zivilprozeßrecht*, 2 Aufl., 1995, at pp.57–59.

[792] And *vice versa* of course; Article 5(1) of the Lugano Convention was the undoubted model for the Swiss Private International Law Act (Bundesgesetz über das Internationale Privatrecht (IPRG)), 18.12.1987, Article 113 '. . . am Erfüllungsort geklagt werden' ('be sued at the place of performance'), when the defendant is in no way connected with Switzerland; and *inter alia*, the Brussels Convention's Article 5(1) has been incorporated, from 1 September 1995, directly into Italian autonomous international civil procedure: Article 3(2) *Riforma del sistema italiano di diritto internazionale privato*, Legge 21 maggio 1995, n.218 and *Corte di Appello di Milano 20.3.1998 Italdecor s.a.s. c/ Yiu's Industries (HK) Ltd* (1998) *Riv. dir. int. priv. e proc.* 170.

[793] *Quaere*, whether a provision of national legislation—with its idiosyncratic concerns for judicial protection of one particular party (below) or other—could ever ideally be suited for transposition, almost *verbatim*, into a multilateral Community Convention.

[794] Nagel, 1991, at p.57; Linke, 1995, at p.58; Schack, 2. Auf., 1996, at pp.102–09; the only difference, according to Schack, 1985, at p.235 para. 338 is in the last two words: 'Der Erfüllungsort des §29 ZPO ist ein rein rechtlicher Begriff'; note *Industrie Tessili Italiana Como v Dunlop AG* (C-12/76) [1976] ECR 1473 has made sure that the place of performance in Article 5(1) has become the same; but Kropholler, 1998 at p.109, para. 21.

[795] This phrase is more precise, conforming to the ruling in *Ets. A. de Bloos S.P.R.L v Soc. en commandite par actions Bouyer* (or more accurately vice versa), than the actual wording of Article 5(1) itself.

[796] *Zivilprozeßordnung, Beck'sche Kurz-Kommentare*, 59 Aufl., 2001, at p.91 following; ('For disputes arising out of a contract and its existence the court which has jurisdiction is the court of the place where the obligation, forming the basis of the proceedings, is to be performed').

An historical excursus of §29 ZPO is undertaken by Schack,[797] and it is clear that as he reviews each constituent element of the article, he could just as well be discussing Article 5(1),[798] so close are the comparisons and solutions. Speaking of the 'obligation in question' ('die streitige Verpflichtung' of §29 ZPO),[799] he notes that cases dating back to around the turn of the century[800] made the same distinction, as would the ECJ years after in *Ets. A. de Bloos* v *Bouyer*, between 'independent' and 'secondary' contractual obligations:

> Bei einer Klage auf Schadenersatz wegen Nicht- oder Schlechterfüllung soll nicht die Schadenersatzpflicht die streitige sein, sondern die verletzte Vertragspflicht[801]

He also draws similar comparisons between §29 ZPO and Article 5(1) with regard to the former's adoption of a 'principal' obligation[802] among a number of obligations.

Yet the most interesting comparisons can be made with regard to the place of performance of (payment) obligations, whose legacy of arbitrariness,[803] varying on the material *lex causae*, still[804] occupies a central position in the debate over the usefulness of Article 5(1) to this day.

Looking back to the time prior to the unified approach to the place of performance of monetary obligations in German material law, §§269–270 BGB,[805] the

---

[797] Schack, 1985, at p.128 onwards; also Spellenberg, U. 'Der Gerichtsstand des Erfüllungsortes im europäischen Gerichtsstands- und Vollstreckungsübereinkommen' (1978) *ZZP* 38, at p.60; for a contemporary account of combining § 29 ZPO and §§ 269, 270 BGB, Fleischer, N. *Der Gerichtsstand des gemeinsamen Erfüllungsortes im deutschen Recht*, 1997, at pp.14–79; *LG München* 12.7.2000 2001 *MDR* 591, *BayObLG* 7.11.2000 2001 NJW-RR 928.

[798] Schack, 1985, at p.224, he does begin to do so.

[799] *RG* 29.3.1893 *Entscheidungen des Reichsgerichts in Zivilsachen*, Band 31, 383, and *RG* 16.12.1890 *Entscheidungen des Reichsgerichts in Zivilsachen*, Band 27, 393.

[800] Schack, 1985, at p.114, n.45: he cites such cases from the *Reichsgericht* in 1907 *RG* 8.3.1907 *Entscheidungen des Reichsgerichts in Zivilsachen*, Band 65, 329 at p.332, citing the *lex causae* in §§269, 270 BGB; and *RG* 29.5.1908 *Entscheidungen des Reichsgerichts in Zivilsachen*, Band 19, 9, and the *OLG Bremen* in 1953, 1952/1953 IPRspr. Nr.291, p.580.

[801] ('In a claim for compensation for non- or mal-performance, it is not the duty to compensate that is in question, but the contractual duty breached.'), Schack, 1985, at p.114, para. 160.

[802] For §29 ZPO, Schack, 1985, at p.119 para. 169; for Article 5(1) *Hassan Shenavai v Klaus Kreischer* (C-266/85) [1987] ECR 239.

[803] Briggs, 1997, at p.107, para. 2.137; for a supreme example of the arbitrary application of the *lex causae*, effecting payment obligations for and against the *forum actoris*: *Cour de Cassation San Carlo Gruppo alimentare SPA c/ SBC Vico* 6.2.1996 (1996) *Rev crit* 504, at p.505, obs. Droz—a three week period, after which the Vienna Sales Convention 1980 would have come into force (in France 1.1.1988) would have given the French plaintiff jurisdiction in France; *Definitely Maybe (Touring) Ltd v Marek Lieberberg Konzertagentur GmbH* [2001] 1 WLR 1745, QBD (Morison J).

[804] Note the recent attacks on the *lex causae* solution by, *inter alia*, Droz, G. 'Delendum est forum contractus? (vingt ans après les arrêts *de Bloos* et *Tessili* interprétant l'article 5.1 de la Convention de Bruxelles du 27 septembre 1968' (1997) *Dalloz*, Chron., p.351, esp. at p.355; and *Sté Comptoir commercial d'Orient c/ Société Medtrafina* 11.3.1997 (1998) *JDI* 129, [1999] I.L.Pr. 336 and *Groupe Concorde et autres c/ Capitaine du Suhadiwarno Panjan et autres* 9.12.1997 (1998) *Rev crit* 117; ECJ's decision (C-440/97) [1999] ECR I-6307.

[805] The BGB came into force on 1.1.1900; in the absence of contrary agreement, and from the surrounding circumstances §269 [I] states: 'so hat die Leistung an dem Orte zu erfolgen, an welchem

various autonomous regions (of what was later to become the Federal Republic) had separate civil codes.[806] These codes either had the rule[807] that the debtor was to seek out his creditor, or vice versa.[808]

Although at that time, the problems associated with this divergence of approach to payment obligations was only internal[809] to 'Germany' herself, we can see that this legacy of combining jurisdiction with material place of performance, outgrew the internal borders, emerging into the international Community arena through the *Industrie Tessili Italiana Como v Dunlop AG*[810] case.

Schack notes what he sees as an arbitrary approach to jurisdiction, its ancient provenance, and the combined jurisdictional effect which such ancient civil codes exercised, when applied together with §29 ZPO:

> So bewirkte §29 ZPO bei Zahlungsklagen zum Beispiel in Bayern,[811] Sachsen,[812] und Preußen[813] einen Gläubigergerichtsstand,[814] in Baden jedoch einen Gerichtsstand am Sitz des Schuldners im Zeitpunkt der Erfüllung.[815]

Transposing[816] §29 ZPO into international jurisdictional situations, the case law demonstrated early on[817] that the place of performance was to be ascertained by using the law applicable to the contract.[818] Subsequent, yet still

---

der Schuldner zur Zeit der Entstehung der Schuldverhätnisses seinen Wohnsitz hatte.' ('performance shall be effected in the place where *the debtor* had his residence at the time the obligation arose'), translation in Goren, S. *The German Civil Code*, 1994, p.45.

[806] For details and texts Schack, 1985, at p.135.

[807] Still in force today in some Contracting States, England and Wales, Italy, Switzerland and Greece among them—for Greece, see the findings in *Raiffeisen Zentralbank Österreich Aktiengesellschaft v National Bank of Greece S.A.* [1999] 1 Lloyd's Rep. 408, at p.413.

[808] In force in the remainder, *inter alia*, France, Belgium, Germany and Austria among them.

[809] Although those autonomous regions necessarily provoked conflict of laws problems.

[810] (C-12/76) [1976] ECR 1473.

[811] Schack's footnote no.50 in the text, at p.135, and *BayOLG* 1888, p.658.

[812] Schack's footnote no.51 in the text, and §707 BGB.

[813] Schack's footnote no. 52 in the text, ALR I 5 §248.

[814] A criticism that is still levelled at Article 5(1) to this day; especially Gothot, P. et Holleaux, D., 1985, at p.41, para. 76: 'En l'absence d'une clause fixant le lieu du paiement, *le for de l'article 5,1 aurait été transformé en un forum actoris au profit des créanciers demandeurs, domiciliés dans les pays où le paiement est portable . . .'.*

[815] ('For example, §29 ZPO created a creditor's *forum actoris* for payment claims in Bavaria, Saxony and Prussia, whereas in Baden, a jurisdiction at the debtor's residence at the time of performance.'), Schack, 1985 at p.135 para. 194.

[816] Note that the German and French procedural codes are 'doppelfunktional', regulating at the same time, international, as well as internal domestic, competence: *LG Hamburg* 26.10.1995 IPRspr. 1995 Nr. 157, at p.321, and *OLG Karlsruhe* 9.10.1992 IPRspr. 1992 Nr. 199, at p.451. The Italian system is different. Apart from jurisdiction internally, Italy now has a new reformed law—as from 1 September 1995: Kindler, P. 'Internationale Zuständigkeit und anwendbares Recht im italienischen IPR-Gesetz von 1995' (1997) *RabelsZ* 227; also Starace, V. 'Le champ de la juridiction selon la loi de réforme du système italien de droit international privé' (1996) *Rev crit* 67, at p.77 onwards.

[817] For example *OLG Stuttgart*, 20.11.1902, OLGZ 6, 381.

[818] Wrangel, P.G. *Der Gerichtsstand des Erfüllungsortes im deutschen, italienischen und europäischen Recht*, 1989, at p.51.

pre-Brussels Convention, cases[819] up to 1973 and thereafter,[820] and the majority view,[821] endorse the *lex causae* qualification.[822] The potential problems that a *lex causae* place of performance could bring to international contractual payment disputes is amply demonstrated in a 1932 decision of the *LG Freiburg*,[823] in which a German creditor could seise his own court for payment against his Swiss debtor, because the Swiss law rule,[824] *lege causae*, states that in payment obligations a debtor must seek out[825] his creditor.

A similar historical picture emerges from a glance at the former provisions of the French and Belgian procedural codes.[826] Both countries had Article 420[827] of their respective *Codes de procédure civile*[828] (in commercial cases), until, in Belgium, the *loi du 25 mars 1876*,[829] Articles 42 (for internal) and 52(3) (for international) contractual actions. Article 52(3) was re-enacted *verbatim* in Article 635(3) of the current Belgian autonomous *Code judiciaire*.[830] Both French and Belgian codes referred, and gave jurisdiction to, 'le lieu dans laquelle l'obligation. . . doit être ou a été executée[831]'. From early to mid-nineteenth century case-law examples up to the present, the courts have had to deal with the obligation in dispute, and especially its place of performance (when the obligation turned out

[819] *LG Freiburg*, JW 1932, 604, reviewed by Volkmar; also quoted by Schack, 1985, at p.153; *LG Zweibrücken* 5.3.1974 IPRspr. 1974 Nr. 148, below; for §29 ZPO used in conjunction with Article 59 of the 1964 Uniform Law on the International Sale of Goods (ULIS), *OLG Frankfurt* 28.1.1987 IPRspr. 1987 Nr. 15.

[820] *LG Hamburg* IPRspr. 1974 Nr.154; the same interpretation has been carried over in Belgian and Italian autonomous procedural law: *Cour d'appel de Bruxelles* 19.3.1987, *Société de droit anglais 'William Timpson Ltd' c/ Société anonyme 'Compagnie Belge Gander Lux Shoe'* 1987 Pas. Belge, II, 111 (Article 635(3) Code judiciaire) and *Corte di Appello di Milano* 20.3.1998 *Italdecor s.a.s. c/ Yiu's Industries (HK) Ltd* (1998) Riv. dir. int. priv. e proc. 170 (Article 3(2) Legge 21 maggio 1995, n.218).

[821] Schack, 2. Auf., 1996, p.151 following.

[822] For example: *OLG Stuttgart* 16.6.1987 IPRspr. 1987 Nr. 130; *OLG Düsseldorf* 15.3.1990 IPRspr. 1990 Nr. 167; and *BGH* 30.9.1976 IPRspr. 1976 Nr. 142.

[823] JW 1932, 604.

[824] Article 74.(2)(1) OR, quoted in Schack, 1985, at p.195; for a relatively early Swiss example applying Article 74 to determine the jurisdictional place of payment, *Obergericht* 23.2.1939, *Blätter für Zürcherische Rechtsprechung*, Band 38, 1939, 365, No. 151, at p.366, col. 1.

[825] What is termed a 'Bringschuld' 'a debt to be brought' (i.e. debtor to seek out creditor) as opposed to a 'Hohlschuld' 'a debt to be sought out' (i.e. creditor to seek out debtor).

[826] Braas, A. *Précis de Procédure Civile, Organisation Judiciaire. Compétence. Procédure Civile*, 2ᵉ éd., 1934, at p.365 onwards.

[827] As early as 1673, in the French *Ordonnance sur le Commerce de 1673* (tit XIX, Article 17) the (commercial) creditor was given the option of suing 'au lieu auquel le paiement doit être fait'('in the place at which payment was to be made'); comments on this and Article 420, Roussel, J. *Les clauses attributives de compétence*, 1933, at pp.75–77.

[828] Esp. *Code de procédure civile*, Milan, 1806, at p.103; Loret, M. *Le Code de procédure civile*, II tome, 1812, esp. p.502, Sirey, J. *Les codes annotés, Code de procédure civile*, 4 ed., 1905, at p.565.

[829] Belgian *Pasinomie, Collection complète des lois, décrets, arrêtés*, Quatrième Série, Tome VIII, 1876, p.121, at p.152; for a commentary on the contractual provisions of this law: Bormans, T. *Code de procédure civile belge*, Livre préliminaire, I, 2ᵉᵐᵉéd., 1877, at pp.466–69, and p.512.

[830] Note the close interpretative links between Article 635(3) and Article 5(1) in *Cour de Travail de Liège* 2.6.1994, *Ramackers c/ Société de droit zaïrois 'Société Nationale des Chemins de fer zaïrois'* 1993 Pas. Belge, II, 97, at p.101.

[831] ('the place where the obligation is or was to be performed').

to be the payment of money). Early Belgian cases determined this place, *lege causae*, in default of choice[832] and contrary surrounding circumstances, under Article 1247 (Belgian) *Code civil*.[833] French cases came to the same result.[834]

What this brief historical excursus into German, French and Belgian civil procedure does show more than anything else is that the drafters of Article 5(1) of the Brussels Convention were not legislating in a vacuum, yet arguably seem to have done so.[835]

If—as the Jenard report mentions—that Article 5(1) was closely modelled on §29 ZPO, the problems, and judicial solutions to them—encountered with §29 ZPO, Article 420 French/Belgian *Code de Procédure civile*, and Articles 42 and 52(3) of the Belgian law of 25.3.1876—were no doubt bound to surface with an almost identically-worded Convention article. Precedents for the likely future interpretation of Article 5(1) had existed for many years; the drafters could, or should, have been alive to the real possibility of importing *mutatis mutandis* the raft of jurisprudence associated with, *inter alia*, §29 ZPO into Article 5(1). This is especially the case with regard to the creation of the *forum actoris*, or more accurately, a creditor's forum, when the place of performance (of a payment obligation)[836] is ascertained *lege causae*, and its material law allows for collection at the creditor's domicile/place of business. The criticism levelled[837] at *Custom Made Commercial Ltd v Stawa Metallbau GmbH*[838] and its use of International Sales Conventions, is at least twenty-six years too late. The warning signs of such an interpretation have been present for over a hundred and fifty years. The Convention could have made special provision in Article 5(1)[839] for payment obligations at the least, but failed to do so.[840]

---

[832] For where a choice was made: *Cassation* 3.9.1891 *Hertogs c/ Preud'Homme* 1893 *Jurisprudence du port d'Anvers*, I, 260 and *Cour de Bruxelles* 8.8.1872 *Wéry c/ Leroy et Co.* 1873 *Jurisprudence du port d'Anvers*, II, 30.

[833] *Comm. Liège* 29.5.1908 *Pieper c/ La Société des Aciéries de Crefeld* 1909 P.P., No.242, 164, at p.164, *Cour de Bruxelles* 22.10.1831 1814–40 *Pas. Belge*, 276 (under Article 420), and *Tribunal de Commerce de Bruxelles* 5.2.1890 *Grumieau c/ Van Wouwe* 1890 *Jurisprudence du port d'Anvers*, II, 65, at p.66.

[834] *Req.* 1894 DP 54, I, 229.

[835] If they did not foresee the possibility of, and draft around, problems of international payment obligations, given their long (Continental) history.

[836] Kennett, W. 'Place of Performance and Predictability' (1995) *YEL* 193.

[837] Schack's concluding remark, 1985, at p.244 para. 353, (that such an important jurisdictional element—the place of performance—should have been left to the vagaries of diverging *leges causae* seems to destroy what §29 ZPO and §§269 270 BGB have tried to maintain 'die Ausgewogenheit des internationalen Zuständigkeitssystems')('the equilibrium of the international jurisdictional system') should have been ringing in the drafters ears at least thirty years ago.

[838] (C-288/92) [1994] ECR I-2913, especially recently in *GIE Groupe Concorde* (C-440/97) [1999] ECR I-6307, AG Colomer's opinion not accepted by the ECJ.

[839] A belated amendment made by the San Sebastian Accession Convention of Spain and Portugal, recognised the need for a special jurisdiction in individual contracts of employment, if only then forced on Article 5(1) by ECJ case law: *Roger Ivenel v Helmut Schwab* (C-133/81) [1982] ECR 1891.

[840] It may be arguable that the Convention's drafters were content to see Article 5(1)'s development proceed along the same lines as the earlier German, French and Belgian jurisprudence; or by ignorance, or otherwise, failed to draft around the obvious problems, or undesirable interpretations, that had manifested themselves with §29 ZPO, and other procedural codes.

1.3.2 The breakdown, and erosion of the protectionist relationship[841] between the Civil Codes and Codes of Civil Procedure[842]

That there has been vociferous criticism of the *Tessili v Dunlop*[843] and *Custom Made Commercial Ltd v Stawa Metallbau GmbH*[844] formula is more understandable in those Contracting States, such as Germany, France, and Italy,[845] which have witnessed a close development, and protectionist[846] interrelationship,[847] between their Civil Codes and Codes of Civil Procedure.[848] This clear interdependence is in evidence[849] between §29 ZPO and §§269, 270 BGB,[850] notably with regard to the protection[851] that domestic debtors[852] receive against the *forum actoris*. The German material law on performance of (monetary) obligations, in

---

[841] Meaning that substantive law provisions should not provide the scaffolding for a *forum actoris*. The protection afforded to potential debtor/defendants from jurisdictional provisions that would upset the 'actor sequitur forum rei' emphasis—any such provisions were neutralised by corresponding provisions of substantive law—§269 BGB/Article 1247 *Code civil*, payment of debts at the debtor's place of residence/domicile. The protection is uniform unless and until Contracting States are introduced with different substantive laws on place of performance, *lege causae*.

[842] Fleischer, 1997, at p.27.

[843] (C-12/76) [1976] ECR 1473.

[844] (C-288/92) [1994] ECR I-2913.

[845] For Italy's (internal) jurisdiction code and Civil code on the place of performance, Schack, 1985, at p.184; Article 1182(3) *codice civile* of course sanctions the *forum actoris* —*Corte di Cassazione* 3.4.2000 *Bellini GmbH contro Stefin SpA* (2001) *Riv. dir. int. priv. e proc.* 395—to have to apply a different *lex causae* would upset this position.

[846] This protectionist interdependence is destroyed when a foreign law, *lege causae*, is introduced. The uniform inter-code relationship breaks down.

[847] On the protectionist aspect of the ZPO, below and esp. Wrangel, 1989, at p.13: 'den untrennbaren Zusammenhang zwischen prozessualer Anknüpfung und materieller Rechtslage' ('the inseparable relationship between procedural connection and material legal position').

[848] Mentioned, *en passant*, by Hertz, 1998, at p.87; he cites an 1899 Proposal in Denmark for a Civil Procedural Code that also recognised the *forum actoris* dangers.

[849] Also in France between Article 46.2 NCPC and Article 1247 Civil Code. Italy has gone the other way and actively promoted the *forum actoris* with regard, at least, to payment obligations in its Civil code and Procedural code—Article 1182(3) *codice civile*: 'al domicilio che il creditore ha al tempo della scadenza' ('at *the domicile of the creditor* at the time the obligation matures'), translated by Beltramo, M. *The Italian Civil Code*, 1969, at p.314; Article 3(2) of the New Italian Private International Law will ensure that this trend continues—and Schack, 1985, at p.184 following.

[850] Lüderitz, A. in 'Fremdbestimmte internationale Zuständigkeit? Versuch einer Neubestimmung von §29 ZPO, Article 5 Nr. 1 EuGVÜ' in *Festschrift für Konrad Zweigert*, 1981, p.233, at p.240: 'gab [der Gesetzgeber] der Zuständigkeitsnorm des (späteren) § 29 ZPO mittelbar einen materiell-rechtlichen Gehalt' '[the legislator] gave to the jurisdictional rule of the (future) §29 ZPO an immediate substantive context').

[851] Wrangel, 1989, at p.84.

[852] Domestic creditors are correspondingly disadvantaged in the international sphere, hence the cases/jurisprudence surrounding commercial agency contracts, below.

the absence of agreement[853] to the contrary, favours, in internal cases[854] at least, the domicile of the debtor.

The historical genesis of the German *Zivilprozeßordnung,* even as early as 1858–1863,[855] shows the legislators' awareness[856] of the need so to draft the place of performance as to protect against a creditor's *forum actoris:*[857]

> Im Hintergrund steht immer der Gedanke an dem GEO[858] und das Bestehen, einen Gläubigergerichtsstand zu vermeiden.[859]

The protectionist relationship,[860] however, completely crumbles[861] in the international context when, applying the *Tessili* formula, the possibility becomes real of a German court having to apply a different[862] *lex causae* under either §29 ZPO, or Article 5(1).

The reported German cases[863] under the Brussels Convention, nevertheless, show

---

[853] Or the circumstances surrounding the case; cf. *Deutsche Rückversicherung AG v La Fondiara Assicurazioni SpA.* [2001] 2 Lloyd's Rep. 621 (David Steel J).

[854] Subject to International Sales Convention cases—under Article 5(1) cases, of course, the place of performance is subject to the vagaries of the *lex causae: LG Freiburg,* JW 1932, 604, and *Industrie Tessili Italiana Como v Dunlop AG* (C-12/76) [1976] ECR 1473.

[855] *Protocolle der Commission zur Beratung eines ADHGB,* Nürnberg, 1858–63, at p.1371, on the development of Article 324 of the ADHGB, the precursor of §269 BGB; and Wrangel, 1989, at p.82.

[856] Note also Von Caemmerer/Schlechtriem, *Kommentar zum Einheitlichen UN-Kaufrecht,* 1990: 'Die Formulierung in §270 IV BGB sollte lediglich vermeiden, daß der Zahlungsort einen Gerichtsstand begründet.'('the drafting of §270 IV BGB had to avoid in principle that the place of payment should form a jurisdictional base.').

[857] The comparatively recent Italian civil code of 1942 which, according to Wrangel, 1989, at p.127, was drafted with a more modern creditor-orientated approach to payment obligations.

[858] Place of performance.

[859] ('In the background always stands a backward glance on the place of performance and the insistence on avoiding a creditor's forum.'), Wrangel, 1989, at p.82.

[860] Note the strong objections of the German negotiating delegation in the Vienna Sales Convention conference, quoted by Von Caemmerer/Schlechtriem, *Kommentar zum Einheitlichen UN-Kaufrecht,* 1990, at p.526, para. 11: 'Um eine solche Verbindung von Zahlungsort und Gerichtsstand zu vermeiden, hatte die Bundesrepublik auf der Wiener Abschlußkonferenz den Antrag gestellt, ausdrücklich klarzustellen, daß *der Zahlungsort keine Gerichtsstand begründet.'*('To avoid such a combination of jurisdiction and place of performance, the Federal Republic of Germany made an application at the Vienna Conference, expressly to clarify that *the place of payment should not form a jurisdictional base.'*); *Cour de Cassation* 26.6.2001 *Anton Huber GmbH & Co c/ Soc. Polyspace,* (2001) *JCP,* IV, 2554, *Cour de Cassation* 26.6.2001 *Sté Ogosa destribuciones c/ SA Madrange* (2001) *JCP,* IV, 2556.

[861] Schack, 2. Auf., 1996, at p.106, para. 269.

[862] I.e. one not oriented to debtor protection.

[863] A small representative number being *BGH* 9.4.1973 (1973) *RIW/AWD* 404; *BGH* 7.7.1980 IPRspr. 1980 Nr. 137b, *Siegfried Zelger v Sebastiano Salinitri* [1981] E.C.C. 191, (1980) *RIW/AWD* 725; *BGH* 26.10.1981 *Re the M/S Hoop* [1982] E.C.C. 533; *BGH* 16.10.1984 *Re a Bank Guarantee* [1987] E.C.C. 26; *BGH* 17.10.1984 IPRspr. (1984) Nr. 146, *Re the recovery of unpaid customs duty* [1985] E.C.C. 331; *BGH* 11.2.1988 *Re Jurisdiction in Tort and Contract* [1988] E.C.C. 415; *BGH* 14.11.1991 IPRspr. (1991) Nr.181; *Re Exchange Control and a Greek Guarantor* [1993] I.L.Pr. 298; *BGH* 26.3.1992 *Custom Made Commercial Ltd v Stawa Metallbau GmbH* [1993] I.L.Pr. 490; *OLG Frankfurt* 28.11.1979 IPRspr. (1979) Nr. 174; *OLG Koblenz* 24.5.1985 (1985) IPRspr. Nr. 139; *OLG Hamm* 27.5.1985 (1985) IPRspr. Nr. 134; *OLG Hamburg* 31.10.1985 1985 IPRspr. Nr. 45; *OLG Hamm* 20.1.1989 (1990) *NJW* 652; *OLG Koblenz* 9.6.1989 *Re a Lawyer's Liability in Jurisdiction Cases* [1991] I.L.Pr. 15; *HOLG* 28.9.1989 *Re a Forwarding Agent's Costs* [1993] I.L.Pr. 49; *OLG Koblenz* 23.2.1990 (1990) *RIW* 316, *Re an Italian Cargo of Adulterated Wine* [1991] I.L.Pr. 473; *OLG Düsseldorf* 28.6.1990 *Re the sublease of a shop* [1991] I.L.Pr. 292; *OLG*

a strict adherence[864] to the *Tessili* formula, and *lex causae* place of performance; the judicial reaction to *Tessili* in France[865], however, has been somewhat different.

The French *Code civil* contains a rule, similar to that of the German code, and a provision in the *Nouveau Code de Procédure Civile*,[866] which also has a long provenance.[867]

As will be demonstrated with the cases for review,[868] notably those dealing with independent payment obligations in commercial agency contracts, the French[869] courts have sought, where possible, to avoid[870] the *Tessili* formula. This, it will be shown,[871] is achieved by localising the place of performance in fact,[872] or by

Hamm 8.3.1991 IPRspr. (1992) Nr. 181a; *OLG Saarbrücken* 2.10.1991 (1992) *IPRax* 165, *Re a Shop fitting contract* [1993] I.L.Pr. 395; *OLG Schleswig-Holstein* 4.6.1992 *Re the Cross-Border Dyeing of Clothes* [1994] I.L.Pr. 202; *OLG Hamm* 25.11.1992 IPRspr. (1992) Nr. 214; *OLG Karlsruhe* 11.2.1993 (1994) *RIW* 1046; *OLG Hamm* 28.1.1994 (1995) NJW-RR 187; *OLG Hamm* 28.6.1994 (1995) NJW-RR 188; *OLG Köln* 19.7.1995 IPRspr. (1995) Nr. 148; *LG Hamburg* 31.1.1984 IPRspr. (1984) Nr. 130; *LG Frankfurt/Main* 13.7.1994 IPRspr. (1995) Nr.139a / *OLG Frankfurt/Main* 23.5.1995 IPRspr. (1995) Nr. 139b; *LG München* 29.5.1995 IPRspr. (1995) Nr. 146; *LG Berlin* 28.9.1995 IPRspr. (1995) Nr. 154; *LG Frankfurt/Main* 5.10.1995 IPRspr. (1995) Nr. 155; *AG Berlin-Tiergarten* 13.3.1997 (1999) *IPRax* 172; BGH 25.2.1999 (1999) *RIW* 456, (2001) *IPRax* 331, [2001] I.L.Pr. 388.

[864] Indeed, the majority of the courts' deliberations concerning Article 5(1) involve ascertaining the *lex causae*: esp. *LG Köln* 5.5.1988 IPRspr. (1988) Nr. 158, *OLG Hamm* 25.11.1992 IPRspr. (1992) Nr. 214. In the latter case, German law as *lex causae*, disadvantaged the German plaintiff/creditor; he had to seek out his debtor in Italy, in §269 BGB; BGH 25.2.1999 (1999) *RIW* 456, (2001) *IPRax* 331, [2001] I.L.Pr. 388.

[865] As will be shown, the reaction has been two-fold: (1) either a direct non-application (via a factual place of performance) or mis-application (*Sté Comptoir commercial d'Orient c/ Société Medtrafina* 11.3.1997, (1998) *JDI* 129, [1999] I.L.Pr. 336 and *Groupe Concorde et autres c/ Capitaine du Suhadiwarno Panjan et autres* 9.12.1997 (1998) *Rev crit* 117) of *Tessili* (section 1.3.6); or (2) a manoeuvring of the obligation in question (above section on commercial agency contracts and the obligation in question); certain Belgian courts have applied *Tessili* to the detriment of Belgian plaintiffs/claimants: *Tribunal de commerce de Liège*, 18.5.1995 (1996) *Rev. dr. comm. belge* 837.

[866] Article 46.2 reads: 'Le demandeur peut saisir à son choix, outre la juridiction du lieu où demeure le défendeur:—en matière contractuelle, la juridiction du lieu de la livraison effective de la chose ou du lieu de l'exécution de la prestation de service; . . .'; *Nouveau Code de Procédure Civile*, Dalloz, 1997, p.62 onwards.

[867] Schack, 1985, at pp.168–69; above at pp.129–130 for its progenitors.

[868] Note especially *Soc. Comptoir des Plastiques de l'Ain c/ Soc. Novamec et autres* 9.2.1994 (1994) *Rev crit* 577, reviewed below at p.145.

[869] The Belgian courts too. These courts have an added incentive to avoid the application of a foreign *lex causae* to the statutory right to compensation under their specially-created law 17.7.1961, below. The Belgian Civil Code does not favour (Belgian) plaintiff/creditors: Article 1247 (Belgian) *Code civil*—note the protectionist aspects of an interpretation of Article 5(1) and the 1961 law in 'Examen de jurisprudence. La loi du 27 juillet 1961 relative à la résiliation unilatérale des concessions de vente exclusive à durée indéterminée (1992 à 1997)' (1998) *Rev. dr. comm. belge* 3, at p.41.

[870] Application, *lege causae*, of the French/Belgian laws on place of performance (of monetary obligations) disadvantages French/Belgian sellers (seeking payment) or commercial agents (seeking compensation or commission).

[871] No better *leitmotiv* for this whole chapter could be the statement of Watt in (1994) *Rev crit* 577, at p.582, reviewing *Soc. Comptoir des Plastiques de l'Ain c/ Soc. Novamec et autres*: 'la méconnaissance de la jurisprudence Tessili *n'est sanctionée que lorsqu'elle a pour effet de priver les tribunaux français de leur compétence internationale*'.

[872] Still evident in the *Cour d'appel de Paris*' decision in *Société anversoise de dépôts et hypothèques c/ Richard*, therefore on appeal a *cassation* for this very reason: *Cour de Cassation* 27.6.2000 (2001) *JDI* 137, (2001) *Rev crit* 152.

choosing an obligation—such as to respect the contract—which, by whatever means, is clearly to be performed in France. Whichever route is chosen, the application of Article 1247 *Code civil lege causae* is avoided, to the benefit of French creditors.

It is now appropriate to turn and look at the German, English, Swiss/Austrian and French cases in a little more detail in the following sections. The impression that will be gleaned is that, on the whole—except perhaps in France—and despite unfavourable material laws, the Contracting States have been faithful to the *Tessili/Custom Made Commercial* jurisprudence.

1.3.3 The application of *Tessili* and *Custom Made Commercial* in German cases

The reported German cases have been exemplary in their application of the *Tessili* formula. Indeed, in some,[873] the majority of argument simply revolves around ascertaining the *lex causae*, according to German conflict of laws rules.[874] Since they provoke little potential non-conformist/protectionist discussion in this area, they will be dealt with briefly. Once the *lex causae* has been identified, the courts have logically applied this in determining the place of performance,[875] more often than not to the detriment[876] of domestic German plaintiffs:

> Nach dem damit geltenden §269 BGB[877] ist Erfüllungsort für den von der Kl. geltend gemachten Anspruch X, [Italien], da die Bekl. dort ihren Sitz hat. §269 BGB gilt nach...§270 IV BGB auch für Geldschulden.[878]

---

[873] For example *OLG Hamm* 25.11.1992 IPRspr. 1992 Nr. 214, at p. 484.

[874] By Articles 27–37 *Einführungsgesetz zum BGB* (as amended), incorporating the 1980 Rome Convention into German law; for an English translation: Goren, S. *The German Civil Code*, 1994, at p.442; a similar conflicts of law route evident in *OGH* 12.11.1998 (2000) *ZfRV* 78 and *Definitely Maybe (Touring) Ltd v Marek Lieberberg Konzertagentur GmbH* [2001] 1 WLR 1745, QBD (Morison J).

[875] Except in cases where a valid place of payment/performance clause was found to exist: *BGH* 17.10.1984 IPRspr. 1984 Nr. 146, at p.357, under §269 I §270 V BGB; *BGH* 25.2.1999 (1999) *RIW* 456 for a construction contract, and *OLG Stuttgart* 7.8.1998 (1999) *RIW* 782.

[876] Recently *OLG Dresden* 24.11.1998 1999 RIW 968, at p.969; exceptionally *LG Frankfurt/Main* 13.7.1994 IPRspr. 1995 Nr.139a and *OLG Frankfurt/Main* 23.5.1995 IPRspr. 1995 Nr. 139b—where the application of Italian law, *lege causae*, helped the German plaintiff to sue in the *forum actoris*; the place of performance determined from the nature of the contractual relationship (a lease) in *OLG Düsseldorf* 28.6.1990 *Re the sublease of a shop* [1991] I.L.Pr. 292, at p.296, para. 4; BGH 25.2.1999 (1999) *RIW* 456, (2001) *IPRax* 331, [2001] I.L.Pr. 388, (place of building site)—Pulkowski, F. (2001) *IPRax* 306, at p.307.

[877] Unless, as in *BGH* 31.1.1991 IPRspr. 1991 Nr. 170, [1992] I.L.Pr. 395, §269 BGB specifies a place of performance in special cases, such as payment of legal fees at the German lawyer's office; *LG München* 12.7.2000 2001 *MDR* 591; also Fleischer, 1997, at p.45 and Hensler, M. 'Der Gerichtsstand des Erfüllungsortes gem. §29 ZPO für die anwaltliche Honorarklage' 1999 *Anwaltsblatt* 186; *BayObLG* 7.11.2000 (2001) NJW-RR 928.

[878] ('The place of performance for the claim advanced by the plaintiff, according to §269 BGB, is X [in Italy], since the defendant has its seat there. §269 BGB is also applicable for monetary debts, in §270 IV BGB'), in *OLG Hamm* 25.11.1992 IPRspr. (1992) Nr. 214, at p.488; lately *LG Stuttgart* 30.4.1996, [1998] I.L.Pr. 100.

Other 'classic' applications of *Tessili* include: *OLG München* 11.11.1976,[879] *LG Kaiserslautern* 5.5.1987,[880] *BGH* 31.1.1991,[881] *BGH* 12.5.1993,[882] *LG Berlin* 28.9.1995,[883] *OLG Dresden* 24.11.1998[884] and *OLG München* 25.6.1999.[885]

It is noteworthy, that even prior to *BGH* 26.3.1992,[886] the German courts had been applying International Sales Conventions to determine the place of performance under Article 5(1) of the Brussels Convention: *OLG Hamm* 3.10.1979.[887] The only squeak of rebellion came from *LG Köln* 5.5.1988,[888] when the *LG* stated that an autonomous place of performance might be sensible, given the potential for the creation of a *forum actoris* with these Sales Conventions:

> erscheint eine *vom nationalen Recht losgelöste, autonome* Begriffsbestimmung im Hinblick auf den internationalen Zuständigkeitseinklang sinnvoll.[889]

Yet the court was quick to point out that it can only be the ECJ[890] that can depart from the jurisprudence built up to date from *Tessili*.

1.3.4 The application of *Tessili* and *Custom Made Commercial* in English cases

Various English courts have considered the place of performance of the obligation in question in detail. In *Royal Bank of Scotland Plc v Cassa di Risparmio delle Province Lombard and others*,[891] the plaintiff RBS, as a confirming bank under a letter of credit transaction was authorised,[892] when adding its confirmation, to seek re-imbursement of payments made to the beneficiary of the credit from the

---

[879] IPRspr. (1976) Nr. 146, at p.420, including a very clear application of the place of performance under German law §269 BGB, as *lex causae*.

[880] IPRspr. (1987) Nr. 128, the reference back in case *Hassan Shenavai v Klaus Kreischer* (C-266/85) [1987] ECR 239, indicating no *forum actoris*: 'entscheidend der Wohnsitz (in den Niederlanden lebenden) Bekl.'('decisively the domicile of the defendant (in The Netherlands)'), at p.314.

[881] IPRspr. (1991) Nr. 170; [1992] I.L.Pr. 395, special place of performance for payment of legal fees.

[882] IPRspr. (1993) Nr. 139, at p.312.

[883] IPRspr. (1995) Nr. 154, at p.313.

[884] (2000) *IPRax* 121, (1999) *RIW* 968.

[885] (2000) *RIW* 142, where the court used §269 BGB to state that the place of performance of a company director's obligations to his company is at its seat.

[886] IPRspr. 1992 Nr. 181b, the German referring court in *Custom Made Commercial Ltd v Stawa Metallbau GmbH* (C-288/92) [1994] ECR I-2913.

[887] IPRspr. (1979) Nr. 168, at p.571 Article 59 of ULIS; also *LG Köln* 5.5.1988 IPRspr. (1988) Nr. 158, *OLG Hamm* 20.5.1977 IPRspr. (1977) Nr. 145, and *OLG Hamm* 27.5.1985 (1985) IPRspr. Nr. 134; in Belgium too, *Cour d'Appel de Bruxelles* 1988 *Ann dr. Liège* 90, at pp.93–94, obs. Van Hecke, G. and after *Custom Made Commercial*, (to the advantage now of Belgian sellers) *Hof van Beroep te Gent* 26.6.1997 (1998) *Rev. dr. comm. belge* 389.

[888] IPRspr. 1988 Nr. 158, at p.339.

[889] ('an *autonomous* concept, *that is divorced from national law* seems sensible, in view of international jurisdictional equilibrium'), IPRspr. 1988 Nr. 158, at p.339.

[890] The French courts have no such reservations, below at pp.143–147.

[891] [1991] I.L.Pr. 411, QBD (Phillips J) affm'd [1992] 1 Bank LR 251, CA.

[892] By the Banco Populare, the issuing bank in the second action.

Manufacturers Hanover Trust Co, in New York. The Trust Co refused payment, after having received instructions to do so from their 'principals', the defendant Italian issuing banks. These banks suspected fraud in the underlying sales transaction. RBS commenced an action directly against the issuing banks under Article 5(1) for failure to fulfil their 're-imbursement' obligation. Phillips J, at first instance, went through the *Tessili/De Bloos/Shenavai* route to find 'the place of performance', 'obligation', and 'principal obligation' respectively. The obligation to reimburse—the basis of the plaintiff's claim—was, by express agreement, the place where the confirming bank had contracted to reimburse itself, and thus the Article 5(1) place of performance:

> the stipulation for the use of an American reimbursing bank made America the place of performance of the reimbursement obligation for the purpose of Article 5(1). . .[893]

The Court of Appeal[894] agreed. According to Mustill LJ, 'the obvious place to start,[895] when searching for a contractual term material to a particular obligation, is the express agreement between the parties'.[896] The enquiry over the place of performance therefore ended when an express place had been stipulated. There was no jurisdiction in England under Article 5(1).

In *Rank Film Distributors Limited v Lanterna Editrice Srl and Banca Nazionale del Lavoro*,[897] an action by Rank against, *inter alia*, Banca Nazionale under a guarantee[898] was governed by a stipulation as to payment—'an undertaking by BNL to pay "according to the obligations undertaken by Lanterna"'. These obligations were to be performed, and amounts due to Rank to be paid, in London.

In *Ocarina Marine Ltd and others v Marcard Stein & Co.*,[899] the plaintiff shipowners sued the defendant German bank under loan agreements to purchase vessels, subject to English law and jurisdiction.[900] A restructuring of these loans had taken place; the plaintiffs alleged that the defendant had orally agreed to provide further finance on conditions. The defendant refused to provide the additional sums, without extra conditions. The plaintiffs' claim under Article 5(1) was, in essence, for damages for repudiation of this further oral agreement. There was

---

[893] [1991] I.L.Pr. 411, at p.423; in 'ordinary' actions under a guarantee, both *Cour de Cassation* 30.1.2001 *ING Bank NV Paris c/ Soc. Mantel Holland Beheer BV* (2001) *Rev crit* 539, at p.542 and *Bank of Scotland v Seitz* (1990) *SLT* 584, at p.594 (Lord Prosser) accept that the performance promised by the guarantor is, in the absence of contrary indication, to be performed at the place where the defaulting debtor should have, but did not, in his turn perform.

[894] [1992] 1 BankLR 251.

[895] *Siegfried Zelger v Sebastino Salinitri* (C-46/79) [1980] ECR 89 demonstrates that a contractually stipulated place of performance clause also implicates the *Tessili* formula.

[896] [1992] 1 BankLR 251, at p.256; followed recently by *Chailease Finance Corporation v Credit Agricole Indosuez* [2000] 1 Lloyd's Rep. 348, CA; Jack, R. *Documentary Credits*, 3rd edn., 2001, at pp.385–86; or implied from the circumstances of the parties' contractual arrangements *inter se*: *Deutsche Rückversicherung AG v La Fondiara Assicurazioni SpA*. [2001] 2 Lloyd's Rep. 621 (David Steel J).

[897] [1992] I.L.Pr. 58, CA.

[898] Governed by Italian law, with no material differences to English law on the point.

[899] [1994] 2 Lloyd's Rep. 524, QBD (Rix J).

[900] Separate points were argued under Article 17 Brussels Convention.

an issue as to the place of performance of the loan, in England, or Germany, which Rix J seems to have determined as a matter of fact—'the probability is that the finance would be provided originally by means of some debiting and/or crediting of accounts in Hamburg'.[901] Unfortunately, the judge made no explicit reference to *Tessili*, although the outcome would have arguably been the same in that event.

In *Medway Packaging Ltd v Meurer Maschinen GmbH & Co. K.G.*,[902] Fox LJ held that the place of performance of an obligation to give notice of termination (of an exclusive distributorship contract) to an English company was to be performed in England.[903] Additionally, the alternative 'negative' obligation not to supply another English distributor could be performed and/or broken in England or[904] the supplier's territory,[905] with equal moment in each case.

In *Boss Group Ltd v Boss France SA*[906] the negative obligation under the disputed exclusive distribution contract not to supply goods to anyone else in the contract's territory, according to Saville LJ, 'was probably performable everywhere, including both here and in France.'[907] This view has not been taken as 'a proposition of general applicability' for negative obligations (outside such exclusivity contracts) by Pumfrey J in *Kenburn Waste Management Ltd v Bergman*.[908] In this case, after strong intimation that proceedings would be taken against the German defendant, Bergman, a so-called 'contract of compromise' was reached between the defendant and claimant, Kenburn Waste Management, whereby in consideration for Kenburn's forbearance of initiating proceedings, Bergman agreed that he would not communicate with any UK companies or individuals complaining to them that the claimant's product violated a British patent. This the claimant alleged he had done in breach of the compromise. The obligation in this case— found by Pumfrey J to be 'a series of ancillary positive steps which must be taken in order to achieve the negative result'—clearly related to *the maintenance of a*

---

[901] [1994] 2 Lloyd's Rep. 524, at p.533, independently of 'the general rule in English law . . . that a bank's obligation to make payment out of an account is an obligation to make payment at the branch where the account is kept: *Richardson v Richardson* [1927] P. 288', at p.533.

[902] [1990] 2 Lloyd's Rep. 112, CA.

[903] *Ibid*, at p.116; persuasive in *Bio-Medical Research Ltd. T/A Slendertone v Delatex S.A.* [2000] 4 IR 307, SC, at p.316 (Fennelly J), coming to the same conclusion as to giving notice.

[904] *Quaere*, whether the obligation *must* be exclusively performed in the jurisdiction and not simultaneously also elsewhere- in Ireland at least *Handbridge Limited v British Aerospace Communications Ltd.* [1993] 3 I.R. 342, HC, SC, at p.358 (Finlay CJ).

[905] [1990] 2 Lloyd's Rep. 112, at p.117.

[906] [1996] 4 All ER 970, CA.

[907] *Ibid*, at p.976; *USF Ltd (t/a USF Memcor) v Aqua Technology Hanson NV/SA* [2001] 1 All ER (Comm) 856. The proposition that jurisdiction under Art.5(1) over a negative obligation can be justified on a 'performable everywhere' basis (as in the English cases), including the *lex fori*, will now have to be reassessed: *S.A. Besix N.V. v WABAG Wasserreinigungsbau Alfred Kretzschmar GmbH* (C-256/00), 19.2.2002, at paras. 28–29, where the ECJ ruled that only *one* place of performance can be indicated by Art.5(1), at para. 34, ie. the obligation must have a 'limitation géographique', at para. 49.

[908] 11.5.2001, Ch.D. (Pumfrey J); affm'd on Art.5(1) point, *Kenburn Waste Management Ltd v Bergman*, 30.1.2002, CA.

state of affairs in the UK—ie non-communication—and so was to be performed within the jurisdiction.[909]

The court in *Raiffeisen Zentralbank Österreich Aktiengesellschaft v National Bank of Greece S.A.*[910] had to hear expert evidence as to the place of performance of an implied term to reimburse sums of money under a loan arrangement on the basis of Greek law, *lege causae*. Although the subject of some debate in the case, this place was, in Article 321 of the Greek Civil Code, found to be at the creditor/plaintiff's place of 'professional establishment', in London.

In *Chailease Finance Corporation v Credit Agricole Indosuez*,[911] the defendant issuing bank under a letter of credit was contractually bound to 'pay [the beneficiary, Chailease] as per [its] instructions'.[912] This it eventually became bound to do under the credit in London. Despite arguments of the defendant that what was termed as a 'floating' place of performance clause was unacceptable in an Article 5(1) case, the CA did not 'see why the rule of jurisdiction . . . should be treated as inapplicable, simply because the parties have agreed that the crystallisation of the obligation as to the place of payment be postponed in that manner.'[913] The plaintiff had a contractual right to stipulate instructions as to a place of payment, and that therefore was an end[914] of the matter.

The application of *Tessili* and *Custom Made Commercial* has caused few, if any, problems in England and Wales. This may, in part, be due to the rule in English law that, in absence of any agreement to the contrary, a debtor must seek out his creditor,[915] or that concessions are made by the parties as to the place of performance in advance.[916]

---

[909] If the negative obligation not to communicate with the UK Co's could *only* be breached within the jurisdiction (a 'limitation géographique'), this would not seem to fall foul of *S.A. Besix N.V. v WABAG Wasserreinigungsbau Alfred Kretzschmar GmbH* (C-256/00), 19.2.2002; *Kenburn Waste Management Ltd v Bergman*, 30.1.2002, CA: '[i]n this case the negative obligation was to achieve a state of affairs within the United Kingdom'.

[910] [1999] 1 Lloyd's Rep. 408, at p.413.

[911] [2000] 1 Lloyd's Rep. 348, CA.

[912] Even if the beneficiary subsequently changed its place of payment instructions to London after two earlier presentations of allegedly non-conforming documents—a distinct situation from that in *Handbridge Limited v British Aerospace Communications*; flexibility in *Deutsche Rückversicherung AG v La Fondiara Assicurazioni SpA.* [2001] 2 Lloyd's Rep. 621 (David Steel J).

[913] [2000] 1 Lloyd's Rep. 348, at p.356; Jack, R. 3rd edn., 2001, at pp.385–86.

[914] Despite an attempt to have the payment instruction clause invalidated as a tacit Article 17 jurisdiction clause: *Mainschiffahrts-Genossenschaft eG (MSG) v Les Gravières Rhénanes SARL* (C-106/95) [1997] ECR I-911.

[915] *Robey & Co. v The Snaefell Mining Company Limited* (1887) 20 QBD 152, and *The Eider* [1893] P. 119, CA.

[916] *AIG Group (UK) Ltd and others v The Ethniki* [1998] 4 All ER 301, QBD (Colman J) affm'd [2000] All ER (Comm) 65, CA.

1.3.5 The application of *Tessili* and *Custom Made Commercial* in Swiss and Austrian cases

The Swiss and Austrian courts,[917] too, have had to come to terms with the *Tessili* jurisprudence under Article 5(1) of the Lugano Convention.[918] The opening indications show that, as with the German courts, they have been completely conformist. Mention should also be made of the fact that the place of performance of payment obligations under Swiss law, *lege causae* in the absence of choice/surrounding circumstances,[919] is at the creditor's seat/place of business.[920]

The Swiss *Bundesgericht* has considered Article 5(1) of the Lugano Convention in a number of reported and unreported[921] decisions. In *Sanft AG v Tasso S.r.l,*[922] the Swiss plaintiff sought payment of the purchase price from the Italian buyer. The place of performance was found by application of Article 57(1)(a) of the 1980 Vienna Sales Convention[923] to be that of the Swiss seller; in the second,[924] *Klara v Bruno*, the Swiss plaintiff Klara demanded repayment of a loan made to Bruno, domiciled in Rome. The court applied Swiss law,[925] *lege causae*, to determine the place of performance of the payment obligation, which—as has been noted—was the creditor's domicile; in the third, *Dames Pfiff & Fanta v Knuff,*[926] the two Swiss ladies claimed commission from the Rome domiciled defendant for having

---

[917] Esp. Volken, P. 'Rechtsprechung zum Lugano-Übereinkommen (1996)' (1997) *SZIER* 335, pp.341–42; and recently the Austrian *OGH* 20.1.1999 1999 *ÖJZ* 504; further details in Klauser, A. *EuGVÜ und EVÜ*, 1999, p.302.

[918] Czernich is in no doubt that Article 5(1) (in combination with Article 57 of the 1980 International Sales Convention) has opened up greater jurisdictional possibilities for Austrian exporters: Czernich, D 'Der Erfüllungsgerichtsstand im Lugano-Übereinkommen' (1996/7) *Anwbl* 426, at p.429; *Corte di Cassazione* 14.12.1999 *Imperial Bathroom company plc. contro Sanitari Pozzi s.p.a.* (2000) *Riv. dir. int. priv. e proc.* 1078; and *OLG Braunschweig* 28.10.1999 IPRspr. 1999 Nr. 130.

[919] Consequently, the *Tribunal cantonal vaudois*, Lausanne 4.7.1994, reported in Volken, P. 'Rechtsprechung zum Lugano-Übereinkommen (1993/94)' (1995) *SZIER* 17, at p.28 Swiss estate agents were able to rely on Article 5(1) to recover fees and commission from an Italian client; also *Tribunal cantonal valaisan*, Sion, 21.10.1994, at p.21.

[920] In the absence of contrary agreement (Article 74(1) OR), Article 74(2)(1) *Obligationenrecht* (OR) states: 'Geldschulden sind am Orte zu zahlen, wo der Gläubiger zur Zeit der Erfüllung seinen Wohnsitz hat...'('monetary debts shall be paid at the creditor's domicile at the time for performance...'); *Bundesgericht* 25.7.2000 *Gerhard Pabst GmbH gegen Ivana Gillar-Kokrda*, unreported; for a recent example of Swiss law *lege causae* applied to the detriment of a French plaintiff: *Cour d'appel de Paris* 13.10.1999 *Soc. Atlantic Ocean Line c/ Soc Tati et Soc AIG Europe* unreported, Lexis; the opposite to Austria, §905 Abs. 1 & 2 ABGB: Austrian *OGH* 9.9.1997 (1998) *ZfRV* 163.

[921] *Bundesgericht* 10.5.2000 *Dame R contre Cour de justice civile du canton de Genève*, 11.7.2000, *Dörken-Gutta Pol gegen Gutta-Werke AG*, 25.7.2000, *Gerhard Pabst GmbH gegen Ivana Gillar-Kokrda*, unreported.

[922] BGE 1996 III, 42; also mentioned in Volken, P. 'Rechtsprechung zum Lugano-Übereinkommen (1996)' (1997) *SZIER* 335, at p.347.

[923] It is unclear from the report on which basis, factual Article 1(1)(a), or legal Article 1(1)(b), the 1980 Vienna Sales Convention applied; in any event, the Italian defendant sought the application of Article 57(1)(a) of the Convention, at BGE 1996 III, 42, at pp.46–48.

[924] BGE 1996 III, 249.

[925] Article 74(2)(1)OR, text noted above.

[926] 23.8.1996 122 BGE III, 298.

introduced a buyer for his apartment in Genf. The Supreme Court followed the *de Bloos/Tessili* route explicitly, eventually finding that the payment obligation was, once again, in Article 74(2)(1) OR, to be performed in Geneva, the ladies' domicile. The *Bundesgericht* was little troubled[927] in any of these cases by the fact that a combination of Article 5(1) Lugano Convention and Article 74(2)(1) OR/International Sales Convention produced a *forum actoris* for the Swiss plaintiff. But the commentator, Volken, is so troubled:

> [b]eunruhigend ist immerhin, daß sich anscheinend niemand daran stört, wenn der Gerichtsstand des Vertragserfüllungsortes manifest als forum actoris eingesetzt ist.[928]

In *A.AG gegen B*,[929] the *Bundesgericht* had to deal with a case of a Swiss sole importer of a Danish defendant manufacturer suing the latter for anticipatory breach of contract by the latter's threat to supply a third party. The court meticulously followed the *Peters v ZNAV/de Bloos/Tessili* routes under Article 5(1) Lugano Convention. Yet it also noted the recent criticisms of Droz to the effect that the place of performance of payment obligations frequently leads to

> Gerichtsstände ohne engere Beziehungen zur Streitsache oder grundsätzlich verpönte Klägergerichtsstände.[930]

Without ECJ authority to the contrary, however, it felt constrained to apply, by giving 'due account' to the recently confirmed *Custom Made Commercial* methodology. Since the appeal court, in its view, had correctly applied Swiss law to the place of performance of the concession contract obligations, Article 74 Abs.2(3) did not give jurisdiction to the Swiss courts[931] in any event. In *Gerhard Pabst GmbH gegen Ivana Gillar-Kokrda*[932] the place of performance of the obligation in question—in the form of an autonomous payment obligation in a contract between Gerhard Pabst and its Swiss sole distributor, expressly in favour of a third party,[933] Gillar—was ascertained using Article 74(2)(1) OR, again favouring retention of jurisdiction in favour of the Swiss claimant, Gillar.

The Austrian courts have also had to grapple with Article 5(1) of the Brussels and Lugano Conventions. The reported cases of the *Oberste Gerichtshof*, the Austrian Supreme Court, show the tri-partite application of Article 5(1) has

---

[927] Volken, (1997) *SZIER* 335, at p.343 is troubled by the advantageous treatment of Swiss plaintiffs.

[928] ('it is nonetheless disconcerting that apparently no-one is disturbed by the fact that jurisdiction at the contractual place of performance is obviously being employed as a *forum actoris*.'), *ibid*, at p.343.

[929] 9.3.1998 124 BGE, III, 188.

[930] ('jurisdiction without any close relationship to the dispute or in essence the much-criticised *forum actoris*'), *ibid*, at p.191.

[931] *Ibid*, at p.192, *in fine*.

[932] *Bundesgericht* 25.7.2000, unreported.

[933] Similar, but not identical to that in *Atlas Shipping Agency (UK) Ltd and United Shipping Services Ltd v Suisse Atlantique Société d'Armement Maritime S.A.* [1995] 2 Lloyd's Rep. 188; also the Contracts (Rights of Third Parties) Act 1999, s 1(1)(a).

caused few problems,[934] and that the jurisprudence of the European Court of Justice, to be given 'due account' under the Declaration to the Lugano Convention 1988,[935] has been precisely followed.

Three cases deserve particular comment: the first OGH 28.10.1997,[936] because of the use of Austrian law to determine the place of performance,[937] and two others[938] for the use of Article 5(1) to obtain jurisdiction to reclaim advance payments made under voidable/mutually cancelled contracts.

The decision in OGH 28.10.1997[939] shows the court dealing with a claim under Article 5(1) by an Austrian hotelier against German guests. These guests had paid their German tour operator in advance, received a voucher to present to the hotel in question, but this was dishonoured on presentation by the hotel. In this case, the legal presumption in §905 Abs.2 of the Austrian ABGB, that the place of performance of a payment obligation is the debtor's place of business, was displaced by a view of the surrounding circumstances of the case that:

> [b]ei einem Beherbergungsvertrag mit Feriengäste entspricht es den Verkehrssitten und den Interessen des Unterkunftgebers, daß auch das vom Gast zu leistende Entgelt am Ort der Beherbergung zu erbringen ist.[940]

In OGH 27.1.1998, the Austrian plaintiff buyers claimed repayment of sums advanced under a contract, the object of which did not correspond to the representations made by German sellers. Contrary to the views of the commentator Tiefenthaler,[941] the court found that the obligation in question was the 'reversed transaction claim' ('Rückabwicklungsanspruch'), which it found—despite de Bloos—was a primary contractual obligation, with its own place of performance:

> Der Rückabwicklungsanspruch tritt nicht an die Stelle einer der beiden vertraglichen Hauptpflichten.[942]

---

[934] OGH 27.1.1998 (1998) JBl 515, in regards to claims for restitution, at p.516, reviewed below; OGH 28.10.1997 Entscheidungen, 70 Band, 1997, No.226, p.617 shows §905 Abs.2 ABGB is detrimental to Austrian plaintiffs seeking payment of debts in Austria.

[935] Note that Austria became a Brussels Convention Contracting State on 1.12.1998.

[936] OGH 28.10.1997 (1998) ÖJZ 264.

[937] Of interest too is OGH 28.7.1998 1999 ÖJZ 70, which, as Austrian law governed the place of performance, lege causae, shows that a post-contractual change of domicile of the debtor (to another Lugano Contracting State) is irrelevant, at p.71.

[938] OGH 27.1.1998 (1998) JBl 515 and 10.3.1998 (1998) ZfRV 161.

[939] (1998) ÖJZ 264.

[940] ('that in a contract for the accommodation of guests, it is customary and in the interests of the host, that the fee due from the guest is to be paid at the place of accommodation'), ibid, at p.265; Fleischer, 1997, at p.76, n.194 reviewing pre-Convention cases, believes, by analogy, that a similar result would obtain under Article 5(1) Brussels Convention in Germany.

[941] Tiefenthaler, S. 'LGVÜ: Gerichtsstand am „Erfüllungsort des Bereicherungsanspruchs'?' (1998) ÖJZ 544, at p.546 who believes the claim was a dependent contractual obligation, dependent on other contractual obligations.

[942] ('the claim for repayment does not take the place of either of the two contractual obligations'), (1998) JBl 515, at p.516.

Unfortunately for the plaintiffs, however, whichever substantive law, Austrian or German were applied to the place of performance of the (re-)payment obligation, neither permitted jurisdiction to be taken on the ground that this 're-imbursement' obligation fell to be performed in Austria.

The application of Swiss law, *lege causae,* came to the aid of the Austrian plaintiff in another reported case of the *OGH,* on 10.3.1998.[943] Again, the plaintiff demanded repayment of sums pre-advanced on the basis of a contract that was eventually terminated by mutual agreement. Again the 'obligation in question' was found to be the independent claim to repayment of sums on mutual termination of the contract. This, by Swiss law,[944] Article 74(2) OR, was found to be Austria.

One of the latest reported Austrian cases[945] shows the inability of an Austrian sole commercial agent to sue his Finnish principal for commission, and compensation for breach of contract in Austria, due to the application of Austrian material law[946] *lege causae.*

1.3.6   The application of *Tessili* and *Custom Made Commercial* in French cases

The greatest departure from the *Tessili* jurisprudence is to be found in France,[947] where the problem of the non- or mis-application of *Tessili* is particularly rife at appeal court level.

The reported cases correctly applying[948] the *lex causae* formula will be dealt with first. Among the 'classic'[949] Article 5(1) cases, reviewing (correctly), in turn, the

---

[943] (1998) *ZfRV* 161.

[944] Although the 1980 Vienna Sales Convention was found to apply, the Convention had a lacuna as regards repayment obligations; Swiss law therefore filled the breach.

[945] *OGH* 20.1.1999 (1999) *ÖJZ* 504; the case is notable in that it *refused* to align sole commercial agency contracts with 'individual contracts of employment' under Article 5(1) second para. of the Lugano Convention: now, of course, *Leathertex Divisione Sintetici SpA v Bodetex BVBA* (C-420/97) [1999] ECR I-6747, AG Léger's opinion 16.3.1999, not followed, and discussed below; *OGH* 28.2.2000 (2000) *ZfRV* 151.

[946] 1999 *ÖJZ* 504, at p.506; §905 Abs. 2 ABGB sent the plaintiff to Finland, the place of the debtor's place of business.

[947] In comparison to the other Contracting States reviewed here.

[948] *Société SPLM, Société anonyme Banque Paribas Belgique Korenmarkt, Société BVBA Finecco* 10.11.1993 (1994) *JDI* 678; *Société Le Crédit Suisse c/ Bouillon et Société pour l'aménagement et la promotion de la station d'Isola 2000* 12.10.1994 (1995) *JDI* 158, *Cassation* 25.2.1997 *Soc. Bateg Delta c/ Soc Ward Group et autre* (1997) *Dalloz,* Juris. 562; *SA Comptoir commercial d'Orient c/ Soc. Medtrafina* 11.3.1997 (1997) *Dalloz,* Juris. 562; 18.3.1997 *Soc. Ernesto Stoppani Spa c/ SARL Stoppani France* (1997) *Dalloz,* Juris. 562; *SCEA GAEC des Beauches c/ Sté Teso Ten Elsen GmbH* 23.10.1996 (1998) *JDI* 125; *Marc Thomas c/ Sté Crédit de l'Est* 17.10.1996 (1998) *JDI* 144, *Cour d'appel de Riom* 3.2.1999 *SA Bourbie c/ Société Thyssen Henschel GmbH* (2000) *JCP,* IV, 1704, at p.772, and the myriad of cases reported on the French database *Juris-data.*

[949] So called, because they follow the *de Bloos/ Tessili/ Shenavai/ Custom Made Commercial* formula for jurisdiction under Article 5(1); also *Promac Sprl v SA Sogeservice* [1993] I.L.Pr. 309; *Soc Eureco v Soc Confezioni Liviam di Crespi Luigi* [1990] I.L.Pr. 50.

obligation in question, and thereafter subjecting it to the *lex causae*, also correctly determined, is *San Carlo Gruppo alimentare SPA c/ SBC Vico.*[950] This was an action for payment by Vico for goods delivered to San Carlo Gruppo in Italy. The applicable law, eventually found to be French,[951] Article 1247 *Code civil*, forced the French plaintiff to seek out its debtor in Italy. As a consequence of this, and other cases, Droz[952] once again criticises the *lex causae* methodology, and wishes to see it abrogated.

Another, and more recent example, from the *Cour de Cassation* is *Sté Stoppani SPA c/ Sté Stoppani France.*[953] This involved an exclusive distribution contract, allegedly breached by the Italian supplier by itself supplying the plaintiff's customers in France. As has been seen,[954] the 'obligation in question' in such contracts has commonly been taken to be the one to 'respect the contract'. The court rebuked the lower appeal court for not having determined its[955] place of performance via the *Tessili* conflict of laws process.[956] In such cases, as the commentator notes, the French jurisprudence

> s'est *presque toujours* abstenue de mettre en œuvre la méthode conflictualiste préconisée par l'arrêt *Tessili.*[957] [958]

The other two cases, *Aujoux et Cie GmbH c/ S.A.R.L. les fils de Henri Ramel*[959] and *Société Julia c/ Société Sodevoc*[960] have not been classified as 'classic' Article 5(1) cases because, one suspects,[961] the only reason *Tessili* was followed, was that the place of payment was found to exist *in favour* of the French *forum actoris*.

A more modern example of the applicable substantive law favouring the *forum actoris* is *SCEA GAEC des Beauches c/ Sté Teso Ten Elsen GmbH.*[962] SCEA overpaid the German defendant Teso Ten for work done and goods supplied by the latter. In a claim for reimbursement, the French company successfully relied on Article 5(1). The *Cour d'appel de Grenoble* followed the conflict of law approach,[963] which

---

[950] 6.2.1996 (1996) *Rev crit* 504.

[951] At p.505, by the rather convoluted route of the Hague Convention 15.6.1955 on the Law Applicable to International Sales.

[952] (1996) *Rev crit* 504, at pp.505–06, the case's reviewer.

[953] 18.3.1997 (1998) *JDI* 129.

[954] Above, at p.84, section 1.2.

[955] No criticism was mentioned of the classification of the 'obligation in question' here.

[956] (1998) *JDI* 129, at p.131.

[957] ('has almost always refrained from applying the conflict of laws methodology advocated by the *Tessili* case').

[958] *Ibid*, at p.130.

[959] 28.2.1979 (1979) *JDI* 104.

[960] 27.11.1979 (1979) *JDI* 333.

[961] Given the level of *Tessili* out-manoeuvring highlighted in this section.

[962] 23.10.1996 (1998) *JDI* 125.

[963] *Ibid*, at p.127. A combination of *Tessili* and Article 1(1)(b) Vienna Convention, thus an express approval of *Custom Made Commercial Ltd v Stawa Metallbau GmbH* (C-288/92) [1994] ECR I-2913; *Cour d'appel d'Orléans* 29.3.2001 *SARL TCE Diffusion c/ Soc. Elettrotecnica Ricci*, http://www.jura.uni-sb.de/CJFA.

eventually lead to the application of the 1980 Vienna Sales Convention, Article 57.1,[964] and the *forum actoris*.[965]

Even in *Société Socomo-Socotub c/ Société Reifenhauser*[966] the *Cour de Cassation* had to reprimand the lower court for not having used the *Tessili* formula. The court of appeal had simply based its decision on a German[967] place of performance clause, without ascertaining the applicable law.

In *Société SPLM, Société anonyme Banque Paribas Belgique Korenmarkt, Société BVBA Finecco*,[968] the Paris court of appeal applied the *lex causae* to a demand of a payment obligation, given in a guarantee[969] by the Belgian defendant bank, to the French seller, SLPM. Article 1247 *Code civil* required the French seller to seek payment from the Belgian debtor/guarantor in Belgium.

In *Société Le Crédit Suisse c/ Bouillon et Société pour l'aménagement et la promotion de la station d'Isola 2000*[970]—an early case of the French courts' application of Article 5(1) Lugano Convention—the French plaintiffs Bouillon, and others, attempted to sue the Swiss bank, Crédit Suisse, in France under a guarantee agreement. Unfortunately for them, the guarantee contained an express choice of Swiss law and an express place[971] of payment clause in Switzerland.

A large number of cases have emerged which, for one reason or another, either omit to apply *Tessili tout court*, preferring a factual[972] place of performance, or, *proprio vigore*, attribute and/or substitute an autonomous[973] place of performance to the 'obligation' in question. A *leitmotiv* that could serve for the cases under

---

[964] Article 57(1)(a) of the UN Convention on the International Sale of Goods (CISG) provides that if 'the buyer is not bound to pay the price at any other particular place, he must pay it to the seller; (a) at the seller's place of business . . .'—*quaere*, whether Article 57 applies to such 'repayment' obligations; *Corte di Cassazione* 14.12.1999 *Imperial Bathroom company plc. contro Sanitari Pozzi s.p.a.* (2000) *Riv. dir. int. priv. e proc.* 1078.

[965] Applied in favour of the *forum actoris* under Article 5(1) in *Tribunal de Grande Instance de Colmar* 18.12.1997 *Soc. Romay AG c/ Soc. Behr France*, unreported; *Cour d'appel de Paris* 15.10.1997 *S.A.R.L. Sodime-la-Rosa c/ Soc. Softlife Design Ltd*, unreported and *Cour d'appel de Paris* 10.11.1993 *SLPM c/ BVVA Finecco* unreported; also *OLG Braunschweig* 28.10.1999 IPRspr. 1999 Nr. 130.

[966] 2.6.1981 (1983) *JDI* 395.

[967] *Quaere*, whether there would have been a *cassation* if the clause had pointed to the French forum *qua forum actoris*.

[968] 10.11.1993 (1994) *JDI* 678; also noted by Gaudement-Tallon H. 'Jurisprudence sur la Convention de Rome du 19 juin 1980' (1994) *Rev. Trim. Dr. eur.* 101, at p.103; [1995] I.L.Pr. 175.

[969] Also *Marc Thomas c/ Sté Crédit de l'Est* 17.10.1996 (1998) *JDI* 144 with the same result under Article 5(1) Lugano Convention.

[970] 12.10.1994 (1995) *JDI* 158.

[971] Article 74(1) of the Swiss *Obligationenrecht* permitted an express choice to be made.

[972] *Quaere*, whether the French and German wording of their versions of Article 5(1) allow for this.

[973] This is rare, but has happened recently, more so, perhaps due to *Custom Made Commercial Ltd v Stawa Metallbau GmbH* (C-288/92) [1994] ECR I-2913; below at p.146 and *Roth c/ Syndicat des copropriétaires de l'immeuble Saint-Georges I et II* 13.6.1989 (1991) JDI 149, *Le Comptoir Commercial d'Orient S.A. c/ Medtrafina S.A. Cassation* 5.4.1994 (1995) *Rev crit* 573, 11.3.1997 (1998) *JDI* 129, and *Groupe Concorde et autres c/ Capitaine du Suhadiwarno Panjan et autres* 9.12.1997 (1998) *Rev crit* 117, (C-440/97) [1999] ECR I-6307.

review, and that introduced section 1.3, here is an impression of Watt, the reviewer of *Soc. Comptoir des Plastiques de l'Ain c/ Soc. Novamec et autres:*[974]

> la méconnaissance de la jurisprudence Tessili *n'est sanctionnée que lorsqu'elle a pour effet de priver les tribunaux français de leur compétence internationale.*[975] [976]

A summation of the cases will attempt to show that there is a perceived impression in this area of such a protectionist abstention from applying *Tessili* in France. In chronological order, the cases that omit any reference to *Tessili* itself and/or localise the obligation by factual circumstances, rather than legal conclusions, start with an early *Cour de Cassation* case of *Etablissements Carl Brehmer und Sohn c/ Baudoin.*[977] The case involved a dispute surrounding an exclusive concession contract for a French exclusive sales agent. Having decided that the obligation in question in the dispute was to deliver the products to the concessionaire in France, the court localised this obligation in fact,[978] without taking the choice of law 'detour'. Gaudemet-Tallon regrets the court's lack of rigour in its reasoning, yet seems to applaud the protectionist result:

> Le *domicile du concessionnaire nous paraît être un chef de compétence digne d'être retenue* . . . il importe de protéger . . . sur le plan de la compétence judiciaire.[979] [980]

Again in *Mosbacher et Société Uniputz c/ Banque nationale de Paris,*[981] certain findings of fact,[982] regarding the place of payment in Paris under a guarantee, enabled the Paris court of appeal to dispense with *Tessili*.

In *Société F.A.BA. c/ dame Pelloux*[983] the *Cour d'appel de Nîmes* simply omitted any reference to locating the place of performance *lege causae*, and opted capriciously for French law, Article 1247 *Code civil*, resulting in its declining jurisdiction.

Ossberger c/ Mauriès,[984] is a case where the *Cour de Cassation* approved a lower court's decision not to research the contract's governing law—the reason? Judicial economy: 'une telle économie du raisonnement conflictualiste'.[985] Again, in *Ets*

---

[974] 9.2.1994 (1994) *Rev crit* 577.

[975] ('ignoring the *Tessili* jurisprudence is only justified when the case has the effect of depriving French courts of their international competence').

[976] *Ibid*, at p.579.

[977] 23.1.1979 (1979) *Rev crit* 816.

[978] *Ibid*, at p.822.

[979] ('the domicile of the concessionnaire appears to us to be a head of jurisdiction worthy of retention [and] protection in the area of judicial competence').

[980] At p.824.

[981] 25.4.1979 (1979) *JDI* 352.

[982] Also the concession contract cases of *Sociétés Rotaprint Export Ehmer et Rotaprint c/ Société Guyot Fourchault* 13.2.1981 (1981) *JDI* 849, and *Société BIG Spielwarenfabrik c/ Compagnie générale du jouet Importation Arbois* 24.6.1982 (1983) *JDI* 404.

[983] 8.10.1980 (1981) *JDI* 851.

[984] 16.2.1982 (1983) *JDI* 393.

[985] *Ibid*, at p.394; AG Colomer's opinion of 16.3.1999 in the recent case *GIE Groupe Concorde* also saw a conflict of laws 'detour' as representing a complex and time-consuming methodology, [1999] ECR

Devriendt c/ Soc Roto Frank[986] involved a French sub-purchaser's action in contract[987] against a Belgian manufacturer. The decision elicits a neglect[988] of the *Tessili* jurisprudence, and a telling comment from Gaudemet-Tallon about the (justified)[989] creation of a *forum actoris* through a manipulation of *Tessili*, in favour of French concessionaires:

> si cette localisation de fait ne soulève guère d'objections *lorsqu'il s'agit de contrat de concession*[990] ou de contrat de travail . . .'[991] [992]

More serious[993] for the uniform application[994] of *Tessili*, and Article 5(1), is the recent tendency of the French courts not only to ignore *Tessili*, but to substitute their own autonomous[995] place of performance criteria.[996] Apart from the recent reference to the ECJ in *Groupe Concorde et autres c/ Capitaine du Suhadiwarno Panjan et autres*,[997] a striking example of this is *Roth c/ Syndicat des copropriétaires de l'immeuble Saint-Georges I et II*,[998] a case outside the specialist area of concession contracts. A syndicate/co-operative of co-owners of a building in France tried to recover (maintenance) charges against one German-domiciled co-owner. Having found, by close analogy with the ECJ decision in *Peters v ZNAV*[999] that the dispute concerned a 'matter relating to a contract', the *Cour d'appel* should have further investigated the law applicable to the co-owners' agreement, to determine

---

I-6307, at p.6317, and pp.6321–22 at paras. 28, 29, 46, respectively, a view not accepted by the ECJ on 28.9.1999.

[986] 28.10.1986 (1987) *Rev crit* 612.

[987] This type of action would now not be successful under Article 5(1): *Jakob Handte & Co. GmbH v Société Traitements Mecano-Chimiques des Surfaces (TMCS)* (C-26/91) [1992] ECR I-3697, but the *lex causae* omission remains.

[988] This neglect is blatant in *Société Adis c/ Société Agredis* 17.11.1988 (1990) *JDI* 150, a sale of goods dispute.

[989] At least in French eyes through French judicial activism.

[990] The French courts appear to have taken it upon themselves to create an autonomous place of performance for such contracts, as the ECJ has done (*Roger Ivenel v Helmut Schwab* (C-133/81) [1982] ECR 1891), and the San Sebastian Accession Convention, 3.10.1989 [1989] OJ L285/1, at p.3, Article 4, has added a new jurisdiction in individual contracts of employment.

[991] ('if this factual localisation does not raise any objection when what is involved is a concession or employment contract').

[992] 28.10.1986 (1987) *Rev crit* 612, at p.615.

[993] Serious, as the protectionism is spreading to contracts in general—Droz, G. 'Delendum est forum contractus? (vingt ans après les arrêts *de Bloos* et *Tessili* interprétant l'article 5.1 de la Convention de Bruxelles du 27 septembre 1968' (1997) *Dalloz*, Chron., 351.

[994] If French plaintiffs are not to be advantaged.

[995] Also *Cour de Cassation* 3.3.1992 *Société Svedex Holding B.V. v B.N.P. et autre* (1993) *Rev crit* 692, obs. Sinay-Clytermann.

[996] Noted by Jacquet *Société SPLM, Société anonyme Banque Paribas Belgique Korenmarkt, Société BVBA Finecco* 10.11.1993 (1994) *JDI* 678, at p.685.

[997] 9.12.1997 (1998) *Rev crit* 117, *Groupe Concorde* (C-440/97) [1999] ECR I-6307, ECJ decision of 28.9.1999, confirming the *Custom Made Commercial lex causae* route.

[998] 13.6.1989 (1991) *JDI* 149, which same result could have been achieved by interpretation of French law in any case.

[999] [1983] ECR 987.

where the charges were payable.[1000] The court did not take this route, but an autonomous one:

> non en fonction de la loi qui lui est applicable en vertu des règles françaises de conflit de lois, *mais en fonction des objectifs*[1001] *de l'article 5–1 . . .*[1002] [1003]

Although *Custom Made Commercial Ltd v Stawa Metallbau GmbH*[1004] has rejected a *forum conveniens* approach to the location of the place of performance under Article 5(1), *Roth c/ Syndicat des copropriétaires*, and several that post-date[1005] *Custom Made Commercial*, show the French courts' reluctance to apply *Tessili* to payment obligations: *Tessili* simply disadvantages French plaintiff/ claimant creditors from suing in the *forum actoris*.

Before these cases are looked at, it is just as well to remind ourselves of the decision in *Custom Made Commercial*.

1.3.7   *Custom Made Commercial* itself, and the triumph of a Convention aim: predictability

There had been murmurs[1006] of disquiet that the *Tessili* formula, in conjunction with certain substantive laws and/or Uniform Sales Convention, had created a *forum actoris*, the Convention's anathema.[1007] The *Bundesgerichtshof* referred such a case under Article 59(1) of ULIS Sales Convention[1008] to the ECJ in *Custom Made Commercial Ltd v Stawa Metallbau GmbH*.[1009] The appeal court in the case, *OLG Hamm*, had found that Article 59(1)(1) of the 1974 Hague Convention (ULIS) applied to determine the place of performance on the facts. The concern of the

---

[1000] One would have thought Germany as French law, *lege causae,* Article 1247 *Code civil,* points to this place.

[1001] Again, influenced by *Peters v ZNAV* (C-34/82) [1983] ECR 987, the place of performance of this payment obligation was deemed to be before the jurisdiction best suited to take cognisance of it—the seat of the syndicate of co-owners in France; also Gaudemet-Tallon, 1996, at p.109, para. 157: this 'relève aussi l'avantage pratique de cette solution: le juge compétent, celui du lieu d'exécution de l'obligation, sera, le plus souvent, celui du siège de l'association.'('highlights the practical advantage of this solution: the judge with jurisdiction, the one at the place of performance of the obligation, will, most often, be the one at the seat of the association').

[1002] ('not according to the law applicable to it by virtue of French conflict of laws rules, *but in accordance with the objectives of* Article *5(1) . . .'*).

[1003] At (1991) *JDI* 149, p.151; the 'objectives' of Article 5(1) were also important for the speeches of Lords Woolf and Cooke in *Agnew and others v Lansförsäkringsbolagens AB* in determining not to limit Article 5(1) obligations to contractual ones, *stictu sensu,* [2001] 1 AC 223, at pp.240–41 (Lord Woolf) and at p.247 (Lord Cooke).

[1004] (C-288/92) [1994] ECR I-2913, reviewed at p.102.

[1005] Droz, (1997) *Dalloz,* Chron., 351.

[1006] Even in Germany, *LG Köln* 5.5.1988 IPRspr. 1988 Nr. 158, and in Switzerland *A.AG gegen B* 9.3.1998 124 BGE, III, 188, at p.191.

[1007] Manifest esp. in Article 3 [II].

[1008] Uniform Law on the International Sale of Goods, annexed to the Hague Convention of 1 July 1964.

[1009] (C-288/92) [1994] ECR I-2913.

BGH was that this Convention could apply either[1010] by the *Tessili, lex causae,* route, or *proprio vigore,*[1011] by the signatories to the Conventions themselves. In the latter case the *BGH* took the view that 'die einheitsrechtlichen Regelungen *unmittelbar*[1012] nach ihrem selbstbestimmten Geltungsbereich anzuwenden [waren]',[1013] so that, in effect, the *lex causae* was shut out.[1014]

The facts before the ECJ are well known and documented.[1015] Stawa Metallbau, the German plaintiff, sought payment in its local courts for the remaining sale price of goods manufactured and sold to Custom Made Commercial, its English customer, and defendant. The German court had held that the place of performance of this payment obligation was, in Article 59 (1)(1) of Hague Convention, at the vendor, Metallbau's, seat in Bielefeld. It also had noted that

> [d]er Gerichtshof hat noch nicht entschieden, wie der Erfüllungsort gemäß Article 5 Nr.1 . . . im Falle von Einheitsrecht, das nationales Kollisionsrecht ausschaltet,[1016] zu bestimmen ist.[1017]

The ECJ was asked whether a Uniform Sales Law could determine the place of performance under Article 5(1) Brussels Convention, such Sales Law being applicable because of[1018] the *lex causae.* The answer given by the ECJ proved to be a gloss on the *Tessili* formula:

> the obligation to pay the price is to be determined pursuant to the substantive law governing the obligation in dispute under the conflicts rules of the court seised,[1019] even

---

[1010] ULIS, Article 1(1)(b).

[1011] Article 1(1)(a).

[1012] In *OLG Hamm* 3.10.1979 IPRspr. 1979 Nr. 168, ULIS was applied because both parties had their seats in two Contracting States; in *LG München* 29.5.1995 IPRspr. 1995 Nr. 146, *OLG Braunschweig* 28.10.1999 IPRspr. 1999 Nr. 130, the court used Article 57(1)(a) 1980 Vienna Sales Convention to ascertain the place of performance. This Convention applied by Article 1(1)(a), *not* under the *Tessili, lex causae,* option of Article 1(1)(b).

[1013] ('that the unified law rules were to be used *directly* form its own self-governing provisions *ratione materiae.*'), *BGH* 1992 NJW 756, at p.757; the incorrect assessment in the review of *Custom Made Commercial Ltd v Stawa Metallbau GmbH* (C-288/92) [1994] ECR I-2913 in the (1994) *Rev crit* 692, at p.699 and p.701.

[1014] (1992) NJW 756, at p.758; the case was not therefore an assault on *Tessili,* but sought confirmation of it.

[1015] In detail Hertz, 1998, at pp.104–10.

[1016] The following footnote for a translation. *Quaere,* does this mean that the *lex causae* is shut out initially, via Article 1(1)(a), or subsequently, after the *lex causae* has pointed to the application of the Uniform Law—Art 1(1)(b)? The *BGH* suggests the former; the English version of the reference suggests the latter interpretation: [1994] ECR I-2913, at p.2916 for the opinion of AG Lenz; Huet on this aspect 1995 *JDI* 461, at p.463: 'le juge d'un Etat contractant doit l'appliquer [the 1980 Vienna Convention], *sans référence aucune à sa règle de conflit*'('the judge of a contracting state must apply [the 1980 Vienna Convention], *without any reference to his conflict of laws rules*').

[1017] ('the Court of Justice has not yet decided how the place of performance is to be found, in cases of Uniform Law that excludes national conflict of laws.'), 1992 NJW 756, at p.758.

[1018] This did not seem to answer the *BGH*'s original concerns; Hertz, 1998, believes 'it saves work to apply the CISG directly, without recourse to choice of law rules', at p.122, para. 4.1.2.

[1019] Confirming *Tessili*

where those rules *refer to the application*[1020] to the contract of provisions such as those of the Uniform Law . . .[1021]

For this treatment, this was not the crux of the case. This proved to be the ECJ's rejection of, by ignoring, AG Lenz's opinion, and thus the triumph[1022] of two related Convention aims that have recently asserted themselves:[1023] foreseeability and legal certainty. To the Advocate General at least, these two latter aims were in collision[1024] with the original *raison d'être* of Article 5, mentioned in the Jenard Report[1025] and *Tessili*[1026] itself: the particularly close relationship between a dispute and the court seised of it. Relying on authorities[1027] from disputes involving employment contracts, he believed that the *lex causae/Tessili* formula had proved not to be an inflexible rule, but could be departed from

> where its application, *in a given case, manifestly* [did] *not square*[1028] *with the aim of* Article 5(1).[1029]

Being somewhat diverted from the *Tessili* route by his conviction that non-payment is ('in most cases'[1030]) linked in some way to 'whether the performance provided by the seller was duly affected',[1031] he thought that the courts best able,[1032]

[1020] An answer if the Uniform Law applies by Article 1(1)(b) of the Hague Convention; what of the case where the Hague Convention applies because of Article 1(1)(a)? The referring court's concerns were not answered here; also Huet, (1995) *JDI* 461, at p.463; *Cour de Cassation* 26.6.2001 *Anton Huber GmbH & Co c/ Soc. Polyspace*, (2001) *JCP*, IV, 2554, *Cour de Cassation* 26.6.2001 *Sté Ogosa destribuciones c/ SA Madrange* (2001) *JCP*, IV, 2556—Vienna Convention applied as part of French law *qua lex causae.*

[1021] *Custom Made Commercial Ltd v Stawa Metallbau GmbH* (C-288/92) [1994] ECR I-2913, at pp.2958–59, para. 29.

[1022] And, it has been subsequently argued, to the detriment of another and fundamental aim of Article 5(1): proximity: *GIE Groupe Concorde e.a.* (C-440/97) [1999] ECR I-6307, AG Colomer's opinion 16.3.1999.

[1023] A clear assertion of their importance comes from *Jakob Handte & Co. GmbH v Société Traitements Mecano-Chimiques des Surfaces (TMCS)* (C-26/91) [1992] ECR I-3697, at p.3995, para. 18, *Mulox IBC Ltd v Hendrick Geels* (C-125/92) [1993] ECR I-4075, at p.4103, para. 11 and *Antonio Marinari v Lloyds Bank Plc and Zubaidi Trading Co.* (C-364/93) [1995] ECR I-2719, at p.2741, para. 19: 'to provide for a clear and certain attribution of jurisdiction'.

[1024] AG Lenz, at p.2931, para. 67 thought that the ECJ had recognised this aspect of Article 5(1)'s weakness in *Hassan Shenavai v Klaus Kreischer* (C-266/85) [1987] ECR 239.

[1025] [1979] OJ C59/22, section 2.

[1026] *Industrie Tessili Italiana Como v Dunlop AG* (C-12/76) [1976] ECR 1473, at p.1485, para. 13.

[1027] *Roger Ivenel v Helmut Schwab* (C-133/81) [1982] ECR 1891 and *Mulox IBC Ltd v Hendrick Geels* (C-125/92) [1993] ECR I-4075.

[1028] He thought that the Bielefeld court, identified as the place of performance of the payment obligation by the Sales Convention, and the *Tessili* route, manifestly did not square with the proximity justification of Article 5(1): the case had closer links with the UK; Gaudemet-Tallon, reviewing *Custom Made Commercial*, at (1994) *Rev crit* 692, at p.700: English negotiations, materials designed for use in English construction, non-payment by English buyer.

[1029] AG Lenz, [1994] ECR I-2913, at p.2929, para. 63, original italics.

[1030] At p.2932 para. 72, *sed quaere.*

[1031] Ibid.

[1032] Briggs (1994) *YEL* 557 at p.576.

geographically, to assess the correct nature of performance would be, in this case,[1033] the place of delivery[1034] in England.

The ECJ did not take up AG Lenz's concerns, but seemed to abandon the original (article) aim of Article 5(1),[1035] proximity,[1036] in favour of a more general aim of the Convention itself,[1037] foreseeability.[1038] Apart from individual contracts of employment, any discretion[1039] to depart from the *Tessili* formula

> might jeopardise the possibility of foreseeing which court will have jurisdiction and for that reason be incompatible with the aim of the Convention.[1040]

This, one would have thought, would be enough to have entrenched the *Tessili lex causae* determination of 'the place of performance of the obligation in question'.[1041] Yet recent decisions[1042] of the French *Cour de Cassation* have again questioned *Tessili*, and now *Custom Made Commercial*'s correctness, by the substitution of their own, autonomous[1043] definition of the place of performance.

1.3.8   The attempted, but failed,[1044] 'rebellion' of the French *Cour de Cassation* against *Tessili/Custom Made Commercial*

The *Cour de Cassation*, in two relatively recent cases,[1045] had manifested an intention to challenge the appropriateness[1046] of the *Tessili/Custom Made lex causae* formula;[1047] instead relying on where performance actually took place,[1048]

[1033] The AG would no doubt have been fortified in his view, by the amended Article 5(1)(b) of the Brussels I Regulation, 'in the case of the sale of goods' the (autonomous) place of performance of the obligation in question is stated to be 'where under the contract the goods were delivered . . .'.

[1034] Gaudemet-Tallon, reviewing *Custom Made Commercial Ltd* (1994) *Rev crit* 692, at p.701.

[1035] Briggs, (1994) *YEL* 557 at pp.575–76.

[1036] [1994] ECR I-2913, at p.2957, para. 21.

[1037] 'the dominant policy aim', according to Briggs, (1994) *YEL* 557 , at p.577.

[1038] In accord with Dietze, J. 'Die aktuelle Rechtsprechung des EuGH zum EuGVÜ' (1995) *EuZW* 359, at p.360.

[1039] Not that there is any discretion in employment contracts—note the post San Sebastian amendments to Article 5(1).

[1040] (C-288/92) [1994] ECR I-2913, at p.2956, para .18.

[1041] Czernich, D. 'Der Erfüllungsgerichtsstand im Lugano-Übereinkommen' (1996/7) *Anwbl* 426, at p.429; *Custom Made Commercial* will clearly advantage Austrian plaintiffs.

[1042] *Sté Comptoir commercial d'Orient c/ Société Medtrafina* 11.3.1997 1998 *JDI* 129, discussed by Droz, (1997) *Dalloz*, Chron., 351.

[1043] Similar in many ways to the approach advocated by AG Lenz.

[1044] Recent cases now conform to the *Tessili* formula: *Cassation* 15.5.2001 *SA Optelec c/ Sté Midtronics BV* (2001) *JCP*, IV, 2249, at p.1395.

[1045] *Sté Comptoir commercial d'Orient c/ Société Medtrafina* 11.3.1997, 1998 *JDI* 129; *Groupe Concorde et autres c/ Capitaine du Suhadiwarno Panjan et autres* 9.12.1997 (1998) *Rev crit* 117.

[1046] The formula's inappropriateness stems latterly from a tendency, also observed and traced by Hill, J. 'Jurisdiction under Article 5(5) of the Brussels Convention' (1996) *CJQ* 94, at p.579, that the original *raison d'être* of Article 5(1) has receded and now disappeared altogether.

[1047] Gaudemet-Tallon, reviewing *Sté Comptoir commercial d'Orient c/ Société Medtrafina* 11.3.1997 (1997) *Rev crit* 585, at p.590 also observes that the *Cassation* in addition disregards the ruling in *Ets. A. de Bloos S.P.R.L v Soc. en commandite par actions Bouyer* (C-15/76) [1976] ECR 1497.

[1048] The French and German versions of Article 5(1) actually allow for this possibility.

or should have taken place, according to vaguer notions of the contractual relationship, and the factual circumstances of the case.[1049] The first, *Sté Comptoir commercial d'Orient c/ Société Medtrafina*,[1050] involved the French court's assessing whether, in an enforcement action, the Greek courts were entitled[1051] to have assumed[1052] jurisdiction under Article 5(1).[1053]

A Liberian plaintiff had initially seised the Greek courts against a French defendant, on 15th June 1987, prior to the Greek Accession Convention's coming into force in Greece on 1st April 1989. The final[1054] appeal court's ruling, the Greek Court of Cassation, was handed down in mid 1990. The Greek judgment would therefore benefit from the recognition and enforcement regime of Title III of the Brussels Convention in France, if, by Article 12(2) of the Greek Accession Convention, '[Greek] jurisdiction [had been] founded upon rules which accorded with the provisions of Title II [of the Brussels Convention]'.[1055] The Liberian plaintiff had claimed payment from the French defendant for goods delivered in Greece. The Paris *Cour d'appel* had localised the obligation.[1056] The *Cour de Cassation* approved the lower court for having ascertained the place of performance, not *lege causae*, but

en fonction de la nature du rapport d'obligation et des circonstances de l'espèce . . .[1057] [1058]

[1049] Perhaps therefore a forum conveniens analysis?

[1050] (1998) *JDI* 129, (1997) *Rev crit* 585.

[1051] As is well known, the general rule in Convention recognition/enforcement actions under Title III of the Brussels Convention, is Article 28 [III]. '[T]he jurisdiction of the court of the State of origin may not be reviewed'. Article 12(2) of the Greek Accession Convention 31.12.1982 [1982] OJ L388/1, at p.3–4, provided for an exception in transitional cases—*Sté Comptoir commercial d'Orient c/ Société Medtrafina* 11.3.1997 (1997) *Rev crit* 585 is such an example.

[1052] The Greek rule actually used to take jurisdiction of the dispute was not reported or discussed. The French courts do not seem to take the wording of Article 12(2) literally. AG Jacobs in *Elsbeth Freifrau von Horn v Kevin Cinnamond* (C-163/95) [1997] ECR I-5451, at p.5464, paras. 34–35 based his opinion on the premise that the recognising court has to look at the actual jurisdiction of the original court and make a comparison with Title II; in this sense his observations at para. 35 '. . . the court seised may not be able to ascertain *the basis on which the court first seised assumed jurisdiction in the absence of a judgment by the latter*'; also Huet in the latter sense (1998) *JDI* 575, at p.578.

[1053] There was no reason to suppose that the *Cassation* interpreted Article 5(1) any differently merely because this was an enforcement action under Article 12(2) of the Greek Accession Convention.

[1054] This final appeal court ruling was taken to be the Article 12(2) 'judgment'; but, apparently, *contra* Briggs, 1997, at p.316, para. 7.09 n.52.

[1055] *Sté Comptoir commercial d'Orient c/ Société Medtrafina* 11.3.1997 (1998) *JDI* 129, at p.131.

[1056] Not *lege causae*, as in *Custom Made Commercial* in *Le Comptoir Commercial d'Orient S.A. c/ Medtrafina S.A.* 5.4.1994 (1995) *Rev Crit* 573, at pp.586–87.

[1057] ('by reference to the nature of the relationship of obligation and the circumstances of the case').

[1058] *Sté Comptoir commercial d'Orient c/ Société Medtrafina* 11.3.1997 (1997) *Rev crit* 585, at p.586; a translation, if needed, for this phrase is provided in the reference to the ECJ by the second *Cassation* case: *Groupe Concorde et autres c/ Capitaine du Suhadiwarno Panjan et autres* 9.12.1997 (1998) *Rev crit* 117; [1998] I.L.Pr. 207, at p.208, ECJ decision (C-440/97) [1999] ECR I-6307 of 28.9.1999; AG's opinion 16.3.1999.

In other words, this effectively locates the place of performance as a matter of fact,[1059] not law. Gaudemet-Tallon, reviewing the case, feels[1060] that its ruling will result in a French court's relying on *Tessili/Custom Made* (if at all), only in circumstances when a factual localisation, according to the rather vague notions quoted above, is not possible.

The operative phrase of *Sté Comptoir commercial d'Orient* was taken up again by the *Cour de Cassation* in *Groupe Concorde et autres c/ Capitaine du Suhadiwarno Panjan et autres.*[1061] The action concerned the plaintiffs, Groupe Concorde, as leading subrogated insurers[1062] suing the German-domiciled carriers Pro Line, the ship's captain, and their respective insurers. The goods in question had been loaded at Le Havre for shipment to Brazil. The lower courts had rejected the French insurers' action against the German defendants on the basis of Article 5(1). They made a factual localisation of the place of performance of the obligation in question in Brazil, without referring[1063] to the *lex causae* of the contract of carriage.

The *Cour de Cassation* therefore referred to the European Court of Justice a (rather presumptuous)[1064] question, *inter alia*, regarding Article 5(1), to determine whether it is legitimate to retain[1065] an autonomous (Community?)[1066] definition of the place of performance, 'having regard to the nature of the relationship creating the obligation and the circumstances of the case'.[1067] The case was a direct attack on, or rebellion[1068] against, the *Tessili/Custom Made* jurisprudence. The case has recently been heard by the ECJ, undermining at a stroke the French courts' position. The disquiet evident in the *Cassation*'s views on Article 5(1) spilled over from the reference to the opinions of the Advocate Generals[1069] however.

[1059] The comment (1998) *Rev crit* 117, at p.120, that such is the preferred method for the French courts to use.

[1060] (1997) *Rev crit* 585, at p.590.

[1061] 9.12.1997 (1998) *Rev crit* 117; AG Colomer's opinion 16.3.1999, not followed by the ECJ, unreported 28.9.1999.

[1062] Of consignees in receipt of damaged cargo.

[1063] As *Industrie Tessili Italiana Como v Dunlop AG* (C-12/76) [1976] ECR 1473 says that they should.

[1064] Given the resounding rejection, by omission, of AG Lenz's opinion by the ECJ in *Custom Made Commercial Ltd v Stawa Metallbau GmbH* (C-288/92) [1994] ECR I-2913.

[1065] *Sté Comptoir commercial d'Orient c/ Société Medtrafina* 11.3.1997 (1998) *JDI* 129.

[1066] At the time it was only a French definition.

[1067] Reported in English at [1998] I.L.Pr. 208.

[1068] Especially Droz, G. '*Delendum est forum contractus*? (vingt ans après les arrêts *De Bloos* et *Tessili* interprétant l'article 5.1 de la Convention de Bruxelles du 27 septembre 1968' (1997) *Dalloz*, Chron., 351, at p.354.

[1069] Also evident in AG Léger's opinion in preliminary reference in *Leathertex Divisione Sintetici SpA v Bodetex BVBA* (C-420/97) [1999] ECR I-6747.

1.3.9 The 'rebellion' against *Tessili/Custom Made Commercial* by the Advocate Generals on the same day

1.3.9(i) AG Ruiz-Jarabo Colomer's opinion in GIE Groupe Concorde e.a. v The master of the vessel 'Suhadiwarno Panjan'[1070]

The French courts' recent unease[1071] with the contemporary development of Article 5(1), and its current interpretation, was condoned by AG Colomer in his recent opinion in *GIE Groupe Concorde e.a.*. He consequently advocated a shift[1072] away from the (by now) 'classic' analysis of the place of performance *lege causae* in *Tessili/Custom Made Commercial*. He justified this stance on the disadvantages which he saw that the *Tessili* interpretation brings to the resolution of contractual disputes in general, and to the specific problems it causes, in the main, for national judges at first instance. Regarding the general disadvantages, he noted that the *Tessili* method of determining the place of performance leads to a fragmentation[1073] of claims, and commonly to the allocation of those claims before Contracting State courts with no real connection with the substance of the dispute.[1074]

Regarding the specific problems encountered by national judges, a *leitmotiv* running through the AG's opinion is that Article 5(1) seems simply too difficult for national courts to apply.[1075] While it is true that Article 5(1) and the *Tessili* approach oblige the judge in 'carry[ing] out three rather painstaking tasks from the legal viewpoint',[1076] this, in his view, leads to a process which is variously described as being of 'a high degree of theoretical thinking'[1077] and of 'fiendish difficulty'.[1078]

[1070] (C-440/97) [1999] ECR I-6307, AG Colomer's opinion 16.3.1999.

[1071] Like the Belgian court in *Leathertex Divisione Sintetici*, the AG felt that this reference was 'un appel désespéré' for change, at para. 96; a Belgian court had already decided against a dispersion: *Tribunal de commerce de Bruxelles*, 22.6.1989, *S.P.R.L. Kheops/ S.A.R.L. Les Créations Ada Tuchbant*, (1990) *Rev. dr. comm. belge* 702.

[1072] At pp.6336–37, paras. 95–100; curiously the French Government resisted any change—it would lead to uncertainty, at para. 20.

[1073] At p.6323, para. 49(b) onwards; a theme that AG Léger will pick up on in *Leathertex Divisione Sintetici SpA v Bodetex BVBA* (C-420/97) [1999] ECR I-6747, at p.6764, onwards.

[1074] At p.6322 and p.6325, paras. 49 and 58, respectively; compare also the views of the *Bundesgericht* in *A.AG gegen B* 9.3.1998 124 BGE, III, 188, at p.191—where the difficulty of application was not one of the criticisms mentioned of Article 5(1).

[1075] At p.6333, para. 84: 'la méthode consacrée dans l'arrêt Tessili . . . complique inutilement la tâche du juge saisi de la demande'.

[1076] At p.6317, para. 28.

[1077] At p.6309, para. 3.

[1078] At p.6336, para. 95, especially n.63 where he reveals that, when questioned, the experts and legal representatives appearing before him could not give a satisfactory answer as to the place of performance under their respective national laws.

The Advocate General showed himself aware of the inappropriateness[1079] of recourse[1080] to choice of law/*lex causae* considerations for what is, under Article 5(1), an essentially jurisdictional question.[1081] In addition, he noted[1082] that Article 5(1) commonly leads to 'a vast *forum actoris* in relation to pecuniary obligations',[1083] which is out of step with the aims for which the article was originally inaugurated: proximity between the court seised and the facts of the dispute.

After outlining these criticisms, he then enumerated the three methods canvassed for determining the place of performance: the *Tessili* method; an autonomous interpretation; and finally that proposed by the referring court, the *Cour de Cassation*, from the circumstances of the case and from the nature of the legal relationship.

For pecuniary obligations/claims,[1084] the Advocate General opted for the autonomous definition of the place of performance, namely the place of performance of 'only the *characteristic obligation* of the contract'.[1085] This was, he believed, sanctioned by reasons of proximity.

For non-pecuniary obligations, he chose the third option advocated by the *Cour de Cassation*:

> reference to *the circumstances of the case in relation to the nature of the obligation in question* should enable the place or places of performance of an obligation to be determined with sufficient reliability in most cases.[1086]

Using his methodology, on the facts before the referring court, the Advocate General concluded that Santos, in Brazil, was the place of performance as the port of delivery mentioned in the bill of lading.

His overhaul of the *Tessili* jurisprudence recommended to the European Court that the place of performance of a contractual obligation henceforth be found

> taking account of the nature of the legal relationship in question, it being understood that it is presumed that that place is the same as the place where the obligation *characterising*[1087] the legal relationship in question . . .[1088]

[1079] Criticised as 'de longues digressions', at para. 107; also the views in *LG Köln* 5.5.1988 IPRspr. 1988 Nr. 158 and *BGH* 12.5.1993 IPRspr. 1993 Nr. 139—also *Firma T S.r.l gegen Firma S.AG* 18.1.1996 122 BGE, III, 43, [1998] I.L.Pr. 77.

[1080] He described this methodology as a 'tendance pernicieuse', at para. 54.

[1081] At p.6323, para. 49(b) onwards.

[1082] Drawing support from Droz's article, (1997) *Dalloz*, Chron., 351.

[1083] At p.6324, para. 55; perhaps selectively vast, as only for those Contracting States with creditor-favourable *leges causae*.

[1084] It is unclear whether he intended all claims of a pecuniary nature, or merely those claims that are 'independent' contractual obligations (as in *de Bloos*), that involve the payment of money.

[1085] At pp.6338–39, para. 103.

[1086] At para. 103.

[1087] An autonomous solution, notable for its previous application to individual contracts of employment: *Roger Ivenel v Helmut Schwab* (C-133/81) [1982] ECR 1891.

[1088] At p.6341, para. 109.

His solution appears to be a confused amalgamation of an autonomous interpretation, as complex and tortuous in its execution as *Tessili* and *Custom Made Commercial* ever were: first, the characteristic performance[1089] of the legal relationship has to be identified; then the place where, having regard to the circumstances of the case and the nature of the relationship creating the obligation, performance is to be effected; *only when* this latter place coincides with the place of the characteristic performance can it be determinative under Article 5(1). No guidance is given when there is no 'coincidence', nor what is to happen in the cases governed[1090] by the 1980 Vienna International Sales Convention. True it is that there have been problems and idiosyncratic interpretations of Article 5(1). Yet to have exacerbated the problem by sweeping away over twenty years of jurisprudence, and to have replaced it with an (equally) complex and less certain[1091] interpretative process was not to be welcomed.

1.3.9(ii)   AG Léger's opinion in Leathertex Divisione Sintetici SpA v Bodetex BVBA[1092]

In an opinion rendered on the same day, in *Leathertex Divisione Sintetici SpA v Bodetex BVBA,*[1093] AG Léger also had the opportunity to review the operation of *Tessili* with regard to international payment obligations.

The main thrust of the case as well as its facts, have been reviewed earlier; but the AG did make some remarks which coincided with the unease felt by AG Colomer in *GIE Groupe Concorde.*

It will be remembered that in *Leathertex,*[1094] the Belgian exclusive concessionnaire was claiming (1) unpaid commission, as well as (2) damages, under Belgian law,[1095] for lack of due notice of termination of the exclusive agreement with its

---

[1089] This will, presumably, amount to the same enquiry as under Art.4(2) of the Rome Convention 1980: *Ferguson Shipbuilders Ltd v Voith Hydro GmbH & Co KG* (2000) *SLT* 229, *Definitely Maybe (Touring) Ltd v Marek Lieberberg Konzertagentur GmbH* [2001] 1 WLR 1745, QBD, *Caledonia Subsea Ltd v Microperi Srl* [2001] SC 716, OH; Moss, (2000) *Nordic Journal of International Law* 379, at p.394; also *Cour de Cassation* 15.5.2001 *SA Optelec c/ Sté Midtronics Bv* (2001) *JCP,* II, 10634, an exclusive distributorship case; *Samcrete Egypt Engineers and Contractors S.A.E. v Land Rover Exports Limited* [2002] CLC 533, CA.

[1090] His interpretation will involve a breach by those Vienna Convention Contracting States of their Treaty obligations under Articles 1(1)(a)(b) and Article 57(1).

[1091] Despite the AG's views on the uncertainty of the place of performance, litigants and their advisors, given an express choice of performance/law clause in their contracts (subject now of course to *Mainschiffahrts-Genossenschaft eG (MSG) v Les Gravières Rhénanes SARL* C-106/95 [1997] ECR I-911), can be reasonably certain whether they will be able to collect (payment) obligations in the *forum actoris* or not; *Chailease Finance Corporation v Credit Agricole Indosuez* [2000] 1 Lloyd's Rep. 348, CA.

[1092] (C-420/97) [1999] ECR I-6747, AG Léger's opinion 16.3.1999.

[1093] *Ibid.*

[1094] The Belgian *Cour de Cassation's* decision is reported at [1998] I.L.Pr. 505.

[1095] Article 3 'Loi relative à la resiliation unilaterale des concessions de vente exclusive à durée indéterminée', 27.7.1961, amended 13.4.1971, *Les Codes Larcier*, I, Ed. 1995, p.650.

Italian principal. AG Léger sympathised with the Belgian appeal court's attempts[1096] to combine the two claims before the one single (Belgian) forum. He shared that court's concern over the fragmentation of certain claims in one and the same action being sent to different Contracting States—often therefore, he remarked, to States with a very tenuous link with the dispute in question as a whole:

> the multiplicity of fora is the result of the differences between the national rules concerning the place of performance of obligations to make payment, as such differences appear following application of the conflict rules.[1097]

His answer to the potential dispersion of payment claims, as we have seen, was partly a review of *De Bloos*, and, here, a recasting of the *Tessili* jurisprudence.[1098] In his reasons for a review of *Tessili*, he was careful to stress that what was needed in the case referred was a single forum[1099] to hear both claims together, even if this meant overturning the methodology of Article 5(1) in *De Bloos* and *Tessili* to achieve it.

As we have seen, in the case referred itself, using the 'classic' *Tessili* approach, one of the 'obligation[s] in question'—to pay commission—was to be performed[1100] in Italy. Only Belgian substantive law, *lege causae*, pointed to Italy, as the place of performance; the rest of the contract itself was almost exclusively concerned with either Belgium or Luxembourg.

One possible solution to avoid the dispersion of the claims—but rejected by the Advocate General—was to give an autonomous interpretation to the place of performance of 'independent' contractual payment obligations themselves: either payments were to be defined as 'quérable'[1101] or 'portable'.[1102] The former solution merely duplicates jurisdiction that (always)[1103] exists under Article 2; while the

---

[1096] [1998] I.L.Pr. 505, at p.509.

[1097] *Leathertex Divisione Sintetici SpA v Bodetex BVBA* (C-420/97) [1999] ECR I-6747, at p.6765, para. 100.

[1098] Again, a direct challenge to the confirming case of *Custom Made Commercial*.

[1099] Where there was a close link between the dispute and the court seised.

[1100] Article 1247 of the Belgian Civil Code points, in default of agreement, to the place of the debtor's establishment, here in Italy.

[1101] I.e., (subject to contrary agreement—*BayObLG* 26.4.2001 (2001) *RIW* 862), collection to be at the *debtor*'s residence, as the substantive laws of, *inter alia*, France (Article 1247 Cc), Germany (§§269 270 BGB), and Austria (§905 Abs. 2 ABGB) currently dictate.

[1102] I.e., (always subject to contrary agreement), collection to be at the *creditor*'s residence, as the following substantive laws dictate: England and Wales, Switzerland (Article 74 Abs.2 1 OR—*Domicrest Ltd v Swiss Bank Corporation* 7.7.1998 [1999] 1 Lloyd's Rep. 80 at pp.86–88), Denmark (Article 1938(3) Cc), Italy (Article 1182(3) Cc), and Greece (Articles 320–21 Civil Code, *Raiffeisen Zentralbank Österreich Aktiengesellschaft v National Bank of Greece S.A.* [1999] 1 Lloyd's Rep. 408, and Stathopoulos, M. *Contract Law in Hellas*, 1995 at p.153); in Denmark, *Østre Landsrets* 1.12.1999 PC *Express AB v Columbus IT Partner A/S* [2001] I.L.Pr. 314.

[1103] Subject to exclusive jurisdiction under Articles 16 and 17 and jurisdiction under Article 57.

latter would consecrate the creation[1104] of a *forum actoris* for the payment of debts.[1105]

As noted earlier, in section 1.2.5, the Advocate General saw a way out of this dilemma by 'demoting' payment obligations to 'dependent' contractual obligations, without a place of performance of their own under Article 5(1). By making them dependent on an 'obligation in question' which was the 'contrepartie' of the payment of commission, the problem of the vagaries of national place of performance laws is avoided.

Released from the shackles of independent payment obligations, as in *De Bloos*, the Advocate General felt himself free to consider *Tessili* afresh, and he concluded that

> it is appropriate to refer to the place where the contested obligation was or must be actually performed.[1106]

In the case of the payment of commission therefore:

> the place of performance to be taken into consideration is that of the agency mandate granted to the commercial agent, whose commission constitutes the consideration therefor . . .[1107]

Since the counter-performance of the obligation to pay commission was the commercial agency itself, undoubtedly to be performed, *inter alia*, in Belgium, that place was to be taken into account when considering the payment of commission.

This solution comes close to those cases[1108] that have ignored the jurisprudence of the European Court of Justice, and merely grouped claims in commercial agency cases at the place where the principal had to 'respect the contract', ie where

---

[1104] Article 59(1) ULIS, and now Article 57(1) of the 1980 Vienna Sales Convention, lead to the same result: *LG München* 29.5.1995 IPRspr. 1995 Nr. 146, *AG Berlin-Tiergarten* 13.3.1997 (1999) *IPRax* 172; *OLG Braunschweig* 28.10.1999 IPRspr. 1999 Nr. 130, and esp. *San Carlo Gruppo alimentare SPA c/ SBC Vico* 6.2.1996 (1996) *Rev crit* 504 and *Zivilgericht des Kantons Basel-Stadt* 10.2.1998 (1999) *SZIER* 190; also *Corte di Cassazione* 14.12.1999 *Imperial Bathroom company plc. contro Sanitari Pozzi s.p.a. (2000) Riv. dir. int. priv. e proc.* 1078.
[1105] The impression given by Thieme, J. 'Notiziarium zur italienischen Rechtsprechung auf dem Gebiet des Internationalen Privat- und Privatverfahrensrechts für die Jahre 1992 und 1993' (1998) *ZfVR* 57, at pp.86–87 reviewing Italian caselaw under the 1980 Vienna Convention; Achilles, W.-A. *Kommentar zum UN-Kaufrechtsübereinkommen (CISG)*, 2000, at p.171.
[1106] [1999] ECR I-6747, at p.6774, para. 163.
[1107] *Ibid*, at p.6777, para. 181.
[1108] *Inter alia*: in France *Cour d'appel d'Amiens Dellinger c/ Société Leppak* 26.4.1978 confirmed by *Cassation Dellinger c/ Société Leppak* 27.11.1979 (1980) JDI 333, *Ets Devriendt c/ Soc Roto Frank* 28.10.1986 (1987) *Rev crit* 612, *Gilbert Mayer c/ Société Charles Wednesbury Limited* 13.9.1995 (1997) JDI 170; in Belgium *Cour de Cassation* 28.6.1979 *Audi-NSU Auto Union AG c Adelin Petit et Cie SA* 1979 *Pas. Belge.* I, 1260, at p.1283, *Tribunal de commerce de Bruxelles*, 29.5.1990, *M.Filipson c/ Gebr.-Herberg K.G.*, (1992) *Rev. dr. comm. belge* 907, at p.911, *semble* Hoge Raad 24.5.1991 *Häcker Küchen GmbH v Bosma Huygen meubelimpex B.V.* [1993] E.C.C. 55; *contra Cour d'appel de Luxembourg* 8.3.1994 *Vesque c/ Badischer Winzerkeller E.G.* 1993–95 *Pas. Lux.* 341.

the agent carried out his commercial activities.[1109] His conclusion was therefore that both claims could be amalgamated and heard together in Belgium, as the appeal court had hoped for.

Acceptance of AG Léger's opinion of finding the counter-performance of (hitherto independent contractual) payment obligations would have represented a radical *volte face* for the European Court of Justice, from its firm stand taken in *Custom Made Commercial*. It would involve undermining not only *Tessili*, but also *Shenavai v Kreischer*, and aligning claims for payment with the solution to the place of performance in individual contracts of employment,[1110] in such authorities as *Ivenel v Schwab*,[1111] *Mulox IBC Ltd v Hendrick Geels*[1112] and *Petrus Wilhelmus Rutten v Cross Medical Ltd*.[1113]

1.3.10   The 'rebellion' is crushed: ECJ decisions in *GIE Groupe Concorde*[1114] and *Leathertex Divisione*[1115]

The European Court has not accepted the task of reforming the interpretation of Article 5(1) in its recent decisions in the above cases. In the former, the Court stressed[1116] that—outside contracts of employment (and only these)—its jurisprudence has consistently upheld the place of performance to be the place designated by the *lex causae*; indeed drew justification for its enduring stance from the (non-)amendments to Article 5(1) during successive Accession Conventions, regarding contracts in general.[1117] Rejecting proposals[1118] for the amendment of the *Tessili* formula suggested by the referring *Cour de Cassation*— a test based on the nature of the obligation and the circumstances of the case[1119]—the Court believed that such a solution would prove, *inter alia*, too uncertain,[1120] and thus contrary to one of the Convention's aims. It is clear from

---

[1109] Above, French section 1.2.1(i) at p.83.
[1110] And, of course, to the post-San Sebastian amendments to Article 5(1) of 3.10.1989, [1989] OJ L284/1.
[1111] (C-133/81) [1982] ECR 1891.
[1112] (C-125/92) [1993] ECR I-4075.
[1113] (C-383/95) [1997] ECR I-57.
[1114] *GIE Groupe Concorde* (C-440/97) [1999] ECR I-6307.
[1115] *Leathertex Divisione Sintetici SpA v Bodetex BVBA* (C-420/97) [1999] ECR I-6747.
[1116] *GIE Groupe Concorde e.a. v Le capitaine commandant le navire «Suhadiwarno Panjan»* (C-440/97) [1999] ECR I-6307, at p.6348, para. 13.
[1117] *Ibid*, at para. 21; it also bore in mind the review of the Brussels Convention that was then underway, culminating in the present form of Article 5(1) Brussels I Regulation.
[1118] *Ibid*, at pp.6351–52, paras. 25 and 29.
[1119] If a particular Contracting State wanted such a solution, it must be found by amending the substantive law of obligations of each particular *lex causae*, at p.6352, para. 31—a *Cour de Cassation* case, decided after *GIE Groupe Concorde*, and expressly citing it, has now reverted to the traditional 'conformist' view in *Tessili* and *Custom Made Commercial*: 14.12.1999 *Soc. de droit allemand Edeka Frucht Kontor c/ Caisse regionale de Credit agricole*, (2001) JDI 133.
[1120] At para. 23.

the tone of the judgment, and the explicit omission of any reference to its Advocate General's opinion, that it was not prepared to sanction a (radical) departure from its earliest jurisprudence in *Tessili,* and confirmed in *Custom Made Commercial.*

The reference in the latter case, *Leathertex Divisione,*[1121] was not a direct attack on the *Tessili* line of reasoning, but in a single paragraph the Court re-affirmed its classic 'place of performance' formula.[1122] In did not make any reference to AG Léger's enthusiasm for an 'effective place of performance' which, in *Leathertex* itself, would have lead to a place where the Belgian exclusive concessionnaire carried out its activities, in, *inter alia,* Belgium.

That a continued interpretation of Article 5(1) was fought out on a teleological battlefront was inevitable: which Convention aims had to prevail[1123]—jurisdictional predictability[1124] or avoiding a *forum actoris*[1125] and the increasingly widening distance/relationship between a dispute and court seised[1126]—was relatively uncertain. Yet it was doubtful, given the current discussions underway for reform, whether the European Court would have sacrificed the former—and its own line of jurisprudence—for the sake of a more uncertain, temporally-limited, albeit teleologically now more justifiable, reading of Article 5(1).

1.4   CONCLUSIONS AND THE REFORMS[1127] TO ARTICLE 5(1)'S PLACE OF PERFORMANCE: BRUSSELS I REGULATION AND THE HAGUE WORLDWIDE JUDGMENTS CONVENTION

Article 5(1)(b) of the Brussels I Regulation has attempted to give autonomous definitions to the place of performance, 'unless otherwise agreed',[1128] in two types

---

[1121] *Leathertex Divisione Sintetici SpA v Bodetex BVBA* (C-420/97) criticised as *Tessili* taken to absurd lengths, Gaudemet-Tallon, at (2000) *Rev crit* 76, at p.84, and notes that Article 5(2)(b) of the Brussels I Regulation offers a solution to this problem.

[1122] [1999] ECR I-6747, at p.6791, para. 33.

[1123] If they seem to be diametrically opposed?

[1124] Predictability for defendants, *Jakob Handte & Co. GmbH v Société Traitements Mecano-Chimiques des Surfaces (TMCS)* (C-26/91) [1992] ECR I-3967, at p.3995, para. 18; for plaintiffs, *Mulox v Geels* (C-125/92) [1993] ECR I-4075, at p.4103, para. 11; and for Article 5 generally, *Antonio Marinari v Lloyds Bank Plc and Zubaidi Trading Co.* (C-364/93) [1995] ECR I-2719, at p.2741, para. 19.

[1125] *Shearson Lehman Hutton Inc. v TVB Treuhandgesellschaft für Vermögensverwaltung und Beteiligungen GmbH* (C-89/91) [1993] ECR I-139, at p.187, para. 17.

[1126] *Lloyd's Register of Shipping v Société Campenon Bernard* (C-439/93) [1995] ECR I-961, at p.981, para. 21 and *Elisabeth Hacker v Euro-Relais GmbH* (C-280/90) [1992] ECR I-1111, at p.1132, para. 12.

[1127] Various solutions had been discussed—*Cheshire and North,* 13th edn., 1999, at p.210.

[1128] On such an aspect, no doubt statements about such agreed places of performance in *Mainschiffahrts-Genossenschaft eG (MSG) v Les Gravières Rhénanes SARL* (C-106/95) [1997] ECR I-911, at p.944 will come into play; not mentioned in a place of delivery case *BayObLG 26.4.2001* (2001) *RIW* 862.

of contractual dispute[1129]—'the sale of goods' and 'the provision of services': the place of delivery or where the services were or should have been provided. In all other cases, according to Article 5(1)(c), the general rule in Article 5(1)(a)—and the current position under Article 5(1) of the Brussels Convention—will prevail. Yet the autonomous nature of the place of performance is linked to the terms of, and/or presumptions of law in, the contract and *lex contractus/causae*. The same inconsistencies that have occurred with the place of payment obligations, will be perpetuated here.[1130]

A similar drafting solution is taken by Article 6 of the Hague draft Worldwide Judgments Convention,[1131] but with a much-reduced ambit[1132] of contracts to which Article 6 applies *ratione materiae*—the supply of goods, the provision of services, and a combination of both, in Article 6(1)(b)(c) respectively.

The value of both AGs' opinions in *GIE Groupe Concorde* and *Leathertex*, is in highlighting the need for a re-appraisal of the Convention's wording. The growing tide of (national) opposition, particularly in France, may soon have become overwhelming.

This chapter has attempted to demonstrate the complexities, problems and controversies surrounding Article 5(1). Together with Article 17, it has provoked the most references, and spawned innumerable reported national caselaw.

The major criticism of Article 5(1), apart from its complexity, was and is that it allows a plaintiff/claimant to sue in the *forum actoris*, legitimately,[1133] by following an interpretation of ECJ jurisprudence, when the circumstances of a given case present little or no connection with the forum. Against this, it is said that the rule is reasonably predictable: with little effort, given an express choice of *lex causae*, a prospective defendant can predict whether, in an action for payment, he can rest solely on Article 2, or will have jurisdiction Article 5(1) alternatively invoked against him in another Contracting State.

Yet the place of performance, *lege causae*, takes no account of the circumstances of the case, and often does destroy Article 5(1)'s originally[1134] optimistic and rather naïve *raison d'être*. The ability of a plaintiff/claimant to rely on Article 5(1)

[1129] AG Alber has stated in his opinion in *S.A. Besix N.V. v WABAG Wasserreinigungsbau Alfred Kretzschmar GmbH* (C-256/00) [2000] OJ C233/25, opinion 27.9.2001, that an exclusive development contract with an non-competition clause will not fall within Article 5(1)(a) of the Brussels I Regulation, unreported at para. 48.

[1130] Cf Harris, J. 'The Brussels Regulation' (2001) 20 *CJQ* 218, at p.220; Markus, (1999) *SZW* 205, at p.213; Piltz, B. 'Vom EuGVÜ zur Brüssel-I-Verordnung' (2002) *NJW* 789, at p.793.

[1131] The version of Article 6 referred to here is that of the Oct. 1999 draft. It now forms an Alternative B in the Commission II's draft interim text. Alternative A is, in one sense less restricted in scope *ratione materiae*, although in another may well not apply to a single dispute relating to a single, one-off contract: it does not refer to a 'place of performance', but to a defendant's frequent and/or significant activity in a particular Contracting State forum, coupled with a necessity for the dispute to be 'based on a contract directly related to' the enumerated 'activities'.

[1132] There is no fall-back provision, as in Article 5(1)(a) of the July 1999 proposal.

[1133] This is to say nothing of the avenue this case law has opened up to protectionist interpretations, touched on above.

[1134] The Jenard Report on the *rationale* for special jurisdiction under Title II, at [1979] OJ C59/22.

to sue in his home forum, in itself, only becomes a *forum actoris* when this jurisdictional *rationale*, as a connecting factor, is absent. Certain national codes allow this, as do the International Sales Conventions. In international payment obligations, it will be rare[1135] for the forum ascertained by Article 5(1) to be other than that of either the plaintiff/claimant or defendant. In this normal scenario:

> Article 5.1. est donc soit inutile lorsqu'il se confond avec le for du défendeur, soit nuisible lorsqu'il ouvre démesurément la porte au forum actoris.[1136] [1137]

Its abolition has therefore been advocated by some, especially Droz, but ultimately has been preserved, in its original and also an amended form, in two special cases by the Brussels I Regulation. In contractual matters, this would shift the emphasis of litigation primarily on to Article 17, if predictability in dispute resolution was to be achieved and maintained.

It is an inescapable consequence of the law of contract that performance of mutual obligations *inter partes*, must be adjudged[1138] by the law governing that contract. This fact takes no account[1139] of jurisdictional issues. For a jurisdictional provision[1140] to intrude into this governing law arena, poach, as it were, 'performance' for its own jurisdictional ends and then expect this concept, alien to jurisdictional considerations, to behave in a jurisdictionally acceptable manner seems extremely naïve. Historical precedent has shown this. All that can be said of the present state[1141] of the law with regard to Article 5(1) is that it is reasonably predictable, albeit disloyal to its original *rationale*.

The English,[1142] German and Swiss jurisprudence have had few problems interpreting and applying the provisions of Article 5(1). The French courts, on the other hand, have proved to be rather inconsistent in their interpretation of the article. They have been keen, on the whole, to preserve a French *forum actoris* for exclusive sales agents, and a chapter of such length bears witness to a jurisdictional provision of some (overwhelming) complexity.

[1135] Droz (1997) *Dalloz*, Chron., 351, at p.355; he strangely does not refer to *Royal Bank of Scotland Plc v Cassa di Risparmio delle Province Lombard and others* [1992] BankLR 251, where this place was outside the Contracting States concerned.

[1136] ('this Article 5(1) is either useless when it merges with the defendant's forum, or harmful when it opens the door excessively to the *forum actoris*').

[1137] Droz, loc. cit., at p.335.

[1138] And sanctioned in Article 10 of the 1980 Rome Convention, except the formalities of (Article 17) jurisdiction clauses: *Francesco Benincasa v Dentalkit Srl* (C-269/95) [1997] ECR I-3767.

[1139] Unless internal to one particular Contracting State, and a protectionist civil code is drawn up, as in Germany, to obviate this unfortunate consequence, above.

[1140] Such as Article 5(1) and §29 ZPO and Article 3(1)(5) of the German Belgian Convention, above; RSC Ord.11 r.1(1)(d)(iii) and CPR 6.20(5), which do not subject performance to the *lex causae*, merely jurisdiction itself to English law *lege causae* more generally.

[1141] It was unlikely that the ECJ would be swayed from its *Custom Made Commercial* jurisprudence by the reference in *Groupe Concorde et autres c/ Capitaine du Suhadiwarno Panjan et autres* 9.12.1997 (1998) *Rev crit* 117, [1999] ECR I-6307.

[1142] Discounting, of course, its scope *ratione materiae*: the meaning of a 'contract', and claims in restitution and pre-contractual duties, above.

2

Article 17

INTRODUCTION

T HIS ARTICLE OF the Brussels Convention allows an examination of a range of issues[1] that face the Convention and the national laws generally: Article 17 represents a great intrusion into the traditional national laws of Contracting States[2] relating to jurisdiction clauses; that this article, like Articles 5(1) and 16(1),[3] has undergone a radical metamorphosis since the original version;[4] that the interpretative case law both from the European Court of Justice[5] and national courts has revealed the essential cleaving of the article—that the

---

[1] More specifically, below, at p.172 and p.209; *Dicey and Morris*, 13th edn., 2000, Vol .I, contrast Rule 32(2) and (3); for specialist works in German on Article 17, Huber, 1994; Staehelin, M. *Gerichts-standsvereinbarungen im internationalen Handelverkehr Europas: Form und Willenseinigungen nach Article 17 EuGVÜ/LÜ*, 1993; Stöve, E. *Gerichtsstandsvereinbarungen nach Handelsbrauch, Article 17 EuGVÜ und §38 ZPO, unter besonderer Berücksichtigung des kaufmännischen Bestätigungsschreiben, des Konnossements und der Faktura*, 1993; Aull, J.M. *Der Geltungsanspruch des EuGVÜ: 'Binnen-sachverhalte' u. internationales Zivilverfahrensrechtt in der Europäischen Union: Zur Auslegung von Article 17 Abs.1 s.1 EuGVÜ*, 1996 Benecke, L. *Die teleologische Reduktion des räumlich-persöhnlichen Anwendungsbereiches von Article 2ff u.Article 17 EuGVÜ*, 1993.
[2] Also Article 48 *Nouveau Code de Procédure Civile*, Dalloz, 93ème éd., Paris, 2001; and *Cour de Cassa-tion* Civ. 1er, 17.12.1985; D.1986, IR, 265, obs. Audit; *Cour de Cassation*, 1er, 12 1997, *M Gianfranco Copelli c/ Société Carofrance Ceramique*, (1998) *JDI* 138; also the former Article 2 of the Italian Civil Code, no longer in force, since 1.9.1995, below, at p.180; as to form §104 (Austrian) Jurisdiktionsnorm *Zivilgerichtliches Verfahren, Kodex des österreichischen Rechts*, 1998, at p.32–33, Heiss, H. 'Die Form internationaler Gerichtsstandsvereinbarungen' (2000) *ZfRV* 202; independence from considerations derived from the *lex causae*: *Francesco Benincasa v Dentalkit Srl* (C-269/95) [1997] ECR I-3767, below at pp.254–258; *Bundesgericht* 7.8.2001 *Notrop Speditions- und Schiffahrtsgesellschaft GmbH gegen Tran-srail AG*, unreported.
[3] In the 1989 San Sebastián amendments, Articles 5(1) and 16(1) underwent amendments to codify and/or amend case law relating to contracts of employment and short-term holiday lets respectively; when the new Brussels I Regulation comes into force on 1.3.2002, these two Articles will undergo change once again—to Articles 5(1)(a)(b)(c), and 22, respectively; above, at pp.116–118, section 1.2.7.
[4] The 'original' Brussels Convention simply referred to agreements 'in writing' or 'oral agreements evidenced in writing'; the original form continues to cause problems in 'battle of the forms' cases: *OLG Karlsruhe* 15.3.2001 (2001) *RIW* 621 (Article 17 Lugano Convention); Article 23, para. 3 of the Brussels I Regulation attempts to keep pace with agreements relating to 'e-commerce'.
[5] The most important jurisprudence discussed here are the following cases: *Ditta Estasis Salotti di Colzano Aima e Giamano Colzano v RÜWA Polstereimaschinen GmbH* (C-24/76), 14.12.1976 [1976] ECR 1831 (*Salotti*); *Galereis Segoura SPRL v Rahim Bonakdarian* (C-25/76) 14.12.1976 [1976] ECR 1851 (*Segoura*); *Partenreederei ms Tilly Russ & Ernst Russ v NV Haven- & Veroerbedriff Nova (The Tilly Russ)* (C-71/83), 19.6.1984 [1984] ECR 2417; *F.Berghöfer GmbH & Co. KG v ASA SA* (C-221/84), 11.7.1985 [1985] ECR 2699; and *Powell Duffryn Plc v Wolfgang Petereit* (C-214/89) [1992] ECR I-1745; *Mainschiffahrts-Genossenschaft e.G (MSG) v Les Gravières Rhénanes SARL* (C-106/95) [1997]

Convention and modern international commercial practice meet head on,[6] prompting suspicions (confirmed by the frequent amendments[7]) that the Convention is arguably a poor instrument in achieving its stated aims:[8] ensuring the free-flow of judgments and the uniform allocation of jurisdiction[9] throughout the European Union. In addition to this, the vagueness or inadequacies[10] of Article 17's drafting, or otherwise, may arguably have allowed a certain amount of alleged court protectionism[11] of their own domestic process. Put simply, the article is not being interpreted uniformly throughout the Conventions' Contracting States. The reasons for these discrepancies, and whether they are avoidable, need to be addressed.

After a brief elucidation of the above issues, this chapter will discuss some of the main themes that have occupied (Continental) commentators. These issues range from the article's scope *ratione materiae*, to its application in relation to non-Contracting State parties,[12] and courts.[13] The ECJ's interpretative case law will be examined briefly, from the position that many of the subsequent national rulings have moulded these judgments to their own advantage. Specific problems that have occurred with the article will then be highlighted: (1) the issue of

---

ECR I-911; *Francesco Benincasa v Dentalkit Srl* (C-269/95) [1997] ECR I-3767; *Società Transporti Castelletti Spedizioni Internazionali SpA v Hugo Trumpy SpA* (C-159/97) [1999] ECR I-1597; *Coreck Maritime GmbH v Handelsveem B.V., and others* (C-387/98) [2000] ECR I-9337, p.9371, at para. 14—Article 17 construed here as 'protect[ing] the wishes of the parties concerned . . . where . . . established'.

[6] For problems regarding Article 17 and jurisdiction clauses' incorporation from one document into another, *AIG Europe (UK) Ltd and others v The Ethniki* [1998] 4 All ER 301, QBD (Colman J) [2000] All ER (Comm) 65, CA and *AIG Europe SA v QBE International Insurance Ltd*, 3.5.2001, (Moore Bick J) (no incorporation of Article 17 jurisdiction clause from primary insurance document into treaty of reinsurance/retrocession by general words of incorporation in the latter—all terms clauses and conditions as 'original').

[7] And the references to the Court of Justice in the previous footnotes.

[8] As in the original Article 220 Treaty of Rome (now Article 293) EC; and Peel, writing about Article 5(1): 'drafted only so as to deal with the paradigmatic claim that the defendant is in breach of a single obligation contained in a contract whose validity and enforceability is not in doubt', Peel, E., [1998] *LMCLQ* 22, at p.27.

[9] Huber, P. *Die englische forum-non-conveniens-Doktrin und ihre Anwendung im Rahmen des Europäischen Gerichtsstands- und Vollstreckungsübereinkommen*, 1994, at p.194; and *Somafer SA v Saar-Ferngas AG* (33/78) [1978] ECR 2183, at pp.2190–1, para. 4, and para. 7, Introduction above at p.39; annotations in Trunk at 'Erste deutsche Rechtsprechung zum Lugano-Übereinkommen: Gerichtsstandsverein-barungen, Gerichtsstand des Erfüllungsorts und intertemporale Fragen' (1996) *IPRax* 249: the Convention represents 'ein in seinen Kernbestandteilen einheitliches europäisches Internationales Zivilprozeßrecht . . .' ('in its central elements, a unified European Law of Civil Procedure'), at p.251.

[10] Especially traditionally regarding transmission to third parties: *The Tilly Russ* (C-71/83) [1984] ECR 2417, and recently *Società Transporti Castelletti Spedizioni Internazionali SpA v Hugo Trumpy SpA* (C-159/97) [1999] ECR I-1597; and (contemporary), regarding 'e-commerce', below at p.276.

[11] Especially Brajeux, G. 'Case note: *The Nagasaki, Cour de Cassation* Nov.1994', Reuter Textline, Lloyd's List, 13.11.1996 at p.3; and Rodger, B. 'Article 17 of the Brussels Convention; Exclusivity is a must?' (1995) 14 *CJQ* 250 at p.254.

[12] Below, at p.191 section 2.1.5 and especially Samtleben, J. 'Europäische Gerichtsstandsvereinbarungen und Drittstaaten—viel Lärm um nichts?' (1995) 59 *RabelsZ* 670.

[13] *Ibid.* and P. Vlas 'Netherlands Judicial decisions regarding the application of the Lugano Convention on jurisdiction and judgments' [1996] *NILR*, p.397, at pp.403–5, for an interesting case study.

'internationality' in relation to Article 17;[14] (2) Article 17 and bills of lading;[15] (3) the tension between Article 17 and Article 21 (in the English courts at least);[16] and (4) the interpretation, *inter alia*, of the amending phrases 'practices'/ 'a usage' 'in international trade or commerce'.[17]

Why has the Convention, and Article 17 in particular, impacted so heavily on commercial practice, international sales of goods, insurance[18] and banking?[19] Perhaps this is best-explained, as it now seems almost traditional to do, by referring back to the Brussels Convention's 'parent' Treaty, the Treaty of Rome, 1957.[20] Article 220 (now Article 293) EC, under which the Brussels Convention was negotiated, read:

Member States shall, so far as is necessary, enter into negotiations . . . to secure . . .

—the simplification of formalities governing the reciprocal recognition and enforcement of judgments . . .

The direct and principal aim of the Convention was *not* initially to unify the rules of 'direct jurisdiction' in civil and commercial matters in the Contracting States: this became merely an adjunct, to ensure the swift and near-automatic recognition and enforcement of judgments rendered by the courts of Contracting States. However, the practical result was that the focus of litigation shifted away from the court requested to enforce the judgment (as had been the position under traditional *conventions simples*[21]) to the courts initially seised, or reputedly seised, of the original cause of action: an aggrieved party is encouraged to seek redress in the original jurisdiction,[22] not in the enforcing court;[23] by then it is too late[24] to object to the original court's jurisdiction. If a Contracting State court is seised of

---

[14] Below, at pp.172 *et seq* section 2.1.
[15] Below, at pp.209 *et seq* section 2.2.
[16] Below, at pp.225 *et seq* section 2.3.
[17] Below, at pp.248 *et seq* section 2.4.
[18] D.Rhidian-Thomas, *The Modern Law of Marine Insurance*, 1996; Jackson, D. *Enforcement of Maritime Claims*, 3rd edn., 1999.
[19] Davenport, B.J. 'Forum shopping in the market' (1995) 111 *LQR* 366, at pp.369–70; the impact of Article 17 in banking/insurance: Swiss *Bundesgericht* 19.9.1998 *Dresdner Forfaitierungs AG gegen Sezione Speciale per l'assicurazione del credito all'esportazione* 124 BGE, III, 436, at p.441, and 20.8.1998 *Banque Bruxelles Lambert (Suisse) SA et huit consorts contre République de Paraguay et Sezione speciale per l'assicurazione del credito all'esportazione* 124 BGE, III, 382, at p.400.
[20] Treaty Establishing the European (Economic) Community as Amended by Subsequent Treaties, Rome, 25 March 1957.
[21] Which allowed the recognising court to scrutinise the jurisdiction taken by the original court: e.g. Article 3 of Schedule to the Reciprocal Enforcement of Foreign Judgments (France) Order in Council 1936, SI 1936/609; Article 1 *Convention entre Belgique et Italie concernant la reconnaissance et l'exécution des décisions judiciaires et d'autres titres exécutoires en matière civile et commerciale*, 6 avril 1962, 490 UNTS, 7161, above, at p.cxix.
[22] *Interdesco S.A. v Nullifire Ltd.* [1992] 1 Lloyd's Rep. 180 (Phillips J) at p.188: 'it will normally be appropriated to leave the defendant to pursue his remedy in the [foreign] jurisdiction'; *SISRO v Ampersand Software* (C-432/93) [1995] ECR I-2269.
[23] But chapter 5, below, at pp.437 *et seq* on Article 27(2).
[24] And besides, in the vast majority of cases, not legitimate either—Article 28 para. 3, and Article 29.

an action against a defendant—domiciled in any Contracting State[25]—under rules common to all the Contracting States,[26] there is little room for complaint[27] possible at the subsequent recognition and enforcement stage. This shift of emphasis thus places an absolute premium[28] on quietly[29] seising, and seising first,[30] the court where the action is best suited for trial for each party. Apart from the 'exclusive' jurisdiction under Article 16, and jurisdiction derived from Article 57,[31] the best way[32] to predict[33] the court to be seised is to use a valid Article 17 jurisdiction clause, rendering the prorogated forum 'exclusively'[34] competent, to the detriment of all lower bases[35] in the hierarchy.[36] In a normal sale of goods transaction,[37] the

---

[25] But not necessarily only domiciled in a Contracting State—as regards defendants not so domiciled, Article 4 allows Contracting States to use their traditional 'extraordinary' bases of jurisdiction.

[26] The rules in Title II to the Brussels and Lugano Conventions, excluding, of course, the exorbitant bases of jurisdiction in Article 3 para. 2.

[27] Note the exhaustive defences to recognition and enforcement in Article 27 and 28(1) (and also Article 59).

[28] The effects of Articles 21/22 in A. Briggs 'Anti-European Teeth for Choice of Court Clauses' (1994) *LMCLQ* p.158, at pp.158–59, 'snatch[ing] the jurisdictional advantage'; important especially if an estoppel *per rem judicatam* may arise from the decision of a foreign tribunal, *qua forum derogatum*, as to whether Article 17 applies or not: *Sté Interholzraimann c/ Sté d'exploitation des établissements Chiaradia* 11.3.1997 (1998) *JDI* 142, obs. Huet.

[29] The saga in *Polly Peck International Plc v Citibank NA and others* [1994] I.L.Pr. 71 and the converse Swiss *Bundesgericht* decision in *A., B. und C. gegen D.* 26.9.1997 123 BGE, III, 414 (inadvisable to send a polite (solicitor's) letter before action, esp. with a fax number); recently *Molins Plc v G.D. S.p.A* [2000] 1 WLR 1741, CA, at p.1749, and *Trustor AB v Barclays Bank Plc (F Van Lanschot Bankiers (Luxembourg) SA (Part 20 Defendant))*, 24.10.2000, Ch.D. Rimer J; also Franzosi, M. [1997] *EIPR* 382, at p.385, regarding patent infringement litigation'; *Knauf UK GmbH v British Gypsum Ltd and another* [2001] 1 WLR 907, CA.

[30] *The owners of cargo lately laden on board the ship 'Tatry' v The Maciej Rataj* (C-406/92) [1994] ECR I-5439; and *Messier-Dowty Ltd and another v Sabena SA & others*, [2000] 1 WLR 2040, at p.2047, (Lord Woolf MR), CA; *Knauf UK GmbH v British Gypsum Ltd and another* [2002] 1 WLR 907, CA, reversing [2001] 2 All ER (Comm) 332, QBD David Steel J; *Phillips and others v Symes and another* [2002] 1 WLR 853, Ch.D, Hart J; *Digit Srl v Apple Computer International*, 5.10.2001, QBD (Goldring J).

[31] This is controversial: *The Bergen* [1997] 1 Lloyd's Rep p.380 (Clarke J); *Doran v Tracy Power* [1995] 2 IR 402, Irish SC; *The Deichland* [1990] 1 QB 361, CA.

[32] Apart, of course, from launching for oneself a jurisdiction—founding, 'prophylactic', pre-emptive action—*The Maciej Rataj* (C-406/92) [1994] ECR I-5439; and Fentiman, R. 'Judgments, purposes and the Brussels Convention' (1994) *CLJ*, p.239, at p.263.

[33] 'Concentration rather than proliferation is the motive behind choice of forum clauses', Polak, M. 'Case note: *Powell Duffryn Plc v Petereit*' (1993) 30 *CMLRev* 406, at p.418.

[34] Care needs to be taken with this phrase; on the relative weakness of Article 17's 'exclusivity' in the hierarchy of the Convention's jurisdictional rules: Briggs, 1997, at pp.64–65, para. 2.82; also contradictory findings as to Article 17's ascendancy over Article 6 in *Hough v P & O Containers Ltd* [1999] Q.B. 834 and *Cassation* 2.3.1999 *Ammerlaan Agro Projecten B.V. v Les Serres de Cosquerou* [1999] I.L.Pr. 627, disregarding its earlier view that Article 17 had ascendancy over Article 6(2) in *Société Voith c/ Société Chantiers et Ateliers de la Perrière et autres* 12.7.1982 (1983) *JDI* 405, at p.406.

[35] Articles 5, 6, and Article 2; as *Sanicentral GmbH v René Collin* (C-25/79) [1979] ECR 3423 has shown, a jurisdiction clause invalid according to national law may be validated by Article 17; for the inverse situation—valid according to national law—Swiss *Bundesgericht* in *Dresdner Forfaitierungs AG gegen Sezione Speciale per l'assicurazione del credito all'esportazione* 124 BGE, III, 436, at p.441, subsequently rendered invalid due to Article 17 III and Article 8.

[36] *Ibid.* and above pp.34–35.

[37] For the (in)validity of Article 17 in consumer cases, *OLG Köln* 16.3.1989 1989 IPRspr. Nr. 187; *LG Berlin* 1.10.1991 (1992) *IPRax* 243; *LG Darmstadt* 2.12.1993 (1995) *IPRax* 318; *OLG Koblenz*

jurisdiction clause becomes especially important.[38] The Convention may allow a number of alternative bases[39] of jurisdiction, Articles 5(1) and (3), Article 6 and Article 2, in this type of situation. Article 17, in theory,[40] neutralises[41] these.

Apart from its practical commercial importance[42] in international trade, an analysis of Article 17 reveals its remarkable metamorphosis.[43] These changes inform of the fact that, firstly, the original drafting of Article 17[44] seemed excessively formalistic and rigid, ill-drafted, or at least ill-suited to certain common commercial situations[45]—a criticism which can be levelled at the Convention in other areas.[46] The original six Civil Law countries responsible for the drafting of the Convention no doubt had the regulation of, then, contemporary disputes in mind: the cross-border sales of goods, and breach of contract actions between commercial agent and exclusive supplier.[47] Even here, however, the original drafting proved highly problematical and inadequate.[48] Secondly, changes made by the 1978 revision[49] reveal the concerns of the Contracting States, notably the

---

9.1.1987 (1987) *RIW* 144; *Société Verkoopconsortium Engels c/ Consorts Couttenier* 19.2.1986 (1986) *JDI* 713.

[38] In view of the jurisdictional base in Article 5(1) and *lex causae*, debtor-based place of payment rules, above at pp.119 *et seq* section 1.3; C. Kohler in 'Internationale Gerichtsstandsvereinbarungen: Liberalität und Rigorismus im EuGVÜ' (1983) *IPRax* 265, at p.265.

[39] Polak, (1993) 30 *CMLRev* 406, at p.411; Rodger, (1995) 14 *CJQ* 250, at p.250.

[40] Problems with the due deference to be accorded to English Article 17 jurisdiction clauses still persists: *OT Africa Line Ltd v Hijazy and others (The 'Kribi')* [2001] 1 Lloyd's Rep. 76 (Aikens J).

[41] Polak, (1993) 30 *CMLRev* 406, at p.418. Curious therefore *Ammerlaan Agro Projecten B.V. v Les Serres de Cosquerou* [1999] I.L.Pr. 627, that gave precedence to Article 6(1) over Article 17, at p.628, para. 2 (the same precedence as is given to a co-defendant under French autonomous law *Cassation* 24.1.1998 *Rafidain Bank et autre c. Soc. Butec et autre* (1999) *Rev crit* 309, at p.310; *contra Hough v P & O Containers Ltd* [1999] QB 834; re contracts of employment *Sicard c/ Société Himolla* 17.12.1997 (1999) *JDI* 195.

[42] Morse, C.G.J. 'Forum-Selection clauses—EEC Style' (1989) 1 *Afr.J.Int'l.L* 539, at p.552.

[43] Gaudemet-Tallon, 1996, at p.75; and below, at pp.258 *et seq* section 2.4.2.

[44] The original Brussels Convention 1968, [1978] OJ L304/36, Article 17 at p.39.

[45] Especially the comments made by AG Tesauro in his opinion in *Mainschiffahrts-Genossenschaft e.G (MSG) v Les Gravières Rhénanes SARL* [1997] ECR I-911, at p.925, para. 23: 'the amendment introduced by the 1978 Accession Convention certainly reflects greater (perhaps necessary) attention and sensitivity to the requirements of international trade and, more generally, to the actual workings of the business world.'

[46] Articles 16(1), and Article 5(1) (contracts of employment) and Article 11 (exclusion for re-insurance)— (*Agnew and others v Lansförsäkringsbolagens AB* [2001] 1 AC 223, HL), for example. No special provision was originally included for the former two; now the amended 1989 Brussels Convention Article 5(1), and Article 16(1)(b).

[47] This has created protectionist problems of its own, Strop, R. 'Internationale Zuständigkeit des Erfüllungsorts bei Verträgen mit französischen Vertretern' (1999) *RIW* 823.

[48] Below, at p.168, and on the necessity for judicial creativity in *Ditta Estasis Salotti di Colzano Aima e Giamano Colzano v RÜWA Polstereimaschinen GmbH* (C-24/76), 14.12.1976 [1976] ECR 1831; *Galereis Segoura SPRL v Rahim Bonakdarian* (C-25/76) 14.12.1976 [1976] ECR 1851 and *The Tilly Russ* (C-71/83) [1984] ECR 2417.

[49] The 1979 Accession Convention, [1978] OJ L304/1, Article 11, at pp.5–6, inserted a new sentence phrase 'or in international trade or commerce, in a form which accords with practices in that trade or commerce of which the parties are or ought to have been aware' into [1978] OJ L304/77 at L304/82; and below, at p.248 *et seq*.

UK,[50] reflecting both this jurisdiction's commercial orientation,[51] and the perceived inadequacies of the original drafting:

> owing to the frequency with which jurisdiction is conferred on UK courts in international trade, the problem takes on considerably greater importance with the UK's accession to the Convention, *than hitherto*.[52]

In perhaps no other area of the Convention has the initial strictness of an article collided so markedly with commercial practice.[53] This is evident from the ECJ's struggle to reconcile two conflicting policies:[54] clear agreement demonstrated between the parties on the jurisdiction clause, and yet an agreement conforming to the demands of the modern business community.[55] This tension was realised[56] in *Galereis Segoura SPRL v Rahim Bonakdarian*[57] and mentioned by commentators:

> Deux préoccupations contradictoires s'affrontent . . . il ne faut pas être rigide au point de bloquer les usages commerciaux qui s'établissent entre professionels . . .[58] [59]

Article 17 shows up these tensions neatly:

> . . . assez rapidement, celle-ci [Article 17] se trouverait confrontée avec la practique et les usages du commerce [60] [61]

and not merely in its relations to trade and commerce, but acted as a paradigm of the almost naivety with which the original Convention was drafted.[62] The fertile[63]

---

[50] Jenard Report [1979] OJ C59/1; Schlosser Report, 6.10.1978, [1979] OJ C59/71 at p.124; AG Franx's observations to this effect in the *Hoge Raad*'s decision in *Transocean Towage Company Limited v Hyundai Construction Co. Limited* [1987] E.C.C. 282, at pp.294–95.

[51] G. Droz 'Entreé en vigeur de la Convention de Bruxelles révisée sur la Convention de Lugano' (1987) *Rev crit* 251, at p.253 speaking of 'surtout de la puissance commerciale, financière et boursière de la *City*'.

[52] Schlosser Report [1979] OJ C59/124, para. 177; the 'problem' referred to is the lack of a provision governing the conferment of jurisdiction on the English High Court by parties, neither of whom were domiciled in Contracting States. This was rectified by the insertion of a new Article 17 para. 2 into the original Brussels Convention.

[53] 'Il était cependant prévisible que, assez rapidement, celle-ci se trouverait confrontée avec la pratique et les usages du commerce . . .' comment by Bischoff on *Salotti v RÜWA* (C-24/76) in (1977) *JDI*, at p.734; Jenard Report, [1979] OJ C59/1, at p.37; note Article 23 of the Brussels I Regulation will allow agreements by electronic means, below at p.276.

[54] Cf. Morse (1989) 1 *Afr.J.Int'l.L* 539, at p.566 on these competing policies.

[55] Cf. Droz 'La Convention de Lugano parallèle à la Convention de Bruxelles concernant la compétence judiciaire des décisions en matière civile et commerciale' (1989) *Rev crit* 1, at p.23 fn.50; Achard, R., 1987 DMF 556 at p.560; Pocar, F. 'Linee di tendenza della convenzione de Bruxelles sulla giurisdizione e l'esecuzione delle sentenze dopo l'adhesione de nuovi stati' (1990) *Riv. dir. internat. priv. e proc.* 5, at p.11.

[56] And informed the drafting of the Lugano Convention.

[57] (C-25/76), 14.12.1976, [1976] ECR 1851.

[58] ('Two contradictory preoccupations clash . . . there must not be rigidity to the point of impeding commercial practices that are set up between professionals').

[59] Droz, (1989) *Rev crit* 1, at p.23.

[60] ('quite quickly, this [Article 17] found itself up against the practice and usages of commerce').

[61] Bischoff, (1977) *JDI*, at p.734.

[62] Morse (1989) 1 *Afr.J.Int'l.L* 539, at p.555.

[63] Cf Moloney, in G.Moloney and N.Robinson (eds) *The Brussels Convention on Jurisdiction and the Enforcement of Judgments: Papers and Precedents from the Joint Conference with the Union des Avocats Europeéns held in Cork, September 1989*, Irish Centre for European Law, 1990, Ch.3 at p.41.

and specialist area of litigation engendered, shows not only the importance and widespread use of such clauses, but the difficulty of accommodating a rigid[64] rule to the vicissitudes of commercial life.

Yet perhaps the most alarming aspect[65] of a study of Article 17 is the opportunity it may provide for judicial protectionism[66] of the prorogated forum courts, and the enhancement of invisible income[67] thereby generated from litigation in these courts. The impression, for it is only such at this stage of investigation, that comes from various cases[68] and comment[69] is that national courts (especially in the UK) are ambivalent[70] towards jurisdiction clauses within Article 17's ambit. On the one hand, if a court is otherwise seised of a case,[71] it is often loath to admit that another Contracting State court has 'exclusive', Article 17 prorogated, jurisdiction;[72] on the other hand, a Contracting State itself prorogated under Article 17 may cling tenaciously[73] to jurisdiction in its own

---

[64] In the original Brussels Convention, an 'agreement in writing or evidenced in writing' *OLG Karlsruhe* 15.3.2001 (2001) *RIW* 621; note now the 'e-commerce' addendum to Art.23 of the Brussels I Regulation; *AIG Europe (UK) Ltd and others v The Ethniki* [1998] 4 All ER 301, QBD (Colman J) [2000] All ER (Comm) 65, CA; *AIG Europe SA v QBE International Insurance Ltd*, [2001] 2 Lloyd's Rep. 268, (Moore-Bick J).

[65] At least for the aims of a unified and harmonious interpretation of this European jurisdictional and enforcement regime.

[66] Cf Rodger, (1995) 14 *CJQ* 250, at p.254.

[67] Cf Davenport, (1995) 111 *LQR* 366, at p.369.

[68] *Continental Bank v Aeakos* [1994] 1 WLR 588; *Phillip Alexander Securities & Futures Ltd v Bamberger*, [1996] CLC 1757 (Waller J) CA at p.1780; *Bankers Trust International Plc v RCS Editori SpA* [1996] CLC 899 (Longmore J); *GIE Réunion européenne c/ Société Plate et Ruys*, Cour de Cassation, Ch. Com., 10.1.1995, (1996) *JDI* 141; or avoid Article 17's application—*Cassation* 2.3.1999 *Ammerlaan Agro Projecten B.V. v Les Serres de Cosquerou* [1999] I.L.Pr. 627; *AIG Europe SA v QBE International Insurance Ltd*, 3.5.2001, (Moore Bick J).

[69] For example Davenport, (1995) 111 *LQR* 366, at p.369; Hamblen, N. 'Injunctions to restrain proceedings brought in breach of English jurisdiction/arbitration clauses.' (1996) *Int. J.Shipping Law*, p.247, at p.249; Palomba, M. 'Arbitration and the Brussels and Lugano Conventions' (1996) *I.C.Lit*, p.36; and 'The English Arbitration Clause and Italian court proceedings—competing forums' (1996) *IHL* p.81.

[70] Especially on the ambivalence aspect Rodger, (1995) 14 *CJQ* 250, at p.254; yet the French *Cour de Cassation* appears to be openly hostile to Article 17 jurisdiction clauses in bills of lading, below, section 2.2.2; note also the English courts' attitude in *Dresser UK Ltd and others v Falcongate Freight Management Ltd and others (The 'Duke of Yare')* [1992] 1 QB 502, *AIG Europe (UK) Ltd and others v The Ethniki* [2000] All ER (Comm) 65, CA; and the caution expressed in regard to anti-suit injunctions in *OT Africa Line Ltd v Hijazy and others (The 'Kribi')* [2001] 1 Lloyd's Rep. 76, at pp.93–94 (Aikens J).

[71] I.e. under Article 5(1), (3) or Article 6, or Article 2.

[72] For the German view: *Declining Jurisdiction in Private International Law*: Reports to the XIVth Congress of the International Academy of Comparative Law, Athens, August 1994 (ed. Fawcett, J.), 1995, at p.201; Sandrock, F.E. *Die Vereinbarung eines 'neutralen' internationalen Gerichtsstandes*, 1997, at pp.67–94; *AIG Europe (UK) Ltd and others v The Ethniki* [2000] All ER (Comm) 65, CA, at pp.74–75; *AIG Europe SA v QBE International Insurance Ltd* [2001] 2 Lloyd's Rep. 268, (Moore-Bick J).

[73] There is no evidence, gleaned so far, which suggests this ambivalence, other than in England and Wales, and Scotland—Rodger, (1995) 14 *CJQ* 250, at p.250 and *Morrison v Panic Link Ltd* (1994) *SLT* 232, and *Kurz v Stella Musical Veranstaltungs GmbH* [1992] 1 All ER 630 and *Dresser v Falcongate Freight Management Ltd and others (The Duke of Yare)* [1992] 2 All ER 450; *Credit Suisse Financial Products v Sociéé Generale d'Entreprises* [1997] CLC 168, CA; although a retreat in *AIG Europe SA v*

favour;[74] this observation can perhaps be expanded and applied, *mutatis mutandis*, to the whole of the Convention.[75] In the UK at least, there is a perceived tendency,[76] amounting almost to a presumption, that once jurisdiction has been invoked (for example under Article 5(1)[77]) that the court will continue to hear the case.

As mentioned in the Introduction, one of the main aims of this work will be to examine the extent to which the Contracting State courts have so interpreted, or misinterpreted, the Convention—in such a way, where possible, as to allow their own jurisdiction[78] invoked under the Convention to proceed. One wonders how far the words of Davenport,[79] writing about the 'first seised' concept in Article 21,[80] have struck a judicial chord. Identifying first the value to the national economy of domestic litigation:

QBE International Insurance Ltd, [2001] 2 Lloyd's Rep. 268, at 273 (Moore-Bick J)—not, at least, in Germany: *OLG Düsseldorf* 16.3.2000 (2001) *RIW* 63 (where a German jurisdiction clause referred to in general conditions in a loan agreement, but not in fact handed to the defendant on contracting held insufficient for Article 17(1)(a) 'in writing'); for reverse side of the coin see *OLG Karlsruhe* 15.3.2001 (2001) *RIW* 621, at p.622; not mentioning interpretative freedom of *Mainschiffahrts Bundesgericht* 28.1.2000 *Elex AG gegen Crig-Hautefaye SARL*, unreported; and *BGH* 22.2.2001 (2001) *RIW* 456 (German jurisdiction clause in personal guarantee application form, as guarantee had not 'signed' the form, only pre-affixed a stamp, at p.457: 'Eine Differenzierung in den Anforderungen an die Schriftform je nachdem, zu wessen Ungunsten sich die Gerichtsstandsklausel auswirken kann, ist dem Übereinkommen fremd' ('a differentiation in the prerequisites in the form for 'a writing' according to whose detriment the jurisdiction clause has effect, is unknown to the Convention')).

[74] This 'suggests a rather insular approach by the English courts, over-zealous in their attempts to retain jurisdiction in cases involving prorogation clauses . . .' Rodger, (1995) 14 *CJQ* 250, at p.254; cf. *Implants International Ltd. v Stratec Medical* [1999] 2 All ER (Comm) 933, (Leeds Mercantile Ct) (Judge McGonigal) at p.949j: 'Before a court removes such existing rights [to sue the defendant in England under Article 5(1)], . . . the court deciding the issue needs to be satisfied at the interlocutory stage that it is *highly likely* that the party alleging that there is 'an agreement conferring jurisdiction' is right'; contrast this with the endorsement on a claim form under r.1.3 of 6PD for service out under CPR 6.19(1)(b)(iii).

[75] Re Article 5(1), chapter 1, above at p.46 *et seq.*

[76] The probability is high that once an attempt is made to gain jurisdiction here, more often than not it is exercised.

[77] Compare the reversal in fortune of pre-contractual, material non disclosure actions (ss.18 and 20(2) Marine Insurance Act 1906) under Article 5(1) from *Trade Indemnity Plc v Fösäkringsaktiebølaget Njord (in liq.)* [1995] 1 All ER 796 (Rix J) to *Agnew v Lansfösäkringsbølagens* [1996] 4 All ER 978 (Mance J), affm'd, [1997] 4 All ER 937, CA, affm'd [2000] 1 All ER 737, HL; *Kenburn Waste Management Ltd v Bergman*, 11.5.2001, Ch.D. (Pumfrey J); admittedly *Fisher and others v Unione Italiana de Riassicurazione SPA* [1998] CLC 682, and *Viskase Ltd and another v Paul Kiefel GmbH* [1999] 1 WLR 1305, not so tenacious.

[78] In this chapter most marked in the *Cour de Cassation*'s bill of lading cases, below, at p.217 *et seq.*

[79] Davenport, (1995) 111 *LQR* 366.

[80] Article 21 requires the court seised second, under certain conditions—which are themselves perhaps open to ambivalent interpretation—to decline jurisdiction if the court first seised's jurisdiction is established; in the UK, the main cases on 'seisure' are *Dresser UK Ltd and others v Falcongate Freight Management Ltd and others (The 'Duke of Yare')* [1992] 1 QB 502 and *Neste Chemicals S.A. and others v DK Line S.A. and Tokumaru Kaiun K.K. (The 'Sargasso')* [1994] 3 All ER 180, CA; it is submitted that CPR Rule 7.2(1) does not alter the position here; *SDL International Ltd v Centre de Co-operation Internationale en Recherche Agronomique pour le Developpement* [2001] CLC 903.

[t]he economy of this country depends significantly upon its ability to provide the essential back-up services . . . such as insurance . . . [and] a first-class dispute resolution machinery . . . One of the chief results of this success of the Commercial Court is a very substantial earner indeed of foreign exchange in the form of invisible earnings . . .[81]

He then asks:

How far are the courts, in practice, prepared to assist in the implementation of this national interest?[82]

Any perturbing inconsistency of approach[83] is marked in the UK;[84] but as will be shown, the French courts too, perhaps not for the same self-serving reasons, seem, at the highest level, hostile to jurisdiction clauses.[85] Indeed, it has been pointed out by some French commentators[86] that the *Cour de Cassation* is misapplying the ECJ's jurisprudence on Article 17.[87] The reasons why are not entirely clear.[88] What is noticeable, however, is that any protectionism will manifest itself most pointedly through Article 17:[89] narrowly construing Article 17's requirements in the case of a foreign jurisdiction clause,[90] and giving a conversely wide interpretation for clauses prorogating the domestic forum.[91]

Most commentators, when dealing with Article 17, divide up its treatment into its (now) lettered sub-paragraphs.[92] On the Continent, it is examined as a series of

---

[81] Davenport, (1995) 111 *LQR* 366, at p.367; *Lafi Office v Meriden Animal Health* [2000] 2 Lloyd's Rep. 51, at pp.59–60, (Symons QC).

[82] *Ibid.*

[83] In requiring different degrees of exclusivity to be expressed for domestic and foreign jurisdiction clauses, above at p.169, and Rodger, (1995) 14 *CJQ* 250; *Continental Bank N.A. v Aeakos Compania Naviera S.A. and others* [1994] 1 WLR 588; *AIG Europe SA v QBE International Insurance Ltd* [2001] 2 Lloyd's Rep. 268, (Moore-Bick J).

[84] Rodger, (1995) 14 *CJQ* 250.

[85] The *Cour de Cassation's* hostility to jurisdiction clauses is legendary: case note *Société Sanicentral GmbH c/ Collin* (1980) *JDI* 429, Huet, at p.429; and at French autonomous law *Cassation* 8.12.1998 *Compagnie d'assurances Helvetia e.a c/ Delmas S.A.* (1999) *ETL* 551; the German and Austrian courts have developed their own theory as to Article 17's application, below, at p.193 and p.204, respectively.

[86] Especially Gaudemet-Tallon (1996) *JDI*, at pp.141-45; i.e. disregarding *The Tilly Russ* [1984] ECR 2417.

[87] Especially *The Tilly Russ* [1984] ECR 2417.

[88] But Brajeux, G. 'Case note: *The Nagasaki, Cour de Cassation* Nov.1994', at p.3.

[89] This treatment will also attempt to discover whether similar divergences emerge in the interpretation of Articles 27(1)(2); Jenard, Rép. Notarial, 1994, Tome XI, livre VI, 3e partie, 1994, believes Germany is engaging in protectionist enforcement manoeuvres under Article 27(2), below, at p.503 Chapter 5.

[90] *Quaere*, whether the courts of Gibraltar are 'foreign' enough in this regard: *The Rothnie* [1996] 2 Lloyd's Rep.202, Creswell J; *The Duke of Yare* [1992] 2 All ER 450; *AIG Europe SA v QBE International Insurance Ltd* [2001] 2 Lloyd's rep. 268, (Moore-Bick J).

[91] Rodger, (1995) 14 *CJQ* 250.

[92] Long-overdue numbering of the whole of Article 17 was introduced by the Lugano Convention: text of Article 17 at [1990] C189/02 at pp.7–8, in force in the UK as from 1.12.1991. The 1989 amendments to the Brussels Convention merely introduced lettering (a), (b), and (c) to the first paragraph of Article 17.

issues, ranging from the scope of its application[93] and the 'internationality' necessary to bring Article 17, and the Convention into play.[94] The conditions as to form, unlike with English authors, receive proportionally less attention in detail. Before the case law is examined, the issue of 'internationality' will be dealt with, primarily because it takes up much of the space in the leading European texts, and has lead to a number of inconsistent Contracting State decisions.

2.1   'INTERNATIONALITY'[95]

The issue of 'internationality'[96]—or more accurately, the degree to which the facts of a given case[97] must have a cross-border element, before Article 17,[98] or indeed the Convention itself,[99] is to apply[100]—is complex[101] and controversial. It is being treated here as a section in its own right simply because of the fact that it has produced so many divergent interpretations in the Contracting State caselaw and commentaries: in similar factual situations, the courts in England,[102] Germany,

---

[93]   Gaudemet-Tallon, 1996, at pp.75–100; Kropholler, 1998 at pp.228–37, paras. 1–20; Briggs, 1997, at pp.64–66. Important issues are the domicile of the parties, and the date for ascertaining this, *Dicey and Morris*, 13th edn, 2000, Vol .I, at p.431, para. 12–088.

[94]   *Ibid.*

[95]   Gaudemet-Tallon, 1996, at pp.76–84; and Kropholler, 1998 at pp.228–32; note Article 2(1)(a)–(c) of the Hague Worldwide Judgments Convention (October 1999 version) clearly deals with the territorial, or 'internationality' issue; it was hoped the ECJ in *Coreck Maritime GmbH* (C387–98) [2000] ECR I-9337, at pp.9372–73, would illuminate the internationality issue—the sufficiency of one Contracting State domiciliary for the application of Article 17—but its recent ruling is not definitive either way in embracing or rejecting a literal interpretation of Article 17, at pp.9372–74, paras. 17–18, and 21; (*obiter*) paras. 41–42, ECJ decision in *Group Josi Reinsurance* (C-412/98) [2000] ECR I-5925, at p.5954; the matter is now uncontroversial in England: *Sinochem International Oil (London) Ltd v Mobil Sales and Supply Corp Ltd (No.2)* [2000] 1 All ER (Comm) 758; *Society of Lloyd's v White and others*, 3.3.2000, QBD, (Creswell J); *OT Africa Line Ltd v Hijazy and others (The 'Kribi')* [2001] 1 Lloyd's Rep. 76 (Aikens J).

[96]   Jenard Report [1979] OJ C59/1 at p.8.

[97]   I.e. the parties' domicile/chosen forum; note the permutations below.

[98]   On the aspect of internationality for Article 17's application, Droz, G. *Compétence judiciaire et effets des jugements dans le marché commun*, 1972.: 'Il convient de souligner immédiatement qu'il s'agit bien là d'une condition d'application de l'Article 17 et *non d'une condition de la validité* de l'accord' (emphasis), at p.117, para. 183; *Cheshire and North*, 13th edn., 1999 at p.236; *Droit International Privé*, B. Audit, 1991, to the same effect at p.437, para. 547.

[99]   'L'internationalité du litige est-elle un critère d'applicabilité matérielle de la Convention et non seul Article 17?' in Born, H. 'Le régime générale des clauses attributives de juridiction dans la Convention de Bruxelles' (1995) *JT* 353, at p.355.

[100]   Kropholler, 1998, and Schlosser Report, 6.10.1978, [1979] OJ C59/71, n.174.

[101]   Apart from the problem of interpretation, the complexity of Article 17 itself stems from the fact that it carries with it, in all, the requirements of form and the effects of the clause; also '[o]n y trouve enfins des règles . . .' neither of form nor effect, but of 'l'application de la disposition elle-même . . . règles relatives au champ d'application de la Convention' Droz, 1972, at pp.115–16, para. 180.

[102]   Especially noticeable in the case where a Contracting State plaintiff/claimant agrees to prorogate his own Contracting State courts with non-Contracting State defendants—Category E, section 2.1.5 below—contrast, in the English cases, *British Aerospace Plc. v Dee Howard Co.* [1993] 1 Lloyd's Rep. 368 with *Mercury Communications Ltd and another v Communication Telesystems International* [1999] 2 All

France, Austria and Switzerland have come to opposite conclusions about the scope, *ratione materiae*, of Article 17. The opening words of the article, which have caused such divergent interpretations, read as follows: 'If the parties, one or more of whom is domiciled in a Contracting State, have agreed . . .'.

Much is made of the issue of internationality by continental writers,[103] especially in Germany,[104] where the jurisprudence of both the *Oberlandesgerichte*[105] and the *Bundesgerichtshof*[106] has contributed to lively and starkly polarised viewpoints.[107] Why is a finding of internationality[108] vital when considering the application of Article 17 to jurisdiction clauses? Traditionally, for whatever reason, some Civil Law countries have been overtly hostile and discriminatory in their procedural codes[109] to jurisdiction clauses derogating from an internal jurisdiction which would otherwise have been well-founded within that country; others, such as France[110] and Germany[111] continue to subject the formal validity of such clauses (that do not enter the EU 'internationality' gateway to Article 17[112]) to more rigorous criteria in their procedural codes—for example regarding the status of persons permitted to prorogate particular courts.[113] A finding of internationality can prove to be vital to the question of whether (discriminatory) national procedural law, or Article 17, will be applied.[114] As will be demonstrated,

---

ER (Comm) 33, (Moore Bick J); *Sinochem International Oil (London) Ltd v Mobil Sales and Supply Corp Ltd (No.2)* [2000] 1 All ER (Comm) 758, at p.770, CA; *Society of Lloyd's v White and others*, 3.3.2000, QBD, (Creswell J).

[103] So much so, that to the substantive issues of Article 17 and its practical, formal application, a disproportionately less amount of ink is dedicated; esp H.Gaudemet-Tallon, 1996, at pp.72–75; and Kropholler, 1998 at pp.228–32.

[104] P. Schlosser *EuGVÜ: Europäisches Gerichtsstands- und Vollstreckungsübereinkommen mit Luganer Übereinkommen*, 1996, at p.100, for extensive references.

[105] Especially *OLG München* 8.3.1989, IPRspr. 1989, Nr.186, [1991] I.L.Pr., p.298; *OLG München* 28.9.1989, IPRspr. 1989, Nr.194; *OLG Hamburg* 30.12.1985, IPRspr. 1985 Nr.36; *OLG Düsseldorf* 15.3.1990, IPRspr. 1990 Nr.167, at p.339; *OLG Hamburg* 31.12.1991, IPRspr. 1991, Nr.184; *OLG Karlsruhe* 9.10.1992, IPRspr. 1992, Nr.199.

[106] *BGH* 4.2.1991 IPRspr. 1991, Nr.171; for an Austrian case following the German view, *OGH* 23.2.1998 *Entscheidungen des österreichischen Obersten Gerichtshofes in Zivil- und Justizverwaltungssachen*, (hereinafter '*Entscheidungen*'), 71 Band, 1998, No.29, p.170, reviewed in section 2.1.5(iv).

[107] Below, at p.193, Samtleben (1995) 59 *RabelsZ* 670, and his opponents below, at pp.191 *et seq*, section 2.1.5(iii), at p.200.

[108] Or more accurately, internationality within the European Union, below, at p.195.

[109] The old Article 2 Italian CpC, now abrogated since 1.9.1995 by Article 4 *Legge 21 Maggio* 1995, N.218 *Le nuove leggi civili commentate*, N.5–6, Anno XIX, settembre-diciembre, p.877, translated by Montanari, A. *Conflict of Laws in Italy*, 1997.

[110] Article 48 NCPC, *Nouveau Code de Procedure Civile*, Dalloz, 93ème éd, 2001, at p.63 with attendant notes; and recently *Cour de Cassation* 1er, 11.2.1997, *Gianfranco Copelli c/ Société Carofrance Ceramique* (1998) JDI 138.

[111] §38 ZPO; and crucially where §38 ZPO governs a case of a German domiciliary and a non-Contracting State domiciliary choosing a German court, below, at p.192; Sandrock, 1997, at pp.67–94.

[112] Where a defendant is not domiciled in a Contracting State, Article 4.

[113] §38 Abs. 2 ZPO.

[114] And also benefit, as a matter of Community law, from the *Kompetenz-Kompetenz* autonomy of *Francesco Benincasa v Dentalkit Srl* (C-269/95) [1997] ECR I-3767, below, at pp.254–8 section 2.4.1(iii);

how[115] internationality is determined, and thus whether Article 17, and the Convention are applied, seems to vary wildly from one Contracting State to another; as does also the amount of critical ink dedicated to its importance.[116]

The discussion of internationality is perhaps most neatly undertaken by dividing it up into a series of factual situations with different permutations, the variables being the respective domiciles/seats of the parties to the contract, the location of the prorogated forum[117] and the court actually seised of the dispute.[118]

Whether or not there are any other additional requirements—or 'ungeschriebene Anwendungsgrenzen'[119] as they are described in the German case law and commentaries—not to the formalities of Article 17 itself, but to the article's very application *ab initio*, will have to be examined.

There is such an amount of confusion over Article 17's application *ratione materiae* for the simple reason that few, thorough, systematic analyses have yet been undertaken.[120] The categories against which internationality, and hence Article 17's application, can be tested are, non-exhaustively as follows:

Category A: Both parties to the contract are domiciled in Contracting State X, and the courts of Contracting State X are exclusively[121] chosen.

Category B: Both parties are as in Category A, yet the courts of Contracting State Y are prorogated instead.

---

also *Bundesgericht* 15.1.1998 *Commune de Macot la Plagne contre Banque X* 124, BGE, III, 134; however, *lex causae* to interpret (scope of) clause itself, however, once agreed upon in an Article 17 'form': *Bundesgericht* 7.8.2001 *Notrop Speditions- und Schiffahrtsgesellschaft GmbH gegen Transrail AG*, unreported.

[115] And whether at all.
[116] Below, at p.193, for extensive German comment.
[117] I.e. within or without the Contracting States.
[118] As either *forum prorogatum* or *derogatum*, as to which below, Category B.
[119] ('unwritten boundaries of application'). The phrase taken from Geimer, R 'Ungeschriebene Anwendungsgrenzen des EuGVÜ: Müssen Berührungspunkte zu mehreren Vertragsstaaten bestehen?' (1991) IPRax 31; *OLG München* 28.9.1989 IPRspr. 1989 Nr. 194, (1991) *IPRax* 46, below, at p.194; recently *Mercury Communications Ltd and another v Communication Telesystems International* [1999] 2 All ER (Comm) 33, (Moore Bick J); *Sinochem International Oil (London) Ltd v Mobil Sales and Supply Corp Ltd (No.2)* [2000] 1 All ER (Comm) 758, at p.770, (Rix J); *Society of Lloyd's v White and others*, 3.3.2000, QBD, (Creswell J).
[120] Exceptionally, O'Malley, S. and Layton, A. *European Civil Practice*, 1989, at pp.554–56; and in more detail, *Internationale Urteilsanerkennung*—Band. I, 1 Halbband: *Das EWG-Übereinkommen über die gerichtliche Zuständigkeit und die Vollstreckung gerichtlicher Entscheidungen in Zivil- und Handelssachen*, R. Geimer and R. Schütze, 1983, at pp.888 *et. seq.*; Aull, 1996; Stöve, 1993.
[121] It will be assumed that all clauses are expressed to be exclusive, Fawcett, J. 'Non-exclusive jurisdiction agreements in private international law' *(2001) LMCLQ* 234; note now that both categories A and B are effectively dealt with by the wording of Article 2 of the Hague Preliminary Draft Worldwide Judgments Convention.

Category C: One contracting party is domiciled in Contracting State X, the other in Contracting State Y and either (i) the Courts of Contracting State X, or (ii) the courts of Contracting State Y are chosen.

Category D:[122] *A non- Contracting State court is chosen and* either (i) both parties are domiciled in Contracting State X; or (ii) one party is domiciled in Contracting State X, the other in Contracting State Y; or (iii) one party is domiciled in Contracting State X, the other *in a non-Contracting State.*

Category E: A party domiciled in Contracting State X agrees with *a non-Contracting State party* to jurisdiction in either (i) the courts of Contracting State X[123] or (ii) the courts of Contracting State Y.

Category F: Both parties are *Non Contracting State* domiciliaries, and Contracting State X's courts are chosen.

Before each category[124] is examined, it is as well to dwell briefly on the Convention's Preamble[125]—the umbilical link the Convention has to the EC Treaty[126]—and bear each in mind when discussing Article 17's requirement of internationality: for the Convention makes it clear that one of its aims is 'to strengthen in the Community the legal protection of persons established therein'[127] and by dint thereof in the Convention 'the international jurisdiction'[128] of the Contracting State courts. These laudable aims neatly nestle under what was Article 220 (now Article 293) EC Treaty, and the supervisory jurisdiction[129] of one of the organs of what is now the European Union, the European Court of Justice.

---

[122] The emboldened phrases in each category emphasise the crucial importance of this particular permutation for the (non-) application of Article 17.

[123] The most controversial aspect, albeit with its own *forum non conveniens* addendum in England in *Mercury Communications Ltd and another v Communication Telesystems International* [1999] 2 All ER (Comm) 33, (Moore Bick J); *Sinochem International Oil (London) Ltd v Mobil Sales and Supply Corp Ltd (No.2)* [2000] 1 All ER (Comm) 758, at p.770, (Rix J).

[124] Due to the confines of space, category C will not be dealt with in any detail, not having provoked widespread comment or contention in this 'internationality' context.

[125] *OLG München,* 28.9.1989 (1991) *IPRax* 47, 'Die Präambel kann und muß aber auch für die übrigen Vorschriften herangezogen werden.'('the preamble can and must however also be brought into play for the remaining provisions'); Samtleben 'Internationale Gerichtsstandsvereinbarungen nach dem EWG-Übereinkommen und nach der Gerichtsstandsnovelle' (1974) NJW 1590, at p.1590: 'Die internationale Zuständigkeit der Gerichte der Vertragsstaaten soll nach der Präambel im Übereinkommen festgelegt werden.'('The international jurisdiction of the Contracting State courts ought to be established by the Convention's preamble').

[126] With the latest amendments by the Treaty of Amsterdam.

[127] 28.7.1990 [1990] C189/2 at p.2; compare the attitude of the Court of Appeal in *In re Harrods (Buenos Aires) Ltd* [1992] Ch 90

[128] *Ibid.*

[129] The Protocol on the interpretation by the Court of Justice of the Convention of 27 September 1968 on jurisdiction and enforcement of judgments in civil and commercial matters 28.7.1990 [1990] C189/25, Article 1.

The Convention then falls strangely silent, in its opening articles, as to any mention of, or need for, internationality in its scope *ratione materiae*. Article 1 merely defines its scope by reference to 'civil and commercial matters',[130] with a subsequent list of exclusions. Many of the ensuing articles in Title II themselves provide for jurisdiction in certain situations, which could only arise in cross-border cases. Indeed, it seems self-evident that the whole area of jurisdiction in the conflict of laws generally only arises when there is a foreign/international element.

The opening words of Article 17, governing whether the article's formal provisions operate at all, are, however, ambiguous:[131]

> If the parties, *one* or more of whom is domiciled in a Contracting State,[132] have agreed ... a court ... of *a* Contracting State ... [,] that court shall have exclusive jurisdiction ... .[133]

From a literal[134] reading, it appears that if one party,[135] domiciled in England, chooses the High Court in London for the resolution of its civil and commercial dispute, the preliminary requirements for Article 17's application *ratione materiae* will have been met.[136] *Prima facie*, then, it matters little whether the other contracting partner is domiciled in England,[137] in France,[138] or in New York.[139] From its wording, the article does not seem to prohibit one party *and* the prorogated forum from being in the same Contracting State: 'a Contracting State' does not

---

[130] For the meaning of 'civil and commercial', *inter alia*, cases cited in the introduction and *Sonntag v Waidmann* (C-172/91) [1993] ECR I-1963.

[131] Especially vis-à-vis Article 4, the crux of the problem in Category E(i) as to whether any element of 'internationality' is needed.

[132] Special care should be taken with Luxembourg domiciliaries: application of Article I of the Protocol in effect in *Tribunal de première instance de Bruxelles* 13.12.1996 *S.A. Bureau Gerard et autres c/ Seligmann et Société de droit luxembourgeois S.A.R.L. Alfred Seligman et cie* 1996 *Pas. Belge*, III, 18; *OGH* 16.1.2001 (2001) *ZfRV* 152.

[133] Jenard Report [1979] OJ C59/1 at p.38, discussing the scope of Article 17; the Schlosser Report tacitly remarks at [1979] OJ C59/71, p.81 para. 21 that 'only international legal relationships are affected'; *Finanziaria Commerciale & Co. SnC v Sago Srl, Corte di Cassazione, Sezioni unite*, No.2243, 1.1.1985, *Digest* I.17.1.1–B22; (1990) *JDI* 676 for the effect of the Italian language version of Article 17, which reads '. . . le parti, di cui almeno una domicilata nel territorio dello Stato contraente', ('the parties, one of whom at least is domiciled in the territory of *the* Contracting State . . .'), in Fazzalari, *Codice di procedura civile e norme complementari*, 1990, at p.503.

[134] D.Rhidian-Thomas, 1996, at p.311; for a list of those commentators who consider Article 17's wording as being self-sufficient Samtleben, (1995) 59 *RabelsZ* 670, at p.672.

[135] Kropholler, 1998 at p.228, para.1: 'es für die Anwendung dieser Vorschrift auf die jeweilige Kläger- oder Beklagtenrolle nicht ankommen soll' ('it should not depend, for the application of this provision, on the respective plaintiff's or defendant's rôle'); Gaudemet-Tallon, 1996, at p.76, para. 106 'Peu importe que la partie domicilieé dans un État contractant soit demandeur ou défendeur'.

[136] *Contra British Aerospace Plc. v Dee Howard Co.* [1993] 1 Lloyd's Rep. 368 (Waller J); *Mercury Communications Ltd and another v Communication Telesystems International* [1999] 2 All ER (Comm) 33, (Moore Bick J); *Sinochem International Oil (London) Ltd v Mobil Sales and Supply Corp Ltd (No.2)* [2000] 1 All ER (Comm) 758, at p.770 (Rix J); *Society of Lloyd's v White and others*, 3.3.2000, QBD (Creswell J).

[137] 2.1.1 below, at pp.177 *et seq*, the situation in Category A.

[138] 2.1.3, the situation in Category C.

[139] 2.1.5(i), the situation in Category E(i).

have tacitly included in it 'a [different] Contracting State';[140] there is no 'in-built' internationality in the provision itself,[141] as in other articles.[142] Internationality has been supplied from the Preamble.[143] It would seem inconsistent, therefore, for a court to apply the Convention to a 'civil and commercial matter'[144] with no reference to internationality, and yet not thereafter also apply Article 17. Either internationality applies at the outset of the Convention's scope, or not at all. However, this is not the view held by the experts responsible for the *travaux préparatoires*[145] in situations of a purely domestic nature, Category A above, reviewed presently; nor has it been the view of certain German appeal courts[146] when a non-Contracting State domiciliary is a party to a jurisdiction clause,[147] in Category E above, reviewed in section 2.1.5.

2.1.1 Category A: Both parties to the contract are domiciled in Contracting State X, and the courts of Contracting State X are chosen[148]

(i) From Contracting State X's perspective—the prorogation aspect

Clearly, at least as far as the courts of Contracting State X are concerned, this is a purely internal/domestic situation, where no reference is necessary to Article 17. The case may well otherwise involve 'civil and commercial' elements, yet the tacit[149] acceptance of the need for internationality means that Article 17 will not be applied. The Convention's aim, as mentioned above, is only to determine 'the international jurisdiction of the courts'.[150] The Schlosser Report echoes the need for a cross-border element:

> only proceedings ... about matters involving international legal relationships are affected.[151]

---

[140] Samtleben, (1995) 59 *RabelsZ* 670, at p.675, 'Ist damit ein anderer Vertragsstaat als der des Wohnsitzes gemeint?'('Is it meant by this, another Contracting State other than the one of the seat?').
[141] But *OLG München*, 28.9.1989, (1991) *IPRax* 47, below, at p.201.
[142] As in Article 5(1) for example.
[143] Droz, 1972, at p.116, para. 181, 'Il faut enfin, mais c'est une portée générale, qu'il s'agisse de *raports internationaux*'.
[144] Where, in Article 1 there is no mention of the Preamble's requirement of internationality.
[145] Below, at n.151.
[146] Especially *OLG München*, 8.3.1989, IPRspr. 1989, Nr.186, [1991] I.L.Pr., p.298; *OLG München* 28.9.1989, IPRspr. 1989, Nr.194.
[147] For a criticism of the unwarranted additions to Article 17's wording by these courts Geimer, (1991) *IPRax* 31.
[148] Schlosser, 1996, at p.104, Article 17 'gilt ... für reine Inlandsfälle nicht'('does not count for purely internal cases').
[149] At least from a combination of the preamble and Article 17, Jenard Report at pp.37–8.
[150] *Ibid.*
[151] Schlosser Report [1979] OJ C59/71; and comments by Huet reviewing *Ollo c/ Caisse de Crédit mutuel de Brest Recouvrance* 27.3.1987 (1988) *JDI* 140, at p.141.

The question we are concerned with here is whether any particular elements of a given case convert a domestic relationship such as in the scenario above, into an international one[152] so as to implicate Article 17: obvious elements would include a dispute involving title to, or rent from, foreign tenancies/land, where the exclusive jurisdiction of Article 16 would, in any event, override[153] any jurisdiction clause. Less certain is the possibility that the parties may have agreed to make delivery[154] to Contracting State Y.[155] Contracting State Y's courts would have jurisdiction over either party as the place of performance of the obligation in question,[156] viz. to deliver. It is generally agreed that where the jurisdiction of another Contracting State is implicated by some other provision of the Convention,[157] an otherwise domestic case, as in Category A, would be elevated into an international one, sufficient[158] to call for the application of Article 17.[159]

(ii)   From Contracting State Y's perspective—the derogation aspect[160]

Clearly, the very fact that the case is able to be heard in Contracting State Y at all, *a fortiori*, stamps the case as international; the courts in Y, where jurisdiction

---

[152] Bonassies, 1995 DMF 1985, p.83 at p.95, Article 17 would not apply here 'même si le litige concerné contient des éléments internationaux, s'agissant, par exemple, d'un transport Italie-France . . .'.

[153] For a choice of another Contracting State court Category B.

[154] Delivery did not make for internationality in *AG Köln*, 6.2.1985, IPRspr. (1985) Nr.133, where two German firms agreed to the jurisdiction of Cologne; the dispute centred on the carriage of goods by road to France; 'Nur Vereinbarungen über die interntionalen Zuständigkeit unterfallen—arg. Abs.4 der Präambel—dem Regelungsbereich des Article 17' ('Only agreements on international jurisdiction—according to para. 4 of the preamble—come under Article 17's sphere of application') IPRspr. 1985, Nr.133, at p.359; *contra* Krings, below, following footnote.

[155] Krings, E. 'Réfexions au sujet de la prorogation de compétence territoriale et du for contractuel' (1978) *Rev. dr. internat. dr. comparé*, p.78, at p.90, 'Deux parties domiciliées dans le même État contractant peuvent avoir un litige qui présente un élément d'extranéité découlant p.ex. du lieu d'exécution du contrat'; Gaudemet-Tallon, 1996, and Kropholler, 1998 at p.229–30; and Hill, J. *The Law Relating to International Commercial Disputes*, 2nd edn., 1998, at pp.107–08, para. 5.3.9 in favour of internationality in this situation.

[156] If the basis of the plaintiff's claim related in some way to delivery, *de Bloos Sprl v Bouyer* (14/76) [1976] ECR 1497 and *Custom Made Commercial Ltd v Stawa Metallbau GmbH* (C-288/92) [1994] ECR I-2913, above, chapter 1, at pp.119–159.

[157] Jackson takes an extremely wide view of Article 17's sphere of application, that is 'to a jurisdiction agreement in any claim involving any foreign element . . . even if the parties are domiciled in the same State, Article 17 may apply whether the court selected is a court of that or any other Contracting State . . .' Jackson, 2nd edn., 1996, at pp.112–113.

[158] Kropholler, 1998 at p.229, para. 2: 'Die Frage der internationalen Zuständigkeit wird bei Vereinbarung eines inländischen Gerichts *immer dann relevant*, wenn dadurch die Zuständigkeit eines ausländischen Gerichts *derogiert wird.*'('the question of international jurisdiction—by agreeing an internal court—*only becomes of relevance*, when the jurisdiction of an external court is *thereby derogated*') and Samtleben, (1995) 59 *RabelsZ* 670, at p.684, and p.695.

[159] Should one of the parties actually commence proceedings in Contracting State Y, in breach of the jurisdiction clause, the question of Article 17's application in this case would be crucial, at least in the current climate in England, with reference to anti-suit injunctions: *Continental Bank v Aeakos* [1994] 1 WLR 588, CA; *OT Africa Line Ltd v Hijazy and others (The 'Kribi')* [2001] 1 Lloyd's Rep. 76 (Aikens J).

[160] Samtleben, (1995) 59 *RabelsZ* 670, at p.695: 'der Derogationseffekt in den übrigen Vertragsstaaten hingegen ist nach Article 17 EuGVÜ zu beurteilen.'('the derogation effect in the remaining Contracting States is, however, to be judged according to Article 17').

would have been possible under, presumably, one of the 'special jurisdiction' bases in Section 2[161] of the Convention, should decline jurisdiction under Article 17, because they are a *forum derogatum*.[162]

2.1.2   Category B: Both parties to the contract are domiciled in Contracting State X, yet the courts of Contracting State Y are chosen[163]

The consensus of (the majority of non-German) academic opinion[164] appears to be that, at least from the perspective of Contracting State X's courts, *qua fora derogata*, a choice of another forum provides the stamp of internationality necessary to move the case into Article 17's sphere of application.[165] The Jenard Report states that Article 17 would be applicable in a Category B case.[166] The Schlosser Report is not specific either way, but seems to think that internationality would not be understood simply by prorogating another Contracting State's courts, even if all the other elements were purely internal to one State.[167] Yet the *OLG Hamm*[168] has recently sided with the Schlosser Report view.[169] Two German companies in Westphalia had agreed to submit any disputes to the 'Swiss courts', and later orally, and more specifically, for those in Zurich. The appeal court refused[170] to apply

---

[161] The only way a defendant, domiciled in Contracting State X, could be sued elsewhere, unless it submits under Article 18, Article 16 applies, or the provisions of Sections 3 or 4 apply.

[162] The similar situation in Category E(i) below, at pp.192 *et seq*, and Droz, 1972, at p.121, para. 191, who, from Contracting State Y's perspective, would 'comme international tout accord . . . qui exclut la compétence normal' under the Convention, i.e. Articles 5 and 6.

[163] Gaudemet-Tallon, 1996, at p.82, para. 113; and Gothot, G. et Holleaux, D. *La Convention de Bruxelles du 27 septembre 1968: compétence judiciaire et effets des jugements dans la CEE*, 1985, at p.99; Schmidt, M. 'Kann Schweigen auf eine Gerichtsstandsklausel in AGB einen Gerichtsstand nach Article 17 EuGVÜ/LuganoÜ begrunden?' (1992) *RIW* 173, at p.176: 'Sobald die Prorogation auf ein Gericht eines Vertragsstaates zur Derogation der Zuständigkeit der Gerichte anderer Vertragsstaaten führt, kann von einer im Rahmen des EuGVÜ "internationalen" Gerichtsstandsvereinbarung gesprochen werden.'('As soon as prorogating a Contracting State court leads to the derogation of another Contracting State court's jurisdiction, can one speak of an 'international' jurisdiction clause in the framework of the Brussels Convention').

[164] Jenard Report, [1979] OJ C59/1, at p.38; *contra* Gaudemet-Tallon, 1996, at p.83, nor the views of *OLG Hamm* 18.9.1997 (1999) *IPRax* 244, at p.245 either.

[165] Strongly supported by Hill, 1998, at p.107, para. 5.3.9; *contra* Huet in (1988) *JDI* 140, at p.141; Article 17 Lugano Convention *not* mentioned in a dispute between two German companies, with a jurisdiction clause in favour of courts of Biel, Switzerland: *OLG Stuttgart* 19.12.2000 (2001) *RIW* 228, at p.229—domestic provisions of §38 Abs. 1 ZPO applied instead (without reasons).

[166] *Ibid.*; as mentioned above, Article 2(1)(a) of the draft Hague Worldwide Judgments Convention appears to have resolved this problem by specific wording to this situation.

[167] Schlosser Report, [1979] OJ C59/71, at pp.123–24.

[168] 18.9.1997 (1999) *IPRax* 244.

[169] This court required more than merely prorogating the courts of another (Lugano) Contracting State in order for Article 17 to be applicable in a Category B case; not reversed on appeal *BGH* 23.7.1998 (1999) *IPRax* 246.

[170] Considered incorrect by Matthias, J. 'Zur isolierten Prorogation nach Article 17 Abs.1 LugÜ' (1999) *IPRax* 226, at p.227; *OLG Stuttgart* 19.11.2000 (2001) *RIW* 228 did *not* even mention Article 17 in a category B case.

Article 17 of the Lugano Convention, in this Category B case. Its reasons were what the court saw as a lack of an international relationship:

> Nach der überwiegenden Literaturmeinung muß zwar ein internationaler Bezug,[171] nicht aber ein Bezug zu einem anderen Vertragsstaat bestehen . . . [und] der internationale Bezug . . . nicht durch die Wahl der Gerichte eines bestimmten Staates in der Gerichtsstandsvereinbarung selbst hergestellt werden [kann].[172]

The reviewer is puzzled why the court did not apply Article 17 of Lugano Convention, because sufficient 'internationality', in his view,[173] was proved by the fact that both *forum prorogatum* and *derogatum* were in different (Lugano) Convention Contracting States.

As far as the courts in Contracting State Y are concerned, should they become seised as *fora prorogata*, it is unarguable that they should decide the jurisdictional issue under Article 17, since the wording *ratione materiae* of Article 17 is clearly fulfilled.[174]

The likelihood of a court being inclined to find internationality and apply Article 17 does indeed seem to depend on whether it is being asked to decline jurisdiction or not: witness two cases, one from Italy, the other German, between the same parties, involving the same cause of action, which illustrate differing conclusions reached according to whether the court is seised as *forum derogatum*[175] or *prorogatum*.[176] The first, a now famous decision of the *Corte di Cassazione*,[177] in April 1985,[178] ruled, as *forum derogatum*, that there was insufficient internationality in a Category B case for the application of Article 17. Two Italian companies had decided[179] to agree, in their contract of share transfer in two Munich companies, to settle their disputes before the courts of Munich. A finding of a lack of internationality meant that Article 2 of the Italian Code of Civil Procedure[180]

---

[171] What the German courts have seen as an *unwritten/tacit prerequisite* for Article 17's application; internationality was not proven by showing that the products in dispute were produced in Turkey.

[172] ('according to overwhelming academic views there must be an international relationship, but not a relation to another Contracting State . . . [and] an international relationship cannot be supplied by the choice of a court in a specific State in the jurisdiction clause'), *OLG Hamm* 18.9.1997 (1999) *IPRax* 244, at p.245.

[173] Matthias, above n. 170, at p.228.

[174] OLG *München* below, at p.200.

[175] The Italian courts: *Finanziaria Commerciale & Co. SnC v Sago Srl Corte di Cassazione, Sezioni unite*, No.2243, 1.1.1985, *Digest* I.17.1.1–B22; (1990) JDI 676; *contra OLG München* 13.2.1985, *Digest* I-21–B10.

[176] The German courts: *OLG München* 13.2.1985, IPRspr. 1985, Nr.133A.

[177] *Finanziaria Commerciale* 1.1.1985, *Digest* I.17.1.1–B22.

[178] Now the (new) Italian Private International Law, 31.5.1995, in force from 1st September 1995, especially Article 4 and 'Internationale Zuständigkeit und anwendbares Recht im italienischen IPR-Gesetz von 1995' Kindler, P. (1997) *RabelsZ* 227; also Starace, V. 'Le champ de la juridiction selon la loi de réforme du système italien de droit international privé' (1996) *Rev crit* 67 at p.77 *et seq.*

[179] Presumably because the contract had been concluded, and the shares held, in Germany.

[180] The non-derogation prohibition in the old, pre 1.5.1995, Article 2 used to prohibit an agreed derogation except in favour of an international dispute—G. Vinci *Il novo codice di procedura civile*, 1994, at p.150.

applied, prohibiting any derogation from the Italian courts.[181] The Supreme Court also went on to hold that the 'protection'[182] afforded to clauses under the Convention should only apply when the Contracting parties are domiciled in different[183] Contracting States.

The case has been criticised;[184] but the impression from reading the report is that the Italian court was loath,[185] as *forum derogatum,* to allow two Italian domiciliaries to evade the application of the domestic prohibition in Article 2 Cpc, merely by prorogating another Contracting State court.

The inverse side of the litigation[186] in Germany produced a different finding as to the application of Article 17:[187] here the article was found to apply

> wenn beide Vertragsparteien ihren Sitz in *einem* Vertragsstaat haben und die Zuständigkeit des Gerichts eines *anderen* Vertragsstaats vereinbaren.[188]

The application of Article 17 should not depend, as these two cases demonstrate, either here or generally, on the forum seised of the dispute;[189] nor its attitude to an Article 17 jurisdiction clause depend on whether it is *forum prorogatum*

---

[181] The liberating innovation in Article 4 II of the new Italian Private International Law, *Legge 21 Maggio 1995,* N.218, which states in the English translation (Montanari, A. *Conflict of Laws in Italy, The Text and an English translation of Italian Law No.218 of May 31, 1995,* 1997), 'Italian jurisdiction may be excluded in favor of a foreign court . . . if the agreement to do so is proved in writing and the matter involves waivable rights'; *Le nuove leggi civili commentate,* N.5–6, Anno XIX, settembre-diciembre, p.877, at p.918, annotations by Carbone S, especially at p.932: 'la sua profonda portata innovata respetto all'abrogato Article 2 CpC'('its profound innovatory effect respecting the abrogation of Article 2 CpC').

[182] An acknowledgment of the harshness of Article 2 CpC, now abrogated since 1.9.1995—'Das anachronistische Derogationsverbot im früheren Article 2 CpC is damit gefallen'('The anachronistic prohibition on derogating in the former Article 2 CpC has gone'), Kindler, P., (1997) *RabelsZ* 227, at p.247.

[183] Admittedly, the Court had to deal with a grammatical solecism in the Italian language version of Article 17, (1990) *JDI* at p.676; other language versions, however, are equally authentic, as provided in Article 68, and were available for consideration.

[184] (1990) *JDI* 676; contrast the opposite conclusion in another case *OLG Köln* 9.2.1990 IPRspr. 1991, Nr.165, at p.320: 'da beide Parteien ihren Sitz innerhalb der Bundesrepublik, also innerhalb eines Vertragstaats . . . und da die Vereinbarung mit der Wahl des Gerichtsstands Rotterdam auch Auslandsberührung hat'('since both parties have their seat inside Germany, that is a Contracting State . . . and since the agreement with a choice of Rotterdam jurisdiction also has an external point of reference'); Article 17 was held by the *OLG Köln* court, as *forum derogatum,* to be applicable when the plaintiff and defendant German domiciliaries respectively, chose the courts of Rotterdam.

[185] The Italian court may be excused because the Italian version of Article 17 reads 'domicile of one of the parties in *the* territory of the Contracting State ['*dello* Stato contraente']' chosen; (1990) *JDI* 676, at p.677.

[186] The German action was for damages and specific performance; the earlier Italian action had been for a negative declaration. The German court's findings that the actions were not the same for Article 21 purposes can no longer be seen as correct in the light of *Gubischmaschinen Fabrik K.G. v Palumbo* (144/86) [1987] ECR 4861; and *The Tatry* (C-406/92) [1994] ECR I-5439.

[187] *Digest* I-21–B9.

[188] ('When both parties have their seat in *one* Contracting State and agree to the jurisdiction of the courts in *another* Contracting State') IPRspr. 1985, Nr.133A, at p.361, a classic example of a Category B case.

[189] Below, at pp.197 *et seq* p.77, Category E(i).

or *derogatum*.[190] The Convention would simply become unworkable if residual national procedural laws could (re-)assert themselves on such a set of facts in one Contracting State, yet be suppressed by another Contracting State, by a criterion that does not even appear in the article itself. The Italian court simply did not apply the Convention at all,[191] yet the German court applied it *in toto*; the only distinction between the two courts being *forum derogatum* and *prorogatum*. The application of the Convention cannot depend[192] in this way on which court is seised.

2.1.3   Category C: One contracting party is domiciled in Contracting State X, the other in Contracting State Y, and the courts of either Contracting State X, Y or Z are chosen

Clearly, this category is the most commonly encountered situation,[193] where the parties have intra-Community dealings. The case of Article 17's actual application in practice in Category C has not been doubted[194] in the innumerable decisions of the Contracting State courts.[195] It does not matter which party appears as plaintiff/claimant or defendant, or which forum is seised, *qua prorogatum* or *derogatum*. In Category C there will always be an element of internationality, either from the wording of Article 17 itself,[196] or from the factual connection[197] between the parties and courts in two Contracting States.

---

[190] *Anema B.V. v Brockman Motorships B.V.* [1991] I.L.Pr. 285, at p.287 where the *Arrondissementsrechtbank* Rotterdam, as *forum derogatum*, Genoa as *prorogatum*, at least judged the clause's validity against Article 17; *OLG Köln* 9.2.1990 IPRspr. 1990 Nr.165, at p.320, as *forum derogatum*, Article 17 was deployed. It was also clear that there was no hint from the German court's judgment of the Italian court's reticence to find any international elements in the case; for more examples of such international elements in Category B, (1989) *IPRax* 80, at p.81.

[191] The Italian case would, after 1.9.1995, be decided under Article 4 of the new Private International Law; due to the drafting solecism of the Italian text of Article 17, however, it is unlikely that Article 17 would be applied.

[192] 'Internationality' has not been solved by Article 23 of the Brussels I Regulation, which retains the current wording of Article 17.

[193] A 'Normalfall' ('normal case') Samtleben, (1995) 59 *RabelsZ* 670, at p.685.

[194] Kropholler, 1998 p.229, para. 3.

[195] In Germany, for example, *OLG Düsseldorf*, 8.2.1979, IPRspr. 1979, Nr.156A; *OLG München*, 11.2.1981, IPRspr. 1981, Nr.154; *OLG Stuttgart*, 9.11.1990, (1992) *IPRax*, p.86, [1992] I.L.Pr. 188; *OLG Saarbrücken* 2.10.1991, (1992) *IPRax* 165; *BGH* 9.3.1994, (1994) *NJW* 2699; *LG München*, 29.5.1995, (1996) *IPRax* 266 (Article 17 Lugano); in France, for example *Cour d'Appel de Paris*, 25.4.1979 (1979) *JDI* 352; *Cour d'Appel de Paris*, 8.6.1988, [1990] I.L.Pr. 102; *Cour de Cassation* 9.1.1996, [1996] I.L.Pr. 495; *Høyesteretts Kjæremålsutvlag* (Norwegian Supreme Court), 3.2.1995, [1996] I.L.Pr. 400; in England *Kurz v Stella Musical Veranstaltungs GmbH* [1992] 1 All ER 630, Ch.D. (Hoffmann J) and *Credit Suisse Financial Products v Société Generale d'Enterprises*, [1997] CLC 168, CA; *OT Africa Line Ltd v Hijazy and others (The 'Kribi')* [2001] 1 Lloyd's Rep. 76 (Aikens J).

[196] The literalists' view of Article 17's scope, below, at p.193.

[197] For the additionalists' reliance on 'ungeschriebene Anwendungsgrenzen' ('unwritten boundaries for applicability'), and their 'Reduktionstheorie' ('reduction/limiting theory') below, at p.194.

In the English case of *Ultisol Transport Contractors Ltd v Bouygues Offshore S.A.*,[198] the plaintiff Bermudan company, managed in The Netherlands and (presumably) domiciled there, agreed with the French defendant company Bouygues in a towage contract for jurisdiction of the English High Court. The interest in the case stems not from the fact that there was any disagreement as to Article 17's application *ratione personae*, but that Article 17 was interpreted in such a way as not to exclude[199] the jurisdiction of a non-Contracting State court, South Africa, the French company having already commenced proceedings for damages there.

The only remaining issue[200] of this section, apart from the formal, substantive prerequisites for exclusivity of the Article 17 jurisdiction clauses themselves, which can only be touched on, is the relevant time 'domicile' is to be measured under Article 17.[201]

The time when the parties' domicile is relevant for Article 17 has not been conclusively decided by the ECJ.[202] The consensus of opinion is that this time is when the jurisdiction clause/contract is concluded.[203] The answer to the question of timing is only dependent on whether one considers, as Samtleben correctly points out,[204] Article 17 to be a judicial 'Prüfungsmaßstab'[205] or a contractual 'Verhaltungsregel'[206]—by which the parties orientate themselves on contracting. There is much to be said that both are relevant—that if, either at the time of contracting or commencement, a party has its domicile in a Contracting State, Article 17 will have its application. If the time of commencement is the unique point in time, it

---

[198] [1996] 2 Lloyd's Rep. 140 (Clarke J); Article 17 not referred to by the CA, [1998] 2 Lloyd's Rep. 461.
[199] *Ibid.* at p.147; Briggs, (1998) *BYBIL* 332, at pp.342–43; the same conclusion was reached in a Category E(i) case in *Mercury Communications Ltd and another v Communication Telesystems International* [1999] 2 All ER (Comm) 33, (Moore Bick J); *Implants International Ltd. v Stratec Medical* [1999] 2 All ER (Comm) 933, (Leeds Mercantile Ct) (Judge McGonigal).
[200] Note that this issue always arises, whatever category is under consideration.
[201] For timing of 'domicile' in other Articles *Canada Trust Co. and others v Stolzenberg and others (Nr. 2)* [2002] 1 AC 1 (on issue of proceedings); other requirements which cannot be dealt with in this section are the self-sufficiency of Art.17 and the effect of additional national law requirements as to a jurisdiction clause's form—again, held to be irrelevant recently by *Hugo Trumpy* (C-159/97) [1999] ECR I-1597, at p.1652, para. 35.
[202] But *Sanicentral GmbH v René Collin* (25/79)[1979] ECR 3423, at p.3429, para. 6, 'such a clause has no legal effect for so long as no judicial proceedings have been commenced and only becomes of consequence at the date when judicial proceedings are set in motion'; this suggests that Article 17 is to be considered as a judicial 'yardstick'—*Dicey and Morris*, 2000, Vol .I, at p.431, para. 12–088.
[203] Droz, 'Entreé en vigeur de la Convention de Bruxelles révisée sur la Convention de Lugano' (1987) *Rev crit* 251, at p.280; but also earlier Droz, 1972., at p.118, para. 184, where either time was considered valid; Gaudemet-Tallon, 1996, at p.84 prefers the proceedings' commencement; but her earlier conflicting comment on *Cour d'Appel de Paris*, 14.11.1990 (1991) *Rev crit* 734, at p.742: 'la clause nous paraît devoir être apprécié *au moment où elle a été conclue*' ('the clause appears to us to be assessed at the moment it was concluded')—*contra*, it seems *OLG Hamm* 22.2.1999 (2000) *RIW* 382, and *LG Bochum* 25.8.1997 (2000) *RIW* 382, where Article 17 was applied to a clause concluded in a contract from 1975 between German claimants and Spanish defendants.
[204] Samtleben, (1995) 59 *RabelsZ* 670, at p.703; *EuGVÜ: Europäisches Gerichtsstands- und Vollstreckungsübereinkommen mit Luganer Übereinkommen*, P. Schlosser, 1996, at p.106.
[205] ('yardstick'), *ibid.* in which case the commencement of proceedings is the relevant time.
[206] ('a behavioural rule'), *ibid.* when the time of contracting is important.

should not be open to a party to evade the exclusivity of Article 17 merely by moving its seat/domicile to a non-Contracting State after the conclusion of the agreement—it is at this latter time that the reciprocal consequences of contracting are realised.[207] Conversely, it would be anomalous not to admit the commencement date as an additional, or alternative, factor—if a party who does not have its seat at the time of contracting subsequently relocates within the European Union, should it not also benefit from the protection of Article 17 and the Convention as a whole?[208]

2.1.4   Category D: A non- Contracting State court is chosen[209] and either: (i) both parties are domiciled in Contracting State X; or (ii) one party is domiciled in Contracting State X,[210] the other in Contracting State Y; or (iii) one party is domiciled in Contracting State X, the other in a non-Contracting State

The wording of Article 17 itself states that the prorogated court must be that of a Contracting State before the article is applicable.[211] The problem of this Category D does not directly reveal a question of the interpretation of Article 17 *per se*. However, important considerations arise regarding jurisdiction clauses and Article 4 of the Convention.

The situation in Category D(i), although otherwise a purely internal matter, could be argued to involve a clash of Convention jurisdiction[212] with the 'foreign' jurisdiction clause, whichever party emerges as the plaintiff/claimant; if this view is not accepted, then, as in England, the normal common law rules on stays[213] will be applicable.

If an action were commenced in England, a Category D(ii) case would involve a clash between the foreign jurisdiction clause and Convention jurisdiction,

---

[207] Droz, 1972, at p.118, para. 184—a 'Verhaltungsregel'.

[208] *Ibid.* at p.118, para. 185, 'eine richterliche Prüfungsnorm' ('a judicial test rule').

[209] Geimer in Geimer, R. and Schütze, R. *Internationale Urteilsanerkennung*, 1983, at p.894; *Cour de Cassation*, 7.12.1983, (1984) *Rev. Crit.* 658, where the courts of Madrid (then a non-Contracting State) were chosen by a French and Spanish plaintiff and defendant respectively. The court held, at p.695, that Article 17 did not apply, and could not be invoked by the defendant, because it did not have its seat in a Contracting State; Gaudemet-Tallon, at p.660, thought that the better solution to Article 17's non-application was that 'les tribunaux désignés ici étant ceux de Madrid, l'Article 17 ne pouvait donc être invoqué' ('the courts designated here were those of Madrid, Article 17 could not be invoked').

[210] For the sake of clarity in Category D, it will be assumed, unless otherwise stated, that the plaintiff is domiciled in Contracting State X, the action is commenced, in breach of the 'foreign' jurisdiction clause, in Contracting State X, and that X is England.

[211] Kropholler, 1998, at pp.233–34, para. 12.

[212] Under Article 2.

[213] At least in England; in Germany especially *BGH* 20.1.1986, IPRspr. (1986) Nr.129; and Roth, G 'Zur Derogation der deutschen Gerichtszuständigkeit' (1987) *IPRax* 141, applying §38 II ZPO, which demands that at least one party 'keinen allgemeinen Gerichtsstand im Inland hat' ('has no general internal jurisdiction'), not the case here; but *contra*, Geimer, (1986) *NJW* 1439, para. 5, who maintains that the Convention applies in this case because the defendant was domiciled in Germany.

Article 2,[214] or potentially between a 'special' Convention jurisdiction, e.g. under Article 5(1).[215] Category D(ii) raises the issue of whether respect for the 'foreign' jurisdiction clause will depend on either the domicile of the plaintiff/claimant, or the Convention article that will be ousted.

A Category D(iii) case involves a clash between the 'foreign' jurisdiction clause and Article 4[216] of the Convention, if the Contracting State X domiciliary appears as plaintiff/claimant.[217] If, however, the non-Contracting State party should appear as plaintiff/claimant, the only caveat is whether he should be treated any differently when commencing proceedings than a Contracting State plaintiff/claimant.

The fundamental question in the English courts is whether there is a discretion to stay[218] proceedings, irrespective of their legal basis, when an action is commenced here in breach of a 'foreign' jurisdiction clause; and whether the Brussels Convention has had any impact[219] on that discretion. This question in turn hinges on the exact scope and function assigned to the Brussels Convention in either a European or global context.[220]

The discretion to stay in Category D(i)—where both parties are domiciled in the same Contracting State—either at common law, or arguably, under any residual discretion under Article 2 of the Convention, will be dealt with presently in Category D(ii).

2.1.4(ii) Category D(ii)[221]—two different Contracting State parties

(a) Plaintiff/claimant domiciled in another Contracting State If, in this context, English and French companies agree to submit their disputes to the courts of New York, what response[222] should an English court give to an action commenced by

---

[214] If the plaintiff is domiciled in Contracting State Y.

[215] If the plaintiff is domiciled in England (X). A defendant domiciled in Contracting State Y may only be sued in X, *inter alia*, under the 'special' rules of jurisdiction in Title II, Section 2 especially Articles 5 and 6, for example in England as the place of performance of the obligation in question, or as a co-defendant under Article 6(1).

[216] Article 4 leaves jurisdiction over non-Contracting State domiciliaries, subject solely to Article 16, to 'the law of that State', including the 'exorbitant' bases of jurisdiction listed in Article 3 para. 2.

[217] Hill, 1998, at p.108, para. 5.3.10 (who correctly believes that Article 17 does not apply); if the non-Contracting State domiciliary appears as plaintiff, the foreign jurisdiction clause will clash with either Article 2, or possibly Article 5.

[218] *Inter alia, The El Amria* [1981] 2 Lloyd's Rep. 119 (Brandon LJ) for pre- and non-Convention cases.

[219] The position with regard to *forum non conveniens In Re Harrods (Buenos Aires) Ltd* [1992] Ch.72; Harman J at p.76, revs'd, CA, at p.90—where there was said still to be a discretion to decline jurisdiction in favour of the courts of a non-Contracting State where jurisdiction is taken under Article 2.

[220] Dillon LJ's views in *Re Harrods* above, *ibid.* at p.97 onwards, that the Convention is merely an agreement between the Contracting State among themselves.

[221] Where the courts of a non-Contracting State are chosen, one party is domiciled in Contracting State X, the other Y; Article 17 is inapplicable, the only question being 'can there be a stay'?

[222] If the domicile of the plaintiff is irrelevant, then there is a strong case for a stay on the grounds enumerated in *El Amria* [1981] 2 Lloyd's Rep. 119; *The Nile Rhapsody* [1994] 1 Lloyd's Rep. 382, CA; if however the fact that the plaintiff is domiciled in a Contracting State has any bearing, the problem

the French company, in England, under Article 2? These facts have received little if any attention.[223] Strictly, Article 17 is of no use, as the article requires the choice of a Contracting State court.[224]

Should an answer to the question of whether a stay may be granted hinge on the plaintiff/claimant's domicile,[225] or on the (expressed) mandatory nature of Article 2? The wording of Article 2 seems explicit on this point. As there are no other provisions of the Convention applicable in this situation, i.e. the '[s]ubject to the provisions of this Convention' requirement of Article 2 does not operate, the English company '*shall . . . be sued*' in England. There appears to be no discretion. Briggs deals with the issue of 'foreign' jurisdiction clauses, and remarks that:

> if the plaintiff[226] seeks to invoke the jurisdiction of the courts of the defendant's domicile, it is not certain that the Court of Justice would permit a court to decline to exercise it.[227]

This is certainly true, but it would seem strange if the ECJ would countenance the taking of jurisdiction under the Convention that would involve the parties in a breach of contract. The answer given by Briggs[228]—(when it is the plaintiff/claimant is domiciled in a non Contracting State[229])—would also seem, by analogy, to be a correct and logical answer[230] where, as here, the plaintiff/claimant is domiciled in France:

---

becomes more acute, and Bingham LJ's views in *Nile Rhapsody* that the Convention's Article 2 does not apply are no longer, or perhaps less, valid.

[223] But Dillon LJ's views in *Re Harrods*, that Article 2 does not have mandatory effect, at p.97, but arguably only with regard to non-Contracting State plaintiffs; Huber, 1994, at p.193 *et seq.*

[224] Briggs, 1997, at p.72, para. 2.92.

[225] As regards the plaintiff's domicile in a non-Contracting State, the answer is fairly certain—Category D(iii) below.

[226] Above n.224; no further identification of the plaintiff's domicile is made, perhaps because it is thought irrelevant, but below, at p.187. The context in which Briggs expresses himself, at p.72 suggests a non-Contracting State plaintiff is meant; Gaudemet-Tallon, 1996, at p.80, para. 111: 'Si les parties ont inséré dans leur contrat une clause attributive de juridiction aux tribunaux des Étas-Unis, . . . et que le demandeur saisit cependant un tribunal d'un État [contractant] . . . au motif que s'y trouve le domicile du défendeur, *ce tribunal devra accueillir l'exception d'incompétence soulevée par le défendeur en faveur des tribunaux américains régulièrement choisis par les parties.*' ('if the parties have inserted a jurisdiction clause into their contract for the courts of the United States, *this court should accept the plea of incompetence raised by the defendant in favour of the American courts properly chosen by the parties*'); '[R]égulièrement' would seem to mean here 'otherwise in accordance with autonomous national law', in casu, Article 48 NCPC or *The El Amria, Dicey and Morris*, 13th edn., 2000, Rule 32(2), at p.424 *et seq.*

[227] Briggs, 1997, at p.72.

[228] *Ibid.* at p.73.

[229] Category D(iii) below.

[230] If the plaintiff's domicile is irrelevant; the 'reflexive effects doctrine', below, at p.188, which could be invoked here.

An English court should be entitled to give effect to a choice of court clause (by staying its proceedings) for a non-contracting state if it, England, has jurisdiction from a provision lower in the hierarchy,[231] such as that given by article 2 or article 4[232]

The rôle of the plaintiff/claimant should, in principle, have little to do with the question, but conversely the links with the Community Convention are *a fortiori* much stronger when both plaintiff/claimant and defendant are domiciled in Contracting States.

It is at least arguable that the conditions under which it is now generally accepted in England, that there is a discretion[233] to stay jurisdiction when plaintiff/claimant and prorogated forum are located in non-contracting states,[234] may *not* be appropriately assimilated to a case where *both* litigants are Contracting State domiciliaries. In the English cases where stays have been ordered, *Re Harrods (Buenos Aires) Ltd*[235] and *The Nile Rhapsody*,[236] the applicant/plaintiffs' respective domiciles in the non-Contracting States of (then) Switzerland[237] and Egypt did not represent what was presumed by the Court of Appeal to be one purpose of the Brussels Convention—'an agreement between the contracting states among themselves'.[238] Whatever the merits of this approach,[239] it is submitted that the Convention's 'mandatory system'[240] is restored when *both* parties are Contracting State domiciliaries.

(b) Plaintiff/claimant domiciled in England and Wales If, in our example, the litigant companies' rôles are reversed—i.e. the English company sues the French company in England under, for e.g. Article 5(1) or 6(2), *in breach* of a New York jurisdiction clause, similar questions arise.

One possible answer to this situation was found by the District Court of Rotterdam on 2 December 1994 in *Dynamex International Shipping & Forwarding BV(Netherlands) v Mediterranean Shipping Co. SA (Switzerland).*[241] The Dutch court had to consider a claim by the Dutch plaintiff consignee,

---

[231] *Quaere,* than Article 17.

[232] *Quaere,* whether Article 17 should even be in the hierarchy in this context, since it does not apply.

[233] Gaudemet-Tallon, below, at p.189 n.259.

[234] *The Nile Rhapsody* [1994] 1 Lloyd's Rep. 382, CA, by analogy, from *Re Harrods (Buenos Aires) Ltd* [1992] Ch.72 .

[235] [1992] Ch.72.

[236] [1994] 1 Lloyd's Rep. 382, CA.

[237] Intercomfinanz S.A., one defendant/respondent to the s 459 Companies Act 1985 unfair prejudice action was also domiciled in Switzerland.

[238] Dillon LJ [1992] Ch.72, at p.97; Collins, L. (1990) 106 *LQR* 535, at pp.538–39 'The contracting states were setting up an intra-Convention mandatory system of jurisdiction'.

[239] When one party and the *forum conveniens/forum prorogatum* are in non-Contracting States.

[240] Collins, L. (1990) 106 *LQR* 535, at pp.538–39.

[241] Noted by Vlas P. in 'Netherlands Judicial decisions regarding the application of the Lugano Convention on jurisdiction and judgments' [1996] *NILR*, p.397, at pp.403–05, co-incidentally a bill of lading case.

Dynamex, against another (Lugano[242]) Contracting State defendant, the Swiss carrier, Mediterranean. A bill of lading contained a jurisdiction clause for the District Courts of New York. The Swiss defendant, Mediterranean, was sued in Holland under Article 5(1) of Lugano Convention.[243] The court gave precedence to neither Article 5, nor to national law,[244] but instead held that the formalities of Article 17 Lugano Convention, though not directly applicable, produced 'reflexive effects'[245] as regards a non-Contracting State jurisdiction clause.

A less controversial answer[246] would seem to be to separate the concept of taking jurisdiction, under the Convention's Articles 2 or 5(1), from the actual exercise of that jurisdiction, once taken.[247] Such conditions for the exercise of jurisdiction have been held to come under the ambit of national law. By analogy, in *Hagen v Zeehaghe*,[248] Article 6(2) was seen by the ECJ as only a pointer to determine which court had jurisdiction, but left the further precise criteria as to the admissibility of the action to national law, 'provided that the effectiveness of the Convention in that regard is not impaired . . .':[249]

> It is . . . necessary to draw a clear distinction between jurisdiction and the conditions governing the admissibility of an action.[250]

Yet as a caveat, relying on its own previous decision in *Duijnstee v Goderbauer*,[251] the Court said:

> a court may not apply conditions of admissibility laid down by national law which would have *the effect of restricting the application* of the rules of jurisdiction laid down in the Convention[252]

The principles of discretionary stays in England, against actions already (incorrectly) brought here in breach of a 'foreign' jurisdiction clause could be described as 'conditions governing the admissibility of'[253] actions, yet also 'have the effect of restricting the application of the [Convention] rules',[254] such as Articles 2 and 5,

---

[242] Article 5(1) Lugano Convention is, for present purposes, identical to Article 5(1) Brussels Convention; Bajons, E. (1993) *ZfRV* 45.

[243] A classic Category D(ii) case.

[244] Article 629 Civil Code (Dutch).

[245] For criticism of applying the 'reflexive effects' doctrine to another Article, Article 16, in Gaudemet-Tallon, 1996, at p.60 para. 84.

[246] Gaudemet-Tallon, who sees no problem in staying in favour of a foreign jurisdiction clause even if both parties are Contracting State domiciliaries: 'Si la clause attributive de juridiction désigne un tribunal étranger à la Communauté . . . l'Article 17 n'intervient pas et le droit commun est libre de décider que la clause ne lie pas impérativement le tribunal désigné' in 'Le "forum non conveniens", une menace pour la convention de Bruxelles?' (1991) *Rev crit*, p.491, at p.512.

[247] Hartley T, (1995) *ELRev* 409.

[248] *Kongress Agentur Hagen GmbH v Zeehaghe B.V.* (C-365/88) [1990] ECR I-1845.

[249] At p.1866, para. 22.

[250] At p.1865.

[251] (288/82) [1983] ECR 3663.

[252] *Kongress Agentur Hagen GmbH v Zeehaghe B.V.* (C-365/88) [1990] ECR I-1845, at p.1866.

[253] At p.1865.

[254] At p.1866.

in our examples. What at first blush seem to be mutually inconsistent statements by the Court in Justice may only be distinguishable by the fact that the national law[255] in *Hagen v Zeehaghe* in some way complemented[256] jurisdiction under Article 6(2); whereas other national rules (such as the English principles of the *El Amria* guidelines) may have the effect of neutralising[257] any jurisdiction under Articles 2 or 5.

Without taking the 'reflexive effects' route of the Dutch court above, the safest solution would seem to be, until resolved[258] by the ECJ, to leave the decision to national law to decide whether a stay is appropriate, irrespective of the parties' domicile, relying on the fact that Article 17 is not applicable.[259]

2.1.4(iii) *Category D(iii)*[260]—*one party domiciled in a Contracting State, the other not*

Much of what has already been said also applies[261] where the other contracting party is domiciled in a non-Contracting State, appearing either as plaintiff/claimant,[262] or defendant:[263] if the non-Contracting State domiciliary appears as defendant, Article 4 allows a Contracting State (X) to take jurisdiction under 'the law of that State',[264] which presumably[265] includes the power, under English law, to stay proceedings.[266]

(a) Plaintiff/claimant domiciled in a non-Contracting State If the non-Contracting State party appears as plaintiff/claimant against a Contracting State defendant, the

---

[255] Governing the admissibility of actions on a guarantee.

[256] In the sense of filling in the precise gaps left by Article 6(2), if the national law criteria are fulfilled; if these criteria are not fulfilled by national law, jurisdiction under Article 6(2) is not taken away, but merely 'left suspended', as it were.

[257] Even though only a stay is granted, and only then to the extent of the stay (which may always be lifted).

[258] *Hamhed El Chaity & Co. v The Thomas Cook Group Ltd (The 'Nile Rhapsody')* [1994] 1 Lloyd's Rep. 382, CA, where the Court of Appeal refused, because of prior delay, to refer the question of what effect a non-Contracting State jurisdiction clause has on a defendant domiciled in England, sued here on the basis of Article 2.

[259] Gaudemet-Tallon, (1991) *Rev crit* 491, at p.512.

[260] Where non-Contracting State courts are chosen, but one party is domiciled in a non-Contracting State; again, Article 17 is inapplicable.

[261] Yet applies with more vigour, Samtleben, (1974) *NJW* 1590, at p.1593: 'eine allgemeine Vereinheitlichung der internationalen Gerichtsstandsvereinbarung war damit nicht bezweckt.'('a general unification of the international jurisdiction clause was not its aim').

[262] Suing Contracting State X defendant under Article 2, or Contracting State Y defendant under, *inter alia*, Article 5(1).

[263] Under Article 4.

[264] Including the exorbitant bases of jurisdiction in Article 3, suppressed as regards Contracting States domiciliaries.

[265] Below, following footnote.

[266] The litigation in *Sarrio v Kuwait Investment Authority* [1996] 1 Lloyd's Rep.650 (Mance J); revs'd, on unconnected grounds, [1997] 1 Lloyd's Rep. 113, where national law under Article 4 was held to include such a power to stay proceedings on *forum non conveniens* grounds.

situation is more controversial.[267] In England at least[268] a discretionary stay has been upheld in these circumstances: *The 'Nile Rhapsody'*.[269] The defendant travel company, Thomas Cook, applied for a stay of English proceedings brought by an Egyptian tourist company, Hamed El Chaity, in breach of what was (eventually) held to be an oral jurisdiction clause[270] in favour of the courts of Egypt. At first instance,[271] a stay was granted on common law grounds by Hirst J. The plaintiff's appeal was dismissed[272] by the Court of Appeal. Crucially, the court declined to exercise its discretion, under the 1971 Interpretation Protocol,[273] to refer the question of whether a discretion to stay[274] under English law was affected by jurisdiction taken under Article 2—even though a decision to the question appeared 'necessary'[275] for the court to give judgment, and that the question seemed not to be 'acte claire'.[276] The case, it was felt, had already involved 'a very substantial delay'.[277] Interestingly,[278] the court's view of the persuasive case of *Re Harrods (Buenos Aires) Ltd*[279] was that:

> Article 2 of the Convention had no application[280] in a case where one of the parties to the contract was domiciled in a non-contracting state.[281]

There is something to be said for the view that there should be no reason to impose the rigid non-discretionary rules of the Convention in a situation where

---

[267] Jurisdiction being claimed under Arts 2 or 5/6.

[268] For the position in Germany Wirth, H-R. 'Gerichtsstandsvereinbarungen im internationalen Handelsverkehr' (1978) *NJW* 460, at pp.461–62: '§38 II [ZPO] findet nur dann Anwendung, wenn eine Partei außerhalb des Gebietes der Vertragsstaaten ... ihren Wohnsitz hat ... wenn also keine Anknüpfungen zu mehreren Vertragsstaaten gegeben sind.'('§38 II [ZPO] is only applicable when one party has its seat outside the area of the Contracting States, when therefore, there are no given links to several Contracting States'); in France *Cour de Cassation*, 1er, 17.12.1985 *Compagnie de signaux c/ C C Sorelec*, (1986) *Dalloz*, 26 *Cahier somm.comm*, p.265, Audit, for a clause in favour of the courts of Libya, not invalidated by Article 48 NCPC.

[269] *Hamhed El Chaity & Co. v The Thomas Cook Group Ltd* (*The 'Nile Rhapsody'*) [1994] 1 Lloyd's Rep. 382, CA (Neill LJ), Staughton and Simon Brown LJJ concurring.

[270] At p.390 (Neill LJ).

[271] [1992] 2 Lloyd's Rep. 399; the authority of *Re Harrods (Buenos Aires) Ltd* obliging Hirst J to find that the Brussels Convention did not affect rules on stays 'where non-Convention countries [were] involved', at p.410.

[272] The impact of *Re Harrods (Buenos Aires) Ltd* [1992] Ch.72 on the application (or ensuing effect) of Article 2 was recognised by the CA, at p.392 (Neill LJ), as being an 'important question'; the more so because of the presence of a jurisdiction clause (not merely a competing available forum).

[273] Under Article 2(2).

[274] Any answer would also have affected stays on *forum non conveniens* grounds.

[275] [1994] 1 Lloyd's Rep. 382, at p.392.

[276] Neill LJ's 'preliminary view', at p.392; Gaudemet-Tallon, (1991) *Rev crit* 491.

[277] At p.392.

[278] And incorrectly, Article 2 only referring to the domicile of the defendant—that of the plaintiff is irrelevant—*Société Group Josi Reinsurance Company SA v Compagnie d'Assurances Universal General Insurance Company (UGIC)*, (C-412/98) [2000] ECR I-5925, at p.5927, para. 59.

[279] *Re Harrods (Buenos Aires) Ltd* [1992] Ch.72.

[280] *Sed quaere*, Introduction, above at p.20.

[281] [1994] 1 Lloyd's Rep. 382, at p.391.

the only link to the Contracting States may be a file at Companies House.[282] Yet if the Convention is seen as an attempt to unify the Contracting States' jurisdictional rules across the 'civil and commercial' spectrum,[283] and not merely to extend to intra-European Union relationships, then there may be some ground for preventing one particular Contracting State from exercising any, or more, leeway[284] in certain areas than in others.

2.1.5   Category E: A party domiciled in Contracting State X agrees with a non-Contracting State party either (i)[285] for the courts of Contracting State X,[286] or (ii)[287] for the courts of Contracting State Y[288]

Of importance to the uniform application of the Convention, and therefore an important aim of this work, is the apparent discrepancy in the interpretation of

---

[282] Dillon LJ's views in *Re Harrods* above, at p.190. The definition of a company's seat in s.42 Civil Jurisdiction and Judgments Act 1982, needs to be tightened up, by eliminating one of the alternatives—perhaps the place of incorporation; for an example of dual domicile, *The Deichland* [1990] 1 QB 361, CA.

[283] Note Samtleben, (1974) *NJW* 1590 who emphatically denies any such unifying rôle for the Convention, at p.1593, thus: 'eine allgemeine Vereinheitlichung des Rechts der internationalen Gerichtsstands . . . war damit nicht bezweckt' ('a comprehensive unification of the law of international jurisdiction was not the aim'), *contra*, for a wider unifying view assigned to the Convention, Basedow, J. 'Das *forum conveniens* der Reeder in EuGVÜ' (1985) *IPRax* 133, at p.135 speaking of Article 17's wide application, a solution which 'kommt dem Wünsch nach einheitlichen zivilprozessualen Außenbeziehungen der EG zu Drittstaaten immerhin ein Stück entgegen.'('at least brings the wish for a civil procedure in foreign relations between the EU and third party States a step closer').

[284] To use *forum non conveniens* considerations for example—cf. dictum in *SISRO v Ampersand Software BV* (C-432/93) [1995] ECR I–2269, defendants brought before one Contracting State should be prevented from 'enjoying greater procedural possibilities' there in comparison to others, at p.2301, para. 41.

[285] Unfortunately, as already mentioned, the ECJ judgment in *Coreck Maritime GmbH* (C-387/98) [2000] ECR I-9337 has not, with sufficient precision, clarified one way or the other the issue as to whether this factual situation satisfies the opening words of Article 17 *ratione personae*.

[286] Samtleben's extensive monograph, devoted almost exclusively to Category E(i): Samtleben, (1995) 59 *RabelsZ* 670; Roth 'Internationalrechtliche Probleme bei Prorogation und Derogation' (1980) *ZZP* 156, at p.159: 'auch zweifelhaft [ist es], ob Rechtsverhältnisse, die ausschließlich einen Vertragsstaat und einen *Drittstaat* berühren, dem Abkommen unterfallen'('[it is] also doubtful whether legal relations that exclusively touch on only a Contracting State and a *non-Contracting State* come under the Convention') (original emphasis); and *OLG Hamburg*, 31.12.1991, IPRspr. 1991, Nr.184, a bill of lading case against a Monrovian carrier, where the German national provision, §38 II ZPO, was used instead—*Dicey and Morris*, 13th edn., 2000, Vol. 1, p.338, para. 11–224; recently Article 17 applied in *OT Africa Line Ltd v Hijazy and others (The 'Kribi')* [2001] 1 Lloyd's Rep. 76 (Aikens J).

[287] Cf. Hill, 1998, who believes Article 17 will be applied in a Category E(ii) case, at p.105, para. 5.3.2; *obiter*, the situation in *Firswood Ltd v Petra Bank* [1996] CLC 608, CA, at p.614, (Schiemann LJ).

[288] A Swiss example applying Article 17 of the Lugano Convention *Sorelec SA contre Saleh Radwan* 23.12.1998 125 BGE, III, 108, at p.112, and an example of a Category E(ii) case mentioned in some detail in Bernasconi, C. 'Der räumlich-persöhnliche Anwendungsbereich des Lugano-Übereinkommens' (1993) SZIER 39, at p.63 ex.(b), the so-called 'Auseinanderfallen von Wohnsitzstaat und Gerichtssaat . . .'('the separation of the domicile State from the forum State'); Kropholler, 1998 p.231, para. 7; Samtleben (1995) 59 *RabelsZ* 670, at p.691; note the interesting permutations given in O'Malley, S. and Layton, A., 1989, at pp.554–55; recently the Court of Appeal has refused to apply Article 17, or the

Article 17's scope *ratione materiae*, revealed most markedly in Category E(i)[289] cases. Indeed, in Germany, and recently in Austria,[290] the factual situation in Category E(i) goes to the very heart of the internationality[291] debate. It has polarised opinion,[292] and lead to some interesting adjuncts to the strict wording of Article 17 in the German and Austrian case law.[293]

It is not clear why so little attention has been devoted to the question in England, and to some extent in France.[294] It may well be that the English courts are relying on the simple, self-sufficient wording of Article 17 itself;[295] or that the treatment accorded to jurisdiction clauses in favour of the forum at common law varies little[296] from the regime under Article 17, so the boundaries between the application of the one or the other need not be so sharply drawn as, perhaps, under §38 ZPO in Germany,[297] or §104 (Austrian) *Jurisdiktionsnorm*.[298]

Convention, to a Category E(ii) case, *Eli Lily & Co. v Novo Nordisk A/S*, unreported Lexis, 9.3.1999 (Morritt LJ) (American plaintiff, Danish defendant, English court *qua forum prorogatum*).

[289] For an overall synopsis, *Internationales Vertragsrecht, Das internationale Privatrecht der Schuldverträge*, (Hrsg. Reithmann, C/Martiny, D.), 5 Aufl., 1996, at p.1602–04, paras. 2119–21.

[290] Decision of the Austrian Supreme Court *OGH* 23.2.1998 (1998) *JBl* 726.

[291] Internationality, in this Category E(i) context, should be refined to mean an intra-European Union internationality—*OLG Düsseldorf* 15.3.1990, IPRspr. 1990, Nr.167, at p.339 'dieses Gemeinschaftsrecht gilt nicht bei Streitigkeiten, *die ihren internationalen Bezug zu anderen Staaten als den GVÜ-Vertragsstaaten haben*'('this community law does not apply to disputes whose *international relationship is only with States other than Brussels Convention Contracting States*'), in this case a (pre-Lugano) Swiss defendant; the basic question for Category E(i), posed by Samtleben, (1995) 59 *RabelsZ* 670, at p.680, is whether Article 17 should apply 'wenn eine Partei im Vertragsstaat des prorogierten Forums und die andere in einem Nicht-Vertragsstaat ihren Wohnsitz hat?'('when only one party is domiciled in the Contracting State of the prorogated court and the other in a non-Contracting State').

[292] The major, diametrically-opposed protagonists are Samtleben, (1995) 59 *RabelsZ* 670, and Basedow, (1985) *IPRax* 133; and (1988) *RabelsZ* 756, at pp.756–57.

[293] Especially *OLG München* 8.3.1989, IPRspr.1989, Nr.186, [1991] I.L.Pr. 298; *OLG München* 28.9.1989, IPRspr. 1989, Nr.194; Austrian *OGH* 23.2.1998 *Entscheidungen*, 71 Band, 1998, No.29, p.170; *contra Handelsgericht Zürich* 9.1.1996 reported in Volken, P. 'Rechtsprechung zum Lugano-Übereinkommen (1996)' (1997) *SZIER* 335, at p.373.

[294] Gaudemet-Tallon, 1996, at p.76, para. 106, seems to favour a literal interpretation and therefore to apply Article 17 in a Category E(i) case; the internationality issue inherent in Category E(i) was not even mentioned in *Cour d'appel de Paris* 14.6.1995 *Soc Przedsiebiorstwo Zagraniczne "Integral" c/ Soc ADS* 1996 *Dalloz*, som com., 169, reviewed below, at p.198.

[295] Yet not so in *British Aerospace Plc. v Dee Howard Co.* [1993] 1 Lloyd's Rep. 368 (Waller J); *contra Mercury Communications Ltd and another v Communication Telesystems International* [1999] 2 All ER (Comm) 33, (Moore Bick J), and *Sinochem International Oil (London) Ltd v Mobil Sales and Supply Corp Ltd (No.2)* [2000] 1 All ER (Comm) 758, but permitting a *forum non conveniens* gloss once Article 17 had been found applicable, another non-Contracting State forum potentially being available.

[296] Clarke J in *The Bergen* [1997] 1 Lloyd's Rep. 380, at p.387; especially as an expression of *pacta sunt servanda*, *Continental Bank v Aeakos* [1994] 1 WLR 588, CA; *Youell and others v Kara Mara Shipping Co. Ltd* [2000] 2 Lloyd's Rep. 102.

[297] §38 III 2 is strict in its application to pre-dispute clauses, '... nur zulässig ... [wenn] 2. ... die Partei ... ihren Wohnsitz ... aus dem Geltungsbereich dieses Gesetzes [hat]'('only admissible ... [when] the party [has] its domicile outside the sphere of application of this law'); Sandrock, 1997.

[298] Stumvoll, H. (ed) *Zivilgerichtliches Verfahren, Kodex des österreichischen Rechts*, 1998, requiring 'documentary' proof of agreement.

Before a more detailed factual examination of the case law is undertaken, it is convenient to set out the problem,[299] the main opposing factions[300] from the German and Swiss doctrinal writings, and consider whether any arguments for, or against, the application of Article 17 in Category E(i) could be assimilated into the English case law.[301]

On the one hand are those commentators who could be called the 'literalists':[302] Basedow,[303] Kropholler,[304] Schlosser,[305] Jenard,[306] Bernasconi,[307] Geimer,[308] Audit,[309] and the Austrian, Bajons,[310] who simply rely on the two explicitly-given criteria in Article 17 itself—a choice of a Contracting State forum, and the domicile of one party[311] in any Contracting State, including, of course, the forum chosen. The literalists opine that the article is, in itself, self-sufficient,[312] and need

---

[299] *Cheshire and North*, 13th edn., 1999, at p.236—referring to the clash between Articles 17 and 4: 'Article 17 will apply if you look only at that Article [in this factual situation]'; despite an early omission to apply Article 17 in *British Aerospace Plc. v Dee Howard Co.* [1993] 1 Lloyd's Rep. 368 (Waller J), the English view now is that Article 17 *will* apply *ratione materiae*; but, on the authority of *Re Harrods (Buenos Aires) Ltd* [1992] Ch 90, with a *forum (non) conveniens* gloss to it thereafter—*Sinochem International Oil (London) Ltd v Mobil Sales and Supply Corp Ltd (No.2)* [2000] Lloyd's Rep. 670.

[300] Summarised by Kropholler, himself a literalist, at pp.230–32.

[301] Schmidt, reviewer of *OLG München*, 8.3.1989, (1990) *ZZP* 84: 'So nimmt denn auch die überwiegende Ansicht an, daß infolge der Zielsetzung des Übereinkommens, den Rechtsverkehr *zwischen den Vertrags*staaten zu erleichtern . . .'('overwhelming opinion accepts that due to the Convention's aim and purpose . . . is to ease the judicial exchange *between the Contracting* States'), at p.93 (original emphasis).

[302] With a literal interpretation of the wording of Article 17: one party (plaintiff/claimant or defendant) a Contracting State domiciliary, and *any* Contracting State prorogated.

[303] Basedow (1988) *RabelsZ* 756, at p.757: 'Der *unmißverständliche Wortlaut von* Article 17 . . . dürfte aber keinen Zweifel daran lassen, das der EGH die Streitfrage zugunsten des GVÜ beantworten würde.' ('the *unmistakable wording of* Article 17 *itself* should leave no room for doubt that the ECJ would answer this legal point in favour of the Convention').

[304] Kropholler, 1998; Briggs, with a comment on (what is now) CPR 6.20(5)(d), places himself with the literalists, 1997, at p.228, para. 4.32; Kröll, (2000) *ZZP* 135, at p.139.

[305] Schlosser, P. *EuGVÜ: Europäisches Gerichtsstands- und Vollstreckungsübereinkommen mit Luganer Übereinkommen*, 1996, especially pp.98–119, at p.105.

[306] Jenard Report, [1979] OJ C59/1, at p.38.

[307] Bernasconi, C 'Der räumlich-persöhnliche Anwendungsbereich des Lugano-Übereinkommens' (1993) *SZIER* 39, at p.65: 'der Wohnsitz einer Partei und die Anrufung eines Gerichts eines Vertragsstaats *einen hinreichenden "Gemeinschaftsbezug"* begründen' ('the domicile of one party and the invocation of a Contracting State court founds a *sufficient Community element*').

[308] Geimer, (1991) *IPRax* 31; and R. Geimer and R. Schütze, 1983, at p.895, saying Article 17 applies in an Category E(i) situation 'auch wenn kein Berührungspunkt zu einem anderen Vertragsstaat vorliegt'('even if there are no points of reference to another Contracting State').

[309] Reviewing *Cour d'appel de Paris* 14.6.1995 *Soc Przedsiebiorstwo Zagraniczne "Integral" c/ Soc ADS* 1996 *Dalloz*, Somm comm., 169, at p.170.

[310] Bajons, E. 'Das Luganer Parallelübereinkommen zum EuGVÜ—der Europäische Jurisdiktionsbereich in österreichischer Perspektive' (1993) *ZfRV*, p.45, at p.49, 'Der Wohnsitz einer der Parteien konstituiert somit hier die europäische Zuständigkeit'('the domicile of one of the parties thereby constitutes the European jurisdiction').

[311] It could be plaintiff or defendant, Kropholler, 1998 at p.228, para. 1—this view has been espoused as the correct one by AG Alber in his opinion, of 23.3.2000, in *Coreck Maritime GmbH* (C387–98), but not dealt with specifically by the ECJ's judgment [2000] ECR I-9337, at pp.9372–73, paras. 17–18, and 21.

[312] Basedow, (1985) *IPRax* 133, at p.134: 'Daher muß Article 17 seine Anwendungsvoraussetzungen *selbst* normieren'('Thus Article 17 *itself* must regulate its own preconditions for applicability').

not be trammelled[313] by extraneous considerations[314] advocated by the so-called 'additionalists'.[315]

These 'additionalists' see the application of Article 17 in a more restricted light,[316] as only regulating intra-Community/European Union relations.[317] They require 'internationality', but of a European kind. The article, they say, should not apply in Category E(i) because the Convention itself has no business in interfering with the mutual relationship between parties from a Contracting and non-Contracting State. The additionalists' essential view of Article 17 is that it should only apply:

> wenn die Gerichtsstandsabrede Berührungspunkte zu *mehreren* Vertragsstaaten aufweist.[318]

Only with these additional points of contact does Article 17 then have any justification to govern, *inter alia*, the formalities of jurisdiction clauses.

These 'points of contact', or references, to several Contracting States, they argue, can be demonstrated either: (1) by undertaking a *forum prorogatum- forum derogatum* analysis[319]—in other words, the jurisdiction clause will be judged in accordance with Article 17 if it *derogates* from another Contracting State's jurisdiction, otherwise potentially available under, for example Articles 5(1) or 6;[320] or alternatively (2), by the fact that the *forum prorogatum* and the domicile of the Contracting State party are in different Contracting States.[321]

---

[313] Bernasconi, a literalist, argues that the opportunity to add an element of internationality to Article 17 would—if desired—have been taken on the occasion of the numerous accessions, 'sollte er [Article 17] wirklich nicht den Intentionen der Vertragsstaaten entsprochen haben'(should it [Article 17] really not have corresponded to the Contracting States' intentions'), at (1993) *SZIER* 39, p.65.

[314] The so-called 'grenzüberschreitend[er] Bezug zu einem anderen Vertragsstaat'('cross-border relationship to another Contracting State'), Geimer, (1991) *IPRax* 31, at p.32; Schmidt, (1992) *RIW* 173.

[315] Or proponents of a more limited application of Article 17, by means of a 'Reduktionstheorie'('a limiting theory')—i.e.. that Article 17 needs *more* of a connection/relationship to the EU than the domicile of 1 of the parties; especially Samtleben (1995) 59 *RabelsZ* 670; Kohler, (1983) *IPRax* 265; and lastly, Wirth, (1978) *NJW* 460.

[316] *Ibid.*

[317] Samtleben's conclusion as to the applicability of Article 17, (1995) 59 *RabelsZ* 670, at p.696: 'Der Richter muß eine Gerichtsstandsvereinbarung nach Article 17 EuGVÜ/ LÜ beurteilen, wenn der Wohnsitz einer Partei ebenso wie das vereinbarte Forum innerhalb der Vertagsstaaten und mindestens eines von beiden *in einen anderen* Vertragsstaat liegt'('the judge must regulate a jurisdiction clause according to Article 17 Brussels/Lugano when the domicile of one party as well as the agreed forum lie within the Contracting States and at least one of which lies *in another* Contracting State').

[318] ('when the jurisdiction agreement reveals points of reference to *several* Contracting States'), Kropholler, 1998, at p.230, para. 6, summarising Samtleben, and the additionalists' main tenet, and the German courts' overwhelming use of national law, under §38 ZPO, in Category E(i).

[319] The method favoured by Samtleben, (1995) 59 *RabelsZ* 670, at p.691.

[320] O'Malley, S. and Layton, A., 1989, at p.553, para. 21.06, agreeing with the 'Reduktionstheorie'; for the theory in a Category B case, one returns to *OLG Hamm* 18.9.1997 (1999) *IPRax* 244, above, at p.179.

[321] The so-called 'Auseinanderfallen von Wohnsitz und Gerichtsstand innerhalb der EG als der eigentliche Regelungsgegenstand', according to Samtleben, (1974) *NJW* 1590, at p.1593, taking the analysis into catetory E(ii), below, at p.202; for example, *OLG Karlsruhe* 30.12.1981 IPRspr. (1981) Nr.171—Austrian (non-Contracting State) plaintiff, German defendant and the courts of Rome

Both camps raise sharp criticism of each other. The literalists are attacked on two fronts: firstly, that the Convention, and especially Article 17, were not designed to unify the Contracting States' laws with regard to persons having no relationship with the Community/European Union itself;[322] and secondly, that a literal interpretation of Article 17 (with regard to non-Contracting State domiciliaries) must also inevitably point to Article 17's application in a purely domestic Contracting State situation.[323]

Indeed, *The Tilly Russ*,[324] on its facts, is an instructive, yet ambiguous case in the context of Article 17's connection with the European Community.[325] The Court spoke of Article 17 governing whether a jurisdiction clause in a bill of lading bound a third party (consignee) if the clause was valid, according to Article 17, as between the original shipper and carrier. In this instance, there was some confusion over the identity of the original parties,[326] both appearing to be US domiciliaries. As the case pre-dated the coming into force of the 1978 amendments to Article 17, it is arguable that the substitution of a Contracting State holder/endorsee for one of the two US parties could not bring Article 17 into play for the original agreement between those two US parties:

> where a holder domiciled in a Member State *is substituted* for one of two contracting parties not so domiciled, the agreement as to jurisdiction *with the holder* does not fall within Article 17[327]

---

prorogated. Article 17 was applied, but its formal requirements were found wanting—*Ultisol Transport Contractors Ltd v Bouygues Offshore S.A.* [1996] 2 Lloyd's Rep. 140, (Clarke J); [1998] 2 Lloyd's Rep. 461, CA.

[322] Samtleben, (1974) *NJW* 1590, at p.1593, point (c); yet Article 16 applies regardless of the domicile of the parties; Moore-Bick J would agree, in *Mercury Communications Ltd and another v Communication Telesystems International* [1999] 2 All ER (Comm) 33, at p.39 but in the context of a *forum non conveniens* argument.

[323] Vociferous is Samtleben, (1995) 59 *RabelsZ* 670, at p.700: '*Darin liegt* aber zugleich *das Eingeständnis*, daß der Wortlaut des Article 17 EuGVÜ/LÜ eben nicht ausreicht, um seinen Anwendungsbereich zu beschreiben.'('*Therein however also lies the admission* that the wording of Article 17 of Brussels/Lugano itself does not suffice to describe its own sphere of application'); but an argument which did not impress the *Handelsgericht Zürich* 9.1.1996 *Thal AG gegen Vilvo N.V.* reported in Volken, (1997) *SZIER* 335, at p.373, reviewed below, at pp.205 *et seq.*

[324] *Partenreederei ms Tilly Russ & Ernst Russ v NV Haven- & Veroerbedriff Nova (The Tilly Russ)* (C-71/83), 19.6.1984 [1984] ECR 2417.

[325] *Hugo Trumpy* seems to suggest some weak support, that in answer to the thirteenth question referred, connection with the European Union is not essential, at [1999] ECR I-1597, p.1654, para. 42; in *Coreck Maritime GmbH* (C-387/98) [2000] ECR I-9337, qu. 2(b) asked whether Article 17 covered the situation described above, but no definitive answer was given in the case by the ECJ—AG Alber, in point 2 of his conclusion, stated that only *one* party need be domiciled in a Contracting State.

[326] AG Sir Gordon Slynn, [1984] ECR 2417, at p.2440; but Schiemann LJ in *Firswood Ltd v Petra Bank* [1996] CLC 608, CA, at p.616, who was able to identify as the only parties to the bill of lading: holder and carrier.

[327] [1984] ECR 2417 at p.2440; this 'tentative view' by the Advocate General could be read to mean that where an original UK shipper and a US carrier agree on the jurisdiction of London, that agreement does not fall within Article 17; conversely, it could also be said to mean the opposite, that it is only *substitution* of a Contracting State holder that negatives Article 17's application—if the Contracting State party was the *original* party, Article 17 would apply; *Navire: "Westfield", Cour d'Appel de Rennes*

For their part the additionalists are criticised, in the main, for introducing into Article 17 itself[328] the vague notion[329] of internationality as one of a number of 'ungeschriebene Anwendungsgrenzen'[330] for the application of this article. The ECJ had repeatedly stressed[331] that it is not for the individual national courts unilaterally to interpret the Convention, by idiosyncratic addition or subtraction of the concepts used in the Convention's articles, so as to undermine its uniform application.[332] This, the literalists argue,[333] is what the additionalists[334] are doing. That other Contracting States also require an additional link[335] to the European Union in a Category E(i) situation has not yet been authoritatively decided.[336]

Further criticism of the additionalists centres on their methodology used to determine these 'unwritten criteria of application': why, the literalists' criticism runs, should Article 17 depend on a Contracting State judge's first embarking[337] on the tortuous task of ascertaining whether there is another Contracting State present as the *forum derogatum*?[338] Indeed, that a judge in Contracting State X should first have to see whether, for example, Article 5(1) gives jurisdiction to

---

23.12.1992, 1993 DMF 298, where the original parties were (pre-Lugano) Norwegian shipper and carrier—the dispute between the Norwegian carrier and the (substituted) French consignee over an English jurisdiction clause in a bill of lading, was decided under Article 17 Brussels Convention.

[328] Ignoring for now even the preamble, which is problematic; but Huber, 1994, who sees little weight in the preamble, at p.193: 'ein allgemein gehaltener Programmsatz in der Präambel kann bei einer Lösung eines speziellen Problems . . . kein großes Gewicht haben.'('a generally held agenda in the preamble can carry no great weight in solving special problems . . . [in the Convention]'); but Schepers, S. 'The Legal Force of the Preamble to the EEC Treaty' (1981) 6 *ELRev* 356, at pp.357–58.

[329] Heß, B. 'Gerichtsstandsvereinbarungen zwischen EuGVÜ und ZPO' (1992) *IPRax* 358.

[330] Geimer, (1991) *IPRax* 31, at p.32; similar, in effect, to arguments brought forward by the Court of Appeal in *Re Harrods (Buenos Aires) Ltd* [1992] Ch 90 to justify the application of *forum non conveniens* in the Brussels Convention context.

[331] Especially *LTU GmbH & Co. K.G. v Eurocontrol* (29/76) [1976] ECR 1541, at pp.1551–52; and *Kalfelis v Bankhaus Schröder* (189/87) [1988] ECR 5565.

[332] *Elefanten Schuh GmbH v Pierre Jacqmain* (C-150/80) [1981] ECR 1671.

[333] Bernasconi, C. 'Der räumlich-persöhnliche Anwendungsbereich des Lugano-Übereinkommens' (1993) *SZIER* 39, at p.67, Article 17 by its terms providing 'einen hinreichenden "Gemeinschaftsbezug"' ('a sufficient "Community reference"').

[334] Also the German jurisprudence, below, at pp.200 *et seq*.

[335] *Quaere*, even what, and how extensive, that link should be; following the German jurisprudence, the Austrian Supreme Court has stated that additional requirements *are* necessary: OGH 23.2.1998 (1998) *JBl* 726; Waller J, in *British Aerospace Plc v Dee Howard Co.* [1993] 1 Lloyd's Rep. 368, did not even hear argument on the potential application of Article 17 in a Category E(i) case; *contra Mercury Communications Ltd* [1999] 2 All ER (Comm) 33, (Moore Bick J).

[336] *Cour de Cassation Société Naviera de Exportacion Agricola c. Société Mory* 7.12.1983, (1984) *Rev crit*, p.658, where a non-Contracting State plaintiff was not able to rely on Article 17 as against a French domiciled defendant; *Cour d'appel de Paris* 18.12.1987 (1998) *Dalloz*, somm., p.343; and *Cour d'Appel de Paris Sieur et Dame Nahas c/ Banque arabe et internationale d'investissement* 14.11.1990, (1991) *JDI* 734—national law applied in Category E(i), not Article 17.

[337] Geimer, (1991) *IPRax* 31, at p.32: 'Eine solche umständliche Rechtsanwendungsprozedur ist für die Praxis unerträglich'('such a tortuous procedure for its legal application is unbearable in practice').

[338] Samtleben recognises this weakness in his own argument at (1995) *RabelsZ* 670, p.691; in any case, the national judge may in fact mis-interpret whether another Contracting State jurisdiction is implicated *qua forum derogatum*, (for example under Article 5(1)). This, argues Schmidt (1990) *ZZP* 84, at pp.95–95 is what occurred in *OLG München*, 8.3.1989 IPRspr. 1989 Nr. 186, [1991] I.L.Pr. 298.

another Contracting State before Article 17 can even be considered to give jurisdiction to Contracting State X as *forum prorogatum*, undermines the very legal
certainty of the Convention itself:

> Erst wenn er [der Richter] jeden Kontakt des Rechtsstreits zu einem anderen
> Vertragsstaat verneint hat, kann er darüber befinden, ob nun europäisches oder
> nationales Zuständigkeit zur Anwendung kommt.[339]

The additionalists' view of Article 17's scope should be rejected.[340] The article's
application cannot depend *in limine* on whether a court has previously embarked
on an examination of the availability of another Contracting State forum under
other Convention articles. The literalists' approach should be preferred; whether,
after mechanically applying Article 17's wording in the factual situation described
above, there is any room for arguments based on *forum non conveniens*, as have
crept into the English cases,[341] is a problem of the Convention's general application towards non-Contracting States, afflicting the Convention as a whole,[342] and
not strictly of Article 17's scope *ratione materiae*. It is a symptom of the ill-liased
linkage between Article 4 and Article 17, perhaps understandable in the original
drafting, but unforgivably left unattended to in the more recent Convention
amendments. Unfortunately, Article 23 Brussels I Regulation[343] does not correct
this solecism, since the recent judgment in *Coreck Maritime GmbH v Handelsveem
B.V.*[344] has *not* put a definite end to the literalist/additionalist debate in Germany.

By way of illustration of the Category E (i) problem, it is instructive to view the
conflicting caselaw from France, England, Germany, Switzerland and Austria
before looking at the proposals for reform in the Brussels I Regulation and the
draft Hague Convention.

2.1.5(i)   *French court decisions on Category E(i)*

Two French courts have been faced with a Category E(i) situation, but on both
occasions the problem of the scope of Article 17 *ratione materiae* was not
discussed. In the first, *Sieur et Dame Nahas c/ Banque arabe et internationale*

---

[339] ('only when [the judge] has first denied any contact of the dispute with another Contracting State,
can he ascertain whether then either European or national jurisdiction comes to be applied'), Geimer
at (1986) *NJW* 1439.
[340] The Nygh/Pocar report on Article 4 of the draft Hague Convention makes it clear that the drafting
of the Article was deliberate in excluding this German view, at p.38.
[341] *Sinochem International Oil (London) Ltd v Mobil Sales and Supply Corp Ltd (No.2)* [2000] 1 All ER
(Comm) 758.
[342] Especially Article 2: *Re Harrods (Buenos Aires) Ltd* [1992] Ch 90; *Haji-Ioannou & ors v Frangos & ors.*
[1999] 2 Lloyd's Rep. 337, CA; *Lubbe v Cape Plc* [2000] 1 WLR 1545, at pp.1561–62 (Lord Bingham of
Cornhill); *ACE Insurance SA-NV v Zurich Insurance Company* [2001] 1 Lloyd's Rep. 618, CA.
[343] Below at pp.206–207.
[344] *Coreck Maritime GmbH v Handelsveem B.V.* (C387–98) [2000] ECR I-9337; qu. 2(b) asked whether
Article 17 covered the situation described above, but no definitive answer was given in the case by the
ECJ.

d'investissement,[345] the French-domiciled bank, Banque arabe, was able to rely on a Paris jurisdiction clause, under (French autonomous law in) Article 48 NCPC, rather than Article 17, in a loan agreement against two Brazilian defendant guarantors, domiciled in Brazil, but resident in Paris. No mention was even made of the possible application of Article 17.

In the second, *Soc Przedsiebiorstwo Zagraniczne «Integral» c/ Soc ADS*,[346] the French company ADS sued a Polish defendant in Paris for non-payment under a sales contract on the basis of a Paris jurisdiction clause. The reviewer, Audit, clearly thinks that the court overlooked the application of Article 17 on these facts:

> c'est donc en principe au regard des autres dispositions de l'article 17 que devaient être appreciées les conditions de validité et les effets de la clause litigieuse.[347] [348]

2.1.5(ii)   English court decisions on Category E(i)

It is only now clear how an English court[349] would resolve the current factual situation in E(i). The scope of Article 17 was not aired[350] in *British Aerospace v Dee Howard*.[351] Here BAe had sought and had been granted leave, *inter alia*, under (what was formerly) RSC Ord.11 r.1(1)(d)(iv)[352] to serve Dee Howard *ex juris*.[353] There was nothing in the report to suggest that Article 17 was considered *ratione materiae* or *personae*. Taking a literal view of the Convention and Article 17, it did seem to apply on the facts:[354] one party, (albeit) the plaintiff, domiciled in a Contracting State, the UK, and a court of a Contracting State was agreed upon.[355]

---

[345]   14.11.1990 (1991) *JDI* 734.

[346]   *Cour d'appel de Paris* 14.6.1995, (1996) *Dalloz*, Som com., 169.

[347]   ('it is in principle therefore in accordance with other provisions of Article 17 that the prerequisites of validity and effects of the disputed clause were to be measured').

[348]   At p.170.

[349]   *The Rewia* [1991] 1 Lloyd's Rep. 69, (Sheen J), (although finding the central management and control of Rewia Shipping to be in Germany for the purposes of s 42(6) CJJA 1982), revs'd, CA, in part on the finding that the defendant's 'principal place of business' was in Hong Kong (it was adjudged on appeal to be Germany), [1991] 2 Lloyd's Rep. 325).

[350]   The Convention was not entirely overlooked: the Italian parent company of Dee Howard, was served out under Article 5(3), [1993] 1 Lloyd's Rep. 368, at p.370.

[351]   [1993] 1 Lloyd's Rep. 368, (Waller J).

[352]   Now CPR 6.20(5)(d).

[353]   CPR 6.22(1), (4)(a) and 6.23(1), (4)(a) now appear to cater for a situation such as *Dee Howard*: periods for, respectively, filing an acknowledgment of service and a defence, where service of the claim form was effected without permission.

[354]   Again, literal interpretation not clearly espoused in *Coreck Maritime GmbH* (C387–98) [2000] ECR I-9337, at pp.9372–73, paras. 17–18, and 21; and the ECJ in *Group Josi* (C-412/98) [2000] ECR I-5925, at pp.5953–54, paras. 41–42.

[355]   Perhaps in England at least, the internationality issue matters little, because, as mentioned earlier, the English court, as *forum prorogatum*, would consider itself competent either under its (English) autonomous rules (n.352, above, with 'permission'), or under Article 17 (no permission required, CPR 6.19(1)(b)(iii)). It is submitted that a literal reading of Article 17 should be adopted, and Article 17 deployed.

This literal view of Article 17 was endorsed in *Mercury Communications Ltd and another v Communication Telesystems International*[356] and *Sinochem International Oil (London) Ltd v Mobil Sales and Supply Corp Ltd (No.2)*.[357] The main issue was not whether the jurisdiction clause had to be assessed under Article 17 or not, but whether a discretion existed thereafter to stay the English proceedings under s.49 CJJA 1982.[358]

In *Mercury Communications*, the plaintiffs had sought and obtained leave to serve the Californian defendants, Communication Telesystems, *ex juris*, on the basis of an English jurisdiction clause. One question was whether leave was strictly necessary, as the wording of Article 17 appeared to be satisfied;[359] the basis of jurisdiction therefore being not under (former) Ord. 11 r.1(1), but r.1(2). The judge agreed with counsel for Mercury that the claim fell within r.1(2).[360] Here, as in *Sinochem International (No.2)*, this was not the end of the matter.[361] Even though Article 17 applied on its wording,[362] the English court still retained the power to stay the action on favour of the courts of a non-Contracting State:[363] the judge thus went on to state that he could see 'nothing to suggest that one of the objects of art 17 was to compel the courts of the contracting states to enforce[364] jurisdiction clauses against defendants domiciled outside their territory'[365] in favour of domestic plaintiffs/claimants.

---

[356] [1999] 2 All ER (Comm) 33.

[357] [2000] 1 All ER (Comm) 758, (Rix J); literal interpretation espoused and Article 17 applied as against an Australian-domiciled respondent in *Society of Lloyd's v White and others*, 3.3.2000, QBD, (Creswell J).

[358] [1999] 2 All ER (Com) 33, at p.39; the judge in *Mercury* believed it would not be inconsistent with the objects of the Convention to consider a stay when the basis of the English jurisdiction was Article 17 (a defendant being domiciled in a non-Contracting State); a stay was not imposed on the facts however—*contra* Peel (1998) *LMCLQ* 182, at p.197.

[359] [2000] 1 All ER (Comm) 758, at p.770, (Rix J) 'Article 17 . . . engaged if at least one of the parties is domiciled in a contracting state . . .'; *Coreck Maritime GmbH* (C387–98) [2000] ECR I-9337, at p.9372, para. 17.

[360] That the English court had a power by virtue of the CJJA 1982 to hear and determine; scope *ratione personae* of Article 17 in this situation not disputed in *OT Africa Line Ltd v Hijazy and others (The 'Kribi')* [2001] 1 Lloyd's Rep. 76 (Aikens J).

[361] A stay was not imposed in *Sinochem International (No.2)* on the facts.

[362] Now *ACE Insurance SA-NV v Zurich Insurance Company* [2000] 2 All ER (Comm) 449 affm'd [2001] 1 Lloyd's Rep. (CA) (Rix LJ) 618, at p.622, presumably, in Article 18 or Article 5(1).

[363] *Mercury Communications Ltd and another v Communication Telesystems International* [1999] 2 All ER (Comm) 33, at p.39, the judge interpreting *Re Harrods (Buenos Aires) Ltd* [1992] Ch 90 as applying to the choice of jurisdiction between the English courts (as *forum prorogatum*) and those of a non-Contracting State.

[364] As in *Re Harrods (Buenos Aires) Ltd* [1992] Ch 90, we therefore have the rather odd spectacle of principles of traditional English jurisdictional practice (notably by analogy, those enumerated in *The El Amria* [1981] 2 Lloyd's Rep. 119) being deployed when the court has jurisdiction under the Convention, this time under Article 17—*Cheshire and North*, 13th edn., 1999, at p. 305, and at n.19: *Citi-March Ltd v Neptune Orient Lines Ltd* [1997] 1 Lloyd's Rep. 72, at p.74 (Colman J), *The 'Vikfrost'* [1980] 1 Lloyd's Rep. 560, at p.568 (Browne LJ), *The 'T.S. Havprins'* [1983] 2 Lloyd's Rep. 356, at p.363, (Staughton J).

[365] [1999] 2 All ER (Com) 33, at p.39; *Sinochem International (No.2)* [2000] 1 All ER (Comm) 758, at p.771.

2.1.5(iii)　German court decisions on Category E(i)

The German courts[366] have been more specific in relation to this category, perhaps due to the more rigorous criteria for the applicability of jurisdiction clauses under national law,[367] rather than under Article 17. A certain and strict discrepancy between national and Convention provisions has produced a correspondingly more detailed response[368] to the issue of applying either national law or Article 17. The cases also demonstrate that the applicability of Article 17 depends in which capacity a German court is seised—as either (a) *forum derogatum*[369] or (b) *forum prorogatum*.[370]

(a) Forum derogatum In the first case,[371] *OLG München*, the plaintiffs were seeking damages against a Luxembourg bank for the wrongful dealing and disposal of the plaintiffs' shares, lodged with the bank and its subsidiaries, as security for a loan. The loan document contained a jurisdiction clause: 'Gerichtsstand ist Luxemburg'.[372] In breach of this clause the plaintiffs sued the bank under Articles 5(1) and (3) in Munich,[373] i.e. in a *forum derogatum*. The appeal court held that the clause was valid according to Article 17, and declined jurisdiction. Clearly the clause was within Article 17 according to the literal wording of that article: both 'the party' (defendant) and chosen court were in Luxembourg. Yet this factual scenario by itself, the court held by implication, was *insufficient* for the application of Article 17. Since the court was seised *qua forum derogatum*, the facts revealed 'eine sogenannte grenzüberschreitende Vereinbarung'[374] simply because of the fact that

---

[366]　Below, at p.201; most recently *OLG Saarbrücken* 13.10.1999 (2000) *NJW* 670, (2000) *JuS* 611.

[367]　§38 ZPO, although a prorogating provision, is also used where the German courts are *fora derogata*. §38 I demands that both parties are 'Kaufleute', or according to §38 II, that at least one contracting party must not have a general jurisdiction (§§12/15) in Germany; in either case, a clause agreed prior to the proceedings' commencement, in §38 III 2, is only permissible when the defendant has its seat or habitual residence outside Germany—*Zivilprozeßordnung*, R.Zöller, 18th edn., 1993, p.140; these domestic provisions are of course overridden when Article 17 applies: *BGH* (1980) *NJW* 2023, and Zöller, 1993, at p.144; Sandrock, 1997, at p.69 *et seq.*

[368]　Clarke J in *The Bergen* [1997] 1 Lloyd's Rep. 380, at p.387: 'the practical result of applying Article 17 on the one hand and . . . English domestic law on the other is likely to be the same in the vast majority of cases'; *BGH* 23.7.1998 1999 NJW-RR 137.

[369]　Compare therefore *OLG München*, 8.3.1989, IPRspr. 1989, Nr.186, [1991] I.L.Pr. 298.

[370]　*OLG München* 28.9.1989, IPRspr. 1989, Nr.194, Geimer (1991) *IPRax* 46.

[371]　*OLG München*, 8.3.1989, IPRspr. 1989, Nr.186; reasoning taken up in *OLG Karlsruhe*, 9.10.1992, IPRspr. 1992, Nr.199, at p.452—German plaintiff, Austrian defendant with the courts of Mannheim, Germany, prorogated—'Article 17 GVÜ solche Fälle nicht erfaßt, in denen keinen Zuständigkeitsbezug zu einem *anderen* Vertragsstaat besteht'('Article 17 Brussels Convention does *not* cover cases in which there is no jurisdictional relationship to *another* Contracting State').

[372]　('jurisdiction is Luxembourg'), 1990 ZZP 84, at p.86.

[373]　*Ibid.* at p.94, Schmidt finding the court's analysis erroneous.

[374]　('a so-called cross-border agreement') *OLG München*, 8.3.1989, (1990) *ZZP* 84, at p.86—*OLG Saarbrücken* 13.10.1999 (2000) *NJW* 670, at p.670: '. . . ist die Vorschrift nur maßgeblich, wenn die Zuständigkeit der Gerichte eines anderen Vertragsstaats begründet werden soll.'('the provision is only applicable when the jurisdiction of the courts of another Contracting State is founded'); again unclear in this factual situation in *Coreck Maritime GmbH* (C387–98) [2000] ECR I-9337.

an action was possible in Munich—i.e. that *forum derogatum* (Munich under Articles 5(1) and (3))[375] and *forum prorogatum* (Article 17, Luxembourg) were in different Contracting States. The court thought the domicile of the plaintiff was irrelevant,[376] when an action with a jurisdiction clause in favour of another Contracting State was initiated in Germany:

> Doch reicht es für die Anwendbarkeit des Article 17 EuGVÜ aus, daß wenigstens *ein* Vertragspartner im Geltungsbereich des Übereinkommens wohnt.[377]

(b) Forum prorogatum The second case,[378] again decided by the *OLG München*,[379] concerned a claim by a German company against its Canadian customer for the price of goods delivered. The plaintiff's general conditions of sale included a jurisdiction clause for the courts of Neu-Ulm, Germany. Relying on this, the plaintiff commenced its action in Germany. The appeal court upheld its jurisdiction, but under national law, §38 I ZPO, not Article 17.[380] According to the literal wording of Article 17, the article appeared to be applicable. In a situation such as Category E(i), however, the court held that Article 17 demanded, *additionally*:

> ein[en] Bezug zu mindestens *einem weiteren* Vertragsstaat'[381]

---

[375] The case reviewer Schmidt, (1990) *ZZP*, at p.94.

[376] *Ibid.*: 'Unerheblich ist in diesem Zusammenhang, ob die Gerichtsstandsvereinbarung einen Bezug zu zwei Vertragsstaaten . . . besitzt'('It is irrelevant in this connection whether the jurisdiction clause possesses a relationship to two Contracting States') This 'Zusammenhang'('connection') was Samtleben's '*forum prorogatum*/derogatum' formula, (1995) 59 *RabelsZ* 670, at p.691.

[377] ('It is however sufficient for the applicability of Article 17, that at least *one* Contracting Party lives within the ambit of the Convention'), (1990) *ZZP* 84, at p.86, Entscheidungsgründe I.1 (emphasis in original text).

[378] The Swiss *Bundesgericht* (but not the Austrian Supreme Court) is uncertain as to the application, or not, of Article 17 Lugano in a Category E (i) situation. Perhaps fortunately for the court, the Convention was found not to apply *ratione temporis* in its decision in *Galerie 3 c/ T.Inc.* 9.9.1993 119 BGE, III, 391, [1995] I.L.Pr. 448; *Sorelec SA contre Saleh Radwan* 23.12.1998 125 BGE, III, 108; in *Galerie X*, a Swiss auction gallery was suing an American purchaser in Berne; the court said 'Ob für die Anwendbarkeit von Article 17 des LÜ der Zuständigkeitsbezug zu *einem* Vertragsstaat ausreicht, kann hier offenbleiben . . .'('whether a jurisdictional relationship to *a single* Contracting State suffices for the applicability of Article 17 of the Lugano Convention, can remain open'), (1994) *SZIER* 488, at p.489 (emphasis original); but *contra* Bernasconi, C. (1993) *SZIER* 39, at p.64 'Der schweizerische Richter dagegen würde *nicht* das Übereinkommen, sondern das IPRG [The Swiss Private International Law Statute] anwenden, da prorogiertes Forum und Sitzstaat beide in der Schweiz liegen.'('The Swiss judge however would *not* use the Convention but the IPRG, since the prorogated forum and the domicile lie in Switzerland').

[379] *OLG München* 28.9.1989, IPRspr. 1989, Nr.194, Geimer; (1991) *IPRax* 46; *Digest*, Issue 5, 1993, D 17.1.1–B.26; criticised as incorrect by Huber, 1994, at p.194.

[380] Article 4 of the Brussels/Lugano Conventions permits this; note now the amendment to similar provision in the Brussels I Regulation, Article 4(1).

[381] ('a connection at least to a *further* Contracting State'), (1991) *IPRax* 46, at p.47 para.2(a) of decision; the essence of the German 'Reduktionstheorie'('limiting theory'; also explained in Gebauer, M. (2001) *ZeuP* 943, at p.952)—literal interpretation not mentioned specifically in *Coreck Maritime GmbH* (C387–98) [2000] ECR I-9337, at p.9372, para. 17.

Using the *forum prorogatum/derogatum* formula,[382] the court found that no other Contracting State was implicated on the facts of this case. Crucially[383] for a uniform application of the Article 17 and the Convention, it advocated that this additional internationality was a defining pre-requisite for the application of Article 17:

> Sinn und Zweck des Übereinkommens kann nur sein und muß als ungeschriebene Tatbestandsvoraussetzungen in Article 17 *hineininterpretiert werden,* daß lediglich die internationale Zuständigkeit im Verhältnis zwischen den Vertragsstaaten erfaßt wird.[384]

A reviewer[385] has pondered whether the English courts would demand an additional element of European Union internationality, were a similar situation to come before these courts as *fora prorogata.*[386] Using the example of a Lloyd's underwriter, suing an Australian assured in the High Court in London, on the basis of a jurisdiction clause in a MAR policy, there is no doubt in Geimer's mind that no such additional standards/prerequisites would be imposed[387] by the High Court, on Article 17, in England:

> Wenn ein australischer Unternehmer seine Industrieanlagen bei *Lloyds* in London versichert, welche Zuständigkeitsbezug besteht dann zu einem *anderen* Vertragsstaat?[388]

---

[382] ('a connection at least to a further Contracting State'), (1991) *IPRax* 46, at p.47 para2(a) of decision; the essence of the German 'Reduktionstheorie'('limiting theory'; also explained in Gebauer, M. (2001) *ZeuP* 943, at p.952)—literal interpretation not mentioned specifically in *Coreck Maritime GmbH* (C387–98) [2000] ECR I-9337, at p.9372, para.17.

[383] Only the Austrian *OGH* 23.2.1998 has explicitly gone as far: *Entscheidungen,* 71 Band, 1998, No.29, p.170, reviewed below, at p.204 section 2.1.5(iv).

[384] ('The aim and object of the Convention is and must be that it only encompasses international jurisdiction between the Contracting States—and this must be *interpreted into* Article 17 as unwritten factual preconditions'), (1991) *IPRax,* at p.48.

[385] Geimer, (1991) *IPRax* 31; Huber, 1994, at p.198.

[386] The application of either Article 17, or CPR 6.20(5)(d) would raise interesting issues if the English court decided to issue an anti-suit injunction. If Article 17 were held to apply, such an injunction could be considered as anti-conventional (despite *Continental Bank v Aeakos* [1994] 1 WLR 588, CA, with a cautionary note sounded in *Phillip Alexander Securities & Futures Ltd v Bamberger,* [1997] I.L.Pr. 73 (Waller J), affm'd, CA, [1997] I.L.Pr. 104 and now *OT Africa Line Ltd v Hijazy and others (The 'Kribi')* [2001] 1 Lloyd's Rep. 76 (Aikens J); *Banker's Trust International Plc v RCS Editori SPA* [1996] ECC p.899 (Longmore J); in English autonomous law, it may well not: *Youell and others v Kara Mara Shipping Co. Ltd* [2000] 2 Lloyd's Rep. 102, (Aikens J).

[387] It is only now clear that the High Court would take jurisdiction under Article 17 (not under CPR 6.20(5)(d)) in this situation, as, under Article 4, an Australian defendant can be sued according to national law. This does not affect the point, however, that if Article 17 were used, no additional criteria would be demanded; but *contra British Aerospace Plc. v Dee Howard Co.* [1993] 1 Lloyd's Rep. 368 (Waller J); now *Mercury Communications Ltd* [1999] 2 All ER (Comm) 33, (Moore Bick J); *Sinochem International Oil (London) Ltd v Mobil Sales and Supply Corp Ltd (No.2)* [2000] 1 All ER (Comm) 758; *Society of Lloyd's v White and others,* 3.3.2000, QBD, (Creswell J).

[388] ('when an Australian business insures its plant and machinery with Lloyd's of London, what jurisdictional relationship then exists with *another* Contracting State'), Geimer (1991) *IPRax* 31, at p.34; also note at p.34, this important observation: 'Träfe die vom OLG München favorisierte Reduktionstheorie zu, wäre Article 12 Nr.4 EuGVÜ n.F. nicht zu deuten.'('If the reduction theory favoured by the *OLG München* were to be applied, Article 12 Nr.4 of the Brussels Convention would have no meaning').

The restrictive application of Article 17 in Category E(i) cases has been confirmed by the *Bundesgerichtshof* in 1991,[389] in a case where a German bank was suing a Greek[390] company director under a loan guarantee, containing a jurisdiction clause for the courts of Düsseldorf. Again, the court decided that the governing provisions were §38 ZPO, and not Article 17. Unfortunately the court also (unusually) declined the invitation to refer the case for interpretation by the ECJ.[391]

This line of reasoning, when the German courts are seised *qua fora prorogata*, has continued recently in *OLG Saarbrücken*, 13.10.1999. Here a German company sought to sue its Polish supplier in Germany for breach of certain delivery obligations. In a Category E(i) case, the court stated that Article 17 was inapplicable:

> Vielmehr ergibt eine teleologische Reduktion, dass sich Article 17 EuGVÜ lediglich mit Zuständigkeitskonkurrenzen zwischen zwei Vertragsstaaten befasst.[392]

The German jurisprudence on the point is clear: only as *fora derogata* will the courts admit the application of Article 17: when one party (either claimant of defendant) and the chosen court are in a Contracting State, but the German courts are otherwise seised of a case *qua fora derogata*.[393]

The application, or not of Article 17, in a Category E(i) case is another example of an oddly idiosyncratic national law interpretation. Putting aside the preamble,[394] 'internationality' is demanded neither by Article 1 nor by Article 17, para.1. The strict wording of Article 17 is clear: it is unjustifiable to add to this, causing the inconsistent application[395] and interpretation of the Convention's provisions.

---

[389] *BGH* 14.11.1991, IPRspr. (1991) Nr.181; [1993] I.L.Pr. 298; *BGH* 4.12.1991, IPRspr. 1991, Nr.171, where Article 17 simply was not mentioned.

[390] Greece was not considered a Contracting State by Germany, since the action had been initiated on 28.2.1989, prior to the Greek Accession Convention's coming into force in Germany on 1.4.1989 (BGBl. II, p.214, 15.2.1989); additionally, of course, the court held that the case lacked a 'further connection' to another Contracting State, (1992) *ZZP* 332.

[391] (1992) *IPRax*, at p.369.

[392] ('Instead there is a teleological restriction, that Article 17 of the Brussels Convention is only concerned with competing jurisdictions between two Contracting States), *OLG Saarbrücken* 13.10.1999 (2000) *NJW* 670, at p.670; again, not a prerequisite mentioned in *Coreck Maritime GmbH* (C387–98) [2000] ECR I-9337, but factual situation not, it seems, *explicitly* dealt with.

[393] This is an alternative to Samtleben's conclusion at (1995) *RabelsZ* 670, p.696; Trunk (1996) *IPRax* 249, at p.252: 'Die Praxis wendet auf Gerichtsstandsvereinbarungen zwischen Inländern und Personen mit Wohnsitz außerhalb der EuGVÜ-Staaten *häufig ohne nähere Begründung* das autonome Recht (. . . §38 ZPO) an' ('Practice—*frequently without more detailed justification*—applies autonomous national law (. . . §38 ZPO) to jurisdiction clauses between persons domiciled within and outside the Brussels Convention Contracting States.

[394] Whose status and application regarding the Brussels Convention is problematic—views of the *Handelsgericht Zürich* 9.1.1996 *Thal AG gegen Vilvo N.V.*, reviewed below, at pp.205 *et seq.*

[395] As far as research has revealed, only the German and Austrian courts have given Article 17 a restrictive interpretation in this way; others in England and France have not confronted the issue in any detail.

2.1.5(iv)   Swiss and Austrian court decisions on Category E(i)

The potential for diverging views as to Article 17's scope under the Lugano Convention is demonstrated by three cases, two from Switzerland,[396] the other from the Supreme Court of Austria.[397]

The German position of requiring additional connecting criteria to the European Union, was followed by the Supreme Court of Austria in a case decided[398] on the 23 February 1998. The Austrian plaintiff sought repayment of overpaid freight costs from a Turkish defendant concerning the transport of loads from Berlin[399] to Taschkent in Turkey. In the contract of transport, the plaintiff alleged[400] that the parties had agreed on Vienna in a jurisdiction clause. Examining the German cases mentioned above, the court found that Article 17 should *not* apply to a situation such as Category E(i). In the interests of judicial harmony under the Lugano Convention, *inter alia*, in Article 1 of Protocol 2 on the uniform interpretation of the Brussels and Lugano Conventions,[401] the court felt that the decisions of other (overwhelmingly German) Lugano Contracting States[402] should only be departed from for compelling reasons.[403] Consequently it held that:

> für die Anwendbarkeit von Article 17 LGVÜ nicht ausreicht, wenn, wie im vorliegenden Fall, eine Partei mit (Wohn-) Sitz in einem Vertragsstaat mit einer solchen, die ihren Sitz außerhalb des Vertragsgebietes hat, die Zuständigkeit der Gerichte *des ersteren* vereinbart . . . Demnach ist es *auch ohne Bedeutung*, daß im vorliegenden Fall der Ladeort in Deutschland . . . lag.[404]

---

[396] *Tribunal cantonal vaudois Lausanne, 17.1.1995 Sonder-Diffusion gegen Res Kofler* reported in Volken, P.'Rechtsprechung zum Lugano-Übereinkommen (1995)' (1996) *SZIER* 69 at p.104; and *Handelsgericht Zürich 9.1.1996 Thal AG gegen Vilvo N.V.* again reported in Volken, P. 'Rechtsprechung zum Lugano-Übereinkommen (1996)' (1997) *SZIER* 335, at p.373.

[397] *OGH* 23.2.1998 30b 380/97, *Entscheidungen*, 71 Band, 1998, No.29, p.170; (1998) *JBl* 726; but a later case, OGH 2.9.1999 (2000) *ZfRV* 32, seems to come to the opposite conclusion—a claimant's domicile in Austria is sufficient connection for the application of Article 17.

[398] Burgsteller, A. 'Probleme der Prorogation nach dem Lugano-Übereinkommen' (1998) *JBl* 691, at p.695, asks why the Austrian court is 'protecting itself' from international disputes in this way.

[399] The fact that another Contracting State, Germany, potentially was 'involved' in the case, was not overlooked.

[400] The Austrian (international) procedural rules governing jurisdiction clauses, in §104 JN, require much stricter evidence of agreement than does Article 17 of the Lugano (and now the Brussels) Convention: for text of §104 JN Stohanzl, R. *Jurisdiktionsnorm und Zivilprozeßordnung*, 14 Aufl., 1990, p.188, and *Zivilgerichtliches Verfahren, Kodex des österreichischen Rechts*, 1998, at pp.32–33; Heiss, H. 'Die Form internationaler Gerichtsstandsvereinbarungen' (2000) *ZfRV* 202.

[401] [1988] OJ L319/9, at L319/31.

[402] Unfortunately, the decision of the Swiss *Handelsgericht Zürich* 9.1.1996 was not cited.

[403] *Entscheidungen* 71 Band, 1998, No.29, p.170, at pp.174–75.

[404] ('that it is not sufficient for the application of Article 17 Lugano Convention, when, as with the case at bar, one party with its domicile/seat in a Contracting State agrees to the jurisdiction *of this first State* with another, which has its seat outside the Contracting State areas . . . Therefore *it is of no import* that in this case the place of delivery was in Germany.') *ibid.*; Austrian autonomous law, §104 JN was applied instead; Huet would have a different view of the fact that a place of performance was in Germany, and would have applied Article 17: reviewing *Ollo c/ Caisse de Crédit mutuel de Brest Recouvrance* 27.3.1987 (1988) *JDI* 140, at p.142.

This, and the German position, may be contrasted with the first instance views of two Swiss courts.

An early decision of the *Tribunal cantonal vaudois Lausanne*, 17.1.1995 in *Sonder-Diffusion gegen Res Kofler*[405] applied Article 17 in a dispute between a Swiss plaintiff company Sonder and (at the time[406]) a non-Lugano Contracting State company, a German undertaking Res Kofler. The court unfortunately did not enter into any reasoned discussion of Article 17 Lugano Convention's scope *ratione materiae* or *personae*; but Volken, the case's reviewer, was in no doubt

[f]ür die Anwendung von Article 17 war der schweizerische Beitritt, genügend[407]

An important, reasoned, first instance decision of the *Handelsgericht Zürich*, *Thal AG v Vilvo N.V.*,[408] has come to the same conclusion. The Swiss plaintiff Thal orally ordered chemicals from the Belgian[409] defendant, Vilvo. The plaintiff then sent a confirmation[410] with its general conditions of purchase, including a Zürich jurisdiction clause, to which the Belgian defendant did not object, nor react. Sued for compensation for late delivery, the Belgian defendant then objected to the jurisdiction of the Zürich courts. In an unusually long judgment, the court set out the arguments for and against applying Article 17 Lugano Convention in a Category E(i) situation, and decided on a wider interpretation, and applied Article 17 on three[411] grounds.

The first reason for rejecting the German[412] 'Reduktionstheorie'—and not applying 'ungeschriebene Anwendungsvoraussetzungen'[413] to the case—was, in its view, the preamble to the Lugano Convention. This Convention, unlike the Brussels Convention, had a greater justified ambit of unifying aims—and unlike the Brussels Convention—was unfettered by the bias of an exclusive European Union background.[414] It would, in the court's view, be unjustified to restrict the

---

[405] Volken, P. 'Rechtsprechung zum Lugano-Übereinkommen (1995)' (1996) *SZIER* 69, at p.104.

[406] Germany only became a Lugano Contracting State on 1.3.1995.

[407] ('sufficient for Article 17's application was Swiss Accession'), (1996) *SZIER* 69, at p.105; i.e. that Article 17 seemed to apply on its own wording.

[408] 9.1.1996 reported in Volken, P. 'Rechtsprechung zum Lugano-Übereinkommen (1996)' (1997) *SZIER* 335, at p.373.

[409] At the time of the commencement of proceedings (i.e. prior to 1 October 1997), Switzerland considered that Belgium was a non-Lugano Contracting State.

[410] A 'classic' *Galereis Segoura SPRL v Rahim Bonakdarian* (C-25/76) 14.12.1976 [1976] ECR 1851 situation.

[411] From the preamble; the strict wording of Article 17 itself, and the confusion caused by applying the (German) notion of 'ungeschriebene Anwendungsvoraussetzungen'.

[412] The *Handelsgericht* did not consider the unifying interpretation provisions of the Protocol, as had the Austrian decision.

[413] ('unwritten/tacit prerequisites (for the application of Article 17)').

[414] Note Articles 60(c) and 62(1)(b) of the Lugano Convention. These Articles do indeed confirm the Lugano's less 'elitist' European stance by opening up at least the possibility of non-European Union States' acceding to the Convention. Poland has recently made use of this: Articles 10(b) and 12 of the CJJA 1982 (Amendment) Order 2000 SI 2000/1824, in force 1 August 2000, amending Sch.3C of the 1982 Act to include Poland among the Lugano Contracting States.

wide wording of a Lugano Convention article by additional[415] tacit requirements. Support for this view the court discovered in differences in the wording[416] of the preambles to the Brussels and Lugano Conventions: the former speaks of the desire to strengthen legal protection 'in the Community'; while the latter is more widely drawn: 'in [the] territories' of the Contracting States. The Lugano Convention was therefore felt to be less '<gemeinschaftsorientiert>'.[417]

The second and third reasons, and '[w]ohl das gewichtigste Argument für eine weite Auslegung[was] aber [Article 17's] *Wortlaut*[418]:[419]

> so sprechen die Aspekte der *Rechtssicherheit und der Voraussehbarkeit* der anzuwendenden Vorschriften eindeutig *gegen* die Annahme eines ungeschriebenen, zusätzlichen Erfordernisses.[420]

The court gave precedence to the parties' intentions in concluding a jurisdiction clause, ensuring predictability would triumph over the uncertain application of Article 17 that the German and Austrian approach would bring.[421]

2.1.5(v)   A solution?[422] The wording of the Brussels I Regulation and the draft Hague Worldwide Judgments Convention

The original Commission proposal for a Council Act[423] to replace/amend the 1968 Brussels Convention contained a re-worded first sentence to Article 17, prorogation of jurisdiction. Any mention of, or pre-requisite for, the domicile of one of the contracting parties in a Contracting State was omitted.[424] The proposed Article 17 read '[i]f the parties have agreed . . .' *simpliciter*.

Article 23 of the Brussels I Regulation, so far as is relevant for present purposes, re-enacts *verbatim*—except for the substitution of 'Member State' for 'Contracting State'—not Article 17 of the earlier December 1997 Commission Proposal, but the wording of the present Article 17(1) Brussels/Lugano Conventions. The

---

[415] Considered by the court to be a convoluted way of applying Article 17, at p.376 of the report.

[416] Not even considered by the Austrian Supreme Court.

[417] ('focussed on the community'), at p.375.

[418] ('really the most important argument for a wide interpretation [was] however [Article 17's] literal wording'); similar arguments could be deployed against the use of *forum non conveniens* when the wording of Article 2 is fulfilled; *contra, In re Harrods (Buenos Aires) Ltd* [1992] Ch 90, CA.

[419] (1997) *SZIER* 335, at p.375.

[420] ('therefore the aspects of *legal certainty and foreability* clearly speak *against* accepting an unwritten additional criterion'), *ibid.*

[421] *Ibid.* at p.377.

[422] The lack of a definitive position on the scope *ratione materiae* of Article 17 in *Coreck Maritime GmbH* (C387–98) [2000] ECR I-9337, underlines the need for redrafting, to exclude a domicile/habitual residence requirement.

[423] Submitted on 22.12.1997, 31.1.1998, [1998] OJ C33/20.

[424] Incidentally the solution taken up by Article 4 of the Hague Draft Worldwide Judgments Convention adopted by the Special Commission on 30.10.1999: http://www.hcch.net/e/conventions/draft36e.html, immediately below.

wording of the Regulation may not therefore[425] offer a solution out of the confusion over the issue of 'internationality in Article 17, especially in a Category E case, where a defendant is domiciled in a non-Contracting State.

The Regulation attempts instead to overcome any problems in this regard by re-drafting Article 4, which reads as follows:

> If the defendant is not domiciled in a Member State, the jurisdiction of the courts of each Member State shall, subject to Articles 22 *and 23*, be determined by the law of that Member State.

This provision will, in future, subject defendants not domiciled in a Member State to the (traditional) laws of that State, except in (now) two cases:[426] firstly, under Article 22, where a court of a Member State has exclusive jurisdiction; and secondly (as an innovation), when a court of a Member State has been prorogated by an Article 23 jurisdiction clause. The explanatory commentary to the July 1999 proposal—whose wording Article 23 of the Brussels I Regulation reproduces—reveals that national jurisdictional law under Article 4 will not 'operate where the defendant, although domiciled in a non-member country, has signed a contract containing a clause conferring jurisdiction on a court in a Member State.'[427]

Prima facie, at least, it appears that the problem of 'internationality' in a Category E case will be resolved by the Regulation; this may be an optimistic view, however. The 'exception' to Article 4 that Article 23 seems to represent will only operate if a Member State finds that Article 23 applies *ratione materiae/ personae*. This therefore once again throws open to individual Member State courts the interpretation of the phrase '[i]f the parties, one or more of whom is domiciled in a Member State, have agreed that a court . . . of a Member State [is] to have jurisdiction . . .'; the current jurisprudence, examined above, will no doubt be brought forward, with predictable idiosyncratic results for a uniform interpretation of the prospective Article 23. That such a solecism in Article 23 has not been redrafted, or even clarified, but left sanguinely for Article 4 to 'correct' is inexcusable.

Given the idiosyncratic and disharmonious interpretation of Article 17 of the Brussels/Lugano Conventions, this solecism is doubly stark when one considers the work that has been underway in the Hague Conference on Private International Law. Article 4 of the Preliminary Draft Worldwide Jurisdiction and Judgments Convention, adopted by the Special Commission on 30.10.1999, omits, in its opening sentence, any reference to—and so excludes the possibility of any irritating exclusionary permutations based on—the domicile of the parties. All that

---

[425] As, for some reason, the necessity of a domicile of one contracting party being in a Member State was *re-introduced*.

[426] Article 4 of the Brussels/Lugano Conventions only provide for an Article 16 exemption, which has been a cause of part of the problem.

[427] [1999] OJ C376 E, p.1, at p.13.

is necessary for its application is that 'the parties have agreed that a court or courts of a Contracting State shall have jurisdiction.' When the Draft Convention eventually comes into force in the UK, if an English claimant agrees with a defendant—wherever this defendant may be 'habitually resident' in the world[428]— that their dispute be heard before the English courts, Article 4 will apply *ratione materiae/personae*. This clarification is of course to be welcomed, as the potential for confusion is greatly multiplied with the possible number of Contracting State accessions to such a worldwide instrument.

2.1.6   Category F: Both parties are non-Contracting State domiciliaries,[429] but the courts of Contracting State X are chosen[430]

Category F cannot be dealt with in any detail. It is at least in its application *ratione materiae*, uncontroversial: should an action be initiated[431] by either non-Contracting State domiciliary in another forum than that specified by the jurisdiction clause, those courts must decline[432] jurisdiction under the unified provisions of Article 17 para. 2, unless and until the prorogated court has itself declined. Article 17 para 2 is a protective mechanism for the prorogated court.[433] The Article avoids the situation that one party could seise the courts of another Contracting State,[434] in which jurisdiction clauses are particularly anathema, whereupon the prorogated court 'second seised' would have to decline jurisdiction under Article 21.[435]

---

[428] Except, of course, in the same Contracting State as the claimant—but exceptions to this statement in Article 2 and Article 2(1)(a) of the Draft Convention.

[429] No definitive answer on the scope *ratione materiae* of Article 17 in *Coreck Maritime GmbH* (C387–98) [2000] ECR I-9337, underlines the need for redrafting, to exclude a domicile/habitual residence requirement.

[430] Article 17 para. 2, the 'abgeschwächte Regelung'('watered-down rule'), Trunk, (1996) *IPRax* 249, at p.252; *Internationales Vertragsrecht*, 5 Aufl., 1996, at p.1599, para. 2113.

[431] Gaudemet-Tallon, 1996, at p.77.

[432] Creating for non-Contracting States an entrance into the '"paradis"' that is the Community system, Droz, 1972, at p.117, para. 183(c).

[433] Inserted, at the UK's insistence, on its accession: Schlosser Report, [1979] OJ C59/71, at p.124 para. 177, to create a unified derogation effect in the other Contracting States—Kropholler, 1998 pp.233–34, paras. 12–13; and Pocar, F.: ' la delegazione britannica chiese e ottenne in sede di negoziato che il testo dell'Article 17 fosse modificato ...', 'the British delegation wanted and obtained at the negotiations that the text of Article 17 be modified in the ... in 'Linee di tendenza della Convenzione de Bruxelles sulla giurisdizione e l'esecuzione delle sentenze dopo l'adesione di nuovi stati' (1990) *Riv. dir. intern. priv. e proc.*, p.5, at p.10.

[434] Under the exorbitant rules of jurisdiction that may be invoked against non-Contracting State defendants in Article 3 para. 2.

[435] Assuming all the prerequisites for Article 21's application are satisfied; controversial in any event in the UK when the parties are Contracting State domiciliaries: *Continental Bank N.A. v Aeakos Compania Naviera S.A. and others* [1994] 1 WLR 588 and *OT Africa Line Ltd v Hijazy and others (The 'Kribi')* [2001] 1 Lloyd's Rep. 76 (Aikens J), below at p.243.

It is important to remember that in the prorogated forum, however, Article 17 has no application,[436] as neither party is domiciled in a Contracting State. In such a case, since either party may be sued as defendant under Article 4, it will be national law,[437] in all its idiosyncratic forms, that will decide whether the court has jurisdiction or not.

2.2   ARTICLE 17 AND BILLS OF LADING

An area that provides evidence that a divergence has occurred between both the jurisprudence of the ECJ and national courts, is in the treatment of third parties[438] in bills of lading cases. The attitude of the French *Cour de Cassation*[439] is especially revealing in this area, and has led to additional idiosyncratic preconditions[440] to Article 17's application in one particular Contracting State. When clauses derogate jurisdiction away from that considered to have been French,[441] Bonassies has graphically remarked that:

> un véritable typhon.. s'est abattu.. sur les clauses attributives de juridiction.[442] [443]

---

[436] Samtleben, (1995) 59 *RabelsZ* 670, at p.678: 'Im vereinbarten Forum dagegen in diesem Fall die Wirksamkeit der Prorogation *allein am nationalen Recht* gemessen'('In the agreed forum, however, in this case the efficacy of the prorogation is measured *solely by national law*').

[437] Samtleben, *ibid.*

[438] I.e. whether they are bound by an Article 17 jurisdiction clause, and the mechanisms to be followed to ascertain this.

[439] Especially *GIE Réunion européenne c/ Société Plate et Ruys, Cour de Cassation*, Ch. Com., 10.1.1995, (1996) *JDI* 141, (1995) *Rev. Crit.* 610 and *Soc. Riunione Adriatica et autres c/ Capitaine du navire Westfield et autres* 4.4.1995 (1995) *Rev. Crit.* 611; for a similar draconian view in French autonomous law *Cassation* 25.11.1997 *Insurance Company of North America and another v Société Intramar and another* [1999] I.L.Pr. 315, at p.319, para. 10.

[440] On the requirement of express acceptance of the clause by a consignee, and possible reasons for this, below, at p.216.

[441] In international shipping disputes, otherwise under other provisions of the Convention or the *Nouveau Code de Procédure civile*.

[442] ('a real hurricane has come crashing down upon jurisdiction clauses').

[443] 1995 DMF at p.197 n.83; for the *Cour de Cassation's* hostility to an Article 17 jurisdiction clause in a Lloyd's insurance policy, *Société d'études d'investissement pour les affaires (SEIA) c/ Souscripteurs des Lloyd's de Londres* 11.3.1997 (1998) *JDI* 139, reviewed below, at p.271; Delebecque explains the current French position 2000 DMF 11, at p.12, that the French consignee resisting application of an Article 17 jurisdiction clause in French proceedings, must specially or expressly accept the (Article 17) jurisdiction clause—simple possession of the bill of lading nor even acceptance of the goods therewith, does *not* amount to acceptance.

Whether this attitude is disguised protectionism[444] or not, is hard to ascertain, but according to Huet, the *Cour de Cassation*'s hostility to jurisdictional clauses in contracts is well known.[445]

Problems have arisen acutely in bills of lading cases, where the bill contains a foreign[446] jurisdiction clause, which a carrier seeks to invoke against (usually) a French consignee, who, in alleged breach of the clause, sues in France.[447] *The Tilly Russ*,[448] *Società Transporti Castelletti Spedizioni Internazionali SpA v Hugo Trumpy SpA*,[449] and now recently *Coreck Maritime GmbH v Handelsveem B.V., V. Berg and Sons Ltd*[450] have dealt squarely with jurisdiction clauses in bills of lading invoked against a third party consignee/holder. In these cases, it was held[451] that so long as the clause was initially valid as between shipper and carrier[452] ('the first limb'), then if, according to the law governing the bill,[453] the third party holder/consignee accedes to the shipper's rights and obligations, the requirements of a valid jurisdiction clause are satisfied as between carrier and that third party ('the second limb'). Allowing the third party to absent itself from the clause in such circumstances, it was said, would be 'alien to the purpose'[454] of Article 17, which is 'to neutralise the effect of jurisdiction clauses that might pass unnoticed in

---

[444] Brajeux thinks that it is 'Casenote: *The Nagasaki, Cour de Cassation* Nov.1994', Reuter Textline, Lloyd's List, 13.11.1996., at p.3; the French *Cour de Cassation* decisions will be harder to justify after *Società Transporti Castelletti Spedizioni Internazionali SpA v Hugo Trumpy SpA* (C-159/97) [1999] ECR I-1597, below, at p.212—unless, of course, French autonomous law regarding third party assignees has changed, below, at p.216; the effect of the ruling in *Coreck Maritime GmbH v Handelsveem B.V., V. Berg and Sons Ltd*, (C387–98) [2000] ECR I-9337, especially statements at p.9375, para. 26 is uncertain.

[445] (1976) *JDI* 143; recent examples, albeit under French autonomous law *Cassation* 25.11.1997 *Insurance Company of North America and another v Société Intramar and another* [1999] I.L.Pr. 315, at p.319, para. 10 (consignee must accept the clause); and *Cassation* 8.12.1998 *Compagnie d'assurances Helvetia e.a. c/ Delmas S.A.* 1999 ETL 551; *contra, Cour d'appel de Paris* 9.9.1999 *Cie Mutuelles du Mans c/ Sté Unison Shipping Private Ltd* 1999 DMF 829, also under autonomous law.

[446] I.e. non-French; cf now the reverse side of the coin in *AIG Europe SA v QBE International Insurance Ltd* [2001] 2 Lloyd's Rep. 268, (Moore-Bick J).

[447] Normally under Article 5(1) or Article 5(3) of the Convention, as the place of performance of the obligation in question (i.e. delivery) or where the damage occurred, subject of course now to the 'undisclosed' carrier/place of damage ruling in *Réunion Européenne SA and others v Spliethoff's Bevrachtingskantoor BV, and the Master of the vessel Alblasgracht V002* (C-51/97) [1998] ECR I-6511, at p.6542, para. 19; cf *OT Africa Line Ltd v Hijazy and others (The 'Kribi')* [2001] 1 Lloyd's Rep. 76 (Aikens J).

[448] *Partenreederei ms Tilly Russ & Ernst Russ v NV Haven- & Veroerbedriff Nova (The Tilly Russ)* (C-71/83), 19.6.1984 [1984] ECR 2417.

[449] (C-159/97) [1999] ECR I-1597, at p.1654, paras. 41–42.

[450] (C387-98) [2000] ECR I-9337.

[451] [1984] ECR 2417, at p.2435, para. 26; and *Hugo Trumpy*, above, at n.444, at p.1654, para. 42.

[452] *Quaere*, whether the original parties' domicile is important in this regard: Morse (1989) 1 *Afr.J.Int'l.L* 539, at p.564; *Coreck Maritime GmbH* (C-387/98) [2000] ECR I-9337, has, once again, reiterated the 'classic' *Tilly Russ* position, at p.9374, paras. 23–24; note that, in *Hugo Trumpy*, the recent amendments to Article 17 (Article 17 I (c)) do not affect the *The Tilly Russ* ruling; they merely make the first limb of *The Tilly Russ* (agreement between the original parties) easier to demonstrate.

[453] But various recent French authorities on this aspect, below, at pp.216–218.

[454] [1984] ECR 2417, at p.2435, para. 24.

contracts.'[455] So long as the clause initially fulfils Article 17's requirements,[456] as between carrier and shipper, it seems[457] that Article 17 thereafter falls away from the enquiry, leaving only the relevant national law[458] to determine whether the consignee is bound.[459] As will be shown, the French courts, at the highest level, have been ignoring this *Tilly Russ* 'formula', and refusing to give effect to what appear to be perfectly valid Article 17 jurisdiction clauses.

Even prior to *Tilly Russ*, there was no help given to the ECJ in the Convention itself to answer this third party problem,[460] but the one advocated was the only possible solution to bill of lading cases, without ruining commercial relations in the free negotiability[461] of bills. That the third party holder himself did not 'agree', within Article 17(1), seemed irrelevant.[462] The solution was eminently of great commercial sense. Ancel[463] does not criticise the ECJ on the inventiveness of its

---

[455] *Ibid.* now much relaxed (with regard to the original contracting parties), *Mainschiffahrts-Genossenschaft e.G (MSG) v Les Gravières Rhénanes SARL* (C-106/95) [1997] ECR I-911 and *Società Transporti Castelletti Spedizioni Internazionali SpA v Hugo Trumpy SpA* (C-159/97) [1999] ECR I-1597, p.1654, para. 43.

[456] *Ibid.*; Gaudemet-Tallon (1985) *Rev. Crit.* 385, at p.396; Kropholler, 1998 therefore incorrect when he states that *Mainsciffahrts* (and presumably now *Hugo Trumpy* and *Coreck Maritime GmbH*) have rendered *The Tilly Russ* obsolete, at pp.252–53, para. 54.

[457] (1996) *JDI* 141 at p.145; and the French reviewer of *The Tilly Russ* in (1985) *JDI* 158, at p.165; and *Glencore International AG v Metro Trading International Inc and others* [1999] 2 All ER (Comm) 899, at pp.915–16, (Moore-Bick J); *obiter* in *Firswood v Petra Bank* [1996] CLC 608, CA, (Schiemann LJ), at p.617—an assignee could take advantage of/be disadvantaged by an Article 17 jurisdiction clause respectively, such documents being frequently assigned; also *OLG Köln* 13.3.1998 1998 IPRspr. Nr.141, at p.260 and *BayObLG* 11.4.2001 (2001) *RIW* 699. The statement in *Coreck Maritime GmbH* (C387–98) [2000] ECR I-9337, at pp.9374–75, paras. 24–26 should not, it is submitted, affect the position of assignees, under Article 17 in England.

[458] *Quaere*, the *lex causae* of the bill, and in England and Wales, the Carriage of Goods by Sea Act 1992, s2(1)(2)—at least the UK Government's position in *Coreck Maritime GmbH* (C387–98) [2000] ECR I-9337—AG Alber's opinion 23.3.2000, at para. 70 and now *OT Africa Line Ltd v Hijazy and others (The 'Kribi')* [2001] 1 Lloyd's Rep. 76 (Aikens J); for Germany §§ 363 364 HGB—von Bernstoff, C. (2001) *RIW* 504, at p.506; *Raiffeisen Zentralbank Österreich AG v Five Star General Trading LLC* [2000] 1 All ER (Comm) 897, at p.903 (Longmore J); the ECJ in *Coreck Maritime GmbH* (C-387/98), at pp.9375–76, paras. 28–32, would not be drawn on this issue; *Cour d'appel de Paris* 9.9.1999 *Cie Mutuelles du Mans Navire Bonastar II* 1999 DMF 829; but Bonassies, apparently in the minority, at 1995 DMF p.93, who thinks this 'national law' should be the *lex fori*; Bernard-Fertier observes that the *Cour de Cassation* is not employing the *lex causae* route, (2001) *Rev crit* 359, at p.372; Takahashi, K. 'Jurisdiction over direct action against sub-carrier under the Brussels Convention' [2001] *LMCLQ* 107, at pp.112–13.

[459] Now confirmed in *Hugo Trumpy SpA* (C-159/97) [1999] ECR I-1597, at p.1654, at para. 41.

[460] Review of *The Tilly Russ* in 1985 *Rev crit*, 385, at p.395.

[461] *Ibid.* at p.396: 'on ne saurait réserver un sort particulier à la clause . . . sans ruiner l'economie d'un système national qui cherche à favouriser au maximum les relations commerciales en ce domaine en assurant une circulation facile du connaissement'; the *obiter* view of Schiemann LJ, in *Firswood Ltd v Petra Bank* [1996] CLC 608, regarding the transmission to third parties under a guarantee, at p.617; also *OLG Köln* 13.3.1998 1998 IPRspr. Nr.141.

[462] But contrast this with the findings in *GIE Réunion européenne c/ Société Plate et Ruys, Cour de Cassation*, Ch. Com., 10.1.1995, (1996) *JDI* 141 discussed below, at p.220.

[463] Ancel, B. 'La Clause attributive de juridiction selon l'Article 17 de la Convention de Bruxelles' (1991) *Riv. dir. intern. priv. e proc.* 263, at p.277.

solution, but condemns the Convention itself for not making any provision for third party transferees.

The European Court of Justice has recently had occasion to revisit this question of the relationship between Article 17, bills of lading, and the transmission of rights and obligations thereunder to third parties in two cases: *Società Transporti Castelletti Spedizioni Internazionali SpA v Hugo Trumpy SpA*[464] and *Coreck Maritime GmbH v Handelsveem B.V., V. Berg and Sons Ltd*[465]. Although the former case itself was concerned with an action under bills of lading, the major tenor of the case[466] has a wider impact on jurisdiction clauses concluded in international trade or commerce[467] than one would first expect. The reason for this is the case's confirmation and application of earlier jurisprudence in *The Tilly Russ*.

At para. 42 of *Hugo Trumpy*, the ECJ ruled again that the only parties who are relevant for Article 17 purposes are the original parties to the bill of lading: the shipper and carrier, who may or may not be Contracting State domiciliaries.[468] If the jurisdiction clause in question satisfies the (now expanded) Article 17 criteria, as is already known, 'it can be pleaded against the third party holding the bill of lading so long as, under the relevant national law, the holder of the bill of lading succeeds to the shipper's rights and obligations.'[469]

So far, this case has not advanced[470] our understanding of Article 17 beyond what—in a bill of lading context[471]—could have been gleaned from *The Tilly Russ*. What the case may in the future highlight will be two things: the scope of Article 17 *ratione personae*, and the rebellion[472] that seems to be underway in the French *Cour de Cassation*, the historical development of which is traced shortly.

In *Hugo Trumpy* itself, as will be recalled, Argentine shippers had (presumably) agreed with Danish carriers, Lauritzen, on the jurisdiction of the English High Court. The scope *ratione personae* of Article 17 is clearly fulfilled on its facts. But situations can be envisaged where a bill of lading contains a principal place of

---

[464] [1999] ECR I-1597.

[465] (C387–98) [2000] ECR I-9337.

[466] The problems specific to bills of lading—the relevant parties—took up only two short paragraphs of the Court's judgment, at p.1654, paras. 41–42; the substantial (material) parts of *Hugo Trumpy* are reviewed below, at pp.274–275, in the sections on 'awareness' of commercial 'usages'.

[467] The relevant sections of this treatment below section 2.4.2.

[468] The *Hoge Raad* asked, in question 2(a) in *Coreck Maritime GmbH v Handelsveem B.V.* (C387–98) [2000] ECR I-9337, the position as regards Article 17 and two non-Contracting State domiciliaries. In the Contracting State seised *qua forum derogatum*, presumably the second paragraph of Article 17 will apply in such a case.

[469] [1999] ECR I-1597, at p.1654, para. 41, adopting almost *verbatim* p.2435 para. 26 of *The Tilly Russ*, 'the second limb'

[470] Gaudemet-Tallon is scathing of the necessity for a reference in *Hugo Trumpy*, (1999) *Rev crit* 559, at p.573.

[471] *Ibid.*

[472] The *Cassation's* jurisprudence will sit uneasily with certain statements in *Hugo Trumpy*; now also by implication the reference to the law governing the bill of lading in *Coreck Maritime GmbH* [2000] ECR I-9337.

business of carrier clause,[473] the carrier is domiciled in a Contracting State, and the shipper is from a non-Contracting State, the Category E(i) problem, discussed above. If an action is commenced by a consignee in either the Contracting State designated in the place of business clause[474] or in another Contracting State, as *forum derogatum*,[475] what would be the position of the (original) parties under Article 17? For the application or not of Article 17 on such a set of facts, reference should be made to section 2.1.5, Category E(i), above, and the divergent answers given in the case law presented therein.

Recently, in *Coreck Maritime GmbH v Handelsveem NV*,[476] German time charterers/carriers, Coreck Maritime, under a bill of lading, agreed to transport goods from China to The Netherlands, presumably with Chinese shippers. The bill contained such a jurisdiction clause, and Coreck's name was printed on the reverse side. Handelsveem and others, as holders of the bill, sued Coreck for damages to the cargo in Rotterdam under Article 5(1) as the place of delivery.

The main aspect,[477] for present purposes, of the decision—especially with regard to the French courts' position, reviewed below, on the transmission to a third party of all, or any, and if so what, rights and obligations under a bill of lading—is the answer the ECJ gave to question 3 submitted,[478] in paras. 22–27.

As expected, the Court followed its previous jurisprudence developed in the *Tilly Russ* and *Hugo Trumpy*—that it is for the 'applicable national law' to ascertain whether a third party consignee/holder has succeeded to the[479] rights and obligations of one of the original contracting parties (the shipper).[480] If he does

---

[473] The exact status of such a clause, as regards the requirement of certainty, was also the subject of questions referred in *Coreck Maritime GmbH* [2000] ECR I-9337—questions 1 and 2; the problem caused to Sheen J by the drafting of such clauses in *The 'Rewia'* [1991] Lloyd's Rep. 69, at p.76—where there was in addition no clause to identify the carrier; cf. the lack of clarity of the clause in *Bundesgericht 28.1.2000 Elex AG gegen Crig-Hautefaye SARL*, unreported.

[474] From the facts of *British Aerospace Plc. v Dee Howard Co.* [1993] 1 Lloyd's Rep. 368, it appears Article 17 would not be employed by the English courts—but the opposite conclusion was reached in *Mercury Communications Ltd and another v Communication Telesystems International* [1999] 2 All ER (Comm) 33, (Moore Bick J).

[475] A German case has already applied Article 17 in a similar scenario: *OLG München* 8.3.1989 IPRspr. 1989 Nr. 186, [1991] I.L.Pr. 298.

[476] *Coreck Maritime GmbH v Handelsveem B.V., V. Berg and Sons Ltd, Man Producten Rotterdam B.V. and The Peoples Insurance Company of China* (C387–98) [2000] ECR I-9337.

[477] The drafting, and clarity, of the Article 17 jurisdiction clause was also an issue: the validity of the 'principal place of business of carrier' jurisdiction clause. The ECJ took a pragmatic stance, and seemed receptive to the autonomy of the parties: Article 17, it was said, 'must be construed in a manner consistent with those wishes [of the parties] where they are established', at p.9371, para.14; cf. *Bundesgericht 28.1.2000 Elex AG gegen Crig-Hautefaye SARL*, unreported.

[478] This had asked, at p.9374, para. 22, whether, and under what (extraneous) circumstances a third party could become bound by a jurisdiction clause, initially found to be valid as between the original contracting parties.

[479] As to whether this means *all* rights and obligations, or merely to *selective ones*, see the next paragraph in the main text. It is submitted that comments of the Court on p.9375, para. 25 hinting at a third party becoming vested with 'all the rights' is merely illustrative of the position when a third party is *already bound*.

[480] At p.9374, para. 24.

so, acceptance of a jurisdiction clause is irrelevant, and presumably therefore no longer a concern of Article 17.[481]

However, it is the next paragraph, para. 26, of the judgment that may be apt to cause confusion, and potentially necessitate a Contracting State court's *de novo* review of a jurisdiction clause under the requirements of Article 17, as between a carrier *and the third party himself*:

> ... if, under the applicable national law, [the third party] did not succeed to the rights and obligations of one of the original parties, the court ... must ascertain ... [under] article 17 ... whether he actually accepted the jurisdiction clause.[482]

The confusion,[483] it is submitted, will stem from whether this 'gloss' on the second limb of the *Tilly Russ* will apply either: (a) if the third party does not, or cannot, succeed to *any*[484] of the rights and obligations, *including* the jurisdiction clause (as when the foreign *lex causae* has no equivalent to s.2 Carriage of Goods by Sea Act 1992 at all); *or* (b) if the third party only succeeds to *a selective number of rights and obligations*—which means for our purposes, all rights and obligations *except* that contained in/represented by an (unfavourable) jurisdiction clause.

The Court was vague as to the answer to this point: if (a) is the correct interpretation of para. 26, the 'gloss' will not apply in England, at least in a bill of lading context;[485] if (b) is the preferred reading of para. 26—and this position may arguably have developed in France as a result of a line of *Cour de Cassation* jurisprudence, reviewed below at p.217 onwards—not only will the French stance have been vindicated, but a *de novo,* 'double' Article 17 enquiry will henceforth be necessary.[486]

For the sake of the unified, certain and sensible application of Article 17 in an already overcomplicated area, meaning (a) is certainly to be embraced. In such a case, it will no doubt be rare—although this is not known for certain—whether any particular Contracting States have a *lacuna* in their law on the transmission of rights and obligations to third party holders/consignees under bills of lading. However, interpretation (b) should be borne in mind when reading the next section, as it may have important repercussions on the French position regarding transmission under bills of lading, hitherto regarded as somewhat idiosyncratic.

---

[481] At p.9375, para. 25.

[482] At p.9375, para. 26.

[483] Especially having regard to what will be discovered in the following French section.

[484] Ie 'the entirety of'.

[485] Cf third party rights outside the bill of lading context, above at n.457 and n.461, and *Firswood Ltd v Petra Bank* [1996] CLC 608, CA.

[486] At least to ameliorate the situation with regard to the acceptance/transmission of jurisdiction clauses to third party consignees under French law: *Cour d'appel de Paris* 29.11.2000 *Soc Hapag Lloyd Container Linie et a c/ La Réunion Européenne et a.* 2001 DMF 684, at p.696, obs. Nicholas; also *Cour de Cassation* 8.12.1998 *Navire Silver Sky* 1999 DMF 1011.

2.2.1   Tracing the historical development of the apparent antipathy in the French cases to jurisdiction clauses in bills of lading

Shortly after the 'original' Brussels Convention came into force in France on 1 February 1973, the French courts were called upon to consider Article 17 in a bill of lading context: *Soc Sopropêche c/ Siekman*.[487] Long before *The Tilly Russ*, the court held that the bill of lading referring expressly to a charterparty, had included the terms thereof, with a jurisdiction clause in favour of the courts of Rotterdam. Indeed,[488] the *Cour de Cassation* itself in *Soc La Concorde et Cie A.I.C.A Lutèce c/ Soc Hamburg-Sudamerkanische*[489]—decided directly after the judgment in *The Tilly Russ*[490]—found that subrogated insurers of consignees could not sue the German carrier in France, but were held bound by a German jurisdiction clause in the bill of lading. Perhaps tellingly in this case, the shipper had expressly signed the bill of lading.

The same line of reasoning was followed in subsequent cases,[491] until a decision of the *Cour d'appel de Rouen*,[492] upheld on appeal to the *Cour de Cassation* in the *Isla-de-la-Plata*.[493]

A case that went through the French appeal court system on the issue of transmission to a consignee, was *Soc Riunione Adriatica c/ Le Capitaine du navire Westfield, The Westfield*.[494] A Norwegian shipper had loaded goods on board the *Westfield* for carriage from Brazil to Nantes. A bill of lading was issued by the carrier, Gearbulk Limited. Damage was noted on arrival by Huet company, the consignees. Huet's insurers sued, *inter alia*, Gearbulk, and these in turn relied on an English High Court jurisdiction clause. The first appeal decision[495] held that:

> il est usage dans le commerce maritime que les conditions générales soient pré-imprimées au verso des connaissements émis par les transporteurs . . .[496] [497]

---

[487]   *Tribunal de Commerce de Valenciennes* 27.11.1973 1974 DMF 173.

[488]   The first instance and appeal court decisions, as is revealed by the reviewer, Nicolas, show an awareness of the necessity for speed, and the lack of formalities.

[489]   *Cassation* 9.10.1984 1985 DMF 733.

[490]   The court did not however follow the *Tilly Russ* 'model' for Article 17, Nicolas, at p.737.

[491]   An example being *Cour d'appel de Paris* 4.12.1987 *Soc Sotrade Française c/ Soc Trois Dimmensions* 1989 DMF 113, and the cases cited therein.

[492]   *Cour d'appel de Rouen* 21.10.1992 *Nedlloyd Lines c/ Union des Assurances De Paris* 1992 DMF 703.

[493]   *Cassation* 15.11.1994 *Soc Nedlloyd Lines c/ UAP* 1995 DMF 357—confirming that the carrier could not point to a practice whereby a jurisdiction clause could bind a shipper (and therefore a consignee) who had not signed the bill of lading; *contra* Tassel, 1995 DMF, at p.361.

[494]   First appeal court decision *Cour d'appel de Rennes* 23.12.1992 1993 DMF 298; *Cassation* 4.4.1995 (1995) *Rev crit* 611; later referred back to *Cour d'appel de Caen* 20.3.1997 1997 DMF 714.

[495]   In 'classic' *Tilly Russ* fashion, without actually citing the case: *Cour d'appel de Rennes* 23.12.1992 1993 DMF 298, at p.300.

[496]   ('it is a usage in maritime commerce that general conditions are pre-printed on the reverse side of bills of lading issued by carriers').

[497]   *Ibid.*; now 'in a form which accords with' in *Hugo Trumpy* [1999] ECR I-1597.

and that therefore the clause could be invoked as against a third party and/or his subrogated insurers. When the case reached the *Cour de Cassation*,[498] the court annulled this decision on the ground that the appeal court had not ascertained whether the consignee, Huet Co., had accepted the clause in writing, according to Article 17.[499] The appeal had unfortunately arrived at the court at a time when the *Cour de Cassation*'s hostility to jurisdiction clauses' binding (French) third parties/insurers was at its zenith: *G.I.E. Réunion européenne c/ Soc. Plate et Ruys et autres*.[500] When the annulled case in *The Westfield* was remitted back to the *Cour d'appel de Caen*,[501] this court followed the *G.I.E. Réunion* decision, to the effect that to bind a consignee/third party holder of a bill of lading, the clause had to be (expressly) accepted by him. As regards the necessary (evidence of) acceptance, the court went one stage further and said

> [e]n prenant possession de la marchandise le destinataire manifeste sa volonté de bénéficier des droits essentiels nés du contrat . . ., *non de consentir à une telle clause*.[502] [503]

Perhaps somewhat drastically, Rèmond-Gouilloud recognises this line of jurisprudence may well have sounded the death-knell for jurisdiction clauses under Article 17 of the Convention;[504] yet subsequent cases have indeed confirmed the court's hostility to jurisdiction clauses.

The current position under French law—which, unless that law as the *lex causae* of bills of lading has undergone a serious *volte-face*,[505] cannot possibly stand in the face of *Hugo Trumpy*—is as follows:

---

[498] *Soc. Riunione Adriatica et autres c/ Capitaine du navire Westfield et autres* 4.4.1995 (1995) *Rev crit* 611.

[499] The *Tilly Russ*, and *Hugo Trumpy*, showed this line of reasoning to be fallacious, unless French law as the *lex causae* requires such a mode of specific acceptance of the jurisdiction clause (Article 37 *décret du 31 décembre 1966*, as amended by *décret du 12 novembre 1987*, 1990 DMF 154); Bernard-Fertier, (2001) *Rev crit* 359, at p.372—(once the clause is initially valid under Article 17 between shipper and carrier, questions of form drop from the picture—'the first limb' of the *Tilly Russ*; the ruling of *Sanicentral GmbH v René Collin* (25/79) [1979] ECR 3423 would have no effect on the second limb, it appears, because this case only affects the conditions as to form); but this may be the only way the French position may be defended, yet see *Cie Mutuelles du Mans* 1999 DMF 829, below at p.219, n.524; that the French law *qua lex causae* has changed is not the view of Rodière, R. *Droit Maritime*, 12ᵉ éd, 1997, at pp.336–7, para. 359: 'le transporteur peut en faire valoir toutes les clauses contre lui [le destinataire]. . .'; French doctrine in favour of the *lex causae* methodolgy: Bernard-Fertier (2001) *Rev crit* 359, at p.372; Takahashi, (2001) *LMCLQ* 107, at pp.112–113; note the recent more favourable view of jurisdiction clauses (at least outside the context of Article 17) by the *Cour de Cassation* in 12.7.2001 *Navire Bonastar II* 2001 DMF 994.

[500] 10.1.1995 (1995) *Rev crit* 610.

[501] *Cour d'appel de Caen* 20.3.1997 *Soc Riunione Adriatica c/ Soc Gearbulk* 1997 DMF 714.

[502] ('by taking possession of the goods the consignee signals his wish to benefit from the essential rights of the contract, not to consent to such a clause').

[503] *Ibid.* at p.714; whether such selectivity is legitimate under Article 17 is to English notions, highly questionable; it is unclear whether *Coreck Maritime GmbH* (C387–98) [2000] ECR I-9337, at p.9375, para.26, will encourage the 'selectivity' of the French position as regards the treatment of transmission of jurisdiction clauses; if it does, the French courts will be permitted to re-examine the agreement between carrier *and third party* under Article 17.

[504] *Ibid.* at p.720; *contra Hugo Trumpy*, at p.1654.

[505] The only possible explanation that Gaudemet-Tallon can find for the position of the *Cour de Cassation*, (1995) *Rev crit* 610, at p.616; but this does not seem to be the answer—note a case where the *lex causae* was ascertained and employed recently in *Cour d'appel de Paris* 9.9.1999 *Cie Mutuelles du*

[p]our être opposable au destinataire, la clause doit été acceptée par lui-même, de manière certaine, l'utilisation du connaissement *ne* suffisant pas à établir cette acceptation . . .[506][507]

2.2.2   The *Cour de Cassation* and bills of lading under Article 17: the position today

It is against this background that the *Cour de Cassation* has dealt with third party holders of bills of lading, resisting jurisdiction clauses, under Article 17.[508] The problems under Article 17 seem to have started in 1992 with its judgment in *Cie Royal Nederland Verzekeringen c/ Société Ethel*.[509] The dispute concerned the inland bill of lading dispute for the shipment of goods down the Rhine. The consignee, Ethel, sued[510] the ultimate carrier, Meijer, domiciled in Belgium and its insurers, Cie Royal Nederland, in the French courts in Strasbourg in breach of a jurisdiction clause in the bill nominating the courts of Duisberg, (Federal Republic of) Germany. The facts in this case were complicated by an agency and subcontract: the original contract of shipment had been concluded between a firm S&F Agency, agents for the shippers Malt, and a head-carrier De Grave. It was De Grave who sub-contracted the actual carriage to the defendants Meijer. It was established that the Agency and De Grave had been in a continuous business relationship using standard forms for ten years.

The defendants, Meijer, contested the French court's jurisdiction on appeal, contending that Ethel, as consignee, was bound by the German jurisdiction clause. The Commercial Chamber dismissed the appeal,[511] holding that Ethel had not *agreed* to the jurisdiction clause:

[u]ne clause attributive de compétence n'est opposable qu'à la partie qui en a eu connaissance et qui l'a acceptée au moment de la formation du contrat.[512][513]

Mans c/ Sté Unison Shipping Private Ltd 1999 DMF 829; *contra*, it appears, Delebecque, 2000 DMF 11, at p.12—the consignee 'n'accepte que les clauses qui font partie de l'économie du contrat, si bien que. . .les clauses de compétences, requièrent *une acceptation spéciale* de sa part.'; *quaere*, now, the position after *Coreck Maritime GmbH* (C387–98) [2000] ECR I-9337, at p.9375, para.26; cf *AIG Europe (UK) Ltd and others v The Ethniki* [2000] All ER (Comm) 65, CA and *AIG Europe SA v QBE International Insurance Ltd* [2001] 2 Lloyd's Rep. 268, (Moore-Bick J).

[506] ('to be able to be binding on the consignee the clause must be accepted by him, in a positive manner; use of the bill of lading does *not* suffice to establish this acceptance . . .').

[507] 1997 DMF 714, at p.720, Rèmond-Gouilloud.

[508] The trilogy of cases reviewed here and below, at pp.220–221 *et seq.*; position neatly summarised by Huet (2000) *JDI*, at pp.85–86.

[509] *Cour de Cassation* (Ch. Com.) 26.5.1992, (1992) *Rev crit* 703.

[510] Under Article 5(1), as the *forum executions*.

[511] From the *Cour d'Appel de Colmar*.

[512] ('a jurisdiction clause is only binding on a party who had knowledge of it and who accepted it when the contract was concluded').

[513] *Cour de Cassation* (Ch. Com.) 26.5.1992, (1992) *Rev crit* 703, at p.705; French Insurance Law, Decree of 12.11.1987, obliges the signature of the bill by the shipper—yet this additional national law

There was no debate, as the issue was simply not considered, as to whether the clause was valid under Article 17 as between shipper and carrier. The court then ignored 'the second limb'[514] of the *Tilly Russ*, without research[515] into the law governing the bill, nor whether a transmission of rights and liabilities had occurred according to that law. The decision is perplexing.[516] It confounds commercial practice, especially when the clause has been found to be binding between the original contracting parties.[517] More worrying for this work, is the fact that the *Tilly Russ* is being mis-applied:[518] the *Cour de Cassation* indicated in this first case its likely future attitude to non-French jurisdiction clauses, and its willingness to side-step *Tilly Russ* in the very aspect dealt with by this case.

The next case, chronologically, which has excited international comment,[519] is undoubtedly infamous—*The Nagasaki*.[520] Unat, a USA insurer, via its Paris-based representative Tour American Inc., sued the carrier Nedlloyd Lines, domiciled in Rotterdam, as a subrogated insurer in a damages action,[521] alleging the faulty carriage of goods aboard the vessel *Nagasaki*. Nelloyd had successfully challenged French jurisdiction before the *Cour d'Appel de Douai*, on the basis of a Rotterdam jurisdiction clause in the bill of lading. The *Chambre Commerciale* overruled this decision. In a totally unwarranted addendum to the *Tilly Russ* 'second limb',[522] the

---

prerequisite should not impact on the applicability of Article 17 however—*Elefanten Schuh GmbH v Jacqmain* (C-150/80) [1981] ECR 1671, and *Hugo Trumpy* (C-159/97) [1999] ECR I-1597, at p.1652, para. 35 and p.1653, para. 38; and 'Des clauses de connaissements maritimes attributant compétence à une juridiction étrangère: essai de démystification' 1995 DMF 1995, p.339, at p.340, Rèmond-Gouilloud.

[514] The 'first limb' being whether the clause is originally binding between shipper and carrier; the 'second limb' being whether under the 'relevant national law', the consignee succeeds to the shipper's rights and obligations; a formula confirmed in *Hugo Trumpy* and *Coreck Maritime GmbH*.

[515] Criticised for this omission by Gaudemet-Tallon, (1992) *Rev crit* 703, at p.707; on this occasion and later in the *GIE Réunion européenne c/ Société Plate et Ruys* case 'la chambre commerciale avait oublié l'Article 17 et l'arrêt Tilly Russ', (1996) *JDI* 141, at p.141.

[516] Cf Gaudemet-Tallon, (1992) *Rev crit* 703, at p.707.

[517] The consent or otherwise of the third party consignee in *The Tilly Russ* and *Hugo Trumpy* was wholly irrelevant; national law on the transmission of the rights and liabilities to the third party holder/consignee is the *only* consideration; however, *Coreck Maritime GmbH* (C-387/98) [2000] ECR I-9337, at p.9375, para. 26, appears to have added an unhelpful 'gloss' to this position, above, at p.214, when the third party does not succeed to (all) rights and obligations.

[518] Unless this line of authorities can be justified by a volte face in French law, as *lex causae*, regarding the transmission of rights and obligations to third party holders. If not, then *Hugo Trumpy* has strengthened the European Court's resolve to continue its *Tilly Russ* jurisprudence; question 3(a) and 4 of *Coreck Maritime GmbH*; Bernard-Fertier (2001) *Rev crit* 359, at p.372.

[519] Cf Brajeux, G. 'Casenote: *The Nagasaki*, Cour de Cassation Nov.1994', Reuter Textline, Lloyd's List, 13.11.1996.

[520] *Unat c/ Nelloyd Lines*, unreported, Cour de Cassation (Ch.Com.), 29.11.1994, Lexis Transcript; Cassation 16.1.1996 *Soc Les Assurances Rhône-Mediterranée et autres c/ Soc China Ocean Shipping Company* 1996 DMF 393; Cassation 25.11.1997 *Insurance Company of North America and another v Société Intramar and another* [1999] I.L.Pr. 315.

[521] The insurers having indemnified the consignee/cargo owners, became entitled to pursue the carrier in negligence/breach of contract.

[522] Above, at p.210; (C-71/83) [1984] ECR 2417, at p.2435, para. 26.

court held that for a jurisdiction clause to be enforceable against a consignee,[523] the clause had to be 'accepted' by the consignee, at the latest, when he adheres to the contract on delivery of the goods.[524] The appeal court had failed to ascertain this and its judgment was therefore quashed.

One can only speculate as to the *Cour de Cassation*'s motives. Has now a discernible trend developed in the *Cassation*'s attitude to jurisdiction clauses? May this not be seen as judicial protectionism and antipathy[525] to foreign jurisdiction clauses? Brajeux[526] notes, and offers one[527] possible reason[528] why, the court is taking such a strict view: that the *Cour de Cassation* is trying to reverse a national trend in the last twenty years of a decline in the French merchant fleet,[529] and to quell the annoyance of French shippers and consignees at finding themselves subject to foreign jurisdiction clauses. By making the conditions for the application of Article 17 that much more strict before the French courts, the *Cour de Cassation* is protecting the domestic consignee/shipper,[530] yet misapplying the *Tilly Russ*, and now, of course *Hugo Trumpy*.

[523] And therefore to be enforceable against its subrogated insurer.

[524] This reasoning cannot now be followed in the face of *Hugo Trumpy SpA* [1999] ECR I-1597, unless—which seems unlikely—French law, as the *lex causae*, on third party rights has itself been altered; Bernard-Fertier (2001) *Rev crit* 359, at p.372. However *Cour d'appel de Paris* 9.9.1999 *Cie Mutuelles du Mans Navire Bonastar II* 1999 DMF 829 shows that the court here had no qualms about finding a French consignee bound by a (Singapore) jurisdiction clause in a bill of lading because the bill was, crucially, not governed by French law, *qua lex causae*, but by the law of Singapore. Despite assertions from Rodière, R. *Droit Maritime*, 12ᵉ éd, 1997, at pp.336–37 this strongly suggests the French substantive law is the source of the problems, (especially Article 37 *décret du 31 décembre 1966*, as amended by *décret du 12 novembre 1987*, 1990 DMF 154 Article 1134 Cc, below at p.223, *Cour d'appel de Paris* 29.11.2000 *Soc Hapag Lloyd Container Linie et a c/ La Réunion Européenne et a.* 2001 DMF 684 (consignee must accept the bill of lading specifically, at p.694, obs. Nicholas); also Takahashi, *(2001)* *LMCLQ* 107, at pp.112–13; now the potential repercussions of *Coreck Maritime GmbH* (C387–98) [2000] ECR I-9337, at p.9375, para. 26, above at p.214, also Nicholas, 2001 DMF 684, at p.696; a similar restrictive application of Article 17 and transmission under Belgian law is reported by Goemans, B. 'Chronique de jurisprudence maritime belge' (2001) *Il diritto marittimo* 1194, at p.1196.

[525] No evidence could be found of any corresponding indulgence towards French jurisdiction clauses in bills of lading.

[526] Brajeux, G. 'Casenote: *The Nagasaki, Cour de Cassation* Nov.1994', Reuter Textline, Lloyd's List, 13.11.1996.

[527] Another reason, albeit unlikely in a Brussels Convention context, may well be that the French courts perhaps consider foreign adjudication of the substantive questions as inappropriate, i.e. an 'ordre public' exception has crept into the Brussels Convention's competence under Article 17— analogous observations in Forde, M. 'The 'ordre public' exception and adjudicative jurisdiction conventions' (1980) *ICLQ* 259, at pp.266, 270, 272—cf *The Hollandia* [1983] 1 AC 565; or an analogous position to that evidenced in the *action directe*, below n.530.

[528] In a related point to the previous footnote, Delebecque, 2000 DMF 11, at p.12, has recently opined that the French courts may be protecting (French) consignees from the lower limits of liability available from other Contracting State courts—cf *The Hollandia* [1983] 1 AC 565—now an impermissible consideration: *Hugo Trumpy SpA* (C-159/97) [1999] ECR I-1597, at p.1656, para. 51.

[529] This attitude by the French court may usefully be contrasted with the German courts' attitude to (a lack of) protection of German domestic share speculators in *LG Darmstadt* 2.12.1993 (1994) NJW-RR 684, at p.686—Article 17 was *not* ousted in this case to protect such individuals.

[530] Again the rights of an *action directe* under French (insurance) law, (L124 -3 *Code des Assurances*), that an injured third party has against the wrongdoer's insurers—particularly acute problems have occurred in French *actions directes* against P & I Clubs: for e.g., *The Charterers Mutual Assurance*

One can easily envisage a situation, which would not be conducive to the uniform application of the Convention, that might occur if the French consignee sues in France in breach of an English jurisdiction clause,[531] which, post *Nagasaki*, it seems easier for such a consignee to do.

One of the more recent cases in this area of the Convention is another decision of the *Chambre Commerciale*[532] on 10.1.1995: *GIE Réunion européenne c/ Société Plate et Ruys*.[533] As we have already seen, this case involved another subrogated insurer's action against a Dutch domiciled carrier, Plate et Ruys, commenced in the *Tribunal de grand instance* in Le Havre. Plate challenged the jurisdiction, contending that a clause in the bill of lading gave exclusive jurisdiction to the courts in Rotterdam. The *Cour d'Appel*[534] again held that the clause could be validly invoked against the consignee because the shipper had signed the bill;[535] again the Commercial Chamber reversed, holding that the lower court was not justified in finding the pre-requisites of Article 17 fulfilled. Rightly censuring the appeal court for only considering the 'first limb' of the *Tilly Russ* satisfied, and for not thereafter ascertaining whether 'by virtue of the relevant national law the third party, upon acquiring the bill succeeded to the shipper's rights and obligations',[536] the *Cour de Cassation* repeated its earlier formulation.[537] It then added that the lower court

---

Association Limited v British & Foreign and T.M.M. Transcap [1998] I.L.Pr. 838, and Fouchier, F. 'L'action directe contre les P & I Clubs' 2000 DMF 3, at pp.8–10; *Cour d'appel de Rouen* 17.12.1987 *Navire Sea Saint* 1988 DMF 477, at pp.485–87 and *Cour d'appel d'Aix-en-Provence* 12.2.1993 *Navire Irini M* 1993 DMF 532; in *Cour d'appel de Paris* 26.1.2000 *SARL Skuld et a.c/ Mutuelle Agricole de Côte d'Ivoire* 2001 DMF 668—arbitration clause adjudged inapplicable between subrogated cargo insurers and owners' P & I Club, and *quaere*, at p.675, obs. Tantin; now *Coreck Maritime GmbH* (C387–98) [2000] ECR I-9337, at p.9375, para. 26, which may perhaps have vindicated, for this type of procedure, a *de novo* examination under Article 17, (potentially in favour of the French third party claimant suing in France as *forum derogatum*).

[531] *The Charterers Mutual Assurance Association Limited* [1998] I.L.Pr. 838; the English courts may well react with an anti-suit injunction: *Continental Bank v Aeakos* [1994] 1 WLR 588 and *OT Africa Line Ltd v Hijazy and others (The 'Kribi')* [2001] 1 Lloyd's Rep. 76 (Aikens J) although the latter sounding a more cautious note in view of the following quoted case—*Phillip Alexander Securities & Futures Ltd v Bamberger*, [1996] CLC, 1757 (Waller J) CA at p.1780; any resulting judgment may also be refused recognition under the public policy exception Article 27(1) (Waller J) *obiter*, at p.1778 'albeit a judgment on the substance of the dispute is a Convention judgment it may well not be recognisable under Article 27 of the Convention if it has been obtained in breach of [a jurisdiction clause or] an arbitration provision', CA concurring at p.1788; *GIE Réunion européenne c/ Société Plate et Ruys, Cour de Cassation*, Ch. Com., 10.1.1995, (1996) *JDI* 141.

[532] Subsequently confirmed six days later by *Navire Chang Ping: Société Les Assurances Rhone-Mediterranée et autres c/ Société China Ocean Shipping Co.* 1996 DMF 393; *The Istanbul Z, Cour de Cassation* 24.1.1995, as yet unreported.

[533] (1996) *JDI* 141, at p.142: 'elle semble bien oublier l'arrêt Tilly Russ (on n'y trouve aucune allusion) . . .'.

[534] Rouen.

[535] (1996) *JDI* 142.

[536] From *Partenreederei ms Tilly Russ & Ernst Russ v NV Haven- & Veroerbedriff Nova (The Tilly Russ)* (C-71/83), 19.6.1984 [1984] ECR 2417, at p.2435, para. 26.

[537] From *Unat c/ Nedlloyd Lines*, unreported, *Cour de Cassation* (Ch.Com.), 29.11.1994, Lexis Transcript.

should have ascertained whether the consignee had *expressly*[538] accepted the clause on delivery.

Express acceptance by the consignee was never a part of *Tilly Russ*, indeed quite the reverse.[539] The consignee could never, until now, evade the jurisdiction clause simply by stating that he had not agreed to it.[540] The French reviewer of *GIE Réunion* correctly explains the true position thus:

> l'article 17 ne se préoccupe pas du consentement du tiers porteur du connaissement . . . [et] paraît tout à fait étranger aux problèmes posés par la transmission . . . Son objet est de déterminer les conditions, de forme et de fond, *qui doive être réspectées ab initio* . . . [*C*]*e qui peut advenir de celle-ci par la suite n'entre pas dans ces prévisions.*[541] [542]

If the *Cour de Cassation*'s views represent this highest court's attitude to jurisdiction clauses, i.e. that express consent of the consignee is needed, then the great majority of bills of lading clauses are in peril.[543] The French reviewers[544] are certainly confused as to why the *Cour de Cassation* has adopted this line of reasoning.

The *Cour de Cassation*'s attitude towards (French) consignees—and the confusion that French courts appear to be labouring under with regard to the two stages of *The Tilly Russ*[545] enquiry—has spread to Article 17 of the Lugano Convention. In a relatively recent *Cour d'appel de Paris* decision, *Soc. Atlantic Ocean Line c/ Soc Tati et Soc. AIG Europe*,[546] French consignees (and their insurers) were able to evade the application of Article 17 of the Lugano Convention (in favour of the prorogated court in Zürich favoured by the carrier, Atlantic Ocean Line). The reason given was simple:

---

[538] (1996) *JDI* 142, at p.142 and p.144, presumably by signing the bill on delivery signifies the consignee's acquiescence to the clause, not merely by being in mere possession of it—*Cour de Cassation* Ch.Com. 29.11.1994, in *Navire Stolt Osprey: CDF Chimie North America c/ Tolt Nelson et Stolt Cormorant* 1995 DMF 218; *Cour d'appel de Caen* 20.3.1997 *Soc Riunione Adriatica c/ Soc Gearbulk* 1997 DMF 714; *Cour d'appel de Paris* 29.11.2000 *Soc Hapag Lloyd Container Linie et a c/ La Réunion Européenne et a.* 2001 DMF 684.

[539] [1984] ECR 2417, para. 24; also Huet (1996) *JDI* at p.142 'l'arrêt Tilly Russ n'a pas dit que l'exigence d'une acceptation de la clause par le destinataire était imposée par l'Article 17'.

[540] *Ibid.* para. 24, if the law governing the bill indicated that rights and duties under it had been transferred to him; if the law governing the bill indicated that (all) rights and duties under it had been transferred to him; but now *Coreck Maritime GmbH* (C387–98) [2000] ECR I-9337, at p.9375, para. 26, may well encourage the French view.

[541] ('Article 17 is not concerned with the agreement of the third party to the bill of lading and appears to be totally unconcerned with problems posed by transference . . . Its object is to determine the conditions of form and substance that must be observed ab initio . . . that which may happen to it in due course does not form part of its further concern').

[542] Huet, (1996) *JDI* 142 quoting from 1985 *JDI* 165; the French reviewers are certainly confused as to why the *Cour de Cassation* has adopted this line of reasoning.

[543] Huet, *Ibid.*; if only under the Convention: *Cour d'appel de Paris Cie Mutuelles du Mans Navire Bonastar II* 1999 DMF 829, (correctly) decided under autonomous law.

[544] (1996) *JDI* 142, at p.144.

[545] And of course, now, *Hugo Trumpy* (C-159/97) [1999] ECR I-1597.

[546] 13.10.1999, unreported, Lexis.

la simple détention de ce document par le destinataire de la marchandise . . . n'emporte pas la preuve de l'acceptation de ladite clause.[547] [548]

Interestingly, the appeal court assessed the validity of the clause between carrier and consignee, Tati, under Article 17(1)(c)[549] of the Lugano Convention—(at least pre-*Coreck Maritime*) an incorrect application of both *The Tilly Russ* and *Hugo Trumpy*. No mention is made in the case—as *Hugo Trumpy* has re-emphasised[550]—that Article 17 is only of relevance to the initial relationship between the original parties to the bill of lading, the carrier and shipper (here an Indian company named Waridhi International).

This antipathy shown towards jurisdiction clauses invoked against French third party consignees is even more marked, and suggests that some sort of hidden agenda has singled these clauses out for especially harsh treatment, when the *Cour de Cassation* case of *Produits Servifrais c/ M. Le Capitaine du navire Monte Cervantès*[551] is examined. This case involved the transmission to a third party of a clause—not a jurisdiction clause—in a bill of lading, stipulating when delivery by ship's hoist by the carrier terminated its liability. Transmission to the third party was held to have occurred, and this clause therefore bound a third party consignee,

sans qu'il soit nécessaire que celui-ci ait spécialement manifesté sa volonté de l'accepter.[552] [553]

The fact that a distinction[554] is being made regarding the acceptance of jurisdiction clauses and acceptance of this type of limitation of liability clause in the same bill of lading—which may go some way in explaining why the *Cour de Cassation* has been so draconian with acceptance of jurisdiction clauses[555]—seems

---

[547] ('simple possession of the document by the consignee of the goods does not amount to proof of acceptance of the aforementioned clause').

[548] *Ibid.*

[549] It was said that since Tati, the consignee, had not signed the bill, its knowledge of the jurisdiction clause could not be demonstrated; neither did the address of the consignee on the bill amount to knowledge of the clause as a commercial usage widely known or regularly observed; *The Tilly Russ* and *Hugo Trumpy* were not referred to, even implicitly, in the decision.

[550] [1999] ECR I-1597, at p.1654, para. 42.

[551] 1996 DMF 627, at p.632 Delebecque P.

[552] ('without it being necessary that the latter expressly manifested its wishes of accepting').

[553] *Ibid.* at p.628.

[554] *Quaere*, whether this distinctive treatment of jurisdiction clauses will be sufficient to allow, after *Coreck Maritime GmbH* (C387–98) [2000] ECR I-9337, at p.9375, para. 26, a reappraisal under Article 17 vis-à-vis the third party.

[555] For harshness in a (marine) insurance context, *Société d'études d'investissement pour les affaires (SEIA) c/ Souscripteurs des Lloyd's de Londres* 11.3.1997 (1998) JDI 139 in section 2.4.4(ii) below, at p.271; criticised in a bill of lading context by Bokalli, 1998 DMF 115, at p.116; Flour, J. *Droit civil, les obligations, I: L'acte juridique*, at para. 458: 'tout se passe donc comme si c'était *le tiers ratifiant qui ait initialement contracté*' ('everything happens as if it was the ratifying third party who had initially contracted').

to stem from the general principles of French contract law,[556] and the freedom of contract[557] vested in the contracting parties in France. The differences in attitude to the clauses, Delebecque explains as follows: certain clauses—among them, this type of delivery clause—belong or participate in what is termed the '«économie»'[558] of the contract; while others—such as jurisdiction clauses—do not so participate.[559] The first type of clauses require no consent, while the latter do. Delebecque later explains, at p.630, that a delivery clause only delimits the extent of the carrier's obligations. Then he states that a delivery clause is

> l'expression de la liberté contractuelle et l'on sait que la liberté contractuelle est l'une des règles de base du droit contractuel[560] [561]

This presupposes therefore that jurisdiction clauses are not an expression of this freedom under French contract law. This distinction may[562] be the cause of the

---

[556] These requirements should be overridden in Article 17 Convention cases in any event; now *Francesco Benincasa v Dentalkit Srl* (C-269/95) [1997] ECR I-3767 and *Hugo Trumpy SpA* (C-159/97) [1999] ECR I-1597, at p.1652, para. 35, and p.1653, para. 38.

[557] All of these (formal) requirements should be overridden in Article 17 Convention cases in any event; now *Benincasa v Dentalkit Srl* (C-269/95) [1997] ECR I-3767 and *Hugo Trumpy* (C-159/97) [1999] ECR I-1597, at p.1652, para. 35, and p.1653, para. 38.

[558] Mazeaud, *Tome II, Obligations*, 1991, appears to state, in the context of assignment, that a jurisdiction clause would be a manifestation of the 'personal relationship' between the original parties, in this case shipper and carrier: 'les *exceptions fondé sur les rapports personnels* du cédé (carrier) et du cédant (shipper) . . . sont inopposables au concessionnaire (consignee)'/('the exceptions founded on the personal relationship of the carrier and the shipper . . . are binding on the consignee'), at p.1291, para. 1271; the discriminatory "économie" treatment meted out to jurisdiction clauses not mentioned, however, in Terré, *Les Obligations*, 6ᵉ ed., 1996, at p.958, para. 1194, p.975, para. 1215; nor in Rodière, R. *Droit Maritime*, 12ᵉ éd, 1997, at pp.335–37, para. 359; cf. in the context of the incorporation of an arbitration clause from one document to another in a reinsurance dispute: *Cigna Life Insurance Co. of Europe SA-NV & ors v Intercaser SA de Seguros y Reaseguros* [2001] CLC 1356, QBD, Morison J (agreement to arbitrate disputes was regarded as personal to the parties).

[559] 'Les stipulations véritablement dérogatoires sont en réalité celles qui ne concerne pas l'économie du contrat et qui ont un caractère procédural plus au moins marqué'/('The strict exception clauses are in reality those that do not involve the 'economy' of the contract and have a more or less obvious procedural character'), 1996 DMF 627, at p.632; jurisdiction clauses 'requiert au contraire une acceptation de la part du destinataire pour qu'elle puisse le lier'/('require on the contrary an acceptance from the consignee to be able to bind him'), at p.629—Article 1134 Cc is brought forward for supporting this stance, which regulates so-called 'clauses abusives'; cf however, *Cour de Cassation* (Ch. com) 7.7.1992 *Soc Belgamar et autres c/ Soc. Cameroon Shipping Lines* 1993 DMF 358; in Cassation 12.7.2001 *Navire Bonastar II* 2001 DMF 994, the *Cour de Cassation* has had a complete *volte face* in a case not governed by Article 17 (i.e. jurisdiction clauses do form part of the 'économie' of the contract); a certain similarity of approach to this can be seen in the question of incorporation, or not, or jurisdiction clauses in original contracts of insurance into treaties of reinsurance by general words such as 'All terms clauses and conditions as original'—*AIG Europe SA v QBE International Insurance Ltd*, [2001] 2 Lloyd's Rep. 268, at p.273 (Moore-Bick J); strict position with regard to acceptance re-iterated in an Article 17 case in *Cour d'appel de Paris* 29.11.2000 *Soc Hapag Lloyd Container Linie et a c/ La Réunion Européenne et a.* 2001 DMF 684, at p.694, obs. Nicholas.

[560] ('the expression of contractual freedom and that is known to be one of the rules based on the law of contract').

[561] *Ibid.* at p.632.

[562] But this does not explain the *Soc Belgamar et autres c/ Soc. Cameroon Shipping Lines* 1993 DMF 358 case.

Cour de Cassation's attitude to jurisdiction clauses regarding third parties.[563] This does not alter the fact, however, that when the Convention applies, it is Article 17, *Tilly Russ* and *Hugo Trumpy* alone which govern whether the requirements of form are satisfied, and whether a third party is bound by the jurisdiction clause.

The difficulties regarding Article 17 and third parties in French law appears to stem from an essential division: when the Convention applies, it is Article 17, *Tilly Russ* and *Hugo Trumpy* alone which govern whether the requirements of form are satisfied, but *not* whether a third party successor is bound by the jurisdiction clause.[564] The source of the problem in this section is French law—if this law, *qua lex causae*, with regard to the transmission of all[565] rights and obligations to third party consignees requires express acceptance, there is nothing in the Convention to prevent this, and nothing to cavil at; however, there is a hint that this rather harsh treatment is being reserved for 'foreign' Article 17 jurisdiction clause cases alone. If this is a correct assessment, it is feared that the French courts will find support from the comments of the ECJ in *Coreck Maritime GmbH v Handelsveem B.V.*, reviewed above at pp.213–214, to the effect that Article 17 may have to be reapplied[566] as between carrier and third party—when, as it appears, French law, *qua lex causae*, does not now permit transmission of (all) rights and obligations under a bill of lading to a third party, in requiring specific acceptance of a jurisdiction clause.

The comment in *Clunet*,[567] at p.145, also makes two further interesting points on the current French position. Firstly, if the consignee's express consent be required, surely the validity of the jurisdiction clause under Article 17 *ab initio*, between shipper and carrier is no longer relevant; and secondly, by speaking of the third party's consent at all,[568] the court is, in addition, demanding an Article 17 agreement[569] from him. Why does such agreement only have to be express? Why also not an agreement valid under Article 17(b) or (c).

---

[563] By maintaining this distinction, the *Cour de Cassation* can single out jurisdiction clauses for special treatment as regards third parties, requiring express consent from the consignee to bind him: *GIE Réunion européenne c/ Société Plate et Ruys, Cour de Cassation*, Ch. Com., 10.1.1995, (1996) JDI 141; now *Coreck Maritime GmbH* (C387–98) [2000] ECR I-9337, at p.9375, para. 26.

[564] *Benincasa v Dentalkit Srl* (C-269/95) [1997] ECR I-3767, at p.3797, para. 25 has recently confirmed the procedural autonomy of Article 17 jurisdiction clauses; cf *Bundesgericht 7.8.2001 Notrop Speditions- und Schiffahrtsgesellschaft GmbH gegen Transrail AG*, unreported.

[565] *Monte Cervantes* 1996 DMF 627, above at p.222, regarding transmission of a non-jurisdiction clause—quaere, now, the consequences of a selective transmission of rights and obligations in *Coreck Maritime GmbH* (C387–98) [2000] ECR I-9337, at p.9375, para. 26, above at p.214.

[566] In contrast therefore, Article 17 will not be reapplied in those Contracting States where *transmission is complete*.

[567] (1996) JDI 145.

[568] Not demanded by *The Tilly Russ* or *Hugo Trumpy* at all; but see now *Coreck Maritime GmbH* (C387–98) [2000] ECR I-9337, at p.9375, para. 26.

[569] I.e. in writing—by admitting one of the prerequisites of Article 17, why not all the others? A position fortified by *Coreck Maritime GmbH*.

Apart from negotiability suffering as a result of its recent decisions, the *Cour de Cassation* appears, for whatever reason, to be blatantly mis-applying,[570] and adding to, the judgment of the ECJ in the *Tilly Russ*.[571]

The Convention is not being uniformly interpreted in this important trade sector. The frequency with which jurisdiction clauses[572] are inserted into bills of lading[573] will be bound to lead to discord between the Contracting State jurisdictions.[574] The approach of the *Cour de Cassation* also raises suspicions[575] about the manner in which the Convention and its jurisprudence are being manipulated,[576] or even ignored, in such a cavalier fashion.

2.3   THE TENSION BETWEEN ARTICLE 17 AND ARTICLE 21[577]

Article 21, one[578] of the *lis pendens* provisions of the Convention, is designed to prevent the unseemly situation of having two Contracting States becoming seised of the same case, and the potential existence of two conflicting/irreconcilable

---

[570] Uncertain therefore the potential influence on the French caselaw of the recent ECJ ruling in *Coreck Maritime GmbH* (C387–98) [2000] ECR I-9337, at p.9375, para. 26.

[571] (1996) *JDI* 145; *Hugo Trumpy*, it appears, may have halted this 'rebellion'.

[572] More often than not carriers' principal place of business clauses, not French jurisdiction.

[573] Wilson, J. *Carriage of Goods by Sea*, 3rd edn., 1998, at pp.148–50 for bills of lading.

[574] Especially with England, where the Court of Appeal has been openly hostile towards jurisdiction-clause breakers, in *Continental Bank v Aeakos* [1994] 1 WLR 588; but note the slight retreat, as regards the grant of anti-suit injunctions suggested by Aikens J in *OT Africa Line Ltd v Hijazy and others (The 'Kribi')* [2001] 1 Lloyd's Rep. 76.

[575] As *Hugo Trumpy* has shown, the Italian *Corte di Cassazione* was a least receptive enough to arguments based on specific assent to foreign jurisdiction clauses (Article 1341 Italian Cc) to request a reference; so far as can be judged, it has not, of its own motion however, side-stepped them like the French cases—Bellagamba, G. and Cariti, G. *Il sistema italiano di diritto internazionale privato*, 2000, at p.10.

[576] By national contractual law considerations; these are not isolated incidents, French cases reviewed below, at pp.219–221.

[577] A UK contribution to a 'perturbation' in the Convention system. As a result of a recent reference to the ECJ by the HL in *Turner v Grovit and others*, [2002] 1 WLR 107, the Court will have the chance to assess the compatibility, generally, of the English practice of issuing restraining orders/anti-suit injunctions with the Brussels Convention system—where a defendant to English proceedings has already commenced, or threatens to commence, proceedings in another Contracting State in breach of an Article 17 exclusive (English) jurisdiction clause (as in this section), or merely to frustrate or obstruct proceedings properly before the English court (as in *Turner v Grovit* itself). In the result, and despite the reference, Lord Hobhouse would have dismissed Grovit's appeal, agreeing with the result of the Court of Appeal's decision. Any judgment of the ECJ will be of more than academic interest, since the only alteration to the status of jurisdiction clauses in the Brussels I Regulation comes in Article 4(1), regarding jurisdiction to be taken over non-Member State domiciliaries. This, it is submitted, is insufficient to make any difference to the attitude of the English courts presented in this section—in all material respects, Articles 23, 27 and 35(1) will inaugurate a similar situation under the Brussels I Regulation. Article 21(1)(6) and Article 26 of the June 2001 Commission II interim text of the Hague Worldwide judgments Convention will, however, render obsolete what most European commentators see as the stark, unilateral protectionist attitude of the English courts under Article 17 presented here: '[t]hese [and other] aspects [of Article 21] of the proposed Hague Convention constitute an important hedge against the risks of strategic behavior [sic]', Burbank, S. (2001) 49 *Am J Comp L* 203, at p.223, and esp at pp.221–22.

[578] Article 22 regulates stays in cases of 'related actions' (*Sarrio SA v Kuwait Investment Authority* [1999] 1 AC 32, HL); Article 23, where two courts may each potentially acquire 'exclusive jurisdiction';

Contracting State judgments.[579] As a result, where the 'same cause of action'[580] is pending between 'the same parties'[581] in any other Contracting State court than the court 'first seised',[582] the former court must stay its proceedings until jurisdiction in the latter is 'established'. Once this occurs, it must thereafter decline jurisdiction.

Tensions potentially exist between the operation of this article, and the views of courts that may become 'second seised' under Article 21, as *fora prorogata* under Article 17. This tension is especially acute in England,[583] where various ways have been found to out-manoeuvre the mandatory application of Article 21.[584] The simplest way was to state that Article 17 gives exclusive jurisdiction to the English courts, and therefore prevails over Article 21;[585] another is to apply in England for a

Article 19 which attempts to pre-empt the application of Article 23—*Coin Controls Ltd v Suzo International (UK) Ltd and others* [1999] Ch. 33, Ch.D (Laddie J).

[579] An Article 27(3) defence caters for 'irreconcilable' judgments; there is no provision, however, for two irreconcilable Contracting State judgments seeking enforcement in a third Contracting State. 'Irreconcilable' involves 'mutually exclusive legal consequences'—paraphrased from *Hoffmann v Krieg* (C-145/86) [1988] ECR 645, at p.668, para. 22, and, by analogy, *Macaulay v. Macaulay* [1991] 1 WLR 179.

[580] For the meaning of the expression, *Gubisch Maschinenfabrik KG v Guilio Palumbo* (C-144/86) [1987] ECR 4861, and *The owners of cargo lately laden on board the ship 'Tatry' v The Maciej Rataj* (C-406/92) [1994] ECR I-5439: a generic term in the English version of the Convention for the same 'cause' (facts and the rule of law relied on as the basis of the action) and 'objet' (what end the action has in view).

[581] For this phrase, again *The Maciej Rataj and Drouot Assurances S.A. v Consoldidated Metallurgical, Protea Assurance and GIE Réunion Européenne* (C-351/96) [1998] ECR I-3075.

[582] The crucial phrase in Article 21—seising first in England and Wales is essential; yet the comparative delays in international service under the 1965 Hague Service Convention *do not* represent 'very special circumstances' nor 'good reason' for ordering internal service by an alternative method (under CPR 6.8(1)) on a defendant domiciled in another Contracting State: *Knauf UK GmbH v British Gypsum Ltd and another* [2002] 1 WLR 907, reversing [2001] 2 All ER (Comm) 332, QBD, (David Steel J). For the meaning of the concept of 'first seisure' in English procedure (arguably unaffected by the changes in the 1998 Civil Procedure Rules), *Dresser UK Ltd and others v Falcongate Freight Management Ltd and others (The 'Duke of Yare')* [1992] 1 QB 502 and *Neste Chemicals S.A. and others v DK Line S.A. and Tokumaru Kaiun K.K. (The 'Sargasso')* [1994] 3 All ER 180, CA; *SDL International Ltd v Centre de Co-operation Internationale en Recherche Agronomique pour le Developpement* [2001] CLC 903; from 1.3.2002, there will be a change in English practice regarding 'first seisure', and a reversal of the current and apparently disadvantageous position: Article 30(1) Brussels I Regulation (*Knauf UK GmbH v British Gypsum Ltd and another* [2002] 1 WLR 907, CA).

[583] Concerns about potential jurisdiction clause/contract breakers is not new, HC debates 24.3.1982, Vol.20, col. 942, at col. 945–46, (Fletcher-Cooke, MP).

[584] Note recently that the use of anti-suit injunctions has perhaps become a wider manifestation of the English courts' malaise/unease (perhaps even mistrust) of the abilities of their Contracting State partners' correctly applying any of the provisions of Title II of the Conventions: *Turner v Grovit* [1999] 3 All ER 616, CA, [2002] 1 WLR 107, HL. The sentiments of the Court of Appeal regarding bad faith in commencing an action in another Contracting State merely to harass a claimant before the English court were echoed in Lord Hobhouse's speech in the House of Lords decision in *Turner v Grovit and others* [2002] 1 WLR 107, esp. at pp.120–1, his Lordship even believing that a 'restraint order' was not incompatible with the Convention (although the legitimacy of an English court's issuing restraining orders in such circumstances was referred to the ECJ); also Fentiman, R. 2000 CLJ 45, at p.47; *Phillips and others v Symes and another* [2002] 1 WLR 853, Ch.D, Hart J; cf Briggs, A. in *Lex Mercatoria: Essays on International Commercial Law in Honour of Francis Reynolds*, (Ed. Rose, F.D.), 2000, p.219, at pp.228–9.

[585] *Kloeckner & Co. A.G. v Gatoil Overseas Inc.* [1990] 1 Lloyd's Rep. 177, at pp.195–6 (not appropriate to 'downgrade' Article 17 in favour of Article 21, (Hirst J)); *IP Metal Ltd. v Ruote OZ S.p.a. (No.2)*

declaration[586] that the Article 17 jurisdiction clause is valid and subsisting, and for an anti-suit injunction[587] to prevent the further continuance[588] of any action in another Contracting State as the *forum derogatum*.[589] This, in turn, involved: examining the principles upon which anti-suit injunctions are granted before English courts,[590] with appropriate adaptation for the context of the Brussels Convention, if any; and distinguishing the 'causes of action' in both *fora* under Article 21, thereby preparing the ground for potential defences in England to recognition and/or enforcement of the 'rogue' foreign judgment under Articles 27(1)[591] and (3).

[1994] 2 Lloyd's Rep. 560, at pp.563–4 ('a stronger moral case' for Article 17's exclusivity, Waller J)); *Gilkes v Venizelos A.N.E.S.A* unreported, 29.10.1999, QBD, (David Steel J); Henry LJ in *Knauf UK GmbH v British Gypsum Ltd and another* [2002] 1 WLR 907, at p.926 conceded that the opposite view obtains in Germany (as to the ascendancy of Article 21 over Article 17).

[586] Or more recently for summary judgment on the issue of whether the respondent is in breach of contract in proceeding in the face of an agreement to the contrary: *National Westminster Bank plc v Utrecht-America Finance Co.* [2001] 3 All ER 733, at p.745, (Clarke LJ); when the *forum derogatum* is in another Contracting State, it is unlikely that special circumstances, such as those in *Union Discount Company Ltd v Robert Zoller and others* [2002] 1 All ER 693, CA, (Schiemann LJ) will exist; (fresh cause of action for re-imbursement of costs in striking out in *forum derogatum*).

[587] On the substantive principles for granting such measures (esp. in breach of a legal right not to be sued (anywhere else but in England)), Briggs, 1997, at p.269, para. 5.28; in *Donohue v Armco Inc and others* [2002] 1 Lloyd's Rep. 425, HL, Lord Bingham of Cornhill summarised (from Lord Goff's speech in the Privy Council in *Société Nationale Industrielle Aérospatiale v Lee Kui Jak*) what are now the undisputed principles to be considered in granting such an injunction; also Lord Hobhouse of Woodborough in *Turner v Grovit and others* [2002] 1 WLR 107, HL, at pp.118–9, who preferred to name such injunctions as restraint orders, so as to emphasise their *in personam* nature; whatever the nomenclature, it was recognised, at p.120, that pending the outcome of the reference, it is legitimate, at least in English procedural law, to issue such an order/injunction on the facts before the Court of Appeal and in the case of an exclusive jurisdiction clause; such an action not being inconsistent with the provisions of the Brussels Convention; *Akai Pty Ltd. v People's Insurance Co. Ltd* [1998] 1 Lloyd's Rep. 90; *Society of Lloyd's v White and others*, 3.3.2000, QBD, (Cresswell J).

[588] 'It would not be . . . an interference [with the exercise of jurisdiction of a court elsewhere] but merely the enforcement of a contractual promise' in *A/S D/S Svendborg and another v Wansa* [1996] 2 Lloyd's Rep. 559, at p.569 (Clark J).

[589] '[t]he continuance of foreign proceedings in breach of contract where the contract provides for exclusive English jurisdiction may well in itself be vexatious or oppressive' in *Sohio Supply Co. v Gatoil (USA) Inc.* [1989] 1 Lloyd's Rep. 588, at p.592 (Staughton LJ), a non-Convention case; in *Donohue v Armco Inc and others* [2002] 1 Lloyd's Rep. 425, HL, Lord Bingham restated the general rule: 'where parties have bound themselves by an exclusive jurisdiction clause effect should *ordinarily* be given to that obligation *in the absence of strong reasons* for departing from it'—such reasons may be that the interests of parties not bound by the clause are involved, a 'single composite trial' therefore proving impossible and a fragmentation of litigation inevitably resulting, were the clause to be upheld; *Turner v Grovit and others* [2002] 1 WLR 107, HL; also *Society of Lloyd's v White and others*, 3.3.2000, QBD, (Cresswell J) for a summation of the relevant principles.

[590] Including human rights aspects of anti-suit injunctions, and the issue of offending the sovereignty of the other Contracting State court: *OT Africa Line Ltd v Hijazy and others (The 'Kribi')* [2001] 1 Lloyd's Rep. 76, (Aikens J); it is clear from *OLG Düsseldorf* 10.1.1996, IPRspr. (1996) Nr. 167, [1997] I.L.Pr. 320, that a German court would feel that its sovereignty would be offended by even serving the application for an anit-suit injunction; confirmed recently by *OLG Frankfurt a.M.* 13.2.2001 (2001) *RIW* 464, 2002 NJW–RR 357.

[591] Below section 4.4.3 on the 'public policy' defence in such cases—*quaere*, post *Dieter Krombach*, public policy can be used to defeat enforcement of judgments that (to English eyes) had been rendered in breach of an Article 17 English jurisdiction clause (or any other 'inferior' Article of the Convention).

2.3.1   Article 17 prevailing over Article 21: the legitimacy of any review[592] by the court second seised of the jurisdiction taken by the court first seised, when deciding whether or not to 'stay its proceedings'[593]

The justifications, if any, for Article 17's ascendancy over Article 21 involve two inter-related aspects of the jurisprudence on Article 21—a comparative examination of the base of jurisdiction in both the court first and second seised, and the meaning to be attached to a certain phrase in *Overseas Union Insurance Ltd & Others v New Hampshire Insurance Company.*[594] In this case, as a departure point and general rule,[595] the European court noted that under Article 21 'the court second seised may, if it does not decline jurisdiction,[596] only stay the proceedings and may not itself examine the jurisdiction of the court first seised.'[597]

The interest for the present section comes from the lacuna left by the Court in this general principle, in the enigmatic phrase 'without prejudice to the case where the court second seised has *exclusive jurisdiction* under the Convention and *in particular*[598] under Article 16 thereof . . . .'[599] What exactly the Court meant by 'exclusive jurisdiction', its scope, and the words 'in particular' has been hotly debated.

Two articles of the Convention are expressed to confer exclusive jurisdiction on the courts of Contracting States, Articles 16 and 17: Article 16, in section 5 of Title II, does so in both its heading, and regardless of domicile; Article 17 does not do so in the heading,[600] and has an additional domicile requirement.[601] The ambit of Article 17's 'exclusivity' in regard to individual contracts of employment,[602] consumer contracts[603] and contracts of insurance[604] is severely curtailed (in comparison to Article 16). Article 18, too, has been interpreted in such a way[605] as to contribute to Article 17's dilution. Yet a court second seised as *forum prorogatum* under Article 17 is still expressed to have 'exclusive' jurisdiction under that

---

[592] Or perhaps better expressed as the ignoring of the jurisdiction taken by the court first seised.

[593] After the amendment to Article 21 effected by the San-Sebastian Convention [1989] OJ L284/1.

[594] (C-351/89) [1991] ECR I-3317.

[595] It is an 'exception' to this general rule (below, at p.232), that has proved to be controversial.

[596] The jurisdiction of the first seised court being contested.

[597] (C-351/89) [1991] ECR I-3317, at p.3351, para. 26.

[598] Tagaras, H. 'Chronique de jurisprudence de la Cour de Justice rélative à la Convention de Bruxelles—Années judiciaires 1990–1991 et 1991–1992' (1993) *Cahiers dr. europ* 653, at p.663.

[599] [1991] ECR I-3317, at p.3351, para. 26.

[600] This may be crucial—Briggs, A. 'Anti-European Teeth for choice of court clauses' (1994) *LMCLQ* 158, at p.161.

[601] At the very least, including other prerequisites.

[602] Article 17, para. 4—Franze, K. (2000) *RIW* 81.

[603] Article 15.

[604] Articles 12 and 12a.

[605] *Elefanten Schuh GmbH v Pierre Jacqmain* (C-150/80) [1981] ECR 1671—the submission argument unsuccessfully deployed in *Toepfer International GmbH v Molino Boschi Srl* [1996] 1 Lloyd's Rep. 510 (Mance J) at pp.514–15.

Article, and could just as easily be seen[606] to drop in the lacuna left in the general rule of non-review in *Overseas Union*.

Another problem surrounding Article 17's pedigree of 'exclusivity' comes from the recognition and enforcement provision of Article 28 I.[607] The link between the necessity to recognise or enforce any eventual Contracting State judgment[608] and the *lis pendens* provisions of Article 21 is re-enforced when reviewing the Court's comments in *Overseas Union*. The exact scope of the *Overseas Union* exception of exclusive jurisdiction, quoted above, is blurred by Article 28 I: an article which stipulates that under certain conditions, a judgment from another Contracting State shall not be recognised or enforced if the adjudicating court took jurisdiction incorrectly under sections 3, 4, or 5 of Title II.[609] When this prohibition is pre-emptively transferred *mutatis mutandis* to the *lis pendens* provision in Article 21, so the argument runs, the court second seised may safely ignore the fact that the court first seised had erroneously assumed jurisdiction in breach of the provisions of the aforementioned sections. Any ensuing judgment will not be entitled to recognition or enforcement in the enforcing, second seised, court (or any other Contracting State court) in any event. Logically, therefore, under these circumstances, a second seised court should not even have to stay its proceedings in favour of the court first seised. From the combined[610] perspective of 'exclusive jurisdiction', and Article 28 I, the question of *Overseas Union* must now be examined.

---

[606] Waller J in *I.P. Metal Ltd v Ruote O.Z. S.p.a* [1993] 2 Lloyd's Rep. 60, at p.62; *IP Metal Ltd. v Ruote OZ S.p.a. (No.2)* [1994] 2 Lloyd's Rep. 560. Note the 'stronger moral case' at p.564 (Waller J) under Article 17 than under even Article 16 to ignore the *lis pendens* requirements in Article 21, presumably on account of a choice having been made/expressed in contractual form.

[607] Implicit in this is also Article 34 II; *Overseas Union* [1991] ECR I-3317, at p.3350, para. 24 mentions that grounds for review of jurisdiction are to be found only in these Articles, suggesting that Article 17 does not have sufficient unalloyed exclusivity; but another ground for potential review introduced, causing 'no lasting injury', albeit in the case of the transitional application of the Convention: *Elsbeth Freifrau von Horn v Kevin Cinnamond* (C-163/95) [1997] ECR I-5451, at p.5476, para. 23.

[608] Note that the draft Hague Worldwide Judgments Convention includes a defence that will encourage the sanctity of the prorogation of jurisdiction. Article 26 of the draft states that '[a] judgment based on a ground of jurisdiction which conflicts with Article [..] 4 [choice of court] . . . shall not be recognised or enforced.' Whether this will stop the English courts issuing anti-suit injunctions is doubtful, but will at least concentrate the minds of the contracting parties, to the possibility of a *brutum fulmen* outside the rendering court *qua forum derogatum.*

[609] Matters relating to insurance, consumers (*OLG Stuttgart* 4.8.2000 2001 NJW-RR 858), or Article 16 exclusive jurisdiction; or the case falls within (an additional exception in) Article 59.

[610] Note, Article 16 is the only Article in the Convention to be blessed with exclusive jurisdiction *and* come within Article 28 I. Whether appearance in the latter suffices, will be examined below, at p.233.

2.3.1(i)   The second seised court believes it has 'exclusive jurisdiction' under Article 16[611]

Most commentators agree[612] that in this situation the court second seised need not decline jurisdiction, nor even stay its proceedings: for there to be a situation of *lis pendens*, two courts must both be competent under the Convention,[613] which, *ex hypothesi*, is not the case[614] if one court[615] has exclusive jurisdiction under Article 16. *Overseas Union* itself makes an express reservation for Article 16 to the general rule that the jurisdiction of the court first seised is not to be examined or ignored under Article 21:

> cette compétence[616] ne peut être établie puisque le second juge a une compétence exclusive.[617]

If one looks at Article 28 I, the Article 16 'reservation' is equally warranted by the fact that any resulting judgment rendered in breach of it must be refused recognition and enforcement in the second seised, or any other, Contracting State court.

2.3.1(ii)   The second seised court believes it has jurisdiction[618] *under section 3 or 4*[619]

Unlike in Article 16, jurisdiction in Article 11 I, relating to assureds among others, or in Article 14 III, relating to consumers, is not expressed by the Convention to be 'exclusive', and so does not seem to come within the precise exception left open in *Overseas Union*. Jurisdiction is said to be exercisable '*only* in the courts of the Contracting State in which the defendant [assured or consumer, respectively] is domiciled'. It is also subject to a number of enumerated exceptions and preconditions. Yet when Articles 11 I or Article 14 III do apply—a qualifying defendant may only be sued in one Contracting State, that of the defendant's domicile—this jurisdiction cannot, in a subsequent recognition and enforcement context, be anything else but 'exclusive'.

---

[611] Article 23 will resolve a dispute if both courts are exclusively competent; but, below, at n.659, *LG Düsseldorf* 27.2.1998 (1998) *GRUR. Int.* 804, re a breach of a European patent, where Article 16(4) was not mentioned.

[612] Droz, 1972, at p.192, para. 311; O'Malley, S. and Layton, A. *European Civil Practice*, 1989, at p.635, para. 23.08; Kropholler, 1998, at p.298, para. 17.

[613] Gaudemet-Tallon, 1996, at p.205, para. 282.

[614] *Ibid.* at p.211, para. 292.

[615] In the case of both courts, Article 23 resolves this problem.

[616] Of the court first seised.

[617] Gaudemet-Tallon, 1996, at p.211, para. 292.

[618] *OLG Köln* 13.12.1990 IPRspr. 1990 Nr. 195, on whether section 3 or 4 jurisdiction is 'exclusive'; in *OLG Stuttgart* 4.8.2000 (2001) NJW-RR 858, Article 13 I expressed by the court to be exclusive, breach of which prevented enforcement of an Austrian judgment under Article 28.

[619] Or that the first seised court may render a judgment in the circumstances envisaged in Article 59.

Considering Article 28 I's influence, as one did for Article 16, any prospective judgment from the court first seised must be refused[620] recognition and enforcement if rendered in breach of, *inter alia*, Articles 11 I and/or Article 14 III. Is this fact alone sufficient to invoke the *Overseas Union* exception? Does Article 28 I, in its entirety, provide a 'defence' to the obligation in Article 21 to decline or stay proceedings? Unfortunately, an answer to these questions may depend on which version of Article 21 applies *ratione temporae*. The earlier, pre-San Sebastian wording of Article 21 may not suffer such an Article 28 I exception, as no mention is made of the jurisdiction of the first court being 'established', but merely contested. The later version of Article 21, merely requires a stay 'until such time as the jurisdiction of the court first seised is established.' *Ex hypothesi*, this jurisdiction ought not be become 'established', if the court second seised has sole jurisdiction under Article 11 or Article 14. The later version, more that the earlier, would appear to permit a court second seised to ignore any prior proceedings by using Article 28 I.

There has at least been one German case that has discussed and ruled on this particular aspect:[621] *OLG Köln* of 13.12.1990.[622] The plaintiff in the German proceedings had insured construction risks involved in building Basrah airport with London-based insurers. At various times, but prior to the German court becoming seised of the present action, the London insurers had issued proceedings before the High Court for negative declarations of liability, and entitlement to avoid the insurance policy. In their turn, the German plaintiffs launched proceedings for declarations that the insurers were bound to indemnify them. The High Court had decided that the English court did not have jurisdiction over the German assureds. The insurers had appealed against this decision. Under Article 21 II of the pre-San Sebastian version, the first instance German court had stayed its proceedings, as it had the option to do,[623] since the English court's jurisdiction was 'contested'. The appeal court, the *OLG Köln*, rejected the appeal against the stay of proceedings, noting that Article 21 did not, unlike German autonomous law, demand a reasonable likelihood of the prospective foreign judgment's enforceability in Germany before accepting a plea of *lis pendens*. The court did, however, accept an exception to the Article 21 duty when the court seised second had exclusive jurisdiction under Article 16:[624] to require a court second seised

---

[620] For examples: *BGH* 2.5.1979 IPRspr. 1979 Nr. 198, 74 BGHZ 248 (breach of Article 12); *Mme Tonnoir c/ Société anonyme Vanherf* 9.2.1989 (1991) JDI 160 (breach of Articles 13 and 14); *Cour d'appel*, Luxembourg 15.5.1991 *Weber -Eurocard Belgium-Luxembourg* 1990–1992 *Pas. Lux.* 157, reported in English at [1993] I.L.Pr. 55 (breach of Articles 13 and 14); *OLG Stuttgart* 4.8.2000 (2001) NJW-RR 858.

[621] Regarding Article 17, and below, at p.233, *BGH* 8.2.1995 IPRspr. 1995 Nr. 165, *Re a Sale of Shares* [1996] I.L.Pr. 292.

[622] IPRspr. 1990 Nr. 195.

[623] IPRspr. 1990 Nr. 195, at p.394, the only alternative to declining jurisdiction.

[624] *Ibid.* at p.396.

with exclusive jurisdiction under Article 16 to decline this jurisdiction would undermine the _rationale_ of the Convention.[625]

As regards jurisdiction in the case before it, and in particular to section 3, insurance disputes, the court did not extend the same 'exclusionary'[626] effect, even though section 3 is included in Article 28 I:

> Eine analoge Anwendung dieser Grundsätze auf den Fall der _nicht ausschließlichen Zuständigkeit nach Article 11 GVÜ_ ist deshalb entgegen der Ansicht der Kl. weder geboten noch auch sachlich vertretbar.[627]

2.3.1(iii)   The second seised court believes it has 'exclusive' jurisdiction under Article 17

This aspect has proved to be the most controversial 'exception'[628] to the _lis pendens_ provision of Article 21. Most (continental)[629] commentators agree that a court second seised as _forum prorogatum_ under Article 17 must nevertheless[630] decline its jurisdiction in favour of the court first seised, regardless of the base of jurisdiction assumed by this latter court. As will be seen, the English courts have decided otherwise.

The ambiguity in the exception expressed in _Overseas Union_—that 'without prejudice to the case where the court second seised has _exclusive jurisdiction . . ._ and _in particular_ under Article 16'[631]—may or may not[632] permit Article 17 to be seen as an exception. Article 17 is clearly a genus of 'exclusive jurisdiction', though not as robust[633] in form as Article 16 'exclusivity'.[634]

The highlighted words from _Overseas Union_ 'in particular' appear to be enumerative[635] only, leaving open the possibility of other exclusive competences. AG

---

[625] IPRspr. 1990 Nr. 195, at p.394, the only alternative to declining jurisdiction.

[626] Cf. now _OLG Stuttgart_ 4.8.2000 (2001) NJW-RR 858.

[627] ('An analogous application of these principles to a case of _non-exclusive jurisdiction under Article 11 of the Brussels Convention_ is, contrary to the plaintiff's view, neither imperative nor objectively sustainable'), _ibid._ at p.396.

[628] If such it is.

[629] Especially Kropholler, 1998, at p.298, para. 18.

[630] Gaudemet-Tallon, reviewing _Overseas Union Insurance Ltd & Others v New Hampshire Insurance Company_ (C-351/89) [1991] ECR I-3317 (1991) _Rev Crit_ 764, at p.776, believing Article 17 to be in the 'exempted' category.

[631] [1991] ECR I-3317, at p.3359, para. 26.

[632] Beaumont, P. _Civil Jurisdiction in Scotland—Brussels and Lugano Conventions,_ 2nd edn, 1995, at p.174 para. 7.39, n.149 believes not.

[633] Article 18 may displace it; and it is also subject to more pre-requisites than Article 16; _contra,_ for Lord Penrose in _The Governor and Company of the Bank of Scotland v S.A. Banque Nationale de Paris_ [1996] I.L. Pr. 668, at p.713, para. 120, where Article 17's differing treatment in the Convention did 'not carry much weight'.

[634] Waller J's view quoted in _IP Metal Ltd. v Ruote OZ S.p.a. (No.2)_ [1994] 2 Lloyd's Rep. 560, CA, at p.564; _contra,_ Briggs, A. in Rose (ed) _Lex Mercatoria etc,_ 2000, p.219, at p.232.

[635] Briggs, A. 'The Brussels Convention casenotes: Overseas; Marc Rich; Van Dalfsen' (1991) _YEL_ 521, at p.527.

van Gerven in his opinion in *Overseas Union* was clearer in believing Article 17 is indeed included in the excepted category of competence:

> Whether Article 16 of the Convention, like other articles (for instance Article 17) which confer exclusive jurisdiction, constitutes an exception [to Article 21, did not, in *Overseas Union*, arise for decision.][636]

Yet Article 17 is not one of the limited bases of jurisdiction that an enforcing court must examine when deciding to refuse recognition or enforcement to another Contracting State judgment under Article 28 I. Indeed, in an Article 17 case, Article 28 III must expressly exclude any power of review at the enforcement stage. In the views of Continental commentators, this translates, at the point of considering whether or not to stay under Article 21, into an obligation to apply Article 21:

> da in diesem Fall die Wertung des Article 28 gegen eine Nachprüfbarkeit der Zuständigkeit des Erstgerichts spricht . . . Article 17 verdrängt den Article 21 nicht.[637]

This view is confirmed by *BGH* 8.2.1995:[638] where the German courts were held obliged to exercise the duty under Article 21 and decline jurisdiction in favour of the Italian courts, even though the parties had agreed, under Article 17, to the exclusive jurisdiction of the courts in Munich.

Even before *Overseas Union*, the English courts had earmarked the inviolability of Article 17, when it conferred 'exclusive' jurisdiction on the English courts: *Kloeckner & Co. A.G. v Gatoil Overseas Inc.*,[639] *The Filiatra Legacy*,[640] *Mark Edmund Denby and others v The Hellenic Mediterranean Lines Co. Ltd.*,[641] and now from *Continental Bank N.A. v Aeakos Compania Naviera S.A. and others*,[642] to *OT Africa Line Ltd v Hijazy and others (The 'Kribi')*.[643] The practical effects of the English courts views will be examined in the following section, 2.3.2.

In *Kloeckner*, Hirst J did not 'think it appropriate to downgrade those two articles [16 and 17] in favour of article 21',[644] and therefore declined to exercise the obligation incumbent upon a court second seised under Article 21 (and ignored

---

[636] [1991] ECR I-3317, at p.3339, para. 13.

[637] ('since in this case, the assessment of Article 28 contradicts a review of the jurisdiction of the original court . . . Article 17 does not oust Article 21'), Kropholler, 1998, pp.298–99, para. 18—but an analogous situation in *Cour d'appel de Paris* 13.10.1999 *Soc Atlantic Ocean Line c/ Soc Tati et Soc AIG Europe*, unreported, Lexis, where the French court took jurisdiction under Article 5(1) of the Lugano Convention, despite the fact that a Swiss domiciled defendant could successfully have resisted enforcement under Article Ia of Protocol 1 to the Lugano Convention.

[638] *BGH* 8.2.1995 IPRspr. 1995 Nr. 165, *Re a Sale of Shares* [1996] I.L.Pr. 292.

[639] [1990] 1 Lloyd's Rep. 177, at pp.195–96, (Hirst J).

[640] [1994] 1 Lloyd's Rep. 513.

[641] [1994] 1 Lloyd's Rep. 320 (Rix J) post- *Overseas Union*.

[642] [1994] 1 WLR 588, CA, post- *Overseas Union*.

[643] [2001] 1 Lloyd's Rep. 76 (Aikens J); *Apple Computers v Digit Srl*, 5.10.2001 (Goldring J): even when purportedly 'competing' Contracting State court (in Italy) not yet 'seised' due to incorrect service under local law and 1965 Hague Convention.

[644] [1990] 1 Lloyd's Rep. 177, at p.195.

the jurisdiction exercised in Germany). He felt himself free to consider his own jurisdiction under Article 17, unencumbered by any *lis pendens* interference. Saville J in *The Filiatra Legacy*[645] was even more forthright in his condemnation of the obligation under Article 21 to decline jurisdiction in favour of a court, which, in his view, *ex hypothesi*, has no jurisdiction:

> To my mind, this is a ludicrous proposition which if adopted would be calculated to cause unnecessary delay and expense for which I can see no justification whatsoever.[646]

His views were followed for the 'good reasons expressed in them'[647] by Rix J in *Denby and others v The Hellenic Mediterranean Lines*. As we shall see, in *Continental Bank N.A. v Aeakos*,[648] this view was taken one stage further by the Court of Appeal. While stating 'the structure and logic of the Convention'[649] point to the fact that 'if article 17 applies its provisions take precedence over the provisions of articles 21 . . .'[650] it confirmed an anti-suit injunction, granted in favour of the Bank against further pursuit of an action in Greece in (what the CA considered as a) clear breach of contract. The continuance of the Greek proceedings in violation of what the court found to be an exclusive jurisdiction clause, valid under Article 17, amounted to vexations and oppressive conduct.[651]

The Article 17 ascendancy view has also found favour in Scotland. Lord Penrose opined in *The Governor and Company of the Bank of Scotland v S.A. Banque Nationale de Paris*[652] that giving precedence to Article 21 by requiring the second-seised court to decline jurisdiction, would frustrate not only the contractual bargain of the parties, but also the presumed confidence reposed in the interpretation that the prorogated court would give to the Article 17 clause. In addition,

> [t]he Convention . . . would have succeeded in introducing wholly unnecessary and unjustified proceedings before the court first seised on an issue which, ex hypothesi, should not have arisen at all . . .[653]

The only (legitimate Community) ground that can be advanced in support of Article 17's ascendancy over Article 21, through the *Overseas Union* 'exception', is

---

[645] And subsequently repeated in *Rank Film Distributors Limited v Lanterna Editrice Srl and Banca Nazionale del Lavoro* [1992] I.L.Pr. 58, at p.72, para. 50.
[646] At p.514.
[647] [1994] 1 Lloyd's Rep. 320, at p.322.
[648] *Continental Bank N.A. v Aeakos Compania Naviera S.A. and others* [1994] 1 WLR 588.
[649] At p.596 (Steyn LJ); in *Alfred C. Toepfer International GmbH v Société Cargill France* [1998] 1 Lloyd's Rep. 379, Phillips LJ acknowledged, at p.386, that *Continental Bank* had provoked criticism, and that it was 'a pity that these proceedings [were] unlikely to provide an occasion for review.'
[650] *Ibid.*
[651] The case has been followed by Mance J in *Toepfer International GmbH v Molino Boschi Srl* [1996] 1 Lloyd's Rep. 510, at p.514, and in subsequent non-Convention cases involving alleged breaches of English jurisdiction/arbitration clauses.
[652] [1996] I.L. Pr. 668, at p.714.
[653] [1996] I.L. Pr. 668, at p.714.

that it has (a species of) expressed 'exclusive' jurisdiction. Yet it does not, like Article 16, have the backing of Article 28 I. If the *Overseas Union* reservation is confined to cases mentioned as having such jurisdiction, and additionally enumerated in Article 28, Article 16 is the only candidate.

2.3.1(iv) Proposals for reform of the Brussels Convention

Article 23 of the Brussels I Regulation, in section 7—'Prorogation of Jurisdiction'—last paragraph, contains similar protective provisions against the insertion of jurisdiction clauses into insurance (Article 13) and consumer contracts (Article 17), together with the familiar 'exclusive' competences, in Article 22. In the recognition and enforcement sphere, Article 42, first paragraph, stipulates that a Member State court 'shall refuse or revoke a declaration of enforceability', if a decision of another Member State court has been granted in breach of these above protective clauses. As with the current Brussels Convention, no mention, nor sanctification, is made of the 'exclusive' competence of Article 23. It appears therefore that the same permutations as rehearsed above will be perpetuated in the above Regulation. It may also safely be assumed that the wording of the Regulation will not divert an English court from its current (at least texturally unjustified) stance on the ascendancy of Article 17 over Article 21.

As has been briefly mentioned in footnote 608, above, the draft Hague Worldwide Judgments Convention *does*, however, provide respite from the tortuous route travelled by the English courts in upholding the inviolability of jurisdiction clauses, in its Article 26—a judgment given in breach of an Article 4 jurisdiction clause must be refused recognition and enforcement.

The current position is that the priorities of the English courts are to protect the sanctity and inviolability of the contractual bargain at the potential expense of having either two Contracting State courts seised of a case and/or the existence of two conflicting Contracting State judgments, which the spirit, if not the letter, of Article 21 (and Article 22) seek to prohibit. Given the European Court's propensity to decide cases on the footing that neither of the above scenarios is desirable nor permissible, it is likely that should an Article 17/Article 21 conflict case ever reach it on a preliminary reference, the Court would rule in favour of the application of Article 21. This would leave the English court to the possible solution in the next section.

2.3.2   The English courts 'second seised' in order to consider declarations that an Article 17 (English) jurisdiction clause is valid and subsisting, and actions in breach of Article 17 initiated first in other Contracting States

2.3.2(i) The 'same cause of action' enquiry in the two sets of proceedings

We have just seen that proceedings already 'pending' abroad in breach of an Article 17 jurisdiction clause[654] in favour of the English courts are no barrier, under Article 21, to the commencement or continuance of an English action. It must now be examined whether such actions here to declare the clause valid and/or[655] the granting of an anti-suit injunction have the 'same cause of action' under Article 21 as the proceedings abroad. Either the English court refuses to apply Article 21, or as here, applies it *ratione materiae*, yet concludes that the application for the anti-suit injunction on the one hand and foreign proceedings on the other do not involve the 'same cause of action'

(a)   The meaning of the same 'cause of action' An essential prerequisite for the court second seised under Article 21 is to ascertain whether the proceedings pending before it and the court 'first seised' involve the 'same cause of action'. If they do, the second seised court must, in theory, stay its proceedings pending any decision the first seised court may make as to its own jurisdiction; if they do not, the court second seised has a discretion under Article 22 to stay if, *inter alia*, the actions are 'related'. Yet the interpretation given by the European Court of Justice to this crucial phrase has not proved to be without its problems for the English courts in this area, and has been criticised[656] on a number of fronts.

The starting point in any consideration of the 'same cause of action' enquiry is, of course, *Gubisch Maschinenfabrik KG v Guilio Palumbo*[657] and *The owners of cargo lately laden on board the ship 'Tatry' v The Maciej Rataj.*[658] In the former case, as is well-known, the Court decided that an action brought by the German company, Gubisch, in Germany for the price of a machine delivered to the Italian company Palumbo, had the same 'cause of action' as the latter's action subsequently brought in Italy for, *inter alia*, a declaration that the aforesaid contract was inoperative. In the latter, *The Tatry*, following a similar line of reasoning, the Court found the same 'cause of action' between a shipowner's action in the Netherlands for a declaration of non-liability for contamination of cargo and those cargo

---

[654] Assuming the foreign proceedings fall within the ambit of the clause.

[655] *Continental Bank N.A. v Aeakos Compania Naviera S.A. and others* [1994] 1 WLR 588, CA.

[656] Especially Gaudemet-Tallon, 1996, at p.207, para. 285, diminishing the scope of Article *22 ratione materiae*; justified by Leipold, 'Internationale Rechtshängigkeit, Streitgegenstand und Rechtsschutzinteresse—Europäisches und Deutsches Zivilprozeßrecht im Vergleich' in Leipold (ed) *Gedächtnisschrift für Peter Arens*, 1993, p.227, at p.236, due to Article 22's vagueness.

[657] C144/86 [1987] ECR 4861.

[658] C406/92 [1994] ECR I-5439.

owners' subsequent action in damages before the English Admiralty court for the loss and damage they allegedly had suffered.

A number of important issues arise from these cases: the interpretative methodology for the phrase (same) 'cause of action' and its *raison d'être*.[659]

Gubisch v Palumbo decided that an interpretation of the phrase could not be arrived at by a comparative law approach of any existing concept in the national laws, but must be reflected in an autonomous Community definition. It drew this conclusion from the inspiration gathered in the aims of what was Article 220 of the Treaty of Rome, from the articles within the Convention itself—especially Article 27(3)—and from the fact that 'the term *lis pendens* as used in the different national legal systems'[660] is not referred to in Article 21 itself.

With a textual and linguistic comparison of the official versions of Article 21, the second part of the French version[661] of 'same cause of action' requires that both sets of proceedings have the same 'cause'. From *Gubisch*, we learn that this is meant to signify where both proceedings 'are based on the same contractual relationship',[662] while in *The Tatry*, it is expressed to comprise 'the facts and the rule of law'[663] relied on as the basis of the action'.[664]

More difficult to extract is whether the two sets of proceedings have the same 'objet'.[665] In *Gubisch*, the action to enforce the contract, and the other seeking its

---

[659] Together with its interpretation by national courts, and the criticism it has received: the phrase does not seem to have provoked a great deal of Continental case law discussing, in any depth, its scope or meaning; but *LG Düsseldorf* 27.1.1998 (1999) *RIW* 147; *LG Düsseldorf* 27.2.1998 (1998) *GRUR. Int.* 804, in both cases relating to patent litigation.

[660] C144/86 [1987] ECR 4861, at p.4874, para. 8.

[661] 'la même cause'.

[662] [1987] ECR 4861, at p.4875, para. 15.

[663] *Quaere*, application of different *lex causae* by the two Contracting State courts: *William Grant & Sons International Ltd v Marie-Brizard & Roger International SA.*, [1997] I.L.Pr. 391, Ct Sess. (Lord Gill). French action in Bordeaux was for this allegedly wrongful termination. The plaintiff/pursuer's claim in Scotland was for economic loss based on an alleged negligent misstatement by the defendant/defender's representation that payments under sales contracts would still be (but were not ultimately) made. This was not considered to be crucial: 'Although the present claim is presented as a claim *ex delicto*, it is not disputed that the damages claimed represent the value of the unpaid invoices . . . in effect a counterclaim to the action for damages for breach of contract raised by the present defenders', [1997] I.L.Pr. 391, at p.399, para. 27; while in *Sarrio S.A. v Kuwait Investment Authority* [1996] 1 Lloyd's Rep. 650, [1997] 1 Lloyd's Rep. 113, CA the difference was important: in English action in tort for negligent misstatement in relation to representations allegedly made by or on behalf of the defendants, inducing the plaintiffs to enter into a sale contract with one of the defendant's subsidiaries. Spanish proceedings 'an attempt, under Spanish legal principles, to "lift the corporate veil"' and to have the KIA held liable for its subsidiary's losses. The Spanish proceedings would concentrate on the relationship between the English defendants KIO/KIA and Grupo Torras/Torraspapel.

[664] [1994] ECR I-5439, at p.5475, para. 39.

[665] *Haji-Ioannou & Ors v Frangos & ors* [1998] CLC 61, Ch.D. (Neuberger J): proceedings in England did not have the same (generic) 'cause of action' as Greek criminal proceedings, with an annexed *partie civile* claim—the plaintiffs in Greece were 'only mounting a civil claim in the proceedings in order to give them locus standi to pursue their complaint . . .', at p.71. Neither when 'objet' of proceedings in the first Contracting State entirely lacking in the proceedings before the other Contracting State: *Grupo Torras S.A. and Torras Hostench London Ltd. v Sheikh Fahad Mohammed al-Sabah and others* [1995] 1 Lloyd's Rep. 374, QBD (Mance J) [1996] 1 Lloyd's Rep. 7, CA: recovery of damages for

rescission did not, at first sight, seem to have the same 'objet'—indeed quite the opposite. Yet the European Court has exhorted national courts to look at the broader picture, to see what[666] 'lies at the heart of the two actions'.[667] If, as in *Gubisch* itself, the later proceedings may be seen 'simply'[668] as a (complete) defence to the earlier, they will have the same 'objet'.

What would happen if this order were reversed? The answer to this was given in *The Tatry*. The case provided an opportunity to see the operation of the *Gubisch* case between two sets of proceedings, the first (in the Netherlands) seeking a negative declaration of liability for damages, while the later, in England, sought to hold the defendants liable for causing loss, and thus liable to pay damages.

From *The Tatry*, it appears that it is the 'end' the proceedings before the court second seised have in view that should be compared[669] to the end in the earlier proceedings. Using this method, the end(s)[670] the second English action had in view was (1) to find the shipowners liable for the contamination of the cargo and (2) the consequent imposition of damages on them for that liability. The prior Dutch action was found to have as its 'end . . . in view' 'a declaration that the plaintiff is not liable for damage.'

The fact that in the English action, a second subsidiary 'end . . . in view' sought damages, should not, according to the Court, have obscured the 'principal object'[671] of this case, the issue of liability. This was 'central to both actions'[672] and the two sets of proceedings therefore had the same 'objet'.

(b) The 'same cause of action' and the injunction under Article 17 Where the matter has been considered at any length whatsoever, the English courts have taken a very restricted view of what the 'cause of action' is in the English proceedings, and

---

conspiracy, breach of trust and directors' duties, would not be considered by the Spanish criminal proceedings; also *Sarrio S.A. v Kuwait Investment Authority* [1996] 1 Lloyd's Rep. 650, [1997] 1 Lloyd's Rep. 113, CA. *The Happy Fellow* [1997] 1 Lloyd's Rep. 130, QBD (Longmore J) affm'd on other grounds [1998] 1 Lloyd's Rep. 13, CA. Earlier French cargo damage liability and Admiralty limitation proceedings. At the heart of both actions was, ultimately, the circumstances surrounding the shipowner's liability for the collision, since 'whether the owners were personally at fault cannot be examined in a vacuum, divorced from the circumstances of the collision itself', at p.16.

[666] Note, in the singular—a common aim.

[667] C144/86 [1987] ECR 4861, at p.4876, para. 16; so it is common factors, or mutually inclusive, yet contradictory, wider aims that we are to identify: as a preliminary question before the German courts in *Gubisch* in the contractual enforcement action would have been the binding nature of the contract; this is exactly what the later Italian action sought to negate. The European Court combined the 'objet' of both actions to find a common denominator—the binding nature of the contract. The later action could said to be subsumed, *qua* defence, in the earlier, answering in the affirmative the question 'whether a finding in the one set of proceedings would [or might] be a conclusive answer to the question raised in the other'.

[668] *Ibid.*

[669] [1994] ECR I-5439, at p.5475–6, paras. 43–44.

[670] If it is correct to say that an action can have more than one end in view for Article 21 purposes?

[671] [1994] ECR I-5439, at p.5476, para. 44.

[672] At para. 43.

have merely made a mechanical comparison between the two actions, without attempting to extract any common denominator, as the European Court seems to exhort in *Gubisch* and *The Tatry*. This is evident from *Toepfer International GmbH v Molino Boschi Srl*:[673] Italian proceedings[674] had been underway for some time, arising from a sale contract, alleging short delivery of the goods. Almost seven years later, Toepfer applied to the English courts for a declaration that the Italian party Boschi, was, *inter alia*, obliged to refer the (or any) dispute to arbitration in accordance with the sale contract, and an anti-suit injunction. Did both actions involve the 'same cause of action'? Mance J thought not:[675] as to their 'objet', the Italian action involved a consideration of the terms and performance of the contract; the English action sought to stop this.[676] As to the 'cause' this was not the same either—again the terms regarding delivery fell for consideration in Italy, while in England 'whether the Italian claims should [have been] determined by arbitration in London'.[677] With respect, the judge's views of the 'cause of action' enquiry are too narrow, given the interpretation of this phrase in both *Gubisch* and *The Tatry*. The 'cause' of both actions in this case is clearly the delivery/sale contract. This is, according to *Gubisch*, entirely sufficient; the relative degree of overlap between issues in the two sets of proceedings—preliminary objections in Italy based on the London arbitration clause—should not be capable of influencing, to this uncertain degree, the determination of the same 'cause'. The European Court, faced with such a dispute, would undoubtedly not pick through the *minutiae* of the dispute to these lengths.

The 'objet' of both proceedings is more difficult to reconcile. As mentioned, in *Gubisch v Palumbo*, the main issue in one set of proceedings—the validity of the contract—was a preliminary issue in the other. Here Toepfer's action for, *inter alia*, a declaration that Molino were obliged to arbitrate in London would be a preliminary issue for decision by the Italian courts. One action is subsumed in the other, and if not stayed, may produce 'a conclusive answer to [a] question raised in the other.'[678]

In a sense, the Italian proceedings in *Gubisch* were designed to prevent the German proceedings from 'taking place', although not, it is true, on a

---

[673] [1996] 1 Lloyd's Rep. 510, QBD (Mance J); the question whether proceedings seeking to buttress the arbitration process—by requesting declarations of a duty to arbitrate—are excluded from the scope of the Convention *ratione materiae*, by Article 1(4) was the subject of a reference to European Court by the Court of Appeal in *Alfred C Toepfer International GmbH v Société Cargill France* [1998] 1 Lloyd's Rep. 379; but the case was not apparently received onto the ECJ's docket.

[674] The most recent decision of the court in Ravenna of 27.9.1996, *inter alia*, on Article 17, is reported at (1998) *Il Diritto Marittimo* 154.

[675] [1996] 1 Lloyd's Rep. 510, at p.513.

[676] And no doubt block enforcement in England (under Article 27(1)(3)) or (*quaere*) in a third country; and/or provide the basis for a breach of contract action.

[677] [1996] 1 Lloyd's Rep. 510, at p.513.

[678] Briggs, 1997, at p.142, para. 2.204.

jurisdictional, but a substantive level. Is this the vital difference that can justifiably distinguish the 'objet' in *Gubisch*, from those[679] in *Molino Boschi SrI*?

Views similar to those of Mance J's in *Molino Boschi Srl* were expressed in *The Charterers Mutual Assurance Association Limited v British & Foreign and T.M.M. Transcap*.[680] In this case, cargo interests[681] had initiated proceedings in France, claiming a (direct) right of indemnity in an *action directe*[682] against the Mutual Association, a P&I Club. Although there was agreement that in these proceedings the French courts would apply English law as the *lex causae*, it was less clear whether they would uphold the arbitration clause in the Association's rules as against the cargo interests—hence the English action seeking declarations that these claims were only to be settled by arbitration, and anti-suit injunctions.[683] Leaving aside, again, the Article 1(4) point, the judge believed 'that the ends[684] in view in the French and English proceedings [were] not the same in the two countries'.

Again, a perhaps too restricted view of 'objet' was taken in *The Charterers Mutual Assurance Association Limited v British & Foreign and T.M.M. Transcap*. Illuminating too is the plural use of 'end[s] the action has in view'. Such methodology distorts the definition of 'objet' in *The Tatry*.[685] It is for one global 'end in view'—'whether two actions have the same object'[686]—that the national court is to seek; not, as here, to compare *two* ends in view. This method,[687] in the vast

---

[679]   *Quaere* whether, like in *Gubisch*, a single unified 'objet' is to be extracted from both sets of proceedings, rather than comparing the two, *The Charterers Mutual Assurance Association Limited v British & Foreign and T.M.M. Transcap* [1998] I.L.Pr. 838.

[680]   [1998] I.L.Pr. 838, at p.855, para. 60 (A. Diamond Q.C.).

[681]   Or, more likely, their subrogated insurers.

[682]   Article L.124–3 *Codes des Assurances*. Cases cited by the court indicated French uncertainty as to whether the subrogated insurers would be bound by any jurisdiction clause in the policy of insurance—Fouchier, F. 'L'action directe contre les P & I Clubs' 2000 DMF 3, at pp.8–10; *Cour d'appel de Rouen* 17.12.1987 *Navire Sea Saint* 1988 DMF 477, at pp.485–87 and *Cour d'appel d'Aix-en-Provence* 12.2.1993 *Navire Irini M* 1993 DMF 532.

[683]   A similar protective action, at English autonomous law, against a similar statute, this time of Louisiana, USA, in *Youell and others v Kara Mara Shipping Co. Ltd* [2000] 2 Lloyd's Rep. 102 (Aikens J).

[684]   *Quaere, The Tatry* requires us to find one 'global' 'end . . . in view'?

[685]   *The owners of cargo lately laden on board the ship 'Tatry' v The Maciej Rataj* (C-406/92) [1994] ECR I-5439, at p.5475, para. 41.

[686]   *Ibid.* at para. 42; Briggs, A. in Rose (ed) *Lex Mercatoria etc*, 2000, p.219, at p.234.

[687]   *Alfred C Toepfer International GmbH v Société Cargill France* [1998] 1 Lloyd's Rep. 379 does not fit easily into this section. The parties had entered into a sale of goods contract on the GAFTA form, which included an arbitration and jurisdiction clause. Cargill claimed non-compliance with the contract and asked in *référé* proceedings in France, for the appointment of an expert to examine the goods. Although Cargill appointed an arbitrator, they also commenced substantive proceedings in the *Tribunal de Commerce de Saint-Nazaire* seeking a claim in damages, in which Toepfer objected to the jurisdiction (under Article 1458 NCPC) on the grounds of the arbitration clause. Toepfer, no doubt to protect its position, issued an originating summons in England, seeking declarations that Cargill were entitled and obliged to arbitrate under the contract. According to Cargill, while objecting to the jurisdiction of the English court to grant such declarations under Article 21, submitted that there were two 'causes of action' in the French proceedings: its substantive claim and Toepfer's objection to the jurisdiction under Article 1458 NCPC. The Court of Appeal was uncertain as to whether 'a procedural objection under the domestic civil code in the French court with a claim for relief based

majority of cases, may well lead to a finding of dissimilarity of 'objet(s)' under Article 21, and therefore the ability of the English courts to proceed under Article 17.

Some believe that the English courts' approach to 'cause of action' under Article 21 in these cases only stops short of protectionism, to express 'sympathy for the individual who has utilised a choice of court[688] clause, only to find it of imperfect effectiveness.'[689] This impression is heightened by statements in *Continental Bank v Aeakos*. As sole justification for the rationale of fortifying Article 17 against Article 21[690] the court held that

> a party will be able to override an exclusive jurisdiction agreement which is governed by article 17, by pre-emptively suing in the courts of another contracting state.[691]

That the English courts are indulging in protectionism in these situations may be putting the matter too high. That they are pre-empting a decision as to the validity and application of an Article 17 jurisdiction clause—which may or may not be raised *sua sponte* by another Contracting State *qua forum derogatum*—is clear.[692]

There is undeniably evidence[693] of a certain (justified)[694] mistrust of the ability, or willingness, of the derogated Contracting State courts to decline proceedings in favour of the UK courts; it is a measure of the weakness, or *lacuna*, in the Convention enforcement system,[695] and the potency of the *lis pendens* provision of Article 21. To see the opportunity for drafting rectification—in some form or other[696]—in the Brussels I Regulation squandered is regrettable.

---

on an allegation of breach of contract in the English court' can either be a 'cause of action', or can be equated as such.

[688] Or arbitration clause.

[689] Briggs, 1997, at p.153, para. 2.211; Hartley, T. 'Casenote: Overseas Union v New Hampshire Insurance' (1992) 17 *ELR* 75, at p.78.

[690] And not by any examination of what a 'cause of action' under Article 21 is.

[691] *Continental Bank N.A. v Aeakos Compania Naviera S.A. and others* [1994] 1 WLR 588, at p.596; correctness or otherwise of this decision not commented upon in *Turner v Grovit and others* [2002] 1 WLR 107, at p.124, HL.

[692] *Gilkes v Venizelos A.N.E.S.A.* unreported, 29.10.1999, QBD (David Steel J).

[693] Generally, with other Convention Articles, *Turner v Grovit* [1999] 3 All ER 616, CA, sentiments and reasoning approved by HL's decision, [2002] 1 WLR 107—but reference made to ECJ in any event on question of legitimacy of issuing restraining orders in a Brussels Convention case; also representations of counsel regarding a misuse of Article 6(1), and Hart J's concession in *Phillips and others v Symes and another* [2002] 1 WLR 853, Ch.D.

[694] Note the *Cour de Cassation's* attitude to jurisdiction clauses, in *Cour de Cassation* 11.3.1997 *Société d'études d'investissement pour les affaires SEIA c/ Souscripteurs des Lloyd's de Londres* (1998) JDI 139, (1997) *Rev Crit* 537.

[695] Having no censure equivalent to Article 26 of the proposed Hague Judgments Convention for the contract-breaking judgment creditor.

[696] Such as a clause mentioned in the previous note.

2.3.2(ii)   Preparing the ground for a defence[697] to recognition and enforcement of the 'rogue' (Contracting State) judgment under Articles 27(1),[698] 27(3)—the pre-emptive grant of an anti-suit injunction for breach of an (Article 17)[699] exclusive English jurisdiction clause[700]

In this section, the English court has passed above and beyond any requirements of staying/declining its jurisdiction under Article 21: be they general, such as the controversial and ambiguous prohibition on assessing the jurisdiction of the court first seised;[701] or specific, as in a consideration of Article 21's 'same cause of action' before both sets of proceedings.

Here we are concerned with the practical effect of the English court's decision that, despite Article 21, it has exclusive jurisdiction under Article 17, and how this view impacts upon the principles[702] under which such an order may be applied for and granted.

---

[697] Lord Hobhouse of Woodborough in *Turner v Grovit and others* [2002] 1 WLR 107, HL at pp.121–2, believed and emphasised that since the restraint order/anti-suit injunction operates *in personam*, there is no question of its grant becoming incompatible with the Brussels Convention system. As other Contracting States are unreceptive to the claim that (anti-suit) injunctions act only *in personam*, some States have refused even to serve them under the 1965 Hague Convention as constituting an infringement of their sole sovereign right to adjudicate upon claims before their courts: *OLG Düsseldorf* 10.1.1996, IPRspr. (1996) Nr. 167, [1997] I.L.Pr. 320, confirmed by reasoning in *OLG Frankfurt a.M.* 13.2.2001 (2001) *RIW* 464, 2002 NJW-RR 357.

[698] Below, 'public policy' chapter, and *Philip Alexander Securities & Futures Ltd v Bamberger & Ors and related action* [1996] CLC 1780, [1997] I.L.Pr. 73, CA; *Toepfer International GmbH v Molino Boschi Srl* [1996] 1 Lloyd's Rep. 510, at p.514 (Mance J); it is uncertain whether the English court would prevent by injunction, prior to the foreign adjudication, ultimate reliance on any judgment subsequently delivered: *Industrial Maritime Carriers (Bahamas) Inc v Sinoca International Inc. (The 'Eastern Trader')* [1996] 2 Lloyd's Rep. 585, at p.602 (Rix J).

[699] This section is equally valid outside the context of the Brussels Convention regarding exclusive English jurisdiction clauses/arbitration clauses and anti-suit injunctions, *Youell and others v Kara Mara Shipping Co. Ltd* [2000] 2 Lloyd's Rep. 102; and the principles and attitudes developed in one appear to be freely interchangeable with Article 17 Brussels Convention; although caution needs to be taken: it may (or should be) a strong factor against the grant of an injunction if either the basis for the English court's jurisdiction is another Article of the Brussels Convention, not expressed to be 'exclusive' (e.g. Article 6(1) in *Société Commerciale de Réassurance and others v Eras International Ltd and others (No.2)* [1995] 2 All ER 278 (Potter J) Briggs, 1997, at p.270, para.5.28), and/or the *forum derogatum* being that of another Contracting State.

[700] A claimant, forced to incur costs in applying to have proceedings struck out in the *forum derogatum* may, in certain circumstances, have a fresh and separate cause of action for damages for breach of contract for re-imbursement of those costs, particularly if they could not be awarded in the foreign striking out action itself: *Union Discount Company Ltd v Robert Zoller and others* [2002] 1 All ER 693, esp. at p.699 (Schiemann LJ), distinguishing especially *Jack L Israel Ltd v Ocean Dynamic Lines SA (The 'Ocean Dynamic')* [1982] 2 Lloyd's Rep. 88. The likelihood of success of this option in a Brussels Convention case, however, may be doubtful, esp. with regard to France, when costs of having proceedings successfully dismissed, due to a valid Article 17 jurisdiction clause, would presumably be awarded to the applicant under Article 700 NCPC; this aspect left open in *Union Discount Company Ltd*, however.

[701] Arguably this implicitly and automatically occurs whenever the English court decides to embark on a pre-emptive assessment of its own jurisdiction under Article 17; for the anti-suit injunction as an Article 24 'provisional, including protective measure', Briggs, 1997, at pp.266–67, para. 5.25.

[702] In general, these were reviewed in *Airbus Industrie GIE v Patel and others* [1999] 1 AC 119, at p.134 onwards by Lord Goff; however, he stressed that he was not, in formulating general principles, 'concern[ed]...with those cases in which the choice of forum has been, directly or indirectly, the subject

Before the substantive issues regarding the grant of an anti-suit injunction can be considered, and therefore any preparation under Article 27(1)(3) likely, *Continental Bank N.A. v Aeakos Compania Naviera S.A. and others*[703] and *OT Africa Line Ltd v Hijazy and others (The 'Kribi')*[704] have shown us that affirmative answers to two questions must be found before the English courts may even proceed to investigate the grant of an anti-suit injunction, under Article 17:

(1)   Disregarding Article 21 for reasons given in the preceding sections, is the Article 17 jurisdiction clause otherwise a formally valid[705] and subsisting one,[706] under the terms of Article 17(1)(a),(b) or (c), thereby conferring 'exclusive' jurisdiction on the English courts? If yes, then:

(2)   Is the dispute in question, underway in the alleged *forum derogatum* first seised, within the terms of the Article 17 exclusive jurisdiction clause?[707] If yes, then:

(3)   The English courts have exclusive jurisdiction and can safely disregard Article 21, as it does not require the English courts to decline jurisdiction.[708] Only then may an English court continue and consider, in its discretion,[709] whether to order the injunction.

Question (1) above, on Article 17's formal prerequisites is not peculiar or exclusive to this section, but arises even in an ordinary case where an English court is deciding jurisdiction; question (2) above is a matter of construction of the clause's wording as a matter of the *lex causae* of the clause/contract in question, and is not directly impacted by the Brussels Convention. So it is to the conclusions of *Continental Bank N.A. v Aeakos* and the discretion to grant the injunction that this section must now concentrate.

---

of choice between the parties', at p.138; also Lord Bingham of Cornhill's summary of the principles in an exclusive jurisdiction clause case in *Donohue v Armco Inc and others* [2002] 1 Lloyd's Rep. 425, HL— *in casu*, setting aside, on terms, the CA's grant of an injunction on the facts, as strong reasons for not enforcing the clause found to exist; also *Turner v Grovit and others* [2002] 1 WLR 107, HL, at pp.118–9.

[703] [1994] 1 WLR 588, CA (Steyn LJ); *Credit Suisse First Boston (Europe) Ltd v MLC (Bermuda) Ltd* [1999] 1 Lloyd's Rep. 767, at pp.775–78, (Rix J).

[704] [2001] 1 Lloyd's Rep. 76 (Aikens J).

[705] Waller J in *Philip Alexander Securities & Futures Ltd v Bamberger & Ors and related action* [1996] CLC 1757, when an (arbitration) clause is found to be invalid.

[706] Note also an application for summary judgment on the issue: *National Westminster Bank plc v Utrecht-America Finance Co.* [2001] 2 All ER (Comm) 7, at pp.19–20 (Clarke LJ).

[707] *Kitechnology BV and others v Unicor GmbH Plastmaschinen and others* [1994] I.L.Pr. 568, at pp.575–76 (Evans LJ).

[708] The conclusion of Steyn LJ in *Continental Bank N.A. v Aeakos Compania Naviera S.A. and others* [1994] 1 WLR 588; the interesting aspect of *OT Africa Line Ltd v Hijazy and others (The 'Kribi')* [2001] 1 Lloyd's Rep. 76 was the attempt to distinguish *Continental Bank*; counsel admitted that if it could not, questions (1) and (2) above would need to be considered.

[709] For the basis of this, Briggs, 1997, at p.268 onwards for general requirements; *Airbus Industrie GIE v Patel and others* [1999] 1 AC 119; *National Westminster Bank plc v Utrecht-America Finance Co.* [2001] 2 All ER (Comm) 7.

(a) Continental Bank N.A. v Aeakos Compania Naviera S.A. and its progeny At
least at and below Court of Appeal level, *Continental Bank N.A. v Aeakos* is authority for the proposition that whenever an English court is second seised under an
otherwise valid Article 17[710] exclusive English jurisdiction clause—and another
Contracting State court is first seised of a dispute which, in the eyes of the English
court, falls within that clause's scope—the English court may disregard its duty
under Article 21 to decline jurisdiction; thereby giving precedence to Article 17.[711]
In addition, it may enjoin by means of an anti-suit injunction pursuit of further
proceedings in the other Contracting State court. Its *ratio* has been followed in
other (Court of Appeal) decisions,[712] reaching to cases outside the scope of the
Brussels Convention, when a recalcitrant defendant, wherever domiciled, has
commenced proceedings in adjudged breach of an English exclusive jurisdiction
clause/arbitration clause in a non-Contracting State.[713] Steyn LJ was no doubt
keen to avoid the ability of a Contracting State party, using the machinery of 'first
seisure' and mandatory stays in Article 21, to set at nought its prior contractual
bargain to sue/be sued under Article 17 in the English courts.[714] This laudable, yet
textually questionable approach was not the most disquieting aspect of the case;[715]

---

[710] Although in the absence of a special factor such as a Convention 'exclusive' jurisdiction, or abuse
of process by harassment/oppression (*Turner v Grovit* [2000] 1 QB 345, CA, sentiments and reasoning
approved by HL's decision [2002] 1 WLR 107—but reference made to ECJ), there appears to be *no*
'right' of a Contracting State defendant only to be sued on the basis of the Convention in a Contracting
State that, *simpliciter*, will ground in an injunction: *Société Commerciale de Réassurance and others v Eras
International Ltd and others (No.2)* [1995] 2 All ER 278, at p.298 (Potter J)—something more, such as
an Article 17 exclusive jurisdiction clause needs to be shown.
[711] Stated simply as a proposition in *Mark Edmund Denby and others v The Hellenic Mediterranean
Lines Co. Ltd.* [1994] 1 Lloyd's Rep. 320 (Rix J); *The Governor and Company of the Bank of Scotland v
S.A. Banque Nationale de Paris* [1996] I.L. Pr. 668, OH (Lord Penrose); *Apple Computers v Digit Srl*,
5.10.2001 (Goldring J).
[712] *Aggeliki Charis Compania Maritima S.A. v Pagnan S.p.A (The 'Angelic Grace')* [1995] 1 Lloyd's Rep.
87; *A/S D/S Svendborg and another v Wansa (t/a Melborne Enterprises Estonian Shipping Co. Ltd)* [1996]
2 Lloyd's Rep. 559; *Turner v Grovit* [2000] 1 QB 345; the HL in *Turner v Grovit and others* [2002] 1 WLR
107 approved the CA's decision (finding the defendants' conduct unconscionable in commencing the
Spanish proceedings) and would have dismissed the appeal but for the perceived necessity of a reference
to the ECJ on the question of issuing restraining orders in a Brussels Convention case; *OT Africa Line Ltd
v Hijazy and others (The 'Kribi')* [2001] 1 Lloyd's Rep. 76; *Alfred C. Toepfer International GmbH v Société
Cargill France* [1998] 1 Lloyd's Rep. 379 (although 'an occasion for its review' missed *in casu*).
[713] *Credit Suisse First Boston (Europe) Ltd* [1999] 1 Lloyd's Rep. 767; *Donohue v Armco Inc and others*
[2000] 1 Lloyd's Rep. 579; CA's grant of an injunction set aside on appeal by HL, [2002] 1 Lloyd's Rep.
425, as, on facts of the case, strong reasons found for *not* giving effect to the exclusive jurisdiction
clause—the appeal was not, however, centred on questions of principle regarding the grant of anti-suit
injunctions'; another alternative—successful on the exceptional facts of *Union Discount Company Ltd
v Robert Zoller and others* [2002] 1 All ER 693, CA, (Schiemann LJ)—is to claim in England for the
costs expended in having the claim struck out in the *forum derogatum* as a separate and fresh cause of
action for breach of contract (presumably in most cases under CPR 6.20(5)(d), or *quaere*, Article 5(1));
the Court of Appeal left open the possibility of maintaining an action here if costs are (partially)
awarded in the striking out procedure abroad; *Youell and others v Kara Mara Shipping Co. Ltd* [2000]
2 Lloyd's Rep. 102; *XL Insurance Ltd v Owens Corning* [2001] 1 All ER (Comm) 530; *Navigation Maritime Bulgare v Rustal Trading Ltd. and others (The 'Ivan Zagubanski')* [2002] 1 Lloyd's Rep. 106.
[714] *Continental Bank N.A. v Aeakos* [1994] 1 WLR 588, at pp.596–97.
[715] Briggs, 1997, at p.153, para. 2.211.

of even more concern to the uniform application of the Convention's rules was the grant of an anti-suit injunction to restrain continuance, or even consideration, of proceedings before another Contracting State court.

(b) The grant of an anti-suit injunction in Continental Bank N.A. v Aeakos, in Brussels Convention cases, and the attempt to distinguish it in OT Africa Line Ltd v Hijazy and others (The 'Kribi'): countervailing factors and a possibly new approach
The precise principles upon which the grant of an anti-suit injunction is based were not expressly spelt out in *Continental Bank v Aeakos*. What Steyn LJ did say was that '[g]iven the total absence of special countervailing factors,[716] this is the paradigm case for the grant of . . . [an injunction]. In our judgment the continuance of the Greek proceedings amount to vexatious and oppressive conduct . . .'.[717] This statement has been rephrased, and adapted by later cases, notably such as by the Court of Appeal in *The 'Angelic Grace'*[718], with regard to an English arbitration clause, that 'the English court need feel no diffidence[719] in granting [such an] injunction, provided that it is sought promptly[720] and before the foreign proceedings are too far advanced';[721] and in *Donohue v Armco Inc and others*[722], being 'in an [exclusive jurisdiction clause] case . . . prima facie oppressive and vexatious to litigate elsewhere than in the agreed forum.'[723]

The approach of *Continental Bank v Aeakos* has attracted some criticism,[724] and a realisation[725] that the other Contracting State enjoined by the English court

---

[716] *Akai Pty Ltd v People's Insurance Co. Ltd* [1998] 1 Lloyd's Rep. 90, at p.105.

[717] [1994] 1 WLR 588, at p.598; the basic principles upon which an anti-suit injunction is granted were summarised by Lord Bingham of Cornhill in *Donohue v Armco Inc and others* [2002] 1 Lloyd's Rep. 425, HL; also Lord Hobhouse in *Turner v Grovit and others* [2002] 1 WLR 107, HL, at pp.118–9.

[718] [1995] 1 Lloyd's Rep. 87.

[719] Toned down somewhat, in the interests of comity in *Credit Suisse First Boston (Europe) Ltd v MLC (Bermuda) Ltd* [1999] 1 Lloyd's Rep. 767, at pp.780–81, (Rix J).

[720] *Toepfer International GmbH v Molino Boschi Srl* [1996] 1 Lloyd's Rep. 510 (Mance J).

[721] [1995] 1 Lloyd's Rep. 87, at p.96 (Millett LJ); '[c]onsiderations of comity . . . [are] considered to be largely irrelevant', Briggs, 1997, at p.269, para. 5.28.

[722] [2000] 1 Lloyd's Rep. 579, [2002] 1 Lloyd's Rep. 425, reversing the CA's grant of an injunction on the facts, as strong reason(s) found for not doing so—together with the imposition of an undertaking not to enforce certain claims against one party (Donohue) in New York proceedings.

[723] At p.589 (Stuart-Smith LJ), on appeal, [2002] 1 Lloyd's Rep. 425, HL, reversing the CA on the facts, Lords Hobhouse and Scott, agreeing with the leading speech of Lord Bingham of Cornhill, both acknowledged that a party who has an exclusive jurisdiction clause in his favour is in a much stronger (though not necessarily unassailable) position to one who has not; *Youell and others v Kara Mara Shipping Co. Ltd* [2000] 2 Lloyd's Rep. 102, at pp.113–4, (Aikens J).

[724] From the CA itself, *Alfred C. Toepfer International GmbH v Société Cargill France* [1998] 1 Lloyd's Rep. 379, at p.388 (Phillips LJ): 'in fundamental conflict with the scheme of the Convention that a defendant before the Court first seised, should, without entering a challenge to jurisdiction in that Court, be able to commence proceedings in a second Court in order to challenge the jurisdiction of the Court first seised.'

[725] *OLG Düsseldorf* 10.1.1996, IPRspr. (1996) Nr. 167, [1997] I.L.Pr. 320; *OLG Frankfurt a.M.* 13.2.2001 (2001) *RIW* 464; *Philip Alexander Securities & Futures Ltd v Bamberger & Ors and related action* [1996] CLC 1780, CA; *OT Africa Line Ltd v Hijazy and others (The 'Kribi')* [2001] 1 Lloyd's Rep. 76; also a comment by Lord Goff in *Airbus Industrie GIE v Patel and others* [1999] 1 AC 119, at p.132, that 'the

would view the grant and eventual application for enforcement of the injunction as an infringement of sovereignty. Attempts were therefore made on a number of fronts to assail *Continental Bank* in *OT Africa Line Ltd v Hijazy and others (The 'Kribi')*.[726] The facts were somewhat involved, but for this section, can be reduced to the following: the claimant English company, OT Africa Line applied for, *inter alia*, an anti-suit injunction to restrain the first defendant, one Hijazy and co-defendant companies owned/controlled by him together with many other defendant consignees from continuing with an action for short delivery, before the Antwerp courts, in breach of Article 17 jurisdiction clauses in several bills of lading, in favour of the English courts.

Aikens J went through the steps (1) and (2), mentioned earlier, for the grant of an injunction, and then had to consider ingenious arguments that *Continental Bank* could be distinguished, and that no injunction should be granted. These arguments were as follows:

(i)   that by granting an anti-suit injunction, this breached the defendants' rights under Article 6(1) ECHR to go before 'an independent and impartial tribunal established by law', incidentally the defendants' preferred choice of the Belgian courts, already first seised under Article 21 of the Convention. Since the 2nd October 2000, the English courts, by ss.3, 1(2), 2 of the Human Rights Act 1998 have been required to read and give effect to 'primary legislation ... in a way which is compatible with Convention rights'. Such arguments based on Article 6(1) ECHR could not have been in their lordships' minds in *Continental Bank*;

(ii)   that s.49 CJJA 1982 does not preserve the power in the English court to grant injunctions;

(iii)   that insufficient account was taken by the Court of Appeal in *Continental Bank v Aeakos* of the European Court of Justice's decision in *Overseas Union Insurance Ltd & Others v New Hampshire Insurance Company*;[727]

(iv)   that since the decision in *Continental Bank*, the wording of Article 21 had changed, not requiring, as previously, an automatic dismissal, but merely a 'stay ... until such time as the jurisdiction of the court first seised is established'; and

(v)   most significantly for the relationship of the grant of an anti-suit injunction and the Brussels Convention regime, that the Belgian courts would consider its grant as an usurpation of its own sovereign function, and may even

---

practical results [of the operation of the Brussels Convention system] are from time to time unwelcome.'; Berti, S. 'Englische Anti-suit Injunctions im europäischen Zivilprozessrecht—A Flourishing species or a Dying breed?' in *Private Law in the International Arena, Liber Amicorum Kurt Siehr*, (Ed. Basedow, J.), 2000, p.33, at p.41, para.15; *OLG Frankfurt* 13.2.2001 2002 NJW-RR 357.

[726] [2001] 1 Lloyd's Rep. 76 (Aikens J).

[727] (C-351/89) [1991] ECR I-3317.

refuse to serve the order,[728] by analogy with the German courts' views, noted in Waller J's judgment in *Philip Alexander Securities & Futures Ltd v Bamberger & Ors and related action.*[729]

As for the Human Rights Act 1998 point, the judge did not consider that the source of the court's power to grant injunctions, s.37 Supreme Court Act 1981, or indeed the exercise of it, curtailed an individual's right to trial before an 'independent and impartial tribunal' in Article 6(1) ECHR. Article 6 in the context of this case, he believed, was not concerned with exactly *where*, so much as the possibility of having the opportunity of appearing *somewhere* before an independent tribunal, albeit one that the defendant would not have preferred; the interpretation of the Brussels Convention, and CJJA 1982 in the light of the duty under s.3 Human Rights Act 1998 did not stretch as far as to credit a defendant with the right to be sued only in the court of his preferred choice (of domicile), especially considering the fact that the Brussels Convention itself lays down alternative (even prorogated) *fora*.

As for the s.49 CJJA 1982 and *Overseas Union* arguments: s.49 was said not to mention injunctions at all, so that s.37 Supreme Court Act 1981 still applied; and the judge was sure *Overseas Union*, and its reservation, had been 'noted and approved'[730] by Steyn LJ in *Continental Bank*. Equally unconvincing for the judge was the change in wording to Article 21, which did not, even in amended form, alter the question whether an English court is bound to impose a stay in the face of a valid Article 17 jurisdiction clause.

The significant aspect of *OT Africa Line Ltd v Hijazy* for present purposes is the effect the potential reaction of the *forum derogatum* may now have on the English court's discretion to grant anti-suit injunctions in Brussels Convention cases. Aikens J was inclined to the view that in a situation where it is clear that the grant of such an order would indeed offend the sovereignty of the other Contracting State court—and it is for the respondent to adduce evidence of this[731]—as had occurred[732] in *Philip Alexander Securities & Futures Ltd v Bamberger & Ors and related action,* 'then this factor would have weighed heavily in this case also.'[733]

---

[728] Evidence already existed of the German courts' attitude to such orders: *OLG Düsseldorf* 10.1.1996, IPRspr. (1996) Nr. 167, [1997] I.L.Pr. 320, *OLG Frankfurt a.M.* 13.2.2001 (2001) *RIW* 464, 2002 NJW-RR 357, at p.357; lack of evidence that French courts would be affronted by the grant of an anti-suit injunction a factor that distinguished *Navigation Maritime Bulgare v Rustal Trading Ltd. and others (The 'Ivan Zagubanski')* [2002] 1 Lloyd's Rep. 106 from the *Philip Alexander Securities & Futures Ltd v Bamberger* case, [2002] 1 Lloyd's Rep. 106, at p.126 (Aikens J).
[729] [1996] CLC 1757.
[730] [2001] 1 Lloyd's Rep. 76, at p.87.
[731] At p.93; the respondents in *OT Africa Line* had failed to show that the Belgian courts (as opposed to the German reaction) would have been affronted by the grant of an injunction in this case; a similar position to *Navigation Maritime Bulgare v Rustal Trading Ltd. and others (The 'Ivan Zagubanski')* [2002] 1 Lloyd's Rep. 106 (Aikens J), at p.126.
[732] The court was aware of failed attempts by the applicants to serve the orders under the 1965 Hague Service Convention: *OLG Düsseldorf* 10.1.1996, IPRspr. (1996) Nr. 167, [1997] I.L.Pr. 320; cf *OLG Frankfurt* 13.2.2001 2002 NJW-RR 357, at p.358, where court re-iterated its concern of a breach of sovereignty.
[733] [2001] 1 Lloyd's Rep. 76, at p.94.

One reading of Aikens J's judgment could be seen, as in *Philip Alexander Securities & Futures Ltd*, to be an awakening of the need for reappraisal of the grounds upon which anti-suit injunctions are granted in Convention cases, and a recognition that other Contracting State courts may justifiably feel aggrieved by the English courts' stance on alleged contract breakers, who initiate proceedings in a *forum derogatum*. Another could be simply a manifestation of the nature or strength of evidence necessary to constitute 'strong reasons' or *Continental Bank* 'special countervailing factors' against granting anti-suit injunctions, especially as they relate to Brussels Convention proceedings.

Clearly if this is the direction the English courts are taking—and there is experience from previous (Contracting State) authorities of an infringement of sovereignty—the better option for a claimant would be to apply for declarations that the Article 17 clause is valid and subsisting and that continuance of the foreign proceedings is therefore in breach of contract and any resulting judgment should not be recognised or enforced as a result.[734]

2.4 THE NEW VERSION OF ARTICLE 17(C): 'AN AGREEMENT . . . IN INTERNATIONAL TRADE OR COMMERCE, IN A FORM WHICH ACCORDS WITH A USAGE OF WHICH THE PARTIES ARE, OR OUGHT TO HAVE BEEN AWARE . . .'[735]

[The] international trade or commerce formality category will be a fertile ground of contention[736]

The formalities of the original version of Article 17 were considered by many,[737] including the UK experts[738] charged with negotiating the UK's accession to the

---

[734] Unfortunately the relationship between prorogation of jurisdiction, in Article 23 of the Brussels I Regulation and *lis pendens* in Article 27(1) has not been clarified; the position discussed above, and the jurisprudence of the English courts, will, until a clarifying preliminary reference, continue after 1 March 2002—cf reference by French first instance court on the English practice of issuing anti-suit injunctions in *Marseille Fret SA v Seatrano Shipping Company Ltd* (C-24/02), 22.1.2002, pending.

[735] For the potential overlap between this form and the Article 17(1)(b) 'established practices' between the parties, Huet reviewing *Société Karl Schaeff c/ Société Patrymat* 14.12.1988, (1990) *JDI* 153, at p.156, and the confusion of the categories by *S.A.Fourmaintraux et Delassus c/ Société Building Adhesives Ltd*, 6.12.1993 (1995) *JDI* 152, at p.154 and *Hof van Beroep te Antwerpen*, 11.10.1994, *Frans Maas/ Logistic Transport*, (1995) *Rev. dr. comm. belge* 385; *Clare Taverns t/a Durty Nelly's v Charles Gill* [2000] 2 ILRM 98, at p.109 (McGuinness J), Irish HC. If there is a hiatus in established practices (when the parties cease to trade *inter se*) and then *resume* commercial relations, a clause in the former trading conditions carried over into the new and distinct relationship will not be valid under Article 17(1)(b): *Knauf UK GmbH v British Gypsum Ltd and another* [2001] 2 All ER (Comm) 332, QBD, at pp.342–3, (David Steel J), *revs'd* on a different point [2002] 1 WLR 907, CA (Henry LJ).

[736] Kaye, *Civil Jurisdiction and Enforcement of Foreign Judgments*, 1987, at p.1062; the new version of Article 17 is being examined here due to recent ECJ case law and the potential that may persist for inconsistent national interpretations.

[737] For example Beraudo J.P. in *Convention de Bruxelles du 27 septembre 1968, Jurisclasseur Europe*, fasc.3000, mars 1988, p.15, para. 37; O'Malley, S. and Layton, A., 1989, at p.595; *Cheshire and North*, 13th ed., 1999, at p.243; AG Tesauro in *Mainschiffahrts-Genossenschaft e.G (MSG) v Les Gravières Rhénanes SARL* (C-106/95) [1997] ECR I-911, at p.925, para. 23: 'The new version of Article 17 seems to have been drawn up precisely because of the excessive formalism of such an approach in regard to international trade'.

[738] ('The provisions of the Article are inconsistent with everyday customs in international commerce'), a phrase encapsulating the strong objections to the original version of Article 17 by the House of Lords,

Brussels Convention 1968, to be too rigid, ill-suited to the demands of modern commercial practice,[739] which dealt at high speed, often on standard terms.[740] The jurisprudence[741] of the European Court suffered the same criticism—Article 17 groaned under excessive formalism.[742] Article 11 of the 1978 Accession Convention[743] recast Article 17, adding to the end of the first paragraph a third possible formal hypothesis[744] with which an agreement on jurisdiction could comply. This hypothesis remained unchanged until Article 7 of the 1989 Accession Convention[745] which paragraphed it to letter (c), and added additional formalities of awareness.[746]

What concerns this present section is how each respective constituent element—'an agreement', 'in international trade or commerce', 'in a form which accords with', 'practices' (1978 version) or a 'usage' (1989 version), and the parties actual or deemed 'awareness'—has been variously interpreted and defined in the light of what seems to be a recurring problem in this area: an orally agreed contract, succeeded by a subsequent jurisdiction clause in letters of confirmation of orders, in standard conditions of sale or invoices, sent to the purchaser, and to which, thereafter, no objection is taken.[747] The importance for the concept of 'an agreement', by fulfilling this third hypothesis, had previously been hinted at,[748] but only recently authoritatively determined—'consensus on the part of the

---

Select Committee on the European Communities, Session 1976–77, 45th Report (Preliminary Draft Convention on the Accession to the Brussels Convention of 27 September 1968) 26 July 1977, pp.8–9, paras. 20–21 and 42; Killias, L. *Die Gerichtsstandsvereinbarungen nach dem Lugano-Übereinkommen*, 1993, at p.148; *Dresser UK Ltd and others v Falcongate Freight Management Ltd and others (The 'Duke of Yare')* [1992] 1 QB 502, at p.511 (Bingham LJ).

[739] (1990) *JDI* 153, at p.154: 'du souci de ne pas entraver les exigences et les practiques du commerce international'; Mezger, M. 'Les grandes lignes de la Convention du 9 octobre 1978' (1980–1981) *Dr Intern Privé*, 15 believes that the new version of Article 17 was a concession to those Contracting States—notably Germany—that regard silence as acceptance of letters of confirmation.

[740] O'Malley, S. and Layton, A., 1989, at p.595.

[741] Especially *Galereis Segoura SPRL v Rahim Bonakdarian* (C-25/76) 14.12.1976 [1976] ECR 1851; Kropholler, 1998, at p.249, para. 46.

[742] Now the effect on an 'agreement' produced by *Mainschiffahrts-Genossenschaft* [1997] ECR I-911, at p.940, para. 19: 'consensus . . . is presumed to exist'; confirmed by Hugo Trumpy [1999] ECR I-1597, at p.1649, para. 21.

[743] [1978] OJ L304/1('The 1978 Accession Convention').

[744] 'in international trade or commerce, in a form which accords with practices in that trade or commerce of which the parties are or ought to have been aware'.

[745] [1989] OJ L284/1.

[746] 'and which in such trade or commerce is widely known to, and regularly observed by, parties to contracts of the type involved in the particular trade or commerce concerned', to align the wording with Article 17 of the Lugano Convention of 16 September 1988, 25.11.1988, [1988] OJ L319/9.

[747] Especially Stöve, 1993, at p.110 onwards.

[748] AG Lenz in *Custom Made Commercial Ltd v Stawa Metallbau GmbH* (C-288/92) [1994] ECR I-2913, at p.2936; Rauscher, (1992) *IPRax* 143, at p.145: 'Auf der Grundlage der Reformziele ergibt sich hieraus nicht nur eine *Form*erleichterung, sondern auch eine Relativierung der vom EuGH geforderten Nachweises der *Vereinbarung*' ('At the heart of the reform's aims proves to be not only a relaxation of *form*, but also a relativisation of the proof of the agreement demanded by the ECJ') (original emphasis).

contracting parties to a jurisdiction clause is presumed to exist'[749] if there is a practice in the relevant branch of trade.[750] The section has also taken on added interest recently, due to two cases on this area from the Court of Justice: *Mainschiffahrts-Genossenschaft eG (MSG) v Les Gravières Rhénanes SARL*[751] and *Società Transporti Castelletti Spedizioni Internazionali SpA v Hugo Trumpy SpA*.[752]

2.4.1   The Article 17(1) 'agreement' and the new Article 17(c)

The opening two sentences of Article 17(1) stress that to confer exclusive jurisdiction, the parties should have 'agreed' to settle any disputes between them on a Contracting State jurisdiction; and such 'agreement' thereafter[753] be in at least one of the 'forms' in paras (a)-(c). Logically, the word 'agreement' appears to be one of the terms which defines Article 17's scope *ratione materiae*—if there be no 'agreement', *a fortiori*, it cannot possibly have a paragraph (a) existence in 'writing', nor a para (b) or (c)[754] 'form'.

This section intends to deal with the problem of the 'agreement' itself—whether or not as a condition precedent to considerations as to its (a)-(c) forms—and how its interpretation may possibly have been effected by recent ECJ jurisprudence, particularly in relation to the interpretation of the new third hypothesis in (c), and its independence/interdependence on the *lex causae*, in *Francesco Benincasa v Dentalkit Srl*.[755]

2.4.1(i)   'Agreement'—its meaning, and assimilation of the meaning of 'a contract'

The early cases to consider Article 17 dealt with the article in its original rigid 1968 Brussels Convention version, where the 'agreement' could only be 'in writing or evidenced in writing'. Form of agreement and 'agreement' itself went

---

[749] *Mainschiffahrts-Genossenschaft e.G (MSG) v Les Gravières Rhénanes SARL* [1997] ECR I-911, at p.940, para. 19; *OT Africa Line Ltd v Hijazy and others (The 'Kribi')* [2001] 1 Lloyd's Rep. 76, at p.90 (Aikens J).

[750] *Ibid.*; AG Lenz, [1994] ECR I-2913, at p.2939, at para. 98.

[751] (C-106/95) [1997] ECR I-911.

[752] (C-159/97) [1999] ECR I-1597; *Coreck Maritime GmbH v Handelsveem B.V.*, (C387–98) [2000] ECR I-9337, concerned the certainty of the Article 17 clause itself, and its potential for transmission to a third party, rather than the interpretation of its constituent elements.

[753] *Quaere*, below, at pp.253–254, whether *Mainschiffahrts-Genossenschaft* has changed the focus of Article 17, with its presumption of consensus in international trade or commerce—finding such a practice/usage first will then raise the presumption of an agreement.

[754] *Ibid.* on a presumption raised in the case of a (c) 'form'.

[755] (C-269/95) [1997] ECR I-3767; cf *Bundesgericht 7.8.2001 Notrop Speditions- und Schiffahrtsgesellschaft GmbH gegen Transrail AG*, unreported; if 'established practices' have been shown to exist regarding the conclusion of clauses at the time of the issue of proceedings, then all clauses retrospectively concluded prior to that point in time will be validated by Article 17(1)(b): *LG Karlsruhe 1.6.2001* (2001) *RIW* 702, at p.704.

hand-in-hand.[756] The concern of these early cases that consensus to a jurisdiction clause be 'clearly and precisely demonstrated'[757] could be fulfilled by looking for 'a writing' or 'evidence[] in writing', as interpreted in those cases. The form dictated an 'agreement' and *vice versa*—both stood or fell together.

It was not until the 1978 amendments that a scission[758] in this mutual inter-dependence occurred, by the introduction of a relaxation to the 'form' an 'agreement' could take. 'Agreement' thereafter seemed to become divorced from form when, in certain circumstances, 'a form which accord[ed]' with certain practices/usages was admissible—although it was not until much later that the effects of the perceived scission were tested before the ECJ in *Mainschiffahrts-Genossenschaft eG (MSG) v Les Gravières Rhénanes SARL.*[759]

Before we move to this case, we should attempt to concentrate on the meaning of the phrase 'agreement conferring jurisdiction' *simpliciter*, in what appears to be the only case which, in part, considered 'agreement' in a context outside the requirements of 'a writing or evidence[] in writing': *Powell Duffryn Plc v Wolfgang Petereit.*[760] The reason for doing this will become apparent, and relevant to the ensuing section reviewing the *Benincasa* case: are the words 'agreement on jurisdiction' in Article 17 to be equated (exactly or vaguely) with the concept of 'a contract' in Article 5(1)?[761]

In other words, if there is *no* contract—as defined autonomously in such cases as *Jakob Handte & Co. GmbH v Société Traitements Mecano-Chimiques des Surfaces (TMCS)*[762] and (now) *Réunion Européenne SA and others v Spliethoff's Bevrachtingskantoor BV, and the Master of the vessel Alblasgracht V002*[763]—can there, *ex hypothesi*, be no 'agreement' as to jurisdiction?[764] And which court is to decide this question, the proto-*forum prorogatum* or *derogatum*?

---

[756] *Salotti v RÜWA* (C-24/76) [1976] ECR 1831, at para. 7; and *Segoura v Bonakdarian* (C-25/76) [1976] ECR 1851, at para. 6; *BGE* 23.11.2001 *X GmbH gegen A*, unreported, where Article 17, by analogy with a contractual agreement, said only to bind the contracting parties and/or their assigns.

[757] Still causing problems of interpretation, when a jurisdiction clause in an insurance contract is argued to have been incorporated into a reinsurance treaty by words in the treaty such as 'all terms, clauses and conditions as original', *AIG Europe SA v QBE International Insurance Ltd*, 3.5.2001, (Moore Bick J).

[758] Briggs, 1997, at p.75, fn.375 talks of the structure of Article 17: an 'agreement', and then to require that agreement to conform to one of the 3 'forms'.

[759] (C-106/95) [1997] ECR I-911; the impression was that 'agreement' was an almost redundant and overlooked concept in Article 17, despite the lip-service paid to the earlier case law.

[760] (C-214/89) [1992] ECR I-1745; *Implants International Ltd. v Stratec Medical* [1999] 2 All ER (Comm) 933, at pp.938–39 (McGonigal J).

[761] For this chapter 1, above and especially section 1.1.5, at pp.64 *et seq*; before *Mainschiffahrts*, there had always been a close assimilation of Article 17 and Article 5(1) in the area of place of performance clauses; now such clauses, formerly valid under Article 5(1), fall, in certain circumstances, into the Article 17 arena.

[762] (C-26/91) [1992] ECR I-3967.

[763] (C-51/97) [1998] ECR I-6511.

[764] A question which Bingham LJ had to deal with in *Dresser UK Ltd and others v Falcongate Freight Management Ltd and others (The 'Duke of Yare')* [1992] 1 QB 502, CA, below, at p.253.

Powell Duffryn Plc involved a dispute as to whether, *inter alia*, a jurisdiction clause in a German company's articles of association could be 'an agreement on jurisdiction' within Article 17, so as to bind an English corporate subscriber for its shares. The latter had not, it argued, 'agreed' to the clause because it had not been a participant in discussions on the drafting changes to those articles,[765] into which the (offending) jurisdiction clause had been inserted. The general and specific tenor of the ECJ's answer[766] was to align the autonomous concept of the 'agreement in writing' to the autonomous meaning[767] the Court had already decided on for a 'contract' in *Peters Bauunternehmung GmbH v Zuid Nederlandse Aannemers Vereniging*:[768]

> the company's statutes must be regarded as a contract covering . . . the relations between the shareholders . . . and the company they set up . . . [i]t follows that a clause conferring jurisdiction in the statutes of a company . . . is an agreement within . . . Article 17[769]

From this statement by the Court, it appears that whenever a jurisdiction clause, which aspires to the status of an Article 17 'agreement on jurisdiction', is part[770] of a relationship between parties freely entered into, it will be an agreement capable of being measured against the requirements of form in paras (a)—(c). Yet this close alignment of 'agreement' and 'contract' runs into at least two difficulties, either when the questions of privity, or even an Article 5(1) 'contract' itself are involved—as in *Handte v (TMCS)* or *Réunion Européenne v Spliethoff's Bevrachtingskantoor BV*—or when there are preliminary objections as to the validity of the contract itself containing the clause, on such grounds as mistake, misrepresentation, (economic) duress, or (with English law *qua* putative *lex causae*), lack of consideration: *Francesco Benincasa v Dentalkit Srl.*

The first difficulty, raised by *Handte* and *Réunion Européenne*, is whether there can be jurisdiction conferred by an 'agreement on jurisdiction' under Article 17, when there is none conferred by Article 5(1), because there is no 'agreement freely entered into'? The answer would appear to be no, if, it is submitted, the autonomous formula employed by *Handte* and *Réunion Européenne* is synonymous with Article 17 'agreement'.[771]

---

[765] Cf s 14 Companies Act 1985.

[766] [1992] ECR I-1745, at pp.1774–75, paras. 15–19.

[767] Care therefore with *Implants International Ltd. v Stratec Medical* [1999] 2 All ER (Comm) 933, at pp.938–39.

[768] (C-34/82) [1983] ECR 987.

[769] (C-214/89) [1992] ECR I-1745, at p.1775, paras. 16–17, strongly suggesting the Article 17 'agreement' analogous to and subsumed within the meaning attributed to 'contract' as a whole.

[770] Unless specifically agreed upon in a separate document, the clause will invariably be one clause as part of a 'contract'; indeed, once the *main contract* has been freely entered into (or joined), Article 17 clauses/agreements already in existence at that time, or (in the case of a company's Articles of association) subsequently added/altered will bind the contracting party whether he specifically agreed thereto or not, *ibid.* at p.1775, paras. 18–19.

[771] It is submitted that Article 17 agreements stand or fall with the autonomous concept of Article 5(1) 'contract'; the French *Cour de Cassation* appears to agree: 23.3.1999 *Soc. Rémi Claeys aluminium*

This was certainly the view of Bingham LJ in *Dresser UK Ltd and others v Falcongate Freight Management Ltd and others (The 'Duke of Yare')*[772] a conclusion which, *ex hypothesi*, after such a case as *Réunion Européenne*, can only have been strengthened. In *Dresser UK Ltd*, the third and forth defendants, Norfolk Line Ltd/B.V., respectively bailees and sub-bailees from, and as regards, the first defendants Falcongate Ltd, (unsuccessfully) attempted to rely on a Rotterdam jurisdiction clause—in a bill of lading issued by the forth defendants—against not the first defendants but the plaintiffs, Dresser UK Ltd, as consignees. Bingham LJ could not accommodate the relationship of bailor and sub-bailee into Article 17:

> the ... relationship between ... bailor and sub-bailee[773] cannot in my view be aptly described as depending on agreement ... a contract[774] is what, I think, the first sentence of article 17 demands.[775]

The person seeking to rely on an Article 17 agreement on jurisdiction must therefore be able to point to its forming an integral part[776] of a wider agreement freely entered into between himself and the person against whom he intends to invoke it. The effect of this proposition in the light of the decision in *Francesco Benincasa v Dentalkit Srl* will be examined shortly.

The discussion should take a short detour to clarify the potential effect the amendment in Article 17(c)—and its interpretation in *Mainschiffahrts* and *Hugo Trumpy*—may have had on the requirement for an 'agreement'.

2.4.1(ii) *'Agreement' and the presumption of agreement in Article 17(c): Mainschiffahrts and Hugo Trumpy*

As we have seen, the early ECJ cases on Article 17 exalted the Contracting State courts to ensure that there was an 'agreement' in existence between the parties,

---

c/ *Soc. Sermit et Soc Roubon* (2000) *Rev crit* 224; *contra* Gebauer, M. *(2001) IPRax* 471, at p.472; the position of a third party consignee is unaffected by this conclusion, however, at least as regards English law, *qua lex causae*, in bills of lading cases: Carriage of Goods by Sea Act 1992, s 2(1)(2) and *Coreck Maritime GmbH* (C387–98) [2000] ECR I-9337.

[772] [1992] 1 QB 502, at p.511; *Implants International Ltd. v Stratec Medical* [1999] 2 All ER (Comm) 933, at p.938.

[773] *Quaere*, no agreement freely entered into; cf Bell, A. 'The place of bailment in the modern law of obligations' in Palmer, N. and McKendrick, E. (eds) *Interests in Goods*, 1998, p.461, at p.467, and *The Pioneer Container* [1994] 2 AC 324, PC, there was 'no direct contractual relationship ... created between the owner and the sub-bailee', at p.339, yet the 'voluntary taking by a sub-bailee of the owner's goods ... of itself results in his owing to the owner the duties of a bailee'; a principal bailor (the owner) is only therefore bound by such terms as he has expressly or impliedly authorised, *in casu*, therefore the owner bound by jurisdiction clause in contract between sub-bailee and bailee, as owners had authorised delegation.

[774] A 'contract' in the 'autonomous' sense of *Handte/Réunion Européenne*, not necessarily, it seems, subsequently a legally enforceable one: *Benincasa*.

[775] [1992] 1 QB 502, at p.511; also the view of Judge McGonigal in *Implants International Ltd. v Stratec Medical* [1999] 2 All ER (Comm) 933, albeit expressed rather in terms of English law concepts of a 'contract'.

[776] Although if the whole contract itself is impugned, *Francesco Benincasa v Dentalkit Srl* (C-269/95) [1997] ECR I-3767 has shown us that the Article 17 jurisdiction clause is (re-)released from the

which meant the courts' embarking on 'clearly and precisely'[777] establishing a 'consensus between the parties'.[778] One question before the ECJ in *Mainschiffahrts* was whether, and if so to what extent, Article 17 third hypothesis had relaxed the need for any 'consensus', as required formerly.

Following what was said in the previous section, the effect of this statement must be that Article 17(c), whatever else it may have changed, does not obviate the need for the existence of 'a contract'—an agreement freely entered into. Although the formation of a contract itself in international trade or commerce by a widely-known trade usage will necessarily mean that any clauses contained therein—including of course the formation of the Article 17 agreement—will have been validly concluded.

Although the Court in *Mainschiffahrts* denied that the changes to Article 17 entailed dispensing with the need for any consensus at all,[779] it introduced a presumption into Article 17, and reversed the order in which Article 17 is interpreted. If the third hypothesis—Article 17(c)—is satisfied, a presumption thereafter is raised that Article 17 *ratione materiae*—and an 'agreement'—have been fulfilled. If commercial practices exist, with the requisite awareness of the parties, and their conduct is consistent with such a practice 'consensus on the part of the contracting parties as to a jurisdiction clause is presumed to exist.'[780]

The result of this and the previous section is that there needs to be a 'contract' into which an Article 17 agreement can embed itself, and (presumably) once there, in international trade or commerce, can be presumed to have been the subject of consensus between the parties.

2.4.1(iii)   The 'agreement' and its independence from the contract's formation/lex causae—Francesco Benincasa v Dentalkit Srl[781]

In *Benincasa*, we glimpsed the ECJ's attitude towards jurisdiction clauses in relation to the context of a contract as a whole. An Italian, (presumably domiciled in Munich), had brought proceedings before the local courts there against Dentalkit, an Italian company, based in Florence, for a declaration that a franchising contract be declared void; the contract, however, contained a jurisdiction clause for the courts of Florence 'to entertain any dispute relating to the interpretation,

---

substantive arguments derived from the putative *lex causae*, below, section 2.4.1(iii); *lex causae* used to interpret meaning and scope of clause however: *Bundesgericht 7.8.2001 Notrop Speditions- und Schiffahrtsgesellschaft GmbH gegen Transrail AG*, unreported.

[777] *Salotti v RÜWA* [1976] ECR 1831, at p.1841, para. 7; *Segoura v Bonakdarian* [1976] ECR 1851, at p.1840, para. 6.
[778] *Ibid.*
[779] [1997] ECR I-911, at p.940, para. 17; followed in *Hugo Trumpy* [1999] ECR I-1597, at pp.1648–49, paras. 19–21.
[780] *Ibid.*
[781] [1997] ECR I-3767—this aspect is considered unimportant by Tagaras, H. 'Chronique de Jurisprudence de la Cour de Justice rélative à la Convention de Bruxelles: Années judiciaires 1996–1997 et 1997–1998' (1999) *Cahiers dr. europ* 159, at p.223.

performance or other aspects of the . . . contract'.[782] One question submitted in the reference was whether -and, if so, assuming that the Article 17 jurisdiction clause were otherwise valid as to form—the German courts had to decline jurisdiction in favour of the courts in Florence, when the action sought to have the whole contract, including the jurisdiction clause, declared void.[783]

In the interests of legal certainty,[784] the Court was eager to divorce substantive arguments as to the whole contract's validity—governed by the *lex causae*[785]—from the jurisdiction clause itself. A jurisdiction clause, it was said, served 'a procedural purpose'[786] and its (formal) validity was governed by the Brussels Convention, untrammelled by the law governing the rest of the contract's provisions.[787]

The essential question after *Benincasa* is where ought a plea of contractual invalidity[788] be properly, and/or exclusively, brought: in either the *forum prorogatum* or a *forum derogatum*? All things being equal, in Brussels Convention and 1980 Rome Convention[789] Contracting States, the same *lex causae* should, in theory, be applied to decide the plea of invalidity—from whatever cause—and wherever the dispute is heard. There is little incentive, in this regard, for one party to engage in forum-shopping to gain a substantive law advantage.

---

[782] *Ibid.* at p.3791, para. 4; included, because the ECJ stated that the interpretation of the scope of the clause was to be undertaken by the national court—(presumably, therefore, the German courts *qua fora derogata*), at p.3798, para. 31.

[783] The crucial issue arising from Benincasa is what possible pleas, if any, (that 'derive [ ] from the applicable substantive law') is it legitimate that the *forum derogatum* may disregard; cf *Bundesgericht* 7.8.2001 *Notrop Speditions- und Schiffahrtsgesellschaft GmbH gegen Transrail AG*, unreported.

[784] [1997] ECR I-3767, at para. 29; the certainty that Article 17 seeks to promote could be jeopardised by a plea by one party.

[785] *Quaere*, whether any pleas (such as *non est factum*), derived from the *lex fori*, are available; this would seem to be the view of *OGH* 29.8.2000 *(2001) ZfRV* 113, albeit, it appears, *obiter*, at p.114: 'Dem innerstaatlichen Recht bleibt nur die Klärung bestimmter Vorfragen (Geschäftsfähigkeit, Stellvertretung, Vorliegen von Willensmängeln etc) vorbehalten . . .' ('Only the clarification of certain preliminary questions—such as contractual capacity, principal and agent, or absence of consent—are reserved to national law').

[786] [1997] ECR I-3767, at p.3797, para. 25.

[787] Now, by analogy with arbitration law, s 30 Arbitration Act 1996, and the power of the arbitrators to decide on their own competence/substantive jurisdiction—termed *Kompetenz—Kompetenz*. Should a Contracting State court not be constrained to examining only procedural requirements, Mankowski believes the opportunities for forum shopping would greatly increase, Mankowski, P. 'Casenote: *Francesco Benincasa v Dentalkit Srl* (C-269/95) [1997] ECR I-3767' (1998) *JZ* 896.

[788] By way of illustration of this point, *Bundesgericht* 15.1.1998 *Commune de Macot la Plagne contre Banque* X 124, BGE, III, 134, where French administrative law was held irrelevant to the question of whether a valid Article 17 Lugano jurisdiction clause had been concluded between the mayor of a French local authority and a Swiss lending institution: '. . . la question de droit étranger litigieuse—soit la validité, au regard de droit administratif français, des conventions de prêt . . .—ne revêt pas un caractère préjudiciel pour l'application de l'Article 17 CL dès lors que cette disposition ne règle pas . . . la question de fond . . .', '(the question of foreign law at issue—viz. the validity of the loan agreements as regards French administrative law—does not assume a prejudicial effect on the application of Article 17 Lugano since this disposition does not govern . . . questions on the merits)', at p.141.

[789] Assuming that the plea of contractual invalidity is different from 'the consequences of nullity of the contract' in Article 10(1)(e) of the Rome Convention, against which the UK has entered a reservation by s 2(2) of the Contracts (Applicable Law) Act 1990.

Conversely, if the plea is one of (economic) duress or misrepresentation—that one party had no choice but to agree to all the contract's clauses, including an unfavourable jurisdiction clause—it can be argued that the *proferetor* cannot be permitted, by using the 'sole determinants'[790] of Article 17 of the Brussels Convention to profit from his illicit conduct, at a minimum, by being able to rely on that clause under Article 17 to defeat the jurisdiction of a *forum derogatum*.

The distinction between the ECJ's invocation of certainty, and the potential for abuse of Article 17 that its separation from the *lex causae* might bring, are hard to reconcile. That the Convention can be entirely deaf to pleas (derived from the *lex causae*)[791] seems to be the result of the ruling in *Benincasa*. However, to prevent more egregious instances of oppressive conduct

> there must be some law by which those issues of validity, which have nothing to do with the empty formality of writing, can be tested.[792]

Yet the decision in *Benincasa* seems to have brought the notion of *Kompetenz—Kompetenz* to Article 17 jurisdiction clauses. That the sanctity of the contractual bargain over a jurisdiction clause is divorced from the remainder of the contract, and any pleas from the *lex fori/causae* to set aside or avoid the latter *ab initio*, has been accepted in other, non-Contracting State jurisdictions,[793] may provide some assistance to the *Benincasa* issue under Article 17.

In *Morrison v The Society of Lloyd's*,[794] a recent Canadian decision, along with a number of cases from the Federal Circuit Court of Appeals in the US (also concerning suits directed against Lloyd's),[795] have tended towards the view that a mere assertion (from whatever grounds) that a contract is void *ab initio* (and therefore dragging the jurisdiction clause down with it) does not take effect 'until a final judgment of the court.'[796] To allow such a plea from the outset to vitiate a jurisdiction clause would be to accept its veracity untested.

US courts have approached the issue in a slightly different, more pragmatic way: a clause will remain effective if the plea is that the contract as a whole has been tainted in some way; conversely 'the claims of fraud or overreaching must be aimed straight at the [jurisdiction] clause in order to succeed'.[797] Whichever route is chosen, under Article 17 of the Brussels Convention, it is clear that a plea that the contract *in toto* has been tainted in some fashion, derived from the *lex causae*, is insufficient to upset the (procedural) 'choice' of forum clause.

---

[790]   Briggs, 1997, at p.75, para. 2.95.
[791]   *Bundesgericht* 15.1.1998 *Commune de Macot la Plagne contre Banque* X 124, BGE, III, 134.
[792]   Briggs, A (1997) *YEL* 515, at p.533.
[793]   Nygh, P. *Autonomy in International Contracts*, 1999, at p.74 on the concept of *Kompetenz—Kompetenz*.
[794]   [2000] I.L.Pr. 92, Court of Queen's Bench, New Brunswick.
[795]   *Bonny v The Society of Lloyd's* 3 F.3d 156 (7th Cir. 1993), at p.160.
[796]   *Ash et al. v Corporation of Lloyd's et al.* (1992) 9 OR (3rd) 755, at p.758 (Carthy JA).
[797]   *Haynsworth et al. v The Corporation, a/k/a Lloyd's of London* 121 F.3d 956 (5th Cir. 1997) at p.963.

That there have been such outspoken reactions to the apparent conclusive ambit of the ruling in *Benincasa*—ie. a differentiation in pleas of invalidity of contract, and even pleas not derived from the *lex causae*—may be a legacy from the leading autonomous English case in *Mackender v Feldia A.G.*[798] As is well-known, the assured diamond merchants argued that service out of an application by the plaintiff Lloyd's insurers (for a declaration, *inter alia*, that the purported insurance was void for illegality) be set aside, due to the presence of a Belgian jurisdiction clause. Diplock LJ, at pp.612–3 of the report, emphasised differences between pleas that a contract was 'void for illegality', and pleas that go to the root of consensus as to the jurisdiction clause:

> It [the claim that a contract is void for illegality] thus raises no dispute about the consensus ad idem of the parties as to the exclusive jurisdiction of the Belgian courts.[799]

The aspect of *Benincasa* that may, however, have the greatest impact on the 'traditional' view of the issue discussed here, is (any) residual rôle of the *lex fori*, and its potential exclusion by *Benincasa*. Diplock LJ foresaw the possibility of a plea, such as *non est factum*, questioning whether there ever had been any consensus ad idem, which might defeat the application of the jurisdiction clause:

> where acts done in England . . . are alleged not to have resulted in an agreement at all (. . . a plea of non est factum) and the question is whether there was any consensus ad idem, it may well be that *this question has to be determined by English law and not by the [putative proper/applicable law]*.[800]

Yet it is probably unworkable, in the Brussels Convention, to attempt to differentiate between different pleas of invalidity—mistake, innocent/negligent misrepresentation, and (economic) duress (in England alone). That some may qualify for subjugation to Article 17, due to the scale of the underlying nefariousness implicit in the plea, while others do not, appears not to be a solution to the *Benincasa* problem. Moreover, such a solution as this may prove to be practically unworkable when, for example, an English court, as a *forum derogatum*, is faced with pleas of invalidity derived from German or French law, unknown to our courts.

In the end the ECJ was, however, adamant that a *forum derogatum* should not 'hav[e] to consider the substance of the case',[801] and that reliance on an Article 17 jurisdiction clause not be frustrated 'simply by claiming that the whole of the contract was void on grounds derived from the applicable substantive law.'[802]

The amendments to Article 17 and the *Mainschiffahrts* ruling have done nothing to alter the effect of the ECJ's ruling in *Benincasa*. A *forum derogatum* must presumably now avoid entering into consideration of any plea 'derived from the

---

[798] [1967] 2 QB 590, CA.
[799] *Ibid*, at p.602.
[800] *Ibid*. at pp.602–03, and therefore not within the *Benincasa* 'exclusion'; cf *Bundesgericht* 7.8.2001 *Notrop Speditions- und Schiffahrtsgesellschaft GmbH gegen Transrail AG*, unreported.
[801] [1997] ECR I-3767, at p.3797, para. 27.
[802] *Ibid*. at p.3798, para. 29.

applicable substantive law' and merely examine whether the clause was 'agreed' to in a form according with an international trade or commercial usage. If it was, such a court must decline jurisdiction, ignoring any pleas of contractual invalidity.

2.4.2 'in international trade or commerce'

Of concern, too, is the lack of coherent guidance from either commentators[803] or the courts[804] as to the exact scope of the 'international trade or commerce' factor: how a usage or practice is to be established, and whether the parties are or ought to have been aware of it.[805]

As far as 'international trade or commerce' is concerned, there appear to have been three views of its scope, one narrow,[806] another the 'institutionalised view', and a third considerably more expansive.[807] The latter, after recent cases from the ECJ,[808] can be seen now as incorrect.

That, prior to *Mainschiffharts*, there could have been a distinction between international trade or commerce in general and specialised sectors of international commerce, seems to have developed[809] from the UK's accession, in that the commercial sectors in the City of London contained many 'institutionalised' multinationals dealing on standard forms, such as Lloyd's.[810] It is such sectors of commerce that the House of Lords Select Committee, in its 45th Report, identified as being at risk if no amendment were made to Article 17, and its restrictive interpretation.[811] Another cause for this restrictive view could be said to be that the only reported English case at present which deals directly[812] with this aspect of the

---

[803] [1997] ECR I-3767; one para. in Gaudemet-Tallon, 1996, at pp.90–91;Vlas, P. 'The EEC Convention on Jurisdiction and Judgments' (1999) *NILR* 87, at p.101 believes that the domiciles of the claimant and defendant are not material in the search for a meaning of 'international trade or commerce'.

[804] (1990) *JDI* 159, the commentator regretting that this term was not defined in the cases, and below, at p.259; *OT Africa Line Ltd v Hijazy and others (The 'Kribi')* [2001] 1 Lloyd's Rep. 76, at p.90 (Aikens J).

[805] Although it seems not to have caused problems for the English courts: *OT Africa Line Ltd v Hijazy* [2001] 1 Lloyd's Rep. 76.

[806] I.e. in a particular trade sector concerned in the dispute, the one endorsed by the ECJ in *Mainschiffahrts-Genossenschaft* (C-106/95) [1997] ECR I–911.

[807] I.e. in international trade generally.

[808] *Mainschiffahrts-Genossenschaft e.G (MSG) v Les Gravières Rhénanes SARL* [1997] ECR I-911, and *Hugo Trumpy* (C-159/97) [1999] ECR I-1597.

[809] AG Lenz echoes this conclusion in *Custom Made Commercial* (C-288/92) [1994] ECR I-2913, at p.2937, para. 91.

[810] A Dutch court's view of London's position in *Transocean Towage Company Limited v Hyundai Construction Co. Limited* [1987] E.C.C. 282, at pp.294–95 (AG Franx).

[811] House of Lords Select Committee, Session 1976–77, 45th Report (Preliminary Draft Convention on the Accession to the Brussels Convention of 27 September 1968) 26 July 1977, at p.9, para. 20.

[812] Although *obiter* comments by Sheen J in *The 'Rewia'* [1991] Lloyd's Rep. 69, at p.76 that a carrier's principal place of business clause in a Conlinebill of lading *does* accord with practices in international trade of which the parties ought to have been aware; third hypothesis held inapplicable without explanation in Irish HC *Holfeld Plastics Limited v ISAP OMV Group SA*, 19.3.1999, unreported, Lexis, but applied in *Clare Taverns t/a Durty Nelly's v Charles Gill* [2000] 2 ILRM 98, at p.109 (Irish HC)

amended Article 17, *M.E.Denby v Hellenic Mediterranean Lines,*[813] concerned international trade connected with a Lloyd's MAR marine insurance policy. Had the case not concerned Lloyd's, (clearly within the international trade or commerce prerequisite), but had been more borderline—a mundane cross-border sale of goods transaction, for example—the judge may well have had to define the exact scope of this third hypothesis.

Although a literal reading of Article 17's wording does not automatically lead to the 'institutionalised' or specialised view of the hypothesis, the English approach can be forgiven for having adopted it. It is all the more surprising that this view was shared by Gaudemet-Tallon,[814] though not by recent decisions of the higher French courts.[815] According to Gaudemet-Tallon, the third hypothesis only covers commerce

'où les échanges internationaux sont plus ou moins institutionalisés . . .'[816] [817]

Such a restrictive 'institutionalised' view of international trade or commerce is not endorsed by the German commentators, nor was it considered correct by AG Lenz in his opinion in *Custom Made Commercial.*[818] His literal, word-for-word analysis[819] must logically be the correct one: cross-border trade by two commercial trading corporations,[820] qualified for the introductory words of the third hypothesis.

Whether or not the particular sector in which these companies operate is 'institutionalised' or not is however, not irrelevant. This fact will have a bearing on the ease or otherwise of demonstrating a practice or usage,[821] and on the presumed knowledge of the parties:[822] the more well known the particular market, the harder it will be to feign ignorance of its practices. AG Lenz argued in *Custom Made Commercial* that the opening words of Article 17 should not

---

(McGuinness J): 'not seriously suggested that . . . practice of printing general conditions . . . on . . . reverse side of invoices . . ., with a reference on the face of the document to the said conditions, was not a common commercial practice in the type of international trade with which we are concerned here'; not seriously doubted in *OT Africa Line Ltd v Hijazy* [2001] 1 Lloyd's Rep. 76, at p.90 (Aikens J).

[813] [1994] 1 Lloyd's Rep. 320 (Rix J).

[814] Gaudemet-Tallon, 1996, at pp.90–91.

[815] *S.A.Fourmaintraux et Delassus c/ Société Building Adhesives Ltd, Cour d'Appel de Colmar,* 6.12.1993, (1995) JDI 152; *Société Microstoff Textiles c/ Société Laines Frères, Cour d'Appel de Paris,* 30.11.1988 (1990) JDI 153, reviewed below, at p.261, adopting a 'specialised sector' approach to international commerce—affirmed in *Hugo Trumpy.*

[816] ('where international trade is more or less institutionalised')

[817] Gaudemet-Tallon, 1996, at p.91, adopting the words of Ch.Kohler in *Diritto del Commercio Internazionale,* 1990, fasc.2 p.611 to p.627, at p.624.

[818] AG Lenz in *Custom Made Commercial Ltd v Stawa Metallbau GmbH* (C-288/92) [1994] ECR I-2913, at p.2937, para. 91: 'The aim of Article 17—which is to prevent jurisdiction clauses in contracts going unnoticed—does not support such an interpretation'.

[819] *Ibid.* at para. 92; this opinion was not referred to in the *Mainschiffahrts-Genossenschaft e.G (MSG)* case.

[820] Doing business on the German seller's standard terms of sale, for the first time.

[821] Below section 2.4.4.

[822] Below section 2.4.5.

be cut down 'from the outset'[823] in this way. Strangely, the Advocate General's opinion was not cited at all by the European Court in *Mainschiffahrts-Genossenschaft e.G (MSG) v Les Gravières Rhénanes SARL*,[824] the recent case concerning, *inter alia*,[825] the application of Article 17 to 'a field such as navigation on the Rhine'.[826] The facts concerned the problem mentioned at the beginning of this section: of an oral (time charter) contract, confirmed in writing by a commercial letter of confirmation containing the jurisdiction clause,[827] with no objection subsequently raised by the other (French) party.[828] Unusually, the Court did not explicitly re-rehearse its much-beloved exhortation for an 'independent' reading[829] of the terms of the Convention, namely 'international trade or commerce'. The Court merely said, at para. 21, that it should indicate 'the objective criteria'[830] in order for the national court to determine whether the third hypothesis applied. This it then patently failed to do in para. 22.[831] Was the answer so obviously an international trade or commerce situation[832] that it did not need stating, or even defining?[833]

2.4.2(i)   French cases on 'international trade or commerce'

The cases from France indicate that it was never seriously argued that the facts of each case—international sales with confirmations unobjected to—were not 'in

---

[823] AG Lenz in *Custom Made Commercial Ltd v Stawa Metallbau GmbH* (C-288/92) [1994] ECR I-2913, at p.2937, para. 91.

[824] [1997] ECR I-911.

[825] Article 5(1) was also discussed in relation to designation of place of performance clauses, at pp.942–44 paras. 26–35.

[826] [1997] ECR I–941, para. 22; it was accepted, without comment, that the facts of *Hugo Trumpy* involved 'international trade or commerce', [1999] ECR I-1597, at p.1649, para. 24.

[827] The jurisdiction clause also featured in a number of invoices which the French charterer consistently paid without objection.

[828] Had this been an isolated transaction, the clause would not have been valid under the pre–1978 Accession Convention version of Article 17: *Galereis Segoura SPRL v Rahim Bonakdarian* (C-25/76) [1976] ECR 1851.

[829] Especially *LTU Lufttransportunternehmen GmbH & Co.KG v Eurocontrol* (29/76) [1976] ECR 1541, at p.1551; *Bertrand v Paul Ott KG* (150/77) [1978] ECR 1431, at p.1445; *Netherlands State v Reinhold Rüffer* (814/79) [1980] ECR 3897; *Martin Peters Bauunternehmung GmbH v Zuid Nederlandse Aaannemers Vereiniging* (34/82) [1983] ECR 987, at p.1002; note AG Lenz in *Custom Made Commercial Ltd v Stawa Metallbau GmbH* (C-288/92) [1994] ECR I-2913, at p.2915, para. 104, said that it 'should give rise to an independent interpretation'.

[830] At p.941, para. 21, possibly an oblique reference to an independent reading of the term.

[831] The guidance, at p.941, on the objective evidence necessary was that '[i]t should first be considered that a contract concluded between two companies established in different Contracting States in a field such as navigation on the Rhine comes under the head of international trade or commerce'—a question of factual evidence *OT Africa Line Ltd v Hijazy* [2001] 1 Lloyd's Rep. 76, at p.90.

[832] AG Tesauro's opinion, delivered on 26 September 1996, in the *Mainschiffahrts-Genossenschaft* case, at para. 29, that since 'the contract in question was a charterparty concluded between traders in the relevant sector there is no doubt that we are in the realm of international trade or commerce.'; *Hugo Trumpy SpA* (C-159/97) [1999] ECR I-1597, at p.1649, para. 24.

[833] AG Lenz in *Custom Made Commercial Ltd* had considered this aspect, [1994] ECR I-2913, at pp.2936–37.

international trade or commerce'. In *S.A.Fourmaintraux et Delassus c/ Société Building Adhesives Ltd*,[834] the parties were operating in the specialised sector of the sale and use of adhesive cement, in *Société Microstoff Textiles c/ Société Laines Frères*,[835] the international sale of yarn, in *Société Karl Schaeff c/ Société Patrymat*,[836] ball bearings. The reviewer of the *Cour de Cassation*'s decision in *Société Stork Colorproofing BV c/ Société Ofmag et Art Nord*[837] approved of the use of the international trade category in *S.A.Fourmaintraux c/ Delassus*. In *Stork Colorproofing* itself, it was simply assumed that the contract between the French buyer and its Dutch seller, *prima facie*,[838] came under the third hypothesis.

Without the authoritative guidance of a definition from the European Court,[839] it appears that the third hypothesis will (always) apply in a wide range of cross-border transactions.[840] At least this is the impression in France,[841] where Article 17 has received a most expansive interpretation, with the probability that any international contract will be included.[842]

2.4.3 'in a form which accords with'

Until raised in the recently-reported case of *Società Transporti Castelletti Spedizioni Internazionali SpA v Hugo Trumpy SpA*,[843] this phrase had received scant attention from the courts and commentators. The referring Italian court in *Hugo Trumpy* had asked[844] for an interpretation of these words in the context of bills of lading, which, in their layout and language, may or may not have been produced[845] and signed in a 'form' which accorded with a usage in the international carriage of goods by sea, but certainly did not comply with particular aspects of

---

[834] *Cour d'Appel de Colmar*, 6.12.1993, (1995) *JDI* 152.
[835] *Cour d'Appel de Paris*, 30.11.1988, (1990) *JDI* 153.
[836] *Cour d'Appel de Paris*, 14.12.1988, (1990) *JDI* 153.
[837] *Cour de Cassation* (1995) *JDI* 154, Huet.
[838] (1995) *JDI* 154, at p.155.
[839] Unfortunately no concrete definition was provided by *Mainschiffahrts-Genossenschaft e.G (MSG) v Les Gravières Rhénanes SARL* (C-106/95) [1997] ECR I-911, at p.941, para. 22; Sheen J in The 'Rewia' [1991] Lloyd's Rep. 69, at p.7; and Aikens J in *OT Africa Line Ltd v Hijazy and others (The 'Kribi')* [2001] 1 Lloyd's Rep. 76, at p.90—the answer seemed obvious in both cases; also obvious in bills of lading case *Cour d'appel de Paris* 29.11.2000 *Soc Hapag Lloyd Container Linie et a c/ La Réunion Européenne et a.* 2001 DMF 684, at p.687.
[840] It would probably not be incorrect to say in every international (sales) contract (that does not involve a 'consumer', nor an assured involved in an Article 12a category).
[841] In Germany, where the third hypothesis was simply applied without definition; Kropholler, 1998 at p.250, at para. 49 that the hypothesis is 'weit aufzufassen'('to be interpreted broadly').
[842] *Contra* Gaudemet-Tallon, 1996, at p.91, para. 126: 'cette dernière forme n'est acceptable que dans "le commerce international" et non dans n'importe quel contrat international.'('this last form is only acceptable 'in international comerce' and not in any international contract whatsoever').
[843] (C-159/97) [1999] ECR I-1597.
[844] In the second, eleventh and tenth questions, [1999] ECR I-1597, at p.1647, para. 15.
[845] By one of the parties only.

the Italian *Codice civile* as regards form and evidence of approval—Article 1341 *Codice civile.*[846]

As surely could have been foreseen, since the European Court re-iterated its jurisprudence in *Elefanten Schuh GmbH v Pierre Jacqmain*[847]—that additional national law pre-requisites are not permitted to reappear in any shape or form as an unwelcome adjunct to Article 17's formal requirements[848]—the arguments based on Article 1341 were bound to fail. Yet the ECJ did align the 'form' in Article 17 with 'practices' which a national court had to ascertain for itself:

> It is therefore for the national court to refer to the commercial usages . . . concerned in order to determine whether, in the case before it, the physical appearance of the jurisdiction clause, including the language in which it is drawn up, and its insertion in a standard form . . . are consistent with forms according with those usages . . .[849]

Thus, if in the particular branch of international trade or commerce concerned, jurisdiction clauses are pre-printed (in English) in very small characters[850] on the reverse side of a bill of lading, signed only by the carrier, it will against this paradigm 'form' that any particular later bill in the *same* sector will have to 'accord', in order to find its validity under Article 17(c) of the Brussels Convention.[851]

This interpretation given in *Hugo Trumpy* will doubtless bring enormous flexibility to the conclusion of jurisdiction clauses in contracts in international trade or commerce. By eschewing a rigid autonomous definition of the term 'a form which accords', and allowing its manifestation to be dictated by commercial usages, themselves incorporated into Article 17 as a paradigm, *Hugo Trumpy* represents an important step in realising the trade fluidity envisaged by the 1978 amendments to the original version of Article 17.

At least at first glance, *Hugo Trumpy* seems finally to have laid to rest the remaining vestiges of national law/civil code opposition to the agreement and formation of jurisdiction clauses, formerly and traditionally manifest in the additional requirements of form, position, consent, objective connection, and language that either clauses, or contracts themselves, had to fulfil.[852] This is of

---

[846] Pescatore, G. and Ruperto, C. *Codice Civile*, 10 ediz., 1997, I, at p.2118; the English version in Beltramo, M *The Italian Civil Code*, 1969, at p.346–47.

[847] (C-150/80) [1981] ECR 1671.

[848] Also the comments of the Court at p.1656, para. 51, that 'substantive rules of liability applicable in the chosen court must not affect the validity of the jurisdiction clause'; cf. now *The Hollandia* [1983] 1 AC 565.

[849] *Hugo Trumpy*, (C-159/97) [1999] ECR I-1597, at p.1653, para. 36.

[850] One defence (under French autonomous insurance law) to which the *Cour de Cassation* was receptive in (potentially) denying application of Article 17 in a Lloyd's policy of insurance in *Société d'études d'investissement pour les affaires (SEIA) c/ Souscripteurs des Lloyd's de Londres* 11.3.1997 (1998) *JDI* 139.

[851] *Ibid.*; incorrect therefore the *Souscripteurs des Lloyd's de Londres* case, 11.3.1997 (1998) *JDI* 139, probably even if the Lloyd's policy is never sent to the French assured—if, as is believed to be the case, this is how Lloyd's underwriters operate (as a well-known 'usage').

[852] (C-159/97) [1999] ECR I-1597, at p.1652, para. 35, at p.1653 para. 38 and at p.1656, paras. 49 and 51.

course to be welcomed. One wonders why—in the face of ECJ authority such as *Elefanten Schuh GmbH v Pierre Jacqmain* and *Sanicentral GmbH v René Collin*[853]— the *Corte di Cassazione* could possibly have been receptive[854] to arguments of nullity derived from its national civil code: Article 1341(2)[855] renders ineffective pre-printed clauses, which, *inter alia*, represent 'derogations from the competence of courts',[856] unless specifically approved in writing. Such a provision has no place in the autonomous, and self-sufficient terms of Article 17. Or so it appears. *Hugo Trumpy*, as is submitted above, has introduced into Article 17 paradigm 'forms' according to which valid jurisdiction clauses may be concluded, over which the European court has, moreover, no (autonomous) control whatsoever. Yet in certain areas of international trade, national provisions have no doubt exerted such a pervasive effect on the formation of contracts, that it may well not be easy for national courts to divorce overnight the traditional influences such provisions have had on international commercial practices. National provisions have to a large extent shaped[857] these paradigm 'forms', and will now continue to exert an (indirect) influence on Article 17, perhaps indefinitely.[858]

2.4.4   Practices/A Usage

The impression gleaned from the cases[859] is that the national courts have been far too easily inclined to find a 'practice' or 'usage' without in fact defining what a 'practice' is:[860] particularly in the case of the effect of silence as to a letter or

---

[853] (C-25/79) [1979] ECR 3423, esp. at p.3429, para. 5.

[854] Asked by Gaudemet-Tallon in (1999) *Rev crit* 559—cf. especially when Article 1341's application had been rejected by its earlier case of *Corte di Cassazione* 4.1.1995 *Soc. Dainvest di Guadalupi contro Soc. Guy Laroche* (1997) *Riv. dir. int. priv. e proc.* 984, at p.984: Article 17 did not require the specific approval of Article 1341 CC.

[855] Beltramo, M *The Italian Civil Code*, 1969, at p.346–47.

[856] *Ibid.*

[857] Schlechtriem, P. *Internationales UN-Kaufrecht*, 1996, *Commentary on the UN Convention on the International Sale of Goods (CISG)*, 2nd edn. (in translation), 1998, p.77 para. 5: 'it is practically impossible for a usage to have arisen that is contrary to mandatory rules of the local applicable law'—yet now a foreign usage, alien to certain local laws, may override them as a result of *Hugo Trumpy*; concurring in this view Garro, A. 'Rule-setting by private organisations, standardisation of contracts and the harmonisation of international sales law' in *Foundations and Perspectives of International Trade Law*, (Fletcher, I./Mistelis, L./Cremona, M. eds.), 2001, Ch.22, p.310, at p.313, para. 22–009.

[858] Killias, 1993, at p.188.

[859] Schmidt, (1992) *RIW* 173; and *OLG Köln* 16.3.1988, (1988) *RIW* 555; *LG Essen* 12.12.1990, (1992) *RIW* 227; *BGH* 9.3.1994, (1994) *RIW* 508; *OLG Hamburg*, 30.7.1992, IPRspr. (1992), Nr.194; *OT Africa Line Ltd v Hijazy and others (The 'Kribi')* [2001] 1 Lloyd's Rep. 76, at p.90.

[860] *Société Karl Schaeff c/ Société Patrymat Cour d'Appel de Paris*, 14.12.1988, (1990) *JDI* 153, at p.159: 'On regrettera cependent que l'arrêt . . . se réfère sans autre précisions aux "usages du commerce international" en général, sans établir leur teneur exacte . . .' ('It is moreover to be regretted that the case refers without further details to usages in international commerce in general without establishing their exact content . . .'); *Cour d'appel de Rennes Navire Westfield*, 23.12.1992, 1993 DMF p.298: 'Il est d'usage dans le commerce maritime que les conditions générales du contrat soit pré-imprimées au verso des

confirmation of contract or sales invoice.[861] AG Lenz[862] thought that the party relying on the existence of a practice should have the burden of proving:

> a de facto usage which is *generally and continuously followed* and *regularly observed* by the parties concerned in commercial transactions . . .[863]

In the *Mainschiffahrts-Genossenschaft* case[864] the European Court said three things about a practice:[865] firstly, it was not to be determined by reference to the law of any particular party,[866] nor did it arise from international trade or commerce generally, but from the particular sector[867] in which the parties are operating; and lastly, a practice was established 'where a particular *course of conduct*[868] is generally and regularly followed by operators in that branch . . .'[869]

In *Società Transporti Castelletti Spedizioni Internazionali SpA v Hugo Trumpy SpA*,[870] the European Court was able to add a gloss to the interpretation it had given to the phrase 'practice' ('usage') in *Mainschiffahrts*. Doubts had been raised by the *Corte di Cassazione* in the questions for reference that there could be a 'practice' if:

(1) it were not proved that the *Mainschiffahrts'* 'course of conduct' existed, *inter alia*, in all the countries of the European Union, or otherwise in a geographically uncertain area;[871] and/or

---

connaissements'('it is a usage in maritime commerce that general conditions of contract are pre-printed on the back of bills of lading'), at p.300 again, without further elucidation; the burden of proof appears to rest on the party seeking to rely on the usage: *Cour d'appel de Paris* 8.6.1988 *Soc.Alusuisse France c/ Soc. Rodwer* (1988) *Dalloz*, IR., p.203, [1990] I.L.Pr. 102.

[861] Perhaps more justifiable was the *OLG Hamburg* 30.7.1992 IPRspr. 1992, Nr.194, finding a practice of inserting a carrier's principal place of business clause in a bill of lading, with the result that the consignee was deemed to know that any litigation would necessarily have to be brought there: '. . . mußte sie auch damit rechnen, daß deren Konnossementsbedingungen eine die Zuständigkeit der Hamburger Gerichte begründende Gerichtsstandsklausel enthielten.'('that it must appreciate that their bill of lading's conditions contained a jurisdiction clause founding jurisdiction of the courts in Hamburg').

[862] In *Custom Made Commercial Ltd v Stawa Metallbau GmbH* (C-288/92) [1994] ECR I-2913.

[863] [1994] ECR I-2913, at p.2939, at paras. 99–100.

[864] *Mainschiffahrts-Genossenschaft e.G (MSG) v Les Gravières Rhénanes SARL* (C-106/95) [1997] ECR I-911, confirmed in *Società Transporti Castelletti Spedizioni Internazionali SpA v Hugo Trumpy SpA* (C-159/97) [1999] ECR I-1597.

[865] [1997] ECR I-911, at p.941, para. 23.

[866] *Ibid.* the German cases on this point must now be considered to be incorrect, below, at p.268.

[867] *Ibid.*; the same point made by AG Lenz in *Custom Made Commercial*, [1994] ECR I-2913, at p.2942, para. 107; in *OT Africa* Line, the merchants plying the West African liner trade.

[868] A phrase refined in *Hugo Trumpy*.

[869] [1997] ECR I-911, at p.941, para. 23; the ECJ left little room for doubt in the post-reference *Mainschiffahrts* court, *OLG Nürnberg* 30.7.1998 (1998) IPRspr. Nr.150, that a 'usage' would be found to exist, at p.280.

[870] [1999] ECR I-1597.

[871] *Ibid.* question 9, at p.1645, para. 9.

(2) it were shown that (presumably Italian) shippers and endorsees had raised objections that such practices existed (by suing in Italian courts *qua fora derogata*[872]); and/or

(3) if it were shown that a practice, or 'course of conduct', was not evidenced by standard forms placed with trade associations or specialised commercial bodies.[873]

In response to (1), the European court stated—as it had in *Mainschiffahrts*—that 'the determining factor', as regards the existence of a practice, continued to be a criterion based on the *dramatis personae* of international trade in question, rather than any particular geographical location:[874]

> whether the course of conduct in question is generally and regularly followed by operators in the branch of international trade in which the parties to the contract operate.[875]

As to (2), the Court had to deal with factors, if any, which might negate a *Mainschiffahrt* course of conduct's achievement of the status of a 'usage'. Again, once a course of conduct is 'generally and regularly followed'—and so becomes an Article 17 usage—the particular factor—*in casu*, suing in a different court than that specified in the jurisdiction clause—was insufficient, as an expression of unilateral action, to destroy such a usage. However, what *would* be sufficient to destroy a 'usage' *ab initio*, or once established, is not discussed; but, by implication, that a usage is no longer 'generally and regularly followed'[876] may well suffice.

As to (3), which concerned not so much the practice itself, but the factual evidence that it is necessary to show for its being 'generally and regularly followed',[877] the European Court would not be drawn in to establishing any minimum preconditions as to the necessary proof of a usage. It merely stated that those examples of publicity[878] (that the appellants were undoubtedly relying on as a *minimum* standard of proof of the existence of a usage) merely 'help[ed] to prove'[879] that a practice is generally and regularly followed, but that 'such publicity [could not] be a [minimum] requirement for establishing the existence of a usage'.[880]

---

[872] *Ibid.* question 8, para. 8; Gaudemet-Tallon, (1999) *Rev crit* 559, at p.575, reviewing *Hugo Trumpy*, thinks the Italian judges were too much influenced by the ruling in *Powell Duffryn* that lodging of the Articles of association were in a public register.

[873] Questions 4 and 5, at p.1644, paras. 4 and 5.

[874] Although it seems common sense to assume that the proximity of merchants *inter se* often results from dealings in a particular location: *OT Africa Line Ltd v Hijazy and others (The 'Kribi')* [2001] 1 Lloyd's Rep. 76 (Aikens J).

[875] At p.1650, para. 27.

[876] At p.1651, para. 29, presumably by falling into disuse.

[877] The same phrase repeated this time at p.1650, in para. 28.

[878] Such as lodging standard form contracts with trade associations; *Société Colorproofing BV c/ Société Ofmag et Art Nord* 23.2.1994 (1995) *JDI* 154, at p.156.

[879] At p.1650, paras. 27 and 28.

[880] *Ibid.* at para. 28.

Hugo Trumpy has strengthened the autonomous[881] and objective interpretation of a usage given in *Mainschiffahrts*. Through constant repetition of the fact,[882] the ECJ has ring-fenced the objectivity of a 'course of conduct which is generally and regularly followed' from any attempt to undermine it, be it from a unilateral act of a particular party, from over-rigid requirements of proof, or from, additionally, restrictions as to the choice of court that may exist in national procedural laws.[883]

In conclusion, once a usage has been established, it will be difficult for the (original) party against whom the clause is invoked[884] to escape from its effects under Article 17, even by claiming ignorance of it.[885] It is now appropriate to turn to the national case law examples of usages/practices[886] to see if any trends in interpretation have emerged.

2.4.4(i)   Practice/Usage in German case law

There have been numerous cases in Germany, admittedly pre-dating[887] *Main-schiffahrts*,[888] *Francesco Benincasa v Dentalkit Srl*[889] and (now) *Hugo Trumpy SpA*,[890] that have considered whether silence by the recipient of a commercial letter of confirmation (of an oral contract containing a jurisdiction clause) represents agreement to it in a form which accords with a practice in international trade or commerce under Article 17(c). All have come to the conclusion that such silence does indeed constitute such a practice. Among the first to do so was the *OLG Köln*,[891] in 1988. A German plaintiff buyer sued his Italian supplier of shoes for non-delivery on the basis of a written confirmation of orders placed with the Italian firm, which made no protestation. The court boldly asserted that:

> das Schweigen auf ein kaufmännischen Bestätigungsschreiben stellen zwar einen internationalen Handelsbrauch dar, der in zahlreichen anderen Vertragsstaaten des EuGVÜ verbreitet ist.[892]

---

[881] Subject to what was said about its 'form' above, at pp.261–262.

[882] Invoked again, at p.1655, para. 45, to show evidence of awareness, presumed or otherwise.

[883] Evident in questions three, six and seven, at para. 51, below, at p.274; cf *The Hollandia* [1983] 1 A.C. 565.

[884] As against third parties (in bills of lading cases), now *Coreck Maritime GmbH v Handelsveem B.V.* (C-387/98) [2000] ECR I-9337, questions 3(a) and 4.

[885] Below, at p.274, and *Hugo Trumpy SpA* (C-159/97) [1999] ECR I-1597, at p.1655, para. 45.

[886] For a recently reported English cases to consider the issue, *OT Africa Line Ltd v Hijazy and others (The 'Kribi')* [2001] 1 Lloyd's Rep. 76 (Aikens J).

[887] Nothing in any ECJ case would alter the outcome should the cases be decided today—indeed their position has been confirmed.

[888] (C-106/95) [1997] ECR I-911.

[889] (C-269/95) [1997] ECR I-3767.

[890] [1999] ECR I-1597.

[891] 16.3.1988 (1988) *RIW* 555.

[892] ('silence to a commercial letter of confirmation indeed represents an international commercial usage, that is widespread in numerous other Contracting States to the Brussels Convention'), (1998) *RIW* 555, at p.557—the clause however failed on the Article 17 'awareness' criterion, below, at p.273 and *OLG Köln* 8.12.1989 (1991) *IPRax* 114.

In *OLG Düsseldorf*,[893] of 6.1.1989, the same approach was in evidence. This line of interpreting a usage was confirmed by the *LG Essen* in 1990,[894] which varied the scope of the practice in Article 17 to include the use of standard conditions— including a jurisdiction clause—in international trade:

> Es ist international üblich und damit internationaler Handelsbrauch, daß Parteien AGB verwenden, die Gerichtsstandsklauseln enthalten.[895]

In the *LG Münster*[896] of 25.9.1991, in facts reminiscent of those in *Custom Made Commercial*, the German plaintiff sent confirmation of orders with general conditions appended on the reverse side to the English defendant buyers, and later invoices with the same conditions. The first instance court found that its jurisdiction had been exclusively prorogated[897] under Article 17(c). It re-iterated the effect that silence has as evidence of an international commercial practice:

> Es ist internationaler Handelsbrauch . . . das Schweigen auf ein kaufmännisches Bestätigungsschreiben als Zustimmung zu verstehen.[898]

In two cases, one from the *OLG Hamburg*[899] and the other from the *OLG Celle*,[900] the practice turned to jurisdiction clauses in bills of lading. In the former, the court recognised that it was usual, in the international carriage of goods by sea, to evidence that contract of carriage by the carrier's issuing a bill of lading containing the conditions of carriage,[901] including a 'principal place of business of carrier' jurisdiction clause. All that was needed to establish a commercial usage in such circumstances was 'die faktische Gebräuchlichkeit einer Form'.[902] In the latter, the *OLG Celle*, the appeal court declined to accept jurisdiction on the ground that a jurisdiction clause in favour of the courts of Rotterdam,

---

[893] 1989 IPRspr. Nr. 180; likewise the clause failed the awareness criterion.

[894] 12.12.1990 (1992) *RIW* 227, at p.228; and also the referring court in the *Custom Made Commercial* case, the *BGH* 26.3.1992 IPRspr. (1992) Nr. 181b, [1993] I.L.Pr. 490.

[895] ('it is internationally usual and therefore an international commercial usage, that parties use standard conditions containing jurisdiction clauses'), (1992) *RIW* 227, at p.228; confirming this view *Clare Taverns t/a Durty Nelly's v Charles Gill* [2000] 2 ILRM 98, at p.109 (Irish HC) (McGuinness J).

[896] 1991 IPRspr. Nr. 168.

[897] Unlike an Italian defendant, the English buyer was not able to claim ignorance of the practice; *dubitante* however *BGH* 26.3.1992 IPRspr. 1992 Nr. 181b, [1993] I.L.Pr. 490.

[898] ('It is an international commercial usage that silence to a commercial letter of confirmation is to be understood as acceptance'), 1991 IPRspr. Nr. 168, at p.339.

[899] 30.7. 1992 IPRspr. (1992) Nr. 194; the form of jurisdiction clause accepted as valid in this case under Article 17, at p.442—was the subject of the reference (on grounds of (in)sufficient certainty) by the Dutch *Hoge Raad* in *Coreck Maritime GmbH v Handelsveem B.V.* (C-387/98) [2000] ECR I-9337 and [1999] I.L.Pr. 721, questions 1 and 2; (compare Sheen J in *The 'Rewia'* [1991] Lloyd's Rep. 69, at p.76–77, ruling on an undefined 'carrier' clause, where he stated that a jurisdiction clause in a bill of lading that did not also identify the carrier was not consistent with practices in the trade in question, at p.77); *Bundesgericht* 28.1.2000 *Elex AG gegen Crig-Hautefaye SARL*, unreported (uncertainty of the clause's wording made Article 17 inapplicable); Briggs, 1997, at p.67, fn.328.

[900] 1.11.1995, IPRspr. 1996 Nr. 138.

[901] IPRspr. 1992 Nr. 194, at p.439.

[902] ('the factual customariness of a form'), *ibid.* at p.440.

drafted in a charterparty, had been included into the bill of lading by reference to a practice in this branch of international trade, even in the absence of an express incorporation:

> Die Klausel ist aber gleichwohl wirksam, weil sie kraft Handelsbrauchs Vertragsinhalt geworden ist.[903]

These cases reviewed above—in which a commercial letter of confirmation follows on the heels of a contract already concluded orally[904]—must be contrasted carefully with a situation where an offer is merely *accepted*, such an acceptance containing standard conditions of sale, including a jurisdiction clause: *BGH*[905] of 9.3.1994 and *OLG Hamburg*[906] 8.3.1996. In the former case, a Belgian company had ordered yarn from a German company. The German company had telexed its acceptance of this offer to buy—by a 'Bestätigungsschreiben'/confirmation of the order—which included a German jurisdiction clause. The *Bundesgerichtshof* denied efficacy to the clause in the acceptance, as it found there was no commercial usage to the effect that a clause could be agreed on in the acceptance of an offer.[907] In the latter case, the general conditions of sale were not included in the acceptance, but in the offer—the order a German company placed with its Danish supplier—itself. The court denied[908] that there was a usage to the effect that clauses could be seen to be agreed upon in such a form. Such a view was reinforced in this area by the *LG Duisburg*,[909] of 17.4.1996 and *OLG Dresden*, of 24.11.1998.[910] Again, general conditions were used in the order form for certain goods by the German party. The Italian supplier did not object:

> Ein internationaler Handelsbrauch, wonach ein solches Schweigen des Vertragspartners die Einbeziehung der AGB des anderen Teils zur Folge hat, ist nicht ersichtlich.[911]

---

[903] ('But the clause is nevertheless valid, because due to commercial usage, it has become incorporated into the contract'), *OLG Celle* 1.11.1995 IPRspr. (1996) Nr. 138, at p.323; contrast *OLG Köln* 27.2.1998 1998 IPRspr. Nr.140, where such usage, in *internal* waterway carriage was said not to have incorporated a jurisdiction clause (without express reference to it in the contract of carriage), at p.257.

[904] The factual situation in *Galereis Segoura SPRL v Rahim Bonakdarian* (C-25/76) 14.12.1976 [1976] ECR 1851.

[905] *BGH* 9.3.1994 (1994) *NJW* 2699, [1995] I.L.Pr. 180.

[906] *OLG Hamburg* 8.3.1996 IPRspr. 1996 Nr. 145.

[907] (1994) *NJW* 2699, at p.2700.

[908] 8.3.1996 IPRspr. 1996 Nr. 145, at p.350.

[909] *LG Duisburg* 17.4.1996 IPRspr. (1996) Nr. 148.

[910] (2000) *IPRax* 121, at p.122: silence equating to acceptance of a clause in standard conditions does not amount to a usage.

[911] ('An international commercial usage whereby such silence on the part of the other contracting party entails the inclusion of general conditions of the other—is not apparent'), IPRspr. 1996 Nr. 148, at p.358.

2.4.4(ii)   Practice/Usage in French case law

As mentioned above, the German courts, as early as 1988, had readily found a practice or usage to the effect that silence[912] as to a commercial letter of confirmation is an indication of tacit assent to the general conditions, including of course the jurisdiction clause contained therein.[913] This view has also been accepted by decisions of the *Cours d'Appel*, of Paris[914] and of Colmar,[915] where the former has held in two cases[916] that there was a usage in international trade and commerce whereby acceptance of the seller's confirmation of order without protestation from the buyer made the clause valid between the parties;[917] the later case of the *Cour d'Appel Colmar*[918] recognised a usage in the specialised area of international adhesive cement sales, to the effect that

> 'la mention d'une clause attributive de juridiction dans les conditions générales de vente figurant au verso des contrats constitue un usage générale dans le commerce international'[919] [920]

However, the *Cour de Cassation* in *Société Stork Colorproofing BV c/ Société Ofmag et Art Nord,*[921] while conceding that there was an international commercial usage according to which international business relations were governed by standard conditions,[922] did not extend this usage to cover a case where the Dutch

---

[912] This practice had originally surfaced in *Galereis Segoura SPRL v Rahim Bonakdarian*—without a continuing business relationship, silence was not seen as acceptance of the clause.

[913] *OLG Köln* 16.3.1988, (1988) *RIW* 555, at p.557: 'Die Regeln über das Schweigen auf ein kaufmännisches Bestätigungsschreiben stellen zwar einen internationalen Handelsbrauch da, der in zahlreichen anderen Vertragsstaaten des EuGVÜ vereinbart ist' ('The rules about silence over a commercial letter of confirmation indeed represents an international commercial practice that is agreed on in numerous other Contracting States'); *BGH* 9.3.1994, (1994) *RIW* 508, at p.510; *OLG Hamburg*, 30.7.1992, IPRspr. 1992, Nr.194; especially *LG Essen* 12.12.1990, (1992) *RIW* 227, at p.228: 'Es ist international üblich und damit internationaler Handelsbrauch, daß Parteien AGB verwenden, die Gerichtsstandsklauseln enthalten' ('It is customary internationally and therefore an international practice, that parties use General Conditions that contain jurisdiction clauses').

[914] (1990) *JDI* 153.

[915] (1995) *JDI* 152.

[916] *Société Microstoff Textiles c/ Société Laines Frères*, Cour d'Appel de Paris, 30.11.1988, (1990) *JDI* 153; *Société Karl Schaeff c/ Société Patrymat* Cour d'appel de Paris, 14.12.1988, (1990) *JDI* 153.

[917] *Société Karl Schaeff c/ Société Patrymat Cour d'appel de Paris*, 14.12.1988, (1990) *JDI* 153: 'Il est néanmoins certain que les usages du commerce international n'exigent pas que les conditions générales du vendeur parmi lesquelles figure une clause de juridiction aient été "acceptées par écrit" par l'acheteur'('it is nonetheless certain that usages of international commerce do not dictate that the seller's general conditions among which a jurisdiction clause figures has been 'accepted in writing' by the buyer'), at p.157.

[918] *S.A.Fourmaintraux et Delassus c/ Société Building Adhesives Ltd, Cour d'Appel de Colmar*, 6.12.1993, (1995) *JDI* 152.

[919] ('the reference to a jurisdiction clause in general conditions of sale on the reverse side of contracts amounts to a general usage in international trade').

[920] *Ibid.* at p.153; previous caselaw, *Ditta Estasis Salotti di Colzano Aima e Giamano Colzano v RÜWA Polstereimaschinen GmbH* (C-24/76) 14.12.1976 [1976] ECR 1831, required express reference to general conditions on the front of the contract.

[921] (1995) *JDI* 154.

[922] *Ibid.* at p.156.

seller's standard conditions were not actually communicated to the French buyer, but instead lodged with a local Dutch chamber of commerce.[923]

A similar view has been expressed as to the effect of silence on receipt of a confirmation of order by the offeror in two cases from the *Cour d'appel de Paris*: *Société Microstoff Textiles c/ Société Laines Frères*,[924] and *Société Karl Schaeff c/ Société Patrymat*.[925]

In a case from the *Cour d'appel de Colmar*, *S.A.Fourmaintraux et Delassus c/ Société Building Adhesives Ltd*,[926] it seems that the necessity for an express reference to the general conditions of sale on the back of a contract,[927] necessitated by *Salotti v RÜWA*[928] has been ameliorated somewhat by the recent version of Article 17(1). The case has been mentioned above; it accepted that it was a 'usage' to have general conditions on the back of contracts. Yet no specific mention was made of the need for 'awareness', perhaps due to the fact that the parties had been in a business relationship for fifteen years.

The change in the wording of Article 17 has been appreciated by the *Cour de Cassation* recently in *Faser c/ Soc. Somestra industries*,[929] on 9.2.1999. Somestra had sued Faser, an Italian company *en référé* in Strasbourg on the basis of a jurisdiction clause in an order form submitted to and signed by the Italian company. There was no express reference to the general conditions printed on the reverse, as would have been required by *Salotti v RÜWA*. One (rejected) ground of the Italian, Faser's, appeal in *cassation* was therefore the fact that 'le bon de commande établi sur papier commercial de Somestra ne contenait aucun renvoi exprès à la clause atttributive de compétence[930] figuarant au recto[931]' of the order. While not referring at all to *Salotti*, the new version of Article 17, nor to *Mainschiffahrts*, the *Cour de Cassation* summarily stated that Faser 'avait eu connaissance de la clause litigieuse'.

---

[923] (1995) *JDI* at p.156: 'il n'y a vraisemblablement pas d'usage du commerce international qui oblige le destinataire des conditions générales à les consulter auprès d'un tiers'('There is not in all probability a usage in international commerce that requires the ultimate recipient of general conditions to have to consult them with a third party'); cf *Credit Suisse Financial Products v Société Generale d'Enterprises*, [1997] CLC 168, CA; in *OLG Karlsruhe* 15.3.2001 (2001) *RIW* 621, the Swiss defendant failed to include its general conditions of sale with its confirmation of order, thereby losing out (under Article 17 Lugano Convention) in the battle of the forms to a German company which *had done so* in its order, at p.622; in *AIG Europe SA v QBE International Insurance Ltd*, [2001] 2 Lloyd's Rep. 268, at p.273 (Moore-Bick J), actual terms referred to need not be with the contracting parties at time of contracting.

[924] 30.11.1988 (1990) *JDI* 153, [1990] I.L.Pr. 364.

[925] (1990) *JDI* 153, at p.158.

[926] 6.12.1993 (1995) *JDI* 152.

[927] None was required.

[928] (C-24/76) [1976] ECR 1831, at p.1842, para. 10.

[929] Unreported, Lexis.

[930] Note, however in favour of the French courts as *forum prorogatum*; whether the *Cassation* would have been so receptive to similar arguments had the clause stated the Italian courts is unknown.

[931] ('the order form set out on the commercial paper of Somestra did not contain any express reference to the jurisdiction clause appearing on the reverse side').

It is all the more strange[932] therefore that the new version of Article 17 was not applied by the *Cour de Cassation* in *Société d'études d'investissement pour les affaires (SEIA) c/ Souscripteurs des Lloyd's de Londres.*[933] The defendant French shipowner, Société d'études, was sued for salvage costs by another French company in Lyon. The defendant joined its Lloyd's underwriters, who via the intermediary of a (French) marine broker, had insured the vessel against such salvage costs. The underwriters objected to French jurisdiction because of the presence of a High Court jurisdiction clause[934] in the insurance policy. This policy, it was found, had not been issued to Société d'études. Both lower courts accepted the plea of a lack of jurisdiction, but the *Cour de Cassation* reversed this. Société d'études advanced various arguments, some based on French (marine) insurance law—regarding the policy/clause's language,[935] and the size of the characters that made up the clause. It also (successfully) objected that it had no knowledge of the policy itself. That the policy had not been delivered was sufficient for the *Cour de Cassation*. Huet, the reviewer, is rightly critical that the court did not even attempt to find whether any of the forms of Article 17 (a)-(c) existed or not.[936] Of concern too, is the fact that the court was receptive to arguments/defences based on French insurance law—but found not to be applicable on the facts—which *Elefanten Schuh GmbH v Pierre Jacqmain* and now *Hugo Trumpy* have shown to be impermissible when Article 17 applies *ratione materiae*. The case is perhaps yet another example of this highest court's antipathy to foreign jurisdiction clauses.[937]

A case from the *Cour d'appel de Paris*, which post-dates the European Court of Justice's decision in *Mainschiffahrts*, but in which no mention is made of this authority,[938] is *Société Marcel Marie v Société Henco.*[939] Here a French jurisdiction clause had been included in General Conditions on the front of invoices submitted by the French seller to the Swiss buyer, over a period of seven years, and were paid without objection. The appeal court confirmed French jurisdiction, in that it

---

[932] The clause, however, would have ousted French jurisdiction.

[933] 11.3.1997 (1998) *JDI* 139, (1997) *Rev crit* 537, 1997 DMF 364; a clause in a Lloyd's of London marine insurance policy stipulated the jurisdiction of the High Court in London.

[934] Although the dispute undoubtedly concerned insurance, Article 12(5) and Article 12a(2)(a) and (3) permitted consideration of a jurisdiction clause under Article 17 in this case.

[935] Despite the earlier ruling against such considerations in *Elefanten Schuh GmbH v Pierre Jacqmain* (C-150/80) [1981] ECR 1671; (and now) *Hugo Trumpy*, [1999] ECR I-1597, at pp.1652–53, paras. 31, 36, 38.

[936] (1998) *JDI* 139, at p.141.

[937] Compare *Cassation* 25.11.1997 *Insurance Company of North America and another v Société Intramar and another* [1999] I.L.Pr. 315.

[938] The case is supported by the conclusions of the court in *Mainschiffahrts* in any event, [1997] ECR I-911, at p.940, para. 20: 'that one of the parties repeatedly paid without objection invoices issued by the other party . . .'; recently, post-*Mainschiffahrts*, in *Cassation* 6.7.1999 *Société de droit italien Graniti Fiandre c/ SA Mothes et autre* 1999 *Dalloz*, IR, 212, which censured the lower court for not considering the alternatives in Article 17.

[939] Currently only available in English at [1998] I.L.Pr. 807.

was held to be 'standard practice[940] in both the national and international sale of goods to incorporate jurisdiction clauses in the general conditions of sale on invoices'.[941]

These cases are a long way from the 'institutionalised' view of Article 17's enlargement, expressed in the House of Lords Select Committee Report.[942] It seems there is a danger that the floodgates may have been opened by the third hypothesis: that national courts, especially in France and Germany, are relying too heavily upon local or national business customs, and imposing them on unsuspecting[943] business clients from other EU countries. This is certainly the impression gleaned from the one-off sales transaction between the German supplier and the English customer in *Custom Made Commercial Ltd v Stawa Metallbau GmbH*,[944] where it is clear that the English company would never have thought that it had to object, somehow, to the jurisdiction clause in the confirmation of order, in default of which it would be taken[945] to have accepted a German jurisdiction clause.

2.4.5   Awareness of the practice/usage

At the second meeting of the joint EEC-EFTA experts charged with the negotiation of the 1988 Lugano Convention, on the 4–5 February 1986,[946] doubts were raised by the Finnish, as *pourparleurs* for the other EFTA State delegations, that Article 17 of the Brussels Convention, in its 1978 version, was too widely drawn,[947] as regards 'awareness' of commercial usages in particular. An ad hoc group, headed by M.Saggio, was set up to consider these concerns in the fourth meeting on 3–4 June 1986.[948] In response to these concerns, working document no.25,[949] presented to the fifth meeting of 16–17 September 1986, introduced the wording which became Article 17(1)(c) of the Lugano Convention, and eventually found its way by re-re-amendment into Article 17(c) of the Brussels Convention.

---

[940] *Contra*, the earlier case of *Cour d'appel de Paris 8.6.1988 Soc.Alusuisse France v Soc. Rodwer* (1988) *Dalloz*, IR., p.203, [1990] I.L.Pr. 102.

[941] [1998] I.L.Pr. 807, at p.810, para. 9.

[942] House of Lords, Select Committee on the European Communities, Session 1976–77, 45th Report (Preliminary Draft Convention on the Accession to the Brussels Convention of 27 September 1968) 26 July 1977, pp.8–9, para. 20: 'Virtually all commodity sales are on the bases of telexes incorporating standard clauses, such as the various *GAFTA forms* . . . There is no risk that the persons who operate in these markets will be taken by surprise by a jurisdiction clause; they are fully acquainted with the terms of these *market conditions*'.

[943] Awareness of the practice, and how to prove it, it is submitted, is the vital piece in the Article 17, third hypothesis' jigsaw; below, at p.274 and Schmidt, (1992) *RIW* 173.

[944] (C-288/92) [1994] ECR I-2913.

[945] By the German courts at least.

[946] In *Convention de Lugano*, II. *Travaux Préparatoires*, Publications de l'Institut suisse de droit comparé, 1991.

[947] *Ibid.* at p.65–66.

[948] *Ibid.* at p.88.

[949] Reproduced, at p.106, *ibid.*

Awareness, then, whichever version of Article 17 Brussels or Lugano Conventions one considers, is the key to the applicability of this hypothesis of Article 17:[950] how to demonstrate it and how to avoid the fiction[951] of being presumed to know of it, however ascertained. Various methods[952] have been suggested as to how to demonstrate the necessary actual or presumed awareness. The approach taken by the German courts,[953] and advocated by AG Lenz in *Custom Made Commercial Ltd*[954] is to judge awareness by whether such a usage exists at the seat[955] or head office, of the relevant party.[956] While this has the merit of a certain simplicity, it also makes the application of the Convention at this point depend on national law eccentricities, undermining the uniform and independent interpretation of its provisions, so often invoked by the European Court: witness the comparative law approach to the issue of the effect of silence in the various Contracting States undertaken by Schmidt,[957] and the result of the case decided by the *OLG Köln*.[958] Although a practice was found to exist,[959] there was no knowledge, actual or presumed, of it simply because the relevant party had its head office in Italy, where no significance[960] was attached to silence regarding a commercial confirmation. Conversely, had the relevant party been domiciled in France, Belgium, Luxembourg, Holland or Denmark,[961] the clause would have been valid, because the law in such Contracting States treats silence in such circumstances as acceptance. Such a solution as to awareness based on the legal position at a particular party's seat is unworkable, and totally inconsistent. The

---

[950] Especially Schmidt, (1992) *RIW* 173, at p.177: 'Diese Frage dürfte in die Zukunft den *Schwerpunkt* der dritten Formvariante in Article 17 Abs.1 Satz 2 bilden. Für die Praxis stellt sich hier die Frage: wie kann man nachweisen, daß ein internationaler Handelsbrauch der anderen Partei bekannt war?' ('This question should in future form the *fulcrum* of the third hypothesis of Article 17(1). Practice should ask itself this question: how can it be proved that an international commercial practice was known to the other party?').

[951] *Ibid.*; the more esoteric or localised a particular international trade practice is shown to be, the less likely the other party 'ought to have been aware' of it.

[952] No research could unearth any suggestion from France as to how to show awareness.

[953] *OLG Köln* 16.3.1988, (1988) *RIW* 555; *LG Essen* 12.12.1990, (1992) *RIW* 227; *BGH* 9.3.1994, (1994) *RIW* 508; *OLG Hamburg*, 30.7.1992, IPRspr. 1992, Nr.194; and *LG Münster* 25.1.1991 (1990) *RIW* 312.

[954] (C-288/92) [1994] ECR I-2913, at p.2945, para. 108.

[955] Especially *OLG Köln* 16.3.1988, (1988) *RIW* 555, at p.557: 'Hinsichtlich des Kennenmüssens kommt es darauf an, ob die Beklagte nach ihrem Wohnsitzrecht damit rechnen müßte, daß ihr Schweigen als Willenserklärung gewertet wird' ('As regards what a party ought to have known, this depends on whether the defendant should have reckoned by the law of its seat that its silence would be counted as acquiescence').

[956] I.e. the one against whom the clause is being invoked; *sed quaere*, or *either* party, at p.1627, in *Internationales Vertragsrecht*, 5 Aufl., 1996.

[957] Schmidt, (1992) *RIW* 173, at p.177.

[958] *OLG Köln* 16.3.1988, (1988) *RIW* 555.

[959] Due in no small measure to the internal practices peculiar to German commercial law.

[960] *OLG Köln* 16.3.1988, (1988) *RIW* 555, at p.557.

[961] Schmidt (1992) *RIW* 173, at p.177.

application or not of the third hypothesis cannot depend in such an arbitrary way on the identity of a particular customer, or its seat.[962]

Thankfully, the European Court in *Mainschiffahrts-Genossenschaft e.G (MSG) v Les Gravières Rhénanes SARL*,[963] and *Società Transporti Castelletti Spedizioni Internazionali SpA v Hugo Trumpy SpA*[964] has given some non-exhaustive guidance[965] as to how to demonstrate actual or presumed awareness, without distinction between the two: firstly, when the parties have 'previously had commercial or trade relations between themselves';[966] secondly, when the parties have 'previously had commercial or trade relations . . . with *other* parties operating in the sector in question'; and lastly when a 'consolidated practice'[967] has been established—in other words when a 'particular course of conduct is sufficiently well-known because it is generally and regularly followed.'[968] It can be assumed that these three criteria apply equally so as to demonstrate both actual or presumptive awareness.[969] Actual knowledge either exists or it does not, from whatever source it happens to come.[970]

As noted earlier, the reference to the ECJ in *Società Transporti Castelletti Spedizioni Internazionali SpA v Hugo Trumpy SpA* gave the Court occasion to refine (by excluding) certain interpretations sought to be place on its earlier decision in *Mainschiffahrts*. The refinements made to the awareness criterion were, unfortunately, fact-specific, driven by the desire to exclude dogmatic expressions, or pre-requisites, of the proof required to demonstrate[971] awareness. In its question twelve, itself in turn referring to the factual conditions (of publicity) in

---

[962] Schmidt (1992) *RIW* 173, at p.178; cf. if the relevant party is a non-Contracting State domiciliary—*Hugo Trumpy* [1999] ECR I-1597, at p.1654, para. 42.

[963] [1997] ECR I-911.

[964] (C-159/97) [1999] ECR I-1597.

[965] [1997] ECR I-911, at p.941, para. 24; *Hugo Trumpy*, [1999] ECR I-1597, at p.1654, para. 43.

[966] This is somewhat of a tautology, because this now forms its own separate sub-para (b), since the San Sebastian amendments: *Knauf UK GmbH v British Gypsum Ltd and another* [2001] 2 All ER (Comm) 332, QBD, (David Steel J), *revs'd* on a different point [2002] 1 WLR 907, CA (Henry LJ).

[967] *Hugo Trumpy* uses the phrase 'established usage', at p.1654, para. 43; nothing may turn on this difference.

[968] *OLG Hamburg*, 30.7.1992, IPRspr. 1992, Nr.194, at p.442: 'Dieser Handelsbrauch muß aber als der Bekl. bekannt angesehen werden, weil sie als am internationalen vekehr teilnemenher Kaufmann weißt, daß die Linienreeder ihren Stückgutfrachtverträgen ihre Konnossementsbedingungen zugrunde zu legen pflegen . . .'('This usage should be known to the defendant, because a businessman participating in international transport by sea knows that liner carriers are in the habit of subjecting their carriage of goods contracts to bill of lading clauses').

[969] The last alternative will be most useful in proving of what a party ought to have been aware.

[970] Should a businessman from one particular market-sector decide to buy some adhesive cement, and he is aware, by whatever means, that there is a practice or usage relating to silence, he will be bound by any jurisdiction clause under the third hypothesis; Kropholler, 1998, at p.251.

[971] Compare the methodology used in *OLG Celle* 1.11.1995 IPRspr. 1996 Nr. 138, at p.323: a questionnaire was sent to participants in the trade in question by the Hamburg Chamber of Commerce, to which over 75% replied that they were aware of a clause's incorporation in the same circumstances as in the case at bar; note also the expert evidence called in the post reference Mainschiffahrts appeal case, *OLG Nürnberg* 30.7.1998 1998 IPRspr. Nr.150—a 'usage', and knowledge of it were found to exist, and jurisdiction was finally asserted, at pp.280–81.

question 5, the referring *Corte di Cassazione* had asked what degree of awareness needed to be shown, and whether it can be demonstrated to exist in the absence of a 'model' contract's residing in a trade association's offices. The European Court answered[972] that it was not essential for a manifestation of awareness that a model contract, including the jurisdiction clause, be so lodged,[973] but would certainly help to prove awareness.

Among other things, what the reference in *Hugo Trumpy* has shown is a Contracting State court struggling to apply the last sentence of the third hypothesis of Article 17. Despite having been in existence in some form for over 13 years, this 'awareness' hypothesis has only recently, with this case, started to be fleshed out. Even while this is occurring, and the scant Contracting State case law increasing, legislative change is underway once more. The lack, until now, of authoritative guidance as to presumed awareness had led certain (German) courts to rely on the shifting lottery of 'awareness' at the defendant's seat—an approach which at least now has been tacitly discouraged in *Hugo Trumpy*.

2.5   AMENDMENTS TO ARTICLE 17, IF ANY, BY THE BRUSSELS I REGULATION[974] AND THE PRELIMINARY DRAFT HAGUE WORLDWIDE JUDGMENTS CONVENTION[975]

As has been mentioned earlier in section 2.1.5(i), Article 23 of the Brussels I Regulation, in conjunction with its Article 4, para. 1, have attempted at least to correct the drafting solecism in, and perpetuated since, the original 1968 Brussels Convention.

Since 1973, the effect of this has been the tension between Article 4 Brussels Convention jurisdiction against non-Contracting State domiciliaries, who also conclude Article 17 jurisdiction clauses with Contracting State partners. The new Article 4 of the Regulation now makes jurisdiction—under national law—against such domiciliaries subject to the application of (additionally) Article 23, jurisdiction clauses. As has also been observed, this may undoubtedly not solve the need to distinguish between various categories of permutations[976] under the new proposed Article 23. The problems highlighted with the German and Austrian jurisprudence will almost certainly be perpetuated.[977]

---

[972]   At p.1654, para. 44.

[973]   Contrast the French case where a contract was lodged with a trade association *Société Colorproofing BV c/ Société Ofmag et Art Nord* 23.2.1994 (1995) *JDI* 154.

[974]   Commission's proposal for a Council Regulation (EC), done at Brussels 14 July 1999 COM(1999) 348 final, 99/0154 (CNS), available on-line at http://europa.eu.int/comm/sg/tfjai/unit/unit3_en.htm.

[975]   *Hague Conference on Private International Law, Preliminary Draft Convention on Jurisdiction and Foreign Judgments in Civil and Commercial Matters*, amended version, adopted by the Special Commission on 30 October 1999, on-line at http://www.hcch.net/e/conventions/draft36e.html.

[976]   Of domicile—now AG Alber in opinion of 23.3.2000 in *Coreck Maritime GmbH*.

[977]   Now *Mercury Communications Ltd and another v Communication Telesystems International* [1999] 2 All ER (Comm) 33, (Moore Bick J).

It is all the more curious therefore that the original wording of Article 17 of the Commission's first proposal for a Council Act, submitted on 22 December 1997, was changed and not adopted. Its opening phrase had been materially different from the form in which it is now drafted in Article 23, with the legacy that such wording will bring with it from Article 17 of the Brussels and Lugano Conventions. This earlier December 1997 proposal had omitted any reference to the domicile of the parties, a solution that has its echo in the proposed drafting of Article 4 of the Hague Conference Draft Worldwide Judgments Convention.[978] If the wording of Article 4 had been used in the Brussels I Regulation, this would, at a stroke, have swept away all the current idiosyncratic interpretations of 'internationality' presented in section 2.1.

That said, however, Article 23 of the proposed draft Regulation, in para.3 does attempt to slot agreements in so-called 'e-commerce', such as by e-mail message, into the 'writing' form in Article 23(a). This will be so, provided that such a communication method 'provides a durable record of the agreement'.[979] Contracts concluded over the internet,[980] and by e-mail, will no doubt satisfy the sufficient degree of durability for the requirement of a 'writing'; but factual situations, currently common with written exchanges of contracts/letters of confirmation, can be envisaged, *mutatis mutandis*, with those in *Salotti v RÜWA* and *Segoura v Bonakdarian* when e-mails of confirmation of orders are sent, and to which no objection nor reaction is taken. If a concluded 'e-contract', for example by e-mail, does not contain an express reference, in the text itself, to a jurisdiction clause, or to general conditions containing such a clause (in an attachment or in earlier offers, previously communicated),[981] it is unlikely that Article 23(a) will be satisfied. Similarly, outside a continuing trading relationship, if a contract is concluded orally, and then confirmed by one party by e-mail with attachments containing general conditions (with a jurisdiction clause), the lack of a reaction to the e-mail will not amount to an agreement in writing within Article 23(a).[982]

Article 23(a) should now be read in conjunction[983] with other initiatives, in the other Articles of the proposed Regulation itself,[984] and more generally at

---

[978] Article 4 of the Hague draft Convention reads as follows: 'If the parties have agreed that a court or courts of a Contracting State shall have jurisdiction . . .'.

[979] COM(1999) 348 final, 99/0154 (CNS), at p.40.

[980] Junker, (1999) *RIW* 809.

[981] *Salotti v RÜWA* (24/76) [1976] ECR 1831, at p.1842, para. 12.

[982] *Segoura v Bonakdarian* (25/76) [1976] ECR 1851, at p.1861, para. 8.

[983] The important links between the July 1999 proposal and these new initiatives were emphasised by the submissions of the London Investment Banking Association in evidence to the *HL Select Committee on the European Union, 14th Report* ('E-commerce: Policy Development and Co-ordination in the EU'), *Evidence*, (HL Paper 1999–2000, 95–I) at p.477.

[984] Article 15(3), jurisdiction over consumer contracts, between 'consumers' and e-businesses which, 'by any means, *directs* [commercial or professional] activities to [the consumer's] State'; Seaman, (2000) *Comp. and Law* 28, at p.29; Omar, (1999) *ICCLR* 148, at pp.148–49; Greggio, (2000) *ICCLR* 193; Powell, (1999) *ICCLR* 361, at p.363; Balonwu, (1999) *Tr Law* 446, at p.448.

Community level,[985] to accommodate and encourage[986] the increase in 'e-commerce'.[987] As part of this progressive shift towards internet-based business in England was the coming into force, on 25.7.2000, of s7[988] Electronic Communications Act 2000, which is designed to facilitate the admissibility of electronic signatures, in relation to the 'authenticity' of electronic communications or data. Section 3, Articles 9–11 of the amended Commission proposal, show the Commission's enthusiasm in actively promoting 'electronic contracts', in particular with regard to consumers, in aspects such as admissibility and when a contract is concluded. The consequences of this for Article 23(a) of the Regulation, and in the meantime, for Article 17 of the Convention will be the extension of the principles and jurisprudence developed thereunder into the electronic realm. If electronic contracts concluded over the internet are permissible, and admissible in evidence, the transition to 'e-commerce', at least for the purposes of 'form' requirements under Article 17, the whole jurisprudence surrounding the article will merely be moved *en bloc* to the electronic arena. As noted, in *Salotti v RÜWA*, jurisdiction clauses in contracts concluded by e-mail will need express reference, if included in attachments, as such do not include a reverse side. As this type of commerce grows, contracts in international trade or commerce, that at one time were concluded in a particular written form, will simply transfer over—without much difficulty, as to form, for regular traders in the particular branch of trade or commerce concerned. Any problems that existed with Article 17 prior to the e-commerce extension to Article 23 will not be solved, but equally not exacerbated by these changes.

2.6   CONCLUSION

The great merit of Article 17 is that of certainty[989]

Article 17 of the Brussels and Lugano Conventions, at first sight simple in terms of its wording and aims,[990] has demonstrated the risks that particular

---

[985] See the *Amended proposal for a European Parliament and Council Directive on certain legal aspects of electronic commerce in the Internal Market*, 17.8.1999, COM (1999) 427 final, 98/0325, especially Preamble 4(a), and section 3, electronic contracts, Article 9 (permissibility) and Article 11 (moment of formation); European Parliament and Council Directive 1999/93/EC on a Community framework for electronic signatures [2000] OJ L13/12, 19.1.2000; Rawson, (1999) *ICCLR* 171; also *UNCITRAL Yearbook*, Vol. XXIX,, 1998, 'Report of the Working Group on Electronic Commerce', 32nd session, 19–30 January 1998, at para. 27 onwards.

[986] Note the comments of HC European Scrutiny Committee, *Eighth Report*, 9.2.2000, HC23–viii, at pp.xxxvi–xl.

[987] The ability to make use of electronic signatures being one such encouragement: Lubbock, M. *E-Commerce, Doing Business Electronically*, 2000, at pp.41–44.

[988] Explanatory notes to the *Electronic Communications Bill*, HL Bill 24-EN, 1999–00, at p.9, states that 'it will be for the court to decide in a particular case whether an electronic signature has been correctly used'.

[989] D.Rhidian-Thomas, 1996, at p.311.

[990] Schlosser Report.

national courts will so construe its terms as to incorporate cherished national law rules[991] and presumptions[992] into the Brussels Convention system, leading to its disharmonious interpretation and the end of the uniform protection of persons established therein. Where certain terms of the Convention remain un- or ill-defined, it is all the more tempting to fall back on familiar national law concepts[993]

If one thing is clear from even a brief overview of only the German, French and English case law on a small, select, area of Article 17 is that choosing a Contracting State court with a jurisdiction clause is no certain guarantee that either the chosen court will take jurisdiction, or, more importantly, that any other Contracting State court will decline jurisdiction.[994]

Article 17 is a 'paradigm'[995] example for exposing the attitude of the domestic Contracting State courts specifically to jurisdiction clauses, and of their potential for protecting domestic economies.[996] Judicial protectionism, if it exists anywhere in the Convention is perhaps nowhere in sharper focus than when considering Article 17.[997]

The article is also one that has undergone most revision through the 1978 and 1989 accessions.[998] This in itself reveals the inadequacies[999] of the original drafting to meet commercial needs—it has also enabled and/or forced the ECJ to indulge in imaginative and often policy-oriented decision-making. The facts in the decided cases were, it seems, simply not foreseen by the Convention's original drafters: oral contracts, (it seems) bills of lading and contracts concluded in ongoing business relationships.

---

[991] Cf. the German courts' ambivalent attitude to the issue of 'internationality', in section 2.1.5(iii), *Mercury Communications Ltd and another v Communication Telesystems International* [1999] 2 All ER (Comm) 33, and *Cour de Cassation* 11.3.1997 *Société d'études d'investissement pour les affaires SEIA c/ Souscripteurs des Lloyd's de Londres* (1998) *JDI* 139.

[992] Cf. the referring court in *Hugo Trumpy*, and the French section on bills of lading, above, at pp.209 *et seq* section 2.2.2.

[993] Also the Rome Convention 1980 and especially Article 4: 'the [Rome] Convention's indeterminate provisions force even impartial judges to resort to pre-Convention techniques', Horlacher 'The Rome Convention and the German paradigm' (1994) *Cornell Int.L.J*, 173, at p.191.

[994] *Continental Bank v Aeakos* [1994] 1 Lloyd's Rep. 505; *Phillip Alexander Securities & Futures Ltd v Bamberger*, [1996] CLC, 1757 (Waller J) CA at p.1780; *GIE Réunion européenne c/ Société Plate et Ruys*, *Cour de Cassation*, Ch. Com., 10.1.1995 (1996) *JDI* 141; *Société d'études d'investissement pour les affaires (SEIA) c/ Souscripteurs des Lloyd's de Londres* 11.3.1997 (1998) *JDI* 139.

[995] Steyn LJ in *Continental Bank v Aeakos* [1994] 1 WLR 588, at p.598.

[996] Davenport, B.J. 'Forum shopping in the market' (1995) 111 *LQR* 366 and Brajeux, G. 'Casenote: *The Nagasaki, Cour de Cassation* Nov.1994', Reuter Textline, Lloyd's List, 13.11.1996.

[997] Although a German commentator, Strop, (1999) *RIW* 823 has written a scathing attack on what he sees as the protectionist attitude of the French courts towards domestic commercial agents under Article 5(1), at p.824, and above, at p.85 chapter 1—and perpetuated now *Cour de Cassation* 8.2.2000 *Figot c/ Sté Leithauser GmbH and Co* (2000) *JCP*, IV, 1544.

[998] Gaudemet-Tallon, 1996, at p.75, para. 104.

[999] And why the House of Lords Select Committee in its 45th Report considered it essential that Article 17 be reworded.

This area of the Brussels Convention has proved fertile[1000] for litigation. It also provides a continuous spool of case decisions[1001] at both European and national level for research.

Indeed, according to Fentiman:

> given its objective of securing legal certainty, the Convention's often delphic wording, and its dependence on the alchemy of purposive interpretation, offers little purchase to litigants . . . [and] encourages disputes and makes their outcome unpredictable, a situation not improved by the European Court's often gnomic pronouncements . . .'[1002]

[1000] *Court of Justice of the European Communities: Digest of Case law Relating to the European Communities*: D Series—Convention of 27 September 1968, Issue 5, 1993, Cases D 17.1–B.1 onwards, covering some sixty pages of national court decisions.

[1001] The latest being *Hugo Trumpy SpA* (C-159/97) [1999] ECR I-1597; and *Coreck Maritime GmbH* (C-387/98) [2000] ECR I-9337, at p.9375, Dutch referring court's decision reported at [1999] I.L.Pr. 721.

[1002] Fentiman, R. 'Judgments, purposes and the Brussels Convention' (1994) *CLJ* 239.

3

Article 24

INTRODUCTION

RECENT CASE-LAW[1] FROM the European Court of Justice has high-lighted issues and uncertainties relating to Article 24, which will no doubt reverberate at both European and national[2] level. This chapter will attempt to explore whether these cases may have encouraged, and fortified, further avenues of domestic protectionism—in the areas of 'interim payments', and the undermining of Article 3 of the Conventions.

The proposed course, and form, which this chapter intends to take will therefore have to reflect these changes; and it is its intention to divide up the examination of Article 24 into two parts: (1) jurisdiction under the article and (2) the meaning of interim relief[3] and/or 'provisional, including protective measures' in its text. An ancillary problem to part (2), which has also received some attention recently from the European Court[4]—and will hereinafter be termed 'the exportability[5] issue'—will also now deserve independent investigation.

Although it is sensible to view Article 24 in its two sections—jurisdiction and substantive interim relief—it will become clear that the type of jurisdiction taken (under Article 24, or the Convention's Title II generally) in order to grant

---

[1] *Van Uden Maritime BV, trading as Van Uden Maritime Africa Line v Kommanditgesellschaft in Firma Deco Line, and another* (C-391/95) [1998] ECR I–7091 and *Hans-Hermann Mietz v Intership Yachting Sneek B.V.* (C-99/96) [1999] ECR I–2277; the whole 'traditional' thinking of Article 24 jurisdiction to order provisional measures may have to be re-assessed in the light of these two cases; *Cheshire and North*, 13th edn, 1999, at p.261.

[2] Post *Van Uden Maritime* decisions of the French *Cour de Cassation* 13.4.1999 *Bachy c/ Soc. Belbetoes* (1999) *Rev crit* 352, [1999] I.L.Pr. 743, *OLG Düsseldorf* 28.1.1999 (1999) *RIW* 873, and the Swiss Supreme Court in *SodaStream Ltd. gegen Urs Jäger AG* 17.9.1999 125 BGE, III, 451; *Hof 's-Gravenhage* 17.7.2000 *F.G.H. Abbing tegen Sibomat N.V.* 2001 *NJ* Nr.87, p.543.

[3] Unless and until this phrase takes on its specialist definition in s 25(7) of the CJJA 1982, it is to mean Article 24 'provisional, including protective measures'; Article 39 of the Conventions also allow the grant of 'protective measures . . . against the property of the party against whom enforcement is sought'—yet the jurisdictional aspects, if any, of Article 39 are uncontroversial and will not be discussed in this chapter, Favre-Bulle, A. 'La mise en œuvre en Suisse de l'Article 39 al.2 de la Convention de Lugano' (1998) *SZIER* 335; *Bundesgericht* 7.7.2000 *Soc S et Soc D contre Cour d'appel du Tribunal cantonal de Fribourg*, 126 BGE, III, 438.

[4] *Hans-Hermann Mietz*, (C-99/96) [1999] ECR I–2277, below, at pp.312 *et seq.*

[5] I.e. whether judgments rendered under Article 24 for interim relief may cross the borders into another Contracting State; worldwide *Mareva*/freezing injunctions and *référé-provision* judgments below, at pp.324 *et seq.*

provisional measures will have a knock-on effect on the type of relief, in fact, available, which will of course, in turn, influence the exportability issue.

The above two divisions should also be borne in mind when scrutiny is undertaken of how the recent ECJ rulings (may) now have filtered down to national procedural level. Again, it will become clear that each Contracting State has had and may still have[6] particular problems with Article 24—be they jurisdictional,[7] as in England and Germany—or be they substantive, as to the meaning of interim relief, as in France and The Netherlands. The recent ECJ rulings will have something to say on each of these issues, to all the Contracting States.

The first half of this chapter will thus be devoted to the jurisdiction of the Contracting States to order interim relief under Article 24. It will begin by outlining the jurisdictional position and problems in the Contracting States prior to the ECJ ruling in *Van Uden Maritime.*[8] To spare any confusion, the beginning will be prefaced by the essential findings of *Van Uden Maritime,* so the reader may be able to compare the current position of the law, and the historical perspective simultaneously.

Then the case of *Van Uden Maritime* itself, and its natural successor, *Hans Herman Mietz,*[9] will be examined in greater detail, together with a re-appraisal of national jurisdictions;[10] and an attempt will be made to evaluate the effects these cases will have on them at the jurisdictional level.

The second half of the chapter will examine the meaning of the phrase 'provisional, including protective measures' in Article 24;[11] in section 3.7, it will look at such measures from one jurisdiction in particular, France, and try to predict the effects that *Van Uden Maritime* and *Hans Herman Mietz* will have not only there, but also in England on interim payments and worldwide *Mareva*/freezing injunctions—the so-called 'exportability issue'.[12]

---

[6] Article 24 procedure prior to *Van Uden Maritime* has *not* diminished; this case's effects, if any, can only be appreciated by an overview of the previous national regimes.

[7] The English court's view of the exclusivity of s 25 of the Civil Jurisdiction and Judgments Act 1982—and not Article 24—as the source of jurisdiction to order provisional measures—from *Alltrans Inc v Interdom Holdings Ltd* [1991] 4 All ER 458, CA, may now have to be revisited, below, section 3.3.3.

[8] (C-391/95) [1998] ECR I–7091.

[9] *Hans-Hermann Mietz v Intership Yachting Sneek B.V.* (C-99/96) [1999] ECR I–2277.

[10] Focussing on English jurisdiction under s 25(1)(2) CJJA 1982, below, section 3.3.4.

[11] Apart from the Propositions A–C, it will be submitted that the full force of the *Van Uden Maritime* ruling will not apply to freezing injunctions, and that illustrative German (and French cases)—albeit with a territorial limitation—prior to *Van Uden Maritime* will remain valid, revealing the dangers of the *référé-provision* at pp.233–34.

[12] A final section will briefly scan the reforms, if any, that will be brought about by the Brussels I Regulation an/or the Hague draft Worldwide Judgments Convention.

Part I

3.1   JURISDICTION OF THE REQUESTED COURT UNDER ARTICLE 24 BRUSSELS/LUGANO CONVENTIONS

3.1.1   Preface to the historical section: propositions from the recent case of *Van Uden Maritime*

When reading the following historical section, it is best that the following three propositions be borne in mind by the reader, which reflect the current position of the law.

Proposition A

The jurisdiction of a Contracting State court, for an application for interim relief under the Conventions, against a particular Contracting State respondent[13] must now *clearly*[14] be derived *either*:[15]

(i)   from Articles 2, 5–18, as a court (simultaneously also) with jurisdiction[16] on the merits, and thus with unfettered power to grant whatever interlocutory relief[17] that may be available; with the resulting opportunity for its enforcement[18] under Title III in other Contracting States

or

(ii)   from Article 24, *and*[19] national law—including Article 3 II provisions—*even as against Contracting State domiciliaries*, thus with a more limited power to order Article 24 'provisional, including protective measures';[20] with a

---

[13] As against non-Contracting State domiciliaries, national law applies in any event—a relatively-recent English example *Refco Inc. and another v Eastern Trading Co. and others* [1999] 1 Lloyd's Rep. 159, CA.

[14] *Hans Herman Mietz* has shown that if the jurisdiction of the rendering court in ordering provisional measures is not clear, it will be presumed that it derived from Article 24, and national law, [1999] ECR I–2277, at para. 55, with its attendant *Van Uden Maritime* restrictions.

[15] For a view that a court 'second seised', but not on the merits, may take jurisdiction under a combination of Article 24 *and* Articles 2, 5–18, Gerhard, F. *L'exécution forcée transfrontière des injonctions extraterritoriales non pécuniaires en droit privé*, 2000, at p.160, and below.

[16] On the point of jurisdiction, below at p.305, and n.217.

[17] Note the general generic use of this term; it is to be distinguished now from 'provisional, including protective measures' (as defined), which are exclusively available only under Article 24.

[18] So long as the measure is granted at an *inter partes* hearing: *Denilauer v Couchet Frères* (125/79) [1980] ECR 1553; *EMI Records Ltd v Modern Music* [1992] 1 QB 115 (Hobhouse J).

[19] This will have an impact, it is believed, on Italian procedure hitherto, according to Cuniberti, 2000, at p.319, para. 432.

[20] Marmisse, A 'Le régime jurisprudentiel des mesures provisiores à la lumière des arrêts *Van Uden Maritime* et *Mietz*' (1999) *Rev Crit* 669, at p.675, has emphasised that this enlargement of jurisdiction to order such measures has increased the importance of their self-limiting definition.

narrower opportunity, if any,[21] for cross-border enforcement under Title III—(the 'exportability issue'),

but not both simultaneously against the same respondent. The basis of jurisdiction against a Contracting State respondent will, in future, prove to be crucial. If a court can, and does, take jurisdiction on the merits, Article 24 is simply not needed.[22]

Proposition B

Jurisdiction under Article 24 is thus a 'special regime', an 'additional' jurisdiction, independent from, and falling outside,[23] the Title II, Articles 2, 5–18[24] system 'on the merits', and is thus unaffected by Article 3.

Proposition C[25]

So long as the application for 'provisional, including protective measures' itself relates to a civil and commercial matter, there is jurisdiction under Article 24,[26] *even if substantive proceedings on the merits under the Convention are otherwise impossible,*[27] *or possibly never even contemplated,*[28] for whatever reason, in any Contracting State.

---

[21] Cf *OLG München* 5.4.2000 (2000) *RIW* 464, which has enforced an interlocutory Greek freezing order, affecting German assets, below at pp.321–322.

[22] *Van Uden Maritime*, at p.7130, para. 19; *quaere*, whether applications under English law to an English court otherwise seised 'on the merits' will *still* involve s 25 CJJA 1982, and now CPR 6.20(4), below at pp.326–327.

[23] At p.7130, para. 20.

[24] Note repercussions on the so-called 'exclusive'/'protective' jurisdictions in Articles 16, 17, 7–12a, 13–15: an application under Article 24 appears possible even against a 'consumer' or assured/policy holder, domiciled in another Contracting State: *OLG Stuttgart* 4.8.2000 (2001) NJW–RR 858.

[25] *Van Uden Maritime*, at p.7133, para. 34; qu.4 in the withdrawn reference in *Boston v Cordis Corp.*(C-186/00) [2000] OJ C233/15 effectively answered in the affirmative by *Van Uden Maritime*— reversing the Court of Appeal's opinion in the same case, *Fort Dodge Animal Health Limited v Akzo Nobel N.V* [1998] FSR 222, at p.246 (Lord Woolf MR).

[26] But jurisdiction is governed by national law, as expansive or restrictive as this may be: *OGH* 13.1.1998 *Entscheidungen*, 71 Band, 1998, No.1, p.3: 'Art 24 EuGVÜ begründet demnach keine Verpflichtung Österreichs zur Ausübung von Gerichtsbarkeit, *es sei denn*, daß eine nationale Zuständigkeit gegeben wäre; ('Article 24 Brussels Convention does not therefore establish an obligation for Austria to exercise jurisdiction, *unless* a national competence is given'); *Hof 's-Gravenhage* 17.7.2000 *F.G.H. Abbing tegen Sibomat N.V.* 2001 *NJ* Nr.87, p.543.

[27] In *Van Uden Maritime*, substantive proceedings impossible in the Netherlands because of an arbitration clause, Article 1(4); it appears none need be instituted at any time; opportunity for ECJ to rule on clash of exclusive jurisdiction and Article 24 lost in qu.4 of withdrawn reference in *Boston v Cordis* (C-186/00) [2000] OJ C233/15. *Van Uden Maritime* seems to have settled the question that no substantive proceedings are necessary.

[28] Even though jurisdiction under s 25(1) CJJA 1982, as extended, appears to require at a minimum that '(a) proceedings *have been or are to be commenced* in a [Brussels or Lugano . . . State] [or now in any State] . . .', whether or not those proceedings' subject matter is within the scope of the Conventions:

3.1.2 Historical overview: the views and caselaw prevailing before *Van Uden Maritime*[29] and *Hans Herman Mietz*[30]

In detailed and carefully thought-out 'conventions doubles' like the Brussels and Lugano Conventions—with examples of permitted and outlawed jurisdictional bases in Title II, Articles 2, 5–18 against persons domiciled in Contracting States[31]—it provokes incredulity[32] that the deceptively simple Article 24 leaves so much out regarding the taking of jurisdiction. One would have thought, given what had gone before in Title II, that some guidance as to how the Contracting State courts were to determine jurisdiction[33] on applications for provisional measures would have been inserted into the text of Article 24 itself, at least for the avoidance to doubt. Various theories[34] had naturally been formulated in the wake of the article's silence. It is the purpose of this section of this chapter to examine these various views,[35] the justifications for them, the critical and judicial acceptance or rejection of them in relation to three[36] jurisdictions in which, tellingly, they have received widespread, or alternatively, scant attention. The ramifications of these views are analysed in the context of the goals that the Brussels/Lugano Conventions seek to achieve. A logical start would seem to be the wording of the text of Article 24 itself:

> Application may be made to the courts of a Contracting State for such provisional, including protective measures as may be available under the law of that State, even if,

---

The Civil Jurisdiction and Judgments Act 1982 (Interim Relief) Order 1997 SI 1997/302—*ICFI Corporate Securities Fund Plc v International Corporation for Finance and Investment*, 17.3.1999: 'case *now* clearly falls within s 25(1) criterion' (Hirst LJ).

[29] (C-391/95) [1998] ECR I–7091 (hereinafter *Van Uden Maritime*); this case was to a large extent presaged by *Verdonck v Algemene Bank Nederland, Arrondissementsrechtbank*, Amsterdam, 15.4.1981, *Digest*, D Series, Issue 5, Feb.1993, I–24–B10—'. . . an exception could be made to the principle laid down in Article 3 that a defendant could not be sued in the courts of a State other than that of his domicile in the cases expressly provided for in the Convention . . . *In view of its wording Article 24 was such an exception*'.

[30] (C-99/96) [1999] ECR I–2277.

[31] As against persons domiciled in non-Contracting States, Article 4 allows jurisdiction to be determined by 'the law of that State' (subject of course to Article 16 and possibly Article 57).

[32] Article 24 has been called a 'Schwachstelle'('weak spot') by both Kropholler, 1998, at p.308, para. 1, and by Jametti Greiner, 130 (1994) *Revue de la Société des juristes bernois*, 694, at p.661.

[33] The provision seems merely to point to substantive issues.

[34] Note the wealth of German comment: Gronstedt, S. *Grenzüberschreitender einstweiliger Rechtsschutz*, 1994; Heiss, B-R. *Einstweiliger Rechtsschutz im europäischen Zivilrechtsverkehr*, 1987; Karl, A-M. *Die Anerkennung von Entscheidungen in Spanien*, 1993; Wastl, U. *Die Vollstreckung deutscher Titel auf der Grundlage des EuGVÜ in Italien*, 1991; Stickler, S. *Das Zusammenwirken von Article 24 EuGVÜ und §§916ff. ZPO*, 1992; Albrecht, C. *Das EuGVÜ und der einstweilige Rechtsschutz in England und in der Bundesrepublik Deutschland*, 1991; Eilers, A. *Maßnahmen des einstweiligen Rechtsschutzes im europäischen Zivilrechtsverkehr*, 1991; Kessedjian, C. *Note on Provisional and Protective Measures in Private International Law and Comparative Law*, Hague Conference on Private International Law, Prel. Doc. No.10 of October 1998.

[35] Below at p.287.

[36] English, French and German jurisdictions have produced a great deal of accessible case law and comment.

under this Convention, the courts of another Contracting State have jurisdiction as to the substance of the matter.

Two courts therefore may, but not necessarily must,[37] be involved, one with 'jurisdiction as to the substance of the matter' 'under this Convention';[38] the other, one in which an application for 'provisional, including protective' measures may be made. Crucially, the measures involved are those 'as may be available under the law of that State';[39] and it is this phrase that has lead to so many interpretative inconsistencies.[40] Just how is a national court to take jurisdiction over a respondent to an application for such measures under Article 24?

Looking at the English version of Article 24 just quoted, the text does not contain any direct indication of how a court, applied to for provisional measures is to have jurisdiction over the application; it merely leaves open the possibility of such an action—under the same conditions as a purely domestic situation—even when[41] a substantive action on the merits is pending, or is possible, in another Contracting State. No mention is made of any jurisdictional base.[42] The word 'such' in Article 24 points only to the various national substantive measures available, not to how a court is to take jurisdiction. Logically and necessarily, however, it seems that a reference to particular provisions must also point to their corresponding national jurisdictional rules governing them.

---

[37] In sharp contrast to what was just noted above at n.28 about jurisdiction under s 25(1) CJJA 1982, *Van Uden Maritime* has shown us that two courts need not be implicated for jurisdiction to be taken under Article 24; this is a stark change of emphasis regarding Article 24, where two courts were assumed to be involved, and Article 24 was seen as merely a defence to a plea under Articles 21/22; however Article 24 must now *not* be read, if it ever was, as if the following emboldened words were implicit in the text: 'Application may be made to the courts of a Contracting State . . ., even if [*and only if*], under this Convention, the courts of another Contracting State have jurisdiction. . .[*and are or will potentially become seised on the merits*]'—cf. *Fox v Fox*, 3.9.1997, CA (Morritt LJ)—cf *ICFI Corporate Securities Fund Plc v International Corporation for Finance and Investment*, 17.3.1999, CA; explicit confirmation of this proposition, pre-*Van Uden Maritime*, in *Trib. prem. instance*, Bruxelles 7.2.1997, unreported: http://194.7.188. 126/cgi_juris/juris_a1; the Court of Appeal's view in *Fort Dodge Animal Health Limited v Akzo Nobel N.V* [1998] FSR 222, at p.246 must, in the light of *Van Uden Maritime*, now be considered incorrect.

[38] As an aside, these three words furnish support for the view that jurisdiction taken under national law against persons domiciled in non-Contracting States, under Article 4, is still 'Convention jurisdiction'.

[39] 'La référence aux mesures 'prévues par la loi d'un Etat contractant' concerne le type de mesure à disposition, *non* la désignation de l'autorité habilitée à les ordonner.' Merkt, O. *Les mesures provisoires en droit international privé*, 1993, at p.112, para. 279.

[40] Below, at p.288.

[41] But *not* 'only when'; and Briggs, A. *Civil Jurisdiction and Judgments*, 2nd edn., 1997, at p.296, para. 6.10; *District Court of the Hague* 6.2.2001 *Therex Limited Partnership v Medtronic BV* [2001] *EIPR* N–121.

[42] Merkt, 1993, at p.112.

Four representative, yet diverse, views can be identified[43] as a jurisdictional base: that Article 24, in and of itself, is sufficient to confer jurisdiction; that[44] from a combination of the reference in Article 24 to the substantive measures 'available under the law of that State' and the silence[45] as to any jurisdictional norm,[46] these naturally point to the national procedural[47] laws of the Contracting States (governing provisional and protective measures);[48] that jurisdiction is derived from

---

[43] From simply reading the article, it seems that two actions, one on the merits, the other for interim relief, are permitted, but, as emphasised above (and illustrated by *Van Uden Maritime*), not a prerequisite—Briggs, 1997, p.296: 'article 24 removed a jurisdictional defence which a defendant might have raised.'; Gerhard, F. *L'exécution forcée transfrontière des injonctions extraterritoriales non pécuniaires en droit privé*, 2000, at pp.145–46, para. 191.

[44] It is Kaye, 1987, at p.1147 (as almost a lone voice with Albrecht, 1991, at p.115) who believe that Article 24, *proprio vigore*, provides jurisdiction to order interim relief: 'Article 24 accords international jurisdiction to courts of all Contracting States . . . to the exclusion *both* of national grounds of international jurisdiction and of the need to satisfy other Convention grounds'; also, against the grain is Alférez-Garcimartín, F. 'Effects of the Brussels Convention upon the Spanish System: Provisional and Protective Measures' in Hommelhoff, Jayme and Mangold (eds) *Europäischer Binnenmarkt, Internationales Privatrecht und Rechtsvergleichung*, 1995, p.129, at p.130: 'Article 24 confers jurisdiction to adopt these measures to [sic] the court of the State where the measures have to be carried out'; these views, though simple, are clearly untenable in the light of the fact that the Conventions are not, in English law at least, self-executing; doubly so when s 25(1) of the Civil Jurisdiction and Judgments Act 1982 represents the (English) national provisions; also the categories at p.33, para. 124 of the *Consultation Paper—The Operation of the Brussels and Lugano Conventions*, Lord Chancellor's Department, April 1997.

[45] Neatly summarised by Merkt, 1993, at p.111: 'S'ils ne sont pas compétents selon les règles expresses de la Convention, leur compétence ne peut résulter que des règles des droits nationaux.'

[46] This view receives the most widespread critical and jurisprudential support, especially in Germany—Gronstedt, 1994, at pp.18–23; Stickler, 1992, at pp.28–47; Eilers, 1991, at pp.196–206; Albrecht, 1991, at pp.81–135; also Dalhuisen, J.H. 'Creditors' Remedies and the Conflicts of Law in The European Community' in *Ius Inter Nationes—Festschrift für Stefan Riesenfeld*, 1983, p.1, at p.9: 'provisional remedies may continue to issue from and be validated by courts exercising local exorbitant-jurisdiction.' The majority view has, post *Van Uden Maritime*, proved to be correct, below, at pp.290–291. In the UK, this view, and the basis of jurisdiction in general, receives poor attention, provoking to date discussion only of s 25(1) and (2) and (what was) RSC Ord.11 r.1(2), and is now CPR Rule 6.20(4); France, on the other hand, has tended towards critical exchanges about the substantive phrase 'provisional, including protective measures'—regarding their special interlocutory procedure known as the *référé-provision*: *Éditions du Juris-Classeur, Procédure Civile*, 1997, Référés-Speciaux, Fasc 235–2 of 1.1997, pp.1–10; also Burgelin/Coulon/Frison-Roche 'Le juge des référés au regard des principes procéduraux' 1995 *Dalloz*, 10e, Chron., p.10, and Part II below, at pp.338 *et seq.*

[47] *Contra*, Merkt, 1993, at p.112, para. 280; Walter, G. 'Die internationale Zuständigkeit schweizerischer Gerichte für 'vorsorgliche Massnahmen'- oder: Article 10 IPRG und seine Geheimnisse' (1992) *AJP* 61, at p.63: 'eine internationale Zuständigkeit für vorsorgliche Massnahmen'(an international jurisdiction for provisional measures').

[48] For the main German view, Geimer, R. and Schütze, R. *Europäisches Zivilverfahrensrech, Kommentar zum EuGVÜ und Lugano-Übereinkommen*, 1997, at p.404, para. 31: 'Erklärtes Ziel dieser Vorschrift ist es, das nationale Zuständigkeitsrecht auf dem Gebiet des einstweiligen Rechtsschutzes nicht zu beschneiden' ('*the express aim* of this provision is not to curtail national jurisdictional rules in the area of provisional and protective measures').

the provisions of Title II of the Conventions themselves;[49] a combination of the last two.[50]

The reason why this issue[51] is so fundamental, are the consequences that naturally ensue from choosing this 'national route'. These interrelated consequences are as follows: do the national jurisdictional rules referred to mean those specifically dedicated to the grant of interim relief,[52] or to all[53] the rules of the Contracting States' procedural codes. (As will be seen these codes, in themselves, may create their own problems impinging on the uniform application[54] of the Conventions). Forming as it does the bulk of critical and judicial comment on this jurisdictional issue, one important consequence is the use of the so-called 'exorbitant' bases of jurisdiction,[55] normally excluded in actions on the merits against defendants domiciled in the Contracting States; and lastly, the ramifications of the availability of such 'exorbitant' bases on the grant of interim relief, especially when combined with sweeping national (substantive) laws.[56]

In the main,[57] three jurisdictions will be looked at. Germany, France and the United Kingdom all deal with 'the national route' in different ways. For the purposes of this chapter, Germany will be discussed first, since most of the specialist

---

[49] Puttfarken (1977) *RIW/AWD* 359, at p.360–61 and Nagel in Harm and Kreuzer (eds) *Internationales Zivilprozeßrecht*, 2nd edn, 1984, at p.83; this view has proved to be erroneous—*Van Uden Maritime*, above, at n.1, at p.7131, para. 22 and Proposition A(i). If a court has jurisdiction under Articles 2, 5–18, it can order unfettered interim relief without reference to Article 24 in any event. But below, at pp.333–334 for *lis pendens* problems.

[50] Appearing in the sections on English (below sections 3.1.2(c), 3.3) and French (below sections 3.1.2(b), 3.5 and Part II) reactions; also *Crédit Suisse Fides Trust SA v Cuoghi* [1998] QB 818, CA (Lord Bingham of Cornhill CJ, Millett and Potter LJJ); and *Mme Mintschukowa et autres c/ SA Bureau Véritas et autres*, TGI de Nanterre, Ord.Ref., 10.3.1997, (1997) *Dalloz*, Juris., 449, obs. Bussy. *Van Uden Maritime* has rendered this view otiose too. As has been mentioned in Proposition A, there is *either* jurisdiction under Articles 2, 5–18, *or* jurisdiction (under traditional national law, at p.7135, para. 42), *not* a combination of both against the same respondent.

[51] I.e. of which jurisdictional rules govern the grant of interim relief.

[52] And s 25 CJJA 1982; especially Zeiler, G 'Europäisches Sicherungsverfahren: Die Regelung der Europäischen Gerichtsstands- und Vollstreckungsübereinkommen über einstweilige Maßnahmen' (1996) *JBl* 635; and Otte, K 'Beschränkte Nachprüfbarkeit internationaler Zuständigkeit im Arrestverfahren' (1991) *ZIP* 1048.

[53] Also the fourth question submitted to the ECJ in *Van Uden Maritime* [1998] ECR I–7091, at pp.7128–29, answered in the affirmative, at p.7135, para. 42.

[54] If Article 14 of the French Civil code can be used, its wording appears to bar reliance on it by, for example an Italian, domiciled in France; *Hof 's-Gravenhage* 17.7.2000 *F.G.H. Abbing tegen Sibomat N.V.* 2001 *NJ* Nr.87, p.543.

[55] *Inter alia*, §23 ZPO and Article 14 CC.

[56] The *référé-provision* in Article 809, alinéa 2, NCPC, immediately springs to mind: 'Dans les cas où l'existence de l'obligation n'est pas sérieusement contestable, il [le président du tribunal de grande instance] peut accorder une provision au créancier . . .' *Nouveau Code de Procedure Civile*, Dalloz, 93ème éd., 2001, at p.409 following; and *Cassation* 13.4.1999 *Bachy c/ Soc. Belbetoes* (1999) *Rev crit* 352, [1999] I.L.Pr. 743.

[57] For a brief attitude in other jurisdictions Alférez-Garcimartín, 1995, p.129; and Honorati, C. 'La Cross-border prohibitory injunction Olandese in Materia di Contraffazione di Brevetti: sulla legittimità dell'inibitoria transfrontaliera alla luce della Convenzione di Bruxelles del 1968' (1997) *Riv. dir. int. priv. e proc.* 301.

commentaries dedicated to provisional relief are from Germany.[58] Ironically, it will become clear that the courts of a country that produces such a wealth of comment on the 'exorbitant' jurisdictional issue under national law in Article 24, have, in the articles of their *Zivilprozeßordnung* itself, no need to rely on these provocative provisions.[59]

(i) Jurisdiction in Germany[60]

As already mentioned as regards Germany,[61] the two articles of the *Zivilprozeß-ordnung* (ZPO) which govern the 'regional' or 'local'[62] jurisdiction of the two most commonly-encountered forms of provisional and protective relief—*Arrest*[63] and

---

[58] Above at p.285 n.34.

[59] § 919 Alt.2 always gives jurisdiction (alternatively) to the *Amtsgericht*; ironic, too, is the dogged insistence on the application of cherished national provisions that are ill-suited, or ill-drafted to complement a reference from Article 24. National law contains, and has provoked, the majority of the problems; *OLG Düsseldorf* 28.1.1999 (1999) *RIW* 873.

[60] An English account in Jacoby, S. 'Extraterritorial English Mareva injunctions in a European context: A comparative approach (England, France and Germany)' (1996) *Annales de droit luxembourgeois* 245, at pp.282–84; and Schlosser 'Protective Measures in various in European Countries' in Goldsmith, J., (ed) *International Dispute Resolution: The regulation of forum selection, 14th Sokol Colloquium,* 1997, p.185, at p.186 onwards.

[61] Various reasons there may be why German commentators have alluded so much to the question of national jurisdiction under Article 24: one could be the fact that even since the coming into force of the Convention in Germany, there had always been specific jurisdictional provisions dealing with the two most common forms of provisional/protective measure: *Arrest* and *einstweilige Verfügung*. German commentators agree Article 24 is a 'Verweisungsnorm'—a remittance rule—to the jurisdictional rules of autonomous (national) law'. Stickler believes 'the granting of provisional measures is remitted *globally* to internal national law'; Gronstedt that Article 24 can only refer to national jurisdictional provisions, to the exclusion of those under the Convention—Gronstedt, 1994, at p.13; *contra* Eilers, 1991, at p.200; also *Mme Mintschukowa et autres c/ SA Bureau Véritas et autres, TGI de Nanterre,* Ord.Ref., 10.3.1997, (1997) *Dalloz,* Juris., 449, obs. Bussy. Perhaps significantly, prior to s 25(1), English law had no specific jurisdictional rules to deal with applications for interim relief in aid of substantive proceedings abroad. Injunctions, known as *Marevas/*freezing injunctions operate *in personam,* by service of a summons; the only *in personam ex juris* service rules extant at that time were service out in an action 'on the merits': *The Siskina* [1979] AC 210, HL at p.243, at p.256 (Lord Diplock). An account of the procedure in English is given by Kessedjian, C. Prel. Doc. No.10 of October 1998, at pp.24–26.

[62] And hence also the international jurisdiction—Geimer *WM* 1975, 910 at p.912; also *OLG Koblenz,* 23.2.1990, (1991) *IPRax* 241, at p.242.

[63] Jurisdiction for an *Arrest* (a type of freezing injunction, similar in effect to a *Mareva* injunction) in §919 ZPO, reads as follows: 'Für die Anordnung des Arrestes ist sowohl *das Gericht der Hauptsache* als das Amtsgericht zuständig, in dessen Bezirk der mit Arrest zu belegende Gegenstand. . .sich befinde[t]'('for the granting of an *Arrest* either *the Court on the merits* or the *Amtsgericht,* in whose district the property to be arrested is found, has jurisdiction'); Cuniberti, 2000 at p.127; Zuckerman, (1996) 1 *ZZPInt* 89, at p.98; recently applied in *OLG Karlsruhe* 2.10.2001 (2002) *IPRax* p.VI, (2002) *RIW* 151.

einstweilige Verfügung[64]—are §§919[65] and 937(1)[66] ZPO respectively. For an *Arrest* there is a choice of jurisdiction; except in cases of emergency, for a 'Verfügung' there is not. Specific jurisdiction to arrest property is given *either* to the court seised of the main substantive proceedings, *or* to the *Amtsgericht* for the district where the property to be arrested is located; for the *Verfügung*, jurisdiction rests solely with the court seised[67] on the merits. It has been this very limitation of jurisdiction to that of 'merits' jurisdiction in §919 Alt.1 and §937(1) that has caused such academic controversy.[68] To use national jurisdictional provisions that give jurisdiction to courts that are expressed[69] to be 'Hauptsachegerichte'—'courts on the merits'—seems to be subverting the very letter of Article 24; in a sense, too, this also threatens the independence of these two separate courts,[70] and may even ultimately lead to a diminished application to German courts under Article 24/§937 ZPO in non-urgent cases.

Not only this, it has been shown that some courts[71] have been deciding an application as if they were the 'Gericht der Hauptsache' under §919 Alt.1 ZPO, and have used §23 ZPO as against Contracting State respondents, feeling themselves freed from the constraints of Article 3 I and II of the Brussels Convention.[72]

---

[64] Jurisdiction for an *einstweilige Verfügung* (a type of provisional order or injunction, such as a disclosure order ancillary to a *Mareva*) in §937(1) ZPO, which reads as follows: 'Für den Erlaß einstweiliger Verfügungen ist *das Gericht der Hauptsache* zuständig'('For the grant of an interlocutory injunction *the Court on the merits* has jurisdiction'); note that *Van Uden Maritime* has shown us that jurisdiction under Article 24 forms a *sui generis* 'special regime' (at p.7135, para. 42), and not a jurisdiction 'on the merits'. Article 1(4) of the Convention precluded any action in that case on the merits in any Contracting State in any event, at p.7131, para. 24.

[65] Above, n.63 for German text.

[66] Above, n.64 for German text; for other measures under Art.24, Kropholler, 2002, at p.362 and p.358, para.7.

[67] Except, by §942(1) ZPO in emergency cases, where the *Amtsgericht* where the assets in issue are located has jurisdiction to order a 'Verfügung'.

[68] And the fabrication of an imaginary/fictitious jurisdiction on the merits; Hanisch, H. 'Internationale Arrestzuständigkeit und EuGVÜ' (1991) *IPRax* 215; favourable Geimer, R. and Schütze, R., 1997, at p.404 para. 31: '§919 ZPO ist eine eigenständige Zuständigkeitsnorm für einstweilige Maßnahmen' ('§919 ZPO is a self-contained jurisdictional rule for interim relief'); it was thought, erroneously, that Article 24 was, after all, an accessory or supplementary jurisdiction, enabling interim relief to be granted while proceedings on the merits are possible, or ongoing, in the courts of another Contracting State; *Van Uden Maritime* has sharpened this distinction.

[69] And what is worse take jurisdiction as a main court on the merits.

[70] Merkt, O., 1993, at p.106: 'L'indépendance des rapports entre mesure provisoire et action au fond, organisée par l'Article 24 Convention, implique que l'attitude procédurale d'une partie dans la procédure de mesure provisoire n'entraîne pas de conséquences dans la procédure au fond.'; Schlosser, 1996, at p.199; also *Winter Maritime Ltd v North End Oil Ltd (The 'Winter')* [2000] 2 Lloyd's Rep. 298.

[71] Below, at p.293; and Geimer and Schütze, 1997, at p.404: 'Das Konventionsrecht derogiert also nicht die Zuständigkeit aus §919 Alt.1 ZPO in Verbindung mit §23 ZPO'('The law of the Convention does not derogate from the jurisdiction under §919 Alt.1 in conjunction with §23 ZPO'); §919 Alt.1 ZPO jurisdiction on presence of assets within the jurisdiction applied under Art.24 in *OLG Karlsruhe* 2.10.2001 (2002) *IPRax* p.VI, (2002) *RIW* 151.

[72] *Van Uden Maritime* has shown that §23 ZPO is now a perfectly legitimate basis on which to found jurisdiction under Article 24, below, at p.310. But this still does not overcome the express wording in §§919 and 937(1) ('on the merits'), and the statement in *Van Uden Maritime* that Article 24 jurisdiction is *not* jurisdiction 'as to the substance of the case', at p.7131, paras. 24–25, and p.7133, para. 34.

Perversely however, these courts do not feel themselves bound to observe Article 3 I and II, because these provisions, they argue, only apply to 'actions on the merits' in the 'Gericht der Hauptsache'.[73]

The following result obtains: should proceedings on the merits be underway or possible in another Contracting State, the German courts are willing, under Article 24, to pair §§919 Alt.1 and 23 ZPO[74] and arrest a Contracting State debtor's property in Germany, as if Title II of the Convention, and Article 3 I and II in particular, did not exist.[75]

One obvious problem occurs with the immediate clash between jurisdiction to order an 'einstweilige Verfügung' under §937(1) ZPO and Article 24. Such interim injunctions, as we have seen, can only be ordered—except in cases of urgency—by the court with jurisdiction on the merits. *Ex hypothesi*, if the German courts did not perceive themselves as a fictitious 'Gericht der Hauptsache', there would simply be no jurisdiction to order such measures.[76]

A more tenable and fundamental justification for the use of exorbitant jurisdictions comes from the view that Article 24 represents a direct 'Verweisungsnorm'[77] to national procedural law governing interim relief. The exclusion of 'exorbitant' jurisdictions in Article 3 II[78] as regards an action on the merits is misleading. Article III is merely a declaratory provision.[79]

---

[73] Even if Title II of the Brussels/Lugano Conventions has no application to the grant of provisional relief because of the 'Verweisungsnorm' in Article 24 to national law—*quaere* because Title II only applies to the 'other' Article 24 court with jurisdiction as to the substance of the matter ('in der Hauptsache')—the granting court cannot, with impunity, take on the mantle of a (fictitious) court 'on the merits' under §919 Alt.2 and §937(1) and yet simultaneously also remain immune from Article 3 I and II. In effect, that is what the German courts are doing here.

[74] This is especially ironic considering the Continental writers' vehement criticisms of the *forum non conveniens* doctrine; the *BGH* has also recently reduced the ambit of § 23 ZPO—an English account in Dannemann G. 'Jurisdiction based on the presence of assets in Germany: a casenote BGH 2.7.1991' (1992) *ICLQ* 632.

[75] Thereby cloaking themselves with a fictitious jurisdiction of the 'Gericht der Hauptsache'; This now does not seem to be a concern under Article 24—the only limitation in place under Article 24—which can be seen as a mode of protection—is a more restrictive meaning to 'provisional, including protective measures', *Van Uden Maritime*, (C-391/95) [1998] ECR I–7091 at p.7135 and p.7137 paras. 40, and 47, discussed below, at pp.310–311; *Hof 's-Gravenhage* 17.7.2000 *F.G.H. Abbing tegen Sibomat N.V.* 2001 *NJ* Nr.87, p.543.

[76] 'Für den Erlaß einstweiliger Verfügungen ist *das Gericht der Hauptsache* zuständig'('For the grant of an interlocutory injunction *the Court on the merits* has jurisdiction'); note *OLG Stuttgart* 19.12.2000 (2001) *RIW* 228 *refused* to order provisional remedy because it did not have jurisdiction under §§ 937 Abs.1, 802 ZPO as the 'Gericht der Hauptsache' because of a jurisdiction clause in favour of the courts of Biel, Switzerland; *OLG Karlsruhe* 2.10.2001 (2002) *IPRax* p.VI, (2002) *RIW* 151.

[77] ('a remittance rule').

[78] At C189/72; also *Verdonck v Algemene Bank Nederland, Digest* I–24–B10—'*Article 24 was such an exception* [to Articles 3 I and II]'.

[79] 'Durch Article 3 I werden bereits die internationalen Zuständigkeitsbestimmungen der Vertragsstaaten ohne Rücksicht darauf, ob sie 'exorbitante' oder 'normale' Anknüpfungen enthalten verdrängt ... Vielmehr kann [Article 24] nur bedeuten, daß einstweilige Maßnahmen nach innerstaatlichem Recht auch dort beantragt werden können, wo das Übereinkommen ... keine Zuständigkeit vorsieht, also immer dann, wenn ein Gericht auch ohne das Übereinkommen nach eigenem Recht zuständig wäre.' ('Through Article 3 I, the international jurisdictional provisions of the

A whole line of more recent commentators[80] support both the view that Article 24 refers to national provisions globally,[81] including those outlawed in Article 3 I and II; and with qualified support,[82] for the fictitious 'Gericht der Hauptsache' jurisdiction that inevitably follows on from this 'global' view. Gronstedt is typically representative of the modern German academic position:

> Nach ganz h.M. sind die nach dem nationalen Rechten eröffneten Zuständigkeiten für einstweilige Verfahren, auf die Article 24 EuGVÜ verweist, nicht durch Article 3 II EuGVÜ beschränkt.[83]

The justification he sees in a wide interpretation of the 'Verweisungsnorm' in Article 24 to national law is that any curtailment of the jurisdiction available to an applicant would seriously endanger any potential judgment creditor's legal protection.[84]

As for the problem of jurisdiction under Article 24, §919 Alt. 1 ZPO and the 'Gericht der Hauptsache', Albrecht[85] believes the court seised of the merits in a Contracting State,[86] and the court applied to for interim relief in another, are seised, as it were, in different degrees.[87] *Ex hypothesi*, an Article 24 provisional court cannot be seised simultaneously on the merits. A jurisdiction, therefore, to

---

Contracting States are already suppressed, irrespective of whether they contain 'exorbitant' or 'normal' connections . . . Moreover, [Article 24] can only mean that provisional measures can even be applied for under domestic law, where the Convention provides no jurisdiction—thus always where a court would be competent under its own law without the Convention.'), Koch, H. 'Neuere Probleme der internationalen Zwangsvollstreckung einschließlich des einstweiligen Rechtsschutzes' in Schlosser, P., (ed) *Materielles Recht und Prozeßrecht und die Auswirkungen der Unterscheidung im Recht der internationalen Zwangsvollstreckung*, 1992, p.171, at p.183; *Van Uden Maritime* has shown this to be the correct view.

[80] Especially Eilers, 1991, at p.195.

[81] Stickler, 1992, at p.38; also Gronstedt, 1994, at p.20: 'Eine Beschränkung auf die Zuständigkeiten nach dem EuGVÜ verkürze den Rechtsschutz des Gläubigers'('A confinement to the jurisdictions in the Brussels Convention is said to curtail the judgment creditor's legal protection').

[82] Stickler, 1992; criticised by Albrecht, 1991 at pp.127 and 135.

[83] Gronstedt, 1994: 'Widespread opinion has it that the jurisdictions available under national laws, to which Art.24 points, are not limited by Article 3 II Brussels Convention'), at p.20; *OLG Karlsruhe* 2.10.2001 (2002) *IPRax* p.VI, (2002) *RIW* 151.

[84] Stickler even goes so far as to argue that the inclusion of §23 ZPO among the provisions available to a potential judgment creditor actually furthers the aim of Article 24, opening up as it does additional available *fora*; conversely, the danger of undermining the Convention's regime on the merits in Title II has also been dealt with in *Van Uden Maritime* and *Mietz* by restricting the meaning of 'provisional, including protective measures', below, at p.310 and Marmisse, (1999) *Rev crit* 669, at p.675.

[85] Albrecht, 1991, at p.135; also Merkt, 1993, at p.115 and Zeiler, (1996) *JBl* 635, at p.635.

[86] This is not an essential prerequisite for Article 24. In principle, even if arbitration were underway in Germany, Article 24 would be available—whether application to the courts, as a matter of German substantive arbitration law, is possible, §1033 ZPO court interim measures in arbitration.

[87] Merkt, 1993, at pp.104–05; cf the English view expressed in *Balkanbank v Taher (No.2)* [1995] 1 WLR 1067 that a respondent to English *Mareva* relief may obtain jurisdiction under Article 4 (or *quaere*, Article 6(3)) to 'counterclaim' against the applicant in England; no apparent change in CPR 20.3(1)—a Part 20 claim (counterclaim) 'shall be treated as if it were a claim', and CPR 20.4(2)(b).

order interim relief in the court fictitiously seised as a 'Gericht der Hauptsache'[88] under §§919 Alt.1 and 937(1) simply cannot exist:

> Soweit das nationale Recht einstweiligen Rechtsschutz in den nationalen Hauptsachegericht vorsieht, sind diese[89] unter Article 24 EuGVÜ grundsätzlich örtlich unzuständig, weil durch sie die Hauptsache wegen Articles 2, 3 EuGVÜ nicht entscheiden werden kann.[90]

The cases[91] show even less consistency of approach. An early case from the *OLG Koblenz*[92] demonstrated that the jurisdiction of the local *Landgericht* for a garnishee *Arrest*, in aid of French substantive proceedings, could not be maintained by a combination of Article 24, §§919 Alt.1 and 23 ZPO. Jurisdiction under §919, it held, was reserved for the main substantive court,[93] here in France. Not only did the court re-inforce the duality of the two courts' rôles, it noted that Article 3 of the Brussels Convention had excluded §23 ZPO from the scope of the Convention,[94] including proceedings for provisional and protective measures.

A contrary ruling was announced by the *OLG Düsseldorf*.[95] This case demonstrates the birth of the so-called fictitious 'Gericht der Hauptsache' or fictitious jurisdiction on the merits: the *Arrest*, this time permitted by a combination of §§919 Alt.1 and 23 ZPO, was of property[96] in Germany belonging to an Italian respondent. Irrespective of the fact that full 'merits jurisdiction' over a dispute between a German commercial agent and his Italian principal lay in Italy, the appeal court found that the *LG Düsseldorf* had correctly taken jurisdiction under Article 24 and the above-mentioned provisions as a fictitious 'Gericht der Hauptsache':

---

[88] A similar restrictive view of the 'Gericht der Hauptsache' shared by Otte, (1991) *ZIP* 1048 and Zeiler, (1996) *JBl* 635: the special 'Eilgerichtstände' of the *Amtsgericht* in §919 Alt.2 provides adequate protection for the judgment creditor, without the court's having to become embroiled in the difficult and self-contradictory 'Gericht der Hauptsache' of §919 Alt.1: 'Article 24 ist daher so zu verstehen, daß er nur auf die Eilgerichtsstände der nationalen Rechte und nicht auch auf deren Hauptsachezuständigkeit verweist.' ('Article 24 is correctly understood as only applying to the summary jurisdiction of national laws and not to those jurisdictional rules on the merits'), Zeiler, at p.639; *OLG Karlsruhe* 2.10.2001 (2002) *IPRax* p.VI, (2002) *RIW* 151.

[89] Including §937(1) ZPO.

[90] 'As far as national law provides for provisional and protective measures in the main court, these courts are not basically competent under Article 24, because the dispute on the merits cannot be decided by them due to Articles 2 and 3 of the Brussels Convention' Albrecht, 1991, at p.135.

[91] *OLG Düsseldorf*, 18.5.1977, 1977 IPRSp. 494, Nr.166; *OLG Koblenz*, 23.2.1990, 1990 IPRsp. 493, Nr.228; *LG Frankfurt a.M.*, 12.4.1989, 1989 IPRsp.581, Nr.229; *OLG Frankfurt a.M.*, 23.9.1980, 1980 IPRsp. 581, Nr.178; *LG Bremen*, 30.5.1978, 1978 IPRsp. 444, Nr.178; *OLG Koblenz*, 2.5.1975, (1977) *RIW/AWD* 359.

[92] (1976) *NJW* 2081.

[93] Also the view of *Hof 's-Gravenhage* 17.7.2000 *F.G.H. Abbing tegen Sibomat N.V.* 2001 *NJ* Nr.87, p.543.

[94] Post *Van Uden Maritime*, now an incorrect approach, below, at p.310. The express exclusion in Article 3 I and II only applies to Articles 2, 5–18, at p.7135 para. 42; *quaere*, are Articles 21/22, excluded too, below, at pp.333–334.

[95] 18.5.1977 (1977) *NJW* 2034.

[96] A legal claim that the respondent company had against a third-party German company in Düsseldorf.

Da insoweit die nationalen Regeln unberuhrt bleiben ... konnte gem.§919 ZPO die Anordnung des Arrestes auch vor dem Gericht beantragt werden, das nach deutschem Recht *als Gericht zur Hauptsache* in Betracht käme[97]

Latterly, the *OLG Koblenz*[98] has retreated from this expanded use of the fictitious merits jurisdiction: the appeal court ruled that merely because an application was 'anhängig'('pending') in the *LG Koblenz*, did not of itself constitute this court a 'Gericht der Hauptsache'; *ex hypothesi*, the court would eventually have to declare itself to be incapable of deciding the case on the merits.[99] This was a novel ruling, in an international case; a review of a *LG's* jurisdiction is not allowed in a domestic case.[100] It did not, however, finally lay to rest the problems concerning §23 ZPO, but simply, and perhaps as a matter of expediency, found that there was no property to arrest in Germany under §23 in any case.[101]

The objections to the German views are therefore based on their use of §23 ZPO, and, more importantly, that they condone a provisional court, requested to issue provisional measures, constituting itself as if it were a court 'on the merits'. The solution to this problem lies at national level, with amendments necessary to the ZPO, or a definitive ruling from the *BGH* on whether §919 Alt.1 is available in Convention cases. *Van Uden Maritime* will only heighten the emphasis on the problem and division between jurisdiction on the merits, and jurisdiction under Article 24.[102]

(ii) Jurisdiction in France[103]

If the German view, and its granting of provisional measures has, in practice, relatively little cross-border impact,[104] except to affirm the use of the 'prohibited' jurisdictions under Article 3 I and II, the same cannot be said for France.[105] It is all the more curious, then, that very scant regard has been paid up until now by the

---

[97] At.p.2034—'since, as such, national rules remain untouched, the application for an *Arrest* can also be made before the court which—according to German law—would be considered as the main court on the merits.'; *OLG Karlsruhe* 2.10.2001 (2002) *IPRax* p.VI, (2002) *RIW* 151.

[98] 23.2.1990, (1990) *RIW* 316.

[99] (1991) *IPRax*, at p.242, para. 2 of judgment.

[100] Hanisch, (1991) *IPRax* 215, at p.216.

[101] *Ibid.*

[102] For the possible effects of *Van Uden Maritime* on German practice, below, section 3.4.

[103] An English overview is provided by Collins, L. 'Provisional and Protective Measures in International Litigation,' (1992) Académie de Droit International, *Recueil des Cours*, III, p.19, at pp.57–59, and Kessidjian, C., Prel. Doc. No.10 of October 1998, at pp.27–35.

[104] It would be rare to have a provisional or protective measure 'exported' from Germany, as *ex hypothesi*, the property arrested and necessary to satisfy any subsequent judgment, is in Germany; *contra* Kessidjian, Prel. Doc. No.10 of October 1998, at p.26, quoting a case from 1972 where an *Arrest* of foreign property was perfectly possible—*OLG Karlsruhe* 26.4.1972 1973 OLGZ 58, No.19, at p.60, where it appears that the respondent did initially have some assets for arrest in Germany; Cuniberti, 2000, at pp.139–40.

[105] Tellingly, France's anathema provision in Article 3 II is not, like §23 ZPO, based on the location of property, but on the French nationality of the plaintiff/applicant, Article 14 *Code civil*; this is potentially therefore overtly discriminatory under Article 24.

French courts and commentators to the exact foundation of a French court in *référé* jurisdiction,[106] under Article 24.

Gaudemet-Tallon is almost alone when she asks whether a French judge should be able to base:

> sa compétence sur l'article 14 du Code civil alors qu'un plaideur français lui demande une mesure conservatoire sur un bien situé en Italie[107] [108]

She answers the question in the negative for the simple reason that if property in Italy is to be affected, the immediacy of conservation orders which Article 24 seeks to promote will be lost in the delays of (even simplified) *exequatur* proceedings (in Italy): the *référé* decision would have to be enforced in Italy in any event.[109] Gothot and Holleaux[110] regret the potential use of Article 3 I and II's national provisions, trying to temper the widespread combination of Article 14 *Code civil* and the *référé* provisions—most commonly the *référé-provision* in Article 809(2)[111] *Nouveau Code de Procédure civile*—by the addition of the pre-condition[112] of urgency to the application, even if urgency is not mentioned in the specific procedural code.[113]

The French case law almost exclusively concerns itself with the actual substantive provisions contained in the NCPC,[114] rather than examining the jurisdictional

---

[106] The literature on these provisional proceedings is voluminous. For a substantive overview of the procedure in English, Baker, W and De Fontbressin, P. 'The French référé procedure—a legal miracle?' (1992–3) *Uni Miami Yrbk Int L* 1—the fact that the substantive, and not the jurisdictional aspects, of the *référé* procedure have dominated the attention is emphasised by Solus et Perrot, *Droit judiciaire privé, Procédure de première instance*, t.3, Sirey, 1991, no.1253, pp.1055–56.

[107] ('its competence on Article 14 Cc when a French plaintiff asks for a protective measure over goods property situated in Italy').

[108] Gaudemet-Tallon, 1996, at p.197, para. 271; this quotation highlights the point just made above, that there is a greater probability in France, than in Germany, that a provisional measure granted under Article 24/Article 14 CC will be 'exported' (to Italy); it also conceals the menace of the *référé-provision*, a common example of which grant interim payments. It is submitted that *Van Uden Maritime* and *Mietz* have quelled these 'exportability' concerns somewhat—[1998] ECR I–7091, at p.7135, para. 40 in general, and at p.7137, para. 47 regarding *référé-provisions* in particular, below, at pp.312 *et seq.*

[109] It would seem more logical to start substantive proceedings in Italy, *sed quaere*

[110] Gothot, P. et Holleaux, D. *La Convention de Bruxelles du 27 septembre 1968: compétence judiciaire et effets des jugements dans la CEE*, 1985, at p.115, para. 203.

[111] Article 809, alinéa 2 NCPC: 'Dans le cas où l'existance de l'obligation *n'est pas sérieusement contestable*, [le président] peut accorder une provision au créancier . . .'; *Nouveau Code de Procedure Civile*, Dalloz, 93ème éd., 2001, at p.409 following.

[112] *Van Uden Maritime*, below, at p.310, has added its own Community gloss (in addition to that already added by *Mario Reichert and others v Dresdner Bank AG* (C-261/90) [1992] ECR I–2149, at p.2184, para. 34) to the phrase 'provisional, including protective measures': a requirement for 'a real connecting link' between measure and Contracting State court, at [1998] ECR I–7091, at p.7135, para. 40.

[113] Gothot et Holleaux, 1985; contested by Vareilles-Sommières, P. de 'La compétence internationale des tribunaux français en matière de mesures provisoires' (1996) *Rev crit* 397, at p.428.

[114] Specifically the issue of whether a *référé-provision* is a provisional or protective measure; the French *Cour de Cassation* in *Bachy c/ Soc. Belbetoes* (1999) *Rev crit* 352, [1999] I.L.Pr. 743 has confirmed that it is.

bases of those provisions. It seems to be taken as indisputable that all the provisions of French national procedural law are applicable.

An early case of the *Tribunal de Grande Instance Nanterre, Tron c/ Société Verkor,*[115] demonstrated the apparent ease with which Article 14 *Code civil* could be used in conjunction with the *référé-provision* in Article 809(2) NCPC. The facts involved an employment dispute between a French employee and his Belgian employer. Having failed[116] to establish jurisdiction in a first action on the merits in a court of his domicile in France, the employee seised the action *en référé* in Nanterre[117] under Article 809, asking for an interim payment, arguing a case 'où l'existence de l'obligation n'est pas sérieusement contestable[118]'.[119] The President of the tribunal declared himself internationally competent and acceded to the *provision*.

The reviewer[120] admits that the only possible basis of international jurisdiction to order such a *provision* could have been Article 14 *Code civil*, and is caused a certain amount of disquiet over this. He is correct in his criticism of the case as tending to fragment the litigation into three *fora*, at the plaintiff's option, rather than promoting judicial certainty: the *référé* in France, its possible *exequatur* in Belgium,[121] and the action (now destined to be abandoned)[122] on the merits in Belgium:

> En dehors de l'article 14, la compétence . . . ne se justifie donc ni en vertu des règles de compétence sur le fond ni par la bonne administration de la justice.[123] [124]

The result of the case is that by a combination of the *forum actoris* in Article 14 *Code civil*, and of Article 809(2) NCPC—which effectively disposes of and stifles the dispute,[125] without a full trial on the merits[126]—it is simply not in the

---

[115] *TGI de Nanterre*, 9.10.1978, (1979) *Rev Crit* 128, obs. Metzger; (1980) *JDI* 894; *Cour d'appel de Versailles*, 27.6.1979, (1980) *JDI* 894, obs. Holleaux.

[116] Article 2 required the Belgian employer to be sued there; this case, from 1979, was prior to the employment amendments by caselaw, and the 1989 San Sebastian Convention additions to Article 5(1).

[117] Metzger's comments, p.131.

[118] ('where the existence of the obligation cannot seriously be disputed').

[119] Article 809, alinéa 2, NCPC.

[120] Metzger, (1979) *Rev crit* 128.

[121] On the 'exportability' aspects of *référé-provisions* post-*Van Uden Maritime* (and *Mietz*), especially at p.7137, para. 47 below, at p.312; Marmisse, (1999) *Rev crit* 669, believes this will now be rare.

[122] Unless the Belgian company wishes to claim, in France, on any guarantee; on the uncertainty of this section 3.2.7 below, at pp.317 *et seq.*

[123] ('Apart from Article 14, jurisdiction is not confirmed either by virtue of rules of jurisdiction on the merits or by the good administration of justice').

[124] *Ibid.*

[125] Below, at pp.360–361, and especially Weber, G. *Die Verdrängung des Hauptsacheverfahrens durch den einstweiligen Rechtsschutz in Deutschland und Frankreich*, 1993, at p.119 following, and sections 3.7.1, 3.7.2, and 3.7.3 below.

[126] One of the criticisms levelled at the *référé-provision*, that it replaces the need for a full trial on the merits—Weber, 1993.

interests[127] of the French applicant fully to pursue his case in the forum designated by Article 2 Brussels Convention, i.e. Belgium.

Diehm c/ Mlle Sicre[128] shows just how little the issue of jurisdiction under Article 14 *Code civil*[129] was considered either by the court or commentator. This case involved injuries caused to a French passenger involved in a car accident which occurred in Germany. The car had been driven by Diehm, a German, and had German insurers. Again, although not specifically mentioned, the only basis of jurisdiction could have been[130] the French nationality of Miss Sicre.

Menegatti c/ Société Mettalurgica Nava Stefano e Guiseppina[131] witnessed the use of a less controversial[132] national law provision of the NCPC, Article 46(2), in order to found jurisdiction for a large *référé-provision*. Menegatti, an Italian,[133] domiciled in France, was the sole commercial agent of an Italian-based company Mettalurgica. He demanded in *référé* proceedings an interim payment[134] representing a large sum as commission, before the *Tribunal de Commerce*, Paris. Although the *Cour d'appel* ultimately declined competence, no doubt in a valiant attempt to halt what it tacitly saw as a *détournement*[135] of the Brussels Convention, the original basis of the jurisdiction had been Article 46(2)[136] NCPC, which allowed the plaintiff[137] to choose 'en matière contractuelle, la juridiction . . . du lieu de l'exécution de la prestation de service.'[138]

Disappointingly, the *Cour de Cassation* in *Société Krupp Widia GmbH c/ Société Schlumberger Industries*[139] did not even mention the international basis of

---

[127] Cf. Albrecht, 1991, at p.134, and at p.133: 'So wird für die örtliche Zuständigkeit an das Interesse des Klägers angeknüpft, den Prozeß nicht im Ausland zu führen.'; ('local jurisdiction is aligned with the interests of the plaintiff not to prosecute an action abroad.').

[128] *Cour d'appel d'Aix-en-Provence*, 4.5.1981, (1983) *Rev crit* 110, obs. Couchez.

[129] Enabling applications *en référé* for the appointment of an expert and an interim payment.

[130] The case's importance lies in its discussion of whether a *référé-provision* is a provisional or protective measure under Article 24; also *Cassation* 13.4.1999 *Bachy c/ Soc. Belbetoes* (1999) *Rev crit* 352, [1999] I.L.Pr. 743.

[131] *Cour d'appel de Paris*, 14e Ch., 17.11.1987, (1989) *JDI* 96, obs. Huet, another *référé-provision* case.

[132] Less controversial, if one is convinced by the Article 3 I and II divisions into normal and exorbitant bases of jurisdiction.

[133] He was therefore unable to invoke Article 14 *Code civil* (Article 4 II Convention), which has lead to criticism of the use of Article 14 *Code civil* in such cases due to discrimination against Community nationals on the grounds of nationality—Article 12 (ex Article 6) EC Treaty.

[134] And for the appointment of an expert. The two usually go hand in glove, *Mme Mintschukowa et autres c/ SA Bureau Véritas et autres, TGI de Nanterre*, Ord.Ref., 10.3.1997, 1997 *Dalloz*, Juris., 449, obs. Bussy; *Cour administrative d'appel de Nantes* 15.4.1999 *Société Mammoet Stoof Vof* (2000) *RFD adm* 1110, at p.1112; cf. *Messier-Dowty Ltd and anor v Sabena S.A. and ors (No.2)* [2000] 1 WLR 2040; *quaere* whether in the future such a case, in the light of *Van Uden Maritime*, will have to be re-evaluated.

[135] Gothot and Holleaux, 1985, at p.116, para. 204: 'l'article 24 pourrait devenir un instrument de subversion d'une grande partie de titre II'—*Van Uden Maritime* has, at least, placed some safeguards to try to ensure the Convention rules on merits are not subverted.

[136] Article 46 is drafted in almost identical terms to Articles 2 and 5(1)(3) Brussels Convention; *Nouveau Code de Procedure Civile*, Dalloz, 93ème éd., 2001, at p.57 following, with attending notes.

[137] And hence an applicant *en référé*—however, Article 46 is clearly intended for actions on the merits.

[138] The commission being payable entirely in Paris.

[139] *Cour de Cassation* Ch. Com., 10.3.1992, (1993) *JDI* 156, obs. Huet.

jurisdiction for the appointment of an expert *en référé*, that, according to the French nationality of the Schlumberger company, again could only have been Article 14 *Code civil*:

> l'article 24 renvoie purement et simplement au droit national du tribunal saisi,[140] en l'occurence à l'article 145 NCPC [141] [142]

More recently,[143] no in depth consideration was given to jurisdiction taken under Article 24 by a head contractor CEFM Facades, and under Article 42(2) NCPC,[144] against co-defendants, one a French company, the other from Luxembourg.

Lastly, litigation arising out of the sinking of the *Estonia* in September 1994 has enabled attempted[145] applications to be made *en référé*,[146] in France, for the appointment of accident investigators. This would have duplicated the work previously undertaken by the inspectors of the Swedish Maritime Administration. Proceedings on the merits against, *inter alia*, the vessel's owners and insurers had already been commenced in Sweden by the few survivors and the victims' personal representatives.

Interestingly for our purposes here, the French *Tribunal* based its competence *en référé* on Article 6(1) of the Lugano Convention:[147]

> Le juge des référés français s'est connu compétent, au plan international . . . en raison de la nationalité français de l'un des défendeurs et des dispositions de la Convention de Lugano relatives tant à la détermination de la juridiction compétente en cas de pluralité de défendeurs (Article 6) . . .[148] [149]

---

[140] *Quaere*, Article 14 *Code civil*?

[141] ('Article 24 refers purely and simply to the national law of the court seised, in this case Article 145 NCPC').

[142] (1993) *JDI*, at p.157; according to *Nouveau Code de Procedure Civile*, Dalloz, 93ème éd., 2001, at p.132, Article 145 does not alter the normal/international competence of the judge *en référé*—for its operation *Messier-Dowty Ltd and anor v Sabena S.A. and ors* [2000] 1 WLR 2040, CA.

[143] In *Société Luxguard c/ Société SN Sitraco et autres, Cour d'appel de Versailles*, 9.4.1993, (1995) *Rev Crit* 80, obs. Couchez.

[144] Article 42, alinéa 2, reads 'S'il y a plusieurs défendeurs, le demandeur saisit, à son choix, la juridiction du lieu où demeure l'un d'eux'; *Nouveau Code de Procedure Civile*, Dalloz, 93ème éd., 2001, at p.54 with attending notes.

[145] Those applications for the *provision* and the appointments failed on the merits.

[146] *Mme Mintschukowa et autres c/ SA Bureau Véritas et autres, TGI de Nanterre*, Ord.Ref., 10.3.1997, (1997) *Dalloz*, Juris., 449, obs. Bussy.

[147] *Quaere*, could the Lugano Convention domiciled 'defendants'/respondents be 'sued' in France, under Article 6(1) Lugano, on the basis of the 'nationality' of the Estonia's French classification society, Bureau Véritas. Yet jurisdiction under Title II had *already* been exercised *on the merits* in Sweden; one is put in mind also of *Crédit Suisse Fides Trust SA v Cuoghi* [1998] QB 818, CA, through Article 2 Lugano (if such was the jurisdiction taken over Mr. Cuoghi), and of Eilers' comments at p.200, in Eilers, 1991; also now *Van Uden Maritime*, at p.7131, para. 22 for a court's unfettered power to order interim relief, when jurisdiction is based, not on Article 24, but 'as to the substance of the case' on one of the heads of jurisdiction under the Convention (presumably in Title II).

[148] ('The French judge *en référé* considered himself to be competent at an international level . . . by reason of the French nationality of one of the defendants and the provisions of the Lugano Convention relating both to determining jurisdiction in the case of multiple defendants (Article 6) . . .').

[149] (1997) *Dalloz*, Juris., 449, obs. Bussy, at p.451.

The upshot of the French cases thus seems to be twofold: the lack of any discussion as to the basis of jurisdiction to order provisional measures, and the lack of criticism[150] of the *référé*-courts' tendency to allow Article 14 *Code civil* to found this jurisdiction. Unfortunately, once it is admitted[151] that Article 24, by silence or otherwise, 'directs' the requested court's jurisdiction over interim relief to national law, a 'double renvoi'[152] occurs, a

> double renvoi au droit national du tribunal saisi d'une demande . . . *à la lex fori*—et non aux règles édictées par les articles 2 à 18 de la Convention[153]—. . . c'est d'autre part la même loi qui détermine les mesures . . . que ce tribunal peut prescrire et les conditions dans lesquelles il peut le faire.[154] [155]

The renvoi to national law seems to mean that the limits on jurisdiction in Article 3 I and II are removed in actions for interim relief.[156] It seems undeniable, therefore, that national provisions, including those of 'exorbitant' jurisdiction, will apply in their entirety.[157] Even if this is accepted,[158] it does seem somewhat surprising that a court *en référé*[159] can rely on an article, Article 6(1)[160] of the Lugano Convention, to found jurisdiction as if it were a court on the merits.[161] It surely could not have been intended by the drafters of Article 24 that the provisional court applied to, not having jurisdiction on the merits, could choose[162] between national or Convention jurisdictional rules, depending on which were fulfilled; if

---

[150] Except the weak protestations of Metzger and Holleaux; Gaudemet-Tallon, (1990) *Rev Arb* 633, at p.646; and 2 paras. in Cuniberti, 2000, at p.332 and p.446; 'L'article 24 est susceptible d'être interpété comme renvoyant aux règles ordinaires de compétence internationale des Etats, mais non aux règles qui établissent des fors exorbitants . . .'('Article 24 is capable of being interpreted as referring to the ordinary State rules of international competence, but not to the rules establishing the exorbitant *fora*') Holleaux, (1980) *JDI*, at p.894.

[151] Perhaps it is futile to resist Article 24's silence as to any jurisdictional guidance.

[152] Huet's phrase, following note.

[153] The correct view, as it turns out: *Van Uden Maritime*, but subject to autonomous limitations on what provisional measures can be ordered, at p.7137 para. 47.

[154] ('a double remittance to the national law of the court seised of the request . . . to the lex fori—and not to the rules laid down in articles 2–18 of the Convention—. . . it is also the same law that determines the measures . . . that this court can prescribe and the conditions under which it may do so').

[155] (1993) *JDI*, at p.156, Huet.

[156] *Van Uden Maritime* has confirmed this under Article 24.

[157] *Ibid.*, and Proposition A(ii) above, at p.283.

[158] As it now must, post-*Van Uden Maritime BV, trading as Van Uden Africa Line v Kommanditgesellschaft in Firma Deco Line, and another* (C-391/95) [1998] ECR I–7091.

[159] Such as *Mme Mintschukowa* (1997) *Dalloz*, Juris., 449, obs. Bussy.

[160] It will be recalled that Proposition A above showed us that a Contracting State court with jurisdiction on the merits can order all types of interim relief; an Article 24 court may only order Article 24 'provisional, including protective measures'.

[161] Similar to the 'Gericht der Hauptsache' theory in Germany—*OLG Karlsruhe* 2.10.2001 (2002) *IPRax* p.VI, (2002) *RIW* 151; *Hof 's-Gravenhage* 17.7.2000 *F.G.H. Abbing tegen Sibomat N.V.* 2001 *NJ* Nr.87, p.543.

[162] *Van Uden Maritime* has shown us that *no* choice is possible—jurisdiction under the special regime inaugurated by Article 24 is under national (exorbitant) provisions alone, not under Title II, Articles 2, 5–18.

any, it should only be the national provisions, with all the problematical ramifications that come riding on their coat-tails.

The picture in France is of the widest possible jurisdictional basis for an Article 24 application, and an almost wilful blindness to the taking of jurisdiction, where applications for *référé-provisions*[163] have been warmly received. The combined effect of jurisdiction and *provision* has undoubtedly lead to forum-shopping opportunities,[164] ruffling the 'level playing field' so earnestly desired by European civil procedural law.[165] Additionally, as will be seen,[166] such a combination may well in a number of cases have the effect of scotching any action on the merits from taking place in the *forum/fora* otherwise presribed by the Convention; i.e. in the courts where 'a normally well-informed defendant'[167] could reasonably predict being sued on the merits:

> ce réquerant pourra être amené à soliciter des mesures provisioires devant l'autorité judiciaire de l'Etat dont le droit lui paraître le plus favourable à sa cause et à requérir l'exequatur de la décision dans l'Etat de l'exécution de la mesure. Le problème a surtout été débattu relativement à l'institution du référé-provision prévu par le droit français.[168] [169]

Perhaps a normally well-informed Contracting State defendant must now expect to be sued *en référé*, if the facts or circumstances of a given case have even the remotest connection with France!

Attempts were made to ameliorate the effects of Article 14 *Code civil* and the *référé-provision*.[170] Recognising the dangers of the combined effect of this 'double renvoi', Gaudemet-Tallon[171] and Gothot and Holleaux[172] had advocated

---

[163] The section dedicated to the *référé-provision*, in Part II, section 3.7.

[164] For a possible case where the worldwide *Mareva*/freezing injunction and associated discovery orders may have had a magnetic effect, *Crédit Suisse Fides Trust SA v Cuoghi* [1998] QB 818, CA, and by analogy, a comment by Collins (1981) 1 *YEL* 249, at p.257; also Donzallaz *La Convention de Lugano*, Vol I, 1996, paras. 1-1736, at p.633 para. 1678: 'Ce vaste choix est dès lors de nature à engendrer un véritable *forum-shopping* . . . chaque tribunal devant apprécier sa compétence d'après sa *lex fori*' ('this vast choice is such as to generate a real forum shopping—each court having to judge its competence according to its *lex fori*'). *Van Uden Maritime* may have eased this concern somewhat, by requiring, at p.7135, para. 40 (in all cases), 'the existence of a real connecting link between the subject-matter of the measures sought and the territorial jurisdiction of the Contracting State . . . before which those measures are sought.'

[165] *Société d'Informatique Service Réalisation Organisation (SISRO) v Ampersand Software BV* (C-432/93) [1995] I–2269, at pp.2300–1, para. 41.

[166] Merkt, 1993, at sections 3.7.1–3.

[167] *Jakob Handte & Co. GmbH v Société Traitements Mecano-Chimiques des Surfaces (TMCS)* (C-26/91) [1992] ECR I–3697, at p.3995, para. 18.

[168] ('this applicant may be lead to demand provisional measures before the judicial authority of the State whose laws appear to him to be the most favourable to his case and to ask for enforcement of the decision. The problem has above all been aired in relation to the introduction of the *référé-provision* provided for by French law').

[169] Emphasising the forum-shopping opportunities, Gaillard, L 'Les mesures provisionelles en droit international privé' (1993) *SJ* 141, at p.158.

[170] Now that *Van Uden Maritime* has condoned the use of Article 3 bases of national jurisdiction, when available, *Hof 's-Gravenhage* 17.7.2000 *F.G.H. Abbing tegen Sibomat N.V.* 2001 *NJ* Nr.87, p.543.

[171] Gaudemet-Tallon, 1996, at p.196, para. 270.

[172] Gothot and Holleaux, 1985, at p.115

the use of judicial creativity to cut back on the potential for abuse, and a perceived *détournement* (at least within the granting Contracting State courts themselves) of the Brussels and Lugano Conventions. They had demanded, firstly, that there be an element of urgency[173] in making the application/demand; secondly that the provision must have been 'territorial'[174] in character, operating only upon assets within France. It should not, they had argued, be used for 'export', in order to gain recognition or enforcement under Title III upon foreign assets, whatever the local provisions of the *Nouveau Code* say.

Gaudemet-Tallon firstly questioned the need to resort to a *provision*, except in a case of urgency:

> A défaut de cette condition, on ne voit pas pourquoi les parties ne devraient pas demander ces mesures au juge compétent au fond.[175] [176]

The same sentiment was shared by Gothot and Holleaux,[177] and by Mamet-Rosenbaum:[178]

> La condition d'urgence justifera l'exception au système de compétence des conventions et la cantonnera à sa seule raison d'être.[179] [180]

The presence of urgency and the grant of a *provision*, they argue, should be to prevent the irremediable;[181] unfortunately, this is not a view shared by the *Cour de Cassation.*[182]

On a more firm footing[183] may be the requirement of only allowing a *provision en référé* if there are actually assets within France on which it can act.[184] A *provision* granted on the basis of Article 14 *Code civil*, should not be allowed to enter the recognition and enforcement machinery of Title III:[185]

---

[173] The earlier numerous bi- and multi-lateral jurisdiction and enforcement Conventions demanded urgency.

[174] This may be more in line with the thoughts of the ECJ in *Bernard Denliauer v S.n.c Couchet Frères* (C-125/79) [1980] ECR 1553, at p.1570, para. 16; this solution is arguably adopted in *Van Uden Maritime*, especially at p.7137, para. 47.

[175] ('In default of this prerequisite, it is not unreasonable that the parties should request these measures from the judge on the merits').

[176] Gaudemet-Tallon, 1996, at p.196, para. 270; local plaintiffs no doubt always prefer their local courts.

[177] Gothot and Holleaux, 1985

[178] Mamet-Rosenbaum, C. *Compétence judiciare et execution des jugements dans le grand espace juridique européen*, Thèse, Doctorat en droit, Panthéon-Assas, Paris-II, 1994, Tomes I and II, at p.409, para. 470.

[179] ('The condition of urgency will justify the exception to the system of competence of the Conventions and confines it to its own *raison d'être*').

[180] *Ibid.*

[181] Gaudemet-Tallon, 1996, at p.196.

[182] *Société Krupp Widia GmbH c/ Société Schlumberger Industries*, Cour de Cassation Ch. Com., 10.3.1992, (1993) *JDI* 156, obs. Huet.

[183] *Denilauer*, which supports the connection theory—*Van Uden Maritime* has entrenched this view, at para. 40.

[184] This may have come about by *Cour de Cassation* 13.4.1999 *Société Bachy c/ Société Belbetoes Fundacoes e Betoes Especiais LDA* (1999) *Rev crit* 352, (2000) *JDI* 83, [1999] I.L.Pr. 743.

[185] '[D]ès lors que sa décision ne pourrait être executée sans passer par le détour d'une procédure d'exequatur' Gaudemet-Tallon, 1996, at p.197, para. 271.

[c]ette nécessité d'une proximité du juge et du lieu de mise en oeurvre de la mesure est à l'origine de l'importante exception réalisée par les Articles 24 . . .[186] [187]

The well-spring of the whole problem in this 'Schwachstelle'[188] of the Convention is that the drafters assuredly never envisaged the possible 'exportability' of provisional and protective *référé-provisions* under Title III of the Convention. This is abundantly clear from the fact that under Article 25, et.seq., the word 'judgment' was, and is, too loosely defined. If 'any judgment . . . whatever the judgment may be called, including a decree, order, decision or writ of execution' was meant to be limited to a 'judgment on the merits',[189] the Convention should have explicitly said as much. At the same time, a phrase should have been inserted into Article 2ff, to demonstrate that court proceedings resulting from jurisdiction taken under Articles 2, 5–18 had as their foundation only provisions designed for the jurisdiction of Contracting States 'on the merits' of a dispute.

(iii)   Jurisdiction in the UK[190]

Until the coming into force of section 25 of the Civil Jurisdiction and Judgments Act 1982,[191] and the 1978 Accession Convention, the English courts had no specific rules[192] dealing with jurisdiction to order provisional or protective relief when substantive litigation was pending outside England and Wales.[193] Indeed,

---

[186] ('the necessity of proximity of the judge and the place of execution of the measure is at the source of the important exception brought about by Articles 24').

[187] Mamet-Rosenbaum, 1994, Tome II, at p.408, para. 468; and confirmed by *Van Uden Maritime.*

[188] '[W]eak spot' Jametti-Greiner, M. 'Der vorsorgliche Rechtsschutz im internationalen Verhältnis' (1994) *Revue de la Société des juristes bernois* 649, at p.661.

[189] Even the definition of 'on the merits' is problematic, admittedly: *Solo Kleinmotoren GmbH v Emilio Boch* (C-414/92) [1994] ECR I–2237, solely to judicial decisions 'emanating from a judicial body . . . on its own authority *on the issues* between the parties', at p.2255, para. 17; the highlighted phrase does not seem to go far enough to exclude provisional/protective measures from Title III—also *Bernard Denilauer v S.n.c. Couchet Frères* (C-125/79) [1980] ECR 1553.

[190] For the Republic of Ireland, the implementing legislation which came into force on the 1st December 1999 is the Jurisdiction of Courts and Enforcement of Judgments Act 1998; its s 13(1), and especially s 13(2), are substantially the same as s 25 CJJA 1982, but *without* the extension, as yet, to the Act similar to s 25(3) CJJA by the Civil Jurisdiction and Judgments Act 1982 (Interim Relief) Order 1997, S.I. 1997, No.302, *Irish Current Law, Statutes Annotated*, 1997–1998, p.52–19; Kessedjian, C. Prel. Doc. No.10 of October 1998, at pp.5–13.

[191] S 25 came into force on 1 Jan 1987 (S.I. 1986/2044); also s 24 (in cases of doubtful jurisdiction), ss 27 and 28 CJJA 1982, dealing with the Court of Session's powers (including under s 1 Administration of Justice (Scotland) Act 1972) to order provisional measures: *Petter Olsen v Forrest Estate Ltd and others*, 14.6.1994, OH (recovery and rendering up of documents under s 1 of the 1972 Act); *Sunderland City Council v Scotsman Publications Ltd* (1999) OHC, unreported, Lexis; and s 2 Arbitration Act 1996.

[192] Unless the defendant came to England and could be served: even this still proves to be problematic: *Mercedes Benz A.G v Leiduck* [1996] 1 AC 284, PC, *Walsh and another v Deloitte & Touche Inc*, 17.12.2001, PC and *Crédit Suisse Fides Trust SA v Cuoghi* [1998] QB 818.

[193] *The Siskina* [1979] AC 243; cf. the 'not subject to the jurisdiction of the English court on the merits' restriction of *The Siskina* loosened (in an international arbitration context) in *Channel Tunnel Group Ltd v Balfour Beatty Construction Ltd* [1993] AC 334, at pp.392–93 (Lord Mustill), when the court could gain jurisdiction by some other means than service out, (presumably by *in personam* jurisdiction, or under s 25(1) CJJA 1982).

The Siskina[194] showed that service out of the document instituting proceedings for the grant of a *Mareva* injunction was impermissible where substantive proceedings on the merits were not possible within the jurisdiction, as there was no cause of action even potentially justiciable before the English courts.

Section 25 CJJA 1982 was drafted[195] so as to give the English court the power to grant interim relief[196] when, *inter alia*, proceedings are, or are to be, commenced[197] in another Brussels/Lugano Contracting State.[198] Unforgivably, however, there proved to be no liaison in the drafting[199] of section 25 and the former Rules of the Supreme Court. The RSC were not specifically amended[200] to incorporate the machinery for service out of an application under section 25, when, as was likely, a foreign respondent needed to be so served.[201]

---

[194] *Ibid.*, and *Mercedes Benz A.G v Leiduck* [1996] 1 AC 284, PC, *Walsh and another v Deloitte & Touche Inc*, 17.12.2001, PC.

[195] *X v Y and another* [1990] 1 QB 220 (Anthony Diamond QC); *Republic of Haiti & others v Duvalier & others* [1990] 1 QB 202, CA; the combination of Article 24 and s 25 CJJA 1982 may be one reason why the impression that under Article 24 two courts are implicated—'two court problem'—has arisen in the UK. It will be rare, after the extension to s 25(1) CJJA 1982 by The Civil Jurisdiction and Judgments Act 1982 (Interim Relief) Order 1997, that consideration in international litigation will *not* have to be given to s 25(1) (and Article 24) *ratione personae/materiae/loci*—cf an exception in *C Inc plc v L and another* [2001] 2 Lloyd's Rep. 459: assets and residence of CPR 6.20(3) co-respondent in Guernsey (and therefore 'made subject to the territorial jurisdiction of the English court'). In such an exceptional case 'a freezing order cannot be entirely 'free-standing'. It has always to be incidental to and dependent upon a claim to enforce a substantive right', at p.475 (Aikens J).

[196] As defined in s 25(7). In this section 'interim relief', in relation to the High Court in England and Wales, means interim relief of any kind which that court has power to grant in proceedings relating to matters within its jurisdiction, other than—(a) a warrant for the arrest of property; or (b) provision for obtaining evidence'; curiously s 25(2) (s 13(2) Ireland) then allows the court, in its discretion, to refuse to grant relief if it is inexpedient to do so, having regard to the fact that the court has no jurisdiction apart from s 25(1).

[197] This wording may have shifted the initial emphasis onto s 25, away from Article 24, and possibly given the (false) impression that two courts had to be involved in the Article 24 process.

[198] Article 25, so far as relevant to this examination, reads as follows: '(1) The High Court in England and Wales . . . shall have power to grant interim relief where—(a) proceedings have been or are to be commenced in a Brussels or Lugano Contracting State other than the United Kingdom . . .; and (b) they are or will be proceedings whose subject-matter is within the scope of the 1968 Convention as determined by Article 1 (whether or not that or any other Convention has effect in relation to the proceedings). (2) On an application for any interim relief under subsection (1) the court may refuse to grant that relief if, in the opinion of the court, the fact that the court has no jurisdiction apart from this section in relation to the subject-matter of the proceedings in question makes it inexpedient for the court of grant it.' In *C Inc plc v L and another* [2001] 2 Lloyd's Rep. 459, it was accepted by the parties, despite s 25's extension, that s 25(1) did not apply in the circumstances of the case to an application for a freezing order before the English courts over assets and a respondent respectively located and resident in Guernsey. Jurisdiction under CPR 6.20(2)(3) was asserted over the respondent in any event, and an application notice (in the existing English action) for a freezing order over Guernsey assets issued and served on respondent.

[199] This solecism was highlighted in *X v Y and another* [1990] 1 QB 220.

[200] Until 1.4.1997, with the coming into force of the Rules of the Supreme Court (Amendment) Order 1997, S.I. 1997/415(L2), which inserted a new r.8A into RSC Ord.11; the current provision, in its own separate head, where 'permission' is needed to serve out, is now CPR Rule 6.20(4) which reads: 'a claim is made for an interim remedy under section 25(1) of the 1982 Act.'.

[201] The problem in the cases proved to stem from inconsistent and ill-liased connecting factors: Article 24 merely refers to Contracting State courts (also *Overseas Union Insurance Ltd & Others v New*

Cases showed that the application had to be clumsily incorporated into (what was) RSC Ord.11 rule 1(2)(a)(b)[202]—where service of a writ out was permissible, without leave, on a 'defendant'/respondent who was domiciled in another Contracting State,[203] and with leave, if domiciled outside the Contracting States. In *X v Y and another*[204] the judge found that the requirements of both Article 24 and section 25 to be satisfied. RSC Ord.11 rule 1(2) could not be used however, as rule 1(2)(a)(ii)—that a defendant be domiciled in another Contracting State— was not fulfilled. The rules therefore demanded[205] that if service out were to be effected, it had to be achieved under rule 1(1). But *The Siskina,*[206] and more recent re-iteration in *Mercedes Benz A.G v Leiduck,*[207] had interpreted the scope of Ord.11 rule 1(1):

> . . . the opening words of rule 1(1) define the extra-territorial jurisdiction by reference to the relief claimed in 'the action begun by the writ' . . . [I]t seems . . . plain that this expression refers to a claim for substantive relief which will be the subject of adjudication in the action initiated by the writ, and not to proceedings *which are merely peripheral.*[208]

However, relying on the fact that the 'broad legislative intent'[209] of section 25 should not be defeated, the judge in *X v Y and another* found that the purpose of Order 11 rule 1(1)(b)—even though cast in exactly the same wording as the earlier rule 1(1)(i), with its *Siskina* interpretation—had changed somehow under section 25's influence, reversing *The Siskina.*[210]

Fortunately,[211] the position has been rectified by the addition of a new CPR rule 6.20(4) dealing specifically with applications for interim relief under section 25(1) CJJA 1982, as extended by the Civil Jurisdiction and Judgments Act 1982 (Interim

---

Hampshire Insurance Company (C-351/89) [1991] ECR I–3317), as does s 25(1) CJJA 1982; yet the former RSC Ord. 11 r.2(a)(iii) (dealing with service of substantive claims by writ without leave) *additionally* required a respondent's Contracting State domicile—yet not mentioned in either of the earlier two provisions.

[202] The claim being one to which 'the Act' otherwise applied, RSC Ord.11 r.2(a).

[203] I.e. RSC Ord.11 r.2.(a)(ii) being satisfied.

[204] *X v Y and another* [1990] 1 QB 220, correctness doubted, with good reason, by Briggs, *Civil Jurisdiction and Judgments,* 1st edn., 1993, at p.231.

[205] It seems that Ord.11 r.1(1) is drafted as a catch-all provision, '*Provided* that the writ . . . is *not* a writ to which paragraph (2) of this rule applies, . . . service is permissible with leave . . .'.

[206] *The Siskina.*

[207] [1996] 1 AC 284, PC.

[208] [1996] 1AC 284, at p.302 (Lord Mustill).

[209] *X v Y and another* [1990] 1 QB 220, at p.229.

[210] With respect, the judge was too much concerned, as was Lord Denning MR in *The Siskina* itself ([1979] AC 225, CA, at p.230), with the wording of the sub-paragraph (i) itself. He had overreached himself, and with it the *Mercedes Benz A.G v Leiduck* interpretation of the opening words of Ord.11 r.1(1) 'the action begun by the writ'; note now that CPR 6.20(4) does not mention 'actions', but service out with permission if 'a *claim* is made for an interim remedy under section 25(1)'; cf *Cool Carriers A.B. and others v HSBC Bank USA and others* [2001] 2 All ER (Comm) 177, at p.189 (Tomlinson J), 'proceedings . . . designed to ascertain the substantive rights of the claimants.

[211] There may well also be financial reasons, as well as for the sake of clarity, why the additions should be applauded, Collins (1981) 1 *YEL* 249, at p.257.

Relief) Order 1997.[212] Wisely, by omission, the domicile of the respondent to the claim under Rule 6.20(4) is shown to be irrelevant, (now) 'permission' for service out being required, it seems,[213] whether the respondent be domiciled in a Contracting State or not.[214]

How do these amendments appear to Continental eyes, bearing in mind what was said about jurisdiction under the German ZPO, Article 14 *Code civil*, and Article 3 I and II of the Brussels Convention? It will be recalled that Article 3 I contains a prohibition on the application of supplementary national jurisdictional rules to a civil and commercial Contracting State action[215]—a prohibition effective when the provisions of Articles 2, 5–18 in Title II apply by virtue of a defendant's domicile in a Contracting State. The declaratory, or exemplary, Article 3 II[216] highlights, for the avoidance of doubt, particularly anathema provisions that do not blend well with the Convention's aim of litigious predictability.[217]

The internal law of England and Wales[218] has now, since the amendments, in its requirement of permission, been put on an equal footing[219] with the remaining list of heads of pre- and non-Brussels Convention traditional rules for service out 'on the merits', under (now) CPR 6.20.[220] Permission for service out under CPR 6.20, 6.21(1)(2A) are provisions which, in proceedings on the merits at least,[221] are prohibited by Article 3 I, as against persons domiciled in Contracting States, in a Convention case *ratione materiae*. CPR 6.20(4) now squarely aligns itself with these

---

[212] S.I. 1997/302.

[213] This is odd—although jurisdiction under Article 24 is still 'Convention jurisdiction', as in Article 1, and would therefore be expected to fall more naturally under CPR 6.19 than CPR 6.20, CPR 6.20(4) is explicit in its requirement of 'permission' in an application to serve out under s 25 CJJA 1982.

[214] The extension by the 1997 Interim Relief Order of the power to order relief wherever the merits jurisdiction be located no doubt prompted this move.

[215] On the merits, as *Van Uden Maritime* has demonstrated.

[216] 'In particular . . .'.

[217] The controversial German view of Article 24, it will be recalled, has it that: 'Nach dem klaren Wortlaut des Article 24 EuGVÜ wird für den Erlaß vorläufiger Maßnahmen *global* auf innerstaatliches Recht verwiesen.' ('From the clear wording of Article 24 Brussels, the granting of provisional measures is remitted globally to internal national law'), Stickler, 1992, at p.38; *Van Uden Maritime* has 'legitimised', *inter alia*, jurisdiction for an application for provisional, including protective relief on either (i) the basis of service of the writ during the respondent's temporary presence in the UK (*quaere* whether then s 25(2) or s 25(7) may operate at all), or (ii) on the basis of the use of the CPR r.6.20(4).

[218] The rules in the Republic of Ireland, even in their current s 13 form, appear not to have been altered.

[219] CPR 6.20(4) and 6.21(2A) ('proper place in which to bring the claim'); *quaere* the enduring authority of *The Spiliada* [1987] 1 AC 460 at p.476, (Lord Goff).

[220] With all its attendant requirements for the granting of permission to serve out. Whether or not this only involves the *forum (non) conveniens* criterion for permission remains to be seen—CPR 6.21(2A) would seem to point to the further application of the principles developed in cases from *The Brabo* [1949] AC 326 to *Seaconsar Far East Ltd. v Bank Markazi Jomhouri Islami Iran* [1994] 1 AC 438. It is also unclear how the *forum (non) conveniens* criterion will interact with, or be subsumed in, the s 25(2) *Cuoghi* 'expediency' enquiry; Briggs, 1997, at p.298, para. 6.13.

[221] But *Van Uden Maritime* has shown us that applications under Article 24 for interim relief are not 'proceedings on the merits', paras. 24 and 25.

general rules in force, regarded as 'exorbitant'[222] or 'extraordinary',[223] even though they are not identified by name in Article 3 II.[224] It would therefore seem somewhat hypocritical to condemn the French or German positions, solely on their use of traditional, 'exorbitant' bases, when CPR rule 6.20(4), 6.21(2a) demand the same. Indeed, as is demonstrated by *Crédit Suisse Fides Trust SA v Cuoghi*,[225] it is at least arguable[226] that to order the grant of a worldwide *Mareva* injunction, the court there used a base of jurisdiction over the respondent, Cuoghi, viz. presence[227]—specifically mentioned in Article 3 II.

In *Cuoghi* the applicant for the worldwide *Mareva* injunction,[228] Crédit Suisse, had commenced proceedings in Switzerland against a Mr. Cuoghi, who was 'domiciled'[229] and 'resident' in England, for his alleged involvement in the fraudulent abstraction of huge sums by one of the applicant's employees. In aid of those proceedings under Article 24 Lugano Convention,[230] Crédit Suisse was granted a worldwide *Mareva* injunction[231] by the English High Court. A question which was unfortunately almost entirely overlooked by the Court of Appeal,[232] and yet which is crucial for the present discussion, is what basis of jurisdiction was being asserted over Cuoghi—traditional or Convention, based on his presence/residence in England, or his domicile[233] here? At one point,[234] Millett LJ re-iterates the 'traditional' common law position, and seems to imply that the basis of jurisdiction taken over Cuoghi was his domicile here, as the case 'involved' the Lugano Convention:

---

[222] *Amin Rasheed Shipping Corporation v Kuwait Insurance Co.* [1984] 1 AC 50, at p.67 (Lord Diplock).

[223] *The Spiliada* [1987] 1 AC 460, at p.481 (Lord Goff).

[224] Which is merely declaratory or exemplary.

[225] [1998] QB 818, CA, Lord Bingham of Cornhill CJ, Millett and Potter LJJ.

[226] It was not clear from the Court of Appeal's judgment which base of jurisdiction was taken over Cuoghi, the respondent.

[227] *Quaere*, if 'presence' was the traditional base of English jurisdiction, why did the court need to invoke the court's jurisdiction under s 25(1), and consider s 25(2)'s 'inexpediency' at length?; CPR 6.20(4) makes this base even clearer.

[228] *Cuoghi* was curiously presaged by an innocuous-looking statement from the German commentator Eilers, 1991, at p.200, musing on whether an Article 24 court applied to could (also) take jurisdiction under any available and applicable provisions of Title II Brussels, Articles 2, 5–18: Proposition A, above, at p.283, has shown this alternative to be fallacious.

[229] But for Articles 21/22, if this was Article 2 'domicile' jurisdiction, the English would have had the power, according to *Van Uden Maritime*, unfettered by any Community definition of 'interim relief' to order such relief under s 25 CJJA; *sed quaere*, whether the court should have taken jurisdiction under Title II in any event, because of the *lis pendens* provisions in Articles 21/22 in favour of the Swiss courts first seised—below, at p.333 on the 'same cause of action' section in 3.3.5; in *The 'Winter'* [2000] 2 Lloyd's Rep. 298, the 'first seised' (Belgian) court was so under Article 24.

[230] Jurisdiction under Article 24 is to be taken by the national court using its national laws, and it seems, only them

[231] And an ancillary disclosure order.

[232] Millett LJ, below, at p.307, referred successively to residence, presence and domicile in England and Wales.

[233] Presumably, under Article 2 (Brussels)/Lugano Conventions—yet arguably the English could not simultaneously, along with the Swiss court, also be (another) Contracting State court with jurisdiction 'on the merits': Articles 21/22 would have prevented this.

[234] *Crédit Suisse Fides Trust SA v Cuoghi* [1998] QB 818, at p.827.

statute and convention apart, jurisdiction of the English court does not depend on domicile but on service. Proceedings may be served on persons temporarily present within the jurisdiction . . .[235]

Then we read:

where the defendant is domiciled within the jurisdiction such an order cannot be regarded as exorbitant or as going beyond what is internationally acceptable.[236]

He continues:

in relation to orders in personam . . . the courts of the state where the person enjoined *resides*[237] [238]

Lastly, we have his belt-and-braces assertion:

Mr Cuoghi is resident and domiciled in England[239]

If Cuoghi is 'domiciled' here, does this mean Article 2 Lugano Convention domicile,[240] relating to substantive proceedings in Title II? If he is present/resident here, is the jurisdictional basis of the power under Article 24 (and section 25(1)), or physical presence at common law?[241] The Court of Appeal did not explain the jurisdictional basis for its order with sufficient precision.

On possible reading of *Cuoghi*[242] appears to be: an English court, using Article 2 of the Conventions, can take jurisdiction over a respondent domiciled in England, even if substantive proceedings are underway in another (Lugano) Contracting State.[243] Extending *Cuoghi*'s reasoning, could it not be argued that jurisdiction could be taken under Articles 5–6? Would then permission be strictly necessary—circumventing the clear wording of CPR rule 6.20(4), as CPR 6.19(1)(b)[244] seems to be satisfied?[245] This outcome could surely not have been intended or foreseen by the Court of Appeal in *Cuoghi*; yet taking Title II Convention jurisdiction—which is after all jurisdiction under Article 2—over a

---

[235] *Ibid.*

[236] *Ibid.*, at p.827, confirmed by *Van Uden Maritime.*

[237] Is this word taken from s 42(1)(a) and (6) or not; if not, whence?

[238] At p.827.

[239] [1998] QB 818, at p.829.

[240] '[can an] applicant . . . apply for the measure in the court seised of the merits *or whether independently of this, he can always apply to one of the jurisdictions made available under Article 2 et.seq. of the Brussels Convention, is not known*', Eilers, 1991, at p.200; this may raise *lis pendens* problems under Articles 21/22, below, at p.333.

[241] I.e. autonomous civil procedural law, similar to §23 ZPO and Article 14 *Code civil.*

[242] *Crédit Suisse Fides Trust SA v Cuoghi* [1998] QB 818.

[243] This view must now be substantially doubted after *Van Uden Maritime*, and the divisions in jurisdiction announced therein.

[244] *Quaere*, what happens to Articles 21 and 22. As with the German courts taking fictitious jurisdiction on the merits under §§919 Alt.1 and 937(1) ZPO, an English court would be taking jurisdiction under Convention provisions designed for jurisdiction on the merits; if so it seems Articles 21/22 should apply? but not CPR 6.19(1)(a).

[245] No, it seems, as CPR 6.19(1)(a) requires there to be 'no proceedings between the parties [pending] concerning the same claim . . . in . . . any other' Contracting State.

respondent to an Article 24/section 25(1) application may lead to this result, despite the clear wording of CPR 6.20(4). This is why it was so vital that the Court of Appeal be precise as to the jurisdictional base used.

It has to be seriously doubted,[246] however, that jurisdiction in Title II should be available to the Article 24 court[247] when only considering applications for *Mareva*/freezing injunction relief. Yet leaving these Title II rules aside, inevitably means that only[248] traditional Contracting State (exorbitant) jurisdictions remain, outlawed by Article 3 I and II, including of course §23 ZPO and Article 14 *Code civil.*

3.2 THE CURRENT POSITION: VAN UDEN MARITIME[249] AND HANS HERMAN MIETZ:[250]—CLARIFICATION OF JURISDICTION TO ORDER 'PROVISIONAL, INCLUDING PROTECTIVE MEASURES' UNDER ARTICLE 24 OF THE BRUSSELS AND LUGANO CONVENTIONS

The facts of *Van Uden Maritime* were the following: Van Uden had applied in Dutch 'kort geding' proceedings[251] for an interim payment of a contractual consideration, agreed between it and the German respondent, Deco Line, under a charter agreement. The dispute on the merits[252] had already been referred by Van Uden to arbitration proceedings[253] in the Netherlands, in accordance with an arbitration agreement in the charter. Unhappy at the delays, Van Uden sought an order, in a truncated procedure known as 'kort geding' proceedings, for payment of the contractual consideration allegedly due to it under the charter. The first instance judge took jurisdiction over Deco Line under a combination of Article 24 and Article 126(3) of the Dutch Code of Civil Procedure,[254] and rejected Deco Line's objection that it could only be sued in Germany on the basis of Article 2.

For present purposes, the *Hoge Raad*'s seventh question in its reference for the preliminary ruling essentially asked whether the phrase 'such . . . measures as may

---

[246] It seems indisputable that Title II was designed for jurisdiction on the merits only.

[247] As a fictitious main court.

[248] Merkt, 1993, at p.111, para. 277: 'S'ils ne sont pas compétents selon les règles expresses de la Convention, leur compétence ne peut résulter que des règles de compétence des droits nationaux'.

[249] *Van Uden Maritime BV, trading as Van Uden Maritime Africa Line v Kommanditgesellschaft in Firma Deco Line, and another* (C-391/95) [1998] ECR I–7091.

[250] *Hans-Hermann Mietz v Intership Yachting Sneek B.V.* (C-99/96) [1999] ECR I–2277.

[251] As to which Kessedjian, C., *Note on Provisional and Protective Measures in Private International Law and Comparative Law, Hague Conference on Private International Law*, Prel. Doc. No.10 of October 1998, at p.36.

[252] *Inter alia*, concerning Deco Line's failure to pay the charter hire.

[253] Under Dutch law, Article 1022(2) of the Code of Civil Procedure, an arbitration clause could not preclude a party's right to seek interim relief before the courts—Hof, J. (1989) *NILR* 180; s 44(1) Arbitration Act 1996.

[254] A provision, otherwise outlawed in Article 3 II, whereby, *inter alia*, a (Dutch) plaintiff can seise the Dutch courts at his domicile if the defendant has no known domicile or place of residence in the Netherlands.

be available under the law of [a Contracting] State' in Article 24 included the power to take jurisdiction under the provisions of its national law, even if outlawed by Article 3 I and II.

In addition, the court also asked in its first three questions whether a court with jurisdiction 'on the merits' under one of the provisions in Title II, Articles 2, 5–18 also had jurisdiction to order interim relief;[255] and if so, whether, in such a case, that relief was subject to any (further) requirements of effectiveness in the court seised. The Court of Justice's answer to the jurisdictional question sharply divided jurisdiction in the court on the merits under Articles 2, 5—18, from jurisdiction under Article 24.[256]

3.2.1   Jurisdiction under Articles 2, 5–18 'on the merits' to order interim relief

As regards a Contracting State court's jurisdiction under Title II, Articles 2, 5–18, the European Court kept the issue of jurisdiction under Title II, and its consequences, entirely separate from jurisdiction under Article 24. A court with jurisdiction simultaneously 'on the merits'[257] has an unfettered power to order any interim relief that national law allows; if a judgment granting such relief is ordered, in *inter partes* proceedings,[258] it is thus capable of enforcement under Title III.

Had the charter contract in *Van Uden Maritime* not[259] contained an arbitration clause, or should a Contracting State court take jurisdiction under the rules in Title II:

the court having jurisdiction[260] as to the substance of a case under one of the heads of jurisdiction laid down in the Convention also has jurisdiction to order provisional or protective measures, *without that jurisdiction being subject to any further conditions* . . .[261]

---

[255] NB, *not* the same as 'provisional, including protective relief' under Article 24.

[256] Proposition A, above, at p.283.

[257] [1998] ECR I–7091, at p.7131, para. 22; König, B. *Einstweilige Verfügungen im Zivilverfahren*, 2 Aufl., 2000, at p.129.

[258] *Bernard Denilauer v S.n.c. Couchet Frères* (C-125/79) [1980] ECR 1553.

[259] Van Uden could (but for the arbitration clause) have taken jurisdiction over Deco Line, for the 'kort geding' interim payment under Article 5(1), as Holland was the place of performance of that contractual obligation in question (payment).

[260] This phrase must be taken to mean (before the effects of Articles 21/22 are felt), that any court which may potentially have jurisdiction under Title II on the merits *has the power* to order such relief, but due to Articles 21/22, *only the court in which an action on the merits is definitively pending (prior to any other) may, in practice, do so.*

[261] *Van Uden Maritime*, at p.7131, para. 22, i.e. without any need for such 'safeguards' as are to be imposed on provisional measures granted under Article 24; for implications on the national systems below, sections 3.3, 3.4, 3.5.

3.2.2   Jurisdiction under Article 24 and national law to order 'provisional, including protective measures'[262]

The Court recognised[263] that its ruling on the use of national law provisions under Article 24 may possibly circumvent the 'normal' rules of jurisdiction under the Brussels Convention,[264] but the Court seems to have preferred to control this potential *détournement* by restricting the interpretation of the phrase 'provisional, including protective measures'. As will be seen in the second part of this chapter, in addition to any substantive requirements laid down at national law level, and to the Court's previous jurisprudence in *Mario Reichert and others v Dresdner Bank AG (No.2)*,[265] the grant of Article 24 measures of whatever kind[266] is now conditional on, *inter alia*, 'the existence of *a real link* between the subject-matter of the measures sought and the territorial jurisdiction of the Contracting State of the court before which those measures are sought'.[267] In *Van Uden Maritime* itself, the interim payments of contractual consideration granted in the case would only[268] come under Article 24's definition if, in addition, repayment of the sum were guaranteed by the plaintiff, and the specific assets affected by the order were, or were to be, located within the jurisdiction of the court making the order.[269]

---

[262] Proposition A(ii) above.

[263] At p.7136, para. 46.

[264] Cf Petrochilos, G. (2000) *LMCLQ* 99, at p.102.

[265] (C-261/90) [1992] ECR I–2149, measures which 'seek to preserve a factual or legal situation', at p.2183, para. 31.

[266] Note, however, that measures which may amount to interim payments of contractual consideration (and therefore possibly also interim payments in tort actions) are, *in addition*, subject to further requirements, at p.7137, para. 47; for these the *référé- provision* section below, at pp.356 *et seq.*—Bloch, A. and Hess, M. (1999) *SZW* 166, at p.174 agree with the view presented here that these additional limitations in *Van Uden Maritime* do *not* apply to *Mareva*/freezing orders; confirmed by *OLG München* (2000) *RIW* 464 (enforcing a Greek freezing injunction), reviewed below at pp.321–322; also agreeing, Schlosser, P. 'Jurisdiction and international judicial and administrative co operation' (2000) 284 *Recueil des Cours* 88, at p.188; *contra* Cuniberti, 2000, at p.334, para.449, where no such differentiation is made.

[267] At p.7135, para. 40; for implications of this under s 25(2) CJJA 1982, below, at pp.320–321 and section 3.3.4—the exact scope of this phrase can only be guessed at—cf Kennett, W. (1999) *ICLQ* 966, at p.972.

[268] *Quaere*, the position in an enforcement case, under Title III as in *Hans-Hermann Mietz v Intership Yachting Sneek B.V.* (C-99/96) [1999] ECR I–2277, where the court takes jurisdiction under Article 24, and disregards the territoriality fetter imposed by *Van Uden Maritime*. Is another Contracting State court obliged to enforce this order? Article 28 I would not seem to be an impediment. This only applies to non-compliance with sections 3, 4, 5 of Title II, or Article 59. *Van Uden Maritime* has told us that Article 24 jurisdiction is special, and not part of Title II. Art 28 III seems to rule out public policy too.

[269] Para. 47; this, it is submitted, may well have a profound impact on cross-border *référé-provision* actions; it is unclear what is to happen if the order under Article 24 is simply an order to pay the contractual consideration—which seems more likely (as happened in *Cour de Cassation* 13.4.1999 *Société Bachy c/ Société Belbetoes Fundacoes e Betoes Especiais LDA* (1999) *Rev crit* 352, [1999] I.L.Pr. 743)—rather than directing the sum to be paid from specific assets of the defendant, wherever located.

The upshot of *Van Uden Maritime* seems to be that so long as a respondent to this type of procedure has, or will have, some assets within the jurisdiction of a particular court,[270] an applicant may ignore any litigation on the merits in any other Contracting State, and any arbitration wheresoever underway, take advantage of exorbitant rules of jurisdiction, and obtain a provisionally enforceable order, in the granting Contracting State.

If, as appears to be the case, this is a correct assessment of the *Van Uden Maritime* decision, the result will be an alarming increase in the application for such interim measures (such as the *référé-provision*) in the *forum actoris*, on (occasionally discriminatory) exorbitant grounds, to the detriment and *détournement* of the protective edifice of Title II, Articles 2, 11, 14, and 17 so carefully erected for actions on the merits. The *Van Uden Maritime* 'safeguards' may prove illusory, if a respondent has (any) assets in the granting Contracting State. A guarantee may prove worthless, or the rights thereunder prohibitorially expensive and time-consuming to vindicate.

3.2.3 Questions left unanswered by *Van Uden Maritime*

Is it possible that there can be *two* (or more) courts taking jurisdiction under Articles 2, 5–17, 18 'on the merits' jurisdictional regime: (i) both able to order unfettered interim relief, or (ii) only the court 'first seised' under Articles 21/22?

At first glance, proposition (i) appears unsustainable, given the *lis pendens* provisions of Articles 21/22. Yet it may be possible that an application may be made to one court with jurisdiction over a defendant on the basis of Article 2,[271] to another on the basis of, for example, Article 17 for interim relief, even if another (third) court in a different Contracting State, on the basis of Article 5(1), is already first seised on the merits of the dispute. *Prima facie*, it seems that Articles 21/22 are designed to prevent a situation of *lis pendens* 'on the merits' of an action, not for interim relief,[272] even if the base of jurisdiction taken in the other two courts derives from separate articles of Title II.

When jurisdiction is taken under Article 24 and national procedural law to order, *inter alia*, interim payment of contractual consideration, or a (worldwide) *Mareva*/freezing injunction, do the restrictions expressed in *Van Uden Maritime* extend to *all*[273] 'provisional, including protective measures' granted

---

[270] At para. 47, and is provided with a suitable (domestic or cross-border?) guarantee of repayment by the applicant/plaintiff if the plaintiff is unsuccessful as regards the substance of his claim; *sed quaere*, what if the plaintiff never initiates an action on the merits? Does the respondent have to do so? below, at pp.317–318.

[271] Arguably what happened in *Crédit Suisse Fides Trust SA v Cuoghi* [1998] QB 818.

[272] The question becomes crucial if this court second seised may order provisional measures equivalent to a judgment on the merits.

[273] It is submitted below, at p.324, that these 'extra' restrictions do *not* apply to *Mareva*/ freezing injunctions—a question asked, but not answered by Marmisse, (1999) *Rev crit* 669, at p.677;

under Article 24, or only to the former 'interim payments', strictly speaking? It is submitted here, and elsewhere that they should not. Support for this view, from the German caselaw, is to be found in the ruling of the *OLG München*[274] case, reviewed at pp.321–322, and in the views of certain commentators.[275]

3.2.4   *Hans-Hermann Mietz*:[276] the 'exportability issue'—the enforcement of Article 24 orders,[277] and *Van Uden Maritime* across borders?

We now know that a Dutch court, not otherwise competent under Title II, Articles 2, 5–18, can take jurisdiction under its national law to order Article 24 'provisional measures'. Such jurisdiction, the ECJ has told[278] us in *Van Uden Maritime*, is additional to the regime in Title II, but falling outside its jurisdictional influence,[279] and hierarchy.[280]

A logical extension of this ruling must therefore be that an applicant under Article 24 may presumably ignore the fact that the (Contracting State) respondent may be: (i) a tenant to a lease of a flat in another[281] Contracting State; (ii) a commercially weaker (domestic) insurance policy-holder, insured, or beneficiary[282]

---

agreeing, Bloch, (1999) *SZW* 166, at p.174; similar distinction view adhered to by Schlosser, P. (2000) 284 *Recueil des Cours* 88, at p.188.

[274] 5.4.2000 (2000) *RIW* 464.

[275] Bloch, A, and Hess, M. (1999) *SZW* 166.

[276] (C-99/96) [1999] ECR I–2277; the German referring court's decision is reported in English at [1996] I.L.Pr. 661.

[277] For the (pre-*Van Uden Maritime*) enforcement in France of a Dutch 'kort geding' patent infringement injunction Mousseron, J.-M. 'Cross-Border Injunctions—a French perspective' 1998 *IIC* 884, at pp.898–99; in detail Véron, P. (2001) *JDI* 805, at pp.813–14; summary of the Dutch practice, Barbosa, C. (2001) *IIC* 729, at pp.736–39; a comparable Swiss injunction condemning unfair competition was held *not* to breach Italian public policy under Article 27(1) in *Corte di Cassazione* 15.9.2000 *I.C.F. s.p.a contro Vitra Collections AG* (2001) *Riv. dir. int. priv. e proc.* 430.

[278] At p.7130, para. 20.

[279] Notably the protection in Article 2 for Contracting State defendants.

[280] Article 16, *quaere* Article 17 and the 'protective' provisions of Article 7–12 and 13–15; in *OLG Düsseldorf* 29.5.2000 (2001) *RIW* 380, the court recognised the jurisdiction under Article 24, in principle, to prevent a Spanish respondent from repossessing a bungalow complex in Spain, but found that jurisdictional competence under German autonomous law (esp.§ 29a ZPO) gave jurisdiction to Spain in any event. The fact that the court on the merits in Spain had exclusive jurisdiction under Article 16(1)(b) did *not* exclude Article 24.

[281] Article 16(1)(b)—or, it seems, the fact that the Article 24 respondent may himself be the applicant in another Contracting State challenging the invalidity of a patent registered there (Article 16(4) and Article 19)—*Fort Dodge Animal Health Limited v Akzo Nobel N.V* [1998] FSR 222, CA, at p.246—question 4 referred not answered, as case withdrawn although, *dubitante*, in recognition and enforcement context in the Contracting State where the property is situated—König, B. *Einstweilige Verfügungen im Zivilverfahren*, 2 Aufl., 2000, at p.172.

[282] Article 11.

domiciled in another Contracting State; or (iii) as in *Hans Herman Mietz* itself,[283] arguably,[284] a consumer (not domiciled in the Netherlands, within Article 13).

The Dutch court may have ordered *internal* enforcement in these situations against domestically-located assets, if any. So long as a guarantee[285] were provided, *Van Uden Maritime* offers no barrier.

What would be the position[286] if, as against such respondents, the Dutch applicant attempted to 'export' the interim judgment to the respondent's domicile, or to another Contracting State: (1) with a guarantee,[287] or (2) with no guarantee,[288] and enforce the judgment against non-Dutch assets.[289] *Prima facie*, it would seem that other Contracting States would be obliged to enforce the order.

Such an issue, *inter alia*, recently came before the European Court in *Hans-Hermann Mietz v Intership Yachting Sneek B.V.*[290] The case can be seen as a logical extension of *Van Uden Maritime*, and the dangers (to the uniform regime of jurisdiction inaugurated by Title II) associated with the potential enforcement of 'kort geding' provisional measures for interim payments under Title III.

In the case, a reference from the German *Bundesgerichtshof* asked among other questions, whether a Dutch court judgment, given in truncated 'kort geding' proceedings, ordering Mietz, a German domiciliary, to pay a contractually agreed sale price, could be enforced in Germany under Title III of the Convention. As the referring court noted, it was impossible to tell from the Dutch judgment on what basis the jurisdiction of the Dutch court was founded, and more particularly whether this court had breached the rules of jurisdiction relating to 'consumers' in Articles 13 and 14.[291]

Under such circumstances, Article 28 I would be an obvious starting place for a defence to enforcement, as it was for Mietz in the German enforcement court

---

[283] The Court has ruled, [1999] ECR I–2277, at p.2315, para. 45 that Mietz's alleged status was no bar to Dutch jurisdiction to order provisional measures under Article 24.

[284] The *Bundesgerichtshof* had referred 3 questions as to Mietz's status as a consumer; the ECJ found that he was not.

[285] If the foreign respondent believes that the 'kort geding' was unjustifiably granted and so wishes to claim on the guarantee, does this mean that he must come to the Netherlands, initiate an action (and not merely apply to have the Article 24 order set aside) under Article 2 on his own account to prove that the Dutch applicant never was so entitled? A Dutch applicant has no interest in commencing an action on the merits. Problems of the enforcement of any cross-border guarantee would also arise. Presumably the respondent, as guarantee, would need to initiate an action under the Convention (Article 5(1)?) against any (Dutch) guarantor.

[286] The facts of *Hans Herman Mietz*, [1999] ECR I–2277.

[287] As noted, problems of the enforcement of a cross-border guarantee would arise. The respondent, as guarantee, would need to initiate an action under the Convention (Article 5(1)) against any (Dutch) guarantor.

[288] In breach of para. 47 of *Van Uden Maritime*.

[289] Again in breach of para. 47.

[290] (C-99/96) [1999] ECR I–2277; [1999] I.L.Pr. 541.

[291] A ground for refusal of recognition and enforcement of a judgment 'on the merits' under Article 28 I and Article 34 II.

system,[292] especially before the *Bundesgerichtshof.* Such a respondent can resist enforcement if the 'kort geding' judgment 'conflicts with the provisions of Sections 3, 4 or 5 of Title II'. *Van Uden Maritime,* however, has held[293] that jurisdiction under Article 24 is outside the established fold of Title II jurisdiction, and so cannot logically 'conflict' with it.[294]

If Article 28 I was unsuccessful as a defence, what of Article 27(1),[295] public policy, read in conjunction with Article 28 III?[296] This defence was not run in the referring case of *Hans-Herman Mietz,* as its referral pre-dated the judgment in *Van Uden Maritime.*

The only obstacle to a defence under Article 27(1) in these circumstances is Article 28 III: 'the *jurisdiction* of the court of the State of origin may not be reviewed' and 'the rules relating to *jurisdiction*' may not be attacked under Article 27(1). But if the 'jurisdiction' under Article 24 is not being attacked by Article 27(1), the 'substance' of the judgment—the fact that it is now being enforced against non-domestic assets—cannot be maligned due to Article 29.[297]

Despite all these objections, the European Court held (as the referring court had acknowledged in its fourth question), that the Dutch court could have still—despite the consumer protection provisions in Articles 12–15—based its decision on Article 24 and Article 136 of the Dutch code of civil procedure to order interim relief.[298] The question for decision was whether such a judgment ordering interim relief was 'provisional, including protective relief' capable of enforcement in another Contracting State under Title III.

Relying on its earlier jurisprudence in *Van Uden Maritime,* the ECJ ruled that a judgment of a (Dutch) Contracting State court in 'kort geding' proceedings,[299] on the basis of Article 24 and national law governing interim relief (Article 126(3) CpC)—*can be* the subject of a Title III enforcement action in another Contracting State if: repayment to the defendant/respondent is guaranteed, and (*quaere*), the

---

[292] *BGH* 29.2.1996 *Hans-Hermann Mietz v Intership Yachting Sneek B.V.* [1996] I.L.Pr. 661, at pp.663–65, paras. 4–9 of the report.
[293] At para. 20.
[294] Yet while being outside the regime in Title II, can it be argued that Article 24 're-enters' the Title II system for recognition and enforcement purposes of Title III and Article 28 I? If this is a tenable position, *Van Uden Maritime* would lose some of its more disquieting aspects.
[295] Prior to *Renault v SpA Maxicar* (C-38/98) [2000] ECR I–2973, Mietz could have attempted to persuade the German court that it would be contrary to German public policy to enforce a decision of another Contracting State's courts, whose effect would be, for whatever reason, a disregard for a ruling of the European Court of Justice, and therefore Community Law under Article 293 EC Treaty (formerly Article 220 Treaty of Rome); *Van Uden Maritime* clearly wishes to prohibit the 'exportability' of 'provisional, including protective' measures granted on exorbitant national grounds under Article 24.
[296] If a defence on the 'substance' of the 'kort geding' judgment is run, it will be doomed to failure because of Article 29: 'Under no circumstances may a foreign judgment be reviewed as to its substance'.
[297] The only possible solution to this problem would seem to be the effect of the judgment itself. If the 'kort geding' judgment is expressed—as *Van Uden Maritime* says it should—to be limited in its application to Dutch assets, this should be an end to its 'exportability'.
[298] At p.2315, para. 45.
[299] That orders the interim payment of contractual consideration.

order is confined to specific assets of the defendant located, or to be located, within the confines of that Contracting State (presumably therefore The Netherlands).

Unfortunately for the Dutch judgment creditor in this case, neither of the two 'safeguards' mentioned in *Van Uden Maritime* was present in its 'kort geding' judgment; rather the creditor had an order for unconditional interim payment, not backed by a guarantee. It could not, in consequence, benefit from the enforcement regime in Title III.[300]

In addition to this ruling, the Court issued a warning to potential judgment creditors. If the Contracting State court which renders any (interim relief) judgment fails[301] to identify, or justify, the grounds for its jurisdiction, any Title III enforcing court will be entitled to presume that the granting court's jurisdiction was founded on its national law governing provisional relief, with the ensuing limitations on that jurisdiction that *Van Uden Maritime* has now imposed.

One immediate question which arises from this case, in conjunction with *Van Uden Maritime*, is whether the European Court has sounded the death knell for the cross-border enforcement of Article 24 'provisional, including protective measures'?[302] At least two possibilities present themselves in this regard, which will be discussed in the next two subsections.

3.2.5 The limitations imposed by *Van Uden Maritime* are complied with

In such a situation, a Dutch or French court, for example, on the basis of Article 126(3) CpC or Article 14 *Code civil*, order, in 'kort geding'/*référé-provision* proceedings, interim payment of contractual consideration, backed by a Dutch or French guarantee, and confined to assets in the Netherlands or France (i.e. in the Contracting States of the granting courts). If the defendant/respondent has sufficient (specific) assets in Holland or France to satisfy this interim order, the question of cross-border enforcement under Title III simply does not arise.

3.2.6 The limitations imposed by *Van Uden Maritime* are not complied with, or are overstepped

If a defendant/respondent has no, or insufficient, assets in the jurisdiction of the granting court, enforcement in another Contracting State may have to be attempted under Title III. Yet now the 'kort geding' or *provision* judgment will be directed at assets other than those specific assets located in the court of origin. *Ex*

---

[300] At p.2318, para. 54.
[301] *Quaere*, or appears to be unsure of its own jurisdiction, *Crédit Suisse Fides Trust SA v Cuoghi* [1998] QB 818; *OLG München* (2000) *RIW* 464.
[302] Van Houtte thinks so, in (1999) *Rev. dr. comm. belge* 134, at p.134.

hypothesi, Van Uden Maritime and *Mietz* have outlawed such provisional judgments under Article 24, and *Mietz* has denied to them the benefit of Title III enforcement.³⁰³ These cases could be said to have confined judgments for interim relief of contractual consideration ordered under Article 24 to the Contracting State in which they were granted.³⁰⁴ This proposition is only correct if the phrase in *Van Uden Maritime*, 'located within the confines of the territorial jurisdiction of the court to which application is made'³⁰⁵ is interpreted as meaning only the territory of the court rendering the provisional measure.

The French commentator³⁰⁶ on *Van Uden Maritime* certainly accepts this interpretation, and the attitude of a recent *Cour de Cassation* case, *Bachy c/ Soc. Belbetoes*,³⁰⁷ would seem to support this view. The French court heard an appeal, in the light of *Van Uden Maritime*—where a *référé-provision* had been granted prior to the decision of the ECJ. Although the case properly belongs in the section devoted to the substantive issues on interim relief, it shows the potential for the use of the *référé-provision* procedure (even) when the *Van Uden Maritime* 'safeguards' are put in place. The French company, Bachy, had obtained a *provision* for payment of certain invoices (allegedly) due to it from a Portuguese company, Belbetoes, in a technology transfer contract. The report states that the *Tribunal de commerce* based its jurisdiction on Article 873(2) NCPC,³⁰⁸ but it was not clear from the report whether the *provision* was backed by a guarantee. As the lower instance decision was handed down on 18.1.1996, before *Van Uden Maritime*, there is no reason to suppose any had been given. There was a *cassation*, not for this reason, but because the lower court had granted the *provision* 'sans rechercher si la condamnation à la provision sollicitée *pouvait être exécutée* en France.'³⁰⁹ ³¹⁰

The (domestic) enforceability or otherwise of such a 'provisional, including protective' measure was not an explicit pre-requisite for its grant under Article 24 and *Van Uden Maritime*, unless this is now the French manifestation of the 'real

---

³⁰³ The conclusions of the *OLG München* (2000) *RIW* 464, at p.465, below, at pp.321 322.

³⁰⁴ Support for a limiting theory on *Van Uden Maritime* type measures comes from the Nygh/Pocar report, to the October 1999 version of the draft Hague Worldwide judgments Convention at p.78 where, under Article 13(3) of the draft Hague Judgments Convention, 'a measure taken . . . is territorially limited in its effect'.

³⁰⁵ *Van Uden Maritime BV, trading as Van Uden Maritime Africa Line v Kommanditgesellschaft in Firma Deco Line, and another* (C-391/95) [1998] ECR I–7091, at p.7137, para. 47.

³⁰⁶ Huet, (1999) *JDI* 613, at p.621—the French courts, according to Huet, are therefore incompetent to order a *saisie-conservatoire* on assets located outside France.

³⁰⁷ 13.4.1999, (1999) *Rev crit* 352, [1999] I.L.Pr. 743.

³⁰⁸ To grant a *référé-provision*; for details of this jurisdiction see the *Nouveau Code de Procedure Civile*, Dalloz, 93ᵉᵐᵉ éd., 2001, at p.437 with attending notes thereon.

³⁰⁹ ('without examining whether the award of the *provision* requested was able to be enforced in France').

³¹⁰ (1999) *Rev crit* 352, at p.353; Heß believes that this domestic enforceability criterion is a function of the *Van Uden Maritime* connecting link 'eine Vollstreckungsmöglichkeit in das inländische Vermögen des Schuldners' ('possible enforcement against the domestic assets of the (judgment) debtor')—Heß, B. 'Die begrenzte Freizügigkeit einstweiliger Maßnahmen nach Article 24 EuGVÜ' zu *Van Uden Maritime BV v Kommanditgesellschaft* (1999) *IPRax* 220, at p.224.

connecting link' for Article 24. The emboldened words can therefore only signify evidence of the *Cour de Cassation*'s willingness to allow a *référé-provision* of contractual consideration, provided that its enforcement is directed only at assets within France—the second condition of *Van Uden Maritime*. A commentator on *Hans Herman Mietz*, Marmisse, believes that, in practice, the strictness of *Van Uden Maritime* safeguards will mean that the cross-border enforcement of 'kort geding'/*référé-provision* judgments will hardly arise:

> l'encadrement des conditions dans lesquelles la compétence du juge des référés peut être exercée, tel qu'édicté par . . . Van Uden rend une telle possibilité fort peu probable.[311] [312]

3.2.7 What is the nature of the guarantee[313] to be given (by a guarantor) on behalf of the claimant/applicant

Initially, to comply with both the jurisdictional and substantive requirements of *Van Uden Maritime*, the applicant for an interim payment of contractual consideration, in order even to ensure its enforceability in the Contracting State which granted it, must procure for the respondent (some sort of) a guarantee that the sum awarded by the interim payment will be repaid 'if the plaintiff is unsuccessful as regards the substance of his claim'.[314]

Yet if the plaintiff/claimant has satisfied his claim, there is no incentive for him to initiate an action on the merits, almost certainly in another Contracting State,[315] with the possibility of another court ultimately[316] finding his claims on the merits to be unfounded. The onus therefore on vindicating the rights or wrongs of the action on the merits seems to fall on the respondent. Only after proving ultimately successful could the respondent hope to claim on any guarantee. It is now to the form and location of this guarantee that this subsection will briefly turn.

---

[311] ('the encapsulation of conditions in which the competence of the *référé* judge can be exercised such as those laid down by . . . Van Uden makes such a possibility highly unlikely').

[312] Marmisse, A. 'Le régime jurisprudentiel des mesures provisiores à la lumière des arrêts *Van Uden Maritime et Mietz*' (1999) *Rev Crit* 669, at p.678–79.

[313] Goode, R. *Commercial Law*, 2nd edn., 1995, at p.821.

[314] [1998] ECR I–7091, at p.7137, para. 47; whether CPR Rule 25.8(2)(a)—regarding the English court's power to order repayment of an interim award, (rather than a pre-existing scheme for repayment)—will satisfy *Van Uden Maritime*, is uncertain; at least the CA decision in *Balkanbank v Taher (No.2)* [1995] 1 WLR 1067 has permitted a respondent to 'counterclaim' in the jurisdiction.

[315] *Ex hypothesi*, Article 24 jurisdiction is used for the simple reason that jurisdiction on the merits could not be asserted by the plaintiff in the *forum actoris* under Title II, Articles 2, 5–18.

[316] Especially long a process if this court happens to be in Belgium, or Italy: *Sepracor Inc. v Hoechst Marrion Roussel Limited* [1999] FSR 746, Pat Ct (Laddie J) at p.750—also litigating in Italy, Vial, E. 'Italian Civil Procedure from a Foreign Party's perspective' in Gessner, V., (ed) *Foreign Courts: Civil Litigation in Foreign Legal Cultures*, 1996, Ch.5, 249, at p.249; Barbosa, C. (2001) *IIC* 729, at pp.736–39.

The ECJ did not specify in *Van Uden Maritime* the Contracting State in which, and by whom, the guarantee is to be given. It is by no means obvious that the guarantee is to be provided by a guarantor domiciled in the Contracting State which granted the interim relief, nor in that of the respondent's domicile. If the former, this would most likely involve the respondent in a cross-border action in another Contracting State, not of his domicile, under Article 2, Article 17 or possibly Article 5(1)—and the *Van Uden Maritime* safeguard proving to be illusory; if the latter, one is put in mind of documentary credit transactions, where the respondent will be the beneficiary under a letter of credit with a confirming bank in the Contracting State of his domicile—with the document to be presented, and therefore triggering payment, a successful decision on the merits!

The form on any such guarantee may also be problematic, so too its period of validity.[317] Additionally, the initially successful applicant may obtain the guarantee from a third party guarantor whose reputation and solvency may be unknown to, or seriously suspected by, the respondent. Yet the respondent appears to be entirely impotent in these matters.

3.3   HOW, IF AT ALL, MAY *VAN UDEN MARITIME* AND *HANS HERMAN MIETZ* AFFECT ENGLISH PRACTICE, SECTION 25 CJJA 1982 AND THE GRANT OF MAREVA/FREEZING INJUNCTIONS?[318]

The potential effects of *Van Uden Maritime* and *Hans Herman Mietz* are best seen by considering (alternatively), the jurisdiction of the English courts on the merits, and then under Article 24 and national, 'exorbitant' rules.

3.3.1   Jurisdiction under Title II

(i)   Jurisdiction under Article 2:

If the English court can take jurisdiction[319] over a defendant/respondent under this article of Title II, simultaneously as the first seised court on the merits, nothing in *Van Uden Maritime* would prevent it from granting the full range of relief

---

[317] A period of validity would force the respondent to commence an action to vindicate his rights on the merits within an equivalent period of time—a problem in some Contracting States, such as Belgium and Italy: *Sepracor Inc. v Hoechst Marrion Roussel Limited* [1999] FSR 746, Pat Ct (Laddie J).
[318] It may be that these cases will shake the English courts out of the complacency that it is only s 25 CJJA that governs applications for interim relief: *Alltrans Inc v Interdom Holdings Ltd* [1991] 4 All ER 458; note it will be assumed throughout this discussion of interim relief and s 25 CJJA 1982, that any relief sought would be warranted if substantive proceedings were brought in England—a concession made in *Crédit Suisse Fides Trust SA v Cuoghi* [1998] QB 818.
[319] Above comment, at p.283.

available under domestic law, including therefore worldwide[320] *Mareva*/freezing injunction relief.

(ii)   Jurisdiction under Articles 5–17, and Article 18,[321] with service ex juris *(with permission?)*

If, for example, England is the place of performance of a contractual obligation in question under Article 5(1) (e.g. payment), a claim form in any action 'on the merits' can now be served out of the jurisdiction on the defendant (in any other Contracting State) 'without permission' under CPR 6.19(1).

Yet under CPR 6.20(4), service of (presumably a separate) claim form[322] in such an action—for an interim remedy—such as a *Mareva*/freezing injunction,[323] *ex juris* under section 25(1) CJJA 1982 needs—in all cases, as it appears—the permission of the court. If such be the case, no advantage is conceded to the English court for the fact that it also has jurisdiction on the merits under Title II. Section 25(2) will also oblige the English court to examine the application's 'inexpediency'. Whether the court will find that it is never 'inexpedient' to allow service out when it is also the court that may take jurisdiction on the merits remains to be seen. *Cuoghi* did not, unfortunately, cover this situation, as the English court did not simultaneously have jurisdiction on the merits,[324] despite indications from the Court of Appeal that Cuoghi was 'domiciled' here under Article 2.

3.3.2   Jurisdiction under Article 24

Cuoghi,[325] it will be remembered, discussed the scope of section 25(2) CJJA 1982: more specifically whether it was 'inexpedient' to grant (worldwide) *Mareva*/freezing injunction relief (against a respondent 'domiciled' and 'resident' in England) when substantive proceedings were taking place in a Lugano Contracting State,

---

[320] For the potential effect of *Van Uden Maritime* on such relief below, section 3.3.4 and Part II.

[321] Article 18 may be a special case within subsection (ii) here. If a defendant confers jurisdiction under Article 18 *after* service *ex juris*, CPR 6.20(4) cannot surely mean that service out be repeated under CPR 6.20: *Credit Suisse First Boston (Europe) Ltd v MLC (Bermuda) Ltd* [1999] 1 Lloyd's Rep. 767, and *Youell v Kara Mara Shipping Co. Ltd* [2000] 2 Lloyd's Rep. 102, at p.120 (Aikens J).

[322] Note a CPR Part 8 claim form in the Commercial Court, N208—*Civil Procedure*, Volume 1, Spring 2001, 2001, at p.131.

[323] These measures represent the culmination of judicial creativity (a foundation now in s 7 Civil Procedure Act 1997), and expansion of such orders since the late 1980's, in particular at Court of Appeal level, in and after the case of *Babanhaft v Bassatne* [1989] 2 WLR 232, CA; for development of their attributes, Devonshire, (2000) *CFILR* 101.

[324] Jurisdiction on the merits lay in Switzerland; but it was not clear on what Convention basis it had (any) civil jurisdiction over Cuoghi, possibly under Article 6(1), or Article 5(4), in *partie civile* proceedings.

[325] *Crédit Suisse Fides Trust SA v Cuoghi* [1998] QB 818, CA.

Switzerland.[326] The Court of Appeal stressed that its rôle was purely an ancillary one.

How may the decision in *Van Uden Maritime* affect cases such as *Cuoghi*, or *Republic of Haiti v Duvalier*[327] for that matter, if at all?

As has been emphasised, one aspect of *Van Uden Maritime* has demonstrated the sharp distinction now to be drawn between the powers of a court with jurisdiction on the merits under Articles 2, 5–17, 18, and a court with jurisdiction under Article 24, and *ex hypothesi*, its national law. In *Cuoghi*, the Swiss court occupied the former, the English court the latter, position. The English court's jurisdiction, it appeared,[328] should therefore have come from the fact that Mr. Cugohi was present in England (and therefore 'properly before the court'[329]), whatever else he otherwise was, such as 'domiciled' or 'resident' here. In such circumstances, *Van Uden Maritime* has emphasised that there be 'a real connecting link'[330] between the subject-matter of the measures sought[331] and the territorial jurisdiction of the English court. The subject-matter[332] of the measures sought (the worldwide *Mareva* injunction and ancillary disclosure order) were the freezing of Mr. Cuoghi's assets (worldwide) and disclosure of those assets.

It is clear that the domestic assets, or the disclosure of them, would satisfy[333] the *Van Uden Maritime* para. 40 'connecting link' limitation; but what of the remaining worldwide assets?[334] Should the English courts' attitude be that since a *Mareva*/freezing injunction acts *in personam*, Mr. Cuoghi himself provides the 'connecting link' between the measures and the territorial jurisdiction? By analogy, this would not appear to be the view of a French commentator, Normand,[335] reviewing *Van Uden Maritime*. He does not speak in such terms,[336] i.e. that the French nationality of the applicant under Article 14 *Code civil* could provide the requisite 'real connecting link', but

> la rattachement à la chose . . . celle du lieu *où se trouve le bien* . . . sans doute, le lieu où la mesure doit être exécutée.[337]

---

[326] Paraphrased from Millett LJ's question at p.826.

[327] [1990] 1 QB 202; below at p.332, Neill LJ's comments in *Cuoghi* [1998] QB 818, at p.827, on the possible inexpediency of restraining a person not resident within the jurisdiction from disposing of his assets outside the jurisdiction.

[328] The Court of Appeal was not entirely clear on this point, reviewed earlier.

[329] [1998] QB 818, at p.826.

[330] [1998] ECR I–7091, at p.7135, at para. 40.

[331] The whole problem of the effect of *Van Uden Maritime* on English practice is that it is asset specific, while the Mareva injunction operates *in personam* against an individual who can be censured before the English courts for contempt; the *location* of assets is an ancillary issue.

[332] Unless the subject matter was, itself, Cuoghi's residence in England *simpliciter*.

[333] If the *in personam* jurisdiction over Cuoghi did not.

[334] Cf *Cheshire and North*, 13th edn., 1999, at p.260, n.5—uncertain on the point regarding assets outside the jurisdiction.

[335] (1999) *Rev crit* 340, at p.362; *contra* Briggs, 2002, at p.90.

[336] Although it is not categorically excluded either.

[337] (1999) *Rev crit* 340, at p.362.

If the *in personam* nature of the order is the decisive connecting factor, *Van Uden Maritime* should effect little change to English practice. The English court's view may very well be that section 25(2) CJJA's test of 'inexpediency'—illuminated by *Cuoghi*—will be sufficient to satisfy[338] (and overlap with) the general concerns about Article 24's provisional relief expressed by paras. 40 and 41 of the ECJ's decision in *Van Uden Maritime*. The safeguards currently included in a worldwide *Mareva*/freezing injunction,[339] such as undertakings in damages and the 'Babanhaft' proviso,[340] may be considered adequate safeguards such as to repel any accusations that the English order[341] is attempting to circumvent the substantive rules of jurisdiction in Title II of the Brussels and Lugano Conventions.

It is submitted that *Van Uden Maritime* should not have as great an impact on the practice of the English courts under Article 24 and section 25 CJJA in granting provisional including protective *Mareva*/freezing injunction relief, as it undoubtedly will on Continental 'kort geding' and *référé-provision* proceedings. One possible reason—and difference—is that *Mareva* injunctions/freezing injunctions, even if granted over assets worldwide, are not, it appears, of the same calibre[342] as the interim measures—such as unconditional interim payment of contractual consideration—ordered by the Dutch courts on the basis of Article 126(3) in *Van Uden Maritime*, and (presumably) *Hans-Herman Mietz*. The additional restrictions these two cases placed on these measures should simply not apply *tout cour* to an entirely different type of order—a *Mareva*/freezing injunction- with different (legal) repercussions.[343]

This differentiation may be due solely to the injunction's *in personam* nature and/or the fact that such a freezing injunction does not have the potential to vary the legal situation of the assets frozen, unlike a provisionally enforceable *référé-provision* order. Such a differentiation view has been endorsed by a recently-reported decision of the *OLG München*.[344] In June 1999, a first instance court in

---

[338] Compare *Kinnear and others v Falconfilms NV and others (Hospital Ruber Internacional and another, third parties)* [1994] 3 All ER 42, QBD, (Phillips J), where the rule in the former RSC Ord. 16 r.1(1) was held sufficient to satisfy the test of special jurisdiction under Article 6(2); Briggs, 2002, at pp.90–91.

[339] An example in the Commercial Court given in *Civil Procedure*, Volume 1, Autumn 2001, 2001, at p.472, onwards.

[340] A provision in a *worldwide* Mareva/freezing injunction to the effect that third parties mentioned in the order are not to be effected by it unless, and to the extent that, the order is enforced by local courts where the assets are located: *Babanhaft International Co. S.A. v Bassatne and another* [1989] 2 WLR 232, CA, (Kerr LJ); and as subsequently developed and refined: *Bank of China v NBN LLC and others*, CA, 18.12.2001.

[341] The essential nature and effect of a *Mareva*/freezing injunction does not affect the respondent's/defendant's assets in the same way and/or to the same extent as, for example, a 'kort geding' judgment/*référé-provision* (which by steps taken in execution divest the respondent of ownership of them); cf Devonshire (2000) *CFILR* 101, at pp.103–04.

[342] A *Mareva* will commonly allow the respondent to draw on a specified account for the payment of ordinary trading/legal expenses—*Civil Procedure*, Volume 1, Autumn 2001, 2001, and the model order therein.

[343] Cf Bloch, (1999) *SZW* 166, at p.174, who agrees; also Schlosser, P. (2000) 284 *Recueil des Cours* 88, at p.188.

[344] 5.4.2000 (2000) *RIW* 464.

Athens had ordered a freezing injunction over the respondent's assets to the value of 2.5 billion drachmas, during arbitration proceedings in Zürich. The applicant was successful in enforcing the injunction as an Article 25 'judgment' under the Brussels Convention in Germany. The appeal court interpreted *Van Uden Maritime* as strictly delineating judgments for provisional measures under Article 24, in the same way as previously suggested above, that the additional 'guarantee' and territorial restriction of *Van Uden Maritime* do not apply to a freezing injunction.

It felt that as a result of *Van Uden Maritime* and *Mietz*, provisional measures ordering interim payments of contractual consideration should be territorially confined, and more generally that 'an 'overall order' for payment that is essentially enforceable against the judgment debtor's entire property should no longer be granted':[345]

> a judgment granting provisional measures in interlocutory proceedings cannot under defined circumstances [esp. granting contractual consideration] be an Article 25 judgment[346]

Conversely, the freezing injunction in this case did not order the judgment debtor to pay a specific sum, but as with a *Mareva*/freezing injunction, only secured any future claim,[347] and could therefore be enforced under the Convention.

3.3.3 Section 25 CJJA 1982 jurisdiction, The *Siskina*, and *Van Uden Maritime*

Whatever effect, if any, *Van Uden Maritime* and *Mietz* arguably may have had on the English practice of granting 'provisional measures'[348] discussed in the previous section, one thing is certain: the jurisdiction to order such relief must now be sharply and strictly delineated. An English court either has jurisdiction to order interim relief (1) as the court simultaneously with jurisdiction on the merits under Title II, Articles 2, 5–17, 18[349] *or*, conversely (2) under Article 24 and

---

[345] 5.4.2000 (2000) *RIW* 464, col. 2.

[346] At p.465.

[347] A freezing injunction is said to ensure the release and return of the judgment debtor's property at any time, at p.465.

[348] At this point the distinction in terminology between interim relief granted under either Articles 2, 5–18, and Article 24 'provisional, including protective measures' (under s 25(1)(7) CJJA 1982) becomes important.

[349] Mentioned above, at p.319; *quaere*, therefore in English procedure when its rules govern this application for interim relief on the merits—either CPR Rule 6.19(1) or Rule 6.20(4); or, under the traditional rules of English civil procedure, *inter alia*, CPR Rule 6.20(2)(3): *C Inc plc v L and another* [2001] 2 Lloyd's Rep. 459, where s 25 CJJA 1982 was conceded by the parties to be inapplicable due, possibly, (i) to the fact that it was simply jurisdictionally redundant or (ii) despite s 25(1)'s extension to proceedings commenced or to be commenced otherwise than in Brussels/Lugano Contracting States, to the inability of claimants' commencing proceedings in Guernsey (as law of Guernsey did not provide for appointment of receiver over local assets), or (iii) the extension to s 25(1) being inapplicable to Bailiwick of Guernsey *sed quaere*, to the fact that Guernsey thus occupies the anomalous position of not being a 'State' for purposes of s 25(1) CJJA 1982 (cf s 52(2) CJJA 1982, and *Chloride*

exorbitant provisions (in conjunction with section 25(1)(2)(7) CJJA 1982) to grant Article 24 'provisional, including protective measures'.

In England and Wales, therefore, as a court without jurisdiction on the merits under Title II of the Convention, Article 24 remits jurisdiction either to (i) where the defendant/respondent was temporarily present within the jurisdiction when the application for such measures was served on him; or (ii) where service of the respondent *ex juris* is possible under a combination, now, of the CPR Rule 6.20(4), 6.21(1),(2A) and section 25 CJJA,[350] with 'permission'. These two Article 24 possibilities will each be examined in turn.

(i)   where the individual defendant was temporarily present, or a corporate entity (oversea company) with its seat[351] in another Contracting State: 'place of business', 'doing business', ss 725, 695, 694A[352] Companies Act 1985, and/or CPR 6.2(2), 6.5(6)[353]

In this situation, it is clear, as the Dutch court itself had proceeded in *Van Uden Maritime*, an English court would be taking jurisdiction on the basis of its own national law, outside the regime of the Conventions' Title II. As we have seen, *Van Uden Maritime* places limits on the 'interim relief' available[354] in this scenario, namely 'the existence of a real connecting link between the subject-matter of the measures sought and the territorial jurisdiction of the Contracting State of the court before which those measures are sought';[355] and a 'need to impose conditions or stipulations such as [a] guarantee'[356] to maintain any such measure's interim nature. How would this affect the grant of an *in personam* (domestic) *Mareva* injunction/freezing injunction or *Anton Piller*[357]/search order?

The nature of a *Mareva* injunction/search order involves no transfer of property to an applicant,[358] nor does it confer any proprietary rights, nor priority in the

---

Industrial Batteries Ltd v F. & W. Freight Ltd [1989] 1 WLR 823, at p.827 (Dillon LJ)), nor is it 'a part of the UK other than that in which the High Court in question exercises jurisdiction.

[350] It has not been aired in the cases whether s 25 exclusively deals with applications for interim relief, even when a Contracting State respondent can be served while temporarily present here.

[351] The provisions of s 42(3) CJJA 1982 not being satisfied, but s 42(7) fulfilled.

[352] Sections listing a number of occasions on which a corporate entity (with a branch) is liable to be served within the jurisdiction—*Saab v Saudi American Bank* [1999] 4 All ER 321, at pp.324–25, at p.326, CA; Enonchong, N. (1999) *ICLQ* 921; Rogerson, P. (2000) *CFILR* 272.

[353] Also *Sea Assets Ltd v PT Garuda Indonesia* [2000] 4 All ER 371, at p.376, (Longmore J).

[354] Or perhaps more accurately the circumstances under which previously extant national provisions may be granted under Article 24—in any event the result becomes the same.

[355] At p.7135, para. 40.

[356] *Ibid.*, at para. 41.

[357] The status and availability of *Anton Piller*/search orders will be discussed in the next subsection; their status under CPR Rule 6.20(4) and s 25(1), (7) is particularly uncertain; compare the position of the Court of Session in Scotland: s.28 CJJA 1982 and *Iomega Corporation v Myrica (U.K.) Limited* (1999) SLT 796, at p.638, *The Laws of Scotland*, vol.4, 1991, p.17; a useful remedy in *Petter Olsen v Forrest Estate Ltd and others*, 14.6.1994, OH.

[358] Or, in the language of *Mario Reichert and others v Dresdner Bank AG* (C-261/90) [1992] ECR I–2149, at p.2184, para. 35, it does not (have even the potential to) '*vary the legal situation* of the assets',

case of bankruptcy or insolvency[359] of the respondent. The anxiety expressed by the European Court in *Van Uden Maritime* and *Mietz*—over unconditional interim payments—simply does not apply in the case of a *Mareva*/freezing injunction:[360] the order is granted subject to an undertaking in damages,[361] and a number of other safeguards for a respondent, including the right to draw on the assets frozen for reasonable living, business and legal expenses.

Whether worldwide *Mareva*/freezing injunctions granted under Article 24— and on the basis of temporary presence/ss 725, 695, 694A[362] Companies Act 1985, and/or CPR 6.2(2), 6.5(6)—will remain unaffected by *Van Uden Maritime* may need more careful examination.[363] However, so long as such an (*inter partes*) *Mareva*/freezing injunction is buttressed by a guarantee in England to compensate any loss to the respondent by the granting of an injunction—so 'guarantee[ing] [its] provisional or protective character'[364]—there is no reason why it should not, in addition,[365] relate to assets of the defendant/respondent in other Contracting States,[366] and be capable of recognition/enforcement in those Contracting States under Title III.[367] This proposition is only sound, and only of any import, if so judged by other Contracting State courts—if one considers that the restrictions on interim payments, in para. 47 of *Van Uden Maritime*, are unique to this type of provisional measure alone, and should *not* extend to freezing injunctions, strictly speaking. Until the (European Court) jurisprudence develops in this area, it is uncertain, and therefore premature, to speculate whether *Van Uden Maritime* has caused the era of the worldwide *Mareva*/freezing injunction to come to an end.[368]

---

to the same extent as a provisionally enforceable *référé-provision* for contractual consideration; *OLG München* (2000) *RIW* 464 agrees with this distinction; also Devonshire (2000) *CFILR* 101, at pp.103–04, and p.110.

[359] *Cretanor Maritime Co. Ltd v Irish Marine Management Ltd* [1978] 1 WLR 966, CA, at p.974 (Buckley LJ): a *Mareva* does not operate as any sort of attachment of the assets frozen; it merely prevents the owner from doing certain things in regard to them; also *C Inc plc v L and another* [2001] 2 Lloyd's Rep. 459, at pp.467–68 (Aikens J).

[360] As a corollary to the previous footnote, the *Mareva*/freezing injunction confers no right on the successful applicant to proceed with measures for domestic and/or foreign execution, unlike a 'kort geding'/*référé-provision* judgment.

[361] Note the applicant's undertakings in Sch.B to the model freezing injunction in *Civil Procedure*, Volume 1, Autumn 2001, 2001, at p.472.

[362] Enonchong, (1999) *ICLQ* 921; Rogerson, P. (2000) *CFILR* 272.

[363] If, contrary to what is the view held here, that worldwide *Marevas* are to be equated with *Van Uden Maritime* interim payments of contractual consideration.

[364] [1998] ECR I–7091, at p.7135, para. 41, presumably up to the full amount of the assets in each particular Contracting State?

[365] Cf *Cheshire and North*'s query on this exact point, 13th edn, 1999, at p.260, n.5.

[366] For the likely reaction of such courts, below section 3.6.4.

[367] At least in Germany, *OLG München* (2000) *RIW* 464, above at pp.321–322.

[368] One would expect, after the *OLG München* case, above at pp.321–322, that German courts and commentators would make a distinction between enforcement in Germany of *Mareva*-type freezing orders and *référé-provision* judgments; the French attitude, after *Bachy c/ Belbetoes*, may well be to confine all provisional measures strictly to the country of origin.

Before leaving this subsection (i)—the first alternative base of English jurisdiction under Article 24—it seems appropriate to examine a subsidiary question that the ruling in *Van Uden Maritime* will almost undoubtedly raise, namely the application or not of section 25 CJJA 1982, in a case of 'undoubted personal jurisdiction' over a defendant served in England, due to either temporary presence, or the provisions of the CPR rule 6 or Companies Act 1985.

The Siskina is authority at common law for the proposition that there are no jurisdictional grounds to serve a respondent to an application for an interlocutory injunction out of the jurisdiction under (what once was)[369] RSC Ord. 11 rule 1(i) unless there be 'a pre-existing cause of action against the defendant arising out of an invasion, actual or threatened, by him of a legal or equitable right of the plaintiff . . .'.[370] *Van Uden Maritime* has held that a Contracting State court may order 'provisional, including protective measures' under Article 24, on the basis of its national law, including any relevant exorbitant bases of jurisdiction in Article 3 II.

In *Cuoghi*, service out of the jurisdiction of the application for a worldwide *Mareva* injunction was not necessary in that case, as Mr. Cuoghi was cumulatively 'present', 'resident' and 'domiciled' in England. *Cuoghi* was a Lugano Convention example of the 'rather uncommon'[371] situation, recognised by Lord Mustill in the Privy Council in *Mercedes Benz v Leiduck*,[372] where there was

> undoubted personal jurisdiction over the defendant but no substantive proceedings . . . brought against him in the court . . . in . . . England . . . [where] an attempt [is being] made to obtain *Mareva* relief in support of a claim pursued [in Switzerland][373]

The Siskina was not concerned with this type of case, nor with that in *Cuoghi*. Its focus was on territorial jurisdiction, *not* the power subsequently properly to 'exercise . . . the injunctive powers of the court'.[374] Yet section 25 CJJA 1982 was enacted to overcome the problem of *The Siskina*, and therefore arguably to enable English courts to grant 'interim relief' under Article 24 of the Conventions, in aid of foreign proceedings, when the respondent was *outside*, and therefore (otherwise) unamenable to English jurisdiction. In the English cases *Republic of Haiti and others v Duvalier and others* and *X v Y and another* decided under Article 24 and section 25, excepting *Cuoghi*, the respondents were domiciled outside[375] the jurisdiction.

---

[369] CPR 6.20, and r.6.20(4) now speak about proceedings for 'claims'.

[370] [1979] AC 210, at p.256, (Lord Diplock).

[371] *Mercedes Benz A.G. v Leiduck* [1996] 1 AC 284, at p.298, *Walsh and another v Deloitte & Touche Inc*, 17.12.2001, PC.

[372] *Ibid.*

[373] *Ibid.*, at p.304.

[374] *Ibid.*, at p.298.

[375] In *Republic of Haiti and others v Duvalier and others* [1989] 1 All ER 456, CA, (reputedly France); in *X v Y and anther* [1990] 1 QB 220 (Diamond QC) (in Saudi Arabia); in *Alltrans Inc v Interdom Holdings Ltd* [1991] 4 All ER 458, the party against whom a *Mareva* injunction was granted—in aid of Dutch proceedings—was a US company Alltrans Inc. but was properly before the English courts as plaintiff suing, *inter alia*, a third party JSA; in *Balkanbank v Taher and others (No.2)* [1995] 1 WLR

It is a slight puzzle therefore why the Court of Appeal in *Cuoghi* so readily took—or needed to take—jurisdiction under section 25(1), when Mr. Cuoghi was 'present', 'resident', and 'domiciled' here. Arguably section 25(1) was jurisdiction-ally redundant,[376] since he could have been, and was served within the jurisdiction. Section 25(1) would only become relevant if Cuoghi was domiciled in Switzerland, another (Lugano/Brussels Convention) Contracting State, (or now) in any other country worldwide. The court did not, but should have, considered whether *in personam* jurisdiction still exists outside the Convention regime,[377] untouched by section 25(1), to order interim relief[378] when a respondent such as Cugohi is properly before the English court.[379]

Had Crédit Suisse applied instead for an *Anton Piller*[380] order against Mr. Cuoghi's (English)[381] home or business premises under his control, no doubt counsel would have raised the above points. The question whether an *Anton Piller* order is available under section 25(1),(7) is authoritatively unsettled, since the definition of 'interim relief' in section 25(7) seems to exclude it, at least in part, as literally 'a provision for obtaining evidence'.[382]

1067, CA unclear where respondents domiciled (but presumably Ireland and Liechtenstein), but no mention was made of the jurisdiction taken, the respondent to a *Mareva* injunction in aid of Irish pro-ceedings was domiciled/present in England in any event; *S & T Bautrading v Nordling* [1997] 3 All ER 718 (in Germany).

[376] Wabwile, (2000) *JBL* 287, at pp.394–95; arguably also why s 25 CJJA 1982 not applicable in *C Inc plc v L and another* [2001] 2 Lloyd's Rep. 459, as jurisdiction could be asserted over, respectively, Bailiwick of Guernsey resident and assets by a *combination* of, *inter alia*, CPR Rule 6.20(2)(3), thereby simultaneously avoiding the 'traditional' *Siskina* restriction to what is now CPR Rule 6.20(2) (the free-standing order) and the need to apply CPR Rule 6.20(4).

[377] Eg s 37 Supreme Court Act 1981; if s 25 CJJA 1982 gives English courts personal jurisdiction where none hitherto existed, what recourse is necessary to it if an action is underway in another Contracting State—on the basis of Article 5(1) or Article 6— as against *an English domiciled* respondent to Article 24 measures present here? Support for the proposition that *in personam* jurisdiction exists outside s 25(1), even as extended, in factual situation in *C Inc plc v L and another* [2001] 2 Lloyd's Rep. 459: com-bination of CPR Rule 6.20(2) and, *inter alia,* 6.20(3) (Guernsey respondent to an English freezing order amendable here, as 'a necessary or proper party' to an application as against his wife for appoint-ment of a receiver), at pp.477–78.

[378] And left untouched by *The Siskina*.

[379] The court may well have found that s 25(1) is an all-embracing provision governing jurisdiction, with no remainder outside the section—the opening words in s 25(1) could be read thus: '[t]he High Court . . . shall have power [where, because of *The Siskina*, there was none before] to grant interim relief . . '. The question (still) needed an answer, especially now in the face of *Van Uden Maritime*.

[380] Jurisdiction now on a statutory basis, s 7 Civil Procedure Act 1997; Dockray, M. 'Anton Piller orders: the new statutory scheme' (1998) *CJQ* 272, at p.274 believes that *Anton Piller*/search orders may be made under the inherent jurisdiction (in the circumstances of *Cuoghi*).

[381] Contrast in Scotland *Iomega Corporation v Myrica (U.K.) Limited* (1999) SLT 796; also *Petter Olsen v Forrest Estate Ltd and others*, 14.6.1994, OH.

[382] *Contra*, Dicey and Morris, 13th edn., 2000, at p.191, para. 8–023; it may be, however, designed to exclude the type of evidence-gathering properly in the ambit now of Council Regulation (EC) 1206/2001 of 28.5.2001 (formerly ss 1, 2(2)(b)–(d) Evidence (Proceedings in other Jurisdictions) Act 1975); in such a case, an *Anton Piller*/search order may be excluded under s 25(7) CJJA 1982; sup-portive the comments in Nygh/Pocar report to the October 1999 version of the draft Hague World-wide judgments Convention at p.75 on Article 13; cf *Iomega Corporation v Myrica (U.K.) Limited*

If an application for such a measure is possible under the inherent jurisdiction of the court -and outside section 25(1)—the objection in section 25(7) simply falls away.[383] Should a residual jurisdiction exist outside the ambit of section 25— when a respondent can be served here—CPR Rule 25.1(1)(c)(i)–(iv) clearly envisages the court's power to order such search orders, wherever the premises to be searched are located.[384] Should an application be made to the court for a search order against a respondent present/domiciled in England in aid of foreign proceedings under Article 24, the distinction—opened up in, and emphasised by *Van Uden Maritime*—will no doubt before long force the English courts to confront this issue.[385]

Whatever the rôle, arguably if any, of section 25 CJJA 1982—where an English court has undoubted personal jurisdiction over a respondent through service within the jurisdiction under (i) above—it assumes vital importance[386] in the next subsection, (ii), discussed presently.

(ii)   Where service of the respondent ex juris is possible under a combination, now, of CPR 6.20(4) and section 25 CJJA, with 'permission'

Since 26 April 1999, the rules governing service out of the jurisdiction of an application—by claim form[387]—for 'interim relief' (as defined in section 25(7) of CJJA 1982)[388] before the English courts are contained in CPR Rule 6.20(4), together with, *inter alios*, Rule 6.21(1), (2A), and section 25(1)(2)(3) CJJA 1982. It appears, *prima facie* at least, that *Van Uden Maritime* and *Mietz* will have little impact on the practice hitherto, such as decisions[389] in *Republic Haiti v Duvalier*.

However, the facts of *Van Uden Maritime*, where a dispute on the merits was impossible in any Contracting State—due to an arbitration clause—would have meant (prior to certain amendments to English procedure) that an application for

---

(1999) *SLT* 796, at p.806; *Coca Cola Bottlers (Ulster) Ltd v The Concentrate Manufacturing Co. of Ireland (t/a Seven-up International)*, 6.4.1990, Ch.D. (Murray LJ).

[383] Cf Wabwile, (2000) *JBL* 287, at pp.394–95, who agrees with this analysis.

[384] S 25 (7) will therefore, if at all, only prevent an *Anton Piller*/search order being granted, for example, in the situation of *Altertext Inc v Advanced Data Communications* [1985] 1 WLR 457, at p.461, (against a Belgian domiciled respondent who could not be served within the jurisdiction).

[385] Left open in *Mercedes Benz A.G. v Leiduck* [1996] 1 AC 284, PC.

[386] Ie in service, under CPR 6.20(4), 6.21(2A) and s 25 CJJA, with 'permission', of a claim form- it appears that in a Commercial Court action a Part 8 claim form is to be used for the application, under the CPR Part 8 procedure;—*Civil Procedure*, Volume 1, Spring 2001, 2001, at p.131.

[387] The only certainty in this rather confusing picture is that under the circumstances of (ii), it appears that a Part 8 claim form is to be used for the application, under the CPR Part 8 procedure—PD 8B, rr.A.1(1), A.2(i) and A.3.

[388] For the uncertainty about *Anton Piller*/search orders, Maher, G. and Rodger, B. 'Provisional and Protective remedies: the British experience of the Brussels Convention' (1999) *ICLQ* 302, at p.321; *quaere*, therefore, statements of Murray LJ in *Coca Cola Bottlers (Ulster) Ltd v The Concentrate Manufacturing Co. of Ireland (t/a Seven-up International)*, 6.4.1990, Ch.D.

[389] Strictly speaking *Crédit Suisse Fides Trust SA v Cuoghi* [1998] QB 818 is not such a case, although it was decided under s 25(1) and s 25(2) CJJA 1982, since Cuoghi was served within the jurisdiction.

service *ex juris* under section 25 CJJA could not have been granted, because section 25(1)(b) would not have been satisfied—*namely in aid of proceedings on the merits* 'whose subject-matter is within the scope of the 1968 Convention'.[390] Recently this lacuna has been filled by rule 2(b) of the Civil Jurisdiction and Judgments Act 1982 (Interim Relief) Order 1997, which now permits applications under section 25 CJJA 1982, even if the substantive proceedings in need of support by interim relief in England are not within the scope of the Conventions *ratione materiae.*

It is unavoidable in the future, due to section 25's now universal ambit *ratione materiae/loci*, that in situations such as described above, section 25(2) will come to greater prominence, and the 'expediency' or otherwise of granting the application, in the case of a *Mareva*/freezing injunction, will need much closer scrutiny.[391]

3.3.4   The meaning and extent of section 25(2) CJJA 1982: 'inexpedient' (in the light of *Van Uden Maritime*) and the grant of (worldwide) *Mareva*/freezing injunctions

There is little doubt that section 25(2) has taken on, and will increasingly continue to take on, an enhanced application.[392] Previously, the section seemed ill-fitting, even superfluous,[393] due to the combined effects of *The Siskina* and Article 24— one excluding, the other enabling, recourse to interim relief where there was no full English jurisdiction on the merits. Indeed, in relation to Convention proceedings, the sub-section made little sense, as an English court requested under Article 24 and section 25(1) to issue interim relief would, in theory,[394] always

---

[390]   Article 1(4) states that the Brussels Convention shall not apply to 'arbitration'.

[391]   Note Binchy's comments in *Irish Current Law (Statutes Annotated)*, Statutes 1988, p.3–01, at p.3–17 in relation to the former Irish equivalent of s 25(2), s 11(2) of the Jurisdiction of Courts and Enforcement of Judgments (European Communities Act) 1988, (1988 *Acts of the Oireachtas*, (as promulgated), No.3 of 1988; replaced *verbatim* from 1.12.1999 by s 13 of the 1998 Act). Of s 11(2) he believed it 'most unlikely that the Irish courts will interpret subsection (2) as warranting a broad 'hands-off' approach . . .' where the court on the merits is another Contracting State court. He wonders whether the discretion involves a rather inflexible 'general judgment' as to the expediency of the High Court making the order, 'apply[ing] the same value-judgment' or, which is more likely, does the court have to proceed on a case-by-case basis? Binchy is undecided, but as a parting comment notes that the absence of any criteria by which to judge 'expediency', militates against the former rigid approach; the latest review of s 13(2) Jurisdiction of Courts and Enforcement of Judgments Act 1998 emphasises the importance of the word 'inexpedient', at p.52–59.

[392]   Due to the extension of the English court's powers under s 25(3) by the Civil Jurisdiction and Judgments Act (Interim Relief) Order 1997, S.I. 1997/302; c.f. Briggs, 1997, at p.297, para. 6.12; *Refco Inc. and another v Eastern Trading Co. and others* [1999] 1 Lloyd's Rep. 159, CA; *Ryan and another v Friction Dynamics Ltd and others* 2.6.2000, Neuberger J; *Bank of China v NBN LLC and others*, CA, 18.12.2001.

[393]   The courts paid lip-service to it *Republic of Haiti & others v Duvalier & others* [1990] 1 QB 202, CA, at p.210–11, and p.216

[394]   But *Continental Bank v Aeakos* [1994] 1 WLR 588.

otherwise have had 'no jurisdiction apart from this section in relation to the subject-matter of the proceedings', due to Articles 16,[395] (*quaere* Article 17), and Articles 21–23 Brussels Convention.[396]

As far as the substantive elements of such worldwide injunctions[397] are concerned, these have been settled, together with the various safeguards for respondents, and provisos incumbent on applicants. Such a worldwide order is now embodied as an example in what is to be termed a 'freezing injunction' in PD25 of the 1998 Civil Procedure Rules.[398] This represents the culmination of judicial creativity, and expansion of such orders since the late 1980's, in particular at Court of Appeal level, in and after the case of *Babanhaft International Co. S.A. v Bassatne and another.*[399]

As far as the effects of such orders are concerned, as has been argued earlier, their unique *in personam* nature takes them outside the type of provisionally enforceable orders for interim payments—and capable of founding court proceedings for execution—exemplified by orders in 'kort geding' or *référé-provision* actions, such as occurred in regard to the former in *Van Uden Maritime* and *Hans Herman Mietz*. The additional restrictions[400] now to be placed on such orders in those cases, while granting 'provisional, including protective relief' (under Article 24 and national law) should, it is submitted,[401] simply not apply to (worldwide) *Mareva*/freezing injunctions.

What *Van Uden Maritime* has demanded of these freezing orders granted under Article 24's jurisdiction, however, is 'a real connecting link between the subject-matter of the measures sought'[402] and the English court's jurisdiction: hence the renewed and invigorated focus on section 25(2) of the 1982 Act. Subsection (2), as we have seen, may prohibit the grant of an application under section 25(1) for interim relief, if, in the court's opinion, 'the fact that [it] has no jurisdiction apart from this section in relation to the subject-matter of the proceedings in question makes it inexpedient for the court to grant it.'[403]

Such cases that have considered interim relief under the Convention—*Alltrans Inc v Interdom Holdings Ltd (Johnson Stevens Agencies Ltd and others, third parties)*,[404] *Republic of Haiti and others v Duvalier and others*,[405] *S & T Bautrading*

---

[395] An example of this *OLG Düsseldorf* 29.5.2000 (2000) *IPRax* 547, (2001) *RIW* 380, regarding Article 16(1)(b).

[396] Article 24 makes it reasonably clear too that, in this case, the 'other' court is the one with full jurisdiction on the merits.

[397] Colman, A. and Lyon, V. *The Practice and Procedure of the Commercial Court*, 1995, at p.101 onwards.

[398] *Civil Procedure*, Volume 1, Autumn 2001, 2001, at p.472, onwards.

[399] [1989] 2 WLR 232, CA.

[400] [1998] ECR I–7091, at p.7135, para. 40, over and above the 'real connecting link'.

[401] *OLG München* (2000) *RIW* 464 now appears to agree, at p.465.

[402] [1998] ECR I-7091, at p.7135; Briggs, 2002, at p.90.

[403] A clearer paraphrased version is provided by Lord Bingham of Cornhill CJ in *Crédit Suisse Fides Trust SA v Cuoghi* [1998] QB 818, at p.831.

[404] [1991] 4 All ER 458, CA.

[405] [1990] 1 QB 202, CA; although Staughton LJ did mention s 25(2) in the 'discretion' section of his judgment, at pp.215–17.

v Nordling[406] and *X v Y and another*[407]—did not consider the inexpediency or otherwise of the applications with any direct precision.

However, in *Crédit Suisse Fides Trust SA v Cuoghi*,[408] the ruling of the Court of Appeal is notable for its stance on the potential ambit of section 25(2). The facts have been rehearsed, above. The main argument before the court centred on the expediency or otherwise of ordering a worldwide *Mareva* injunction and disclosure order against Cuoghi, a Swiss national, domiciled and resident in England, in aid of substantive fraud proceedings in Switzerland. It was admitted that a similar order,[409] affecting the disclosure of assets outside the (Swiss) jurisdiction was unavailable before a Swiss court.

The result of the Court's views is, it seems, twofold, discussed in (A) and (B):

(A) The first finding in *Cuoghi*—it would (normally) be 'inexpedient' under section 25(2) to grant relief such as a *Mareva* injunction/freezing or disclosure order in aid of Brussels/Lugano proceedings on the merits: (i) where the 'primary court' has similar remedies available to it but has refused to grant them;[410] and/or (ii) where auch orders may otherwise obstruct or hamper the case in the foreign court, or result in inconsistent[411] or overlapping orders.

These above two aspects in (i) and (ii) have been further discussed, in *obiter*[412] observations, in a relatively recent, yet still pre-*Van Uden Maritime*, Court of Appeal decision in *Refco Inc. and another v Eastern Trading Co. and others*.[413] The case was not concerned with jurisdiction under Article 24—the court seised of the merits being a non-Contracting State court, in the USA—but under the extension to section 25 CJJA 1982's ambit, brought about by the Civil Jurisdiction and Judgments Act 1982 (Interim Relief) Order 1997.[414] The case is nonetheless of interest to applications under Article 24 and section 25(2) in Convention cases because Morritt LJ did not see why 'there should be any different approach in non-Convention country cases'[415] (and presumably *vice-versa*).

As to the first aspect (i) in *Refco Inc.*, above—that the primary court has similar remedies to those applied for here, but has declined to exercise them—Potter

---

[406] [1997] 3 All ER 718, CA.

[407] [1990] 1 QB 220 (A. Diamond QC).

[408] [1998] Q.B. 818, CA, (Lord Bingham of Cornhill CJ, Millett and Potter LJJ).

[409] Irrelevant under s 27 CJJA 1982 in Scotland: *Stancroft Securities Ltd v McDowell* (1990) *SLT* 746, at p.748; but compare the position under s 28 CJJA 1982 in *Union Carbide Corporation v BP Chemicals Ltd* (1995) *SLT* 972, at p.977.

[410] Millett LJ at p.829; Lord Bingham at pp.831–32. This aspect was discussed in the later case of *Refco Inc. and another v Eastern Trading Co. and others* [1999] 1 Lloyd's Rep. 159, CA, discussed on this page.

[411] *State of Brunei Darussalam v Bolkiah*, *The Times*, 5.9.2000, Ch.D. (Jacob J): inconsistent orders under s 25 CJJA 1982 should generally be avoided.

[412] The applicant Refco, counterclaimant in the Illinois proceedings, could not show that there would be a real risk of the dissipation of the respondents' English-based assets.

[413] [1999] 1 Lloyd's Rep. 159.

[414] S.I. 1997/302, in force 1.4.1997; for Scotland The Civil Jurisdiction and Judgments Act 1982 (Provisional and Protective Measures) (Scotland) Order 1997 SI 1997/2780.

[415] [1999] 1 Lloyd's Rep. 159, at p.172.

LJ[416] did not think that this, in some absolute way, made an application in England automatically 'inexpedient' under section 25(2).[417] For him, the question becomes whether the primary court would view the English application as an aid, or an hindrance, to its own proceedings. In the case before them, there was, unusually, evidence from a judge in Illinois conceding that the court there on the merits would be unconcerned with any interlocutory activity before the English court. Morritt LJ also agreed that any rejection to exercise similar remedies before the primary court necessarily (always) rendered inexpedient a section 25 application for *Mareva* relief. To him, the reasons, and grounds for the rejection were important.[418] If, in this case, the Illinois court had applied the same principles to the rejected application[419] as would an English court, this would point to inexpediency under section 25(2):[420]

> [i]n that event, the grant by the latter [English court] of relief which has been refused by the former [Illinois court] would be to ignore the subordinate role of the [English court] and to set up conflicting decisions.[421]

As to (ii), above—the risk of treading on the toes of the foreign court[422]—Potter LJ entirely agreed[423] with the statements to this effect by Lord Cornhill of Bingham CJ in *Cuoghi*. By implication so, too, did Morritt LJ:

> the grant of interim relief here would not trench at all on the management of the case in Illinois . . .[424]

(B) The second finding in *Cuoghi*—it would not be inexpedient to grant such injunctions where the *in personam* jurisdiction of the English court can be invoked against a respondent as a result of his/her presence, residence, or domicile in England,[425] whose

---

[416] At first instance, Rix J, and in the Court of Appeal, Millett LJ, did not concur with this view; Millett LJ thought it a very significant factor, pointing therefore towards inexpediency, that an English court would be granting relief where the primary court would not, even against one of its residents, at p.174, and at p.175.

[417] Also in *Ryan v Friction Dynamics Ltd* 2.6.2000, *Times Law Reports*, 14 June 2000 459 (Neuberger J).

[418] [1999] 1 Lloyd's Rep. 159, at p.173.

[419] It had not; the application was rejected because 'it sought advice from the Court', *ibid*.

[420] Not always so—the High Court could grant a freezing order even where foreign court had refused to do so: *Ryan v Friction Dynamics Ltd*; cf *Union Carbide Corporation v BP Chemicals Ltd* (1995) SLT 972, at pp.976–77 (Lord President (Hope)), and at p.979 (Lord Cullen) on s 28 CJJA 1982: the court must be careful 'not to be drawn into a situation . . . to grant a discretionary remedy which the other court, possessed of a similar power . . . would not provide in the same circumstances.'

[421] *Ibid*.

[422] Where overlapping injunctions have been made (ie abroad, *and* applied for in England), the English order should in normal circumstances replicate the foreign order: *Ryan v Friction Dynamics Ltd* (Neuberger J).

[423] At p.174.

[424] At pp.173–74.

[425] At p.829 (Millett LJ); at p.832 (Lord Bingham CJ).

courts [are] best able to make their orders effective . . . ; in relation to orders *in personam*, including orders for disclosure, this means the courts of the state where the person enjoined resides.[426]

Clearly, then, in *Cuoghi*, the case for exercise of the discretion to refuse under section 25(2) would have been that much stronger had Cuoghi been domiciled in another Contracting State:

> It is a strong thing to restrain a defendant who is not resident within the jurisdiction from disposing of assets outside the jurisdiction.[427]

But this is not to say categorically that a worldwide *Mareva*/freezing injunction will never[428] be granted in aid of foreign proceedings under Article 24 and/or section 25 CJJA 1982, against a respondent domiciled outside the United Kingdom:[429] exceptional cases may exist, such as in *Republic of Haiti and others v Duvalier and others*.[430] Some think[431] the current position in England will remain unaffected by *Van Uden Maritime*. The true position may lie somewhere in between: future cases based on facts similar to those in *Republic of Haiti* and *X v Y* will require more careful assessment, and re-appraisal, in the light of *Van Uden Maritime* and section 25(2). After all, Millett LJ had observed in *Cuoghi* that '[i]t would be a very different matter if we were being asked to make a worldwide order against [Mr Cuoghi's alleged co-conspirator] Mr Voellmin, [domiciled in Switzerland].'[432]

The seriousness of the charges and case against the respondent and/or co-conspirators in the foreign forum, the vast sums involved in any alleged wrongdoing, and/or the commercial sophistication and (proven or suspected) nefariousness[433] of any prospective respondent may, in the English court's view, continue to override any concerns as to section 25(2)'s inexpediency, or for that matter, the requirements of a *Van Uden Maritime* 'real connecting link'[434] to the English court.

---

[426] At p.827; the State where the person resides is presumably therefore the best place to ensure that an *in personam* order is complied with.

[427] At p.827; strengthened by *Van Uden Maritime*, previous footnote.

[428] *Contra* Millett LJ in *Refco*, expressing the minority *obiter* opinion, who thought that in such cases as these, the 'long-arm jurisdiction against foreign residents' under s 25(1) may well be inexpedient, especially if the primary court would have rejected a similar application against one of its own citizens, at p.174; also *Union Carbide Corporation v BP Chemicals Ltd* (1995) *SLT* 972, at p.977.

[429] *Quaere*, whether the domicile of the respondent in, alternatively, a non-Contracting State or a Contracting State may well alter the balance of expediency, and any factors relevant to its determination.

[430] [1990] 1 QB 202, CA, the extent and nefarious nature of the alleged fraud was an important factor in the English court's buttressing rôle to litigation abroad; Peel E. (1998) *YEL* 689, at pp.696 98.

[431] *Dicey and Morris, The Conflict of Laws*, 13th edn., 2000, at p.193, para. 8–027.

[432] [1998] QB 818, at p.829.

[433] Neuberger J in *Ryan v Friction Dynamics Ltd*, thought factors such as comity and the need to discourage international fraud, may override s 25 (2) concerns—it appears a court will have to delve into the merits to a certain extent, to undergo the s 25(2) inexpediency enquiry.

[434] Such a link has been shown to exist where England is the only effective jurisdiction available to make such freezing/disclosure orders, *Dicey and Morris*, 13th edn., 2000, at p.193, para. 8–027.

In conclusion therefore, it appears as yet that *Van Uden Maritime* will have little[435] direct impact on the practice of granting (worldwide) *Mareva* relief and ancillary disclosure orders. What the case may, or should have done, is to focus the minds of judges more sharply on to an examination of 'inexpediency' under section 25(2) of the CJJA 1982.

3.3.5   The possible consequences of *Van Uden Maritime* on the *lis pendens* provisions in Articles 21/22[436]

Van Uden Maritime has demonstrated that a court with jurisdiction 'on the substance'[437] of a case under one of the provisions of Title II, Articles 2, 5–18, 'also'[438] has jurisdiction to order unfettered[439] provisional measures. Yet where, for example, an arbitration clause deprives a court, or any court, under Article 1(4), of jurisdiction on the merits, no jurisdiction logically exists under Title II to order such measures, and the special regime in Article 24 must[440] be resorted to.

Article 21 does, and Article 22 may, under the conditions described in those articles,[441] deprive one court which may potentially take 'merits' jurisdiction and order unfettered interim relief, if another Contracting State court is 'seised' earlier in time. If 'the same cause of action'—for example, for a negative declaration of liability to pay contractual consideration—is already underway in Germany on Article 2 grounds, it is all but unarguable that one party cannot[442] thereafter claim for payment by means of 'kort geding' proceedings in the Netherlands on the

---

[435]   The attitude expressed by Leggatt LJ in *Alltrans Inc v Interdom Holdings Ltd (Johnson Stevens Agencies Ltd and others, third parties)* [1991] 4 All ER 458, CA, at p.469, that the *fons et origo* of interim relief applications is s 25 and not Article 24, perhaps will soften *Van Uden Maritime*'s impact.

[436]   For a discussion of the problem under Article 10 (Swiss) IPRG, which is in all material respects, drafted identically to Article 24, Walter, G. 'Die internationale Zuständigkeit schweizerischer Gerichte für 'vorsorgliche Massnahmen'- oder: Article 10 IPRG und seine Geheimnisse' (1992) *AJP* 61, esp. p.63.

[437]   [1998] ECR I–7091, at p.7131, para. 22; *District Court of the Hague* 6.2.2001 *Therex Limited Partnership v Medtronic BV* [2001] *EIPR* N–121; Thomas J in *Winter Maritime Ltd v North End Oil Ltd (The 'Winter')* [2000] 2 Lloyd's Rep. 298, at p.302 has observed that Articles 21/22 will *normally* have no application in the Article 24 court, *quaere* whether first or second seised, as 'the provisional measures . . . taken will not be determining anything of a substantive nature between the parties'; but the Article 24 court may, on occasion, determine issues of substance, a particularly strong suggestion that Articles 21/22 *should apply* to the Article 24 court (second seised) ordering a *référé-provision*.

[438]   [1998] ECR I–7091, at p.7131, para. 22.

[439]   *Ibid.*, at para. 20; contrast this with its somewhat more limited power to order 'provisional, including protective measures' under national jurisdiction and Article 24, paras. 40, and 47.

[440]   *Ibid.*, at para. 25.

[441]   Article 21 requires any court seised second (except possibly with exclusive jurisdiction under Article 16: *Overseas Union Insurance Ltd & Others v New Hampshire Insurance Company* (351/89) [1991] ECR I–3317, and Article 17 in England *Continental Bank N.A. v Aeakos* [1994] 1 WLR 588) to decline jurisdiction if an action with the same 'cause of action' between 'the same parties' is definitively pending in the court first seised, or may do so, if proceedings in both courts are 'related', under Article 22— *The Maciej Rataj* (C-406/92) [1994] ECR I–5439; also *OT Africa Line Ltd v Hijazy and others (The 'Kribi')* [2001] CLC 148, at p.162 (Aikens J).

[442]   *Ibid.*, by analogy, Article 24 would have to be used.

ground that the payment was to be made (in Amsterdam) under Article 5(1). Article 21 would appear to prohibit this.[443]

Instead of claiming payment on the merits, under Article 5(1), an applicant attempts an application by 'kort geding' under Article 24 and Dutch national procedural law.[444] Would either Article 21 or Article 22 prevent this? Clearly not,[445] as the express wording of Article 24 points to the situation where 'under this Convention, the courts of another Contracting State have jurisdiction as to the substance of the matter'.[446]

The problem of the 'kort geding'/*référé-provision* application under Article 24 for interim payment of contractual consideration is that it is so similar to an action on the merits as to attract the attention of Article 21,[447] should a negative declaration action already be underway in another Contracting State.

The relationship of Article 21 to Article 24 should be interpreted to mean that a court 'second seised', under Article 24, should decline jurisdiction (even if such jurisdiction is technically not 'on the merits') when the Article 24 provisional measure potentially may involve the 'same cause of action'[448] as a prior action strictly on the merits elsewhere. An Article 24 'kort geding'/*référé-provision* application for payment of contractual consideration should be held to have the same 'objet'[449] as a declaration of non-liability. Common sense would suggest that an Article 24 applicant cannot undermine a negative declaration action already underway in a court of another Contracting State first seised on the merits, by an application for the disputed amount in the *forum actoris*, under national law. Article 21 ought to prevent this.[450]

Changing the facts, could the same applicant, whether or not substantive proceedings were underway in Germany, simultaneously apply for: a 'kort geding' interim payment under Article 126(3) of the Dutch Code of Civil Procedure; a *Mareva*/freezing injunction[451] in England and Wales under section 25 CJJA 1982 and CPR 6.20(4) and CPR 25.1(f), for a *référé-provision* in France for the same

---

[443]   *The Maciej Rataj* (C-406/92) [1994] ECR I–5439.

[444]   As happened in *Van Uden Maritime BV* (C-391/95) [1998] ECR I–7091.

[445]   The 'classic' view of Article 24 as a shield—national jurisdiction under Article 24 is outside the regime of Title II, including presumably Articles 21/22; *contra* Gerhard, F. *L'exécution forcée transfrontière des injonctions extraterritoriales non pécuniaires en droit privé*, 2000, at p.146, where both actions initiated by the claimant, as in *Cuoghi* itself.

[446]   The result would be an unsightly rush to judgment which the 'kort geding' judgment creditor would undoubtedly win, until the (eventually) successful applicant for a negative declaration could insist on repayment of the amount awarded in the 'kort geding'—a highly unsatisfactory result.

[447]   This view confirmed in *Winter Maritime Ltd v North End Oil Ltd (The 'Winter')* [2000] 2 Lloyd's Rep. 298, at p.302, col.2 (Thomas J).

[448]   For the meaning of this term, *Gubisch v Palumbo* (144/86) [1987] ECR 4861 and *The Maciej Rataj* (C-406/92) [1994] ECR I–5439; cf *The 'Winter'* [2000] 2 Lloyd's Rep. 298, at p.302, where 'substantive matters in respect of which the decision will be decisive . . .'.

[449]   *The Maciej Rataj* (C-406/92) [1994] ECR I–5439.

[450]   If Article 21 is not confined to Article 2 actions 'on the merits'.

[451]   There would probably be no *lis pendens* problem in England here under Article 21 in the case of a *Mareva* injunction.

contractual consideration under Article 809(2) NCPC on the (possible) basis of Article 46(3) NCPC;[452] and finally for similar relief in Belgium under either Article 635(5), or Article 638 of the Belgian *Code Judiciare*? Having obtained all or any of these interim measures, could[453] the applicant then have them recognised and enforced[454] in Germany, or in any other, or all, Contracting States?[455]

Before this stage under Title III is reached,[456] could a respondent successfully advance a plea of *lis pendens* under Articles 21/22 in any of the subsequent courts applied to under Article 24? In other words, does section 8, regulating *lis pendens*, apply to Article 24 in section 9 at all?

The general tenor of *Van Uden Maritime* would seem to imply that it would not. In para. 20 of the judgment, the Court states that Article 24 'adds a rule of jurisdiction falling outside[457] the system set out in Article 2, and 5 to 18',[458] i.e. what was previously assumed (rightly or wrongly) to be the (entire)[459] Convention jurisdiction system. On the other hand, the Court was keen to stress[460] its earlier jurisprudence in *Jacques de Cavel v Luise de Cavel*[461] that 'the nature of the rights which [the Article 24 measures] serve to protect'[462] must fall with the scope *ratione materiae* of the Convention. To discover this, necessitates a court examining the underlying cause of action ('the nature of the rights') which must fall within Article 1, first sentence, and outside Article 1, second sentence, and Article 1(1)–(4).

---

[452] Note, the exorbitant jurisdiction in Article 14 *Code Civil* is only available to French nationals; *Van Uden Maritime*'s effect is that Article 2 II and, on its wording, Article 4 II are inapplicable to jurisdiction under Article 24.

[453] Note, disregard for the jurisdictional provisions, except in Sections 3, 4, 5, in Title II, is no bar to enforcement of a 'normal' judgment; yet Article 24 is a special separate regime vis-à-vis Title II, and is not mentioned in Article 28 I.

[454] Below, at pp.354–355, for an Article 27(1) public policy argument (breach of Community law) and the non-application of Article 28 III; a French court has used this ground in the past *TGI de Troyes* 4.10.1978, *Société anonyme Almacoa c/ Société anonyme Etablissements Moteurs Cères*, (1979) *Gaz. Pal.*, Juris., p.131 to deny enforcement; but not permitted now, *SA Régie Nationale des Usines Renault v SpA Maxicar and Orazio Formento* (C-38/98) [2000] ECR I–2973, below, chapter 4, at pp.402 *et seq.*

[455] Assuming all the application hearings were *inter partes*—*Bernard Denilauer v S.n.c. Couchet Frères* (C-125/79) [1980] ECR 1553; *Normaco v Lundman*, Ch. D, 6.1.1999, (Carnwath, J); note, care must be taken in *not* applying first to a jurisdiction under Art.24 that may possibly be (procedurally) unreceptive, or the most unreceptive, to an application for provisional measures—*Italian Leather SpA v WECO Polstermöbel GmbH & Co.* (C-80/00), [2000] OJ C149/22, AG Léger's opinion 21.2.2002, pending (an unfavourable, irreconcilable *res judicata* may be created under Article 27(3)/Article 34(3) Brussels I Regulation).

[456] On this aspect and the recent reference in *Hans-Hermann Mietz v Intership Yachting Sneek B.V.* (C-99/96) [1999] ECR I–2277, below, at pp.350–351.

[457] This would seem to mean that the Article 24 court can disregard Articles 11, 13, 14 and 16 for jurisdictional purposes, main text above pp.312–313—paras. 24 and 24 by analogy—an Article 24 court could not have jurisdiction on the merits if another court was exclusively competent under Article 16. Does the same follow for Title III, and especially Article 28 III, *Hans-Hermann Mietz v Intership Yachting Sneek B.V.* (C-99/96) [1999] ECR I–2277?

[458] [1998] ECR I–7091, at p.7130.

[459] With isolated exceptions, such as Article 57 of the Conventions.

[460] Paras. 30 and 34.

[461] *Jacques de Cavel v Luise de Cavel* (C-143/78) [1979] ECR 1055.

[462] *Ibid.*, at p.1066, para. 8.

If, in interim relief proceedings under Article 24, this process has to be undergone for Article 1 in each Contracting State court applied to, is there any logic for not applying also Articles 21/22? If a 'kort geding' and a *référé-provision* both award the exact same amount for the same contractual consideration, the nature of the rights, and undeniably, the 'cause of action'[463] under Article 21 are the same.[464] The Article 24 court 'second seised' should, it seems, decline jurisdiction.

However, if the Article 21/22 duty to decline is applicable to Articles 2, 5–18 'merits jurisdiction', the obligation under any *lis pendens* provision is not entirely clear with regard to Article 24. If, as *Van Uden Maritime* suggests, Article 24 is indeed a special provision, it should theoretically be possible to seise as many Contracting State jurisdictions as make available interim payment relief[465] under expansive, exorbitant grounds of jurisdiction, at least until one such order is completed by domestic execution. This is clearly unwarranted; the opportunities for harassing respondents that such a release from Articles 21/22 represents, should be curtailed. Articles 21/22 should prevent such a situation.

3.4 HOW, IF AT ALL, MAY *VAN UDEN MARITIME* AND *HANS HERMAN MIETZ* AFFECT THE GERMAN PRACTICE OF GRANTING INTERIM RELIEF?

3.4.1 §919 ZPO jurisdiction and the availability of, *inter alia*, §23 ZPO

Jurisdiction to order an *Arrest*, as we have seen, lies either with the court on the merits, or the local *Amtsgericht*. *Van Uden Maritime* has now made it clear that jurisdiction under Article 24 and national law is not 'merits' jurisdiction under Title II. The case could therefore be said to have ended the confusion as to whether a German court can henceforward consider itself as a fictitious 'Gericht der Hauptsache'[466] (i.e. on the merits). As the alternative base of jurisdiction under §919 ZPO is a *forum arresti* in any event, the asset-specific nature, and proximity requirements of *Van Uden Maritime* may not be affected.

---

[463] If 'cause of action' and proceedings only refer to merits jurisdiction, the same could not be said for an English *Mareva* injunction; *The 'Winter'* [2000] 2 Lloyd's Rep. 298, at p.302; this case does envisage Articles 21/22 applying under Article 24, when questions of a 'cause of action' are implicated in both *fora*.

[464] *Contra*, Walter, (1992) *AJP* 61, at p.63: under Article 24 'können gleichzeitig bei Gerichten verschiedener Staaten vorläufige Massnahmen beantragt werden, ohne dass dem Article 21 des Übereinkommens entgegenstünde'('provisional measures can be applied for simultaneously to courts in various states without Article 21 standing in their way').

[465] According to Thomas J in *The 'Winter'* [2000] 2 Lloyd's Rep. 298, if substantive matters may be decided in the 'second seised' Article 24 court, Articles 21/22 should in principle apply, at p.302.

[466] By-passed by the case reviewed, below, following page; §§23, and 919 ZPO duplicate the *forum arresti* in any event; *OLG Karlsruhe* 2.10.2001 (2002) *IPRax* p.VI, (2002) *RIW* 151.

3.4.2 §937 ZPO jurisdiction and the availability of, *inter alia*, §23 ZPO [467]

The real change effected by *Van Uden Maritime* to German practice may well result from the unique[468] 'Gericht der Hauptsache'[469] base in German procedure to order interim injunctions under §937 ZPO. The German courts will have to confront the issue of their jurisdiction as the courts (fictitiously) 'on the merits', when *ex hypothesi*, *Van Uden Maritime* has shown that Article 24's jurisdiction is clearly not such jurisdiction. This occurred in *OLG Düsseldorf* 28.1.1999.[470] In this case, the applicant (for a prohibitory injunction against a Spanish Co. from claiming under a letter of guarantee) was able to rely on §23 ZPO, in conjunction with the above jurisdictional provision. While stating that jurisdiction under Article 24 did not exclude the use of exorbitant grounds of jurisdiction, unfortunately no mention was made of *Van Uden Maritime*. The issue of the 'Gericht der Hauptsache' was touched on, but glossed over, simply by stating that Article 24 jurisdiction would admit of no restriction, apparently not even those of national law:

> Die Regelung [Article 24] soll gewährleisten, daß das nationale Zuständigkeitsrecht auf dem Gebiet des einstweiligen Rechtsschutzes nicht beschnitten wird.[471]

The issue of the 'Gericht der Hauptsache' did not need to be dealt with head on in this case, as jurisdiction of the German courts was given in any event from §23 ZPO. Whether as a result of *Van Uden Maritime* or otherwise, it is likely that in the area of provisional and protective measures, we are likely to see an increase, not only in Germany, of the use of 'exorbitant', and other, bases of jurisdiction, that the Convention has so successfully sought to repress in courts with jurisdiction on the merits.

---

[467] Obviously, on the facts of a particular case, if the German court cannot find a provision of its autonomous code, the ZPO, otherwise applicable under Article 24, there is no jurisdiction in any event: no jurisdiction under, *inter alia*, § 23 ZPO and none therefore under Article 24 in *OLG Karlsruhe* 10.11.1997 IPRspr. (1997) Nr. 161, nor in *OLG Düsseldorf* 29.5.2000 (2000) *IPRax* 547, (2001) *RIW* 380; *Hof 's-Gravenhage* 17.7.2000 *F.G.H. Abbing tegen Sibomat N.V.* 2001 *NJ* Nr.87, p.543; jurisdiction, however, in *OLG Karlsruhe* 2.10.2001 (2002) *IPRax* p.VI, (2002) *RIW* 151.

[469] The Dutch courts have held under a similar court 'on the merits' jurisdiction, that no jurisdiction under Article 24 exists when another Contracting State court does in fact have jurisdiction on the merits under the Convention (similar to the position in UK before 1987 and *The Siskina* [1979] AC 210, HL: *Hof 's-Gravenhage* 17.7.2000 *F.G.H. Abbing tegen Sibomat N.V.* 2001 *NJ* Nr.87, p.543.

[470] (1999) *RIW* 873.

[471] ('The rule [Article 24] should guarantee that the national jurisdictional law in the area of provisional measures is not curtailed'), at p.874.

3.5   HOW, IF AT ALL, *VAN UDEN MARITIME* AND *HANS HERMAN MIETZ* AFFECT THE FRENCH PRACTICE OF GRANTING INTERIM RELIEF?

As regards the jurisdictional aspects of *Van Uden Maritime*, the French practice of combining the provisions of the NCPC, *inter alia*, Articles 809(2) and 873(2), with earlier articles governing internal jurisdiction, together with Article 14 *Code civil*, has been sanctioned by the European Court in *Van Uden Maritime*. *Bachy c/ Soc. Belbetoes*[472] has shown that the *Cour de Cassation* did not censure that part of the appeal court's judgment dealing with jurisdiction, under Article 873(2) NCPC (in conjunction with, presumably,[473] Article 14 *Code Civil*, and/or Article 46(2) NCPC) to order a *provision* against a Portuguese company for the payment of invoices. What *Van Uden Maritime* may have done—and is borne out in the decision in *Bachy*—is to confine[474] enforcement of the *provision* to assets of the defendant located in France, if any. Failure to do this may well now result in a successful *cassation* against the grant of such a measure.

Part II

3.6   'PROVISIONAL, INCLUDING PROTECTIVE MEASURES' THEMSELVES, AND THE FRENCH RÉFÉRÉ-PROVISION IN ARTICLE 809(2) NCPC[475]

As will be seen,[476] it is important for a number of reasons, to have a definition, autonomous or otherwise, of the phrase 'provisional, including protective measures' in Article 24. That one is not forthcoming in the Convention itself is no surprise.[477] This omission could, in part, be explained by the remittance of such measures to those 'as may be available' under the law of the Contracting State applied to; national law provides the definition, type and conditions for their grant.[478] That there are national variations in the substantive and procedural

---

[472] *Cassation* 13.4.1999, (1999) *Rev crit* 352, [1999] I.L.Pr. 743.

[473] *Mietz* has ruled that we may make such a presumption.

[474] *OLG München* (2000) *RIW* 464 will *not* regard a cross-border *provision* as an Article 25 'judgment' under Title III.

[475] For detailed explanation of this jurisdiction the *Nouveau Code de Procedure Civile* should be consulted: Dalloz, 93ème éd., 2001, at p.409 following; for a comparative European excursus into interim relief generally Morbach, B. *Einstweiliger Rechtsschutz in Zivilsachen—Eine rechtsvergleichende Untersuchung*, 1988, and Eilers, 1991, at pp.67–199.

[476] Below, at pp.339–340.

[477] *Industrie Tessili Italiana Como v Dunlop AG* (C-12/76) [1976] ECR 1473-defining the 'place of performance'; *Martin Peters Bauunternehmung GmbH v Zuid Nederlandse Aannemers Vereniging* (C-34/82) [1983] ECR 987 and *Jakob Handte & Co. GmbH v Société Traitements Mecano-Chimiques des Surfaces (TMCS)* (C-26/91) [1992] ECR I–3697-matters relating to a 'contract'; and *Siegfried Zelger v Sebastino Salinitri* (C-129/83) [1984] ECR 2397—providing a definition of 'first seised' for Articles 21/22.

[478] Within the limits set down by the ECJ jurisprudence, including now *Van Uden Maritime*; in England and Wales CPR Part 25, esp. Rule 25.1.

requirements seems to be inevitable. According to Jenard,[479] had the framers tried to harmonise national laws relating to the grant of such measures, and to distil this effort into Article 24 itself, the Convention would never have been completed.

The importance of a unified definition of provisional measures is revealed by the (original)[480] purpose and effect of Article 24 itself: should such relief be applied for in one Contracting State,[481] Article 24 acts as a bar[482] or hurdle[483] to a defendant/respondent's objecting[484] to the jurisdiction of this court. Conversely,

> in any case where the relief does *not* fall within article 24, the defendant *will be* entitled to object to the jurisdiction of [for eg. an English] court . . .[485]

While paying lip-service to the principle that the Convention does not seek to regulate matters of internal Contracting State procedure,[486] it is conducive to the uniform protection of persons within the Contracting States that Article 24's removal of any jurisdictional objection should be available, or indeed imposed, equally throughout all the Contracting States.[487]

Other commentators[488] seek to justify a uniform interpretation from a different viewpoint on Article 24: that the granting court is not fettered,[489] under Article 24, by the earlier provisions of Articles 2, 3 [I] [II], 5–17, 18,[490] but may[491] take

---

[479] Jenard, P. *La Convention de Bruxelles du 27 septembre 1968 et ses prolongements*, Rép. Notarial, 1994, Tome XI, livre VI, 3e partie, 1994, p.156.

[480] *Van Uden Maritime* has shown that Article 24 has another, more aggressive rôle than the one assigned to it here.

[481] '[E]ven though' substantive proceedings are, or may be, pending in another.

[482] Briggs, 1997, at p.300, para. 6.14; *Republic of Haiti and others v Duvalier and others* [1990] 1 QB 202, at p.212 (Staughton LJ); note this bar's removal in the submissions of Deco Line in the referring court in *Van Uden Maritime Africa Line v Kommanditgesellschaft in Firma Deco Line* [1996] I.L.Pr. 269, at p.271 para. [10].

[483] Also *Mietz v Intership Yachting Sneek B.V.* (C-99/96) [1999] ECR I–2277. If there were no 'provisional, including protective measures' under Article 24, Articles 28[I], 13 and 14[II] would have assisted the respondent Mietz, but above, at p.313.

[484] Also Grundmann, S. *Anerkennung und Vollstreckung ausländischer einstweiliger Maßnahmen nach IPRG und Lugano-Übereinkommen*, 1996, p.108: 'Diese Einrede wird jedoch verunmöglicht, wenn sich das Gericht auf eine (aufgrund einer 'misbräuchlichen' Bestimmung des Begriffs der einstweiligen Maßnahme) über Article 24 LugÜ gewonnene Zuständigkeit abstützen kann.'('this objection [to the jurisdiction] can be dismissed when the court may rely on a jurisdiction provided for in Article 24, on the grounds of a misconceived interpretation of the concept of provisional measure').

[485] Briggs, 1997, at pp.300–01, para. 6.14.

[486] *Kongress Agentur Hagen GmbH v Zeehaghe B.V.* (C-365/88) [1990] ECR I–1845.

[487] *Société d'Informatique Service Réalisation Organisation (SISRO) v Ampersand Software BV* (C-432/93) [1995] I–2269, at p.2301, para. 41 has shown us that parties should not enjoy 'greater procedural possibilities' in one Contracting State than another.

[488] Geimer and Schütze, 1997, at p.398.

[489] Note also that these provisional and protective measures also benefit from the simplified recognition and enforcement regime in Title III—*Bernard Denilauer v S.n.c. Couchet Frères* (C-125/79) [1980] ECR 1553 and *Luise de Cavel v Jaques de Cavel* (C-120/79) [1980] ECR 731; and also Heiss, 1987, at p.43.

[490] As announced in *Van Uden Maritime*, above, at p.283, and Proposition A(i) in Part I.

[491] But cannot, under Article 24, if no jurisdiction exists under these autonomous regimes: *OLG Karlsruhe* 10.11.1997 IPRspr. (1997) Nr. 161, *OLG Düsseldorf* 29.5.2000 (2000) *IPRax* 547, (2001) *RIW* 380; *Hof 's-Gravenhage* 17.7.2000 *F.G.H. Abbing tegen Sibomat N.V.* 2001 *NJ* Nr.87, p.543.

jurisdiction under national rules, including those outlawed in Article 3 [I] [II]. If such a drastic remission to national jurisdictional rules[492] is to be countenanced at all, thereby circumventing Article 2 and Articles 5–18, surely it can only occur throughout the Contracting States on the coat-tails of a common definition of 'interim relief' in Article 24:

> Article 24 EuGVÜ eine Durchbrechung der Zuständigkeitsordnung des Übereinkommens vorsieht ... Eine solche muß aber *klar bestimmt sein*, um nicht Rechtsunsicherheit, Ungleichbehandlung[493] und die Umgehung des Übereinkommens zu ermöglichen.[494]

Obviously, too, a uniform interpretation may go some way to relieving what is unavoidable[495] in a system with such diverse procedural devices for interim relief proceedings: forum-shopping[496] for the most effective or comprehensive provisional measures.[497]

---

[492] Heiss, 1987, at p.37 speaking of a 'Durchbrechung des Zuständigkeitskatalogs' of the Convention; *Van Uden Maritime* and *Mietz*, too, have emphasised the potential for a *détournement* of the Convention under Article 24.

[493] A respondent to Article 24 measures in a Contracting State with a restrictive definition of Article 24 would enjoy 'greater procedural possibilities' of objection than a respondent in another (in France, for example).

[494] ('Article 24 of the Brussels Convention provides a way past the jurisdictional provisions of the Convention ... such a way *must however be clearly delineated*, in order not to facilitate legal uncertainty, discrimination and a *détournement* of the Convention') Albrecht, 1991, at p.102; also Damjanovic, D. *Les mesures provisoires ou conservatoires dans le cadre de la Convention de Bruxelles*, 1996, at p.4.

[495] Yet due to this lack of intra-Community coherence, one rule of the *Nouveau Code de Procédure Civile* has almost single-handedly thrown doubt on this *laissez-faire* remittance in Article 24, and had prompted calls for the European Court of Justice to intervene with a Community definition; the 'kort geding' procedure of Dutch law has similar effects, yet, outside intellectual property disputes, had not reached the same level of international notoriety until *Van Uden Maritime*: Brinkhof (1997) *Grur.Int.* 489; Zonderland, P. (1977) *ZZP* 225 and Gauci, (1998) *ICLit* 32; Mousseron, (1998) *IIC* 884; Véron, P. (2001) *JDI* 805, at p.812–13; Barbosa, C. (2001) *IIC* 729, at pp.736–39.

[496] For the relative attractiveness of French procedure, especially Vareilles-Sommières, (1996) *Rev crit* 397, at p.400: 'le plaideur aura alors intérêt à solliciter du juge français une mesure provisoire exécutoire en France, *plutôt qu'attendre le jugement étranger sur le fond* et son exequatur incertain par nos juridictions'('the plaintiff will thus be interested in requesting from the French judge a provisionally enforceable measure in France, rather than awaiting a foreign judgment on the merits and its uncertain enforcement by our jurisdictions'); for the allure of England, *Crédit Suisse Fides Trust SA v Cuoghi* [1998] QB 818, CA and other English cases—*Ryan and another v Friction Dynamics Ltd and others* 2.6.2000, Times Law Reports 14 June 2000 459 (Neuberger J) and *State of Brunei Darussalam v Bolkiah*, The Times, 5.9.2000 (Jacob J).

[497] Also Gaillard, 1993 *SJ* 141, at p.158, para. 33: an applicant may request measures 'dont le droit lui paraîtra le plus favorable à sa cause et à requérir l'exequatur de la décision dans l'Etat de l'exécution de la mesure. Le problème a surtout été débattu relativement à l'institution du référé-provision prévu par le droit français'.

3.6.1   A definition of Article 24's 'provisional, including protective relief'?

Most commentators[498] agree that the procedure for obtaining provisional relief is a necessary antidote to the delays commonly encountered[499] between the initiation of proceedings and final judgment on the merits; indeed, even beyond this, to the processes for its eventual enforcement.[500] Frequently, some sort of pre-judgment or pre-service security measures are applied for swiftly to prevent a recalcitrant opponent from spiriting assets out of the reach of easy domestic enforcement, so backing up any (eventual) trial on the merits. Other measures can include interlocutory injunctions to force, or prevent, a certain conduct that cannot wait on a full trial, or even mean that there will be no full trial. The common thread running through this necessarily vague overview is that these measures are 'provisional' in the sense of being temporary, and prior to, judgment on the merits; 'protective', in the sense of preserving the status quo pending trial and judgment, presupposing that they are granted in support, and anticipation, of a full trial.

This last aspect—of two courts,[501] separated by different functions[502]—is re-inforced in Article 24 itself, and will prove crucial in the review of the *référé-provision*. This cleaving of the two courts' separate rôles, their relationship *inter se*, and the requested court's subordinate, bolstering function, are highlighted by the Swiss commentator, Pellet, thus:

> Mesures provisoires, *accessoires à un procès sur le fond*, [sont] prises dans une procédure rapide et sommaire . . . afin de protéger les droits . . . *jusqu'à décision définitive*.[503] [504]

Albrecht provides quite a succinct and workable definition of provisional including protective measures in Article 24: both as to what they should, and should not accomplish:

> um Streitgegenstand, Beweismittel oder Vermögen . . . bis zur Hauptsacheentscheidung oder zur Vollsteckung . . . zu sichern, zu regeln oder vorläufig zu befriedigen, *ohne in das*

---

[498] Merkt, O., 1993; Albrecht, 1991; Collins, L. *Essays in International Litigation and the Conflict of Laws*, 1994, at p.7.

[499] Meier, I. 'Besondere Vollstreckungstitel nach dem Lugano-Übereinkommen' in Schwander (ed) *Das Lugano-Übereinkommen*, 1990, p.157, at p.159.

[500] Article 39 of the Conventions.

[501] Emphatically on this point Eilers, 1991, at p.193: 'macht der Wortlaut die *Trennung von Hauptsacheverfahren und einstweiligen Verfahren* deutlich' ('the wording makes clear the *separation of proceedings on the merits from interlocutory proceedings*'); also Kaye, P. *Law of the European Judgments Convention*, Vol. 4, 1999, at p.3030.

[502] *Van Uden Maritime* has now demonstrated that there need not be two courts, an action on the merits under Article 2, 5–18 proving impossible in any Contracting State due, *inter alia*, to Article 1(4) arbitration exclusion.

[503] ('provisional measures, incidental to an action on the merits [are] taken in a rapid and summary procedure in order to protect rights until a final decision').

[504] Pellet, V. *Mesures provisionelles: Droit fédérale ou cantonal—Reglementation fédérale des mesures provisionelles et procédure civile cantonale contentieuse*, 1987, at p.4.

Hauptsacheverfahren einzugehen, seine Durchführung unmöglich zu machen oder es zu präjudizieren.[505]

The important aspect, for present purposes, in this definition, is the fact that the requested court should make no pre-emptive value judgment on the merits or demerits of the underlying cause of action[506] on the merits in the main court proceedings under Title II, if any. This, it is submitted, is vital to preserve any application's sobriquet of 'provisional, including protective' relief;[507] additionally it is this aspect, *inter alia,* that singles out the *référé-provision* in Article 809(2) NCPC for special vilification.[508]

The position in England and Wales[509] is complicated[510] by the intercession of section 25 Civil Jurisdiction and Judgments Act 1982, and its definitional subsection (7). The upshot in England, at least, is that an English court may order, under Article 24, 'provisional, including protective measures as may be available under the law of'[511] England; which law encompasses 'interim relief of any kind which the court has power to grant',[512] excepting four cases of relief. Two are (English) statutory[513] exceptions, two from ECJ case law.[514]

Exceptionally therefore, an English court arguably may *not* order any of the following: a warrant for the arrest of property;[515] (it appears) provisions for the

---

[505] ('in order to secure, to control or provisionally satisfy the subject matter of the dispute, the evidence or property, until a decision on the merits or enforcement, *without intruding into the main proceedings* so as to prejudice it or make its prosecution impossible') , Albrecht, 1991, at pp.109–10; not taken up directly by *Van Uden Maritime.*

[506] Now CPR Rule 25.7(1)(c) for orders for interim payments—yet 'inexpediency' is England's watchword under s 25(2) CJJA 1982, above at pp.328–333.

[507] Cf Huet (1993) *JDI* 461 at p.464: 'l'article 24 impose une distinction rigoureuse des mesures provisoires ou conservatoires et des mesures touchant au fond, de sorte qu'une mesure concernant le fond ne peut pas être qualifiée en même temps de mesure provisoire . . .' ('Article 24 imposes a rigorous distinction between provisional or protective measures from those concerning the merits in such a way that a measure on the merits cannot simultaneously be qualified as a provisional measure').

[508] Below section 3.7.

[509] Note powers of Scottish courts under ss 27, 28 CJJA 1982 to order, *inter alia,* inspection of documents—*Iomega Corporation v Myrica (U.K.) Limited* 1998 SC 636.

[510] Briggs, 1997, at p.299.

[511] Article 24—if jurisdiction of the English court is based upon service within the jurisdiction, it is unclear whether s 25 CJJA need be invoked at all, above section 3.3.3(i); CPR 6.20(4) appears to confirm this.

[512] S 25(1) CJJA 1982—for applications made on or after 26.4.1999, CPR Rule 25.1 provides a non-exhaustive (CPR Rule 25.3) list of interim remedies, some of the conditions to the granting of which are ill-drafted and/or unsuitable for use in international, (Article 24) cases—for interim payments, CPR Rule 25.6(1), below, at pp.352–353.

[513] S 25(7)(a) and (b), uncertain as the scope is; cf Court of Session's powers under s 28 CJJA 1982; in operation in *Petter Olsen v Forrest Estate Ltd and others,* 14.6.1994, OH.

[514] As will be seen presently, *Mario Reichert and others v Dresdner Bank AG* (C-261/90) [1992] ECR I–2149 at p.2184, para. 34; *Van Uden Maritime* has added an additional 'Community' restriction to 'provisional, including protective measures' generally (at para. 40), and to interim payments of contractual consideration in particular (at para. 47)—this distinction acknowledged in *OLG München* (2000) *RIW* 464, at p.465, col. 1, above at pp.321–322.

[515] Under s 25(7)(a); controversial, if there is any residual jurisdiction outside s 25.

obtaining of evidence;[516] measures which do not 'maintain or preserve a factual situation pending judgment . . .';[517] nor any measures which do not demonstrate 'the existence of a real connecting link between the subject matter of [those] measures'[518] and the jurisdiction of the court granting them. The ECJ has added a definitional gloss to interim relief, howsoever that phrase may now be diversely interpreted[519] throughout the Contracting States.

3.6.2 The necessity of a Community definition of 'provisional, including protective measures'

(i) Historical precedents?

By way of a short historical aside, it is interesting to investigate the position taken with regard to Britain's bilateral Treaty relations, prior to its EEC accession, with France, Germany and others. If it can be shown that little comment is provoked by the area of the cross-border enforcement of provisional measures under earlier bilateral Conventions, and only appears after February 1973, it may be a safe assertion to state that the Brussels Convention—and esp. its Article 2—may be to blame for the increase in such measures.

A cursory glance at the Orders in Council,[520] made under the Foreign Judgments (Reciprocal Enforcement) Act 1933 shows that judgments from France and Germany were singled out for special treatment. Why should this be so?

The Reciprocal Enforcement of Foreign Judgments Orders for Italy, The Netherlands, Norway and for Belgium[521] each defined the word 'judgment' slightly differently, but in essence, made no mention, nor exclusion, of provisional or protective measures. This is to be contrasted with the definition in the Orders for France and Germany.[522] For France, '[t]he word 'judgment' . . . [did] not

---

[516] s 25(7)(b), again controversial for the same reason; as to whether *Anton Piller*/search orders (under CPR Rule 25.1(h), s 7 Civil Procedure Act 1997) are outlawed, Briggs, 1997, at p.299 para. 6.14; not, it seems, if comment by Murray LJ in *Coca Cola Bottlers (Ulster) Ltd v The Concentrate Manufacturing Co. of Ireland (t/a Seven-up International)*, 6.4.1990, Ch.D., is applied.

[517] Briggs (1992) YEL 657, at p.663, paraphrasing; the operative phrase from the ECJ decision in *Reichert* in full, with added emphasis is, at p.2184, para. 34: 'measures which, in matters within the scope of the Convention, *are intended to preserve a factual or legal situation so as to safeguard rights* the recognition of which is sought *elsewhere from the court having jurisdiction as to the substance of the matter.*' This seems to have been overlooked somewhat in *Van Uden Maritime.*

[518] *Van Uden Maritime*, [1998] ECR I–7091, at p.7135, para. 40 together with conditions that preserve their provisional character.

[519] Such as Huet the reviewer of *Van Uden Maritime*—only measures against property in France, (1999) *JDI* 613, at p.621.

[520] Now reduced almost to the point of extinction by the Brussels and Lugano Conventions.

[521] Of 1973, S.I. 1973/1894, Sch.1 Article 1(2); of 1969, S.I. 1969/1063, Sch.1 Article 1(2); of 1962, S.I. 1962/636, Sch.1 Article 1(2); of 1936, S.I. 1936/1169, Sch.1 Article 1(4) respectively.

[522] Of 1936, S.I. 1936/609, Sch.1 Article 1(4), (incidentally the same year as Belgium, but with a different definitional treatment); and of 1961, S.I. 1961/1199, Sch.1 Article 1(3), respectively.

include (in particular) provisional, interlocutory or preparatory judgments';[523] for Germany it did not include 'orders for anticipatory seizure (Arrestbefehle), or other decisions by which only a provisional security is obtained for a claim *or other interlocutory orders*'.[524] Why should it be that the negotiators of these Conventions were aware of a special danger of cross-border measures with respect to France and Germany,[525] if such measures had not already attained a certain level of notoriety within and without those countries?[526]

What is therefore all the more striking is the drafting of other bilateral Conventions[527] of the six original Brussels Convention Contracting States *inter se*. A good example is the 1962 Recognition and Enforcement Convention between Germany and the Netherlands.[528] Its Article 1(1)[529] expressly included German 'Arreste und einstweilige Verfügungen' in its judgment-defining section; in addition, its Article 18(2), like Article 24 Brussels Convention, provided for the case[530] that provisional measures could be granted despite full merits jurisdiction belonging to the courts in the other Contracting State Party.[531]

---

[523] Article 1(4).

[524] Article 1(3), for the catch-all phrase, passed over with little comment concerning their exclusion in 1971 by Geimer and Schütze *Internationale Urteilsanerkennung*—Band. II, at p.363, para. 5.

[525] The addition of such an exclusionary definition is curious for Germany, unless the intention of the bilateral Convention was to outlaw the international *Mahnverfahren* procedure.

[526] The revealing comment on Article 1(4) of the Anglo-French Convention by Gutteridge, H-C. 'La Convention Franco-Britannique pour l'exécution réciproque des jugements' (1937) *Rev Crit* 369, at p.377: 'C'est là une mesure de sauvegarde qui . . . n'a pas besoin d'être commentée, car jamais un pays ne fera exécuter les jugements provisoires des tribunaux d'un autre pays' ('Here is a protective measure that needs no comment, because one country will never enforce provisional judgments of the courts of another'); no comment on the article by Audinet, E. 'L'exécution des jugements étrangers en Angleterre d'après la loi du 13 avril 1933 et la convention franco-britannique du 18 janvier 1934' (1935) *JDI* 805.

[527] Note, as early as 1899, the Convention between Belgium and France relative to the Enforcement of Judgments, Parry (ed) *Consolidated Treaty Series*, 187 (1898–1899), p.378, Article 9. That the furore over cross-border relief seems only to have arisen since 1973 strongly suggests the French orders *en référé* under Article 809(2) NCPC in conjunction with Article 24 of the Brussels Convention are to blame.

[528] BGBl.1965, II, 27 at p.27 and p.32; for an overview of these and other Conventions Al Mulla, H. *The recognition and enforcement of foreign civil and commercial judgments under multilateral and bilateral conventions*, Ph.D Thesis, Cambridge University.

[529] Additionally, Article 1(1) of the 1958 Recognition and Enforcement Convention between Germany and Belgium, BGBl. 1959, II, 766 explicitly states that '. . . einstweilige Anordnungen, die auf eine Geldleistung lauten, anerkannt [werden]'('provisional orders, granting pecuniary performance are to be recognised'); again, its Article 15(2) is also almost identical to Article 24 Brussels Convention.

[530] Despite a refusal ground of two inconsistent judgments, similar to Article 27(3).

[531] Apart from the requirement of urgency, Article 18(1)'s wording bears an uncanny resemblance to Article 24 Brussels Convention: 'Jedoch können die zuständigen Behörden jedes Staates *in Eilfällen* die in ihrem innerstaatlichen Recht vorgesehenen einstweiligen Maßnahmen anordnen, einschließlich solcher, die auf eine Sicherung gerichtet sind, und zwar ohne Rücksicht darauf, welches Gericht mit der Hauptsache befaßt ist.'('Nonetheless, the competent authorities of each State may, *in urgent cases*, order provisional measures as provided for in their internal law, including those granting a seisure, irrespective of what court is seised on the merits').

From this brief glimpse, historical precedent exists for the possibility of cross-border exchange[532] of interim relief. No excuse remains, either for the (arguably incomplete) drafting of Article 24[533] or Article 25,[534] nor for the surprise that, for example, French interlocutory judgments affecting foreign assets were sought under the Brussels Convention in France.[535] It is true that Article 809(2) NCPC only came to the fore[536] after the Convention's coming into force, yet the drafters ought to have been alive to the possibility of the 'exportability' of provisional measures. No doubt insufficient attention[537] was paid to the short-circuiting effects that certain national law provisions might have had; provisions which, in the heady days of integration, were not sought to be regulated by the Brussels Convention in any event.

(ii)   The current position today

By the time of writing, seven[538] cases of the ECJ will have dealt with, or touched on, interim relief under Article 24,[539] with varying degrees of relevance: from the *De Cavel*[540] cases to *Mario Reichert and others v Dresdner Bank AG*,[541] *Van Uden Maritime Africa Line v Kommanditgesellschaft in Firma Deco Line*,[542] and *Hans-Hermann Mietz v Intership Yachting Sneek B.V.*[543] At present, only *Reichert v Dresdner Bank AG* has given a clear 'definition' of interim relief under Article 24.

---

[532] Or refusal in Britain's relations with France and Germany; old French and Belgian cases suggest that some exchange did go on: Belgian *Cour de Cassation* 6.6.1907 (1908) *Rev crit* 294 and Paris 24.7.1908, 1909 *JDI* 1070; generally Batiffol, H. *Traité élémentaire de droit international privé*, 2ème éd., 1955, at p.875.

[533] Regarding urgency—it should have been a reasonably foreseeable side-effect of (the rather draconian rule in) Article 2 of the Convention that a plaintiff/claimant would, wherever and whenever possible, seek a provisionally enforceable judgment in the *forum actoris* under Article 24.

[534] By excluding, if necessary, provisional orders from Title III's enforcement scheme.

[535] Arguably, *Van Uden Maritime* and *Hans Herman Mietz* may have put a stop to the cross-border exchange of foreign interlocutory orders.

[536] Or perhaps because of the Convention; a French applicant under Article 24 was no longer fettered by the inconvenient *actor sequitur forum rei* rule in Article 2, nor by Article 3 II.

[537] Cf Bermann, G. 'Provisional Relief in Transnational Litigation' (1997) *Col J Transnat L* 553, at p.556.

[538] *Mund & Fester v Hatrex Internationaal Transport* (C-398/92) [1994] ECR I–467 is not relevant for present purposes, showing only a German domestic *Arrest*.

[539] The latest *Hans-Hermann Mietz v Intership Yachting Sneek B.V.* (C-99/96) [1999] ECR I–2277, [1999] I.L.Pr. 541 deals, *inter alia*, with the question of cross-border enforcement under Article 24 of a 'kort geding' judgment for payment of contractual consideration; under Article 50 TRIPS Agreement in *Hermès International v FHT Marketing Choice BV* (C-53/96) [1998] ECR I–3603, the ECJ has held that an immediately enforceable measure of a Dutch court was a 'provisional measure' despite the fact that the decision was usually accepted by the parties as a final resolution of their dispute, at p.3652, para. 45; also *V.O.F. Schieving-Nijstad and others v Robert Groeneveld* (C-89/99), AG Jacob's opinion 15.2.2001, at paras. 36–37—Article 50(6), however, unlike Article 24 provides for a lapse of the measures taken, on request, if proceedings on the merits are not initiated within a given time.

[540] *Jacques de Cavel v Luise de Cavel* (C-143/78) [1979] ECR 1055; *Luise de Cavel v Jaques de Cavel* (C-120/79) [1980] ECR 731.

[541] (C-261/90) [1992] ECR I–2149.

[542] (C-391/95) [1998] ECR I–7091.

[543] (C-99/96) [1999] ECR I–2277, reference case *BGH* 29.2.1996 [1996] I.L.Pr. 661.

The interest for present purposes[544] in the *De Cavel* cases, is in the 'exportability' of provisional freezing injunctions—granted *inter partes*—in one Contracting State, affecting property located in another. The objection found by the Court in *Jacques de Cavel v Luise de Cavel*[545] was not to the French order's freezing, *per se*, of the flat's chattels and the bank account located in Frankfuhrt,[546] but to the fact that the orders were granted in divorce proceedings—which of course are excluded from the Convention's scope in any event, by Article 1(2)(1)

It is hard to gauge whether the Convention's framers ever had it in mind that provisional measures should have had such trans-frontier effects. A rather naïve hope is expressed by Droz,[547] when speaking of such orders, that 'dans la plupart des cas, de telles mesures seront prises en effet au lieu de situation des biens[548]'.[549] He also adds what comes close to a *forum conveniens* gloss, that measures should be sought from the courts best-placed to order the measures.[550]

The framers seem to have been rather short-sightedly looking to the effect[551] that Article 24 was going to have upon the 'normal' rules of competence *inter se* under the Brussels Convention. They no doubt saw that Article 24 was to be a Convention exception to Articles 2 and 21–23, rather than considering the wider repercussions at national level, within the Contracting States themselves, once an action for protective relief had been initiated nationally.[552]

---

[544] Article 24 was not strictly in issue at all, the granting court in Aix being also seised on the merits of the divorce; the *Maxwell Report* is a model of clarity on this point *Report of the Scottish Committee on Jurisdiction and Enforcement*, 1980, p.101 para. 5.233. After speaking of Article 24, the report states: [Article 24] is not to be confused with the case where a person litigating in a court of one Contracting State obtains an order for provisional . . . measures *from that court* and seeks to have the order enforced in another Contracting State. That is a case of enforcement under Title III . . .'—a view confirmed by *Van Uden Maritime.*

[545] (C-143/78) [1979] ECR 1055.

[546] Again in *Bernard Denilauer v S.n.c. Couchet Frères* (C-125/79) [1980] ECR 1553, it was the *ex parte* nature of the proceedings, not the orders themselves, which were repugnant to the Court.

[547] Droz, G. *Compétence judiciaire et effets des jugements dans le marché commun*, 1972, at p.200, para. 331.

[548] ('in the majority of cases, such measures will be taken at the place where the assets are').

[549] *Ibid.*; also Alférez-Garcimartín, 1995, p.129, at p.134, giving an example of where a French court made a seizure order over a villa in southern Spain. He regrets that post San-Sebastian Convention courts will now have to recognise the decision, subject of course to Article 27(1) and *Van Uden Maritime.*

[550] *Van Uden Maritime* has now stipulated that to grant such measures under Article 24, there must be the 'existence of a real connecting link' between the 'subject-matter' of the relief and the court concerned, at para. 40; how this is to be shown—(location of property to be seised)—is uncertain as yet.

[551] Cf Bermann, (1997) *Col J Transnat L* 553, at p.556.

[552] They could not, however, have known of the 17 December 1973 changes to French law, by Décret no.73–112 du 17 décembre 1973, adding the *référé-provision* to the battery of French provisional measures, below, at pp.356–357. That there is little cross-border activity in provisional relief prior to 1973 (either 1 February 1973 or December) is mirrored by the sudden increase of reported French cases on, *inter alia*, Article 809(2) after 1973.

Bernard Denilauer v S.n.c. Couchet Frères,[553] was another case not directly concerned[554] with Article 24. Couchet Frères sought the enforcement in the *LG Wiesbaden* of a seizure order granted *ex parte* in France by the *TGI de Montbrison,* the court incidentally also seised of the underlying dispute.[555] The order affected a bank account in Frankfurt. Rather than ruling, as it could have done,[556] that Article 25 did not extend to provisional or protective measures,[557] the ECJ did not in principle rule[558] out Title III's benefit to such measures,[559] but insisted that they must be granted, at a minimum, on an *inter partes* hearing. It chose an unsatisfactory half-way position, recognised by the UK Government[560] as likely to destroy their effectiveness. The Court reiterated the rather naïve hope expressed seven years earlier by Droz,[561] that 'exportability' under Article 24 might not arise. Instead it issued encouragement that such measures should therefore be requested from the Contracting State courts 'where the assets subject to the measures sought [were] located';[562] those being the 'best able to assess the circumstances which may lead to [their] . . . grant or refusal'.[563]

In *C.H.W v G.J.H*[564] an application before a Dutch court for the delivery up of a 'codicil' document in divorce proceedings in those courts was held not to fall within the scope of the Convention *ratione materiae* in any event; Article 24 could therefore not apply to the application. Yet the ECJ, in a curt reply taken from its jurisprudence in *De Cavel (1),*[565] did seem to give the impression that two courts were necessarily involved under Article 24, 'in which provisional measures are ordered in a contracting State where 'under this Convention' a court of another contracting State has jurisdiction as to the substance of the matter.' In the light of *Van Uden Maritime,* this impression of Article 24 has proved to be fallacious.

---

[553] (C-125/79) [1980] ECR 1553; also preceding footnote. This case shows that an applicant, given the legislative opportunity and encouragement, will stay at home for his enforcement measures rather than going, under Article 24, to the Contracting State (Germany) where the assets to be seized are located.

[554] Despite the *OLG Frankfuhrt*'s third question, the *TGI de Montbrison,* which had ordered the *ex parte saisie-arrêt,* was *also* seised of the underlying contract of carriage dispute.

[555] A perfectly legitimate proceeding; *Van Uden Maritime* has changed our outlook here; the case has made a clear demarcation of jurisdictional regimes, one under Title II, Articles 2, 5–18, and the other under national law in Article 24.

[556] This would then have forced reliance on Article 24 in each and every Contracting State.

[557] Whether granted under Article 24 or, as here, not.

[558] Only that the order had to be made *inter partes.*

[559] And as a consequence, unfortunately also to provisional relief under Article 24; also Collins (1981) 1 *YEL* 249, at p.265: 'This . . . would be a development which could not have been intended by the Convention and one which, when it arises for decision, should be resisted by the Court'.

[560] (C-125/79) [1980] ECR 1553, at p.1567, para. 6.

[561] Droz, 1972, at p.200.

[562] (C-125/79) [1980] ECR 1553, at p.1570, para. 16, echoing Droz.

[563] *Ibid.*; this has now become a pre-requisite in *Van Uden Maritime,* below, at pp.349–350.

[564] (C-25/81) [1982] ECR 1189.

[565] [1979] ECR 1055.

Only with *Mario Reichert and others v Dresdner Bank AG*[566] is a definition, albeit *en passant*, of provisional, including protective measures finally given. The German bank sought to invoke jurisdiction in France against the defendants, the Reicherts, also domiciled in Germany. The measure Dresdner Bank was so anxious to have declared provisional[567] was an order in proceedings known as an *action paulienne*, the effect of which, the ECJ found, was to 'vary the legal situation of the assets'[568] of the debtor 'by ordering the revocation [of the transaction]'[569] as against *inter alia*, the creditor. Whatever the action's legal nature, the Court considered that it was not 'intended to preserve a factual or legal situation so as to safeguard rights the recognition of which . . . [was] sought *elsewhere from the court having jurisdiction as to the substance of the matter*'.[570]

The bank should therefore have been hoist by its own petard. By relying so vehemently on various other Convention articles[571]—Article 16(1),[572] Article 5(3) and Article 16(5) to seise the French courts—this fact should have been enough to disqualify them from relying on Article 24 in the *same* (French)[573] Contracting State courts. They were attempting simultaneously[574] to seise a court both for the merits and for provisional measures under Article 24.

What, however, does emerge from *Mario Reichert and others v Dresdner Bank AG* is that Article 24 now has an autonomous Community meaning. Its effect? It will mean that the national stamp put upon a measure by domestic law is no longer relevant. Supporters of the *référé-provision* can therefore no longer hide behind the national definition of orders *en référé* under Article 484 NCPC.[575]

In the light of *Reichert* alone, it must seriously be doubted,[576] in addition to the other objections regarding Article 809(2) NCPC, whether this article can now be seen as preserving or safeguarding rights under consideration on the merits in

---

[566] (C-261/90) [1992] ECR I–2149, again the bank's reliance on other articles show even this case was not, *strictu sensu*, an Article 24 case; only upon the bank's failure to invoke jurisdiction on the merits in France under Articles 5(3) and 16, did Article 24, and its definition of provisional, including protective measures become vital.

[567] After failure to gain French jurisdiction on the merits.

[568] (C-261/90) [1992] ECR I–2149, at p.2184, para. 35; *quaere*, a 'kort geding' or *référé-provision* judgment, consequent upon (domestic or foreign) execution proceedings being taken on their basis, would also 'vary the legal situation of the assets'—by depriving the defendant/respondent of them! This aspect appeared to be overlooked in *Van Uden Maritime*.

[569] [1992] ECR I–2149, at p.2184.

[570] *Ibid.*; this case also gave (a false) impression that two courts were necessarily 'involved' under Article 24—*Van Uden Maritime* seems to have answered in the affirmative question 4 in the withdrawn reference in the reference in *Boston Scientific Ltd v Cordis Corp.*(C-186/00) [2000] OJ C233/15.

[571] Articles which indisputably seise a court 'on the merits'.

[572] As in *Mario P.A. Reichert & Others v Dresdner Bank (No.1)* (C-115/88) [1990] ECR I–27.

[573] Now, above at p.283, Proposition A, and the division of competence brought by *Van Uden Maritime* between Title II and Article 24.

[574] *Ibid.*

[575] As to which the *référé*-section below, at p.357.

[576] Not doubted, however, by the *Cour de Cassation* in 13.4.1999 *Société Bachy c. Société Belbetoes Fundacoes e Betoes Especiais LDA* (1999) Rev Crit 352, [1999] I.L.Pr. 743, (2000) JDI 83.

another Contracting State.[577] As we shall see, Article 809(2) does the opposite; it obviates the need for a Frenchman[578] to be put to the trouble of suing *ex juris* on the merits, as Article 2, (and possibly Articles 7–12, 13–15, 16, and 17) say he must.[579] But *Reichert* is not the end of the story.

Van Uden Maritime BV, trading as Van Uden Africa Line v Kommanditgesellschaft in Firma Deco Line, and another[580] is an important recent case for present purposes. The *Hoge Raad* referred questions[581] on the interpretation of Article 24, the answers to which from the European Court have finally laid to rest one aspect[582] of the controversy surrounding the *référé-provision*.[583]

Van Uden, seated in The Netherlands, had brought arbitration proceedings in the Netherlands against Deco-Line, seated in Germany, over disputed, and late, freight payments. Fearing a lack of Deco's assets in Holland, and its intransigence over nominating an arbitrator,[584] Van Uden applied in The Netherlands for an interim payment order[585] of nearly 405,000 marks which, at first instance, was substantially granted.

The ECJ unfortunately did not define Article 24 'provisional, including protective measures' in this case, but merely stipulated that whatever measures are granted under Article 24's jurisdiction—and hence to come under Article 24's jurisdiction—had to represent 'a real connecting link'[586] between the subject-matter of the order and the granting court. The European court was clear that its interpretation of Article 24 would not countenance a *détournement* of the Convention by permitting unconditional (and provisionally enforceable) interim judgments of contractual consideration to be obtained under Article 24 in

---

[577] Paraphrased from [1992] ECR I–2149, p.2184.

[578] This point has been made before: jurisdiction under Article 14 *Code civil* (a provision available under Article 24), rests on the French nationality of the plaintiff; as against defendants/respondents domiciled in other Contracting States, a German or Italian national domiciled in France, cannot therefore benefit from Article 14 *Code civil* under Article 24.

[579] As to which below, at p.360.

[580] (C-391/95) [1998] ECR I–7091; prior to this case, in *Hermès International v FHT Marketing Choice BV* [1998] ECR I–3603, the ECJ had already interpreted the words 'provisional measures' in Article 50 of the TRIPS agreement to include measures which, *inter alia*, were classed by the *lex fori* as provisional, and which usually disposed of any dispute on the merits, at p.3650, para. 33 and p.3652, para. 45.

[581] The referring court proceedings are reported in English at [1996] I.L.Pr. 269.

[582] As to whether a *référé-provision* granting interim payment of contractual consideration is a 'provisional, including protective' measure under Article 24—it is also subject to further conditions, however.

[583] It appears to have done so, *Cassation* 13.4.1999 *Bachy c/ Soc. Belbetoes* (1999) *Rev crit* 352, [1999] I.L.Pr. 743, (2000) *JDI* 83.

[584] *Quaere*, it should not matter for the application of Article 1(4) Brussels Convention that by Dutch law—as the *lex loci arbitri*—no arbitration proceedings as a matter of law could be said to be under-way; *Marc Rich & Co. AG v Società Italiana Impianti PA* (C-109/89) [1991] ECR I–3855.

[585] In so-called 'kort geding' proceedings, similar in procedure and effect to Article 809(2) NCPC; Véron, P. (2001) *JDI* 805, at p.812.

[586] [1998] ECR I–7091, at p.7135, para. 40.

conjunction with national exorbitant rules. As a result, it made the grant of such[587] measures conditional on the provision of a guarantee, and their geographical confinement to assets located within the jurisdiction of the (granting) court. This radical solution seems, at a stroke, to have removed the 'exportability' cases like *De Cavel (1)* and *C.H.W v G.J.H*,[588] and encourage an applicant to seise each and every Contracting State where assets are located under Article 24.

The latest case to have been referred on the interpretation of Article 24 is *Hans-Hermann Mietz v Intership Yachting Sneek B.V.*[589] Here there was a dispute over the payment of late instalments owed to the Dutch boat builder, Sneek, by the German defendant, Mietz. The contract had been to customise a boat that Mietz was to acquire, with unique specifications. Sneek obtained a 'kort geding' judgment from a Dutch court for the sum of all instalments, and sought its enforcement in Germany, in the *LG Lüneberg*. It is not clear from the report whether the Dutch court had acted under Article 24,[590] or as the court on the merits.[591]

The issues raised on the reference were as follows: did the Dutch court take jurisdiction under (exorbitant) national rules (under Article 24) to grant the 'kort geding' payment; this, in turn, depended on whether the order in such a 'kort geding' procedure was an Article 24 'provisional, including protective' measure. If it was, the payment order seemed to be *prima facie* enforceable. If it was not such a measure, Article 24 dropped from the picture and the case would become an 'ordinary' enforcement case,[592] similar to *Denilauer v S.n.c. Couchet Frères.*

For present purposes, the *Bundesgerichtshof* referred a question as to the exact status of the 'kort geding' under Article 24. Unfortunately, *Hans Herman Mietz* offered no answer to the vexed question of what measures are, or are not, to be included in Article 24's definition of 'provisional, including protective measures'; it merely re-iterated the concerns expressed in *Van Uden Maritime* over unconditional interim payments of contractual consideration, but in the context of proceedings for the enforcement of such orders in another Contracting State, Germany.

What the court did say was that such proceedings as the 'kort geding' (and therefore by implication also the *référé-provision*) procedure are the types of

---

[587] And it is submitted only such measures. This restriction may be significant for worldwide *Mareva*/freezing injunctions—Bloch, (1999) *SZW* 166, at p.174 agrees: *OLG München* 5.4.2000 (2000) *RIW* 464; Schlosser, P. (2000) 284 *Recueil des Cours* 88, at p.188.

[588] (C-25/81) [1982] ECR 1189.

[589] (C-99/96) [1999] ECR I–2277; [1999] I.L.Pr. 541.

[590] Hence question 4, below, at p.351; the *BGH* did comment on the 'kort geding' procedure however—it 'appear[ed] to have replaced proceedings on the substantive issues to a relatively wide extent in Holland', [1996] I.L.Pr., at p.666; Véron, P. (2001) *JDI* 805, at p.812.

[591] *Van Uden Maritime* has made this distinction vital: the territorial scope of the measures granted will depend on whether the court took jurisdiction under Title II (in which case Article 28 I may well have been breached), *or* Article 24; it may be (but was unclear whether) the Dutch court took jurisdiction under Article 5(1).

[592] *Maxwell Report, Report of the Scottish Committee on Jurisdiction and Enforcement*, HMSO, Edinburgh, 1980, at p.101 para. 5.233.

proceedings envisaged under Article 24.[593] Where the ruling went beyond what could be gleaned from *Van Uden Maritime*, was the opinion the ECJ had as to the extent to which it was possible to seek enforcement of such orders, delivered under the auspices of Article 24, in another Contracting State. This ruling makes it clear that where the order or judgment purporting to grant interim relief does not possess the *Van Uden Maritime* 'safeguards' of territorial limitation and a guarantee, the enforcing court will be justified in taking the view that such an order cannot benefit from Title III's enforcement regime.[594]

It would have been far simpler to have stated categorically that orders in the 'kort geding'/*référé-provision* truncated procedure, that lead to a provisionally enforceable interim judgment for contractual consideration, must be strictly territorial,[595] and thus are incapable of enforcement in any other Contracting State under Title III. *Ex hypothesi*, if an order granting interim payment—albeit conforming domestically with the *Van Uden Maritime* safeguards—crosses a Contracting State border for enforcement in another Contracting State against assets there, it will no longer 'relat[e] only to specific assets of [a] defendant located . . . within the confines of the territorial jurisdiction of the court to which application [was originally] made'.[596]

The post *Van Uden Maritime* decision[597] of the *Cour de Cassation* in *Bachy c/ Soc. Belbetoes*[598] unfortunately did not involve cross-border enforcement of a *provision* granted in *référé* proceedings against a Portuguese company. Yet the commentary spoke in terms of the order's territorial confinement[599] to the respondent company's assets, if any, in France.

It is to be hoped that (un)conditional measures for the interim payment of contractual consideration are rigorously ring-fenced within the territorial confines of the Contracting State which granted them; otherwise the exclusive jurisdictional provisions (Articles 16 and 17) and protective rules (Articles 7—12a, Articles 13—15) will be completely undermined[600] by applications on the basis of the very 'exorbitant' national provisions that Article 3 I and II sought to outlaw.

---

[593] [1999] ECR I–2277, at p.2313, para. 38.

[594] *Ibid.*, at p.2318, para. 54; now *OLG München* (2000) *RIW* 464.

[595] If this is not what *Van Uden Maritime* limitations already mean.

[596] At p.2318, para. 53; if this is how this phrase of the second *Van Uden Maritime* safeguard is to be understood; the confusion caused by this somewhat anomalous position may well take another visit to the European Court to resolve.

[597] *OLG München* (2000) *RIW* 464, involved enforcement of a Greek freezing order, not an interim payment, reviewed above, at pp.321–322.

[598] (1999) *Rev crit* 352, [1999] I.L.Pr. 743; also *OLG Düsseldorf* 28.1.1999 (1999) *RIW* 873.

[599] (1999) *Rev crit* 352, at p.621, (Huet): the French court being 'incompétent, en dépit de la nationalité française d'une partie . . ., si le bien se trouve à l'étranger'.

[600] Especially regarding provisionally enforceable *référé-provision*/'kort geding' judgments—despite their territorial restriction (*Bachy c/ Belbetoes* (1999) *Rev crit* 352, (2000) *JDI* 83), objections can still be raised against them: that they stifle any action on the merits, award a provisionally enforceable judgment in interlocutory proceedings, and necessitate claiming under any guarantee—*Cassation* 4.10.2000 (2000) *Dalloz*, IR, 264.

The Swiss *Bundesgericht* has also recently had the opportunity of assessing the impact of *Van Uden Maritime* and *Hans Herman Mietz* on Swiss practice in *SodaStream Ltd. gegen Urs Jäger AG.*[601] SodaStream had appointed the Swiss company Urs Jäger as its products distributor in Switzerland. In essence, it terminated the agreement and solicited other distributors. Urs sought provisional measures[602] ordering SodaStream to continue the supply of goods,[603] and also an injunction preventing it from supplying anyone else. The court recognised that it did not have jurisdiction[604] on the merits over the distribution agreement. After considering *Van Uden Maritime* and *Mietz,* the court did not accept that provisional measures ordering the respondent to perform some task—such as continuing supplies—were automatically excluded from the scope of Article 24. Yet it did stress the concerns expressed in the two recent ECJ cases, and held that jurisdiction to order provisional measures was only justified

> wenn das in der Hauptsache zuständige Gericht nicht in der Lage ist, rechtzeitig vorsorgliche Massnahmen zu erlassen, die sicherstellen, dass der praktische Wert der im Hauptverfahren geltend zu machenden Ansprüche erhalten bleibt, bis ein rechtskräftiges Haupturteil vorliegt.[605]

The fact that the court scrutinised the provision of security (under §306 ZPO Aargau) bears witness to the effect *Van Uden Maritime* has had, and will continue to have, on the grant of such measures on (Lugano) Contracting State civil (Cantonal) procedure.

3.6.3   Interim Relief/Payments in England and Wales, and section 25 CJJA 1982, post *Van Uden Maritime*

(i)   *CPR Part 25 interim remedies*

Interim payments are now grouped together with, *inter alia,* what are now known as 'freezing injunctions'[606] and 'search orders'[607] in the Civil Procedure Rules, Part 25. The definition of an 'order for interim payment' under CPR Rule 25.1(1)(k) is wide enough[608] to include what the *Van Uden Maritime* case would term 'unconditional interim payments of contractual consideration'. The

---

[601]   17.9.1999 125 BGE, III, 451.
[602]   On the basis of (the Canton of) Aargau civil procedure §302 Abs. 1(b) ZPO.
[603]   A 'Leistungsmassnahme'.
[604]   Article 17 Lugano Convention gave exclusive jurisdiction to the English courts.
[605]   ('when the court with jurisdiction on the merits is unable quickly to grant provisional measures that ensure that the practical worth of the claims being made on the merits are preserved until a binding judgment on the merits is available'), 125 BGE, III, 451, at p.457—the necessity for an indemnity was also in place here.
[606]   Supplemented by Practice Direction 25.
[607]   *Ibid.*
[608]   'payment . . . on account of any damages, debt or other sum . . .'.

individual *minutiae*[609] of the interim payment procedure itself are to be found in CPR Rule 25.6, and the conditions to be satisfied—which are taken from the old RSC Ord.29[610]—in Rule 25.7. The wording of the new rule, however, reveals at a glance that it was not drafted[611] with any cross-border influence and/or application (under Article 24 or otherwise) in mind—indeed, in a contractual consideration case, such an application for an order for interim payment is likely, if at all, only to fulfil CPR Rule 25.7(1)(c),[612] where an English court would have to make an assessment of the applicant's likely success in any 'foreign' trial.

Assuming that an Article 24 application for provisional measures can somehow clumsily be accommodated into CPR Rules 25.6—10, it is clear that the definition of interim payments will be enough to attract the censure of *Van Uden Maritime.* The order eventually granted will have to 'relate to'[613] assets only in England and Wales, and be backed by a guarantee. CPR Rule 25.8(2)(a)[614]—regarding a repayment—may well be insufficient to quell any doubts expressed in *Van Uden Maritime* about the need for a guarantee.

Although some of the uncertainties of the old RSC Ord.29[615] have gone, it is likely that most attention for CPR interim remedies will no doubt focus on CPR Rule 25.1(1)(f) 'freezing injunctions', and to a lesser extent, Rule 25.1(1)(h) 'search orders'.[616]

---

[609] Over and above CPR Part 23 or CPR Rule 8 in the Commercial Court—'The Commercial Court Guide' and generally *Civil Procedure, Vol.1, Spring 2001,* 2001.

[610] Apart from the same arguments as to pre-empting a merits decision made against Article 809(2) NCPC—esp. Ord 29 r.11(1)(c) 'the plaintiff would obtain judgment for substantial damages' and *British and Commonwealth Holdings Plc. v Quadrex Holdings Inc.* [1989] 1 QB 842, CA, at p.866, (Sir Nicholas Browne-Wilkinson V.C.) 'the court . . . [must] be satisfied that the plaintiff *will* succeed and the burden is a high one.' (original emphasis).

[611] Esp. CPR Rule 25.7(4).

[612] The comments in *The Civil Procedure Rules 1999,* at p.299, para. 25.7.10.

[613] This presumably means therefore 'be available for execution against'.

[614] Only relating, *inter alia,* to a subsequent court order for repayment by the applicant: (no grounds or circumstances are mentioned)—this is, however, not an equivalent safeguard for a respondent represented by an independent third party guarantee.

[615] I.e. whether 'interim payments' were included or not—suggested by the insertion of the old r.8A in Ord.29 itself. The position of r.8A in the Order was to be noted, and especially its wording: the application by originating summons, under s 25(1) CJJA 1982 and Ord.29, for 'interim relief' generally, was said to be subject to 'the *foregoing* provisions of this Order [29](except rules 5,6 and 7(2)'; interim payments on the other hand were governed by rules which *followed* r.8A.

[616] *Quaere,* whether these are available in any event under s 25(7) CJJA 1982; *Coca Cola Bottlers (Ulster) Ltd v The Concentrate Manufacturing Co. of Ireland (t/a Seven-up International),* 6.4.1990, Ch.D. (Murray LJ); s 28 CJJA 1982 for Court of Session; eg. *Petter Olsen v Forrest Estate Ltd and others,* 14.6.1994, OH.

3.6.4   The likely reaction, post *Van Uden Maritime* and *Hans Herman Mietz*, of other Contracting State courts to an application under Title III of the Brussels Convention, for the enforcement of a worldwide Mareva/freezing injunction issued by the English courts under Article 24/section 25 CJJA 1982

The procedure for applications under Article 24 on or after 26.4.1999 for *Mareva*/freezing injunctions before the English courts, is governed by a rather confused amalgam of the CJJA 1982, as amended, and, *inter alia*, the CPR Part 25. Sections 25(1), (2) and (7) CJJA 1982 provide the statutory authority necessary for the implementation of the policy behind Article 24, and the CPR the domestic framework. The interim remedy of a *Mareva* injunction, now known as a 'freezing injunction', may be granted and served, if necessary, *ex juris* under CPR Rule 25.1(f)(i), (ii), in conjunction with CPR Rule 25.4(a), Articles 23 and 8, and CPR Rule 6.20(4), 6.21(1)(2A).

Should all the above provisions have been complied with—and most notably the test of 'expediency' in section 25(2) CJJA 1982 not prevent[617] its grant—the successful applicant will now attempt to implement the breadth of the freezing injunction by its terms, under Title III of the Brussels Convention, and prevent 'a party [the respondent] from dealing with any assets . . . located . . . [for e.g. in France, or Switzerland]'[618] in those jurisdictions. What will be the likely reaction of the French or Swiss courts to the application for enforcement of such an order under Title III?

All things being equal,[619] it seems the only possible defence[620] a respondent may have is under Article 27(1), that the freezing order breaches 'public policy'.[621] A defendant's line of attack, in its widest terms, may well run that the English freezing injunction breaches each respective Contracting State's sovereignty, itself to

---

[617] *Crédit Suisse Fides Trust SA v Cuoghi* [1998] QB 818; *Refco Inc. and another v Eastern Trading Co. and others* [1999] 1 Lloyd's Rep. 159, CA; *Ryan v Friction Dynamics Ltd* 2.6.2000 (Neuberger J) mentioned above at p.331.

[618] CPR Rule 25.1(f)(ii).

[619] Assuming the order is not otherwise impeachable, *inaudita alterem partem*: *Bernard Denilauer v S.n.c. Couchet Frères* (C-125/79) [1980] ECR 1553.

[620] Assuming again that: the freezing injunction is considered as an Article 25 judgment (*OLG München* (2000) *RIW* 464) the respondent had been duly served in sufficient time with the claim form applying for the order, and no irreconcilable foreign/domestic judgment exists; *Normaco and anor v Lundman and ors*, Ch. D. (Carnwath, J) *The Times Law Reports*, 6.1.1999.

[621] Note, in *OLG Karlsruhe* IPRspr. 1995 Nr. 166, (the rejection of) the potential for a worldwide *Mareva* injunction to offend, under Article 27(1), German public policy of proportionality, at p.338—public policy in this case inapplicable, however, due to a business proviso in the order— (also a protective proviso for third party banks subject to the jurisdiction with subsidiaries outside the jurisdiction—*Bank of China v NBN LLC and others*, CA, 18.12.2001). The real problem in the case, and not strictly a concern to the Convention, is how a *Mareva*/freezing injunction was to be translated into an effective, comparable order locally—Zuckerman, (1996) 1 *ZZPInt* 89, at pp.98–100; cf *Högsta Domstolens* 12.9.1995 *G.N. Preziosi di Gori & Nibi S.D.F. v Swiss Gold Imports Plc (In Bankruptcy)* [1997] I.L.Pr. 509, at pp.512–13, (conversion into a 'comparable' order under Swedish law).

regulate the fate of 'assets' within its own borders.[622] Alternatively, it may be that other[623] Contracting State courts may consider it a breach of public policy to enforce a judgment which, potentially, contravenes the restrictions placed upon it by rulings of the ECJ,[624] viz. *Van Uden Maritime* and *Hans Herman Mietz*. This merits closer attention.

A cross-border worldwide freezing injunction granted under Article 24 and section 25 CJJA 1982, and affecting assets beyond the UK, it may be argued, does not represent a 'real connecting link between the subject-matter of the measures sought and the territorial jurisdiction [of the English court] . . . before which those measures [were] sought.'[625] The foreign court may also not distinguish between the general[626] and specific[627] restrictions in post-*Van Uden Maritime* provisional measures, and therefore scrutinise the freezing injunction to see, in addition, whether it relates only[628] to assets in the UK,[629] and is backed by a guarantee.[630] If such a distinction is not made, the worldwide injunction will clearly fail to relate only to domestic assets.

Even despite the recent ruling on the limited extent of the defence of public policy in Article 27(1) in *Dieter Krombach v Andre Bamberski*[631] and *SA Régie Nationale des Usines Renault v SpA Maxicar and Orazio Formento*,[632] it appears more likely than not that another Contracting State court will not look kindly[633] on an application to enforce an Article 24 worldwide freezing order, despite Title III and Article 25's exhortation to the contrary.

The early indications are that, at least in Germany and Switzerland, a differentiation has been made between the type of provisional measures granted in *Van Uden Maritime* and in *Mietz* from the freezing-type injunction typified by a *Mareva*/freezing injunction. In Germany, the *OLG München* has stated that Article 24 measures such as provisional payment orders, without all the safeguards

---

[622] A particularly acute concern in Germany: *OLG Düsseldorf* 10.1.1996 1997 (1997) *IPRax* 176, [1997] I.L.Pr. 320.

[623] And *vice versa* for an English court confronted with enforcement under Title III of a cross-border 'kort geding' or *référé-provision* judgment.

[624] Or 'Community Law' in general—*SA Régie Nationale des Usines Renault v SpA Maxicar and Orazio Formento* (C-38/98) [2000] ECR I–2973; not an argument that impressed the ECJ.

[625] *Van Uden Maritime BV, trading as Van Uden Maritime Africa Line v Kommanditgesellschaft in Firma Deco Line, and another* (C-391/95) [1998] ECR I–7091, at p.7135, para. 40—it is unclear whether another Contracting State court would regard the *in personam* nature of a *Mareva*/freezing injunction as a, or the, 'real connecting link'.

[626] The 'real connecting link' between subject-matter and granting court, *ibid.*

[627] That the order be backed by a guarantee, and 'relates only to specific assets' of the defendant in the territory of the granting court.

[628] Cf *Cheshire and North*, 13th edn., 1999, at p.260 n.5.

[629] The rôle of Article 29 is unclear in this instance.

[630] Even though Practice Direction 25 provides in Sch.B a suggested model clause for the issuance of a guarantee at the behest of the applicant.

[631] (C-7/98), unreported, 28.3.2000, AG Antonio Saggio's opinion 23.9.1999.

[632] (C-38/98) [2000] ECR I–2973.

[633] Perhaps not in Switzerland, according to Bloch, (1999) *SZW* 166, at p.175, the only problem over the domestic enforcement of a *Mareva*/freezing injunction is such an order's local equivalent.

therein, are simply not Article 25 judgments capable of recognition under Title III.[634] As regards freezing injunctions[635] *simplicter*, it has enforced such a Greek order. Bloch, a Swiss commentator, has stated with regard to *Van Uden Maritime*, that those safeguarding 'considerations . . . do not apply to measures which are only intended to protect the status quo (such as a Mareva injunction).'[636]

The French reaction to an English Article 24 freezing injunction affecting French assets is more uncertain: the *Bachy* decision has suggested a territorial limitation to French *saisie* orders, and it might be confidently stated that a foreign injunction would be expected likewise to be similarly confined to assets within England and Wales.

3.7   THE RÉFÉRÉ-PROVISION ITSELF[637]

. . . on imagine qu'un créancier réclame et obtienne d'un juge français des référés— estimé compétent en vertu de l'article 24—. . . une provision à 100%, alors qu'en vertu des articles 2 et 5–1 . . . (ou de l'article 17) le fond du litige relève de la compétence de juridictions allemandes ou italiennes.[638] [639]

The jurisdiction of the French courts *en référé* in general, is of ancient origin, dating from the practices of the *lieutenant civil du Châtelet de Paris*, recognised by royal decree of 1685,[640] and later incorporated into Articles 806–11 of the *Code de procédure civil* of 1806.[641] Today, a ruling of a judge *en référé* is, according to Article

---

[634] A pre-*Van Uden Maritime* case had already enforced the effects of a *Mareva* injunction, *OLG Karlsruhe* IPRspr. 1995 Nr. 166: reviewed Zuckerman (1996) 1 *ZZPInt* 89; provided the usual business expenditure provisos are included, the German courts will, it is submitted, even after *Van Uden Maritime*, find nothing to cavil at in a *Mareva*/freezing order.

[635] Not clear from report in *OLG München* 5.4.2000 (2000) *RIW* 464, whether, as in *OLG Karlsruhe* IPRspr. (1995) Nr. 166, provisos were included in the Greek freezing order to stave off a defence of specificity under Article 27(1).

[636] (1999) *SZW* 166, at p.174, col.2.

[637] Especially Damjanovic, 1996; and Baker, W. and De Fontbressin, P. 'The French référé procedure— a legal miracle?' (1992–3) *Uni Miami Yrbk Int L* 1; as *Cheshire and North* is forced to admit, all the following must be read subject to, and with a critical eye upon, *Van Uden Maritime*; Weber, G. *Die Verdrängung des Hauptsacheverfahrens durch den einstweiligen Rechtsschutz in Deutschland und Frankreich*, 1993, at pp.82–88; for general introduction to procedure Baker W. and de Fontbressen, P. (1998) 25 *Syracuse J. Int'l L. and Com.* 61, at p.72–75.

[638] ('it is foreseeable that a creditor claims and obtains from a French *référé* judge—considered to have jurisdiction by virtue of Article 24—. . . a 100% *provision*, while by virtue of Articles 2 and 5(1) . . . (or Article 17) jurisdiction on the merits is a matter for German or Italian jurisdiction').

[639] Huet (1989) *JDI* 96, at p.98; post *Van Uden Maritime* now a legitimate fear if the respondent to the *provision* has assets located, or to be located, in France—*Cour de Cassation* 13.4.1999 *Société Bachy c/ Société Belbetoes Fundacoes e Betoes Especiais LDA* (1999) *Rev Crit* 352, (2000) *JDI* 83, [1999] I.L.Pr. 743.

[640] For a reference to a copy of this edict in French, with an English translation, the preface to the article devoted to the *référé* procedure by Baker, W. and De Fontbressin, P. (1992–3) *Uni Miami Yrbk Int L* 1, at p.1.

[641] For its historical origins, generally Cadiet, L. *Droit Judiciaire Privé*, 1992, at p.524 and refs.

484 NCPC, termed as 'une décision *provisoire*[642] . . . dans les cas où la loi confière à un juge *qui n'est pas saisi du principal . . .*'[643]

Curiously,[644] considering such a long *provenance*, the *référé-provision* procedure itself was only introduced into the NCPC in December 1973,[645] becoming Article 809(2) NCPC as regards the powers of the president of the *Tribunal de Grande Instance*.[646] Its nearest English equivalent is to the interim payment[647] (now) found in CPR Rule 25.1(k), and Rule 25.6. A French judge may order a *provision*, or interim payment, quickly,[648] in cases where the (underlying) obligation is not 'sérieusement contestable[649]'.[650]

Despite the contrary rulings of French courts,[651] there are features[652] of the procedure which, on the one hand, make it particularly unsuitable to come within Article 24,[653] and on the other, leave it considerable scope to by-pass the 'normal' jurisdictional rules of the Brussels Convention, Articles 2, 5–18.[654] Although these features will be treated separately in what follows, in conjunction they work an injustice[655] which is hard to countenance.

---

[642] Commentators defending Article 809(2)'s provisional status rigidly plead Article 484's— national—definition of a measure *en référé*: Couchez is typical—'En droit, l'on est donc indiscutablement en présence d'une mesure provisoire'('By law, a provisional measure is undeniably at issue') (1983) *Rev Crit* at p.115. Whether this tenacity is now strictly legitimate in the face of *Mario Reichert and others v Dresdner Bank AG* (C-261/90) [1992] ECR I–2149, remains open, below, at p.358, n.664.

[643] ('a provisional decision . . . in the cases where the law confers on a judge who is not seised on the merits'); *Nouveau Code de Procedure Civile*, Dalloz, 93ème éd., 2001, at p.252, following, with attending explanatory notes.

[644] If one believes in accidents of timing.

[645] By Décret no. 73–112 du 7 décembre 1973—prior to this, according to Weber, 1993, at p.82, the French courts had been reticent to order a provisionally enforceable judgment in *référé* proceedings.

[646] For the powers of the *Tribunal de Commerce*, Article 873(2) NCPC; *Nouveau Code de Procedure Civile*, Dalloz, 93ème éd., 2001, at p.437 following.

[647] As to the provisional nature of which under the old RSC Ord.29 rr.10–11, Briggs, 1997, at p.300.

[648] In cases of urgency, even at the judge's home, *porte ouverte*—Article 485(2); Vincent, J. and Guinchard, S. *Procédure Civile*, 22nd edn., 1991, p.424.

[649] ('seriously arguable').

[650] Also limited opportunities to appeal against a finding of not 'sérieusement contestable': *Cassation* 4.10.2000, (2000) *Dalloz*, IR., 264; Boujeka, A. (2001) *Dalloz*, com., 1580.

[651] *Société Krupp Widia GmbH c/ Société Schlumberger Industries, Cour de Cassation* Ch. Com., 10.3.1992, (1993) *JDI* 156, obs. Huet; *Tron c/ Société Verkor, TGI de Nanterre*, 9.10.1978, (1979) *Rev Crit* 128, obs. Metzger; (1980) *JDI* 894; *Cour d'appel de Versailles*, 27.6.1979, (1980) *JDI* 894, obs. Holleaux; *Diehm c/ Mlle Sicre, Cour d'appel d'Aix-en-Provence*, 4.5.1981, (1983) *Rev Crit* 110, obs. Couchez; *Menegatti c/ Société Mettalurgica Nava Stefano e Guiseppina, Cour d'appel de Paris*, 14e Ch., 17.11.1987, (1989) *JDI* 96, obs. Huet; *SARL Yakari Italie c/ S.A. Gondrand et Société Vinco, Cour d'appel de Chambéry*, 2.3.1992, (1994) *JDI* 173, obs. Huet; *Société Luxguard c/ Société SN Sitraco et autres, Cour d'appel de Versailles*, 9.4.1993, (1995) *Rev. crit* 80, obs. Couchez.

[652] As to which in greater detail below, at pp.359 *et seq.*

[653] That the *référé-provision* is now an Article 24 measure is undeniable, *Van Uden Maritime* and *Cour de Cassation* 13.4.1999 *Bachy c/ Soc. Belbetoes* (1999) *Rev crit* 352.

[654] Article 24 may by-pass the 'ordinary' Convention jurisdictional rules, but the (cross-border) scope of 'provisional, including protective measures' has been somewhat curtailed by *Van Uden Maritime*.

[655] To anyone without French domicile/nationality, or who cannot otherwise seise the French courts (under Article 14 *Code civil*).

The *référé-provision* will be briefly treated in the following eight non-exhaustive categories: that the *référé-provision* prejudges, and pre-empts the court on the merits, by assessing the underlying cause of action; that provisional, including protective relief, whether under Article 24 or otherwise, is never intended to allow full recovery of the claim;[656] that Article 809(2) therefore dispenses with the need for a full judgment on the merits; that this procedure reverses certain aspects of the litigation,[657] especially damaging for a respondent in international cases;[658] that, having paid the applicant, the risk of the applicant's insolvency is unfairly cast onto the respondent,[659] should any trial court on the merits decide that the *provision* should not have been paid; the exportability aspects of the *provision*, and its enforcement under Title III; and as a consequence of all these previous characteristics, that Article 809(2) represents a *détournement* of the Brussels Convention; the *provision* will then be considered in the light of arbitration proceedings, as well as litigation. The solutions to the problem offered by commentators will then briefly be touched on.

The idiosyncratic nature of this one *référés-spéciaux* is demonstrated by a characteristic which other interim measures would not be expected to possess. The 'assignation' *en référé* actually has a suspensory effect on the limitation period running in the underlying cause of action.[660] It is hard to see that a measure, which claims to be of an interim type,[661] should exert such a wide influence on the underlying cause of action. Giverdon[662] concedes that the *référé* in general exhibits characteristics that make this a distinct procedure *sui generis*, unattached to any jurisdiction on the merits, despite the wording of Article 484,[663] and *Reichert v Dresdner Bank AG*.[664]

---

[656] Via a provisionally enforceable order on which measures of execution can be taken, something a *Mareva*/freezing injunction does *not* do.

[657] Requiring a prejudiced respondent to claim on any guarantee.

[658] Especially now since *Van Uden Maritime*, the need to claim under a guarantee (in another jurisdiction).

[659] According to Baker, W. and De Fontbressin, P. (1992–3) *Uni Miami Yrbk Int L* 1, at p.26, a guarantee does not have to be provided as a matter of French substantive law; for measures granted under Article 24, however, the position is now different, para. 47 of *Van Uden Maritime*; yet CPR Rule 25.8(2)(a) may well prove insufficient.

[660] *Éditions du Juris-Classeur*, 1997, 'Référés-spéciaux', Fasc. 235–2, janvier 1997, p.9 para. 48; *Cassation* 4.10.2000 (2000) *Dalloz*, IR, 264.

[661] As in Article 484 NCPC.

[662] The commentator for the *Éditions du Juris-Classeur*, 1997.

[663] *Éditions du Juris-Classeur*, 1995, 'Référés', mars 1995, Fasc.232, p.7 para. 27; the provision that adjudges an *ordonnance de référé* as a provisional judgment.

[664] (C-261/90) [1992] ECR I–2149.

3.7.1 The *référé-provision* prejudging, and pre-empting the court on the merits[665]

Yet for some, the most pernicious aspect[666] of the *référé-provision* is the fact that its grant involves a consideration of the underlying cause of action—which must not be 'sérieusement contestable'.[667] This fact alone is unlike what could be described as the traditional remit of interim relief: to support and assist the action on the merits, not to usurp, pre-judge nor emasculate it. Indeed, according to Couchez,[668] the consideration of the underlying merits is only done on the most cursory of evidence.

The view that the *référé-provision* somehow represents an intrusion into and value-judgment on the merits of a dispute, properly under the auspices of another Contracting State's jurisdiction, litters the comments and comparative law treatments of French interim relief. Typical is the view of Bermann:[669]

> it is one thing for the court that is hearing the main action (and that will eventually decide the case on the merits) to order provisional payment, but quite another for the court of a different jurisdiction to do so.[670]

Contributing to the perniciousness is the fact that the *référé-provision* is couched within the protective wording of Article 24, is available[671] on exorbitant grounds of jurisdiction, otherwise outlawed in Article 3 [I] [II], such as Article 14 *Code civil*, which then *de facto* renders superfluous[672] and nugatory any necessity for a successful applicant to initiate a subsequent action[673] on the merits:

---

[665] Dalhuisen, 'Creditors' Remedies and the Conflicts of Law in The European Community' in *Festschrift für Stefan Riesenfeld*, 1983, at p.21, for this reason, wishes that these types of measures be outlawed under Article 24; the concerns over such measures' potential for prejudicing the main action in *Cour d'appel de Rennes* 4.11.1992 *Zinser Fleisch Import & Export Handelsgesellschaft v S.A. Salaisons du Jet Jean Laurent* [1994] I.L.Pr. 237, at p.240, para. 4.

[666] If one concedes, as Article 24's wording forces a concession, that another Contracting State court (properly) with jurisdiction on the merits has to consider the exact same question on the underlying claim. In conjunction with Article 24, the *référé-provision* represents an international usurpation of functions.

[667] It should be noted that the *Cour de Cassation*'s ability to reverse lower courts' decisions on whether a cause of action is not 'sérieusement contestable' has been strictly limited: *Cour de Cassation* 4.10.2000, Boujeka, A. (2001) *Dalloz*, com., 1580.

[668] Couchez, G. 'Le référé-provision: mesure ou démesure' in *Mélanges offerts à Pierre Raynaud*, 1985 162, at p.167; also Morbach, 1988, at p.151.

[669] Bermann, (1997) *Col J Transnat L* 553, at p.611.

[670] *Ibid.*, especially on exorbitant grounds of jurisdiction.

[671] Unless the applicant happens not to be French or is not domiciled in France.

[672] '[P]uisque l'on cherche . . . à obtenir immédiatement cela même que le juge du fond pourrait nous donner si l'on agissait au principal' ('since what was sought the same immediate measure that the judge on the merits could grant us as if we were suing on the merits')(Vareilles-Sommières), (1996) *Rev crit* 397, at p.406.

[673] As to which below section 3.7.3.

Les avocats ont insensiblement poussé le juge des référés à *s'arroger* un pouvoir d'intervention qui n'est pas très loin de celui . . . du juge au fond.[674] [675]

Such measures could surely not have been intended by the Convention's framers to be included in the Article 24 definition. One therefore wonders at the propitious[676] introduction[677] of this measure by the December 1973 decree.[678]

Any measure resulting in a provisionally enforceable judgment, which involves second-guessing[679] the main trial court should not be considered to be provisional:

Le référé-provision est devenu une sorte de "pré-jugement au fond"[680] [681]

3.7.2   Full recovery of the claim

This and the next (inter-linked) property of the *référé-provision*, one following on naturally from the other, also display strong reasons for its not being allowed in under Article 24. The *Cour de Cassation* has ruled[682] that the level of the *provision* can equal[683] the amount that would ultimately have been claimed in an action on the merits—a far cry from an *Arrest* under §§916ff ZPO or a *Mareva*/freezing injunction. According to Grandcourt,[684] there is no

simple mesure provisoire, dès lors que . . . le référé-provision peut porter sur la totalité de la créance . . . et conduire à un payment immédiat.[685] [686]

The levels of claims generated in this way *en référé* are staggering.[687] Allowing full recovery almost certainly dispenses with the need to 're-litigate' the matter at

---

[674] ('Lawyers have imperceptibly forced the *référé* judge to assume a power of involvement that is not far off from that of the judge on the merits').

[675] Burgelin, J-F. 'Le juge des référés au regard des principes procéduraux' 1995 *Dalloz*, 10e., Chron., p.67, at p.67.

[676] Merkt, 1993, at p.31, para. 72.

[677] Gaudemet-Tallon, (1990) *Rev Arb* 633, at p.647 makes an oblique reference to the timing of its introduction thus: 'Le droit français est resté longtemps sans connaitre le référé-provision'('French law for a long time remained without the *référé-provision*').

[678] Merkt, 1993, makes no comment on its appearance ten months after the coming into force of the Brussels Convention, at pp.31–32.

[679] Collins, 1994, at pp.37–38; rather than outlawing such orders *tout cour*, *Van Uden Maritime* and *Hans Herman Mietz* have merely made them territorially-restricted.

[680] ('The *référé-provision* has become a sort of "interlocutory judgment on the merits"').

[681] Hohl, F. *La réalisation du droit et les procédures rapides*, 1994, at p.194.

[682] Ch. Comm. 20.1.1981, 1981 Bull.Civ. IV no.40, p.30.

[683] A fact which makes the reviewer Couchez hesitate, at (1983) *Rev Crit* p.115, to include Article 809(2) in Article 24.

[684] Grandcourt, J. 'Les compétences respectives du juge des référés et de l'arbitre international' in *L'internationalisation du droit, Mélanges en l'honneur de Yvon Loussouarn*, 1994, 203.

[685] ('no simple provisional measure, due to the fact that the *référé-provision* can be aimed a the whole of the debt and leads to an immediate payment').

[686] *Ibid.*, at p.209.

[687] *Cour de Cassation* 1er Ch. Civ. 29.11.1989 *Société Balenciaga c/ Société Allieri et Giovanozzi* (1990) *Rev Arb* 633 (where the sum in dispute was 42.5 million lire); TGI Paris (Réf) 21.2.1986 *Maeght et*

full trial (in another Contracting State), on the merits. Rose is not alone in doubting that any such measures as allow for full compensation are provisional or protective:

> [i]f the relief granted under Article 24 would fully satisfy the plaintiff's cause of action then it is not provisional.[688]

3.7.3   Dispensing with the need for a full trial[689]

The rule-of-thumb characteristic that is normally associated with interim relief is that it ensures there is a fund available, against which execution of a trial judgment on the merits can be levied, not that it *replaces* this full trial:

> Ziel des einstweiligen Rechtsschutzes sei, die . . . Sicherung des Anspruchs oder des Rechtsverhältnisses und *zwar die reale Sicherung der realen Durchfuhrung der Zwangsvollstreckung.*[690]

Naturally, if the applicant has been fully compensated in his home forum,[691] there is no incentive to litigate abroad.[692]

3.7.4   A reversal of certain aspects of the litigation

The short, yet important point is made by Perrot,[693] that an unsuccessful respondent, should he wish to escape the unfortunate consequences of Article 809(2), instead of merely defending his corner—normally under Article 2 of the Brussels Convention—is put to the trouble: either of appealing in France against the *provision*; or, worse still, of taking the initiative of launching an action

---

autres c/ Société Galerie Maeght-elong (1986) *Rev Arb* 565, at p.577 (5.2 million francs)—both cases where *provisions* were sought during an international arbitration—recently *Cour de Cassation* 29.6.1999 (1999) *Dalloz*, Com., 649.

[688] Rose, N. *Pre-emptive remedies in Europe*, 1992, at p.21.

[689] Esp. Merkt, 1993, at p.33, para. 76: 'la procédure du référé-provision est en réalité une procédure au fond, qui permet, en fait sinon en droit, de trancher définitivement certains litiges . . .'('the *référé* provisional procedure is, in reality, a procedure on the merits, that allows in fact if not in law, a resolution of certain disputes and can, in effect settle the dispute once and for all by granting to the creditor all the sum due'); also Donzallaz, Y. *La Convention de Lugano*, Vol I, 1996, paras. 1-1736, at p.622, para. 1645; 'le référé-provision peut, en effet, vider totalement le litige en allouant au créancier tout son dû'; Najjar, I reviewing *Cour de Cassation* 29.6.1999 (1999) *Dalloz*, Com., 649.

[690] Morbach, 1988, at p.9.

[691] Statistical analysis undertaken by Weber, 1993, by questionnaire, submitted to various French courts, demonstrates that the grant of a *provision* in 80–90% of cases settles the matter on the merits, at pp.132–33, and is the most effective procedure for doing so, at p.130.

[692] Geimer and Schütze, 1997 p.402, para. 22.

[693] Perrot, R. 'Les mesures provisoires en droit français' in Tarzia (ed) *Les mesures provisoires en procédure civile*, 1985, p.149, at p.169 para. 24.

of non-liability, and then, it successful, trying to recoup any money he may have been forced to pay over.[694] This therefore in effect 'renverse ainsi le contentieu[695]'.[696]

3.7.5 The risk of the applicant's ensuing insolvency[697]

This disadvantage is always present if, subsequent to payment, the respondent shows that the underlying dispute was, *ab initio*, 'sérieusement contestable':

> Qu'arrivera-t-il lorsque les juges du fond statueront dans un sens différent et que la victime devenue entre-temps insolvable ne pourra plus rien rembourser?[698] [699]

3.7.6 A *détournement* of the Convention and the issue of 'exportability'[700]

Lastly, due to the combination of: (1) Article 24's remittance rule to national law;[701] (2) the definition of 'judgment' in Article 25 which includes provisional and protective relief; (3) the ruling in *Denilauer v Couchet Frères*[702] and therefore the exportability,[703] if necessary of an *ordonnance en référé*, the very protective jurisdictional regime of Articles 2ff of the Brussels Convention could be undermined.[704] A Frenchman,[705] on the basis of Article 14 *Code civil* can obtain *en référé* a *provision* up to the full amount of his claim against a respondent domiciled in another Contracting State;[706] should the latter have no assets in France, the *provision* would appear to be[707] recognisable and enforceable in England under Article 25 and Article 31 in Part III of the Brussels Convention.[708] This result, which defies

---

[694] Or to enforce a *Van Uden Maritime* guarantee in another Contracting State.

[695] ('this reverses the litigation').

[696] Perrot, R. 1985, at p.169.

[697] Baker, W. and De Fontbressin, P. (1992–3) *Uni Miami Yrbk Int L* 1, at p.26—however the former practice of not providing a guarantee may have to change after *Van Uden Maritime*.

[698] ('What would happen if the judges on the merits were to give judgment in a different way and in the meantime the victim had become bankrupt and could not re-imburse anything').

[699] Tendler, R. 'Le juge des référés, une «procédure ordinaire»?' in *Dalloz*, (1991), Chron., A–21, at p.139; also Baker, W. and De Fontbressin, at p.26; ameliorated somewhat by a (bank) guarantee.

[700] Delaporte, V. 'Les mesures provisoires en droit international privé' in *Droit international privé* 1987–1988, p.147, at p.148: 'il faut que la mesure . . . soit prise par le juge . . . où elle doit être exécutée' ('It is necessary that the measure is taken by the judge where it is to be enforced').

[701] Above, at pp.283–284; *Van Uden Maritime* has confirmed this.

[702] *Bernard Denilauer v S.n.c. Couchet Frères* (C-125/79) [1980] ECR 1553.

[703] *OLG München* (2000) *RIW* 464 has, however, stated that such a payment order is *not* an Article 25 'judgment'.

[704] The ECJ in *Hans Herman Mietz* was alive to these dangers.

[705] An no-one else.

[706] Even in the face of an Article 17 jurisdiction clause, and, it is thought Article 16; Beraudo, example quoted by Gaudemet-Tallon, 1996, at p.195, n.10.

[707] *Quaere*, the effect of *Van Uden Maritime* and *Société Bachy c/ Société Belbetoes Fundacoes e Betoes Especiais LDA* (1999) *Rev crit* 352, (2000) *JDI* 83, [1999] I.L.Pr. 743; *OLG München* (2000) *RIW* 464.

[708] This bold assertion now has to be tempered by the decision in *Mietz*; but for enforcement internally in France itself, a *détournement* there undeniably has been.

the logical framework and ideals of the Convention, is what is known as its *détournement:*[709]

> Ainsi, en particulier, la procédure française du référé-provision . . . pourrait-elle être employée pour méconnaître les règles de compétence de la Convention.[710] [711]

3.7.7 The discussion in the cases, and a comparison with the *référé* granted in international commercial arbitration

Two cases, one from the *Cour d'Appel de Rouen,*[712] the other the *Cour d'Appel de Paris*[713] have had to consider the question of whether Article 809(2) is a 'mesure provisoire ou conservatoire'[714] in the context of an application under Article 8(5) of the ICC rules in an international arbitration,[715] which was underway.[716] In the former case, *Société Engrais de Saint-Wandrille*, the court was at pains to point out that a judge *en référé* considers the merits of a case when deciding an application, and thus such an in-depth analysis was properly in the remit of the appointed arbitrators:

> pour statuer sur de telles prétensions la juridiction des référés doit nécessairement examiner le fond du litige et prendre inévitablement parti au moins sur certains éléments de celui-ci . . . *le référé-provision ne saurait être assimilé aux mesures provisoires ou conservatoires* prévus par [8(5)] comme compatible avec la poursuite de l'instance arbitrale.[717] [718]

A similar conclusion was reached by the Paris Court of Appeal in *Société industrielle d'acide phosphorique* that 'une telle demande ne peut être assimilée à celle d'une simple mesure conservatoire[719]'.[720] These pronouncements were made in the

---

[709] From Gaillard, (1993) *SJ* 141, at p.141; also Albrecht, 1991, at p.103; also Bermann, (1997) *Col J Transnat L* 553, at p.558 'transnational provisional relief is both an imperative of, and a potential threat to, contemporary international litigation.'

[710] ('Thus, in particular, the French *référé-provision* procedure . . . may be deployed to circumvent the jurisdiction rules of the Convention').

[711] Gaudemet-Tallon, 1996, at p.195, para. 269.

[712] *Société Engrais de Saint-Wandrille «E.S.W.» c/ Société Trans Agricultrual Investment «T.A.I»*, (1986) *Rev Arb* 565, at p.566.

[713] *Société industrielle d'acide phosphorique et d'engrais c/ Société Industrie engrais commerce* (1986) *Rev Arb* 565, at p.574.

[714] Incidentally the same words used *verbatim ac litteratim* as in Article 24.

[715] Mentioned in Collins, 1994, at p.38–39.

[716] When the *ad hoc* tribunal is not constituted, *Cour de Cassation* Ch.Civ., 6.3.1990, (1990) *Rev. Arb.* 633, at p.636.

[717] ('to decide on such claims the *référé* jurisdiction must of necessity examine the merits of the dispute and inevitably take a stand on certain aspects of it . . . *the référé-provision cannot be compared with provisional and protective measure* laid down in [8(5)] as being compatible with the arbitration proceedings').

[718] (1986) *Rev Arb* p.573.

[719] ('such an application cannot be compared to one for a simple protective measure').

[720] (1986) *Rev Arb*, at p.579.

context of arbitrations already underway, subject also to the rules of the ICC. Yet it would seem at best inconsistent, fervently to classify the *référé-provision* as not belonging to the provisional and protective measures under Article 8(5) ICC rules, yet not to adopt the same reasoning and classification to the identical words in Article 24 Brussels Convention,[721] even if litigation were not underway in another Contracting State.

More inconsistency follows when the arbitration tribunal has not yet been constituted. The *Cour de Cassation*[722] has allowed recourse to a *provision*,[723] despite the presence of an arbitration clause. When there is an unconstituted tribunal, this fact

> n'exclut pas, en cas d'urgence . . . la compétence exceptionnelle du juge des référés[724] [725]

Leaving aside the constituted/unconstituted arbitration argument, it is clear from the earlier cases that the courts thought, at least with regard to arbitration, that the intrusion into a consideration on the merits usurped the arbitrators' remit and disqualified Article 809(2) from consideration as a provisional or protective measure. It is therefore, again, inconsistent that, *a fortiori*, the same question as to Article 809(2)'s inclusion in Article 24 in the litigation context is not more forthrightly and squarely answered in the negative. As regards the *référé-provision* under Article 24 of the Brussels Convention, the facts of the cases involving Article 24 have been rehearsed earlier in relation to jurisdiction.

In one of the earliest 'litigation' cases *Tron c/ Société Verkor*,[726] a *provision* was granted in favour of a French employee against his erstwhile Belgian employer.[727] Holleaux,[728] the commentator, recognised at an early stage, the danger of combining Article 24 and Article 809(2) in an international Brussels Convention context:

> la mesure en question constitue *une anticipation de la décision au fond* . . . dans le cadre de la Convention de Bruxelles, on s'étonne qu'elle puisse être décidée par un autre juge que celui compétent au principal, suivant les règles conventionelles.[729] [730]

---

[721] Unfortunately not the case, the *Cour de Cassation* 13.4.1999 *Bachy c/ Soc. Belbetoes* (1999) *Rev Crit* 352; and *Hermès International v FHT Marketing Choice BV* [1998] ECR I–3603.

[722] *Société Horeva c/ Société Sitas*, 1re Ch. Civ., 6.3.1990, (1990) *Rev Arb* 633, at p.636.

[723] Additionally the Court required urgency to be shown; this is not an explicit requirement in the wording of Article 809(2) itself.

[724] ('does not, in cases of urgency . . . exclude the special jurisdiction of the *référé* judge').

[725] *Ibid.*

[726] *TGI de Nanterre*, 9.10.1978, (1979) *Rev Crit* 128, obs. Metzger; (1980) *JDI* 894; *Cour d'appel de Versailles*, 27.6.1979, (1980) *JDI* 894, obs. Holleaux; the order was reversed on appeal, simply because the claim was 'sérieusement contestable'; also *Cassation* (2000) *Dalloz*, IR, 264.

[727] The French courts would now have jurisdiction on the merits under post-San-Sebastian Article 5(1) amendments in any case.

[728] Metzger, too, at (1979) *Rev crit* 128, at p.132, thought that 809(2) was not 'provisoire au sens habituel'.

[729] ('the measure in question amounts to pre-empting the decision on the merits . . . within the Brussels Convention system, it is remarkable that it may be granted by a judge other than that with jurisdiction on the merits according to the rules of the Convention').

[730] (1980) *JDI* 894, at p.895.

Again, in *Diehm c/ Mlle Sicre*[731] a *provision* was granted[732] to Mlle. Sicre against a German driver and his insurers over an accident that had occurred in Germany. The reviewer wonders whether this remedy is a 'simple mesure provisoire'.[733] Later in *Menegatti c/ Société Mettalurgica Nava Stefano e Guiseppina*[734] a payment of 380,000Fr was awarded to an Italian, domiciled in France, against Mettalurgica, domiciled in Italy. Huet is critical of this decision which misconceives of the wording of Article 24 and of the Brussels Convention system.[735] Yet the most ringing endorsement of the use of Article 809(2) comes from a brace of cases, one the *Cour d'Appel de Chambéry,*[736] the other from the *Cour d'Appel de Rennes.*[737] Perhaps, with respect, being blinkered by a national provision in the NCPC, Article 484 (which announces the blanket sobriquet of 'provisioire' for all orders *en référé*) these courts held with regard to Article 809(2), that the *référé-provision*:

entre *parfaitement* dans le champ d'application de l'article 24 de la Convention[738] [739]

The post-*Van Uden Maritime Cour de Cassation* case of *Bachy c/ Belbetoes*[740] has put any argument beyond doubt. As has been mentioned, the *provision* granted to a French company against its Portuguese contracting party under Article 873(2) NCPC in the Paris first instance court was an Article 24 provisional measure, albeit with a requirement for domestic enforceability.

These cases show Article 809(2) being used liberally in Brussels Convention cases under Article 24, and the *provision* itself being accommodated into the definition of 'provisional, including protective measures'. Conversely, with the exception of Vareilles-Sommières[741] and Couchez,[742] commentators[743] believe either that Article 809(2), for the sake of a uniform interpretation of Article 24, should be

---

[731] *Cour d'appel d'Aix-en-Provence*, 4.5.1981, (1983) *Rev crit* 110, obs. Couchez.

[732] (1983) *Rev crit* 110, at p.112, a sum of 15,000Fr.

[733] *Ibid.*, at p.116, but Couchez finally concedes that it is such a measure; a stricter regime regarding the classification of such measures should reign in the Article 24 context; and thinks urgency should be required.

[734] *Cour d'appel de Paris*, 14e Ch., 17.11.1987, (1989) *JDI* 96, obs. Huet.

[735] (1989) *JDI* 96, at p.98.

[736] *SARL Yakari Italie c/ S.A. Gondrand et Société Vinco*, 2.3.1992 (1994) *JDI* 173, obs. Huet.

[737] *Société Zinser Fleisch Handelsgesellschaft c/ S.A. Salaisons du JET Jean Laurent* (1994) *JDI* 173, (1993) *JCP*, IV, Juris 179, no.1519; the case came to a strange conclusion, yet was not directly concerned with Article 24.

[738] ('fits precisely into the scope of the application of Article 24').

[739] (1994) *JDI*, at p.174.

[740] (1999) *Rev crit* 352.

[741] Vareilles-Sommières, (1996) *Rev crit* 397.

[742] In *Mélanges offerts à Pierre Raynaud*, 1985, p.161.

[743] Gaudemet-Tallon, 1996, at p.196; Gothot, P. et Holleaux, D., 1985, at p.117; Mamet-Rosenbaum, 1994, Tome II at p.410, para. 470.

excluded in its entirety,[744] or at the very least, be subjected to an additional requirement of urgency.[745]

The preponderance of French decisions under Article 809(2), demonstrate the potential concerns expressed in *Hans Herman Mietz* of Article 24, and reveal the naivety of those[746] who thought that measures would be requested from the courts closest to where those measures were to be carried out. Article 809(2) has neatly shown that an applicant does not have to go to each and every Contracting State where a respondent has assets; he can simply obtain an order in the *forum actoris*, under the now exposed anathema grounds in Article 3[I][II]. Prior to *Van Uden Maritime* and *Hans Herman Mietz*, it was believed an applicant could also seek its enforcement under the simplified provisions of Title III. As long as the respondent has assets in France, *Van Uden Maritime* and *Hans Herman Mietz* at the least will not prevent an applicant obtaining a provisionally-enforceable *référé-provision* there.

3.8   THE BRUSSELS I REGULATION AND THE HAGUE CONFERENCE DRAFT WORLDWIDE JUDGMENTS CONVENTION

In section 6a of the first Commission proposal of December 1997, entitled 'Jurisdiction in respect of provisional, including protective measures', the Commission had proposed a redrafting of Article 24, in a new Article 18a(1)(2). Any measures sought had to find 'enforce[ment] in [the] territory' of the court addressed, 'irrespective of the place where they produce[d] their effects' under similar circumstances as under the old Article 24. Article 18a(2) would have provided a definition of provisional measures, meaning, *inter alia*, 'urgent measures for the examination of a dispute, for the preservation of evidence or of property . . .'.[747]

However, the Brussels I Regulation, will not take up[748] the amendments proposed by the earlier Commission document, but has retained the original wording of Article 24 of the Brussels/Lugano Conventions, *mutatis mutandis*, for a

---

[744] Or as advocated earlier, should not receive the benefit of recognition under Title III—*Van Uden Maritime* and *Hans Herman Mietz* may now have quietened the concerns of cross-border enforcement somewhat.

[745] As the *Cour de Cassation* had done in the arbitration case of *Société Horeva c/ Société Sitas*, 1re Ch. Civ., 6.3.1990, (1990) *Rev Arb* 633, above, at p.364; Gothot and Holleaux, 1985, say '[l]es verifications consécutives à la condition d'urgence auraient donc suffit à éviter que les juges français *ne mettent en péril l'équilibre des compétences* . . . en applicant l'article 809 . . . sous le couvert de l'article 24' ('the enquiries following on from the requirement of urgency would have been sufficient to avoid the fact that French judges should imperil the balance of jurisdiction by applying Article 809, under the pretext of Article 24'), at p.117.

[746] Droz, 1972, at p.200.

[747] This definition would have been sufficiently narrow to exclude interim judgments for the payment of contractual consideration.

[748] It could be remarked that the *verbatim* re-adoption in Article 31 acknowledges approbation of *Van Uden Maritime*.

Community instrument. It continues in the same form as Article 24, in Article 31 of the Brussels I Regulation.

As the Commission pointed out in the explanatory memorandum to the July 1999 proposal, at p.20, Article 31, cast in identical terms to the previous Article 24, 'must be read in the light of preliminary rulings given by the Court of Justice under the Protocol to the Brussels Convention'. This means that the jurisprudence of the ECJ, notably *Van Uden Maritime* and *Hans Herman Mietz*, will continue to govern the interpretation of the new Article 31 from 1.3.2002.[749] This reversion must indicate tacit approval of the way the ECJ itself, in its jurisprudence, has shaped the development of provisional measures under Article 24, and condones the imposition of the 'safeguards' set out in the above two cases.

As far as the work of the Hague Conference on Private International Law is concerned, the 'Preliminary Draft Convention on Jurisdiction and Foreign Judgments in Civil and Commercial Matters'[750] adopted at the meeting of the Special Commission on 25–30 October 1999, dealt with provisional and protective measures in its Article 13. Subject to further agreement on the scope *ratione materiae* of provisional and/or protective measures in Article 1(2)(k)[751] of the re-negotiated Hague Special Commission II interim text, Article 13 of the former version will survive in this latter instrument, although in a much amended form. In what follows, both versions of Article 13 will be compared side by side.

Reading the original manifestation of Article 13's construction, it is no doubt clear that it delineated jurisdiction to order provisional and protective measures, as had the ECJ decision in *Van Uden Maritime*, since it unambiguously reflected the ECJ's division of competence under Article 24 of the Brussels Convention,[752] and corresponding powers of a national court to order interim relief. Article 13(1) stated that a court with jurisdiction on the merits under any of the foregoing articles of the October 1999 Draft Convention (i.e. under Articles 3–12) may have ordered, in unfettered fashion, any interim relief (that may be available[753] to the domestic court). Such a decision under Article 13(1) was also capable of recognition and enforcement under Chapter III—the cross-border effects of

---

[749] The issue of cross-border enforcement should have been addressed specifically.

[750] Again available on-line at http://www.hcch.net/e/conventions/draft36e.html

[751] Article 1(2)(k), Alternative A, if adopted, would *not* subject jurisdiction to order provisional and protective measures to the limitations of the Convention's jurisdictional scheme, *except* in the case of 'interim payment orders'; these, as has been seen above, have been controversial in the context of Article 24 of the Brussels Convention, (and see the comment in footnote 9 to the text of Alternative A); Alternative B, if adopted, would either exclude this area of practice from the Convention in its entirety or force the inclusion into the draft Convention's scheme of provisional or protective measures, 'mentioned in', ie. defined by Articles 13 and 23A—while, *a contrario*, excluding any that did not so fall from the regime. Unhelpfully, no consensus is said to have existed among the delegates at the June 2001 conference as to the exclusion or inclusion of such measures *ratione materiae*.

[752] This difference in Proposition A(i) and A(ii) above, at p.283.

[753] Note US Supreme Court practice, *Grupo Mexicano de Desarrollo S.A. v Alliance Bond Fund, Inc.* 527 US—, 144 L Ed. 2d 319, at p.338–39.

interlocutory orders emanating from courts with jurisdiction on the merits was preserved in the definition of 'judgment' given in Article 23(b).

The underlying rationale of Article 13(1), Alternative A[754] of the draft Commission II interim text, is a direct yet more restrictive reprise of the earlier version of Article 13:

> A court seised and having jurisdiction under Articles [in the white list] to determine the merits of the case has jurisdiction to order provisional and protective measures.[755]

Only minor comments need be made on the differences. The inclusion of the word 'seised', as a past participle, without a qualification of 'or about to be seised', would seem to suggest that any English claim form commencing proceedings on the merits of a action on one or more grounds of jurisdiction in Articles 4, 7, 8, 11, 12, and 13 has already been 'lodged with the court.'[756] This restriction on pre-commencement interlocutory activity was not evident at all in the earlier version of Article 13(1). Of note too, in footnote 92 to the main text of the interim draft, should be the 'cumulative'[757] definition of 'provisional *and* protective measures', again not evident from the 'alternative' expression in the earlier version. As with the earlier version, measures emanating, under Article 13(1), from a court seised on the merits are, subject always to the permitted defences, to be recognised and enforced in other Contracting States under Article 23A, Alternative A; with the *caveat* that they must fall within the definitional section of Article 23A(2)(a)(b)(c).[758] The fact that a definitional restriction is subsequently place in Article 23A(2) on the, presumably, cross-border aspects of Article 13(1) provisional and protective measures reflects no doubt the delegates' concern over the 'exportability' of such measures outside the jurisdiction of the Contracting State which granted them.

Article 13(2) of the October 1999 draft was property-specific, permitting any provisional measures to have been taken in the courts of the State where that

---

[754] Its Alternative B is a far simpler version of the whole of Alternative A, and would restrict the grant of provisional and protective measures to *the court which is simultaneously also seised of a claim on the merits*: 'A court which is or is about to be seised of a claim *and* which has jurisdiction under Articles [3 to 15] to determine the merits thereof may order provisional and protective measures, intended to preserve the subject-matter of the claim.'

[755] Internal footnotes omitted.

[756] This expression will, it is submitted, be borrowed from the 'autonomous' definition, for English civil procedure, in Article 21(5)(a) of the interim text relating to 'first seisure' and *lis pendens*.

[757] This, it is submitted, may still not suffice to exclude the types of procedures and orders witnessed in the *référé-provision* section of this chapter; from the current text of Article 13(1), provisional and protective measures granted thereunder are not subject to the definitional limitation of Article 13(4)(a)(b)(c); however, applicants seeking such measures would be advised to seek to ensure they do so if they wish to benefit from the recognition and enforcement regime of the Convention's Article 23A, and following footnote.

[758] These are identical to the definition of a 'provisional and protective measure' for the purpose of Article 13(3), set out in Article 13(4): both read as follows: '(a) a measure to maintain the status quo pending determination of the issues at trial; or (b) a measure providing a preliminary means of securing assets out of which an ultimate judgment may be satisfied; or (c) a measure to refrain conduct by a defendant to prevent current or imminent future harm'.

property was located. This sub-paragraph would thus have permitted an English court to have taken jurisdiction over a non-domiciled defendant/respondent to a *Mareva*[759]/freezing injunction, where the property or assets to be frozen were located (in England); the same may be said of the *Arrest* option given to the German courts under §919 ZPO, or the extreme urgency for an *einstweilige Verfügung* under § 942 ZPO. It may also have been the case that the French courts would have considered themselves competent to order *en référé* a *provision* of contractual consideration—or, indeed, the Dutch courts an order in 'kort geding' proceedings—where the defendant had property located in France or The Netherlands.

The underlying purpose of Article 13(2), Alternative A, of the Commission II interim text is also a property-specific provision, but is now expressed in a more convoluted, expansive, and detailed way:

> A court of a Contracting State [may] [has jurisdiction to], even where it does not have jurisdiction to determine the merits of a claim, order a provisional and protective measure in respect of property in that State or the enforcement of which is limited to the territory of that State, to protect on an interim basis a claim on the merits which is pending or to be brought by the requesting party in a Contracting State which has jurisdiction to determine that claim under Articles [in the white list].

Although implicit in the older Article 13(2), the new Article 13(2) makes it clear that the court concerned here will *not* have[760] 'jurisdiction[761] to determine the merits of a claim'. What may[762] now be ordered in such a court is a provisional and protective measure:[763]

(i)   'in respect of property in that State';[764] or
(ii)   'the enforcement of which is limited to the territory of that State',[765]

in each case to protect 'on an interim basis'[766] the substantive action 'pending[767] or to be brought' by the applicant in another Contracting State, which has (or

---

[759] Article 13(2) was fairly clear in its language that a *worldwide Mareva*/freezing injunction may not have been sanctioned here.

[760] In the expression in Article 13(2) 'even where'; the Article 13(1) court is clearly a court with jurisdiction on the merits.

[761] *Quaere*, jurisdiction under national law, and on bases of jurisdiction in the Convention excluded from the so-called 'white list'.

[762] The comment in footnote 94 to the main text of Article 13(2) does not, since s 25 CJJA 1982, (as extended by The Civil Jurisdiction and Judgments Act 1982 (Interim Relief) Order 1997 SI 1997/302), apply to interim relief practice in the UK.

[763] Again, at this (jurisdictional) stage, without any definitional limitation in the text.

[764] This is similar to the provision in the older Article 13(2); reference should therefore be made to the comments on this, and also to the footnote numbered 94.

[765] This would provide a basis for the grant of a *Mareva*/freezing injunction, and possibly also for the grant of a *référé-provision* over French located assets.

[766] As we have seen in the section on the French *référé-provision*, such measures are not granted on an interim basis; nothing will probably turn on this expression in practice though.

[767] A different expression than 'seised' in Article 13(1), and potentially at a later stage in the proceedings; however, it is emasculated by the subsequent wording 'or to be brought' in any event.

potentially may have) jurisdiction under[768] Articles 4, 7, 8, 11, 12, and 13. Although it has more elements to it, much of what has already been said with regard to the older version of Article 13(2) need not be repeated here.

As far as recognition and enforcement of Article 13(2) measures are concerned, Article 23A, Alternative A,[769] would provide *no* basis for such steps, since, *ex hypothesi*, they would have been rendered by a court other than one seised on the merits.

Under Article 13(3) of the October 1999 draft, there was a (limited) catch-all provision when a court was neither seised on the merits under Article 13(1), nor had property within its jurisdiction in respect of which measures under Article 13(2) could have been taken. Under Article 13(3), a court may have ordered provisional measures only if[770] 'their enforcement [was] limited to the territory of that State', per Article 13(3)(a) *and* 'their purpose[771] [was] to protect on an interim basis a claim on the merits which [was] pending . . . by the requesting party', per Article 13(3)(b).

Unlike the French *référé-provision*, worldwide *Mareva*/freezing injunctions did not have the potential to offend Article 13(3)(b); their problem stemmed from Article 13(3)(a), where, as we have seen, 'their enforcement [must have been] limited to the [granting] territory'. Article 13(3) concentrated on the measures themselves, rather than—as do English interlocutory orders such as *Marevas*—on their *in personam* nature. This characteristic meant that the party enjoined from carrying out the provisions of such orders was before the English court,[772] and sanctionable with contempt if in breach. If 'enforcement' in Article 13(3)(a) related—as it seemed—to the *Mareva*/freezing injunction itself, and not the respondent over whom the court had *in personam* jurisdiction, such a *Mareva*/freezing injunction would have been limited to 'the territory of that State'.[773]

As for the French *référé-provision*, even if enforcement had been limited to France, clearly this would not have satisfied the buttressing (and definitional) rôle that was envisaged for provisional measures by Article 13(3)(b).[774] Article 13, it

---

[768] One of the two aspects which differentiates jurisdiction (of the court on the merits) under Article 13(2) from that under Article 13(3), below.

[769] 'A decision ordering a provisional and protective measure, which has been taken by a court seised-with the claim on the merits, shall be recognised and enforced in Contracting States in accordance with Articles [25, 27–34].' There is, however, an Alternative B to Article 23A; this, conversely, if adopted, on its wording alone, would allow measures granted under *the whole spectrum of Article 13* to enter the scheme set up under the interim text of the Convention; note also the comment in footnote 141 to the text of Article 23A.

[770] Expressed as 'provided that'.

[771] The ancillary nature of the court's jurisdiction under Article 13(3)(b) had been even clearer in the earlier version of the Draft Convention adopted by the Special Commission on 18 June 1999: 'their [sole] purpose [was] to protect . . .'.

[772] Even if served *ex juris*.

[773] Article 13(3)(a) jurisdiction would have therefore overlapped considerably with Article 13(2) jurisdiction.

[774] Again the Nygh/Pocar report, in its wording ('cannot seriously contest') would have excluded the *provision* under Article 809(2).

seems, was clear in its attempt to stifle the cross-border circulation of provisional measures.

Article 13(3) and Article 13(4),[775] Alternative A, of the Commission II interim draft, should be read together:

> Nothing in this Convention shall prevent a court in a Contracting State from ordering a provisional and protective measure for the purpose of protecting on an interim basis a claim on the merits which is pending or to [be] brought by the requesting party in another State.

These two articles represent, in practice, a residual, catch-all category for jurisdiction in one Contracting State to order provisional and protective measures,[776] 'on an interim basis' in aid of a claim on the merits pending, or to be brought in, another State. What immediately differentiates Article 13(3) from Article 13(2), apart from the limitation of the measures available in Article 13(4), is that the Contracting State court in which a claim on the merits may be pending (or threatened) need not intend to take (or have taken) jurisdiction under the 'acceptable' 'white list' of Articles 4, 7, 8, 11, 12 and 13: hence the attempted reigning in of the provisional measures that may be sought by a (rather widely-drawn) definitional section Article 13(4).[777] Under the current wording of Article 13(3), as presented, both courts, on the merits and ordering such Article 13(4) measures, may take jurisdiction on bases of jurisdiction otherwise anathematised by Article 18, and to some extent Article 17.

The immediate dangers inherent in Article 13(3), especially in conjunction with measures under Article 13(4)(c), will be obvious, and have been explored with regard to Article 24 Brussels Convention and the section on the French *référé-provision*, in both its jurisdictional and substantive aspects. The same points may be re-iterated here, especially if Article 23A, Alternative B[778]—regarding the recognition and enforcement of (all) Article 13 measures—were to be adopted.

3.9 CONCLUSION

There is little doubt that the practice of granting provisional, including protective measures, will, in future, gain much greater prominence than hitherto: certainty over the jurisdictional base to grant them having been provided in *Van Uden Maritime*. Overt approval of the current development in Article 24 jurisprudence is witnessed by the reintroduction of Article 24's wording into Article 31 of the Brussels I Regulation. Whether such a move will turn out to be complacency, in

---

[775] A definitional section, identical to Article 23A(2), Alternative A, quoted above at n.769.
[776] As defined in Article 13(4).
[777] This has already been mentioned in regard to the recognition and enforcement provisions of Article 23A, Alternative A in Article 23A(2), above n.769.
[778] Previously quoted above, at n.754.

the light of this chapter's attempt to emphasise the dangers of individual Contracting State's procedures in granting provisional measures, is a matter for debate. Real danger exists, however, of a *détournement* of the Brussels Convention's jurisdictional regime on the merits, when combining the expanded possibilities offered by Article 24—a provisionally enforceable judgment granted in truncated proceedings (on the basis of the applicant's nationality), even if enforcement of it is not sought abroad.

While the jurisdictional base has become certain, queries exist over the exact scope of the safeguards put in place by *Van Uden Maritime*: the nature of the connecting link between the measures sought and the granting court, and whether *Van Uden Maritime* and *Mietz* have effectively blocked cross-border enforcement of Article 24 provisional measures once and for all. If this is so, these cases will have all but partitioned up the Contracting States into a series of provisional, including protective judicial 'areas', with an assessment of the relative (un-)attractiveness of each an attendant result.

As far as English practice of granting *Mareva*/freezing injunctions and other provisional measures is concerned, the effect and scope of the *Van Uden Maritime* 'safeguards' is uncertain. Can an English court now grant a worldwide *Mareva*/freezing injunction under Article 24, and section 25 CJJA 1982, over assets of the respondent located in other Contracting States, and will these States now be compelled to recognise and/or enforce it? An answer to this question is contingent on whether the additional 'safeguards' mentioned in *Van Uden Maritime* and *Mietz*—for provisional judgments of contractual consideration, also bite on temporary freezing injunctions, even over overseas assets.[779]

That there is any form of protectionism at work in Contracting State jurisdictions may (now) be hard to distinguish from that built-in to the civil procedure codes and substantive law/practice on interim relief itself—*Van Uden Maritime* will simply have brought any such advantageous positions to the fore. It we have to direct our gaze anywhere, it should be to France, to find out the impact of *Van Uden Maritime* on the *référé-provision* procedure.

---

[779] *OLG München* 5.4.2000 (2000) *RIW* 464, reviewed above, at pp.321–322.

4

Article 27(1): Public Policy

INTRODUCTION

THE 'UNRULY HORSE' of public policy[1] has had a long history[2] in bilateral[3] and multilateral[4] recognition and enforcement Conventions, not only with regard to judgments, but also to arbitral awards.[5] It was, and is, present in the autonomous laws of those Contracting States[6] which had a (or any) developed recognition and enforcement law. It would come as no surprise therefore to discover that this veteran defence made an appearance[7] in Articles 27(1) of the Brussels and Lugano Conventions. Droz,[8] in his early work on the Brussels Convention, was of the opinion that public policy was included not so much as a defence provision *simpliciter*, but more as a 'soupape de sûreté'[9][10] for those

---

[1] Burrough LJ's view of the defence in *Richardson v Mellish* (1824) 2 Bing. 229, at p.252: 'It is never argued at all but when other points fail'; Nourissat, C. (2001) *JCP*, II, 10607, at p.1899, quoting the views of Bartin on the subject; Smith, D. 9 POF3d 687, at p.732: 'a catch-all provision'.

[2] Cf Beaumont, P. *Civil Jurisdiction in Scotland: Brussels and Lugano Conventions*, 2nd edn., 1995, at p.186, para. 8.13; Bülow, A. and Böckstiegel, K.-H., *Der Internationale Rechtsverkehr in Zivil- und Handelssachen*, Band I, II, 1985; and ECJ in *Eco Swiss China Time Ltd v Benetton International NV* (C–126/97) [1999] ECR I–3055, at p.3093, para. 39.

[3] Among them being Article III(i)(c) of *Abkommen zwischen der Bundesrepublik Deutschland und dem Vereinigten Königreich Großbritannein und Nordirland über die gegenseitige Anerkennung und Vollstreckung von gerichtlichen Entscheidungen in Zivil- und Handelssachen*, 14.7.1960, (1961) BGBl, II, 302, in force 15.7.1961; also Article 7(a) of the aborted UK-US Convention on the Reciprocal Recognition and Enforcement of Judgments in civil and commercial matters, (1977) *ILM* 71.

[4] For example Article 5(1) of the 1971 Hague Convention on the Recognition and Enforcement of Foreign Judgments in civil and commercial matters—1.2.1971, 144 UNTS 249, and (1966) *Annuaire suisse de droit international* 267.

[5] Article V(2)(b) of The New York Convention 1958, 330 UNTS 38 (1958) no.4739, in force June 7 1959—where public policy has been described as 'a defense without meaningful definition,... pragmatically useless if not altogether nonexistent', Berglin, H. 4 *Dick. J Int'l L* 167, at p.169.

[6] Considered by Bruns, A. 'Der anerkennungsrechtliche ordre public in Europa und den USA' (1999) *JZ* 278, at p.278 to be an essential defence, recognised worldwide; Lenz, C. *Amerikanische Punitive Damages vor dem Schweizer Richter*, 1992, at pp.140–50.

[7] Criticised early on by esp. Bellet, P. 'L'élaboration d'une convention sur la reconnaissance des jugements dans le cadre du Marché Commun' (1965) *JDI* 833 at p.840; retained by Article 34(1) of the Brussels I Regulation as '*manifestly* contrary to public policy'.

[8] Droz, 1972, at p.309, para. 487.

[9] ('a safety valve').

[10] Weser, M. 'Faut-it réviser la Convention franco-italienne du 3 juin 1930 sur l'exécution des jugements?' (1954) *Rev crit* 451, at p.470.

Contracting States in which the provisions of Title III, and especially Articles 28 and 29, would prove to be a radical departure[11] from national procedures hitherto:

> la clause d'ordre public [était] d'abord comme un élément tendant à faciliter la ratification du Traité, en 'rassurant' les Etats contractants[12] [13]

Its exact scope[14] is controversial,[15] and its parameters between an international and domestic application, uncertain.[16] It is a fluid concept, varying in meaning and extent in the temporal, economic and socio-legal context.[17]

The Jenard Report[18] is brief on what Article 27(1) in fact comprises, merely stating, unhelpfully, that 'this clause ought to operate only in exceptional circumstances';[19] and that Article 27(1) represents a ground 'for refusal, not of the foreign judgment itself, but if recognition of it is contrary to public policy'[20] in the State addressed. The Schlosser Report[21] is slightly more specific in its mention of the defence of fraud's qualification for inclusion in Article 27(1), but provides no more concrete[22] guidelines.

---

[11] Common in the autonomous enforcement regimes of the Contracting States is an examination of the jurisdiction of the rendering court.

[12] ('the public policy clause [was] at first like a measure as it were to ease the ratification of the Treaty by 'reassuring' the Contracting States'.

[13] (1954) *Rev crit* 451, at p.470.

[14] A non-exhaustive attempt will be made to define this, below, at pp.376–377; for what it does not cover, Kaye, P. *Civil Jurisdiction and Enforcement of Judgments*, 1987, at p.1439, and Article 28 III.

[15] Schmidt, M.J. *Die internationale Durchsetzung von Rechtsanwaltshonoraren nach EuGVÜ, Lugano-Übereinkommen und anderen Verträgen*, 1991, at pp.131–94—the outer limits set by the ECJ to its meaning, within which the individual Contracting States are free to develop its application, in *Dieter Krombach v Andre Bamberski* (C–7/98), 28.3.2000, at para. 37.

[16] Comments of the Belgian *Cour de Cassation* on this point—*S. c/ C.* 27.2.1986, (1989) *Rev crit Juris. belge*, 56, at p.59: 'loi d'ordre public interne n'est d'ordre public international privé que pour autant que le législatuer ait entendu consacrer . . . un principe qu'il considère *comme essentiel à l'ordre moral, politique ou économique* . . .'('internal public policy is not international public policy unless the legislature was to be understood as inaugurating a principle that it considers as essential to the moral, political or economic order').

[17] Compare the German futures trading cases BGH 4.6.1975 (1975) *NJW* 1600 with BGH 21.4.1998 (1999) *IPRax* 466, [1999] I.L.Pr. 758, below; Swiss *Bundesgericht G Ltd contre K* 19.9.2000 126 BGE III, 534, below; Kessedjian, C. *La reconnaissance et l'exécution des jugements en droit international privé aus Etats-Unis*, 1987, at p.305, para. 507; *Scarpetta v Lowenfeld* (1911) 27 TLR 509.

[18] 5.3.1979, [1979] OJ C59/1.

[19] *Ibid.*, at p.44; confirmed by *Hoffmann v Krieg* (C–145/86) [1988] ECR 645, at p.668 para. 21; now *Dieter Krombach v Andre Bamberski* (C–7/98), 28.3.2000, and *SA Régie Nationale des Usines Renault v SpA Maxicar and Orazio Formento* (C–38/98) [2000] ECR I–2973.

[20] *Ibid.*; the difference may be hard to draw in practice, Briggs, 1997, at p.321, para. 7.15; and on this point *BGH* 16.9.1993, IPRspr. (1993) Nr. 178, the post-reference decision in *Volker Sonntag v Hans Waidmann and others* (C–172/91) [1993] ECR I–1963, below, at pp.427–428.

[21] [1979] OJ C59/71, at p.128, para. 192.

[22] General principles will have to be extracted from individual cases under the Convention, and arguably, under autonomous enforcement law; cf. also Schmidt, 1991, at p.166, below, at p.377—but AG Alber's view in *SA Régie Nationale des Usines Renault v SpA Maxicar and Orazio Formento* (C–38/98) [2000] ECR I–2973, opinion 22.6.1999 that a definition of *ordre public* is *not* to be left entirely to national law; confirmed by ECJ's judgment at p. 3020, para. 28.

Despite the limited attention dedicated to public policy—as will be seen at Community level at least[23]—the defence has been run under the Convention on a number of occasions in France,[24] the UK,[25] Germany[26] and other Contracting States[27]—in the vast majority[28] of cases without success.

---

[23] Many believed that public policy in Article 27(1) was not a matter for the European Court of Justice: especially the early attitude of the *BGH* in 26.9.1979, 75 BGHZ, 167, at p.171: 'Diese Frage berüht allein das nationale Recht. Sie kann nur durch die deutschen Gerichte entscheiden werden; denn der Europäische Gerichtshof ist nicht dazu berufen, den Begriff der öffentlichen Ordnung in den einzelnen Mitgliedstaaten für deren Gerichte bindend zu definieren'('This question concerns only national law. It can only be decided by the German courts, for the ECJ is not called upon to give a binding definition to the concept of public policy for the individual courts of the Member States'): a reference was therefore refused; *contra*, ECJ decision *SA Régie Nationale des Usines Renault* (C–38/98) [2000] ECR I–2973, at p. 3020, para. 28, an entirely national definition would lead to an excessively large concept of the defence; also *Dieter Krombach v Andre Bamberski* (C–7/98), 28.3.2000; on the review by the ECJ of the application of public policy by the national courts/authorities, recently also AG Jacobs' opinion of 14.6.2001 in *Kingdom of the Netherlands v European Parliament and Council of the European Union* (C–377/98), unreported, at para. 101.

[24] Representative examples being *Vanclef c/ Société Trans Traide International* 17.5.1978 / *Etienne c/ Société Handelsonderneming Claessen B.V.* 24.11.1977 / *Theillol c/ Office de la jeunesse de Fribourg* 18.4.1978 (1979) *JDI* 380; *Almacoa c/ Etablissement Moteurs Ceres* 4.10.1978 (1979) *JDI* 623; *Société France International Représentation c/ héritiers Baas* 16.3.1979 (1980) *Rev crit* 121, 10.3.1981 (1981) *Rev crit* 553; *Dame Py c/ dame Diamedo* 18.1.1980 (1981) *Rev crit* 113; *Klopp et autres c/ Holder* 7.10.1982 (1985) *Rev crit* 131 / *Klopp et autres c/ Holder* 28.2.1984 (1985) *Rev crit* 131; *S.A. La Signalisation c/ Société C.A.E Electronica* 15.12.1987 (1989) *JDI* 102; *Société Polypétrol c/ Société générale routière* 9.10.1991 (1993) *JDI* 157, (1992) *Rev crit* 516, [1993] I.L.Pr. 107; *Cassation* 5.5.1993 *Times Newspapers Limited v Gustave Pordea* 1994 Gaz. Pal., Juris., p.382, [1994] I.L.Pr. 96; *Cour d'appel de Poitiers*, 1.6.1994 *Sté de transports internationaux Dehbashi c/ Sté Gerling Konsern* (1994) *JCP*, IV, 2520, [1996] I.L.Pr. 104; *Cassation* 16.3.1999 *Sieur Pordéa c/ Société Times Newspapers Limited* (1999) *JDI* 773; *Cour de Cassation* 17.11.1999 *Mme T. c/ Mme H* (2000) *Rev crit* 52.

[25] In relation to fraud under Article 27(1) *Interdesco v Nullifire* [1992] 1 Lloyd's Rep. 180, *SISRO v Ampersand* [1994] I.L.Pr 55; *Artic Fish Sales Co. Ltd. v Adam (No.2)* 7.6.1995 (1996) SLT 970, OH (Lord Cameron of Lochbroom); *Clarke v Fennoscandia Limited* [1998] SC 464; unrelated to fraud *Philip Alexander Securities & Futures Ltd. v Bamberger & others* [1996] CLC 1757, QBD, 1780 CA.

[26] From the vast wealth of German public policy cases, the most representative being: *BGH* 26.9.1979 IPRspr.(1979) Nr. 204; *BGH* 22.6.1983, IPRspr. (1983) Nr. 176; *BGH* 10.7.1986 IPRspr. (1986) Nr. 182; *OLG Saarbrücken* 3.8.1987 IPRspr. (1987) Nr. 156; *BGH* 21.3.1990, IPRspr. (1990) Nr. 207; *BGH* 4.6.1992 (1993) *IPRax* 310; *BGH* 16.9.1993, IPRspr. (1993) Nr. 178; *OLG Düsseldorf* 7.12.1994 (1995) *RIW* 324, *OLG Karlsruhe* 19.12.1994 IPRspr. (1995) Nr. 166; *OLG Köln* 16.9.1996, IPRspr. (1996) Nr. 180; *OLG Düsseldorf* 13.11.1996, IPRspr. (1996) Nr. 182; *OLG Stuttgart* 15.5.1997 (1997) *RIW* 684 and *Dieter Krombach v Andre Bamberski* (C–7/98), 28.3.2000, AG Antonio Saggio's opinion 23.9.1999—post-reference decision in *BGH* 29.6.2000, *Krombach v Bamberski* (2000) *RIW* 797, (2001) *IPRax* 50.

[27] From Belgium especially *Tribunal de première instance de Liège* 9.10.1995 (1996) *Act Dr* 80; from Italy *Malanca Motori SpA v Société des Etablisements B Savoye*, *Corte d'appello di Bologna*, 19.4.1983 (1984) *Giur. Comm*, II, 76, noted in Vigitori, V. 'Recent developments in the Recognition and Execution of Foreign Judgments and Arbitral Awards in Italy' (1987) *CJQ* 248, at p.256; Swiss *Bundesgericht G Ltd contre K* 19.9.2000 126 BGE III, 534, below, regarding an English judgment for gaming debts; *Bundesgericht* 5.7.2001 *X contrre l'arrêt rendu le 11.1.2001 . . . Y Ltd*, unreported, *Bundesgericht* 23.7.2001 *M.R. gegen H AG*, unreported.

[28] Notable for their rarity therefore are *BGH* 16.9.1993 IPRspr. (1993) Nr. 178, and *BGH* 10.7.1986 IPRspr. (1986) Nr. 182, *OLG Düsseldorf* 29.11.1999 (2000) *IPRax* 527, [2002] I.L.Pr. 71, at p.173, para. 10, explicit in *OLG Köln* 7.3.2001 2001 NJW-RR 1576, at p.1577 (re service by *remise au parquet*); and especially *Société Polypétrol c/ Société générale routière* 9.10.1991 (1993) *JDI* 157; (1992) *Rev crit* 516, [1993] I.L.Pr. 107, and relatively-recent *Cassation* 16.3.1999 *Sieur Pordéa c/ Société Times Newspapers Limited* (1999) *JDI* 773.

In terms of one of the aims of this work—that there may be hidden protectionist[29] leanings in the operation of public policy under the Brussels and Lugano Conventions—may simply not be the case, or at least may be impossible to discern; yet the defence in Article 27(1) would seem at first sight to be an ideal opportunity for idiosyncratic, or nationalistic, preconceptions to come to the fore. As will be seen, the case law and jurisprudence, in the main, simply do not evidence any such uprising; indeed quite the opposite.[30]

To deal with the topic in greater detail, it will be necessary to divide up this section into the following parts. An attempt will be made, first, briefly to define public policy and to distinguish between the various sub-categories evidenced from the case law. Then the development of the defence of public policy in earlier bilateral and multilateral Conventions, and from the autonomous recognition and enforcement laws of selected Contracting States will be examined.[31] The European Court of Justice's views in the recent cases of *Dieter Krombach v Andre Bamberski*[32] and *SA Régie Nationale des Usines Renault*,[33] will then be discussed. Then appearances of the defence will be examined, either successful or unsuccessful, in France, the UK, Germany and elsewhere, including the concept and reception of fraud under the Brussels Convention. Lastly, the Commission's July 1999 proposals, the new Brussels I Regulation, and the work at the Hague Conference, will be mentioned briefly.

4.1   'MATERIAL' AND 'PROCEDURAL' PUBLIC POLICY[34]

At its simplest, public policy, in the sphere[35] of recognition and enforcement of judgments, can be divided[36] into 'procedural'[37] and 'material' public policy, often with an 'international' prefix added, where necessary.[38] The former[39] seeks

---

[29] Schmidt, 1991, at p.160, and below, at p.379.

[30] Compared to Article 27(2), especially reticent—despite public policy's frequent invocation—are the German cases, above, at p.376, n.26; for discussions of them below section 4.4.4.

[31] For the reasons of an historical analysis below, at p.379, and esp. Schmidt, 1991, at p.166.

[32] (C–7/98), 28.3.2000, AG Antonio Saggio's opinion 23.9.1999.

[33] (C–38/98) [2000] ECR I–2973.

[34] On the differentiation in Rechberger, W. 'Das Anerkennungs- und Vollstreckungsabkommen zwischen Österreich und Italien' (1975) *ZfRV* 17, at p.30.

[35] A 'public policy' exclusion also exists in the choice of law process, with reference to contracts—the EEC Convention on the Law Applicable to Contractual Obligations 1980 ('The Rome Convention 1980') Article 16, given force of law in the UK, as from 1.4.1991, by the Contracts (Applicable Law) Act 1990, s 2(1).

[36] Cf also Kessedjian, C. in *Société Polypétrol c/ Société générale routière* 9.10.1991 (1992) *Rev crit* 516, at p.523; a workable starting point for the distinctions in interpretation (albeit in an international arbitration context): *Bundesgericht* 11.6.2001 *A contre UEFA et autres*, unreported; what was *not* sufficient for a breach of (procedural) public policy in that case was, *inter alia*, that evidence was misapplied.

[37] This procedural defence has been most frequently invoked in Germany.

[38] Especially in France—the international prefix denotes that certain provisions of national, or purely domestic, public policy are considered important enough to be elevated to the private international law recognition and enforcement arena—Lalive, P. 'Transnational (or truly international) Public Policy and International Arbitration' in *Comparative Arbitration Practice and Public Policy in Arbitration* ICCA 8th Congress 1986 (ed. Sanders), 1987, p.257, at pp.260–69.

[39] Kessidjian, (1992) *Rev crit* 516, at p.523, believes Article 27(1) should not cover procedural public policy; Othenin-Girard, S. *La réserve d'ordre public en droit international privé suisse*, 1999, at pp.92–95.

to regulate, in a broad way, the procedures followed in the rendering forum from initial service[40] to the judgment's delivery, and any appeal. This is to ensure that the defendant be given a fair hearing,[41] and an opportunity of presenting his case.[42] It arises from the inescapable fact, at present, that the civil procedure systems of the Contracting States differ: even though the correct procedure was followed in the rendering court, this often does not accord with that which would have been followed if the trial had been held in the court addressed.[43]

'Material' public policy is aimed not at the foreign procedure itself, but at the effects[44] which recognition or enforcement of the judgment would produce in the State addressed.[45] A breach here most often occurs when the foreign court has applied a different[46] *lex causae* to the dispute in issue, and this in itself, part of it, or an omission to apply a mandatory rule[47] of the Contracting State addressed, is so repugnant, or an affront to, certain cherished[48] principles of the latter that no effect can be given to the judgment containing it. One of the problems with this category is that certain (sometimes obscure)[49] provisions of a particular

---

[40] Although in the Brussels Convention context, this particular function has been overtaken by Article 27(2)—*Berhandus Hendrikman and Maria Feyen* v *Magenta Druck & Verlag GmbH* C–78/95 [1996] ECR I–4943, p.4958, para. 57, (AG Jacobs); *contra*, the German case *OLG Karlsruhe* 12.3.1999 (1999) *RIW* 538, [2001] I.L. Pr. 208—although recently there has been a conscious elision between Article 27(1) procedural public policy and Article 27(2) 'due service' in *OLG Köln* 7.3.2001 (2001) NJW-RR 1576, at p.1577, both *remise au parquet* cases.

[41] Cf. Geimer's categories in Geimer, R. and Schütze, R. *Europäisches Zivilverfahrensrech, Kommentar zum EuGVÜ und Lugano-Übereinkommen*, 1997, at p.460, para. 25: independence and impartiality of the court; a fair hearing (*audi alterem partem*); equal treatment of the parties; and a fair trial.

[42] What amounts, at English common law, to the generic term, 'substantial justice'—*Adams and others* v *Cape Industries Plc. and another* [1990] 1 Ch. 433, at p.566 (Slade LJ, *obiter*), and *Minemetals Germany GmbH v Ferco Steel Ltd* [1999] CLC 647, re enforcement of an foreign (Chinese) arbitration award, at pp.659–62, esp. p.661; also important for the ECJ was Article 6 European Convention on Human Rights, in *Dieter Krombach v Andre Bamberski* (C–7/98).

[43] Schmidt, 1991, at p.135; not, of itself, sufficient, according to AG Saggio in *Dieter Krombach v Andre Bamberski* (C–7/98) at para. 22 to implicate Article 27(1)—the ECJ agreed, at para. 32, *even if* the rendering court mis-applied the jurisdictional provisions of the Convention (outside Article 28).

[44] Beck, H. *Die Anerkennung und Vollstreckung ausländischer gerichtlicher Entscheidungen in Zivilsachen nach den Staatsverträgen mit Belgien, Österreich, Grossbritannien und Griechenland*, Inaugural Dissertation, Universität des Saarlandes, 1967, at p.102.

[45] No doubt, in this sense, the Jenard Report, [1979] OJ C59/1, at p.44.

[46] But Article 27(4); *quaere*, whether the rendering court must correctly apply the *lex causae* of the State addressed—yes, (in breach of Article 29), according to *OLG Hamm* 19.7.1985 IPRspr. (1985) Nr. 187, at p.514; no, at English common law, *Goddard v Gray* (1870) LR QB 139, at p.151 (Blackburn J), and of course now, Article 29—in *SA Régie Nationale des Usines Renault v SpA Maxicar and Orazio Formento* (C–38/98) [2000] ECR I–2973, Article 27(1) invoked to block enforcement of a French judgment in Italy (in contravention of and/or mis-applying Community law), the ECJ did *not* consider the correct application of the *lex causae*/Community law to be an essential pre-requisite to recognition and enforcement, and therefore a cause for censure under Article 27(1), at p. 3022, para. 33.

[47] In the sense of the Rome Convention 1980, Article 16; also the *Terruzzi* litigation (*Wilson, Smithett & Cope Ltd. v Terruzzi* [1976] 1 QB 683, *Corte di Cassazione* 2.7.1981 (1982) *Riv.dir.int.priv. e proc.* 107) and Abbatescianni, G. 'Recognition of English Judgments in Italy: the *Terruzzi* case' (1985) *NLJ* 179.

[48] Especially *Sonntag v Waidman*, post-reference below, at pp.430–431 *BGH* 16.9.1993, IPRspr. (1993) Nr. 178; s 32 CJJA 1982 may also have been elevated to such a status, Briggs, 1997, at p.323 para. 7.15— *quaere* whether, post *Dieter Krombach*, simple divergences of Contracting State procedural (and material) laws will be sufficient excuse to deploy Article 27(1).

[49] If, as in the post-reference case of *Sonntag v Waidman*, the provisions eventually relied on under Article 27(1) to defeat enforcement the Italian *partie civile* judgment were part of German public

Contracting State's law—and potentially unknown to the rendering court (and the claimant)—will be considered by that enforcing State as being important enough to be promoted[50] to the status of a (material) public policy provision, with an attendant application under Article 27(1).

4.2   PRE-BRUSSELS AND LUGANO CONVENTION DEFINITIONS IN THE CONTRACTING STATES

As has already been observed, in many of the former[51] bilateral recognition and enforcement Treaties[52] concluded between the Contracting States to the Brussels and Lugano Conventions, provision was commonly made for judgments to be refused domestic efficacy on the ground(s) of a breach of 'public policy'. This was, and is, also the case under many autonomous recognition and enforcement laws.[53]

The question, apart from the historical interest, which concerns this section, is whether definitions of public policy, or instances of its application derived from State relations prior to the Brussels and Lugano Conventions could, or should, be carried across to the new recognition and enforcement regime, and atmosphere, introduced by Title III of these Conventions. If, as is generally believed, the Brussels Convention, and its Articles 28, 29, 31, and 34 represent a more liberal recognition and enforcement regime throughout the European Union, what place remains[54] for pre-Convention definitions derived from earlier Conventions, and often more stringent national[55] enforcement laws?

policy, why was this fact not picked up and submitted at first instance, rather than producing the protracted course of the case, and the reference under Article 27(2)?

[50] Demotion is also possible: the early case of *BGH* 4.6.1975 (1975) *NJW* 1600, where public policy was held to have been breached, and the change of attitude recently in *BGH* 21.4.1998 (1998) *WM* 1176, regarding BörsG §§ 53, 58, 61, the German futures trading law; Bugstaller, (2000) *ZfRV* 83, at pp.90–91.

[51] In the sense of having been replaced *ratione materiae* and *ratione temporis* by the Brussels and Lugano Conventions.

[52] For example, *Convention Franco-Suisse* of 15 June 1869, Article 17(3); Reciprocal Enforcement of Foreign Judgments (France) Order in Council 1936, S.I. 1936/609, incorporating UK/French Convention, Article 3(1)(c); and *Vertrag zwischen der Bundesrepublik Deutschland und dem Königreich Norwegen über die gegenseitige Anerkennung und Vollstreckung gerichtlicher Entscheidungen und anderer Schuldtitel in Zivil- und Handelssachen,* 17.6.1977, (1981) BGBl., II, 342, in force 3.10.1981, Article 6(1)(1); further examples in Al Mulla, H. *The recognition and enforcement of foreign civil and commercial judgments under multilateral and bilateral conventions,* Ph.D Thesis, Cambridge University, 1992.

[53] As to which, for example § 328 I Nr.4 (German) ZPO; Article 27(1) (Swiss) IPRG; Article 570(1) (Belgian) *Code Judiciaire*; Article 64(1)(g) of the (Italian) l.31 maggio 1995, n.218 *Riforma del sistema italiano di diritto internazionale privato,* below, at p.393.

[54] The possibility of exchanging meanings of public policy between Article 27(1) Lugano and Article 27(1) of the Swiss IPRG by Walder, H. 'Anerkennung und Vollstreckung von Entscheidungen' in Schwander (ed) *Das Lugano-Übereinkommen,* 1990, p.135, at p.139; the view that in a more liberal enforcement climate, more succour should be found in public policy, was not the initial view of the December 1997 proposal for a review of the Brussels Convention: which omitted the defence in its entirety. This proved to be a step too far however, below, at p.433.

[55] Linke, H. *Internationales Zivilprozeßrecht,* 2 Auf., 1995, at p.161, para. 424 believes it is dangerous to use the same concepts of public policy forged in the atmosphere of national law under Article 27(1).

Schmidt,[56] for one, feels that a pre-Convention definitional legacy will be hard to shake off, especially for those[57] Contracting States with an expansive concept of public policy:

> Sollte sich in einem Land ein großzügiger[58] Umgang mit dem ordre public feststellen lassen, so könnte man daraus folgern,[59] daß die dortigen Gerichte geneigt sind, auch in Zukunft unter der Geltung des EuGVÜ die ihnen vertrauten, für das frühere Recht geltenden Maßstäbe anzuwenden . . .[60]

It is to selected Contracting State laws that we shall now turn.

4.2.1 The public policy defence under German 'autonomous' law[61]

A clear example of a pre-Convention concept of public policy which has survived[62] and flourished under Article 27(1) comes from German case law. The enduring definition of (procedural)[63] public policy (for the purposes of Article III (1)(c) of the Anglo-German Recognition and Enforcement Convention of 14 July 1960[64]) was given by the *Bundesgerichtshof* in 1967.[65] The case demonstrates, and

---

[56] Schmidt, 1991, at p.160.

[57] *Ibid.*, at p.160, with particular focus on France and Portugal: France's requirements of a reasoned judgment: *Klein c/ Niedermann Trib. civ. Seine* 15.10.1931 (1932) *JDI* 678; similarly in Belgium *Misseghers c/ Craet Trib. civ. Termonde* 3.3.1931 (1932) *Rev crit* 589, Luxembourg (1971) *JDI* 153, at p.155, and *Cassazione* 18.5.1995, n.5451 reported in Bellagamba, G. and Cariti, G. *Il sistema italiano di diritto internazionale privato*, 2000, at p.194.

[58] ('expansive'). A restricted autonomous definition, *a contrario*, would thus be expected to continue under Article 27(1).

[59] Yet he does not feel that this tendency will continue with regards to Article 27(1) in Spain, Schmidt, 1991, at p.190.

[60] ('If in one country an expansive relationship with public policy is perceived, then the conclusion can be drawn that their courts will, in the future, tend to use the trusted former yardstick of the old law in the application of the Brussels Convention'), Schmidt, at p.166.

[61] Wuppermann, M. *Die deutsche Rechtsprechung zum Vorbehalt des ordre public im Internationalen Privatrecht seit 1945*, 1977, pp.9–27; Campbell, D. (1994) 18 *Southern Illinois U. L. J.* 517, at p.542; Geimer, R. in Walter, G. and Baumgartner, S. (eds) *Recognition and Enforcement of foreign judgments outside the scope of the Brussels and Lugano Conventions*, 2000, at pp.240–42; note Karl, A-M. *Die Anerkennung von Entscheidungen in Spanien*, 1993, at p.152 believes that due to the strong constitutional guarantees in both Germany and Spain, public policy will rarely be invoked in German/Spanish relations (under now Article 27(1)), in what was then Article 5(1)(i) German Spanish Recognition and Enforcement Convention of 14.1.1987, (1987) BGBl., II, 35.

[62] The argument regarding the Swiss cases below, at pp.387–390, that the restricted application under autonomous law will also be transferred to the Lugano Convention.

[63] Specifically designated as such in the case headnote, of *BGH* 18.10.1967 (1968) *NJW* 354; for an example of denying recognition and enforcement of foreign arbitral awards under §1044 Abs.2 Nr.2 ZPO (now amended, 1.1.1998 in §1061 ZPO) and the 1958 New York Convention, Marx, L. *Der verfahrensrechtliche ordre public bei der Anerkennung und Vollstreckung ausländischer Schiedssprüche in Deutschland*, 1994, at p.88 and pp.91–122; Haas, U. (2001) *IPRax* 195, at p.200.

[64] *Abkommen zwischen der Bundesrepublik Deutschland und dem Vereinigten Königreich Großbritannien und Nordirland über die gegenseitige Anerkennung und Vollstreckung von gerichtlichen Entscheidungen in Zivil- und Handelssachen*, 14.7.1960, (1961) BGBl, II, 302, in force 15.7.1961; English version in the Reciprocal Enforcement of Foreign Judgments (Germany) Order, 1961, S.I. 1961/1199.

[65] *BGH* 18.10.1967 48 BGHZ 327; and applied *verbatim* under Article 27(1) of the Brussels Convention in *BGH* 19.9.1977 (1978) *NJW* 1114; *BGH* 21.3.1990 IPRspr. (1990) Nr. 207; *OLG Hamm* 27.6.1996 (1998) *IPRax* 202.

anticipates, the restricted use that the German courts will make of an alleged breach of (procedural) public policy.[66] As will be seen, too, the definition has been carried across *verbatim* to cases under Article 27(1).[67] In the case itself, a wife tried to enforce an English High Court interim payment order in the *LG Berlin*, which the husband opposed on the ground that, due to an earlier contempt of court order, he had been prohibited[68] from participating in the deliberations. His defence under Article III (1)(c) failed. The court set the tone for the application of (procedural) public policy in this case: merely because the procedure adopted in the foreign court does not accord exactly with that under the *Zivilprozeßord-nung*, this is no reason, of itself, to deny enforcement under the public policy defence. Only when the foreign procedure:

> von den Grundprinzipien des deutschen Verfahrenrechts in einem solchen Maße abweicht, daß nach der deutschen Rechtsordnung das Urteil *nicht in einem geordneten, rechtstaatlichen*[69] *Verfahren* ergangen angesehen werden kann[70]

may public policy intervene and deny enforcement.

For examples of a breach of 'material' public policy, and the fluidity of such a concept, we must also look to autonomous German enforcement law.[71] This is

---

[66] Even though had a German court been hearing the case, a breach of the German Constitution would have occurred: comments on this case by Schack, H. *Internationales Zivilverfahrensrecht*, 2.Auf., 1996, at p.335, para. 864: 'Obwohl hier ein schwerer Verstoß gegen den von Article 103 I GG garantierten Grundsatz des rechtlichen Gehörs vorliegt . . .'('although here there is a serious breach of the principle of the right to a fair hearing, guaranteed by Article 103 I of the Constitution'); also the less generous French case of *Cassation* 5.5.1993 *Times Newspapers Limited v Gustave Pordea* (1994) *Gaz. Pal.*, Juris., p.382, [1994] I.L.Pr. 96, and *Cassation* 16.3.1999 *sub nom. Sieur Pordéa c/ Société Times Newspapers Limited* (1999) *JDI* 773, both below, at p.410.

[67] Notably, *BGH* 21.3.1990 IPRspr. (1990) Nr. 207; *OLG Hamm* 27.6.1996 (1998) *IPRax* 202; Kropholler, 2002, acknowledges that borrowing interpretations from autonomous law is possible under Art.27(1), at p.394, para. 11.

[68] The court viewed the sanction as self-imposed; *contra* Schack, 2.Auf., 1996, at p.335, para. 864; note the potential French attitude under Article 27(1) to striking out an action for non-compliance with an English security for costs order: *Sieur Pordéa c/ Société Times Newspapers Limited* (1999) *JDI* 773 16.3.1999, discussed below, at p.410; and the potential for problems under Article 27(1) with security for costs in the English appeals procedure in *Federal Bank of the Middle East v Hadkinson*, *The Times* 7.12.1999, CA.

[69] ('the rule of law'). This concept was explained in a later case, again on the scope of Article III (1)(c) *BGH* 19.9.1977 (1978) *NJW* 1114, at p.1115: (1) the court must not prejudge the issue or reach a decision before the parties have had a chance to put their case; (2) the inviolability of basic human rights to participate in the proceedings. Also in *Dieter Krombach v Bamberski*, the AG held Article 630 of the French *Code de Procédure pénale* violated the right to be heard, at para. 28; the ECJ agreed, at paras. 40, and 45; the European Court of Human Rights also found a breach, *inter alia*, of Article 6(1) ECHR in *Affaire Krombach c. France* (No.29731/96) of 13.1.2001.

[70] ('diverges from the basic principles of German procedural law to such an extent that, according to the German legal system, the judgment cannot be said to have been given in *a well-ordered procedure in accordance with the rule of law*'), BGH 18.10.1967 48 BGHZ 327, at p.331, (an alternative translation in *OLG Frankfuhrt/M* 8.5.1992 *Re Enforcement of an Italian judgment* [1993] I.L.Pr. 353, at p.355, para. 5. The emboldened words are the essence, to German eyes, of (procedural) public policy, now under Article 27(1) Brussels Convention. This is perhaps why this procedural defence has failed on so many occasions, below, at pp.421 *et seq.*

[71] For a brief overview in English, Campbell, D. *Enforcement of Foreign Judgments*, 1997, at pp.195–96.

governed by three provisions of the ZPO, §§§ 722,[72] 723[73] and 328 I Nr.4.[74] Two cases[75] have considered the position under these provisions of 'amateur' German 'futures' traders,[76] having suffered losses on foreign investment stock-markets. Having been sued abroad for these losses, the judgment debtors set up a defence of public policy under domestic trading legislation. Due to a change in German domestic law on private traders on the Stock Exchange, in *BGH* 21.4.1998,[77] an Austrian judgment was declared enforceable, under the 1959 Austro-German Convention, and did not offend against German 'material' public policy,[78] as had been the case under the consumer protection provisions of the former version of the German Stock Exchange Act.[79]

Provisions which were once considered part of public policy have, due to this change,[80] subsequently been removed from the public policy prohibition. The definition, however, remains the same. In the above case law examples, it is not the fact that a particular foreign judge applied a different *lex causae*[81] than would a German judge in the same situation, but whether:

> das Ergebnis der Anwendung ausländischen Rechts im konkreten Fall zu den Grundgedanken der deutschen Regelungen und den in ihnen enthaltenden Gerechtigkeitsvorstellungen in so starkem Widerspruch steht, daß es nach deutscher Vorstellung untragbar erscheint.[82]

---

[72] Enforcement can only follow on from an *exequatur* procedure leading to a 'Vollstreckungsurteil' (an enforcement judgment), § 722 (1) ZPO.

[73] § 723(1) prohibits a review of substance of the foreign judgment; §723(2) states that the foreign judgment must have acquired the status of *res judicata* in the State of origin, and that the provisions of §328 do not exclude its recognition.

[74] Contains the substantive defences to recognition, among which, § 328 I Nr.4 reads 'wenn die Anerkennung des Urteils zu einem Ergebnis führt, das mit wesentlichen Grundsätzen des deutschen Rechts offensichtlich unvereinbar ist, insbesondere wenn die Anerkennung mit den Grundrechten unvereinbar ist; . . .' ('when recognition would result in manifest incompatibility with the fundamental principles of German law, esp. when recognition is incompatible with constitutional rights'); post *Krombach* decision in *BGH* 29.6.2000 (2000) *RIW* 797, at p.798, has ruled that provisions of the German Constitution are a matter of public policy under Article 27(1).

[75] The earlier one finding a breach of German (material) public policy: *BGH* 4.6.1975 (1975) *NJW* 1600.

[76] *OLG Düsseldorf* 8.3.1996 IPRspr. (1996) Nr. 144, [1998] I.L.Pr. 327; protection of these 'traders' as was evident from *Philip Alexander Securities & Futures Ltd. v Bamberger & others* [1996] CLC 1757, QBD, 1780 CA; also similar to the position in the *Terruzzi* litigation, below, section 4.3.4.

[77] *BGH* 21.4.1998 (1999) *IPRax* 466, [1999] I.L.Pr. 758, prior to the Lugano Convention's entry into force.

[78] A departure from earlier established case law principles (*BGH* 4.6.1975 (1975) *WM* 676, *BGH* 25.5.1981 (1981) *WM* 758) was therefore warranted here; instructive, too, the German courts' attitude to public policy in regard to Article V(2)(b) New York Convention 1958, Racine, J-B. *L'arbitrage commercial international et l'ordre public*, 1999, at p.507 onwards.

[79] (1999) *IPRax* 466, at p.468, [1999] I.L.Pr. 758, at p.764, paras. 16–17.

[80] Also the effect on Swiss (material) public policy under Article 27(1) of a change in the gaming laws in Switzerland: *Bundesgericht G Ltd contre K* 19.9.2000 126 BGE III, 534, below.

[81] *Quaere* therefore the statements in *OLG Hamm* 19.7.1985 IPRspr. (1985) Nr. 187, reviewed below, at p.427 questionable now, *SA Régie Nationale des Usines Renault v SpA Maxicar and Orazio Formento* (C–38/98) [2000] ECR I–2973; Moura Ramos, R. M. (2000) *Yearbook of Private International Law* 25, at p.32.

[82] ('that the result of applying the foreign law in the actual case stands in such sharp contrast to the basic principles of German law and concepts of justice contained therein, that it appears unacceptable

Also considered by the *Bundesgerichtshof*[83] recently is the issue[84] of the enforcement of US punitive damages claims,[85] and public policy, under §328 I Nr.4 ZPO. In this case, the court refused to enforce a $400,000 award of punitive damages of a Californian State court on the ground that 'es mit wesentlichen Grundsätzen des deutschen Rechts offensichtlich unvereinbar, *pauschal*[86] *zuerkannten* Strafschadenersatz von nicht unerheblicher Höhe im Inland zu vollstrecken.'[87]

One of these 'Grundsätzen' that would have been offended by the recognition of punitive damages is that of 'Verhältnismäßigkeit'—proportionality. Under German law, the award of damages was also said to be compensatory,[88] not penal.[89] Penal sanctions lie in the proper and exclusive remit of the State in criminal proceedings and therefore

> erscheint es unerträglich, in einem Zivilurteil eine erhebliche Geldzahlung aufzuerlegen, die nicht dem Schadensausgleich dient, sondern wesentlich nach dem Interesse der Allgemeinheit bemessen wird . . .[90]

to German notions'), *BGH* 21.4.1998 (1998) *WM* 1176, at p.1177; this 'formula' had been used in the earlier case of *BGH* 4.6.1975 (1975) *NJW* 1600.

[83] *BGH* 4.6.1992 (1992) *NJW* 3096, [1994] I.L.Pr. 602.

[84] Also Zekoll, J. 'The enforceability of American money judgments abroad: a landmark decision by the German Federal Supreme Court' (1992) *Col J Transnat L* 641; and Brockmeier, D. *Punitive damages, multiple damages und deutscher ordre public*, 1999, at pp.105–14; for a Swiss view of non-recognition/enforcement of punitive damages judgments, Lenz, C. *Amerikanische Punitive Damages vor dem Schweizer Richter*, 1992, at p.140 onwards.

[85] For US anti-trust treble damages claims, Zekoll, J. 'US-amerikanische Antitrust-Treble-Damages-Urteile und deutscher ordre public' (1999) *JZ* 384, esp. p.392; Heb, B. 'Die Anerkennung eines Class Action Settlement in Deutschland' (2000) *JZ* 373; *obiter* observation of *LG Stuttgart* 24.11.1999 IPRspr. (1999) Nr. 150, at p.358, that in a class action, an active participation in the proceedings by both defendant(s) and claimant(s) necessary to ensure compliance with German public policy.

[86] Compare the similar approach to the unreasoned (i.e. no judicial assessment of the) award of damages in *Adams and others v Cape Industries Plc. and another* [1990] 1 Ch. 433, at p.571, (Slade LJ, *obiter*); *Masters v Leaver* [2000] I.L.Pr. 387.

[87] ('it is obviously irreconcilable with fundamental principles of German law to enforce in Germany *globally-awarded* punitive damages of a not inconsiderable amount'), (1992) *NJW* 3096, at p.3104, [1994] I.L.Pr. 602, at p.633 para. 82.

[88] Cf Zekoll, (1992) *Col J Transnat L* 641, at p.656; Brockmeier, 1999; in more detail on the aspect of proportionality of damages, Müller, P. *Punitive Damages und deutsches Schadenersatzrecht*, 2000, at pp.364–65.

[89] A decision of the *Bundesverfassungsgericht* of 8.3.2000, (2000) *NJW* 2187, esp. p.2188, which has sounded a conciliatory note to the idea of a preventative, deterrent effect of a damages award, has led the reviewer Müller to believe that US punitive damages awards may no longer be resisted under the public policy defence in § 328 Abs.1 Nr.4 ZPO: Müller, P. 'Sind US-amerikanische Punitive-damages-Urteile in Deutschland vollstreckbar?' (2001) *Der Betrieb* 83, at p.83; the position is therefore now unclear in Germany; cf the abandonning of the 'cause of action' test for the award of exemplary damages in England: *Kuddus (AP) v Chief Constable of Leicestershire Constabulary* [2001] 2 WLR 1789, HL.

[90] ('it appears to be unsupportable to impose a large award in a civil judgment that does not serve a compensatory aim but is fundamentally assessed to be for the general welfare'), (1992) *NJW* 3096, at p.3104; note the motivation for the award of punitive damages recently by the United States District Court for the District of Columbia in *Thomas M. Sutherland v Islamic Republic of Iran* 151 F.Supp.2d 27 (D.D.C. 2001), at p.53: 'the failure to impose substantial punitive damages after several previous impositions might be considered by MOIS as a capitulation by the United States in the debate over the legitimacy of hostage-taking'.

In accordance with Schmidt's thesis of those Contracting States with restricted scope for public policy under their autonomous law, one would expect that a similar restrictive trend to continue under Article 27(1) of the Brussels Convention. It is clear that, in the main, the German courts under their bilateral treaties, and §328 I Nr. 4 ZPO, have sought to restrict public policy to egregious violations of accepted norms of procedural fairness and substantial justice.[91] Whether similar tendencies have been carried across to Article 27(1) remains[92] to be demonstrated.

4.2.2   The public policy defence in England and Wales at common law[93]

Rule 44 of *Dicey and Morris*[94] tells us that a 'foreign judgment is impeachable on the ground that its enforcement, or as the case may be, recognition, would be contrary to public policy'. Individual defences to enforcement which, on the Continent, would fall under the broader head of 'public policy', have been treated separately at common law in England and Wales: rules 43[95] and 45 of *Dicey and Morris*—'fraud' and 'natural justice'[96] respectively.

What examples there are of public policy,[97] in the main, come from aspects of family law, from cases such as *Re Macartney*,[98] *Phrantzes v Argenti*[99] and *Armitage v Nanchen*.[100] Whether any of the principles enunciated therein would be carried across, holus bolus, without appropriate amendment, to conform to the Title III enforcement regime is doubtful. *A fortiori*, a case such as *Israel Discount Bank v Hadjipateras*[101]—although demonstrating that a judgment from a Greek, French or Spanish court may arguably come under Article 27(1), if obtained by 'undue

---

[91] A view recently confirmed in *Dieter Krombach v Andre Bamberski* (C–7/98), 28.3.2000.

[92] Below section 4.4.4.

[93] Registration is similarly excluded under s 1(2)(b) of the Administration of Justice Act 1920, ss 4(1)(a)(v) and 8(1)(2) of the Foreign Judgments (Reciprocal Enforcement) Act 1933, and the Conventions concluded thereunder, on the ground of a breach of public policy.

[94] *Dicey and Morris on the Conflict of Laws*, 13th edn., 2000, Vol.I, at p.525.

[95] *Ibid.*, at p.518 onwards.

[96] *Ibid.*, at p.527, which would equate to the German view of 'procedural' public policy, above, at p.380; in the context of the enforcement of an arbitration award, *Minemetals v Ferco Steel* [1999] CLC 647, has equated 'public policy' in s 103(3) Arbitration Act 1996 with the defence of natural/substantial justice at common law; other examples of public policy (in its manifestation of illegality) in *Soleimany v Soleimany* [1999] QB 785 (Beth Din award not enforced due to acknowledged illegal object of underlying contract), and *Westacre Investments Inc v Jugoimport-SPDR Holding* [2000] QB 288, CA, (ICC award enforced after arbitrators had found no illegality on underlying contract).

[97] No doubt the *Vervaeke v Smith* [1983] AC 145 defence, at p.164 onwards, *inter alia*, of irreconcilable judgments has been subsumed within Article 27(3).

[98] [1921] 1 Ch. 552; also *Gray (orse. Formosa) v Formosa* [1963] P 259, CA, at p.269 (Lord Denning MR).

[99] [1960] 2 QB 19, not an enforcement case, but a cause of action unknown under English law.

[100] (1983) 4 FLR 293, at p.300 (Sir John Arnold P), which is curiously almost a *verbatim* translation of the German material public policy criterion, above, at p.381.

[101] [1984] 1 WLR 137.

influence, duress or coercion'—would, like the defence of fraud,[102] be subject to the provisions of Article 29; and the necessity of seeking redress, primarily,[103] and if possible, from the local court.

Whether or not, at common law at least, the enforcement of 'punitive damages'[104]/multiple damages judgments would contravene public policy may not now need a decision, as section 5(1) of the Protection of Trading Interests Act 1980[105] now prohibits enforcement of multiple damages *per se*, whether or not[106] as an expression of public policy.

Recently, (procedural) public policy has been considered by Colman J, when enforcement was attempted of a Chinese arbitral award under the 1958 New York Convention in *Minemetals Germany GmbH v Ferco Steel Ltd.*[107] Enforcement was resisted under Article V(2)(b) of the Convention, and section 103(3) of the Arbitration Act 1996,[108] on the ground that, *inter alia*, the Chinese arbitrators had failed to provide the respondents, Ferco Steel, with an opportunity to make certain submissions. To succeed with regard to the public policy defence, Colman J held that the award had to be 'contrary to the requirements of substantial justice'[109] as interpreted in *Adams v Cape Industries.*[110] Although the case involved the enforcement of an arbitration award, the fact that it was to be accomplished against the background of an international enforcement Convention perhaps[111] makes the summary of the judge of more than passing interest to enforcement under Article 27(1) of the Brussels Convention. Applying the judge's remarks, *mutatis mutandis*, to the Brussels Convention, we find that an enforcing court should normally consider '(1) the nature of the procedural injustice,[112] ...

---

[102] As to which: *Interdesco S.A. v Nullifire Ltd.* [1992] 1 Lloyd's Rep. 180 (Phillips J) and *Artic Fish Sales Co. Ltd. v Adam (No.2)* (1996) *SLT* 970, below, at pp.418–420.

[103] The approach of Phillips J in *Interdesco*—of the practical exhaustion of local remedies—finds its supporters among the German commentators, Geimer and Schütze, 1997, at p.741, para. 2955; *contra* Schack, 2.Auf., 1996, at p.334, para. 866.

[104] Considerably relaxed in *Kuddus (AP) v Chief Constable of Leicestershire Constabulary* [2001] 2 WLR 1789, HL.

[105] The *raison d'être* of which has been reviewed earlier, in the Introduction, at p.29, n.221.

[106] Cf Stone, P. *The Conflict of Laws*, 1996, at p.336 no doubt sees s 5 as a 'crystallisation of English public policy'; another example may well be the sanctity of jurisdiction/arbitration clauses, s 32 Civil Jurisdiction and Judgments Act 1982, Briggs, 1997, at p.323, para. 7.15.

[107] [1999] CLC 647; (material) public policy and the New York Convention 1958, *Deutsche Schachtbau* [1987] 2 All ER 769, CA, revs'd on other grounds [1990] 1 AC 295; *Westacre Investments Inc v Jugoimport-SPDR Holding* [1999] QB 740—enforcement of an award, valid by the curial law, not contrary to public policy, even though the underlying contract shown to be illegal in Kuwait.

[108] *Cheshire and North*, 13th edn., 1999, at p.528; also *Russell on Arbitration*, 21st edn., 1997, at p.409, para. 8–022.

[109] [1999] CLC 647, at p.659.

[110] [1990] Ch 433.

[111] Although Waller LJ in the CA in *Westacre Investments Inc v Jugoimport-SPDR Holding Co. Ltd* [2000] 1 QB 288, at p.309 was not receptive to importing ideas from the Brussels Convention enforcement regime to the enforcement of international arbitration awards under the 1958 New York Convention; caution should therefore be expressed vice-versa.

[112] ECJ authority (*Hoffmann v Krieg* (145/86) [1988] ECR 645, *Hendrikman v Magenta Druck* (C–78/95) [1996] ECR I-4943, at p.4957–58, para. 56 (Advocate-General Jacobs)) has shown us that if

(3) whether a remedy was available under that jurisdiction . . . [and] (5) if the enforcee [sic] has failed to invoke that remedial jurisdiction, for what reason and in particular whether he was acting reasonably in failing to do so.'[113] The analogy with the position under Article 27(1) and *Interdesco v Nullifire*[114] may become more marked.

4.2.3 The public policy defence under French 'autonomous' law

The principles or conditions for the recognition and enforcement of foreign judgments at French autonomous law are curiously[115] not governed by the *Code civil*, nor the *Nouveau Code de Procédure Civile*. For these we must look to the seminal case of the *Cour de Cassation* in the *Munzer*[116] decision, of 7.1.1964. One of the current prerequisites[117] for the pronouncement of an *exequatur* is that the foreign judgment conforms to 'l'ordre public international'.[118] Other subsequent

such 'injustice' consists of not being duly served with the document which institutes proceedings in sufficient time to arrange a defence, redress should be sought under Article 27(2); 'injustices' occurring outside, or after, service of such a document fall under Article 27(1)—endorsed by *OLG Köln* (2000) *IPRax* 528, at p.529; a breach of Article 27(2) found using similar language as procedural public policy under Article 27(1) in *OLG Köln* 7.3.2001 (2001) NJW-RR 1576, at p.1577: 'i.S. des Article 27 Nr. 2 EuGVÜ als nicht ordnungsgemäß zu beurteilen, wenn darin ein Vertoß gegen die verfahrensrechtliche deutsche öffentliche Ordnung, den ordre public läge, und mithin die Entscheidung auf Grund eines Verfahrens ergangen ist, das von den Grundprinzipien des deutschen Verfahrensrechts in einem solchen Ausmaß abweicht, dass sie nicht als in einem geordneten, rechtsstaatlichen Verfahren ergangen angesehen werden kann'('judged in the sense of Article 27(2) Brussels Convention as not "due", when there proves to be a breach of procedural German public policy, or *ordre public*, and thereby a judgment has been reached on the basis of proceedings that diverge from the basic principles of German procedural law to such an extent that it cannot be said to have been given in a well-ordered procedure in accordance with the rule of law').

[113] [1999] CLC 647, at p.661; refined by Waller LJ in the CA, [2000] 1 QB 288, at p.309, regarding adducing the evidence of fraud: '. . . evidence to establish the fraud was not available to the party alleging fraud at the time of the hearing . . . and . . . where perjury is the fraud alleged . . . the evidence must be so strong that it would reasonablz be expected to be decisive at a hearing, and if unanswered must have that result'.

[114] Below section 4.4.3.

[115] Article 509 NCPC and Article 2123 *Code civil* only appear to have a laconic, declaratory effect; compare the position in Belgium: Article 570 of the *Code judiciaire* contains the defences, among which Article 570(1) is the 'ordre public' defence, *Les Codes Larcier*, Tome I, *Droit civil et judiciaire*, 1998, p.266.

[116] (1964) *JDI* 302; (1964) *Rev Crit* 344, refined also by *Cassation* 4.10.1967 *Bachir c/ Dame Bachir* (1968) *Rev Crit* 98.

[117] Loussouarn, Y. and Bourel, P. *Droit international privé*, 6ème éd, 1999, at p.591, and pp.597–99; although Mayer and Heuzé, *Droit International Privé*, 7ème éd, 2001, at p.247, para. 366 list five prerequisites, but nothing here turns on this; Kessedjian, C. in Walter and Baumgartner (eds) *Recognition and Enforcement of foreign judgments outside the scope of the Brussels and Lugano Conventions*, 2000, at pp.196–204; Béraudo, (2001) *JDI* 1033, at p.1070; Lelièvre-Boucharat, M. (2001) *JDI* 1130, at p.1145.

[118] In *Bachir c/ Dame Bachir* subsumed an examination of the procedure followed by the rendering court into the (procedural) public policy defence; *International Execution against Judgment Debtors: France*, Release 98–1, at p.6 and p.11 for public policy; contrast *Cour de Cassation* 17.11.1999 *Mme T.*

cases have brought under this head the regulation of the procedure before the foreign judge, and the 'irreconcilable judgments' defence.[119] What is clear from the comments on the case, is that material public policy is included.

As far as cases that reveal any lingering tendencies to interpret public policy in an idiosyncratic[120] way, under the various bi-lateral Conventions that France has concluded with Great Britain,[121] Belgium,[122] Italy[123] or Switzerland,[124] there is very little relevant material to work with. Under the Anglo-French Convention of 18.1.1934, there is a case[125] that stresses that differences in the limitations periods for the prosecution of a libel action in England will not amount to a breach of French public policy. Of more interest for a future interpretation under the Brussels Convention is the French courts' approach to the issue of a 'reasoned' judgment in *Blunt c/ Miles,*[126] where, in spite of attempts to enforce what was seen as an unreasoned English judgment, the reference in it to the statement of claim prevented a breach of French public policy under Article 3(1)(c) of the Anglo-French Convention. Under the *Traité Franco-Suisse* of 5 June 1869, there are many instances of the mutual application of public policy in the areas of adoption, guardianship and divorce. Of more immediate interest, is an important example of the likely French attitude under Article 27(1) of the Brussels Convention to the recognition of an English anti-suit injunction: *Dame H c/ Dr. H.*[127] Here the husband sought to enforce, in France, an order by a Swiss court to the effect that Dame H was enjoined from continuing with her French action. This, the court held, was incontestably contrary to the right to 'agir en justice'[128] in France, and therefore contrary to public policy:

---

c/ Mme H (2000) *Rev crit* 52, where an appeal court was said *not* to have to raise the defence under Article 27(1) Brussels Convention of its own motion, at p.53.

[119] Audit, B. *Droit International Privé*, 1991, at p.384.

[120] In the case of the 'unreasoned' foreign judgment, the early case of *Klein c/ Niedermann Trib. civ. Seine* 15.10.1931, (1932) *JDI* 678, and the criticism provoked by it at p.680, and below, at pp.408–409.

[121] *Convention Franco-Britannique du 18 Janvier 1934,* Article 3(1)(c), *Juris-Classeur, Droit Int.,* Fasc.593–2, 1989, Lipstein and Gaudement-Tallon, esp. at p.8, para. 53 following.

[122] *Convention Franco-Belge du 8 Juillet 1899,* Article 11(1), *Juris-Classeur, Droit Int.,* Fasc.591, 1990 Watté; also Ropers, J.-L. 'La reconnaissance et l'exécution reciproque des décisions de justice à l'intérieur du Marché Commun' (1962) *JCP,* I, Doctr., 1679 for examples.

[123] *Convention Franco-Italienne du 3 Juin 1930,* Article 1(2), *Juris-Classeur, Droit Int.,* Fasc.592, 1988, Hanine.

[124] *Convention Franco-Suisse du 15 Juin 1869,* Article 17(3), *Juris-Classeur, Droit Int,* Fasc. 590, 1952–3, Flattet, esp. paras. 147–71; Vögli, N. *Die Vollstreckung schweizerischer Zivilurteile in Frankreich,* 1959, Ch.4, p.72, onwards in paternity cases; Escher, A. *Neuere Probleme aus der Rechtsprechung zum französisch-schweizerischen Gerichtsstandsvertrag vom 15. Juni 1869,* 1937, at p.155 onwards, merely noting the French tendency to use the defence more than the Swiss.

[125] *TGI Behune General Anders c/ Kwiatowski et Gas* 31.1.1961, (1961) *JDI* 1126.

[126] *Trib. civ. Corbeil* 5.3.1952, (1953) *JDI* 128.

[127] *Trib. civ. Montpellier* 11.12.1935, (1936) *JDI* 364, obs. Valéry.

[128] ('be able to have access to a court of law').

l'ordre public français s'oppose également à l'exécution en France d'une décision étrangère à un plaideur d'avoir à se désister en faveur de son adversaire d'un procès qu'il avait intenté à ce dernier.[129] [130]

The attitude of the French courts—especially concerning those elements of French national procedure which a French judgment itself must fulfil to be valid—has been to elevate their courts, *mutatis mutandis*, almost to a rôle of a court of appeal on the foreign judgment, using its own national procedure as a 'public policy' yardstick. This function arrogated to itself—especially when the foreign court had delivered judgment in accordance with its own procedure—had its critics even as early as 1932:

> le jugement dit que l'absence de motifs empêcherait le contrôle par le juge français..Ce serait faire du juge d'exquatur une espèce de juge de cassation.[131] [132]

It would be a worrying development if this trend[133] were to continue under Article 27(1) of the Brussels Convention.

4.2.4 The public policy defence under Swiss 'autonomous' law[134]

Although until quite recently[135] there were no Swiss higher court decisions on public policy under Article 27(1), there is a wealth of cases concerning the interpretation of public policy[136] under various bi-lateral Conventions,[137] indicating the likely attitude[138] the Swiss courts will take to the defence under the Lugano Convention.

---

[129] ('French public policy is equally opposed to the enforcement in France of a foreign judgment directed at a plaintiff to have to refrain, in favour of his opponent, from an action that he had brought against the latter').

[130] *Ibid.*, at p.365.

[131] ('the judgment states that the lack of reasoning would prevent control by the French judge . . . This would make the enforcement judge a type of appeal judge').

[132] *Klein c/ Niedermann*, 15.10.1931, (1932) *JDI* 678, at p.680; contrast *Bundesgericht 23.7.2001 M.R. gegen H AG*, unreported, where an unmotived (default) judgment does not, *per se*, breach Swiss public policy under Article 27(1) Lugano Convention.

[133] Unfortunately, this trend has continued, below at the French section 4.4.1.

[134] In regard to punitive damages, Lenz, C. *Amerikanische Punitive Damages vor dem Schweizer Richter*, 1992; Walther, F. in Walter and Baumgartner (eds) *Recognition and Enforcement of foreign judgments outside the scope of the Brussels and Lugano Conventions*, 2000, at p.555; Othenin-Girard, S. *La réserve d'ordre public en droit international privé suisse*, 1999, at p.92 onwards.

[135] *Bundesgericht G Ltd contre K* 19.9.2000 126 BGE III, 534, reviewed in this section.

[136] The tendency not to use public policy to censure the foreign procedure has a long history: *Bundesgericht Constantin Mavromati c/ Vacher, syndic de faillité*, 18.2.1938, (1938) *Rev Crit* 508, at p.516—also comments on Swiss bilateral Convention in Alexander, E. 'Die internationale Vollstreckung von Zivilurteilen insbesondere im Verhältnis zu den Nachbarstaaten' (1931) *ZBJV* 1, at p.15.

[137] *Recueil Systématique des lois et ordonnances*, 1848–1947, 12ᵉ vol., 1953; for a pre-IPRG overview, Niedermann, M. *Die ordre-public Klauseln in den Vollstreckungsverträgen des Bundes und den kantonalen Zivilprozessgesetzen*, 1976; Bülow, A and Böckstiegel, K-H., *Der Internationale Rechtsverkehr in Zivil- und Handelssachen*, Band I, p.660, BII.

[138] Past restrictive attitude to public policy will be continued, according to Siehr, K. in Symeonides (ed) *Private International Law at the End of the 20ᵗʰ Century: Progress or Regress?*, 2000, p.383, at p.403; yet, *dubitante, Bundesgericht G Ltd contre K* 19.9.2000 126 BGE III, 534.

As far as non-Convention law is concerned, recognition and enforcement of civil and commercial judgments in (the various Cantons of) Switzerland[139] is governed[140] by the relatively recent Private International Law Statute,[141] the *Bundesgesetz vom 18 Dezember 1987 über das Internationale Privatrecht*, (IPRG).[142] Article 27(1) IPRG[143] provides a defence if recognition would be manifestly[144] incompatible 'with Swiss public policy'. Article 27(2) lists other grounds, relating to the reception of proper notice of the proceedings, and tellingly, in Article 27(2)(b), *inter alia*, the necessity of 'das rechtliche Gehör'('a fair hearing').[145]

There are examples of this court's reviewing public policy under its own law, which may form guidelines for its eventual attitude to Article 27(1) of Lugano Convention:[146] in *Rostuca Holdings c/ Polo et autre*,[147] Rostuca sought the recognition of a New York default judgment in Geneva. It was resisted under Article 27(2) IPRG on the grounds that the default judgment itself was not served, nor contained any reasoning on the merits. Tellingly for any future interpretation of Article 27(1) Lugano, the *Bundesgericht* reviewed earlier decisions which had given a restricted[148] interpretation to 'ordre public' under earlier bilateral Conventions and ruled equally in this case that

---

[139] Generally Bucher, A. *Droit international privé suisse*, Tome I/1: *Partie générale—Conflits de juridictions*, 1998, pp.212–17; Niedermann, 1976, at p.89 onwards; Article 401 *Code de procédure civile du canton de Berne*, §§271; 280 ZPO Kanton Uri; §424(2) ZPO Kanton Aargau; §258 I, II ZPO Kanton Basel-Stadt.

[140] In Articles 25–29.

[141] For an English translation, if necessary, Karrer, P., Arnold, K., Patocchi, P., *Switzerland's Private International Law*, 2nd edn., 1994.

[142] AS 1988, 1776, as amended in 1993 and 1995; generally Samuel, A. 'The New Swiss Private International Law Act' (1988) *ICLQ* 681; an account in English, Hochstrasser, D. *Commercial Litigation and Enforcement of Foreign Judgments in Switzerland*, 1995, at p.80 following.

[143] Article 27(1) reads as follows: 'Eine im Ausland ergangene Entscheidung wird in der Schweiz nicht erkannt, wenn die Anerkennung mit dem schweizerischen Ordre public offensichtlich unvereinbar wäre'('a decision rendered abroad will not be recognised in Switzerland if recognition would be manifestly incompatible with Swiss public policy').

[144] Walder, in *Das Lugano-Übereinkommen*, (Hrsg Schwander, I.,), 1990, p.135, at p.139 thinks that nothing turns on the fact that the word 'manifestly' was omitted from the wording of Article 27(1) Lugano Convention; Walter, G. *Internationales Zivilprozessrecht der Schweiz*, Ein Lehrbuch, 2 Aufl., 1998, at p.354.

[145] In *G gegen B* 19.11.1994 120 BGE,III, 83, at p.85 the Swiss Federal Court stated that the defences in Article 27(2) IPRG: 'dem formellen oder prozessualen ordre public zugerechnet wird, [und sind] restriktiv anzuwenden,' ('is attributed to formal or procedural ordre public, [and are] to be applied restrictively', which can only mean that 'public policy' in Article 27(1) IPRG refers to 'material' public policy; for procedural *ordre public*, Article 4 of the Swiss Constitution and Donzallaz, Y. *La Convention de Lugano*, Vol II, 1997, paras. 1737–4238, at p.423, para. 2844 onwards.

[146] Dörig, A. *Anerkennung und Vollstreckung US-amerikanischer Entscheidungen in der Schweiz*, 1998, at pp.349–74 regarding punitive damages, and at p.367 uncertain, regarding judgments for contingency fees; Bucher, 1998, who believes under the Lugano Convention that Article 27(1) will be used rarely, at p.215, para. 690.

[147] 116 BGE, II, 625.

[148] Cf also Piantino, Y. 'Switzerland's Treatment of U.S. Money Judgments' (1998) *Am J Comp L* 181, at p.187.

[c]*ette jurisprudence doit être maintenue* en tout cas pour les jugements par défaut et à la condition que la partie défaillante ait été invitée sans succès . . .[149] [150]

Yet perhaps the most revealing cases—that one would have expected[151] to form the basis for the future interpretation of public policy under Article 27(1) Lugano Convention in Switzerland—are those decided under bilateral Treaties with Germany,[152] and Italy:[153] for example under Article 4 I[154] of the German-Swiss Recognition and Enforcement Convention of 2 November 1929:[155] *Anton Bertl c/ Deutsche Bau- und Bodenbank AG.*[156] A default judgment against Bertl was found to contain no statement as to facts, nor any reasoning[157] on the merits. What is remarkable about the judgment is its receptive[158] attitude to enforcement, and its willingness, faced with the court's Treaty obligations, to restrict as much as possible, recourse to a defence that would thwart the aims of recognition and

---

[149] ('these ruling should be preserved in cases of default judgments and on condition that the party in default had been summoned without success').

[150] 19.12.1990 116 BGE, II, 625, at p.632.

[151] Unfortunately, the restrictive attitude to the invocation of public policy expressed in the cases reviewed here was not, however, evident in the application of Article 27(1) Lugano Convention in *Bundesgericht G Ltd contre K* 19.9.2000 126 BGE III, 534, below.

[152] *Abkommen zwischen dem Deutschen Reich und der Schweizerischen Eidgenossenschaft über die gegenseitige Anerkennung und Vollstreckung von gerichtlichen Entscheidungen und Schiedsprüchen*, 2.11.1929, RGBl, 1930, II, 1066, in force 1.12.1930, Article 4(1); *Pfister-Grüebler gegen Firma Obpacher GmbH* 19.5.1976 102 BGE, Ia, 308, at pp.313–14, also *Ligna Aussenhandelsunternehmen gegen Baumgartner & Co. A.G.* 12.2.1958 84 BGE, I, 39, at pp.48–49, under the Swiss-Czech Convention of 21.12.1926.

[153] Jellinek, W. *Die zweiseitigen Staatsverträge über Anerkennung ausländischer Zivilurteile*, Zweites Heft: Vertragstexte und Register, 1953; 1848—1947 AS, Bd. 12, p.338, Article 1(1)(2); *Nicolini contro Gatti* 20.9.1972 98 BGE, Ia, 527, at p.533, *Hagen gegen Gritschneder* 29.3.1961 87 BGE, I, 73, under the 1933 Italian-Swiss Convention, Article 1(2).

[154] Recognition could be denied if the judgment was contrary to the 'öffentliche Ordnung' of either country.

[155] *Abkommen zwischen dem Deutschen Reich und der Schweizerischen Eidgenossenschaft über die gegenseitige Anerkennung und Vollstreckung von gerichtlichen Entscheidungen und Schiedsprüchen*, 2.11.1929, RGBl, 1930, II, 1066, in force 1.12.1930.

[156] (1979) *JT*, II, 98.

[157] Compare the draconian attitude to such judgments by the French courts under Article 27(1) of the Brussels Convention: *Vanclef c/ Société Trans Traide International* 17.5.1978 / *Etienne c/ Société Handelsonderneming Claessen B.V.* 24.11.1977/*Theillol c/ Office de la jeunesse de Fribourg* 18.4.1978 (1979) *JDI* 380; *Société Polypétrol c/ Société générale routière* 9.10.1991 (1993) *JDI* 157; (1992) *Rev Crit* 516, below, at p.409.

[158] (1979) *JT*, II, 98, at p.101: 'Il ne convient donc pas qu'en se réclamant de l'ordre public suisse, l'application de cette réglementation conventionelle soit pratiquement mise en échec et que *les effets du Traité international, dont le but est précisément de reconnaître l'existence de sytèmes juridiques différents et de les coordonner*, soient contrecarrés.'('it is not therefore appropriate that by relying on Swiss public policy, the application of this convention rule should be set at nought and that the effects of an international Treaty, whose aim is precisely to recognise the existence of different judicial regimes and to harmonise them, should be subverted'); also *Bundesgericht* 1.7.1983 *Dame B contre B*, 109 BGE, Ib, 232, at p.235: 'La teneur étroite de l'art 4 al..1 de la convention germano-suisse a pour objet d'empêcher que la réserve d'ordre public *ne prenne une extension exagérée* . . .'('the narrow content of Article 4(1) of the German-Swiss Convention is aimed at preventing the public policy exemption from attaining an extended ambit').

enforcement. Bertl's 'public policy' defence of the lack of a reasoned judgment therefore failed.[159]

The Federal Court has stressed that the meaning of public policy in the recognition and enforcement context must be interpreted in a narrower way[160] than in its application to choice of law issues.[161] In addition, it is clear that, as with the German jurisprudence, the Swiss courts will undoubtedly divide[162] up Article 27(1) Lugano Convention public policy into its material and procedural manifestations.[163]

Another revealing attitude in a further important case, *Hoepffner gegen Wollner*,[164] again decided under Article 4(1) of the German-Swiss Convention of 1929, is the lack of necessity to institute an appeal, or of exhausting all local remedies (in the rendering court) before relying on public policy in Switzerland. There seems to be little doubt that this attitude may have to change under Article 27(1) of Lugano Convention. The court held in this case that instituting such measures of appeal in the original court were not necessary: Wollner had not done so in Germany. Reliance on public policy in Switzerland, it was observed

> setzt nicht voraus, dass der Verurteilte im Ausland die gegen das Urteil zur Verfügung stehenden ordentlichen Rechtsmittel ergriffen hat. Die in der Schweiz wohnhafte Partei, der gegenüber im Ausland ein gegen den schweizerischen ordre public verstossenes Urteil ergeht, *darf dessen Vollstreckung . . . abwarten und den Mangel dann geltend machen*.[165]

---

[159] (1979) *JT*, II, 98, at p.104.

[160] *Consortium de transports commerciaux S.A.* 13.5.1964 90 BGE, I, 113, at p.118, under Article 1(2) of the Italian-Swiss Convention.

[161] Also *Dame B contre B* 1.7.1983 109 BGE, Ib, 232, under Article 4(1) of the German -Swiss Convention.

[162] *Hoepffner gegen Wollner* 21.1.1959 85 BGE, I, 39, at p.47, under Article 4(1) of the German-Swiss Convention.

[163] Also in line with the German view is the fact that mere differences in the procedure between the Contracting States will not constitute an assault on Swiss public policy: *Hagen gegen Gritschneder* 29.3.1961 87 BGE, I, 73, at pp.78–79, decided under Article 4(1) of the German-Swiss Convention; equally when the two laws contain similar provisions: *Consortium de transports commerciaux S.A.* 13.5.1964 90 BGE, I, 113, at p.119; *Bundesgericht* 5.7.2001 *X contrre l'arrêt rendu le 11.1.2001 . . . Y Ltd*, unreported: 'en droit suisse également, l'autorité n'est tenue de prendre en considération que les preuves régulièrement offertes" ('equally in Swiss law, the legal authorities are only bound to take into account properly proffered evidence'); also, in stark contrast to the French position under Article 27(1), *Bundesgericht* 23.7.2001 *M.R. gegen H AG*, unreported, enforcement of an 'unmotivated' Austrian default judgment not refused on Article 27(1) grounds: 'die Anerkennung eines Versäumnisurteiles, das weder eine Sachverhaltsdarstellung noch Entscheidungsgründe enthält, den schweizerischen Ordre public nicht verletzt, wenn die säumige Partei Gelegenheit zur Verteidigung gehabt hat'('the recognition of a default judgment that contains neither a presentation of the factual situation nor the grounds of the decision does not offend Swiss public policy when the party in default has had an opportunity of presenting a defence').

[164] 21.1.1959 85 BGE, I, 39.

[165] ('does not presuppose that the judgment debtor has resorted abroad to the appeal procedure ordinarily available against the judgment. The party resident in Switzerland against whom a judgment abroad has been given, which is contrary to Swiss public policy, *may await its enforcement and then rely on this fault*.') 85 BGE, I, 39, at p.50.

There was no reason to suppose that these attitudes,[166] which, after all, had developed in the context of recognition and enforcement Conventions dating back to the 1920s, would have failed to provide a restrictive legacy when the *Bundesgericht* came to consider a similar question against the background of the Lugano Convention.

On 19.9.2000, the *Bundesgericht* decided the appeal in *G Ltd contre K*.[167] An English company owning a licensed casino in the UK had obtained from the QBD a judgment against K for gambling debts, and attempted to enforce it against him in Geneva. Lower instance courts had already dismissed K's defence of a breach of Swiss public policy under Article 27(1) Lugano Convention in enforcing gaming debts in Switzerland. The *Bundesgericht* in turn rejected the defence. The judgment is notable for a least two reasons:

(1) firstly, and of slight concern, the explicit exhortations against an extensive, or extended use of public policy witnessed in the earlier Treaties—which might have been predicted from the examples such as *Bertl gegen Deutsche Bau- und Bodenbank AG*[168]—were absent. One would have thought that under the Lugano Convention, they would have applied *a fortiori*: all that was said on this score was that by becoming party to such an international Treaty, the legislature had recognised that foreign judgments *may* be based on substantive laws that will differ from those under Swiss (federal) law.[169] Nor was there any reference to other Lugano Contracting State caselaw, to any *travaux préparatoires*, nor even a terse acknowledgement of *SA Régie Nationale des Usines Renault v SpA Maxicar and Orazio Formento*.[170]

Accordingly, under Article 27(1), the Swiss judge is to ascertain:

si le jugement [anglais], qui condamne à payer une dette de jeu, heurte de manière choquante les principes les plus essentiels de l'ordre juridique, tel qu'il est conçu en Suisse.[171] [172]

---

[166] Yet the approach of the French courts to unreasoned (default) judgments will almost certainly not be followed in Switzerland: statements to this effect also in *Hagen gegen Gritschneder* 29.3.1961 87 BGE, I, 73, again under Article 4(1) of the German-Swiss Convention, at p.78.

[167] 126 BGE III, 534.

[168] 9.2.1977 103 BGE, Ia, 199.

[169] 126 BGE III, 534, at p.538, para. (c); nor was there any espousal of a truly 'international' public policy, but a rather parochial view, Donzallaz, Y. 'Le renouveau de l'ordre public dans la CB/CL au regard des ACJCE *Krombach* et *Renault* et de la révision de ces traités' (2001) *AJP* 160, at p.169.

[170] Under the Declaration to the 1988 Lugano Convention, Switzerland declared that its courts would 'pay due account' to such matters when interpreting, *inter alia*, Article 27(1), [1988] OJ L319/40.

[171] ('if the [English] judgment ordering the payment of a gaming debt, offends in an egregious way the most important principles of the judicial order, as understood in Switzerland'); Swiss (procedural) public policy demands 'respect des garanties fondamentales de procédure déduites de la Constitution . . . le droit à un procès équitable et le droit d'être entendu' ('respect for fundamental guarantees of procedure derived from the Constitution . . . the right to a fair procedure and the right to be heard'): *Bundesgericht* 5.7.2001 *X contrre l'arrêt rendu le 11.1.2001 . . . Y Ltd*, unreported.

[172] 126 BGE III, 534, at p.538.

(2) secondly, and in order ascertain this, the *Bundesgericht*'s judgment reveals the fluidity of the concept of public policy, relative as it is in a socio-legal, and temporal, context. Had this case come before the court prior to early 1993, cases dating from 1935 had shown the opposition of the legislature to the opening and running of casinos in Switzerland. By a plebiscite of 1993, this attitude had changed; and on 1.4.2000 an amendment to the *Code des Obligations* permitted an exception to recovery of gaming debts from licensed gambling premises. Enforcement of the English judgment could no longer therefore be said to run counter to Swiss notions of public policy under Article 27(1).[173]

4.2.5 The public policy defence under Belgian, Italian, Austrian, and Spanish[174] 'autonomous' law

At least from as early[175] as Article 10(1) of the law of 25 March 1876, Belgium has had a provision for the (non-)recognition of foreign decisions, if, *inter alia*, they contain anything contrary to Belgian 'ordre public'. This provision has, since 1970, been perpetuated almost *verbatim* in Article 570(1) of the *Code Judiciaire*.[176] Various cases[177] have been collected[178] in which the issue of public policy has been aired; yet (in comparison to the German position), it appears that no comprehensive, consistent concept has emerged in Belgian recognition and enforcement

---

[173] Cf the 'amateur' German 'futures' traders, having suffered losses on foreign investment stock-markets: finding a breach of German (material) public policy: *BGH* 4.6.1975 (1975) *NJW* 1600, later *BGH* 21.4.1998, a departure from earlier established case law principles (*BGH* 4.6.1975 (1975) *WM* 676, *BGH* 25.5.1981 (1981) *WM* 758) was warranted; *Scarpetta v Lowenfeld* (1911) 27 T.L.R. 509, at p.510 (Lawrence J); Article 27(1) inapplicable to an English judgment, disallowing judgment debtor's evidence not in affidavit form—as debtor had been given opportunity to participate in English proceedings but had not done so: *Bundesgericht 5.7.2001 X contrre l'arrêt rendu le 11.1.2001 . . . Y Ltd*, unreported.

[174] Esp. Karl, A-M. *Die Anerkennung von Entscheidungen in Spanien*, 1993, at pp.61–62, and Article 954(3) *Ley de Enjuiciamiento civil* (civil procedure code) in combination with Article 12(3) *Código civil*; for Greece, Article 323(5) Code of Civil Procedure, and Yessiou-Faltsi, P. *Civil Procedure in Hellas*, 1998, at p.440 ('not . . . of particular practical significance'); Anthimos (2000) *IPRax* 327, at p.331 (restricted use); Maridakis, *Enforcement of Foreign Judgments*, 3rd edn., (in Greek); Anthimos, 1995 *Dike* p. 1099ff (in Greek); for The Netherlands, despite Article 431 Cpc (Dutch), Kokkini-Iatridou, D. and Verheul, J.P. *Les effets des jugements et sentences étrangers aux Pays-Bas*, 1970, at pp.13–15.

[175] For the law prior to this date, Article 546 CPC and Article 2123 *Code civil*, Bormans, T. *Code de procédure civile belge*, Livre I, Titre premier, 2ᵉ éd, 1877, at p.302.

[176] *Les Codes Larcier*, I, 1998, at p.266; Fevery, D. in Walter and Baumgartner (eds) *Recognition and Enforcement of foreign judgments outside the scope of the Brussels and Lugano Conventions* 2000, at pp.95–96.

[177] A breach of promise case *Cour d'appel de Bruxelles* 4.11.1882 1883 *Pas. Belge*, II, 35; *Tribunal civil de Bruxelles* 6.3.1970 *S.A.R.L. de droit français Groslambert c/ Madame Veuve Eugène Hunin* (1971) *JDI* 894; *Cassation* 4.5.1950 *Vigouroux c Vigoouroux* 1950 *Pas. Belge*, I, 624; *Cassation* 28.3.1952 *État Belge c État Suédois* 1952 *Pas. Belge*, I, 483.

[178] *Répertoire Décennal de la Jurisprudence Belge*, Tome 2ᵉᵐᵉ, 1900–1910, at p.396, no.108; *Répertoire Décennal*, 1966–1977, at p.20, no.27; *Répertoire Décennal*, 1947–1955, at p.97, no.45 (a situation similar to the facts of *Israel Discount Bank v Hadjipateras*).

law[179] that could have said to have been carried across under Article 27(1) of the Brussels Convention.

Italy and Austria, too, have similar defences to recognition and enforcement. In the former case, Article 797(7) of the *Codice di procedura civile*,[180] and, since 1.1.1997, Article 64(1)(g) of the law of 31ˢᵗ May 1995[181] subject foreign judgments to compliance with Italian 'ordine publico'.[182] In the latter, Austria's autonomous recognition and enforcement law is to be found in §§79–86 *Executionsordnung* (EO) of 27.5.1896, as amended.[183] Its §81(3) EO[184] currently prohibits recognition and enforcement of judgments against 'd[ie] öffentliche[] Ordnung' or 'd[ie] Sittlichkeit'. Recently, an Austrian Supreme Court decision has had to consider public policy in the context of the enforcement of a (domestic) arbitration award, and provisions of §595 Abs.1 of the Austrian ZPO. This in turn has led commentators[185] to speculate on the rôle of public policy under Article 27(1) of (now) the Brussels Convention. These believe—contrary to the decision of the *BGH* in the *Sonntag* case—that mandatory provisions of national law should *not* prevent the recognition and enforcement of other (Lugano) Contracting State judgments.

4.3 THE COMMUNITY DIMENSION TO PUBLIC POLICY, AND THE RÔLE OF THE EUROPEAN COURT OF JUSTICE[186]

Up until the cases of *SA Régie Nationale des Usines Renault v SpA Maxicar and Orazio Formento*[187] and *Dieter Krombach v Andre Bamberski*,[188] the European Court has not had to deal squarely with the issue of 'public policy' under Article 27(1) of the Brussels Convention. As a defence in Title III of the Convention it is,

---

[179] For the exclusion of foreign law due to public policy: *Cour de Cassation* 27.2.1986 *S.C.C.* (1989) *Rev crit juris belge* 56.

[180] Satta, S. *Commentario al Codice di Procedura Civile*, IV, 1971, at p.133; Bellagamba, G. and Cariti, G. *Il sistema italiano di diritto internazionale privato*, 2000, at pp.193–97.

[181] *Legge 21 Maggio 1995*, N.218 *Le nuove leggi civili commentate*, N.5-6, Anno XIX, settembre-diciembre, p.877, translated by Montanari, A. *Conflict of Laws in Italy, The Text and an English translation of Italian Law No.218 of May 31, 1995*, 1997.

[182] Lupoi, M. in Walter and Baumgartner (eds) *Recognition and Enforcement of foreign judgments outside the scope of the Brussels and Lugano Conventions*, 2000, at p.358—notion appears to vary according to whether judgment to be recognised/enforced involves an Italian citizen or not.

[183] RGBl 1896/79; now Stumvoll, H. (ed) *Zivilgerichtliches Verfahren, Kodex des österreichischen Rechts*, 1998.

[184] Angst, P., Jakusch, W., Pimmer, H. (eds) *Executionsordnung, samt Einführungsgesetz, Nebengesetzen, und sonstigen einschlägigen Vorschriften*, 13 Aufl., 1995, at p.431 for definitions; Rechberger, W. in Walter and Baumgartner (eds) *Recognition and Enforcement of foreign judgments outside the scope of the Brussels and Lugano Conventions*, 2000, at pp.59–60.

[185] Achatz, M. 'Ordre public, Unionsrecht und Steuerrecht' *OGH* 5.5.1998 (1999) *JBl* 390, at p.403–04.

[186] In some detail Donzallaz, Y. 'Le renouveau de l'ordre public dans la CB/CL au regard des ACJCE *Krombach* et *Renault* et de la révision de ces traités' (2001) *AJP* 160.

[187] (C–38/98) [2000] ECR I–2973; *Eco Swiss China Time Ltd v Benetton International NV* (C–126/97) [(1999)] ECR I–3055 at p.3093, para. 39.

[188] (C–7/98), 28.3.2000 from the German BGH 4.12.1997 (1999) *EuZW* 26, [1998] I.L.Pr. 681, discussed below, at p.398, AG Antonio Saggio's opinion 23.9.1999.

as such, capable of forming the legitimate basis for a competent court to request a ruling on its meaning from the European Court under either Articles 2 or 3 of the Protocol on the interpretation of the Convention. So whether the interpretation given by the Court in *Dieter Krombach* was justified, providing as it did a framework[189] Community 'autonomous' definition,[190] or whether the entire matter was best remitted to national law, will no doubt be a matter of some debate.

The majority view,[191] prior to *Dieter Krombach*, of this issue was that it was in the sole competence of the individual Contracting States to define their own notions of 'public policy' in a national context.[192] There was much to be said, at a domestic level, for this approach as upholding the last bastion of national concern in an increasingly autonomous and integrated system of jurisdiction and recognition of judgments. Several German courts shared this attitude. Early on in 1979,[193] the *BGH* decided[194] that public policy was not a matter for the European Court at all, and refused[195] to allow a reference to be made on the subject.

It seems, however, inconceivable that the European Court could not at least set the boundaries[196] for the application of this defence, within which national considerations will be allowed a free rein:[197] an approach that is similar to that which it has demonstrated in regard to the meaning of 'provisional, including protective

---

[189] Within which the Contracting States are free to apply public policy.

[190] Any autonomous interpretation was likely to be so vague that it will permit the pre-existing national interpretations to remain in any event—framework recently enhanced in *SA Régie Nationale des Usines Renault*, at para. 28.

[191] Against the Court's interference in a definition of public policy Kropholler, J. *Europäisches Zivilprozeßrecht*: Kommentar zu EuGVÜ und Lugano-Übereinkommen, 6 Aufl., 1998, at p.343, para. 4; Briggs, 1997, at p.321, para. 7.15; Gothot and Holleaux, 1985, at p.147, para. 256; *contra*, AG Alber in *SA Régie Nationale des Usines Renault*, (C–38/98) [2000] ECR I–2973, at para. 58.

[192] Cf AG Darmon in *Hoffmann v Krieg* (C–145/86) [1988] ECR 645, at p.656 para. 16 *in fine*: public policy is a matter for the national courts alone; confirmed by AG Saggio in *Dieter Krombach*, at para. 24.

[193] Although the *BGH* made a reference on the scope of public policy in *Dieter Krombach*, its 'national' view of this matter has not changed: [d]ie Anwendung der nationalen öffentlichen Ordnung obliegt im Rahmen des Article 27 Nr.1 EuGVÜ regelmäßig allein den Gerichten des Anerkennungsstaates' ('the application of national public policy in the framework of Article 27(1) of the Brussels Convention is the regular responsibility solely of the courts of the recognising State'), (1999) *EuZW* 26, at p.28; English at [1998] I.L.Pr. 681, p.687—the scope of the definition in *Dieter Krombach* has left the Contracting State courts enough latitude to quell domestic concerns, however; *BGH* 75 BGHZ 167, at p.171 and post-reference decision *BGH* 29.6.2000, *Krombach v Bamberski* (2000) *RIW* 797, (2001) *IPRax* 50.

[194] *BGH* 26.9.1979 75 BGHZ 167, at p.171: 'Diese Frage berührt allein das nationale Recht. Sie kann nur durch die deutschen Gerichte entscheiden werden . . .' ('This question involves only national law. It can only be resolved by the German courts'); however, the court in this case also believed that 'irreconcilability' for Article 27(3) purposes was a matter for national law. *Hoffmann v Krieg* (C–145/86) [1988] ECR 645 proved it wrong.

[195] Unusually for this court, which to date has made the overwhelming number of references, 31 in all (of which 2 were withdrawn).

[196] Kropholler, 1998, at p.343 para. 4; what *Dicey and Morris on the Conflict of Laws*, 12th edn., 1993, Vol.I., referred to as 'a possible check' at p.536.

[197] Cf Gaudemet-Tallon, 1996, at p.256, para. 355; Cheshire and North, 13th edn., 1999, at p.495—this indeed was the ECJ's view in *Dieter Krombach*, at para. 22.

measures' under Article 24. As has been seen in the previous chapter, the measures that may be granted under that article are those 'as may be available under national law'. This fact alone—that the Convention's wording remits the matter to national law—did not prevent the Court from setting limits[198] within which a national court is to grant those measures. The same interpretation has followed on in Article 27(1).

4.3.1 The AG Saggio's opinion in *Dieter Krombach v Andre Bamberski*

The European Court has recently dealt with public policy in Article 27(1) in the case *Dieter Krombach v Andre Bamberski*,[199] a reference from the *Bundesgerichtshof* in 4.12.1997.[200] If, as was generally believed,[201] public policy's definition was not a matter for the ECJ, nor of any autonomous Community meaning, at least one aspect[202] of the French judgment, given in *partie civile* proceedings before a Paris criminal court, will offend German public policy:[203] that at every stage in both civil and criminal proceedings in Germany, a defendant/accused has a constitutionally-guaranteed right to be represented by a lawyer, and to state his case 'with regard to the claim for damages'.[204] In this case, the Paris criminal court had tried and convicted Krombach *in absentia*. Various provisions of the French criminal procedural code[205] forbade the criminal court from permitting defence lawyers from appearing on behalf of an absent defendant/accused.

AG Saggio delivered his opinion on the 23rd September 1999, in *Dieter Krombach*.[206] The Advocate General reiterated the view of his colleague AG Darmon in *Horst Ludwig Martin Hoffman v Adelheid Krieg*[207] that the definition and content of the concept of public policy was a matter solely for the national judge:

> Generally speaking, it is not for the Community judicature, but for the national court, to identify the internal provisions which have the force of principles of 'public policy in the national legal system.[208]

---

[198] *Mario Reichert and others v Dresdner Bank AG* (C–261/90) [1992] ECR I– 2149, and *Van Uden* (C–391/95) [1998] ECR I–7091.

[199] (C–7/98), 28.3.2000.

[200] (1999) *EuZW* 26, [1998] I.L.Pr. 681.

[201] Briggs, 1997, at p.321, para. 7.15; *contra*, ECJ in *Dieter Krombach*.

[202] One aspect, relating to the jurisdiction taken by the criminal court is prohibited by Article 28 III.

[203] As the referring court, the *BGH*, had already found (1999) *EuZW* 26, at p.27, point 2: 4.12.1997, *Dieter Krombach v Andre Bamberski* [1998] I.L.Pr. 681; confirmed a breach of (German procedural) public policy: BGH 29.6.2000, (2000) *RIW* 797, (2001) *IPRax* 50, reviewed below at p.428.

[204] [1998] I.L.Pr. 681, at p.686, para. 16.

[205] Article 630 of which provides: 'Aucun "avocat" ne peut se présenter pour l'accusé contumax'; facts and French proceedings reviewed in detail in *Affaire Krombach c. France* (No.29731/96) of 13.1.2001, before the European Court of Human Rights (breach, *inter alia*, of Art.6(1) ECHR).

[206] (C–7/98), AG Antonio Saggio's opinion 23.9.1999; for the material parts of his opinion, below, at p.397.

[207] (C–145/86) [1988] ECR 645.

[208] *Dieter Krombach*, at para. 24, not taken up by the ECJ, however.

Interestingly, however, he viewed the reference from the *BGH* not as seeking justification to define public policy on the national level, but to ascertain whether the European Court intended to impose, at Community level, any, and if so what, limitation on the defence of public policy in Article 27(1).[209] According to AG Saggio, as we shall see, a breach of Article 27(1) can only occur in 'grave[s] . . . manifeste[s]'[210] and extreme cases, breaching one of the fundamental rights of the parties. It seems, therefore, as predicted earlier, the Advocate General has added (as would the ECJ after him) a European definitional 'gloss' to what is essentially a matter for the legal systems of each individual Contracting State.

Returning to the order for reference itself, the German court had considered, in addition, that there was a breach of public policy in circumstances when an alleged offence was committed in Germany, and the alleged perpetrator can (under French criminal jurisdictional rules) be compelled to answer for damages in the *partie civile* proceedings in France on the basis of the victim's French nationality.[211] This latter ground failed to impress the European Court.[212] After all, Article 28 III tells us quite clearly that 'the test of public policy referred to in point 1 of Article 27 may not be applied to the rules relating to jurisdiction'. But Article 28 III arguable only relates to jurisdiction taken in 'civil and commercial matters' under Article 1 of the Convention. Could it be used to override a sanction against jurisdiction taken by a Contracting State's criminal courts?

Article 5(4) complicates the matter still further. This article foresees the possibility of a *partie civile* action before the criminal courts of one Contracting State against a person domiciled in another. '[T]o the extent that that [criminal] court has jurisdiction under its own law to entertain civil proceedings',[213] the jurisdictional basis of the criminal proceedings appears to be irrelevant; that, in *Dieter Krombach*, the Paris criminal court took jurisdiction over the accused on the basis of the deceased victim's French nationality is not, *per se*, sanctionable under Article 27(1). Hartley, reviewing[214] a similar[215] case of *Rinkau*,[216] neatly summarises the position under Article 5(4) thus:

> [Article 5(4)] gives a special advantage to the *partie civile*: even if the courts of the country in question would not have had jurisdiction if the civil action had been brought on its own . . . [,]jurisdiction may nevertheless be obtained if a criminal prosecution [can be and] is brought.[217]

[209] At para. 25.
[210] At para. 27.
[211] The 'mirror principle'; German recognition and enforcement law, §328 I Nr.1 ZPO requires jurisdiction to have been taken in the rendering court along similar lines, and under similar provisions, as would a German court hearing the case under its own jurisdictional provisions of the ZPO.
[212] 28.3.2000, at para. 32.
[213] Article 5(4) *in fine*.
[214] (1982) *ELR* 483.
[215] The only difference being that in *Dieter Krombach*, Krombach had been charged and convicted of an intentional offence, and so Article II of the Protocol did not apply.
[216] *Criminal Proceedings against Siegfried Ewald Rinkau* (C–157/80) [1981] ECR 1391.
[217] (1982) *ELR* 483, at p.484.

Advocate General Saggio in the material part of his opinion in *Dieter Krombach v Andre Bamberski* itself, preferred to distil the issues raised in the above paragraphs, and by the *BGH*—of (French) jurisdiction being given to the court of the victim, and the suppression of the rights of the defence in cases of an accused *in absentia*—into a relatively simple question. This was whether differences in the procedural laws of the Contracting States—where, as here, in Germany comparable jurisdictional rules to those in the French criminal procedure/*partie civile* proceedings did not exist, but the right to be heard was constitutionally guaranteed—could have an ostracising effect on ensuing judgments under Article 27(1).

As far as the objection taken by the *BGH* to the French rule in the criminal code allowing jurisdiction to be taken on the basis of the victim's French nationality, the Advocate General was keen to stress that a recognising/enforcing court should not refuse to give effect to a judgment rendered in another Contracting State merely because the jurisdictional rule employed by the adjudicating court was different from,[218] or non-existent in, the State court addressed.[219] Indeed, he was adamant that no review of an adjudicating court's jurisdiction should be undertaken under Article 27(1) at all. In these views he was strengthened by the text of Title III itself: Article 28 III/Article 34 II explicitly prohibit a review of jurisdiction at all, including under the auspices of Article 27(1).[220] He also drew support from the text of Article 5(4).[221]

This was, however, not the only divergence between the French and German rules that were (or would have been) applicable in this case: Article 630 of the French code of criminal procedure prevented an accused *in absentia*/in default from legal representation before the trial court—a right to legal representation in similar circumstances being guaranteed by the German Constitution. The secondary question for the Advocate General therefore became whether a *partie civile* judgment based on differences in Contracting State procedure[222]—a divergence in approach to rules governing an accused *in absentia*—could justify the application of Article 27(1).[223] He again stressed that Article 27(1) should not, in general, be used as a mechanism to control the jurisdiction of the adjudicating court, but in 'cas extrêmes de violation des droits fondamentaux'[224]—which needed to be 'grave et manifeste'[225]—a judge addressed in recognition/enforcement proceedings was entitled to find a breach of the rules of national public policy under

---

[218] At para. 17.
[219] The European Court itself preferred to prohibit any review by an enforcing court of the (even erroneous) jurisdiction taken by a rendering court, even in breach of Title II's provisions, at para. 32; exception, however, in Article 28 I.
[220] At paras. 14 and 16, *in fine*.
[221] At para. 18.
[222] Again, below, the Court preferred censure under more general principles enshrined in Article 6 ECHR, the right to a fair hearing, and legal assistance of one's own choosing.
[223] At para. 22.
[224] At para. 27.
[225] *Ibid.*

Article 27(1). According to the Advocate General, the Brussels Convention, after all, did not go so far in its inauguration of a swift and simple Title III recognition/ enforcement procedure as to ride rough-shod over the basic principles of any Contracting State's national jurisdictional order.[226]

While he did not take up the bold assertion in some French decisions—which have directly invoked Article 6 ECHR for application under Article 27(1)[227]—the AG did note the referring court's awareness of the former article's protection of the right to be heard, and concluded that to recognise the French judgment would implicate a violation of a superior right[228] and could be refused under Article 27(1) as a breach of (German) public policy.

As will be seen, it was almost certain that the ECJ would follow their Advocate General in ruling as he did on the first two aspects of the reference. The Court was anxious to dampen any tendency to censure a rendering court's jurisdiction under Article 27(1), but did not expect the Convention to be interpreted as an instrument that might undermine the rights of the defence, already enshrined in the Brussels Convention itself,[229] or in any other international instrument such as other Community Treaties and the European Convention on Human Rights.[230]

4.3.2   The ECJ's decision in *Dieter Krombach v Andre Bamberski*

In a judgment that can be reviewed briefly here, the ECJ left little doubt that a Contracting State court would be justified in invoking Article 27(1) to block enforcement of the particular (*partie civile*) judgment given *in absentia* in the circumstances of this case: it brought out the full range of ordinance from other areas of (Community) law (at paragraphs 25–26), and the European Convention on Human Rights, to censure the French criminal procedure's treatment of the (German) judgment debtor/accused; it was keen to stress that the enforcement provisions of Title III of the Brussels Convention were not isolated from other concerns of Community law, and could not be construed as undermining the rights of the defence.

---

[226] *Isabelle Lancray S.A. v Firma Peters und Sickert KG* (C–305/88) [1990] ECR I– 2725, at p.2748, para. 20 and *Leon Emile Gaston Carlos Debaecker and Berthe Plouvier v Cornelius Gerrit Bouwman* (C–49/84) [1985] ECR 1779, at p.1796, para. 10, sentiments echoed by the ECJ itself in *Dieter Krombach*, at para. 43.

[227] A recent example being *Cassation 16.3.1999 Sieur Pordéa c/ Société Times Newspapers Limited* (1999) *JDI* 773 against an English order for security for costs—now a legitimated approach, *Dieter Krombach*, ECJ.

[228] *Dieter Krombach* at para. 28.

[229] *Lancray* [1990] ECR I– 2725, at p.2748, para. 20 *Debaecker v Bouwman* [1985] ECR 1779, at p.1796, para. 10.

[230] Emphasised by the European Court in *Dieter Krombach*, at paras. 39–43, quoting the European Court of Human Rights cases in *Eur. Court HR, Poitrimol v France judgment of 23 November 1993, Series A no.277–A*, and *Eur. Court HR, Pelladoah v the Netherlands judgment of 22 September 1994, Series A no.297–B*, one of the fundamental features of a fair trial; also judgment in *Affaire Krombach c.*

Yet the most telling part of its recent ruling, for our purposes, is the view as to when recourse to the defence of public policy may be available under Article 27(1). A judgment of another Contracting State will only contravene Article 27(1) when it

> would be at variance to an unacceptable degree with the legal order of [the enforcing Court] inasmuch as it infringes a fundamental principle . . . [T]he infringement would have to constitute a manifest breach of a rule of law regarded as essential in the legal order of [the enforcing Court] . . . or a right recognised as being fundamental . . .'[231]

When another Contracting State judgment is so at variance with the legal order of the enforcing court is left to the judicial assessment of the latter.

What may be of some interest to observers of Brussels Convention practice, in *Dieter Krombach*, is the strength and nature of the mutual trust, reposed by each Contracting State, in the ability and willingness of the individual Contracting State partners correctly to apply the jurisdictional provisions of the Convention, especially the prohibitions on the use of exorbitant jurisdictions enumerated in Article 3. The concrete manifestation of this trust appears in Article 28, third paragraph of Title III—the exclusion of a review of jurisdiction taken by the rendering court, notably on public policy grounds. The potency of this exclusion has been emphasised in *Dieter Krombach*.

Of itself, the fact that a rendering Contracting State court mis-applied the rules of the Convention[232] is irrelevant, (at least outside the Contracting State of that court) under Title III. Public policy cannot block recognition and enforcement 'solely on the ground that the court of origin failed to comply with the rules of the Convention which relate to jurisdiction.'[233] The German enforcing court would therefore have to ignore that aspect of the case in which the French criminal court, sitting in the *partie civile* action, took its jurisdiction[234] from the French nationality of the deceased victim.

The only question that remains, and that was not considered by the Court, is Article 27(1)'s (residual) relationship to the other defences in Article 27, and now, to Article II of the Protocol.[235]

Many autonomous recognition and enforcement regimes subsumed the distinct defences now contained in Articles 27(2), 27(3), 27(4), and 27(5) within the

---

France (No.29731/96) of 13.1.2001, European Court of Human Rights also finding a breach, *inter alia*, of Article 6(1) ECHR.

[231] *Ibid.*, at para. 37, close in its tone to the German notion of public policy, quoted above; applied *SA Régie Nationale des Usines Renault* (C–38/98) [2000] ECR I–2973, at p. 3021, para. 30.

[232] There are exceptions of course in Article 28 I—a misapplication of Article 16, Section 3 (insurance matters), Section 4 (consumer contracts) and Article 59 (not strictly a mis-application defence, however).

[233] At para. 32.

[234] Article 5(4) reveals that the jurisdiction of the criminal court was arguably legitimate in any event; this article allowed a criminal court to sue another Contracting State domiciliary 'to the extent that that court [had] jurisdiction under its own law to entertain civil proceedings.'

[235] *Dieter Krombach* 4.12.1997 (1999) *EuZW* 26, the second question referred—this specific provision could not exclude the general right to be represented before a Contracting State court, at para. 44.

general 'umbrella' of public policy, in Article 27(1). It would have come as no surprise therefore to discover that problems over the respective competences of each
defence *ratione materiae* would eventually arise. In *Horst Ludwig Martin Hoffman v
Adelheid Krieg*,[236] the question of the compatibility of a domestic and foreign judgment was resolved under the specific defence of Article 27(3), 'irreconcilability' and
not (also) under Article 27(1):

> the public-policy clause . . . is in any event precluded when, as here, . . . the issue must
> be resolved on the basis of the specific provision[237]

This was followed by the Court in *Berhandus Hendrikman and Maria Feyen v
Magenta Druck & Verlag GmbH*.[238] The second question referred in the case concerned the application of Article 27(1) to a judgment where the losing party was
allegedly not validly represented, nor had any knowledge of the proceedings until
after judgment had been rendered;[239] the third question involved the application
of Article 27(2) to the same set of facts. AG Jacobs had no hesitation[240] in applying *Hoffmann v Krieg*'s reasoning to the relationship between Article 27(1) and
Article 27(2).[241]

The cases, however, do not deal with Article 27(1)'s residual rôle—if such it is—
and the extent of its exclusion when the facts at issue are specifically dealt with in
another Article 27 article, or of the Protocol.[242] Does the 'mutual exclusivity' criterion laid down in *Hoffmann v Krieg* mean that whenever a particular situation
is, *prima facie*, (loosely) covered *ratione materiae* by another Article 27 case, that
Article 27(1) is excluded for all time?[243] This would, of course, deny a 'catch-all'
function to Article 27(1).[244] Should the enforcing court find, on reviewing the particular elements, that, for example, the defendant was not 'in default of appearance'[245] after all, or the judgments were not 'irreconcilable', can it then proceed to

---

[236] (C–145/86) [1988] ECR 645.
[237] *Ibid.*, at p.668, para. 21.
[238] C–78/95 [1996] ECR I-4943, at p.4968, para. 23.
[239] *Ibid.*, at p.4948; compare therefore *OLG Köln* 12.4.1989 IPRspr. (1989) Nr. 213, [1991] I.L.Pr. 483,
which resolved issues similar to the facts of *Hendrikman* under Article 27(1).
[240] At p.4958, at para. 57.
[241] Curious, and incorrect therefore seems to be the exclusionary statement of the *Cour d'appel de Paris*
in *SA Eurosensory c/ Sté F.J. Tieman BV*, 1994, *Dalloz*, IR, 66; the approach of recent German cases
under Article 27(2) is to amalgamate due service (in the context of service by *remise au parquet* or its
equivalent) with the form and definitional content of procedural public policy, and Article 103 *GG*, the
right to a fair hearing: *OLG Köln* 7.3.2001 (2001) NJW-RR 1576.
[242] Para. 44 of *Dieter Krombach*.
[243] Possibly the meaning of Beaumont, 2nd edn, 1995, at p.187, para. 8.13.
[244] In this sense *OLG Hamm* 28.12.1993 (1994) *RIW* 243, at p.244: '[Article 27(1)] kann nicht auf
diejenigen Verfahrensmängel gestützt werden, die die Antragsgegnerin zur Begründung des Anerken-
nungshindernisses des Article 27 Nr.2 . . . vorgetragen hat'('[Article 27(1)] cannot be based on the
same procedural errors that the judgment debtor submitted in support of the barrier to enforcement
under Article 27(2)').
[245] *OLG Köln* 6.10.1994, (1995) NJW-RR 446, at p.447, where 'in sufficient time' (of Article 27(2)) was
fulfilled, but *subsequent* defects in procedure could be censured under Article 27(1).

judge the issue, which has eventually filtered through Articles 27(2)(3) down to Article 27(1) under public policy?[246]

What the court in *Hoffmann v Krieg* must have meant is that defences traditionally associated with public policy have emerged from beneath its general cover—in other words, if, under Article 27(3), judgments are not 'irreconcilable', a court cannot then proceed, under its own notions of public policy in Article 27(1), to judge irreconcilability under any autonomous notions.[247] Support for this view would seem to come from the post-reference decision of the *Bundesgerichtshof* in the *Sonntag v Waidmann* case. Here the attack on the Italian judgment came, under Article 27(1), not from the fact that Sonntag had been denied[248] a fair hearing, but on other (material) public policy grounds.

At paragraph 27, *in fine*, of his opinion in *Dieter Krombach v Andre Bamberski*, AG Saggio did seem to distance himself from the (Commission's) view that when a particular defence is explicitly dealt with in Article 27—such as Article 27(2)— this necessarily prevents a residual rôle for Article 27(1)'s application to those areas not specifically dealt with:

> There is no support for the Commission's view that the existence of a specific rule . . . means that no other violations of that right or of other subjective rights of the parties can be relevant.[249]

As to the problem raised in the Protocol, in *Dieter Krombach v Andre Bamberski*, as the *Bundesgerichtshof* found on the facts, a defence to enforcement in Article II of the Protocol to the Brussels Convention did not apply *ratione materiae*: Krombach had been charged with, and convicted of, a crime 'intentionally committed' in the French criminal proceedings. Yet this fact alone could not seriously mean that the right to a fair hearing in German public policy under Article 27(1) was suppressed. The German court did not believe so.[250]

Article 27(1) must have a catch-all sphere of competence. In situations not expressly covered by the other Convention defences, it steps into the breach. This seems uncontroversial since *Hoffmann v Krieg*. Whether, thereafter, under autonomous notions of public policy under Article 27(1), a similar defence can be run that would have, or did, fail under Articles 27(2)(3)(4)(5) seems more problematic.

---

[246] The *Bundesgerichtshof*, in the post-reference decision in *Volker Sonntag v Hans Waidmann and others* (C–172/91), clearly thought so -IPRspr. (1993) Nr. 178: reference under Article 27(2), subsequently decided under Article 27(1).

[247] Compare this with Waller J in *Philip Alexander Securities & Futures Ltd. v Bamberger & others* [1996] CLC 1757, QBD, 1780 CA, at p.1780.

[248] If his lawyer's indolence, and the brief 'document which instituted the [*partie civile*] proceedings' could amount to such.

[249] At para. 27.

[250] 4.12.1997 (1999) *EuZW* 26, at p.27: 'Die Vollstreckbarerklärung eines so zustande gekommenen Versäumnisurteils verletzt die deutsche öffentliche Ordnung' ('the enforcement of a default judgment delivered in this way offends German public policy'); [1998] I.L.Pr. 681; the European Court agreed, at para. 42.

4.3.3   The ECJ's decision and AG Alber's opinion in *SA Régie Nationale des Usines Renault v SpA Maxicar and Orazio Formento*[251]

In this case, the ECJ considered the effect of public policy under Article 27(1) when a judgment of a Contracting State (allegedly) misinterprets, or fails correctly to apply, Community law—*in casu*, a French judgment misinterpreting and/or not applying Articles 28–30 (ex Articles 30–36) and Article 82 (ex Article 86) EC Treaty. AG Alber considered in his opinion of 22.6.1999 that such a judgment could not be censured under Article 27(1). Discussing the issue of whether the notion of public policy could be left entirely to the competence of national courts, he believed such an approach would lead to 'une interprétation excessivement large'[252] and would set at nought the edifice of the Convention. He opined that an erroneous interpretation of the law by a particular Contracting State, even if of Community law, is not a ground for refusing recognition and enforcement under Article 27(1).[253] As to what public policy did encompass, he stated that it

> doit donc intégrer les principes fondamentaux et la reconnaissance ne peut être refusée à ce titre que dans les cas où l'exécution serait absolument incompatible avec ses principes.[254] [255]

The ECJ decision itself substantially re-iterated and followed its findings and observations in *Krombach*, with no distinction nor alteration to the framework public policy definition, merely because 'material' public policy was under consideration. The Court therefore repeated the need to review the outer limits of Article 27(1), within which the individual Contracting States have a degree of autonomy and possibility of adaptation for local political and social idiosyncrasies; the ambit of Article 29, prohibiting a review of findings of fact or law. Since the Court did not consider that an (alleged) error of law (in misapplying Community law) constituted 'a manifest breach of a rule of law',[256] a Contracting State could not refuse recognition and enforcement 'solely on the ground that it considers that national or Community law[257] was misapplied'[258] in the rendering court's decision.

---

[251] (C–38/98) [2000] ECR I–2973, substantially re-iterating its views in *Dieter Krombach*, at pp.3020–21, paras. 27–30.

[252] At para. 58.

[253] At paras. 62 and 67; *contra*, it appears, ECJ in *Eco Swiss China* (C–126/97) [1999] ECR I–3055: arbitration award contrary to Article 82 EC (ex. Article 85) may be annulled by national court as contrary to public policy (at p.3093, para. 37).

[254] ('must therefore include fundamental principles and recognition can only be refused on this ground in cases where enforcement would be totally incompatible with its principles').

[255] At para. 63; the ECJ reiterated its 'framework' definition of public policy from *Dieter Krombach*, at para. 30.

[256] At para. 34.

[257] The solution to mis-application to be found in the rendering court, via appeal or preliminary reference under EU law.

[258] At para. 33.

What the opinion does show, and has sought to emphasise, is that, under Articles 29 and 34(3), the enforcing court is not entitled to review the substance of the case before the rendering court. The proper recourse, if at all possible, was to institute an appeal in the rendering Contracting State appeal system.

4.3.4 Article 27(1) and the restrictions under Articles 28 and 29[259]/ Article 34 II, III

The third paragraph of Article 28 reminds the enforcing[260] court that its reviewing powers over the jurisdiction taken by the rendering court,[261] is strictly and exhaustively limited to ensuring compliance with only[262] Articles 7–16[263] and Article 59. Public policy is not to be used (at all) to censure the jurisdiction taken by the foreign court.[264] We will see that on the whole, Article 27(1) has been invoked—mostly without success—to attack the rendering court's system of internal civil[265] procedure. This escapes the confines of Article 28 III, last section. But Article 27(1) has also been used, in Germany at least, in its manifestation of (material) public policy, to prevent enforcement of an Italian judgment which conflicted with cherished principles of German social/compulsory insurance law.[266] Does Article 29 prevent such a review under Article 27(1)?[267] Its wording is clear and draconian—'[u]nder no circumstances may a foreign judgment be

---

[259] Whenever Articles 28 or 29 are referred to, they are to be taken as including a reference to Article 34.

[260] Or recognising court; note the effectively diametrically-opposed views on the scope of Article 28 in two cases, the first Waller J's in *Philip Alexander Securities & Futures Ltd. v Bamberger & others* [1996] CLC 1757, at p.1778, and the second in *OLG Hamm* 28.12.1993 (1995) NJW-RR 189, at p.190.

[261] In contrast to the Contracting States' autonomous law, and under various bi-lateral treaties.

[262] And not even Article I of the Protocol—*Weinor v SARL Wirion Mod'enfants*, 11.11.1975 D-Series I–28-B1; *Tribunal d'arrondissement de Luxembourg* 1.11.1974 / *Cour supérieure de justice de Luxembourg* 5.3.1974 (1975) *Rev crit* 660, at p.667, *Cour d'appel Luxembourg* 20.5.1999 *Entreprise de Constructions Pedinotti c/ Sollase* (2000) *Pas. Lux.* 200.

[263] Instances of where this has been done are relatively rare: *Mme Tonnoir c/ Société anonyme Vanherf* 9.2.1989 (1991) *JDI* 160, 9.2.1989; *BGH* 2.5.1979 IPRspr. (1979) Nr. 198; *Weber c/ Eurocard Belgium-Luxembourg Cour d'appel de Luxembourg*, 15.5.1991, (1990–1992) *Pas. Lux.*, 157.

[264] If this is a correct paraphrase of the words 'may not be applied to the rules relating to jurisdiction'; Waller J's observations in *Philip Alexander Securities & Futures Ltd. v Bamberger & others* [1996] CLC 1757, QBD, 1780 CA must be read in this light; also ECJ in *Dieter Krombach*—Article 27(1) cannot be raised 'solely on the ground that the court of origin failed to comply with the rules of the Convention which relate to jurisdiction', at para. 32.

[265] In *Dieter Krombach v Andre Bamberski* (C–7/98), the judgment debtor attacked the criminal procedure of the French courts relating to an absent accused, and their taking jurisdiction over him on the basis of the victim's French nationality; the ECJ and AG in *Dieter Krombach* have confined breaches of the enforcing court's notions of procedural public policy to extreme cases of a breach of fundamental rights, at para. 37.

[266] The case in the post-reference decision of *Sonntag v Waidmann*, BGH 16.9.1993 (1994) *IPRax* 118, IPRspr. (1993) Nr. 178, 123 BGHZ 268; *Bundesgericht G Ltd contre K* 19.9.2000 126 BGE III, 534.

[267] Article 29 applied in the *Tribunal de première instance*, Brussels in *Gronowska v Pfeiffer*, 18.12.1979, D-Series I–29-B2; and *Cour de Cassation*, 29.5.1985, *M. et Mme Yun c/ Soc. Seibo*, (1986) *Rev crit* 520.

reviewed as to its substance'. To what extent is Article 27(1) an exception to this prohibition?

Some believe[268] that a review of a foreign judgment under the material public policy of the State addressed under Article 27(1) inevitably involves a review of the substance of the judgment,[269] and is therefore prohibited by Article 29. But this may be going too far, or at least may reflect an unsubtle reading of the article.[270] The crucial word in Article 29 and Article 34 III is 'reviewed'. It defines the articles' scope, and the permitted, or impermissible, extent to which the recognising court may look behind the face[271] of the judgment. What is reasonably clear is that the enforcing court may not comment on, nor, for the purposes of denying recognition or enforcement, examine whether the rendering court made mistakes in its civil procedure, in its ascertaining of facts, nor in its application of its own private international law, or material *lex causae*.[272] What the enforcing court may do under Article 29 is less well-defined.

Logically, for Article 27(1) to be effective, and not emasculated, this court must therefore be able to look behind[273] the mere stark assertion that one party is ordered to pay a certain sum to another for a breach of contract or tort committed. In certain judgments of the Italian courts in the *Terruzzi*[274] litigation and subsequently, there is evidence that the courts have overstepped their function when considering the public policy exception, and entered the prohibition in Article 29. As is known in the *Terruzzi* case, a High Court judgment had ordered an Italian national, Terruzzi, to pay to the plaintiff London Metal brokers a sum representing the sale of certain metals on the London market. After unsuccessfully pleading before the English courts that such 'exchange contracts'[275] were unlawful and

---

[268] Gevrey, S. *L'exequatur communautaire: Titre III de la Convention de Bruxelles*, 1990–1991, Collection, Paris I, at p.153; also Kaye, 1987, at p.1448.

[269] The dangers of reviewing the judgment as to its substance is not novel: the *Cour d'appel de Paris Bensa c/ Coleman* 4.7.1958 (1959) *JDI* 1122, at p.1130—Ponsard, who hopes, in the context of the Anglo-French Convention that 'le biais du caractère d'ordre public attaché à certains principes . . ., la jurisprudence ne tienne pas en échec le principe d'exclusions de la revision au fond des décisions étrangères'('the bias of the nature of public policy linked to certain principles . . . the caselaw should not block the principle of excluding the review of the merits of the foreign judgment'); sentiments that may also resound under Article 27(1); *Bundesgericht G Ltd contre K* 19.9.2000 126 BGE III, 534.

[270] Abbatescianni, (1985) *NLJ* 179, at p.181.

[271] The face of the judgment is assumed to be 'B is hereby ordered to pay X amount to A for [a breach of contract]'; also *Cour de Cassation*, 29.5.1985, *M. et Mme Yun c/ Soc. Seibo*, (1986) *Rev crit* 520, a mis-identification of the judgment debtor on the face of the judgment could be corrected by the enforcing court and censured under Article 27(1).

[272] Also Kaye, 1987, at p.1560, fn.9; and Kropholler, 1998, at p.378, para. 2; confirmed by the ECJ in *SA Régie Nationale des Usines Renault*, at p.33.

[273] In the context of Article 27(2), AG Jacobs in *Hendrikman* v *Magenta Druck* C–78/95 [1996] ECR I-4943, at p.4995, para. 39, allowed the enforcing court to perform a 'comparative preliminary appraisal' to ensure that the party was truly in default; a similar appraisal is only logical under Article 27(1).

[274] The English rendering court's decision is reported as *Wilson, Smithett & Cope Ltd.* v *Terruzzi* [1976] 1 QB 683, the Italian case *Corte di Cassazione* 2.7.1981 (1982) *Riv. dir. int. priv. e proc.* 107); also *Malanca Motori SpA v Société des Etablisements B Savoye*, Corte d'appello di Bologna, 19.4.1983 (1984) *Giur. Comm*, II, 76.

[275] [1976] 1 QB 683, at p.714, (Lord Denning MR).

unenforceable by Italian law, Terruzzi eventually succeeded in resisting enforcement of the English judgment in Italy under Italian public policy,[276] the judgment being null and void, due to a breach of Italian Exchange Control regulations. Would the Italian court, under the Brussels Convention, have breached Article 29 by 'review[ing the judgment] as to its substance', had this case[277] been decided under the Brussels Convention? According to Abbatescianni, it would have done so:

> when the Court of Cassation declines the recognition of a foreign judgment because the contract is considered in breach of Exchange Control regulations it *re-examines*[278] the substance of the case in order to assert that the contract is null and void under Italian law.[279]

Can the Italian courts be said to have 'reviewed' the English or a French judgments, and thus breached Article 29, merely because they have come to a different conclusion as to the application of the very provisions[280] which the English courts found not to apply? If the answer to this question is yes, then the scope for the defence of a breach of material public policy—in the form of mandatory rules of the forum[281]—under Article 27(1) has all but disappeared. If this is the case, the word 'review' in Article 29, in this sense, must then mean that Article 29 represents a wide-ranging prohibition: there must be *no* failure to attribute to certain, or any, issues decided in the foreign proceedings the (prospective) status of *res judicata*.

Similarly in the *Sonntag* litigation, the *Bundesgerichtshof* refused to enforce an Italian judgment on the grounds of a breach of German material public policy. What is unclear, but considered unimportant by the German court in the event, is whether the Italian courts considered, then mis-applied, or even ignored, the German provisions as to compulsory social security insurance. In a sense, the German court is 'reviewing' the Italian court's decision on the substance: an application of Article 27(1) to the facts and legal issues in the case is impossible without 'looking at' the Italian judgment. To be effective Article 27(1) must, in its

---

[276] Under the former Italian recognition and enforcement rules in, *inter alia*, Article 797(7) Cpc; Bellagamba, G. and Cariti, G. *Il sistema italiano di diritto internazionale privato*, 2000.

[277] A later court of appeal decision followed this court's reasoning in *Malanca Motori SpA v Société des Etablisements B Savoye, Corte d'appello di Bologna*, 19.4.1983 (1984) *Giur. Comm*, II, 76.

[278] This is different from merely a (neutral) examination of the substantive law governing a cause of action in order to judge its compatibility with domestic public policy—*Bundesgericht G Ltd contre K* 19.9.2000 126 BGE III, 534.

[279] Abbatescianni, (1985) *NLJ* 179, at p.181; the post-reference decision of the *BGH* in the *Sonntag* case would suggest this view here is incorrect, below, at pp.430–431.

[280] As to the meaning and scope of 'exchange contracts'.

[281] As will be seen in the material public policy section of German law, 4.4.4(ii), below, it is more or less certain that included in (German notions of) Article 27(1) would be those nebulous group of rules which, in a choice of law context—such as in contract under Article 7(2) of the 1980 Rome Convention—command application irrespective of the law otherwise applicable. It is doubtful whether such an analogy, without some differentiation, could be made for the UK: the framework definition of Article 27(1) public policy given in *Dieter Krombach*, above, at p.399, section 4.3.2— *inter alia*, a 'manifest breach of a rule of law' may make borrowing concepts from the choice of law process dangerous.

relationship with Article 29, deny a pre-emptive *res judicata* effect to the very issues in the judgment that the judgment debtor considers as being contrary to public policy. This is a different assertion from maintaining that the Italian or English courts made mistakes in interpreting, or applying the material *lex causae*.[282]

4.4 EXAMPLES OF CONTRACTING STATE CASE LAW APPLYING ARTICLE 27(1) BRUSSELS CONVENTION[283]

4.4.1 French case law under Article 27(1) and the reception of fraud

Under French autonomous recognition and enforcement law, it is one of the pre-requisites for an *exequatur* of the foreign judgment that it conforms to 'l'ordre public international'.[284] Kessedjian has attempted to define the scope of this in the context of Article 27(1) Brussels Convention, commenting on a case[285] that had refused enforcement of a German judgment because it failed to provide a 'reasoned basis' for the decision.

Within the Brussels Convention, she divides public policy into its well-known manifestations of 'material' and 'procedural', the former controlling the effect the judgment's recognition and enforcement will eventually have on the French territory, while the latter is said to uphold the rights of the defence.[286] Such latter rights have three aspects: 'l'assignation doit avoir été loyale et réelle; le défendeur doit avoir eu les moyens de se défendre; les modes de preuve utilisés par le juge étranger ne doivent pas heurter nos principes fondamenteux.[287],[288] She questions whether procedural public policy has a place under Article 27(1), and believes that the article should be exclusively reserved for material public policy alone. This, it is submitted cannot be correct. A court that, in rendering a judgment, refuses the defendant an opportunity to be heard,[289] or is in some way biased,

---

[282] Irrelevant for Article 27(1) purposes, according to the ECJ in *SA Régie Nationale des Usines Renault* (C–38/98) [2000] ECR I–2973.

[283] Examples here were decided prior to *Krombach* and *Renault v SpA Maxicar*, but facts finding breach of public policy so egregious that these cases will have little impact on the line of authorities.

[284] The *Munzer* case, above, at p.385; as for fraud under Article 27(1), *Signalisation c/ C.A.E Electronica* (1989) *JDI* 102, (alleged failure of Italian creditor to inform the Milan court of the full facts of the case: the best course for the rendering court was a stay to encourage the judgment debtor to pursue an extraordinary appeal before the rendering court).

[285] *Société Polypétrol c/ Société générale routière* 9.10.1991 (1992) *Rev crit* 516, [1993] I.L.Pr. 107 and *Soc. Laboratoire France Parfum c/ Soc. Codipar* 26.9.1991 (1992) *Rev crit* 517.

[286] (1992) *Rev crit* 516, at p.523.

[287] ('service must have been fair and real, the defendant must have had the means for his defence; the methods of proof used by the foreign judge must not offend our fundamental principles').

[288] *Ibid.*; cf. *Scarpetta v Lowenfeld* (1911) 27 T.L.R. 509, at p.510 (Lawrence J).

[289] Confirmed by *Dieter Krombach v Andre Bamberski* (C–7/98), AG Saggio' opinion, at para. 28; Article 27(2) inapplicable as refusal of an opportunity to be heard occurred *after* (presumably) valid service of the document that instituted the (*partie civile*) proceedings; *BGH* 29.6.2000 (2000) *RIW* 797.

cannot expect that judgment to escape censure in another Contracting State under Article 27(1).

The overwhelming majority of French cases where the defence of public policy has been run have dealt with issues of procedural public policy of the State addressed and consider a defence to enforcement under Article 27(1) where the foreign procedures were, at best different,[290] at worst, allegedly[291] contrary to basic human rights.[292]

The single most obvious stumbling block to enforcement of judgments in France under Article 27(1) of the Brussels Convention has been the 'unreasoned' judgment.[293] This defence has a relatively long provence in autonomous French recognition and enforcement law, and it seems that from the cases to be discussed shortly, the legacy from this autonomous view has been carried across into Article 27(1) of the Brussels Convention. In 1931 the *Tribunal de la Seine*[294] had refused *exequatur* to an unreasoned judgment for being contrary to public policy. The reasons the court gave would later have their echo in the *Cour de Cassation*'s decisions under Article 27(1). Even at this early stage, the impression was that the French court was, in a way, sitting as an appeal court on the foreign judgment:

---

[290] Unlike the *Cour d'appel de Bordeaux* in the case, the *Cour de Cassation* 8.2.2000 in *Abadia Otin c/ SA Ateliers de la Chainette* (2000) *JCP*, IV, 1546, did *not* consider sufficient the fact that there was only a limited right to engage Spanish appellate procedures—on the facts of the case in an employment dispute—any reason to implicate Article 27(1); simply because (Dutch) foreign procedure allows a court to give interlocutory (kort geding) judgment in circumstances where French procedural law would not—an action on the merits subsequently essential—does not warrant application of Article 27(1): *Cour d'appel de Paris* 28.1.1994 *Eurosensory c/ Tieman et Blind Equipment Europe* (1995) *RD prop. intell.* 13, n° 57, Véron, P. (2001) *JDI* 805, at p.814; in *Cour de Cassation* 11.3.1997 *Copraf SARL c/ Savict sas* (1997) *RJDA* 488, no.733, the fact that an Italian court had indexed the amount of damages in (non-French) currency not a breach of international public policy in Article 27(1).

[291] *Ibid.,*—one (successful) argument run before the European Court in *Dieter Krombach v Andre Bamberski* was that the French criminal court had breached Article 6 ECHR; Donzallaz, Y. (2001) *AJP* 160: 'Article 27(2) n'est que l'instrument permettant de mettre en oeuvre les règles minimales essentielles de la CEDH, jugées supérieures'.

[292] Also *Cassation* 5.5.1993 *Times Newspapers Limited v Gustave Pordea* (1994) *Gaz. Pal.*, Juris., p.382, [1994] I.L.Pr. 96, where unavoidable non-compliance with an English security of costs order by a French libel plaintiff caused his action to founder in England; the resulting defendant's order for costs was refused recognition in France, at appeal court level; the case was annulled on other grounds, below; now *Cassation* 16.3.1999 *Sieur Pordéa c/ Société Times Newspapers Limited* (1999) *JDI* 773, applying Article 27(1).

[293] However, (English) 'decision' on taxation of costs of procedure need not be 'motivée': *Cour de Cassation* 13.1.1998 *Jean Pierre Mailliez c/ Soc. Norgrips et Soc. Redland plasterboard overseas Ltd*, unreported, http://curia.eu.int/common/recdoc/convention/en/1999/45–1999.htm; contrast attitude of Swiss courts towards unmotivated judgments in *Bundesgericht* 23.7.2001 *M.R. gegen H AG*, unreported. Not a problem encountered with Switzerland: *Bertl contre Deutsche Bau- und Bodenbank AG* 9.2.1977 (1979) *Journal des Tribunaux,* II, 98, discussed above, at p.389—also relying on evidence from on 1 interested party, (unsuccessful *in casu*), *Cour de Cassation* 17.11.1999 *Mme T. c/ Mme H* (2000) *Rev crit* 52, at p.54 and examples given by Ancel; Pluyette G, in *Etudes offertes à Pierre Bellet*, 1991, p.427, at p.433.

[294] *Klein c/ Niedermann*, 15.10.1931, (1932) *JDI* 678.

[c]e serait faire du juge d'exequatur une espèce de juge de cassation, alors que son droit de réviser complètement au fond l'apparente plutôt à un juge d'appel[295] [296]

It will be seen that this tendency has continued: from early cases under the Convention such as *Vanclef c/ Société Trans Traide International*[297] to *Sté de transports internationaux Dehbashi c/ Sté Gerling Konsern*,[298] it is apparent that principles derived from French procedural law,[299] focussing on the need for a reasoned judgment, have been elevated[300] to the realm of (international procedural) public policy, and have found their way into Article 27(1).[301]

According to the *Nouveau Code de Procédure Civile*, an unreasoned French judgment violates Article 455 NCPC, and is therefore a nullity,[302] under Article 458.[303] The same fate, it appears, awaits foreign judgments from other Contracting States under Article 27(1).[304] This was made clear in the *Vanclef* judgment, where the *Cour de Cassation* refused to enforce a Belgian default judgment for not being 'reasoned':[305]

qu'est au contraire à la conception française de l'ordre public international la reconnaissance d'une décision étrangère non motivée lorsque ne sont produits des documents de nature à servir d'équivalent à la motivation défaillante . . .[306] [307]

---

[295] ('this would turn the enforcing judge into an appeal judge, since his right to a complete review of the merits assimilates him rather with an appeal judge').

[296] *Ibid.*, at p.680.

[297] 17.5.1978 (1979) *JDI* 380 along with *Etienne c/ Société Handelsonderneming Claessen B.V.* 24.11.1977 and *Theillol c/ Office de la jeunesse de Fribourg* 18.4.1978 (1979) *JDI* 380.

[298] *Cour d'appel de Poitiers*, 1.6.1994 *Sté de transports internationaux Dehbashi c/ Sté Gerling Konsern* (1994) *JCP*, IV, 2520, [1996] I.L.Pr. 104.

[299] Also the influential article by Motulsky requiring a reasoned judgment, quoted by Pluyette, G., 'La Convention de Bruxelles et les droits de la défence' in *Etudes offertes à Pierre Bellet*, 1991, p.427, at p.433 *in fine*.

[300] Early examples of the French and Belgian courts doing so have been quoted by Jellinek, *Erstes Heft: Abhandlung*, 1953, at p.190 onwards: *Tribunal de la Seine* 15.10.1932, (1932) *JDI* 678.

[301] Observed by Holleaux in *Vanclef c/ Société Trans Traide International* 17.5.1978 (1979) *JDI* 380, at p.390.

[302] The rule is not absolute, however; the applicant can provide evidence, *aliunde*, that fills in the *lacuna(e)* in the judgment's reasoning, enforcement will be allowed.

[303] The explicit reasoning used under Article 27(1) by the Poitiers court to reject enforcement *Sté de transports internationaux Dehbashi c/ Sté Gerling Konsern* (1994) *JCP*, IV, 2520.

[304] The tendency of the French courts to look at the actual contents and drafting of the judgment itself is confirmed by *Roche c/ Direction générale des aéroports de l'État d'Ankara* 1996 *Dalloz*, IR, 210: but generously, French public policy 'n'exige pas . . . que la notification de la décision comporte l'indication des voies de recours ouvertes dans l'État d'origine'('does not require that the information about the decision contain any indication of the means of appeal in the State of origin').

[305] According to the court, the Belgian proceedings had relied on presumptions of the plaintiff's evidence as the defendant had been in default.

[306] ('that it is contrary to the notion of international French public policy to recognise an unreasoned foreign judgment when the documents equivalent to the missing reasoning are not produced').

[307] *Vanclef c/ Société Trans Traide International* 17.5.1978 (1979) *JDI* 380; reasoning applied *verbatim* to censure another Belgian judgment in *Cassation* 12.01.1994 *SARL Audio-Prestique c/ Soc. Nexon Distribution*, reported in *Collection of jurisprudence of the European Court of Justice and of the highest courts of the States Parties concerning the Lugano Convention*, Vol.III, 1994, Publications of the Swiss Institute of Comparative Law, 1998, at p.515; Kodeck, (1999) *ZZPInt* 250; cf Jolowicz, (2000) *CLJ* 263, where a general duty is owed by a judge to give reasons.

In *Dame Py c/ dame Diamedo*[308] the same approach was adopted, but the applicant seeking enforcement was able to submit evidence[309] equivalent to the missing reasons of the rendering court. The principle has now been followed by another *Cour de Cassation* decision, in *Société Polypétrol c/ Société générale routière*.[310]

In a later case from the *Cour d'appel de Poitiers*, in *Sté de transports internationaux Dehbashi c/ Sté Gerling Konsern*,[311] the court explained the reason for taking this rather draconian stance under the Brussels Convention. The absence of any reasoning in the judgment 'ne permet pas de vérifier à quel titre le tribunal étranger a pu retenir sa compétence et le défendeur est donc en droit de contester devant le juge d'exequatur [article 28 de la Convention].[312]'[313] If there is insufficient information before the enforcing court to enable it to determine whether the provisions of sections 3, 4 or 5 have been complied with, there is some justification for the French position: these sections have a mandatory character in Article 28 I. Yet there remains the argument that sufficient trust by the enforcing court should be reposed in the capabilities of the rendering court correctly to apply sections 3, 4 or 5. The French position does, in part, smack of a lack of confidence in its Convention partners.[314] It may well be better to sanction such an unreasoned 'judgment' under Articles 46, 47 and 48, rather than as an attack on, and breach of, French public policy under Article 27(1).

In the case of *Times Newspapers Limited v Gustave Pordea*,[315] an English costs order had been granted against a French libel plaintiff in England. He could not satisfy a security for costs order made by the defendant newspaper, and his action was therefore halted. In the event, in this case there was a *cassation* because the *Cour d'appel* had incorrectly applied the Franco-British Convention[316] to the judgment. But it seems that the lower court's views as to a breach of public policy in the case—Pordea had allegedly been deprived, 'for reasons of personal wealth

---

[308] 18.1.1980 (1981) *Rev crit* 113.

[309] (1981) *Rev crit* 113, and Holleaux: '[g]râce aux éléments fournis, la Cour . . . put reconstituer la nature du litige, [et] le raisonnement du juge'('thanks to the facts adduced, the Court could reconstruct the nature of the dispute and the judge's reasoning'), at p.114.

[310] 9.10.1991 (1993) *JDI* 157; (1992) *Rev crit* 516.

[311] 1.6.1994, (1994) *JCP*, IV, 2520, [1996] I.L.Pr. 104.

[312] ('does not permit a verification of what basis the foreign court could take jurisdiction and the defendant is therefore right to object before the enforcing judge').

[313] *Ibid.*, at p.330; such a check evident by *Cour de Cassation* in *Soc. Bertrand v Paul Ott KG* (150/77) [1978] ECR 1431, at p.1444, para.7.

[314] Compare this attitude to an early Italian case of *Corte d'appello Genoa*, 21.4.1976 *Thiesen KG v Bertella D-Series* I–34-B2, where the point of an unreasoned German judgment did *not* prevent enforcement; cf. the position at autonomous Italian law: Bellagamba and Cariti *Il sistema italiano di diritto internazionale privato*, 2000, at p.196.

[315] *Cassation* 5.5.1993 *Times Newspapers Limited v Gustave Pordea* (1994) *Gaz. Pal.*, Juris., p.382, [1994] I.L.Pr. 96; also *European Case Law on the Judgments Convention*, (ed. Kaye, P.), 1998, p.442, case 430.

[316] Annexed to the Reciprocal Enforcement of foreign judgments (France) Order in Council 1936 SI 1936/609; if applicable, Article 5(2) would have allowed application for a sum representing 10% of costs actually awarded.

or status, of his right to a fair hearing'[317]—would have been the same, had the enforcement mechanism been under Title III of the Brussels Convention instead.

When this case eventually returned to the *Cour de Cassation,* in March of 1999, *sub. nom. Sieur Pordéa c/ Société Times Newspapers Limited,*[318] the court ruled that there had been a breach of Article 27(1), in its manifestation of 'l'ordre public international'. It found that Pordea had been denied a fair hearing (guaranteed by Article 6 ECHR) when his 1986 English libel action had been struck out for non-payment of (for him an exorbitant) order for security for costs; the ensuing High Court judgment awarding taxed costs to the defendant in the aborted action could therefore not be enforced in France due to Article 27(1).

The importance of the decision lies in the court's scrutiny of the foreign (English) procedure against the benchmark of Article 6 ECHR,[319] and the use of Article 27(1) to chastise any departure from the provisions of the former. By incorporating Article 6 ECHR directly into Article 27(1)'s public policy—it 'relève de l'ordre public international au sens de l'article 27, 1°'[320]—Article 27(1)'s potential application to a greater array of procedural situations will be opened up, perhaps to an extent not originally envisaged by the Convention's framers.[321] The hybridisation of Article 6 ECHR and Article 27(1) greatly increases the scope for the use of a breach of (procedural) public policy as a defence under the Convention. Huet,[322] the reviewer, is the first to recognise this fact. Among other issues raised by the direct incorporation of Article 6 ECHR into the Brussels Convention, he believes that the *Cassation*'s judgment, in France, may have a profound effect on procedures which were (hitherto) impossible to prohibit under Article 27(2), because procedural irregularities occurred outside (and after) service of 'the document which instituted the proceedings'[323] under Article 27(2).[324]

That Article 6 ECHR's influence can be felt in an enforcement context in Article 27(1) has already been noted in the ECJ's judgment in *Dieter Krombach v Andre Bamberski.*[325] While the Court does not go as far as to elide both articles together,

---

[317] [1994] I.L.Pr. 96, at p.98.

[318] *Cassation* 16.3.1999 *Sieur Pordéa c/ Société Times Newspapers Limited* (1999) JDI 773.

[319] A stance recently confirmed by the ECJ in *Dieter Krombach*, at para. 39; Van Dijk, P. and Van Hoof, G. *Theory and Practice of the European Convention on Human Rights,* 1998, pp.391–479, esp. at p.434.

[320] (1999) JDI 773, at p.774.

[321] Although now Article 1(8)(a) of the Treaty of Amsterdam, which has, from 1.5.1999, replaced Article F of the Treaty of European Union with a new re-numbered Article 6(1) to reflect a fundamental tenet, that 'The Union is founded on the principles of liberty, democracy, *respect for human rights* and fundamental freedoms, *and the rule of law,* principles which are common to the Member States'—the ECJ has recently confirmed in *Dieter Krombach* that the Community instruments and law are founded on, and incorporate, basic principles of human rights, at paras. 25–26.

[322] At pp.774–75.

[323] For when this occurs, see below chapter 5.

[324] 'un procès équitable, notamment du *principe du contradictoire* et des *droits fondamentaux de la défense* . . .'('a fair procedure, notably the right to be heard and the fundamental rights of the defence'), (1999) JDI 773, at p.780; the reach of a challenge under Article 27(1)/Article 6 ECHR may even be extended, he argues, to the decisions (in the appeal procedure) of the enforcing court under Articles 37/40 Brussels Convention, *sed quaere.*

[325] (C–7/98), AG Antonio Saggio's opinion 23.9.1999.

it clearly took note of the concerns of the *BGH*, that a breach of Article 6 had occurred in Krombach's treatment before the French criminal court,[326] citing cases decided by the European Court of Human Rights in 1993 and 1994,[327] one, coincidentally, against France.

Whether *Pordéa c/ Société Times Newspapers Limited* will cause (French or all Contracting State) commercial conflicts lawyers scurrying to textbooks on the European System for the protection of Human Rights may be too early to discern.[328] The advice of AG Saggio to the effect that a breach of Article 27(1) public policy must be 'grave et manifeste',[329] suggested that perhaps not the entire raft of jurisprudence built up around Article 6 ECHR—of (procedural) rights would come under Article 27(1). The European Court's judgment seems to counsel otherwise, noting that the interpretation of the Brussels Convention is based on respect for fundamental human rights generally, embodied in the ECHR.[330]

There seems to be little express indication from the French courts that the more liberal recognition and enforcement regime of Title III of the Brussels Convention has had a constraining effect on the use of 'procedural' public policy under Article 27(1),[331] or whether the pre-Convention uses of public policy have been tempered in order smoothly to elide with that article.

As far as fraud is concerned, *S.A. La Signalisation c/ Société C.A.E Electronica*[332] is a reported example of the defence of fraud being invoked in France under Article 27(1). The French debtor alleged that it was fraudulent for an Italian company to sue it for the price of goods delivered in a Milan court that would not have jurisdiction under the Convention because the creditor failed to inform the Milan court of the full facts of the case. The commentator, Huet,[333] believes that the court (implicitly) adopted the views[334] of Droz:[335] that the best course for the

---

[326] '[A] manifest breach of a fundamental right', at para. 40.

[327] *Eur. Court HR, Poitrimol v France judgment of 23 November 1993, Series A no.277-A*, and *Eur. Court HR, Pelladoah v the Netherlands judgment of 22 September 1994, Series A no.297-B*.

[328] Cf Droz (2000) *Rev crit* 181, at p.188 who thinks the amalgamation of Article 6 ECHR and Article 27(1) is complete; Van Dijk, 1998, esp. at p.434; on current English appeal procedure, and security for costs, esp. CPR 25.13(2)(a)(ii) (making a repeat of *Pordea* impossible), *Nasser v United Bank of Kuwait*, 11.4.2001, CA (Mance LJ); since 2 October 2000, English legislation has had to be interpreted in conformity with ECHR in any event.

[329] AG Antonio Saggio's opinion 23.9.1999, at para. 27.

[330] As from 2.10.2000, s 2(1) Human Rights Act 1998 has ensured that, under Article 27(1) Brussels Convention, an English enforcing judge must 'take into account', *inter alia*, decisions of the European Court of Human Rights (on Article 6(1) ECHR), when 'determining a question . . . in connection with a [European] Convention right'; an unsuccessful attempt to employ Article 6(1) has already been made under Title II of the Brussels Convention: *OT Africa Line Ltd v Hijazy and others (The 'Kribi')* [2001] 1 Lloyd's Rep. 76 (Aikens J).

[331] One difference being, however, that Article 27(1) need not be raised by an appeal court *sua sponte*: *Cour de Cassation* 17.11.1999 *Mme T. c/ Mme H* (2000) *Rev crit* 52.

[332] 15.12.1987 (1989) *JDI* 102.

[333] *Ibid.*, at pp.103–04.

[334] A similar approach to fraud as Phillips J in *Interdesco S.A. v Nullifire Ltd.* [1992] 1 Lloyd's Rep. 180.

[335] Droz, 1972, at p.312, para. 496.

rendering court is a stay[336] to encourage the judgment debtor to pursue an extraordinary appeal in the rendering court.

4.4.2   Belgian case law under Article 27(1)

Statements from certain Belgian cases have shown a willingness to adapt and restrain[337] the use of public policy,[338] when used in the Brussels Convention context. In 1987 the *Tribunal de première instance de Bruxelles*, in *De Bruyne c/ Collard*,[339] refused to allow a defence of public policy to block enforcement of a French judgment, when it had disregarded the *res judicata* effect in the French proceedings of an earlier Belgian judgment.[340] All barriers to an *exequatur* of EEC judgments, it was said, must be construed 'strictement et restrictivement'.[341] This attitude was taken up again by the *Tribunal de première instance de Liège*,[342] where a German judgment was attacked, *inter alia*, on public policy grounds[343] for having failed to apply to its decision what the judgment debtor considered to be part of Belgian public policy: the mandatory influence of the law on the cancellation of sales concession contracts of 1961.[344] 'International' public policy, it was held,

---

[336] Yet the Convention only allows a stay of enforcement proceedings under Article 38 when the appeal is an *Industrial Diamond Supplies v Luigi Riva* (C–43/77) [1977] ECR 2175 'ordinary appeal'; fraud requires an 'extraordinary' one.

[337] (1992) *JT*, at p.435.

[338] Interestingly, the Belgian courts also, prior to the Brussels Convention, had used, it seems incorrectly, the 'motivation/reasoned' judgment rule: for an example of its operation under Article 11(1) of the *Traité Franco-Belge de 8 juillet 1899*, Tribunal civil de Termonde, 3.3.1931, 1931 *Rev crit* 589, criticised by Baccara, at p.592: 'elles [requirements for motivation] n'ont point le caractère de dispositions d'ordre public international et absolue qui s'imposent même aux décisions rendues sous l'empire d'une autre législation'('they [requirements for reasons] do not have the characteristics of dispositions of international and rigid public policy that even applies to decisions rendered under the rule of another legal system').

[339] 1987 *Pas. Belge*, III, 80; also *Civ. Bruxelles* 28.3.1989 (1989) *JLMB* 1098—public policy not applicable to a Swiss order for lawyer's fees (under Article 1(1)(a) of 1959 Swiss/Belgian Convention).

[340] No mention appears in the report as to the possible application of Article 27(3); cf. *Philip Alexander Securities & Futures Ltd v Bamberger & Ors and related action* [1996] CLC 1780, [1997] I.L.Pr. 73, CA.

[341] *Ibid.*, at p.81.

[342] *Tribunal de première instance de Liège* 9.10.1995 (1996) *Act Dr* 80.

[343] This defence seemed optimistic as an earlier, pre-Brussels Convention case had ruled similarly in 1970: *S.A.R.L. de droit français Groslambert c/ Madame Hunin* (1970) *JT* 298 that there could be no review of the substance of the French decision—cf. now ECJ in *SA Régie Nationale des Usines Renault* (C–38/98) [2000] ECR I–2973, Advocate-General Alber, at p.2991, para. 60, and *Dieter Krombach*.

[344] *Les Codes Larcier*, I, Ed. 1995, p.650.

doit s'interpréter de manière *paticulièrement restrictive* dans le cadre de la Convention de Bruxelles . . . en tenant compte de la *confiance réciproque*[345] qui caractérise les relations entres tous les Etats[346] [347]

of the Convention.

The court decided that the French disregard for the 1961 law did not amount to a breach of Belgian public policy under Article 27(1). Interestingly, too, and in contrast to the French case of *Société anonyme Almacoa c/ Société anonyme Etablissements Moteurs Cères*,[348] the Belgian court observed that a review of the German decision's conformity or non-conformity with Community law was a prohibited exercise under Articles 29 and 34.

It appears that the French courts are using Article 28 I—the requirements of conformity with sections 3, 4 or 5 of Title II—as a means to perpetuate long-held[349] domestic views about a motivated judgment. Although Belgium had a similar rule at autonomous law, the same problems have not surfaced under the Brussels Convention in Belgium, nor have such tendencies continued under Article 27(1).

4.4.3   UK case law under Article 27(1)[350] and the reception of fraud

A number of times[351] in proceedings within a Brussels Convention context, the English courts have granted so-called 'anti-suit' injunctions against parties[352] enjoining them from commencing, or continuing with, proceedings in other

---

[345] As sentiment expressed by Droz, 1972, at p.313, para. 497; contrast *Turner v Grovit* [2000] 1 QB 345, CA, [2002] 1 WLR 107, HL, reference to ECJ made.

[346] ('must be interpreted in a particularly restrictive way in the sphere of the Brussels Convention . . . taking into account the *reciprocal trust* which characterises relations between all the States').

[347] (1996) *Act Dr* 80, at p.91; also the similar attitude of the Swiss court to public policy in *Anton Bertl c/ Deutsche Bau- und Bodenbank AG* (1979) *JT*, II, 98, above, at p.389.

[348] *TGI de Troyes* 4.10.1978, (1979) *Gaz. Pal.*, Juris., p.131; incorrect now *SA Régie Nationale des Usines Renault.*

[349] The requirement stems back to the post Ancien Régime euphoria of legislation; a decree in *loi 16–24 août 1790*, V, Article 5 demonstrates the history of the legacy felt today under Article 27(1) regarding the motivation of a judgment.

[350] Recently, the CA has revealed that in giving judgment on the merits, it may cast a prospective eye on the potential application of public policy under Article 27(1) to its own judgment in another Contracting State (in Greece regarding the issue of quantum of damages): *Johnson and another v Coburn*, 24.11.1999, (Kennedy LJ).

[351] Most notably in *Continental Bank N.A. v Aeakos Compania Naviera S.A. and others* [1994] 1 WLR 588, *Turner v Grovit* [2000] 1 QB 345, CA; legitimacy of CA's approach upheld by Lord Hobhouse in *Turner v Grovit and others* [2002] 1 WLR 107, HL, but a reference on the question of the compatibility of issuing restraining orders with the Brussels Convention system referred to ECJ; and a noticeable retreat in *OT Africa Line Ltd v Hijazy and others (The 'Kribi')* [2001] 1 Lloyd's Rep. 76 (Aikens J).

[352] The English courts stress that the order acts *in personam*; it is in no way directed at the foreign court itself, above at chapter 2, Article 17, section 2.3.2(ii). Unfortunately the Continental courts do not share this separation of roles, below, at pp.414–415 and *Dame H c/ Dr. H Trib. civ. Montpellier* 11.12.1935, (1936) *JDI* 364, obs. Valéry; also the adverse reaction of the *OLG Düsseldorf* 10.1.1996, IPRspr. (1996) Nr. 167, [1997] I.L.Pr. 320, *OLG Frankfurt a.M.* 13.2.2001 (2001) *RIW* 464, at p.465.

(Contracting) States—commonly in breach of an (English) jurisdiction[353] or arbitration[354] clause. The practice is controversial,[355] and has provoked disquiet and consternation[356] on the Continent. The 'conventional view' that such injunctions only operate *in personam*,[357] and not as an interference with the sovereignty of the foreign court has done little, in Germany at least, to convince their courts that there is no attack on their independence to adjudicate: *OLG Düsseldorf*[358] of 10 January 1996. Here the appeal court refused even to serve an English application[359] for such an injunction under Article 13 I of the 1965 Hague Service Convention, as being an infringement of German sovereignty.[360] The court held[361] that German courts alone have exclusive jurisdiction to judge their own competence.

There seems no doubt then that enforcement of the anti-suit injunction itself, *a fortiori*, would be considered to be contrary to German public policy;[362] yet it seems that by granting such an order, it is not ultimately the applicant's intention in the English action ever to have the foreign proceedings enjoined by the enforcement of the order abroad, but merely to prepare the ground[363] to enable the non-German opponents to resist enforcement of the 'rogue' (German) judgment in England under Article 27(1), or even Article 27(3).[364] It appears that the natural

---

[353] After cases such as *Continental Bank N.A. v Aeakos Compania Naviera S.A. and others* [1994] 1 WLR 588, and *Donohue v Armco Inc and others* [2000] 1 Lloyd's Rep. 579 *revs'd* on facts, HL, [2002] 1 Lloyd's Rep. 425, an injunction will be granted unless 'special countervailing factors' or good/strong reasons/cause be shown why it should not: for possible examples of this, *Philip Alexander Securities & Futures Ltd v Bamberger & Ors and related action* [1996] CLC 1780, CA, *OT Africa Line Ltd v Hijazy and others (The 'Kribi')* [2001] 1 Lloyd's Rep. 76, at pp.91–94 (Aikens J) and *Donohue v Armco Inc and others* [2002] 1 Lloyd's Rep. 425, HL, (Lord Bingham of Cornhill). It remains to be seen whether the decision in *Francesco Benincasa v Dentalkit Srl* (C-269/95) [1997] ECR I-3767 will have an effect on the English courts' attitude; at least the Article 17 enquiry, rightly or wrongly, has been released from hostile *leges causae*; but also *Minister for Agriculture, Food and Forestry v Alte Leipziger Versicherung Aktiengesellschaft*, 6.3.1998, Irish High Court.

[354] *Philip Alexander Securities & Futures Ltd. v Bamberger & others* [1996] CLC 1757, QBD, 1780 CA; *The Angelic Grace* [1995] 1 Lloyd's Rep. 87, at p.96, (Dillon LJ).

[355] Briggs, A. 'Anti-European Teeth for Choice of Court Clauses' (1994) *LMCLQ* 158; Rogerson, P. 'English interference in Greek affairs' (1994) *CLJ* 241.

[356] Hau, W. (1996) *IPRax* 44; Mansel, H.-P. 'Grenzüberschreitende Prozeßführungsverbote (antisuit injunctions) und Zustellungsverweigerung *OLG Düsseldorf* (1996) *EuZW* 335.

[357] Eg *Ellerman Lines Ltd v Read* [1928] 2 KB 144, CA, at p.151 (Scrutton LJ); (Lord Bingham of Cornhill) in *Donohue v Armco Inc and others* [2002] 1 Lloyd's Rep. 425, HL.

[358] *OLG Düsseldorf* 10.1.1996, IPRspr. (1996) Nr. 167, [1997] I.L.Pr. 320; confirmed by *OLG Frankfurt a.M.* 13.2.2001 (2001) *RIW* 464, 2002 NJW-RR 357.

[359] But not, it seems an application for punitive damages: *BVGe* 7.12.1994 *Re the Service of an American Writ in a claim for punitive damages* [1997] I.L.Pr. 325; *OLG Frankfurt a.M.* 13.2.2001 (2001) *RIW* 464, 2002 NJW-RR 357; yet the *BGH* has refused to enforce such judgments under national law: *BGH* (1992) *NJW* 3096, above.

[360] The French courts too, under the *Traité Franco-Suisse*, have traditionally refused to enforce a similar order from a Swiss court: *Dame H c/ Dr. H Trib. civ. Montpellier* 11.12.1935, (1936) *JDI* 364, obs. Valéry.

[361] IPRspr. (1996) Nr. 167, at p.177.

[362] Lenebach, (1998) *Loyola Int'l and Comp. L.J* 257, at p.277.

[363] Mansel's view of the situation in *OLG Düsseldorf*, (1996) *EuZW* 335, at p.338.

[364] Mance J in *Alfred C. Toepfer International GmbH v Molino Boschi Srl* [1996] CLC 738, at p.742; also *Philip Alexander Securities & Futures Ltd v Bamberger & Ors and related action* [1996] CLC 1757, at p.1778 (Waller J) and [1996] CLC 1780, at p.1788, CA (Leggatt LJ).

and ineluctable legacy of the 'early' anti-suit injunction cases of *The Angelic Grace*[365] and *Continental Bank N.A. v Aeakos Compania Naviera S.A. and others*,[366] has been a shift of emphasis onto English public policy[367] under Article 27(1).

The undesirability of this position, and the unseemly jockeying[368] for proce-dural advantage in two jurisdictions, can be seen from the reverse side of the battle line to the *OLG Düsseldorf* in *Philip Alexander Securities & Futures Ltd v Bamberger & Ors and related action*.[369] Here interim injunctions had been granted in favour of the plaintiffs, PASF, against certain German customers restraining them from pursuing actions in their local German courts, allegedly in breach of a London arbitration clause. Various German parties had had 'notice' of these injunctions, but despite this proceeded to judgment in Germany. Evidently fearful of enforce-ment in England, PASF sought further assurances at first instance from Waller J in the form of declarations that the arbitration agreements were valid and enforce-able, and declarations that the German judgments were to be denied enforcement in England. These the judge denied. Of present interest to this section, is the con-cept of English 'public policy' under Article 27(1).[370] The trial judge took the view, first,[371] that a judgment of another Contracting State delivered in defiance of an arbitration provision should not be recognised and enforced under Article 27(1) if an injunction, of which the recalcitrant party was aware,[372] had been granted to restrain those foreign 'rogue' proceedings. Secondly, he went further, and saw 'some force in the submission that it should not really depend on whether an injunction, or . . . a declaration'[373] had first been granted for the application of public policy in Article 27(1).[374] The Court of Appeal agreed with the judge's first view that a foreign judgment obtained in breach[375] of an English anti-suit injunc-tion should not be enforced here as being contrary to English public policy.[376] It made no express views as to the judge's second assertion.

---

[365]   [1995] 1 Lloyd's Rep. 87.

[366]   [1994] 1 WLR 588.

[367]   Cf in a non-Convention context, but with equal moment for Title III, *E.I. Du Pont de Nemours v I.C. Agnew (No.2)* [1988] 2 Lloyd's Rep. 240: on the facts (no breach of English exclusive jurisdiction clause) an unsuccessful application for an injunction to prevent a party, bent on litigation abroad, from relying on any eventual favourable judgment in English proceedings by way of issue estoppel, at p.243 (Dillon LJ); also *OT Africa Line Ltd v Hijazy and others (The 'Kribi')* [2001] 1 Lloyd's Rep. 76 (Aikens J).

[368]   At least as a potential breach of Articles 21/22, above.

[369]   [1996] CLC 1757, QBD, 1780 CA.

[370]   Different attitude to contract-breakers in *OLG Hamm* (1994) *RIW* 243, where Article 28 III was said to *prohibit* a review under Article 27(1).

[371]   At p.1778.

[372]   Otherwise than by actual service, as this method had failed.

[373]   At p.1778.

[374]   The German courts have taken a different view as to jurisdiction taken in breach of an arbitration clause: *OLG Hamm* 28.12.1993 (1994) *RIW* 243, where Article 28 III was said to prohibit a review under Article 27(1).

[375]   *Quaere*, whether these facts are better dealt with under the express provision of Article 27(3), or that *Hoffmann* forces this conclusion.

[376]   Leggatt LJ, at p.1788; Mance J came to a similar point of view in *Alfred C Toepfer International GmbH v Molino Boschi SRL* [1996] CLC 738, at p.742H—critical, Peel, E. 'Exclusive jurisdiction

Although observance of a court order, or perhaps more accurately the effects of its non-observance, implicate matters of domestic public policy, it is not so clear-cut that non-observance of a contractual bargain[377]—and the doctrine of *pacta sunt servanda*—should represent a breach of public policy under Article 27(1) in a Brussels Convention context. While it is true that section 32 of the Civil Jurisdiction and Judgments Act 1982[378] has a certain claim to represent the inviolable sanctity,[379] to English eyes, of jurisdiction and arbitration clauses—after all, it merely replaced from 24.8.1982 what had earlier been section 4(3)(b)[380] of the Foreign Judgments (Reciprocal Enforcement) Act 1933—there may be some doubt, under the Brussels Convention,[381] that such a section represents, or has been elevated to, the status of public policy.[382] It surely cannot be correct to say that a breach of contract[383] has become a matter of public policy. But this, after all, is what section 32 demands. *Benincasa v Dentalkit*[384] has shown us, rightly or wrongly, the special position of jurisdiction clauses within the contract for Article 17 purposes, divorced, to the extent of their formal validity,[385] from the *lex causae*:

> [a] jurisdiction clause, which serves a procedural purpose,[386] is governed by the provisions of the Convention ... In contrast, the substantive provisions of the main contract in which that clause is incorporated ... are governed by the *lex causae* ...[387]

Breach of a jurisdiction clause cannot therefore, on *Benincasa*'s ruling, equate to a breach of the (other) material provisions/terms of the contract. Waller J's view

---

agreements: purity and pragmatism in the conflict of laws' (1998) *LMCLQ* 182, at p.208, as a refusal under Article 27(1) would be an indirect out-manoeuvring of the prohibition under Article 28 III.

[377] Why stop at jurisdiction/arbitration clauses? Taken to its logical conclusion, any breach of contract by the party suing abroad should entitle the English court to invoke public policy.

[378] S 32(4), in a circular argument, however states that s 32(1) is not (adversely) to affect judgments 'required to be enforced' under the Conventions.

[379] Subject to s 32(2); contrast the position in *Cour de Cassation* 14.11.2000 *Soc. Assurances générales de France et autres c/ M. Karl Goettgens* (2001) *Rev crit* 172, (2001) *Rev de l'Arb*. 507, obs. Idot, (2001) *JCP*, Juris., II, 10597, where a German judgment was enforced in France, despite the German court's seisure in the face of a (German) arbitration clause requiring disputed questions of medical evidence to be referred to a doctor/arbitrator. While the reviewer, Kaplan, (2001) *JCP*, Juris., II, 10597 admits that the French autonomous recognition and enforcement position is similar to that under s 32 CJJA 1982, he does *not* emphatically raise an Article 27(1) point in regard to enforcement of such a judgment under Title III (as in *Philip Alexander Securities & Futures Ltd v Bamberger & Ors and related action* [1996] CLC 1757 (Waller J), but reduces the arbitration clause issue to whether the judgment debtor raised objections to seisin before the rendering Contracting State court, at p.1789.

[380] Although s 4(3)(b) had a different emphasis: to state that the foreign court was deemed not to have had jurisdiction.

[381] S 32(4) of the CJJA 1982; and Article 28 I: breach of Article 17 is not a ground for refusal to recognise or enforce.

[382] Or even if it has, whether Article 28 III prohibits its use in any event.

[383] Whether of an express term (such as a jurisdiction clause) or implied term.

[384] *Francesco Benincasa v Dentalkit Srl* (C–269/95) [1997] ECR I–3767.

[385] Controversially thereafter, their scope of application to the dispute is to be judged by the *lex causae*, at p.3798, para. 31.

[386] But public policy under Article 27(1) is being used here not to attack the foreign procedure itself, but the taking of jurisdiction by the foreign court, outlawed by Article 28 III.

[387] [1997] ECR I–3767, at p.3797, para. 25.

that without the scaffolding of an injunction to that effect, breach of a jurisdiction/
arbitration clause will contravene Article 27(1) may well go too far.

Whatever the answer to the question of section 32 CJJA 1982 as a free-standing,
public policy defence under Article 27(1), the better solution is to rely on a breach
of a court order—an anti-suit injunction and any declaration.[388]

As far as the reception of fraud is concerned, it seems to have been more problematic in England than the other Contracting States. This may be because of the
special place fraud traditionally occupies as a defence at common law, 'an unjustified and chauvinistic rule . . . disfigur[ing] the law',[389] whereby the merits of the
case, and the defence can be re-litigated in enforcement proceedings here.

On the rare occasions when (collateral)[390] fraud has been invoked as a defence
to enforcement under part III of the Brussels Convention, differences in attitude
of the French,[391] German[392] and English[393] courts have been observed. Before the
cases are examined in greater detail, some short remarks should be made about
traditional autonomous attitudes to the defence of fraud. In England and France
at least, the defence is a *sui generis*[394] part of the law[395] on recognition and enforcement of judgments. This independence from the other defences of public policy,
or natural justice, at English common law, had important repercussions on raising the plea of fraud before the English courts: namely when the matter of fraud
had already been placed before the foreign court, or raised[396] in the foreign proceedings. The defendant/judgment debtor could re-litigate the fraud issue[397] in
England even when this meant re-opening the merits of the foreign proceedings.
This liberality was not extended[398] to defences of public policy and natural
justice:[399] if the latter two defences were substantially the same as at English law,

---

[388] As in *E.I. Du Pont de Nemours v I.C. Agnew (No.2)* [1988] 2 Lloyd's Rep. 240, at p.243 (Dillon LJ);
but now *OT Africa Line Ltd v Hijazy and others (The 'Kribi')* [2001] 1 Lloyd's Rep. 76 (Aikens J).

[389] According to Collier, J. (1992) *CLJ* 441, at p.442; *Abouloff v Oppenheimer & Co.* (1882) 10 QBD 295,
CA; *Owens Bank Ltd v Bracco* [1992] 2 AC 443 (no fresh evidence necessary for plea as a bar before the
English courts).

[390] Fraud, not of the court itself, but in the presentation of evidence to it.

[391] *S.A. La Signalisation c/ Société C.A.E Electronica* 15.12.1987 (1989) *JDI* 102.

[392] *BGH* 10.7.1986, IPRspr. (1986) Nr. 182.

[393] *Interdesco S.A. v Nullifire Ltd.* [1992] 1 Lloyd's Rep. 180 (Phillips J), *SISRO v Ampersand Software*,
[1994] I.L.Pr. 55, CA; in Scotland *Artic Fish Sales Co. Ltd. v Adam (No.2)* 7.6.1995 (1996) *SLT* 970—for
a Scottish case, under s 18 and Sch.6, para. 9 CJJA 1982, analogous to the factual situation in *House of
Spring Gardens v Waite* [1991] 1 QB 241, *Clarke v Fennoscandia Limited* [1998] SC 464.

[394] O'Malley, S. and Layton, A. *European Civil Practice*, 1989, at p.697, para. 27.20.

[395] In England cases from *Abouloff v Oppenheimer* (1882) 10 QBD 295 to *House of Spring Gardens v
Waite* [1991] 1 QB 241 and *Owens Bank v Bracco* [1992] 2 AC 443; in France the third prerequisite of
the *Munzer* decision, above, at p.385.

[396] *Abouloff v Oppenheimer* (1882) 10 QBD 295, CA and *Syal v Heyward* [1948] 2 KB 433, CA.

[397] Not it seems *ad infinitum*, however, *Owens Bank v Etoile* [1995] 1 WLR 44, PC, in which *Abouloff*
was not regarded with much enthusiasm.

[398] *Ellis v M'Henry* (1871) LR 6 CP 228, at p.238; *Israel Discount Bank New York v Hadjipateras and
another* [1983] 3 All ER 129.

[399] *Adams and others v Cape Industries Plc. and another* [1990] 1 Ch. 433; *obiter*, the defendants could
however have relied on the natural justice defence, as they were unaware of circumstances that would
have enabled them to raise the defence before the rendering Texas court; also *Masters v Leaver* [2000]

were available, and were not raised before the foreign court—or were raised but were rejected—the defendant was barred from re-litigating on the same issue in England.

When a defence of fraud therefore came before Phillips J in *Interdesco v Nullifire*[400] under Article 27(1), it was quite clear that the judge required a change[401] of emphasis from the common law position.[402] Nullifire had appealed against the Master's order authorising enforcement of a French judgment on the ground that it had been procured by fraud relating to certain evidence[403] of test results in the French action. As was noted above, had an action been brought[404] on the judgment at common law, the judge could have reconsidered *de novo* the issue of fraud, even if available, and raised abroad. However the judge ruled that Articles 29 and 34 III had altered the common law position in *Abouloff v Openheimer*,[405] at least 'in its most extreme formulation':[406] reviewing again the fraud issue already decided by the foreign court.[407] In view of Article 29, this approach must be correct.

The judge's solution to the 'more difficult question'[408]—where, as in *Interdesco* itself, the foreign court had *not* had an opportunity[409] to consider the alleged fraud—also represented a departure from the pre-Convention position, that may be called 'the exhaustion of local remedies'.[410] In such a case as the one before the judge, he considered it expedient[411] that:

I.L.Pr. 387, at p.397, para. 41, (Morritt LJ); *Habib Bank Ltd v Ahmed* 12.10.2000 (Carnwath J), *The Times* 2.11.2000; *dubitante, Jet Holdings Inc. v Patel* [1990] 1 QB 335, at p.345 (Staughton LJ), decided on fraud grounds.

[400] [1992] 1 Lloyd's Rep. 180.

[401] *Quaere*, whether the change has been wrought by Title III in general, or by Articles 29/34 in particular; whichever it is, change there has been—the view in the case of international arbitration award in *Westacre Investments Inc v Jugoimport-SPDR Holding* [2000] QB 288, at p.309 (Waller LJ).

[402] The analysis in *Cheshire and North*, 13th edn., 1999, at p.496.

[403] As Nullifire alleged, 'a deliberately false averment in a document in the nature of a pleading'.

[404] Or more accurately registration of the judgment, in the case of France, under the Foreign Proceedings (Reciprocal Judgments) Act 1933 and the Reciprocal Enforcement of Foreign Judgments (France) Order in Council 1936, S.I. 1936/609, incorporating the *Convention between His Majesty in respect of the United Kingdom and the President of the French Republic providing for the reciprocal enforcement of judgments in civil and commercial matters, with Protocol*, esp. Article 3(1)(c)(ii).

[405] And German cases, below, at pp.423–424.

[406] [1992] 1 Lloyd's Rep. 180, at p.187.

[407] Cf *Westacre Investments Inc v Jugoimport-SPDR Holding* [1999] QB 740—a 'strong argument for the policy of the enforcement court [under the 1958 New York Convention] being less willing than that of a domestic court . . . to permit the reopening of an award on issues of fraud', at p.782 (Colman J), but see Waller LJ in [2000] QB 288, CA, at p.309; abuse of process to insist on defence in *Owens Bank Ltd v Etoile Commerciale S.A.* [1995] 1 WLR 44, at p.51, PC (Lord Templeman).

[408] *Ibid.*

[409] Because evidence had only been discovered after judgment.

[410] A stance favoured by the German courts and commentators for other aspects of public policy, apart, ironically, from fraud, above, at pp.423–424, and *BGH* 10.7.1986, IPRspr. (1986) Nr. 182, discussed below, at pp.428–429; the justification for this exhaustion of local remedies appears to rest on the mistaken assumption that the 'remedy' is the equivalent of the plea of fraud at common law.

[411] For the sake of the spirit of co-operation in the Convention and the efficacy of the investigation of the alleged fraud.

the English Court should first consider whether a remedy[412] lies . . . in the foreign jurisdiction in question. If so,[413] it will normally be appropriate to leave the defendant to pursue his remedy in that jurisdiction.[414]

It is submitted that two different situations must be distinguished, where the other Contracting State court has had *no* opportunity to examine the question of fraud. Either:

(1) it has not done so because fresh evidence of such conduct has only come to light after judgment has been pronounced; or

(2) because of the judgment debtor's negligence or inadvertence in submitting evidence of fraud in the original proceedings when it was possible to do so, and the debtor now for the first time raises the defence under Article 27(1) before the English court. The section of Phillip J's judgment just quoted is aimed, rightly or wrongly at the first situation. The second situation implicates the rule in *Henderson v Henderson*.[415]

In addition in *Interdesco*, as a future general rule[416] for the use of Article 27(1) and fraud, the judge said that the principles as to reviewing Brussels/Lugano Convention judgments have been equated with those[417] which would cause an English court to review, or decline to review, one of its own judgments.[418]

The judge's approach in this case has been approved by the Court of Appeal in *SISRO v Ampersand Software*.[419] Here Ampersand resisted enforcement, again, of a French judgment on the ground of an alleged fraud in a nominated expert's report. Unlike the *Interdesco* case, the issue of this fraud was raised in the French trial, but rejected.[420] Again, unlike *Interdesco*, Ampersand had appealed against

---

[412] The possibility of having the judgment overturned in the foreign forum by a form of (extraordinary) appeal; but the 'remedy' in the foreign jurisdiction (unlike the traditional *Abouloff* fraud defence to enforcement in England) is to upset the first judgment, having it set aside, under stricter conditions, requiring fresh evidence; the 'same' fraud argument, as is available in England, may therefore prove to be unavailable, or woefully inadequate, in the foreign jurisdiction.

[413] *Quaere*, if there is no such remedy; and Hill, J. *The Law Relating to International Commercial Disputes*, 2nd edn., 1998, at p.387, para. 13.3.17, where 'there is no means of recourse under the law of the state of origin'.

[414] [1992] 1 Lloyd's Rep. 180, at p.188; and Briggs, 2002, at p.123.

[415] Barnett, P. *Res judicata, estoppel, and foreign judgments*, 2001, at p.227 and p.291.

[416] Note the judge's statement in the penultimate paragraph, in the second column on p.188.

[417] According to Barnett, P., 2001, at p.185 and esp. p.228 onwards, erroneously equated with, it appears, '[t]he specific plea of abuse of process', and/or the rule in *Henderson v Henderson* (1843) 3 Hare 100, at p.114–15 (Sir Thomas Wigram VC): except in exceptional circumstances (which may include fraud), submissions/aspects of case not brought forward 'from negligence, inadvertence, or even accident'; assimilated and accepted in a 1958 New York Convention context (as to finality of Convention awards) as a correct statement of law in *Westacre Investments Inc v Jugoimport-SPDR Holding* [1999] QB 740, at p.783–84, (Colman J), but care in this assimilation in CA, [2000] QB 288, CA, at p.309 (Waller LJ).

[418] [1992] 1 Lloyd's Rep. 180, at p.188, penultimate paragraph, *in fine*.

[419] [1994] I.L.Pr. 55, at p.60, (Dillon LJ).

[420] *Interdesco*'s 'most extreme formulation'.

this outcome to the Paris Court of Appeal. To allow the defence of fraud under Article 27(1)—and refuse enforcement— in circumstances where this issue was before a foreign appeal court—which may dismiss[421] the allegation—seemed to the judge to be 'stupid and highly undesirable'.[422] It appears that if the judgment debtor either raises the issue of fraud in the foreign proceedings, or appeals against its rejection, Article 27(1) will be unavailable in England.[423] Once the debtor embarks upon (forlorn) exhaustion of local remedies, as *Interdesco* encourages him to do, the defence appears to be lost.

The approach in *Interdesco* has been followed in Scotland, in *Artic Fish Sales Co. Ltd. v Adam (No.2)*,[424] but where neither *Interdesco* nor *SISRO* was cited. An Irish judgment, it was argued, had been 'impetrated' by fraud. The judge rejected the Article 27(1) defence thus:

> it is not for this court to assess the matter but for the Irish courts. It was not suggested that the remedy of reduction was not available[425] to the appellant in the Irish courts.[426]

The approach of Phillips J in *Interdesco*, and that of Droz is to be commended. It is certainly not appropriate in the Brussels/Lugano Convention context to treat a judgment from another Contracting State in a prejudicial fashion, by not equating the effects of fraud on it any more harshly than on a domestic judgment. That there can be any review of the circumstances surrounding an allegation of fraud, once examined in the rendering court, is no longer in any doubt. Article 29 expressly forbids this. To engender a spirit of mutual trust and cooperation between the courts of the Contracting States,[427] it was essential that the local rendering court, or an appeal court, be given the first opportunity to remedy any alleged impropriety, and not suffer the affront of censure from another Contracting State. Litigants[428] are to be encouraged 'durch aktive Teilnahme am Verfahren auf die Vermeidung sie benachteiligender Fehler des

---

[421] If the allegation is accepted, there would be no judgment to enforce in England in any event, at p.60.

[422] [1994] I.L.Pr. 55, at p.60.

[423] There are statements in *Soleimany v Soleimany* [1999] QB 785 (failed application for enforcement of an arbitration award on the basis of a contract recognised as illegal) that whether an appeal is possible, or would be successful, on illegality grounds, is of no concern to the issue of illegality in English enforcement proceedings, at p.804 (Waller LJ)

[424] 7.6.1995 (1996) *SLT* 970, OH, Lord Cameron of Lochbroom.

[425] Presumably then, if no remedy is 'available' abroad, the defence will be available in Scotland.

[426] (1996) *SLT* 970, at p.973.

[427] As Droz saw, 1972, at p.313.

[428] Whether Droz is over-optimistic in believing that reciprocity will be encouraged by such an attitude, at p.313, para. 497 *in fine*: 'ils comprondront vite que le meilleur moyen d'assurer l'autorité de leur propres décisions est encore de respecter au maximum celles de leurs collègues étrangers'('they will quickly come to appreciate that the best way to assure the binding nature of their own decisions is also to respect as much as possible those of their foreign colleagues').

Gerichts hinzuwirken oder hierwegen ein Rechtsmittel einzulegen.'[429] What is true in the case of potential defects in the foreign procedure,[430] is, *a fortiori*, doubly so in the case of fraud:

> Il vaut beaucoup mieux . . . que le juge du pays requis surseoie à statuer et incite la partie intéressée à se pouvoir en recours extraordinaire devant le juge étranger compétent[431] [432]

4.4.4   German case law under Article 27(1), the reception of fraud and the procedural/material public policy issue

The numerous examples where this defence has been invoked by German judgment debtors under the Convention enables a reviewer to divide up the analysis into 'procedural' and 'material' public policy defences. The former by far outweigh the latter, and will be dealt with first.

4.4.4(i)   Procedural public policy[433]

The cases from Germany demonstrate their courts' willingness to recognise that foreign procedural law may not always correspond[434] to the standards expected of the German trial process. For the most part,[435] the procedural[436] public policy defence has been unsuccessful[437] under Article 27(1). The definition of this defence has been bequeathed by two pre-Convention cases[438] decided under the Anglo-German recognition and enforcement Convention, discussed earlier, and

---

[429] ('by active participation in the procedure to work towards the avoidance of disadvantageous mistakes of the court or to put in an appeal against them'), taken from *BGH* 21.3.1990 (1990) *FamRZ* 868, at pp.869–90, but not in the context of fraud; the German attitude to fraud is less tolerant, and absolute, in next subsection.

[430] The Luxembourg case of *Reicherz-Roth* 17.7.1997, (1997) *Pas. Lux.*, 340 must therefore be incorrect in this respect.

[431] ('It would be better . . . if the requesting judge stays proceedings and encourages the interested party to institute an extraordinary appeal before the competent foreign judge').

[432] Droz., 1972, at p.312, para. 496.

[433] Exceptionally, success in *Krombach* (C-7/98), 28.3.2000; breach of Article 6 ECHR already found in referring case, reported (1999) *EuZW* 26, at p.27, post-reference decision *BGH* 29.6.2000, (2000) *RIW* 797, (2001) *IPRax* 50, and *OLG Köln* 12.4.1989 IPRspr. (1989) Nr. 213, (1990) *RIW* 229, [1991] I.L.Pr. 483, discussed below, at pp.428–429; Kropholler, 2002, at pp.392–400, and at p.396, para. 15.

[434] Direct equivalence has been held to be unnecessary, *BGH* 26.9.1979 IPRspr. (1979) Nr. 204; Kropholler, 2002, at p.395, para. 13.

[435] *Dieter Krombach v Andre Bamberski* (C–7/98), 28.3.2000, AG Antonio Saggio's opinion 23.9.1999; the *BGH* decision had already stated that it considered the French criminal procedure in that case as being contrary to German procedural public policy and Article 6 ECHR, 4.12.1997 (1999) *EuZW* 26, at p.27, [1998] I.L.Pr. 681.

[436] For examples of the material defence, especially *BGH* 22.6.1983, IPRspr. (1983) Nr. 176, below, at p.430.

[437] A rare exception is *OLG Köln* 12.4.1989 IPRspr. (1989) Nr. 213, [1991] I.L.Pr. 483, discussed below, at pp.426–427.

[438] Esp. *BGH* 18.10.1967 (1968) *NJW* 354; *BGH* 19.9.1977 (1978) *NJW* 1114.

has been frequently re-iterated[439] ever since. A decision cannot be refused recognition and enforcement simply because, had a German court been hearing the case, a different set of procedures would have been employed. Procedural public policy will only intervene to prevent recognition and enforcement of a judgment when the procedure followed in the foreign court 'nicht als in einem geordneten, rechtstaatlichen Verfahren ergangen angesehen werden kann'.[440]

Proceedings that may not represent such a 'geordneten, rechtstaatlichen Verfahren' would include[441] a breach of certain provisions of the German Constitution, especially[442] Article 103 I *Grundgesetz*—the right to a fair hearing, and the right to be heard (at all).[443]

The concrete examples of when procedural public policy has been invoked are the following cases: in a rather complex case, in *OLG Hamm* 27.6.1996,[444] a German company was sued and initially held liable as a third party in French proceedings between French litigants, on the basis of an expert's report (the 'original report'). The French trial court, the *Tribunal de Commerce de Versailles*, rejected the Germany company's plea of a lack of jurisdiction and limitation, and applied French law. An appeal by the German company resulted in the separation of the main trial and third party proceedings, and the ordering of a fresh experts report. In the meantime, in the main action, the French defendant's liability to the French plaintiff was established, without the German company's participation. The appeal court in Versailles ordered the German company to indemnify the French defendant on the basis of the original report, following issues in the main proceedings in which the German company had taken no part. Its appeal in *cassation* was rejected.[445] The pre-emptory nature of the appeal court's decision was cause for complaint under Article 27(1) when the third party judgment was registered for enforcement in Germany. The appeal to the *OLG Hamm* was unsuccessful.[446] The court rehearsed the pre-Brussels Convention definition of (procedural) public policy, now a feature of Article 27(1), and came to the conclusion, amounting almost to a presumption that

---

[439] *OLG Koblenz* 8.2.1996 IPRspr. (1996) Nr. 139; *OLG Hamm* 19.7.1985 IPRspr. (1985) Nr. 187; and *BGH* 21.3.1990, IPRspr. (1990) Nr. 207.

[440] ('cannot be considered to have been rendered in a well-ordered procedure in accordance with the rule of law'), *BGH* 19.9.1977 (1978) *NJW* 1114, at p.1115; *verbatim* repetition in *OLG Hamm* 28.12.1993 (1995) NJW-RR 189, at p.190.

[441] *BGH* 19.9.1977 (1978) *NJW* 1114, at p.1115 also included issues such as the right to participate in the proceedings, and the impartiality of the court.

[442] *OLG Hamm* 19.7.1985 IPRspr. (1985) Nr. 187; also *Bundesgericht* 5.7.2001 *X contre l'arrêt rendu le 11.1.2001 . . . Y Ltd*, unreported.

[443] Confirmed recently by ECJ, at para. 45 in *Dieter Krombach v Andre Bamberski*, (C–7/98), AG Saggio also opined that the right to be heard was a matter of public policy.

[444] *OLG Hamm* 27.6.1996, IPRspr. (1996) Nr. 178.

[445] On the necessity of exhausting local remedies under Article 27(1) generally, and in relation to fraud, below at p.424.

[446] The company had initially been given an opportunity to be heard.

[b]esonders selten sind Verstöße gegen den verfahrensrechtlichen ordre public, weil Entscheidungen im Sinne des Article 25 EuGVÜ in allen Vertragsstaaten *regelmäßig* in einem rechtstaatlichen Verfahren ergehen.[447]

Geimer, commenting on the case,[448] acknowledges that German respondents to enforcement under Title III of the Brussels Convention will only in 'extremen Ausnahmesituationen'[449] have any chance of resisting enforcement under procedural public policy, in Article 27(1).

Again, in *OLG Düsseldorf,*[450] a German judgment debtor unsuccessfully sought to block enforcement of a Netherlands judgment under Article 27(1) on two grounds. Firstly, that the Arnhem rendering court was not competent;[451] and secondly that, due to the civil procedure in the rendering court, an appeal was excluded in the circumstances.[452] As to the second objection, the court stated that:

> Fehlen einer Rechtsmittelinstanz stellt keine Verletzung wesentlicher Grundsätze des deutschen Rechts dar.[453]

In *BGH* 21.3.1990,[454] also to be discussed in relation to Article 27(2) *infra*, the enforcement of an Italian divorce judgment for maintenance was resisted, *inter alia*, under Article 27(1), on the ground that an Italian appeal court had awarded maintenance, when this fact had not initially been included in the original petition for divorce. There was some doubt, also, as a matter of Italian internal procedure, whether fresh proceedings had to be initiated for such a maintenance order, and not, as had happened, *sua sponte* by the appeal court. The *BGH* was not impressed by either objection, and held that there was not such a serious breach of German procedural public policy as to warrant a refusal of enforcement. In an argument reminiscent of that used by Phillips J in relation to fraud in *Interdesco S.A. v Nullifire Ltd.,*[455] the court stated

---

[447] ('Breaches of procedural public policy are *especially rare,* because decisions within the meaning of Article 25 Brussels Convention are *usually* given in all Contracting States in a procedure governed by the rule of law'), *OLG Hamm* 27.6.1996 (1998) *IPRax* 202, at p.203—a presumption of regularity?

[448] Geimer, R. 'Härtetest für deutsche Dienstleister im Ausland' zu *OLG Hamm* 27.6.1996 und *BGH* 18.9.1997 (1998) *IPRax* 175, at p.177.

[449] ('extremely exceptional circumstances'), *ibid.*

[450] 7.12.1994 (1995) *RIW* 324.

[451] Articles 34 II and 28 III show this submission was doomed to failure.

[452] Also *OLG Düsseldorf* 21.2.2001 (2001) *RIW* 620: no breach of German (procedural) public policy by an Italian summary judgment, where review of decision available in same court, although rights of further appeal limited; cf. *Cour de Cassation* 6.3.1996 *Bernard Marc Guittienne v Soc. Nationale de Credit a L'Industrie S.C.I* [1997] I.L.Pr. 522.

[453] ('Lack of an appeal procedure does not represent an affront to fundamental principles of German law'), (1995) *RIW* 324, at p.325; similar sentiments expressed in *Cour de Cassation* 10.7.1996 *Roche c/ Direction générale des aéroports de l'État d'Ankara* (1996), *Dalloz*, IR, 210.

[454] IPRspr. (1990) Nr. 207.

[455] [1992] 1 Lloyd's Rep. 180, discussed above, at pp.418–419.

daß es in erster Linie Sache der Parteien ist, durch aktive Teilnahme am Verfahren auf die Vermeidung sie benachteiligender Fehler des Gerichts hinzuwirken oder hierwegen ein Rechtsmittel einzulegen.[456]

The view that it is up to the parties to exhaust all local remedies of appeal in the rendering court, and not to rely on mistakes of foreign procedure under Article 27(1) in the enforcing court receives almost[457] universal[458] support from commentators. The view is logical: the enforcing court does not (and should not), under Article 27(1), sit as an appeal court on the way the foreign procedure has been conducted.[459] It is simply not in the best position to rule on questions of foreign procedural law;[460] that is best left to an appeal in the Contracting State of origin. This is not an absolute rule however, although Article 29 seems to prevent the enforcing court from reviewing the internal substance of the foreign decision.

In *OLG Karlsruhe*,[461] enforcement of an English *Mareva* injunction was resisted under Article 27(1) because of the non-specific, general nature[462] of the freezing injunction. Without re-iterating whether German procedural public policy was directly in issue, the court made an important statement[463] concerning the atmosphere of enforcement under Title III of the Brussels Convention, and rejected the defence. The German courts, it found, are obliged 'bei der Vollsteckung europäis-

---

[456] ('That it is up to the parties in the first place, by active participation in the procedure, to work towards the avoidance of disadvantageous mistakes of the court, or to lodge an appeal against them'), 1990 FamRZ, 868, at p.869–70; *OLG Düsseldorf* 21.2.2001 (2001) *RIW* 620; or even when there has been no mistake in the foreign proceedings: *Bundesgericht* 5.7.2001 *X contrre l'arrêt rendu le 11.1.2001 ... Y Ltd*, unreported; *BGH* 18.9.2001 (2002) *RIW* 238 (mistake in date printed on Dutch initiating document) not fatal under Article 27(1).

[457] Schack, 2.Auf., 1996, at p.336 para. 866 thinks it is wrong to expect a defendant to an unfair and unfamiliar procedure abroad, in which the defendant no doubt has lost all confidence, to waste money on participation, or an appeal.

[458] A vociferous supporter is Geimer, in Geimer, R. and Schütze, R. 1997, at p.741, para. 2955; also Hill's conclusions, 2nd edn., 1998, at p.387 para. 13.3.17.

[459] *OLG Köln* 6.10.1994 (1995) NJW-RR 446, at p.447: a fundamental breach in procedure is necessary. The fact that the foreign court has not followed its own procedure is irrelevant; compare at English common law *Pemberton v Hughes* [1899] 1 Ch. 781, at p.792, (Lindley MR).

[460] An isolated case, *OLG Hamm* 19.7.1985 IPRspr. (1985) Nr. 187 shows that this view is not absolute in every instance.

[461] 19.12.1994 IPRspr. (1995) Nr. 166—it first appeared that cross-border enforcement of a *Mareva*/freezing injunction may have needed re-appraisal in the light of *Van Uden* (Article 24 orders such as the interim payments in that case, should be territorially confined), but note *OLG München* (2000) *RIW* 464, reviewed above at pp.321–322, allowing enforcement in Germany of a Greek freezing order; *contra*, Kropholler, 2002, at p.359, para. 8 who believes that cross-border *Mareva*/freezing injunctions are unenforceable.

[462] Allegedly contrary to Articles 2 & 14 *Grundgesetz*: 'Die Bestimmtheit des Vollstreckungstitels ist Bestandteil des deutschen ordre public'('the specificity of the judgment is a part of German public policy'), IPRspr. (1995) Nr. 166, at p.338; *inter partes Mareva* injunction *sufficiently* precise in wording in *OLG Frankfurt/Main* 27.3.1998 (1998) IPRspr. Nr.182a, at p.360.

[463] Entirely consistent with the Belgian court's attitude in *Tribunal de première instance de Liège* 9.10.1995 (1996) *Act Dr* 80, above, at pp.412–413.

chen Titeln möglichst Bestandteil des deutschen Geltung zu verschaffen, auch wenn sie deutschen Bestimmtheitsanforderungen nicht voll genügen'.[464]

A slightly different objection was taken to a French decision in *OLG Saarbrücken*.[465] Here the German debtor objected that the decision had been given by lay judges of the Paris Commercial Court. The defence predictably failed. The public policy 'formula' was paraphrased slightly, applying

> nur in ganz krassen Fällen entgegen . . . und setzt voraus, daß grundlegende Werte der zweitstaatlichen Rechtsordnung oder elementare staatspolitische Zielsetzungen des Zweitstaates in Frage gestellt würde.[466]

While admitting that Article 27(1) could never be excluded from applying to a foreign procedure, in this case there was not such a flagrant disregard for the basic principles of German procedure, in that the lay judge system had an integral part in the French first instance court structure.

Other cases illustrating reliance on Article 27(1) have been to challenge enforcement by the way the rendering court calculated, or estimated[467] the level of damages. An early unsuccessful attempt is exemplified by *BGH* 26.9.1979.[468] Here the Paris Commercial Court had awarded an estimated amount of damages. Although there were differences[469] in the methods of assessing the scale of damages in the two Contracting States, an impermissible affront to German public policy had not been established. It was part of the foreign procedural *lex fori* that left to the court the assessment of damages on an estimated basis, without specific proof of itemised loss.[470]

In *OLG Koblenz*[471] and *OLG Köln*,[472] again, odious comparisons between the law of evidence[473] in Germany and Italy were avoided, where, in the Italian proceedings before the local courts in Bari and Brescia respectively, certain evidence

---

[464] ('when enforcing European orders to create for them as much as possible a part of German validity, even if they do not fulfil German notions of specificity'), IPRspr. (1995) Nr. 166, at p.338; now post *Van Uden Maritime v Kommanditgesellschaft in Firma Deco Line, and another* (C–391/95) [1998] ECR I–7091—*OLG München* (2000) *RIW* 464, reviewed above at pp.321–322.

[465] 3.8.1987, IPRspr. (1987) Nr. 156.

[466] ('only in quite egregious cases, and presupposes that basic values of the requested State's legal system, or that this State's fundamental governmental or political aims, would be called into question'), IPRspr. (1987) Nr. 156, at p.391.

[467] Cf at English common law: *Adams and others v Cape Industries Plc. and another* [1990] 1 Ch. 433, at p.568, (Slade LJ), *obiter*, where the Texas judge had made no apparent 'judicial' assessment of damages, despite US federal procedure rules directing him to do so; also *European Case Law on the Judgments Convention*, (ed. Kaye, P.), 1998, at pp.551–52.

[468] IPRspr. (1979) Nr. 204.

[469] Similarly, *OLG Hamburg* 5.11.1991 IPRspr. (1991) Nr. 211; since German law had provisions dealing with the award of compound interest, an English judgment confirming a GAFTA arbitration award, with compound interest, could not be attacked on Article 27(1) grounds.

[470] IPRspr. (1979) Nr. 204, at p.665.

[471] 8.2.1996 IPRspr. (1996) Nr. 139.

[472] 16.9.1996 (1998) *IPRax* 116.

[473] That a German judge, hearing the same case, would have been considered to have breached fundamental German procedural laws of evidence was held to be irrelevant, (1997) *RIW* 328, at p.329.

(of German directors of the defendant company, in the first case) was not examined by the rendering courts. Even though the German courts accepted that as a matter of Italian procedural law of evidence, there had been a mistake, this fact, of itself,[474] was insufficient to breach German public policy:

> Verfahrensfehler des Gerichts begründen aber nicht schon die Annahme, die nachfolgende Entscheidung sei nicht in einem geordneten, rechtstaatlichen Verfahren ergangen.[475]

A successful, and therefore isolated, example of procedural public policy under Article 27(1)[476] is shown by *OLG Köln*.[477] Here a Belgian default judgment had been given in the defendant's absence. The document instituting the proceedings, initially served by *remise au parquet*[478] on the local Belgian court officer,[479] only came to the German defendant's attention after judgment had been rendered. This, it was found, was rendered

---

[474] The general view was accepted that use was to be made of the Italian appeal procedure, (1998) *IPRax* 116, at p.116 in such cases.

[475] ('Procedural blunders of the court do not raise the presumption that the ensuing judgment was not given in a well-ordered procedure according to the rule of law'), (1998) *IPRax* 116, at p.116; also *OLG Köln* (2000) *IPRax* 528, at p.529; a 'well-ordered' procedure now appears to include correct service according to (German) procedural law: *OLG Düsseldorf* 29.11.1999 (2000) *IPRax* 527, at p.528, [2002] I.L.Pr. 71, at p.73.

[476] Article 27(2) was used in conjunction with public policy: *contra Hoffmann v Krieg* (C–145/86) [1988] ECR 645 which shows us that a factual situation falling within a specific defence under Article 27 cannot also fall within Article 27(1).

[477] 12.4.1989 IPRspr. (1989) Nr. 213, [1991] I.L.Pr. 483; Article 27(2) seemed the more appropriate defence, but Article 27(1) was seen as a better way of dealing with service by *remise au parquet*: also Roth, (2000) *IPRax* 497, at p.498; in *OLG Köln* 7.3.2001 (2001) NJW-RR 1576, where the service of Italian document—by a method similar to the *remise au parquet*—was held not to be 'due service' for Article 27(2), simply because of the fact that such service was, *inter alia*, impermissible under similar circumstances under German procedural law.

[478] Exemplified by French Article 684(1) NCPC: '[l]a signification d'un acte destiné à une personne domiciliée à l'étranger est faite au parquet.'('service of a certificate bound for a person domiciled abroad is accomplished at the local public prosecutor's office'—for details *Nouveau Code de Procedure Civile*, Dalloz, 93ème éd., 2001, at p.367 following with notes). Thereafter, in Article 686, a certified copy of the document is then transmitted/sent (note, *not served*, as this has already occurred internally—the 'Schlunk exception' to mandatory 'service' under the 1965 Hague Service Convention: *Volkswagenwerk Aktiengesellschaft v. Herwig J. Schlunk* (1988) 486 US 694, at p.707, (O'Connor J)) by registered post to the recipient abroad. Although not new in its operation—Nagel, 1971, at pp.97 onwards, (for its historical effects *Cour de Douai* 25.1.1935 *Hoedhaar c/ Faill. Mallet* (1936) *JDI* 606)—this method of service has caused trouble in Germany: eg *OLG Saarland* (1998) *RIW* 632, *OLG Karlsruhe* (1999) *RIW* 538 and probably will do so in Switzerland: Dörig, 1998, at p.382, fn. 2179, and p.394; note changes to this service regime by Article 14 Council Service Regulation 1348/2000, and the Commission *communiqués* submitted thereunder, below chapter 5.

[479] Also vociferous in condemnation of the circumvention of the 1965 Hague Service Convention: *OLG Karlsruhe* (1999) *RIW* 538, *OLG Köln* 7.3.2001 (2001) *IPRax*, Issue 6, p.V (French) service by *remise au parquet* censured under Art.27(1) (and Art.27(2)); *OLG Köln* 7.3.2001 2001 NJW-RR 1576; cf Henry LJ in *Knauf UK GmbH v British Gypsum Ltd and another* [2002] 1 WLR 907, (reversing [2001] 2 All ER (Comm) 332, (David Steel J)), who found *no* 'good reason' for ordering, by an alternative method (CPR 6.8(1)), internal service on a German defendant's solicitors 'when such an order [for service] subverts, and is designed to subvert, in the absence of any difficulty about effecting service, the principles on which service and jurisdiction are regulated by agreement [ie., *inter alia*, under the 1965 Hague Convention]', [2002] 1 WLR 907, at p.924; *Phillips and others v Symes and another*

unter Verletzung des Grundsatzes des rechtlichen Gehörs . . . und somit den inländischen ordre public verletzt.[480]

Interestingly, no definition of public policy was presented, as would have been expected; neither was there any suggestion that the respondent should have sought redress, primarily, before the Belgian courts, and attempt to have the default judgment set aside![481]

To conclude this section are two cases from the *OLG Hamm*[482] and the post-reference decision of the *BGH*[483] in *Krombach v Bamberski*. The first deals with the *Brennero v Wendel GmbH*[484] saga. As is well-known, the case concerned the enforcement in Germany of an Italian freezing injunction in proceedings in Verona between an Italian shoe-manufacturer and German respondent. The order was enforced at first instance, the Italian company proceeding with attachments in Germany. The respondent appealed to the *OLG*, which ordered conditional enforcement under Article 38 II, as an appeal against the freezing injunction had been lodged in Italy. The *OLG*'s order was appealed to the *BGH*, and the reference made in *Brennero v Wendel*. After the reference, the German respondent disputed the enforceability of the Italian order, *inter alia*, on the grounds that the Italian judge had applied, and incorrectly interpreted,[485] German law as the *lex causae*. As would be expected, the appeal court quoted Article 29 of the Brussels Convention, stating '[u]nder no circumstances' is a review of the substance of the foreign judgment permitted. This is what the German respondent was asking for. That would have been enough to end the matter there and then. Curiously, however, the appeal court in this case unilaterally abrogated to itself a German public exemption[486] to Article 29:

[2002] 1 WLR 853, at p.861, Ch.D., (Hart J), finding service of Greek action on Greek public prosecutor *not* good service (as a matter of English law) for Art.21 purposes of 'first seisure'.

[480] ('in breach of the fundamental principle of the right to a legal hearing. . .and is therefore contrary to public policy in this country'), IPRspr. (1989) Nr. 213, at p.481, [1991] I.L.Pr. 483, at p.486, para. 8; Article 27(1) deployed because of difficulties German judgment debtors have with demonstrating lack of 'due service' by *remise au parquet*; also trenchant criticism in *OLG Düsseldorf* (1999) *RIW* 464; Article 27(1) also available to censure Dutch proceedings by a *remise au parquet* service (thereby avoiding 1965 Hague Convention) in *OLG Düsseldorf* 29.11.1999 (2000) *IPRax* 527, [2002] I.L.Pr. 71, at p.73, para.10; Article 27(2) deployed, but *rationale* and wording of a comparable breach of German procedural public policy under Article 27(1) invoked, to censure an Italian default judgment served by comparable Italian method of service by *remise au parquet* in circumstances where similar service prohibited by German law in *OLG Köln* 7.3.2001 2001 NJW-RR 1576.

[481] Note now Article 19(4) Service Regulation 1348/2000 on default judgments, below, at pp.463–465.

[482] The first *OLG Hamm* 19.7.1985 IPRspr. (1985) Nr. 187; the second *OLG Hamm* 28.12.1993 (1995) NJW-RR 189.

[483] *BGH* 29.6.2000 (2000) *RIW* 797, (2001) *IPRax* 50.

[484] *Calzaturificio Brennero sas v Wendel GmbH Schuhproduktion International* (C–258/83) [1984] ECR 3971.

[485] At English common law, the case of *Godard and another v Gray and another* (1870) LR 6 QB 139, especially at p.151, (Blackburn J); now ECJ in *SA Régie Nationale des Usines Renault* (C–38/98) [2000] ECR I–2973.

[486] Not, however, applicable on the facts of this case.

Eine Ausnahme[487] kommt allenfalls dann in Betracht, wenn die Rechtsanwendung durch das ausländische Gericht *so fehlerhaft ist*, daß das Ergebnis der Entscheidung als Verstoß gegen den ordre public des Vollstreckungsstaats anzusehen wäre (Art 27 Nr.1 EuGVÜ).[488]

The second, *OLG Hamm* 28.12.1993,[489] deals with the enforcement of a French provisional order, where the French court had taken jurisdiction despite[490] the presence of an arbitration clause. This, the German court held, was irrelevant. Arts 28 III and 34 III forbade the German court from examining the jurisdiction of the rendering court under the public policy objection. Even a crass disregard for internal French procedural law in ignoring the arbitration clause could not be the subject of censure in Germany:

> solche Unrichtigkeiten können aber vom Zweitrichter nicht nachgeprüft werden, sondern unterfallen dem Verbot der Gesetzmäßigkeitsprüfung des Article 28 III EuGVÜ.[491]

As could have been predicted, the *BGH*[492] has refused, under Article 27(1), to enforce the French *partie civile* judgment, the subject of the reference in *Krombach v Bamberski*. The court repeated the fact that the judgment breached Article 103 Abs.1 *GG*, the right to a fair hearing. Unusually, however, the court did not test whether the Constitution could be fitted into the framework definition of public policy from the ECJ judgment, as perhaps the answer seemed obvious; nor did it appeal to Article 6(1) ECHR: all that was said is that a breach of the (German) Constitution implicated a matter of public policy.

As for fraud, in *BGH* 10.7.1986,[493] an Italian judgment creditor had obtained, by allegedly fraudulent means, a judgment from a court in Pisa, by stating to the German judgment debtor that he needed the judgment for unrelated credit-rating purposes, and that it would never be enforced. On the strength of this assurance, a default judgment was issued.[494] Enforcement of 'ein durch Täuschung des ausländischen Gerichts erschlichenes Urteil'[495] in Germany was refused under

---

[487] This statement must be incorrect: Article 29 is quite specific and unequivocal 'under no circumstances'.

[488] ('*An exception*, if need be, can then be considered, when the application of law by the foreign court is *so erroneous* that the result of the decision can be seen to be a breach of the public policy of the enforcing court (Article 27(1) of Brussels Convention'), *OLG Hamm* 19.7.1985 IPRspr. (1985) Nr. 187, at p.514; what degree of incorrectness is not mentioned.

[489] (1995) NJW-RR 189, and *OLG Hamburg* 5.8.1993 IPRspr. (1993) Nr. 177; also ECJ *SA Régie Nationale des Usines Renault* (C–38/98) [2000] ECR I–2973.

[490] Now *Van Uden Maritime BV, trading as Van Uden Africa Line v Kommanditgesellschaft in Firma Deco Line, and another* (C–391/95) [1998] ECR I–7091.

[491] ('Such mistakes cannot be reviewed by the enforcing judge, but come within the prohibition on a revision of the jurisdiction of the State of origin in Article 28 III Brussels Convention'), (1995) NJW-RR 189, at p.190.

[492] *BGH* 29.6.2000 (2000) *RIW* 797.

[493] *BGH* 10.7.1986 IPRspr. (1986) Nr. 182; also *BGH* 15.10.1992 (1993) *NJW* 1270, at p.1272, [1994] I.L.Pr. 470.

[494] Compare *Wyatt v Palmer* [1899] 2 QB 106, at pp.109–10, (Lindley MR).

[495] ('a judgment connived at by the duping of the foreign court'), IPRspr. (1986) Nr. 182, at p.418.

Article 27(1). Interestingly, in the context of the need to seek a remedy in the Contracting State of origin, nothing was said about this issue by the *Bundesgerichtshof.* Outside the context of fraud, the courts and commentators, as has been observed, are keen to promote the exhaustion of local remedies. Why nothing was said in this case about the sensitive issue of a foreign court's having been misled by one of the parties, is unknown. It may well be that, from a historical point of view, the 'global' defence of public policy under autonomous German law, §328 I Nr.4, and under the bilateral Conventions, made no distinction between fraud, public policy or natural justice in the English sense of those terms.

To sum up the German procedural public policy position, the cases show that the German courts, except in the most extreme cases of a blatant violation of the rights of the defence,[496] are, almost without exception, unreceptive to arguments that the rendering Contracting State procedure breaches German public policy. Unlike the French courts, they do not demand compliance with national procedures which commonly, in the circumstances, simply do not exist in the foreign procedural system: this is only to be expected. To an almost overwhelming degree, the German courts proceed from the basis that all the Contracting States are placed by the Brussels Convention's jurisdictional and enforcement regime on an equal footing *inter se.* They accept that national procedural regimes regarding the parties, the evidence, and the assessment of damages will inevitably differ. There is absolutely no evidence of any kind of domestic debtor protectionism[497] under Article 27(1); quite the reverse. As the *OLG Saarbrücken*[498] observed in 1987:

> Abweichungen des Gerichtsverfassungs- und Verfahrensrechts des Erststaates von dem des Zweitstaates[499] vermögen auch deshalb grundsätzlich keine ordre-public-Widrigkeit zu begründen, weil sich die Gesetzgebung in allen Vertragsstaaten des GVÜ auf einem rechtsstaatlichen Niveau bewegt.[500]

---

[496] *BGH* in *Dieter Krombach v Andre Bamberski*; also *OLG Köln* 12.4.1989 IPRspr. (1989) Nr. 213, [1991] I.L.Pr. 483.

[497] *OLG Düsseldorf* (2000) *IPRax* 527 only seems to have ensured that the *remise au parquet* does not circumvent what has been held to be the mandatory nature of the 1965 Hague Service Convention; also now Henry LJ's views in *Knauf UK GmbH v British Gypsum Ltd and another* [2002] 1 WLR 907, CA esp. at p.921, that CPR 6.8(1) should *not* be permitted to circumvent the applicable international service agreements merely in order to secure 'first seisure' in England; also a similar view, it seems, *Phillips and others v Symes and another* [2002] 1 WLR 853, Ch.D., (Hart J).

[498] 3.8.1987 IPRspr. (1987) Nr. 156, at p.392.

[499] Yet, under Article 27(2), the German courts are more than ready to condemn these differences, often in foreign service requirements (esp. *remise au parquet*): *LG Hamburg* IPRspr. (1991) Nr. 205; *OLG Hamm* (1993) *IPRax* 395; *OLG Düsseldorf* (2000) *IPRax* 527; *BGH* IPRspr. (1993) Nr. 169 (post *Minalmet*) and the (often shorter) foreign procedures for preventing default judgments; *OLG Koblenz* (1988) *RIW* 476, *OLG Koblenz* (1992) *IPRax* 35; and esp. *OLG Düsseldorf* (1999) *RIW* 464; also *OLG Köln* 7.3.2001 (2001) NJW-RR 1576, where Italian service by such a method (when not permitted in similar circumstances under German law) held to amount to a breach of the right to a fair hearing.

[500] ('Discrepancies between the court procedure and civil procedure of the rendering and enforcing courts cannot in principle thereby found a breach of public policy because the legislation in all the Contracting States operates on the level of the rule of law.') 3.8.1987 IPRspr. (1987) Nr. 156, at p.392.

4.4.4(ii)   Material public policy[501]

Three German cases, one from 1983,[502] another[503] the post-reference decision in *Sonntag v Waidmann,*[504] and the *BGH* in 24.2.1999,[505] have dealt with defences based on German material public policy: all demonstrate the highest court's attitude to foreign judgments based on causes of action unknown to,[506] different from, or excluded/protected by,[507] domestic German law. In the first, the *Bundesgerichtshof* was confronted by a judgment of an Italian court in favour of an injured car passenger, a German, against both the German driver and the German car owner. The driver's negligence had caused an accident on an Italian motorway. Yet recovery of damages against the car owner in these circumstances, had the accident occurred in Germany, was much more limited under German law, than Italian. The court did not find a breach of material public policy. This would only occur when

> das Ergebnis der Anwendung des ausländischen Rechts zu den Grundgedanken der deutschen gesetzlichen Regelung und den in ihnen liegenden Gerechtigkeitsvorstellungen in so starkem Widerspruch stehen würde, daß es von uns für untragbar gehalten würde.[508]

The only obvious difference in this case from the post-reference decision in *Sonntag* (the second case), is that the cause of action against the vehicle's owner, although unknown, was not prohibited, (only limited) by a provision of national law, elevated to the status of public policy.

This elevation of domestic law occurred in the second case *BGH* 16.9.1993, the reference in *Sonntag v Waidmann.*[509] Here the *Bundesgerichtshof* refused to order enforcement of an Italian judgment on the ground that its effects would be to conflict with provisions of German public policy under Article 27(1).[510] As will be

---

[501] Kaye, 1987, at p.1442 believes that the entire raft of provisions that excludes the application of foreign law in the choice of law process will also be applicable under Article 27(1); Kropholler, 2002, at p.398, para. 17 following.

[502] *BGH* 22.6.1983, IPRspr. (1983) Nr. 176.

[503] *BGH* 16.9.1993, IPRspr. (1993) Nr. 178.

[504] *Volker Sonntag v Hans Waidmann and others* (C–172/91) [1993] ECR I–1963, left no room for doubt that a defence under Article 27(2) would fail because the German accused was adjudged to have 'appeared' (through his counsel) in the *partie civile* 'section' of proceedings in Italy.

[505] *BGH* 24.2.1999 (1999) *IPRax* 371, now reported in English [2001] I.L.Pr. 425; comment Schulze, G. (1999) *IPRax* 342.

[506] The earliest case.

[507] In *Sonntag v Waidmann*.

[508] ('the result of the application of the foreign law stands in such a marked contrast to the fundamental principles of the German legal order and the notions of justice contained therein, that it would be considered unsupportable for us.'), IPRspr. (1983) Nr. 176, at p.460; applied in *OLG Brandenburg* 27.8.1998 (1998) IPRspr. Nr.190, at p.386.

[509] IPRspr. (1993) Nr. 178, heavily criticised as to the result and the court's findings, by Haas, U. 'Unfallversicherungsschutz und ordre public' zu *BGH* 16.9.1993 *Volker Sonntag v Waidmann and others* (1995) *ZZP* 219.

[510] Care, Kaye *European Case Law on the Judgments Convention*, (ed. Kaye, P.), 1998, at p.548 'case principle' statement on case 521 needs careful reading.

remembered from the reference itself, the Waidmanns had obtained an Italian *partie civile* judgment against the German teacher, employed by the German State school, of which the deceased German schoolboy was a pupil. Certain provisions of German compulsory insurance law barred a (private) cause of action for a civil claim in damages between a state school pupil and (his) school, including its employees.[511] According to the court's findings, this exclusion in '§§636ff RVO gehört zum Inhalt der deutschen öffentlichen Ordnung,[512] weil er ein wesentliches Element des Gesamtsystems der gesetzlichen Unfallversicherung ist.'[513] Circumvention of this statutory exclusion by an action abroad would, it was felt, consist in an unacceptable affront[514] to German notions of domestic 'material' public policy.

In *BGH* 24.2.1999, Article 27(1) was (unsuccessfully) invoked before the German Supreme Court in order to avoid enforcement of a French judgment awarding payment under a guarantee. The initially successful French bank had taken the guarantee, according to the report, from a (young, commercially-inexperienced) French guarantor, now domiciled in Germany, for debts incurred to the bank by the guarantor's sister. In 'family' situations such as these—similar in many ways to English notions of undue influence,[515] reposing trust and confidence—the German Constitution and provisions of the BGB have been interpreted to ensure that there was equality of bargaining power between the guarantor/guarantee: that the bank must fully explain the nature of the guarantor's potential liability, and that the third party (principal debtor) had not exerted undue influence on the guarantor. After long deliberation the court eventually found that there had been no breach of the above provisions, so (on this occasion) public policy could not be invoked under Article 27(1);[516] but the case does demonstrate the German courts' receptiveness,[517] under national public policy, in considering arguments based on a potential breach of what could, in more extreme circumstances, have been certain consumer protection provisions—had the case been decided by a German court.

---

[511] Haas, (1995) *ZZP* 219, at p.225 and p.231.

[512] Haas, *ibid.*, disputes whether this provision is part of public policy, at p.237.

[513] ('Article 636 of the RVO [Federal Insurance Order] belongs to the category of German public policy, because it is a basic part of the overall system of compulsory accident insurance.').

[514] Haas, (1995) *ZZP* 219.

[515] *Barclays Bank Plc v O'Brien and another* [1994] 1 AC 180, HL, 'Class 2(b)' at pp.189–90 (Lord Browne-Wilkinson), where a creditor is put on enquiry when, *inter alia*, the (loan) transaction is not to the financial advantage of the surety; *C.I.C.B. Mortgages Plc v Pitt and another* [1994] 1 AC 200, HL; Treitel, G.H. *The Law of Contract*, 10th edn., 1999, esp. at pp.387–88.

[516] However, Article 27(2) denied enforcement, since the guarantor in default and his sister had been represented by the same lawyer, and the guarantor had not had a free choice in his counsel: *Berhandus Hendrikman and Maria Feyen v Magenta Druck & Verlag GmbH* C–78/95 [1996] ECR I-4943, below, at p.470.

[517] A useful weapon, according to Bruns, (1999) *JZ* 278, at p.279.

It is almost impossible to argue, and there is no real evidence, that the German courts are indulging in protectionism in the application of Article 27(1);[518] even if a hidden protectionist agenda is operating, the cause is not a mis-application of the provisions of the Convention. Article 27(1)'s traditional wording of 'public policy' permits considerable latitude for domestic manoeuvring, and cross-application of concepts traditionally employed under earlier Treaties. The German courts have shown restraint in the procedural sphere;[519] yet the material public policy section leaves the impression that a judgment (commonly) rendered under a different material law will be minutely scrutinised to ensure compliance with German substantive law,[520] applicable if the case had come before these courts on the merits.

4.5   THE BRUSSELS I REGULATION, AND THE DRAFT HAGUE WORLDWIDE JUDGMENTS CONVENTION

The Commission, in its first proposal[521] to the European Council in December 1997, had advocated omitting any reference to public policy.[522] In its accompanying communication[523] to the Council and European Parliament, aimed at a revision of the Brussels Convention, and the greater internal free circulation of European Union judgments, the Commission believed that public policy was an anachronistic stumbling block to the eventual erection of a European judicial area. It noted that changes were necessary to the current defences in Article 27 'and, in particular, the public policy ground, which does not sit well with the European integration process or the civil and commercial matters concerned here.'[524] This is as may be. But what is clear, and slightly alarming, in the *communiqué* is the standpoint from which these changes had been advocated. On page three of the report it was made clear that the Commission, in a sense, was still

---

[518] There are suspicions under Article 27(2), however: draconian view the German courts take towards 'due service' and the curing thereof—*OLG Karlsruhe* IPRspr. (1996) Nr. 174, *OLG Karlsruhe* (1999) *RIW* 538; and 'sufficiency of time', *OLG Hamm* IPRspr. (1987) Nr. 155, *OLG Köln* IPRspr. (1989) Nr. 213, [1991] I.L.Pr. 483; cf Jenard, Rép. Notarial, 1994, Tome XI, livre VI, 3e partie, 1994, at p.167 speaking of Germany as an enforcement 'fortress' under Article 27(2); on the temporally-limited shelf-life of 'due service' under Article 27(2) and Council Service Regulation 1348/2000, below at pp.507–510.

[519] The French courts appear to be stricter in their attitude to the reasoned judgment, above at p.408; likely German courts would deploy Article 6(1) ECHR in a *Pordéa c/ Times Newspapers Limited* situation, where an action had been halted due to inability of one party to satisfy a security for costs order; there is no real evidence of the blatant manipulation of Article 27(1) for protectionist ends in this situation.

[520] A worrying development therefore *BGH* (1999) *RIW* 457, 140 BGHZ 396.

[521] Commission's *Proposal for a Council Act establishing the Convention on Jurisdiction and Recognition and Enforcement of Judgments in Civil and Commercial Matters in the Member States of the European Union*, submitted on 22.12.1997, 31.1.1998, [1998] OJ C33/20, Article 37(a)(1)(1).

[522] Criticised by Bruns, (1999) *JZ* 278, at p.287.

[523] *Commission Communication to the Council and the European Parliament 'towards greater efficiency in obtaining and enforcing judgments in the European Union'* 31.1.1998, [1998] OJ C33/3.

[524] [1998] OJ C33/3, at p.9, para. 20.

blinkered by the problems in consumer litigation, and the fact that cross-border purchases of consumer goods are being heavily hampered by difficulties in the cross-border litigation process.

Removing public policy totally may well have been too draconian[525] a measure. From an overall impression of the cases in which it has been seen to succeed, there are only a handful of instances, mostly from France and Germany. For the avoidance of doubt, it would be far better, using explicit drafting, to remove from Article 27(1) those defences of a procedural nature that have proved to be so unsuccessful in the German courts, and have caused certain provisions of French law to be elevated to Convention-thwarting status. Concerns for basic principles of human rights—the right to a fair hearing—are, however, indispensable. To remove this aspect, as the ECJ has recently shown in *Dieter Krombach v Andre Bamberski*, weakens the potential defence of a right enshrined in Article 6 ECHR.

In the Brussels I Regulation, which will replace the Brussels Convention on 1 March 2002, public policy makes a re-appearance[526] in Article 34(1). Recognition in Article 33 will be refused—or, as in Article 45(1), the 'declaration of enforceability' shall be revoked—'if such recognition [sic] is *manifestly* contrary to public policy in the State in which recognition is sought'.[527] The addition of the adverb 'manifestly' brings the wording of the Article 34(1) defence into line with that of Article 5(1) of the 1966 Hague Convention, and as is evident from the explanatory memorandum accompanying the July 1999 Draft Council Regulation,[528] it is intended to 'underscore[] the exceptional nature of the public policy ground'.[529]

The exceptional nature of the current Article 27(1) has recently been emphasised in the ECJ's judgments and AGs' opinions in *SA Régie Nationale des Usines Renault v SpA Maxicar and Orazio Formento* and *Dieter Krombach*, where only 'en présence des cas extrêmes de violation de droits fondamentaux des parties'[530] may (procedural) public policy prevent recognition and enforcement. Since the decision in *Dieter Krombach*, Article 34(1) of the Brussels I Regulation will not represent any major change to the current practice under Article 27(1).

---

[525] As *BGH* 16.9.1993, IPRspr. (1993) Nr. 178, the post-reference decision in *Volker Sonntag v Hans Waidmann and others* (C–172/91) [1993] ECR I–1963, has demonstrated.

[526] No doubt an absolute abolition was considered a step too far.

[527] Draft in COM(1999) 348 final, 99/0154 (CNS), at p.45, added emphasis, now embodied in Article 34(1) Brussels I Regulation, [2001] OJ L12/1; for a pre-Convention view on the meaning of this adverb Niedermann, M. *Die ordre public-Klauseln in den Vollstreckungsverträgen des Bundes und den kantonalen Zivilprozessgesetzen*, 1976, at p.95 who sees it as a judicial reminder '[f]ür kleinlichen Chauvinismus ist kein Platz' ('there is no room for petty chauvinism').

[528] COM(1999) 348 final, 99/0154 (CNS), at p.22.

[529] Also the Economic and Social Committee of the EU's opinion on the draft proposed Regulation, [2000] OJ C–117/02, at para. 2.2.6—this has been done in any event in *Krombach*: *BGH* 29.6.2000 (2000) *RIW* 797.

[530] *Dieter Krombach v Andre Bamberski* (C–7/98), 28.3.2000, AG Antonio Saggio's opinion 23.9.1999, at para. 27.

As far as Article 28 of the October 1999 draft and the June 2001 Commission II interim text version of the Hague Worldwide Judgments Convention is concerned, public policy[531] has been split,[532] into what appears to be: (1) respect for 'procedural' public policy, in Article 28(1)(c)—'proceedings incompatible with fundamental principles of procedure';[533] (2) 'fraud',[534] under Article 28(1)(e); and (3) 'material' public policy, in Article 28(1)(f)—'manifestly incompatible with the public policy of the State addressed'.[535]

The fact that the defence has endured so long, and has manifested itself in so many international instruments, points to its importance, yet not to its

---

[531] As the Contracting States to the Brussels Convention would understand the term.

[532] Possibly due to US influence, which, in §4(a)(1)(2)(3) of the 1962 Uniform Foreign Money-Judgments Recognition Act (UFMJRA) has such separate, representative defences—as enacted by (currently) 29 States, the District of Columbia and the Virgin Islands; 13 Uniform Laws Annotated 263 (1986, and 2000 supplement); by way of example *McKinneys' Consolidated Laws of New York Annotated* CPLR §5304(a)(1) (New York, adopted 1.9.1970); Texas VTCA *Civil Practice and Remedies Code*, §36.005(a)(1) (adopted 17.6.1981); Illinois SHA 735 ILCS 5/12—627(a)(1)(2) (approved 15.7.1963); Weinschenk, F. *Die Anerkennung und Vollstreckung bundesdeutscher Urteile in den Vereinigten Staaten unter den „Foreign Country Money Judgment Recognition Acts'*, 1988, at pp.122–39, covering all representative defences; Kessedjian, C. *La reconnaissance et l'exécution des jugements en droit international privé aus Etats-Unis*, 1987, at pp.296–309; Brand, R., (ed) *Enforcing Foreign Judgments in the United States and United States Judgments Abroad*, 1992, at pp.17–18; Harder, E. *Die Anerkennung und Vollstreckung deutscher Urteile, insbesondere deutscher Ehescheidungsurteile und Schiedsprüche in New York*, 1967, at pp.96–102; Weintraub, R. *International Litigation and Arbitration, Practice and Planning*, 3rd ed., 2001, at pp.253–54.

[533] '[. . . [T]he [judgment results from] proceedings [in the State of origin were][|] incompatible with fundamental principles of procedure of the State addressed, [including the right of each party to be heard by an impartial and independent tribunal];][|]—drafting in brackets not agreed upon, but no doubt inspired by certain (US) State court examples of this defence, *Manches & Co. v Gilbey* (1995) 646 N.E2d 86 (Massachusetts MGLA c.235 §23A); *Dart v Dart* (1997) 568 N.W2d 358, appeal granted 586 N.W2d 744 (Michigan MCLA §691.1154(2)(b)); also Newman, L. 'Due process and the recognition of foreign judgments' (1995) *New York LJ* 3, esp. at p.7.

[534] 'Fraud in connection with a matter of procedure'; the current English approach to the latitude of the fraud defence had not been followed in Canada—*Beals et al v Saldanha et al.; Kelly, Third Party* 202 DLR (4th) 630 (2001), at pp.644–45

[535] For the reception of foreign (English libel) judgments in the US and public policy, esp. Minehan, K. 'The public policy exception to the Enforcement of Foreign Judgments—Necessary or Nemesis?' (1996) *Loyola Int'l and Comp. L.J.* 796, and *Bachchan v India Abroad Publications, Inc.* 585 N.Y.S.2d 661 (Sup.Ct., N.Y. County, 1992); *Telnikoff v Matusevitch* 702 A.2d 230 (1997) (*Maryland Code, Courts and Judicial Proceedings*, §10—704(b)(2)); Youm, K. 'The interaction between American and foreign libel law: US courts refuse to enforce English libel judgments' (2000) 49 *ICLQ* 131; also Müller, R. *Anerkennung und Vollstreckung schweizerische Zivilurteile in den USA*, 1994, at pp.116–25; *Southwest Livestock and Trucking Company, Inc. v R. Ramón* 169 F.3d 317 (5th Cir. 1999), esp. at p.321; Silberman, L. 'A different challenge for the ALI: Herein of Foreign Country Judgments, and International Treaty, and an American Statute' (2000) *Ind LR* 635, at pp.644–45 and n.68 suggests that a federal implementing statute may well develop a less parochial public policy standard (mirroring the US experience under the 1958 New York Arbitration Convention), and 9 U.S.C.A. §§201–307: *The Society of Lloyds v James Duncan Webb* 156 F.Supp.2d 632 (N.D.Tex.2001), at p.643; *Scherk v Alberto-Culver Company* 417 US 506, 41 L.Ed. 2d 270 (1974), *Parsons & Whittemore Overseas Co., Inc. v Societe Generale de L'industrie du Papier (RAKTA)* 508 F.2d 969 (1974), and *Fotochrome, Inc. v Copal Co., Ltd.* 517 F.2d 512 (1975); Superior Court of Justice, Ontario 7.3.2000 *The Society of Lloyd's v Paul F. Saunders* [2001] I.L.Pr. 217, at pp.230–34, (Swinton J).

widespread use. The approach of the French courts[536]—in censuring a perfectly legitimate foreign procedure by recourse to national considerations—is to be discouraged.[537] Only the most flagrant breach of the rule of law and/or fundamental human rights ought to suffice to activate the defence under Article 27(1).

4.6 CONCLUSION

Article 27(1)'s appearance represents a chink in the armour of mutual trust, equivalence and confidence[538] reputedly reposed in each Contracting State's civil and commercial procedure, and an undermining of the monolith edifice inaugurated by Title III of the Conventions.

The potential application of Article 27(1) in Germany, as in France, is rare, but to an extent, uncertain. While lip-service is apparently paid to notions of restraint, of respect for fundamental aspects of procedure and basic principles of the rule of law, isolated cases, normally unforeseen[539] in the rendering court, arise. Commonly they stem from cherished national views (which differ from those elsewhere in other Contracting States) to thwart the recognition and enforcement of judgments under Article 27(1). These instances are scarce, so their appearance tends to excite comment and disapprobation. What can be gleaned from the national cases, and from *Dieter Krombach*, is that a Contracting State should not be obliged to enforce a judgment that may potentially be in conflict with basic human rights, e.g. the right to a fair hearing under Article 6 ECHR;[540] conversely, differences in the procedure between the Contracting States and/or the (erroneous) decision-making process in one particular court ought not to provoke censure under Article 27(1) in another:[541] that one Contracting State may have misapplied its own law, whether or not *qua lex causae*, or even Community law, is irrelevant.

As to any evidence of (party or court) protectionism, it is impossible[542] to conclude that such is the motivation in any of the decisions, where Article 27(1) has been considered or applied. That judgment debtors have invoked the defence so

---

[536] The approach of the English courts to breaches of jurisdiction and arbitration clauses may well be counted herein.

[537] *Dieter Krombach v Andre Bamberski* (C–7/98), AG Antonio Saggio's opinion 23.9.1999.

[538] *De Bruyne c/ Collard* 1987 *Pas. Belge*, III, 80, Article 27(1) 'doit s'interpréter de manière *paticulière-ment restrictive* . . . en tenant compte de la *confiance réciproque* qui caractérise les relations' within the EU; also *Liège* (1996) *Act Dr* 80, at p.91.

[539] Note however, CA, 24.11.1999, *Johnson and another v Coburn*, (Kennedy LJ).

[540] *Ibid.*, at paras. 39–40; *Cour de Cassation* 16.3.1999 *Sieur Pordéa c/ Société Times Newspapers Limited* (1999) *JDI* 773, (2000) *Rev crit* 223, [2000] I.L.Pr 763.

[541] AG Alber in *SA Régie Nationale des Usines Renault* (C–38/98) [2000] ECR I–2973, at pp.2991–92.

[542] The only possible evidence is the post-reference case of *Sonntag v Waidmann*, *BGH* IPRspr. (1993) Nr. 178 (possible protection of State employee statutory insurance scheme) and *BGH* 24.2.1999 (1999) *IPRax* 371, [2001] I.L.Pr. 425 (possibly protection from undue influence).

unsuccessfully in Germany may either be a function of the restrictive legacy of a pre-Convention definition, and/or a recognition of the special enforcement atmosphere engendered by Title III. The article's elision with concepts derived from international instruments for the protection of fundamental human rights, may in future, if not already, lead to a conclusion of some degree of (justified) protectionism—yet the evidence suggests that Article 27(1)'s application would be uniform throughout the Contracting States,[543] even when applied in those circumstances in any one of them.

---

[543] Yet unimpeachable 'protectionism' from a breach of the Constitution in *BGH* 29.6.2000 (2000) *RIW* 797, *Krombach v Bamberski.*

5

Article 27(2)[1]

5.1 INTRODUCTION

ARTICLE 27(2) OF the Brussels and Lugano Conventions has proved to be a controversial[2] article in many respects: its intricacies have rendered it a potent defence[3] in some Contracting States, especially Germany, when quantitative comparisons are made as to the number of occasions the article is (successfully) invoked. The essential problem with the article, which will become readily apparent from this chapter, is the number, nature and complexity of its constituent elements,[4] together with the potential protean amalgam of 19 Contracting State default judgment procedures.[5]

Other problems associated with the article, which are peripheral in a sense, also create uncertainty, and an uneven application of such an important defence. Such

---

[1]   This defence currently reads as follows: 'where [a judgment] was given in default of appearance, if the defendant was not duly served with the document which instituted the proceedings or with an equivalent document in sufficient time to enable him to arrange for his defence'; for the future amendment in Art. 34(2) of the Brussels I Regulation, below.

[2]   The initially rather naïve position of the Swiss *Botschaft betreffend das Lugano-Übereinkommen über die gerichtliche Zuständigkeit und die Vollstreckung gerichtlicher Entscheidungen in Zivil- und Handelssachen vom 21 Februar 1990, Bundesblatt* Nr.16 Band II, 142 Jahrgang, 24 April 1990, p.265, at p.320, para. 234.2 that Art. 27(2) 'sollte eigentlich selten zum Zug kommen'('should rarely make its mark') certainly has not been realised. It is, without doubt, the most complex, and frequently invoked defence to recognition and enforcement under the Conventions: Kondring, J. *Die Heilung von Zustellungsfehlern im internationalen Zivilrechtsverkehr*, 1995, at p.324 and Fahl, C. *Die Stellung des Gläubigers und des Schuldners bei der Vollstreckung ausländischer Entscheidungen nach dem EuGVÜ*, 1993, at p.21.

[3]   The greatest potential danger in Art. 27(2) will be shown to be *a latent defect in service, especially in service according to the lex fori of the rendering court*. Such other mistakes may range from the representation allowed, in the document instituting proceedings, and especially regarding 'due service' (under the Hague Service Conventions)—may ultimately only become apparent in the enforcing court after the expense of trial; a plaintiff is then left with a *brutum fulmen*. Art. 20 Brussels Convention does not appear to have been successful in filtering out such mistakes; between 31.5.2001 and 1.3.2002, these dangers will potentially be perpetuated by, *inter alia*, Art. 7(1) Council Service Regulation 1348/2000, discussed below.

[4]   Note that Art. 34(2) of the Brussels I Regulation will cut out 'due' service altogether, but will introduce other problems of 'initiating appeals', below; as previously mentioned, an interregnum period until 1.3.2001 will see 'due service' under Art. 27(2) combined with a new service regime within the Member States (except Denmark) under Council Regulation (EC) 1348/2000 of 29 May 2000 on the service in the Member States of judicial and extrajudicial documents in civil or commercial matters [2000] OJ160/37, which came into force on 31.5.2001, (the 'Service Regulation').

[5]   For an overview of the setting aside procedure: Jolowicz, J. and van Rhee, C.H. (eds) *Recourse against Judgments in the European Union*, 1999.

particular non-exhaustive aspects[6] include[7] whether a recognising or enforcing court is to apply the article of its own motion;[8] the fact that, in its interpretation, it is merely, *pars pro toto*, a manifestation of a more general defence of the right to a fair hearing;[9] its historical progenitors in earlier bi-lateral conventions; and finally, of course, the proposed alterations on 1 March 2002 to Article 27(2) by Article 34(2)[10] of the Brussels I Regulation, and eventually by the Hague draft Worldwide Judgments Convention.[11]

After a number of preliminary matters have been touched on—notably the problems that have arisen historically with the defence in earlier bilateral instruments—Article 27(2) will be divided up in to its constituent elements, and an examination undertaken, where necessary, either of its effects on civil procedure in England and Wales, or (which is crucial) the perceived impression that some Contracting States,[12] for whatever reason, are making more use of the defence than others. At each juncture, the future text of the defence in Article 34(2) of the Brussels I Regulation, and draft Hague worldwide judgments Convention will be inserted and scrutinised in order to compare any changes to the current form of Article 27(2) that these will eventually herald.

---

[6] Also of note should be the *verbatim* changes wrought by Art. 27(2) on §328 I Nr.2 (German) ZPO, surely a sign of approbation in wishing to incorporate the wording and interpretation of Art. 27(2) into (German) autonomous recognition and enforcement law; and on Italian law, the new Art. 64 (1)(b) of l.31 maggio 1995, n.218, *Riforma del sistema italiano di diritto internazionale privato*, in *Le nuove leggi civili commentate*, N.5–6, Anno XIX, settembre-diciembre, p.877, at p.1460 following, esp. p.1473, as from 1.1.1997.

[7] For a breakdown into its constituent elements: 'in default of appearance', section 5.2; 'the document which instituted the proceedings', section 5.3; 'due service', section 5.4; and 'sufficient service', section 5.5, below.

[8] Not according to the *Cour de Cassation* 17.11.1999 *Mme T. c/ Mme H* (2000) *Rev crit* 52; cf Art. 27(1); Art. 41 of Brussels I Regulation makes it clear that the first instance court applied to cannot take this or any other Art. 34/35 defence into consideration.

[9] This has repercussions on the tension between, on the one hand, the plaintiff/claimant's (and Conventions') interest in the free movement of judgments, and on the other, the effective protection of a defendant's interests (in a fair hearing).

[10] The changes read as follows: 'where [a judgment] was given in default of appearance, if the defendant was not served with the document which instituted the proceedings or with an equivalent document in sufficient time and *in such a way as to enable him to arrange for his defence, unless the defendant failed to commence proceedings to challenge the judgment when it was possible for him to do so;*' the italicised words represent the innovation from the current version of Art. 27(2), effectively overruling *Firma Minalmet GmbH v Firma Brandeis Ltd* (C–123/91) [1992] ECR I–5661, but raising the profile of *Debaecker v Bouwman* (C–49/84) [1985] ECR 1779, esp. at p.1787, fn.10 (Advocate General Van Themaat) and necessitating the commencement of proceedings to set aside any default judgment.

[11] Art. 28(1)(d) of the October 1999 draft read: '. . . (d) the document which instituted the proceedings or an equivalent document, including the essentials of the claim, was not notified to the defendant in sufficient time and in such a way as to enable him to arrange for his defence;'.

[12] Especially Germany.

5.1.1 Article 27(2)'s historical origins

One does not have to look very far to find the historical progenitors of Article 27(2) of the Brussels and Lugano Conventions. Such a defence to recognition and enforcement, worded in more or less closely corresponding ways[13] has been a feature of many bilateral recognition and enforcement conventions; and even of various autonomous recognition and enforcement provisions of the Contracting States. Even a brief overview will show that many of the (interpretative) problems associated with Article 27(2) have quite a long provenance.

Among these bilateral Conventions concluded by the United Kingdom, which have a defence to registration of a judgment based on the due and adequate citation of a defaulting defendant are: with France, in Article 3(1)(b); with Belgium, in Article 3(1)(b); with The Netherlands, Article III(2)(b) and Norway, Article 3(2)(b).[14]

Of greater antiquity are: Article 17(2) of the *Traité franco-suisse* of 15 June 1869,[15] which required, *inter alia*, that the defendant be 'dûment cité[]'[16]; and Article 11(4)[17] of the *Traité franco-belge* of 8 July 1899, with slightly different wording, 'légalement cité[]'[18].[19]

The bilateral Conventions concluded between Germany[20] and Italy, Article 4(3); Belgium, Article 2(1)(2); Norway, Article 6(2)(1),(2); and Spain, Article 5(2)(1)(2),[21] all speak of a defendant not 'appearing in proceedings', of 'a

---

[13] Based on the need for an enforcing court to scrutinise whether the defaulting defendant's rights of defence were upheld by the rendering court—by correct/due summons before it in adequate time for a defence.

[14] Reciprocal Enforcement of Foreign Judgments Orders in Council with France, Belgium, the Netherlands and Norway, 1936, S.I. 1936/609, 1936 S.I. 1936/1169, S.I. 1969/1063, S.I. 1962/636, respectively.

[15] Convention between France and the Swiss Confederation respecting Jurisdiction and the Execution of Civil Judgments, 15 June 1869, 1869 *Cons. Treaty Series*, 329.

[16] ('duly served').

[17] Also Art. 11(4) of *Convention entre La Belgique et Les Pays-Bas sur la compétence judiciaire territoriale, sur la faillite, ainsi que sur l'autorité et l'exécution des décisions judiciaires, des sentences arbitrales et des actes authentiques*, Signée à Bruxelles le 28 Mars 1925, (1929–1930) *L.N.T.S.*, XCIII, 432, requiring a defendant to have been 'légalement cité[]'.

[18] ('legally served').

[19] An early example being *Weyl Frères et Cie c/ C.F. Freneys* 8.6.1910, 1911 *Pas. Belge*, III, 229 at p.230; Vroonen, E. *De la force extraterritoriale des jugements étrangers et des conditions extrinsèques de validité des actes étrangers en Belgique*, 1920, at pp.147–49, para.4; Weiss, A. *Traité théorique et pratique de droit international privé*, Librairie de la Société du Receuil, Paris, 1905, at p.657 onwards.

[20] These of all the provisions bear the closest similarities with Art. 27(2)—in some detail Linke, H. *Die Versäumnisentscheidungen im deutschen, österreichischen, belgischen und englischen Recht—Ihre Anerkennung und Vollstreckbarerklärung*, 1972, pp.127–31 (Austria); pp.134–37 (Belgium); pp.142–51 (England).

[21] Of 9.3.1936, (1937) RGBl., II, 145, in force 19.6.1937, and again (post-war) on 1.10.1952 until 1.2.1973—for an example under the Franco-Italian Convention Ropers, J.-L. 'La reconnaissance et l'exécution reciproque des décisions de justice à l'intérieur du Marché Commun' (1962) *JCP*, I, Doctr., 1679, at p.1679; of 26.6.1959, (1959) BGBl., II, 766, from 27.1.1961 until 1.2.1973; of 17.6.1977, 1981 BGBl., II, 342, in force 3.10.1981 to 1.3.1995; of 14.1.1987, 1987 BGBl., II, 35 between 15.1.1987 and 1.12.1994, respectively; and Karl, A.-M. *Die Anerkennung von Entscheidungen in Spanien*, 1993.

document initiating the proceedings', and 'sufficient time'.[22] Along similar lines are Austria's Conventions[23] concluded with France, Article 4(4);[24] Luxembourg, Article 4(4)[25] and Sweden, Article 4(e);[26] and Switzerland's concluded with Belgium, Article 1(1)(d),[27] Austria, Article 1(4),[28] and Germany.[29]

Of the autonomous laws, mention has already been made of the German autonomous recognition law §328 Nr.2 ZPO.[30] Of similar provenance, and in force between 1876 and 1970,[31] was Article 10(4) of the Belgian *Code de Procédure civile*, law of 25 March 1876,[32] which required that 'les droits de la défense [avaient] été respectés'.[33]

Much of the vast amount of caselaw and commentaries[34] generated under these Treaties and procedural codes is instructive, in view of the fact that certain issues relating to the interpretation of Article 27(2) of the Brussels and Lugano Conventions, have previously arisen under these older regimes. Of note here will thus be

---

[22] The German wording—'nicht eingelassen' , 'die den Rechtsstreit einleitende Ladung' and 'nicht oder nicht so (recht)zeitig' almost identical under these provisions to Art. 27(2).

[23] Linke, 1972, p.127 onwards.

[24] *Abkommen zwischen der Republik Österreich und der Französischen Republik über die Anerkennung und Vollstreckung von gerichtlichen Entscheidungen und öffentlichen Urkunden auf dem Gebiet des Zivil- und Handelsrechtes*, 1967 BBl, 288, refusing enforcement 'si le défendeur défaillant n'a pas pu avoir connaissance . . . *en temps utile'*—echoes heard now in Art. 27(2) 'in sufficient time'.

[25] *Abkommen zwischen der Republik Österreich und dem Großherzogtum Luxemburg über die Anerkennung und die Vollstreckung von gerichtlichen Entscheidungen und öffentlichen Urkunden auf dem Gebiet des Zivil- und Handelsrechtes*, 1975 BBl, 610.

[26] *Abkommen zwischen der Republik Österreich und dem Königreich Schweden über die Anerkennung und Vollstreckung von Entscheidungen in Zivilsachen*, 1983 BBl 556.

[27] *Abkommen zwischen der Schweiz und Belgien über die Anerkennung und Vollstreckung von gerichtlichen Entscheidungen und Schiedssprüchen*, 29.4.1959, AS 1962, 893, in force 15.10.1962.

[28] *Vertrag zwischen der Schweizerischen Eidgenossenschaft und der Republik Österreich über die Anerkennung und Vollstreckung gerichtlicher Entscheidungen*, 16.12.1960, AS 1962, 263, in force 12.5.1962.

[29] *Convention entre la Confédération suisse et le Reich allemand*, 2.11.1929 *Recueil Systématique des lois et ordonnances*, 1848–1947, 12ᵉ vol., 1953, at p.327, in force 1.12.1930.

[30] Noteworthy application, regarding the necessary content of 'the document which instituted proceedings': BGH 29.4.1999 (1999) *RIW* 698, (1999) *ZZP* 473, (2001) *IPRax* 230, Haas, (2001) *IPRax* 195—similarly aligned to Art. 27(2) (but must be pleaded); also the Swiss federal recognition and enforcement law, Art. 27(1)(a) IPRG and the rather generous case of 31.10.1996 *M.R. gegen A.SA und D Establishment* BGE 122, III, 439, at p.447; prior to this the individual Swiss Cantons had similar provisions; for a case illustrating the application of §323 Abs. 2(c) ZPO of the Canton of Solothurn ('gesetzlich vorgeladen' ('legally cited')), *Bundesgericht* 4.5.1979 *Lawrence Jusko gegen Fortis-Uhren AG* BGE 105 Ia, 307, at p.311.

[31] For the (present) Belgian autonomous recognition and enforcement regime see Art. 570(2) *Code judiciaire, Les Codes Larcier*, I, 1998, p.266, (a precise re-enactment).

[32] *Pasinomie, Collection complète des lois, décrets, arrêtés*, Quatrième Série, Tome XI, 1879, p.121, at p.130.

[33] *Cour d'appel de Bruxelles* 26.1.1906 1906 *Pas. Belge*, II, 129 and *Répertoire Décennal de la Jurisprudence Belge*, Tome 2ᵉᵐᵉ, 1900–1910, p.389 no.57; *Tribunal de Bruxelles* 9.1.1900, (1900) *Pas. Belge*, III, 157; Vroonen, E., 1920, at p.149.

[34] Readily accessible accounts for the modern reader, from the Swiss perspective, are Dutoit, Knoepler, Lalive, and Mercier *Répertoire de droit international privé suisse*, Vol II 1983 and Jellinek, Erstes Heft: Abhandlung, Zweites Heft: *Vertragstexte und Register*, 1953; Leresche, A. *L'Exécution des jugements civils étrangers en Suisse*, 1927, at p.34 onwards.

cases under Article 17(2) of the *Traité franco-suisse* of 1869 regarding service of the initiating document by the (currently controversial)[35] method of *remise au parquet:*[36] *Bundesgericht* in *Behrendt et Cie gegen Lehher*[37] and *Bröniman contre Soc. Universelle de Films.*[38] While not outlawing this type of service, the decisions show the courts having to come to terms with the sufficiency of the delay— between (internally fictitious) service[39] and judgment—that a party must have so as to be able to defend himself adequately. The above cases ruled that the time (*in casu* 1 month) to appear did not even begin to run until actual receipt by the defendant of the notice.[40]

A question which a Belgian court had to decide in 1930[41] under Article 10(4) of its law of 25 March 1876—and the Swiss *Bundesgericht* under Article 17(2) of the *Traité franco-suisse* 1869[42]—was the effect of a defendant's being represented before the rendering court by counsel not appointed, nor consented to, by him. This case gave the same answer as would the European Court many years later: that the rights of the defence had not been observed by allowing the defendant to be represented by a lawyer without[43] instructions from his/her client. In the latter, the court observed that

---

[35] Especially in Germany, *OLG Karlsruhe* 12.3.1999 (1999) *RIW* 538, [2001] I.L.Pr. 208, below, at pp.504–505 section 5.4.3(a) stating, *inter alia*, that such a method of service under French law is a breach of Art. 6 (now Art. 12) EC Treaty under Art. 27(2).

[36] This method has also been doubted in the Swiss-Italian Convention, *Répertoire*, Vol II, 1983, at p.222; certain German courts, via Art.27(2), have *refused* to permit such a method to circumvent the 1965 Hague Service Convention—*OLG Karlsruhe* 12.3.1999 (1999) *RIW* 538, [2001] I.L.Pr. 208; as has been mentioned, in *Knauf UK GmbH v Gypsum Ltd and another* [2002] 1 WLR 907, CA (reversing [2001] 2 All ER (Comm) 332, (David Steel J)), the Court of Appeal did not permit, in the circumstances, service of claim form on a German company's solicitors by alternative means *within* the jurisdiction, merely so as to steal a march on German party, and to obviate the need, initially, for protracted service under 1965 Hague Convention, below; *Phillips and others v Symes and another* [2002] 1 WLR 853, Ch.D., (Hart J): service (of document commencing Greek proceedings) *must* be in accordance with Art.IV of Protocol to the Brussels Convention (which in practice means the 1965 Hague Service Convention and supplementary agreements).

[37] Of 24.10.1912, AFT 38, I, 543.

[38] Of 23.6.1949, BGE 75, I, 146 at p.150 and p.152; (1952) *Rev crit* 98.

[39] The problems that postal service will later encounter with German courts under Art. 27(2) and the Hague Service Conventions can be seen developing in AFT 94 III, 35 and AFT 94, I, 235.

[40] The problems of international postal service had already been revealed under the 1899 *Traité franco-belge* in two French cases: *Trib. Civ de la Seine* 26.2.1924 *Meuter c/ Sander Van de Smet* (1925) *Rev Dr. Int. Privé* 63, at p.67 and *Trib Civ. De Lille* 11.12.1906 *Soc. Des Hauts-Fourneaux d'Anvers c/ Herbaumetz* (1907) *Rev Dr. Int. Privé* 394.

[41] *Trib. Civ., d'Anvers*, 10.7.1930 *Paul Buonasorte c/ Evrard Havenith* (1930) *Pas. Belge*, III, 149.

[42] *Dame Lanvin c/Dame Quellien* (1933) *JDI* 237 and which would surface again in the case of *Berhandus Hendrikman and Maria Feyen* v *Magenta Druck & Verlag GmbH* (C–78/95) [1996] ECR I–4943, reviewed below, section 5.2.2(d); and BGH 24.2.1999 (1999) *IPRax* 371, 140 BGHZ 396, now reported in English [2001] I.L.Pr. 425.

[43] In the Belgian case, the defendant had become disillusioned with his Italian counsel, and *withdrawn* instructions, *Buonasorte c/ Havenith* (1930) *Pas. Belge*, III, 149, at p.150; Vroonen, E., 1920, at pp.147–49.

[l]e fait que dame Quellien *paraît avoir été representée* dans l'instance par un avoué *constitué et jugée contradictoirement* ne suffit pas pour justifier l'exécution du jugement en Suisse.[44][45]

The problems of international service, and the absence of a translation affecting due service, surfaced in another early case of the Swiss *Bundesgericht* in 1924,[46] again under Article 17(2) of the same *Traité*. The French *citation*, written in French, was served on the Swiss defendant in a German-speaking Canton, without a translation. The court made it clear that had the defendant not 'cured' the defective service by accepting the document, it would not have been 'dûment citée' under Article 17(2).

Firma Minalmet GmbH v Firma Brandeis Ltd[47] has historical echoes in a decision of the Zürich *Cour de Cassation* in 1930, again under the *Traité franco-suisse*:

[i]l est dès lors sans importance que le défendeur ait omis d'utiliser les voies de recours que lui donne la procédure française du chef d'insuffisance du délai de comparution de l'irrégularité du mode d'assignation.[48][49]

A case which had to deal with the meaning of the phrase 'document which instituted the proceedings' is another from the Swiss *Bundesgericht* in 1976[50] *Pfister-Grüebler gegen Firma Obpacher GmbH*, under the 1929 Swiss-German Convention. There the court held that subsequent documents in the proceedings could not be subject to the 'due service' requirement, a conclusion that will prove a legacy in the German jurisprudence,[51] below.

What this brief historical excursus shows is that many of the problems that have surfaced with regard to Article 27(2)—in default of appearance, representation, service by *remise au parquet*, and appealing—are not new. That the drafters of the Conventions could not have foreseen that an almost *verbatim reprise* of the wording of earlier defences in bilateral conventions would not thereafter reveal similar problems under Article 27(2) is unlikely; that no clarification, until now,[52] was forthcoming is hard to comprehend.

Another issue of concern with the defences to recognition and enforcement is the relationship between Article 27(1), 'public policy' and Article 27(2).

---

[44] ('the fact that lady Quellien appears to have been represented at first instance by a selected lawyer and found to be *inter partes* does not suffice to justify enforcement of the judgment in Switzerland').

[45] (1933) *JDI* 237, at p.240, according to Leresche; the similarities with the facts of *Hendrikman* are surprising.

[46] *Geiger et Cie c/ Bigorre* 17.10.1924, (1926) *JDI* 1114.

[47] (C–123/91) [1992] ECR I–5661, with regard to the necessity of appealing in the rendering court.

[48] ('it is from then on unimportant that the defendant omitted to use the methods of appeal that French procedure affords on the basis of insufficiency of time for appearance and the mistake in the method of service').

[49] (1931) *JDI* 778, at p.779.

[50] 19.5.1976 BGE 102 Ia, 308, at p.311; also *Grabowsky gegen Bultot* 27.3.1979 BGE 105 Ib, 45, at p.47.

[51] Most recently in *BGH* 10.11.1998 (1999) *RIW* 295.

[52] On 1.3.2002, Art. 41(1) of the Brussels I Regulation will alter the position on initiating an appeal, and will delete the need for the problematic formalities of 'due' service.

5.1.2   The mutual exclusivity of Article 27(2) and Article 27(1)

As with so much of this area of the Conventions, a certain amount of controversy exists as to the exact position Articles 27(1) and (2) take *inter se*. It is clear they are both[53] a manifestation of the wider principle of the right to a fair hearing. Dicta[54] from the European Court have clarified the position of Article 27(2) vis-à-vis Article 27(1), but not *vice versa*. In *Berhandus Hendrikman and Maria Feyen v Magenta Druck & Verlag GmbH*,[55] AG Jacobs[56] used *Hoffman v Krieg*,[57] by analogy, to confirm that when Article 27(2) applies *ratione materiae*,[58] there is no call for reliance on (procedural) public policy in Article 27(1). Also quoted[59] by AG Jacobs was a section of AG Capotorti's opinion in *Établissements Rohr Société anonyme v Dina Ossberger*[60] to the effect that in Article 27(2), 'a *particular aspect*[61] of the rights of the defence has been ensured by the authors of the Brussels Convention by means of a provision other than that concerning public policy.'[62]

Here the problems start. If Article 27(2) is a 'subset' of the wider aspect of (procedural) public policy in Article 27(1), and Article 27(1) has no application in the very specific ambit of Article 27(2), does this mean that procedural irregularities outside Article 27(2)—where the defendant has 'appeared'—cannot be regulated by the enforcing court under Article 27(1)? In other words, does Article 27(2), and it alone, deal with procedural irregularities?[63] This view has been aired[64] in some quarters. Two recent cases, one from France, the other from Luxembourg, provide support for this rather startling standpoint of Article 27(2)'s exclusivity in procedural matters. In *Reichertz-Roth*,[65] the Luxembourg *Cour d'appel*, in the face of a defence to enforcement under both Articles 27(1) and (2) on the same facts[66] held that

---

[53] Art. 27(1) also covers substantive as well as procedural public policy, above, at pp.376–377.

[54] From a comparison of the relationship between Art. 27(3) and Art. 27(1) in *Hoffmann v Krieg* (C–145/86) [1988] ECR 645.

[55] (C–78/95) [1996] ECR I–4943.

[56] *Ibid.*, at p.4957–58, para. 56.

[57] (C–145/86) [1988] ECR 645.

[58] I.e. when a defendant is 'in default of appearance', below, at pp.455 *et seq.*

[59] [1996] ECR I–4943, at p.4958, para. 58.

[60] (C–27/81) [1981] 2431; the Commission's view, at p.2437, that Art. 27(2) makes it clear that only this article may censure the foreign procedure: 'Art. 27(2) constitutes the only ground based on an infringement of the rights of the defence for refusing to recognise a judgment.'

[61] *Quaere*, whether this aspect deals exhaustively with the rights of the defence?

[62] *Rohr v Ossberger* (C–27/81) [1981] 2431, at p.2444, para. 5.

[63] Cf the Commission's observations in *Rohr v Ossberger* (C–27/81) [1981] 2431, at p.2436 para. 2.

[64] *Maxwell Report*, *Report of the Scottish Committee on Jurisdiction and Enforcement*, 1980, at p.118; and Schmidt's view of the French jurisprudence, below, at p.444, in Schmidt, M.J. *Die internationale Durchsetzung von Rechtsanwaltshonoraren nach EuGVÜ, Lugano-Übereinkommen und anderen Verträgen*, 1991, at p.133; *contra*, post-*Dieter Krombach* observation in (2001) *JDI* 690, at p.696: 'l'article 27–1° est susceptible de relayer . . . l'article 27–2° qui ne protège que certains droits de la défense'('Art. 27(1) is likely to take over from Art. 27(2), that only protects certain rights of the defence').

[65] 17.7.1997, (1997) *Pas. Lux.*, 340.

[66] Enforcement of a German order for costs.

l'intention des auteurs de la Convention . . . ayant été de restreindre autant que possible le recours à l'ordre public, abstraction faite de 27-2 . . . le contrôle de la regularité de la procédure suivie à l'étranger au regard de l'ordre public . . . n'est pas autorisé par l'article 27-1.[67] [68]

A similar conclusion was reached by the *Cour d'appel de Paris* in *SA Eurosensory c/ Sté F.J. Tiefman B.V. et autre*:[69] outside Article 27(2)'s limited sphere, the foreign proceedings are not to be scrutinised under Article 27(1). Other French courts[70] have considered this issue. The *Cour d'appel de Paris*, in *S.A.R.L. Manubut Holding*[71] had to decide whether an alleged procedural irregularity[72] of an Italian court—outside the scope *ratione materiae* of Article 27(2)—had violated the rights of the defence. The court seemed to adhere to the view quoted above in the Luxembourg decision, that the only sanction possible at the recognition and enforcement stage for procedural irregularities[73] was under Article 27(2); public policy could not be invoked.

The French *Cour de Cassation* has clearly taken a different line. In *Société Polypétrol c/ Société générale routière*,[74] it used *both* Article 27(1) and 27(2) to chastise the same German judgment. For Article 27(2), and the rights of the defendant to be respected, it found that[75] the document instituting the proceedings should, 'par définition, contenir des indications suffisantes sur l'objet de la demande';[76] in addition, the judgment itself must contain sufficiently reasoned argument for the recognising/enforcing judge to gauge whether Article 28 [I] has been complied with:

[E]st contraire à la conception française de l'ordre public international la reconnaissance d'une décision étrangère non motivée[77] . . .[78]

---

[67] ('the intention of the framers of the Convention . . . having been to restrain as much as possible recourse to public policy, apart from Art. 27(2) . . . the control of the legality of the procedure followed abroad in regard to public policy . . . is not authorised by Art. 27(1)'.

[68] (1997) *Pas. Lux.*, 340, at p.342; also Kaye, 1987, at p.1441—this cannot now stand in the light of *Dieter Krombach*.

[69] 28.1.1994, (1994) *Dalloz*, IR, 66.

[70] Especially *Société Polypétrol c/ Société générale routière* 9.10.1991 (1993) *JDI* 157; (1992) *Rev crit* 516.

[71] *S.A.R.L. Manubat Holding c/ Société Impresa generale construzioni M.B.M Meregaglia* 2.10.1987 / *Betito c/ Société Deritex* 13.11.1987 (1989) *JDI* 100.

[72] The Italian court had relied on expert evidence in prior criminal proceedings to which the French company had not been a party.

[73] These would encompass, *inter alia*, mistakes in the procedural process of the *lex fori*, such as omissions in serving certain documents.

[74] 9.10.1991 (1993) *JDI* 157; (1992) *Rev crit* 516.

[75] (1992) *Rev crit* 516, at p.517.

[76] *Ibid.*; cf service of a 'generally endorsed/particularised' claim form in Commercial Court action, below, at p.481.

[77] ('It is contrary to notions of French public policy to recognise an unreasoned foreign judgment'). Except (from a principle of French autonomous enforcement law), where such reasoning appears from other documents, *aliunde*, that Art. 28[I] has been respected, above chapter 4, at pp.407–408.

[78] (1992) *Rev crit* 516, at p.517.

The court uses both articles in close juxtaposition,[79] Article 27(1) filling any lacuna in this case left by the rather limited sphere of Article 27(2).

Both German commentary[80] and case law support the wider view that Article 27(1), public policy, is applicable whenever there may have been a breach of procedure outside[81] the initial service of the document that instituted the proceedings. In *OLG Hamm*,[82] 28.12.1993, the question of the residual application of Article 27(1) was not sufficiently touched upon for any judicial standpoint to be extracted. The case merely re-iterated, at p.244, what is already known[83] that Article 27(1) does not intrude into an area already covered[84] by Article 27(2):

> Für das Stadium der Verfahrenseinleitung d.h. für die Eröffnung der Möglichkeit am Verfahren nach angemessener Vorbereitung teilzunehmen, stellt Article 27 Nr.2 ... jedoch einen Spezialtatbestand dar, der die Anwendbarkeit des Article 27 Nr.1 ... insoweit einschränkt.[85]

On 21.3.1990,[86] the *BGH* came to the same conclusion as the *Cour de Cassation* in *Société Polypétrol*, that Article 27(1) was to take a subsidiary, lacunae-filling function, *ensuring further compliance* with the right to a fair hearing:

> Soweit diesem Grundsatz durch *das sonstige Verfahren* nicht genügt worden ist, kann die Vollstreckbarerklärung nur aufgrund ... Article 27 Nr.1 ... abgelehnt werden.[87]

Certain earlier cases, *OLG Köln*[88] in 12.4.1989, for example, have showed the courts' using Article 27(1) and (2) in parallel. It would seem fanciful for an enforcing court to have to accept a flagrant breach of the right to a fair hearing otherwise impeachable under Article 27(1)—after due and timeous service—by the rather weak argument that the only aspect of procedural public policy that may be scrutinised under the Conventions would be under Article 27(2).

A further subsidiary issue, which has received greater comment on the Continent than in England and Wales is whether an enforcing court, and if so which court, can, or is in any position to raise the defences under Article 27, and in particular under Article 27(2).

---

[79] *Ibid.*, at p.159.
[80] Braun, S. *Der Bekagtenschutz nach Article 27 Nr.2 EuGVÜ*, 1992, at p.183.
[81] Roth, H. 'Herausbildung von Prinzipien im europäischen Vollstreckungsrecht' zu *OLG Saarbrücken* 3.8.1987 (1989) *IPRax* 14, at p.17.
[82] (1994) *RIW* 243
[83] From *Établissements Rohr Société anonyme v Dina Ossberger* (C–27/81) [1981] ECR 2431.
[84] *In casu*, the German defendant was held to have submitted to the French court.
[85] ('For the commencement of proceedings stage, i.e. opening the possibility of participation in the proceedings after adequate preparation, Art. 27(2) represents a special set of circumstances that limits Art. 27(1)'s application in this respect'), *OLG Hamm* 28.12.1993 (1994) *RIW* 243, at p.244.
[86] IPRspr. (1990) Nr. 207.
[87] ('As far as this principle is not fulfilled by *the remaining proceedings*, enforcement can only be refused on Art. 27(1) grounds'), IPRspr. (1990) Nr. 207, at p.430.
[88] IPRspr. (1989) Nr. 213.

5.1.3   Raising the defence of Article 27(2) by the court of its own motion[89]

This question which seems to have detained continental commentators unduly is the extent to which both[90] the first instance enforcing court,[91] in Article 32 and Article 34, and the first appeal court, in Article 36 and Article 37(1), must, of their own motion,[92] verify that the requirements of Articles 27 and 28 II have been complied with. The general consensus has it that at the initial *ex parte* application stage at least,[93] the examination[94] must be *sua sponte*. Before the first instance court, without the judgment debtor's participation, the verification, it seems,[95] is limited to formal compliance with certain documentary[96] evidence, which in itself, has been relaxed by *Van der Linden v Berufsgenossenschaft der Feinmechanik und Elektrotechnik.*[97]

This court's function, at this stage, is merely a reflection of the 'bedrock principle'[98] of the whole Convention, that recognition and enforcement goes almost automatically. Thus in England and Wales, registration can be completed, and conservatory measures granted,[99] merely on the production[100] of the certificates provided by Articles 46 and 47. To suggest that, at this stage, anything more than a cursory examination is undertaken—rather than second-guess what a

---

[89]   Note here that from 1.3.2002, Art. 41 of the Brussels I Regulation will allow recourse to this and any other 'defence' *only* at the 'appeal court' level, in England and Wales, therefore, before the High Court, Art. 43(2) and Annex III.

[90]   The question here is which court, if any, and at what stage of the enforcement process, must raise the defence under Art. 27(2) of its own motion.

[91]   A clear distinction in the hierarchy is not always made by the commentators; from *TSN Kunststoffrecycling GmbH v Jurgens*, QBD, 16.2.2001, Jack J, it is clear that it is the Art. 36/37 'appeal court' that is meant.

[92]   Only evidence at first instance is *LG Mönchengladbach* 20.7.1987, IPRspr. (1987) Nr. 154, below, at p.448.

[93]   For the appeal stage, Wiehe, H. *Zustellungen, Zustellungsmängel und Urteilsanerkennung am Beispiel fiktiver Inlandszustellungen in Deutschland, Frankreich und den USA*, 1993, at p.213.

[94]   The declaration of enforceability in the Art. 31 court 'shall' be given if the judgment creditor produces the Art. 46(1)(2) evidence and the Art. 47(1), (and if necessary the Art. 47(2)), documents; whether the applicant must state s (*quaere*, where?) that the judgment debtor may have a defence, under Art. 27(2) is doubtful; no indication to this effect is given in the witness statement/affidavit in support of the application for registration under s 4 CJJA 1982, and (now) CPR Sch.1 RSC Ord. 71 r.28.

[95]   A first instance court refusing to enforce on 'insufficient time' grounds is *LG Mönchengladbach* 20.7.1987 IPRspr. (1987) Nr. 154, at p.386; also statements in *OLG Frankfurt* 21.2.1991 IPRspr. (1991) Nr. 202, at p.424 and *OLG Koblenz* 10.6.1991 IPRspr. (1991) Nr. 207, at p.439, referring to the checking of Arts. 46 and 47 certificates only.

[96]   Arts.46 and 47; and in some detail Keßler, A. *Die Vollstreckbarkeit und ihr Beweis gem. Article 31 und 47 Nr.1 EuGVÜ*, 1998.

[97]   (C–275/94) [1996] ECR I–1393; relaxed some years prior to *Van den Linden* by the German courts: *OLG Köln* 10.2.1976 IPRspr. (1976) Nr. 164.

[98]   *Berhandus Hendrikman and Maria Feyen v Magenta Druck & Verlag GmbH* (C–78/95) [1996] ECR I–4943, at p.4957, para. 51, (AG Jacobs).

[99]   Art. 39.

[100]   Now CPR Sch. 1 RSC Ord.71 r.28(2)(a), (b) and (c) which allow a certain relaxation of the formalities too.

respondent/judgment debtor may possibly raise[101] in Article 36 appeal proceedings—would be to undermine the Convention's enforcement system. In England and Wales at least,[102] in (CPR Sch.1) RSC Ord. 71 rule 28, the belief that the Queen's Bench Division Master[103] will have sufficient evidence before him from the applicant's[104] affidavit[105] to be in a position to foresee what a judgment debtor may, in (any) appeal proceedings, subsequently raise, seems fanciful. Rule 28(1)(a) merely reproduces what formal documents are required[106] by Articles 46 and 47. The only possible section of Rule 28 that could give the slightest indication of the opponent's case is rule 28(1)(d)(i), where the deponent, in the affidavit, must state 'to the best of [his] information or belief . . . (i) the grounds on which the right to enforce the judgment is vested in the party making the application.'[107] This, it is submitted, is no more than a requirement for the judgment creditor to swear, how and why, the judgment creditor is an Article 31 'interested party', entitled to recognition and enforcement. The first instance court, apart from reviewing the adequacy of the documentary evidence in support of the application is simply not[108] in a position to take any stance on its merits. It cannot therefore raise a defence under Article 27(2) of its own motion. The court will only be aware, from Article 46(2) and CPR 1998, Sch. 1 RSC Ord.71 rule 28(1)(a)(ii), that it is being asked to enforce a default judgment; there would simply be no evidence before the (English) court so as to suppose that it will examine due service, or the sufficiency thereof.[109]

Although the commentators fail to make this important and obvious distinction between *ex parte* enforcement, and the appeal stage, when they speak of a court raising possible defences[110] of its own motion, it seems logical[111] to suppose that only the appeal stage can be meant. The number of decisions at the Article 37(1), first appeal level, bear witness to the fact that defences which

---

[101] Below, at p.448; there may be *no* information before the court for it to be able to predict what a defendant may raise in these appeal proceedings—a prime example is the *Sonntag v Waidmann* litigation, where a subsequent Art. 27(1) plea was ultimately successful.

[102] Not including the consideration that at this stage, the application is made *ex parte*.

[103] *Civil Procedure*, Vol 1, Spring 2001, 2001, at p.1275 onwards; CPR Sch.1 RSC Ord. 71 r.25 onwards—*TSN Kunststoffrecycling GmbH v Jurgens*, QBD, 16.2.2001 (Jack J).

[104] Or, more likely the deponent solicitor for the applicant.

[105] (CPR Sch.1) RSC Ord. 71 r. 28(1).

[106] And may be waived, in r. 28(2)(c) in any case.

[107] Prior to 26.4.1999, the *Supreme Court Practice*, 1998, at p.1348; Practice Form No.PF 159, affidavit para. 7 merely showed that the purpose of r.28(1)(d)(i) was correctly to identify the applicant for enforcement, nothing more: 'the right to enforce the Judgment is vested in the plaintiff on the grounds that the Court pronounced Judgment in his favour . . .'; there is no evidence to show this has changed under the CPR; Dutoit, Knoepler, Lalive and Mercier, *Répertoire de droit international privé suisse*, Vol II 1983, at pp.109–10.

[108] *Contra* LG Mönchengladbach 20.7.1987, IPRspr. (1987) Nr. 154, where the time period between service and hearing—4 days, with an intervening weekend—was so blatantly insufficient even from the documentary evidence as to warrant a dismissal.

[109] *Quaere*, a patently insufficient time between the date of service and date of judgment.

[110] Whether the position is the same for public policy, under Art. 27(1), is another matter, above, at p.424 chapter 4.

[111] From the points made in the preceding paragraph; *Cassation Wagner c/ Tettweiler* 9.11.1983 (1984) *Rev crit* 501: 'la cour n'était pas tenue de contrôler d'office la condition prévue à l'article 27–2 . . .'; also

appellant/judgment debtors thought worthy of being raised, were not considered *sua sponte* by the Article 32 first instance courts, at the *ex parte* stage.

The statistics of German decisions[112] show that the *Landgerichte* are, in the vast majority of cases, not raising the defences at all. In the approximately 71 reported *Oberlandesgericht*[113] cases on recognition and enforcement, the evidence that the lower courts are not raising defences, under Article 27(2), (of their own motion) will be demonstrated where a judgment debtor has successfully appealed[114] under Article 37(1) against the lower court's decision. This has happened in 26 cases. Of these, judgment debtors successfully appealed on Article 27(2) grounds in 22[115] of them.

There are, however, an isolated number[116] of German first instance decisions[117] which have considered of their own motion[118] whether to enforce on grounds other than missing certificates[119] in Articles 46 and 47. Two early[120] decisions of the *LG Hamburg*,[121] in 8.1.1975 and 20.3.1975 demonstrate this first instance court reviewing whether the document instituting the proceedings had been

---

Goetz, A. *Anerkennungshindernisse nach dem EuGVÜ, dargestellt unter besonderer Berücksichtigung der französischen Rechtspraxis,* Inaugural-Dissertation, Friedrich-Alexander Universität, Nürnberg, 1997, at p.131 following.

[112] The large number of these allow for statistics to be complied.

[113] The *Oberlandesgericht* is the first appeal court under Art. 37(1).

[114] 8 *Oberlandesgericht* cases, under Art. 40, show that the *Landgerichte* had refused to enforce at first instance.

[115] *OLG Köln* 10.2.1976 IPRspr. (1976) Nr. 164; *OLG Stuttgart* 16.8.1977 IPRspr. (1977) Nr. 149; *OLG Hamm* 12.12.1977 (1980) *RIW/AWD* 62; *OLG Düsseldorf* 4.4.1978 (1979) *RIW/AWD* 570; *OLG Hamm* 10.9.1979 IPRspr. (1979) Nr. 203; *OLG Stuttgart* 3.2.1983 IPRspr. (1983) Nr. 173; *OLG Düsseldorf* 13.12.1984 IPRspr. (1984) Nr. 182, [1986] E.C.C. 478; *OLG Koblenz* 25.2.1987 (1988) *RIW* 476; *OLG Hamm* 3.8.1987, IPRspr. (1987) Nr. 155; *OLG Hamm* 27.11.1987 IPRspr. (1987) Nr. 159; *OLG Köln* 25.5.1990 IPRspr. (1990) Nr. 199; *OLG Frankfuhrt* 21.2.1991, IPRspr. (1991) Nr. 202; *OLG Düsseldorf* 10.6.1992 IPRspr. (1992) Nr. 221; *OLG Hamm* 25.9.1992 (1993) *IPRax* 395; *OLG Saarbrücken* 1.10.1993 (1995) *IPRax* 35; *OLG Köln* 20.4.1995 IPRspr. (1995) Nr. 172; *OLG Düsseldorf* 23.8.1995 IPRspr. (1995) Nr. 168; *OLG Düsseldorf* 2.9.1998 (1999) *RIW* 464; *OLG Karlsruhe* 12.3.1999 (1999) *RIW* 538, [2001] I.L.Pr. 208; *OLG Düsseldorf* 11.10.1999 (2000) *RIW* 230; *OLG Düsseldorf* 29.11.1999 IPRspr. (1999) Nr. 164, (2000) *IPRax* 527, [2002] I.L.Pr. 71; *OLG Düsseldorf* 8.11.2000 (2001) *RIW* 143.

[116] However, this relatively low figure suggests that apart from reviewing the adequacy of the Arts. 46/47 certificates, the German first instance courts are not reviewing, of their own motion, Art. 27(2) as a substantive due and sufficient service defence.

[117] *LG Hamburg* 8.1.1975 IPRspr. (1975) Nr. 160; *LG Hamburg* 20.3.1975 IPRspr. (1975) Nr. 162.

[118] *OLG Koblenz* 10.6.1991 IPRspr. (1991) Nr. 207 reported in English at [1993] I.L.Pr. 289, at p.293: 'The absence of the necessary documents (Arts. 33(3), 46 and 47 . . .) is also a ground for refusal. The court of the State of enforcement has to consider *of its own motion* whether there are grounds for refusal under the above-mentioned provisions.'

[119] For rejection on the ground of a lack of certificates, *LG Münster* 21.6.1978 IPRspr. (1978) Nr. 153 at p.369; also the first instance decision reported by the *OLG Köln* 10.2.1976 IPRspr. (1976) Nr. 164.

[120] The fact of being transitional cases under Art. 54 I, may have had a bearing on these cases.

[121] 8.1.1975 IPRspr. (1975) Nr. 160, at p.392: 'Anerkennungshindernisse im Sinne von Art. 27, 28 GVÜ, die eine Vollstreckbarerklärung gemäß Art. 34 II entgegenstehen, sind nicht ersichtlich' ('there are obviously no barriers to enforcement in the sense of Art. 27, 28 that prohibit enforcement according to Art. 34 II'); same conclusion *LG Hamburg* 20.3.1975 IPRspr. (1975) Nr. 162.

served in sufficient time or not. A lone example that supports those commentators' view that the Article 31/32 court, on the *ex parte* application, must examine the pre-requisites of Article 27(2) of its own motion is the *LG Mönchengladbach*.[122] Here the court did find that insufficient time[123] had been given to a German defendant in order for him to prepare for his defence in The Netherlands. The only explanation for this case can be that this information must have been *prima facie* evident from the Article 46 and 47 certificates, and the time so blatantly inadequate, as to call the court's attention to this fact. Whatever the cause, the court is clearly reviewing the adequacy of service. This is normally associated with grounds for rejecting enforcement by an *Oberlandesgericht*, Article 37(1) appeal court.

When commentators therefore speak of a court raising the Article 27(2) defence of its own motion, the case law of the *OLG* appeal courts logically shows that only the Article 36, 37 appeal court level can be meant. Otherwise the first instance courts would have rejected applications for enforcement in a much higher proportion of cases, and at an earlier stage. Fahl[124] disagrees, but the empirical evidence contradicts his assertion.[125] Paetzold[126] is imprecise about the exact stage she is referring to when she speaks of a court raising the Article 27(2) defence of its own motion. Wiehe[127] is more specific:

> Im Vollstreckungsverfahren erster Instanz ohne Anhörung des Urteilschuldners gemäß Article 34 Abs.1 . . . sei von Amts wegen zu prüfen,[128] während es im kontradiktorischen Beschwerdeverfahren der Article 36,40 . . . einer Rüge bedürfe.[129]

A statement by AG Jacobs in *Berhandus Hendrikman and Maria Feyen v Magenta Druck & Verlag GmbH,*[130] in this regard, merits closer attention. In this case the defendants were held not to have 'appeared' in ostensibly *inter partes* proceedings before a German adjudicating court, despite the fact that they had been represented—without their knowledge or approval—in those proceedings. In circumstances such as these, according to the Advocate General, the court[131] may be required 'to undertake a comparable preliminary appraisal . . . to ascertain whether the provision [Article 27(2)] applies'.[132] This language does suggest that a *sua sponte* investigation, at some stage of enforcement proceedings, is warranted.

---

[122] 20.7.1987, IPRspr. (1987) Nr. 154.

[123] 4 days.

[124] Fahl, 1993.

[125] *Ibid.*, at p.53.

[126] Paetzold, V. *Vollstreckung schweizerischer Entscheidungen nach dem Lugano-Übereinkommen in Deutschland,* 1995, at p.21, para. 5.

[127] Wiehe, 1993, at p.213.

[128] This, it is submitted must be wrong; common sense and the statistics show it to be.

[129] ('*ex parte* enforcement proceedings at first instance, in Art. 34(1), must be tested of its own motion, while an objection is necessary in the *inter partes* appeal proceedings in Art. 36/40') Wiehe, 1993, at p.213.

[130] (C–78/95) [1996] ECR I–4943.

[131] Again, he does not specify which court, but could be taken to mean either.

[132] (C–78/95) [1996] ECR I–4943, at p.4955, para. 39.

On this procedure, Article 41 of the Brussels I Regulation will have a welcome clarifying impact. Under this article, the focus of defences to enforcement proceedings will shift squarely up the court hierarchy to the appeal court level. The current first instance court under the Brussels Convention will, in future,[133] be deprived under Article 41 of any review of the merits of the application, and confined to a mere administrative function: '[t]he judgment shall be declared enforceable immediately on completion of the formalities in Article 53 without any review under Articles 34 and 35.'

5.1.4   The equipoise between a judgment creditor's and debtor's interests, and the right to a fair hearing

Both Article 27(1) and (2) protect the defendant/judgment debtor's rights to a fair hearing. Article 27(1) is said to do so only in 'exceptional circumstances'.[134] Article 27(2), however, due partly to the interpretation it has received from the European Court of Justice, and, in addition, its links to supplementary conventions[135] on service abroad of judicial documents—as we shall see—has become a potent weapon[136] in avoiding recognition and enforcement of judgments (particularly in Germany). The article represents a direct attack on the very purposes of the Brussels and Lugano Conventions—the free movement of judgments throughout the EU and (the remaining) EFTA States. Two competing principles are thus vying for ascendancy within the Convention—the interests of a plaintiff/judgment creditor in seeing the fruits of his litigation realised, and of a defendant/judgment debtor's right to receive a fair hearing.

The feeling obtained from reading the Court of Justice[137] (and German) cases strongly suggests that the latter's rights have gained the upper hand. There is an overwhelming impression that Article 27(2) has been favourably interpreted against the background[138] of the defendant's right to a fair hearing. Whenever an

---

[133] The competent first instance authority will remain the same, Art. 39(1) of the Brussels I Regulation, and Annex II.

[134] Jenard Report, (lip service only) OJ [1979] C59/1, as various cases have refused on this ground, above, at pp.428–429 and now *SA Régie Nationale des Usines Renault v SpA Maxicar and Orazio Formento* (C–38/98) [2000] ECR I–2973, *Dieter Krombach* (C–7/98) unreported, 28.3.2000.

[135] Section 5.4 on 'due service', below, at p.492; now, except *vis-à-vis* Denmark, Council Service Regulation 1348/2000.

[136] Cf Schack, H. *Internationales Zivilverfahrensrecht*, 2.Auf., 1996, at p.328, para. 842; comments in the explanatory memorandum (to the July 1999 proposal for the Council Regulation (EC)—Art. 27(2) will be modified by Art. 34(2) of the Brussels I Regulation to 'avoid abuses of procedure', at http://europa.eu.int/comm/sg/tfjai/unit/unit3_en.htm, at p.22.

[137] *Isabelle Lancray S.A. v Firma Peters und Sickert KG* (C–305/88) [1990] ECR I–2725, the cumulative interpretation of Art. 27(2), and allowing the defendant to send back the writ/claim form to the adjudicating court; and *Firma Minalmet GmbH c. Firma Brandeis Ltd* (C–123/91) [1992] ECR I–5661, unnecessary to institute an appeal, even if time to do so in Contracting State of origin.

[138] Recently, *Berhandus Hendrikman and Maria Feyen v Magenta Druck & Verlag GmbH* (C–78/95) [1996] ECR I–4943, has continued the trend, at p.4966, para. 15.

interpretation more beneficial to plaintiffs/claimants[139] could be applied, it is abandoned[140] in the interests of a fair hearing. The jurisprudence of the ECJ frequently invokes this wider principle: it is evident[141] in the time[142] between service of the document instituting the proceedings and the adjudicating court's rendering a judgment capable of being enforced under the Convention.[143] This attitude is clear in the statement in *Debaecker v Bouwman*[144] that the aim[145] of the free movement of judgments 'cannot . . . be attained by undermining *in any way* the right to a fair hearing.'[146] More generally, in *Bernard Denilauer v S.n.c. Couchet Frères*[147] and *Hengst Import BV v Anna Maria Campese*,[148] it is observed that the entire Convention has a defence-orientated bias:

> Title II . . . and III on recognition and enforcement manifest an intention to ensure that, within the scope and objectives of the Convention, proceedings culminating in judicial decisions are conducted in such a way that the rights of the defence are observed.[149]

The respect for such rights extends[150] to having a lawyer of the defendant's own choice and appointment representing him before the foreign tribunal; in default of which 'such a person is quite powerless to defend himself.'[151]

It is against this background[152] that the interpretation[153] of Article 27(2) must

---

[139] For example the necessity of appealing in the country of origin, as in *Firma Minalmet GmbH v Firma Brandeis Ltd* (C–123/91) [1992] ECR I–5661—compare the attitude of this case to that under Art.2(2)(a)(b) of the German-Austrian Convention of 6 June 1959, in Geimer and Schütze, *Internationale Urteilsanerkennung*—Band. II, 1971, at p.100.

[140] *Hendrikman v Magenta Druck* [1996] ECR I–4943, at p.4966–67, paras. 16–17.

[141] In that this period is seen as the best, and perhaps only, time, from a procedural point of view, for a defendant to defend himself.

[142] Paramount and inviolate, *Firma Minalmet GmbH v Firma Brandeis Ltd* (C–123/91) [1992] ECR I–5661, at p.5679, para. 19.

[143] *Peter Klomps v Karl Michel* (C–166/80) [1981] ECR 1593, at p.1605, paras. 7 and 9.

[144] (C–49/84) [1985] ECR 1779.

[145] The provisions of the Brussels Convention, we are told, are designed to ensure that the defendant's rights are effectively protected: *Pendy Plastic Products BV v Pluspunkt Handelsgesellschaft GmbH* (C–228/81) [1982] ECR 2723, at p.2736, para. 13.

[146] (C–49/84) [1985] ECR 1779, at p.1796, para. 10; and *Isabelle Lancray S.A. v Firma Peters und Sickert KG* (C–305/88) [1990] ECR I–2725, at p.2748, para. 21.

[147] (C–125/79) [1980] ECR 1553.

[148] (C–474/93) [1995] ECR I–2113.

[149] *Ibid.*, at p.2127, para. 16.

[150] No criticism is intended; it is merely illustrative.

[151] *Berhandus Hendrikman and Maria Feyen v Magenta Druck & Verlag GmbH* (C–78/95) [1996] ECR I–4943, at p.4967, para. 18—with an uncertain ambit, Briggs, A. (1996) *YEL* 601, at p.608; *BGH* 24.2.1999 (1999) *RIW* 457, 140 BGHZ 396, (1999) *RIW* 536, (1999) *IPRax* 371, [2001] I.L.Pr. 425, at p.432 (solicitor not instructed by defendant).

[152] *Société Polypétrol c/ Société générale routière* 9.10.1991 (1992) *Rev crit* 516, at p.517: 'l'acte introductif d'instance . . ., *doit, par définition*, contenir des indications suffisantes sur l'objet de la demande, à défaut desquelles les droits de la défense ne sont pas respectés' ('the document which began the proceedings . . . must by definition contain sufficient particulars of the subject-matter of the claim, in default of which the right to a fair hearing has not been safeguarded'), translation from English report in [1993] I.L.Pr. 107, at p.108, para. 4.

[153] The four sections, on, respectively, 'in default of appearance', 'the document which instituted the proceedings', 'due service' and 'in sufficient time'.

be viewed. Commentators have made the point[154] that two competing interests are at work in the Convention, and the European Court of Justice has a difficult task in balancing[155] them together.

Geimer, an ardent supporter of a judgment's enforceability in practically every aspect of Article 27's interpretation,[156] naturally feels the balance has unjustifiably inclined towards (indolent) defendants;[157] so too does Jenard:[158]

> On peut constater que la cour a de plus en plus nettement pris position en faveur du défendeur défaillant . . .[159][160]

Others are more forthright,[161] arguing that the Convention's aim of ensuring the free movement of judgments is simply no longer an 'entscheidendes Auslegungskriterium'[162] in the interpretation of Article 27(2),

> und dadurch den *gleichrangigen* Justizgewährungsanspruch des Klägers in unvertretbarem Ausmaß beeinträchtigt hat.[163]

An unsatisfactory aspect of the defence in Article 27(2)—which will receive at least some curative attention[164] in Article 34(2) of the Brussels I Regulation—is the current necessity, or lack of it, incumbent on a defaulting defendant to take any steps—even after being advised of, or served with, a judgment in default—to seek to have it set aside. This aspect will be discussed presently.

5.1.5   The necessity of 'appealing'[165] against the default judgment in the state of origin under Article 27(2)?

The final section to be dealt with here, before the constituent elements of Article 27(2) are dealt with in greater detail, will do nothing to dispel the impression that

---

[154] Braun, 1992, at p.39: 'neben dem Beklagtenschutz auch die Freizügigkeit der ausländischen Entscheidungen bezweckt, muß der Umfang des Beklagtenschutzes stets im Bezug zu dem Klägerinteresse an erleichterter Anerkennung gestezt werden.' ('Being aimed equally at the rights of the defence, as much as the free movement of foreign judgments, the scope of the rights of the defence must always be seen in relation to the plaintiff's interest in easier recognition').

[155] The comment of AG Jacobs in *Hendrikman* v *Magenta Druck* (C–78/95) [1996] ECR I–4943, at p.4952, para. 31: 'the proper balance to be struck'.

[156] He has traditionally always been so, Geimer and Schütze, Band. II, 1971, at p.88.

[157] Geimer and Schütze, *Europäisches Zivilverfahrensrech, Kommentar zum EuGVÜ und Lugano-Übereinkommen*, München, 1997, at pp.470–71.

[158] Jenard, P. *La Convention de Bruxelles du 27 septembre 1968 et ses prolongements*, Rép. Notarial, 1994, Tome XI, livre VI, 3e partie, at p.466.

[159] ('We must admit that the court has increasingly taken a position in favouring a defendant in default').

[160] Jenard, P. *ibid.*, at p.466.

[161] Schmidt-Parzefall, T. *Die Auslegung des Parallelübereinkommens von Lugano*, 1995, at pp.51–52.

[162] ('a decisive interpretative method'), *ibid.*, at p.52.

[163] ('and thereby has prejudiced, to an unjustifiable extent, the plaintiff's equally valid right to justice'), *ibid.*

[164] For new problems created by Art. 34(2), below.

[165] Or, more accurately, take steps to have the default judgment set aside— Jolowicz, J. and van Rhee, C.H. (eds) *Recourse against judgments in the European Union*, 1999 above, at p.437.

Article 27(2), in its current form, is inclined towards protecting recalcitrant and/or indolent defendants.

Many years prior to *Firma Minalmet GmbH v Firma Brandeis Ltd*,[166]—which decided that a defaulting defendant did not have to 'appeal' against the default judgment in the state of origin for Article 27(2) to apply—the German courts had unilaterally[167] come to a similar conclusion.[168] In *OLG Stuttgart*, on 16.8.1977,[169] an Italian default judgment, of which enforcement was sought, was successfully resisted on the grounds of Article 27(2), lack of due service. The judgment creditor argued, on the basis of, and by analogy with, a provision[170] in a 1962 bilateral recognition and enforcement convention between Germany and The Netherlands,[171] that due/defective service could be cured by the fact that the judgment debtor had not 'appealed' on this, or any other, ground to the Italian adjudicating court. The *OLG*, like the European Court in *Minalmet*, was unimpressed by this isolated[172] concession[173] to a judgment creditor:

> Diese Regelung kann jedoch entgegen der Ansicht von Geimer[174] nicht als Ausdruck eines allgemeinen Rechtssatzes . . .[175]

The absence from the Brussels Convention's Article 27(2) of any necessity to take action in the adjudicating court encouraged the *OLG Hamm*, on 10.9.1979,[176] in its view that the requirements of due and timely service were cumulative. The German appeal court in *Minalmet* itself did not take a position on the question of appeals because it found[177] that service had been due, and in sufficient time. Prior

---

[166] (C–123/91) [1992] ECR I–5661; although, as early as 1978, the German courts had been troubled by the issue in the withdrawn case: *Prost-International SARL v Firma Sägemühle Emil Brodbeck* (C–254/78) [1978] OJ C311/16, removed on 13.12.1978 [1979] OJ C35/13.

[167] For another anticipatory judgment—this time *Isabelle Lancray S.A. v Firma Peters und Sickert KG* (C–305/88) [1990] ECR I–2725—*OLG Hamm* 12.12.1977 (1980) *RIW/AWD* 62, and *OLG Hamm* 10.9.1979 IPRspr. (1979) Nr. 203.

[168] Also Braun, 1992, at p.167.

[169] IPRspr. 1977 Nr. 149.

[170] Art. 2(c)2: 'dies [the defence similar to Art. 27(2) Brussels Convention] gilt jedoch nicht, wenn der Kläger nachweist, daß der Beklagte gegen die Entscheidung keinen Rechtsmittel eingelegt hat, obwohl er von ihr Kenntnis erhalten hat.'('this does not apply when the plaintiff proves that the defendant has not lodged an appeal against the decision, although he has knowledge of it.').

[171] *Vertrag zwischen der Bundesrepublik Deutschland und dem Königreich der Niederlande über die gegenseitige Anerkennung und Vollstreckung gerichtlicher Entscheidungen und anderer Schuldtitel in Zivil- und Handelssachen* 30 August 1962, BGBl 1965, II, 27.

[172] Also a similar 'defence' in Art. 10(6) of the Hague Convention on the Recognition and Enforcement of Foreign Judgments in civil and commercial matters, and supplementary protocol, 1.2.1971.

[173] Its omission from the Brussels Convention's Art. 27(2) showed the exact opposite must have been intended.

[174] Geimer and Schütze, 1997, who have still clung to this view today.

[175] ('this rule cannot, despite Geimer's view, be taken as an expression of a general legal principle') in *OLG Stuttgart* 16.8.1977 IPRspr. (1977) Nr. 149, at p.439.

[176] *OLG Hamm* 10.9.1979 IPRspr. (1979) Nr. 203.

[177] As the *BGH*, the referring court in *Minalmet v Brandeis*, informs us BGH 4.4.1991 IPRspr. (1991) Nr. 203.

to the European Court's decision in *Minalmet*, however, the *OLG Düsseldorf*[178] thought that allowing the necessity of an appeal to restrict the application of Article 27(2) would eventually lead to an undermining of the service requirements of the adjudicating court—an intolerable position, so long as the judgment debtor could be informed *ex post facto* of the judgment and could 'appeal', no harm would be done to the rights of the defence.[179]

Geimer's view, as we know, is very much in the minority, in the face of domestic decisions, *Minalmet* itself, and now AG Jacobs in *Berhandus Hendrikman and Maria Feyen* v *Magenta Druck & Verlag GmbH*.[180]

Fortunately, changes to Article 27(2) of the Brussels Convention will occur on 1st March 2002, in Article 34(2) of the Brussels I Regulation, where the necessity of initiating an action to challenge the default judgment has been introduced, as a pre-requisite for reliance on the sufficiency of service,[181] and probably even the defence in general. It is worded as a condition precedent[182] thus:

> unless the defendant failed to commence proceedings to challenge the judgment when it was possible for him to do so.[183]

In conclusion, even before the constituent elements of the defence are examined in greater detail, the impression may be gained that Article 27(2) is a powerful weapon in a defaulting defendant's armoury.[184] The uncertainty over its precise ambit and—it will be shown—the technical nature of the defence, relying as it does on the vicissitudes of 'due', international service, contribute to its complexity. The balance of competing aims—of the rights of defence and the free movement of judgments—seems to have come down firmly on the side of a defaulting defendant (esp. in Germany).

---

[178]   *OLG Düsseldorf* 10.6.1992 IPRspr. (1992) Nr. 221.

[179]   *Ibid.*, at p.538.

[180]   (C–78/95) [1996] ECR I–4943, at p.4967, para. 20; also at p.4955, para. 10

[181]   The current requirement of 'due' service has been omitted; Art. 28(1)(d) of the June 2001 draft interim text of the Hague Worldwide Judgments Convention does not mention any necessity for 'appealing' against any default judgment—for the changes, see section 5.2.1(ii), below.

[182]   Béraudo, (2001) *JDI* 1033, at p.1072, para.57.

[183]   Art. 34(2), final sub-clause—the effects of which are dealt with below, at pp.461–465, section 5.2.1(ii)—note also now the provision in Art. 19(4) Council Service Directive 1348/2000 of 29 May 2000 [2000] OJ 160/37, in force 31.5.2001, allowing a defaulting defendant to appeal out of time if certain conditions are met from the date of the default judgment; for the various time limits within which this may be possible, the information communicated under Art. 23 of Council Regulation (EC) (No 1348/2000), [2001] OJ C151/4 should be consulted, and below at p.464.

[184]   There is insufficient case law in the UK to form a view in this jurisdiction, but German section below, at pp.494 *et seq.*

5.2   IN DEFAULT OF APPEARANCE[185]

For the Article 27(2) shield to be effective *ratione materiae*, it is essential the judgment be given in proceedings to which the defendant was 'in default of appearance'.[186] If the defendant 'appears'[187] the shield is lost.[188]

The European Court has been called upon to deal directly with the scope of Article 27(2) in three cases: *Peter Klomps v Karl Michel*,[189] *Volker Sonntag v Hans Waidmann and others*,[190] and *Berhandus Hendrikman and Maria Feyen v Magenta Druck & Verlag GmbH*.[191]

It appears to be logical to divide up what constitutes 'appearance' into two time periods—'appearance' after, and 'appearance' before, a 'default judgment'[192] has been rendered.

---

[185] Art. 34(2) of Brussels I Regulation contains identical opening wording to the scope of the current defence in Art. 27(2) *ratione materiae*; Art. 28(1)(d) of the Commission II draft interim text of the proposed Hague Worldwide Judgments Convention will permit a judgment debtor to resist recognition and enforcement in far wider circumstances than that currently in Art. 27(2). The Art. 28(1)(d) shield will only be lost (in a combination of three circumstances (provided the *lex fori* of the rendering court allows it): (i) the defendant must have 'entered and appearance'; and (ii) the defendant must also have 'presented his case'; and (iii) 'without contesting the matter of notification'. These elements appear to be cumulative and sufficient: any communication with the rendering court, if it is to be attempted, should be confined at a minimum to objecting to the method of service/notification *and nothing more*—objecting to jurisdiction *simpliciter* may mean the protection of Art. 28(1)(d) will be lost.

[186] It is submitted that *less* is required of a defendant to 'appear' in proceedings (and therefore lose the right to Art.27(2)) than to 'submit', under Art.18, in them; even though the German version uses the same term in both: ('der sich auf das Verfahren nicht *eingelassen* hat'; and, in Art.18, 'wenn sich der Beklagte...auf das Verfahren *einläßt*'); the French text of the Conventions has in its Art.27(2) the phrase 'défendeur défaillant'; the defence can apply, irrespective of where the defendant is domiciled; Kropholler, 2002, at p.401, para. 24.

[187] For 'appearance' in English procedure, see below.

[188] Cf Briggs, 1997, p.323, para. 7.16.

[189] (C–166/80) [1981] ECR 1593.

[190] (C–172/91) [1993] ECR I–1963.

[191] (C–78/95) [1996] ECR I–4943.

[192] To English procedural lawyers, at least as it may apply to Art. 27(2), this phrase must be defined under CPR Rule 12(1)(a) (and the former RSC Ord 13, esp. r.7B) specifically as 'a judgment given in default for a defendant's *failure to file an acknowledgment of service*'—not, it seems, under CPR Rule 12(1)(b), where a defendant fails to file a defence. By then, it is submitted, another Contracting State court will be justified in considering that a defendant has already 'appeared' for purposes of Art. 27(2). In the enforcement court, however, appearance has an autonomous meaning: *Volker Sonntag v Hans Waidmann and others* (C–172/91) [1993] ECR I–1963; what the other Contracting State courts may make of CPR 12.1, 12.2, and 12.3 (together with Arts.19(1)(2) Council Service Regulation) is awaited, as to dispute jurisdiction (at all) a defendant must first acknowledge service under CPR Part 11.

5.2.1 'Appearance' after[193] judgment in default has been given?[194]

Klomps v Michel concerned, *inter alia*, the case where, after judgment had been given in default, the defendant had 'appealed'[195] against it, but out of time. The adjudicating court had rejected the appeal/application to set aside on this ground, as inadmissible. The European Court held in such a case as this—that where the judgment in default remains intact—Article 27(2) 'remains applicable'.[196] This immediately begs the question of how the defendant can be deprived of Article 27(2)'s protection by taking any, and if so what, steps in any 'appeal/application procedure' *after* judgment has been rendered? In other words, can it be argued[197] that there can possibly be an *ex post facto* legitimisation[198] of the default judgment by a defendant's timely (and therefore detrimental) objection,[199] or appeal?

The procedural example in *Klomps* was perhaps not of the best, and, it is submitted, is not of general application to 'normal' civil proceedings,[200] so that any general rule cannot be extracted from the case itself. The truncated, summary *Mahnverfahren* procedure in *Klomps* is *sui generis*, and cannot be regarded as serving as a paradigm for general 'writ/claim form-defence-judgment' actions. Indeed, as the Swiss *Bundesgericht* has shown, had the defendant appealed in time, the *Mahnverfahren* procedure would have ended, and a 'normal' *inter partes* action

---

[193] Appearance in this section appears to be a question of degree. You may be said to have 'appeared': (i) by taking any steps to have judgment set aside, or (ii) by a timely application to set aside, but it is rejected. You may be said *not* to have 'appeared', (i) if you are in time with the application, but are under a burden in the application which would not otherwise have been yours in normal adversarial proceedings, or (ii) if you are out of time in the application (as in *Klomps v Michel*).

[194] *Dicey and Morris on the Conflict of Laws*, 13th edn., 2000, Vol .I, at p.553, para. 14–210; also *TSN Kunststoffrecycling GmbH v Jurgens*, QBD, 16.2.2001 (Jack J), below n.200; a comparatively rare occurrence in practice—if a defendant is initially in default, *a fortiori*, he may probably not then apply to set aside.

[195] Or more accurately, attempted to lodge an objection to the *Mahnbescheid* under §694(1) and §696(1) German ZPO; for the English procedure of applying to set aside a default judgment (not appealing), which of course it will be for another Contracting State to consider under Art. 27(2), RSC Ord. 13 r.9 and now CPR Part 13, esp. Rule 13.3, and below, at pp.472–3 section 5.2.3; for a national case where a timely objection *was* lodged in *Klomps* circumstances, *X. Financial Services GmbH gegen W. Bundesgericht* (Swiss) 12.7.1997, 123 BGE, III, 374.

[196] (C–166/80) [1981] ECR 1593, at p.1607, para. 13.

[197] Below, at p.457, and Briggs, 1997, at p.323, para. 7.16.

[198] By reason of an objection, which the adjudicating court then decides against the defendant, the defendant is thereafter no longer considered by any court to be in default? At least in England, this may well depend (in the eyes of a foreign court) on the grounds on which the defendant's application to set aside the English default judgment was dismissed.

[199] *X. Financial Services GmbH gegen W. Bundesgericht* (Swiss) 12.7.1997, 123 BGE, III, 374.

[200] Yet in *TSN Kunststoffrecycling GmbH v Jurgens*, QBD, 16.2.2001 (Jack J) the fact that judgment debtor unsuccessfully 'appealed' in the German action—the appeal court had rejected the 'appeal' as being out of time—did not dis-entitle Jurgens from relying on Art. 27(2) before the English court.

could have[201] continued.[202] Objecting[203] in the *Mahnverfahren*, contrary to what *Klomps* suggests,[204] cannot mean[205] that the defendant has renounced his Article 27(2) defence in any contentious proceedings that may follow.

Other commentators[206] legitimately approach the question of the effect of an appeal/application against the default judgment from a different angle, with subtler[207] conclusions. According to Briggs:

> [i]f the defendant, in seeking to have [the default judgment] set aside, is under a burden[208] . . . by reason of the [judgment] itself . . . the judgment will retain its original default character.[209]

Under *Klomps* itself, the defendant who lodged an 'appeal' was under no 'burden', as the rules of procedure for an appeal in the *Mahnverfahren* laid down strict time limits within which this step had to be taken. These rules had to be applied by the court of its own motion. Yet the summary rejection of the defendant's appeal did not mean that he no longer remained 'in default'.

The European Court's attitude to the sacrosanct time-period between service of 'the document which instituted the proceedings' and the giving of a judgment, is well-known.[210] In *Firma Minalmet GmbH v Firma Brandeis Ltd*,[211] the Court

---

[201] On the application of either party; in that case a 'normal' *inter partes*, though ultimately default, proceedings did continue.

[202] Continue is somewhat misleading; the plaintiff/applicant in the *Mahnverfahren* is required to re-commence (§697(1) ZPO) his action by substantiating his claim—an account of the German procedure in English can be found in Koch, H. and Diedrich, F. *Civil procedure in Germany*, 1998, at pp.115–16.

[203] Objecting in the *Mahnverfahren* procedure does not place any burdens (of proof) on the defendant in any case.

[204] The implication being that had the objection been in time, the defendant would have lost his status of being 'in default'.

[205] Unsuccessfully applying to have the judgment in default set aside in 'normal' proceedings should be considered afresh: the Convention itself does, after all, envisage, under Art. 38[I], that the defendant may have lodged an 'ordinary appeal' in the State of origin against the 'judgment'. An argument can therefore be made that the Convention's articles should work in harmony, and not pull in opposite directions. That one article envisages an 'ordinary appeal' being lodged should not have an exclusion-ary impact on the application of any other, including of course, Art. 27(2)—the conclusion reached by the *Bundesgericht* above, at p.456, n.199.

[206] Briggs, 1997, at p.323 para. 7.16.

[207] This solution may be too subtle for the Convention system; and in any event, it may be contrary to its prevailing autonomous spirit—again *Industrial Diamond Supplies* (C–43/77) [1977] ECR 2175, at p.2188, para. 24 and *Société d'Informatique Service Réalisation Organisation (SISRO) v Ampersand Software BV* (C–432/93) [1995] ECR I–2269.

[208] Such as now perhaps having the burden of proof on the application to set aside. This would be the case in the vast majority of situations under RSC Ord.13 r.9 and CPR Rule 13.3, except perhaps under CPR Rule 13.2(a) in conjunction with Rule 12.3(1)(a), below, at p.481—whether the 'burden' referred to is any burden (of proof) *simpliciter*, or more specifically, a burden that would not otherwise have been on a defendant in the normal course of an *inter partes* procedure, is unclear.

[209] Briggs, 1997, at p.323, para. 7.16, and Briggs, 2002, at p.125, rather generous to applicants.

[210] Note the statements that this is perhaps the best, and only time, that a defendant may effectively defend himself: *Berhandus Hendrikman and Maria Feyen v Magenta Druck & Verlag GmbH* (C–78/95) [1996] ECR I–4943, at p.4967, para. 20.

[211] (C–123/91) [1992] ECR I–5661.

reiterated its desire to see the defendant given a proper opportunity for a defence at the most effective time, *viz.,* when proceedings are commenced:

> [r]ecourse, at a later stage, to a legal remedy against a judgment given in default . . . cannot constitute an *equally effective alternative* to defending . . . before judgment[212]

It is worth looking at the English default judgment (and applications to set it aside) in the light of the above, bearing in mind the 'shift in burden of proof' test, and the fact that it will most likely be another Article 32/37 recognising or enforcing court that will be considering these issues.

5.2.1(i)[213] *'Appearance' to have the default judgment set aside in England, under CPR Rule 13 and Article 19(4) Council Service Regulation 1348/2000*[214]

Applications to set aside existing proceedings[215] made/submitted on or after 26 April 1999[216] must be under Part 13 of the 1998 Civil Procedure Rules.[217]

As for a time limit for doing so in England under the new regime, the answer is revealed after a rather tortuous route has been taken through the Civil Procedure Rules. Although no express time limit is mentioned in CPR Part 13 itself,[218] it appears that a defendant to a default judgment under Part 13 has 7 days after

---

[212] (C–123/91) [1992] ECR I–5661, at p.5679, para. 19.

[213] At this stage, in section 5.2.1(i), we are only concerned with whether another Contracting State court may consider a defaulting judgment debtor to have 'appeared' under Art. 27(2) by engaging the setting aside procedure in Part 13 within the time allowed by Art. 19(4) Council Service Regulation.

[214] CPR 13.3(2) subjects the rather strict time limits in internal domestic procedure to Art. 19(4) Council Service Regulation when the 'time limit for appealing has expired'; at this 'setting aside' stage, the questions arising under Art. 19(4) are a matter for the domestic (English) judge. After 1.3.2002, in Art. 34(2) Brussels I Regulation, at any future recognition and enforcement stage, for when another Member State court may need to review or 'double check' whether it was still possible for a judgment debtor to challenge an English default judgment, see section 5.2.1(ii).

[215] Proceedings commenced after 26 April 1999 will of course be subject to CPR Rule 13 in any event.

[216] For applications before 26.4.1999, RSC Ord. 13 r.9 stated in a simple and perfunctory way that 'the Court may, on such terms as it thinks just, set aside or vary any judgment entered' in default under Ord.13. Whether or not another Contracting State enforcing court will continue to view a defendant as still being 'in default of appearance' under Art. 27(2) in these circumstances, may of course, depend on the reason(s) why a defendant's application to set aside under Ord.13 r. 9 was dismissed. Unfortunately, the reasons why this may have occurred are not fixed, but unconditional, and wholly discretionary. Delay in making the application may be one (summary) reason why a dismissal was the outcome; so too (commonly) may have been a lack of 'a real prospect of success' of the defence: *Alpine Bulk Transport Co.Inc. v Saudi Eagle Shipping Co. Inc. (The 'Saudi Eagle')* [1986] 2 Lloyd's Rep. 221, CA; it is submitted that if the English court rejected the defendant's application to set aside on the ground that the defendant had failed to show a prospect of success (despite a reversal of the burden of proof), an Art. 32 enforcing court will doubtless find that the defendant has 'appeared' and the Art. 27(2) shield lost. No other Contracting State authorities could be unearthed for this proposition, however.

[217] The transitional provisions of Practice Direction 51, Rule 7(4); as stated above, under the general provisions of the new rules governing applications for court orders generally (Part 23 (Form N244)), Rule 23.10(2) appears to give a defaulting defendant 7 days within which to do so (after the judgment is served on him, Rule 23.9)—but such a stringently short time period will be ameliorated by Art. 19(4) of the Service Directive (1348/2000), discussed below at p.464.

[218] The claimant will presumably have filed an application notice for a judgment in default under CPR Rule 12.10(b)(i), without notice, Rule 12.11(4) in conjunction with Part 23 itself and PD 23 r.3(6).

service on him of the order within which to apply to have it set aside. In any event, such a defendant in default will therefore be under a burden,[219] *inter alia*, in setting aside proceedings, to show that he has applied as promptly as possible. CPR Rule 13.3(2), in tandem with Article 19(4) Council Service Regulation,[220] makes it clear that when considering a defaulting judgment debtor's application to set aside, the English court must have regard to whether he 'made an application to do so promptly'.[221]

As for the substantive requirements, CPR Rule 13 then contains 3 germane instances when the English court must, or may, set aside a (Part 12) 'default judgment'. For our purposes, it *must* do so, under Rule 13.2, if judgment in default of an acknowledgment of service was granted *before* the 21 day[222] period for filing such an acknowledgment had expired.

Conversely, the court *may* set aside, under Rule 13.3 if (a)[223] the defendant has a real prospect of successfully defending the claim, or (b) there is some other good reason to do so.[224] In any case, Rule 13.3(2) makes it clear that the application under Rule 13.3 must be made 'promptly'.

A third ground is innovative: Rule 13.5 obliges the *claimant* to apply to have his own default judgment set aside if he has good reason to believe[225] that the particulars of claim did not reach the defendant before judgment in default was entered.

What then is another Contracting State enforcing court to make of the procedure on an unsuccessful application to set aside under CPR 13.2, 13.3 and Article 19(4) Council Service Regulation? The English court's rejection of the application (and refusal to set aside) under Rule 13.2(1)(a) may well still entitle a defendant to claim the protection of Article 27(2) before a foreign enforcing court; yet a potential refusal under Rule 13.3(1)(a) or (b) may be more problematic. Using the 'burden shifting to the defaulting defendant'[226] test, under both Rule 13.3(1)(a) and (b), the burden will be on the defendant to show why the defaulting judgment should be set aside—he should therefore continue to be considered still in default.

---

[219] It is the foreign Art. 32 enforcing court's view of the matter that counts, below, at p.466 section 5.2.2.

[220] Note also the Information communicated by Member States under Art. 23 of Council Regulation (EC) No 1348/2000) of 29 May 2000 on the service in the Member States of judicial and extrajudicial documents in civil or commercial matters, 22 May 2001, [2001] OJ C151/4, at p.15.

[221] *Ibid.*, for Scotland, the relevant time limit is 1 year from the date of the decree.

[222] If (for the sake of simplicity) the defendant is domiciled in a European territory of another Contracting State.

[223] Legislative approval of the conclusion in *The 'Saudi Eagle'* [1986] 2 Lloyd's Rep. 221, CA.

[224] Despite Art. 19(1)(2) Council Service Regulation, that a judgment in default of acknowledgement of service has been entered when the defendant had not received the claim form and/or particulars of claim, will normally justify a setting aside under CPR 13.3(1)(b), unless it is pointless to do so (if defendant has no defence)—*obiter* observations in *Godwin v Swindon Borough Council* [2001] 4 All ER 641, at p.658 (May LJ), CA.

[225] Perhaps, for example, if the claimant receives information *aliunde*, by letter from the defendant, asking for the particulars, or stating that he received them late in the day.

[226] Advocated by Briggs, 1997, at p.323, para. 7.16; it is uncertain, however, that another Contracting State court will use this test under Art. 27(2).

In summary, either the 'appeal'/application against the judgment in default does, or does not, represent 'an equally effective alternative' to defending the action prior to judgment: for example where the burden of proof shifts to the defendant to adduce evidence that may have come to light since the judgment; or further additional facts, after judgment may be necessary for setting aside. In this latter case the appellant still be considered to be 'in default of appearance'. The defendant—if placed under a burden that would not have been his in the course of 'normal' proceedings,[227] but has shifted to him because of his status as an appellant/applicant—should be considered to be still 'in default of appearance'.

Using the 'equally effective alternative' test as applied to the *Mahnverfahren* procedure, the lodging of an objection appears[228] to nullify what has gone before, and necessitates the plaintiff, as it were, in recommencing afresh;[229] this fact, it is believed, amounts to an appearance.[230] Yet deriving general conclusions from *Klomps* may ultimately be apt to lead astray.

The best that can be extracted from the foregoing confusion is that *Klomps* is not at all suited to serve as a general principle regarding appeals after judgment. It was unfortunate in that case that a *sui generis* procedure formed the background to the reference. One possible resolution[231] to the conundrum may be the 'equally effective remedy' test. If the appellant, on lodging an appeal after judgment, is not prejudiced[232] in any way as regards setting aside, and the adjudicating court thereafter, again, rules against him, Article 27(2) will no longer apply *ratione materiae*;[233] conversely, if he is so prejudiced, Article 27(2) will continue to protect him before the enforcing court.

Another solution may simply be to say that an ultimately unsuccessful 'ordinary appeal' having been lodged under Article 36, should not, whatever the respective shifting burdens of proof between the protagonists, adversely oust a defence under Article 27(2). This has a certain allure of simplicity, and is divorced[234] in the eyes of an enforcing court, from the peculiarities of the various Contracting State appeal procedures.

---

[227] A 7 day time limit within which to convince an English court why a default judgment should not have been entered against him under CPR Part 12, is such a severe burden on (another Contracting State) defendant—Art. 19(4) Service Regulation 1348/2000, below.

[228] Koch, H. and Diedrich, F. 1998, at p.115: 'A timely objection bars the issuing of a writ of execution and brings the whole collection proceedings [the *Mahnverfahren*] to a halt.'; also a similar view in *X. Financial Services GmbH gegen W. Bundesgericht* (Swiss) 12.7.1997, 123 BGE, III, 374.

[229] The burden of proof remains on the plaintiff in his claim.

[230] *Contra X. Financial Services GmbH gegen W. Bundesgericht* (Swiss) 12.7.1997, 123 BGE, III, 374.

[231] Paraphrasing Briggs, 1997, at p.323, para. 7.16.

[232] Allowing the application of Art. 27(2) to balance on national procedural rules on burdens of proof in appeal proceedings may not seem the best solution to this problem either.

[233] Jolowicz, J. and van Rhee, C.H. (eds) *Recourse against judgments in the European Union*, 1999, above at p.457.

[234] *Société d'Informatique Service Réalisation Organisation (SISRO) v Ampersand Software BV* (C–432/93) [1995] ECR I–2269, at pp.2300–01, para. 41.

5.2.1(ii)   Legislative clarification of 'appealing' against a default judgment: Article 34(2) of the Brussels I Regulation and 'challenging the judgment'

Fortunately, the above uncertainty may have a limited life in any event. Ever-present in the examination of the Brussels and Lugano Conventions is the Brussels I Regulation, establishing a streamlined Brussels Convention, under what are now Articles 61(c) and 65 EC Treaty. The Regulation, and (all) the changes that it will herald on 1.3.2002, can be seen as a manifestation of the European Union's present dissatisfaction[235] with the current version of the Brussels Convention, and the interpretations it has received at the hands of the ECJ. Of importance, for present purposes, is the last sub-clause of the proposed Article 34(2), a newly-drafted version of the current defence in Article 27(2). Article 34(2) will provide that the defence of sufficient time for service, and the concomitant (in)ability of arranging a defence, shall be available to a judgment debtor unless:

> the defendant failed to commence proceedings to challenge the judgment *when it was possible for him to do so.*[236]

This whole phrase has a number of elements which merit brief mention here. Clearly the necessity of 'commenc[ing] proceedings'[237] refers to the individual procedural mechanisms[238] of each Contracting State, if any, to challenge the grant of the default judgment.[239] The procedural pre-requisites—such as time limits and forms—and the substantive requirements for a challenge, must clearly be judged (by the enforcing court) by reference to the procedural laws/codes of the adjudicating court.[240]

This much appears to be uncontroversial.[241] So, too, is the second element 'challeng[ing] the judgment'.[242] The lack of a prospect of success appears to be

---

[235] Esp. the comments in the explanatory memorandum to the July 1999 Draft Council Regulation, on the interpretation of the current Art.27(2), at p.22; Geimer, R. (2002) *IPRax* 69, at p.73, and Briggs, 2002, at p.125.

[236] This sub-clause will provide a review, or 'double check' by a recognising/enforcing judge in one Member State of the time limits in the setting aside/appealing procedures (under Art. 19(4)) of another.

[237] Béraudo, (2001) *JDI* 1033, at p.1072 on possible French appellate procedure, and below at n.238; Kropholler, 2002, at p.408, believes that the 'duty' of commencing proceedings to challenge the judgment should only be based on the limited grounds of sufficiency of time or method of service (and not any and all setting aside grounds available under national procedural laws in general).

[238] Note in many Contracting States this procedure is not an appeal mechanism, but by *opposition*, or objecting to the grant of a default judgment, or motion to set aside the judgment: Jolowicz, J. and van Rhee, C.H. (eds) *Recourse against judgments in the European Union*, 1999, at pp.131–32 (France), p.168 (Germany), p.251 (Netherlands); consideration must also be given to the changes to the procedures in all Contracting States by Art. 19(4) Service Regulation 1348/2000, below.

[239] In England and Wales, CPR Rule 13.1, 13.2, 13.3 and Art. 19(4) Council Service Regulation.

[240] *Kongress Agentur Hagen GmbH v Zeehaghe BV* (C–365/88) [1990] ECR I–1845; Art. 19(4) Service Regulation 1348/2000 and *communiqués* to EC Commission.

[241] Although those Contracting States with a generous/wide 'appeals' procedure may, under Art.34(2), inevitably disadvantage defendants from other Contracting States with a restricted right of appeal, below, at p.464; a simpler test envisioned by Briggs, 2002, at p.125.

[242] At least as it appears in English procedure of an application to set aside—the French phrase (*recours à l'encontre de la décision*) seems to be more problematic, and redolent of the whole edifice of the

irrelevant, as is the necessity of determining whether there has been a shift in the burden of proof to the defendant.

It is the last segment 'when it [is] possible for [a defendant] to do so' which may cause the most problems. One can envisage, as with the term 'first seised' under Article 21, that 'when it [is] possible' to mount an 'appeal' will be given an autonomous meaning, but left to national procedural law of the rendering court to decide when such a valid challenge to set aside/appeal against the default judgment may be made.

This, of course, in turn, raises the protean spectre of time limits under the Contracting States' procedural codes,[243] if any, and when these limits commence, and end.[244] Commonly under the Continental codes,[245] the time limit to apply to have the default judgment set aside commences with service of the judgment[246] on the defendant. Commencement of such time periods then involves the time either on the occasion of internal service,[247] service under the Hague Service Conventions, or (from 31.5.2001) the Council Service Regulation 1348/2000. This may lead to a situation where—by the rendering court's procedural law—the time limit (of whatever length) has expired, yet a defendant domiciled in another Contracting State will continue to be ignorant of the fact that a default judgment has been entered against him: in these circumstances it will therefore no longer be 'possible' for such a defendant to commence proceedings, and the defence under Article 34(2) will presumably remain open.

As had been mentioned, the procedures and time limits[248] under the CPR for setting aside a default judgment is now governed by CPR Rule 13.2(a), or Rule

appellate structure of French procedure—according to Béraudo, (2001) *JDI* 1033, at p.1072, the Brussels I Regulation 'ne distingue pas entre les recours ordinaires et extraordinaires, il y a lieu d'inclure . . . un pourvoi en cassation' ('does not differentiate between ordinary and extraordinary appeals, there is room to include . . . an appeal *en cassation*'). The possibility that another Member State judgment debtor, of a French default judgment, will be prevented from relying on Art. 34(2) until exhausting all avenues of appeal in France, including *en cassation*, will not be welcome.

[243] Note the application of Art. 19(4) of Council Service Directive 1348/2000, below at pp.464–465.

[244] As with procedural differences in the laws of the Contracting States regarding 'first seisure' under Art. 21, similar differences between when and how it may be 'possible' to initiate proceedings to challenge the default judgment will exist. Even under Art. 19(4) Service Regulation 1348/2000, this could lead to certain defendants either (if the rendering court's procedure for setting aside is particularly strict or circumspect) benefiting from, or (a generous setting aside procedure (at any time) *preventing* reliance on Art. 34(2), as it theoretically will always remain possible to 'appeal') being prejudiced by, the future defence in Art. 34(2) Brussels I Regulation.

[245] Before the application of Art. 19(4) in those Contracting States that have made a declaration thereunder: Jolowicz, J. and van Rhee, C.H. (eds), *Recourse against judgments in the European Union*, 1999 (The Netherlands within 8 weeks of officicial notification of the default judgment on a defaulting defendant outside the Netherlands, at p.251 onwards; France 1 month from service of default judgment, Art. 538 NCPC, at pp.131–32; Greece 15 days from service of default judgment, at p.184).

[246] This is also presumably the position under CPR Rule 13.3 and Art. 19(4) Council Service Regulation.

[247] Note German §175 ZPO (fictitious internal service of judgments); also the CPR Rule 12.11(4) and Practice Direction 12 r.5.1 do not require a claimant/applicant to give notice of the Part 23 'application notice' for a default judgment to another Contracting State domiciled defendant.

[248] No time limits are expressly mentioned in Part 13 itself—reference must be made to the general provisions of Part 23—*Civil Procedure*, Volume 1, Autumn 2001, at pp.382–83.

13.3,[249] in conjunction with Part 23 (general rules about applications for court orders),[250] and Article 19(4)[251] of the Council Service Regulation 1348/2000. Fortunately Article 19(4)'s wording and effects may in many cases[252] ameliorate the uneven situation of varying time limits just mentioned above.

In situations where the Service Regulation now applies,[253] and transmission 'for the purpose of service' is to be effected thereunder, a rendering judge, having pronounced judgment against a defendant who did not appear, 'shall have the power to relieve the defendant from the effects of *the expiration of time for appeal* from the [default] judgment', provided two conditions are met. These are given in Article 19(4)(a) and (b): sub-paragraph (a) relates to the reasons for a defendant's lack of knowledge of either the 'writ of summons' or 'judgment', in sufficient time to act accordingly, by responding or appealing, respectively; and sub-paragraph (b) relates to the merits of a defence.

Of greater importance for default judgments under Article 34(2) of Brussels I Regulation, (and the possibility of challenging them contained therein), are the last two unnumbered paragraphs of Article 19(4): the time limit within which a defaulting defendant must apply in Article 19(4) for relief. The first unnumbered para. states this time to be within 'a reasonable time after the defendant has knowledge of the judgment',[254] which the Member States *may* (in the second

---

[249] CPR Rule 13.3 now contains a statement in parenthesis, inserted by r.10 of Civil Procedure (Amendment No.2) Rules 2001, on 31.5.2001, that Art. 19(4) 'applies to applications to appeal a judgment in default when the time limit for appealing has expired'.

[250] Rule 23.10(1)(2) states that the time limit is 7 days: 'An application under this rule [Rule 23.10] must be made within 7 days after the date on which the order [granting the application for the default judgment] was served on the person making the application.'

[251] This reads as follows: 'When a writ of summons . . . has had to be transmitted to another Member State for the purpose of service, under the provisions of this Regulation, and a judgment has been entered against a defendant who has not appeared, the judge shall have the power to relieve the defendant from the effects of the expiration of the time for appeal from the judgment if the following conditions are fulfilled: (a) the defendant, without any fault on his part, did not have knowledge of the document in sufficient time to defend, or knowledge of the judgment in sufficient time to appeal; and (b) the defendant has disclosed a prima facie defence to the action on the merits. An application for relief may be filed only within a reasonable time after the defendant has knowledge of the judgment. Each Member State may make it known, in accordance with Art. 23(1), that such application will not be entertained if it is filed after the expiration of a time to be stated by it in that communication, but which shall in no case be less than one year following the date of the judgment.'

[252] Except perhaps the problem of the *remise au parquet*, as Art.19(4) is premised on the fact that transmission of a 'writ of summons' was made 'for the purpose of service'—a problem for those Continental courts that allow it—cf *Knauf UK GmbH v Gypsum Ltd and another* [2002] 1 WLR 907, CA (reversing [2001] 2 All ER (Comm) 332, (David Steel J)). The Court of Appeal appeared to incline strongly to the view that, as a matter of English law on service overseas, the 1965 Hague Convention, in the circumstances, was mandatory; also *Phillips and others v Symes and another* [2002] 1 WLR 853, at p.861, Ch.D.: Hart J accepted Greek service by its form of *remise au parquet* (for 'first seisure' purposes of Art.21) was *not* good service for Brussels Convention; cf Schlosser, P. 'Jurisdiction and international judicial and administrative co-operation' 284 *Recueil des Cours* 88 (2000), at p.107.

[253] For this in more detail, and the scope of the amendments to the Civil Procedure Rules 1998, *inter alia*, in Rules 6.25(5) and 6.26A (as inserted on 31 May 2001 by r.8 The Civil Procedure (Amendment No.2) Rules 2001, SI 2001/1388), *Civil Procedure*, Volume 1, Autumn 2001, 2001, at p.141 onwards.

[254] *Quaere* then, whether a reasonable time may be less than 1 year, if a Member State has made no declaration under Art. 19(4), last para., such as in England and Wales, N. Ireland and Gibraltar.

unnumbered para.) declare to be a stated period, of not less than 1 year from the date of the default judgment.[255]

According to the *communiqués* of information to the European Commission under Article 23 of the Service Regulation,[256] Belgium, Spain, France, Luxembourg, The Netherlands, Portugal and Germany,[257] have all made declarations under Article 19(4) that the above-mentioned stated period is one year from the date of judgment.[258] Not surprisingly, the UK (except Scotland) and Ireland have not made a dogmatic statement.[259] Austria and Finland have not yet made declarations under Article 19(4); Italy does not intend to make one.[260]

The future, and crucial, interaction between the defence under Article 34(2) of the Brussels I Regulation and Article 19(4) of the Service Regulation (affecting the notion of the 'possibility' of appealing), will, it is submitted, rest on three interrelated factors—the subjective or objective interpretation of 'possible' under Article 34(2); whether a 1 year minimum declaration has been made under Article 19(4) in a particular Member State; and the time, if at all, when a defendant first becomes aware a default judgment has been entered against him. If—as has happened in the cases under the Brussels Convention—a defendant only first learns that a default judgment has been rendered when served with the Article 42(2) 'declaration of enforceability' in Brussels I Regulation, is the Article 34(2) shield lost? All other elements of Article 34(2) being present, the question then becomes is it (still), or was it 'possible' to commence proceedings?

If the rendering Member State has made the 1 year declaration, it may not (still) be possible; if no declaration be made, in Article 19(4) Service Regulation 1348/2000, an application may still be filed 'within a reasonable time.' If a

---

[255] Presumably an absolute cut-off period, irrespective of whether a defendant knows of the judgment or not; if a defendant becomes aware of a default judgment and does nothing in the adjudicating court within this 1 year to apply for relief, an Art. 45 enforcing court in another Member State will in future be entitled to conclude that the Art. 34(2) defence is unavailable, as the defendant failed to commence proceedings to challenge the judgment when it was possible for him to do so.

[256] Of 22 May 2001, [2001] OJ C151/4, as amended by updates of the information communicated, 18 July 2001, [2001] OJ C202/10.

[257] Third update of the information communicated by Member States under Art. 23 of Council Regulation (EC) No 1348/2000) of 29 May 2000 on the service in the Member States of judicial and extra-judicial documents in civil or commercial matters, 17 January 2002, [2002] OJ C13/2, at p.5: 'No application may be entertained [in Germany] for the restoration of the original situation within the meaning of Art. 19(4) . . . more than *one year after the end of the missed deadline*'.

[258] Greece has made a declaration of *3 years* after a judgment is rendered, a considerable period which prevents reliance on Art. 34(2)); in Scotland, the period is 1 year.

[259] In Ireland, the court has to be satisfied that the application was made 'within a reasonable time after defendant had knowledge of the judgment', and, in England and Wales/Northern Ireland whether the application was made 'promptly'. Taking a cynical and protectionist view, to ensure that a default judgment, rendered in the UK courts against other Member State domiciliaries attain maximum efficacy in those other Member States, means effectively, from the earliest point in time, to deprive another Member State judgment debtor of the ability to rely on Art. 34(2) (for as long as possible). A 'circumstances of the case' or 'promptly' test may be impossible for another Member State Art. 45 appeal court to apply: (*Neste Chemicals S.A. and others v DK Line S.A. and Tokumaru Kaiun K.K. (The 'Sargasso')* [1994] 3 All ER 180, CA).

[260] [2001] OJ C202/14.

judgment debtor becomes aware, *prior* to the Article 42(2) declaration of enforce-ability of the judgment, the likelihood of a loss of the Article 34(2) shield will increase. Again, in a Member State with a 1 year declaration, if the debtor is made aware within this time and does nothing, the last paragraph of Article 34(2) will mean that the Article 34(2) shield will be cast away.[261] If no declaration be made, the time-frame within which the risk of forfeiting the Article 34(2) shield continues, and is considerably more uncertain and possibly greater.

In conclusion therefore, a few tentative observations are now offered, distilled from the above discussion as to the effect of the last paragraph of Article 34(2) Brussels I Regulation:

(1) Whether the time within which it is, or was,[262] still 'possible' for a defaulting defendant to initiate proceedings will be a matter of fact. The time limit for doing so should be considered to run from the date of service of the default judgment on the judgment debtor until the time, under the procedural law of the rendering court, when it is no longer 'possible' to do so: whether this be 1 year, or a 'reasonable time', or 'promptly'.[263] An answer to this question therefore crucially hinges on *whether at all, and if so at what point within* the above time frame, the judgment debtor was served with the judgment.

(2) If service on the defaulting defendant was *not effected at all* within the time frame, the defendant could not have failed in his duty under Article 34(2) last sentence, and the remaining elements of the defence will be available.

(3) If service on the defaulting defendant *was effected*, the question becomes *at what point in time* this happened: (i) in sufficient time before the expiration of the period, or (ii) in insufficient time before its expiration to be able to commence proceedings. Unfortunately, it will be apparent from this, that sufficiency[264] of time from the current version of Article 27(2) Brussels Convention will, it is submitted, be carried across into the possibility of ini-tiating proceedings: if a judgment debtor is only made aware of the default judgment against him, for example 2 weeks before a 1 year declared period of time expires, the enforcing court may be entitled to take the view that it was not, from that point in time, (subjectively) possible for him to initiate proceedings to challenge the judgment.

---

[261] As 'the defendant failed to commence proceedings . . . when it was possible . . . to do so'.

[262] The more likely expression, as an enforcing court will no doubt be looking back over a period of time that will have by then expired.

[263] As currently is the practice under Art. 27(2), the view of the rendering court—should a defaulting judgment debtor initiate proceedings—that this step was taken within a reasonable time, or promptly, will not necessarily be the conclusion of the Art. 34(2) enforcing court, nor should be binding on it.

[264] The methodology of service of the default judgment will have an impact on the 'possibility' of being able to initiate proceedings.

5.2.2 'Appearance' before judgment[265]

There have been various views[266] as to what will constitute an 'appearance' prior to judgment, for Article 27(2) purposes. That the concept has an 'autonomous' meaning[267] has certain adherents;[268] although the ECJ has yet to define the term comprehensively, merely contenting itself, on a piecemeal basis,[269] with circumstances which will,[270] or will not[271] amount to an 'appearance'. It has been left to certain commentators, and national courts[272] to adopt either narrow,[273] or wide,[274] views of what behaviour on the part of a defendant will preclude reliance on Article 27(2). In the narrow category, which seems to represent the majority opinion,[275] and the attitude of the German courts,[276] any action on the part of the defendant before the adjudicating court, *other than* submitting an objection[277] to due or timely service of the 'document instituting the proceedings', will amount to an 'appearance':

> jedes Verhandeln gelten aus dem ergibt, daß der Beklagte von dem gegen ihn eingeleiteten Verfahren Kenntnis erlangt . . . es sei denn sein Vorbringen hat sich nur darauf beschränkt, den Fortgang des Verfahrens zu rügen, weil die Zustellung nicht ordnungsgemäß oder nicht rechtzeitig erfolgt sei[278]

[265] Still an important concept, as it is not dealt with separately in the defence under Art. 34(2) Brussels I Regulation.

[266] Pfennig, G. *Die internationale Zustellung in Zivil- und Handelssachen*, 1988, at p.85 onwards.

[267] Here the amalgamation of 'appearance' with that concept in Art. 18 may be apt to lead astray, section 5.2.2(i) below, at p.467.

[268] Esp. Kropholler, 1998, at p.352, para. 22.

[269] Cf Boularbah, (1997) *Rev. dr. comm. belge* 512, p.520, para. 14: '[l]a notion communautaire de 'comparution' devait dès lors [post *Hendrikman*] être entendue comme étant *la possibilité de se défendre devant le juge d'origine*' ('the Community idea of appearance must since then be understood as being the possibility of defending oneself before the rendering court'), at para. 39.

[270] *Volker Sonntag v Hans Waidmann and others* (C–172/91) [1993] ECR I–1963, below, at pp.470–471, having counsel of one's choice appear only in the criminal procedure part of collective (*partie civile*) proceedings, but not in others amounts to 'appearance'.

[271] *Hendrikman v Magenta Druck* (C–78/95) [1996] ECR I–4943, below, at pp.470–471, no representation by counsel of one's choice: tacitly no 'appearance' in other circumstances, re posting the writ back to the rendering court: *Lancray v Peters* (C–305/88) [1990] ECR I–2725, at p.2727, para. 5, and p.2744, para. 5.

[272] Especially *OLG Hamm* 27.11.1987 IPRspr. (1987) Nr. 159; and the recent case of *OLG Frankfurt a. M* 11.11.1998 (1999) *RIW* 146: the German defendant had submitted to the Dutch default proceedings by making written and oral submissions.

[273] Certain behaviour is permitted, which will still allow the defendant to remain in default, (in comparison to the wide view, below, following footnote).

[274] *Any* behaviour on the part of the defendant which evidences the fact that he knows of the proceedings, (such as sending the document back to the court for an explanation, as has happened with some German defendants).

[275] Kropholler, 1998, at p.352 para. 22; also Pfennig, 1988, at p.85, and Linke, H. 'Aspekte des Beklagtenschutzes im Exequaturverfahren' zu *OLG Köln* 8.12.1989 (1991) *IPRax* 92.

[276] *OLG Köln* 8.12.1989 IPRspr. (1989) Nr. 218; tacitly, *OLG Hamm* 27.11.1987 IPRspr. (1987) Nr. 159 and *OLG Stuttgart* 3.2.1983 IPRspr. (1983) Nr. 173, at p.449.

[277] But *not* by asking for a stay of the foreign proceedings, as in *OLG Köln* 8.12.1989 IPRspr. (1989) Nr. 218, at p.491.

[278] ('every action from which it is apparent that the defendant has knowledge of the proceedings commenced against him, unless his pleading is limited to an objection to proceedings continuing because

5.2.2(i)   Article 27(2) appearance (before judgment) and 'communicating' with the rendering court

(a) The narrow view What is to be the effect under Article 27(2) of merely sending the writ/claim form back to the rendering (serving) court, as happened in *Lancray v Peters*?[279]

In the area of communicating with the rendering court, the attitude of the early decisions of the *OLG Hamm*[280] and the *OLG Stuttgart*[281] has been carried through from the later decision in *OLG Hamm (Isabelle Lancray S.A. v Firma Peters und Sickert KG*[282]), to the answer eventually given by the referring court.[283] No point was taken before the ECJ in *Isabelle Lancray S.A. v Firma Peters und Sickert KG* itself, the post-reference appeal court, nor by the *OLG Stuttgart*,[284] as to the effect on Article 27(2) that a defendant's sending the (untranslated) writ/claim form back to the adjudicating court may have on the concept of 'appearance'.[285] However in the *OLG Hamm*,[286] of 20.5.1977, the German enforcing court took a firm stance by permitting a German defendant to ask for a translation from the adjudicating court, without being considered to have appeared[287] under Article 27(2).[288]

---

service was not duly effected, or in sufficient time'), according to Kropholler, 1998, at p.352, para. 22, adopted *verbatim* by *OLG Düsseldorf* 18.9.1996 (1996) *RIW* 1043, at p.1043—*in casu*, the defendant was held to have appeared by objecting to jurisdiction, and advancing a counterclaim; also now a formulaic phrase in *OLG Zweibrücken* 14.9.1999 (2001) NJW-RR 144, at p.144 (German defendants having submitted in Austrian proceedings).

[279] (C–305/88) [1990] ECR I–2725; the point was *not* taken before the English court in *TSN Kunststoffrecycling GmbH v Jurgens*, QBD, 16.2.2001 (Jack J), that the judgment debtor could be argued to have appeared *via* a communication with the rendering German court; the European Court has allowed a quite generous plea under Art. 27(2) *ratione materiae* before the enforcing court.

[280] *OLG Hamm* 20.5.1977 IPRspr. (1977) Nr. 145.

[281] 3.2.1983 IPRspr. (1983) Nr. 173.

[282] 27.11.1987 IPRspr. (1987) Nr. 159.

[283] Enforcement was refused in the post-reference decision in *Lancray: BGH* 20.9.1990 IPRspr. (1990) Nr. 200.

[284] 3.2.1983 IPRspr. (1983) Nr. 173, where an Italian *decreto ingiunctivo* was sent back to the Italian court in Brescia on the same day as service was received—at p.449: 'ihre bloße Erklärung, der Mahnbescheid sei in Form und Inhalt unverständlich, *ist gerade die Verweigerung einer Einlassung . . .*' ('the mere assertion that the decreto was incomprehensible in form and content *is exactly the denial of submission*').

[285] Now also *TSN Kunststoffrecycling GmbH v Jurgens*, QBD, 16.2.2001 (Jack J).

[286] IPRspr. 1977 Nr. 145, at pp.431–32.

[287] '[W]enn der Schuldner wegen Sprachschwierigkeiten zunächst lediglich um eine Übersetzung bittet, um feststellen zu können, welchen Inhalt die ihm zugesandten Schriftstücke haben.'('when initially the judgment debtor merely asks, due to linguistic difficulties, for a translation, in order to be able to ascertain what the writ sent to him contains'), *ibid.*., at p.432.

[288] Yet in the *OLG Köln* 8.12.1989 IPRspr. (1989) Nr. 218, the German defendant/judgment debtor had gone *one stage further* and had actually asked for a stay before the Belgian rendering courts, with the result that: '[d]ies kann jedoch nicht als Nichteinlassung im Sinne von Art. 27(2) . . . angesehen werden, da die Vertagung *nicht wegen eines Zustellungsmangels* beantragt wurde, sondern wegen der Abwesenheit des von den Ag. beauftragten Rechtsanwalts.' ('however this cannot be considered as "non-appearance" for the purposes of Art. 27(2), since the stay was requested *not because of a defect in service*, but because of the absence of the defendant's appointed lawyer'), at p.491.

The decision of the *OLG Hamm*[289] in 1993 is also instructive, in that it points out a defendant's dilemma in either defending or staying away. The defendant was found to have cast away his shield[290] by appearing in French *référé* proceedings for a vast sum; the reason being, that in the appeal lodged before the rendering *Cour d'appel de Versailles*,

> stützt die Antragsgegnerin eine ihrer Verfahrensrügen darauf, daß der Richter der ersten Instanz ihren Sachvertrag ungeachtet seiner minutiösen Darlegung nicht berücksichtigt habe.[291]

The stark dilemma of whether to defend an action on the merits, or remain indolent, has been highlighted by Article 27(2), increasing the criticism[292] that it behoves defendants not to defend proceedings in any way, 'mit der sicherem Aussicht, die Vollstreckung (in der Bundesrepublik) . . . über Art 27 Nr.2 . . . abwehren zu können';[293] by objecting to certain technicalities at first instance, the defendant/judgment debtor in the *OLG Hamm* case threw away his shield.

(b) The wide view Alternatively, a wide view of 'appearance' for the purposes of Article 27(2) is supported by Geimer and Schütze,[294] almost loan voices[295] in this respect. For them, any steps taken by a defendant which demonstrate[296] that he has knowledge of the foreign[297] proceedings will amount to an 'appearance' under Article 27(2). According to their view therefore, in *Isabelle Lancray S.A. v Firma Peters und Sickert KG*,[298] the defendant Peters and Sickert would have been deemed to have appeared,[299] from evidence that the defendant company sent the untranslated writ/claim form back to the French court. Certain weak support for

---

[289] *OLG Hamm* 28.12.1993 1994 *RIW* 243; also *OLG Brandenburg* 23.4.1998 (1998) IPRspr. Nr.186, where German judgment debtor knew, in Austrian truncated proceedings, of substance and extent of claim, denying both, at p.375.

[290] *Ibid.*, at p.244.

[291] ('the respondent relied on one of its procedural objections—that the first instance court had taken into account the facts, but had ignored its detailed submissions'), *ibid.*

[292] Especially Droz, in (1993) *Rev crit* 81, at p.86, commenting on *Firma Minalmet GmbH v. Firma Brandeis Ltd* (C–123/91) [1992] ECR I–5661, a position remedied somewhat by Art. 34(2) of Brussels I Regulation.

[293] ('secure in the prospect of being able to defend enforcement (in Germany) under Art. 27(2)'), in *OLG Hamm* 28.12.1993 (1994) *RIW* 243, at p.244.

[294] Geimer and Schütze, 1997, at p.477, para. 103, a view that they have traditionally held, even under pre-Convention bilateral recognition and enforcement Treaties.

[295] AG Jacobs in *Hendrikman v Magenta Druck* (C–78/95) [1996] ECR I–4943, below, at pp.470–471.

[296] To the adjudicating court, such as receiving a communication.

[297] Of course, *Peter Klomps v Karl Michel* (C–166/80) [1981] ECR 1593 and *Leon Emile Gaston Carlos Debaecker and Berthe Plouvier v Cornelius Gerrit Bouwman* (C–49/84) [1985] ECR 1779 have shown us that the same principles apply when the defendant is sued before the courts in the Contracting State of his domicile.

[298] (C–305/88) [1990] ECR I–2725.

[299] *Contra OLG Hamm* 20.5.1977 IPRspr. (1977) Nr. 145.

this 'wide' approach can be gleaned from AG Jacobs in *Berhandus Hendrikman and Maria Feyen* v *Magenta Druck & Verlag GmbH:*[300]

> the essence of an *inter partes hearing*[301] before a court is that '[t]he defendant, or his counsel, had the opportunity before that court to object that the document instituting the proceedings was defective . . .'[302]

It is hoped that Article 34(2) of the Brussels I Regulation will sweep away the confusion over the appearance before judgment. Even though the addendum to what is now Article 27(2) in the last sub-clause of Article 34(2) does nothing to alter the article's scope *ratione materiae*, even a defendant who communicates with the adjudicating court and therefore remains in default will, in future, be encouraged 'to commence proceedings to challenge the judgment'.

5.2.2(ii)   Appearance before judgment in related/partie civile proceedings[303]

In *Volker Sonntag v Hans Waidmann and others,*[304] the defendant, Sonntag, was held to have 'appeared' to the *partie civile*[305] portion of Italian criminal proceedings by having his own appointed[306] lawyer answer the criminal charge, while standing tacitly by while the *partie civile* claim unfolded. Whether any general notion of 'appearance' for present purposes can be gathered from this case is doubtful; unless one sees the mere fact of awareness of the *partie civile* proceedings as sufficient to show in the defendant a desire not to rely on Article 27(2).

Until the European Court rules definitively on the issue of exactly what procedural steps can be taken in the adjudicating court before Article 27(2)'s protection is lost, any (such) action remains a risk.[307]

---

[300] (C–78/95) [1996] ECR I–4943, at p.4953, para. 36, quoting from AG Darmon in *Volker Sonntag v Hans Waidmann and others* (C–172/91) [1993] ECR I–1963.

[301] Thus a technical objection that the writ is untranslated and/or not duly served would form the basis of an *inter partes* hearing and would therefore amount to an 'appearance'.

[302] (C–78/95) [1996] ECR I–4943, at p.4953, para. 36; therefore objecting does constitute an *inter partes* hearing.

[303] For problems of qualification of 'related' proceedings—such as an order for costs in German proceedings (§19 BRAGO): *OGH* 20.9.2000 (2001) *ZfRV* 114, at p.117: 'Bei bloßen AnnexE, die wie etwa Kostenfestsetzungs- oder Kostenerstattungsbeschlüsse *im Anschluss an ein Hauptverfahren* ergehen, . . . ist für eine Versagung der Anerkennung nach Art 27 Nr 2 kein Raum.' ('For purely related decisions—such as those issued for the taxation of costs or orders for costs *in conjunction with proceedings on the merits*—there is no room for a denial of recognition under Art. 27(2)).

[304] (C–172/91) [1993] ECR I–1963; for the non-recognition of the Italian judgment, under Art. 27(1), on the case's return to the *Bundesgerichtshof BGH* 16.9.1993 IPRspr. (1993) Nr. 178 and critical Haas, (1995) *ZZP* 219, above at pp.430–431.

[305] For the special problem involving 'the document which instituted [*partie civile*] proceedings' under Art. 27(2) below, at pp.486–487, section 5.3.4; for problems under Art. 27(1) above, at p.428, and *Dieter Krombach v Andre Bamberski* (C–7/98).

[306] This point was crucial as it turned out in *Berhandus Hendrikman and Maria Feyen* v *Magenta Druck & Verlag GmbH* (C–78/95) [1996] ECR I–4943; historical examples in 10.7.1930 *Tribunal Civil d'Anvers* 10.7.1930 *Paul Buonasorte c/ Évrard Havenith* (1930) *Pas. Belge*, III, 149; *BGH* 24.2.1999 140 BGHZ 396, [2001] I.L.Pr. 425.

[307] Whether it is safe to rely on Art. 18's definition of 'submission' for Art. 27(2) is highly doubtful; Geimer and Schütze 1997, at p.477 para. 103 think that if would not; nor Braun, 1992, at p.87.

5.2.2(iii) 'Appearance' considered as fulfilled under the procedural law of the rendering court

Unfortunately, the latest case to consider 'appearance' in Article 27(2), *Berhandus Hendrikman and Maria Feyen v Magenta Druck & Verlag GmbH*[308] does not advance the search for a definition of the term 'appearance' much further. There it was found by the referring court that the Hendrikmans: (1) were not declared to be 'in default of appearance' by the German adjudicating court; (2) were not validly represented;[309] and (3) were not aware at any stage[310] that proceedings in Germany had been commenced against them. By a process of elimination,[311] the essential element of *Hendrikman* appears to be that a defendant, whatever else he does, does not 'appear' unless he has consented to representation by his own counsel.[312] As to (1), by analogy with *Pendy Plastic Products BV v Pluspunkt Handelsgesellschaft GmbH*,[313] whether or not the adjudicating court declares[314] the defendant to have been in default, has no bearing on the recognising/enforcing court; as to (3), *Klomps* has already shown[315] us that for the application of Article 27(2), it is not essential that 'the document instituting the proceedings' actually come to the defendant's attention.[316]

The Court in *Hendrikman* found that the defendants were powerless to defend themselves; they had had no knowledge of, nor say in, the counsel who were appointed to represent them. Nor were they declared to be in default by the

---

[308] (C–78/95) [1996] ECR I–4943.

[309] This proved to be crucial; for a potential abuse Boularbah, (1997) *Rev. dr. comm. belge* 512, at p.521, para. 51.

[310] Except of course when, under Art. 36 I and II, the Dutch order declaring the German judgment to be enforceable was served on them as judgment debtors.

[311] Of points (1) and (3); the (procedural) law of the adjudicating court, generally, or in the special circumstances of the case being irrelevant as to a finding of being in default cf Briggs (1996) *YEL* 601, at p.608.

[312] As we have seen above, at p.441, this issue is not a novel one recognition and enforcement Conventions, *Trib. Civ., d'Anvers*, 10.7.1930 *Paul Buonasorte c/ Evrard Havenith* (1930) *Pas. Belge*, III, 149 dealt with this problem; also Geimer and Schütze, Band. II, 1971, at p.88 n.5—there cannot be an 'appearance' when a defendant is '[represented] . . . durch einen *vom Erstgericht ohne Wissen des Beklagten aufgestellten* Vertreter oder Prokurator'('[represented] by a representative or agent *engaged by the rendering court without the knowledge of the defendant*'), quoting a case of the Bavarian Appeal Court in 1890—how far this statement of principle may be taken is unknown—Briggs (1996) *YEL* 601, at p.609 for possible examples.

[313] (C–228/81) [1982] ECR 2723.

[314] This point (1) was only taken because of a statement by AG Darmon in *Volker Sonntag v Hans Waidmann and others* (C–172/91) [1993] ECR I–1963, at p.1987, para. 82 that for Art. 27(2), the defendant must be found to be in default by the adjudicating court. This was rejected by AG Jacobs in *Hendrikman v Magenta Druck* (C–78/95) [1996] ECR I–4943, at p.4951, para. 27 and implicitly rejected by the Court itself pp.4966–67, paras. 16–17; *contra*, and therefore probably incorrectly now *Coverbat S.A. v Jackson* 31.1.1997, unreported, CA (Swinton Thomas LJ), and Kaye P. (ed) *European Case Law on the Judgments Convention*, 1998, Case 353 at p.358–59.

[315] *Peter Klomps v Karl Michel* (C–166/80) [1981] ECR 1593, at p.1608 para. 19.

[316] *TSN Kunststoffrecycling GmbH v Jurgens*, QBD, 16.2.2001 (Jack J).

German adjudicating court. The wider implications of the case, if any such may be gleaned, are uncertain.[317]

On one level, despite the fact that to the German court, the proceedings were ostensibly *inter partes*, the Article 27(2) enforcing court is able to undertake an unfettered 'comparable preliminary appraisal'[318] of the circumstances surrounding the judgment's handing down, in order to ascertain whether they are so exceptional as to warrant censure[319] under the article. It appears that the procedural law of the rendering *lex fori* is not exclusively relevant[320] in the (now) autonomous definition of 'in default of appearance'. The scope of the case, on a wider level, would seem to turn on whether the defendant was in a position to defend himself, a state which admits of many permutations: what of a defendant who (un)reasonably dismisses[321] his legal team, or, due to financial constraints, abandons a promising defence? How long is the 'powerlessness' to defend oneself (and consequently the ability to rely on Article 27(2)) to last? Presumably from service of the initiating document until first instance (default) judgment? As a consequence of the judgment in *Hendrikman*, must a plaintiff/claimant now regularly seek irrevocable undertakings, at each stage of the litigious process, that the defendant's (supposed) legal team has authority to act on the defendant's behalf?[322] Surely the scope of Article 27(2) was not intended to extend so far?

Tagaras has noted that allowing defendants to plead before the enforcing court exceptional circumstances which nevertheless maintain Article 27(2)'s scope *ratione materiae* will open the door to dilatory tactics from judgment debtors, ready to latch on to (even self-induced) faults in the rendering court's procedure:

> les plus 'malins' prépareront même à l'avance leur défense d'une manière qui leur permettra par la suite de faire valoir des arguments analogues à ceux des défendeurs dans l'affaire du principal.[323] [324]

---

[317] Cf the necessity of independent representation under Art. 27(2) in *BGH* 24.2.1999 140 BGHZ 396, [2001] I.L.Pr. 425: the guarantor in default and his sister had been represented by the same lawyer before a French court, and the guarantor had *not* had a free choice in his counsel. Enforcement was refused.

[318] [1996] ECR I–4943, at p.4955, para. 39, (AG Jacobs); situations of ostensible representation in certain German cases may need closer scrutiny: *OLG Saarland* 24.11.1997 (1998) *RIW* 632, *OLG Frankfurt a. M* 11.11.1998 (1999) *RIW* 146.

[319] Although the opening words of Art. 27(2) define the article's scope, and do not imply any words of censure.

[320] Which, according to Briggs, 'The Brussels Convention' (1996) *YEL* 601, at p.608, renders the scope of Art. 27(2) harder to predict.

[321] As happened in *Trib. Civ., d'Anvers*, 10.7.1930 *Paul Buonasorte c/ Evrard Havenith* (1930) *Pas. Belge*, III, 149.

[322] And would this in any event satisfy an enforcement court under Art. 27(2).

[323] ('the most «nefarious» will even prepare their defence in advance in such a way so as to permit them later to rely on arguments similar to those that a defendant in the case on the merits could make').

[324] Tagaras, H. 'Chronique de Jurisprudence de la Cour de Justice rélative à la Convention de Bruxelles: Années judiciaires 1996–1997 et 1997–1998' (1999) *Cahiers Dr. Euro* 159, at p.171.

In the meantime, it strongly behoves plaintiff/claimants' legal advisors, more than ever, to ensure that their opposite numbers—if any—have clear, valid, unequivocal and irrevocable authority from their clients to act on their behalf in the relevant litigation before any (further) steps[325] are taken in the litigation. To proceed without this may expose a judgment creditor to a situation comparable to that in *Hendrikman,* and prevent enforcement of any eventual (and ostensibly) default judgment.

5.2.3   'Appearance' in cases outside Germany

The infrequency with which the reported French decisions[326] have dealt with Article 27(2) *in toto,* makes it impossible to glean any tendencies in their courts' attitude towards the notion of a 'défendeur défaillant'. Those that have dealt with Article 27(2) have concerned other aspects, notably the problem of raising the defence *sua sponte, Wagner c/ Tettweiler*[327] and timely service, *Société B.V. Rosco c/ S.A.R.L. Fraisgel,*[328] *Josiane Vieira v Jean-Claude Scherer.*[329] The position is the same with English jurisprudence on the matter. The 'appearance' point did not directly arise for decision in *Thierry Noirhomme v David Walklate,*[330] in *EMI Records Ltd v Modern Music Karl Ulrich Walterbach GmbH,*[331] nor in *TSN Kunststoffrecycling GmbH v Jurgens.*[332]

In concluding this section, various problems have arisen with the notion of a defendant in default of appearance: after a default judgment has been given, a defendant takes action to have it set aside, the necessity and/or advisability of doing so; prior to judgment, communicating with the court, or ostensibly being represented before it, and its handing down of a *prima facie inter partes* judgment. Of most concern is the exact scope of the ruling in *Hendrikman.* When litigating

---

[325] As far as applying for judgment in default of acknowledgment of service under English civil procedure is concerned, the representation point does not arise.

[326] A selection of the more noteworthy are *Cassation,* 26.1.1994, *B c/Mme K,* (1994) *JCP,* IV, 839; *Cassation,* 17.4.1985, *Drakides,* (1985) *JCP,* IV, p.226; *Cassation,* 11.6.1991, *Sté Biomécanique intégrée c/ Sté Fabrique nationale de Herstal,* (1991) *JCP,* IV, p.317; *Cassation,* 9.10.1991, *SARL Polypétrol c/ Sté Générale routière,* (1993) *JDI* 157; (1992) *Rev crit* 516, (1991) *JCP,* IV, p.427; *Vanclef c/ Société Trans Traide International* 17.5.1978 / *Etienne c/ Société Handelsonderneming Claessen B.V.* 24.11.1977 / *Theillol c/ Office de la jeunesse de Fribourg* 18.4.1978 (1979) *JDI* 380; *Cour d'appel de Poitiers,* 1.6.1994 *Société de Transports Internationaux Dehbashi v Gerling Konzern* [1996] I.L.Pr. 104; *Cassation* 19.7.1989 *Josiane Vieira v Jean-Claude Scherer* [1990] I.L.Pr. 252; *Cassation* 11.6.1991 *Soc. Biomechanique Integree v Fabrique Nationale de Herstal SA* [1993] I.L.Pr. 127.

[327] 9.11.1983 (1984) *Rev crit* 501.

[328] *TGI Paris,* 2.11.1984, (1985) *Gaz. Pal.,* Juris., p.61.

[329] *Cassation* 19.7.1989 [1990] I.L.Pr. 252.

[330] [1992] 1 Lloyd's Rep. 427 (Judge Kershaw QC).

[331] [1992] 1 QB 115 (Hobhouse J).

[332] QBD, 16.2.2001, Jack J, even though the judgment debtor, Jurgens, had communicated with the rendering German court prior to judgment, and had unsuccessfully appealed to the relevant *Oberlandesgericht;* note the dangers for the defendant when the claimant agrees to an extension of time: *Midland Resources Ltd v Gonvarri Industrial SA and another* [2002] I.L.Pr. 74, at pp.76–77, (Chambers QC).

abroad, it behoves the claimant's advisers to obtain confirmation that the defendant's advisers have (continuing) authority to act on behalf of their clients.

5.2.4   'Appearance' before judgment in England and Wales: when may another Contracting State court consider a defendant to have 'appeared'?

In this situation, we are not dealing with the consequences of a defendant's failure to file an acknowledgment of service under CPR 10.2, when the claimant will no doubt proceed to obtain a default judgment under CPR Part 12.[333]

Here—in the eyes of an enforcing court—we are concerned with what actions, if any, a defendant may take before the English courts that will preclude him from relying on Article 27(2) in enforcement proceedings in another Contracting State, due to an 'appearance' in English proceedings; and more specifically, what are the repercussions,[334] under Article 27(2) to a defendant's disputing jurisdiction under CPR 11?

Rule 11(1) allows the possibility of an application to challenge the assertion of the English court's jurisdiction, and Rule 11(2) makes clear that a 'defendant who wishes to make such an application [for an order declaring that the English court has no jurisdiction] must first file an acknowledgment of service in accordance with Part 10 [i.e. within 21 days[335] after service of any claim form, or within 21 days after service of any separate particulars of claim].' Although CPR Rule 11(3) states that by taking this step (of filing an acknowledgment of service), a defendant does not thereby lose the right to challenge the jurisdiction, it is *not* for the purposes of 'submission',[336] under Article 18, that this step is to be measured. It should be reasonably arguable[337] therefore that by acknowledging service a (Contracting State) defendant should lose the right to rely on Article 27(2) before another Contracting State court, due to his 'appearance' before the English courts: this should be so irrespective of whether one adheres to the narrow or wide view of 'appearance'; filing the correct form of acknowledgment of service shows to the rendering court that the defendant has received the claim form and is in a position both to assert his rights of defence and/or refrain from exercising them by letting judgment go by default.[338]

---

[333] The 'domestic' conditions to be satisfied for the issue of a default judgment under CPR 12.3 must presumably be read, cumulatively, with Art. 19(1) Council Service Regulation, and now also Art. 19(2) (as the information communicated under Art. 23 of the same Regulation, [2001] OJ C151/4, at p.15 informs us).

[334] And another Contracting State's attitude?

[335] Assuming the defendant to be domiciled in the European territory of another Contracting State, 31 days otherwise PD 6B rules 7.3 and 7.4.

[336] *Hewden Stuart Heavy Cranes Ltd v Leo Gottwald Kommanditgesellschaft & others*, 13.5.1992, CA.

[337] Although it will be in the decision of another Contracting State court.

[338] Arts.19(1) and (2) Council Service Regulation 1348/2000, governing the circumstances under which a rendering court may enter judgment in default when the defendant does not enter an appearance, should not apply here, *ex hypothesi*, because the defendant *has* 'appeared'.

5.3 'THE DOCUMENT WHICH INSTITUTED THE PROCEEDINGS'[339]

It is important to identify this or these[340] items of the rendering court's procedural process. For it will be only[341] to this 'document'[342] that the cumulative severity[343] of the due and timely service requirements will be subjected.[344] Only this document sets in motion the sacrosanct[345] time period during which the defendant can effectively assert his rights of defence; only this document is subject to the complex vagaries of international service.[346]

Until *Hengst Import BV v Anna Maria Campese*,[347] the only perceived problem in defining this term came from certain summary debt collection actions,[348] exemplified by the German *Mahnverfahren* procedure in §§688 ff ZPO.[349]

---

[339] For a comparative overview of European procedure, Frank, M. *Das verfahrenseinleitende Schriftstück in Article 27 Nr.2 EuGVÜ, Lugano-Übereinkommen und in Article 6 Haager Unterhalt-sübereinkommen 1973*, 1998; Art. 34(2) of Brussels I Regulation retains this phrase and therefore the statements made in this section will have continued relevance beyond 1.3.2002.

[340] Collectively which may now add up to this document, *Hengst Import BV v Anna Maria Campese* (C–474/93) [1995] ECR I–2113.

[341] For example the statements, below, at pp.487 *et seq* from *BGH* 10.7.1986 IPRspr. (1986) Nr. 182 at p.417 and *BGH* 20.9.1990 IPRspr. (1990) Nr. 200, *Cassation* 11.6.1991 *Soc. Biomechanique Integree v Fabrique Nationale de Herstal SA* (1991) *JCP*, IV, Juris, 317; [1993] I.L.Pr. 127; and *BGH* 21.3.1990 (1990) *FamRZ*, 868, at p.869, *BGH* 10.11.1998 (1999) *RIW* 295, at p.298, and below, also section 5.3.5.

[342] Now a collective noun: *Hengst v Campese* (C–474/93) [1995] ECR I–2113; it is the document which instituted the proceedings that must be duly served, not the ensuing judgment itself—Cour de Cassation 24.10.2000 *Gregori Sud-est S.A. v Ferruccio Ziliani trading as Cave Ferruccio Ziliani* [2001] I.L.Pr. 717.

[343] If, with Jenard, the 'forteresse' of the German jurisprudence on Art. 27(2) is given even cursory scrutiny, Jenard, P. Rép. Notarial, 1994, Tome XI, livre VI, 3e partie, 1994, at p.167.

[344] *OLG Saarland* 24.11.1997 (1998) *RIW* 632.

[345] AG Jacobs in *Firma Minalmet GmbH v Firma Brandeis Ltd* (C–123/91) [1992] ECR I–5661, at p.5673, para. 11, and the Court at p.5679, para. 19; also *Hendrikman v Magenta Druck & Verlag GmbH* (C–78/95) [1996] ECR I–4943, at p.4967, para. 20.

[346] Below, at pp.492 *et seq*, section 5.4 on 'due' service, from now until 1.3.2002, except with regard to Denmark, under the Service Regulation (1348/2000), below; *Knauf UK GmbH v British Gypsum Ltd and another* [2002] 1 WLR 907, CA, reversing [2001] 2 All ER (Comm) 332, QBD, (David Steel J); the case demonstrates the Court of Appeal's attitude to service under international Conventions/agreements.

[347] (C–474/93) [1995] ECR I–2113.

[348] Although the Italian procedure in *Hengst* was the equivalent of the German procedure in *Klomps*; also now similar procedure introduced into Spanish civil proceedings, Arts.812-818 LEC.

[349] On this procedure's international dimension, Wagner, R. 'Verfahrensrechtliche Probleme im Auslandsmahnverfahren' (1995) *RIW* 89; also in detail Zöller, R. *Zivilprozeßordnung*, 18th edn., 1993, at p.1582 onwards.

5.3.1   The 'document which instituted the proceedings' and uncontradicted summary (debt collection) actions

5.3.1(i)   The Mahnverfahren procedure[350] and Peter Klomps v Karl Michel

A brief excursus into this procedure[351] will be necessary for a more thorough understanding of *Klomps*, and of the Contracting State courts' responses to it.[352] In German truncated debt collection procedure, by §690 ZPO, an application may be made by a creditor to the appropriate *Landgericht* for the grant of a *Mahnbescheid*. This application itself is not served on the debtor; it is granted if certain formal requirements are met,[353] and a *Mahnbescheid* is then issued. This *Mahnbescheid* is the document which *is* served on the debtor, and sets in motion the one month time period[354] for lodging an objection. After expiration of this time, in §694 ZPO and §699(1) ZPO, an enforceable (§700 ZPO) *Vollstreckungsbescheid*, can be granted, should the debtor not have lodged an objection to the *Mahnbescheid*, in §694 ZPO, within that one month period. The question in this procedure, as it was in *Peter Klomps v Karl Michel*,[355] is, what is 'the document which instituted the proceedings' that sets running the 1 month period of time, if no objection is lodged within that time[356]—the *Mahnbescheid* or the *Vollstreckungsbescheid*?

The European Court in *Klomps* chose the former *Mahnbescheid*,[357] and defined the document which instituted the proceedings as the one[358] which enables the

---

[350] French law provides an analogous procedure, the *injonction de payer*, in Title IV, 1st chapter, 1st section, of the NCPC, arts.1405-25 NCPC, *Nouveau Code de Procedure Civile*, Dalloz, 93ᵉᵐᵉ éd., 2001, at p.575 onwards—where, as in *Klomps*, the document which instituted the proceedings has been treated as not the initial *requête*/request under art.1407, but the decision itself, the *ordonnance portant injonction de payer*, OLG Saarbrücken 5.3.1992 IPRspr. (1992) Nr. 219, at p.533; service of this *ordonnance* stops limitation periods running, art.1411; for analogous Italian procedure, Oberto, G. 'La gestion de l'urgence dans le procès civil italien' (2001) *Rev Int dr Comparé* 709, at pp.714–16.

[351] For an overview in English see Koch, H. and Diedrich, F. 1998, at p.115, onwards.

[352] A case worthy of close scrutiny is *X. Financial Services GmbH gegen W*, *Bundesgericht* (Swiss) 12.7.1997, 123 BGE, III, 374.

[353] §690 ZPO.

[354] In Brussels Convention/international cases, for defendants to the *Mahnbescheid* domiciled in Contracting States, from 1.3.2001, §32(3) AVAG, as amended, 2001 BGBl, I, 288, roughly the equivalent of CPR Sch.1 RSC Ord.71 rr.25; during this period, an objection may be lodged; similar time period in French procedure; no concession, it appears, being made if defendant domiciled in another Contracting State, art.1416.

[355] (C–166/80) [1981] ECR 1593.

[356] When it is so lodged, *X. Financial Services* reported above.

[357] The *ordonnance portant injonction de payer* most closely resembles the form, (with regard to the necessary information in art.1413 NCPC) and function of a writ/claim form; it is the document which first summons a defendant to answer for the art.1405 (normally contractual and fixed) debt, stops the limitation period running, and from service (art.1416), starts a 1 month period for objection; for reception of comparative Austrian procedure and ensuing judgment in Germany: OLG Brandenburg 23.4.1998 (1998) IPRspr. Nr.186, at p.373.

[358] The definition of Kropholler—and the one adopted by the German courts (*BGH* 21.3.1990 (1992) *IPRax* 33)—is not therefore (strictly) in accordance with *Klomps* (and *Hengst v Campese*), although the

plaintiff/claimant to obtain an Article 25 'judgment', capable of recognition and enforcement, should the defendant not take appropriate steps[359] (presumably to have it, or service of it, set aside). It was irrelevant, in that case,[360] what procedural activity on the plaintiff's side had preceded the *Mahnbescheid*'s service; likewise after its service, one part at least of Article 27(2) was fulfilled. Other questions, such as the defendant's appearance (by raising an objection) would then have to be dealt with.

5.3.1(ii)   The decreto ingiunctivo[361] and Hengst Import BV v Anna Maria Campese[362]

In *Hengst v Campese*, the position was complicated by the fact that, under a similar summary debt collection procedure under the Italian *Codice Civile*,[363] both the application *and* the summary decision had to be served on the debtor, and thus,[364] collectively, represented the 'document' that instituted proceedings. The case has added a gloss[365] to *Klomps*, and has introduced a certain amount of uncertainty[366] in the area of such 'documents'. This is as a result of the fact that joint service of the Italian *decreto ingiunctivo and* the preceding application was prescribed by the Court to set time running. One document, it was said,[367] was not comprehensible[368] to a defendant without the other. The Article 27(2) 'document which insti-

---

same result commonly obtains when it is applied. He believes it is the one which informs the defendant of the institution of proceedings for the first time, Kropholler, 1998, at p.352, *in fine*, para. 24.

[359] [1981] ECR 1593, at p.1606, para. 11

[360] But now *Hengst Import BV v Anna Maria Campese* (C–474/93) [1995] ECR I–2113.

[361] As from 8.1.2001, a similar summary procedure has been introduced into Spanish procedural law: arts. 812–18 *LEC*, Fröhlingsdorf, J. 'Das neue spanische Zivilprossgesetz (LEC) (2001) *RIW* 357, at p.359. It is not known whether, like the Italian procedure, the Spanish is confined to debtors domiciled in Spain.

[362] (C–474/93) [1995] ECR I–2113.

[363] Arts 633–56 CPC, *Codice di Procedura Civile e Norme complementari*, Fazzalari, E., 1998, pp.169–74.

[364] Per the *Klomps* formula, *both* had to have been served as a requirement of Italian law before the plaintiff/applicant could obtain, under Italian law, an Art. 25 enforceable judgment; the French *injonction de payer* appears to follow the Italian procedure: art.1411 NCPC states: 'Une copie certifiée conforme de la requête *et* de l'ordonnance est signifiée . . . à chacun des débiteurs'('a certified copy conforming to the request *and* the order must be served . . . on each of the debtors').

[365] A 'comprehensibility' requirement, below, at pp.480 *et seq*.

[366] As when, for example, as in English procedure, at least before the Commercial Court, pleadings may be served separately with intervals of weeks in between—this distinction may be in sharp relief currently when, as from 31 May 2001, the rules on international service within the European Union are in a state of transition—from the regime under the 1965 Hague Convention to the Service Regulation 1348/2000. CPR Rule 6.26A(1) clearly only envisages the service of a 'claim form' under the Service Regulation; nothing is said in the rules about service of a separate 'document which instituted the proceedings', such as particulars of claim.

[367] [1995] ECR I–2113, at p.2128, para. 21.

[368] *Quaere*, whether the French *ordonnance portant injonction de payer* is comprehensible without the preceding art.1407 *requête*, or allows a defendant to assert his rights; for details of this procedure, *Nouveau Code de Procedure Civile*, Dalloz, 93ème éd., 2001, at p.576 following and attending notes.

tuted the proceedings' is therefore extended beyond the definition in *Klomps*, to include:

> the document *or documents* which must be duly and timeously served on the defendant in order to *enable him to assert his rights*.[369]

Although nothing in the case seemed to turn[370] on which document was to be considered as the 'document which instituted the proceedings', the reference by the European Court to article 643 of the Italian *Codice di Procedura civile*, appears to give the lie to any autonomous definition of the phrase 'document which instituted the proceedings'. In *Klomps*, and under §693(1) ZPO, only the *Mahnbescheid* alone needed to be served; in *Hengst*, both application and *ingiunctivo* did. It is therefore the national *lex fori*, it seems, which dictates, according to its own procedure, what will be considered as fulfilling the requirements of this 'document'.[371] *Hengst* itself revealed no particular problems in this regard. Different cases can be imagined, however, where one or more documents may be served at different times: the first informing the defendant that proceedings have been commenced against him;[372] while a later document may expand[373] the basis of the plaintiff/claimant's claim in greater detail. One such document on its own[374] may not be intelligible, nor sufficiently informative of the plaintiff/claimant's claim, to achieve the status of the 'document which instituted the proceedings'—consequences which will be examined presently.

5.3.2   The potential impact of *Hengst v Campese*

The impact that *Hengst* may have on the practice, in English procedure, of issuing[375] and serving a writ/claim form with only a 'general endorsement' thereon is uncertain.

---

[369] At p.2128, para. 21; also question 3 submitted by the *Bundesgerichtshof*—but left unanswered—in *Volker Sonntag v Hans Waidmann and others* (C–172/91) [1993] ECR I–1963, at p.1967: 'although the [criminal proceedings document] in question *gives no additional details of the civil claim* which is to be made, is such a document capable of being treated as a 'document which instituted the proceedings' . . .'; on the absence of detail from this document, also *Cassation Société Polypétrol c/ Société générale routière* 9.10.1991 (1993) *JDI* 157, Huet at p.159.

[370] For when it could do so, in English proceedings, where a generally or specifically endorsed/particularised writ/claim form is issued, in the former case, with the necessity of serving an attendant statement of claim, as to which below, at pp.480 *et seq.*

[371] Compare the position now after 26.4.1999, under English law, when a 'particularised' claim form is served; particulars of claim must follow later, below, at pp.480 *et seq.*

[372] Following the German definition, according to Kropholler, this would be considered the relevant 'document'.

[373] Under the CPR 1998, the particulars of claim. If, following *Hengst*, the first is not intelligible without this second document, it will be the second document which 'instituted the proceedings', even though the defendant already knows that a (or some sort of ill-defined) claim has been commenced against him.

[374] If, as in *Hengst*, one document is not sufficiently detailed enough to enable the defendant to assert his rights.

[375] Formerly RSC Ord. 6 r.2(1)(a); and CPR Rule 7.2.

If one poses the question of what (in the view of an Article 32 enforcing court) in English procedure is 'the document which instituted the proceedings', the answer will likely be, it depends. It may turn on whether the enforcing court under Article 27(2) considers this document merely to be any, or an amalgamation of, all the following:

(1) the document which first informs the defendant that an action has been commenced against him,[376] and/or
(2) as in *Klomps,* 'any document . . . service of which enables the plaintiff [under English law] . . . to obtain, in default [of filing an acknowledgment of service[377]] a decision'[378] capable of enforcement under Part III of the Convention, and/or
(3) now, as in *Hengst,* 'the document or documents which must be duly and timeously served . . . to enable [the defendant] to assert his rights before an enforceable judgment is given.'[379]

The answer given by the enforcing court will, it is submitted, therefore critically depend on how the English action was commenced: by generally[380] or specifically endorsed writ/particularised claim form, discussed presently.

5.3.2(i)   The potential impact of Hengst on English proceedings which were instituted by a document before 26 April 1999[381]

Proceedings commenced in the High Court before this date were commonly done so by the issue and service of a 'generally' or 'specifically' endorsed writ. The *Supreme Court Practice*[382] told us, at p.39, that a 'concise statement of the nature of the claim made or the relief or remedy required' was to be endorsed[383] on the back of the writ. It did not need to be a précis[384] of any subsequent statement of claim, but 'must [have] give[n] sufficient information to enable the recipient to identify the occasion [for example] when the breach of contract . . . is alleged to have occurred.'[385] If this had not been done, or the information was insufficient,

---

[376] This may be an unparticularised claim form, but it may be unlikely a foreign court would take this view.
[377] CPR rules 12.1 and 12.11; note not judgment in default of defence, which presupposes that the defendant has acknowledged service, and (will therefore presumably be considered by a foreign court) no longer to be 'in default' under Art. 27(2).
[378] (C–166/80) [1981] ECR 1593, at p.1606, para. 11; this is no longer possible under the CPR.
[379] (C–474/93) [1995] ECR I–2113, at p.2128, para. 19; a likely view, if a generally particularised claim form used in a Commercial Court action, with particulars of claim which subsequently follow.
[380] *The Supreme Court Practice 1999,* Vol. 1, 1998, and RSC Ord. 6 r. 2 and pp.38–39.
[381] Under the old regime of the Rules of the Supreme Court, in force prior to 26.4.1999.
[382] *The Supreme Court Practice 1999,* 1998.
[383] If a specific endorsement was not made.
[384] *Supreme Court Practice, 1999,* 1998, p.39, para. 6/2/3.
[385] *Ibid.,* reviewing *The Jangmi* [1988] 2 Lloyd's Rep. 462.

or had been endorsed—but was considered inadequate[386] by the enforcing court using *Hengst*—any subsequent English default judgment may (still) be in peril.

As far as concerned the procedure after service for the defendant, such a party served with a generally-endorsed writ in the (European)[387] territory of another Contracting State had 21 days to acknowledge service of the writ,[388] and may have given notice of intention to defend, if he had wished; whereupon, within 14 days[389] after the defendant had given this notice, the plaintiff must have served his statement of claim. However, if the defendant did not return the acknowledgment of service within this 'prescribed time'[390]—i.e. 21 days—the plaintiff could have applied, *ex parte*, with the court's leave, for judgment in default to be entered against the defendant for failure to give notice of intention to defend.[391] It is against exactly this type of default judgment that Article 27(2) is aimed.

Conversely, if, as is perfectly possible, the defendant *did* return the acknowledgment of service, but it 'contain[ed] a statement that the defendant [did] not intend to contest the claim',[392] the defendant would no doubt have been considered by another Contracting State enforcing court to have 'appeared' for the purposes of the article, and to have cast away his Article 27(2) shield.

For Article 27(2) therefore, under the old Rules of the Supreme Court, an Article 27(2) judgment given 'in default of appearance' can only be taken to mean,[393] in the narrow sense, simply failing to return any acknowledgment of service within 21 days.

If, in these circumstances, the English court had given leave under RSC Ord. 13 rule 7B to enter judgment in default, what, to another Contracting State enforcing court, would have been the 'document which instituted [these] proceedings'? The answer may seem obvious—the writ.[394] But what if the writ was only generally

---

[386] This may be likely to occur in France; the *Cassation*'s attitude to such insufficiently-drafted documents in *Société Polypétrol c/ Société générale routière* 9.10.1991 (1993) *JDI* 157, (1992) *Rev crit* 516, [1993] I.L.Pr. 107; but Commission's view of the matter in *Sonntag v Waidmann* (C–172/91) [1993] ECR I–1963, at p.1974, para. 3 below, at p.484; the German courts appear to be uncharacteristically more generous in this area than the French: *BGH* 29.4.1999 (1999) *RIW* 698, (1999) *ZZP* 473, (2001) *IPRax* 230; Haas, U. 'Zur Anerkennung US-amerikanischer Urteile in der Bundesrepublik Deutschland' (2001) *IPRax* 195, at p.199: 'wenn der Beklagte aufgrund der Angaben im einleitenden Schriftstück in die Lage versetzt wird, die Entscheidung sachgerecht zu treffen, ob er sich auf das Verfahren einläßt oder nicht'('when, due to the statements in the document initiating the proceedings, the defendant is put in the position *to make an informed decision* whether or not he will appear in the proceedings').

[387] Note, some Contracting States have *not* extended the geographical reach of the Brussels Convention to their non-European territories.

[388] RSC Ord. 11 r.(3)(a).

[389] RSC Ord. 18 r.1.

[390] RSC Ord. 13 r.6A.

[391] RSC Ord. 13 r.7B, for Convention cases.

[392] *Supreme Court Practice, 1999*, 1998, Vol. I, p.139, para. 13/0/13.

[393] The 1998 Civil Procedure Rules make this distinction clearer.

[394] The point was never raised in those German cases which have dealt with the enforcement of English judgments: *OLG Frankfuhrt* 21.2.1991, IPRspr. (1991) Nr. 202; *OLG Hamm* 5.8.1992 (1993) *RIW* 148.

endorsed? Whether or not the defendant had actually received such a document, would it have been considered sufficiently detailed, or 'comprehensible',[395] to qualify at all as such a document under *Hengst*? Yet service of a more detailed statement of claim had never been a condition precedent[396] to a plaintiff's applying for leave to enter judgment in default of acknowledgment of service under RSC Ord.13 rule 7B. Nothing in *Hengst* would seem to have required a reversal of, or addendum to, the English procedure of obtaining a default judgment.

5.3.2(ii)   *The potential impact of Hengst v Campese on English proceedings which were instituted by a document/claim form on or after 26 April 1999*

For present purposes, civil and commercial actions commenced, or to be commenced, on or after 26 April 1999, are now governed by the 1998 Civil Procedure Rules. These rules have changed the nomenclature of the pleadings procedure (now called statements of case) for initiating, *inter alia*, High Court actions.

In contrast to the practice of the Commercial Court,[397] in the Queen's Bench Division, Part 7, Rule 7.2(1) and Practice direction 7, Rule 3.1 now provide that proceedings are started when the court issues 'a claim form'.[398] Rule 7.4(a)(b)[399] must now be read with some caution in the Brussels Convention context, and subject to the Queen's Bench Guide,[400] which states that 'where a Claim Form is to be served out of the jurisdiction,[401] the particulars of claim *must accompany* the Claim Form.'

---

[395] *Hengst v Campese* [1995] ECR I–2113, at p.2128, para. 21.

[396] Compare this to the position now under the 1998 Civil Procedure Rules, esp. Rule 7.4(a)(b), below, at n.399; all that was required was due service of the writ, expiry of the time period to acknowledge service, an affidavit of service, and finally leave under Ord. 13 r.7B.

[397] Special, idiosyncratic and adapted rules and practice directions, apply for Commercial Court actions, with which a large majority of Brussels Convention cases will be concerned; separate and careful reference therefore needs to be made to these rules in claims governed by them: esp. the practice guide called 'The Commercial Court Guide' in *Civil Procedure*, Volume 2, 2001, and to the comments therein on *separate* service of claim form and particulars of claim at pp.374–75, esp. paras. 2C–60–61, and PD6B rule 1.5.

[398] In most cases for our purposes, in Form N1, including, in Practice Direction 6B rules 1.1, 1.2., 1.3 (as appropriate)—supplementing section III of CPR Part 6—a Civil Jurisdiction and Judgments Act 1982 endorsement; in such cases, the claim form for service out of the jurisdiction has a six month validity period for service.

[399] Stating that 'particulars of claim' *must* either (a) be contained in or served with this claim form, or (b) be served on the defendant within 14 days of the service of this claim form; according to the Commercial Court guide, *Civil Procedure*, Volume 2, 2001, at p.374, para. 2C-61, this time limit of 14 days does not apply to Commercial Court actions—this relatively short period of 14 days is seen as unrealistic; service of the particulars of claim in these actions is extended, and to be accomplished within *28 days after acknowledgment of service.*

[400] *Civil Procedure*, Volume 2, 2001, at p.79.

[401] Cf *Knauf UK GmbH v British Gypsum Ltd and another* [2002] 1 WLR 907, CA. The advantage of service by an alternative means, under CPR 6.8(1), of a claim form, in a Brussels Convention case (Arts. 21/22), on a German company's solicitors *within* jurisdiction *not* permissible. The claimant's attempt, as David Steel J had found at first instance 'to forestall any attempt by [German defendant] Peters to take advantage of the disparity in periods needed to accomplish service. . .' [2001] 2 All ER

If the defendant fails to acknowledge service (of the claim form), the claimant may proceed to obtain[402] (an Article 27(2)) default judgment.[403]

The procedure to be followed by the claimant in such a case is given in Part 12 of the CPR. Rule 12.3(1)(a)(b) provides that the claimant may only obtain judgment in default if (a) the defendant has not filed an acknowledgment of service *and* (b) the relevant time period for doing so has expired. This period (for a European Contracting State domiciled defendant), is 21 days after (i) service of a 'fully endorsed'[404] claim form, or, if not, 21 days after (ii) service of the particulars of claim, when served separately (in Commercial Court actions).[405]

In stark contrast to the position under the former Rules of the Supreme Court, a default judgment cannot be obtained under the CPR on service of a non-particularised claim form *simpliciter*. Why is this? Rule 7.4(1)(b) provides the answer. At least in QBD actions, this provision is mandatory in requiring particulars of claim to be served: '[p]articulars of claim *must . . .* (b) *. . .* be served on the defendant by the claimant within 14 days after the service of the claim form.' Until the particulars of claim are served, the 21 day time limit for acknowledging service does not start to run against the defendant, and the claimant is therefore unable to apply for judgment in default.

What will be the most likely attitude of an enforcing court in another Contracting State to the new claim form/particulars of claim procedure, and ensuing default judgments under Article 27(2)? If a non-particularised claim form is served in a Commercial Court[406] action, the Article 27(2) 'document which instituted the proceedings'[407]—on either view of the matter in *Klomps*[408] or, arguably *Hengst*,[409]—will no doubt be considered to be service of the particulars of claim, *not* the non-particularised claim form. In this case, the crucially 'sufficient' period of time for the purposes of Article 27(2)—ie. that available to the defendant for the purposes of preventing the issue of a default judgment—will be the minimum 21 day period between service of the particulars of claim and the claimant's ability

---

(Comm) 332, at p.339, was considered by the Court of Appeal to be an impermissible subversion of the regime of international service agreements.

[402] Note the UK's declaration in the Information communicated by Member States under Art. 23 of Council Regulation (EC) No 1348/2000) of 29 May 2000 on the service in the Member States of judicial and extrajudicial documents in civil or commercial matters, 22 May 2001, [2001] OJ C151/4, at p.15, in conjunction with the prerequisites in Arts.19(1)(2) Council Service Regulation.

[403] I.e. a judgment in default of an acknowledgment of service under Rule 12.3(1)(a).

[404] I.e. one in which the particulars are contained in, or served with, the claim form, as *must* occur in a QBD action.

[405] PD6B rule 1.5.

[406] This problem does not appear to affect Queen's Bench Division actions.

[407] And which sets the 'sufficient' time period running.

[408] I.e., service only of a generally-endorsed claim form does not allow the claimant to obtain a judgment in default, capable of enforcement under Part III of the Conventions.

[409] I.e., a generally-endorsed claim form may not contain sufficient information about the claim to qualify as the 'document which institutes the proceedings'.

to apply for judgment in default.[410] Whether this time will prove to be 'sufficient'[411] will be a matter of fact for the enforcing court, a separate question dealt with below in its own subsection.

Following *Hengst*, then, it may well be considered by other Contracting State enforcing courts that time only begins to run, in a Commercial Court action, on service of the second document (the particulars of claim); it may be that only from the time of service of the particulars of claim will the defendant be able 'to assert his rights';[412] only on service of the particulars of claim may 'the document which instituted the proceedings' be fully constituted.[413] This will have important repercussions which will be readily appreciated: both the generally particularised claim form and particulars of claim may be subject to the vagaries[414] of international service under the 1965 Hague Service Convention[415] and now Council Service Regulation 1348/2000. Time, as that period to be considered as sufficient, will be counted[416] by an enforcing court, from the particulars of claim's service, not the claim form's. Yet, crucially, sufficient time, as far as the claimant may view matters, may well have been calculated by him with reference to service of the claim form. A defendant may also abscond, or disappear in the interim period[417] between valid

---

[410] Assuming the pre-requisites of CPR 12.3(3) and Art. 19(1) Council Service Regulation have otherwise been observed, i.e. (a) that the claim form/particulars of claim were served in accordance with the domestic law of the Member State addressed (for, presumably purely domestic actions) or (b) that the claim form/particulars of claim were actually delivered to the defendant or to his residence in accordance with the provisions of the Service Regulation, and that in either case sufficient time was allowed for the defendant to defend himself. The UK has made a declaration that, notwithstanding Art. 19(1), its courts may also give judgment in default if the requirements of Art. 19(2) have been met: Information communicated by Member States under Art. 23 of Council Regulation [2001] OJ C151/4, at p.15.

[411] Below, at pp.510 *et seq*, section 5.5.

[412] *Ibid.*,—this may happen in the Commercial Court, as it has been pointed out that the particulars of claim only need be served on a (Contracting State) defendant 28 days after this defendant returns the acknowledgment of service, if at all—Commercial Court Guide, *Civil Procedure*, Volume 2, 2001, at p.374.

[413] *Hengst Import BV v Anna Maria Campese* (C–474/93) [1995] ECR I–2113, at p.2128 para. 21.

[414] And this doubles the chance that, as happened in *Minalmet* or *Lancray*, Contracting State postal authorities may make service mistakes, reprehensible (and incurable) under the other additional 'due service' requirements of Art. 27(2).

[415] Since 31 May 2001 and for some months thereafter, we may be confronted with the anomalous situation of (in)valid service of a claim form under the 1965 Hague Service Convention prior to that date, and/or (in)valid service of particulars of claim under the Service Regulation 1348/2000, *even though* CPR Rule 6.26A(1) only subjects service of 'a claim form' to the regime under the Service Regulation. Note also, however, that the information regarding the UK in Annex II to Commission Decision of 25 September 2001 adopting a manual of receiving agencies and a glossary of documents that may be served under Council Regulation (EC) No 1348/2000 [2001] OJ L298/1, at p.476, omits to enumerate the particulars of claim as a 'document[] which may be served'. If *both* claim form and particulars of claim generically form 'the document which instituted proceedings', (at least in the eyes of other enforcing Contracting States), due service of the particulars of claim *must be regulated* under Service Regulation, in default of any other mechanism.

[416] In the case of a generally-endorsed claim form.

[417] Precisely what happened in *X. Financial Services GmbH gegen W. Bundesgericht* (Swiss) 12.7.1997, 123 BGE, III, 374, below, at pp.489–492.

service of the claim form and (perhaps now invalid) substituted service of the particulars of claim.

The problems that *Hengst* has introduced need careful attention when initiating an action in the Commercial Court—if an eventual default judgment creditor is not potentially to be robbed of the fruits of his litigation in other Contracting States. As far as English procedure is concerned, the ruling in *Hengst* should be taken as strong advice to (have) serve(d) the writ/claim form and statement/particulars of claim together (formerly under RSC Ord. 18 rule 1) and CPR Rules 6.26A and 7.4(1)(a), and not to send the two independently. More generally, and until the European Court rules on the point, as much detail as possible should be included in the document which institutes proceedings, so as to avoid the type of censure[418] meted out to the *Mahnverfahren* procedure by the *Cour de Cassation* in *Société Polypétrol c/ Société générale routière*.[419] The safest answer would seem to be to serve both (a correctly translated) claim form and particulars of claim together, if possible.[420]

5.3.3   The precise and/or sufficient contents of 'the document which instituted the proceedings'

A related problem[421] to the foregoing section is what detail the document which starts proceedings must contain to qualify as such under Article 27(2). The European Court missed the opportunity[422] for clarification of this particular issue[423] in *Volker Sonntag v Hans Waidmann and others*.[424] According to the report for the hearing[425] in this case, apart from being made aware of the criminal proceedings,[426] Mr Sonntag, the accused, was served with a document on (or by) the

---

[418] For insufficient information in the document instituting the proceedings, next section.

[419] 9.10.1991 (1993) *JDI* 157, (1992) *Rev crit* 516, [1993] I.L.Pr. 107.

[420] With a distant glance on the possible problems of enforcement in another Contracting State under Art. 27(2), as happened in similar circumstances *Berliner Bank A.G. v Karageorgis & another* [1996] 1 Lloyd's Rep. 426 (Colman J), where a full trial was conducted, despite the opportunity for proceedings to go by default.

[421] Of special concern to English practitioners in the Commercial Court, who may not initially serve a 'particularised' claim form.

[422] Not dealt with either in *Dieter Krombach v Andre Bamberski* (C–7/98) judgment 28.3.2000, nor in AG Saggio's opinion.

[423] The exact content a document must possess in order to qualify as a 'document' instituting proceedings; Art. 28(1)(d) of the Commission II interim text of the draft Hague Worldwide Judgments Convention states that the document which instituted the proceedings is to include 'the essential elements of the claim'; if this aspect was not already implicit in both Art. 27(2) and/or Art. 34(2) Brussels I Regulation, it is spelt out here.

[424] (C–172/91) [1993] ECR I–1963.

[425] *Ibid.*, at p.1965, para. 1.

[426] Two cases reported in *Digest*, D Series, Convention of 27 September 1968, Issue 5 Feb. 1993, D-I–27.2-B17 and D-I–27.2-B19 deal with a related problem of whether a 'document', whatever its contents, needs to be issued at all in criminal/*partie civile* proceedings; with opposite conclusions, below, at p.487.

16 February 1987, stating *simpliciter*[427] that the Waidmanns (as plaintiffs in the ensuing civil litigation) had become *parties civiles* in the Italian criminal proceedings. In its question 3, the referring *Bundesgerichtshof* asked whether this February document was sufficiently detailed so as to qualify as the 'document which instituted the proceedings'. Unfortunately, the Court considered that Sonntag had submitted/'appeared' in any event, and so did not deal with the point.[428] AG Darmon, too, although he raised our particular concern[429] in his opinion, became lost in his amalgamation of this question with the issue of appearance.[430] The Italian Government, at the hearing, simply submitted, in accordance with Italian law,[431] that the quantum of *partie civile* damages need not have been specified in the application.

The Commission did at least propose an answer. In regard to the necessary detail, it pointed out that a defendant must be given

> at least *a general idea of the nature of the claim* made and of the proceedings brought . . . even though the document in question gives no more precise details of the magnitude[432] of the civil claim . . .[433]

From this it is expected that, outside the context of *partie civile* proceedings (annexed to a criminal charge),[434] the 'general idea' to be given in 'normal' civil proceedings should, *a fortiori*, be more detailed. No doubt, in such a situation, the European Court will be tempted to fall back on general principles, so beloved by it, in the interpretation of Article 27(2) generally: that the defendant be given an adequate opportunity to defend himself.[435] This may have a narrow or broad interpretation, depending, no doubt, on the complexity of the dispute. At the narrow end of the spectrum, all that may be necessary is a cursory statement that an action has been commenced, without more;[436] conversely, in more complex cases,[437] more detailed point-by-point pleadings may be required for the defendant adequately to prepare his defence. This was the finding of the only case, to

---

[427] One complaint was, *inter alia*, that the amount claimed was not mentioned, [1993] ECR I–1963, at p.1966, para. 4, sub-para. 4 *in fine*.

[428] At p.2001, para. 43.

[429] At p.1986, para. 78.

[430] At p.1987, para. 80.

[431] This fact may be relevant; yet an autonomous definition of what the document must contain, despite *Hengst*, is preferable; cf art.1413 NCPC, above, which stipulates the information that the *ordonnance* must contain to avoid a sanction of nullity.

[432] *Quaere*, whether this extends beyond mere quantum to more expansive information?

[433] At p.1974, para. 3; Gaudemet-Tallon, in (1994) *Rev crit* 96, at p.114, thinks that this 'Community' definition will be taken up by the European Court in the future; cf definition at German autonomous recognition and enforcement law under § 328 Abs.1 Nr.2 ZPO in *BGH* 29.4.1999 (1999) *RIW* 698, (1999) *ZZP* 473, (2001) *IPRax* 230, incidentally drafted in precise terms of Art. 27(2).

[434] An accused may well have a better idea of what he has, or has not, allegedly done.

[435] The conclusion reached in *Société Polypétrol c/ Société générale routière* 9.10.1991 (1993) *JDI* 157, (1992) *Rev crit* 516, [1993] I.L.Pr. 107.

[436] In a case of an undisputed debt, in summary proceedings.

[437] It may be safe to assume that most cases before the English Commercial Court will fall into this category.

the writer's knowledge, that has dealt squarely with this problem under the Convention:[438] *Société Polypétrol c/ Société générale routière.*[439] In this case the *Cour de Cassation* found[440] that the rights of the defence had been adversely prejudiced under Article 27(2), by an insufficiently drafted[441] 'document which instituted the proceedings':

> l'acte introductif d'instance . . . doit, par définition, contenir *des indications suffisantes, sur l'objet de la demande,* à défaut desquelles les droits de la défense ne sont pas respectés . . .[442] [443]

The commentator on the case is unsure whether the *Cassation* is reviewing the sufficiency of grounds in the document as a function of 'due service', the sufficiency of the document itself, or a wider concept of the rights of the defence generally.[444] Reading the above quotation, it seems that it is the last option which is meant. The commentator points out, however, that the Convention does not allow for the control of the procedure undertaken in the adjudicating court, except in clearly defined and exhaustive circumstances:

> Il n'y avait donc pas lieu de vérifier la régularité de l'acte introductif d'instance . . .[445] [446]

Clues can be gained as to the likely attitude of the German courts as to the sufficiency aspect of the document which instituted the proceedings from the relatively recent *Bundesgerichtshof* decision under German autonomous recognition and enforcement law, §328 Abs.1 Nr.2.[447] The case concerned the enforcement of a US district court default judgment. The court acknowledged,[448] and did not censure, the fact that certain US State procedural systems only require the delivery of detailed, enumerated claims once the defendant has indicated his willingness to defend the action. If this attitude is carried across[449] to Article 27(2), there is no reason to suppose that a non-particularised English claim form will be attacked on the grounds of insufficiency in Germany:

---

[438] Again at German autonomous law *BGH* 29.4.1999 (1999) *RIW* 698, (2001) *IPRax* 230, noted by Haas, U. (2001) *IPRax* 195, below, this and following page.

[439] *Cassation* 9.10.1991 (1992) *Rev crit* 516; (1993) *JDI* 157.

[440] (1992) *Rev crit* 516, at p.517.

[441] Or 'motivé' as the French court has it; for cases where it is the *judgment* itself that is 'non-motivé' and therefore against Art. 27(1), public policy above, at pp.407 *et seq*, section 4.4.1.

[442] ('the document instituting the proceedings must, by definition, contain sufficient details as to the basis of the claim, in default of which the rights to the defence will not have been respected').

[443] (1992) *Rev crit* 516.

[444] (1993) *JDI* 157, at p.159, paras. 3, and 4 respectively, Huet.

[445] ('there is not place for verifying the correctness of the document instituting the proceedings').

[446] *Ibid.*, at p.159.

[447] *BGH* 29.4.1999 (1999) *RIW* 698, commentary by Roth (1999) *ZZP* 473, at p.483; §328 Abs. 1 Nr.2 provides in identical terms to Art. 27(2) for 'das verfahrenseinleitende Schriftstück' ('the document which instituted the proceedings').

[448] (1999) *RIW* 698, at p.700, col. 2.

[449] ECJ authorities on Art. 27(2) were considered by the court in interpreting their autonomous law.

Es is ausreichend, wenn der Beklagte über die *wesentlichen Elemente* des Rechtsstreits in Kenntnis gesetzt ist.[450]

5.3.4   *Partie civile* actions[451] themselves and the document instituting the proceedings

An issue related to the detail necessarily to be included in the document instituting the proceedings is how Article 27(2) interacts with *partie civile* actions—where a civil compensation claim is made during[452] criminal proceedings. The question centres around whether the 'document which instituted the proceedings' is either the criminal charge/summons itself, served on the accused/perpetrator, or the summons containing a statement that *parties civiles* have been joined[453] thereto, or a fresh independent writ/claim form and statement/particulars of claim as in 'normal' adversarial civil litigation.

Geimer,[454] for one, is no doubt correct when he states that the criminal charge *simpliciter* is insufficient to make the accused aware that a civil claim will be made against him:

Zustellung der Strafklage genügt nicht, wenn für den Beklagten nicht deutlich[455] gemacht wird, daß im Strafverfahren auch zivilrechtliche Ansprüche erhoben sind.[456]

Implicitly, too, the comparison to normal civil proceedings is rejected.

Whether conclusions can be drawn from the fact that, in *Sonntag v Waidman*, no objection was taken in the case to the 'document which instituted the proceedings' in the form that was served on Sonntag, is unclear. The rôle of national

---

[450] ('it is sufficient that the defendant is made aware of the *essential elements* of the dispute') (1999) *ZZP* 490, Roth, original emphasis.

[451] A *vague* approximation, and a considerably weaker mechanism in England and Wales to these actions, is the making of a compensation order against convicted persons under s 130 Powers of Criminal Courts (Sentencing) Act 2000—by s 130(1) an order may be made 'on application or otherwise': *Archibold, Criminal Pleading, Evidence and Practice,* 2001, at p.679 does not provide any elucidation of the (application) procedure, nor the necessary detail for any comparison to the *partie civile* procedure to be made; such approximation *dubitante* editors of *The Laws of Scotland,* 1991, Vol.4, 'Civil Jurisdiction', at p.26, para. 38—'there is no "claim" in any sense'.

[452] Notable in enforcement sphere have been *Black v Yates* [1992] QB 526 (at common law, 'automatic' *partie civile* proceedings unless reservation made, in Spain); in Italy, *Volker Sonntag v Hans Waidmann and others* (C–172/91) [1993] ECR I–1963 and in France *Dieter Krombach v Andre Bamberski* (C–7/98), judgment unreported 28.3.2000; for referring case, *BGH* 4.12.1997, (1998) *IPRax* 205, [1998] I.L.Pr. 681.

[453] As happened in *Sonntag v Waidmann* (C–172/91) [1993] ECR I–1963 itself; the report of the judgment of the European Court of Human Rights in *Affaire Krombach c. France* (No.29731/96) of 13.1.2001, reveals that the complainant Krombach submitted to the Court that he had not received any information as to the particulars of claim or conclusions in the *partie civile* action itself, at para.47.

[454] Geimer and Schütze, 1997, p.479, para. 109.

[455] *Contra, Gerechtshof s'- Hertogenbosch* 25.6.1981, *Digest,* D Series, Convention of 27 September 1968, Issue 5 Feb. 1993, D- I–27.2-B17, stating that nothing but the criminal summons is necessary.

[456] ('service of the criminal summons itself is insufficient, when it is not made clear to the defendant that in the criminal proceedings additional civil claims will be raised'), *ibid.*

procedural rules[457] in the enquiry also needs clarification, especially in the light of certain statements by the European Court in *Hengst Import BV v Anna Maria Campese.*[458]

Two cases reported in the *European Court Digest*[459] that have considered the sufficiency aspect of *partie civile* actions, come to opposite conclusions on this topic. However, the translated transcripts are so scant as to make comparisons, or even the drawing of conclusions, doubtful. The earlier of the two, *Centrale Suikermaatschappij BV and Mahijssen v De Deugd,*[460] from the *Gerechtshof 's-Hertogenbosch*, states that 'Article 27 of the Convention did not require it to be mentioned in the document instituting proceedings that the injured parties would be pursuing a claim for damages under civil law'; a German court, the *LG Münster,*[461] came to the opposite conclusion. In this case there was no enforcement ordered of a Belgian judgment since there was 'no proof that the respondents had been duly informed that a civil claim was to be pursued in the course of criminal proceedings.'

In the recent European Court case of *Dieter Krombach v Andre Bamberski,*[462] the question of the enforcement of a *partie civile* judgment again came before the European Court. As we have seen, in French criminal proceedings against a German citizen, Krombach, a civil claim was simultaneously[463] served with the criminal indictment on him, in Germany, on 5.6.1993. No doubt, had this *partie civile* claim not been served at all, his defence would have taken the point, and additional questions[464] would have been submitted. The safest answer to the question of whether to inform the accused of a concurrent civil claim is in the affirmative, perhaps even in as great a detail as the national (criminal) procedural rules allow and/or require.

5.3.5   The subsequent service of other, additional documents in the proceedings, and any requirements of Article 27(2)

There are those[465] who view the plaintiff/claimant's strict Article 27(2) service requirements as encompassing no more than informing the defendant, for the first time, that proceedings have been commenced against him; thereafter,

---

[457] Above, at pp.480 *et seq.*
[458] (C–474/93) [1995] ECR I–2113, at p.2128, para. 21, *in fine*: 'the requirement for joint service . . . is confirmed by Art. 643 . . .'.
[459] *Digest*, D Series, Convention of 27 September 1968, Issue 5 Feb. 1993.
[460] *Digest*, I–27.2.—B17, of 25.6.1981.
[461] *Digest*, I–27.2.—B19, of 5.4.1982; *contra*, Kropholler, 2002, at p.401, para. 26.
[462] Referring court reference at *BGH* 4.12.1997 (1998) *IPRax* 205, [1998] I.L.Pr. 681.
[463] (1998) *IPRax* 205, at p.205, [1998] I.L.Pr. 681, at p.683, para. 3.
[464] For the public policy points under Art. 27(1) referred to the Court, above, at pp.395 *et seq*, public policy section.
[465] Geimer, R. and Schütze, R. 1997, wholly outspoken in this area of recognition and enforcement law.

subsequent summonses,[466] extending, or altering the proceedings,[467] although of course requiring service, are not subject to Article 27(2)'s rigours:

> Article 27 Nr.2 EuGVÜ will eben die rechtzeitige Kenntnis vom ausländischen Verfahren als solchen gewährleisten, nicht dessen genauen Inhalt.[468]

The wording of Article 27(2) is specific, and would support such a conclusion. It bites only on a document[469] that 'institutes' the proceedings, not on subsequent summonses. So long as the parties remain the same,[470] the continuing development of the proceedings does not concern Article 27(2).[471]

Few cases outside Germany have had to deal with this problem. In *BGH* 10.7.1986,[472] (notable also for its acceptance of a plea of fraud under Article 27(1)[473]), the Italian plaintiff/judgment creditor, after service of the instituting document, increased the size of her claim, without further service of the amended amount on the German defendant. The 'document which instituted the proceedings', with the lower figure, had been validly served. The *Bundesgerichtshof* acknowledged that only this latter document was subject to Article 27(2):

> Derartige Fehler bei der Zustellung späterer Schriftsätze rechtfertigen [the application of Article 27(2)] nicht.[474]

Again, in *BGH* 21.3.1990,[475] in divorce proceedings in Italy, an Italian wife had petitioned for divorce, and requested maintenance for the children. This petition was duly served on the Italian husband, domiciled in Germany, and relief was granted. The husband did not appear at first instance in Italy, nor in appeal proceedings, in which an additional lump sum, not initially pleaded in the petition,[476] was awarded[477] to the wife. In enforcement proceedings in Germany, both lower

---

[466] On this point *Cassation*, 11.6.1991, *Sté Biomécanique intégrée c. Sté Fabrique nationale de Herstal*, (1991) *JCP*, IV, p.317, 'seul l'acte introductif d'instance est à prendre en considération'; *Efeteio Thessaloniki* 18.12.2000 *Re Recognition of an Italian judgment* [2002] I.L.Pr. 165, at p.169.

[467] In some detail Frank, M. *Das verfahrenseinleitende Schriftstück in Article 27 Nr.2 EuGVÜ, Lugano-Übereinkommen und in Article 6 Haager Unterhaltsübereinkommen 1973*, 1998.

[468] ('Art. 27(2) Brussels Convention only serves to give timely knowledge of the foreign proceedings, not their exact content'), according to Braun, 1992, at p.71.

[469] Or a combination of such documents, *Hengst Import BV v Anna Maria Campese* (C–474/93) [1995] ECR I–2113.

[470] Geimer and Schütze, 1997, at p.479, para. 10.

[471] It may, however, involve the application of Art. 27(1), above, at pp.429 *et seq.*

[472] *BGH* 10.7.1986 IPRspr. (1986) Nr. 182.

[473] Above, at pp.421 *et seq*, section 4.4.4, on Art. 27(1).

[474] ('such defects in service of later documents do not justify [the application of Art. 27(2)]'), in *BGH* 10.7.1986 IPRspr. 1986 Nr. 182, at p.417.

[475] (1990) *FamRZ* 868.

[476] Although it should have been irrelevant (Art. 28 I), there was some discussion in the case, whether, under Italian law, a fresh cause of action was necessary to grant the lump sum, or even whether an Italian appeal court had jurisdiction to award it *sua sponte*.

[477] The fact that the appellate Italian court had allegedly breached its own internal rules in doing so was also held to be irrelevant: now for confirmation of this view, *Hengst Import BV v Anna Maria Campese* (C–474/93) [1995] ECR I–2113, at p.2129, para. 24 (where service out of the application for the *decreto ingiunctivo* should not have taken place), (compare at (English) common law *Pemberton v*

courts[478] took the view that service of an application for the additional lump sum was necessary under Article 27(2), but was not forthcoming, and the judgment for the additional sum could therefore not be enforced. The *BGH* reversed this, finding

> Article 27 Nr.2 . . . verlangt aber . . . nur in den von dieser Vorschrift genannten Kernpunkten die Gewährung des rechtlichen Gehörs.[479]

The husband had been duly and timeously notified of the document instituting proceedings, the petition. This, it was held, was as far as the defence of a fair hearing in Article 27(2) went. Service of any additional documents,[480] extending the claim to a lump sum could not be challenged under Article 27(2). That was the remit[481] of Article 27(1).

As a tentative conclusion, the issue of the document instituting the proceedings appears to be governed in part by the need for a fair hearing in the eyes of the enforcing court, and also by the procedural law of the *lex fori*. A survey of the above cases seems to point out the need in this document to be as detailed as the national procedural law will allow,[482] so as to avoid any possible censure from an enforcing court under Article 27(2)—that such a document was not detailed enough to enable the defendant to assert his rights.

Bearing the rights of the defence in mind, manifest in Article 27(2), the new Civil Procedure Rules, as adapted by the Commercial Court, may well highlight the risky practice of merely serving a claim form, waiting for an acknowledgment of service before serving particulars of claim, and in default of which, applying for judgment in default of acknowledgment of service.

5.3.6   Contested summary (debt collection) actions: the Mahnverfahren and the lodging of an objection—the effect on 'the document which instituted the proceedings'

In *Peter Klomps v Karl Michel*[483] and in *Hengst Import BV v Anna Maria Campese*,[484] the defendants to the summary proceedings did not lodge an objection under, respectively, §§694 and 696 ZPO against the *Mahnbescheid*, and under

---

Hughes [1899] 1 Ch. 781); for enforcement in Germany of an Italian *decreto*, after erroneous service *ex juris*: OLG München 24.3.1999 IPRspr. (1999) Nr. 159, at p.378: such a *decreto*, applying Italian civil procedure and despite the glaring error, not found to be a complete nullity.

[478] (1990) *FamRZ* 868, at p.869.

[479] ('Art. 27(2) demands access to a fair hearing only in respect of the essentials laid down in the article itself'), *ibid.*

[480] *Ibid.*, at p.869, relying on its earlier jurisprudence.

[481] The mutual exclusivity section, above, at pp.443 *et seq*, section 5.1.2.

[482] Cf *Berliner Bank A.G. v Karageorgis & anor.* [1996] 1 Lloyd's Rep. 426: 'the defendant has taken no part in the proceedings . . . [and] the court in giving judgment in this automatic way has not reviewed the merits of the claim' at p.427 (Colman J).

[483] (C–166/80) [1981] ECR 1593.

[484] (C–474/93) [1995] ECR I–2113.

Article 641 of the Italian procedural code,[485] against the *decreto ingiunctivo*. Provisionally enforceable decisions potentially recognisable under Article 25 and Title III, were issued upon their default of appearance. However, this section is concerned with the question of what would have been the position under Article 27(2) if objections had been lodged in time? Would an enforcing court consider, in such circumstances, that the defendants had cast away their shield? If not, would the document instituting the proceedings subsequently still be considered[486] to be service of the first document/documents which notified the defendants of actions instituted against them?[487] Would a fresh writ/claim form have to be duly and timeously re-served, under pain of nullity under Article 27(2), as if the original *Mahnverfahren* or *ingiunctivo* proceedings had never taken place?

The Swiss *Bundesgericht* has had to deal with the enforcement of a contradicted *Mahnverfahren* judgment in *X. Financial Services GmbH v W*[488] under Article 27(2) of the Lugano Convention. X.FS had demanded over DM 116,000 against a Mr. W in purely domestic German *Mahnverfahren* proceedings. The *Mahnbescheid*[489] was served on the debtor W on 31.3.1994 at his home in Germany. On 7.4.1994, W lodged an objection, indicating that he knew of the proceedings. Under the *Mahnverfahren* procedure, the lodging of an objection prevents the issue of the provisionally enforceable judgment from being granted;[490] either party, under §696(1), can thereupon demand an *inter partes* procedure, via a 'Streitantrag'. The applicant for this *inter partes* procedure must substantiate his claim,[491] and deliver to the court a document to this effect (an 'Anspruchsbegründung') under §697(1), which is served in the normal way—i.e. as a 'normal' writ ('Klageschrift') would be. X. FS therefore tried to serve its 'Anspruchsbegründung', but W had, in the meantime, left Germany for Zürich. Substituted service of this 'new' claim on W occurred in March 1995 in Germany. On 13 June 1995, the *LG Stuttgart* issued a default judgment, which was also served by substituted service. After eventually locating W in Zürich, X. FS attempted to enforce the default judgment there, which succeeded at first instance. W appealed and was successful. X. FS appealed to the *Bundesgericht*. The appeal court[492] had taken the view that the document that instituted proceedings could vary according to whether or not an objection

---

[485] Cf Arts.1412, 1415-16 NCPC.

[486] The document instituting the proceedings, whether defined autonomously (*Klomps*) or not (*Hengst*), can only be but inextricably linked to the procedure in the summary proceedings themselves, as the decision discussed here demonstrates.

[487] It would if Kropholler's definition, above, at p.466, is accepted.

[488] 12.7.1997, 123 BGE, III, 374.

[489] The pure procedural formalities for its issue having been satisfied.

[490] Although, technically, the whole process ends with the application to continue with contentious proceedings, if the creditor wishes to pursue the claim further; also Koch and Diedrich, 1998, at p.115.

[491] In a similar way to serving detailed statement/particulars of claim in English procedural law.

[492] *X. Financial Services GmbH gegen W. Bundesgericht* (Swiss) 12.7.1997, 123 BGE, III, 374, at p.379, point 3.

was lodged. If—as had happened—such an objection *was* lodged in due time, the proceedings became contentious:[493]

> Mahnverfahren und streitiges Verfahren bilden somit keine Verfahrenseinheit, weshalb der Mahnbescheid *grundsätzlich nicht zugleich* verfahrenseinleitendes Schriftstück bezuglich des streitigen Verfahrens sein könne.[494]

The *Bundesgericht* took due account of the European Court's decisions in *Hengst*[495] and left it open whether, in the light of *Hengst*, *Klomps'* view that the *Mahnbescheid* is the document which instituted the proceedings is still correct, in an uncontradicted case. The *Mahnbescheid* may not be sufficiently detailed enough to satisfy the *Hengst*, additional, requirement of 'comprehensibility'.[496]

On the facts before it, and reviewing German procedural law, the Federal court found that on lodging an objection '[d]as Verfahren tritt damit in ein neues Stadium':[497]

> Die Zustellung des Mahnbescheids versetzt den Beklagten nur in die Lage, seine Rechte innerhalb *dieses* Verfahren wahrzunehmen. Weder weisst er zu jenem Zeitpunkt, ob der Kläger seinen behaupteten Anspruch überhaupt weiterfolgen wird, *noch auf welche Grundlage* dieser die Forderung stützt.[498]

It confirmed that the appeal court was correct to deprive the *Mahnbescheid*, in a *contradicted* case, of its quality as the 'document instituting the proceedings'. Relying on the general principle which Article 27(2) represents—the right to a fair hearing—the Federal Court found that this principle is only guaranteed

> wenn er auch von dem Forseztungsantrag und der Anspruchsbegründung des Klägers Kenntnis erhalten hat, so dass er nun seinerseits in der Lage ist, die *Fundiertheit* des klägerischen Anspruchs zu beurteilen und sich mit einer begründeten Eingabe zu verteidigen.[499]

The impression from the attitude of the highest Swiss court in this case, is that a distinctly hostile[500] reaction to the German *Mahnverfahren* procedure has

---

[493] According to German procedural law—Koch and Diedrich, 1998, at p.115.

[494] ('*Mahnverfahren* and contentious proceedings do not form a unified procedure, so that the *Mahnbescheid cannot, in essence, simultaneously* be the 'document which instituted the proceedings' as regards the contentious proceedings'), 123 BGE, III, 374, p.382.

[495] Especially at para. 21 thereof and Grunsky, W. 'Das verfahrenseinleitende Schriftstück beim Mahnverfahren' zu *Hengst Import BV v Anna Maria Campese* 1996 *IPRax* 245.

[496] Above, at pp.477 *et seq.*

[497] ('the proceedings enter a new phase'), in 123 BGE, III, 374, p.382.

[498] ('Service of the *Mahnbescheid* only puts the defendant in a position to defend himself in those proceedings. He neither knows at this time whether the plaintiff will continue with his claim, as made, nor on what basis it is founded.'), *ibid.*

[499] ('when he is also aware of both the plaintiff's application to continue with the proceedings ('Fortsetzungsantrag') and the basis of the plaintiff's claim ('Anspruchsbegründung'), so that he is in a position to judge the strengths and weaknesses of the plaintiff's case, and be able to defend himself with a reasoned submission'), *ibid.*, at p.383.

[500] No doubt for the same reason the French *Cassation* is so adverse to decisions which are not reasoned in *Mahnverfahren* procedures: *Société Polypétrol c/ Société générale routière* 9.10.1991 (1993) *JDI* 157.

emerged. This is even more surprising in that Swiss procedural law provides for an almost identical form of proceeding.

Having discarded the *Mahnverfahren,* (which was correctly served), as the document instituting the proceedings, the court did not find it necessary to subject the 'Anspruchsbegründung' to Article 27(2), because the judgment itself was not sufficiently reasoned (as to jurisdiction) for the court to be able to judge its conformity with the transitional provisions of Article 54(2) Lugano Convention.

In conclusion, the form that a document instituting proceedings may take is as polymorphic as the number of different civil and commercial proceedings in any one Contracting State. In 'normal' civil proceedings, that there could be any confusion over what document is (adequately) constituted by this phrase appeared to be uncontroversial. Yet the sufficiency of detail necessary, and the possibility that the document which instituted proceedings can be seen as a collective noun has introduced unwarranted and unwelcome confusion into this area. It has been the specialised, truncated debt collection actions, exemplified by the *Mahnverfahren* and *decreto ingiunctivo* procedures, that have created the problems, and provoked the definitions. As has been demonstrated, uncertainties have arisen, under the Civil Procedure Rules, for judgments in default of acknowlegment of service— where claim form and particulars of claim are issued and served separately, if at all.

5.4   'DUE SERVICE' UNDER ARTICLE 27(2)[501]

This aspect of Article 27(2) has proved to be most problematic, even from the outset.[502] Early German[503] cases demonstrated the problems. They gave adverse[504] and hostile interpretative solutions to Article 27(2), which would later[505] only be

---

[501] Fortunately, a requirement of 'due' service will be omitted, as from 1.3.2002 (except for Denmark), in Art. 34(2) Brussels I Regulation; Art. 66(2)(a) of the Brussels I Regulation—a transitional provision *ratione temporis* for enforcement of judgments—will ensure that 'due' service (under Art. 27(2) of the Conventions) does not have any transitional life-span after this date; until then, the former regime of the 1965 Hague Convention, and from 31.5.2001, Service Regulation 1348/2000 need to be consulted for the 'due' service requirements of the Member States of the EU, (excepting, again, Denmark).

[502] Droz, 1972, pp.316–17, para. 503; and *OLG Stuttgart* 16.8.1977 IPRspr. (1977) Nr. 149, on postal service under the 1954 Hague Service Convention; implications summarised in Brand, P-A. 'Fehlerhafte Auslandszustellung' (2001) *IPRax* 173.

[503] In UK, France, Belgium and Switzerland the problem is not so nearly as acute as in Germany; contrast the postal service cases in Germany, below, with facts of *TSN Kunststoffrecycling GmbH v Jurgens,* QBD, 16.2.2001 (Jack J) (held 'due' service of German document instituting proceedings on an English domiciled defendant/judgment debtor under 1965 Hague Service Convention by postal service through letterbox at defendant's home address).

[504] To the free movement of judgments, at least.

[505] Section 5.1.1 on the historical aspects of Art. 27(2), and whether these problems should have been foreseen under the 1968 and 1988 Conventions.

confirmed by the European Court in both *Isabelle Lancray S.A. v Firma Peters und Sickert KG*[506] and *Firma Minalmet GmbH v Firma Brandeis Ltd.*[507]

The tone that was set early on (in Germany), and that has prevailed, is amply demonstrated by *OLG Stuttgart*, 16.8.1977,[508] and the *OLG Hamm* 12.12.1977[509] as regards due service.[510] This tendency has continued, during and after the various references to the European Court in *Klomps* and *Debaecker v Bouwman*[511] through *Lancray*[512] and *Minalmet* to the present.

The crux of the problem in interpreting the 'due' service aspect of Article 27(2) was, and continues to be, the *renvoi*[513] of the Brussels Convention to other international Conventions on the 'service'[514] of judicial documents abroad. Not only did[515] these Service Conventions need to be understood and interpreted, but so did a myriad of supplementary Conventions[516] which elaborate on these 'parent' service Conventions. As if this were not bad enough, the methods of service envisaged by these Conventions, and employed by the adjudicating court, often involved transmission of the documents to be served on a Central Authority in the Contracting State where the defendant was domiciled. This was often accompanied by a request that they be served in accordance[517] with the law of this recipient State.[518]

The law employed on these occasions was commonly not the *lex fori simpliciter*, but that embellished by the aforementioned supplementary agreements, which

---

[506] (C–305/88) [1990] ECR I–2725; *OLG Hamm* 12.12.1977 (1980) *RIW*/AWD 62 which stated early on that the two requirements of Art. 27(2) were cumulative; *OLG Frankfurt a.M.* 21.8.1978 (1980) *RIW*/AWD 63; also the withdrawn reference of the *BGH* of 17.12.1987, case (C–36/88) *Carl Schilling v Merbes Sprimont Travaux* [1988] OJ C79/4, which asked the same question as *Lancray*.

[507] (C–123/91) [1992] ECR I–5661; in *OLG Stuttgart* 16.8.1977 IPRspr. (1977) Nr. 149.

[508] IPRspr. 1977 Nr. 149.

[509] (1980) *RIW*/AWD 62.

[510] The latter court commenting on the cumulative aspects of Art. 27(2).

[511] (C–49/84) [1985] ECR 1779.

[512] The appeal court's hostile attitude to enforcement in *Lancray*: *OLG Hamm* 27.11.1987 IPRspr. (1987) Nr. 159.

[513] Art. IV of the Protocol, and Art. 20: for relationships: Wiehe, 1993, at p.31; also Kennett, W. 'Service of documents in Europe' (1998) *CJQ* 284, at p.297.

[514] Note the scope of these service Conventions themselves are controversial, in *remise au parquet* section; Schlosser, P. (2000) 284 *Recueil des Cours* 88, at pp.93–94, and p.107; as already mentioned, since 31 May 2001, the former regime of service of judicial documents throughout the Member States of the European Union (except Denmark) has been replaced by Service Regulation 1348/2000—see for the English reception of the Service Regulation, The Civil Procedure (Amendment No.2) Rules 2001, SI 2001/1388, rules 1(c), and 2–11 inclusive, and below at pp.507 *et seq* for a discussion of its effects on 'due' service.

[515] The former service rules under, *inter alia*, the 1965 Hague Service Convention, continue to apply to Denmark.

[516] In Germany's relations, *inter alia*, with many other 1954 and 1965 Hague Convention countries: cf *Molins Plc v G.D. S.p.A.* [2000] 1 WLR 1741; now *Knauf UK GmbH v British Gypsum Ltd and another* [2002] 1 WLR 907, CA (Henry LJ).

[517] As happened in *Lancray* and *Minalmet*, but proved to contain latent defects *ex post facto*; although notorious, the same problem, it is submitted, has been perpetuated in Art. 7(1) Service Regulation 1348/2000, below, at p.509.

[518] And may thus involve the enforcing court reviewing 'due service' (more scrupulously) under its own procedural law.

often contained essential and additional prerequisites[519] for due service. The upshot for the plaintiff/claimant was often, despite being in possession of a valid certificate of service,[520] latent ignorance of the true position of defective service,[521] when continuing with his action to judgment, and ultimate enforcement.

As with most other features of Article 27(2), it is to the wealth of German caselaw on the issue that the examination of 'due service' must now turn, to see the potential pitfalls that a plaintiff/claimant must overcome.[522]

5.4.1   The German position with regard to 'due service'

The case law history of due service in Germany is a litany of complex service arrangements, of which many foreign courts and legal advisers seem to have been unaware.[523] Although it is beyond the purlieu[524] of this treatment to enter into a detailed analysis of the Hague Service Conventions of 1905, 1954 1965 and/or now the Council Service Regulation 1348/2000,[525] a review of defective, as opposed to due, service in the Brussels Convention context is incomplete without mentioning the lesser-known, and ironically-entitled, 'additional' bilateral agreements for the further simplification of service under these instruments. Germany has concluded[526] such agreements with Luxembourg, Sweden, Denmark, Belgium, Austria, France, the Netherlands and Norway.[527] With Britain and Greece,

---

[519] Most notably, the need for a translation, in the event of substituted service—especially §3 *Gesetz zur Ausführung des Haager Übereinkommens vom 15. November 1965*, 1977 BGBl, I, 3105 and the ZRHO.

[520] From Hague Convention 1965, Art. 6 I, and Art. 46 (2) of the Brussels Convention; Brand, P-A. 'Fehlerhafte Auslandszustellung' (2001) *IPRax* 173, at p.173.

[521] This may well ultimately have been the case with the Italian court in *Molins Plc v G.D. S.p.A.* [2000] 1 WLR 1741, CA.

[522] There is no reason to suppose that the legal position has been changed by the Service Regulation 1348/2000; the Regulation contains no provision for curing defective service.

[523] Part of the problem (and beyond the control of legal advisers)—that of postal service—stems from the related topic of service by *remise au parquet* internally in some other Contracting States, notably France, below, at pp.500 *et seq*, and the German courts' adverse reactions to it: a relatively recent example being *OLG Karlsruhe* 12.3.1999 (1999) *RIW* 538, [2001] I.L.Pr. 208, below, at pp.504–505; and recently the censure meted out to an Italian default judgment in *OLG Köln* 7.3.2001 2001 NJW-RR 1576. A comparable English version, service by an alternative method under CPR 6.8(1), not permissible in Brussels Convention context, except in 'very special circumstances' : *Knauf UK GmbH v British Gypsum Ltd and another* [2002] 1 WLR 907, CA (Henry LJ); also the reverse side of the coin in *Phillips and others v Symes and another* [2002] 1 WLR 853, Ch.D., Hart J (Greek *remise au parquet simpliciter*, for purpose of 'first seisure' under Art.21 service not accepted).

[524] For more detailed views, Wiehe, 1993, at p.58.

[525] Council Regulation (EC) 1348/2000 of 29 May 2000 on the service in the Member States of judicial and extrajudicial documents in civil or commercial matters [2000] OJ160/37, which came into force on 31 May 2001; until 1.3.2002, comments in this section on the position under the 1965 Hague Convention will still have validity in transitional cases under the Brussels Convention.

[526] For a detailed account, Pfennig, 1988, at p.58 onwards.

[527] Of 2 August 1909, RGBl 1909, 910; RGBl 1910, 455; BGBl, 1932, II, 20; BGBl, 1959, II, 1525— *Tribunal de commerce de Bruxelles*, 29.5.1990, *M.Filipson / Gebr.Herberg K.G.*, (1992) *Rev. dr. comm. belge* 907 where service was considered as having taken place when the document was *received* by the

mention is made in the cases of two[528] bi-lateral Conventions concluded with these States. Together with these, finally, comes a non-legislative document, the *Rechtshilfeordnung für Zivilsachen*[529] of 19 October 1956, in its second, 1976 edition. This curious supplementary interpretative aid's aim[530] is to fill in the gaps left by the legislative instruments.[531]

One of the most common[532] errors committed by foreign courts, or the plaintiff/claimant's advisers, is postal service of the document instituting the proceedings under the Hague Conventions on a German domiciled defendant. Under Article 6(1)(i) of the 1954, and Article 10 of the 1965 Hague Service Conventions, Germany entered a reservation,[533] prohibiting the simple and informal 'transmission' of, *inter alia*, such documents by post to a German domiciled recipient. Courts[534] in The Netherlands,[535] Italy,[536] France,[537] Belgium[538] and Luxembourg,[539] and presumably, legal advisors in England and Wales,[540] have all fallen foul of this requirement. All these judgments became *brutum fulmen* in Germany.[541] Illustrative examples of the confusion will be briefly given. In *OLG Stuttgart* of

competent German authorities, at p.909; BGBl 1959, II, 1523; BGBl 1961, II, 1041; BGBl 1964, II, 468; BGBl 1979, II, 1292, respectively.

[528] RGBl 1928, II, 623; RGBl 1939, II, 848, respectively.

[529] Reprinted in Bülow, A. and Böckstiegel, K-H., *Der Internationale Rechtsverkehr in Zivil- und Handelssachen*, Band II, 1985, G1, esp. at pp.900–06, and §68; also Wiehe, 1993, at p.33 and at p.119 for an example of its operation.

[530] For example for a 'förmliche Zustellung', §67(1)(2) (via the procedures laid out in the ZPO), under the Hague Conventions, §71(1)(2) a translation *must be provided*; the Third update of the information communicated by Member States under Art. 23 of Council Regulation (EC) No 1348/2000 of 29 May 2000 on the service in the Member States of judicial and extra-judicial documents in civil or commercial matters, 17 January 2002, [2002] OJ C13/2 informs us that Germany *will indeed* accept postal service within the meaning of Art. 14(1) of the Service Regulation *provided* that the documents to be served are 'in the form of a registered letter with advice of delivery' translated into German, or are in the language of the transmitting state if the addressee is such a national.

[531] *OLG Düsseldorf* 4.4.1978 (1979) *RIW/AWD* 570, at p.571.

[532] Cf Pfennig, 1988, at p.87; again the 'error' is compounded by the fact that the civil procedure of some Contracting States—art.686 French NCPC—require a copy of the document served internally *au parquet* to be transmitted to the defendant by registered mail—German courts require 'service' be obligatory and accomplished under the Hague Service Conventions.

[533] Breach of this reservation by postal service has had important repercussions on the curing of defective service, below; since 31.5.2001 now only of concern to Danish practitioners; under Art. 14(2) Service Regulation 1348/2000, the 'provisional situation' now in Germany is that they will accept direct service of documents by post by registered letter with acknowledgment of receipt, translated into German, [2001] OJ C151/5.

[534] The injustice to the plaintiff is all the greater, in that service is taken out of the plaintiff's control and (ultimately) given to the local courts at the defendant's domicile.

[535] *OLG Düsseldorf* 23.8.1995, IPRspr. (1995) Nr. 168; *OLG Köln* 25.5.1990 IPRspr. (1990) Nr. 199.

[536] *OLG Stuttgart* 3.2.1983 IPRspr. (1983) Nr. 173; *OLG Stuttgart* 16.8.1977 IPRspr. (1977) Nr. 149; *OLG Hamm* 12.12.1977 (1980) *RIW/AWD* 62.

[537] *OLG Düsseldorf* 10.6.1992 IPRspr. (1992) Nr. 221.

[538] *OLG Düsseldorf* 4.4.1978 (1979) *RIW/AWD* 570.

[539] *OLG Hamm* 10.9.1979 IPRspr. (1979) Nr. 203.

[540] *OLG Frankfuhrt* 21.2.1991, IPRspr. (1991) Nr. 202.

[541] Also the procedure in operation in German autonomous law in *OLG Köln* 1.6.1994 *Re Enforcement of an Israeli Judgment* [1996] I.L.Pr. 573, at p.575, paras. 8–9—also actual receipt of the document does *not* cure defective service—as it was not spelt out as a method in the 1965 Hague Service Convention.

16.8.1977,[542] the Italian courts seemed to have been unaware of Germany's Article 6(1)(i) 1954 Hague Convention reservation concerning postal service; in *OLG Stuttgart* 3.2.1983,[543] they were equally ignorant of a similar reservation in Article 10(a) of the 1965 Convention. All the more unforgivable therefore is the case of *OLG Düsseldorf* of 23.8.1995,[544] in which the local court in Utrecht, The Netherlands, used postal service. The familiar rejection of due service under Article 27(2) was presaged by now the repetitive formulaic statement:

> weil die Bundesrepublik . . . der Anwendung von Article 10 . . . widersprochen hat, ist die formlose Übersendung eines Schriftstücks durch einfachen Brief an einem in Deutschland wohnhaften Empfänger keine vertragsgerechte Zustellungsform.[545]

A supreme example of the confusion that can be caused by the combination of postal service, the 1965 Hague Convention and the additional bilateral Conventions is *OLG Frankfurt*, in 21.2.1991.[546] An English High Court writ had been sent by post to a German recipient. Although it was acknowledged[547] in the case that this was a valid means of service within England and Wales, the German reservation to Article 10 of the 1965 Hague Convention prohibited this method. Yet postal service could be agreed upon in additional bilateral Conventions, such as in a supplementary Convention dating back to 1928.[548] Article 6 of this Convention provides:

> Documents may also be transmitted by post in cases where this method of transmission is permitted by the law of the country from which the document emanates.[549]

The *OLG Frankfurt* then came full circle by finding that the law of England and Wales, as the 'law of the country from which the document' emanated, included the 1965 Hague Convention—which of course, prohibits postal service on German recipients.[550] A more convoluted line of reasoning, and overburdened use of obscure laws on service can hardly be imagined; until further (German) cases on substituted service, and the requirements of a translation, are examined.

---

[542] *OLG Stuttgart* 16.8.1977 IPRspr. (1977) Nr. 149, at p.439
[543] *OLG Stuttgart* 3.2.1983 IPRspr. (1983) Nr. 173
[544] *OLG Düsseldorf* 23.8.1995 IPRspr. (1995) Nr. 168
[545] ('since Germany has entered a reservation to Art. 10's application, service by informal transmission of a writ by post on a German domiciled recipient is not an agreed method of service'), at 1996 *RIW* 67, at p.68.
[546] *OLG Frankfuhrt* 21.2.1991, IPRspr. (1991) Nr. 202.
[547] IPRspr. (1991) Nr. 202, at p.425.
[548] *Reichsgesetzblatt* 1928, II, 623, at p.626.
[549] *Ibid.*, English/German version in Art. 6 of the original.
[550] This case would have provided a salutary warning for any eventual judgment in *Knauf UK GmbH v Gypsum Ltd and another*, had the first instance judge's views on service by an alternative method under CPR 6.8(1) prevailed before the Court of Appeal, [2002] 1 WLR 907.

The general rule on this aspect in Germany appears to be that 'informal service'[551] (by simple delivery/handing over of the document[552]) to a willing recipient[553] *does not need* to be accompanied by a translation[554]—subject to the important proviso that the recipient understands its contents, or is in a position to obtain a translation (§69(3) ZRHO). This presumably gives the recipient the opportunity to reject the document, if need be.

Formal service[555] is a completely different matter. If formal service is necessary,[556] in Article 5(1)(a) of the 1965 Hague Convention, or requested, in Article 5(1)(b), then, according to the explanatory BGBl 1977,[557] I, 3105, §3, and §71(1) ZRHO, a translation *must*[558] *be provided*:

> Eine förmliche Zustellung (Artikel 5 Abs.1 des Übereinkommens) ist nur zulässig, wenn das zuzustellende Schriftstück in deutscher Sprache abgefaßt oder in diese Sprache übersetzt ist.[559]

In addition therefore to the vicissitudes[560] of German law on domestic service, must be added this supplementary law interpreting the 1965 Hague Convention, with its requirement of a translation. Many cases illustrate judgments being refused under Article 27(2) for lack of a pre-requisite translation into German. *OLG Hamm* 27.11.1987[561] is a good example of this.

The necessity of a translation is not over-burdensome (in a large cross-border claim) in itself. Problems arise in regard to the need for translations when one method of (informal) service fails, and, presumably unknown to the claimant's advisers, where formal service is attempted in its place, but *without* a translation.

---

[551] An incorrect translation of §67(1)(1) 'formlose Zustellung'; for the differences in terminology under the 1965 Hague Service Convention, Kennett, W. 'Service of documents in Europe' (1998) *CJQ* 284, at pp.299–300.

[552] §67(1)(1) ZRHO.

[553] §68(2); §69(3) ZRHO requires additional time for the recipient to examine the document to see whether he will accept or reject it, together with the procedural consequences of ignoring the document—all of which must be certified as having taken place: §69(3) ZRHO.

[554] *OLG Koblenz* 3.12.1990 IPRspr. (1990) Nr. 203.

[555] §67(1)(2) 'förmliche Zustellung', means service, *inter alia*, under the domestic German provisions for service under the ZPO, where there appears to be no opportunity to reject documents.

[556] Or *ex post facto*, is deemed to have been so: the debacle in *Isabelle Lancray S.A. v Firma Peters und Sickert KG* (C–305/88) [1990] ECR I–2725 was caused by such a belated finding.

[557] An explanatory law on, *inter alia*, the 1965 Hague Convention: *Gesetz zur Ausführung des Haager Übereinkommens von 15. November 1965 über die Zustellung gerichtlicher und außergerichtlicher Schriftstücke im Ausland in Zivil- oder Handelssachen und des Haager Übereinkommens vom 18 März 1970 über die Beweisaufnahme im Ausland in Zivil- oder Handelssachen*, 22.12.1977 BGBl 1977, I, 3105.

[558] Otherwise, service will not be 'due' under Art. 27(2) Brussels Convention: an example *OLG München* 22.6.1992 IPRspr. (1992) Nr. 223.

[559] ('formal service (Art. 5(1) of the Convention) is only permitted when the document to be served is rendered in German, or so translated'), in §3.

[560] The fate of the writ in *Firma Minalmet GmbH v Firma Brandeis Ltd* (C–123/91) [1992] ECR I–5661, and its post-reference decision in *BGH* 18.2.1993 IPRspr. (1993) Nr. 169, [1995] I.L.Pr. 523.

[561] IPRspr. (1987) Nr. 159.

This, of course, happened in *Lancray v Peters*.[562] The unfairness to the French plaintiff in this case stems from the fact that the due service requirement in Article 27(2) is adjudged *ex post facto*, in the light of what form of service was actually employed, rather than the form originally envisaged/requested by the plaintiff. What was, no doubt, intended by the French plaintiff under Article 5(1)(a) of the 1965 Hague Service Convention was the *informal service* (by simple handing over) of the untranslated document on a willing recipient, *in casu*, the defendant's managing director;[563] what, in fact, occurred was *formal service* by way of substituted service on a secretary at the company's offices. *Ex post facto*, service was not duly effected because no translation was provided, which fell foul of §3 of the *Gesetz zur Ausführung des Haager Übereinkommens von 15. November 1965*[564] and §71(1) ZRHO.

Even this brief, yet complex, overview of international service between Germany and its Brussels Convention Contracting State partners, reveals the legal minefield[565] that awaits claimants/plaintiffs hoping to secure enforcement of judgments initially started by documents served under the Hague Conventions[566] and (German)[567] national procedural laws. The best that can be said is that a more thorough knowledge of the reservations Germany has made, and the additional bilateral agreements concluded, is essential.

The strictness of the due service requirement as interpreted by the courts in Germany, has provoked criticism.[568] Even prior to the decision in *Lancray*—which held that the requirements of due and timely service were cumulative[569]—the German courts had come[570] to the same conclusion. In *OLG Hamm* 10.9.1979,[571]

---

[562] (C–305/88) [1990] ECR I–2725; the post-reference decision of the *BGH* is reported at *BGH* 20.9.1990 IPRspr. (1990) Nr. 200, Kaye P. (ed) *European Case Law on the Judgments Convention*, 1998, p.556, case no. 528.

[563] The whole edifice of recognition and enforcement under Part III and Art. 27(2) of the Brussels Convention 1968 turned on the managing director's (un)fortuitous absence from the company's offices; also *Evgenia Papadopoulo NV (Trading as 'Interexpress') v G.J. Van der Vaart Beheer BV (Trading as 'All Transport Rotterdam BV')* Gerechtshof, The Hague, 18.7.1996 [1998] I.L.Pr. 782, where a Greek plaintiff had continued his action, armed with a Dutch certificate of due service, only to find that the Dutch enforcing court unearthed *ex post facto* a breach of Dutch service rules.

[564] 22.12.1977 BGBl 1977, I, 3105, above, at p.494.

[565] Also the statement by Jenard in Rép. Notarial, 1994, Tome XI, livre VI, 3e partie, 1994: 'les autres jugements allemandes metionés . . . donnent la nette impression que l'on se trouve, pour faire exécuter un jugement en Allemagne, en présence d'une véritable «forteresse» . . .', at p.167.

[566] It is submitted that the position has altered little under Council Service Regulation 1348/2000, although caselaw is awaited to contradict this assertion.

[567] A breach by the German postal authorities of their *own* service rules proved fatal for Brandeis Ltd in *Firma Minalmet GmbH v Firma Brandeis Ltd* (C–123/91) [1992] ECR I–5661.

[568] Linke, H. 'Die Kontrolle ausländischer Versäumnisverfahren im Rahmen des EG-Gerichtsstands- und Vollstreckungsübereinkommens—Des Guten zuviel?' (1986) *RIW* 409, at p.413.

[569] *Isabelle Lancray S.A. v Firma Peters und Sickert KG* (C–305/88) [1990] ECR I–2725, at p.2748–49, para. 23.

[570] As early as 1979 in *OLG Hamm* 10.9.1979 IPRspr. (1979) Nr. 203.

[571] *Ibid.*

the court used almost identical words in 1979 that would be taken up later in *Lancray*[572] itself, to justify a cumulative interpretation:

> Der vom Article 27 Nr.2 GVÜ bezweckte Schutz ... würde weitgehend entwertet, wenn der Gläubiger geltend machen könnte, der Schuldner habe das zuzustellende Schriftstück rechtzeitig *auf andere Weise* erhalten oder von dem Verfahren von anderer Seite so rechtzeitig Kenntnis bekommen, daß ihm eine Verteidigung ... möglich gewesen sei.[573]

Indeed, the appeal court in the *Lancray* saga was,[574] again, the *OLG Hamm*. There the court accepted as a matter of course[575] that due service was a cumulative factor to be considered along with the sufficiency of service.

Geimer is critical of the draconian, yet perfectly legitimate way, a seemingly trivial defect in formal service—even when the defendant has actual knowledge of the proceedings—can upset the whole enforcement process system under the Brussels Convention.[576] So long as there has been sufficient time made available to a defendant, he argues,[577] Article 27(2)'s strictness should not apply to deny enforcement:

> auch wenn die Zustellung nach dem maßgeblichen Zustellungsrecht des Erststaates[578] mängelbehaftet war.[579]

Whatever method of service that a plaintiff envisages under Article 5(1) of the 1965 Hague Service Convention, experience shows that a translation into German is an extremely prudent and necessary adjunct, in all cases.

The complexity of the German position has no doubt allowed the impression that a certain amount of protectionism[580] is flourishing. Although not directly as a result of Article 27(2) of the Brussels Convention, the continual *renvoi* to more and more obscure service agreements does nothing to ease clarity, the international service of documents, nor, crucially, the free movement of judgments that

---

[572] [1990] ECR I–2725, at p.2748, para. 20.

[573] ('The protection envisaged in Art. 27(2) would be considerably weakened, if the judgment creditor could claim that the debtor had received the writ in due time *but by another method*, or that he had knowledge from his opponent in time, so that a defence was possible for him'), IPRspr. (1979) Nr. 203.

[574] *OLG Hamm* 27.11.1987 IPRspr. (1987) Nr.159.

[575] IPRspr. (1987) Nr.159, at p.405.

[576] Certainly a reason why 'due' service will be taken out of the defence in Art. 34(2) Brussels I Regulation.

[577] Geimer and Schütze, 1997, at p.473, para. 86.

[578] It is often not this law which has been breached, but a Service Convention, or even the national procedural service law of the recipient's/enforcing court itself under Art. 5(1)(b) 1965 Hague Service Convention.

[579] ('even if service were defective according to the applicable law on service of the adjudicating court'), Geimer and Schütze, 1997, at p.473, para. 86.

[580] Although not of the German courts own making; but see the section on 'sufficient time' for examples of this—and *LG Mönchengladbach* 20.7.1987, IPRspr. (1987) Nr. 154 and *OLG Hamm* 3.8.1987, IPRspr. (1987) Nr. 155; Geimer, R. 'Über die Kunst der Interessenabwägung auch im internationalen Verfahrensrecht, dargestellt am rechten Maß des beklagtenschutzes gemäß Art. 27 Nr.2 EuGVÜ' zu *OLG Hamm* 3.8.1987 und *LG Mönchengladbach* 20.7.1987 (1988) *IPRax* 271.

the Brussels Convention is so keen to foster. Whether Council Service Regulation 1348/2000 on service within the European Member States[581] will alter this position remains to be seen. A few tentative suggestions are proffered at the end of this section.

5.4.2   Other Contracting States' positions with regard to 'due service'

In France and England and Wales, the 'due service' segment of Article 27(2) has caused fewer difficulties.[582] The absence of a translation was held not to be a barrier to enforcement of a German default judgment in *Cour d'appel de Lyon* in *Theillol c/ Office de la jeunesse de Fribourg*,[583] at p.385, nor by *Cour de Cassation* in *Vanclef c/ Société Trans Traide International*.[584]

In *Thierry Noirhomme v David Walklate*,[585] the High Court rejected a construction of Article IV of the Protocol to the Brussels Convention put forward by the respondent (facing enforcement) to the effect that postal service between Belgium and England was not 'laid down'[586] in the 1965 Hague Convention, and was therefore impermissible.[587] Such a method was merely permitted in Article 10(1); equally, this was found to be 'laid down', or 'provided for', in the 1965 Convention. Kaye, in his casebook,[588] reports decisions of the Danish courts regarding the requirements of a translation. The reports are so brief, however, as to make critical comment almost impossible.

5.4.3   'Due Service' by the *remise au parquet*, and Article 27(2)?[589]

This type of internal service[590]—exemplified by service by *remise au parquet* under article 684(1) of the French *Nouveau Code de Procédure civile*—has

---

[581] Except for Denmark.

[582] In *Selco Ltd v Mercier* 21.5.1996, (1996) *SLT* 1247, at p.1252 (Lord Colsfield), OH, the Scottish court set aside registration of a Belgian judgment in the absence of 'due service' under Belgian law, where, in Belgian civil procedure, service had been effected in Belgium rather than at the defender's domicile in Scotland; 'due' service by post at defendant's home address in England not a problem in *TSN Kunststoffrecycling GmbH v Jurgens*, QBD, 16.2.2001 (Jack J).

[583] 18.4.1978 (1979) *JDI* 380.

[584] *Ibid.*, at p.381.

[585] [1992] 1 Lloyd's Rep. 427 (Judge Kershaw QC).

[586] *Ibid.*, at p.430; the judge held that these words meant 'provided for'; also Kaye P. (ed) *European Case Law on the Judgments Convention*, 1998, at p.385, case no.380.

[587] Postal service was 'due' service in *TSN Kunststoffrecycling GmbH v Jurgens*, QBD, 16.2.2001, Jack J, affm'd [2002] 1 All ER (Comm) 282, CA.

[588] Kaye, *ibid.*, at p.71, case no.75, and at pp.73–74, case no.80.

[589] In some detail Pfennig, 1988, at p.128 onwards; Nagel, H. *Nationlale und internationale Rechtshilfe im Zivilprozeß; das europäische Modell*, 1971, at p.97 following; on its historical effects *Cour de Douai* 25.1.1935 *Hoedhaar c/ Faill. Mallet* (1936) *JDI* 606; cf Stadler, A. (2001) *IPRrax* 514, at p.516.

[590] The option, or not, validly to serve process *within* the jurisdiction is what, in US parlance, would be called the 'Schlunk exception' to mandatory 'service' under the 1965 Hague Service Convention: *Volkswagenwerk Aktiengesellschaft v Herwig J. Schlunk* (1988) 486 US 694, at p.707, (O'Connor J)—

recently[591] been the subject of conflicting Contracting State court decisions[592] under Article 27(2) of the Brussels and Lugano Conventions; and for this reason should detain our attention.[593]

As we have seen, the validity of service under Article 27(2) is to be measured by the enforcing court's own independent view, against the benchmark of the procedural law of the rendering court, including any relevant, additional international service conventions binding on the latter.[594] It is in the relationship between the ambit of national service rules,[595] and the scope of these service Conventions *ratione materiae* that tensions have arisen. As will be seen, it is whether these Conventions are mandatory in their application, whenever a judicial document must be transmitted abroad, by way of service or otherwise.

Various Continental civil procedural laws[596]—of France,[597] Belgium,[598] Luxembourg,[599] and Italy[600]—(in essence) provide that if the defendant/recipient

---

'[w]here service on a domestic agent is valid and complete under both state law and the Due Process Clause, our inquiry ends and the [1965] Convention has no further implications.'; Schlosser, P. 284 *Recueil des Cours* 88 (2000), at p.94, and p.107; now in England, service by an alternative method under CPR 6.8(1) *not* permissible, under the circumstances (merely a desire for speed), in a 1965 Hague Convention case in *Knauf UK GmbH v British Gypsum Ltd and another* [2002] 1 WLR 907, CA (Henry LJ); *Phillips and others v Symes and another* [2002] 1 WLR 853, Ch.D., (Hart J).

[591] Although the issue of service by *remise au parquet* is not a new one: Alexander, E. 'Die internationale Vollstreckung von Zivilurteilen insbesondere im Verhältnis zu den Nachbarstaaten' (1931) *ZBJ* 1, at p.16; as mentioned in previous note, in English procedure, CPR Rule 6.8 (service by alternative means) could not, in the circumstances, be deployed to obtain a *lis alibi pendens* tactical advantage over service of corresponding proceedings in a competing German action: *Knauf UK GmbH v Gypsum Ltd and another* [2002] 1 WLR 907, CA; the German enforcing courts (even if their adjudicating courts decline jurisdiction in favour of the first seised English courts, under Art.21) were *not* likely to countenance any circumvention of the 1965 Hague Convention, and *may* well have reacted adversely under Art.27(2) by declaring the English document *not* duly served; a current draconian view of Art.27(2) and such a method of service is provided by *OLG Köln* 7.3.2001 2001 NJW-RR 1576.

[592] Finnish Supreme Court 17.6.1998, reviewed in Paanila, R. 'Anerkennungsantrag nach dem Lugano-Übereinkommen—Versagungsgrund nach Article 27 Nr.2 LugÜ' (1999) *Dalloz* 358, contrasted with draconian attitude in *OLG Karlsruhe* 12.3.1999 (1999) *RIW* 538, [2001] I.L.Pr. 208.

[593] Esp. because the scope *ratione materiae* of Service Regulation 1348/2000, Art. 1(1) is drafted in very similar terms as Art. 1 of the 1965 Hague Convention: 'This Regulation shall apply in civil and commercial matters where a judicial or extrajudicial document *has to be transmitted* from one Member State to another *for service there.*'

[594] Dörig, A. *Anerkennung und Vollstreckung US-amerikanischer Entscheidungen in der Schweiz*, 1998, at p.382, n. 2179, and p.394—like the Germans, the Swiss attitude to service under the 1965 Hague Convention, upon ratification, was that it is *exclusively competent.*

[595] Which may state that international service on a defendant domiciled outside the territory is deemed to be effected when service is made internally.

[596] These provisions make no distinction between service of the document which institutes the proceedings and any later documents for service—conversely (and a potential cause of tension), fictitious service in Germany—§175 ZPO—is *not* permissible for the document which institutes the proceedings: *OLG München* 28.9.1988 IPRspr. (1988) Nr. 176, at p.390 and *BGH* 3.2.1999 (1999) *RIW* 454, at p.456.

[597] Arts.684-87 NCPC, *Nouveau Code de Procedure Civile*, Dalloz, 93ème éd., 2001, at pp.367–68.

[598] Now in Art.40(1)(2) *Code Judiciare.*

[599] Arts.102(7), 156-57 *Nouveau Code de Procédure civile* of 16 September 1998.

[600] Art. 142(1)(2) and Art. 143(3) *Codice di Procedura civile*, but its scope is now much reduced, in Art. 143(3): this method is only permissible if service under the 1965 Hague Conventions has proved impossible; Wiehe, 1993, at p.65.

of a judicial document for service is domiciled/resident outside the jurisdiction, service on such a party within the jurisdiction will be considered to have been validly effected when service is made internally—commonly on the public prosecutor's office attached to the local court where the suit is/will become pending: termed in French a *remise au parquet.*

A paradigm example of this procedure is article 684(1) NCPC,[601] in which '[l]a signification d'un acte destiné à une personne domiciliée à l'étranger est faite au parquet.'[602] Thereafter, in article 686, a certified copy of the document is then transmitted/sent[603] by registered post to the recipient abroad.

How does this type of procedure impact on international service under the 1954 and 1965 Hague Service Conventions? As far as the 1965 Convention is concerned, Article 1(1) defines its scope to that of occasions, in civil and commercial matters, where there is to be transmission of judicial documents 'for service abroad.'[604] If the Convention is applicable, and the documents to be served are transmitted to the Central Authority of the recipient's domicile under Article 5, various formalities commonly arise, notably the need for a translation. Notable, too, is the reservation under Article 10 entered by some Contracting States to postal service.

The questions that concern us, and the enforcing court, here are whether the Article 27(2) document which instituted the proceedings is 'duly served' under this provision by the mere *remise au parquet*; and whether, on the contrary, in the view of the enforcing court,[605] 'service' must be effected exclusively under the 1965 Hague Service Convention. These questions take on added force when the particular enforcing court happens to be in a Brussels/Lugano[606] Contracting State that has taken an overtly robust stance to international service.

Unfortunately, the answers are not consistent, creating uncertainty for aspirant judgment creditors who seek to have the fruits of their litigation realised in other Contracting States. Again, it is German caselaw that provides most of the material for examination here.

---

[601] Curiously, the *Nouveau Code* gives litigants before a French court a choice between this type of service and service under the Hague Service Conventions, art.683(3) NCPC and art.684 NCPC.

[602] ('service of a certificate bound for a person domiciled abroad is accomplished at the local public prosecutor's office').

[603] Note, *not served*, as this has already occurred internally.

[604] As mentioned, Art. 1(1) Service Regulation is drafted in all material respects in the same terms, so what is stated here has continuing validity after 31 May 2001.

[605] The rendering court may have taken a different view and posted the untranslated document directly to the recipient, for example as art.686 NCPC prescribes—the essential problem.

[606] Switzerland, it seems, will be as draconian under Art. 27(2) Lugano Convention as is Germany at present: Dörig, A. *Anerkennung und Vollstreckung US-amerikanischer Entscheidungen in der Schweiz*, 1998, p.382 onwards.

5.4.3(i)   German caselaw on the remise au parquet

An inconsistent line of German (appeal court) cases[607] will demonstrate whether the service by *remise au parquet* has a place[608] within the scheme of 'due service' under Article 27(2). There are early decisions that have regarded the 'due service' requirement of the article fulfilled by an untranslated French or Belgian 'writ' being sent[609] directly to the German defendant by registered post, despite Germany's reservation to such a method (of service) under Article 10(a) of the 1965 Hague Service Convention: *OLG Düsseldorf* 19.10.1984.[610] In this case enforcement was sought of a Paris court judgment. The court held that the 'cases in which 'service' must take place in the foreign country are determined solely in accordance with the law of the court before which the action is pending.'[611] As service had been validly effected internally in France, by *remise au parquet,* without the need for a translation, due service had been complied with for the purposes of Article 27(2). It was considered irrelevant that Article 5 of the 1965 Hague Convention would have required a translation, and that the reservation to such direct postal 'service' had been clearly communicated by the German authorities.

A similar conclusion was reached recently by *OLG Saarland* 24.11.1997,[612] albeit in regard to the service of the judgment itself. The French judgment creditor sought enforcement of a default judgment, and the judgment debtor objected to the fact that the judgment had been served by *remise au parquet.* The court focussed on the scope *ratione materiae* of Article 1 of the 1965 Hague Service Convention, and concluded that whether service was or was not to be effected 'abroad' hinged on the provisions of French law. This law, unlike German law,[613] gives the judgment creditor a valid choice[614] between service under the 1965

---

[607] Of the 12 or more reported cases, 2 have specifically endorsed, 10 rejected, the *remise au parquet* as a legitimate method of service; likely English (recognition/enforcement) reaction, at least as is discernible from the context of Art.21: *Phillips and others v Symes and another* [2002] 1 WLR 853, Ch.D., (Hart J).

[608] Some German courts have avoided confronting the due service requirement, preferring to censure the *remise au parquet* under the 'sufficient' time criterion, below; Schlosser, P. (2000) 284 *Recueil des Cours* 88, at p.109: 'It is a matter of course that this act [service by *remise au parquet*] in itself can never be completed 'in sufficient time' . . .; this would seem the solution the Austrian courts would prefer to adopt with such methods of service: *OGH* 20.9.2000 (2001) *ZfRV* 114, at p.116. 'Eine solche fiktive Zustellung kann jedoch ohne Hinzutreten weiterer Umständen niemals rechtzeitig sein' ('such a fictitious method of service cannot however, without the involvement of further circumstances, ever be in sufficient time').

[609] Note, not 'served', the 'Schlunk exception' in operation.

[610] (1985) *RIW* 493, [1986] E.C.C. 472.

[611] Translation taken from the English version of the case at [1986] E.C.C. 472, p.475, para. 11.

[612] (1998) *RIW* 632.

[613] Although German law, §175 would have allowed substituted service of *the judgment* (but not the document instituting the proceedings) in this case too.

[614] This choice, available to plaintiffs in French proceedings, (and not to Germans in German proceedings) was thus anathema to another German court: *OLG Karlsruhe* 12.3.1999 (1999) *RIW* 538, [2001] I.L.Pr. 208 reviewed below, at p.505.

Hague Convention[615] and internal service, by *remise au parquet*, under article 684 NCPC. If the judgment creditor chooses the latter method, there is no cause for complaint in the enforcing court.

As an aside, this line of reasoning has also been followed in Finland, where for the first time, the Finnish Supreme Court[616] of 17.6.1998, has had to decide on the compatibility of the *remise au parquet* procedure with due service under Article 27(2). Again, at issue, was, *inter alia*, whether 'due service' of the initiating documents had been effected in France under article 684 NCPC, before they crossed the border into Finland. It was important to ascertain this point, as the Finnish law of 19 March 1992, no.211 supplementing the 1965 Hague Service Convention (would have) required a translation of the documents into either Finnish or Swedish. This had not been done in the present case. Nonetheless, the court decided that 'due service', according to French law, occurred internally on the *remise au parquet.*[617]

More numerous are the (German) cases that object[618] to this fictitious method of internal service procedure. Early examples[619] come from the *OLG Hamm*[620] and *OLG Frankfurt.*[621] More recent examples have avoided the *remise au parquet's* compatibility with 'due service' under Article 27(2) altogether, preferring instead to censure this procedure under the cumulative requirement of the sufficiency of time:[622] *OLG Koblenz,*[623] *OLG Hamm,*[624] and *OLG Köln.*[625]

Yet the most vehement criticism of this system of service has come recently from two decisions of the *OLG Karlsruhe*, in 22.1.1996[626] and 12.3.1999.[627] The more instructive, and vituperative is the latter: the judgment creditor sought the enforcement in Germany of a *référé* judgment of the *Tribunal de Commerce de Colmar*. The document(s) which instituted the proceedings had been 'served' by *remise au parquet*, under article 684 NCPC, on the court lawyers' offices in

---

[615] Art. 683(3) NCPC; *Nouveau Code de Procedure Civile*, Dalloz, 93ème éd., 2001, '"Les dispositions du présent article *ne préjudicient pas* à l'application des traités prévoyant *une autre forme de notification*"'

[616] *Korkein oikeus*, 17.6.1998 *Oy Valkom Stevedoring Co AB / Amstelstraat Management Co*, http://www.curia.eu.int/common/recdoc/convention/en/1999/70–1999.htm reviewed by Paanila, R. 'Anerkennungsantrag nach dem Lugano-Übereinkommen—Versagungsgrund nach Art. 27 Nr.2 LugÜ' (1999) *RIW* 358.

[617] *Ibid.*, at p.360.

[618] *OLG Düsseldorf* 29.11.1999, has censured a Dutch judgment served by this method under Art.27(1), (2000) *IPRax* 527, [2002] I.L.Pr. 71.

[619] The European Court of Justice has yet to rule on the matter.

[620] 20.5.1977 IPRspr. (1977) Nr. 145.

[621] 21.8.1978 IPRspr. (1978) Nr. 164.

[622] Note, traditionally this is how the Swiss *Bundesgericht* has handled the *remise au parquet* default judgments under Art. 17 Abs. 1(2) *Traité franco-suisse 1869—Behrendt & Cie gegen Lehner* 24.10.1912, 38 BGE, I, 543, at p.549 and *Brönimann contre Soc. Universelle de Films* 23.6.1949, 75 BGE, I, 146; *OGH* 20.9.2000 (2001) *ZfRV* 114, at p.116.

[623] 25.2.1987 (1988) *RIW* 476.

[624] 3.8.1987 IPRspr. (1987) Nr. 155.

[625] 12.4.1989 IPRspr. (1989) Nr. 213, [1991] I.L.Pr. 483.

[626] 22.1.1996 IPRspr. 1996 Nr. 174.

[627] 12.3.1999 (1999) *RIW* 538, [2001] I.L.Pr. 208.

Colmar, on 21.5.1996, thence by registered post to the German defendant, and were received on 25.5.1996.

After an exposition of this French procedure, the court came to the stark conclusion that 'die remise au parquet vom 21.5.1996 . . . erfüllt nach Auffassung des Senats nicht die Voraussetzung ordnungsgemäßer Zustellung.'[628]

On the following page of its judgment, the court noted that article 684's intention was simply the need to obviate a French plaintiff/claimant's necessity for service abroad. The *remise au parquet*, it felt, assured that such a plaintiff/claimant was spared[629] the difficulties and delays[630] encountered by German plaintiffs/claimants under the Hague Service Conventions. The French procedure was therefore considered to be a breach not only of Article 27(2), excluding enforcement under the Brussels Convention, but of Article 6 (now Article 12) EC Treaty[631] and even of Article 6 of the European Convention on Human Rights:

> Die 'remise au parquet' führt im Extremfall dazu, daß ein EU-Bürger mit einer postalisch übersandten Klage in fremder Sprache überzogen wird . . .[632]

Whether other German courts will now follow this reasoning is not yet known, but it seems likely that French and Belgian parties[633] would be well-advised to seek service under the 1965 Hague Convention, if enforcement is sought from the majority of courts in Germany.[634]

The essence of the antipathy towards such methods of service lies not in the method itself, but in the fact that, under Article 27(2) and Article IV of the Protocol, this type of service represents a circumvention of the (protective)

---

[628] ('in the opinion of this Chamber, the *remise au parquet* of 21.5.1996 does not fulfil the prerequisite of due service'), (1999) *RIW* 538, at p.538, [2001] I.L.Pr. 208, at p.212, para. 8; also Schlosser, P. (2000) 284 *Recueil des Cours* 88, at p.109; recently the *OLG Köln* 7.3.2001 (2001) NJW-RR 1576 has used Art. 27(2) in conjunction, *inter alia*, with Art. 103 GG (the right to a fair hearing) to ensure default judgments decided after service of the initiating document has been made by *remise au parquet* (or its Italian equivalent) do not qualify for 'due service' enforcement under the Convention.

[629] The court likened the Art.684 NCPC procedure to the favourable jurisdictional treatment French parties traditionally enjoyed under Art.14 *Code civil*, now of course abrogated within the EU/EFTA states by Art.3 II of the Conventions, [2001] I.L.Pr. 208, at p.214, para.13; cf *Knauf UK GmbH v British Gypsum Ltd and another* [2002] 1 WLR 907, CA; *Phillips and others v Symes and another* [2002] 1 WLR 853, Ch.D., (Hart J).

[630] For evidence of such, Vial, E. *Die Gerichtsstandswahl und der Zugang zum internationalen Zivilprozeß im deutsch- italienischen Rechtsverkehr*, 1999, at p.43, p.53, p.67.

[631] The non-discrimination provision, (1999) *RIW* 538, at p.539.

[632] ('In extreme cases, the *remise au parquet* leads to a case where a writ served by post in a foreign language may be brought against an EU citizen'), *ibid.*, at p.539.

[633] Even if service is a matter for the local court.

[634] By analogy with the cases on the *remise au parquet*, and had not the case been reversed on appeal, a German enforcing court may well have considered the eventual judgment in *Knauf UK GmbH v Gypsum Ltd and another* [2001] 2 All ER (Comm) 332, (David Steel J), to have not been *duly* served (at all and/or in sufficient time). The recent Court of Appeal judgment, [2002] 1 WLR 907, has not permitted the international service Conventions in place between the UK and Germany to be bypassed, under CPR 6.8(1), merely to obtain a 'first seisure' advantage in English proceedings under Arts. 21/22.

control the German (and Swiss)[635] authorities seek to exert over the means of service, which in these jurisdictions is a manifestation of sovereign State authority.

The effect of accepting as valid a method such as service by *remise au parquet* is that control is lost over service of the document that instituted the proceedings on their State defendants as regards method and formalities (the need for a translation), so carefully preserved under the 1954 and 1965 Hague Service Conventions. Although there are as yet no direct cases in point under Article 27(2) from the Swiss *Bundesgericht*, Dörig[636] is of the opinion that its attitude to the use of the 1965 Hague Convention will be obligatory, and will consequently not allow circumvention of its provisions—especially its reservation to Article 10(a), postal service—by fictitious internal service by *remise au parquet* in, *inter alia*, France, Belgium and Italy.

5.4.4　The limited future of 'due service' under the Brussels I Regulation[637] (and Council Service Regulation 1348/2000 of 29 May 2000 on service in the Member States of judicial and extra-judicial documents in civil and commercial matters)[638]

'Due' service has thankfully been entirely omitted from Article 34(2) of Brussels I Regulation; instead, the document which instituted the proceedings has merely to be 'served', *inter alia*, 'in such a way as to enable [the defendant] to arrange for his defence'.[639] While this may well overcome some of the more trivial objections and *minutiae* of (German) procedural laws on service, the redrafting may provide other avenues of attack—the new wording being, it seems, a legislative acceptance and expansion of the ECJ's judgment in *Debaecker v Bouwman*.[640] This case held

---

[635] Below, last para of text.

[636] Dörig, A., 1998, at p.394 onwards.

[637] Changes will be made from 1.3.2002 to Art. 27(2) to avoid 'abuses of procedure' as set out in the explanatory memorandum to the July 1999 draft Council Regulation; Art. 66(2) Brussels I Regulation, a transitional provision, will ensure that on or after 1.3.2002, Chapter III of the Regulation—without a 'due' service requirement—*must* be resorted to for recognition and enforcement of judgments given after 1.3.2002, when initiated (under the Brussels/Lugano Convention) before that date; Gaudemet-Tallon, (2001) *JDI* 381, at p.411.

[638] [2000] OJ L160/37.

[639] An important innovation; this will eliminate the all-too-common situation of when a defendant only becomes aware that proceedings have been commenced against him when he is presented with the *fait accompli* of the Art. 36 decision to allow enforcement—*ex hypothesi*, the document could not have been served 'in such a way as to enable [him] to arrange . . . [a] defence'; there will be opportunities for Member State courts to consider the extent of this last phrase before 1.3.2001, as a similarly-worded defence appears in Art. 15(1)(b) and (2)(c) of Council Regulation 1347/2000 of 29 May 2000 on jurisdiction and the recognition and enforcement of judgments in matrimonial matters and in matters of parental responsibility for children of both spouses [2000] OJ160/19; this has been in force since 1 March 2001; Gaudemet-Tallon, (2001) *JDI* 381, at p.411; also Helms, T. (2001) *FamRZ* 257, at p.264.

[640] (C–49/84) [1985] ECR 1779.

that despite, and after, 'due' service, the enforcing court was able to apportion blame on each respective party for the failure of the 'sufficient time' criterion to run, or for circumstances leading to its interruption. This, it seems, has been perpetuated in Article 34(2).

As to service itself, it is unclear whether faults that are currently sanctionable under Article 27(2) will remain so under the new version of Article 34(2). Recently, as will be noted in the next section, in information provided to the Commission[641] by the Member States under Article 23 of Council Service Regulation 1348/2000, Germany—until legislation is passed implementing the Regulation[642]—now will accept postal service of judicial documents, under certain conditions, as permitted under Article 14 of the Service Regulation. This is in stark contrast to those cases in which other Member State courts were formerly in breach of Germany's reservation under Article 10 of the 1965 Hague Service Convention.

5.4.4 (i)   Council Service Regulation 1348/2000[643] and the limited future of 'due service' from 31 May 2001 until 1 March 2002

The Council of the European Union had, by an Act of 26 May 1997, proposed a new Service Convention for the EU Member States in civil and commercial matters. It was overtaken somewhat by events (notably the coming into force of the Amsterdam Treaty amendments to the various EU Treaties), and received no ratifications. It had, of course, similarities[644] with the current 1965 Hague Service Convention. Most striking was its Article 1, defining the Convention's scope *ratione materiae*. Like the Hague Convention before it, it would have applied 'in civil and commercial matters where a judicial . . . document has to be transmitted from one Member State to another *for service* there.'[645] It seemed, therefore, that the highlighted words would have perpetuated the problems and inconsistencies

---

[641] [2001] OJ C151/4.

[642] §2 ZustDG, 2001 BGBl, I, 1536 has now provided the machinery of postal service in Germany, and the ZPO has been amended to accommodate it—§183 Abs.1 Nr.1 ZPO, as recently amended, permits this form of service—Stadler, A. (2001) *IPRax* 514, at p.516; Third update of the information communicated by Member States under Art. 23 of Council Regulation (EC) No 1348/2000) [2002] OJ C13/2—Germany accepts postal service provided that the documents to be served are 'in the form of a registered letter with advice of delivery' translated into German, or are in the language of the transmitting state if the addressee is such a national.

[643] For the history of this Regulation see the earlier document of 4.5.1999, COM (1999) 219 final, 99/0102 (CNS), replacing an earlier *Convention drawn up on the basis of Article K.3 of the Treaty on European Union, on the service in the Member States of the European Union of judicial and extrajudicial documents in civil or commercial matters* [1997] OJ C261/2.

[644] It is clear that the Convention was not drawn up to deal with the problems made specifically manifest in Art.27(2); Kropholler, 2002, at p.407, para. 39, believes that 'due service' will not become entirely obsolete, but should still be the first port of call under Art.34(2)—it will be hard for any defendant to demonstrate that he was not served 'in such a way as to enable him to arrange' a defence if the documents are served by a method (under Council Service Regulation 1348/2000) that would formerly have been considered 'due service' under Art.27(2).

[645] *Ibid.*, Art. 1.

encountered, above, with regard to the fictitious service procedure of the *remise au parquet*, in those Member States where service, by the law of the rendering court, is deemed to have been effected internally. If therefore a document is to be transmitted to another Member State for purposes other than service, the Convention appeared not to apply.[646]

On 31 May 2001, its current form, the Service Regulation 1348/2000[647] came into force throughout the Member States of the European Union,[648] except for Denmark. As an effect of this, during the short 'interregnum' period—a little over 8 months—from then until the end of Thursday 28 February 2002 (after which 'due service' will be deleted from its current position in Article 27(2) Brussels Convention by Article 34(2) Brussels I Regulation) the 'legality' of service has now to be adjudged anew[649] against the background of expedited and simplified Member State service rules, at least in comparison with the 1965 Hague Service Convention system.

When the Service Regulation applies, Articles 2 and 3 set up a structure of transmitting[650] and receiving agencies,[651] with a central body in each Member State overseeing the efficient function of document exchange. The formalities of this particular part of the Service Regulation are outside the scope of the 'due service' consideration of this chapter and should not detain this enquiry further.

Bearing in mind what has already been witnessed in regard to 'due service' in the previous section with regard to Article 27(2) and the Hague Service

---

[646] This issue is not dealt with in the explanatory report, [1997] C261/26, at p.28; cf Stadler, A. (2001) *IPRax* 514, at p.516.

[647] For the history of this Regulation see the earlier document of 4.5.1999, COM(1999) 219 final, 99/0102 (CNS), replacing an earlier *Convention drawn up on the basis of Article K.3 of the Treaty on European Union, on the service in the Member States of the European Union of judicial and extrajudicial documents in civil or commercial matters* [1997] OJ C261/2.

[648] The Service Regulation was accommodated notably from 31 May 2001 into the existing service regime in Civil Procedure Rules 1998, Rule 6 by various provisions in The Civil Procedure (Amendment No.2) Rules 2001, SI 2001/1388, notably inserting a new rule 6.26A regarding service of a claim form in accordance with the Service Regulation.

[649] The scope *ratione temporis* of the Service Regulation is not governed by any transitional provisions in the Regulation itself; but it is submitted that it will not only apply to claim forms issued on or after 31 May 2001, but to those issued before that date which have yet to enter the 'machinery of service' under the old Hague Convention regime—ie not yet transmitted to the former agencies for service.

[650] Information as to the various transmitting agencies has been provided by a EU communiqué— *Information communicated by Member States under Article 23 of Council Regulation (EC) No 1348/2000) of 29 May 2000 on the service in the Member States of judicial and extrajudicial documents in civil or commercial matters*, 22 May 2001, [2001] OJ C151/4, as to the identity and addresses of these bodies.

[651] An enormous document, entitled Commission Decision of 25 September 2001 adopting a manual of receiving agencies and a glossary of documents that may be served under Council Regulation (EC) No 1348/2000 on the service in the Member States of judicial and extrajudicial documents in civil or commercial matters, 15.11.2001, [2001] OJ L298/1, sets out, in Annexes, a manual and glossary of information on receiving agencies under Art. 2 of the Council Service Regulation—it, and the inevitable updates, should be consulted online at the European Commission's website at http://europa.eu.int/comm/justice_home/unit/civil_reg1348_en.htm.

Conventions, it will be of interest to examine where the potential service pitfalls[652] under the new Service Regulation arise.[653]

Leaving aside for now the controversy that will inevitably be provoked by the Service Regulation's (non-)mandatory scope, in Article 1, and service by *remise au parquet*, the following non-exhaustive list of circumstances under which, until 1.3.2002, a defence of a lack of 'due service' under Article 27(2) may be sustained, is still alarmingly long:

(1) *Article 6(3) Service Regulation*—manifestly outside scope of Regulation/ impossibility defence: that the receiving agency in the Member State where the defendant to be served is domiciled, goes ahead and serves the documents, consequently failing in its duty under Article 6(3) to return the documents despite 'the request for service [being] manifestly outside the scope of [the] Regulation or if non-compliance [sic] with the conditions required [making] service impossible.'

(2) *Article 6(4) Service Regulation*—incorrect service *ratione loci*: similarly, a receiving agency serves the documents, despite being territorially incompetent to do so, and thereafter fails in its duty under Article 6(4) to forward the documents to the correct agency, and inform the transmitting agency of the errors.

(3) *Article 7 Service Regulation*—*ex post facto* incorrect or incompatible service with law of Member State addressed: the receiving agency, under Article 7 *purportedly* serves, or has the documents served, either: (i) 'in accordance with the law of the Member State addressed' and despite the existence of an Article 10 certificate, this method is adjudged, *ex post facto*, by the enforcing court under Article 27(2) Brussels Convention to have been defective service all along;[654] or (ii) 'in a particular form' requested by the transmitting agency, even though such a method of purported service 'is incompatible with the law of that Member State [addressed]'.[655]

---

[652] Unfortunately, it is submitted these will remain as marked as ever, since the Service Regulation contains no provisions for curing defective service—notable in the post-reference decision of *Isabelle Lancray S.A. v Firma Peters und Sickert KG, BGH* 20.9.1990 IPRspr. (1990) Nr. 200, (1991) *NJW* 641, (1990) *RIW* 1010, [1992] I.L.Pr. 52.

[653] An obvious initial stumbling block that was evident under the older Hague Convention regimes was the confusion over the necessity of recourse to the Hague Conventions at all, especially if internal fictitious service (by *remise au parquet*) was a valid method of service by the *lex fori* of the rendering court—certain (German) courts took exception to the bypassing of the Hague Conventions, and this attitude will no doubt continue, since recourse to the Service Regulation will be viewed as compulsory, cf Schlosser, P. 284 Recueil des Cours 88 (2000), at pp.108–9—cf current English position under CPR 6.24(1)(b)(ii) and CPR 6.26A(1) in *Knauf UK GmbH v British Gypsum Ltd and another* [2002] 1 WLR 907, CA (alternative service, on English solicitors of German party not permitted, and set aside).

[654] The same problem that was encountered in *Firma Minalmet GmbH v Firma Brandeis Ltd* (C–123/91) [1992] ECR I–5661; also *Molins Plc v G.D. S.p.A.* [2000] 1 WLR 1741, CA; *Knauf UK GmbH v British Gypsum Ltd and another* [2002] 1 WLR 907, CA; *Phillips and others v Symes and another* [2002] 1 WLR 853, Ch.D. (Hart J).

[655] Again, cf *Molins Plc v G.D. S.p.A.* [2000] 1 WLR 1741, CA.

(4) *Article 8 Service Regulation*—refusal right and untranslated documents: the defendant/addressee, on being served, is *not* informed of his/her/its right to refuse to accept the documents: (i) if they are *not* correctly translated into the official language(s) of the Member State addressed, or, if different (ii) if they are drawn up in a language (of the Member State of transmission) not understood by the defendant/addressee, in Article 8(1); and/or, under Article 8(2), the receiving agency fails to alert all concerned about the addressee's refusal to accept, and the rendering court blithely proceeds to judgment in ignorance of the true picture.

(5) *Articles 12, 13 Service Regulation*—incorrect service by consular or diplomatic channels/agents and/or when opposition to such a method has been expressed.

(6) *Article 14 Service Regulation*—service incorrect by post: service is *purportedly* effected by post upon persons in another Member State under Article 14, but 'the conditions under which . . . service of judicial documents by post' is permitted in this latter Member State *have not been complied with and/or were overstepped,* Article 14(2).[656]

(7) *Article 15 Service Regulation*—direct service defence: 'direct service' through the relevant judicial officers/officials/other competent persons of the Member State addressed is *purportedly* undertaken in the face of such a Member State's objection to this method of service under Article 15(2).[657]

(8) *Article 20(2) Service Regulation*—incorrect service under a supplementary agreement or arrangement between the Member States involved.[658]

5.5: 'IN SUFFICIENT TIME'[659]

The second, and additional,[660] criterion, that the document which instituted the proceedings must demonstrate under Article 27(2), is that it was 'served . . . in *sufficient time* to enable [the defendant] to arrange for his defence.'

---

[656] The German courts will no doubt be watchful of this provision; the Third update of the information communicated by Member States under Article 23 of Council Regulation (EC) No 1348/2000) [2002] OJ C13/2 confirms that Germany will indeed accept postal service within the meaning of Art.14(1) of the Service Regulation provided that the documents to be served are 'in the form of a registered letter with advice of delivery' translated into German, or are in the language of the transmitting state if the addressee is such a national; Spain has indicated (*Second update of the information communicated by Member States under Article 23 of Council Regulation (EC) No 1348/2000) of 29 May 2000 on the service in the Member States of judicial and extrajudicial documents in civil or commercial matters,* 6 October 2001, [2001] OJ C282/2) that it accepts service of judicial documents by post, provided the translation rules in Arts.5 & 8 of Council Service Regulation 1348/2000 are complied with.

[657] The Official Journal should be consulted and carefully scrutinised to discover these objections, Art.23(2), also http://europa.eu.int/comm/justice_home/unit/civil_reg1348_en.htm.

[658] Again, *Molins Plc v G.D. S.p.A.* [2000] 1 WLR 1741, CA; and now caution in *Phillips and others v Symes and another* [2002] 1 WLR 853, at p.860, Ch.D. Hart J; *Digit Srl v Apple Computer International,* 5.10.2001, QBD Goldring J.

[659] This aspect of Art.27(2) will also survive the changes in Art.34(2) Brussels I Regulation on 1.3.2002.

[660] This is a cumulative requirement with due service: *Isabelle Lancray S.A. v Firma Peters und Sickert KG* (C–305/88) [1990] ECR I–2725; the time between 'service' and 'default judgment' emphasised in

The case law of the European Court has shown us that the time period under scrutiny is that beginning[661] with service of the document which instituted the proceedings,[662] and ending with the day on which a judgment, capable of being enforced under Part III of the Convention, was rendered.[663]

It is irrelevant in the eyes of the recognising/enforcing court that, from whatever source,[664] the adjudicating court came to the conclusion[665] under Article 20, that service *had been* effected in sufficient time.[666] The scrutiny under this aspect of Article 27(2) gives the enforcing court, for good or ill, totally free rein[667] to consider all[668] the facts[669] of the case in its assessment of the sufficiency of time left to the defendant to prepare for his defence.

5.5.1 Insufficient time despite due service

As a result of the relatively recent case of *TSN Kunststoffrecycling GmbH v Jurgens,*[670] this section, which hitherto merited only a footnote and a brief review of *Debaecker v Bouwman*[671] needs slightly more attention. It concerns the approach an enforcing court is to take under Article 27(2) when the judgment debtor has clearly been duly served, according to the procedures described in the previous section 5.4; but despite this, the document instituting the proceedings—for reasons of the valid *method* of service effected—did *still* not come to

---

Court of Appeal in *TSN Kunststoffrecycling GmbH v Jurgens,* [2002] EWCA Civ 11, 25.1.2002, CA (Rix LJ)—the fact that some other step, prior to the moment of rendering judgment had to be, or could have been, accomplished according to the *lex fori* of the rendering court (such as entering and appearance within a short time limit) does not affect the general rule as to the computation of the sufficiency of time allowed for Art.27(2) purposes.

[661] For circumstances which may cause a hiatus in, or non-commencement of, this time period: *Peter Klomps v Karl Michel* (C–166/80) [1981] ECR 1593 and *Debaecker v Bouwman* (C–49/84) [1985] ECR 1779, especially AG Verloren Van Themaat, at p.1787, fn.10.

[662] It is of course essential to know which document or documents set this (rather vague) period of time running, above section 5.3.

[663] *Klomps v Karl Michel* [1981] ECR 1593, at p.1606, para. 11.

[664] National procedural law, as in *Klomps v Michel,* or the various Hague Service Conventions.

[665] Erroneous therefore the view of the Court of Appeal in *Coverbat SA v Jackson,* 31.1.1997, unreported—*European Case Law on the Judgments Convention,* (ed. Kaye, P), 1998, at pp.358–9, case no.353.

[666] *Pendy Plastic Products BV v Pluspunkt Handelsgesellschaft GmbH* (C–228/81) [1982] ECR 2723, at p.2136, para. 13—Art.27(2) operates for Contracting State defendants as a double check on the rights of the defence.

[667] Applauded by Walter, G. 'Die zu kurz bemessene Einlassungsfrist' zu *BGH* 23.1.1986 (1986) *IPRax* 349, at p.350: '[i]nsoweit ist es ein Tribut,. . .wenn man dem Zivilrichter keine feste Grenzen geben kann, sondern ihm einen Beurteilsspielraum einräumen läbt'('thus it is a tribute that no rigid boundaries are set for the judge, but a free margin of appreciation'), *sed quaere.*

[668] *OLG Koblenz* 19.6.1990 (1992) *IPRax* 35, at p.37.

[669] The European Court has told us that sufficiency of service is a matter of fact.

[670] QBD, 16.2.2001, (Jack J), appeal on a different point dismissed by CA, 25.1.2002, (Rix LJ); also *Artic Fish Sales Co. Ltd v Adam (no.2)* 1996 SLT 970, OH.

[671] (C–49/84) [1985] ECR 1779.

defendant's attention in sufficient time. Thus the mode of service has an effect on the sufficiency of time.

The defendant, Bouwman, in *Debaecker v Bouwman,* had left the rented premises in Antwerp, without a forwarding address. Service was duly effected at an Antwerp police station. The claimants' advisor became aware, after service, that the defendant had a new address (for service) in Essen, Belgium, but did nothing to notify the defendant of proceedings. The questions arose, *inter alia,* whether the enforcing court could take account of special circumstances—*in casu,* intervening after service—in computing the sufficiency of time; and whether blame could be apportioned between the parties, as to whether to apply such 'special circumstances': on the claimant's side, such as circumstances that would prevent time running against the defendant; on the defendant's side, as being the author of this own misfortune. The Court answered in the affirmative to both questions.[672]

The facts of *TSN Kunststoffrecycling GmbH v Jurgens*[673] provide an illustration of the application of the special circumstances of *Debaecker v Bouwman* before the English court. Jurgens, a Dutch national, had been duly[674] served in England with German proceedings under the Hague Convention, by post at his home address. He claimed to have been away at the time. Five weeks elapsed between this event and the German court giving a default judgment. Jack J reviewed both *Peter Klomps v Karl Michel* and *Debaecker v Bouwman*—which he thought unhelpful in this regard—and emphasised that *the mode of service* can have an effect on the sufficiency of time, when the defendant claims not to have seen the document. If, therefore,

> 'service is effected at an address . . . [business or home], where in the ordinary course it should come to his attention[675] . . . it will normally be immaterial that such service did not bring the proceedings to his attention.'[676]

In contrast to this circumstance,

> 'if service is effected at an address which may not, or is unlikely to,[677] bring the proceedings to the defendant's attention [only then can the special factors, such as those in *Debaecker v Bouwman* be taken into account].'

---

[672] (C–49/84) [1985] ECR 1779, at p.1799, para. 20.

[673] QBD, 16.2.2001, (Jack J), appeal dismissed, CA, 25.1.2002, on the issue, unexplored at first instance, as to how to calculate the time frame for 'sufficiency' purposes. Rix LJ, *obiter,* did state, however, that if a 2 week period had been considered as the relevant period under enquiry he would 'not have placed any limitation' on the examination of the 'special circumstances' raised by the appellant, Jurgens.

[674] Jack J had found this.

[675] In sufficient time in any event, in the case 5 weeks.

[676] I.e. the *Debaecker v Bouwman* 'special factors' irrelevant.

[677] E.g. *Artic Fish Sales Co. Ltd v Adam (no.2)* 1996 SLT 970, at pp.975–6, (Lord Cameron of Lochbroom), when there is a mis-identification of the actual defendant (via a trading name) and service therefore unlikely to come to the defendant's attention at place of service.

5.5.2 Examples of 'sufficiency'

Since the considerations of sufficient time are of a purely factual[678] nature, it is impossible to glean any general principles from the cases, which may vary infinitely one from another. There are, however, discernible trends.

Pendy Plastic Products BV v Pluspunkt Handelsgesellschaft GmbH[679] has already shown us that the enforcing court is not bound by the findings of sufficient time from the adjudicating court, either under its own internal procedural time limits, nor under the Hague Service Conventions. Case law has extended this independence from procedural law, even to time limits[680] laid down under the law of the enforcing court:

> 'Auch an die Bestimmungen des Prozeßrechts des Urteilstaates und die *des eignen Prozeßrechts* ist das Gericht des Vollstreckungsstaates insoweit nicht gebunden.'[681]

Like the rest of the elements of Article 27(2), it is clear that this factual appraisal is taken against the background of the right to a fair hearing,[682] and the ability of a defendant to defend himself adequately.[683] Sufficient time must be granted to a defendant to set in motion all necessary steps to prevent a default judgment, *prima facie* enforceable under Title III of the Convention, being given against him. The number and complexity of these steps will, of course, vary from case to case, and from procedure to procedure,[684] leading to the particular judgment in default; so will a correspondent increase or decrease, as the case may be, of the time considered to be adequate.

---

[678] *Debaecker v Bouwman* [1985] ECR 1779, at p.1800, para. 27; also Briggs, 1997, at p.324, para. 7.16; also Kropholler, 1998, at p.357, para. 34; *OLG Koblenz* 25.2.1987 (1988) *RIW* 476; *OLG Koblenz* 19.6.1990 (1992) *IPRax* 35, at p.37; obviously, if the document which instituted the proceedings only comes to the defendant's attention *after* the date of the first hearing, insufficient time will have been accorded: *Cour de Cassation* 7.4.1998 *Société Breevast VN c/ Société Brunot immobiliers et autres*, http://curia.eu.int/common/recdoc/convention/en/1998/98de29br.htm.

[679] (C–228/81) [1982] ECR 2723.

[680] '[N]och ist das Fristenrecht des Vollstreckungsstaates mabgebend' (neither is the time limit of the enforcing court applicable'), in *OLG Koblenz* 19.6.1990 (1992) *IPRax* 35, p.37; but *contra*, it seems, *BGH* 23.1.1986 IPRspr. (1986) Nr. 171.

[681] ('the enforcing court is not bound by the provisions of *lex fori* of the adjudicating court, *nor of its own procedural law*'), *OLG Hamm* 3.8.1987 (1988) *IPRax* 289, at p.290; also *Cassation* 3.11.1977 *Bull.Civ.*, I, n.401, p.320: '...sans être liée par les délais par le droit interne français'; *Corte di Cassazione* 25.9.1998 *Vlachakis s.n.c. contro Gamba* (1999) *Riv. dir int. priv e proc.*983 (both sets of procedural rules irrelevant in this assessment); *Dicey & Morris*, 13th edn, 2000, Vol .I, at p.554, para. 14–212.

[682] *BGH* 21.3.1990 (1992) *IPRax* 33.

[683] *OLG Koblenz* 19.6.1990 (1992) *IPRax* 35.

[684] *OLG Düsseldorf* 19.10.1984 (1985) *RIW* 493—very little needed to be done to prevent a default judgment from being issued in French summary proceedings in this case.

5.5.3   German case law and sufficiency of time

Among the non-exhaustive factors[685] which these courts have been brought[686] into this factual determination of (in)sufficiency have been: the status,[687] economic and legal sophistication,[688] of the defendant; the defendant's ability to understand the document's language,[689] and (as a result) the need to consult a translator;[690] the physical location[691] of the defendant and his consequent (in)ability to consult qualified legal help;[692] the pending threat of legal proceedings, and any previous letters before action;[693] whether the document could reasonably be interpreted as a 'writ',[694] or is in the least sense intelligible;[695] the nature of the proceedings in the adjudicating court;[696] the day of the week on which the docu-

---

[685] Pluyette, in *Etudes offertes à Pierre Bellet*, 1991, p.427, at pp.448–51; and also Schack, 2.Auf., 1996, at p.330, para. 850.

[686] Compare the factors mentioned by Kallmann, F. *Anerkennung und Vollstreckung ausländischer Zivilurteile und gerichtlicher Vergleiche*, 1946, regarding Art.4 III of the German-Swiss Convention, at pp.299–300.

[687] Gevrey, S. *L'exequatur communautaire: Titre III de la Convention de Bruxelles*, 1990–1991, Collection DEA, Universitaire Jean Moulin, Lyon III, at p.182: 'Les juges seront moins indulgents en présence de défendeurs rompus aux relations commerciales suivies et à la pratique du contentieux international, disposant pour ce faire d'une infrastructure juridique appropriée pour réagir rapidement.'.

[688] *OLG Düsseldorf* 19.10.1984 (1985) *RIW* 493, at p.494—an international corporate defendant (with its own in-house legal team) would therefore be considered to have sufficient time in circumstances where an economically weaker individual may need more time (to consult legal advice); recently in *OLG Düsseldorf* 8.11.2000 (2001) *RIW* 143, despite the fact that the judgment debtor engaged in cross-border commerce, the period of 9 days from service of a 6-sided document in Dutch was considered insufficent, as it would have involved the German debtor in 'extraordinary efforts', at p.144.

[689] *Corte di Appello di Milan Officina costruzioni Meccaniche OCM c/ SA Établissement J.Ivens* (1983) *JDI* 199; *BGH* 23.1.1986 IPRspr. (1986) Nr. 171, at p.390; *OLG Koblenz* 25.2.1987 (1988) *RIW* 476; *OLG Hamm* 3.8.1987 IPRspr. (1987) Nr. 155; sufficient time to engage legal help in *OLG Koblenz* 10.6.1991 IPRspr. (1991) Nr. 207, [1993] I.L.Pr. 289.

[690] Important in *OLG Düsseldorf* 11.10.1999 (2000) *RIW* 230—8 days considered insufficient to seek a translation of a 2-page document; 9 days *insufficient, inter alia*, to find a Dutch translator in *OLG Düsseldorf* 8.11.2000 (2001) *RIW* 143.

[691] Compare a court near to defendant's domicile in *OLG Koblenz* 19.6.1990 (1992) *IPRax* 35, with the (controversial) case of *OLG Hamm* 3.8.1987 (1988) *IPRax* 289, the defendant's domicile being in a 'sleepy backwater' in S.W.Westphalia, at p.290; proximity permitted enforcement in *Gerechtshof s'-Hertogenbosch* 4.3.1982, *D Series*, I- 27.2-B18, despite a fairly curt period.

[692] *Ibid.*,—surprisingly this factor has been brought into the equation.

[693] *OLG Koblenz* 25.2.1987 (1988) *RIW* 476, at p.477; *BGH* 2.10.1991 IPRspr. (1991) Nr. 210 at pp.447–8, where the court found the defendant must have been aware that proceedings (to call in a fixed-term loan) would have been initiated at the end of the term.

[694] *OLG Hamm* 3.8.1987 (1988) *IPRax* 289; Belgian document found not to resemble anything like a formal document commencing legal proceedings; cf a similar French document in *OLG Koblenz* 25.2.1987 (1988) *RIW* 476: '[i]nsbesondere besagt das Schreiben nicht,...ein einstweiliges Verfügungsverfahren bei dem Handelsgericht in Marseille einzuleiten'('for a start the document does not say that a *référé* has been lodged in the Commercial Court in Marseille'), at p.477; translated (English) writ in *OLG Hamm* 5.8.1992 (1993) *RIW* 148.

[695] *OLG Koblenz* 25.2.1987 (1988) *RIW* 476, at p.477: 'Die Antragsgegnerin konnte zudem dem Aufforderungsschreiben nicht entnehmen, wann und wo die Klage eingereicht werden würde'('the judgment debtor could not glean from the letter of request where and when the claim would be adduced'), therefore more time was needed.

[696] *OLG Düsseldorf* 19.10.1984 (1985) *RIW* 493, and above, at n.684; *OLG Koblenz* 25.2.1987 (1988) *RIW* 476, at p.477.

ment was served, and any intervening weekends when legal advice may have been more difficult to obtain;[697] the time limits under national law for comparable domestic proceedings;[698] and the status of the relationship between the parties,[699] particularly if, in this deteriorated state, the defendant should have been aware[700] that legal proceedings may have been initiated against him.

Depending on all these factors, it is difficult to predict that any given time period will, or will not, be adjudged to be sufficient. However, a detailed study of this aspect by Wiehe[701] has revealed that he notices what he terms a 'kritische Punkt'[702] of between 10 and 25 days. At either side of this 'grey period', respectively, the presence of any, or all, of the above factors seems to be irrelevant: thus a period of less than 10 days will normally be considered[703] insufficient whatever the circumstances of the case; conversely, a period over 25 days will normally be held to be sufficient in the vast majority of cases.[704] Therefore the above factors will play a crucial rôle in this intervening 'grey' period.

An important factor which seems to lower the pre-requisite sufficiency of time is the nature of the foreign proceedings—*Mahnverfahren*, or *référé* proceedings. These may require less work, or intellectual expenditure, and consequently less time, to prevent an enforceable default judgment.[705] Conversely, in a legally complex, or fiercely contested dispute, the need to consult translators and qualified (competent) lawyers[706] may demand that more time be given. This seemed to be one crucial fact taken into account by the *OLG Hamm*,[707] reviewed below. From reading the above factors, it appears that the German courts are, in the main,

---

[697] *LG Mönchengladbach* 20.7.1987 (1988) *IPRax* 291: service on a Friday afternoon, hearing fixed in Belgium for the following Tuesday. The intervening weekend, it was found, made it almost impossible to obtain legal consultation; also *OLG Koblenz* 25.2.1987 (1988) *RIW* 476, above, at n.695.

[698] This is generally believed to be irrelevant, but a comparison between domestic procedure *was* considered in *OLG Koblenz* 25.2.1987 (1988) *RIW* 476, in *OLG Köln* 8.3.1999 (2000) *IPRax* 528, and in *OLG Düsseldorf* 8.11.2000 (2001) *RIW* 143 as a factor in judging sufficiency; in *OLG Köln* 2.3.2001 (2002) NJW-RR 360 domestic procedure considered irrelevant.

[699] AG van Themaat in *Leon Emile Gaston Carlos Debaecker and Berthe Plouvier v Cornelius Gerrit Bouwman* (C–49/84) [1985] ECR 1779.

[700] *OLG Köln* 19.6.1990 (1992) *IPRax* 35; and therefore a generous case, *OLG Köln* 10.2.1993 IPRspr. (1993) Nr. 168, at p.374: 'Wenn sich der Schuldner. . .im Zeitpunkt der Zustellung für eine gewisse Zeit im Ausland befand, so oblag es ihm, dafür zu sorgen, dab ihn die in der Zwischenzeit an seinem Wohnsitz eingehende Post rechtzeitig erreichte.'('when the judgment debtor, at the time of service, was abroad for a certain period, it behove him to make sure that post arriving at this residence in this interim period reached him in good time').

[701] Wiehe, 1993, at p.219.

[702] ('a critical time period'), *ibid.*, at p.218—from the recent decision *OLG Düsseldorf* 11.10.1999 (2000) *RIW* 230, at p.231 it appears that a German court will scrutinise minutely (and suspiciously) time periods of less than 2 weeks, the time allowed for comparable procedure under German law.

[703] Since an inactive weekend may intervene.

[704] 5 weeks interval in *TSN Kunststoffrecycling GmbH v Jurgens*, QBD, 16.2.2001, Jack J not, in itself objected to by the parties nor the court as being insufficient.

[705] Cf Wiehe, 1993, at p.221 and pp.223–4.

[706] Who, in turn, may have to liase with foreign colleagues.

[707] 3.8.1987, IPRspr. 1987, seen as an egregious example of protectionism.

comparatively indulgent and patient in accepting a multitude of excuses from domestic judgment debtors. Other Contracting State courts do not share this leniency.

5.5.4   Italian case law and the sufficiency of time[708]

Wastl[709] has conveniently collected a number of early cases from the Italian courts which, in the main,[710] are generously orientated towards recognition and enforcement in this area:

> 'die italienische Rechtsprechung, soweit ersichtlich, keineswegs dazu neigt, durch eine extensive Auslegung . . . [,]die..Vollstreckbarerklärung zu erschweren.'[711]

5.5.5   French case law and sufficiency of time

The French case law on this area is scant; but periods of 10[712] days up to 6 months[713] have been considered sufficient. Curiously, they seem less[714] sympathetic towards a defendant's indolence than the German courts. Among the features looked at by the *Tribunal de grande instance*, Paris in *Société B.V. Rosco c/ S.A.R.L. Fraisgel* was 'notamment, les dilligences accomplies par le défendeur pour faire connaître ses moyens de défense.'[715] [716]

5.5.6   A Protectionist vein in Article 27(2)?

The more notable German cases are the ones which reveal (what in the outcome of the case can only be explained away by) a certain protectionist vein in their generous stance towards defaulting domestic debtors.

---

[708] Capotorti, F. & Starace, V. *La giurisprudenza italiana di diritto internazionale privato e processuale, Repertorio 1967–1990*, 1991, section VIII Ca, at pp.503–506; Bellagamba, G. & Cariti, G. *Il sistema italiano di diritto internazionale privato*, 2000.

[709] Wastl, U. *Die Vollstreckung deutscher Titel auf der Grundlage des EuGVÜ in Italien*, 1991, at pp.335–9.

[710] Unless the period is clearly short—6 days in *Corte d'Appello di Milano Standers & Zoon p.v.b.a. c/ Legati Rep. Foro it.* 1981, 709, n.2.

[711] ('the Italian case law, as far as can be seen, in no way tends to hinder enforcement via a restrictive interpretation') Wastl, 1991, at p.49; 20 days sufficient in *Corte d'appello di Napoli* 11.3.1999 *Industria Confetti Nicola Tortora S.n.c contro Adrian Pujol S.A.* (2001) *Il Diritto Marittimo* 1464.

[712] *Cassation* 3.11.1977 *Bull.Civ.*, I, n.401, p.320.

[713] Sufficient 1 month *Betito c/ Société Deritex* 13.11.1987 (1989) *JDI* 100; sufficient 3(months in *TGI Paris*, 2.11.1984, *Société B.V. Rosco c/ S.A.R.L. Fraisgel*, 1985 *Gaz. Pal.*, Juris., p.61.

[714] *Société B.V. Rosco c/ S.A.R.L. Fraisgel*, 1985 *Gaz. Pal.*, Juris., p.61.

[715] ('notably how quickly the defendant undertook the means by which he could become aware of the means to defend himself').

[716] *Ibid.*, at p.67.

A supreme example of this attitude is *OLG Hamm.*[717] Service of a Belgian document, in Flemish, instituting the proceedings on the German defendant gave him 20 days before the hearing (at which the default judgment was handed down) in order for him to prepare for his defence. In the circumstances,[718] this the *OLG* found to be insufficient time. The criticism[719] the case has provoked, centres on the protection the German judgment debtor received due to his physical location:

> 'Schon das Auffinden eines derartigen Übersetzers war für die nicht im deutsch-niederländischen Grenzgebiet, sondern in einer eher entlegenen ostwestfälischen Kleinstadt ansässige Ag. mit Schwierigkeiten und benachtlichem Zeitaufwand verbunden.'[720]

This location, it has been argued,[721] was no initial barrier to the judgment debtor's entering into commercial negotiations for the sale of the disputed product to the Belgian plaintiff; why this then[722] becomes such a hurdle at the enforcement stage can only be from protectionist motives.

All that can be said of the factual appraisal of 'sufficient time' is that a minimum period of two weeks is probably the safest time period to leave before applying for a default judgment.

5.6   CONCLUSION TO ARTICLE 27(2)

The great disadvantage from an (English) claimants point of view in the current version of Article 27(2) is its uncertain application, coupled with the many pitfalls—some engendered by the civil procedure rules themselves (article 620 NCPC or a generally endorsed writ/non-particularised claim form)—that may even open up *ex post facto*: from the article's application *ratione materiae*, to defective service under the 1965 Hague Service Convention/Council Service Regulation 1348/2000, and uncertainty as to the pre-requisite detail to satisfy a foreign enforcing court. Article 34(2) Brussels I Regulation will address some of these

---

[717] *OLG Hamm* 3.8.1987 (1988) *IPRax* 289, IPRspr. (1987) Nr. 155, (1987) *RIW* 871.

[718] Apart from the necessity of finding a translator; the nature of the document; and the defendant's lowly commercial status.

[719] Naturally from Geimer, R. 'Über die Kunst der Interessenabwägung auch im internationalen Verfahrensrecht, dargestellt am rechten Mab des beklagtenschutzes gemäb Art.27 Nr.2 EuGVÜ' zu *OLG Hamm* 3.8.1987 und *LG Mönchengladbach* 20.7.1987 (1988) *IPRax* 271.

[720] ('Even locating such a translator produced difficulties and a disadvantageous expenditure of time for a respondent not domiciled in the Germano-Dutch area, but rather in a remote village in Eastern Westphalia'): *OLG Hamm* 3.8.1987 (1988) *IPRax* 289.

[721] Geimer is caustic, (1988) *IPRax* 271, at p.275 'Idylle einer Kleinstadt in Ost-Westfalen'(the idyll of a village in East Westphalia').

[722] Van Venrooy, G. 'Nochmals: Über die Kunst der Interessenabwägung auch im internationalen Verfahrensrecht, dargestellt am rechten Mab des beklagtenschutzes gemäb Art.27 Nr.2 EuGVÜ' (1989) *IPRax* 137, explains that a German defendant would not be aware legal documents would be drawn up in Flemish.

concerns, but leaves others intact, unearthing novel ones along the way. It is the writer's belief that in the future, Article 34(2) of Brussels I Regulation will remain just as potent a tool for recalcitrant defendants, and provide as many opportunities for abuse as does the current Article 27(2).

Conclusion

It is remarkable in the Community-wide implementation of the Brussels and Lugano Conventions that more 'perturbations', even amongst the limited number of Articles[1] reviewed in the preceding pages, have not come to the fore; but this review has revealed certain important discrepancies.[2] The causes may be harder to identify—some inevitable,[3] some inadvertent,[4] and even perhaps (rare) instances of deliberate circumvention,[5] from whatever motivation.

Much of the success of the Brussels Convention in providing (as far as possible) a uniform jurisdictional code in civil and commercial matters can be attributed to the interpretative rôle assigned to the ECJ under the Brussels reference Protocol,[6] and the ensuing 'autonomous' definitions of many of the concepts used in the Convention.[7] Conversely, areas where discrepancies and controversy still exist could be seen as an indirect result of an unwillingness on the part of some Contracting State courts[8] to make clarifying preliminary references.

In chapter 1, Art.5(1), we saw problems encountered by national courts in interpreting the tripartite structure of an article that has produced voluminous case law,[9] and ECJ references. Except in the area of individual contracts of employment, it has also shown the ECJ taking an uncharacteristic non-interventionist stance, hide-bound by its own jurisprudence.[10] Of note have been certain Contracting State interpretations of (the principal) 'obligation in question', and

---

[1] For Art.2, *Re Harrods (Buenos Aires) Ltd* [1992] Ch 90; *ACE Insurance SA-NV v Zurich Insurance Company* [2001] 1 Lloyd's Rep. 618, CA; for Art.27(2), the German case law section below, at pp.LVIII–LXI, esp. *OLG Hamm* (1988) *IPRax* 289, *BGH* (1999) *RIW* 454, *BGH* 140 BGHZ 396, *OLG München* (2000) *RIW* 464, *OLG Karlsruhe* (1999) *RIW* 538

[2] Many will continue after 1.3.2002 in the Brussels I Regulation

[3] Where an autonomous interpretation of terms is rejected, and/or a *renvoi* to national law, or International Convention is made

[4] Inexperience and/or complexity of certain Articles, notably Art.5(1), in *Concorde* (C-440/97) [1999] ECR I-6307, at p.6314, para. 20, p.6322, para. 46, p.6336, para. 95, (Advocate-General Colomer)

[5] The *Cour de Cassation* in sections on bills of lading, above at pp.209 *et seq.*, and place of performance, sub-sections 1.3.6 and 1.3.8, above at pp.142 *et seq.*, and pp.150 *et seq.*, respectively.

[6] And also Art.1 Protocol 2 of Lugano Convention, [1998] OJ L319/31 & 40; Swiss *Bundesgericht A., B. und C. gegen D.* 123 BGE, III, 414, in the *Polly Peck* litigation, taking account of the observations of English notions of 'definitively pending' in *Dresser v Falcongate* [1992] 1 QB 502

[7] Cf *Cour de Cassation Donovan Data Systems* (2000) *Rev crit* 67, at p.69, Pataut

[8] Acute, it seems in the English CA: *Firswood v Petra Bank* [1996] CLC 608, CA, at p.619, (Schiemann LJ); *In re Harrods (Buenos Aires) Ltd* [1992] Ch 90, at p.98, (Dillon LJ); also *Jordan Grand Prix Ltd* [1999] 2 AC 127, at p.135 (Lord Steyn); cf *Lubbe v Cape Plc* [2000] 1 WLR 1545, at pp.1561–2 (Lord Bingham of Cornhill)

[9] Case list below, pp.xxvi–xxvii (Belgian), pp.xxxiv–xxxvii (French), pp.liv–lvi (German), pp.lxxiii–lxxiv (Italian, Dutch, Spanish), pp.lxxx–lxxi (Swiss and Austrian), and pp.lxxxvii–lxxix (UK and Irish).

[10] *Tessili v Dunlop* (C-12/76) [1976] ECR 1473 being re-applied in *Concorde* (C-440/97) [1999] ECR I-6307

what appeared to be the outright 'rebellion' of the French *Cour de Cassation*[11] over Art.5(1)'s place of performance, particularly ones involving payment obligations. The historical section has shown that the interpretative problems associated with Art.5(1) are not new; and that the autonomous amendments in the Brussels I Regulation and Worldwide Judgments Convention will be welcome.

In chapter 2, devoted to Art.17 jurisdiction clauses, we saw inconsistent interpretations as to its scope *ratione materiae* (re. the domicile of the parties), particularly as between German, Swiss and Austrian case law, extending even to English decisions.[12] The reasons for this are not entirely clear, but appear to stem from the rôle of the Convention as a whole, and the Preamble's self-limiting scope. The future amendments to the Convention that both the Brussels I Regulation and draft Hague Worldwide Judgments Convention will bring have either perpetuated, or nullified these inconsistencies.

In the section on bills of lading, we saw the reaction of a Contracting State, France, to case law from the ECJ[13] which has, no doubt, been perceived as injurious to national interests. Whether this attitude translates to protectionism is harder to discern, but has justifiably been the view of some commentators. Again, recent ECJ case law—notably *Hugo Trumpy*[14]—should ameliorate this situation in the future. The last substantive section is a comparative review of ECJ and national case law on the amendments to Art.17, in the 'international trade or commerce' form of jurisdiction clause.

Chapter 3, Art.24 'provisional, including protective measures', is interesting not so much for inconsistencies and uncertainties that have been erased,[15] but for the future potential of a (possibly protectionist) undermining of the Brussels Convention's Title II, with regard to interim orders, based on traditionally anathematised, exorbitant grounds of jurisdiction—the initiative for this upsurge surprisingly not coming from national courts, but from case law of the ECJ itself.[16] Although controversial in scope, the effect of such interim orders (symbolised here by the French *référé-provision* procedure for contractual payments) has been perpetuated in the Council Regulation (EC), and, to some extent, in the draft Hague Convention.

Chapter 4, 'public policy' under Art.27(1) is perhaps where idiosyncratic manifestations of particular Contracting State concerns would have been expected to arise more often and clearly than in any other article; in fact, the conclusion is, in

---

[11] *Cour de Cassation La Réunion européenne* (1997) *Rev crit* 101, [1997] I.L.Pr.711; *Comptoir commercial d'Orient* (1998) *JDI* 129, (1997) *Rev crit* 585; [1999] I.L.Pr.336
[12] *British Aerospace v Dee Howard* [1993] 1 Lloyd's Rep. 368 and *Mercury Communications Ltd* [1999] 2 All ER (Comm) 33 and *Sinochem International (No.2)* [2000] 1 All ER (Comm) 758
[13] *The Tilly Russ* (C-71/83) [1984] ECR 2417, *Mainschiffahrts* (C-106/95) [1997] ECR I-911
[14] (C-159/97) [1999] ECR I-1597; and *Coreck* (C–387–98), Advocate-General Alber's opinion 23.3.2000
[15] Ie whether Art.3 II exorbitant bases of jurisdiction could be used under Art.24
[16] *Van Uden* (C-391/95) [1998] ECR I-7091 and *Mietz* (C–99/96) [1999] ECR I-2277

the vast majority of cases,[17] that no protectionism is in evidence, despite, until now,[18] a lack of a 'framework', or working definition of Art.27(1) 'public policy'. Two recent decisions of the ECJ will raise the interest in Art.27(1), containing as they do (now) references to other EC instruments and the European Convention of Human Rights. The defence persists in both future amendments to the Brussels Convention.

Chapter 5, Art.27(2), the right to a fair hearing, has shown the potency of this potential defence, especially in its 'due service' aspects (in Germany)—and those that will continue under its partial amendment in Art.34(2) Brussels I Regulation in March 2002. Other issues regarding the exact nature of the phrase 'document which instituted the proceedings' have been explored, as have the uncertainties of the factual determination of the 'sufficiency of time' and the concept of 'appearance' in relation to general and specific/specialised civil and commercial proceedings. Attention has been drawn to the addition, in Art.34(2) Brussels I Regulation, of the necessity to commence proceedings to have any default judgment set aside, as a prerequisite for future reliance on the defence; and the potential ramifications this may have in different Contracting States via the Council Service Regulation 1348/2000. The chapter, in the round, has sought to highlight all the major pitfalls that may await a default judgment creditor in other Contracting States.

Without making a bold assertion that inconsistencies do not exist in other Convention articles,[19] the Convention's success can be measured by the way the remainder have produced correspondingly fewer anomalous reported decisions, and critical comment. Some of the inconsistencies highlighted throughout the text will, no doubt, be swept away, when the ECJ (eventually) comes to rule on a particular issue; many have been so, when recent case law filters down to national application. Future amendments may go some way in ensuring the tensions in certain Contracting State positions, yet, as has been mentioned, further clarifying amendments could have been undertaken. So long as Contracting State judgments are rendered in *inter partes* hearings, there appears little in the Convention to prevent the attainment of its primary *desideratum*—the free movement of judgments. A lasting legacy of the Convention's success is the framework it has provided for the work currently underway at the Hague Conference on Private International Law.

---

[17] With very isolated exceptions, *BGH* IPRspr. (1993) Nr. 178 and *BGH* (1999) *IPRax* 371

[18] But now *Krombach* (C–7/98), 28.3.2000, Advocate-General Antonio Saggio's opinion 23.9.1999 and *Renault v SpA Maxicar* (C–38/98), 11.5.2000, Advocate-General Alber's opinion 22.6.1999

[19] Notably the existence and availability of the discretion in English law of applying *forum non conveniens* in a case governed by the Brussels Convention: *Re Harrods (Buenos Aires) Ltd* [1992] Ch 90, *The 'Xin Yang'* [1996] 2 Lloyd's Rep. 217, *Mercury Communications Ltd* [1999] 2 All ER (Comm) 33, *Sinochem International v Mobil Sales (No.2)* [2000] 1 All ER (Comm) 758

Bibliography—Books

Access to civil procedure abroad (ed. Snijders, H.), Sweet & Maxwell, London, 1996

Achilles, W-A. *Kommentar zum UN-Kaufrechtsübereinkommen (CISG)*, H.Luchterhand Verlag GmbH, Neuwied, 2000

Aird, RE and Jameson, WS. *The Scots Dimension to Cross-Border Litigation*, Sweet & Maxwell, Edinburgh, 1996

Albrecht, C. *Vollstreckbarkeit von Urteilen und Schiedssprüchen im deutsch-italienischen Rechtsverkehr*, Paul Evert Verlag, Hamburg, 1937

—— *Das EuGVÜ und der einstweilige Rechtsschutz in England und in der Bundesrepublik Deutschland*, Carl Winter Universitätsverlag, Heidelberg, 1991

Alférez-Garcimartín, F. 'Effects of the Brussels Convention upon the Spanish System: Provisional and Protective Measures' in *Europäischer Binnenmarkt, Internationales Privatrecht und Rechtsvergleichung* (Hrsg Hommelhoff/Jayme/Mangold), C.F. Müller Juristischer Verlag, Heidelberg, 1995, p.129

Al Mulla, H. *The recognition and enforcement of foreign civil and commercial judgments under multilateral and bilateral conventions*, Ph.D Thesis, Cambridge University, 1992

Ameli, F. *La saisie-arrêt en droit international privé*, Thèse, Paris I, 1990

Angeli, F. *La convenzione giudiziaria di Bruxelles del 1968 e la riforma del processo civile italiano*, Franco Angeli Libri, Milano, 1985

Anderson, D. *References to the European Court*, Sweet & Maxwell, London, 1995

Annales de l'Association internationale pour le Progrès des sciences sociales, première session, 1863, A. Lacroix, Bruxelles et Leipzig, 1863

Annales de l'Association internationale pour le Progrès des sciences sociales, deuxième session, A. Lacroix, Bruxelles et Leipzig, 1864

Annales de l'Association internationale pour le Progrès des sciences sociales, troisième session, 1865, Bols-Wittouck, Bruxelles, 1865

Article 177 EEC: Experiences and Problems (eds. Schermers/Timmermans/Kellermann/ Watson), Elsevier Science Publishers B.V., Amsterdam, 1987

Audit, B. *Droit International Privé*, Economica, Paris, 1991

Aull, JM. *Der Geltungsanspruch des EuGVÜ: 'Binnensachverhalte' u. internationales Zivilverfahrensrecht in der Europäischen Union: Zur Auslegung von Art.17 Abs.1 s.1 EuGVÜ*, Peter Lang, Frankfurt am Main, 1996

Baeck, P. *The General Civil Code of Austria*, Oceana Publications, New York, 1972

Barnett, P. *Res judicata, estoppel, and foreign judgments*, Oxford University Press, Oxford, 2001

Bartin, E. *Principes de droit international privé*, Éditions Domat-Montchrestien, Paris, 1930

Batiffol, H. *Traité élémentaire de droit international privé*, 2ème éd., LGDJ, Paris, 1955

Bauer, H. *Compétence judiciaire internationale des tribunaux civils français et allemands*, Librairie Dalloz, Paris, 1965

Bauer, P. *Die internationale Zuständigkeit bei gesellschaftsrechtlichen Klagen unter besonderer Berücksichtigung des EuGVÜ*, Hartung-Gorre, Konstanz, 2000

Beaumont, P. *Civil Jurisdiction in Scotland – Brussels and Lugano Conventions*, 2nd edn, Sweet & Maxwell, Edinburgh, 1995

Beck, H. *Die Anerkennung und Vollstreckung ausländischer gerichtlicher Entscheidungen in Zivilsachen nach den Staatsverträgen mit Belgien, Österreich, Grossbritannien und Griechenland*, Inaugural Dissertation, Universität des Saarlandes, 1967

Beiso, I. *Le forum non conveniens*, Mémoire pour le DEA, Paris II, Bibliothèque interuniversitaire Cujas, 1996

Bell, J and Boyron, S and Whittaker, S. *Principles of French Law*, Oxford University Press, Oxford, 1998

Bellagamba, G and Cariti, G. *Il sistema italiano di diritto internazionale privato*, Dott. A Giuffrè Editore, Milano, 2000

Beltramo, M. *The Italian Civil Code*, Oceana Publications, New York, 1969

Benecke, L. *Die teleologische Reduktion des räumlich-persöhnlichen Anwendungsbereiches von Art.2ff u.Art.17 EuGVÜ*, Dissertation, Universität Bielefeld, 1993

Benot, AR. *Los acuerdos atributivos de competencia judicial internacional en derecho comunitario europeo*, Ediciones Beramar, S.L. Eurolex, Madrid, 1994

Bernard, M. *De la compétence des tribunaux français à l'égard des étrangers et de l'exécution des jugements étrangers en France*, Maison L. Larose & Forcel, Paris, 1900

Berti, S. 'Gedanken zur Klageerhebung vor schweizerischen Gerichten nach Artikel 21–23 des Lugano-Übereinkommens' in *Recht und Durchsetzung, Festschrift für Hans Ulrich Walder*, Schulthess Polygraphischer Verlag, Zürich, 1994, at p.307

—— 'Englische Anti-suit Injunctions im europäischen Zivilprozessrecht – A Flourishing species or a Dying breed?' in *Private Law in the International Arena, Liber Amicorum Kurt Siehr*, (ed. Basedow, J.), TMC Asser Press, The Hague, 2000, p.33

Besse, D. *Die Vergemeinschaftung des EuGVÜ*, 1 Aufl., Nomos Verlag, Baden-Baden, 2001

Bincy, W. *Irish Conflicts of Law*, Butterworths (Ireland) Ltd, 1988

Bischof, P. *Produkthaftung und Vertrag in der EU*, Verlag Stämpfli & Cie AG, Bern, 1994

Bischof, T. *Die Zustellung im internationalen Rechtsverkehr in Zivil-oder Handelssachen*, Schulthess Polygraphischer Verlag, Zürich, 1997

Bittighofer, A. *Der internationale Gerichtsstand des Vermögens*, Peter Lang, Frankfurt am Main, 1994

Blum, CP. *Forum non conveniens*, Schulthess Polygraphischer Verlag, Zürich, 1979

Bonner Grundgesetz, Das, 4er Aufl., Band 3,: Artikel 79–146 (Starck, C. Hrsg.), Verlag Franz Vahlen GmbH, München, 2001

Bormans, T. *Code de procédure civile belge*, 2e éd, Larcier, Bruxelles, 1877

Botschaft betreffend das Lugano-Übereinkommen über die gerichtliche Zuständigkeit und die Vollstreckung gerichtlicher Entscheidungen in Zivil-und Handelssachen vom 21 Februar 1990, Bundesblatt Nr.16 Band II, 142 Jahrgang, 24 April 1990, p.265

Braas, A. *Précis de Procédure Civile, Organisation Judiciaire. Compétence. Procédure Civile*, 2ème éd., Emile Bruylant, Bruxelles, 1934

Brandenberg Brandl, B. *Direkte Zuständigkeit der Schweiz im internationalen Schuldrecht*, Dike-Verlag AG, St.Gallen, 1991

Brandes, F. *Der gemeinsame Gerichtsstand, Die Zuständigkeit im europäischen Mehrparteienprozeß nach Art.6 Nr.1 EuGVÜ/LÜ*, Peter Lang, Frankfurt am Main, 1998

Braun, S. *Der Bekagtenschutz nach Art.27 Nr.2 EuGVÜ*, Duncker & Humblot, Berlin, 1992

Bridge, M. *The International Sale of Goods, Law and Practice*, Oxford University Press, Oxford, 1999

Briggs, A. *Civil Jurisdiction and Judgments*, 1st edn., 1993, 2nd edn., Lloyd's of London Press, London, 1997

Briggs, A. 'Anti-Suit Injunctions in a Complex World' in *Lex Mercatoria: Essays on International Commercial Law in Honour of Francis Reynolds*, (ed. Rose, F.D.), Lloyd's of London Press, London, 2000, p.219

—— *The Conflict of Laws*, Oxford University Press, Oxford, 2002

Brocher, C. *Nouveau Traité de droit international privé*, H. Georg, Libraire-Éditeur, Genève, Bale, Lyon, 1876

Brockmeier, D. *Punitive damages, multiple damages und deutscher ordre public*, Mohr Siebeck, Tübingen, 1999

Broggini, G. 'Zuständigkeit am Ort der Vertragserfülllung' in *Das Lugano-Übereinkommen*, (Hrsg Schwander, I.), Dike-Verlag AG, St.Gallen, 1990, p.111

Brulhart, V. *La compétence internationale en matière d'assurances dans l'espace judiciaire européen*, Dike Verlag AG, St.Gallen/Lachen, 1997

Bucher, A. *Droit international privé, Loi fédéral et Conventions internationales*, Recueil de Textes, 1994

—— *Droit international privé suisse*, Tome I/1: *Partie générale – Conflits de juridictions*, Helbing & Lichtenhahn, Bâle, 1998

Buhiges, JLI. 'Competencia judicial y ejecucion de sentencias en Europa' in *El Derecho Comunitario Europeo y su aplicacion judicial* (ed.Rodriguez-Iglesias, G.C.), Editorial Civitas, Madrid, 1993, p.1047

Bülow, A and Böckstiegel, K-H., *Der Internationale Rechtsverkehr in Zivil- und Handelssachen*, Band I, II, Verlag C.H. Beck, München, 1985

Burst, S. *Pönale Momente im ausländischen Privatrecht und deutscher ordre public*, Peter Lang, Frankfurt am Main, 1994

Buschmann, A. *Rechtshängigkeit im Ausland als Verfahrenshindernis*, Verlag V. Florentz GmbH, München, 1996

Byrne, R and Binchy, W. *Annual Review of Irish Law 1997*, Round Hall, Sweet & Maxwell, London, 1998

The Brussels Convention on Jurisdiction and the Enforcement of Judgments: Papers and Precedents from the Joint Conference with the Union des Avocats Europeéns held in Cork, September 1989, (G Moloney and N Robinson eds.), Irish Centre for European Law, 1990

Caffrey, B. *International Jurisdiction and the Recognition and Enforcement of Foreign Judgments*, CCH Australia Limited, Sydney, 1985

Camacho, V.F. *Las Medidas provisionales y cautelares en el espacio judicial europeo*, Eurolex, Madrid, 1996

Campbell, D. *Enforcement of Foreign Judgments*, Lloyd's of London Press, London, 1997

Campeis, G. *Il processo civile italiano e lo Straniero*, Giuffrè Editore, Milano, 1996

Capotorti, F and Starace, V. *La giurisprudenza italiana di diritto internazionale privato e processuale, Repertorio 1967–1990*, Giuffrè Editore, Milano, 1991

Carbone, S. *Lo spazio giudiziario europea*, G.Giappichelli Editore, Torino, 1997

Carey Miller, DL. *The Option of Litigating in Europe*, The United Kingdom National Committee of Comparative Law, London, Vol. 14, 1993

Cattaneo, F. *La convenzione tra la Svizzera e l'Italia circa il riconoscimento e l'esecuzione delle decisioni giudiziarie del 3 gennaio 1933*, Rezzonico-Pedrini, Lugano, 1939

Cebecioglu, T. *Stellung des Ausländers im Zivilprozeß*, Peter Lang, Frankfurt am Main, 2000

Cheshire, GC. *Private International Law*, Clarendon Press, Oxford, 1935

Cheshire GC. *Cheshire and North's Private International Law*, 12th edn., Butterworths, London, 1992

Cheshire and North's Private International Law (eds. North, P. and Fawcett, J.), 13th edn., Butterworths, London, 1999

Cieslik, H-W. *Die Methode des Gerichtshofs der Europäischen Gemeinschaften bei der Auslegung des Europäischen Gerichtsstands- und Vollstreckungsübereinkommens*, Dissertation, Universität Bayreuth, 1992

Civil Jurisdiction and Judgments in Europe – Proceedings of the Colloquium on the Interpretation of the Brussels Convention by the Court of Justice considered in the context of the European Judicial Area, Luxembourg, 11 and 12 March 1991, Butterworths, 1992

Civil Procedure, Volumes 1 and 2, Autumn 2001, Sweet & Maxwell, London, 2001

Code Civil Suisse et Code des Obligations Annotés (Scyboz et Gilliéron), Editions Payot, Lausanne, 1993

Code de Procédure Civile, Ann., Griolet, G, 1904

—— 44ème éd Dalloz, 1948

—— 62ème éd Dalloz, 1966

—— 67ème éd Dalloz, 197–1971

Codice di Procedura Civile e norme complementari, Fazzalari, E and Luiso, F., Dott. A Giuffrè Editore, Milano, 1998

Coipel-Cordonnier, N. *Les conventions d'arbitrage et d'élection de for en droit international privé*, LGDJ, Paris, 1999

Collection of jurisprudence of the European Court of Justice and of the highest courts of the States Parties concerning the Lugano Convention, Vol.1, 1992, Vol.II, 1993, Vol.III, 1994, Publications of the Swiss Institute of Comparative Law, Schulthess Polygraphischer Verlag, Zürich (*Collection*)

Collier, JG. *Conflict of Laws*, 2nd edn., Cambridge University Press, Cambridge, 1994

Collins, L. *The Civil Jurisdiction and Judgments Act 1982*, Butterworths, London, 1983

—— 'Provisional and Protective Measures in International Litigation' in *Academie de droit international, Recueil des Cours* 1992, III, Tome 234, Martinus Nijhoff Publishers, Dordrecht, Boston, London, 1993, p.19

—— *Essays in International Litigation and the Conflict of Laws*, Clarendon Press, Oxford, 1994

Colloque de Fribourg relatif au projet suisse de loi fédérale sur le droit international privé, Schweizer Studien zum internationalen Recht, Band 14, Schulthess Polygraphischer Verlag AG, Zürich, 1979

Colman, A. *The Practice and Procedure of the Commercial Court*, . Lloyd's of London Press, London, 1995

Commercial Operations in Europe (eds. Goode/Simmonds), A.W. Sijthoff, Leiden/Boston, 1978

Comparability and Evaluation, Essays on comparative law in Honour of Dimitra Kokkini-Iatridou, (eds. Boele-Woelki/Grosheide/Hondius/Steenhoff), Martinus Nijhoff Publishers, Dordrecht/Boston, 1994

Conférence de La Haye de droit international privé, *Actes et documents de la Session extraordinaire 13 au 26 avril 1966, Exécution des jugements*, Imprimerie Nationale, La Haye, 1969

Contuzzi, FP. *Commentaire Théorique et Pratique des Conventions de la Haye concernant la codification du droit international privé*, Tome I, Librarie Maresq Ainé, Paris, 1904

Convention de Lugano, II. *Travaux Préparatoires*, Publications de l'Institut suisse de droit comparé, Schulthess Polygraphischer Verlag, Zürich, 1991

Convention de Lugano de 1988 – La compétence judiciaire internationale et l'exécution des décisions étrangères, Journées d'étude de droit international des 27 et 28 juin 1991 Friboug, University of Fribourg, Switzerland 1991

Cramer-Frank, B. *Auslegung und Qualifikation bilateraler Anerkennungs-und Vollstreckungsverträge mit Nicht-EG-Staaten*, Verlag V.Florentz GmbH, München, 1987

Cuniberti, G. *Les mesures conservatoires portant sur des biens situés à l'étranger*, LGDJ, Paris, 2000

Curti, E. *Der Staatsvertrag zwischen der Schweiz und Frankreich betreffend den Gerichtsstand und die Urtheilsvollziehung vom 15. Juni 1869*, Druck von Zürcher und Furrer, Zürich, 1879

Cypra, P. *Die Rechtsbehelfe im Verfahren der Vollstreckbarerklärung nach dem EuGVÜ, unter besonderer Berücksichtigung der Ausgestaltung in Deutschland und Frankreich*, Peter Lang, Frankfurt am Main, 1996

Czempiel, B. *Das bestimmbare Deliktsstatut*, Duncker & Humblot, Berlin, 1991

Dalhuisen, JH. 'Creditors' Remedies and the Conflicts of Law in The European Community' in *Ius Inter Nationes – Festschrift für Stefan Riesenfeld*, C.F. Müller Juristischer Verlag, Heidelberg, 1983

Damjanovic, D. *Les mesures provisoires ou conservatoires dans le cadre de la Convention de Bruxelles*, Mémoire de DEA, Bibliothèque Interuniversiaire Cujas, 1996

Das Lugano-Übereinkommen (Hrsg Schwander, I), Dike-Verlag AG, St.Gallen, 1990

Das Lugano-Übereinkommen von 1988, Studientag, 1991

Däubler, W. *Internationale Arbeits- und Sozialordnung*, Bund-Verlag, Köln, 1994

David, C-H. and Maier, H-J. *Die Vollstreckung von gerichtlichen Entscheidungen und Schiedssprüchen im Verhältnis zwischen der Bundesrepublik Deutschland und der Schweiz*, unpublished, Library of Congress Collection, 1970

De Bavier, J-C., *L'application en Italie de la Convention Italo-Suisse du 3 Janvier 1933*, M.Audin, Lyon, 1948

De Bra, P. *Verbraucherschutz durch Gerichtsstandsregelungen im deutschen u. europäischen Zivilprozeßrecht*, Peter Lang, Frankfurt am Main, 1992

De Cock, H. *Études sur la Convention Franco-belge du 8 juillet 1899*, I, A. Rousseau, Paris, 1912

De Lapuerta, RS. *El procedimiento ante el Tribunal de Justicia de las Comunidades Europeas*, Distribuciones de La Ley, Madrid, 1993

De Sousa, M and Vicente, D. *Comentário à Convenção de Bruxelas de 27 de setembro de 1968 relativa à competência judiciária e à ececução de decisões em matéria civil e comercial e textos eompelentares*, Lex Idiçóes Jurídicas, Lisboa, 1994

Despagnet, F. *Précis de droit international privé*, 3ème Éd, Librairie de la Société du Receuil, Paris, 1899

Diab, N-A. *Le tribunal internationalement compétent en droits libanais et français*, LGDJ, Paris, 1992

Di Blase, A. *Connessione e litispendenza nella Convenzione di Bruxelles*, CEDAM, Milano, 1993

Dicey, AV. *A digest of the Law of England with reference to the Conflict of Laws*, Sweet & Maxwell, London, 1896

—— *A Digest of the Law of England with reference to The Conflict of Laws*, 2nd edn., Sweet & Maxwell, London, 1908

Dicey's Conflict of Laws, 7th edn. (ed. Morris, J), Stevens & Sons Ltd., London, 1958

Dicey and Morris on the Conflict of Laws, 9th edn., Stevens & Sons Ltd, London, 1973

—— 12th edn., Sweet & Maxwell, London, 1993, Vol.I.

Dicey and Morris on the Conflict of Laws, 13th edn., Sweet & Maxwell, London, 2000, Vol.I

Die Übereinkommen von Brüssel und Lugano, Der Einfluß der Europäischen Gerichtsstands- und Vollstreckungsübereinkommen auf den österreichischen Zivilprozeß, (Hrsg. Bajons/Mayr/Zeiler), Verlag Österreich, Wien, 1997

Digest of case-law relating to the European Communities, D Series, Convention of 27 September 1968, Issue 5 Feb. 1993, 1995

Dohm, C. *Die Einrede ausländischer Rechtshängigkeit im deutschen internationalen Zivilprozeßrecht*, Duncker & Humblot, Berlin, 1996

Donzallaz, Y. *La Convention de Lugano*, Vol I, 1996, paras. 1–1736, Vol II, 1997, paras. 1737–4238, Vol III, 1998 paras.4239–7164, Stæmpfli Editions S.A., Berne

Dörig, A. *Anerkennung und Vollstreckung US-amerikanischer Entscheidungen in der Schweiz*, Dike Verlag AG., St.Gallen, 1998

Dorsel, C. *Forum non conveniens, richterliche Beschränkung der Wahl des Gerichtsstandes im deutschen und amerikanischen Recht*, Duncker & Humblot, Berlin, 1996

Droz, G. *Compétence judiciaire et effets des jugements dans le marché commun*, Dalloz, Paris, 1972

—— *Pratique de la Convention de Bruxelles*, Dalloz, Paris, 1973

Drobnig, U. *American-German Private International Law*, Oceana Publications, New York, 1972

Dutilleul, F and Delebeque, P. *Contrats civils et commerciaux*, 3ᵉ éd, Dalloz, Paris, 1996

Eichenhofer, E. 'Zwei Aufgaben des Internationalen Privatrechts' in *Festschrift für Günther Jahr*, J.C.B. Mohr (Paul Siebeck), Tübingen, 1993, p.435

Eickhoff, W. *Inländische Gerichtsbarkeit und internationale Zuständigkeit für Aufrechnung und Widerklage*, Duncker & Humblot, Berlin, 1985

Eilers, A. *Maßnahmen des einstweiligen Rechtsschutzes im europäischen Zivilrechtsverkehr*, Verlag Ernst und Verner Giesking, Bielefeld, 1991

Ein internationales Zivilverfahrensrecht für Gesamteuropa, EuGVÜ, LÜ (Hrsg. Jayme), C.F. Müller Juristischer Verlag, Heidelberg, 1992

Elias, O. *Judicial remedies in the Conflict of Laws*, Hart Publishing, Oxford, 2001

Endres, P. *Die französische Prozeßrechtslehre vom Code de procédure civile (1806) bis zum beginnenden 20. Jahrhundert*, J.C.B. Mohr (Paul Siebeck), Tübingen, 1985

Enforcing foreign judgments in the United States and United States Judgments Abroad, (ed. Brand, R.), American Bar Association, 1992

Epe, A. *Die Funktion des Ordre Public im deutschen internationalen Privatrecht*, Druckerei Stehle, 1983

E Pluribus Unum, Liber Amicorum Georges A.L. Droz, (eds. Borrás/Bucher/Struycken/ Verwilghen), Martinus Nijhoff Publishers, The Hague, 1996

Erauw, J. *Bronnen van Internationaal Privaatrecht*, Maklu Uitgevers, Antwerpen, 1994

—— and Watté, N. *Les Sources du droit international privé belge et communautaire*, Emile Bruylant, Bruxelles, 1993

Erwand, C. *Forum non Conveniens und EuGVÜ*, Peter Lang, Frankfurt am Main, 1996

Escher, A. *Neuere Probleme aus der Rechtsprechung zum französisch-schweizerischen Gerichtsstandsvertrag vom 15. Juni 1869*, Verlag H.R. Sauerländer & Co., Aarau, 1937

Estévez, J. *Reconocimiento y ejecución de resoluciones judiciales en el ordenamiento positivo español en el Convenio de Bruselas de 27 de Septiembre de 1968*, Promociones y Publicaciones Universitarias, S.A., Barcelona, 1987

Etudes offertes à Pierre Bellet, Litec, Paris, 1991

Le droit des relations économiques internationales, Etudes offertes à Berthold Goldman, Litec, Paris, 1983

Etudes dédiées à Alex Weill, Dalloz, Paris, 1983

Europäischer Binnenmarkt, Internationales Privatrecht und Rechtsangleichung (Hrsg. Hommelhoff/ Jayme/Mangold), C.F. Müller Juristischer Verlag, Heidelberg, 1995

Europäisches Kollisionsrecht: Die Konventionen von Brüssel, Lugano und Rom (Hrsg. Reichelt), Peter Lang, Frankfurt am Main, 1993

European Case Law on the Judgments Convention (ed. Kaye, P), John Wiley & Sons, Chichester, 1998

Executionsordnung, Gesetz vom 27.Mai 1896, Zweite Auflage, Druck und Verlag der Österreichischen Staatsdruckerei, Wien, 1932

Executionsordnung, samt Einführungsgesetz, Nebengesetzen, und sonstigen einschlägigen Vorschriften (Hrsg. Angst, P/Jakusch, W./Pimmer, H.), 13 Aufl., Manzsche Verlags-und Universitätsbuchhandlung, Wien, 1995

Fahl, C. *Die Stellung des Gläubigers und des Schuldners bei der Vollstreckung ausländischer Entscheidungen nach dem EuGVÜ*, Nomos Verlagsgesellschaft, Baden-Baden, 1993

Fasching, H. *Kommentar zu den Zivilprozessgesetzen, III Band, Zivilprozessordnung §§ 226–460,* Manzsche Verlags-und Universitätsbuchhandlung, Wien, 1966

—— *Kommentar zu den Zivilprozessgesetzen, I Band, Jurisdiktionsnorm,* Manzsche Verlags-und Universitätsbuchhandlung, Wien, 1959

—— *Lehrbuch des österreichischen Zivilprozeßrechts*, Manzsche Verlags-und Universitätsbuchhandlung, Wien, 1990

—— *Kommentar zu den Zivilprozeßgesetzen in vier Bänden:* 1.Band *EGJN, JN samt EuGVÜ/LGVÜ,* 2 völlig neu. Aufl., Manzsche Verlags-und Universitätsbuchhandlung, Wien, 2000

Fawcett, JJ. *Declining jurisdiction in private international law*, Clarendon Press, Oxford, 1995

Fawcett, J and Torremans, P. *Intellectual Property and Private International Law*, Clarendon Press, Oxford, 1998

Festschrift für Gottfried Baumgärtel (Hrsg.Prütting), Carl Heymanns Verlag AG, Köln, Berlin, Bonn, München, 1990

Festschrift für Arthur Bülow (Hrsg. Böckstiegel/Glossner), Carl Heymanns Verlag AG, Köln, Berlin, Bonn, München,1981

Festschrift für Ulrich Everling, Nomos Verlagsgesellschaft, Baden-Baden, 1995

Festschrift für Karl Firsching (Hrsg. Henrich/Von Hoffmann), C.H. Beck'sche Verlagsbuchandlung, München, 1985

Neues zum Gesellschafts- und Wirtschaftsrecht, Festschrift für Peter Forstmoser, Schulthess Polygraphischer Verlag, Zürich, 1993

Festschrift für Wilhelm G. Grewe (Hrsg. Kroneck/Oppermann), Nomos Verlagsgesellschaft, Baden-Baden, 1981

Festschrift für Wolfram Henckel, Walter de Gruyter, Berlin/New York, 1995

Internationales Privatrecht und Rechtsvergleichung im Ausgang des 20. Jahrhunderts, Bewahrung oder Wende? Festschrift für Gerhard Kegel, (Hrsg. Lüderitz/Schröder), A. Metzner Verlag, Fankfurt am Main, 1977

Festschrift für Winfried Kralik (Hrsg. Rechenberger/Welser), Manzsche Verlags-und Universitätsbuchhandlung, Wien, 1986

Festschrift für Franz Matscher, Manzsche Verlags-und Universitätsbuchhandlung, Wien, 1993

Festschrift für Klemens Pleyer (Hrsg. Hofmann/Meyer-Cording/Wiedemann), Carl Heymanns Verlag AG, Köln, Berlin, Bonn, München,1986, p.371

Festschrift für Murad Ferid (Hrsg. Heldrich, A/Sonnenberger, H.), Verlag für Standesamtswesen, Frankfurt am Main, 1988

Ius Inter Nationes – Festschrift für Stefan Riesenfeld, C.F. Müller Juristischer Verlag, Heidelberg, 1983

Festschrift für Otto Sandrock, Verlag Recht und Wirtschaft GmbH, Heidelberg,

Festschrift für Karl Heinz Schwab (Hrsg.Gottwald/Prütting), C.H. Beck'sche Verlagsbuchandlung, München, 1990

Foundations and Perspectives of International Trade Law, (Fletcher, I./Mistelis, L./Cremona, M. eds.), Sweet & Maxwell, London, 2001

Europa im Aufbruch, Festschrift für Fritz Schwind, Manzsche Verlags-und Universitätsbuchhandlung, Wien, 1993

Festschrift für Ernst Steindorf, Walter de Gruyter, Berlin, 1990

Beiträge zum schweizerischen und internationalen Zivilprozessrecht, Festschrift für Oskar Vogel, Universitätsverlag Freiburg, Schweiz, 1991

Festschrift für Konrad Zweigert, J.C.B. Mohr (Paul Siebeck), Tübingen, 1981

Festskrift Till Stig Strömlolm, Vol. II, Författarna och Iustus Förlag AG, Göteborg, 1997

Firsching, K and von Hoffmann, B. *Internationales Privatrecht,* 5 Aufl., C.H. Beck'sche Verlagsbuchhandlung, München, 1997

Fleischer, N. *Der Gerichtsstand des gemeinsamen Erfüllungsortes im deutschen Recht*, Inaugural-Dissertation, Bonn, 1997

Foreign Courts, Civil Litigation in Foreign Legal Cultures (ed. Gessner, V), Dartmouth Publishing Co. Ltd, Aldershot, 1996

Frank, M. *Das verfahrenseinleitende Schriftstück in Art.27 Nr.2 EuGVÜ, Lugano-Übereinkommen und in Art.6 Haager Unterhaltsübereinkommen 1973*, Duncker & Humblot, Berlin, 1998

Franzen, M. 'Internationale Gerichtsstandsvereinbarungen in Arbeitsverträgen zwischen EuGVÜ und autonomem internationalem Zivilprozeßrecht' 2000 *RIW* 81

Freedman, W. *Foreign plaintiffs in products liability actions*, Quorum Books, New York, 1988

Frick, J. *Culpa in contrahendo – Eine rechtsvergleichende und kollisionsrechtliche Studie*, Schulthess Polyraphischer Verlag, Zürich, 1992

Fricke, M. *Die autonome Anerkennungszuständigkeitsregel im deutschen Recht des 19. Jahrhunderts*, J.C.B. Mohr (Paul Siebeck), Tübingen, 1993

—— *Anerkennungszuständigkeit zwischen Spiegelbildgrundsatz und Generalklausel*, Verlag Ernst und Werner Gieseking, Bielefeld, 1990

Gabriel, H. *Practitioner's Guide to The Convention on Contracts for the International Sale of Goods (CISG) and The Uniform Commercial Code (UCC)*, Oceana Publications, New York, 1994

Gärtner, J. *Probleme der Auslandsvollstreckung von Nichtgeldleistungsentscheidungen im Bereich der Europäischen Gemeinschaft*, Verlag V. Florentz, München, 1991

Gassmann, R. *Arrest im internationalen Rechtsverkehr*, Schulthess Polygraphischer Verlag, Zürich, 1998

Gaudemet-Tallon, H. *Recherches sur les origines de l'article 14 du Code civil*, Presses Universitaires de France, Paris, 1964

—— 'La litispendence internationale dans la jurisprudence française' in *Mélanges dédiés à Dominique Holleaux*, Litec, Paris, 1990, p.121

—— *Les Conventions de Bruxelles et de Lugano*, 1^{ier} éd., 1993, 2ème éd., LGDJ, Montchrestien, Paris, 1996

Gauthier, M. *La Convention de Bruxelles et les droits de propriété intéllectuelle*, 1994–5, Paris I, Bibliothèque Interuniversiaire Cujas

Gedächtnisschrift für Peter Arens (Hrsg. Leipold), C.H. Beck'sche Verlagsbuchhandlung, München, 1993

Gedächtnisschrift für Rudolf Bruns (Hrsg.Baltzer/Baumgärtel/Peters/Pieper), Verlag Franz Vahlen, München, 1980

Geimer, R. *Zur Prüfung der Gerichtsbarkeit und der internationalen Zuständigkeit bei der Anerkennung ausländischer Urteile*, Verlag Ernst und Werner Gieseking, Bielefeld, 1966

—— 'Kompetenzkonflikte im System des Europäischen Gerichtsstands- und Vollstreckungsübereinkommens' in *Festschrift für Winfried Kralik* (Hrsg. Rechenberger/ Welser), Manzsche Verlags-und Universitätsbuchhandlung, Wien, 1986, p.179

—— 'Anerkennung ausländischer Entscheidungen auf dem Gebiet der freiwilligen Gerichtsbarkeit' in *Festschrift für Murad Ferid*, (Hrsg. Heldrich, A./Sonnenberger, H.), Verlag für Standesamtswesen, Frankfurt am Main, 1988, p.89

—— *Anerkennung ausländischer Entscheidungen in Deutschland*, Verlag C.H. Beck, München, 1995

—— *Internationales Zivilprozeßrecht*, 3 neu. Auf., Verlag Dr.Otto Schmidt, Köln, 1997

—— and Schütze, R. *Europäisches Zivilverfahrensrecht, Kommentar zum EuGVÜ und Lugano-Übereinkommen*, C.H. Beck'sche Verlagsbuchhandlung, München, 1997

—— and Schütze, R. *Internationale Urteilsanerkennung* – Band. II, C.H. Beck'sche Verlagsbuchhandlung, München, 1971

—— and Schütze, R. *Internationale Urteilsanerkennung*– Band. I, 1 Halbband: *Das EWG-Übereinkommen über die gerichtliche Zuständigkeit und die Vollstreckung gerichtlicher Entscheidungen in Zivil-und Handelssachen*, C.H. Beck'sche Verlagsbuchhandlung, München, 1983

Gerhard, F. *L'exécution forcée transfrontière des injonctions extraterritoriales non pécuniaires en droit privé*, Schulthess Juristische Medien, SA., Zürich, 2000

Gevrey, S. *L'exequatur communautaire: Titre III de la Convention de Bruxelles*, 1990–1991, Collection DEA, Universitaire Jean Moulin, Lyon III

Girerd, P. *Aspects juridiques du Traité Communauté Européenne*, Editions L'Harmattan, Paris, 1996

Girsberger, D. 'Erfold mit dem Erfolgsort bei Vermögensdelikten?' in *Private Law in the International Arena, Liber Amicorum Kurt Siehr,* (Ed. Basedow, J.), TMC Asser Press, The Hague, 2000, p.219

Gloge, A. *Die Darlegung und Sachverhaltsuntersuchung im einstweiligen Rechtsschutzverfahren,* Verlag V. Florentz GmbH, München, 1991

Goetz, A. *Anerkennungshindernisse nach dem EuGVÜ, dargestellt unter besonderer Berücksichtigung der französischen Rechtspraxis,* Inaugural-Dissertation, Friedrich-Alexander Universität, Nürnberg, 1997

Good Faith in European Contract Law (Zimmermann, R./Whittaker, S. eds.), Cambridge University Press, Cambridge, 2000

Goode, R. *Commercial Law,* 2nd edn., Penguin Books, London, 1995

Goren, S. *The German Commercial Code,* 2nd edn., F.B. Rothman & Co., Littleton, Col, 1998

Gotanda, J. *Supplemental Damages in Private International Law,* Kluwer Law International, The Hague, 1998

Gothot, P et Holleaux, D. *La Convention de Bruxelles du 27 septembre 1968: compétence judiciaire et effets des jugements dans la CEE,* Editions Jupiter, Paris, 1985

Gottwald, P. *Revision des EuGVÜ – Neues Schiedsverfahrensrecht,* Gieseking, Bielefeld, 2000

Gronstedt, S. *Grenzüberschreitender einstweiliger Rechtsschutz,* Peter Lang, Frankfurt am Main, 1994

Gruebler, R. *Die Vollstreckung ausländischer Civilurteile in der Schweiz,* Helbing & Lichtenhahn, Basel, 1906

Grundriß des österreichischen Zivilprozeßrechts, Erkenntnisverfahren, Rechberger, W. & Simotta, D., 4 Aufl., Manzsche Verlags-und Universitätsbuchhandlung, Wien, 1994

Grunert, J. *Die 'world-wide' Mareva Injunction,* Nomos Verlagsgesellschaft, Baden-Baden, 1998

Dashwood, A and Bacon, R and White, R. *A Guide to the Civil Jurisdiction and Judgments Convention,* Kluwer Law and Taxation Publishers, Deventer/London, 1987

Grundmann, S. Anerkennung und Vollstreckung ausländischer einstweiliger Maßnahmen nach IPRG und Lugano-Übereinkommen, Helbing & Lichtenhahn, Basel/Frankfurt am Main, 1996

Gschnitzer, F. *Österreichisches Schuldrecht, Allgemeiner Teil,* 2 Aufl., Springer-Verlag, Wien, 1985

Guldner, M. *Das internationale und interkantonale Zivilprozeßrecht der Schweiz,* Schulthess, & Co., Zürich, 1951

Gutteridge, HC. *The Codification of Private International Law,* Jackson, Son & Co., Glasgow, 1951

Haas, H. *Die prorogatio fori,* Verlag Von Stämpfli & Cie, Bern, 1943

Habscheid, WJ. 'Les mesures provisoires en procédure civile: droits allemand et suisse' in *Les Mesures Provisoires en Procédure Civile* (ed. Tarzia), Dott.A Giuffrè Editore, Milano, 1985, p.33

Hackenberg, U. *Der Erfüllungsort von Leistungspflichten unter Berücksichtigung des Wirkungsortes von Erklärungen im UN-Kaufrecht und der Gerichtsstand des Erfüllungsortes im deutschen und euro-päischen Zivilprozeßrecht,* Kovac Verlag, Hamburg, 2000

Haffner, G. 'Some comments on the Lugano Convention – the International Law perspective' in *Creating a European Economic Space: Legal Aspects of EC-EFTA Relations,* Papers from the Dublin Conference, October 1989 (ed. Robinson/Findlater), The Irish Centre for European Law Ltd., Dublin, 1990, p.139

Handbook of the National Conference of Commissioners on Uniform State Laws and Proceedings of the 42nd Annual Conference, Washington, D.C., October 4–10 1932

Harder, E. *Die Anerkennung und Vollstreckung deutscher Urteile, insbesondere deutscher Ehescheidung-surteile und Schiedssprüche in New York,* Frankfurt am Main, 1967

Hau, WJ. *Positive Kompetenzkonflikte im Internationalen Zivilprozeßrecht,* Peter Lang, Frankfurt am Main, 1996

Hauschild, M. *Gerichtsstandsvereinbarungen in Spanien und Portugal und das Beitrittsübereinkommen zum EuGVÜ von San Sebastián,* Dissertation, Universität Hamburg, 1995

Hausmaninger, H. *The Austrian Legal System,* Manzsche Verlags-und Universitätsbuchhandlung, Wien, 1998

Hay, P. 'On Comity, Reciprocity, and Public Policy in U.S. and German Judgments Recognition Practice' in *Private Law in the International Arena, Liber Amicorum Kurt Siehr* (ed. Basedow, J.), TMC Asser Press, The Hague, 2000, p.237

Heidinger, F and Hubalek, A. *Europäisches Gerichtsstands- und Vollstreckungsrecht,* Verlag Orac, Wien, 1998

Heldrich, A. *Internationale Zuständigkeit und anwendbares Recht*, Walter de Gruyter & Co., Berlin, 1969

Hertz, K. *Jurisdiction in Contract and Tort under the Brussels Convention*, Jurist-og Økonomforbundets Forlag, Copenhagen, 1998

Hill, J. *The Law Relating to International Commercial Disputes*, 2nd edn., Lloyd's of London Press, London, 1998

Heiss, B-R. *Einstweiliger Rechtsschutz im europäischen Zivilrechtsverkehr*, Duncker & Humblot, Berlin, 1987

Hernandez-Breton, E. *Internationale Gerichtsstandsklauseln in Allgemeinen Geschäftsbedingungen*, Peter Lang, Frankfurt am main, 1993

Hochstrasser, D. *Commercial Litigation and Enforcement of Foreign Judgments in Switzerland*, Helbing & Lichtenhahn, Basel, 1995

Hofstetter-Schnellmann, M. *Die Gerichtsstandsvereinbarung nach dem Lugano-Übereinkommen*, Inaugural-Dissertation, Universitäts Bibliothek, Basel, 1992

Hohl, F. *La réalisation du droit et les procédures rapides*, Éditions Universitaires Friboug Suisse, 1994

Hollatz, R. *Formularmäßige Gerichtsstandsvereinbarungen im vollkaufmännischen Geschäftsverkehr*, Universitätsverlag Dr. N. Brockmeyer, Bochum, 1993

Holleaux, D. *Compétence du juge étranger et reconnaissance des jugements*, Dalloz, Paris, 1970

Honnold, J. *Uniform Law for International Sales under the 1980 United Nations Convention*, 2nd edn., 1991, 3rd edn., Kluwer Law International, The Hague, 1999

Huber, P. *Die englische forum-non-conveniens-Doktrin und ihre Anwendung im Rahmen des Europäischen Gerichtsstands- und Vollstreckungsübereinkommen*, Duncker & Humblot, Berlin, 1994

Hübner, H. *Kodifikation und Entscheidungsfreiheit des Richters in der Geschichte des Privatrechts*, Peter Hanstein Verlag GmbH, Königstein, 1980

International American Conference, *Reports of Committees and Discussions Thereon*, Vol.II, Washington, 1890

International Dispute Resolution: The regulation of forum selection, 14th Sokol Colloquium (ed. Goldsmith, J), Transnational Publishers, Inc., New York, 1997

International Commercial Litigation (Fellas, J.), Practising Law Institute, New York, 1999

International Judicial Assistance in Civil Matters (Campbell, D gen.ed.), Transnational Publishers, Inc., New York, 1999

International Jurisdiction and Judgments Project, Report April 14, 2000, American Law Institute

Internationales Vertragsrecht, Das internationale Privatrecht der Schuldverträge, (Hrsg. Reithmann, C/Martiny, D.), 5 Aufl., Verlag Dr.Otto Schmidt, Köln, 1996

Internationales Zivilverfahrensrecht (Hrsg. Burgstaller, A), Verlag Orac, Wien, 2000

Internet Which Court decides? Which Law applies?, Proceedings of the International Colloquium in honour of Michel Pelichet, (Eds. Boele-Woelki, K/Kessedjian, C.), Kluwer Law International, The Hague, 1998

Isenburg-Epple, S. *Die Berücksichtigung ausländischer Rechtshängigkeit nach dem Europäischen Gerichtsstands- und Vollstreckungsübereinkommen von 27.9.1968*, Peter Lang, Frankfurt am Main, 1992

Jack, R. *Documentary Credits*, 3rd edn., Butterworths, London, 2001

Jackson, DC. *Enforcement of Maritime Claims*, 3rd edn., Lloyd's of London Press, London, 2000

Jametti Greiner, M. *Der Begriff der Entscheidung im schweizerischen internationalen Zivilverfahrensrecht*, Helbing & Lichtenhahn, Basel, 1998

Jasper, D. *Forum shopping in England und Deutschland*, Duncker & Humblot, Berlin, 1990

Jaspert, A. *EuGVÜ-Gerichtsstände und Anspruchsdurchsetzung gegen ausländische herrschende Unternehmen*, Inauguraldissertation, Universität Bielefeld, 1995

Jayme, E. 'Subunternehmervertrag und Europäisches Gerichtsstands-und Vollstreckungsübereinkommen (EuGVÜ)' in *Festschrift für Klemens Pleyer* (Hrsg. Hofmann/ Meyer-Cording/Wiedemann), Carl Heymanns Verlag AG, Köln, Berlin, Bonn, München, 1986, p.371

—— *Nationale ordre public und europäische Integration*, Vorlesungen und Vorträge – Ludwig Boltzmann Institut für Europarecht, Wien, 2000

—— *Wiener Vorträge: Internationales Privat- und Verfahrensrecht Rechtsvergleichung Kunst-und Kulturrecht*, Manzsche Verlags- und Universitätsbuchhandlung, Wien, 2001

Jellinek, W. *Die zweiseitigen Staatsverträge über Anerkennung ausländischer Zivilurteile*, Erstes Heft: Abhandlung, Zweites Heft: Vertragstexte und Register, Walter de Gruyter & Co., Berlin, 1953

Jenard, P. *La Convention de Bruxelles du 27 septembre 1968 et ses prolongements*, Rép. Notarial, 1994, Tome XI, livre VI, 3e partie, Maison Larcier, Bruxelles, 1994

Jiménez, AS. *Ejecución de sentencias extranjeras en España: Convenio de Bruselas de 1968 y procedimiento interno*, Editorial Comares S.L., Granada, 1998

Johner, E. *Die direkte Zuständigkeit der Schweiz bei internationalen Arbeitsverhältnissen*, Helbing & Lichtenhahn, Basel und Frankfurt am Main, 1995

Jolowicz, JA. *On Civil Procedure*, Cambridge University Press, Cambridge, 2000

Jones, J. *The Treaty approach to recognition and enforcement of foreign judgments: The proposed Convention between the United States and the United Kingdom*, unpublished Thesis, George Washington University, 1978

Jung, H. *Vereinbarungen über die internationale Zuständigkeit nach dem EWG-Gerichtsstands-und Vollstreckungsübereinkommen und nach §38 Abs.2 ZPO*, Studienverlag R.N. Brockmeyer, Bochum, 1980

Jurisdiktionsnorm und Zivilprozeßordnung, Stohanzl, R., 14 Aufl., Manzsche Verlags-und Universitätsbuchhandlung, Wien, 1990

Kahn-Freund, O. *A Source-Book on French Law*, Clarendon Press, Oxford, 1991

Kallmann, F. *Anerkennung und Vollstreckung ausländischer Zivilurteile und gerichtlicher Vergleiche*, Helbing & Lichtenhahn, Basel, 1946

Karl, A-M. *Die Anerkennung von Entscheidungen in Spanien*, J.C.B. Mohr (Paul Siebeck), Tübingen, 1993

Kaufmann, MO. *Einstweiliger Rechtsschutz: Die Rechtskraft im einstweiligen Verfahren und das Verhältnis zum definitiven Rechtsschutz*, Stämpfli & Cie AG, Bern, 1993

Kaye, P. *Civil Jurisdiction and Enforcement of Judgments*, Professional Books Ltd, Oxford, 1987

—— *Law of the European Judgments Convention*, Vols. 1–5, Barry Rose Publishers Ltd, Chichester, 1999

Kegel, G. *Internationales Privatrecht*, 7 Aufl., C.H. Beck'sche Verlagsbuchhandlung, München, 1995

Kennett, W. *Enforcement of Judgments in Europe*, Oxford University Press, Oxford, 2000

Kerameus, KD. 'Das Brüsseler Gerichtsstandsübereinkommen und das griechische Recht der internationalen Zuständigkeit' in *Festschrift für Gottfried Baumgärtel* (Hrsg. Prütting), Carl Heymanns Verlag AG, Köln, Berlin, Bonn, München, 1990, p.215

—— 'Rechtsvergleichende Bemerkungen zur internationalen Rechtshängigkeit' in *Festschrift für Karl Heinz Schwab* (Hrsg.Gottwald/Prütting), C.H. Beck'sche Verlagsbuchandlung, München, 1990, p.257

—— and Kozyris, P. *Introduction to Greek Law*, 2nd edn., Kluwer Law and Taxation Publishers, Deventer/Boston, 1993

Kessedjian, C. *La reconnaissance et l'exécution des jugements en droit international privé aus Etats-Unis*, Economica, Paris, 1987

Kessedjian, C. 'Jurisdiction and foreign judgments in civil and commercial matters: the Draft Convention proposed by the Hague Conference on Private International Law' 26 (2000) Forum Internazionale 43

Keßler, A. *Die Vollstreckbarkeit und ihr Beweis gem. Art.31 und 47 Nr.1 EuGVÜ*, Duncker & Humblot, Berlin, 1998

Killias, L. *Die Gerichtsstandsvereinbarungen nach dem Lugano-Übereinkommen*, Schulthess Polygraphischer Verlag, Zürich, 1993

Kim, C. *Selected writings on comparative and private international law*, F.B. Rothman & Co., Littleton, Colorado, 1995

Kim, YJ. *Internationale Gerichtsstandsvereinbarungen*, Peter Lang, Frankfurt am Main, 1995

Klauser, A. *EuGVÜ und EVÜ*, Manzsche Verlags-und Universitätsbuchhandlung, Wien, 1999

Koch, H. 'Neuere Probleme der internationalen Zwangsvollstreckung einschließlich des einstweiligen Rechtsschutzes' in *Materielles Recht und Prozeßrecht und die Auswirkungen der Unterscheidung im Recht der internationalen Zwangsvollstreckung* (Hrsg. Schlosser, P.), Gieseking Verlag, Bielefeld, 1992, p.171

—— *Unvereinbare Entscheidungen i.S.d. Art.27 Nr.3 u. 5 EuGVÜ und ihre Vermeidungen*, Peter Lang, Frankfurt am Main, 1993

Koch, H and Diedrich, F. *Civil procedure in Germany*, C.H. Beck, München, 1998

Kohler, C. 'Anwendbarkeit des Europäischen Gerichtsstands- und Vollstreckungsübereinkommen vom 27. September 1968 in Rechtsstreitigkeiten wegen grenzüberschreitender Umweltbelastungen' in *Rechtsfragen grenzüberschreitender Umweltbelastungen*, Fachtagung, Saarbrücken vom 13–15 Mai 1982 (Hrsg. Bothe/Prieur/Ress), Erich Schmidt Verlag, Berlin, 1984, p.159

—— 'Staatsvertragliche Bindungen bei der Ausübung internationaler Zuständigkeit und richterliches Ermessen – Bemerkungen zur *Harrods*-Entscheidung des englischen Court of Appeal' in *Festschrift für Franz Matscher*, Manzsche Verlags-und Universitätsbuchhandlung, Wien, 1993, 251

Kokkini-Iatridou, D and Verheul, JP. *Les effets des jugements et sentences étrangers aux Pays-Bas*, Kluwer, Deventer, 1970

Kommentar zur ZPO (Hrsg. Rechberger, W.), Springer-Verlag, Wien, 1994

Kommentar zum Schweizerischen Zivilgesetzbuch, (Hrsg. Egger/Escher/Haab, Oser), V. Band: *Das Obligationenrecht, Erster Halbband*, Schulthess & Co., Zürich, 1929

Kommentar zur Züricherischen Zivilprozessordnung, (Sträuli/Messmer), 2 Aufl., Schulthess Polygraphischer Verlag, Zürich, 1982

Kondring, J. *Die Heilung von Zustellungsfehlern im internationalen Zivilrechtsverkehr*, Duncker & Humblot, Berlin, 1995

König, B. *Einstweilige Verfügungen im Zivilverfahren*, 2 Aufl., Manzsche Verlags-und Universitätsbuchhandlung, Wien, 2000

Kropholler, J. 'Problematische Schranken der europäischen Zuständigkeitsordnung gegenüber Drittstaaten' in *Festschrift für Murad Ferid* (Hrsg. Heldrich, A./Sonnenberger, H.), Verlag für Standesamtswesen, Frankfurt am Main, 1988, p.239

—— *Europäisches Zivilprozeßrecht*: Kommentar zu EuGVÜ und Lugano-Übereinkommen, 6 Aufl., Verlag Recht und Wirtschaft GmbH, Heidelberg, 1998

—— *Europäisches Zivilprozeßrecht*: Kommentar zu EuGVO und Lugano-Übereinkommen, 7. Aufl., Verlag Recht und Wirtschaft GmbH, Heidelberg, 2002

—— *Internationales Privatrecht*, 4. Aufl., Mohr Siebeck, Tübingen, 2001

Kurth, J. *Inländischer Rechtsschutz gegen Verfahren vor ausländischen Gerichten*, Duncker & Humblot, Berlin, 1989

Kußmaul, R. *Zur Vorgeschichte der Vorschriften der ZPO über einstweiligen und beschleunigten Rechtsschutz*, Inaugural-Dissertation, Eberhard-Karls-Universität, Tübingen, 1989

Lachau, C. *De l'exécution des jugements étrangers d'après la jurisprudence française avec le texte des principaux arrêts et jugements*, L.Larose et Forcel, Paris,1889

Lagarde, P. '*Perpetuatio fori* et litispendence en matière international' in *Mélanges dédiés à Dominique Holleaux*, Litec, Paris, 1990, p.237

Lando, O. 'Comparative Aspects of the jurisdiction rules of the Brussels and Lugano Conventions' in *Creating a European Economic Space: Legal Aspects of EC-EFTA Relations*, Papers from the Dublin Conference, October 1989 (ed. Robinson/Findlater), The Irish Centre for European Law Ltd., Dublin, 1990, p.117

La revisión de los Convenios de Bruselas de 1968 y Lugano de 1988 sobre competencia judicial y ejecución de resoluciones judiciales: una reflexión preliminar española, (ed. Borrás, A.), Marcial Pons, Ediciones Jurídicas y Sociales SA, Madrid, 1998

Lasok, D and Stone, P. *Conflict of Laws in the European Community*, Professional Books, Abingdon, 1987

Law and Reality, Essays on national and international procedural law in Honour of Cornelis Carel Albert Voskuil, (ed. Sumampouw), Martinus Nijhoff Publishers, Dordrecht/Boston, 1992

Law of the European Convention on Human Rights, (eds.Harris/O'Boyle/Warbrick), Butterworths, London, 1995

Lawyers Committee for Human Rights, *Draft Convention on Jurisdiction and Judgments: Human Rights Concerns*, June 1999

Laufer, H. *La libre circulation des jugements dans une union judiciaire*, Peter Lang, Berne/Berlin/New York, 1992

Lechner, M and Mayr, P. *Das Übereinkommen von Lugano*, WUV-Universitätsverlag, Wien, 1996

Legislación básica de Derecho internacional privado (Rodriguez/Vidal/Campos/Soriano), 6 edición, Editorial Tecnos SA, Madrid, 1996

Lehrbuch des österreichischen Zivilprozeßrechts, Fasching, H., 2 Aufl., Manzsche Verlags-und Universitätsbuchhandlung, Wien, 1990

Le nuove legge civili commentate, settembre-diciembre, 1996, Anno XIX, fasc.N.5–6, p.877 et seq

Lenz, C. *Amerikanische Punitive Damages vor dem Schweizer Richter*, Schulthess Polyraphischer Verlag, Zürich, 1992

Leresche, A. *L'Exécution des jugements civils étrangers en Suisse*, H.R. Sauerländer & Cie., Aarau, 1927

L'espace judiciaire européen – La Convention de Lugano du 16 septembre 1988 (édité par Gillard), CEDIDAC, Lausanne, 1992

Linke, H. *Die Versäumnisentscheidungen im deutschen, österreichischen, belgischen und englischen Recht – Ihre Anerkennung und Vollstreckbarerklärung*, Verlag Enrst und Werner Giesking, Bielefeld, 1972

—— *Internationales Zivilprozeßrecht*, 3 Auf., Dr.Otto Schmidt Verlag, Köln, 2001

Lohse, M. *Das Verhältnis von Vertrag u. Delikt – eine rechtsvergleichende Studie zur vertragsautonomen Auslegung von Art.5 Nr.1 u. Art.5 Nr.3 GVÜ*, Verlag V.Florentz GmbH, München, 1991

Lookofsky. JM. *Transnational Litigation and Commercial Arbitration – A Comparative analysis of American, European and International Law*, Transnational Juris Publications, New York, 1992

Lopez, AM. *Derecho internacional privado español*, I, Parte General, 9 ed., Copias Coca, Granada, 1994

Loret, M. *Le Code de Procédure civile*, II tome, J. Gratiot, Paris, 1812

Loussouarn, Y and Bourel, P. *Droit international privé*, 6ème éd, Dalloz, Paris, 1999

Lowenfeld, A. *International Litigation and the Quest for Reasonableness*, Clarendon Press, Oxford, 1996

Lüpfert, JA. *Konnexität im EuGVÜ, Rechtsvergleichende Studie mit einem Vorschlag zur Weiterentwicklung des deutschen Rechts*, Duncker & Humblot, Berlin, 1997

Lupoi, M. *Il luogo dell'esecuzione del contratto come criterio di collegamento giurisdizione*, Dott.A Giuffrè Editore, Milano, 1978

Luther, G. *Das deutsch-italienische Vollstreckungsabkommen und seine zukünftige Gestaltung*, Verlag C.F. Müller, Karlsruhe, 1966

Lyssy, P. *Die Rechtshängigkeit im Zivilprozess der Kantone Basel-Stadt und Basel-Landschaft*, Helbing & Lichtenhahn, Basel, 1987

Majoros, F. *Les Conventions Internationales en matière de droit privé*, II, Editions A. Pedone, Paris, 1980

Mamet-Rosenbaum, C. *Compétence judiciare et execution des jugements dans le grand espace juridique européen*, Thèse, Doctorat en droit, Panthéon-Assas, Paris-II, 1994, Tomes I & II

Markesinis, BS. *A Comparative Introduction to the German Law of Torts*, 3rd edn., Clarendon Press, Oxford, 1994

——/Lorenz, W/Dannemann, G. *The German Law of Obligations*, Volume 1, *The Law of Contracts and Restitution: A comparative Introduction*, Clarendon Press, Oxford, 1997

Markus, A. *Lugano- Übereinkommen und SchKG – Zuständigkeiten: provisorische Rechtsöffnung, Aberkennungsklage und Zahlungsbefehl*, Helbing & Lichtenhahn, Basel, 1996

Mair, L. *Il diritto processuale civile della Convenzione di Bruxelles*, Cedam, Padova, 1999

Marx, L. *Der verfahrensrechtliche ordre public bei der Anerkennung und Vollstreckung ausländischer Schiedsprüche in Deutschland*, Peter Lang, Frankfurt am Main, 1994

Materielles Recht und Prozeßrecht und die Auswirkungen der Unterscheidung im Recht der internationalen Zwangsvollstreckung, (Hrsg. Schlosser, P.), Gieseking Verlag, Bielefeld, 1992, p.171

Maxwell Report, Report of the Scottish Committee on Jurisdiction and Enforcement, HMSO, Edinburgh, 1980

Mayer, P et Heuzé, V. *Droit International Privé*, 7ème éd, Montchrestien, Paris, 2001

Mayr, P. *EuGVÜ und LGVÜ*, WUV Universitätsverlag, Wien, 2001

Mayss, A and Reed, A. *European Business Litigation*, Dartmouth Publishing Co. Ltd, Aldershot, 1998

Mazeaud, H. *Leçons de Droit Civil, Tome II, Obligations*, Montchrestien, Paris, 1991

McGregor, H. *McGregor on Damages*, 16th edn., Sweet & Maxwell, London, 1997

McLachlan, C. *Transnational Tort Litigation: Jurisdictional Principles*, Clarendon Press, Oxford, 1996

Meier, I. 'Besondere Vollstreckungstitel nach dem Lugano-Übereinkommen' in *Das Lugano-Übereinkommen* (Hrsg Schwander), Dike-Verlag AG, St.Gallen, 1990, p.157

Meier, M. *Grenzüberschreitende Drittbeteiligung*, Peter Lang, Frankfurt am Main, 1994

Mélanges dédiés à Dominique Holleaux, Litec, Paris, 1990

Mélanges en l'honneur de Jacques-Michel Grossen, Editions Helbing & Lichtenhahn, Bâle, 1992

L'Internationalisation du droit, Mélanges en l'honneur de Yvon Loussouarn, Éditions Dalloz, Paris, 1994

Mélanges en l'honneur d'Alfred E. von Overbeck, Editions Universitaires Fribourg Suisse, Fribourg, 1990

Nouveaux juges, nouveaux pouvoirs? Mélanges en l'honneur de Roger Perrot, Éditions Dalloz, Paris, 1996

Mélanges offerts à Pierre Hébraud, Université des sciences sociales de Toulouse, Toulouse, 1981

Mélanges offerts à Pierre Raynaud, Dalloz, Paris, 1985

Mennie, A. *Civil Jurisdiction and Enforcement of Judgments in Scotland*, Ph.D. Thesis, Edinburgh, 1991

Mercier, P and Dutoit, B. *L'Europe judiciaire: les Conventions de Bruxelles et de Lugano*, Helbing & Lichtenhahn, Bâle, 1991

—— *Effets internationaux des jugements dans les Etats du Marché Commun*, Librairie Droz, Genève, 1965

Merkin, R. *Insurance Contract Law*, Kluwer, London, 1988–, section D.4.1

Merkt, H. *Abwehr der Zustellung von 'punitive damages' – Klagen*, Verlag Recht und Wirtschaft GmbH, Heidelberg, 1995

Merkt, O. *Les mesures provisioires en droit international privé*, Schulthess Polygraphischer Verlag, Zürich, 1993

Mezger, E. 'Über einige Lücken des EuGVÜ (Brüssel 1968) und des deutschen Ausfürungsgesetzes' in *Rechtsvergleichung, Europarecht und Staatenintegrationen, Gedächtnisschrift für Léontin-Jean Constantinesco* (Hrsg. Lüke/Ress/Will), Carl Heymanns Verlag AG, Köln, Berlin, Bonn, München,1983, p.503

Miele, A. *La Cosa Giudicata Straniera – Esecuzione e riconoscimento delle sentenze nel diritto commune europeo*, Padova, CEDAM, 1989

Möller, G. 'Provisions on jurisdiction in the Lugano, Brussels and San Sebastian Conventions and how to seek uniform interpretation of the three Conventions' in *Creating a European Economic Space: Legal Aspects of EC-EFTA Relations*, Papers from the Dublin Conference, October 1989 (ed. Robinson/ Findlater), The Irish Centre for European Law Ltd., Dublin, 1990, p.131

Montanari, A. *Conflict of Laws in Italy, The Text and an English translation of Italian Law No.218 of May 31, 1995*, Kluwer Law International, The Hague, 1997

Moor, L. *Das italienische internationale Gesellschaftsrecht, Ein Vergleich mit dem schweizerischen IPRG und zu Problemen des schweizerisch-italienischen Rechtsverkehrs*, Schulthess Polygraphischer Verlag AG, Zürich, 1997

Morbach, B. *Einstweiliger Rechtsschutz in Zivilsachen – Eine rechtsvergleichende Untersuchung*, Peter Lang, Frankfurt am Main, 1988

Moreau, F. *Effets internationaux des jugements en matière civile*, L. Larose & Forcel, Paris, 1884

Müller, H.B. *Die Umsetzung der europäischen Übereinkommen von Rom und Brüssel in das Recht der Mitgliedstaaten*, Peter Lang, Frankfurt am Main, 1997

Müller, M. *Die internationale Zuständigkeit bei grenzüberschreitenden Umweltbeeinträchtigungen*, Helbing & Lichtenhahn, Basel und Frankfurt am Main, 1994

Müller, P. *Punitive Damages und deutsches Schadenersatzrecht*, Walter de Gruyter, Berlin, 2000

Müller, R. *Anerkennung und Vollstreckung schweizerische Zivilurteile in den USA*, Helbing & Lichten-hahn, Basel, 1994

Muñoz, MD. *El Proceso civil con elemento extranjero y la cooperación internacional*, 1995

Munz, C. *Das spanische System der internationalen Zuständigkeiten und seine künftige Einfügung in das EuGVÜ*, Inaugural Dissertation, Universität Bonn, 1984

Nagel, H. *Internationales Zivilprozeßrecht*, 3 Aufl., Aschendorff, Münster, 1991

—— *Nationale und internationale Rechtshilfe im Zivilprozeß; das europäische Modell*, Nomos Verlags-gesellschaft, Baden-Baden, 1971

—— and Gottwald, P. *Internationales Zivilprozeßrecht*, 4 Auf, Aschendorff Rechtsverlag, Münster, 1997

Nelle, A. *Anspruch, Titel und Vollstreckung im internationalen Rechtsverkehr*, Mohr Siebeck, Tübingen, 2000

Neuner, R. *Internationale Zuständigkeit*, J.Bensheimer, Mannhem, 1929

Niedermann, M. *Die ordre public-Klauseln in den Vollstreckungsverträgen des Bundes und den kantonalen Zivilprozeßgesetzen*, Schulthess Polygraphischer Verlag AG, Zürich, 1976

Niegisch, M. *Mehrspurigkeit des internationalen Zivilverfahrensrechts in den Mitgliedstaaten der EuG am Beispiel des Vereinigten Königreiches – Die doktrin forum non conveniens und das EuGVÜ*, Inaugural Dissertation, Universität Heidelberg, 1993

North, P. 'La liberté d'appréciation de la compétence (jurisdictional discretion) selon la Convention de Bruxelles) in *Nouveaux Itinéraires en droit Hommage à François Rigaux*, Bruylant, Bruxelles, 1993, p.373

Nouveau Code de Procedure Civile, Dalloz, 89ème éd., Paris, 1997, pp.627–705

—— 90ème éd., Paris, 1998, pp.685–715

—— 92ème éd., Paris, 2000, pp.628–674

—— 93ème éd., Paris, 2001

Nygh, P. *Autonomy in International Contracts*, Clarendon Press, Oxford, 1999

Obligationenrecht I, Art.1 – 529 OR, *Kommentar zum schweizerischen Privatrecht* (Hrsg. Honsell/Vogt/ Wiegland), Helbing & Lichtenhahn, Basel, 1992

O'Malley, S and Layton, A. *European Civil Practice*, Sweet & Maxwell, London, 1989

Omar, P. *Procedures to enforce foreign judgments*, Ashgate, Dartmouth, 2002

Ong, C. *Cross-Border Litigation within ASEAN*, Kluwer Law International, The Hague, 1997

Op Recht, Bundel opstellen, aangeboden aan prof.mr.A.V.M. Struycken (Kortmann/ Maeijer/Nuytinck/ Perrrick), W.E.J. Tjeenk Willink Zwolle, Den Haag, 1996

Osterwalder, P. *Die Rechtshängigkeit im schweizerischen Zivilprozessrecht*, Juris Druck & Verlag, Zürich, 1981

Othenin-Girard, S. *La réserve d'ordre public en droit international privé suisse*, Schulthess, 1999

Paetzold, V. *Vollstreckung schweizerischer Entscheidungen nach dem Lugano-Übereinkommen in Deutschland*, Handelskammer Deutschland-Schweiz, Zürich, 1995

Panagopoulos, G. *Restitution in Private International Law*, Hart Publishing, Oxford, 2000

Pasinomie, Collection complète des lois, décrets, arrêtés, Quatrième Série, Tome VIII, 1876, p.121, E. Bruylant, Bruxelles, 1876

Pålsson, L. 'Lis pendens under the Brussels and Lugano Conventions' in *Festskrift Till Stig Strömlolm*, Vol. II, Författarna och Iustus Förlag AG, Göteborg, 1997, at p.709

—— 'Interim Relief under the Brussels and Lugano Conventions' in *Private Law in the International Arena, Liber Amicorum Kurt Siehr* (ed. Basedow, J.), TMC Asser Press, The Hague, 2000, p.621

Perret, R. *La reconnaissance et l'exécution des jugements étrangers aux Etats-Unis*, Imprimerie Centrale S.A., Lausanne, 1951

Perrot, R. 'Les mesures provisoires en droit français' in *Les Mesures Provisoires en Procédure Civile* (ed. Tarzia), Dott.A Giuffrè Editore, Milano, 1985, p.149

Petitpierre, M *La reconnaissance et l'exécution des jugements civils étrangers en Suisse*, LGDJ, Paris, 1924

Petschek, G. *Der österreichische Zivilprozeß, eine systematische Darstellung*, Manzsche Verlags-und Universitätsbuchhandlung, Wien, 1963

Pfeiffer, T. *Internationale Zuständigkeit und prozessuale Gerechtigkeit*, Vittorio Klostermann, Frankfurt am Main, 1995

Pfennig, G. *Die internationale Zustellung in Zivil-und Handelssachen*, Carl Heymanns Verlag AG, Köln, Berlin, Bonn, München, 1988

Picone, P. *Codice del diritto internazionale privato*, Grafitalia, Napoli, 1996

Piggott, F. *Service out of the Jurisdiction*, William Clowes and Sons, London, 1892

—— *Foreign Judgments and Jurisdiction*, I, *Foreign Judgments Jurisdiction*, Butterworth & Co., London, 1908

Pillet, A. *Les Conventions internationales relatives à la compétence judiciaire et à l'exécution des jugements*, Recueil Sirey, Paris, 1913

Pirrung, J. '"Parallelübereinkommen" zum Brüsseler Gerichtsstands-und Vollstreckungsübereinkommen zwischen den EG-und den EFTA-Staaten von Lugano vom 16 September 1988 sowie das Übereinkommen über den Beitritt Spaniens und Portugals zum GVÜ von Donastia-San Sebastian vom 26 Mai 1989' in *Stellungnahmen und Gutachten zum Europäischen internationalen Zivilverfahrens-und Versicherungsrecht* (Hrsg. Stoll), J.C.B. Mohr (Paul Siebeck), Tübingen, 1991, p.161

Pocar, F. *Codice delle Convenzioni sulla Giurisdizione e l'Esecuzione delle sentenze straniere nella C.E.E.*, Giuffrè Editore, Milano, 1983

Private International Law at the End of the 20th Century: Progress or Regress? (ed. Symeonides, S), Kluwer Law International, The Hague, 2000

Probst, R. *Die Vollstreckung ausländischer Zivilurteile in der Schweiz nach den geltenden Staatsverträgen*, Verlag Von Stämpfli & Cie, Bern, 1936

Proctor, C. *International Payment Obligations – a Legal Perspective*, Butterworths, London, 1997

Prütting, H. 'Auf dem Weg zu einer Europäischen Zivilprozeßordnung' in *Festschrift für Gottfried Baumgärtel* (Hrsg.Prütting), Carl Heymanns Verlag AG, Köln, Berlin, Bonn, München, 1990, p.457

Racine, J-B. *L'arbitrage commercial international et l'ordre public*, LGDJ, Paris, 1999

Rahmann, D. *Ausschluß staatlicher Gerichtszuständigkeit)*, Carl Heymanns Verlag AG, Köln, Berlin, Bonn, München,1984

Rammeloo, S. *Corporations in Private International Law*, Oxford University Press, Oxford, 2000

Rauscher, T. *Verpflichtung und Erfüllungsort in Art.5(1) EuGVÜ*, Verlag V Florentz GmbH, München, 1984

Rechberger, W. *Kommentar zur ZPO Jurisdiktionsnorm und Zivilprozeßordnung samt den Einführungsgesetzen*, 1994, 2 Aufl., Springer Verlag, Wien, 2000

—— *Kommentar zur ZPO Jurisdiktionsnorm inklusive EuGVÜ und LGVÜ*, 2., überarbeitete und erweiterte Aufl., Springer-Verlag, Wien, 2000

Rechtsfragen grenzüberschreitender Umweltbelastungen, Fachtagung, Saarbrücken vom 13.-15 Mai 1982, (Hrsg. Bothe/Prieur/Ress), Erich Schmidt Verlag, Berlin,1984

Rechtskollisionen, Festschrift für Anton Heini (Hrsg. Meier/Siehr), Schulthess Polygraphischer Verlag AG, Zürich, 1995

Rechtsvergleichung, Europarecht und Staatenintegrationen, Gedächtnisschrift für Léontin-Jean Constantinesco (Hrsg. Lüke/Ress/Will), Carl Heymanns Verlag AG, Köln, Berlin, Bonn, München, 1983

Recognition and Enforcement of foreign judgments outside the scope of the Brussels and Lugano Conventions (eds.Walter, G and Baumgartner, S), Kluwer Law International, The Hague, 2000

Record of the Association of the Bar of the City of New York, 1953, Vol.8, No.6, pp.302–310

Recourse against judgments in the European Union (eds. Jolowicz, J and van Rhee, CH), Kluwer Law International, The Hague, 1999

Reimann, M. *Conflict of Laws in Western Europe*, Transnational Publishers, Inc., Irvington New York, 1995

Reinsurance Law, Issue 51, March 2001 (eds. Butler, J/Merkin, R), Sweet & Maxwell, London

Reiser, H. *Gerichtsstandsvereinbarungen nach dem IPR-Gesetz*, Schulthess Polygraphischer Verlag, Zürich, 1989

—— *Gerichtsstandsvereinbarungen nach dem IPR-Gesetz und Lugano–Übereinkommen*, Schulthess Polygraphischer Verlag, Zürich, 1990

The International Law Association's Report of the Sixty-Seventh Conference, held at Helsinki, Finland, 12–17 August 1996, London, 1996

Répertoire de droit international privé suisse, Vol.II, *Les Conventions bilatérales sur les conflits de juridictions, la reconnaissance et l'exécution des jugements étrangers*, (Dutoit/Knoepler/Lalive/Mercier), Editions Stæmpfli & Cie, Berne, 1983

Ress, G. 'Die Entscheidungserheblichkeit im Vorlageverfahren nach Art.177 EWG-Vertrag im Vergleich zu Vorlageverfahren nach Art.100 Abs.1 GG' in *Festschrift für Günther Jahr*, J.C.B. Mohr (Paul Siebeck), Tübingen, 1993, p.339

Restitution and the Conflict of Laws (ed. Rose, F.), Mansfield Press, Oxford, 1995

Rhidian Thomas, D. *The Modern Law of Marine Insurance*, Lloyd's of London Press, London, 1996

Rideau, J. *Code de procédures européennes*, Litec, Paris, 1990

—— *Droit institutionnel de l'Union et des Communautés européennes*, LGDJ, Paris, 1994

—— *Code de procédures communautaires*, Litec, Paris, 1994

Rigaux, F. *Droit International Privé – Tome I: Théorie Générale*, Larcier, Bruxelles, 1977

—— and Fallon, M. *Droit International Privé – Tome II: Droit Positif Belge*, Larcier, Bruxelles, 1993

Rijavec, V. 'Der Einfluß des Brüsseler Gerichtsstands- und Vollstreckungsübereinkommen (EuGVÜ) auf nationales Recht' in *Die internationale Dimension des Rechts, Festschrift für Willibald Posch* (Hrsg. Terlitaz/Schwarzenegger/Boric´), Österreichische Staatsdruckerei, Wien, 1996, p.289

Robles, CT. *La competencia judicial en la Unión Europea, Comentarios al Convenio de Bruselas*, Editorial Bosch, Barcelona, 1995

Rochaix, M. *Internationale Produkthaftung*, Schulthess Polygraphischer Verlag, Zürich, 1995

Rodière, R. *Droit Maritime*, 12ᵉ éd, Dalloz, Paris, 1997

Roguin, E. *Conflits des Lois Suisse en matière internationale et intercantonale*, R. Rouge, Lausanne, 1891

Rose, N. *Pre-emptive remedies in Europe*, Longman, London, 1992

Roussel, J. *Les clauses attributives de compétence*, Imprimerie Douriez-Bataille, Lille, 1933

Rummel, P. *Kommentar zum Allgemeinen bürgerlichen Gesetzbuch*, Manzsche Verlags-und Universitätsbuchhandlung, Wien, 1990

Salerno, F. *La giurisdizione italiana in materia cautelare*, CEDAM, Milano, 1993

Sandrock, FE. *Die Vereinbarung eines „neutralen" internationalen Gerichtsstandes*, Verlag Recht und Wirtschaft GmbH, Heidelberg, 1997

Satta, S. *Commentario al Codice di Procedura Civile*, IV, 1971

Schack, H. *Der Erfüllungsort im deutschen, ausländischen und internationalen Privat- und Zivilprozeßrecht*, Alfred Metzner Verlag, Frankfurt am Main, 1985

—— *Internationales Zivilverfahrensrecht*, 2.Auf., C.H. Beck'sche Verlagsbuchhandlung, München, 1996

Schaunig-Kandut, G. 'Verbraucherschutz im österreichischen Internationalen Privatrecht, illustriert am Beispiel Teleshopping' in *Die internationale Dimension des Rechts, Festschrift für Willibald Posch* (Hrsg. Terlitaz/Schwarzenegger/Boric´), Österreichische Staatsdruckerei, Wien, 1996, p.303

Schauwecker, H. *Die Einrede der Litispendenz im eidgenössischen und züricherischen internationalen Zivilprozeßrecht*, Polygraphischer Verlag, Zürich, 1943

Schemmer, F. *Der ordre public-Vorbehalt unter der Geltung des Grundgesetzes*, Peter Lang, Frankfurt am Main, 1995

Schlafen, H-D. *Der Anwendungsbereich des EWG-Gerichtsstands- und Vollstreckungsübereinkommens vom 27.9.1968*, Inaugural-Dissertation, Universität Köln, 1979

Schlechtriem, P. *Internationales UN-Kaufrecht*, J.C.B. Mohr (Paul Siebeck), Tübingen, 1996, *Commentary on the UN Convention on the International Sale of Goods (CISG)*, 2nd edn. (in translation), Clarendon Press, Oxford, 1998

Schlosser, P. 'Vertragsautonome Auslegung, nationales Recht, Rechtsvergleichung und das EuGVÜ' in *Gedächtnisschrift für Rudolf Bruns* (Hrsg.Baltzer/Baumgärtel/Peters/Pieper), Verlag Franz Vahlen, München, 1980, p.45

—— 'Das internationale Zivilprozeßrecht der Europäischen Wirtschaftsgemeinschaft und Österreich' in *Festschrift für Winfried Kralik* (Hrsg. Rechenberger/Welser), Manzsche Verlags-und Universitätsbuchhandlung, Wien, 1986, p.287

—— *EuGVÜ: Europäisches Gerichtsstands-und Vollstreckungsübereinkommen mit Luganer Übereinkommen*, Verlag C.H. Beck, München, 1996

Schmelcher, G. *Der Erfüllungsort von Geldschulden (Der Zahlungsort) – Eine rechtsvergleichende Darstellung*, unpublished Dissertation, University of Basel, 1972

Schmidt, MJ. *Die internationale Durchsetzung von Rechtsanwaltshonoraren nach EuGVÜ, Lugano-Übereinkommen und anderen Verträgen*, Verlag Recht und Wirtschaft GmbH, Heidelberg, 1991

Schmidt-Parzefall, T. *Die Auslegung des Parallelübereinkommens von Lugano*, J.C.B. Mohr (Paul Siebeck), Tübingen, 1995

Scholz, I. *Das Problem der autonomen Auslegung des EuGVÜ*, Mohr Siebeck, Tübingen, 1998

Schönberger, T. *Das Tatortsprinzip und seine Auflockerung im deutschen internationalen Deliktsrecht*, 1990

Schubert, W. *Entstehung und Quellen der Civilprozeßordnung von 1877*, Erster Halbband, Vittorio Klostermann, Frankfurt am Main, 1987

Schulte-Beckhausen, S. *Internationale Zuständigkeit durch rügelose Einlassung im europäischen Zivilprozeßrecht*, Verlag Ernst und Werner Gieseking, Bielefeld, 1994

Schumann, E. 'Internationale Rechtshängigkeit (Streitanhängigkeit)' in *Festschrift für Winfried Kralik* (Hrsg. Rechenberger/Welser), Manzsche Verlags-und Universitätsbuchhandlung, Wien, 1986, p.301

Schuschke and Walker *Vollstreckung und Vorläufiger Rechtsschutz*, Band II, Arrest u. Einstweilige Verfügung §§916–945 ZPO, Carl Heymanns Verlag AG, Köln, Berlin, Bonn, München, 1995

Schütze, R. *Deutsch-amerikanische Urteilsanerkennung*, Walter de Gruyter, Berlin, 1992

Schwarz, I. 'Übereinkommen zwischen der EG-Staaten: Völkerrecht oder Gemeinschaftsrecht?' in *Im Dienste Deutschlands und des Rechts, Festschrift für Wilhelm G. Grewe* (Hrsg. Kroneck/Oppermann), Nomos Verlagsgesellschaft, Baden-Baden, 1981

Schwarz, M. *Der Gerichtsstand der unerlaubten Handlung nach deutschem und europäischem Prozeßrecht*, Peter Lang, Frankfurt am Main, 1991

Scoles, E and Hay, P. *Conflict of Laws*, 3rd edn., West Publishing Co., St. Paul, Minn., 2000

Siegel, D. *New York Practice*, 3rd edn., West Group, Minnesota, 1999

Sikora, D. *Die Anerkennung und Vollstreckung US-amerikanischer Urteile in England*, Lit Verlag, Münster, 1998

Silberberg, H. *The German Standard Contracts Act*, Bilingual Edition, Fritz Knapp Verlag, Frankfurt am Main, 1979

Soltész, U. *Der Begriff der Zivilsache im Europäischen Zivilprozeßrecht: zur Auslegung von Art.1 Abs. 1 EuGVÜ*, Peter Lang, Frankfurt am Main, 1998

Sperl, H. *Vereinbarung der Zuständigkeit und Gerichtsstand des Erfüllungsortes nach dem neuesten österreichischen Civilprozessrecht*, Leuschner & Lubensky's, Graz, 1897

Spühler, K. 'Art.21 LugÜ: Zum Beispiel BGE 123 III 414 - und die schweizerischen Interessen?' in *Der Einfluss des europäischen Rechts auf die Schweiz: Festschrift für Professor Roger Zäch zum 60. Geburtstag*, (Hrsg. Forstmoser/von der Crone/Weber/Zobl), Schulthess Polygraphischer Verlag, Zürich, 1999, p.847

Staehelin, M. *Gerichtsstandsvereinbarungen im internationalen Handelverkehr Europas: Form und Willenseinigungen nach Art.17 EuGVÜ/LÜ*, Helbing & Lichtenhahn, Basel, 1993

Stathopoulos, M. *Contract Law in Hellas*, Kluwer Law International, The Hague, 1995

Stein-Hobohm, V. *Der einstweilige Rechtsschutz im Recht der Bundesrepublik Deutschland und im Recht des Staates New York*, Dissertation, Universität Mainz, 1985

Stein, F and Jonas M. *Kommentar zur Zivilprozeßordnung*, 21 Aufl., Band 1, §§1–90, J.C.B. Mohr, Tübingen, 1993

Stellungnahmen und Gutachten zum Europäischen internationalen Zivilverfahrens-und Versicherungsrecht (Hrsg. Stoll), J.C.B. Mohr (Paul Siebeck), Tübingen, 1991

Stickler, S. *Das Zusammenwirken von Art.24 EuGVÜ und §§916ff. ZPO*, Duncker & Humblot, Berlin, 1992

Stone, P. *The Conflict of Laws*, Longman, London/New York, 1996

Story, J. *Commentaries on the Conflict of Laws*, 7th edn., Little, Brown & Co., Boston, 1872

Stöve, E. *Gerichtsstandsvereinbarungen nach Handelsbrauch, Art.17 EuGVÜ und §38 ZPO, unter besonderer Berücksichtigung der kaufmännischen Bestätigungsschreiben, des Konnossements und der Faktura*, R.v. Decker's Verlag, G. Schenck, Heidelberg, 1993

Studi in onore di Vittorio Denti, Vol I, CEDAM, Milano, 1994

Stumberg, G. *Principles of Conflict of Laws*, The Foundation Press, New York, 1951

Switzerland's Private International Law (Karrer, P/Arnold, K/Patocchi, P), 2nd edn., Kluwer Law and Taxation Publishers, Deventer/Boston1994

Takahashi, K. *Claims for contribution and Reimbursement in an international context*, Oxford University Press, Oxford, 2000

Taliadoros, C. *Greek Civil Code*, Astikos Kodix, Athens, 1982

Tebbens, H. 'The English Court of Appeal in *Re Harrods*: An unwelcome interpretation of the Brussels Convention' in *Law and Reality*, Essays on national and international procedural law in Honour of Cornelis Carel Albert Voskuil (ed. Sumampouw), Martinus Nijhoff Publishers, Dordrecht/Boston, 1992, 47

Teitz, L. *Transnational Litigation*, Michie Law Publishers, Virginia, 1996

Terré, F and Simler, P. *Droit Civil, Les Obligations*, 6ᵉ ed., Dalloz, Paris, 1996

The Civil Court Practice 2000, Vol.1, October 2000 Reissue (gen. eds. Thompson, P and di Mambro, L)

Torture as Tort, Comparative Perspectives on the Development of Transnational Human Rights Litigation, (Scott, C. ed.), Hart Publishing, Oxford, 2001

Tosi, U. *EuGVÜ und Drittstaaten*, Peter Lang, Frankfurt am Main, 1988

Transnationales Prozeßrecht, Transnational Aspects of Procedural Law (Hrsg. Gilles, P), Nomos Verlagsgesellschaft, Baden-Baden, 1995

Trunk, A. *Die Erweiterung des EuGVÜ- Systems am Vorabend des Europäischen Binnenmarktes*, C.H. Beck'sche Verlagsbuchhandlung, München, 1991

Uhl, L. *Internationale Zuständigkeit gemäss Art.5 Nr.3 des Brüsseler und Lugano-Übereinkommens*, Peter Lang, Frankfurt am Main, 2000

Unification, and comparative law in theory and practice, Contributions in honour of Jean Georges Sauveplanne, Kluwer Law and Taxation Publishers, Deventer, 1984

Valery, J. *Manuel de droit international privé*, Fonemoing et Cie, Paris, 1914

Valloni, LW. *Der Gerichtsstand des Erfüllungsortes nach Lugano- und Brüsseler-Übereinkommen*, Schulthess Polygraphischer Verlag, Zürich, 1998

Vander Elst, R. *Droit international privé*, 4ème éd, Presses Universitaires de Bruxelles, Bruxelles, 1976–1977

—— and Weser, M. *Droit international privé belge*, Tome II, *Conflits de Juridictions*, Bruylant, Bruxelles, 1985

Van Dijk, P and Van Hoof, G. *Theory and Practice of the European Convention on Human Rights*, Kluwer Law International, The Hague, 1998

Van Rooij, R and Polak, M. *Private International Law in the Netherlands*, Kluwer Law and Taxation Publishers, Deventer/London, 1987, Supplement, Kluwer Law International, The Hague, 1995

Verfahrensrecht am Ausgang des 20.Jahrhunderts, Festschrift für Gerhard Lüke, C.H. Beck'sche Verlagsbuchandlung, München, 1997

Vial, E. *Die Gerichtsstandswahl und der Zugang zum internationalen Zivilprozeß im deutsch- italienischen Rechtsverkehr*, Nomos Verlagsgesellschaft, Baden-Baden, 1999

Vicente, J. *Derecho procesal civil internacional*, Editorial Tecnos, 1993

—— 'Competencia judicial y reconocimiento y ejecución de resoluciones judiciales en materia civil y mercantil en el ámbito de la comunidad europea' in *Hacia un Neuvo Orden Internacional y Europeo, Estudios en Homenaje al Profesor Velasco*, Editorial Tecnos, Madrid, 1993, p.865

Vincent, J and Guinchard, S. *Procédure civile*, 24ème éd, Dalloz, Paris, 1996

Vögeli, N. *Die Vollstreckung schweizerischer Zivilurteile in Frankreich*, Verlag P.G. Keller, Winterthur, 1959

Volken, P. 'The Lugano Convention in the framework of Legal Unification in Europe' in *Creating a European Economic Space: Legal Aspects of EC-EFTA Relations*, Papers from the Dublin Conference, October 1989 (ed. Robinson/Findlater), The Irish Centre for European Law Ltd., Dublin, 1990, p.145

—— *Die internationale Rechtshilfe in Zivilsachen*, Schulthess Polygraphischer Verlag, Zürich, 1996

Volz, G. *Harmonisierung des Rechts der individuellen Rechtswahl, der Gerichtsstandsvereinbarung und der Schiedsvereinbarung im Europäischen Wirtschaftsraum (EWR)*, Kartung-Gorre Verlag, Konstanz, 1993

Von Bar, CL. *Theorie und Praxis des internationalen Privatrechts*, Band 2, Scientia Verlag, Aalen, 1966

Von Bazan, UB. *Der Gerichtsstand des Sachzusammenhangs im EuGVÜ, dem LÜ und im deutschen Recht*, Peter Lang, Frankfurt am Main, 1995

Von Caemmerer/Schlechtriem, *Kommentar zum Einheitlichen UN-Kaufrecht*, Beck, 1990

Von Fürstl, C. *Die österreichischen Civilprocessgesetze*, Band II, *Executionsordnung*, Verlag Von Mortiz Perles, Wien, 1899

Von Mehren, A 'The transmogrification of defendants into plaintiffs' in *Festschrift für Ulrich Drobnig* (Hrsg. Basedow/Hopt/Kötz), Mohr Siebeck, Tübingen, 1998, p.409

Von Rönn, K. *Die Anwendung des Europäischen Gerichtsstands- und Vollstreckungsübereinkommens im Vereinigten Königreich*, Peter Lang, Frankfurt am Main, 1996

Von Savigny, FC. *A Treatise on The Conflict of Laws*, Stevens & Sons, London, 1869 (Transl. Guthrie, W)

Vroonen, E. *De la force extraterritoriale des jugements étrangers et des conditions extrinsèques de validité des actes étrangers en Belgique*, M. Lamertin, Bruxelles, 1920

Wadlow, C. *Enforcement of Intellectual Property in European and International Law*, Sweet & Maxwell, London, 1998

Wahl, N. *The Lugano Convention and Legal Integration*, Juristförlaget, Stockholm, 1990

Walder, HU. *Einführung in das Internationale Zivilprozessrecht der Schweiz*, Schulthess Polygraphischer Verlag, Zürich, 1989

Walder-Richli, HU. *Zivilprozessrecht nach den Gesetzen des Bundes und des Kantons Zürich unter Berücksichtigung anderer Zivilprozessordnungen*, 4 Auf., Schulthess Polygraphischer Verlag, Zürich, 1996

Walter, G. *Internationales Zivilprozessrecht der Schweiz*, Ein Lehrbuch, 2 Aufl., Verlag Paul Haupt, Bern, 1998

Wastl, U. *Die Vollstreckung deutscher Titel auf der Grundlage des EuGVÜ in Italien*, Verlag V.Florentz GmbH, München, 1991

Weber, G. *Die Verdrängung des Hauptsacheverfahrens durch den einstweiligen Rechtsschutz in Deutschland und Frankreich*, Bundesanzeiger Verlagsges., Köln, 1993

Weinschenk, F. *Die Anerkennung und Vollstreckung bundesdeutscher Urteile in den Vereinigten Staaten unter den „Foreign Country Money Judgment Recognition Acts"*, Duncker & Humblot, Belin, 1988

Weintraub, R. *Commentary on the Conflict of Laws*, 4th edn., Foundation Press, New York, 2001

—— *International Litigation and Arbitration, Practice and Planning*, 3rd edn., Carolina Academic Press, Durham, N.Carolina, 2001

Weiß, J. *Die Konkretisierung der Gerichtsstandsregeln des EuGVÜ durch den EuGH*, Peter Lang, Frankfurt am Main, 1997

Weiss, A. *Traité théorique et pratique de droit international privé*, Tome V, *L'étranger et la Justice*, Librairie de la Société du Receuil L.Larose & Forcel, Paris, 1905

Weser, M. *Traité Franco-belge du 8 Juillet 1899*, Recueil Sirey, Paris, 1952

—— *Convention communautaire sur la compétence judiciaire et l'exécution des décisions*, CIDC, Bruxelles/Editions A. Pedone, Paris, 1975

Westlake, J. *A Treatise on Private International Law*, 7th edn., Sweet & Maxwell Ltd, London, 1925

Wharton, F. *A Treatise on the Conflict of Laws*, Kay & Brother, Philadelphia, 1872

Whinchop, M. *Policy and Pragmatism in the Conflict of laws*, Ashgate, Dartmouth, 2001

Wiehe, H. *Zustellungen, Zustellungsmängel und Urteilsanerkennung am Beispiel fiktiver Inlandszustellungen in Deutschland, Frankreich und den USA*, WF Verlag, München, 1993

Wittibschlager, M. *Rechtshängigkeit in internationalen Verhältnissen*, Helbing & Lichtenhahn, Basel und Frankfurt am Main, 1994

Wolf, M. 'Einheitliche Urteilsgeltung im EuGVÜ' in *Festschrift für Karl Heinz Schwab* (Hrsg.Gottwald/Prütting), C.H. Beck'sche Verlagsbuchhandlung, München, 1990, p.561

Woloniecki, J. 'The road to Byzantium – an examination of the impact of the 1968 Brussels Convention upon English law and the implications of the 1988 Lugano Convention' in *Creating a European Economic Space: Legal Aspects of EC-EFTA Relations*, Papers from the Dublin Conference, October 1989 (ed. Robinson/Findlater), The Irish Centre for European Law Ltd., Dublin, 1990, p.157

Wrangel, PG. *Der Gerichtsstand des Erfüllungsortes im deutschen, italienischen und europäischen Recht*, Verlag V. Florentz GmbH, München, 1989

Wuppermann, M. *Die deutsche Rechtsprechung zum Vorbehalt des ordre public im Internationalen Privatrecht seit 1945*, Verlag für Standesamtswesen, Frankfurt am Main, 1977

Wyss, R. *Der Gerichtsstand der unerlaubten Handlung*, Dike Verlag AG, Lachen/St.Gallen, 1997

Yearly Supreme Court Practice 1920, Vol.1 (Chitty, W), Butterworth & Co., London, 1920

—— *1921*, Vol.1 (Chitty, W), Butterworth & Co., London, 1921

Yessiou-Faltsi, P. *Civil Procedure in Hellas*, Ant. N. Sakkoulas Publishers, Athens, 1998

Zaragoza, J de M. 'Notas sobre los convenios de Bruselas y Lugano sobre competencia judicial y ejecucion de resoluciones judiciales en materia civil y mercantil' in *Convenios multilaterales relativos a la competencia judicial y a la ejecucion de resoluciones judiciales en materia civil y mercantil*, Artes Gráficas Suárez Barcala, Madrid, 1989

Zeiler, G. *Internationales Sicherungsverfahren*, Verlag Österreich, Wien, 1996

Zeuner, A. 'Zum Verhältnis zwischen internationaler Rechtshängigkeit nach Art.21 EuGVÜ und Rechtshängigkeit nach den Regeln der ZPO' in *Verfahrensrecht am Ausgang des 20.Jahrhunderts, Festschrift für Gerhard Lüke*, C.H. Beck'sche Verlagsbuchhandlung, München, 1997, p.1003

Zivilgerichtliches Verfahren, Stumvoll, H., Verlag Orac, Wien, 1995

Zivilprozeßordnung mit Gerichtsverfassungsgesetz, Sydow & Busch, 9 Aufl., Verlagsbuchhandlung J. Guttentag, Berlin, 1901

Zivilprozeßordnung für das deutsche Reich, Stein F and Jonas M, 12 Aufl., J.C.B. Mohr, Tübingen, 1925

Zivilprozeßordnung, Beck'sche Kurz-Kommentare, Baumbach-Lauterbach, 28 Aufl., C.H. Beck'sche Verlagsbuchhandlung, München, 1965

—— Baumbach-Lauterbach, 30 Aufl, C.H. Beck'sche Verlagsbuchhandlung, München, 1970

—— Baumbach-Lauterbach, 37 Aufl., C.H. Beck'sche Verlagsbuchhandlung, München, 1979

—— Baumbach-Lauterbach, 56 Aufl., C.H. Beck'sche Verlagsbuchhandlung, München, 1998

—— Baumbach-Lauterbach, 59 Aufl., C.H. Beck'sche Verlagsbuchhandlung, München, 2001

Zöller, R. *Zivilprozeßordnung*, 18 Aufl., Verlag Dr.Otto Schmidt, Köln, 1993

Bibliography—Articles

Abbatescianni, G. 'Recognition of English Judgments in Italy: the Terruzzi case' 1985 *NLJ* 179

Abbott, R. 'The emerging doctrine of forum non conveniens: a comparison of the Scottish, English and United States applications' 1985 *Vanderbilt J Transnat'l L* 111

Achard, R. 'Entrée en vigueur de la Convention de Luxembourg du 9 octobre 1978' 1987 *DMF* 557

—— 'Connaissements. Clauses de juridiction. Convention CEE de Bruxelles de 1968–1978, art.17. Recours en interprétation' 1998 *DMF* 339

Adams, M. 'The conflicts of jurisdictions – an economic analysis of pre-trial discovery, fact gathering and cost shifting rules in the United States and Germany' 1995 *ERPL* 53

Addis, F. 'La conferma per iscritto della proroga verbale di competenza (art.17 della convenzione di Bruxelles)' 1998 *Riv trim dir & proc civ* 831

Adolphsen, J. 'Revision des EuGVÜ und neues deutsches Schiedsverfahrensrecht' 2000 *ZZP* 85

Ahrens, H-J. 'Ausschüttungsgarantien des Kapitalanlagevermittlers im IPR – Neue Kollisionsnormbildung für den Kapitalmarkt?' zu *BGH* 13.6.1996 1998 *IPRax* 93

Aird, R. 'The Scottish arrestment and the English freezing order' 2002 *ICLQ* 155

Akers, F. 'Enforcement of intellectual property rights in Scotland' 1995 *IHL* 16

Albrecht, C. 'Artikel 24 EuGVÜ und die Entwicklung des einstweiligen Rechtsschutzes in England seit 1988' 1992 *IPRax* 184

Aldous, W. 'The Brussels Convention: a New Convention impinging on disputes on jurisdiction including those relating to intellectual property litigation' 9 *Federal Circuit Bar Journal* 523 (1999)

Alexander, E. 'Die internationale Vollstreckung von Zivilurteilen insbesondere im Verhältnis zu den Nachbarstaaten' 1931 *ZBJV* 1

Alexander, K. 'The Mareva injunction and Anton Piller order: the nuclear weapons of English commercial litigation' 1997 *Florida Journal of International Law* 487

Alexiou, A Grammatickaki- 'Casenotes international civil procedure in Greece' 1992 *Rev Hellén Dr Int* 241

Allarousse, V. 'A comparative approach to the Conflict of Characterisation in Private International Law' 1991 *Case W Res J Int'l L* 479

Allen & Overy 'Casenote: *Royal Bank of Scotland v Cassa di Risparmio*' 1992 *BJIB & FL* 142

—— 'Casenote: *Marinari v Lloyd's Bank Plc*' 1995 *BJIB & FL* 514

Allwood, W. 'Casenote: *Iveco v Van Hool*' 12 (1987) *ELR* 461

—— 'Casenote: *Schotte v Rothschild*' 12 (1987) *ELR* 213

—— 'Casenote: *Shenavai v Kreischer*' 13 (1988) *ELR* 60

—— 'Casenote: *Arcado v Haviland*' 13 (1988) *ELR* 366

Amodeo, G. 'Deciding conflicts of jurisdiction within the United Kingdom: the Cumming decision' 1995 *ML & P* 145

Ancel, B. 'La Clause attributive de juridiction selon l'article 17 de la Convention de Bruxelles' 1991 *Riv. dir. int. priv. e proc.* 27

Ancel, B and Muir Watt, H. 'La désunion européenne: le Règlement dit "Bruxelles II"' 2001 *Rev. crit.* 403

Andrews, N. 'A good arguable case about what?' 1994 *CLJ* 244

—— 'Mareva relief cannot stand alone: further judicial reflections upon the Siskina principle' 1996 *CLJ* 12

Anthimos, A. 'Der verfahrensrechtliche ordre public im internationalen Zivilprozeßrechts Griechenlands' 2000 *IPRax* 327

Anton, A. 'Casenote: *Overseas Union*' 1994 *SLJ* (News) A2 13

—— 'Casenote: *Powell Duffryn v Petereit*' 1994 *SLJ* A4 35

Arnaldez, J-J. 'Le règlement de référé pré-arbitral de la Chambre de Commerce Internationale' 1990 *Rev de l'Arb.* 835

Arnold, H. 'Die Entwurf eines Gerichtsstands-und Vollstreckungsabkommens für die Europäische Wirtschaftsgemeinschaft' 1965 *AWD* 321
—— 'Das EWG-Gerichtsstands und Vollstreckungsübereinkommen vom 27.9.1968' 1969 AWD 89
—— 'Ist Artikel 34 des EWG-Gerichtsstands-und Vollstreckungsübereinkommens mit Artikel 103 Abs.1 GG vereinbar?' 1972 *RIW* 389
—— 'Anerkennungs- und Vollstreckungsabkommen in Zivil-und Handelssachen nach der Deutschen Einigung' 1991 *BB* 2240
Arter, O. 'Zuständigkeit und anwendbares Recht bei internationalen Rechtsgeschäften mittels Internet unter Berücksichtigung unerlaubter Handlungen' 2000 *AJP* 277
Asser, T-M-C. 'De l'effet ou de l'exécution des jugements rendus à l'étranger en matière civile et commerciale' 1 *Rev. dr. intern. dr. comparé* 82 (1869)
Atalah, A. 'Quelques rélexions sur le développement du "forum shopping"' 2001 DMF 867
Atteslander-Dürrenmatt, A. 'Sicherungsmittel 'à discrétion'? Zur Umsetzung von Art.39 LugÜ in der Schweiz' 2001 *AJP* 180
Auchter, G. 'Jurisprudence récente' 1995 DMF 567
Audinet, E. 'L'éxecution des jugements étrangers en Angleterre d'après la loi du 13 avril 1933 et la convention franco-britannique du 18 janvier 1934' 1935 *JDI* 805
Audit, B. 'Arbitration and the Brussels Convention' 1993 *Arb. Int.* 1
Baatz, Y. 'Jurisdiction agreements and multiple proceedings in Europe' 1998 ITLQ 269
—— 'Objective test of validity of jurisdiction clauses under the Brussels Convention on Jurisdiction' 2000 *ITLQ* 44
Baccara, R. 'A propos de l'exécution en Belgique des sentences arbitrales étrangères' 1928 *Rev. dr. intern. dr. comparé* 121
Bachmann, B. 'Der Gerichtsstand der unerlaubten Handlung im Internet' zu *LG München* 17.10.1996 1998 *IPRax* 179
Bajons, E. 'Das Luganer Parallelübereinkommen zum EuGVÜ - der Europäische Jurisdiktionsbereich in österreichischer Perspektive' 1993 *ZfRV* 45
Baker, W. 'The French référé procedure – a legal miracle?' 1992–3 U *Miami Yrbk Int'l L* 1
—— and De Fontbressin, P. 'The French référé procedure and conflicts of Human Rights' 1998 *Syracuse Journal of International Law and Commerce* 69
Balonwu, S. 'Consumer v. Industry The e-commerce frontier: jurisdiction and applicable law' 1999 *Tr Law* 446
Bamodu, G. 'Jurisdiction and applicable law in Transnational dispute resolution before the Nigerian courts' 1995 *Int'l Law* 555
Barbosa, C. 'From Brussels to The Hague – the ongoing process towards effective multinational patent enforcement' 2001 *IIC* 729
Bariatti, S. 'What are judgments under the 1968 Brussels Convention' 2001 *Riv. dir. int. priv. e proc.* 5
Bartlett, L. 'Full faith and credit comes to the Common Market: an analysis of the provisions of the Convention on Jurisdiction and Enforcement of Judgments in Civil and Commercial Matters' 1975 *ICLQ* 44
Basedow, J. 'Das forum conveniens der Reeder im EuGVÜ' zu *Partenreederei ms Tilly Russ and Ernest Russ v NV Haven- & Vervoerbedrijf Nova and NV Goeminne Hout* C71/83 [1984] 2417 1985 *IPRax* 133
—— 'Haftungsersetzung durch Versicherungsschutz-ein Stück ordre public?' zu *BGH* 16.9.1993 1994 *IPRax* 85
—— 'Primer Encuentro Jurídico Argentino-Germano (Bs.As.) 5–8 April 1988' 1988 *RabelsZ* 756
Bassindale, J. 'Title to sue under Bills of Lading: The Carriage of Goods by Sea Act 1992' 1992 *JIBL* 414
Beaumont, P. 'European Court of Justice and Jurisdiction and Enforcement of Judgments in Civil and Commercial Matters' 1992 *ICLQ* 206
—— 'Private International Law of the Environment' 1995 *Jur Rev* 28
—— 'European Court of Justice and Jurisdiction and Enforcement of Judgments' 1995 *ICLQ* 218
—— 'Brussels Convention II: A new private international law instrument' 20 (1995) *ELR* 268
—— 'Brussels and Lugano Conventions' 1997 *ICLQ* 211
Beck, A. 'Casenote: Data Delecta Aktiebolag, Security for costs' 1996 *Corp Brief* 20

Beck, A. 'Casenote: The "Tatry"' 1996 *Corp Brief* 19

—— 'Casenote: *Sarrio v Kuwait Investment Authority*' 1996 *Corp Brief* 18

Behr, V. 'Internationale Tatortzuständigkeit für vorbeugende Unterlassungsklagen bei Wettbewerbverstößen' 1992 *Grur. Int.* 604

Bell, A. 'Anti-suit injunctions and the Brussels Convention' 1994 *LQR* 204

—— 'The negative declaration in Transnational Litigation' 1995 *LQR* 674

Bell, R. 'Casenote: Trade Indemnity' 1994 *Int ILR* G-181

Bellet, P. 'L'élaboration d'une convention sur la reconnaissance des jugements dans le cadre du Marché Commun' 1965 *JDI* 833

Béraudo, J-P. 'Du bon usage des règles de compétence spéciales des Conventions de Bruxelles et de Lugano pour plaider chez soi' 2001 *JCP*, Doctr., 417

—— 'Le Règlement (CE) du Conseil du 22 décembre 2000 concernant la compétence judiciaire, la reconnaissance et l'exécution des décisions en matière civile et commerciale' 2001 *JDI* 1033

Berger, D. 'Zuständigkeit und forum non conveniens im amerikanischen Zivilprozeß' 1977 RabelsZ 39

Berlingieri, F. 'The scope of application of the 1952 Brussels Convention on the Arrest of ships' 1991 *J Mar L & C* 405

—— 'Coéxistence entre la Convention de Bruxelles et la Convention de Hambourg' 1993 *Dir mar* 351

—— 'Italian Private International Law Rules' 1997 *I J O S L* 33

Bermann, G. 'The Use of Anti-suit injunctions in International Litigation' 1990 *Colum J Transnat'l Law* 589

—— 'Provisional relief in transnational litigation' 1997 *Colum J Transnat'l Law* 553

Bernasconi, C. 'Der räumlich-persönliche Anwendungsbereich des Lugano-Übereinkommens' 1993 *SZIER* 39

—— 'La théorie du forum non conveniens – un regard suisse' 1994 *IPRax* 3

Bernet, M. 'Recognition and Enforcement of Foreign Civil Judgments in Switzerland' 1993 *Int'l Law* 317

Bernheim, M. 'Rechtshängigkeit und im Zusammenhang stehende Verfahren nach dem Lugano-Übereinkommen' 1994 *SJZ* 133

Bernstein, H. 'International contracts in European courts: jurisdiction under article 5(1) of the Brussels Convention' 1996 *Tul Euro Civil L F* 31

Berti, S. 'Das Lugano- Übereinkommen und die Ausdehnung des Europäischen Zivilprozessrechts' 1992 *Schw Treu* 198

Besson, S. 'A propos de deux arrêts du tribunal cantonal: exequatur d'un jugement comportant une condamnation pécuniaire selon la Convention de Lugano' 1996 *JT*, III, 6

Betlem, G. 'Cross-border water pollution: two paradigmatic Dutch cases' 1996 *ERPL* 159

Beucher, K. 'United States punitive damage awards in German courts: the evolving German position on service and enforcement' 1991 *Vanderbilt J Transnat'l L* 967

Biavati, P. 'La funzione unificatrice della Corte di giustizia delle Comunità europea' 1995 *Riv trim dir & proc civ* 273

—— 'Le prospettive di riforma della convenzione di Bruxelles' 1999 *Riv trim dir & proc civ* 1201

Bird, J. 'Choice of law rule for priority disputes in relation to shares' 1997 *LMCLQ* 57

Bisset-Johnson, A. 'The efficacy of choice of jurisdiction clauses in international contracts in English and Australian Law' 1970 *ICLQ* 541

Black, D. 'Enforcement of judgments and the Brussels Convention' 1993 *SJ* 225

Black, E. 'Casenote: *Trivelloni-Lorenzi v Pan American World Airways*' 1988 *Suffolk Transnat'l LJ* 173

Black, R. 'Enforcement of Scottish decrees outside Scotland and of Non-Scottish decrees within Scotland' 1987 *JLSS* 10

Blair, W. 'Insulating perceived risks and the role of choice-of-law in cross-border financings' 1995 *NAFTA L Bus R Am* 60

Blaisse, A. 'Quo vadis référé?' 1982 *JCP*., Doctr., 3083

Blanc, G. 'L'application de l'article 5–1 de la Convention de Bruxelles dans les contrats de distribution' 2000 *Dalloz, Juris.* 741

Blobel, F. 'Zum Entwicklungsstand der Lehre vom "forum non conveniens" in England' 2001 *RIW* 598

Bloch, A and Hess, M. 'Discussion of the protective measures available under Swiss law' 1999 *SZW* 166

Boele-Woelki, K. 'Brüssel II: Die Verordnung über die Zuständigkeit und die Anerkennung von Entscheidungen in Ehesachen' 2001 *ZfRV* 121

Böhmer, C. 'Vollstreckbarerklärung ausländischer Unterhaltstitel, insbesondere österreichischer Titel' zu *BGH* 31.1.1990 1991 *IPRax* 90

Bohner, H Walder- 'Vorsorgliche Massnahmen ausländischer Gerichte unter dem neuen IPR-Gesetz' 1987 *SJZ* 238

Bonassies, P. 'La fin de l'affaire du 'Nagasaki Spirit': une espérence déçue' 1997 *DMF* 451

Borchers, P. 'Introductory remarks: Symposium "Could a treaty trump Supreme Court jurisdictional doctrine?"' 1998 *Alb L R* 1159

—— 'Judgments Convention and minimum contacts' 1998 *Alb L R* 1161

Born, G. 'Reflections on judicial jurisdiction in international cases' 1987 *Ga J Int'l Comp L* 1

Born, H. 'Droit judiciaire international (1978–1982)' 1983 *JT* 197

—— 'L'article 5,1 de la Convention de Bruxelles du 27 septembre et l'arrêt de la Cour de Cassation du 19 janvier 1984' 1985 *JT* 497

—— 'La Convention de Bruxelles du 27 septembre 1968' 1987 *JT* 461

—— 'Casenote Tribunal civil de Marche-en-Famenne' 1988 *Ann dr. Liège* 100

—— 'La Convention de Bruxelles du 27 septembre 1968' 1992 *JT* 408

—— 'Les règles communautaires de compétence judiciaire internationale relatives au recouvrement des créances commerciales' 1994 *Ann dr. Liège* 9

—— 'Le régime générale des clauses attributives de juridiction dans la Convention de Bruxelles' 1995 *JT* 353

Boschiero, N. 'Die Reform des italienischen IPR-Systems' 1996 *ZfRV* 143

Boujeka, A. 'L'étendue du contrôle de la Cour de cassation en matière de référé-provision' 2001 *Dalloz, Som com.* 1580

Bourlarbah, H. 'Casenote: *Drouot Assurances S.A. v Consoldidated Metallurgical, Protea Assurance and GIE Réunion Européenne* (C-351/96)' 1998 *JT* 772

Bradley, C. 'The Treaty power and American Federalism' 97 *Mich. L R* 390 (1998)

Brajeux, G. 'Casenote: The Nagasaki, Cass. Nov. 1994' 1996 Reuter Textline: Lloyd's List Nov.13 1996

Brand, P-A. 'Fehlerhafte Auslandszustellung' 2001 *IPRax* 173

Brand, R. 'Punitive damages and the recognition of judgments' 1996 *NILR* 143

—— 'Due process, jurisdiction and a Hague Judgments Convention' 1999 *University of Pittsburgh Law Review* 661

Braslow, N. 'The recognition and enforcement of common law punitive damages in a civil law system: some reflections on the Japanese experience' 1999 *Arizona Journal of International and Comparative Law* 285

Brenscheidt, M. 'The recognition and enforcement of foreign money judgments in the Federal Republic of Germany' (1977) 11 *Int'l L* 261

Brenton, T. 'Casenote: Union de Remorquage' 1997 *Int Mar L* 3

Brereton, P. 'Forum non conveniens in Australia: a case note on *Voth v Manildra Flour Mills*' 1991 *ICLQ* 895

Briggs, A. 'The Brussels Convention: Casenotes Hoffman; Arcado; Scherrens; Kalfelis' 1988 *YEL* 265

—— 'Conflict of Laws; postponing the future?' 1989 *OJLS* 250

—— 'Forum non conveniens in Australia' 1989 *LQR* 200

—— 'The Brussels Convention: Casenote Six Constructions' 1989 *YEL* 323

—— 'The Brussels Convention: Casenotes Reichert; Dumez; Hagen; Lancray' 1990 *YEL* 481

—— 'Forum non conveniens and the Brussels Convention' 1991 *LQR* 180

—— 'The Brussels Convention: Casenotes Overseas; Marc Rich; Van Dalfsen' 1991 *YEL* 521

—— 'Get your writs out?' 1992 *LMCLQ* 150

—— 'The Brussels Convention: Casenotes Hacker; Reichert; Powell Duffryn; Handte; Minalmet' 1992 *YEL* 657

—— 'The Brussels Convention: Casenotes Shearson; Sonntag; Mulox' 1993 *YEL* 511

—— 'Anti-European Teeth for choice of court clauses' 1994 *LMCLQ* 158

—— 'How soon is an English court seised (revisited)?' 1994 *LMCLQ* 476

—— 'The Brussels Convention: Casenotes Owens Bank; Mund & Fester; Webb; Solo; Lieber; Custom Made; Brenner; Tatry' 1994 *YEL* 557

Briggs, A. 'Restitution meets the Conflict of Laws: *Macmillan v Bishopsgate Investment Trust*' 1995 *RLR* 94

—— 'The Brussels Convention: Casenotes Shevill; Kleinwort; Lloyd's Register; Danvaern; Hengst; SISRO; Marinari' 1995 *YEL* 487

—— 'The Brussels Convention tames the Arrest Convention' 1995 *LMCLQ* 161

—— 'Choice of law in tort and delict' 1995 *LMCLQ* 519

—— 'The Brussels Convention: *Van der Linden v Berufsgenossenschaft der Feinmechanik und Elektro-technik*' 1996 *YEL* 601

—— 'Decisions of British courts during 1996 – B. Private International Law' 1996 *BYIL* 577

—— 'The uncertainty of special jurisdiction' 1996 *LMCLQ* 27

—— 'Two undesirable side-effects of the Brussels Convention?' 1997 *LQR* 364

—— 'The unrestrained reach of an anti-suit injunction: a pause for thought' 1997 *LMCLQ* 90

—— 'The Brussels Convention: Rutten; Mainschiffahrts; Van den Boogaard; Farrell; Benincasa; Von Horn' 1997 *YEL* 515

—— 'Decisions of British courts during 1997 – B. Private International Law' 1997 *BYIL* 331

—— 'Decisions of British courts during 1998 – B. Private International Law' 1998 *BYIL* 332

—— 'Claims against sea carriers and the Brussels Convention' 1999 *LMCLQ* 333

—— 'Decisions of British courts during 1999 – B. Private International Law' 1999 *BYIL* 319

Brinkhof, J. 'Could the President of the district court of The Hague take measures concerning the infringement of foreign patents?' 1994 *EIPR* 360

—— 'Geht das grenzüberschreitende Verletzungsverbot im niederländischen einstweiligen Verfü-gungsverfahren zu weit?' 1997 *Grur. Int.* 489

Brown, K. 'Your court or mine?' 1996 *SJ* 78

Brulhart, V. 'Casenote: Bundesgericht 19.8.1998 *Dresdner Forfaitierungs AG gegen Sezione Speciale per l'assicurazione del credito all'esportazione* 124 BGE, III, 436' 1999 *AJP* 213

—— 'Casenote: Bundesgericht 20.8.1998 *Banque Bruxelles Lambert Suisse SA et huit consorts contre République de Paraguay et Sezione speciale per l'assicurazione del credito all'esportazione* 124 BGE, III, 382' 1999 *AJP* 216

Bruneau, C. 'L'interprétation, par la CJCE, de l'article 5–1° de la Convention de Bruxelles: . . . persiste et signe!' 2000 *JCP, Juris.*, II, 10354

—— 'Les règles européennes de compétence en matière civile et commerciale' 2001 *JCP, Doctr.*, I, 304

—— 'L'obtention des preuves en matière civile et commerciale au sein de L'Union Européenne' 2001 *JCP, Doctr*, I, 349

Brunner, R. 'Zur Auslegung des französisch-schweizerischen Staatsvertrages vom Jahr 1869' 1885 *ZBJV* 501

Bruns, A. 'Der anerkennungsrechtliche ordre public in Europa und den USA' 1999 *JZ* 278

Bucher, A. 'Vers une convention mondiale sur la compétence et les jugements étrangers' 2000 *SJ* 77

Buhler, P. 'Forum selection and choice of law clauses in international contracts: a United States viewpoint with particular reference to maritime contracts and Bills of Lading' 1995 *U Miami Int-Am LR* 1

Bülow, A. 'Vereinheitliches Internationales Zivilprozeßrecht in der Europäischen Wirtschaftsgemein-schaft' 1965 *RabelsZ* 473

Buonaiuti, F. 'Forum non conveniens facing the prospective Hague Convention and E.C. Regulation on jurisdiction and the enforcement of judgments in civil and commercial matters' 1999 *Riv dir europeo* 3

Burbank, S. 'Jurisdictional Equilibrium, the proposed Hague Convention and progress in national law' 49 *Am J Comp L* 203 (2001)

Burgelin, J-F. 'Le juge des référés au regard des principes procéduraux' 1995 *Dalloz, Chron.* 67

Burgstaller, A. 'Probleme der Prorogation nach dem Lugano-Übereinkommen' 1998 *JBl* 691

—— 'Vollstreckung ausländischer Schiedssprüche in Österreich' 2000 *ZfRV* 83

Busl, P. 'Deutsches "internationales" Mahnverfahren - §§ 688 ff. ZPO und EuGVÜ' 1986 *IPRax* 270

Buttimore, J. 'Service out of the jurisdiction and the Brussels Convention: *Short v Ireland*' 1996 *Bar Rev* 86

Byrne, P. 'Casenote: *Marc Rich v Impianti*' 1992 *ILT* 286

Byrne, P. 'Recent cases on the EEC Convention on Jurisdiction and the Enforcement of Judgments' 1993 *ILT* 63

—— 'Casenote: *Van Dalfsen v Van Loon*' 1993 *ILT* 246

—— 'Casenote: *Hacker v Euro-Relais*' 1993 *ILT* 276

—— 'The application of the Brussels Judgments Convention by the Irish courts 1988–1993 (II)' 1994 *IJEL* 128

—— 'Casenote: *Powell Duffryn v Petereit*' 1994 *ILT* 4

Campbell, D. 'Enforcing American Money Judgments in the United Kingdom and Germany' 18 Southern *Illinois U L J* 517 (1994)

Capper, D. 'Worldwide Mareva injunctions' 1991 *MLR*

—— 'The Trans-jurisdictional effects of Mareva injunctions' 1996 *CJQ* 211

—— 'Further trans-jurisdictional effects of Mareva injunctions' 1998 *CJQ* 35

Carl, B. 'The Common Market Judgments Convention – Its threat and challenge to Americans' 1974 *Int Law* 446

Carpi, F. 'Riflessioni sull'armonizzazione del diritto processuale civile in Europa in relazione alla convenzione di Bruxelles del 1968' 1993 *Riv trim dir & proc civ* 1037

Carr, I. 'Forum non conveniens and the Warsaw Convention' 1996 *JBL* 518

Carter, P. 'Casenotes: Private International Law, Decisions of British Courts during 1972–3' 1973 *BYIL* 428

—— 'Casenotes: Private International Law, Decisions of British Courts during 1985–6' 1986 *BYIL* 429

—— 'Casenotes: Private International Law, Decisions of British Courts during 1988' 1988 *BYIL* 342

—— 'Casenote: Shearson Lehmann Hutton' 1993 *BYIL* 557

—— 'Casenotes: Private International Law, Decisions of British Courts during 1993' 1993 *BYIL* 467

—— 'The Private International Law (Miscellaneous Provisions) Act 1995' 1996 *LQR* 190

Casey, S. 'Notes on the 1968 European Communities (Judgments) Convention' 1989 *GILSI* 101

Castel, J-G. 'Back to the future! Is the 'new' rigid choice of law rule for interprovincial torts constitutionally mandated?' 1995 *Osgoode Hall L J* 35

Cathala, T. 'L'intterprétation uniforme des conventions conclues entre États membres de la C.E.E. en matière de droit privé' 1972 *Dalloz, Chron.* 10

Cebrian, M. 'Reconocimiento y exequatur de decisiones judiciales en la CEE' 1986 *Rev Insti Euro* 29

Cerina, P. 'In tema di rapporti tra litispendenza e Art.57 nella Convenzione di Bruxelles del 27 settembre 1968' 1991 *Riv. dir. int. priv. e proc.* 953

Chaloupka, R. 'International E-commerce jurisdiction and taxation issues' 2001 *International Quarterly* 157

Charkham, G. 'Casenote: *Viskase Ltd and another v Paul Kiefel GmbH*' 2000 *ITLQ* 59

Chatterjee, C. 'The legal effect of the exclusive jurisdiction clause in the Brussels Convention in relation to Banking Matters' 1995 *JIBL* 334

Ching, J. 'Get it on account: the interim payment in commercial cases' 1997 *Lit* 177

Christians, LL. 'Casenote: Tribunal de commerce de Liège 1996 *Ann dr. Liège* 275

Clare, J. 'Enforcement of foreign judgments in Spain' (1975) 9 *Int'l L.* 509

Clavel, S. 'Anti-suit injunctions et arbitrage' 2001 *Rev de l'Arb.* 669

Clermont, K. Exorcising the evil of forum-shopping 1995 *Cornell LR* 1507

—— 'Jurisdiction salvation and the Hague Treaty' 1999 *Cornell LR* 89

Coester-Waltjen, D. 'Die Bedeutung des Art.6 Nr.2 EuGVÜ' zu *Kongress Agentur Hagen GmbH v Zeehaghe BV* (C-365/88) [1990] ECR I-1845 1992 *IPRax* 290

Coffin, C. 'Casenote: *Royal Bank of Scotland v Cassa di Risparmio*' 1992 *JIBL* 111

Cohen, S. 'Jurisdiction over Cross-Border Internet infringements' 1998 *EIPR* 294

Cole, M. '*Doe v Amour* – Forum (non) conveniens or political decision' 1994 *ILT* 267

Collier, J. 'Sorry, the Court of Appeal cannot stay' 1996 *CLJ* 9

—— 'The surprised bank clerk and the Italian customer - competing jurisdictions' 1996 *CLJ* 216

Collin, K. 'Casenote: forum – Lugano Convention' 1994 *Int ILR* G-88

Collins, L. 'Arbitration Clauses and Forum Selection Clauses in the Conflict of Laws: Some recent developments in England' 1971 *JMLC* 363

—— 'Provisional Measures, the Conflict of Laws and the Brussels Convention' 1981 *YEL* 249

Collins, L. 'Forum non conveniens and the Brussels Convention' 1990 *LQR* 535
—— 'Provisional and Protective Measures in International Litigation' 1992 *Recueil* 19
—— 'The Brussels Convention within the United Kingdom' 1995 *LQR* 541
—— 'The Siskina again: an opportunity missed' 1996 *LQR* 8
Contaldi, G. 'Le clausole di proroga della giurisdizione contenute in polizze di carico ed il nuovo testo dell'art.17 della Convenzione di Bruxelles del 1968' 1998 *Riv. dir. int. priv. e proc.* 79
Cox, S. 'Why properly construed due process limits on personal jurisdiction must always trump contrary treaty provisions' 1998 *Alb L R* 1177
Creswell, C. 'Arresting ships in England and Wales' 1996 *I J O S L* 186
—— 'The English Commercial Court' 1996 *ICLit* 12
Cromie, S. 'The Brussels Convention. Forum non conveniens revived or why Harrods gives you a choice' 1991 *LE* 7
—— 'A choice between evils' 1996 *NLJ* (Practitioner) 1244
Culhane, J. 'The limits of product liability reform within a consumer expectation model: a comparison of approaches taken by the United States and the European Union' 1995 *Hastings Int'l & Comp L R* 1
Czernich, D. 'Der Erfüllungsgerichtsstand im Lugano- Übereinkommen' 1996/7 *AnwBl* 426
—— 'Kauf- und Dienstleistungsverträge im Internet' 1996 Ecolex 82
—— 'Zu den Voraussetzungen der Anerkennung und Vollstreckung fremder Entscheidungen nach autonomen Recht (§79 EO)' 1996 *JBl* 495
—— 'Neue Aspekte im internationalen Verfahrensrecht durch den Beitritt Österreichs zum EuGVÜ' 1998 *JBl* 745
Dageförde, C. 'Aufrechnung und Internationale Zuständigkeit' 1990 *RIW* 873
Dahl, B. 'Consumer protection and the provisions on jurisdiction in the 1968–EEC Judgments Convention' 1977 *Nord Tids Int Ret* 104
Dannemann, G. 'Jurisdiction based on the presence of assets in Germany: a casenote *BGH* 2.7.1991' 1992 *ICLQ* 632
Davenport, B. 'Injustice just avoided' 1994 *LQR* 25
—— 'Forum shopping in the market' 1995 *LQR* 366
Davies, C. 'Internet Contracts' 1996 *Comm Law* 50
De Bournonville, P. 'L'article 1er Septembre 27, 1968 sur la compétence judiciaire et l'exécution des décisions en matière civile et commerciale' 1977 *JT* 249
De Cristofaro, M. 'Presupposti e rimedi per il Provvedimento che "sospende" l'opposizione all'exequatur o il riconoscimento di sentenza comunitaria' 1998 *Riv. dir. int. priv. e proc.* 745
—— 'Critical remarks on the Vienna Sales Convention's impact on jurisdiction' 2000 *Rev. dr. unif.* 43
De Groote, B. 'Quelques changements importants aux règles de compétence internationale de la Convention de Bruxelles' 2000 *Afri J Int'l Comp L* 31
Deketelaere, Y. 'Casenote: Leathertex' 2001 *Rev gén dr civ belge* 384
De Leval, G. 'Reconnaissance et exécution dans la Convention de Bruxelles du 27 septembre 1968' 1994 *Act Dr* 73
Demetriou, M. 'When is the House of Lords not a judicial remedy?' 20 (1995) *ELR* 628
De Sousa, 'Die neue internationale Zuständigkeitsregelung im portugiesischen Zivilprozeßbuch und die Brüsseler und Luganer Übereinkommen: Einige vergleichende Bermerkungen' 1997 *IPRax* 352
Devers, A. 'De Vienne à Grenobles en passant par Bruxelles: Cour d'appel de Grenoble, 6.11.2000' 2001 *Dalloz, Jurisp.*, 2547
De Vries, H. 'Jurisdiction in personal actions – a comparison of civil law views' 1959 *Iowa L R* 306
De Winter, L. 'Excessive Jurisdiction in Private International Law' 1968 *ICLQ* 706
Debattista, C. 'Carriage Conventions and their interpretation in English Courts' 1997 *JBL* 130
Decker, M. 'Contract or tort: Handte 1993 *ICLQ* 366
Delany, H. 'Security for costs and plaintiffs resident outside the jurisdiction' 1996 *ILT* 119
Delaporte, V. 'Les mesures provisoires et conservatoires en droit international privé 1987–1988' *Dr Intern Privé* 147
Deli, M. 'Criteri di giurisdizione e convenzione di Bruxelles del 1968 nelle vendite a catena' 1993 *Riv. dir. int. priv. e proc.* 305

Dellebecque, P. 'Casenote: Navire Monte Cervantes Cass.Ch.Com. 16.1.96' 1996 DMF 627

Denning, S. 'Choice of Forum Clauses in Bills of Lading' 1970 *JMLC* 17

Denson, J. 'Casenote: *Denilauer v Couchet Frères*' 1982 *Tex Int'l L J* 252

Deprez, J. 'Les clauses relatives au règlement des litiges dans le contrat de travail international' 1990 *Rev. dr. Aff Intern* 833

Deringer, A. 'Europäisches Gemeinschaftsrecht' 1976 *NJW* 453

Desmazieres, A. 'EEC Jurisdiction and Judgments: A French perspective' 1987 *JLSS* 309

Dessemontet, F. 'La responsabilité des organes en droit international privé – Aspects du droit international des sociétés' 1994 *Jour Suiss dr. int* 149

—— 'Internet le droit d'auteur et le droit international privé' 1996 *SJZ* 285

Deville, R. 'Der gewöhnliche Aufenthalt als ausschließliches Anknüpfungsmerkmal im internationalen Verkehrsunfallrecht' zu *OLG Düsseldorf* 8.7.1996 1997 *IPRax* 409

Devonshire, P. 'Freezing injunctions as security' 2000 *CFILR* 101

Di Brozolo, LG. Radicati, 'International Payments and Conflicts of laws' 48 *Am J. Com. L.* 307 (2000)

Dickinson, A. 'Restitution and the Conflict of Laws in the House of Lords' 1998 *RLR* 104

Dietze, J. 'Die aktuelle Rechtsprechung des EuGH zum EuGVÜ' 1995 *EuZW* 359

—— 'Die aktuelle Rechtsprechung des EuGH zum EuGVÜ' 1997 *EuZW* 459

—— 'Die aktuelle Rechtsprechung des EuGH zum EuGVÜ' 1998 *EuZW* 485

Diloy, C. 'Compétence judiciaire internationale et contrats de distribution' 2002 *Dalloz, Juris.*, 198

Dockray, M. 'Anton Piller orders: the new statutory scheme' 1998 *CJQ* 272

Dodge, W. 'Antitrust and the draft Hague Judgments Convention' (2001) 32 *Law & Policy in International Business* 363

Donzallaz, Y. 'L'interpretation de la Convention de Lugano (CL) par le Tribunal fédéral: étude de jurisprudence' 1999 *ZschweizR* 11

—— 'Le for contractuel de l'art.5 ch.1 CL dans la jurisprudence du Tribunal fédéral' (1999) 135 *ZBJV* 381

—— 'Les mesures provisoires et conservatoires dans les Conventions de Bruxelles et de Lugano' 2000 *AJP* 956

—— 'Convention de Lugano (CL) et Loi fédérale sur les fors (Lfors)' 2000 *AJP* 1259

—— 'Le renouveau de l'ordre public dans la CB/CL au regard des ACJCE *Krombach* et *Renault* et de la révision de ces traités' 2001 *AJP* 160

Dörig, A. 'The finality of U.S. Judgments in Civil Matters as a Prerequisite for Recognition and Enforcement in Switzerland' 1997 *Tex Int'l L J* 271

Dörner, H. 'Internationale Zuständigkeit – Vertragsstaatenbezug, rügelose Einlassung und Gerichtsstandsklausel' zu *BGH* 21.11.1996 1999 *IPRax* 338

Dreyfuss, RC. 'An alert to the intellectual property bar: The Hague Judgments Convention' 2001 *U. Ill. L R* 421

Droz, G. 'Le récent projet de Convention de la Haye sur la reconnaissance et l'exécution des jugements étrangers en matière civile et commerciale' 1966 *NILR* 225

—— 'Entreé en vigeur de la Convention de Bruxelles' 1973 *Rev. crit.* 21

—— 'Réflexions pour une réforme des articles 14 et 15 du Code civil français' 1975 Rev. crit. 1

—— 'Entreé en vigeur de la Convention de Bruxelles révisée sur la Convention de Lugano' 1987 *Rev. crit.* 251

—— 'La Convention de Lugano parallèle à la Convention de Bruxelles concernant la compétence judiciaire des décisions en matière civile et commerciale' 1989 *Rev. crit.* 1

—— 'Le traité franco-suisse de 1869 à la lumière de la Convention de Lugano' 1989 *Jour Soc Légis Comp* 541

—— 'La Convention de San Sebastian alignant la Convention de Bruxelles sur la Convention de Lugano' 1990 *Rev. crit.* 1

—— 'Le bouleversement des relations franco-suisses: entrée en vigueur de la Convention de Lugano et abrogation de la Convention du 15 juin 1869' 1992 *Jour Notaires et Avocats* 417

—— 'Delendum est forum contractus? (vingt ans après les arrêts *De Bloos* et *Tessili* interprétant l'article 5.1 de la Convention de Bruxelles du 27 septembre 1968' 1997 *Dalloz, Chron.* 351

—— 'Variations Pordea' 2000 *Rev. crit.* 181

Droz, G. & Gaudemet-Tallon, H. 'La transformation de la Convention de Bruxelles du 27 septembre 1968 en Règlement du Conseil concernant la compétence judiciaire, la reconnaissance et l'exécution des décisions en matière civile et commerciale' 2001 *Rev. crit.* 601

Dutson, S. 'The Internet, the Conflict of Laws, international litigation and intellectual property: the implications of the international scope of the Internet on intellectual property infringements' 1997 *JBL* 495

—— 'The Characterisation of Product Liability Claims in Private International Law in England and Australia' 1997 *Univ Qld LJ* 215

—— 'Actions for Infringement of a Foreign Intellectual Property right in an English court: The court's new jurisdiction' 1998 *Constr LJ* 161

—— 'International E-commerce' [2000] *C.T.L.R.* 76

Eadie, G. 'Application of EEC Convention – grim news for newspapers' 1994 *ML & P* 64

Edwards, J. 'Exclusive jurisdiction clauses and forum non conveniens' 1998 *I J O S L* 193

Egan, T. 'The case for a EU Convention causebook and Judgment registry database' 1996 *Bar Rev* 14

Egli, F. 'Die Anerkennung und Vollstreckung deutscher, österreichischer und liechtensteinischer Gerichtsentscheidungen in Zivil- und Handelssachen in der Schweiz' 1991 *RIW* 977

Ehrenzeller, S. 'Vorläufiger Rechtsschutz im internationalen Verhältnis' 1998 *SZIER* 177

Ehricke, U. 'Gerichtsstandsvereinbarungen in Allgemeinen Geschäftsbedingungen im vollkaufmännischen Geschäftsverkehr, insbesondere im Hinblick auf §32 ZPO' 1998 *ZZP* 145

Eidenmüller, H. 'Europäische Verordnung über Insolvenzverfahren und zukünftiges deutsches internationales Insolvenzrecht' 2001 *IPRax* 2

Ekelmans, M. 'Casenote: *Caron*' 1986 *JT* 665

—— 'Casenote: *Leon Emile Gaston Carlos Debaecker and Berthe Plouvier v Cornelius Gerrit Bouwman* (C49/84) [1985] ECR 1779' 1985 *JT* 158

—— 'Casenote *Kalfelis*' 1988 *JT* 214

Endler, M. 'Urlaubsfreuden: Ferienhausvermittlung und Art.16 Nr.1 EuGVÜ' zu *LG Frankfurt/Main* 6.9.1991 und *LG Berlin* 1.10.1991 1992 *IPRax* 212

English, R. 'Forum non conveniens – the legal aid factor' 1996 *CLJ* 214

Enonchong, N. 'Public policy in the Conflict of Laws: a Chinese wall around little England?' 1996 *ICLQ* 633

—— 'Service of process in England on overseas companies and Article 5(5) of the Brussels Convention' 1999 *ICLQ* 921

—— 'The enforcement of foreign arbitral awards based on illegal contracts' 2000 *LMCLQ* 495

Ernst, M. 'Recognition and Enforcement of Foreign Money Judgments in the US and UK in light of currency conversion problems' 1988 *J of Int'l Dis Res* 59

Ernster, P. 'Recognition and Enforcement of foreign money-judgments: a clear position for New Jersey' 1968 *Rutgers Law Review* 327

Everling, U. 'Rechtsvereinheitlichung durch Richterrecht in der Europäischen Gemeinschaft' 1986 *RabelsZ* 193

Fallon, M. 'Le référé international en matière civile et commerciale' 1993 Revue de droit de l'Université libre de Bruxelles 43

Fastiff, E. 'The Proposed Hague Convention on the Recognition and Enforcement of Civil and Commercial Judgments: A solution to Butch Reynold's Jurisdiction and Enforcement Problems' 1995 *Cornell Int'l L J* 469

Favre-Bulle, A. 'La mise en œuvre en Suisse de l'art.39 al.2 de la Convention de Lugano' 1998 *SZIER* 335

Fawcett, J. 'Multi-party litigation in Private International Law' 1995 *ICLQ* 744

—— 'Non-exclusive jurisdiction agreements in private international law' 2001 *LMCLQ* 234

Fentiman, R. 'Jurisdiction, Discretion and the Brussels Convention' 1993 *Cornell Int'l L J* 59

—— 'Judgments, Purposes and the Brussels Convention' 1994 *CLJ* 239

—— 'Tactical Declarations and the Brussels Convention' 1995 *CLJ* 261

—— 'Antisuit injunctions and the appropriate forum' 1997 *CLJ* 46

—— 'Antisuit injunctions and the Brussels Convention' 2000 *CLJ* 45

—— 'Commercial Expectations and The Rome Convention' [2002] *CLJ* 50

Ferrari, F. '"Forum shopping" trotz internationaler Einheitssachrechtskonventionen' 2002 *RIW* 169

Finnegan, E. 'Casenote: *Kleinwort Benson*' 1995 *ICLit* 43

—— 'Casenote: *Marinari v Lloyd's Bank Ltd.*' 1995 *ICLit* 44

Fitzpartick, J. 'The Lugano Convention and Western European Integration: a comparative analysis of jurisdiction and judgments in Europe and the United States' 1993 *Conn J Int'l L* 695

Flécheux, G. 'L'application des conventions internationales en droit interne français' 1995 *Jour Soc Légis Comp* 19

Fleischhauser, J. 'Unkenntnis schützt Ausländer vor Fristversämnis nicht' zu *BGH* 10.11.1998 2000 *IPRax* 13

Fletcher, I. 'The European Union Convention on Insolvency Proceedings: Choice-of-Law provisions' 1998 *Tex Int'l L J* 119

Flynn, L. 'Interim relief in national courts pending the outcome of a preliminary reference' 1996 *ILT* 206

Focsaneanu, L. 'Convention de Bruxelles du 27 septembre 1968 concernant la compétence judiciaire et l'exécution des décisions en matière civile et commerciale' 1987 *Rev Marché Com* 207

Forde, M. 'The "ordre public" exception and adjudicative jurisdiction conventions' 1980 *ICLQ* 259

Forner, J. 'Special jurisdiction in commercial contacts: From the 1968 Brussels Convention to 'Brussels-one-Regulation" [2002] *I.C.C.L.R.* 131

Forsyth, C. 'Defamation under the Brussels Convention: a forum shopper's charter' 1995 *CLJ* 515

—— 'Brussels Convention Jurisdiction "in matters relating to a contract" when the plaintiff denies the existence of a contract' 1996 *LMCLQ* 329

—— 'The Impact of the applicable law of contract on the law of jurisdiction under the European Conventions' 1996 *ICLQ* 190

—— 'Characterisation revisited: an essay in the theory and practice of the English Conflict of Laws' 1998 *LQR* 141

Foss, M and Bygrave, L. 'International consumer purchases through the internet: jurisdictional issues pursuant to European law' 2000 *International Journal of Law and Information Technology* 99

Foulkes, S. 'Forum shopping – a thing of the past?' 1993 *Int ILR* 335

Foussard, D. 'Entre exequatur et exécution forcée' 1996–1997 *Droit int. privé* 175

Francescakis, P. 'Le contrôle de la compétence du juge étranger après l'arrêt "Simitch" de la Cour de Cassation' 1985 *Rev. crit.* 243

Franzosi, M. 'Article 5(5) of the Brussels Convention and the rules on groups of companies in Italy: a new approach?' 1996 *ICCLR* 261

—— 'Worldwide patent litigation and the Italian torpedo' [1997] *EIPR* 382

—— 'Torpedoes are here to stay' 2002 *IIC* 154

Frauenberger-Pfeiler, U. 'Lugano-Abkommen: Anerkennung und Vollstreckung ausländischer Entscheidungen' 1996 *Ecolex* 735

Freedman, C. 'E-Commerce: the U.K.'s Draft Electronic Commerce Bill' [1999] *JIBL* 377

Freeman, E. 'The EEC Convention on Jurisdiction and Enforcement of Civil and Commercial Judgments' 1981 *Northwest J Int'l L & Bus* 496

Fricke, M. 'Internationale Zuständigkeit und Anerkennungszuständigkeit in Versicherungssachen nach europäischem und deutschem Recht' 1997 *VersicherungsR* 399

Friedman, P. 'Jurisdiction and Beyond' 1995 *NLJ* 1158

Fröhlingsdorf, J. 'Das neue spanische Zivilprossgesetz (LEC) 2001 *RIW* 357

Fuchs, A. '§917 Abs.2 ZPO erneut auf dem Prüfstand' zu *LG Hamburg* 14.8.1996 1998 *IPRax* 25

—— 'Begriff "Unterhaltsberechtiger" in Art.5 Nr.2 EuGVÜ geklärt' 1998 *IPRax* 327

Fucik, R. 'Die Zuständigkeit nach dem LGVÜ' 1996 *ÖRZ* 241

Furtak, O. 'Wechselrückgriff und Art.5 Nr.1 EuGVÜ' zu *LG Bayreuth* 29.6.1988 1989 *IPRax* 212

Gaillard, L. 'Les mesures provisionelles en droit international privé' 1993 *SJ* 141

Gaja, G. 'Le convenzione internazionali e le nuove norme sulla giurisdizione e sul riconoscimento delle sentenze straniere' 1996 *Riv trim dir & proc civ* 823

Gallant, S. '"Abroad, that large home of ruined reputations": why Scottish libel plaintiffs will be suing south of the border, *Foxen v The Scotsman Publications*' 1995 *Ent LR* 31

Gandara, R. 'Forum non conveniens y Convenio de Bruselas: quiebras de un modelo de atribucion de competencia judicial internacional' 1995 *REDI* 55

Garcia, R. 'Tratamiento jurisprudencial del ámbito del aplicación de los foros de protección en materia de contratos de consumidores del convenio de Bruselas de 1968' 1996 *REDI* 39

Garcimartín-Alférez, F. 'The first application of the EEC Judgments Convention by the Spanish Tribunal Supremo' 1993 *IPRax* 426

—— 'Caben reducciones teleologicas o "abuso de derecho" en las normas sobre competencia judicial internacional?' 1995 *REDI* 121

Gardner, M. 'Formation of international contracts – finding the right choice of law rule' 1989 *Aust L J* 751

Gauci, G. 'Beware of the danger which lurks in the Netherlands: The pan-European injunction' 1998 *EIPR* 361

—— 'Why the ECJ must stop pan-European injunctions' 1998 *ICLit* 32

Gaudemet-Tallon, H. 'Le Règlement nº 1347/2000 du Conseil du 29 mai 2000: "Compétence, reconnaissance et exécution des décisions en matière matrimoniale et en matière de responsabilité parentale des enfants communs"' 2001 *JDI* 381

—— 'L'incompétence internationale discrétionnaire du juge anglais et ses limites' 1974 *Rev. crit.* 607

—— 'Compétence internationale et dettes de monnaie étrangère devant la Chambre de Lords Nouveaux développements' 1979 *Rev. crit.* 25

—— 'La Convention de Rome de 1980 sur la loi applicable aux obligations contractuelles' 1985 *Jour Soc Légis Comp* 287

—— 'Le "forum non conveniens" une menace pour la convention de Bruxelles?' 1991 *Rev. crit.* 491

—— 'Signature de la Convention d'adhésion de l'Espagne et du Portugal à la Convention de Rome du 19 juin 1980' 1993 *Rev trim dr euro* 61

—— 'Les régimes relatifs au refus d'exercer la compétence juridictionelle en matière civile et commerciale: forum non conveniens, lis pendens' 1994 *Rev Int dr Comparé* 423

—— 'Jurisprudence sur la Convention de Rome du 19 juin 1980' 1994 *Rev trim dr euro* 101

Gebauer, M. 'Internationale Zuständigkeit und Prozeßaufrechnung' zu *LG Berlin* 30.1.1996 1998 *IPRax* 79

—— 'Zur Drittwirkung von Gerichtsstandsvereinbarungen bei Vertragsketten' 2001 *IPRax* 471

—— 'Drittstaaten- und Gemeinschaftsbezug im europäischen Recht der internationalen Zuständigkeit' 2001 *ZeuP* 943

Gee, S. 'Mareva injunctions – the reforms of the law made by its soul' 1998 *Int J IL* 133

Geimer, R. 'Die Vollstreckbarerklärung ausländischer Urteile' 1965 *NJW* 1413

—— 'Anerkennung und Vollstreckbarerklärung französischer Garantieurteile in der Bundesrepublik Deutschland' 1972 *ZZP* 196

—— 'Nichtanerkennung ausländischer Urteile wegen nichgehöriger Ladung zum Erstprozeß' 1973 *NJW* 2138

—— 'Einige Zweifelsfragen zur Abgrenzung nach dem EWG-Übereinkommen vom 27.9.1968' 1975 *RIW* 81

—— 'Anerkennung gerichtlicher Entscheidungen nach dem EWG-Übereinkommen vom 27.9.1968' 1976 *RIW/AWD* 139

—— 'Das Anerkennungsverfahren gemäß Art.26 Abs.2 des EWG-Übereinkommens vom 27. September 1968' 1977 *JZ* 145

—— 'Fora connexitatis: Der Sachzusammenhang als Grundlage der internationalen Zuständigkeit' 1979 *WM* 350

—— 'Nachprüfung der internationalen Zuständigkeit des Urteilsstaates in Versicherungs-und Verbrauchersachen' zu *BGH* 2.5.1979 1980 *RIW/AWD* 305

—— 'Beachtung ausländischer Rechtshängigkeit und Justizhewährungsanspruch' 1984 *NJW* 527

—— 'Zuständigkeitsvereinbarungen zugunsten und zu Lasten Dritter' 1985 *NJW* 533

—— 'Der doppelte Schutz des Beklagten, der sich auf den Erstprozeß nicht eingelassen hat, gemäß Art.20 II-III und Art.27 Nr.2 EuGVÜ' zu *EuGH* 15.7.1982 228/81 1985 *IPRax* 6

—— 'Das Nebeneinander und Miteinander von europäischem und nationalem Zivilprozeßrecht' 1986 *NJW* 2991

—— 'EuGVÜ und Aufrechnung: Keine Erweiterung der internationalen Entscheidungszuständigkeit – Aufrechnungsverbot bei Abweisung der Klage wegen internationaler Unzuständigkeit' zu *A.S Autoteile Service GmbH v Malhé* (C-220/84) [1985] ECR 2267 und *OLG Hamm* 25.9.1985 1986 *IPRax* 208

Geimer, R. 'Das neue Gesetz zur Ausfürung zwischenstaatlicher Anerkennungs-und Vollstreckungs-verträge in Zivil-und Handelssachen (Anerkennungs- und Vollstreckungsausführungsgesetz – AVAG)' 1988 *NJW* 2157

—— 'Über die Kunst der Interessenabwägung auch im internationalen Verfahrensrecht, dargestellt am rechten Maß des beklagtenschutzes gemäß Art.27 Nr.2 EuGVÜ' zu *OLG Hamm* 3.8.1987 und *LG Mönchengladbach* 20.7.1987 1988 *IPRax* 271

—— 'Ungeschriebene Anwendungsgrenzen des EuGVÜ: Müssen Berührungspunkte zu mehreren Ver-tragsstaaten bestehen?' 1991 *IPRax* 31

—— 'Anerkennung und Vollstreckbarerklärung von ex parte-Unterhaltsentscheidungen aus EuGVÜ-Vertragstaaten' zu *BGH* 21.3.1990 und *OLG Koblenz* 19.6.1990 1992 *IPRax* 5

—— 'Zur internationalen Gerichtspflichtigkeit im Vermögensgerichtsstand' zu *OLG München* 7.10.1992 1993 *IPRax* 216

—— 'Zur internationalkompetenzrechtlichen Perspektive der Prozeßaufrechnung: die internationale Zuständigkeit Deutschlands für die Aufrechnungsforderung als Voraussetzung für die Beachtung der Aufrechnung im deutschen Prozeß' zu *BGH* 4.2.1993 und *BGH* 12.5.1993 1994 *IPRax* 82

—— 'Härtetest für deutsche Dienstleister im Ausland' zu *OLG Hamm* 27.6.1996 und *BGH* 18.9.1997 1998 *IPRax* 175

—— 'Schwedische Bank im deutschen Grundbuch: Grundschuld zur Sicherung einer ausländischem Recht unterliegenden Forderung' zu *HansOLG Hamburg* 6.2.1998 1999 *IPRax* 152

—— 'Freizügigkeit vollstreckbarer Urkunden im Europäischen Wirtschaftsraum' zu *Unibank A/S v Flemming G. Christiensen* 2000 *IPRax* 366

—— 'Casenote *Dieter Krombach*' 2000 *ZIP* 859

—— 'Entscheidungsharmonie in Europa per Entscheidungsstop' zu OLG Frankfuhrt 19.6.2000 2001 *IPRax* 191

—— 'Salut für die Verordnung (EG) Nr.44/2001 (Brüssel I-VO)' 2002 *IPRax* 69

Geller, P. 'International Intellectual Property, Conflicts of Laws and Internet Remedies' [2000] *EIPR* 125

Gentinetta, J. 'Befreiung der internationalen Handelsschiedsgerichtbarkeit von der nationalen Umklammerung' 1969 *AWD* 46

Gerhard, F. 'La compétence du juge d'appui pour prononcer des mesures provisoires extraterritoriales' 1999 *SZIER* 97

Giardina, A. 'The European Court and the Brussels Convention on Jurisdiction and Judgments' 1978 *ICLQ* 263

Gilardi, AV. 'Clausola di proroga di giurisdizione: concenso effettivo o presunto?' 2001 *Riv trim dir & proc civ* 487

Gill, A. 'The EEC Convention on the Law Applicable to Contractual Obligations' 1982–3 *JISEL* 1

Gilliéron, P-R. 'L'exequatur des décisions étrangères condamnant à une prestation pécuniaire ou à la prestation de sûretés selon la Convention de Lugano' 1992 *SJZ* 117

—— 'Itérativement: L'exécution des décisions rendues dans un Etat partie à la Convention de Lugano, portant condamnation à payer une somme d'argent ou à la prestation de sûretés' 1994 *SJZ* 73

Gillies, L. 'Rules of jurisdiction for electronic consumer contracts: Scottish perspectives' 6 *Scottish Law and Practice Quarterly* (2001) 124

Girsberger, D. 'Gerichtsstandsklausel im Konnossement: Der EuGH und der internationale Handels-brauch' zu *Hugo Trumpy* 2000 *IPRax* 87

Giverdon, C. 'La procédure de règlement des exceptions d'incompétence, de litispendence et de con-nexité d'après le décret no 72–684 du 20 juillet 1972' *Dalloz, Chron.* 155

Gleiss, A. 'Die Gefahren des US-Antitrustrechts für europäische Unternehmen' 1969 *AWD/RIW* 499

Glenn, HP. 'Harmonization of law, foreign law and private international law' 1993 *ERPL* 47

Goemans, B. 'Chronique de jurisprudence maritime belge' 2001 *Il diritto marittimo* 1194

Golden, A. 'Casenote: *Webb v Webb*, CA' 1992 *EG* 34

Goldman, B. 'Un Traité fédérateur: La Convention entre les Etats membres de la C.E.E. sur la recon-naissance et l'exécution des décisions en matière civile et commerciale' 1971 *Rev trim dr euro* 1

Golomb, A. 'Recognition of foreign money judgments: a goal-oriented approach' 43 *St.John's L Rev* 604 (1969)

Gothot, P. 'La Convention entre les Etats membres de la Communauté économique européenne sur la compétence judiciaire et l'exécution des décisions en matière civile et commerciale' 1972 *JDI* 747
—— 'L'espace judiciaire européen délimité par la convention de Bruxelles du 27 septembre 1968' 1985 *Ann dr. Louvain* 51
Gottwald, P. 'Streitiger Vertragsschluß und Gerichtsstand des Erfüllungsortes (Art.5 Nr.1 EuGVÜ)' 1983 *IPRax* 13
—— 'Die Prozeßaufrechnung im europäischen Zivilprozeß' zu *Hannelore Spitzley v Sommer Exploitation S.A.* C48/84 [1985] ECR 787 1986 *IPRax* 10
—— 'Die einseitig bindende Prorogation nach Art.17 Abs.3 EuGVÜ' zu *Rudolf Anterist v Crédit Lyonnais* C22/85 [1986] ECR 1951 und *BGH* 18.9.1986 1987 *IPRax* 81
—— 'Grundfragen der Anerkennung und Vollstreckung ausländischer Entscheidungen in Zivilsachen' 1990 *ZZP* 257
—— 'Die internationale Zwangsvollstreckung' 1991 *IPRax* 285
—— and Baumann, T. 'Zur Derogation der deutschen internationalen Zuständigkeit' zu BGH 18.3.1997 1998 *IPRax* 445
Grainger, I. 'The Brussels Convention: Sarrio' 1995 *Commercial Lawyer* 8
Graupner, R. 'Die Durchsetzung des Schadensersatzanspruchs gegen einen englischen receiver vor deutschen Gerichten' 1994 *RIW* 109
Greggio, F. 'The Competent Jurisdiction in B2C Contracts' [2000] *ICCLR* 193
Grothe, H. '"Exorbitante" Gerichtszuständigkeiten im Rechtsverkehr zwischen Deutschland und den USA' 1994 *RabelsZ* 686
—— '"Exorbitant" territorial jurisdiction in Legal relations between Germany and the United States' 1994 *RabelsZ* 724
Grube, L. 'Deutsch-spanische Gerichtsstandsvereinbarungen' 1992 *EuZW* 17
Gruber, J. 'Sind französische Urteile über die Haftung von Gesellschaftsorganen im Konkurs nach dem EuGVÜ anerkennungsfähig?' 1994 *EWS* 190
Gruber, U. 'Die neue "europäische Rechtshängigkeit" bei Scheidungsverfahren' 2000 *FamRZ* 1129
Grundmann, S. 'Zur internationalen Zuständigkeit der Gerichte von Drittstaaten nach Art.16 EuGVÜ' 1985 *IPRax* 249
Grunert, J. 'Interlocutory remedies in England and Germany: a comparative perspective' 1996 *CJQ* 18
Grunsky, W. 'Probleme des EWG-Übereinkommen über die gerichtliche Zuständigkeit und die Vollstreckung gerichtlicher Entscheidungen in Zivil-und Handelssachen' 1973 *JZ* 641
—— 'EWG-Übereinkommen über die gerichtliche Zuständigkeit und die Vollstreckung gerichtlicher Entscheidungen in Zivil-und Handelssachen im deutsch-italienischen Rechtsverkehr' 1977 *RIW* 1
—— 'Zur Vollstreckung eines im Ausland erschlichenen rechtskräftigen Urteils' zu *BGH* 10.7.1986 1987 *IPRax* 219
—— 'Voraussetzungen für die Anordnung von Maßnahmen des Beschwerdegerichts nach Art.38 EuGVÜ' zu *BGH* 21.4.1994 1995 *IPRax* 218
—— 'Das verfahrenseinleitende Schriftstück beim Mahnverfahren' zu *Hengst Import BV v Anna Maria Campese* 1996 *IPRax* 245
Gutteridge, H-C. 'La Convention Franco-Britannique pour l'exécution réciproque des jugements' 1937 *Rev. crit.* 1
Haas, U. 'Der Ausschluß der Schiedsgerichtsbarkeit vom Anwendungsbereich des EuGVÜ' zu *Marc Rich & Co. AG v Società Italiana Impianti PA* C109/89 [1991] ECR I-3855 1992 *IPRax* 292
—— 'Beginn der Sicherungs(zwangs)vollstreckung nach Art.39 Abs. 1 EuGVÜ' zu *OLG Saarbrücken* 5.1.1994 1995 *IPRax* 223
—— 'Unfallversicherungsschutz und ordre public' zu *BGH* 16.9.993 *Volker Sonntag v Waidmann and others* 1995 *ZZP* 219
—— 'Zur Anerkennung US-amerikanischer Urteile in der Bundesrepublik Deutschland' zu BGH 29.4.1999 2001 *IPRax* 195
Habscheid, W. 'Schütze, R. 'Die Berücksichtigung der Rechtshängigkeit eines ausländischen Verfahrens' 1967 *RabelsZ* 254
—— 'Anerkennung und Vollstreckung von Urteilen aus EWG- Staaten in der Bundesrepublik Deutschland' 1973 *ZfRV* 262

Hackl, C. 'Örtliche Zuständigkeit gemäß Art.5(1) und (3) des Brüsseler EG-Übereinkommens vom 27.9.1968 über die gerichtliche Zuständigkeit und die Vollstreckung gerichtlicher Entscheidungen in Zivil-und Handelssachen' 1984 *ZfRV* 1

Hackspiel, S. 'Berichtigende Auslegung von Art.22 EuGVÜ durch die französische Cour de Cassation – ein nachahmenswertes Beispiel?' Zu Cass. 27.10.1992 1996 *IPRax* 214

Hall, E. 'Who is suing whom?' 1995 *GILSI* 225

Halpern, J. '"Exorbitant Jurisdiction" and the Brussels Convention: Toward a theory of restraint' 1983 *Yale J World P O* 369

Hamblen, N. 'Injunctions to restrain proceedings brought in breach of English jurisdiction/ arbitration clauses' 1996 *I J O S L* 247

Handley, KR. '*Res judicata* in the European Court' 2000 *LQR* 191

Hanisch, H. Internationale Arrestzuständigkeit und EuGVÜ' 1991 *IPRax* 215

Hanotiau, B. 1998 *Ann dr. Louvain* 296

Hanson, J. 'Cutting through the confusion? The rights of third parties under insurance and reinsurance contracts' 1997 *Int J IL* 50

Hardenberg, L. 'First demand guarantees: Recent developments in the Netherlands' 1996 *IBL* 380

Harries, H. 'Das Deutsch-Belgische Anerkennungs-und Vollstreckungsabkommen' 1961 *RabelsZ* 629

Harris, J. 'The ambivalent plaintiff and the scope of forum non conveniens: *Advanced Portfolio Technologies v Ainsworth*' 1996 *CJQ* 279

—— 'Rights *in rem* and the Brussels Convention: *Re Hayward*' 21 (1997) *ELR* 179

—— 'Related actions and the Brussels Convention: *Sarrio v Kuwait Investment Authority*' 1998 *LMCLQ* 145

—— 'Jurisdiction clauses and void contracts: Benincasa' 22 (1998) *ELR* 279

—— 'Justiciability, choice of law and the Brussels Convention' 1999 *LMCLQ*

—— 'Ordering the sale of land situated overseas, *Ashurst v Pollard*' 2001 *LMCLQ* 205

—— 'The Brussels Regulation' (2001) 20 *CJQ* 218

Hartley, T. 'Casenote: *Tessili v Dunlop*' 2 (1977) *ELR* 57

—— 'Casenote: *Bier v Mines de Potasse*' 2 (1977) *ELR* 143

—— 'Casenote: *De Wolf v Cox*' 2 (1977) *ELR* 146

—— 'Casenote: *Salotti v RÜWA* and *Segoura v Bonakdarian*' 2 (1977) *ELR* 148

—— 'Casenote: *Bavaria Fluggesellschaft v Eurocontrol*' 2 (1977) *ELR* 461

—— 'Casenote: *Diamond Supplies v Riva*' 3 (1978) *ELR* 160

—— 'Casenote: *Sanders v Van der Putte*' 3 (1978) *ELR* 164

—— 'Casenote: *Bertrand v Ott*' 4 (1979) *ELR* 47

—— 'Casenote: *Meeth v Glacetal*' 4 (1979) *ELR* 125

—— 'Casenote: *Somafer v Saar-Ferngas*' 4 (1979) *ELR* 127

—— 'Casenote: *De Cavel v De Cavel*' 4 (1979) *ELR* 222

—— 'Casenote: *Gourdain v Nadler*' 4 (1979) *ELR* 482

—— 'Casenote: *Sanicentral v Collin*' 5 (1980) *ELR* 73

—— 'Casenote: *Denilauer v Couchet Freres*' 6 (1981) *ELR* 59

—— 'Casenote: *Porta-Leasing v Prestige International*' 6 (1981) *ELR* 62

—— 'Casenote: *Netherlands State v Ruffer*' 6 (1981) *ELR* 215

—— 'Casenote: *Blanckaert v Trost*' 6 (1981) *ELR* 481

—— 'Casenote: *Effer v Kantner*' 7 (1982) *ELR* 235

—— 'Casenote: *Elefanten Schuh v Jacqmain*' 7 (1982) *ELR* 237

—— 'Casenote: *Peters v ZNAV*' 7 (1982) *ELR* 262

—— 'Casenote: *Ivenel v Schwab*' 7 (1982) *ELR* 328

—— 'Casenote: *Klomps v Michel*' 7 (1982) *ELR* 419

—— 'Casenote: *Gerling v Tesoro*' 8 (1983) *ELR* 264

—— 'Casenote: *Duijnstee v Goderbauer*' 9 (1984) *ELR* 64

—— 'Casenote: *The Tilly Russ*' 9 (1984) *ELR* 456

—— 'Casenote: *Zelger v Salinitri*' 10 (1985) *ELR* 56

—— 'Casenote: *P. v K.*' 10 (1985) *ELR* 233

—— 'Casenote: *Rösler v Rottwinkel*' 10 (1985) *ELR* 361

Hartley, T. 'Casenote: *Brennero v Wendel*' 11 (1986) *ELR* 95
—— 'Casenote: *Berghöfer v ASA*' 11 (1986) *ELR* 470
—— 'Casenote: *Carron v Germany*' 12 (1987) *ELR* 64
—— 'Casenote: *Debaecker v Bowmann*' 12 (1987) *ELR* 121
—— 'Casenote: *Gubisch v Palumbo*' 13 (1988) *ELR* 216
—— 'Casenote: *Minster Investments v Hyundai*' 13 (1988) *ELR* 217
—— 'Casenote: *Scherrens v Maenhout*' 14 (1989) *ELR* 57
—— 'Casenote: *Overseas Union v New Hampshire*, QBD' 14 (1989) *ELR* 58
—— 'Casenote: *Kalfelis v Banhaus Schroder*' 14 (1989) *ELR* 172
—— 'Casenote: *Six Constructions v Humbert*' 14 (1989) *ELR* 236
—— 'Casenotes: *Hoffmann v Krieg*; *Reichert*; *Dumez France*; *Kongress Agentur*' 16 (1991) *ELR* 64
—— 'Casenote: *Marc Rich v Impianti*' 16 (1991) *ELR* 529
—— 'Casenote: *Overseas Union v New Hampshire Insurance*' 17 (1992) *ELR* 75
—— 'Casenote: *Powell Duffryn Plc v Petereit*' 17 (1992) *ELR* 225
—— 'Casenote: *Shevill v Presse Alliance*' 17 (1992) *ELR* 274
—— 'Casenote: *Hacker v Euro-Relais*' 17 (1992) *ELR* 550
—— 'Casenote: *Re Harrods (Buenos Aires) Ltd.*' 17 (1992) *ELR* 553
—— 'Casenote: *Powell Duffryn v Petereit*' 18 (1993) *ELR* 225
—— 'Unnecessary Europeanisation under the Brussels Jurisdiction and Judgments Convention: the case of the dissatisfied sub-purchaser' 18 (1993) *ELR* 506
—— 'Casenote: *Minalmet v Brandeis*' 19 (1994) *ELR* 535
—— 'Casenote: *Shearson Lehmann Hutton v TVB*' 19 (1994) *ELR* 537
—— 'Casenote: *Sonntag v Waidmann*' 19 (1994) *ELR* 538
—— 'Casenote: *Webb v Webb*' 19 (1994) *ELR* 547
—— 'Casenote: *Continental Bank v Aeakos*' 19 (1994) *ELR* 549
—— 'Enforcement of third-country judgments: *Owens Bank*' 19 (1994) *ELR* 545
—— 'Casenote: *The Tatry*' 20 (1995) *ELR* 409
—— 'Jurisdiction under competing Conventions' 1995 *LMCLQ* 31
—— 'Casenote: *Lloyd's Register of Shipping*' 21 (1996) *ELR* 162
—— 'Casenote: *Marinari v Lloyd's Bank*' 21 (1996) *ELR* 164
—— 'Casenote: *Danvaern Production*' 21 (1996) *ELR* 166
—— 'Casenote: *SISRO v Ampersand*' 21 (1996) *ELR* 169
—— 'Pleading and proof of foreign law: the major European systems compared' 1996 *ICLQ* 271
—— 'Article 17 of the Brussels Convention: Jurisdiction agreements, Mainschiffahrts' 22 (1997) *ELR* 360
—— 'Article 27(2) of the Brussels Convention: Judgments in default of appearance, *Hendrikman*' 22 (1997) *ELR* 364
—— 'Antisuit Injunctions and the Brussels Jurisdiction and Judgments Convention' 2000 *ICLQ* 166
Hartwieg, O. 'Forum Shopping zwischen Forum non Conveniens und "hinreichendem Inlandsbezug"' 1996 *JZ* 109
Haß, D. 'Zur internationalen Gerichtsstandsvereinbarung in einer Patronserklärung' zu LG Berlin 18.2.2000 2000 *IPRax* 494
Hascher, D. 'Recognition and Enforcement of Arbitration awards and the Brussels Convention' 1996 *Arb Int* 233
Hau, W. 'Durchsetzung von Zuständigkeits-und Schiedsvereinbarungen mittels Prozeßführungsverboten im EuGVÜ: Neuere Rechtsprechung des Court of Appeal zu obligation-based antisuit injunctions' zu *Continental Bank N.A. v Aeakos Compania Naviera S.A. and others* [1994] 1 WLR 588 1996 *IPRax* 44
—— 'Zum Rechtsschutz gegen die Vollstreckbarerklärung gemäß Artt.36 bis 38 EuGVÜ' zu *(SISRO) v Ampersand Software BV* 1996 *IPRax* 322
—— 'Probleme der abredewidrigen Streitverkündung im europäischen Zivilrechtsverkehr' 1997 *RIW* 89
—— 'Zustellung ausländischer Prozeßführungsverbote: Zwischen Verpflichtung zur Rechtshilfe und Schutz inländischer Hoheitsrechte' zu *OLG Düsseldorf* 10.1.1996 1997 *IPRax* 161

Hau, W. 'Die einseitige Erledigungserklärung im Exequaturverfahren' zu *OLG Düsseldorf* 10.7.1996 1998 *IPRax* 255

—— 'Europäische Rechtshilfe, endgültige Rechtshängigkeit, effektiver Rechtsschutz' zu *LG München II* 6.3.1997 1998 *IPRax* 456

—— 'Zur schriftlichen Bestätigung mündlicher Gerichtsstandsvereinbarungen' zu *OLG Düsseldorf* 2.10.1997 1999 *IPRax* 24

—— 'Der Vertragsgerichtsstand zwischen judizieller Konsolidierung und legislativer Neukonzeption' 2000 *IPRax* 354

Haubold, J. 'Internationale Zuständigkeit für gesellschaftsrechtliche und konzerngesellschaftsrechtliche Haftungsansprüche nach EuGVÜ und LugÜ' zu *OLG München* 25.6.1999 2000 *IPRax* 375

Hauschild, W. 'L'importance des conventions communautaires pour la création d'un droit communautaire' 1975 *Rev trim dr euro* 4

Hauschka, C. 'Central Issues of Business Litigation in West German civil courts' 1988 *Cal W Int'l L J* 47

Hausmann, R. 'Zur Anerkennung und Vollstreckung von Maßnahmen des einstweiligen Rechtsschutzes im Rahmen des EG-Gerichtsstands-und Vollstreckungsübereinkommens' zu *Bernard Denilauer v S.n.c. Couchet Frères* (C125/79) [1980] ECR 1553 1981 *IPRax* 79

Hay, P. 'The Common Market Preliminary Draft Convention on the Recognition and Enforcement of Judgments – some considerations of policy and Interpretation' 1968 *Am J Int'l L* 149

—— 'The proposed Recognition-of-Judgments Convention between the United States and the United Kingdom' 1976 *Tex Int'l L J* 421

—— 'The proposed U.S.–U.K. Recognition-of-Judgments Convention: another perspective' 1978 *Virg J Int'l L* 753

—— 'The case for federalizing rules of civil jurisdiction in the European Community' 1984 *Mich L Rev* 1323

—— 'Nichtermittelbarkeit ausländischen Rechts und Forum non Conveniens' 1998 *RIW* 760

Hayer, H. 'Die Anknüpfung des privaten Darlehensvertrages' 1996 *ZfRV* 221

Hayer, R. 'Die Anerkennung und Vollstreckung schweizerischer Schiedsgerichts-und Gerichtsurteile in Spanien' 1994 *IPRax* 391

Heerstrassen, F. 'Die künftige Rolle von Präjudizien des EuGH im Verfahren des Luganer Übereinkommens' 1993 *RIW* 179

Heidneberger, P. 'Vollstreckung deutscher Urteile in den Vereinigten Staaten' 1953 *NJW* 1117

—— 'Zustellung amerikanischer Punitive-damages-Klagen weiterhin ein Problem' 1995 *RIW* 705

Heiderhoff, B. 'Diskussionsbericht zu Streitgegenstandslehre und EuGH' 1998 *ZZP* 455

—— 'Widerklage und ausländische Streitanhängigkeit' zu *OGH* 12.2.1997 1999 *IPRax* 392

Heinrich, D. 'Internationale Zuständigkeit und korrigierende Anknüpfungen in Unterhaltssachen' 2001 *IPRax* 437

Heiss, H. 'Neuerungen im österreichischen internationalen Verfahrens- und Vertragsrecht' 1999 *IPRax* 305

—— 'Die Form internationaler Gerichtsstandsvereinbarungen' 2000 *ZfRV* 202

Helms, T. 'Die Anerkennung ausländischer Entscheidungen im Europäischen Eheverfahrensrecht' 2001 *FamRZ* 257

Henrich, D. 'Zur Anerkennung und Vollstreckung einer deutschen Entscheidung über den Versorgungsausgleich in Österreich' zu *Landesgericht Innsbruck* 12.9.1997 1998 *IPRax* 396

Henssler, M. 'Der Gerichtsstand des Erfüllungsortes gem. §29 ZPO für die anwaltliche Honorarklage' 1999 *AnwBl* 186

Herbert, F. 'Belgian caselaw on the Brussels Convention' 1 (1976) *ELR* 165

—— 'Belgian caselaw on the Brussels Convention' 2 (1977) *ELR* 72

—— 'Belgian caselaw on the Brussels Convention' 3 (1978) *ELR* 83

—— 'Luxembourg caselaw on the Brussels Convention' 3 (1978) *ELR* 91

—— 'Belgian caselaw on the Brussels Convention' 4 (1979) *ELR* 402

—— 'Belgian caselaw on the Brussels Convention' 5 (1980) *ELR* 419

—— 'Belgian caselaw on the Brussels Convention' 6 (1981) *ELR* 405

Herbots, J. 'La Convention Parallele concernant la compétence judiciaire et l'exécution des décisions en matières civiles et commerciales' 1988–9 *Dr Intern Privé* 3

Herzog, P. 'The Common Market Convention on Jurisdiction and the Enforcement of Judgments: An interim update' 1977 *Virg J Int'l L* 417
—— 'Brussels and Lugano, Should you race to the Courthouse or Race for a Judgment?' 1995 *Am J Comp Law* 379
Heß, B. 'Gerichtsstandsvereinbarungen zwischen EuGVÜ und ZPO' zu *BGH* 14.11.1991 1992 *IPRax* 358
—— 'Amtshaftung als "Zivilsache" im Sinne von Art.1 Abs.1 EuGVÜ' zu *Volker Sonntag v Hans Waidmann and others* (C-172/91) [1993] ECR I-1963 1994 *IPRax* 10
—— 'Die begrenzte Freizügigkeit einstweiliger Maßnahmen nach Art.24 EuGVÜ' zu *Van Uden Maritime BV v Kommanditgesellschaft* 1999 *IPRax* 220
—— 'Die Anerkennung eines Class Action Settlement in Deutschland' 2000 *JZ* 373
—— 'Die begrenzte Freizügigkeit einstweiliger Maßnahmen im Binnenmarkt II – weitere Klarstellungen des Europäischen Gerichtshofs' zu *Hans Herman Mietz* 2000 *IPRax* 370
—— 'Die Zustellung von Schriftstücken im europäischen Justizraum' 2001 *NJW* 15
—— 'Die Integrationsfunktion des Europäischen Zivilverfahrensrechts' 2001 *IPRax* 389
Heusler, A. 'Das forum contractus und das schweizerisches Bundesrecht' 1881 *ZschweizR* 23
Heuzé, V. 'La notion de contrat en droit international privé' 1995–1998 *Dr Intern Privé* 319
—— 'De quelques infirmités congénitales du droit uniforme: l'exemple de l'article 5.1 de la Convention de Bruxelles du 27 septembre 1968' 2000 *Rev. crit.* 595
Hill, J. 'Jurisdiction in matters relating to a contract under the Brussels Convention' 1995 *ICLQ* 591
—— 'Jurisdiction under Art.5(5) of the Brussels Convention' 1996 *CJQ* 94
—— 'Illegality under the law of the place of performance and the enforcement of arbitration awards' [2000] *LMCLQ* 311
Ho, HL. 'Policies underlying the Enforcement of Foreign Commercial Judgments' 1997 *ICLQ* 443
Hoffmann, B. 'Das EWG-Übereinkommen über die gerichtliche Zuständigkeit und die Vollstreckung gerichtlicher Entscheidungen in Zivil- und Handelssachen' 1973 *AWD* 57
Hoffmann, E. 'Zustellung und Vollstreckung deutscher Urteile in Belgien aus Sicht eines deutschen Antragstellers' 2000 *AnwBl* 114
Hogan, G. 'The Judgments Convention and Mareva Injunctions in the United Kingdom and Ireland' 1989 *JBL* 191
—— 'Procedure and Practice and the Judgments Convention: some further developments' 1992 *IJEL* 82
—— 'Casenote: *Dresser v Falcongate*' 17 (1992) *ELR* 555
—— 'The Brussels Convention, forum non conveniens and the connecting factor problem' 20 (1995) *ELR* 471
Holl, V. 'Der Gerichtsstand des Erfüllungsortes gemäß Art.5 Nr.1 EuGVÜ' 1995 *WB* 462
—— 'Der Gerichtsstand des Erfüllungsortes nach Art.5 Nr.1 EuGVÜ bei individuellen Arbeitsverträgen: *Mulox v Geels*' 1997 *IPRax* 88
—— 'Kehrtwende in der Rechtsprechung des EuGH zur Auslegungszuständigkeit im Vorabentscheidungsverfahren?' zu *Kleinwort Benson Ltd v City of Glasgow District Council* (C346/93) [1995] ECR I-615 1996 *IPRax* 174
Holleaux, D. 'La Convention de Bruxelles du 27 septembre 1968 sur la compétence judiciaire et l'exécution des décisions en matière civile et commerciale: cinq années d'application en France' 1978 *Rev. crit.* 520
—— 'La Convention de Bruxelles du 27 septembre 1969' 1978 *JDI* 520
—— 'Casenote: *Zelger v Salinitri*' 1985 *Rev. crit.* 374
Hohloch, G. 'Ordre public i.S. des Art.27 Nr. 1 EuGVÜ' 1997 *JuS* 755
—— 'Erfolgsort und Schadensort – Abgrenzung bei Ansprüchen auf Ersatz von (primären und sonstigen) Vermögensschäden' zu *Antonio Marinari v Lloyds Bank Plc and Zubaidi Trading Co.* (C364/93) [1995] ECR I-2719 1997 *IPRax* 312
Hondius, E. 'European Private Law' 1993 *ERPL* 1
Honorati, C. 'Concorso di reponsablità contrattuale ed extracontrattuale e giurisdizione ai sensi della Convenzione di Bruxelles del 1969' 1994 *Riv. dir. int. priv. e proc.* 281
—— 'La *Cross-border prohibitory injunction* Olandese in Materia di Contraffazione di Brevetti: sulla legittimità dell'inibitoria transfrontaliera alla luce della Convenzione di Bruxelles del 1968' 1997 *Riv. dir. int. priv. e proc.* 301

Hornung, U. 'Auswirkungen der Einschränkung des Vermögengerichtsstandes auf die internationale Zuständigkeit im dinglichen Arrestverfahren' 1996 *ZfRV* 305

Hoyer, H. 'Zur Streitanhängigkeit im österreichischen internationalen Zivilprozeßrecht' 1969 *ZfRV* 241

Hoyer, V. 'Bemerkungen zur Geschichte der Vollstreckung ausländischer Entscheidungen in Österreich im 19. Jahrhundert' 1964 *ZfRV* 94

Hoyle, M. 'The Mareva injunction and overseas assets' 1989 *JIBL* 15

Hu Zhenjie '*Forum non conveniens*: an unjustified doctrine' 2001 *NILR* 143

Hub, T. 'Die Neuregelung der Anerkennung und Vollstreckung in Zivil- und Handelssachen und das familienrechtliche Anerkennungs- und Vollstreckungsverfahren' 2001 *NJW* 3145

Huber, P. 'Verleumdungsklagen und Art.5 Nr.3 EuGVÜ vor englischen Gerichten' zu *Shevill and others v Presse Alliance S.A* [1992] 2 WLR 1, CA 1992 *IPRax* 263

—— 'Forum non conveniens und EuGVÜ' 1993 *RIW* 977

—— 'Neues aus England zu Artt.21, 22 EuGVÜ' zu *Dresser UK v Falcongate* 1993 *IPRax* 114

—— 'Art.21 EuGVÜ und Rechtshängigkeit in England – Ende der Debatte?' zu .*Neste Chemicals S.A. and others v DK Line S.A. and Tokumaru Kaiun K.K. (The 'Sargasso')* [1994] 3 All ER 180, CA 1995 *IPRax* 332

—— 'Forum non conveniens – the other way round' zu *SC Ireland* [1994] 1 IRLM 416 1996 *IPRax* 48

—— 'Revision des EuGVÜ und neues Schiedsverfahrensrecht' 1999 *IPRax* 298

Hudault, J. 'Sens et portée de la compétence du juge naturel dans l'ancien droit français' 1972 *Rev. crit.* 27

Hudleston, S. 'Preserving Free speech in a global courtroom: The proposed Hague Convention and the First Amendment' 10 *Minn. J. Global Trade* 403 (2001)

Huet, A. 'La marque communautaire: la compétence des juridictions des Etats membres pour connaître de sa validité et de sa contrefaçon (Règlement (CE) no. 40/97 du Conseil, du 20 décembre 1993' 1994 *JDI* 623

Hunter, R. 'Reinsurance litigation and the Civil Jurisdiction and Judgments Act 1982' 1987 *JBL* 344

Huskisson, I. 'Casenote: Domicrest Ltd' 1998 *JIBL* N-105

Hüßtege, R. 'Internationale Zuständigkeit deutscher Gerichte bei der Überlassung von Räumen im Ausland' 1990 *NJW* 622

—— 'Internationale Zustellung – Probleme ohne Ende?' zu *OLG Düsseldorf* 2.9.1998 2000 *IPRax* 289

—— 'Ferienwohnungen im Ausland als Spielball der Gerichte' zu EuGH Dansommer 2001 *IPRax* 31

Inglis, B. 'Jurisdiction, the doctrine of forum conveniens, and choice of law in conflict of laws' 1965 *LQR* 380

Isenburg-Epple, S. 'Grenzen des Ermessens in Art.21 II des Europäischen Gerichtsstands-und Vollstreckungsübereinkommens vom 27.9.1968' zu *OLG Köln* 13.12.1990 1992 *IPRax* 69

Jackson, D. 'Fitting English maritime jurisdiction into Europe – or vice versa?' 2001 *LMCLQ* 219

Jacoby, S. 'Extraterritorial English Mareva injunctions in a European context: A comparative approach (England, France and Germany)' 1996 *Ann dr. Lux* 245

Jaksic, A. 'Die Beachtung ausländischer Rechtshängigkeit in Ehesachen' 2001 *ZfRV* 161

Jametti-Greiner, M. 'Der vorsorgliche Rechtsschutz im internationalen Verhältnis' 1994 *ZBJV* 649

—— 'Die Revision des Brüsseler und des Lugano-Übereinkommens' 1999 *AJP* 1135

Janssens, T. 'Casenote: Shearson Lehmann Hutton' 1995 *ERPL* 605

Jayme, E. 'Reziproke Gerichtsstandsklauseln EuGVÜ und Drittstaaten' zu *OLG München* 8.8.1984 1985 *IPRax* 323

—— 'Zur Anwendbarkeit des Art.17 EuGVÜ bei Wohnsitz beider Parteien in demselben Vertragsstaat' zu *Cass.* 1.4.1985 und *OLG München* 13.2.1985 1989 *IPRax* 80

—— 'Grundfragen zum Anwendungsbereich des EuGVÜ – Zwei Vorlagen an den EuGH' zu House of Lords *Ladenimor S.A.* 1992 *IPRax* 357

—— 'L'interaction des règles de conflit contenues dans le droit dérivé de la Communauté européenne et des Conventions de Bruxelles et de Rom' 1995 *Rev. crit.* 1

—— 'Prozessuale Hindernisse für Timesharing-Anbieter in Auslandsfällen' zu *LG Essen* 10.3.1994 und *LG Darmstadt* 23.8.1995 1996 *IPRax* 87

—— 'Europäisches Kollisionsrecht 1996 – Anpassung und Transformation der nationalen Rechte' 1996 *IPRax* 377

Jayme, E. 'Neues Internationales Privatrecht für Timesharing-Verträge – zum Teilzeit-Wohnrechtegesetz vom 20.12.1996' 1997 *IPRax* 149

—— 'Ein Europäisches Zivilgesetzbuch: Die Initiative der Niederlande' 1997 *IPRax* 375

—— 'Europäisches Kollisionsrecht 1998: Kulturelle Unterschiede und Parallelaktionen' 1998 *IPRax* 417

—— 'Europäisches Kollisionsrecht 2000: Interlokales Privatrecht oder universelles Gemeinschaftsrecht?' 2000 *IPRax* 454

—— 'Europäisches Kollisionsrecht 2001: Anerkennungsprinzip statt IPR?' 2001 *IPRax* 501

——/Kohler, C. 'Zum Stand des internationalen Privat-und Verfahrensrecht der Europäischen Gemeinschaft' 1985 *IPRax* 65

——/Kohler, C. 'Das Internationale Privat-und Verfahrensrecht der Europäischen Gemeinschaft – Jüngste Entwicklungen' 1988 *IPRax* 133

——/Kohler, C. 'Das Internationale Privat-und Verfahrensrecht der EG – Stand 1989' 1989 *IPRax* 337

——/Kohler, C. 'Das Internationale Privat-und Verfahrensrecht der EG 1991 – Harmonisierungsmodell oder Mehrspurigkeit des Kollisionsrechts' 1991 *IPRax* 361

——/Kohler, C. 'Das Internationale Privat-und Verfahrensrecht der EG nach Maastricht' 1992 *IPRax* 346

——/Kohler, C. 'Das Internationale Privat-und Verfahrensrecht der EG 1993 Spannung zwischen Staatsverträgen und Richtlinien' 1993 *IPRax* 357

——/Kohler, C. 'Europäisches Kollisionsrecht 1994: Quellenpluralismus und offene Kontraste' 1994 *IPRax* 405

Jeantet, F-C. 'Un droit européen des conflits de juridiction de compétence judiciaire et de l'exécution des décisions en matière civile et commerciale' 1966–69 *Dr Intern Privé* 375

Jefferson, M. 'Casenotes' 1993 *SLR* 11

Jegher, G. 'Mit schweizerischer negativer Feststellungsklage ins europäische Forum Running – (Gedanken anlässlich BGE 123 III 414)' 1999 *ZschweizR* 31

—— 'Rechtshängigkeit in der Schweiz nach Art.21 Lugano-Übereinkommen' zu *BG* 26.9.1997 2000 *IPRax* 143

Jenard, P. 'Les développements attendus et inattendus de la Convention de Bruxelles du 27 septembre 1968 concernant la compétence judiciaire et l'exécution des décisions en matière civile et commerciale' 1989 *JT* 173

Jestaedt, E. 'Internationale Zuständigkeit eines deutschen Vollstreckungsgerichts bei alleinigen Wohnsitz des Drittschuldners im Inland?' 2001 *IPRax* 438

Johnson, B. 'Defending forum shopping by foreign plaintiffs' 1994 *PLI* 136

Juenger, F. 'La Convention de Bruxelles du 27 septembre 1968 et la courtoisie internationale' 1983 *Rev. crit.* 37

Juenger, F. 'Localising provisions in international contracts: efficacy, utility and the limitation of international risk' 1994 *Aust L J* 649

Jung, H. 'The Brussels and Lugano Conventions: The European Court's jurisdiction; its procedure and methods' 1992 *CJQ* 38

Jung, K. 'How punitive damage awards affect U.S. businesses in the international arena' 17 *Wis. Int'l LJ* 489 (1999)

Jünger, F. 'Der Kampf ums Forum' 1982 *RabelsZ* 708

Junker, A. 'Von Citoyen zum Consommateur-Entwicklungen des internationalen Verbraucherschutzrechts' 1998 *IPRax* 65

Junker, A. 'Internationales Vertragsrecht im Internet' 1999 *RIW* 809

Kaczorowski, A. 'Foreign torts in the United Kingdom and Ireland – a new Eurofan perspective' 1996 *IJEL* 20

Kaiser, E. 'Rechtshängigkeit im Ausland nach ausländischem Prozeßrecht?' 1983 *RIW* 667

Kaiser, T. 'Neuere Entwicklungen zur Mareva Injunction' 1985 *ZfRV* 254

—— 'Mareva Injunction: Höhepunkt überschritten' 1988 *ZfRV* 194

Kamper, S. 'Casenote *OLG Düsseldorf* 23.8.1995 – Dutch costs award not enforceable' 1996 *ICLit* 43

Karet, I. 'Intellectual Property Litigation – Jurisdiction in Europe' 1998 *IPQ* 317

—— 'Suit, Anti-suit' [1998] *EIPR* 76

Kargados, P. 'Rules for declining to exercise jurisdiction on civil and commercial matters in Greece: forum non conveniens and foreign choice of jurisdiction clauses' 1994 *Rev Hellén Dr Int* 161

Kartzke, U. 'Verträgen mit gewerblichen Ferienhausanbietern' 1994 *NJW* 823

Kaufmann-Kohler, G. 'Commandemicht de payer, mainlevée provisoire, action en libération de dette et Convention de Lugano. Réflexions à l'occasion d'un arrêt du tribunal fédéral' 1995 *SJ* 537

—— 'Convention de Lugano et contentieux bancaire' 1996 *Rev. dr. Aff. Intern* 961

Kautz, T. 'Casenote: *Shevill v Presse Alliance*' 1995 *ICLit* 46

—— 'Casenote: *BGH*, court can assist in punitive damages complaint' 1995 *ICLit* 46

Kaye, P. 'Nationality and the European Convention' 1988 *ICLQ* 268

—— 'Transitional scope of the Jurisdiction and Judgments Convention' 1988 *CJQ* 53

—— 'Convention rules for the determination of domicile in a Contracting State' 1988 *NILR* 183

—— 'L'exécution dans le Royaume-Uni de Grande-Bretagne et d'Irlande des décisions rendues par les tribunaux belges en application de la Convention de Bruxelles de 1968 sur la compétence judiciaire et l'exécution des décisions en matière civile et commerciale' 1989 *JT* 137

—— 'Der Beitritt des Vereinigten Königreichs zum Brüsseler Übereinkommen von 1968 über die gerichtliche Zuständigkeit und die Vollstreckung gerichtlicher Entscheidungen in Zivil- und Handelssachen' 1989 *IPRax* 403

—— 'Business Insurance and Reinsurance under the European Judgments Convention' 1990 *JBL* 517

—— 'Stay of Enforcement proceedings under the European Judgments Convention: Factors relevant to the exercise of discretion' 1991 *JBL* 261

—— 'Corporate jurisdiction under the European Judgments Convention' 1991 *CJQ* 220

—— 'The EEC Judgments Convention and the outer world: goodbye to forum non conveniens?' 1992 *JBL* 47

—— 'The EEC and Arbitration' 1993 *Arb Int* 27

—— 'Do the courts possess a jurisdictional discretion in intra-United Kingdom cases?' 1994 *PILMR* 151

—— 'The date upon which an English court becomes "seised" of Proceedings under the Brussels Convention: Issue or Service of Process?' 1995 *JBL* 217

—— 'A further limitation by the European Court upon the scope of application of the Brussels Convention' on *Owens Bank Ltd v Fluvio Bracco & Others (No.2)* C129/92 [1994] ECR I-117 1995 *IPRax* 214

—— 'Creation of an English resulting trust of immovables held to fall outside Article 16(1) of the European Judgments Convention' on *George Lawrence Webb v Lawrence Desmond Webb* C294/92 [1994] ECR I-1717 1995 *IPRax* 286

Kegel, G. 'The Conflict-of-Laws Machine – Zusammenhang im Allgemeinen Teil des IPR' 1996 *IPRax* 309

Kehrli, J. 'Neuerungen auf dem Gebiete der Zwangsvollstreckung ausländischer Zivilurteile in der Schweiz' 1942 ZBJV 21

Kellermann, A. 'French cases on the Brussels Convention' 2 (1977) *ELR* 389

Kennett, W. 'Reviewing service: Double check or double fault?' 1992 *CJQ* 115

—— 'Harmonization and the Judgments Convention: Historical influences' 1993 *ERPL* 83

—— 'Forum non conveniens in Europe' 1995 *CLJ* 552

—— 'Place of performance and predictability' 1995 *YEL* 193

—— 'Service of documents in Europe' 1998 *CJQ* 284

—— 'Current Developments Private International Law' 1999 *ICLQ* 966

—— 'Current Developments Private International Law: the Brussels I Regulation' 2001 *ICLQ* 725

Kerameus, K. 'La compétence internationale en matière délictuelle dans la Convention de Bruxelles' 1992–1993 *Dr Intern Privé* 255

—— 'Angleichung des Zivilprozeßrechts in Europa' 66 *RabelsZ* 1 (2002)

Kerr, M. 'The EEC Judgments Convention: some repercussions beyond the EEC' 1980 *Europarecht* 353

Kessedjian, C. 'Mesures provisoires et conservatoires: A propos d'une resolution adoptée par l'Association de droit international' 1997 *JDI* 103

Kessel, C. 'Practical Issues in the conduct of litigation subject to German law before English courts' 1996 *ICCLR* 425

Kidner, R. 'Jurisdiction and choice of law in international trade disputes' 1994 *ILJ* 109
—— 'Jurisdiction in European Contracts of Employment' 1998 *ILJ* 103
—— 'The place of a tort under the Brussels Convention on jurisdiction' 2000 *ITLQ* 3
Kieninger, E. 'Internationale Zuständigkeit bei der Verletzung ausländischer Immaterialgüterrechte: Common Law auf dem Prüfstand des EuGVÜ' 1998 *Grur. Int.* 280
Keithe, K. 'Internationale Tatortzuständigkeit bei unerlaubter Handlung – die Problematik des Vermögensschadens' 1994 *NJW* 222
—— 'Die Zustellung von Urteilen im Ausland – Keine gerichtliche Hinweispflicht' 1999 *RIW* 249
Killias, L. 'Internationale Zuständigkeit für Arrest- und Arrestprosequierungsverfahren in der Schweiz' 1996 *RIW* 1005
Killmann, B. 'Die Wirksamkeit österreichischer Gerichtsentscheidungen in Italien nach dem 1.1.1997' 1997 *ÖJZ* 525
Kindler, P. 'Internationale Zuständigkeit und anwendbares Recht im italienischen IPR-Gesetz von 1995' 1997 *RabelsZ* 227
Koch, H. 'Zweimal amerikanische punitive damages' vor deutschen Gerichten' zu *OLG München* 15.7.1992 und *BGH* 4.6.1992 1993 *IPRax* 288
—— 'Private International Law: a "soft" alternative to the harmonisation of Private Law?' 1995 *ERPL* 329
—— 'Verbrauchergerichtsstand nach dem EuGVÜ und Vermögensgerichtsstand nach der ZPO für Termingeschäfte?' zu *Sherson Lehman Hutton Inc. v TVB Treuhandgesellschaft für Vermögensverwaltung und Beteiligungen mbH* C89/91 [1993] ECR I-139 1995 *IPRax* 71
—— 'Anmerkung *Mainschiffahrts-Genossenschaft eG (MSG) v Les Gravières Rhénanes SARL* C-106/95' 1997 *JZ* 839
—— 'Rechtsvergleichung im Internationalen Privatrecht' 1997 *RabelsZ* 623
—— 'AGB-Klauseln über Gerichtsstand und Erfüllungsort im europäischen Zivilrechtsverkehr: Größere Gerechtigkeit ohne Parteivereinbarung?' zu *BGH* 28.3.199 und *OLG Celle* 1.11.1995 und *HansOLG* 8.3.1996 1997 *IPRax* 405
—— 'Europäische Vertrags-und Deliktsgerichtsstände für Seetransportschäden ("Weiche Birnen")' zu *Réunion européenne SA* 2000 *IPRax* 186
Koch, R. 'Der besondere Gerichtsstand des Klägers/Verkäufers im Anwendungsbereich des UN-Kaufrechts' zu *Custom Made Commercial Ltd v Stawa Metallbau GmbH* (C288/92) [1994] ECR I-2913 1996 *RIW* 379
—— 'Zur Vereinbarkeit des Erfordernisses "hinreichender Inlandsbezug des Rechtsstreits" gemäß §23 ZPO mit dem Gemeinschaftsrecht' 1997 *IPRax* 145
Koetsier, J. 'Arresting of ships in the Netherlands' 1996 *I J O S L* 240
Koh, P. 'Foreign judgments in ASEAN – a proposal' 1996 *ICLQ* 844
Kohl, A. 'Les modifications à la Convention C.E.E. du 27 septembre 1968' 1988 *JT* 151
Kohlegger, G. 'Ein Vergleich zwischen EuGVÜ und LGVÜ' 1999 *ÖJZ* 41
Kohler, C. 'Internationale Gerichtsstandsvereinbarungen: Liberalität und Rigorismus im EuGVÜ' 1983 *IPRax* 265
—— 'La jurisprudence de la Cour de Justice des Communautés européennes sur la Convention (CEE) du 28 septembre 1968 concernant la compétence judiciaire et l'exécution des décisions en matière civile et commerciale' 1983 *Ann dr. Louvain* 177
—— 'Practical Experience of the Brussels Jurisdiction and Judgments Convention in the Six original Contracting States' 1985 *ICLQ* 563
—— 'Pathologisches im EuGVÜ: Hinkende Gerichtsstandsvereinbarungen nach Art.17 Abs.3' 1986 *IPRax* 340
——/Winterhoff, K. 'Neuregelung der internationalen und örtlichen Zuständigkeit in Dänemark' 1988 *IPRax* 53
—— 'Die zweite Revision des Europäischen Gerichtsstands-und Vollstreckungsübereinkommens' 1991 *EuZW* 303
—— 'Gerichtsstandsklauseln in fremdsprachigen AGB: Das Clair-obscur des Art.17 EuGVÜ' zu *OLG Hamm* 10.10.1988 und *BGH* 31.10.1989 1991 *IPRax* 299
—— 'La Cour de Justice des Communautés européennes et le droit international privé' 1993–1994 Dr Intern Privé 71

Kondring, J. 'Die Bestimmung des sachlichen Anwendungsbereiches des EuGVÜ im Urteils-und Vollstreckungsverfahren' 1995 *EWS* 217

Koppenol-Laforce, M. 'Casenote: Dutch Supreme Court Art.12 Rome Convention' 1998 *NILR* 129

Kort, M. 'Zur europarechtlichen Zulässigkeit von Abkommen der Mitgliedstaaten untereinander' 1997 *JZ* 640

Kotuby, C. 'External competence of the European Community in the Hague Conference on private international law: Community harmonization and Worldwide unification' 2001 *NILR* 1

Kötz, H. 'Rechtsvereinheitlichung - Nutzen, Kosten, Methoden, Ziele' 1986 *RabelsZ* 1

Kourtis, V. 'Private International Law (Greece), Casenotes' 1993 *Rev Hellén Dr Int* 297

Koutaïssoff, P. 'Des mesures provisionelles et du séquestre dans les relations franco-suisses' 1937–38 *SJZ* 56

Kozyris, P. 'Multinational litigation and the notion of forum non conveniens as a remedy against jurisdictional abuse' 1992 *Rev Hellén Dr Int* 7

Kreuzer, K. 'Die *Shevill*-Entscheidung des EuGH: Abschaffung des Deliktsortsgerichtsstands des Art.5 Nr.3 EuGVÜ für ehrverletzende Streudelikte' 1997 *IPRax* 90

Krings, E. 'Réfexions au sujet de la prorogation de compétence territoriale et du for contractuel' 1978 *Rev. dr. intern. dr. privé* 78

Krohn, W. 'Casenote: Marc Rich' 1992 *Am J Int'l L* 134

Kröll, S. 'Gerichtsstandsvereinbarungen aufgrund Handelsbrauchs im Rahmen des GVÜ' 2000 *ZZP* 135

—— 'Kollidierende Allgemeine Geschäfts-bedingungen in internationalen Kaufverträgen' 2001 *RIW* 736

Kronke, H. 'Neue Entwicklungen im englischen Recht der internationalen Zuständigkeit' 1977 *RIW* 613

Kropholler, J. 'Neues europäisches Zivilprozeßrecht' 1986 *RIW* 929

—— 'Review Eickhoff' 1987 *ZZP* 352

Kruis, F. 'Anerkennung und Vollstreckung eines italiensichen Mahnbescheids (decreto ingiuntivo) in Deutschland' 2001 *IPRax* 56

Kubis, S. 'Gerichtspflicht durch Schweigen? – Prorogation, Erfüllungsortsvereinbarung und internationale Handelsbräuche' zu *Mainschiffahrts-Genossenschaft eG (MSG) v Les Gravières Rhénanes SARL* C-106/95 [1997] ECR I 911 1999 *IPRax* 10

—— 'Internationale Gläubigeranfechtung – vor und nach Inkrafttreten der Insolvenzrechtsreform' zu BGH 17.12.1998 und OLG Düsseldorf 25.8.1999 2000 *IPRax* 501

—— 'Gerichtsstand am Erfühlungsort: Erneute Enttäuschung aus Luxemburg' 2001 *ZeuP* 737

Kullmann, H. 'Die Rechtsprechung des *BGH* zum Produkthaftpflichtrecht in den Jahren 1989/90' 1991 *NJW* 675

Kulms, R. 'Qualifizierte faktische GmbH-Konzerne und Außenhaftung: (k)ein Fall fürArt.5 Nr.1 EuGVÜ' zu *OLG Frankfurt a.M.* 9.9.1999 2000 IPRax 525 2000 *IPRax* 488

Kur, A. 'International Hague Convention on Jurisdiction and Foreign Judgments; a way forward for I.P.?' [2002] *E.I.P.R.* 175

Kwaw, E. 'Sovereign Immunity and jurisdiction clauses in international lending: The Canadian Perspective' 1996 *BFLR* 27

Laforce, ME. 'Casenotes: Dumez France' 1990 *NILR* 233

Lagarde, P. 'Les limites objectives de la Convention de Rome (Conflits de lois, primauté du droit communautaire, rapports avec les autres conventions)' 1993 *Riv. dir. int. priv. e proc.* 33

Landau, J. 'The effect of multi-media communication on jurisdiction and enforcement' 1996 *Comm L* 58

Lando, O. 'Lex fori in Foro Proprio' 1995 *MJ* 359

—— 'Some issues relating to the law applicable to contractual obligations' 1996–7 *KCLJ* 55

Lane, S. 'Free movement of judgments within the EEC' 1986 *ICLQ* 629

Lasok, P. 'Casenote: *Reichert v Dresdener Bank*' 1990 *JIBL* N-131

Layton, A. 'The interpretation of the Brussels Convention by the European Court and English courts' 1992 *CJQ* 28

Le Clercq, H. 'De quelques abus dans l'application de la Convention franco-belge de 1899' 1909 *JDI* 416

Leclerc, F. 'Les chaînes de contrats en droit international privé' 1995 *JDI* 267

Ledoux, R. 'Les concessions de vente en Belgique et règles de compétence de la C.E.E.' 1975 *JT* 217

—— 'L'application de l'article 5,1 et 5 de la Convention de Bruxelles en matière de concession de vente' 1975 *JT* 581

Leipold, D. 'Zuständigkeitsvereinbarungen und rügelose Einlassung nach dem Europäischen Gerichtsstands- und Vollstreckungsübereinkommen' 1982 *IPRax* 222

Lenaerts, K. 'Belgian caselaw on the Brussels Convention' 14 (1989) *ELR* 453

—— 'Belgian caselaw on the Brussels Convention' 17 (1992) *ELR* 463

Lenenbach, M. 'Gerichtsstand des Sachzusammenhangs nach Art.21 EuGVÜ?' 1995 *EWS* 361

—— 'Antisuit Injunctions in England, Germany and the United States' 1998 *Loy. L.A. Int'l & Comp. L.J* 257

Lenhardt, I. 'Service of U.S. punitive damages complaint passes constitutional muster in Germany' (1996) 29 *Vanderbilt J Transnat L* 291

Lepa, M. 'Die Haftungsersetzung gemäß §§636, 637 RVO in der Rechtsprechung des Bundesgerichtshofs' 1985 *VersicherungsR* 8

Leslie, J. 'The jurisdiction of the English courts' 1996 *ICLit* 26

Leue, J. 'Die grenzüberschreitende „reine Mietzinsklage" beim Ferienhaus' zu *LG Offenburg* 16.11.1982 1983 *NJW* 1242

Leutner, G. 'Casenote: *BGH* 26.6.1997, Art.32 Eu GVÜ' 1998 *ZZP* 89

Levis, O. 'Der Wohnsitzbegriff im Schweizerisch-Deutschen Vollstreckungsabkommen' 1935/6 *SJZ* 62

—— 'Die Vollstreckung schweizerischer Urteile und das Deutsche Vollstreckungs-Mißbrauch-Gesetz' 1937/8 *SJZ* 373

Lewis, X. 'Casenote: *Mulox v Geels*' 1994 *ILJ* 262

Lindacher, W. 'Europäisches Zustellungsrecht' 2001 *ZZP* 179

Lindblom, H. 'Complex litigation – a comparative perspective' 1993 *CJQ* 33

Linke, H. 'Zur Berücksichtigung ausländischer Rechtshängigkeit eines Scheidungsverfahrens vor deutschen Gerichten' zu *OLG Frankfurt* 1.12.1981 1982 *IPRax* 229

—— 'EG-Gerichtsstands- und Vollstreckungsübereinkommen' 1985 *RIW* 1

—— 'Die Kontrolle ausländischer Versäumnisverfahren im Rahmen des EG-Gerichtsstands- und Vollstreckungsübereinkommens – Des Gutes zuviel?' 1986 *RIW* 409

—— 'Aspekte des Beklagtenschutzes im Exequaturverfahren' zu *OLG Köln* 8.12.1989 1991 *IPRax* 92

—— 'EG-Gerichtsstands- und Vollstreckungsübereinkommen' 1991 *RIW* 5 Beilage, 1

—— 'Verbundzuständigkeit – anderweitige Rechtshängigkeit – res iudicata' zu *OLG München* 26.6.1991 1992 *IPRax* 159

—— 'Zur Rechtzeitigkeit fiktiver Zustellungen im Sinne von Art.27 Nr.2 EuGVÜ' zu *BGH* 2.10.1991 1993 *IPRax* 295

—— 'Anderweitige Rechtshängigkeit im Ausland und inländischer Justizgewährungsanspruch' zu *BGH* 12.2.1992 1994 *IPRax* 17

—— 'Zur grenzüberschreitenden Wirkung konkursbedingter Vollstreckungsbeschränkungen, insbesondere nach Art.169 des französischen Insolvenzgesetzes vom 25.1.1985' zu *Eric Coursier v Fortis Bank and Martine Coursier, née Bellami* (C-267/97) [1999] ECR I – 2543 2000 *IPRax* 8

Lipstein, K. 'Enforcement of judgments under the Jurisdiction and Judgments Convention: safeguards' 1987 *ICLQ* 873

Lloyd, K. 'Developments in European jurisdiction – part one and two' 1994 *NLJ* (Practitioner) 1482

Loimer, B. 'Grundsätzliches zur grenzüberschreitenden Durchsetzung von zivilrechtlich begründeten Honoraransprüchen gegen den eigenen Mandanten nach EuGVÜ bzw LGVÜ' 1996 *AnwBl* 661

Looschelders, D. 'Der Klägergerichtsstand am Wohnsitz des Versicherungsnehmers nach Art.8 Abs.1 Nr.2 EuGVÜ' zu *LG Stuttgart* 9.2.1996 1998 *IPRax* 86

Lorenz, W. 'Kollisionsrecht des Verbraucherschutzes: Anwendbares Recht und internationale Zuständigkeit' zu *BGH* 26.10.1993 1994 *IPRax* 429

Löwe, W. 'Das neue Recht der Gerichtsstandsvereinbarung' 1974 *NJW* 473

Lucchini, A. 'Questioni di diritto intertemporale nella Convenzione di Lugano del 16 settembre 1988' 1996 *Riv. dir. int. priv. e proc.* 67

Lundstedt, L. 'Jurisdiction and the principle of territoriality in intellectual property law: Has the pendulum swung too far in the other direction?' 2001 *IIC* 124

Lupoi, M. 'La competenza in materia contrattuale nella convenzione di Bruxelles del 27 settembre 1968' 1994 *Riv trim dir & proc civ* 1263

—— 'Convenzione di Bruxelles ed esercizio discrezionale della giurisdizione' 1995 *Riv trim dir & proc civ* 997

—— 'Esercizio discrezionale della giurisdizione: "forum (non) conveniens" ed altro ancora' 1996 *Riv trim dir & proc civ* 601

—— 'Esercizio discrezionale della giurisdizione: "forum (non) conveniens" ed altro ancora: parte seconda' 1996 *Riv trim dir & proc civ* 875

—— 'Convenzione di Bruxelles del 1968 e conflitti di giurisdizioni tra Stati membri e Stati terzi' 1998 *Riv trim dir & proc civ* 965

—— 'Litispendenza internazionale e riconoscimiento delle sentenze straniere in Italia: due normative allo specchio' 1998 *Riv trim dir & proc civ* 1215

Luther, G. 'Zur Auslegung von Art.39 des europäischen Gerichtsstands- und Vollstreckungsübereinkommens von 1968' zu *OLG Turin* 18.4.1980 1982 *IPRax* 120

—— 'Die Grenzen der Sperrwirkung einer ausländischen Rechtshängigkeit' zu *BGH* 26.1.1983 1984 *IPRax* 141

Lutz, P. 'Auslegung der Art. 13 ff. EuGVÜ auf Realkredite' 1999 *RIW* 827

Lutz, R. 'Bibliography: Enforcement of Foreign Judgments, Part I' 1993 *Int'l Law* 471

—— 'Bibliography: Enforcement of foreign judgments, Part II' 1993 *Int'l Law* 1029

Macdonald, C. 'Declining of Jurisdiction- Brussels Convention Article 21 – When English court seised' 1994 *Int Mar L* 19

—— 'Casenote: The Indian Grace' 1994 *Int Mar L* 50

—— 'Casenote: *Atlas Shipping Agency v Suisse Atlantique*' 1995 *Int Mar L* 141

—— 'Collision in Holland – English court first seised – *The Xin Yang*' 1996 *Int Mar L* 183

—— 'Casenote: The Owners of the Ship Kapitan Shvetsov: Supreme Court, HK' 1997 *Int Mar L* 18

Macfarlane, N. 'Limits to forum shopping in European cases: *Coin Controls Ltd. v Suzo International*' 1997 *ICLit* 22

MacGillavry, O. 'Casenote Scherrens' 1988 *JT* 714

MacMillan, C. 'Casenote: *Webb v Webb*' 1996 *Conv* 125

Maggione, M. 'Le prime pronunce interpretative della corte comunitaria sulla convenzione di Bruxelles del 1968 relativa alla competenza giurisdizionale e all'esecuzione delle sentenze' 1977 *Rivista di diritto civile* 667

Maher, G. 'Casenote: Kleinwort Benson, HL' 1998 *Jur Rev* 131

—— and Rodger, B. 'Provisional and Protective remedies: the British experience of the Brussels Convention' 1999 *ICLQ* 302

Maier, H. 'A Hague Conference Judgments Convention and United States Courts: a problem and a possibility' 1998 *Alb L R* 1207

Majoros, F. 'A propos de la procédure simplifiée de l'exequatur' 1978 *Rev. crit.* 45

—— 'Konflikte zwischen Staatsvertägen auf dem Gebiete des Privatrechts' 1982 *RabelsZ* 84

Majumdar, S. Casenote: '*Agnew and ors v Lansförsäkringsbolagens AB*' [2000] *IJIL* 345

Malatesta, A. 'Litispendenzia e riconoscibilità di sentenze nella convenzione di Bruxelles del 1968' 1994 *Riv. dir. int. priv. e proc.* 511

Malaure, M. 'Le référé-concurrence' 1993 *JCP., Doctr.* 3637

Malaurie, P. 'Droit comparé et droit international privé France' 1984 *Jour Soc Légis Comp* 341

Mankowski, P. 'Casenote The Tatry' 1996 *EWS* 301

—— 'Zu einigen internationalprivat-und internationalprozeßrechtlichen Aspekten bei Börsentermingeschäften' zu *OLG Düsseldorf* 26.5.1995 u. *OLG Düsseldorf* 8.3.1996 1996 *RIW* 1001

—— 'Casenote: Danvaern Production C-341/93' 1996 *ZZP* 373

—— 'Zur Auslegung des Art.13 EuGVÜ' 1997 *RIW* 990

—— 'Casenote: *Francesco Benincasa v Dentalkit Srl* (C-269/95) [1997] ECR I-3767' 1998 *Juristen-Zeitung* 896

—— 'Die österreichischen Gerichtsstände der Streitgenossenschaft, des Vermögens und der inländischen Vertretung mit Blick auf das Lugano-Übereinkommen' zu *OGH* 13.3.1996 1998 *IPRax* 122

Mankowski, P. 'Fiscus non conveniens – oder: Einzug der Lehre vom forum non conveniens in das deutsche Recht der Prozeßkostenhilfe' zu *OLG Celle* 5.1.1998 1999 *IPRax* 155

—— 'Der gewöhnliche Arbeitsort im Internationalen Privat-und Prozeßrecht' zu *Petrus Wilhelmus Rutten v Cross Medical Ltd* C383/95 1999 *IPRax* 332

—— 'Im Dschungel der für die Vollstreckbarerklärung ausländischer Unterhaltsentscheidungen einschlägigen Abkommen und ihrer Ausführungsgesetze' zu *OLG Rostock* 9.11.1998 2000 *IPRax* 188

—— 'Keine örtliche Ersatzzuständigkeit der Hauptsachegerichte für Verbrauchersachen unter dem EuGVÜ – oder: Tod einer Theorie in Berlin' zu *KG* 13.1.2000 2001 *IPRax* 33

Mansel, H-P. 'Vollstreckung eines französischen Garantieurteils bei gesellschaftsrechtlicher Rechtsnachfolge und andere vollstreckungsrechtliche Fragen des EuGVÜ' zu *HansOLG Hamburg* 5.8.1993 1995 *IPRax* 362

—— 'Grenzüberschreitende Prozeßfürungsverbote (antisuit injunctions) und Zustellungsverweigerung *OLG Düsseldorf* 1996 *EuZW* 335

—— 'Gerichtsstandsvereinbarungen und Ausschluß der Streitverkündung durch Prozeßvertrag' 1996 *ZZP* 61

Marasinghe, L. 'International Litigation: Choice of forum' 1993 *WALR* 264

Margolis, R. 'Staying an action because the foreign law is ambiguous: The Planeta' 1994 *LMCLQ* 30

Marino, D. 'European Parliament and Council Draft Directive on Electronic Commerce' [2000] *C.T.L.R.* 45

Markesinis, B. 'Caparo & Murphy: How two recent decisions of the House of Lords look from the other side of the Channel' 1993 *ERPL* 201

—— 'Judicial style and judicial reasoning in England and Germany' 2000 *CLJ* 294

Markus, A. 'Der schweizerische Vorbehalt nach Protokoll Nr.1 Lugano-Übereinkommen: Vollstreckungsaufschub oder Vollstreckungshindernis?' (1999) 135 *ZBJV* 57

—— 'Revidierte Übereinkommen von Brüssel und Lugano: Zu den Hauptpunkten' 1999 *SZW* 205

Marmisse, A. & Wilderspin, M. 'Le régime jurisprudentiel des mesures provisiores à la lumière des arrêts *Van Uden* et *Mietz*' 1999 *Rev. crit.* 669

Martin, G. 'La responsabilité civile pour les dommages à l'environnement et la Convention de Lugano' 1994 *R J E* 121

Martin, M. 'Enforcement of foreign judgments in Spain' 1994–5 *Litigation* 194

Martinez, MC. 'Fundamentos y limites del forum shopping: modelos europeo y angloamericano' 1998 *Riv. dir. int. priv. e proc.* 521

Martiny, D. 'Autonome und einheitliche Auslegung im Europäischen Internationalen Zivilprozeßrecht' 1981 *RabelsZ* 427

Martiny, D. 'Recognition and Enforcement of Foreign Money judgments in the Federal Republic of Germany' 1987 *Am J Comp L* 721

—— 'Der Beitritt Polens zum Luganer Übereinkommen' 2001 *IPRax* 29

Mathers, I. 'The Brussels Convention of 1968: its implementation in the United Kingdom' 1983 *YEL* 49

Masia, EF. 'Convención de Bruselas. Interpretación del artículo 5.1.' 1995 *Rev Gen Der* 7129

—— 'Las relaciones entre el Convenio de Bruselas de 1968 y las Convenciones Internacionales en materias particulares: aplicación de los articulos 21 y 22 relativos a la litispendencia y a la conexidad' 1995 *Rev Gen Der* 13079

Matscher, F. 'Vollstreckung im Auslandsverkehr von vorläufig vollstreckbaren Entscheidungen und von Maßnahmen des provisorischen Rechtsschutzes' 1982 *ZZP* 170

—— 'Vollstreckung im Auslandsverkehr von vorläufig vollstreckbaren Entscheidungen und von Maßnahmen des provisorischen Rechtsschutzes' 1982 *ZZP* 170

—— 'Walder, U. 'Grundfragen der Anerkennung und Vollstreckung ausländischer Entscheidungen in Zivilsachen aus österreichischer Sicht' 1990 *ZZP* 294

—— 'Die Indikationentheorie an der Schwelle der Integration des österreichischen in das europäische Zivilprozeßrecht' 1996 *JBl* 277

—— 'Sprache der Auslandszustellung und Art.6 EMRK' zu *OGH* 16.6.1998 1999 *IPRax* 274

—— 'Der verfahrensrechtliche ordre public im Spannungsfeld von EMKR und Gemeinschaftsrecht' 2001 *IPRax* 428

Matthews, P. 'Security for costs and European Law' 1994 *LMCLQ* 454

—— 'Provisional and protective measures in England and Ireland at common law and under the conventions: a comparative study' 1995 *CJQ* 190

Matthias, J. 'Zur isolierten Prorogation nach Art.17 Abs.1 LugÜ' zu *OLG Hamm* 18.9.1997 1999 *IPRax* 226

Mattick, R. 'English court declines jurisdiction over misrepresentation and non-disclosure claim' 1995 *Int ILR* 67

Mauro, J. 'Quand les traducteurs vont un peu vite – Incompétence territoriale en France et Convention de Bruxelles sur la compétence de l'exécution des jugements' 1975 *Gaz. Pal., Doctr.*, p.370

—— 'De quelques aspects mathématiques de la convention de Bruxelles sur la compétence et l'exécution des jugements' 1987 *Gaz. Pal., Doctr.*, 146

Mayr, P. 'Das "Europäische Zivilprozeßrecht" und Österreich' 1997 *ÖJZ* 847

Mayss, A. 'Casenote: *Lynch v Halifax Building Society and Royal Bank of Scotland*: Art.16(1)' 1996 *Consumer Law Journal* CS59

McAuley, E. 'An introduction to the Jurisdiction of Courts and Enforcement of Judgments (European Communities) Act 1988' 1989 *GILSI* 94

McCaffrey, E. 'The Lugano and San Sebastian Conventions: General Effects' 1992 *CJQ* 12

McCarthy, E. 2Networking in cyberspace: electronic defamation and the potential for international forum shopping' 1995 *U of Pa J Int'l BL* 527

McClellan, A. 'Choice of Jurisdiction Clauses under the EEC Judgments Convention' 1994 *JBL* 445

McEvoy, T. 'The implication for Australia of the Brussels Convention on Jurisdiction and the Enforcement of Judgments in Civil and Commercial Matters' 1994 *Aust L J* 576

McGrath, P. '*Kleinwort Benson v Glasgow City Council*: A simple point of jurisdiction' 1999 *CJQ* 41

McIntosh, D. 'Faced by Counsel in insurance cases' 1993 *Def Couns J* 194

McKenzie, D. 'The EC Convention on Insolvency Proceedings' 1996 *ERPL* 181

McKie, D, 'The Arrest Convention bites back? Arrest confers merits jurisdiction despite exclusive jurisdiction clause' 1998 *I J O S L* 185

McLachlan, C. 'The jurisdictional limits of disclosure orders in transnational fraud litigation' 1998 *ICLQ* 3

Meibom, W. 'Cross-border injunctions in international patent infringement proceedings' 1997 *EIPR* 469

Mendes, E. 'The troublesome workings of the Judgments Convention of the European Economic Community' 1980 *Vanderbilt J Transnat'l L* 75

Mennicke, P. 'Berücksichtigung einer Schutzschrift des Antragsgegners bei der Entscheidung über die Vollstreckbarerklärung nach EuGVÜ' zu *LG Darmstadt* 8.12.1998 2000 *IPRax* 294

—— 'Vollziehung einer Unterlassungsverfügung durch Zustellung in einem anderen Vertragsstaat des EuGVÜ' zu *KG* 4.9.1998 2001 *IPRax* 202

Mennie, A. 'The Brussels Convention and the Scottish courts' discretion to decline jurisdiction' 1989 *Jur Rev* 150

Meo, F. 'Reform des italienischen Internationalen Privatrechts' 1996 *ZfRV* 46

Mercier, P. 'Le projet de Convention du Marché Commun sur la procédure civile internationale et les États tiers' 1967 *Cahiers dr. europ* 367

—— 'La Convention de la C.E.E sur la compétence et l'exécution des jugements en matière civile et commerciale ou une étape vers la fedération européenne' 1969–70 *Riv. dir. intern.* 89

Merkelbach, R. 'La Convention de Lugano sur la compétence judiciaire et l'exécution des décisions en matière civile et commerciale: son importance pour les entreprises d'assurances' 1994 *Rev gén ass terr* 45

Metzger, E. 'Die Ausschließlichkeit des gewählten Gerichtsstands (Art.17 EuGVÜ) aus französischer Sicht' 1984 *IPRax* 331

Meyer, J. 'Europäisches Übereinkommen über die Zustellung gerichtlicher und außergerichtlicher Schriftstücke in Zivil-und Handelssachen in den Mitgliedstaaten der Europäischen Union' 1997 *IPRax* 401

Meyer, S. 'Vollstreckung spanischer Gerichtsentscheidungen in der Bundesrepublik vor dem Hintergrund des deutsch-spanischen Vollstreckungsvertrages' 1991 *IPRax* 292

Mezger, E. 'Drei Jahre EG-Zuständigkeits-und Vollstreckungsübereinkommen in Frankreich' 1976 *RIW/AWD* 345

—— 'Gerichtsstands- und andere Klauseln im Geschäftsverkehr mit Frankreich 1974' *RIW/AWD* 377

—— 'L'unification du lieu du paiement des obligations monétaires' 1967 *Clunet* 584

—— 'Anerkennung deutscher Vaterschafts- und Unterhaltsurteile in Frankreich' 1981 *IPRax* 103

—— 'Das Haager Übereinkommen vom 15.11.1965 als Hindernis der Vollstreckung von Versäumnisurteilen (zu einem Urteil des französischen Kassationshofs vom 16.12.1980)' 1982 *IPRax* 30

—— 'Die Ausschließlichkeit des gewählten Gerichtsstands (Art.17 EuGVÜ) aus französisher Sicht' 1984 *IPRax* 331

—— 'Umrechnung einer Verurteilung in ausländischer Währung zum Zwecke der Vollsreckung nach dem EuGVÜ im Inland' zu *BGH* 21.2.1985 1986 *IPRax* 142

—— 'Nochmals: Zur Umrechnung bei Vollstreckung eines auf ausländische Währung lautenden Urteils' zu *OLG Karlsruhe* 29.1.1986 u. *BGH* 10.7.1986 1987 *IPRax* 146

—— 'Zur Bestimmung des Erfüllungsorts im Sinne von Art.5 Nr.1 EuGVÜ bei einem gegenseitigen Vertrag' zu *LG Kaiserslautern* 5.5.1987 1987 *IPRax* 346

Mezger, M. 'Les grandes lignes de la Convention du 9 octobre 1978' 1980 *Dr Intern Privé* 15

Michinel Álvarez, MA. 'Sobre la interpretación del artículo 6.3 del Convenio de Bruselas de 27 de septiembre de 1968' 1997 *REDI* 47

Mildred, M. 'The use of the Brussels Convention in Group Actions' 1996 *JPIL* 121

Milionis, A. 'Praxis der Vollstreckung deutscher Titel in Griechenland nach dem EuGVÜ' 1991 *RIW* 100

Miner, R. 'The reception of foreign law in the US federal courts' 1995 *Am J Comp L* 581

Minor, J. 'The Lugano Convention: Some Problems of Interpretation' 1990 *CMLRev.* 507

Moccia, L. 'La ratifica italiana della convenzione di Lugano' 1993 *Riv trim dir & proc civ* 261

Mok, M. 'The Interpretation by the European Court of Justice of Special Conventions concluded between the Member States' 1971 *CMLRev.* 485

Moons, E. 'Zustellung im deutsch-belgischen Rechtsverkehr' 1989 *RIW* 903

Moore, C. 'Our fragmented federation: forum bias and forum shopping in Australia' 1994 *Federal Law Review* 171

Morse, CGJ. 'Forum-Selection clauses - EEC Style' 1989 *Afri J Int'l Comp L* 539

—— 'International Shoe v Brussels and Lugano: principles and pitfalls in the law of personal jurisdiction' 1995 *U C Davis L R* 999

Mosconi, F. 'Un confronto tra la disciplina del riconoscimento e dell'esecuzione delle decisioni straniere nei recenti regolamenti comunitari' 2001 *Riv. dir. int. priv. e proc.* 545

Moss, GC. 'Performance of obligations as the basis of jurisdiction and choice of law (Lugano and Brussels Conventions Article 5(1) and Rome Convention Article 4) 2000 *Nordic Journal of International Law* 379

Moura Ramos, RM. 'La Convention de Bruxelles après la Convention de San Sebastian concernant l'adhésion du Portugal et de l'Espagne' 1991 *Rev Hellén Dr Int* 165

—— 'Public policy in the framework of the Brussels Convention' 2000 *Yearbook of Private International Law* 25

Mourre, A. 'La compétence juridictionnelle dans les litiges relatifs à la rupture d'un contrat de concession exclusive' 1992 *Gaz. Pal., Chron.* 920

—— 'À propos de l'application de l'art.5–1 de la Convention de Bruxelles aux litiges nés de la rupture d'un contrat de représentation' 1994 *Gaz. Pal., Doctr.*, 849

—— 'Trente ans après la Convention de Bruxelles' 1999 *Rev. dr. Aff. Intern* 385

Mousseron, J-M. 'Cross-Border Injunctions – a French perspective' 1998 *IIC* 884

Moustaira, E. 'Rules for declining to exercise jurisdiction in civil and commercial matters' 1994 *Rev Hellén Dr Int* 173

Muchlinski, P. 'Corporations in international litigation: Problems of jurisdiction and the United Kingdom asbestos cases' 2001 *ICLQ* 1

Müller, P. 'Sind US-amerikanische Punitive-damages-Urteile in Deutschland vollstreckbar?' 2001 *Der Betrieb* 83

Münch, J. 'Ausländische Tenorierungsgewohnheiten kontra inländische Bestimmtheitsanforderungen' 1989 *RIW* 18

Nacimiento, P. 'The application of the Lugano Convention in France' 1996 *ICLit* 33

Nadelmann, K. 'The United States of America and Agreements on reciprocal enforcement of foreign judgments' 1 *Ned. Tidj. Int. Recht* 156 (1954)

—— 'Ignored State Interests: The federal government and international efforts to unify rules of private law' 102 *Uni. Pen. L. Rev.* 323 (1954)

—— 'Non-recognition of American money judgments abroad and what to do about it' 1957 *Iowa L R* 236

—— 'Common Market assimilation of laws and the outer world' 1964 *Am J Int'l L* 724

—— 'The Extraordinary Session of the Hague Conference on Private International Law' 1966 *Am J Int'l L* 803

—— 'Jurisdictionally improper fora in Treaties on recognition of judgments: The Common Market draft' 1967 *Colum L R* 995

—— 'The Common Market Judgments Convention and a Hague Conference Recommendation: what steps next?' 1969 *Harvard LR* 1282

Nagel, B. 'Internationales Produkthaftungsrecht im transatlantischen Konflikt der Rechtsordnungen' 2001 *Der Betrieb* 1075

Nagel, H. 'Die gegenseitige Anerkennung und Vollstreckung gerichtlicher Urteile in der Europäischen Wirtschaftsgemeinschaft' 1960 *NJW* 985

—— 'Der Umrechnungszeitpunkt bei Vollstreckung eines französischen Urteils' zu *BGH* 28.6.1984 1985 *IPRax* 83

Naschitz, P. 'Forum non conveniens in Israel, England, and the United States: a comparative note' 1988 *JMLC* 551

Nassall, W. 'Verbraucherschutz durch europäisches Verfahrensrecht – Anmerkungen zum Vorlagebeschluß des *BGH* WM 1993, 1215' 1993 *WM* 1950

Neumann, S. 'Ein Lehrstück zu Art.13 EuGVÜ?' zu Cour d'appel de Colmar 24.2.1999 2001 *IPRax* 257

Newman, L and Burrows, M. 'Proposed Hague Convention on Judgments' 1998 *New York LJ* 3

Newton, J. 'Forum non conveniens in Europe (again)' 1997 *LMCLQ* 337

Nguyen, KD. 'Invisibly radiated: Federalism principles and the proposed Hague Convention on jurisdiction and foreign judgments' 28 *Hastings Constitutional Law Quarterly* 145 (2001)

Ngwasiri, C. 'The role of the judge in French civil proceedings' 1990 *CJQ* 167

—— 'Pre-trial civil proceedings in England and France: a comparative study' 1991 *CJQ* 289

Nicolaidis, S. 'Greek courts' decisions on jurisdiction under the Brussels Convention' 1996 *I J O S L* 47

Niemeyer, F. 'Die Vollstreckung deutscher Gerichtsentscheidungen in Spanien im Hinblick auf das EuGVÜ' 1992 *IPRax* 265

Normand, J. 'Juridiction Arbitrage et référé provision' 1985 *Rev trim dr civ* 208

—— 'La compétence territoriale en matière contractuelle. Le concept de "livraison effective de la chose"' 1987 *Rev trim dr civ* 395

—— 'Jurisprudence française en matière de droit international privé' 1987 *Rev trim dr civ* 794

North, P. 'The Brussels Convention and Forum non Conveniens' 1992 *IPRax* 183

Nourissat, C. 'Interprétation de la notion d'"ordre public de l'État requis" visée à l'article 27, point 1, de la Convention de Bruxelles du 27 septembre 1968' 2001 *JCP*, II, 10607

Novy, D. 'Article 5(1) of the Brussels Convention' (2000) 1 *Hibernian Law Journal* 69

Nussbaum, A. 'Public policy and the political crisis in the conflict of laws' (1940) 49 *Yale LJ* 1027

Nuyts, A. 'L'application des lois de police dans l'espace' 1999 *Rev. crit.* 31

Nygh, P. 'Choice-of-law rules and forum shopping in Australia' 1995 *South Carolina Law Review* 899

Oberhammer, P. 'Internationale Gerichtsstandsvereinbarungen: Konkurrierende oder ausschließliche Zuständigkeit?' 1997 *JBl* 434

—— 'Zwangsarbeiter vor deutschen Gerichten' zu LG Stuttgart 24.11.1999 2001 *IPRax* 211

Oberto, G. 'La gestion de l'urgence dans le procès civil italien' 2001 *Rev Int dr Comparé* 709

O'Connor, L. 'Research Essay' 1995 *Cornell Int'l L J* 417

Odeke, A. 'The EC conflict of laws regime for insurance contracts' 1996 *Professional Negligence* 7

Oliver, G. 'Future interpretations of Article 17 of the Convention on Jurisdiction and the Enforcement of Judgments in the European Communities' 1985 *Cornell LR* 289

Omar, P. 'The special status of consumer and employment contracts in the Brussels Convention' 1996 *EBLR* 90

Ondo, G. 'Gerichtsstandsklauseln, Rechtswahl und Schidsgerichtsbarkeit in Rückversicherungsverträgen' 1995 *SchweizVZ* 3

Ong, C. 'The ASEAN Free Trade Area and the necessity for the creation of a Legal Mechanism for resolving private disputes of an international nature' 1998 *JBL* 213

Otte, K. 'Beschränkte Nachprüfbarkeit internationaler Zuständigkeit im Arrestverfahren' 1991 *ZIP* 1048

—— 'The GROTIUS Program: Proposals for amending Article 21 and 22 of the Brussels Convention' 2000 *ERPL* 257

—— 'Vertragspflichten nach Seefrachtrecht (Haager-Visby-Regeln) – gerichtsstandsweisende Kraft für Art.5 Nr.1 EuGVÜ?' 2002 *IPRax* 132

Ottomann, R. 'Der Arrest' 1996 *ZschweizR* 241

Paanila, R. 'Anerkennungsantrag nach dem Lugano-Übereinkommen – Versagungsgrund nach Art.27 Nr.2 LugÜ' 1999 *RIW* 358

Pabst, H. 'Das internationale Zivilprozeßrecht des Mercosur' 1999 *IPRax* 76

Padberg, M. 'When is a bill of lading holder bound by charterparty terms? Principals and agents' 1999 *I J O S L* 143

Paipetis, A. 'Recognition of foreign arbitration and foreign jurisdiction clauses' 1998 *I J O S L* 297

Palomba, M. 'Arbitration and the Brussels and Lugano Conventions' 1996 *ICLit* 36

Pålsson, L. 'The Institute of Lis pendens in international civil procedure' 1970 *Scandinavian Studies in Law* 59

—— 'The Lugano Convention in Sweden' 1999 *IPRax* 52

Panagopoulos, G. 'Jurisdiction in relation to a contract split between two States' 2000 *LMCLQ* 150

Pauckstadt, U. 'Zur Vollstreckbarerkäurng schweizerischer Kostenentscheidungen' zu *OLG Frankfurt* 12.1.1983 1984 *IPRax* 17

Pearl, S. 'Forum shopping in the EEC' 1987 *IBL* 391

Pearson, N. 'Reconciling conflicting provisions of the Brussels Convention' 1998 *Sol J* 624

Peel, E. 'Recognition and Enforcement under the Brussels Convention' 1994 *LQR* 386

—— 'Non-admissibility and Restitution in the European Court of Justice' 1996 *LMCLQ* 8

—— 'Jurisdiction over restitutionary claims' 1998 *LMCLQ* 22

—— 'Exclusive jurisdiction agreements: purity and pragmatism in the conflict of laws' 1998 *LMCLQ* 182

—— 'The Brussels Convention' 1998 *YEL* 689

Pellis, L. 'The Lugano Convention: Protocols and Declarations' 1990 *NILR* 390

—— 'All roads lead to Brussels: Towards a Uniform European Civil Procedure' 1990 *NILR* 372

—— 'The Lugano Convention: Recognition and enforcement provisions' 1990 *NILR* 387

—— 'Purpose of amendments the Brussels Convention 1968' 1990 *NILR* 391

Perrot, R. 'Voies d'exécution et mesures provisoires' 1987 *Rev trim dr civ* 155

Peruzzetto, S. 'L'ordre public international en droit communautaire: Eco Swiss China' 2000 *JDI* 299

Pesce, A. 'Le Convenzioni internazionali in materie particolari ed il conflitto con la Convenzione di Bruxelles 27 settembre 1968 e con la convenzione di Lugano 19 settembre 1988 in materia di litispendenza' 1993 *Dir mar* 675

—— 'Die Reform des italienischen Internationalen Privat-und Verfahrensrechts' 1995 *RIW* 977

Pester, I. 'Reinsurance, Good faith and Art.5(1) of the Brussels Convention' 2000 *LMCLQ* 289

Peter, A. 'Ersatz von Inkassokosten im grenzüberschreitenden Rechtsverkehr nach UN-Kaufrecht?' zu *AG Berlin-Tiergarten* 13.3.1997 1999 *IPRax* 159

Peterson, C. 'Choice of law and forum clauses and the recognition of foreign country judgments revisited through the Lloyd's of London cases' (2000) 60 *Louisiana Law Review* 1259

Petrochilos, G. 'Arbitration and interim measures: in the twilight of the Brussels Convention' 2000 *LMCLQ* 99

Peukert, W. 'Verfahrensgarantien und Zivilprozeß (Art.6 EMRK)' 1999 *RabelsZ* 600

Pfeiffer, T. 'BGH –Rechtsprechung aktuell: Internationales Zivilprozeßrecht' 1994 *NJW* 1634

—— 'BGH –Rechtsprechung aktuell: Internationales Zivilprozeßrecht' 1994 *NJW* 1454

—— 'Halbseitig fakultative Gerichtsstandsvereinbarungen in stillschweigend vereinbarten AGB?' zu *OLG Frankfuhrt* 17.10.1995 1998 *IPRax* 17

Pfund, P. 'The Hague Conference celebrates its 100th Anniversary' 1993 *Tex Int'l L J* 531

Philip, A. 'Set-Offs and counterclaims under the Brussels Convention: Danværn Production' 1997 *IPRax* 97

Piantino, Y. 'Switzerland's Treatment of U.S. Money Judgments' 1998 *Am J Comp L* 181

Picone, P. 'La riforma italiana del diritto internazionale privato' 1996 *REDI* 9

Piekenbrock, A. 'Ordre-public-Verstoß durch Inanspruchnahme exorbitanter Zuständigkeit und Verurteilung im strafrechtlichen Abwesenheitsverfahren?' zu *BGH* 4.12.1997 1998 *IPRax* 177

—— 'Kann der Ausschluß des ordre public in Art.28 Abs.3 EuGVÜ ausnahmlos gelten?' 2000 *IPRax* 364

Pieri, S. 'The 1968 Brussels Convention: The evolution of the text and the case law of the Court of Justice over the last four years' 1992 *CMLRev.* 537

Piltz, B. 'Die Zuständigkeitsordnung nach dem EWG- Gerichtsstands- und Vollstreckungsübereinkommen' 1979 *NJW* 1071

—— 'Der Gerichtsstand des Erfüllungsortes nach dem EuGVÜ' 1981 *NJW* 1876

—— 'Vom EuGVÜ zur Brüssel-I-Verordnung' 2002 *NJW* 789

Pirrung, J. 'Vom Überraschungseffekt – Voraussetzungen der Sicherungsvollstreckung nach Art.39 GVÜ' zu *LG Stuttgart* 28.3.1988 1989 *IPRax* 18

Pittam, N. 'Casenote: *SISRO v Ampersand*' 1995 *ICLit* 43

Pocar, F. 'Jurisdiction and the Enforcement of judgments under the EC Convention of 1968' 1978 *RabelsZ* 405

—— 'Linee di tendenza della Convenzione de Bruxelles sulla giurisdizione e l'esecuzione delle sentenze dopo l'adesione di nuovi stati' 1990 *Riv. dir. int. priv. e proc.* 5

—— 'Das neue italiensiche Internationale Privatrecht' 1997 *IPRax* 145

—— 'La giurisdizione sulle controversie marittime nello sviluppo della convenzione di Bruxelles del 1968' 1999 *Dir mar* 183

Polak, M. 'Casenote: *Powell Duffryn Plc v Petereit*' 1993 *CMLRev.* 406

Poulain, B. 'L'opposabilité de la clause attributive de juridiction au porteur – communautaire? – du connaissement' 2001 *Unif. L. Rev.* 649

Powell, J. 'Brussels and Lugano Conventions: What they are, what they do' 1994 *Def Couns J* 371

Powell, M. 'Putting the e- in Brussels and Rome' [1999] *ICCLR* 361

Prinzing, G. 'Internationale Gerichtsstandsvereinbarung nach §38 ZPO' zu *OLG Bamberg* 22.9.1988 1990 *IPRax* 83

Proctor, C. 'Breach of international payment obligations, Part 1' 1998 *BJIB & FL* 146

Prütting, H. 'Probleme des europäischen Vollstreckungsrechts' zu *BGH* 13.4.1983 und *BGH* 16.5.1983 1985 *IPRax* 137

Pryles, M. 'Liberalising the rule on staying actions – towards the doctrine of forum non conveniens' 1978 *Aust L J* 678

Pryles, M. 'Forum non conveniens – the next chapter' 1991 *Aust L J* 442

Pulkowski, F. 'Internationale Zuständigkeit und anwendbares Recht bei Streitigkeiten aus grenzüberschreitenden Bauverträgen' 2001 *IPRax* 306

Purves, R. 'Article 4 of the Rome Convention and the law applicable to international contracts of insurance and reinsurance' 1997 *Int J IL* 138

Quadri, R. 'Il forum solutionis e la Convenzione italo-svizzera sull'esecuzione delle sentenze' 1937 *Riv. dir. intern.* 88

Queirolo, I. 'Art.17 della Convenzione di Bruxelles e clausola attributiva di competenza contenuta in uno statuo societario' 1993 *Riv. dir. int. priv. e proc.* 69

—— 'Forum non conveniens e Convenzione di Bruxelles: un rapporto possibile?' 1996 *Riv. dir. int. priv. e proc.* 763

—— 'Accordi sulla competenza giurisdiziionale: riflessioni a margine di alcune recenti decisioni' 2001 *Il Diritto Marittimo* 32

Querzola, L. 'Tutela cautelare e convenzione di Bruxelles nell'esperienza della Corte di giustizia delle Comunità europee' 2000 *Riv trim dir & proc civ* 805

Rabe, D. 'Casenote: *BGH* Art.23 ZPO' 1996 *Int Mar L* 154

Rabkin, J. 'Universal justice: the role of federal courts in international litigation' 1995 *Colum L R* 2120

Radtke, C. 'L'exécution des décisions exécutoires par provision en vertu de la Convention de Bruxelles du 27 septembre 1968' 1988 *Gaz. Pal., Doctr.* 216

Rasir, R. 'L'Europe judiciare entre l'efficacité et le droit de défense' 1995 *JT* 417

Rasmussen, H. 'A New Generation of Community Law? Reflections on the handling by the Court of Justice of the Protocol of 1971 relating to the Interpretation of the Brussels Convention on Jurisdiction and Enforcement of Judgments' 1978 *CMLRev.* 249

Ratliff, J. 'Civil procedure in Germany' 1983 *CJQ* 257

Rau, M. 'Schadenersatzklagen wegen extraterritorial begangener Menschenrechtsverletzungen: der US-amerikanische Alien Tort Claims Act' 2000 *IPRax* 558

Rauscher, T. 'Rechtshängigkeit nach dem EuGVÜ' zu *OLG München* 31.10.1984 1985 *IPRax* 317

—— 'Strikter Beklagtenschutz durch Art.27 Nr.2 EuGVÜ' zu *Isabelle Lancray S.A. v Firma Peters und Sickert KG* (C-305/88) [1990] ECR I- 2725 1991 *IPRax* 155

—— 'Gerichtsstandsbeeinflussende AGB im Geltungsbereich des EuGVÜ' 1991 *ZZP* 271

—— 'Zustellung durch Brief und Art.27 EuGVÜ' zu *OLG Frankfurt* 21.2.1991 1992 *IPRax* 71

—— 'Prorogation und Vertragsgerichtsstand gegen Rechtsscheinhaftende' zu *OLG Saarbrücken* 2.10.1991 1992 *IPRax* 143

—— 'Keine EuGVÜ-Anerkennung ohne ordnungsgemäße Zustellung' zu *EuGH* 12.11.1992 und *OLG Hamm* 25.9.1992 und *BGH* 18.2.1993 1993 *IPRax* 376

—— 'Rechtshängigkeitseinwand bei belgischem Parallelverfahren' zu *OLG Celle* 21.10.1992 1994 *IPRax* 188

—— 'Prozessualer Verbraucherschutz im EuGVÜ?' zu *Wolfgang Brenner and Peter Noller v Dean Witter Reynolds Inc.* C-318/93 [1994] ECR I-4275 1995 *IPRax* 289

—— 'Neue Fragen zu Art.27 Nr.2 EuGVÜ' zu *Berhandus Hendrikman and Maria Feyen v Magenta Druck & Verlag GmbH* C-78/95 [1996] ECR I-4943 1997 *IPRax* 314

—— 'Intertemporale Anwendung des Art.21 EuGVÜ' zu *Von Horn v Cinnamond* 1999 IPRax 80

Rawlinson, W. 'A common market for court judgments' 1986 *Int F L R* 16

Rawson, S. 'An Emerging Framework for Electronic Commerce: The E.U. Electronic Commerce Directive and Related Developments' [1999] *ICCLR* 171

Raynard, J. 'Contrat international de distribution' 2001 *JCP*, II, 10364

Ready, N. 'The enforcement in the United Kingdom of foreign authentic instruments under the Brussels Convention of 1968 and the Lugano Convention of 1988' 1995 *Int Mar L* 218

Rechberger, W. 'Das Anerkennungs-und Vollstreckungsabkommen zwischen Österreich und Italien' 1975 *ZfRV* 17

—— 'Das Anerkennungs-und Vollstreckungsabkommen zwischen Österreich und dem Fürstentum Liechtenstein' 1975 *ZfRV* 122

Reeb, B. 'Les mesures provisioires dans la procédure de poursuite' 1997 *ZschweizR* 1

Reed, A. 'Forum non conveniens and the Brussels Convention' 1995 *NLJ* 1697

—— 'Non-recognition of transnational divorces' 1995 *ILT* 265

—— 'International torts and Shevill: the ghost of forum shopping yet to come' 1996 *LMCLQ* 108

—— 'Jurisprudential support for exemplary damage awards' 1996 *J of Transnat'l L & P* 459

—— 'Article 5(1) of the Brussels Convention, restitutionary claims and the need for a new approach' 1997 *NILQ* 243

—— 'Special Jurisdiction and the Convention: the Case of *Domicrest Ltd v Swiss Bank Corporation*' 1999 *CJQ* 218

—— 'To be or not to be: The forum non conveniens performance acted out on Anglo-American courtroom stages' (2000) 29 *Ga. J. Int'l & Comp. L* 31

Reinmüller, B. 'Zur Vollstreckung von titulierten deutschen Anwaltsgebühren in Frankreich' zu franz. Cass.28.2.1984 1985 *IPRax* 56

—— 'Zur Feststellung der Kosten eines französischen Verkehrsanwalts' zu *OLG Koblenz* 5.11.1985 1987 *IPRax* 10

—— 'Zur Vollstreckbarkeit französischer Anwaltsgebühren in der Bundesrepublik Deutschland (Artt.31 ff. EuGVÜ)' zu *LG Hamburg* 31.8.1987 1989 *IPRax* 142

—— 'Zur Vollstreckung von Zustellungs- und Gerichtsvollzieherkosten im Rahmen des EuGVÜ' zu *OLG Saarbrücken* 11.8.1989 1990 *IPRax* 207

Reinmüller, B. 'Zur Vollstreckbarkeit französischer Anwaltsgebühren in der Bundesrepublik Deutschland (Artt.31 ff. EuGVÜ) 1992 *IPRax* 73
—— 'Vollstreckung eines französischen Garantieurteils gegen einen deutschen Gesamtschuldner' zu OLG Düsseldorf 27.11.196 1998 *IPRax* 460
—— 'Die "Urkunde" eines französischen Gerichtsvollziehers ("huissier") und ihre Vollstreckung nach dem EuGVÜ' zu OLG Saarbrücken 6.7.1998 2001 *IPRax* 207
Rèmond-Gouillard, M. 'Des clauses de connaissements maritimes attribuant compétence à une juridiction étrangère' 1995 DMF
Reuland, R. 'The recognition of judgments in the European Community: The twenty-fifth anniversay of the Brussels Convention' 1993 *Mich J Int'l L* 559
Reus, A. 'Die "forum non conveniens-doctrine" in Großbritannien und den USA in Zukunft auch im deutschen Prozeß?' 1991 *RIW* 542
Reymond, J-M. 'For de la connexité au lieu de situation de l'immeuble et exception de litispendence selon la Convention de Lugano' 1996 *JT*, III, 42
Reynolds, F. 'Forum non conveniens in Australia' 1989 *LQR* 40
—— 'Overriding policy of the forum: Casenote *Akai v People's Insurance*' 1997 *LMCLQ* 177
—— 'Overriding policy of the forum: the other side of the coin' 1998 *LMCLQ* 1
Richter, A. 'Das EWG-Übereinkommen über die gerichtliche Zuständigkeit und die Vollstreckung in Zivil- und Handelssachen aus versicherungsrechtlicher Sicht' 1978 *VersicherungsR* 801
Rigaux, F. 'Vers une nouvelle politique belge de ratification des traités de droit international privé' 1995 *Rev belge dr int* 306
Rigaux, R. 'New problems of Private International Law in the Single Market' 1993–4 *KCLJ* 23
Riley, J. 'Void contracts, restitution and jurisdiction' 1996 *LMCLQ* 182
Robertson, D. 'Forum non conveniens in America and England: 'a rather fantastic fiction'' 1987 *LQR* 398
—— 'The federal doctrine of forum non conveniens: 'an object lesson in uncontrolled discretion'' 1994 *Tex Int'l L J* 353
Rodger, A. 'International insurance disputes: where will they be heard?' 1994 *Ins L & P* 58
Rodger, B. 'Article 17 of the Brussels Convention; Exclusivity is a must?' 1995 *CJQ* 250
—— 'Ascertaining the Statutory Lex loci delicti: certain difficulties under the Private International Law (Miscellaneous Provisions) Act 1995' 1998 *ICLQ* 205
—— 'The communitarisation of international private law: reform of the Brussels Convention by regulation' 2001 *The Juridical Review* 59, and 69
—— 'Developments in International Private Law in 2000' 6 *Scottish Law and Practice Quarterly* (2001) 293
Rodière, R. 'La compétence des tribunaux français en matière d'abordage et la Convention de Bruxelles de 1968' 1979 *Rev. crit.* 341
Rogerson, P. 'English interference in Greek affairs' 1994 *CLJ* 241
—— 'Equity, rights in rem and the Brussels Convention' 1994 *CLJ* 462
—— 'Issue estoppel and abuse of process in foreign judgments' 1998 *CJQ* 91
—— 'Habitual Residence: the new domicile?' 2000 *ICLQ* 86
—— 'English courts' jurisdiction over companies: how important is service of the claim form in England?' [2000] *CFILR* 272
Rogge, M. 'Towards transnational corporate accountability in the global economy' 36 (2001) *Tex Int'l L J* 299
Roland, R. 'La clause de juridiction dans les connaissements devant l'article 17 de la Convention C.E.E. du 27 septembre 1968' 1983 *JT* 301
Romy, I. 'Class actions américaines droit international privé suisse' 1999 *AJP* 783
Ropers, J-L. 'La reconnaissance et l'exécution reciproque des décisions de justice à l'intérieur du Marché Commun' 1962 *JCP*, I, Doctr., 1679
Roquette, A and Nordemann-Schiffel, A. 'Zur Einklagbarkeit von Spielschulden im deutschen und Internationalen Privatrecht' 2000 *ZvglRWiss* 444
Rosenow, R. 'La compétence du juge da la mainlevée provisoire selon la Convention de Lugano' 1995 *SZIER* 51

Roth, G. 'Internationalrechtliche Probleme bei Prorogation und Derogation' 1980 *ZZP* 156
—— 'Zulässiges forum shopping?' zu *BGH* 22.6.1983 1984 *IPRax* 183
—— 'Zur Derogation der deutschen Gerichtszuständigkeit' zu *BGH* 20.1.1986 1987 *IPRax* 141
Roth, H. 'Gerichtsstand kraft Sachzusammenhangs in dem Vollstreckbarerklärungsverfahren des europäischen Zivilprozeßrechts' 1987 *RIW* 814
—— 'Herausbildung von Prinzipien im europäischen Vollstreckungsrecht' zu *OLG Saarbrücken* 3.8.1987 1989 *IPRax* 14
—— 'Vollziehung von Arrestbefehlen gegen ausländischen Schuldner' 1990 *IPRax* 161
—— 'Gerichtsstandsvereinbarungen nach Art.17 EuGVÜ und kartellrechtliches Derogationsverbot' zu *OLG Stuttgart* 9.11.1990 1992 *IPRax* 67
—— 'Konkretisierung unbestimmter ausländischer Titel' zu *BGH* 4.3.1993 1994 *IPRax* 350
—— 'Die Vorschläge der Kommission für ein europäisches Zivilprozeßgesetzbuch – das Erkenntnisverfahren' 1996 *ZZP* 271
—— 'Fehlerhafte Urteilszustellung im europäischen Zivilprozeßrecht' zu *OLG Hamm* 11.2.1997 1997 *IPRax* 407
—— 'Aufrechung und internationale Zuständigkeit nach deutschem und europäischem Prozeßrecht' 1999 *RIW* 819
—— 'Casenote *BGH* 29.4.1999' 1999 *ZZP* 473
—— 'Die negative Feststellungsklage zur Abwehr drohender Zwangsvollstreckung als Anwendungsfall von Art.16 Nr. 5 Lugano-Übereinkommen' zu IP.322 *OGH* 5.1.1998 1999 *IPRax* 50
—— 'Remise au parquet und Auslandszustellung nach dem Haager Zustellungsübereinkommen von 1965' zu *OLG Düsseldorf* 29.11.1999 2000 IPRax 527 und *OLG Köln* 8.3.1999 2000 IPRax 528 2000 *IPRax* 497
Rozas, JC. 'Jurisprudencia española y comunitaria de derecho internacional privado' 1996 *REDI* 287
—— 'Jurisprudencia española y comunitaria de derecho internacional privado' 1996 *REDI* 251
Rüfner, T. '*Lis alibi pendens* under the CMR' [2001] *LMCLQ* 460
Ruiz, E. 'Law and jurisdiction in insurance contracts: Limited freedom of choice in the EC' 1995 Int *ILR* 156
Ruitinga, P. 'Dutch jurisdiction in transportation matters' 1997 *JMLC* 61
Russell, K. 'Exorbitant jurisdiction and enforcement of judgments: the Brussels system as an impetus for United States action' 1993 *Syracuse J Int'l L & Com* 57
Rüßmann, H. 'Negative Feststellungsklage und Leistungsklage sowie der Zeitpunkt der endgültigen Rechtshängigkeit im Rahmen des EuGVÜ – Entscheidungs- und Klärungsbedarf durch den EuGH' zu *OLG Hamm* 3.12.1993 1995 *IPRax* 76
—— 'Die Streitgegenstandslehre und die Rechtsprechung des EuGH – nationales Recht unter gemeineuropäischem Einfluß?' 1998 *ZZP* 399
Saenger, I. 'Internationale Gerichtsstandsvereinbarungen nach Eu GVÜ und LugÜ' 1997 *ZZP* 477
Saggio, A. 'European judicial area for civil and commercial matters: The Brussels and Lugano Conventions' 1991 *Riv dir europeo* 617
Salerno, F. 'L'incidenza del diritto applicabile nell'accertamento del forum destinatae solutionis' 1995 *Riv. dir. intern.* 76
Salesi, A. 'Casenote: Chang Ping' 1997 *Dir mar* 209
Samtleben, J. 'Internationale Gerichtsstandsvereinbarungen nach dem EWG- Übereinkommen und nach der Gerichtsstandsnovelle' 1974 *NJW* 1590
—— 'Forum fixing' 1982 *RabelsZ* 716
—— 'Europäische Gerichtsstandsvereinbarungen und Drittstaaten - viel Lärm um nichts? Zum räumlichen Anwendungsbereich des Art.17 I EuGVÜ/LugÜ' 1995 *RabelsZ* 670
—— 'Ein Gerichtsstandsübereinkommen für den Südamerikanischen Gemeinsamen Markt (MERCOSUR)' 1995 *IPRax* 129
Sandrock, O. 'Die Prorogation der internationalen Zuständigkeit eines Gerichts durch hilfsweise Sacheinlassung des Beklagten, Art.18(2)' 1979 *ZVGlRWISS* 177
—— 'Prejudgment Attachments: Securing international loans or other claims for Money' 1987 *Int Law* 1

Schack, H. 'Vermögensbelegenheit als Zuständigkeitsgrund – Exorbitant oder sinnvoll?' – §23 ZPO in rechtsvergleichender Perspektive' 1984 *ZZP* 46

—— 'Widersprechende Urteile: Vorbeugen ist besser als Heilen' zu EuGH 8.12.1987 1989 *IPRax* 139

—— 'Rechtshängigkeit in England und Art.21 EuGVÜ' zu *Kloeckner & Co. AG v Gatoil Overseas Inc.*1991 *IPRax* 270

—— 'Perspektiven eines weltweiten Anerkennungs- und Vollstreckungsübereinkommens' 1993 *ZEuP* 306

—— 'Wechselwirkung zwischen europäischem und nationalem Zivilprozeßrecht' 1994 *ZZP* 279

—— 'Die Versagung der deutschen internationalen Zuständigkeit wegen forum non conveniens und lis alibi pendens' 1994 *RabelsZ* 40

—— 'Gerechtigkeit durch weniger Verfahren' zu *The owners of cargo lately laden on board the ship 'Tatry' v The Maciej Rataj* C406/92 [1994] ECR I-5439 1996 *IPRax* 80

—— 'Zur Anerkennung ausländischer Forderungspfändungen' zu *BAG* 19.3.1996 und *OLG Oldenburg* 25.4.1995 1997 *IPRax* 318

—— 'Entscheidungszuständigkeiten in einem weltweiten Gerichtsstands- und Vollstreckungsübereinkommen' 1998 *ZEuP* 931

Scheider, E, 'Wann ist die Rechtshängigkeit ausländischer Verfahren zu beachten?' 1959 *NJW* 88

Schepers, S. 'The legal force of the Preamble to the EEC Treaty' 6 *ELR* (1981) 356

Schlosser, P. 'Neue Zuständigkeit des Gerichtshofs der Europäischen Gemeinschaften' 1975 *RIW/AWD* 534

—— 'Neues Primärrecht der Europäischen Gemeinschaft' 1975 *NJW* 2132

—— 'Zum Begriff „Zivil- und Handelssachen" in Art.1 Abs.1 EuGVÜ' zu *Eurocontrol* 1981 *IPRax* 154

—— 'Europäisch-autonome Interpretation des Begriffs „Vertrag oder Ansprüche aus einem Vertrag" i.S. v. Art.5 Nr.1 EuGVÜ?' 1984 *IPRax* 65

—— 'Gerichtsstandsklausel in einem Konnossement' 1984 *RIW* 909

—— 'Jurisdiction in international litigation – the issue of Human Rights in relation to national law and to the Brussels Convention' 1991 *Riv. dir. intern.* 5

—— 'Einschränkung des Vermögengerichtsstandes' zu *BGH* 2.7.1991 1992 *IPRax* 140

—— '*Airbus Industrie GIE v Patel*' 1999 *IPRax* 115

Schmandt, P. 'The long arm of French law' 1995 International Commercial Litigation 22

Schmidt, H. 'Casenote on *OLG München* 8.3.1989' 1990 *ZZP* 84

Schmidt, M. 'Wann sind Anwaltshonorare nach EuGVÜ und Lugano-Übereinkommen vollstreckbar?' zu *LG Karlsruhe* 7.12.1990 1991 *RIW* 626

—— 'Kann Schweigen auf eine Gerichtsstandsklausel in AGB einen Gerichtsstand nach Art.17 EuGVÜ/LuganoÜ begründen?' 1992 *RIW* 173

Schneider, E. 'Der Eintritt der Rechtshängigkeit nach Mahnverfahren' 1981 *MDR* 460

Schnichels, D. 'Die aktuelle Rechtsprechung des EuGH zum EuGVÜ' 1994 *EuZW* 370

Schnyder, A. '"Der Kampf ums Forum": Reziproke Prorogation und Flip-Flop-Klauseln' 1983 *RabelsZ* 340

Schockweiler, F. 'Jurisprudence récente de la Cour en matière de conflits de compétence judiciaire et d'exécution des décisions' 1996 *ERPL* 1

Schoibl, N. 'Die Zuständigkeit für Verbrauchersachen nach europäischem Zivilverfahrensrecht des Brüsseler und des Luganer Übereinkommens (EuGVÜ/LGVÜ)' 1998 *JBl* 700

—— 'Zum zeitlichen Anwendungsbereich und zum Ratifikationsstand des Brüsseler Übereinkommens und zum Konkurrenzverhältnis der beiden Europäischen Gerichtsstands-und Vollstreckungsübereinkommen EuVÜ-LGVÜ' 2000 *ÖJZ* 481

Schrage, E. 'Unjustified enrichment – recent Dutch developments from a comparative and historical perspective' 1999 *NILR* 57

Schultz, J. 'Zwischenbilanz des europäischen Gerichtsstands- und Vollstreckungsübereinkommens' 1983 *IPRax* 97

Schulz, A. 'Einstweilige Maßnahmen nach dem Brüsseler Gerichtsstands-und Vollstreckungsübereinkommen in der Rechtsprechung des Gerichtshofs der Europäischen Gemeinschaften (EuGH)' 2001 *ZeuP* 805

Schulz, C. 'Englisches internationales Deliktsrecht im Umbruch' 1996 *RIW* 468

Schulze, G. 'Internationale Annexzuständigkeit nach dem EuGVÜ' zu *KG* 17.11.1997 1999 *IPRax* 21
—— 'Der pathologische Fall – die Gerichtsstandsvereinbarung nach Art.17 Abs.4 LugÜ/EuGVÜ' zu *BGH* 23.7.1998 1999 *IPRax* 229
—— 'Anerkennung einer ausländischen Entscheidung bei Einwand strukturell ungleicher Verhandlungsstärke und nicht wirksame Vertretung im Erstverfahren (Art.27 Nr.1 und Nr. 2 EuGVÜ) zu *BGH* 24.2.1999 1999 *IPRax* 342
Schütze, R. 'Die Berücsichtigung der Rechtshängigkeit eines ausländischen Verfahrens' 1967 *RabelsZ* 233
—— 'Zur partiellen Verbürgung der Gegenseitigkeit bei der Anerkennung ausländischer Zivilurteile' 1973 *NJW* 2143
—— 'Die Nachprüfung der internationalen Zuständigkeit nach dem EWG-Übereinkommen über die gerichtliche Zuständigkeit und die Vollstreckung gerichtlicher Entscheidungen' 1974 *RIW* 428
—— 'Die Berücsichtigung der Rechtshängigkeit eines ausländischen Verfahrens nach dem EWG-Übereinkommen über die gerichtliche Zuständigkeit und die Vollstreckung gerichtlicher Entscheidungen' 1975 *RIW* 78
—— 'Die Berücsichtigung der Konnexität nach dem EWG-Übereinkommen über die gerichtliche Zuständigkeit und die Vollstreckung gerichtlicher Entscheidungen' 1975 *RIW* 543
—— 'Zur Bedeutung der rügelose Einlassung im internationalen Zivilprozeßrecht' 1979 *RIW/AWD* 590
—— 'Die Wirkung ausländischer Rechtshängigkeit in inländischen Verfahren' 1991 *ZZP* 136
—— 'Formlose Zustellung im internationalen Rechtsverkehr' 2000 *RIW* 20
—— 'Aussetzung des Verfahrens wegen konnexer Verfahren nach Art.22 EuGVÜ' zu OLG Stuttgart 24.11.1999 2000 *RIW* 939
Schwander, I. 'Rechtsprechung zum internationalen Schuld- und Gesellschaftsrecht' 1994 SZIER 475
—— 'Casenote: Mund & Fester' 1994 *AJP* 795
Schwarz, A. 'In re Harrods Ltd: The Brussels Convention and the proper application of forum non conveniens to non-Contracting States' 1991–2 *Fordham Int'l LJ* 174
Schwenzer, I. 'Internationaler Gerichtsstand für die Kaufpreisklage' zu *LG Köln* 5.5.1988 1989 *IPRax* 274
Seaman, A. 'E-Commerce, Jurisdiction and Choice of Law' 2000 *Comp. & Law* 28
Seatzu, F. 'Jurisdiction agreements under article 17(1)(c) of the Brussels Convention' 1998 *NILQ* 327
—— 'Materia fiscale e convenzione di Bruxelles del 27 settembre 1968' 2001 *Riv. dir. int. priv. e proc.* 621
Sedlacek, W. 'Die Neuregelung der Zwangsvollstreckung zwischen der Republik Österreich und der Bundesrepublik Deutschland' 1960 *ZfRV* 58
Sessler, A. 'Die Anwendbarkeit des §917 Abs.2 Satz 1 ZPO auf Urteile aus EuGVÜ-Staaten' 2001 WM 497
Sieg, K. 'Blick vom Exequaturverfahren auf das französische Arbeitsunfallrecht' zu *OLG Hamburg* 18.6.1993 1994 *RIW* 973
Sieg, O. 'Internationale Anerkennungszuständigkeit bei US-amerikanischen Urteilen' 1996 *IPRax* 77
—— 'Internationale Gerichtsstands- und Schiedsklauseln in allgemeinen Geschäftsbedingungen' 1998 *RIW* 102
Siegenthaler, T. 'Für eine vorläufige Vollstreckung nicht rechtskraftiger Urteile betreffend Geldforderungen – ein Diskussionsbeitrag' 2000 *AJP* 172
Siehr, K. 'Ehrenzweigs Lex-fori-Theorie und ihre Bedeutung für des amerikanische und deutsche Kollisionsrecht' 1970 *RabelsZ* 585
—— '"Forum shopping" im internationalen Rechtsverkehr' 1984 *ZfRV* 124
—— 'Zur Anerkennung und Vollstreckung ausländischer Verurteilungen zu "punitive damages"' 1991 *RIW* 705
—— 'Entwicklungen im schweizerischen internationalen Privatrecht' 1998 *SJZ* 86
—— 'Entwicklungen im schweizerischen internationalen Privatrecht' 1999 *SJZ* 70
Silberman, L. 'Developments in jurisdiction and forum non conveniens in international litigation: thoughts on reform and a proposal for a uniform standard' 1993 *Tex Int'l L J* 501
—— and Lowenfeld, A. 'A different challenge for the ALI: Herein of Foreign Country Judgments, and International Treaty, and an American Statute' 2000 *Ind. L. R.* 635

Silva, E. 'Practical views on stemming the tide of foreign plaintiffs and concluding Mid-Atlantic settlements' 1993 *Tex Int'l L J* 479

Simeone, J. 'The recognition and enforceability of foreign country judgments' 1993 *St Louis U L J* 341

Sinagra, A. 'I rapporti di famiglia nella Convenzione di Bruxelles del 27 settembre 1968, concernente la competenza giurisdizionale e l'esecuzione delle decisioni in materia civile e commerciale' 1995 *Dir Fam e Pers* 1539

Sinclair, A. 'Funding decisive: Asbestos group action to proceed in England, *Lubbe v Cape*' 2001 *LMCLQ* 197

Skene, M. 'Commercial Litigation beyond the pale: a comparison of extraterritorial antisuit and Mareva jurisdiction exercised by the courts of England and British Columbia in commercial disputes' 1996 *U B C L R* 1

Slater, A. 'Forum non conveniens: a view from the shop floor' 1988 *LQR* 554

Smart, P. 'Corporate domicile and multiple incorporation in English private international law' 1990 *JBL* 126

—— 'Insolvency proceedings and the Civil Jurisdiction and Judgments Act 1982' 1998 *CJQ* 149

—— 'The rule against foreign revenue laws: *QRS1 v Frandsen*' (2000) 116 *LQR* 360

Smit, H. 'The proposed United States–United Kingdom Convention on Recognition and Enforcement of Judgments: A Prototype for the future?' 1977 *Virg J Int'l L* 443

Smith, L. 'Antitrust injunctions, Forum non Conveniens und International Comity' 1993 *RIW* 802

Smith, R. 'International Employment Contracts – The applicable law' 1993 *ILJ* 1

Solimine, ME. 'Forum selection clauses and the Privatisation of Procedure' 1992 *Cornell Int'l L J* 51

Speck, P. 'Forum non conveniens and Choice of Law in Admiralty: Time for an overhaul' 1987 *JMLC* 185

Speer, C. 'The continued use of forum non conveniens: is it still justified?' 1993 *J Air LC* 845

Spellenberg, U. 'Der Gerichtsstand des Erfüllungsortes im europäischen Gerichtsstands- und Vollstreckungsübereinkommen' 1978 *ZZP* 38

—— 'Drittbeteilung im Zivilprozeß in rechtsvergleichender Sicht' 1993 *ZZP* 283

Sperl, H. 'Ein Staatsvertrag über die Vollstreckungshilfe zwischen Oesterreich und Deutschland' 1910 *NiemeyersZ* 57

—— 'Der Rechtsschutz-und Rechtshilfevertrag zwischen Österreich und Deutschland vom 21. Juni 1923' 1924 *ZöR* 299

Spickhoff, A. 'Verjährungsunterbrechung durch ausländische Beweissicherungsverfahren ' zu LG Hamburg 15.9.1998 2001 *IPRax* 37

Sprung, R. '„Einlassung zur Hauptsache" im österreichischen zivilgerichtlichen Verfahrensrecht' 1975 *ZfRV* 36

Stade, S. 'Die ordnungsgemäße und rechtzeitige Zustellung des verfahrenseinleitenden Schriftstücks für die Anerkennung eines Versäumnisurteils nach Art.27 Nr.2 EuGVÜ' 1993 *NJW* 184

Stadler, A. 'Die internationale Durchsetzung von Gegendarstellungsansprüchen' 1994 *JZ* 642

—— 'Schuldnerschutz nach Artt. 38,39 EuGVÜ und seine Voraussetzungen' zu BGH 21.4.1994 1995 *IPRax* 220

—— 'Neues europäisches Zustellungsrecht' 2001 *IPRax* 514

Starace, V. 'Le champ de la juridiction selon la loi de réforme du système italien de droit international privé' 1996 *Rev. crit.* 67

Stauder, D. 'Grenzüberschreitender Rechtsschutz für europäische Patente' 1997 *Grur Int.* 859

—— 'Grenzüberschreitende Verletzungsverbote im gewerblichen Rechtsschutz und das EuGVÜ' 1998 *IPRax* 317

Steiner, M. 'London as a forum for dispute resolution' 1997 *ICLit* 34

Stevens, J. 'No foot in Minorca? The jurisdiction of the English courts in claims of title to foreign land: *Re Hayward (deceased)*' 1998 *Conv* 145

Stevens, R. 'The law applicable to priority in shares' 1996 *LQR* 198

—— 'Restitution and the Brussels Convention' 1996 *LQR* 391

—— 'Restitution and the Rome Convention' 1997 *LQR* 249

Stoffel, WA. 'Das Verfahren zur Anerkennung handelsrechtlicher Entscheide nach dem Lugano-Übereinkommen' 1993 *SZW* 107

Stoll, D. 'Die britische Mareva-Injunction als Gegenstand eines Vollstreckungsbegehrens unter dem Lugano-Übereinkommen' 1996 *SJZ* 104

Stone, PA. 'Problems with the forum loci solutionis' 1983 *Anglo-Am L R* 52

Stone, W. 'Jurisdiction of the foreign corporations' 1962 *Alb L R* 61

Storme, M. 'Rechtsvereinheitlichung in Europa – Ein Plädoyer für ein einheitliches europäisches Prozeßrecht' 1992 *RabelsZ* 290

Storp, R. 'Internationale Zuständigkeit des Erfüllungsorts bei Verträgen mit französischen Vertretern' 1999 *RIW* 823

Stotz, R. 'Hinweise des EuGH Zur Vorlage von Vorabentscheidungsersuchen durch die innerstaatlichen Gerichte' 1997 *EuZW* 129

Straub, P. 'Englische Mareva Injunctions und Anton Piller Orders' 1992 *SZIER* 525

Stauder, D. 'Die Anwendung des EWG-Gerichtsstands- und Vollstreckungsübereinkommens auf Klagen im gewerblichen Rechtsschutz und Urheberrecht' 1976 *Grur. Int.* 465

—— 'Die Anwendung des EWG-Gerichtsstands- und Vollstreckungsübereinkommens auf Klagen im gewerblichen Rechtsschutz und Urheberrecht – Zweiter Teil' 1976 *Grur. Int.* 510

Staudinger, A. 'Rom, Brüssel, Berlin und Amsterdam' 2000 *ZfRV* 93

—— 'Vertragsstaatenbezug und Rückversicherungsverträge im EuGVÜ' zu *Société Group Josi Reinsurance Company SA v Compagnie d'Assurances Universal General Insurance Company (UGIC)* 2000 *IPRax* 483

Strauss, A. 'Beyond national law: the neglected role of the international law of personal jurisdiction in domestic courts' 1995 *Harvard Int'l LJ* 373

—— 'Where America ends and the International order begins' 1998 *Alb L R* 1237

Struycken, A.V.M. 'The rules of jurisdiction in the EEC Convention on Jurisdiction and the Enforcement of Judgments in Civil and Commercial Matters' 1978 *NILR* 354

Struycken, THD. 'Some Dutch judicial reflections on the Rome Convention, Art.4(5)' 1996 *LMCLQ* 18

Stückelberg, M. '*Lis pendens* and *forum non conveniens* at the Hague Conference' 26 Brook. *J. Int'l. L.* 949 (2001)

Stürner, H. 'Casenote *OLG Düsseldorf* 10.1.96' 1996 *ZZP* 221

Stürner, R. 'Förmlichkeit und Billigkeit bei der Klagzustellung im Europäischen Zivilprozeßrecht' 1992 *JZ* 325

—— 'Rechtliches Gehör und Klauselerteilung im Europäischen Vollstreckungsverfahren' zu *EuGH* 12.7.1984 1985 *IPRax* 254

Sturlèse, B. 'Les nouvelles règles du droit international privé européen du divorce: Règlement (CE) n° 1347/2000 du Conseil' 2001 *JCP, Doctr.*, I, 292

Swadling, W. 'A Claim in Restitution' 1996 *LMCLQ* 63

Tagaras, H. 'L'applicabilité des Conventions de la Haye dans le cadre de la Convention de Bruxelles' 1991 *Rev belge dr int* 479

—— 'Chronique de jurisprudence de la Cour de Justice rélative à la Convention de Bruxelles – Années judiciaires 1990–1991 et 1991–1992' 1993 *Cahiers dr. europ.* 653

—— 'Chronique de jurisprudence de la Cour de Justice rélative à la Convention de Bruxelles – Années judiciaires 1992–1993 et 1993–1994' 1995 *Cahiers dr. europ.* 157

—— 'Chronique de jurisprudence de la Cour de Justice rélative à la Convention de Bruxelles – Années judiciaires 1994–1995 et 1995–1996' 1997 *Cahiers dr. europ.* 141

—— 'Chronique de Jurisprudence de la Cour de Justice rélative à la Convention de Bruxelles: Années judiciaires 1996–1997 et 1997–1998' 1999 *Cahiers dr. europ.* 159

Takahashi, K. 'Jurisdiction over direct action against sub-carrier under the Brussels Convention' [2001] *LMCLQ* 107

—— 'Forum non conveniens discretion in third party proceedings' 2002 *ICLQ* 127

Tarzia, G. 'Les mesures provisoires dans les pays de la C.E.E' 1996 *Ann dr. Louvain* 163

Tassel, Y. 'Doit-on craindre l'application de la Convention de Bruxelles sur la saisie conservatoire de navire?' 1987 *Ann dr. Marit. & Aéro-Spat* 127

—— 'Casenote: Cour de Cassation "Ruminski"' 1998 *DMF* 1111

Teare, N. 'The Court of Appeal, the European Court and the Admiralty action *in rem*' 1997 *Int Mar L* 149

Tebbens, H. 'The European Jurisdiction and Enforcement Convention: Interpretations, Concurrence and Prospects' 1993 *NILR* 471

Teizeira de Sousa, M. 'Die neue internationale Zuständigkeitsregelung im portugiesischen Zivil-prozeßgesetzbuch und die Brüsseler und Luganer Übereinkommen: Einige vergleichende Bemerkungen' 1997 *IPRax* 352

Tendler, R. 'Le juge des référés, une "procédure ordinaire"?' 1991 *Dalloz. Chron.* 139

Tessiore, M. '"Forum solutionis", Convenzione di Bruxelles des 27 settembre 1968 e giurisprudenza italiana' 1980 *Riv trim dir & proc civ* 113

Tetley, W. 'Jurisdiction clauses – forum non conveniens' 1986 *ETL* 287

—— '"Shipowners" limitation of liability and Conflicts of Law: The properly applicable law' 1992 *JMLC* 585

—— 'Conflicts of Law between the Bankruptcy courts in Admiralty: Canada, United Kingdom, United States and France' 1996 *Tul Mar L J* 257

—— 'New development in Private International Law: *Tolofson v Jensen* and *Gagnon v Lucas*' 1996 *Am J Comp L* 647

Theis, W. 'Admiralty proceedings and the proposed Hague Convention on Jurisdiction and Judgments' 2001 *J Mar L & C* 59

Theiss, A. 'Enforcement of foreign awards, Austria' 1996 *ICLit* 44

Thieffry, P. 'European Integration and Transnational Litigation' 1990 *Boston Coll Int'l & Comp L R* 339

Thiele, C. 'Erfüllungsort bei der Rückabwicklung von Vertragspflichten nach Art.81 UN-Kaufrecht – ein Plädoyer gegen die herrschende Meinung' 2000 *RIW* 892

Thieme, J. 'Notiziarium zur italienischen Rechtsprechung auf dem Gebiet des Internationalen Privat- und Privatverfahrensrechts für die Jahre 1992 und 1993' 1998 *ZVGlRWISSR* 57

Thorn, K. 'Verbrauchergerichtsstand nach EuGVÜ und örtliche Zuständigkeit' zu *LG Konstanz* 24.8.1992 1994 *IPRax* 426

—— 'Grenzüberschreitende Gerichtsstandsvereinbarungen in Kreditverträgen zur Finanzierung von Börsenspekulationen' zu *LG Darmstadt* 2.12.1993 1995 *IPRax* 294

Thümmel, R. 'Casenote: *Mund & Fester v Hatrex*' 1994 *EuZW* 242

—— 'Einstweiliger Rechtsschutz im Auslandsrechtsvekehr' 1996 *NJW* 1930

Tichadou, E. 'Casenote: Custom Made Commercial 29 juin 1994' 1995 *Rev trim dr euro* 83

Tiedemann, A. 'Primer encuentro juridico Argentino-Germano' 1988 *RabelsZ* 756

Tiefenthaler, S. 'LGVÜ: Gerichtsstand am "Erfüllungsort des Bereicherungsanspruchs"?' 1998 *ÖJZ* 544

Trappe, J. 'The Arbitration clause in a bill of lading' 1999 *LMCLQ* 337

Trittmann, R. 'Die Durchsetzbarkeit des Anwaltsvergleiches gemäß §§796 a ff. ZPO im Rahmen des EuGVÜ/LugÜ' 2001 *IPRax* 178

Trooboff, PD. 'International Law The Hague Conference' *The National Law Journal*, 23.7.2001, A19

Trunk, A. 'EuGVÜ und Osteuropa' 1991 *IPRax* 278

—— 'Erste deutsche Rechtsprechung zum Lugano-Übereinkommen: Gerichtsstandsvereinbarungen, Gerichtsstand des Erfüllungsorts und intertemporale Fragen' 1996 *IPRax* 249

—— 'Derogationswirkung von Gerichtsstandsvereinbarungen im deutsch-polnischen Rechtsverkehr: Doppelrelevante Tatsachen und sittenwidrige Schädigung' zu *OLG Köln* 9.9.1996 1998 *IPRax* 448

Tsouca, C. 'Conflit des juridictions' 1999 *RHDI* 554

Tub, T. 'Die Neuregelung der Anerkennung und Vollstreckung in Zivil- und Handelssachen und das familienrechtliche Anerkennungs- und Vollstreckungsverfahren' 2001 NJW 3145

Turkki, I. 'Casenote: *Boss Group v Boss France*' 21 (1996) *ELR* 419

—— 'Interpretation of Modified Convention: Kleinwort Benson, CA' 21 (1996) *ELR* 422

Tugendhat, M. 'Media Law and the Brussels Convention: *Pearce v Ove Arup*' 1997 *LQR* 360

Tweeddale, A. 'Enforcing arbitration awards contrary to public policy in England' 2000 *International Construction Law Review* 159

Ulmer, M. 'Neue Tendenzen bei der Auslegung des Art.16 Nr.1 EuGVÜ' zu *Norbert Lieber v Willi S Göbel & Siegrid Göbel* C292/93 [1994] ECR I-2535 1995 *IPRax* 72

Underhill, D. 'Denying Enforcement of a foreign country injunction: Solution or symptom?' Pilkington Bros 1985 *Conn LR* 703

Vandencasteele, A. 'La reconnaissance et l'exécution des mesures provisiores et conservatoires dans la Convention sur la compétence judiciaire et l'exécution des décisions en matières civile et commerciale du 27 septembre 1968' 1980 *JT* 737

Vanderbloemen, T. 'Assessing the potential impact of the proposed Hague Jurisdiction and Judgments Convention on Human Rights litigation in the United States' 50 (2000) *Duke Law Journal* 917

Van Gent, EM. 'Casenote Supreme Court, 2.2.1996 Choice of domicile' 1996 *NILR* 387

Van Hecke, G. 'Casenote: Cour d'Appel de Bruxelles' 1988 *Ann dr. Liège* 90

Van Hille, P. 'Concessions de vente en Belgique et règles de compétence de la Convention C.E.E. du 27 septembre 1968' 1976 *JT* 733

Van Houtte, H. 'May court judgments that disregard arbitration clauses and awards be enforced under the Brussels and Lugano Conventions?' 1997 *Arb Int* 85

Van Leeuwen, M. 'Casenote: The Skadarlija: Art.17' 1994 *Int Mar L* 68

Van Loon, J. 'Hague Conference on Private International Law work in 1994' 1994 *Hague Yrbk Int L* 325

—— 'Hague Conference on Private International Law work in 1995' 1995 *Hague Yrbk Int L* 209

Van Rossum, M. 'The Principles of European Contract Law' 1996 *MJ* 69

Van Schaack, B. 'In defense of civil redress: the domestic enforcement of Human Rights norms in the context of the proposed Hague Judgments Convention' 2001 *Harvard International Law Journal* 141

Van Venrooy, G. 'Nochmals: Über die Kunst der Interessenabwägung auch im internationalen Verfahrensrecht, dargestellt am rechten Maß des beklagtenschutzes gemäß Art.27 Nr.2 EuGVÜ' 1989 *IPRax* 137

Vareilles-Sommières, P. de 'La compétence internationale des tribunaux français en matière de mesures provisoires' 1996 *Rev. crit.* 397

Verbeek, FH. 'Die Staatsverträge über die Vollstreckung ausländischer Zivilurteile' 1931 *NiemeyersZ* 1

Verheul, H. 'Casenote *Gubisch v Palumbo*' 1988 *NILR* 80

Verheul, JP. 'The EEC Convention on jurisdiction and judgments of 27 September 1968 in Netherlands Legal Practice' 1976 *NILR* 347

Verheul, J. 'The Convention relating to the Arrest of Seagoing ships of 1952. Some questions' 1983 *NILR* 383

—— 'The forum (non) conveniens in English and Dutch law under some international conventions' 1986 *ICLQ* 413

Véron, P. 'Trente ans d'application de la Convention de Bruxelles à l'action en contrefaçon de brevet d'invention' 2001 *JDI* 805

Verwilghen, M. 'Les règles de droit international privé européen régissant les conflits individuels du travail' 1991 *Rev gén dr* 79

Viatte, J. 'A propos de la litispendence' 1976 *Gaz. Pal., Doctr*, 354

Vigitori, V. 'Recent developments in the Recognition and Execution of Foreign Judgments and Arbitral Awards in Italy' 1987 *CJQ* 248

Virgo, G. 'Restitution and Private International Law – Square pegs and round holes' 1996 *RLR* 109

Vivant, M. 'Das Europäische Gerichtsstands- und Vollstreckungsübereinkommen und die gewerblichen Schutzrechte' 1991 *RIW* 26

Vlas, P. 'The Protocol on interpretation of the EEC Convention on Jurisdiction and Enforcement of Judgments: over ten years in legal practice (1975–1985)' 1986 *NILR* 84

—— 'Casenotes: *Handte v TMCS*; *Reichert*; *Shearson Lehmann*; *Hacker*; *Powell Duffryn*; *Minalmet*' 1993 *NILR* 497

—— 'The EEC Convention on jurisdiction and Judgments' 1994 *NILR* 333

—— 'Casenote: *Marinari v Lloyd's Bank*' 1995 *NILR* 420

—— 'Casenote: *Shevill v Presse Alliance*' 1995 *NILR* 413

—— 'Casenote: Lloyd's Register of Shipping' 1995 *NILR* 425

—— 'Netherlands Judicial decisions regarding the application of the Lugano Convention on jurisdiction and judgments' 1996 *NILR* 397

—— 'The EEC Convention on Jurisdiction and Judgments' 1999 *NILR* 87

Vogel, H. 'Aus der Vollstreckungspraxis auf Grund der Staatsverträge mit dem Deutschen Reich und Oesterreich' 1933 *SJZ* 129

Vogel, O. 'Der Eintritt der Rechtshängigkeit nach Art.21 und 22 des Lugano-Übereinkommens' 1994 *SJZ* 301

—— 'Lugano –Übereinkommen' (1999) 135 *ZBJV* 426

Vogenauer, S. 'Zur Begründung des Mehrparteiengerichtsstands aus Art.6 Nr.1 LugÜ in England un Schottland' zu *Canada Trust Co. and others v Stolzenberg and others (No.2)* [2000] 3 WLR 1376, [2000] 4 All ER 481 2001 *IPRax* 253

Volken, P. 'Rechtsprechung zum Lugano-Übereinkommen (1991)' 1992 *SZIER* 223

—— 'Der EuGH knackt den Ausländerarrest' 1994 *SZIER* 1

—— 'Rechtsprechung zum Lugano-Übereinkommen (1993)' 1994 *SZIER* 393

—— 'Rechtsprechung zum Lugano-Übereinkommen (1993/94)' 1995 *SZIER* 17

—— 'Rechtsprechung zum Lugano-Übereinkommen (1995)' 1996 *SZIER* 69

—— 'Rechtsprechung zum Lugano-Übereinkommen (1996)' 1997 *SZIER* 335

—— 'Rechtsprechung zum Lugano-Übereinkommen (1996/1997)' 1998 *SZIER* 91

—— 'Rechtsprechung zum Lugano-Übereinkommen (1998)' 1999 *SZIER* 441

Volkovitsch, M. 'When is litigation arbitration: *Marc Rich v Impianti*' 1991 *Am Rev Int'l Arb* 501

Von Hippel, E. 'Schadenersatzklagen gegen deutsche Produzenten in den Vereinigten Staaten' 1971 *AWD/RIW* 61

Von Hoffmann, B. 'Empfiehlt es sich, das EG-Übereinkommen über das auf vertragliche Schuldver-hältnisse anzuwendende Recht in das deutsche IPR-Gesetz zu inkorporieren?' 1984 *IPRax* 10

—— 'Deutscher Prozeßvergleich kein Anerkennungshindernis nach Art.27 Nr.3 EuGVÜ' zu *Solo Kleinmotoren GmbH v Emilio Boch* (C414/92) [1994] ECR I-2237 1995 *IPRax* 217

—— 'Probleme der abredewidrigen Streitverkündung im Europäischen Zivilrechtsverkehr' 1997 *RIW* 89

—— 'Zur internationalen Anerkennungszuständigkeit US-amerikanischer Zivilgerichte' 1998 *RIW* 344

Von Mehren, A. 'Recognition and Enforcement of Sister-State judgments' 1981 *Colum L R* 1044

—— 'The case for a Convention-mixte Approach to Jurisdiction to adjudicate and Recognition and Enforcement of Foreign Judgments' 1997 *RabelsZ* 86

—— 'Recognition and enforcement of foreign judgments: a new approach for the Hague Conference?' 1994 *Law and Contemporary Problems* 271

—— 'The Hague Jurisdiction and Enforcement Convention Project faces an impasse: a diagnosis and guidelines for a cure' 2000 *IPRax* 465

—— 'La rédaction d'une convention universellement acceptable sur la compétence judiciaire interna-tionale et les effets des jugements étrangers: Le projet de la Conférence de la Haye peut-il aboutir?' 2001 *Rev. crit.* 85

—— 'Drafting a Convention on International Jurisdiction and the effects of foreign judgments accept-able World-wide: Can the Hague Conference project succeed?' 49 *Am J Comp L* 191 (2001)

Von Meibom, W. 'Die europäische "Transborderrechtsprechung" stößt an ihre Grenzen' 1998 *Grur. Int.* 765

—— 'Cross-border jurisdiction in Europe from a German perspective' 1998 *Patent World* 28

Vortisch, F. 'Die Anerkennung der schweizerischen Gerichtsentscheidungen in Ehesachen in der Bundesrepublik Deutschland nach den zwischen ihr und der Schweizerischen Eidgenossenschaft bestehenden Staatsverträgen' 1964 *SJZ* 281

Vuitton, X. 'Le référé-provision et l'article 24 de la Convention de Bruxelles' 1999 *Dalloz, Juris.*, 545

Wabwile, M. 'Anton Piller orders revisited' 2000 *JBL* 387

Wagner, G. 'Ehrenschutz und Pressefreiheit im europäischen Zivilverfahrens- und Internationalen Privatrecht' 1998 *RabelsZ* 243

—— 'Die Aufrechnung im Europäischen Zivilprozeß' 1999 *IPRax* 65

Wagner, R. 'Zum zeitlichen Anwendungsbereich des Lugano-Übereinkommens' 1994 *ZIP* 81

—— 'Verfahrensrechtliche Probleme im Auslandsmahnverfahren' 1995 *RIW* 89

—— 'Der Beitritt Österreichs, Finnlands und Schwedens zum Brüsseler Gerichtsstands- und Voll-streckungsübereinkommen vom 27.9.1968' 1998 *RIW* 590

—— 'Die geplante Reform des Brüsseler und des Lugano-Übereinkommens' 1998 *IPRax* 241

—— 'Die Anerkennung und Vollstreckung von Entscheidungen nach der Brüssel II-Verordnung' 2001 *IPRax* 73

Wagner, R. 'Die Bemühungen der Haager Konferenz für Internationales Privatrecht um ein Übereinkommen über die gerichtliche Zuständigkeit und ausländische Entscheidungen in Zivil- und Handelssachen' 2001 *IPRax* 533

—— 'Vom Brüsseler Übereinkommen über die Brüssel I-Verordnung zum Europäischen Wollstreckungstitel' 2002 *IPRax* 75

Walder, U. 'Grundfragen der Anerkennung und Vollstreckung ausländischer Urteile unter besonderer Berücksichtigung schweizerische Sicht' 1990 *ZZP* 322

Walker, W-D, 'Die Streitgegenstandslehre und die Rechtsprechung des EuGH – nationales Recht unter gemein-europäischem Einfluß*' 1998 *ZZP* 429

Waller, S. 'A unified theory of transnational procedure' 1993 *Cornell Int'l L J* 101

Walter, G. 'Die zu kurz bemessene Einlassungsfrist' zu *BGH* 23.1.1986 1986 *IPRax* 349

—— 'Die internationale Zuständigkeit schweizerischer Gerichte für 'vorsorgliche Massnahmen'- oder: Art.10 IPRG und seine Geheimnisse' 1992 *AJP* 61

—— 'Zur Sicherungsvollstreckung gemäß Art.39 des Lugano-Übereinkommens' 1992 *ZBJV* 90

—— 'Wechselwirkungen zwischen europäischem und nationalem Zivilprozeßrecht: Lugano-Übereinkommen und Schweizer Recht' 1994 *ZZP* 301

—— 'Aspetti internazionali del diritto processuale' 1996 *Riv trim dir & proc civ* 1159

Warlomont, R. 'L'Exécution des jugements et des sentences, rendus à l'étranger, au regard de la notion de l'ordre public et des bonnes mœurs' 1953 *Rev. dr. intern. dr. comparé* 84

Washington, J. 'The impact of *Piper Aircraft Co. v Reyno* on the foreign plaintiff in the forum non conveniens analysis' 1989 *J Air LC* 303

Watson, H. 'Transnational Maritime Litigation: Selected problems' 1983 *Mar L* 87

Watt, H. 'Extraterritorialité des mesures conservatoires in personam (à propos de l'arrêt de la Court of Appeal, *Crédit suisse Fides Trust v Cuoghi*)' 1998 *Rev. crit.* 27

Weatherill, S. 'The scope of Article 7 EEC' 15 (1990) *ELR* 334

—— 'Prospects for the development of European Private Law through "europeanisation" in the European Court – the case of the Directive on Unfair Terms in Consumer Contracts' 1995 *ERPL* 307

Weber-Rey, D. 'Casenote: *Oberlandesgericht Düsseldorf* 15.12.94 1996 *JIBL* N-73

Weigland, F. 'Der Beitritt Spaniens und Portugals zum EuGVÜ' 1991 *RIW* 717

Weintraub, R. 'International Litigation and Forum non conveniens' 1994 *Tex Int'l L J* 321

—— 'Negotiating the tort long-arm provisions of the Judgments Convention' 1998 *Alb L R* 1269

Weller, M. 'Zur Abgrenzung von ehelichem Güterrecht und Unterhaltsrecht im EuGVÜ' zu *Antonius van den Boogaard v Paula Laumen* C-220/95 [1997] ECR I-1147 1999 *IPRax* 14

—— 'Zur Handlungsortsbestimmung im internationalen Kapitalanlegerprozeß bei arbeitsteiliger Deliktsverwirklichung' zu *OLG Bremen* 21.11.1997 2000 *IPRax* 202

Weser, M. 'Faut-il réviser la Convention franco-italienne du 3 juin 1930 sur l'exécution des jugements?' 1954 *Rev. crit.* 451

—— 'Bases of judicial jurisdiction in the Common Market countries' 1961 *Am J Comp L* 323

—— 'Litigation on the Common Market Level' 1964 *Am J Int'l L* 44

—— 'Some reflections on the Draft Treaty on Execution of Judgments in the E.E.C.' 1965 *Int Tr & Inv* 771

—— 'La libre circulation des jugements dans le Marché Commun' 1969 *Dr Intern Privé* 353

—— 'La Convention communautaire sur la compétence judiciaire et l'exécution des décisions réalise-t-elle la libre circulation des jugements dans le Marché commun?' 1973 *JT* 229

—— 'L'article 5, alinéa 1er de la Convention de Bruxelles du 27 septembre 1968 et la concession de vente exclusive' 1976 *JT* 323

Westin, D. 'Interim Relief awarded by U.S. and German courts in support of foreign proceedings' 1990 *Colum J Transnat'l Law* 723

Wetter, J. 'The case for international law schools and an international legal profession' 1980 *ICLQ* 206

White, R. 'The Government role: Negotiation, legislation and litigation' 1992 *CJQ* 52

Whiteley, A. 'Forum shopping in Ontario' 1995 *ICCLR* 76

Wilbraham, A. 'Casenote: *Bankers Trust Co. and another v P.T Jakarta International Hotels*' [2000] *ITLQ* 112

Wilderspin, M. 'Casenote: *The Tilly Russ*' 1984 *ELR* 456

Wilkins, J. 'Application of Admiralty jurisdiction to Aviation disasters on the High Seas' 1996 *Tul Mar L J* 465

Williams, J. 'Bringing proceedings in the U.S. for English plaintiffs – the obstacle of forum non conveniens' 1996 *JPIL* 2

Wilske, S. 'Gerichtsstandsvereinbarungen nach Rechtshängigkeit' 2000 *NJW* 3549

Wilson, J. 'Anti-suit injunctions' 1997 *JBL* 424

Windahl, J. 'Nordic jurisdiction over cases against sub-carriers' 2001 *Il diritto marittimo* 1002

Wirth, H-R. 'Gerichtsstandsvereinbarungen im internationalen Handelsverkehr' 1978 *NJW* 460

Withers, C. 'Jurisdiction clauses and the Unfair terms in consumer contracts regulations' [2002] *LMCLQ* 56

—— 'Jurisdiction and applicable law in antitrust tort claims' [2002] *JBL* 250

Witz, C. 'Die neuere Rechtsprechung französischer Gerichte zum Einheitlichen UN- Kaufrecht' 1998 *RIW* 278

—— 'Droit uniforme de la vente internationale de marchandises' 2002 *Dalloz, Juris.*, 313

Wolf, A. 'Das Ausführungsgesetz zu dem EWG-Gerichtsstands- und Vollstreckungsübereinkommen' 1973 *NJW* 397

Wolf, C. 'Rechtshängigkeit und Verfahrenskonnexität nach EuGVÜ: The Tatry' 1995 *EuZW* 365

—— 'Feststellungsklage und Anspruchsgrundlagenkonkurrenz im Rahmen von Art.5 Nr.1 und Nr.3 LugÜ' zu *OLG Stuttgart 7.8.1998* 1999 *IPRax* 82

Woloniecki, J. 'Off-shore reinsurance disputes: forum shopping and insolvency' 1993 *Def Couns J* 205

Woodward, S. 'Casenote: *Kleinwort Benson*' 1995 *JIBL* N-154

Wouters, J. 'Conflict of Laws and the Single Market for Financial Services' 1997 *MJ* 161

Wu, M. 'Should a national standard govern recognition and enforcement of foreign country judgments in the United States?' 1998 *Glendale Law Review* 65

Youm, KH. 'The Interaction between American and Foreign Libel Law: US Courts refuse to enforce English libel judgments' 2000 *ICLQ* 131

Yseux, V. 'La Litispendence dans les relations internationaux' 1892 *JDI* 862

Zapater, M. 'El articulo 5.1 del Convenio de Bruselas de 27 de septiembre de 1968 y su interpretacion jurisprudencial por el tribunal de justicia de las Comunidades Europeas' 1985 *Rev Inst Euro* 399

Zeiler, G. 'Europäisches Sicherungsverfahren: Die Regelung der Europäischen Gerichtsstands und Vollstreckungsübereinkommen über einstweilige Maßnahmen' 1996 *JBl* 635

Zekoll, J. 'The enforceability of American money judgments abroad: a landmark decision by the German Federal Supreme Court' 1992 *Colum J Transnat'l Law* 641

—— 'The role and status of American law in the Hague Judgments Convention project' 1998 *Alb L R* 1283

—— 'US-amerikanische Antitrust-Treble-Damages-Urteile und deutscher ordre public' 1999 *JZ* 384

Zonderland, P. 'Einstweilige Verfügungen in den Niederlanden' 1977 *ZZP* 225

Zuckerman, A. 'Dispensation with undertaking in damages – An elemetary injustice' 1993 *CJQ* 268

—— and Grunert, J. 'Casenote: *European Consulting Unternehmensberatung AG v Refco Overseas Limited: OLG Karlsruhe 19.12.1994*' (1996) 1 *ZZPInt* 89

Index